THE **Building Christian English** SERIES

Building

Christian English

Building Securely

Grade 7

Teacher's Manual

Rod and Staff Publishers, Inc.
Hwy. 172, Crockett, Kentucky 41413
Telephone: (606) 522-4348

Acknowledgments

We are indebted first and most of all to God, whose blessing made possible the writing and publishing of this book.

We express gratitude to each one who was involved in this work. The original edition was written by Lela Birky, and the revision by Bruce Good. Marvin Eicher and Ernest Wine were the editors, H. Lynn Martin and various others were reviewers, and the artwork was done by Lester Miller. Eugene Campbell supplied the photograph on page 479. We are also indebted to the teachers who used the material on a laboratory basis in their classrooms, as well as to numerous people who assisted along the way by providing finances, by encouraging those directly involved in the work, and by interceding in prayer for the work.

Various reference books were consulted in accomplishing this task, such as English handbooks, other English textbooks, encyclopedias, and dictionaries. For these too we are grateful. We have chosen to favor the more conservative schools of thought that are considered authoritative in correct English usage.

—The Publishers

Copyright, 1996

First edition, copyright 1972

by

Rod and Staff Publishers, Inc.

Hwy. 172, Crockett, Kentucky 41413

Printed in U.S.A

ISBN 978-07399-0529-6

Catalog no. 12797.3

7   8   9   10   11   12   —   23   22   21   20   19   18   17   16   15   14

Table of Contents
(Stars indicate Written Composition and Oral English lessons.)

Chapter 1   Sentence Parts
Writing Character Sketches

Chapter 2   Sentence Construction
Writing Paragraphs

Chapter 3   Nouns
Developing Paragraphs

Chapter 4 Verbs
Writing Outlines

Chapter 5 Verb Usage
Writing Letters

Chapter 6 Pronouns
Giving Oral Reports

Chapter 7 Adjectives
Writing Descriptions

Chapter 8 Adverbs
Giving Book Reports and Explanations

Chapter 9 Prepositions, Conjunctions, and Interjections
Studying Poetry

Chapter 10 Capitalization and Punctuation
Writing Stories

Chapter 11 Using Reference Books
Writing Effective Sentences

Worksheets

Tests

To the Teacher

This English course is designed for approximately 120 minutes of class time per week (four classes per week of 30 minutes each). The course includes a pupil's book, a teacher's guide, a worksheets booklet, and a test booklet. For a schedule with five classes per week, some lessons may be divided—especially the chapter reviews—or the worksheets may be used more often.

The Pupil's Book

The lesson text explains and illustrates the new concepts. The **Class Practice** exercises provide oral work to make the concepts of the lesson stick. If your schedule does not allow enough time for all the oral drill, try to cover at least several exercises in each section. You could also assign some of the Class Practice as written work.

The written work usually includes both **Written Exercises** (on the present lesson) and **Review Exercises** (on concepts taught previously). Depending on your students' abilities and other circumstances, you may not always be able to assign all of these exercises. Rather than omitting entire sections, you should consider assigning parts of each section.

A Chapter Review at the end of each chapter provides a review of the material taught in that chapter. The test booklet has a test for each chapter.

Note: This course intersperses lessons on oral and written composition throughout the textbook. This arrangement facilitates the teaching of a balance of grammar and composition throughout the year, rather than having the whole "composition load" in one large block. For simple reference, each of these composition lessons is marked with a string of pencils along the margin. Each chapter review and chapter test covers the composition material taught in that chapter.

A number of sentences used as illustrations or exercises are quotations from the Bible or other sources. All such quotations would normally be enclosed in quotation marks; but to avoid confusion, quotation marks are used only with Bible verses.

> **Examples:**
> "A friend loveth at all times." (Bible proverb)
> A friend in need is a friend indeed. (other proverb)

The Teacher's Guide

Each lesson in the teacher's guide begins by stating the **Purpose** of the lesson. A star indicates that the lesson introduces a new concept for this English series. If a concept was previously taught only to a certain degree, a note usually describes the extent of that previous experience.

Following the Purpose, some lessons have a part called **Teacher.** This is not a main part of the lesson but is rather for the teacher's information and awareness.

An **Oral Review** follows the Purpose. Use it to begin the class period. Generally, the first exercises deal with concepts from recent lessons to get the pupils' minds "in gear" for the new English lesson. The remaining exercises deal with less recent concepts (some from previous grades), usually to prepare the students for the written Review Exercises in the new lesson. If you wish, you may duplicate the Oral Review exercises and hand them to the students for personal study, especially if you have slow students or a tight schedule.

The **Lesson Introduction** suggests a way to introduce the lesson, and the **Lesson Outline** lists the specific points taught in the lesson. If a subpoint in the Lesson Outline is marked with a number or letter in double parentheses, such as (1) or (a), it matches the number or letter of a rule in the pupil's lesson.

Drill and Review

This course is designed to provide sufficient drill and review of all the English concepts taught. If the Class Practice, Written Exercises, and Review Exercises are used, the average pupil's mastery of the concepts should be satisfactory for this grade level.

For thorough mastery, however, overlearning the material by repeated drill and review is helpful (especially for slow students). This is the purpose of the Oral Reviews in the teacher's guide, and it is also one purpose of the Worksheets. If time allows, or if the pupils need further drill and review, the teacher is strongly encouraged to use these extra materials; however, they may be omitted if time is limited. **The Worksheets and the Oral Reviews are not required in order to teach this English course successfully.**

General Teaching Suggestions

Use the chalkboard frequently in demonstrating ideas. Keep a brisk pace, and do not waste precious class time to "major on minors." Students should follow along with open books during class discussion. Although thoroughly teaching the lesson may crowd the schedule, the time it will save over answering many student questions later is worthwhile.

Most of the written work, especially in grammar lessons, should be checked in class. Instruct students to use red ink pens for checking. Their checking should be done neatly, without unnecessary scribbling or doodling. If you read the answers clearly, and if you train your students to follow carefully, this should normally require only a few minutes.

Plan ahead so that you will complete the book. Make a schedule for the year, showing how many lessons you should cover each week and where you should be in the book at the end of each marking period. Then stick to your schedule as much as possible.

Develop a grading system that provides an accurate picture of the students' progress but does not bog you down with time-consuming work. Do not give full credit when students fail to follow directions.

It is also a good policy to grade on class participation. Students need to pay attention, follow along in their books, show interest in what is being said, and participate in answering questions during class discussion.

Check the class average periodically. If it is higher than a B, you may be moving too slowly through the book or grading too leniently. If it is much lower, you may be moving too fast or grading too strictly. This is only a general guide; every class has different abilities. Comparing your class records with those from previous years may prove helpful.

The **Worksheets** may be used for remedial practice or simply for extra drill on various concepts. They may be reproduced as needed in teaching this course.

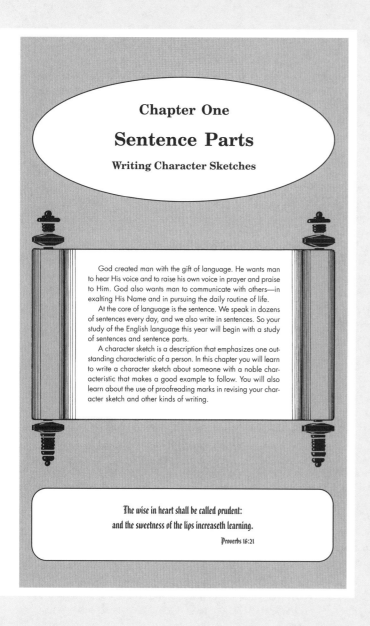

Chapter One

Sentence Parts

Writing Character Sketches

God created man with the gift of language. He wants man to hear His voice and to raise his own voice in prayer and praise to Him. God also wants man to communicate with others—in exalting His Name and in pursuing the daily routine of life.

At the core of language is the sentence. We speak in dozens of sentences every day, and we also write in sentences. So your study of the English language this year will begin with a study of sentences and sentence parts.

A character sketch is a description that emphasizes one outstanding characteristic of a person. In this chapter you will learn to write a character sketch about someone with a noble characteristic that makes a good example to follow. You will also learn about the use of proofreading marks in revising your character sketch and other kinds of writing.

The wise in heart shall be called prudent:
and the sweetness of the lips increaseth learning.

Proverbs 16:21

1. The English Language

Lesson Survey
- Language is a gift from God.
- We can understand English because it follows certain rules. We study these rules so that our communication will be as effective as possible.

Language is a gift from God. He created man with the ability to communicate on a much higher level than that of any other creature on earth. Of course, animals also communicate with each other. Perhaps you have heard a pair of quails calling back and forth across the meadow. And, no doubt, you have heard the neighborhood dogs howling to each other!

Many animals even communicate with man. If you have a pet dog or cat, you certainly will agree. Yet all that communication is very limited. Animals form no sentences intelligibly. They have no ability to communicate abstract ideas. They cannot express ideas in writing.

Man is the crown of creation. He fills a unique place in God's world. One aspect of his uniqueness is his ability to communicate with God. God wants man to understand the riches of His truth as revealed in His Word and to share that truth with others. So He gave man the gift of language.

Many thousands of languages have grown from the languages that God sent into the human family at the Tower of Babel. In any language, people can understand each other because languages follow certain rules. If English is your native tongue, you learned most English rules when you were quite young. Long before you went to school, you understood the difference between *John saw the cat* and *The cat saw John.* You did not know anything about complete sentences, subjects and verbs, or direct objects. But you did know how to talk.

Even though you could communicate quite well before you entered school, you have had many English lessons in school. These lessons have helped you to understand how the language works. For example, you have studied the eight parts of speech, the basic parts of sentences, and the parts of written compositions. Most likely you have also had to unlearn some things that you had learned wrong. The following examples may illustrate a few of these.

Incorrect: I <u>set</u> in my seat.
Correct: I <u>sit</u> in my seat.

Incorrect: I <u>have went</u> through six grades in school.
Correct: I <u>have gone</u> through six grades in school.

Lesson 1

Purpose: To show the value of a structured language, and the importance of studying language for effective communication.

Oral Review:

(Some Oral Review items deal with concepts taught in previous grades, to help prepare students for the written reviews.)

1. Name the part of speech described by each sentence.
   a. It names a person, place, thing, or idea. (noun)
   b. It modifies a noun or pronoun. (adjective)
   c. It modifies a verb, an adjective, or an adverb. (adverb)
   d. It shows action or being. (verb)
   e. It takes the place of a noun. (pronoun)
   f. It joins words, phrases, or clauses. (conjunction)
   g. It shows the relationship between its object and some other word. (preposition)
   h. It expresses strong feeling. (interjection)
2. Name the sentence part described by each sentence.
   a. It receives the action of a verb. (direct object)
   b. It tells *who* or *what* a sentence is about. (subject)
   c. It follows a linking verb and renames the subject. (predicate nominative)
   d. It comes between a verb and a direct object and tells *to whom or what* or *for whom or what* something is done. (indirect object)
   e. It follows a linking verb and describes the subject. (predicate adjective)
   f. It tells what a subject does or is. (predicate)

Lesson Introduction: Ask your students why they never expect the sun to rise in the west. What would

Incorrect: The prodigal was the <u>youngest</u> of the two sons.
Correct: The prodigal was the <u>younger</u> of the two sons.

Learning to speak correct English is more like learning to ride a bicycle than like solving a long division problem or naming the parts of an insect. Language is a complex system of habits. A person says certain words or phrases over and over until it becomes natural. Because this is so, a person can use poor English and think that good English sounds strange and wrong. Poor English is a matter of poor habits; good English is a matter of good habits. And habits are built or changed by repetition and practice.

Like clothes, manners, and habits of work and play, a person's use of language shows others something about himself. Others soon learn that a certain person says certain things in certain ways. They will judge what kind of person he is partly by what he says and how he says it.

Doubtless, you have heard older people lament their lack of skill in reading, speaking, or writing. They may observe that their opportunities were limited when they were young. Or they may confess that they wasted good opportunities. Today is *your* day of opportunity. Will you recognize the importance of mastering good English, or will you wish all your life that you could speak and write better English?

Class Practice

Answer these questions.
1. In what ways is the communication of animals limited?
2. Why did God give man the gift of language?
3. Why can people of a language understand each other?
4. Why do we study English in school?
5. How is learning to speak correct English more like learning to ride a bicycle than like learning history dates?
6. Why can a person use poor English and think it sounds correct?
7. By what things do people identify you?
8. What must you do to change poor English into good English?

Written Exercises

These exercises test how well you remember English concepts that you learned in previous grades.
A. Rewrite each sentence, correcting the mistakes.
1. The balloon busted with a loud bang.
2. The pair of socks are on the line.
3. Ray's dog laid in the shade all morning.
4. The multitude sang their hosannas to Jesus but the chief priests sought to kill Him.
5. Do you still live along Redwood drive?

life be like if we never knew when to expect summer or winter? God has established a dependable order in the solar system. Language, too, must maintain order to avoid confusion. Our study of the English language will help us to understand that order and thus to communicate more effectively.

Lesson Outline:
1. *Language is a gift from God.*
   a. God created man with the ability to communicate on a much higher level than that of any other creature.
   b. God wants to communicate with man through His Word.
2. *We can understand English because it follows certain rules.*
   a. Most English rules are learned when we are young.

Lesson 1 Answers

Class Practice

1. They cannot communicate with God, form intelligible sentences, communicate abstract ideas, or express ideas in writing.
2. God wants to communicate with man. He wants man to understand the riches of His revealed truth and to share that truth with others.
3. Each language follows certain rules.
4. to learn how the language works, and to unlearn some things that we learned wrong
5. It involves a complex system of habits.
6. It feels natural to him because he has used it over and over.
7. by clothes, manners, habits of work and play, and speech
8. Recognize the importance of the change, and use present opportunities to learn good English.

Written Exercises

A. (Corrections are underlined.)
1. The balloon <u>burst</u> with a loud bang.
2. The pair of socks <u>is</u> on the line.
3. Ray's dog <u>lay</u> in the shade all morning.
4. The multitude sang their hosannas to Jesus<u>,</u> but the chief priests sought to kill Him.
5. Do you still live along Redwood <u>D</u>rive?

b. English instruction is necessary to help us learn how the language works and to help us unlearn things that we may have learned wrong.
3. *Language is a complex system of habits.*
   a. Saying certain words or phrases over and over makes them feel natural.
   b. Either poor or good English becomes a matter of habit.
4. *A person's use of language reveals something about himself.*

6. Who's book is on the floor?
7. These flowers come from Rachel and I.
8. This don't look like my pencil.
9. Us boys will need to work fast to get the chores done.
10. Jerry can sing tenor very good.

B. Read each italicized sentence, and answer the questions following it.

Before Jesus was born, Joseph and Mary went to Bethlehem.
1. What is the prepositional phrase in this sentence?
2. Do the first four words make an adverb or an adjective clause?
3. What part of speech is *and*?
4. What part of speech is *was*?

Jesus taught the disciples clearly, but they did not always understand His words.
5. Is this sentence simple, compound, or complex?
6. What part of speech is *clearly*?
7. What part of speech is *they*?
8. What is the subject of the first part of the sentence?
9. What is the verb phrase in the second part of the sentence?
10. What is the direct object in the second part of the sentence?

6. <u>Whose</u> book is on the floor?
7. These flowers come from Rachel and <u>me</u>.
8. This <u>doesn't</u> look like my pencil.
9. <u>We</u> boys will need to work fast to get the chores done.
10. Jerry can sing tenor very <u>well</u>.

B. 1. to Bethlehem
2. adverb clause
3. conjunction
4. verb
5. compound
6. adverb
7. pronoun
8. Jesus
9. did understand
10. words

---

2. Sentences

> **Lesson Survey**
> * A **sentence** is a group of words that expresses a complete thought.
> * A **fragment** is a group of words that does not express a complete thought.
> * A **run-on error** results from writing two or more sentences together as one.

We use words every day to communicate with each other. When we communicate by writing words, we normally divide the words into sentences. Writing is difficult to read if there are no sentence divisions.

When Saul was on his way to Damascus a bright light suddenly shone around him Saul fell to the ground and heard a voice asking Saul Saul why persecutest thou me in response he asked who art thou Lord the voice identified itself as Jesus the one whom he was

Lesson 2

Purpose: To teach the definitions of a sentence, a fragment, and a run-on error.

Oral Review:
1. In what ways is man's communication superior to that of animals? (Man can communicate with God, form intelligible sentences, communicate abstract ideas, and express ideas in writing.)
2. Why did God give man the gift of language? (He wants man to understand the riches of His revealed truth and to share that truth with others.)
3. Why can people who speak the same language understand each other? (Languages follow certain rules.)
4. Why must we study English in school? (to learn how the language works and to unlearn some things that we learned wrong)

5. Why might good English sound strange or wrong? (A person may be so accustomed to poor English that good English sounds unnatural.)
6. What must you do to change poor English into good English? (Recognize the importance of the change. Use present opportunities to learn good English.)

Lesson Introduction: Read the following sets of dialogue.

"Did you hear what we're going to do?"
"No; what are we going to do?"
"We're going to the zoo!"
"Are we really going to the zoo? When are we going?"
"We're going to the zoo on Wednesday."
        *   *   *   *   *
"Did you hear what we're going to do?"
"No; what?"
"Go to the zoo!"
"Really? When?"
"On Wednesday."

persecuting in humble submission Saul asked what wilt thou have me to do.

This paragraph is hard to read, not because the words are unfamiliar, but because the units of thought are hard to follow. In conversation our expressions, gestures, and pauses help to convey the meaning. In written communication, we depend on punctuation and the distinct structure of sentences to show the units of thought.

A *sentence* is a group of words that expresses a complete thought. Every sentence can be divided into two parts: the complete subject, which tells *who* or *what* the sentence is about, and the complete predicate, which tells what the subject does or is.

<u>The Lord</u> <u>called Jeremiah to be a prophet.</u>
subject   predicate

<u>Did</u> Jeremiah <u>prophesy to Israel or to Judah?</u>

This dedicated man of God <u>is called the weeping prophet.</u>

A *fragment* is a group of words that does not express a complete thought. It may be short or long. It may be just a subject or just a predicate. It may have neither a subject nor a predicate, or it may contain both.

The boy. (subject only)
The boy with five barley loaves and two small fish. (subject only)
The habit of good study. (subject only)
Is best learned in school. (predicate only)
Past the soldiers, through the iron gate, and right into the street.
   (neither a subject nor a predicate)
When <u>Jesus</u> <u>came</u> into the world.
   (This word group has both a subject and a predicate. But the thought is not complete, because the words do not tell what happened when Jesus came into the world. This fragment is an adverb clause.)
For whom <u>Jesus</u> <u>died</u>.
   (This word group has both a subject and a predicate. But the thought is not complete, because the words do not identify the ones for whom Jesus died. This fragment is an adjective clause.)

If two or more sentences are incorrectly written together, the result is a *run-on error*. Inserting a comma does not correct the error; it produces a comma splice. A run-on error can be corrected in the following three ways.
1. By dividing the sentence and using proper capitalization and end punctuation.

Discuss the difference between these two examples. Point out how unnatural the first example sounds. When we talk, we use many incomplete sentences and we are usually understood clearly. But in writing (other than dialogue), we need complete sentences to communicate clearly.

Lesson Outline:

1. A sentence is a group of words that expresses a complete thought. Every sentence can be divided into a complete subject and a complete predicate. (*Teacher:* Most seventh graders will know these two facts from previous years. You need not spend much time on them unless they seem unfamiliar to your class.)

2. A fragment is a group of words that does not express a complete thought.
   a. A fragment may be short or long.
   b. A fragment may be just a subject or just a predicate.
   c. A fragment may have neither a subject nor a predicate, or it may contain both.

3. A run-on error is two or more sentences incorrectly written as one. There may be no punctuation at all between the sentences, or they may be separated by only a comma (resulting in a comma splice).

2. By using a comma and a conjunction between the two sentences.
3. By using a semicolon between the two sentences.

Run-on: We went to the zoo last summer it was such fun!
Correct: We went to the zoo last summer. It was such fun!
We went to the zoo last summer, and it was such fun!

Run-on: We enjoyed watching the orangutan, he sat on his crate watching the zookeeper. (comma splice)
Correct: We enjoyed watching the orangutan. He sat on his crate watching the zookeeper.
We enjoyed watching the orangutan; he sat on his crate watching the zookeeper.

Class Practice

A. Identify each word group as a *sentence,* a *fragment,* or a *run-on error.*
  1. Emily propped her head she was deep in thought.
  2. The poem for tomorrow's English class.
  3. Was proving to be a hard assignment.
  4. She had already finished one stanza now her inspiration seemed to have dried up.
  5. If she came back to it later, perhaps her thoughts would flow again.

B. Tell whether each fragment is a *subject,* is a *predicate,* has *neither* a subject nor a predicate, or has *both* a subject and a predicate. Then add words to make a complete sentence.
  1. Daniel and his three friends
  2. Had a dream about a magnificent image
  3. Although the furnace was heated seven times hotter than usual
  4. In the lions' den all night
  5. Because Darius loved Daniel

Written Exercises

A. Label each word group *S* for sentence, *F* for fragment, or *R* for run-on error.
  1. The crows in a big black swarm.
  2. Descended on the corn patch.
  3. They squawked and cawed, they ate the corn.
  4. Which was almost ready to be picked.
  5. The three boys were in the barn.
  6. When they heard the commotion.
  7. They dashed outside, for a moment they stood in astonishment.
  8. Then they waved their arms they shouted at the top of their voices.
  9. The crows, hungry for corn, refused to fly away.
  10. They just flew to the other end of the patch.

Lesson 2 Answers

Class Practice

A. 1. run-on error   4. run-on error
   2. fragment   5. sentence
   3. fragment

B. (Suggestions are in parentheses.)
  1. subject; Daniel and his three friends (were faithful to the Lord).
  2. predicate; (Nebuchadnezzar) had a dream about a magnificent image.
  3. both; Although the furnace was heated seven times hotter than usual, (the three Hebrews were not hurt by the fire).
  4. neither; (God protected Daniel) in the lions' den all night.
  5. both; Because Darius loved Daniel, (he tried hard to deliver him).

Written Exercises

A. 1. F   6. F
   2. F   7. R
   3. R   8. R
   4. F   9. S
   5. S   10. S

B. The paragraphs below are not divided into sentences. Show how to correct them by writing the first word and the last word of each sentence, with three dots (...) between them. Use proper capitalization and end punctuation.

Example:

The snow fell thick and fast all night by early morning the wind was forming huge drifts in the back yard was a drift eight feet deep we had to dig a tunnel through it to get to the barn.

Answer:

The... night. By... drifts. In... deep! We... barn.

1.   From the top of the hill, we could see down into the valley many things were happening people were going about their daily business wagons drawn by horses rumbled along the roads smoke was rising from the chimneys the morning sun illuminated everything gloriously watching over all was our kind Father in heaven above.

2.   We had an interesting devotional meditation this morning Brother Jacob, home from Guatemala for a visit, impressed on our minds the power of God's Word after prayer, he described the little school where he teaches and showed us some pictures of his students he also had pictures of the mountainous scenery around the mission on a large map of Guatemala, he pointed out the different mission locations.

Review Exercises

These exercises review things that you studied in previous grades. Use the index in the back of this book if you need help.

A. Match the parts of speech to the descriptions. Some answers will be used more than once.

noun   adjective   conjunction
pronoun   adverb   interjection
verb   preposition

1. It modifies a noun or pronoun.
2. It names a person, place, thing, or idea.
3. It modifies a verb, an adjective, or an adverb.
4. It takes the place of a noun.
5. It shows action or being.
6. It expresses strong feeling.
7. It shows the relationship between its object and some other word.
8. It connects words, phrases, or clauses.
9. It tells *how, when, where,* or *to what degree.*
10. It tells *which, whose, how many,* or *what kind of.*

B. Write the correct plural form of each noun.

B. 1. From ... valley. Many ... happening. People ... business. Wagons ... roads. Smoke ... chimneys. The ... gloriously. Watching ... above.
   2. We ... morning. Brother ... Word. After ... students. He ... mission. On ... locations.

Review Exercises

(*Teacher:* You may prefer not to take grades on exercises that review concepts from previous years, or you might assign them for extra credit.)

A. 1. adjective   6. interjection
   2. noun   7. preposition
   3. adverb   8. conjunction
   4. pronoun   9. adverb
   5. verb   10. adjective

1. knife	5. brick	9. blotch		
2. island	6. roof	10. sheep		
3. deer	7. volcano	11. fox		
4. candy	8. chimney	12. house		

B. 1. knives   7. volcanoes *or* volcanos
   2. islands   8. chimneys
   3. deer   9. blotches
   4. candies   10. sheep
   5. bricks   11. foxes
   6. roofs   12. houses

---

3. Subjects and Predicates

> **Lesson Survey**
> - A **subject** tells *who* or *what* a sentence is about. The **simple subject** is the main part of the **complete subject.**
> - A **predicate** tells what the subject does or is. The **simple predicate** is the main part of the **complete predicate.**
> - A **sentence skeleton** consists of a simple subject and a simple predicate.

In Lesson 2 you were reminded that a sentence is a group of words that expresses a complete thought. To express a complete thought, a sentence must include two main parts: the *complete subject* and the *complete predicate*.

Normally, the subject comes first in the sentence. It is literally the *subject* (the topic) of the sentence. Since the subject tells *who* or *what* the sentence is about, you can easily identify it by finding the verb and asking *who* or *what* about it.

Leon grew corn, beans, and tomatoes to sell.
  (The verb is *grew. Who* grew? Leon.)
The three kittens were playing in the yard.
  (The verb is *were playing. What* were playing? The three kittens.)

The *simple subject* is the main part of the *complete subject*. It is usually a single noun or pronoun. However, it may also be a noun phrase or a compound noun. Every word in a proper noun phrase, such as a name or a title, is part of the simple subject. This includes the small words that are not capitalized. The simple subjects of these sentences are underlined.

The street was littered with tree branches after the storm.
Main Street was littered with tree branches after the storm.

This book is a gripping story about persecuted Anabaptists.
Evangelists in Chains is a gripping story about persecuted Anabaptists.

Lesson 3

Purpose: To teach the definitions of a complete subject, a complete predicate, a simple subject, a simple predicate, and a sentence skeleton.

Oral Review:

1. What is a sentence? (a group of words that expresses a complete thought)
2. What two parts does every sentence have? (subject, predicate)
3. Can a fragment have both a subject and a predicate? Explain. (yes, if it is an adjective or adverb clause)
4. What is a run-on error? (two or more sentences incorrectly written as one)
5. Name the twenty-three helping verbs. (am, is, are, was, were, be, been, being; have, has, had; do, does, did; may, might, must; can—could, shall—should, will—would)

Lesson Introduction: The skeleton of an animal provides its basic shape and support. A skeleton alone is lifeless. On the other hand, the muscle and skin tissues without a skeleton would be limp and useless. Likewise, the skeleton of a sentence provides the basic framework of the sentence. A sentence skeleton alone usually has little life. But the other parts of the sentence have little meaning if they are not attached to the sentence skeleton.

Lesson Outline:

   1. The subject of a sentence tells **who** *or* **what** *the sentence is about.*

   2. The simple subject is the main part of the complete subject.
      a. The simple subject may be a single noun or pronoun, or it may be a noun phrase or

A <u>blue jay</u> is a beautiful but aggressive bird.
<u>This</u> is a beautiful but aggressive bird.

The simple subject is often modified by adjectives. These adjectives may be words, phrases, or clauses. The simple subject and all its modifiers make the complete subject. In the following examples, the simple subject is *watermelons*. But notice the modifiers that are included in the complete subject.

<u>*Watermelons*</u> grow well in wet, sandy soil. (no adjectives)
The juicy, red <u>*watermelons*</u> taste delicious. (one-word adjectives)
The <u>*watermelons* on the counter</u> are for dessert. (adjective phrase)
The <u>*watermelons* that we planted</u> have grown well. (adjective clause)

Remember that the subject of a sentence is never found in a prepositional phrase. Sometimes it seems quite reasonable to say that the object of a preposition is the subject. In fact, the object of a preposition may sound more sensible than the real subject. (Look at the second and third examples below.) But the fact remains that the subject is *never* in a prepositional phrase.

The <u>Lord</u> (of glory) will bless His people.
   (Who will bless His people—the Lord or glory? The subject is *Lord.*)
This <u>piece</u> (of chicken) is well done.
   (What is well done—the piece or the chicken? Both make sense. But since *chicken* is the object of a preposition, the subject must be *piece.*)
A <u>glass</u> (of cold water) is appreciated on a warm day.
   (What is appreciated—the glass or the water? *Water* is sensible, but it is the object of a preposition. The subject is *glass,* which in this case means the container full of cold water.)

The *predicate* of a sentence tells what the subject does or is. In most sentences, the predicate immediately follows the subject. You can easily identify the predicate by finding the verb and all the words associated with it.

Janet <u>drew this picture</u>.
   (The verb is *drew.* The predicate is *drew this picture.*)
The girls in the yard <u>are my cousins</u>.
   (The verb is *are.* The predicate is *are my cousins.*)

The *simple predicate* is the main part of the *complete predicate*. It is the verb or verb phrase. In each of the following examples, the simple predicate is *will obey*. But notice how the complete predicate may include

a compound noun. In a proper noun phrase (such as a name or a title), every word is part of the simple subject.

  b. The simple subject is never in a prepositional phrase.

3. The predicate tells what the subject does or is.

4. The simple predicate is the main part of the complete predicate. It is the verb or verb phrase.

5. The sentence skeleton consists of the simple subject and the simple predicate. The subject, the predicate, or both may be compound.

  a. Modifiers and direct objects are often attached to the sentence skeleton to add interest and meaning.

  b. The sentence skeleton is diagramed on a horizontal line, with a vertical line between the simple subject and the simple predicate.

  c. Compound parts are diagramed on a fork, with the conjunction on a broken line between the two subjects or verbs.

adverb modifiers or direct objects.

> I <u>*will obey*</u>.
> I <u>*will obey*</u> <u>promptly and completely</u>.
> I <u>*will obey*</u> the Bible.

The two most important parts of a sentence are the simple subject and the simple predicate. These two make up the *sentence skeleton*. Modifiers and direct objects are often attached to the sentence skeleton to add interest and meaning.

> <u>Hezekiah</u> <u>read</u>. (skeleton)
> <u>Hezekiah</u> <u>read</u> the letter from Sennacherib.
>   (skeleton with added words)
>
> <u>Army</u> <u>was slain</u>. (skeleton)
> The <u>army</u> of Sennacherib <u>was slain</u> by the angel of the Lord.
>   (skeleton with added words)

A sentence skeleton may have a *compound subject* (more than one simple subject) or a *compound predicate* (more than one simple predicate). It may even have both a compound subject and a compound predicate.

> <u>Abraham</u>, <u>Isaac</u>, and <u>Jacob</u> are called the patriarchs. (compound subject)
> Abraham <u>built</u> an altar and <u>worshiped</u> the Lord. (compound predicate)
> <u>Esau</u> and <u>Jacob</u> <u>made</u> peace and then <u>went</u> their separate ways.
>   (compound subject and compound predicate)

A sentence skeleton is diagramed on a horizontal line, with a vertical line between the simple subject and the simple predicate.

> The wicked Queen Jezebel was judged severely.
>
> | Queen Jezebel | was judged |

Compound parts are diagramed on a fork. The conjunction is placed on a broken line between the two subjects or verbs.

Joseph and Mary found no room at the inn.

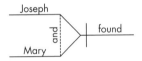

They went to a stable and lodged there.

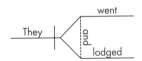

The shepherds and the wise men came and worshiped the Messiah.

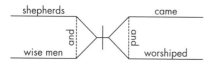

Class Practice

A. Identify the complete subject and the complete predicate in each sentence.
1. The new songbooks are in the racks.
2. All the cousins are playing prisoner's base.
3. The long line of covered wagons started over the hills.
4. Great herds of bison roamed the Great Plains.
5. Aunt Kathryn hoed the weeds in the garden.

B. Read the skeleton of each sentence.
1. The Appalachian Trail runs from Maine to Georgia.
2. Many people have been hiking this trail every year.
3. Kangaroos and opossums are marsupials.
4. The children worked in the garden and mowed the lawn.
5. This pretty flower is called a larkspur.

C. On the chalkboard, diagram the skeletons of the sentences in Part B.

Written Exercises

A. Copy each sentence, and draw a vertical line to divide the complete subject from the complete predicate.
1. Nehemiah served as the king's cupbearer.
2. This godly man heard sad news from Jerusalem.
3. King Artaxerxes noticed his sad countenance.
4. He inquired about the reason for Nehemiah's sadness.
5. Nehemiah's answer revealed the deep longing of his heart.
6. The city of Jerusalem lay in ruins.
7. Its walls and its temple had been destroyed.
8. The Lord God of Israel used Nehemiah in a mighty way.
9. The people of Jerusalem had a mind to work.
10. The construction of the walls was done in fifty-two days.

B. Diagram the skeleton of each sentence. Watch for noun and verb phrases and for compound parts.
1. Elijah the prophet lay wearily under a juniper tree.
2. Athaliah usurped the throne and killed most of the kingly line.
3. Peter and John were going to the temple.
4. The lame man was laid daily at the Beautiful Gate.

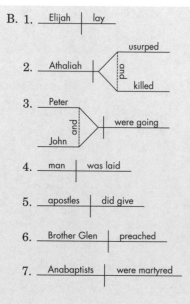

Lesson 3 Answers

Class Practice

A. 1. The new songbooks | are in the racks.
2. All the cousins | are playing prisoner's base.
3. The long line of covered wagons | started over the hills.
4. Great herds of bison | roamed the Great Plains.
5. Aunt Kathryn | hoed the weeds in the garden.

B. 1. Appalachian Trail runs
2. people have been hiking
3. Kangaroos (and) opossums are
4. children worked (and) mowed
5. flower is called

C.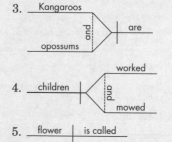

Written Exercises

A. 1. Nehemiah | served as the king's cupbearer.
2. This godly man | heard sad news from Jerusalem.
3. King Artaxerxes | noticed his sad countenance.
4. He | inquired about the reason for Nehemiah's sadness.
5. Nehemiah's answer | revealed the deep longing of his heart.
6. The city of Jerusalem | lay in ruins.
7. Its walls and its temple | had been destroyed.
8. The Lord God of Israel | used Nehemiah in a mighty way.
9. The people of Jerusalem | had a mind to work.
10. The construction of the walls | was done in fifty-two days.

5. The two apostles of Christ did not give him any money.
6. Brother Glen preached a stirring sermon.
7. Many Anabaptists were martyred for their faith.
8. Some Catholics and Protestants persecuted and killed sincere Christians.
9. Menno Simons and Pilgram Marpeck were not martyred.
10. Christians of all ages have been standing loyal to the Lord.
11. Young people today need the same determination to be true.
12. The Lord will abundantly bless His faithful followers.
13. The best rewards for faithfulness will be given in heaven.
14. Our talents and opportunities are given by the Lord.
15. The widow's barrel of meal always contained enough.
16. Moses and Aaron stood before Pharaoh and proclaimed God's message.

Review Exercises

Write a more descriptive word for each underlined word, as you learned in previous grades.

1. After recess, we went back inside the <u>building</u>.
2. Darvin <u>said</u>, "The cows are out!"
3. Yesterday was a <u>nice</u> day for our hike.
4. Harvey Martin will <u>go</u> to Paraguay by jet.
5. Jay carried five <u>containers</u> of feed to the calf pens.
6. The frisky little <u>animals</u> playfully nipped at each other.
7. This cake tastes <u>good</u>.
8. Miriam felt <u>bad</u> after eating the green apples.
9. The crippled man <u>walked</u> down the street.
10. Leonard <u>took</u> the box of jars to the basement.
11. Naomi <u>looked</u> in amazement at the huge elephant.
12. The horses <u>ran</u> across the pasture.
13. Where did Margaret <u>get</u> her new stationery?
14. Put the flowers into that <u>thing</u> on the counter top.
15. The half-starved dog <u>ate</u> the meat scraps.

4. Writing a Character Sketch

Lesson Survey

- A **character sketch** is a description that emphasizes one outstanding characteristic of an individual.
- Be careful to follow the Golden Rule when you write a character sketch.

Lesson 4

Purpose: To teach *writing a description that emphasizes one outstanding characteristic of an individual.

Oral Review

1. What are some rules about story writing that you remember from other grades?
   (a. Write about a problem that must be solved.
   b. Know the facts.
   c. Put things in proper order.
   d. Include all the important information.
   e. Stick to the main idea of the story.
   f. Use complete sentences.
   g. Vary the length and the word order of sentences.
   h. Use good grammar, proper spelling, correct punctuation, and neat handwriting.)
2. What are some ways to develop paragraphs? (by

(Numbers 5–7 are on page 22.)

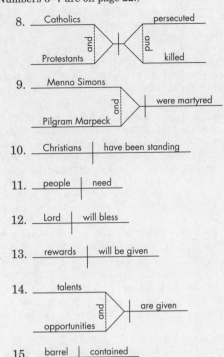

Review Exercises

(Sample answers.)

1. school
2. shouted, called
3. pleasant, beautiful
4. fly, travel
5. buckets, bags
6. puppies, foxes
7. delicious
8. sick, nauseated
9. limped, shuffled, hobbled
10. carried
11. gazed, stared
12. galloped, trotted
13. buy, purchase
14. vase, jar
15. devoured, gulped, wolfed

using details, by using examples and illustrations, by using comparison or contrast)

3. Give some rules of good outline form.
   (a. Use Roman numerals for topics, capital letters for subtopics, and Arabic numerals for points. Place a period after each numeral or letter.
   b. Have at least two items in each group—no *A* without a *B*, no *1* without a *2*, and so on.
   c. Make all the items in each group as nearly parallel as possible.
   d. Indent each subtopic and each point.
   e. Begin each item with a capital letter.)

Have you ever watched a skilled artist sketching a person's face? With a few quick strokes, the outline of the head appeared on the paper. A few more strokes and a bit of shading brought the face into full view. Even the person's expression seemed to live in the picture.

This lesson is about a different kind of sketch. Instead of drawing a sketch of a person's appearance, you will learn to write a sketch of his character. A *character sketch* is a description that emphasizes one outstanding characteristic of an individual. The following steps explain how to write a character sketch.

1. *Decide whom you will write about and what characteristic you will emphasize.* Think of a person whom you know very well. Then think: What is one characteristic that stands out? Is it the person's friendliness? Or perhaps he is very active, always seeming to be bustling about his work. Maybe his cheerfulness is outstanding. Or he may be so calm and unruffled that nothing ever seems to disturb him.

Of course, no individual is always cheerful or always busily working. A person may display several characteristics that you could write about. But you must be selective, like an artist drawing a sketch. What single thing about the person's character stands out as you think about him? That one characteristic will be the theme of your character sketch.

2. *List a number of events or examples that illustrate the characteristic you want to emphasize.* Suppose your theme could be expressed in the following sentence: John Weaver is a friendly person. Now think: What are some specific things that show his friendliness? Does he always have a smile and a cheery greeting for you? Is he usually the first one to welcome visitors at church? Can you think of some incident that illustrates his friendliness especially well? You need a list of these specific events or examples so that you have details to put into your character sketch.

A character sketch is a special kind of report. Like any other report, it must have an introduction, a body, and a conclusion.

3. *Write the introduction of your character sketch.* The introduction should be brief and catchy. You may begin by placing the character in a setting that either reflects or contrasts the characteristic you want to emphasize.

Setting that reflects a characteristic:

> I first became acquainted with Lynette two years ago when I went to my cousin Darlene's house to help with peaches. Lynette is Darlene's cousin on the other side of the family, and she was spending several days with Uncle Lloyd's. Even before I saw her, I heard her voice and Darlene's blending in song. As I entered the kitchen, I was immediately impressed by her smiling eyes and pleasant tone of voice.

Lesson Introduction: Have you ever described a good friend to someone else? Perhaps you mentioned a few things about how he looks. But unless you were trying to point him out so that the other person would recognize him, you likely said more about what your friend does than about how he looks. Inner character, after all, is more important than outer appearance.

Lesson Outline:

1. A character sketch is a description that emphasizes one outstanding characteristic of an individual.

2. To write a character sketch, use the following steps.

(1) *Decide whom you will write about and what characteristic you will emphasize.*

   a) You must be well acquainted with the person you describe.

   b) You must choose one main characteristic to emphasize.

(2) *List a number of events or examples that illustrate the characteristic you want to emphasize.* You must select only the details that contribute to your theme.

(3) *Write the introduction of your character sketch.*

   a) You may place the character in a setting that either reflects or contrasts the characteristic you want to emphasize.

   b) You may give a first impression, followed by a description of how different you found the person to be when you learned to know him better.

(4) *Write the body of your character sketch.*

   a) Make the person come to life by having him say and do things.

Lynette Graybill is one of the most cheerful people I know. . . .

Setting that contrasts a characteristic:

Robert Compton has been coming along with our family to church ever since he was five years old. His parents have never come to church, however, and his two older brothers quit coming when he was about ten.

Now fifteen years old, Robert often challenges me with his determination to do what is right. . . .

You may also introduce a character sketch by describing a first impression and then showing how different you found the person to be when you learned to know him better. A stern face, for example, may mask a kind heart.

Last summer when we moved into this community, I did not know what to think the first time I heard Brother Melvin preach. As he stood before the congregation, his six-foot frame and broad shoulders seemed to dwarf the small pulpit. His booming voice sounded across the auditorium with no need of an amplifier.

A few weeks later, we invited his family to our home for Sunday dinner. . . .

4. *Write the body of your character sketch.* The body of a character sketch should *show* rather than merely *tell about* the individual's character. Using your list of details, make the person come to life by having him say and do things. Write with specific words and picturesque language. Remember to include only those details that illustrate the characteristic you have chosen to emphasize.

5. *Write the conclusion of your character sketch.* The conclusion should briefly summarize your main emphasis. You may describe some way in which the person has been blessed because of the characteristic in focus. Or you may say that you want to cultivate the characteristic you have seen in that person.

In writing a character sketch, be sure to follow the Golden Rule. You must never write something that would embarrass or insult another person. But you must also avoid empty flattery. Not every person you know will be a suitable subject for a character sketch. Choose someone with a noble characteristic that you can lift up as a good example to follow.

Sample character sketch:

A Surprisingly Gentle Man

Last summer when we moved into this community, I did not know what to think the first time I heard Brother Melvin preach. As he stood before the congregation, his six-foot frame and broad

b) Use specific words and picturesque language.

(5) *Write the conclusion of your character sketch.*

a) Briefly summarize your main emphasis.

b) You may show how the person has been blessed because of the characteristic in focus.

c) You may express your desire to follow the character's example.

3. Be careful to follow the Golden Rule when you write a character sketch.

a. Do not write something that would embarrass or insult another person.

b. Avoid empty flattery.

c. Write about a person of noble character who is a good example to follow.

shoulders seemed to dwarf the small pulpit. His booming voice sounded across the auditorium with no need of an amplifier.

A few weeks later, we invited his family to our home for Sunday dinner. When Brother Melvin shook my hand, his voice sounded surprisingly gentle as he asked, "What's your name again?" Then he knelt down right beside Eldon, who was building a truck with his blocks. "You have a mighty fine truck there, my boy," he said.

When we walked outside after dinner, Brother Melvin's love for animals quickly became evident. The puppies' playful tumblings made him chuckle. He put his shoe to Spot's mouth and said, "G-r-r-r. Do you have a rat? Shake it! Shake it!" In the barn, he spied the kittens almost right away. His huge hand practically swallowed the tiny kitten he picked up, but he stroked it gently. He actually made soft, purring noises in his throat.

The other Sunday, when Brother Melvin preached with his usual enthusiasm on "The Power of the Gospel," I thought again about my first impression of him. He still has the same powerful voice, but now I know what to think. Though I will probably never be six feet tall, I surely would like to grow into a man of gentleness like Brother Melvin.

Class Practice

Suppose you are to write a character sketch of David as he is portrayed in 1 Samuel 17. The main characteristic you want to emphasize is David's loyalty to God. Do the following exercises.

1. The introduction could describe the army of Israel in 1 Samuel 17:10, 11. Would this reflect or contrast the characteristic you want to emphasize?
2. What information about David's physical appearance is given in verse 42? Would this information contribute to the theme of your character sketch?
3. From the following verses, give details that could be used to develop the theme of this character sketch.
   a. verses 17, 20, 28   d. verses 34–37   f. verse 45
   b. verse 26   e. verses 39, 40   g. verse 46
   c. verse 32
4. How could you use 1 Samuel 17:55–18:5 as an effective conclusion?

Written Exercises

Write a character sketch of a person with whom you are well acquainted. A number of suggestions are listed here.

Lesson 4 Answers

Class Practice

1. contrast
2. David was "ruddy [red], and of a fair countenance."

   Yes, this information contributes to the theme. It suggests that David was a pure young man; his face was free from all traces of sinful living.
3. a. He readily obeyed his father even though he may have suspected his brother's resentment toward him.
   b. He recognized Goliath not only as a fearsome giant but also as a wicked man defying God.
   c. He offered to fight Goliath.
   d. He testified of past experiences when God had helped him.
   e. He used only the weapons that he knew God could bless.
   f. He met Goliath in the Name of the Lord.
   g. He expressed confidence that God would enable him to overcome.
4. These verses show that David was rewarded with the friendship of Jonathan, an honored position in King Saul's army, and the respect of others.

Written Exercises

(Individual work.)

Persons:
 father, mother, brother, sister, grandfather, grandmother, uncle, aunt, cousin, neighbor, minister

Characteristics:
 carefulness, kindness, cheerfulness, patience, efficiency, humility, tenderheartedness

IMPORTANT: Keep your character sketch for use in a later lesson.

---

5. Direct and Indirect Objects

> **Lesson Survey**
> - A **direct object** is a noun or pronoun that completes a sentence skeleton by receiving the action of a verb.
> - An **indirect object** is a noun or pronoun that helps to complete a sentence skeleton by telling *to whom or what* or *for whom or what* an action is performed.
> - Direct and indirect objects are **object complements.**

Every complete sentence is based on a sentence skeleton, which contains a simple subject and a simple predicate. In many sentences, however, additional words are needed to complete the sentence skeleton.

A *direct object* is a noun or pronoun that follows a verb and receives its action *directly*. Only action verbs can have direct objects because only action verbs can pass action to a receiver. Of course, not all action verbs are followed by direct objects.

> Jesus Christ <u>is</u> the Messiah. (no action verb; no direct object)
> Jesus <u>came</u> for our salvation. (action verb followed by a prepositional phrase but no direct object)
> Jesus <u>shed</u> His *blood*. (action verb followed by direct object *blood*)

To find a direct object, say the sentence skeleton and ask *whom* or *what*.

> Isaiah saw the Lord in a vision. (Isaiah saw *whom*? Lord.)
> Jeremiah bought a field in Anathoth. (Jeremiah bought *what*? Field.)
> Children should work willingly.
> (Children should work *what*? *Willingly* is an adverb that tells *how,* not *what.* There is no direct object.)

Lesson 5

Purpose: (1) To show that some sentence skeletons are completed by direct objects and indirect objects. (2) To teach that direct objects and indirect objects are *object complements.

Oral Review:

1. What is a sentence skeleton? (the simple subject and simple predicate of a sentence)
2. What question can you ask to find the subject of a sentence? (*who* or *what*)
3. What does the predicate of a sentence tell? (what the subject does or is)
4. Two or more sentences incorrectly written as one are ———. (a run-on error)
5. A group of words that does not express a complete thought is a ———. (fragment)

Lesson Introduction: Write the following items on the board.

> Henry found.
> The Gehmans raise.
> The Sanhedrin condemned.

Although these word groups have skeletons, they do not seem like complete sentences. They need *complements* to complete their thoughts. (Note the relationship between *complete* and *complement.* A complement is a "complete-ment.") Now finish the sentences by adding direct objects.

> Henry found his missing paper.
> The Gehmans raise watermelons and cantaloupes.
> The Sanhedrin condemned Jesus.

Since the direct object is used to complete the sentence skeleton, it is diagramed on the horizontal line after the skeleton. The direct object is separated from the verb by a vertical line that rests on the horizontal line. The following examples show how to diagram the previous sample sentences. Notice again that the last one has no direct object.

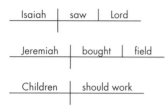

A skeleton may be followed by a *compound direct object* (more than one direct object). A compound direct object is diagramed on a fork, after the vertical line that separates the direct object from the verb.

Rebecca writes good
stories and poems.

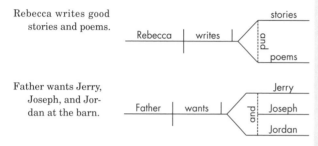

Father wants Jerry,
Joseph, and Jor-
dan at the barn.

Note: The conjunction may be placed on either side of the broken vertical line. It is usually placed on the side away from the fork because there is more space on that side, except when the compound part has three items.

If there is a compound predicate, each verb may have its own direct object. Then the compound predicate is diagramed as usual, and each direct object is placed after the appropriate verb.

Jesus loves righteousness and hates iniquity.

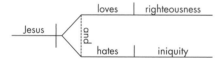

Lesson Outline:

1. A direct object is a noun or pronoun that completes a sentence skeleton by receiving the action of a verb. Only action verbs can have direct objects. However, not all action verbs have direct objects.

    a. A direct object can be found by saying the sentence skeleton and asking *whom* or *what.*

    b. On a sentence diagram, the direct object is placed on the horizontal line after the sentence skeleton. It is separated from the verb by a vertical line that rests on the horizontal line.

    c. Two or more direct objects may follow the same verb. In a compound predicate, each verb may have its own direct object.

2. An indirect object is a noun or pronoun that helps to complete the sentence skeleton by telling to whom or what *or* for whom or what *an action is performed.* An indirect object normally comes between the verb and the direct object.

    a. Only a sentence with a direct object can have an indirect object. But not every sentence with a direct object has an indirect object.

    b. An indirect object can be found by saying the skeleton and the direct object, and then asking *to whom or what* or *for whom or what.*

    (*Teacher:* Emphasize the position of the indirect object between the verb and the direct object. Give practice in finding these objects by steps. Have the pupils pick out the skeleton first, then the direct object, and finally the indirect object. Emphasize

Another word that helps to complete the sentence skeleton is the *indirect object*. An indirect object is a noun or pronoun that comes between a verb and a direct object. It receives action *indirectly* by telling *to whom or what* or *for whom or what* an action is performed. Only a sentence with a direct object can have an indirect object. But many sentences with direct objects do not have indirect objects.

> Marvin <u>writes</u> neatly. (no direct object; no indirect object)
> Marvin <u>writes</u> interesting *letters*. (direct object—*letters;* no indirect object)
> Marvin <u>writes</u> his *friends* interesting *letters*. (direct object—*letters;* indirect object—*friends*)

To find an indirect object, say the skeleton and the direct object. Then ask *to whom or what* or *for whom or what*. Remember that an indirect object normally comes between the verb and the direct object.

> Carla gave the story her best effort.
> (Carla gave *what*? effort; *to what*? story.)
> Christ is preparing His people a heavenly home.
> (Christ is preparing *what*? home; *for whom*? people.)

When a sentence has both a direct object and an indirect object, take special care to first identify the direct object correctly. At first glance, you may decide that *story* and *people* are the direct objects in the examples above. But *story* does not name the thing that Carla gave. *People* does not name the ones Christ is preparing. These words do not answer the questions *whom* or *what*.

On a diagram, an indirect object is placed on a horizontal line below the skeleton, with a slanted line connecting it to the verb. The following examples show how to diagram the sentences above.

Any word that *completes* the sentence skeleton is called a *complement*. A complement that follows the verb and receives its action is an *object complement*. Direct objects and indirect objects are object complements.

the difference between the direct object questions and the indirect object questions. This should help students avoid labeling the indirect object as the direct object.)

c. An indirect object is diagramed on a horizontal line below the skeleton, with a slanted line connecting it to the verb.

3. Direct objects and indirect objects are called object complements. A complement is a word that completes the sentence skeleton.

★ *EXTRA PRACTICE*
Worksheet 1 (*Direct and Indirect Objects*)

Class Practice

A. Name the direct objects in these sentences. Watch for compound parts. Not every sentence has a direct object.
1. The rain was falling in torrents.
2. Father eyed the swollen creek soberly.
3. The creek was now a raging river.
4. We committed our lives and our farm to the Lord.
5. God promises wisdom and gives grace for trying times.

B. Find each object complement, and tell whether it is a *direct object* or an *indirect object*. Not every sentence has an indirect object.
1. The Lord gives His angels a charge.
2. God promises His grace and provides a way of escape.
3. Jonathan gave David his robe and his sword.
4. God sent manna for Israel in the wilderness.
5. Jael brought Sisera some milk.

C. On the chalkboard, diagram the skeletons and the object complements of the sentences in Part B.

Written Exercises

A. Copy the direct objects in these sentences. Watch for compound parts. If a sentence does not have a direct object, write *none.*
1. Dallas read every book on the list.
2. Mother is not feeling well.
3. The boys will wash the dishes this evening.
4. Floyd painted the picnic table, the benches, and the swings.
5. Brother Richard raises pigs and sheep.

B. Copy each object complement, and label it *DO* for direct object or *IO* for indirect object. There are fifteen direct objects and five indirect objects. (Not every sentence has an object.)
1. You should brush your teeth and wash your face every morning.
2. The men gave the porch a new floor.
3. The tour guide handed each person a brochure and a map.
4. Brother Myron's will provide us some help.
5. The children formed their letters and numbers carefully.
6. Sister Dorcas is walking across the lawn.
7. This car has given her some trouble.
8. Father can probably help her.
9. We put the toolbox, the booster cables, and the gas can into the pickup.
10. Father gave the car a quick inspection and found the problem.

C. Diagram the skeletons and the object complements of these sentences. Watch for compound parts.

Lesson 5 Answers

Class Practice

A. 1. (no direct object)
2. creek
3. (no direct object)
4. lives, farm
5. wisdom, grace

B. 1. angels—indirect object; charge—direct object
2. grace—direct object; way—direct object
3. David—indirect object; robe—direct object; sword—direct object
4. manna—direct object
5. Sisera—indirect object; milk—direct object

C. 1.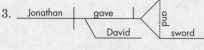
2.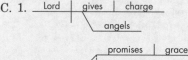
3.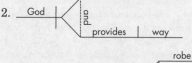
4.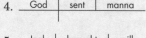
5. Jael | brought | milk / Sisera

Written Exercises

A. 1. book
2. none
3. dishes
4. (picnic) table, benches, swings
5. pigs, sheep

B. 1. teeth—DO; face—DO
2. porch—IO; floor—DO
3. person—IO; brochure—DO; map—DO
4. us—IO; help—DO
5. letters—DO; numbers—DO
6. (none)
7. her—IO; trouble—DO
8. her—DO
9. toolbox—DO; (booster) cables—DO; (gas) can—DO
10. car—IO; inspection—DO; problem—DO

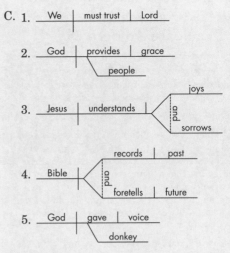

1. We must trust the Lord.
2. God provides His people the grace for faithful living.
3. Jesus understands our joys and our sorrows.
4. The Bible records the past and foretells the future.
5. God gave Balaam's donkey a voice.

Review Exercises

A. Label each item *S* for sentence, *F* for fragment, or *R* for run-on error. [2] (Turn to the lesson number in brackets if you need help.)
   1. Moses was adopted by Pharaoh's daughter.
   2. And was educated in the learning of the Egyptians.
   3. When Moses struck the rock.
   4. Water came gushing out, the people drank thirstily.
   5. Moses' arms grew tired Aaron and Hur held them up.
   6. Because the people had broken the commandments.
   7. Moses threw down the tables of stone and broke them.
   8. From Mount Pisgah, Moses viewed the good land.
   9. Which God had promised to the children of Israel.
   10. Moses died on Mount Pisgah, God buried him there.

B. These sentences have run-on errors and comma splices. Show how to correct them by writing the first word and the last word of each sentence, with three dots (. . .) between them. Use proper capitalization and end punctuation. [2]

   Example: I was reading about Roger Williams, he was a minister in New England.
   Answer: I. . . Williams. He. . . England.

   1. In 1636 Roger Williams founded a settlement in Rhode Island he offered freedom to people of any religion.
   2. Maryland also offered religious freedom the Act of Toleration in 1649 granted freedom to all who believed in Christ's deity.
   3. Pennsylvania was established by William Penn in 1682, it soon gained a reputation for religious freedom.
   4. In 1786 Virginia passed the Statute for Religious Freedom this law, which was proposed by Thomas Jefferson, provided complete freedom of religion.
   5. Several states had official churches, in 1833 Massachusetts became the last state to end this practice.

C.

Review Exercises

A. 1. S   6. F
   2. F   7. S
   3. F   8. S
   4. R   9. F
   5. R   10. R

B. 1. In . . . Island. He . . . religion.
   2. Maryland . . . freedom. The . . . deity.
   3. Pennsylvania . . . 1682. It . . . freedom.
   4. In . . . Freedom. This . . . religion.
   5. Several . . . churches. In . . . practice.

6. Predicate Nominatives and Predicate Adjectives

> **Lesson Survey**
> - A **predicate nominative** is a noun or pronoun that follows a linking verb and renames the subject.
> - A **predicate adjective** follows a linking verb and modifies the subject.
> - Predicate nominatives and predicate adjectives are **subjective complements.**

You have learned that in many sentences, additional words are needed to complete the meaning of the sentence skeleton. Many action verbs need complements, and linking verbs also require them. In former grades, you learned the following three groups of linking verbs.

Forms of *be*:
 am, is, are, was, were, be, been, being
Verbs of sense:
 taste, feel, smell, sound, look, appear
Other linking verbs:
 grow, seem, stay, become, remain

A *predicate nominative* is a noun or pronoun that follows a linking verb and renames the subject. It refers to the same person or thing as the subject. Sometimes a predicate nominative is compound.

The <u>Lord</u> is the true *God.*
 (*Lord* and *God* name the same person.)
This small <u>building</u> was our *church* and *school.*
 (*Building, church,* and *school* name the same thing.)

Since the subject and the predicate nominative name the same person or thing, the linking verb can be considered an equal sign. The subject equals the predicate nominative.

Lord = God
building = church and *school*

Usually the two nouns or pronouns can be exchanged and the sentence has the same meaning. The examples above can be rewritten to illustrate this.

The true <u>God</u> is the <u>Lord.</u>
Our <u>church</u> and <u>school</u> was this small <u>building.</u>

Lesson 6

Purpose: (1) To show that some sentence skeletons are completed by predicate nominatives and predicate adjectives. (2) To teach that predicate nominatives and predicate adjectives are *subjective complements.

Teacher: Direct and indirect objects are called *object* complements, but predicate nominatives and predicate adjectives are called *subjective* complements. These terms are used because there are actually six kinds of complements, as shown below.

Object complements: Complements that are objects
 Mr. Arnold built a <u>house.</u> (direct object)
 Mr. Arnold built <u>himself</u> a house. (indirect object)

Subjective complements: Complements that rename or modify subjects
 The house was his <u>home.</u> (predicate nominative)
 The house was <u>large.</u> (predicate adjective)

Objective complements: Complements that rename or modify objects
 He called the house his <u>castle.</u> (noun renaming the direct object)
 He painted the house <u>white.</u> (adjective modifying the direct object)

According to the pattern above, a subjective complement *relates* to a subject, and an objective complement *relates* to an object. An object complement *is* an object. But no complement *is* a subject; so the term *subject complement* is not used.

However, not all subjects and predicate nominatives are interchangeable. If the subject is specific and the predicate nominative is general, exchanging them often sounds awkward. It may also sound awkward if the verb is modified by a negative word. If the verb is *become,* exchanging the two will completely change the meaning and usually make a statement that is not true.

Saskatchewan is a province of Canada. (sensible)
A province of Canada is Saskatchewan. (awkward)

She was not a lazy girl. (sensible)
A lazy girl was not she. (awkward)

Jesus became the crucified Saviour. (sensible)
The crucified Saviour became Jesus. (meaning changed; untrue statement)

A *predicate adjective* follows a linking verb and modifies the subject. Predicate adjectives may also be compound. Since the predicate adjective modifies the subject, it is usually sensible to say the adjective before the subject.

The <u>manna</u> from heaven tasted *sweet.* (sweet manna)
This <u>box</u> is too *heavy* and *cumbersome.* (heavy, cumbersome box)

If the subject is a pronoun, saying the adjective before the subject may sound right only if the pronoun is replaced with its antecedent.

<u>I</u> felt *worried* until Father came.
   (*Worried I* does not sound right, but *worried person* does.)
<u>She</u> usually seems *contented.*
   (*Contented she* does not sound right, but *contented girl* does.)

Of course, a predicate nominative must be a noun or pronoun, and a predicate adjective must be an adjective. Sometimes other sentence parts follow the same verbs that may be linking verbs. Before you decide what sentence part a word is, test it carefully with the two questions below. The word is a predicate nominative or predicate adjective only if the answers to both questions are yes.

1. Is it truly a noun or pronoun that renames the subject, or an adjective that modifies the subject?
2. Does the verb express being instead of action?

The dessert was pie.
   (*Pie* is a noun that renames *dessert;* dessert = pie. *Was* expresses being. So *pie* is a predicate nominative.)
We tasted the pie.
   (*Pie* does not rename *we. Tasted* expresses action, not being. So

Oral Review:
1. What is a complement? (a word that completes the sentence skeleton)
2. Name the two kinds of object complements. (direct object, indirect object)
3. What kind of complement tells *to whom or what* or *for whom or what* an action is performed? (indirect object)
4. What kind of complement receives the action of a verb? (direct object)
5. What two parts make up a sentence skeleton? (simple subject, simple predicate)
6. Choose the correct verbs, as you learned in previous grades. (Correct verbs are underlined.)
   a. Someone's coat is (laying, <u>lying</u>) on the floor.
   b. The balloon (raised, <u>rose</u>) into the sky.
   c. That car has (set, <u>sat</u>) beside the road all week.
   d. Father (<u>let</u>, left) us go fishing yesterday.
   e. He said we (can, <u>may</u>) use his fishing rod.
   f. Father (<u>taught</u>, learned) me how to tie a bowline knot.

Lesson Introduction: Write the following sentences on the board.

God created the world in six days.
Man is the crown of God's creation.
Adam and Eve were happy in the Garden of Eden.

Have someone read the skeleton and the complement in the first sentence. Identify the complement as a direct object. Then see if someone can read the skeleton and the complement in the second sentence. Ask if this complement is also a direct object. How can they tell that it is not? (It does not follow an action verb; it does not receive action.) Do the same for the third sentence. Ask if someone can tell

pie is not a predicate nominative; it is a direct object.)
The pie tasted good.
>   (*Good* is an adjective that modifies *pie; good pie* is sensible. *Tasted*
>   expresses being. So *good* is a predicate adjective.)

The trumpet sounded loudly across the valley.
>   (*Loudly* does not modify *trumpet; loudly trumpet* is not sensible.
>   *Sounded* expresses action, not being. So *loudly* is not a pred-
>   icate adjective; it is an adverb.)

Your story sounds interesting.
>   (*Interesting* is an adjective that modifies *story; interesting story*
>   is sensible. *Sounds* expresses being. So *interesting* is a pred-
>   icate adjective.)

Like direct objects and indirect objects, predicate nominatives and predicate adjectives are *complements;* they complete sentence skeletons. Because
these complements refer directly to *subjects,* they are called *subjective com-*
plements.

A subjective complement is diagramed on the horizontal line after the
sentence skeleton, the same as a direct object. However, since a subjective
complement refers to the subject, the line separating it from the verb slants
back toward the subject.

David became the king of   David | became \ king
    all Israel.

The stars appear unusually   stars | appear \ bright
    bright tonight.

A compound predicate nominative or predicate adjective is diagramed
on a fork, the same as a compound direct object.

Jesus Christ is Lord and Saviour.

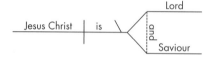

The cornfields looked green, lush, and fruitful.

what these complements are called. (predicate nominative, predicate adjective)

Lesson Outline:

> *1. A predicate nominative is a noun or pro-*
> *noun that follows a linking verb and renames*
> *the subject.* The predicate nominative refers to the
> same person or thing as the subject.

>   a. The linking verb acts like an equal sign be-
>   tween the subject and the predicate nom-
>   inative.

>   b. Usually the subject and the predicate nom-
>   inative can be exchanged, and the sentence
>   means the same. But this may not work if
>   the subject is specific and the predicate nom-
>   inative is general, if the verb is modified by
>   a negative word, or if the verb is *become.*

> *2. A predicate adjective follows a linking*

> *verb and modifies the subject.* It is usually sen-
> sible to say the predicate adjective before the sub-
> ject. But if the subject is a pronoun, saying the
> adjective before the subject may sound right only if
> the pronoun is replaced with its antecedent.

> *3. Predicate nominatives and predicate ad-*
> *jectives are called subjective complements.*

> *4. A subjective complement is diagramed on*
> *the horizontal line after the skeleton.* Since it
> refers to the subject, the line separating it from the
> verb slants toward the subject. A compound predi-
> cate nominative or predicate adjective is diagramed
> on a fork, the same as a compound direct object.

★ *EXTRA PRACTICE*
>   Worksheet 2 (*Predicate Nominatives and*
>   *Predicate Adjectives*)

Class Practice

A. Name the predicate nominatives in these sentences. Identify each as a *noun* or a *pronoun*.
1. Jesus has become the Saviour of the world.
2. A man of sorrows was He.
3. He has always been a faithful friend to the penitent.
4. Judas had been Jesus' disciple.
5. He became a thief and a traitor.

B. Name the predicate adjectives in these sentences.
1. You must be creative and diligent to write good poems.
2. Uncle Clarence is feeble with age.
3. These biscuits taste delicious.
4. The hay in the mow was old and musty.
5. Our dog seems afraid of thunderstorms.

C. Name the subjective complements in these sentences. Identify each as a *predicate nominative* or a *predicate adjective*. (Some sentences have none.)
1. The fruit looked pleasant and desirable to Eve.
2. Eve tasted the forbidden fruit.
3. Satan has been a liar from the beginning.
4. Adam and Eve did not become gods.
5. The Bible will forever remain God's Word.
6. Your circumstances may seem completely hopeless.
7. But the promises of God should be our inspiration.
8. Brother Lynn sounded a clear warning from God's Word.
9. The pages in Grandfather's Bible are brown and brittle with age.
10. His Bible is in the bookcase in his room.

D. On the chalkboard, diagram the skeletons and complements of the sentences in Parts A and B.

Written Exercises

A. Copy the subjective complements in these sentences. Write *PN* after each predicate nominative and *PA* after each predicate adjective. If a sentence has no subjective complement, write *none*.
1. The orbit of a planet is an ellipse.
2. The largest planets are Jupiter and Saturn.
3. George seems perplexed with his math problem.
4. You should be kind and merciful to others.
5. The singing should sound melodious with so many voices.
6. The engineer should sound his whistle at each crossing.

Written Exercises
A. 1. ellipse—PN
   2. Jupiter—PN; Saturn—PN
   3. perplexed—PA
   4. kind—PA; merciful—PA
   5. melodious—PA
   6. none

Lesson 6 Answers

Class Practice
A. 1. Saviour—noun
   2. He—pronoun
   3. friend—noun
   4. disciple—noun
   5. thief—noun; traitor—noun

B. 1. creative, diligent
   2. feeble
   3. delicious
   4. old, musty
   5. afraid

C. 1. pleasant—predicate adjective; desirable—predicate adjective
   2. (none)
   3. liar—predicate nominative
   4. gods—predicate nominative
   5. Word—predicate nominative
   6. hopeless—predicate adjective
   7. inspiration—predicate nominative
   8. (none)
   9. brown—predicate adjective; brittle—predicate adjective
   10. (none)

D. (Sentences from Part A.)

1. Jesus | has become \ Saviour

2. man | was \ He

3. He | has been \ friend

4. Judas | had been \ disciple

5.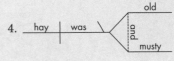
He | became \ thief and traitor

(Sentences from Part B.)

1.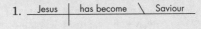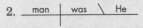
You | must be \ creative and diligent

2. Uncle Clarence | is \ feeble

3. biscuits | taste \ delicious

4.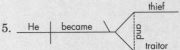
hay | was \ old and musty

5. dog | seems \ afraid

7. The children have not been careful with the paint.
8. The first arrivals have usually been they.
9. Brother Clair will be the substitute teacher.
10. The plane will appear at any moment.
11. A tropical forest is warm and moist.
12. Jungle growth becomes dense and tangled.
13. A desert may appear lifeless.
14. Yet a cactus may be the home of several animals.
15. A high mountaintop may remain a frozen wilderness all year.
16. They were natural barriers to man's movement.
17. The Great Plains was a vast grassland.
18. This region has become an important agricultural and industrial area.

B. Diagram the skeletons and the complements of these sentences.
1. Gideon was a brave leader and judge of Israel.
2. Samson was not strong in overcoming temptation.
3. Ehud was quite clever.
4. Some lesser known judges were Tola and Jair.
5. Samuel was a judge, prophet, and priest.

Review Exercises

Write the correct verbs in parentheses, as you learned in previous grades.
1. Did your mother (teach, learn) you to bake bread?
2. The baby is (laying, lying) in the crib.
3. The red ball of the sun (raised, rose) into the hazy sky.
4. Did Sister Helen say that we (can, may) eat outside?
5. Please (set, sit) the egg crate down carefully.
6. God (raised, rose) Jesus from the dead.
7. The masons (laid, lay) the blocks yesterday morning.
8. After arriving in Mexico, Marla (taught, learned) Spanish quickly.
9. Did Aunt Sue (let, leave) you look at her scrapbook?
10. Brother David was (setting, sitting) beside Brother Ira.
11. Charlene said that she (can, may) draw horses fairly well.
12. Yesterday the sick calf just (laid, lay) around.
13. The students (set, sat) in respectful silence.
14. The paintings had (laid, lain) in the artist's basement.
15. With relief, we (let, left) the swamp behind.
16. The smoke from the pioneers' campfire was (raising, rising) into the morning air.
17. Marie (can, may) choose the menu for dinner.
18. (Let, Leave) Loretta help with the project.

7. careful—PA
8. they—PN
9. teacher—PN
10. none
11. warm—PA; moist—PA
12. dense—PA; tangled—PA
13. lifeless—PA
14. home—PN
15. wilderness—PN
16. barriers—PN
17. grassland—PN
18. area—PN

B. 1.

2.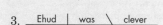

3. Ehud | was \ clever

4.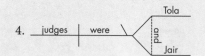

5.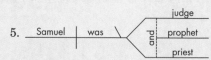

Review Exercises

1. teach
2. lying
3. rose
4. may
5. set
6. raised
7. laid
8. learned
9. let
10. sitting
11. can
12. lay
13. sat
14. lain
15. left
16. rising
17. may
18. Let

19. Curvin (taught, learned) me a new song.
20. Father has (let, left) me drive the new tractor before.

19. taught
20. let

---

7. Nouns of Direct Address and Nouns Used as Appositives

> **Lesson Survey**
> - A **noun of direct address** names the person or thing to whom one is speaking.
> - An **appositive** is a noun or pronoun that immediately follows another noun or pronoun to identify or explain it.

Sometimes you greet a person by name or use his name to get his attention. When you *directly address* someone in this way, you are using a *noun of direct address*. The noun may be either a name or a title.

Thomas, do we have any gasoline on hand? (name of person)
Star, you are quite a handsome colt! (name of animal)
Mister, please come inside and enjoy the service. (title)

A noun of direct address is never the subject of a sentence. Look again at the examples above. Their skeletons are diagramed here.

You will be most likely to mistake a noun of direct address as the subject when the subject is *you* understood.

Gerald, feed the calves now.
Betty, clear the table quickly.

You can show in several ways that *Gerald* and *Betty* are not the subjects. First, the sentences are still complete even if you remove these names. Second, if you pair the names with the verbs as the sentence skeletons, they do not sound right. *Gerald feed* and *Betty clear* are not sensible skeletons. You would need to say *Gerald feeds* and *Betty clears*.

Lesson 7

Purpose: (1) To teach nouns of direct address and nouns used as appositives. (2) To show *how these nouns are related to the rest of the sentence.

Oral Review:
1. Name the two kinds of subjective complements. (predicate nominative, predicate adjective)
2. How is a subjective complement diagramed differently than a direct object? (A direct object is placed after a vertical line, but a subjective complement is placed after a line that slants toward the subject.)
3. What kind of object complement tells *to whom or what* or *for whom or what* an action is performed? (indirect object)
4. Where is an indirect object normally found in a sentence? (between the verb and the direct object)

5. Choose the correct words, as you learned in previous grades.
   a. Resisting temptation is up to you and (I, me) individually.
   b. (We, Us) older ones are an influence on younger children.
   c. The man in charge is (he, him).
   d. Little Jason has been walking (good, well) for several weeks.
   e. Of the two men, Grandfather is (older, oldest).
   f. Let's go (in, into) the house and warm up.
   g. We parked the car (between, among) two vans.

Lesson Introduction: When we speak to someone, we may address him by name. Sometimes this is done out of respect.

Father, may we go out to the tree house now?

Sometimes we need to address a person in order to get his attention.

A noun of direct address may be modified by a word, a phrase, or even a clause. Then the whole unit is considered a noun of direct address. In the following examples, the nouns of direct address are underlined. (Note that the main "noun" of direct address may actually be a pronoun like *you* or *ye*.)

"Good Master, what shall I do to inherit eternal life?"
"Ye men of Israel, hear these words."
"Ye that fear the Lord, trust in the Lord."

A noun of direct address must be set off from the rest of the sentence. If it is at the beginning or end of the sentence, use one comma. If it is in the middle, use two commas.

Brother Leon, do you know where we are going on our hike?
Do you know where we are going on our hike, Brother Leon?
Do you know, Brother Leon, where we are going on our hike?

A noun of direct address is diagramed on a separate line to the left of the main base line. If modifiers are included, place them in their usual position under the noun.

Rover, did you catch another woodchuck?

Do your work carefully, young man.

My dear little girl, are you lost?

An *appositive* is a noun or pronoun that immediately follows another noun or pronoun to identify or explain it. It may follow a noun or pronoun in any part of the sentence. If the noun or pronoun is modified by one-word adjectives or adjective phrases, the whole unit is called an appositive.

The prophet Nathan warned David of Adonijah's scheme.
   (appositive to a subject)

Susan, did you hear what Cheryl just said?

A public speaker may address his audience to communicate a sense of urgency.

We must heed the Scriptures, my dear brethren.

Parents may also use direct address to communicate a sense of urgency or of deep interest.

Now, James, that was completely out of place.
We are interested, Joy, in seeing you develop good habits.

Nouns of direct address are used in all these examples.

Lesson Outline:

1. A noun of direct address names the person or thing to whom one is speaking. Such a noun is used to *direct*ly *address* someone.

a. A noun of direct address is never the subject of a sentence. Special care is needed when the subject is *you* understood.

b. A noun of direct address must be set off from the rest of the sentence with one or two commas.

c. A noun of direct address is diagramed on a separate line to the left of the main base line. If the noun is modified by adjectives, place them in their usual position under the noun.

2. An appositive is a noun or pronoun that immediately follows another noun or pronoun to identify or explain it.

a. An appositive may follow a noun or pronoun in any part of the sentence.

b. If the noun or pronoun has modifiers, the whole unit is called an appositive.

The next king would be Solomon, the wisest man.
    (appositive to a predicate nominative)
King David called Zadok, the priest of the Lord.
    (appositive to a direct object)
David gave his son Solomon the right to the throne.
    (appositive to an indirect object)
Zadok anointed Solomon at Gihon, a spring near Jerusalem.
    (appositive to the object of a preposition)

If an appositive includes two or more words, it is usually set off with commas. The commas may be omitted if the appositive is a single word that is closely related to the preceding word. Notice the commas that set off the appositives in the second, third, and fifth examples above. The first and fourth sentences have no commas because each appositive is a single word that is closely related to the word it follows.

An appositive is diagrammed in parentheses after the noun or pronoun that it explains.

Paul, a faithful apostle, preached Christ, the Saviour of mankind.

This is my brother Leroy.

Class Practice

A. Give the nouns of direct address and the subjects in these sentences.
   1. Mother, the clothes are dry now.
   2. Do you have some tape, Sister Minerva, for this torn page?
   3. Girls, clean the upstairs this morning.

B. Read each appositive, and tell what word it explains.
   1. Alfonso, a visitor from Guatemala, will be here for two months.
   2. We visited my uncle Levi.
   3. Give the goats, Susie and Molly, their hay.

C. Tell where commas are needed in each sentence, and whether they set off a *noun of direct address* or an *appositive*.
   1. Son work in my vineyard today.
   2. Jesus endured the cross a symbol of shame and glorified it my friend.

    c. If an appositive includes two or more words, it is usually set off with commas. The commas may be omitted if the appositive is a single word that is closely related to the preceding word.
    d. An appositive is diagrammed in parentheses after the noun or pronoun that it explains.

★ *EXTRA PRACTICE*
    Worksheet 3 (*Appositives and Nouns of Direct Address*)

3. David the sweet psalmist of Israel spent much time with the sheep.

D. On the chalkboard, diagram the skeletons, complements, appositives, and nouns of direct address in the sentences in Part C. Remember to include all the modifiers that go with an appositive or a noun of direct address.

Written Exercises

A. Write the nouns of direct address and the subjects in these sentences. Identify each one by writing *D* or *S* after it. If a subject is *you* understood, put parentheses around it.
   1. You are blessed of the Lord, Abigail, for your sound advice.
   2. Nancy, read 1 John 3:1.
   3. We need all the help available, my friend.
   4. "Get thee behind me, Satan."
   5. My son, I have already blessed Jacob.

B. Copy each appositive and the noun that it explains.
   1. My teacher, Brother Harold, told us an interesting story.
   2. Many people moved to North America, a haven of freedom.
   3. Our aunt Mabel gave us a bicycle.
   4. The lady in that car is Annette Zimmerman, our neighbor.
   5. Portugal, a small European country, sent the first sailors around Africa, the dark continent.

C. Write *A* or *D* to tell whether each sentence contains an appositive or a noun of direct address. Then copy each word that should be followed by a comma, and add the comma.
   1. Eli the priest of the Lord was an old man.
   2. Eli did you call me?
   3. You must listen Samuel for the Lord's voice.
   4. Jesus appeared to Saul a zealous Pharisee.
   5. Saul of Tarsus is praying Ananias.

D. Diagram the skeletons, complements, appositives, and nouns of direct address. Remember to include all the modifiers that go with an appositive or a noun of direct address.
   1. This Book, the Bible, reveals the nature of God.
   2. Daughters of Jerusalem, do not weep for me.
   3. Hear, heavenly Father, our prayer.
   4. Psalm 23, the Shepherd Psalm, is one of the most familiar psalms.
   5. Ahab hated Micaiah, a faithful prophet of God.

Review Exercises

These exercises review things that you studied in previous grades. Use the index in the back of this book if you need help.

3. David, Israel,—appositive

D. 1.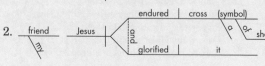

2.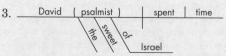

3.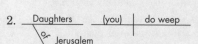

Written Exercises

A. 1. You—S; Abigail—D
   2. Nancy—D; (you)—S
   3. We—S; my friend—D
   4. (you)—S; Satan—D
   5. My son—D; I—S

B. 1. Brother Harold, teacher
   2. a haven of freedom, North America
   3. Mabel, aunt
   4. our neighbor, Annette Zimmerman
   5. a small European country, Portugal; the dark continent, Africa

C. 1. A; Eli, Lord,   4. A; Saul,
   2. D; Eli,   5. D; praying,
   3. D; listen, Samuel,

D. 1.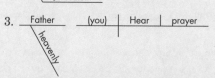

2.

3.

4.

5.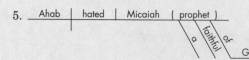

A. Each sentence contains one mistake in pronoun usage. Write the correct form of the pronoun in error.
1. Harriet and her are doing their chores.
2. Us older students are making a surprise for Sister Erma and them.
3. This book belongs to him; the rest are our's.
4. He is just the person who I need right now.
5. The one who helped us children is him.
6. We boys saw a robin sitting on it's nest.

B. Each sentence contains one mistake in adjective or adverb usage. Write the correct word to replace the modifier in error. If the mistake is an unnecessary word, copy that word and draw a line through it.
1. Linford does good at drawing pictures.
2. Them apple trees produce delicious apples.
3. Duke is the baddest little puppy I ever saw.
4. Of the two storms, the second one was worst.
5. Kenneth is the most fastest runner in our class.
6. Stephen didn't bring no lunch today.

C. Each sentence contains one mistake in preposition usage. Write the correct word to replace the preposition in error. If the mistake is an unnecessary word, copy that word and draw a line through it.
1. Myron left the playground and went in the schoolhouse for a drink.
2. Father fell off of the ladder while he was putting on siding.
3. While we were inside of the cave, the lights went off for a short time.
4. Mother said that we may divide the cookies between us four boys.
5. All of the family accept Edwin will go and visit Aunt Hetty.
6. The boy sitting besides Eugene is my cousin from Manitoba.

Review Exercises

A.
1.	she	4.	whom
2.	We	5.	he
3.	ours	6.	its

B.
1.	well	4.	worse
2.	Those	5.	~~most~~
3.	worst	6.	any

C.
1.	into	4.	among
2.	~~of~~	5.	except
3.	~~of~~	6.	beside

8. Proofreading Your Writing

> **Lesson Survey**
> - Proofreading a composition includes the following things.
>   1. Checking for mistakes in spelling, capitalization, punctuation, and grammar.
>   2. Deleting unnecessary material.
>   3. Checking for missing words.
>   4. Correcting any transpositions.
>   5. Dividing the composition properly into paragraphs.

Lesson 8

Purpose: To introduce *proofreading marks.

Oral Review:
1. Should a character sketch emphasize one or several characteristics of an individual? (one)
2. What are some good ways to introduce a character sketch? (You may place the person in a setting that either reflects or contrasts the characteristic to be emphasized. You may give a first impression, followed by a description of how different the person is when one learns to know him better.)
3. What are some ways to *show* rather than merely *tell* about a person's character? (Have the person speak and act. Use specific words and picturesque language.)
4. List the basic steps involved in planning a report.
   (a. Choose a suitable topic.
   b. Take notes from several sources.
   c. Make a brief outline.)
5. Give some rules of good outline form.
   (a. Use Roman numerals for topics, capital letters for subtopics, and Arabic numerals for points. Place a period after each numeral or letter.
   b. Have at least two items in each group—no A without a B, no 1 without a 2, and so on.
   c. Make all the items in each group as nearly parallel as possible.
   d. Indent each subtopic and each point.)

Lesson Introduction: A mechanic test-drives a car before telling the customer that it is ready to go. A brick layer occasionally stands back and eyes the wall he is building. A seamstress tries on a dress several times as she makes it. A cook, before sliding a

Very few good writers, if any, produce their best compositions without proofreading and rewriting. In fact, many professional writers admit that they rewrite their stories and articles many times before they are satisfied. As a beginning writer, you should never omit this important step on the road to effective writing.

Careful proofreading takes time. Do not try to proofread a composition right after you have written it. Put it aside, and do something else for a while. When you come back to it later, you will be able to catch mistakes more easily. Also, do not try to find all the weaknesses in your composition at one time. Read through it several times, concentrating on only one or two things each time. The following paragraphs tell about specific things to look for.

1. *Check for mistakes in spelling, capitalization, punctuation, and grammar.* Cross out a wrong letter or word, and write the correction above it. A caret (∧) may be used to show where something is inserted.

Pay close attention to spelling mistakes that you know you often make. Double-check the *ei* and *ie* spellings. Make sure you have the right choice of homonyms like *their—there—they're, its—it's,* and *whose—who's.* Use a dictionary freely to check any word about which you are not sure.

If you know that you frequently make a certain mistake in grammar, be sure to check for that error. Make sure that your subjects and verbs agree, especially when a prepositional phrase comes between the subject and the verb, when the verb or part of the verb precedes the subject, and when there is a compound subject.

> The <u>dish</u> of potatoes ~~were~~ *was* <u>steaming</u> pleasantly on the table.
>
> There ~~is~~ *are* many <u>occasions</u> to test our honesty.
>
> Either <u>discontentment</u> or <u>covetousness</u> <u>make</u>*s* a person unthankful.

Be sure that the pronouns agree with their antecedents.

> Every <u>child</u> said ~~their~~ *his* Bible verses correctly.
>
> All <u>students</u> are to provide ~~your~~ *their* own paper.

Do not shift verb tenses unnecessarily.

> As the boys <u>lined</u> up at the door John suddenly <u>shout</u>*ed*~~s~~, "Look at the deer in Brother Ray's field!"

2. *Delete unnecessary material.* Show a deletion by drawing a neat line through the words that you want to remove. Watch especially for the following unnecessary items.

cake into the oven, double-checks to be sure that she missed none of the ingredients. And a good writer proofreads his story before he is satisfied that he has done his best. Each of these is interested in a job well done, a worthwhile finished product. Each of them puts time and thought into evaluating his own work.

Lesson Outline:

Proofreading a composition includes a number of things.

(1) *Check for mistakes in spelling, capitalization, punctuation, and grammar.* Cross out a wrong letter or word, and write the correction above it. A caret (∧) may be used to show where something is inserted.

(2) *Delete unnecessary material.* A deletion can be marked by drawing a neat line through the words to be removed.

(a) Watch for unnecessary adjectives and adverbs.

(b) Be alert for repetitious words and phrases.

(c) Check for ideas that do not contribute to the theme of the composition.

(3) *Check for missing words in the composition.* Use a caret to show where those words should be inserted.

(4) *Correct any transpositions.* Mark transposed letters, words, phrases, or clauses to show the correct order.

(5) *Be sure the composition is properly divided into paragraphs.* The symbol ¶ is used to show where a new paragraph should start.

a) In conversation, paragraph divisions are marked by changes in speakers.

a. Adjectives and adverbs that are more distracting than meaningful.

> The three ~~soft, yellow, playful,~~ fluffy kittens purred softly. (The deleted words are distracting. One or two adjectives are enough in a sentence like this.)

> Father read from the Bible ~~clearly, carefully, and~~ distinctly. (The deleted adverbs add little meaning.)

b. Repetitious words and phrases.

> Balaam persisted stubbornly ~~and obstinately~~ on his way. (*Stubbornly* and *obstinately* are synonyms.)

> The ~~light of the~~ full moon softly illuminated the ~~night~~ scene of deer feeding in the cornfield. (If something illuminates, it must be a light. If the full moon is shining, it is night.)

c. Ideas that do not contribute to the theme of the composition.

> Everything seemed to be going wrong that morning. Sherrie must have forgotten to set her alarm, so we had to wait for her at breakfast time. Just after we had prayed, the electricity went off. Father went to check that out while Mother served the oatmeal. ~~We usually have oatmeal or eggs for breakfast.~~
>
> (The deleted sentence does not contribute to the theme of everything seeming to go wrong.)

3. *Check for missing words in the composition.* Use a caret to show where those words should be inserted.

> "I noticed our thermometer showed thirty-five degrees," Father commented. "This light rain might might ^*be* freezing on Eagle Mountain."
>
> "It's good that we left in plenty of time then," Mother said.
>
> I shivered as I thought of the steep ^*climb* up the mountain. The road from Oakdale to Eagleton had one sharp curve after another.

b) In other writing, paragraph divisions should generally be parallel to the divisions on the outline.

NOTE: It would be good to make copies of the original stories in Class Practice and in Written Exercises to give to the students.

★ **EXTRA PRACTICE**
Worksheet 4 (*Proofreading a Story*)

4. *Correct any transpositions.* A transposition is two letters or words that are transposed; that is, they are switched from their correct order. Sometimes two phrases or clauses are transposed, resulting in an awkward or absurd sentence. The following sentences illustrate the symbol to use for marking transpositions.

I beli*ei*ve it is starting to snow!

Had I known ⌐would ⌐what⌐ happen, I would never have gone.

The box ⌐puzzled us students⌐ that the teacher put on her desk⌐.

5. *Be sure the composition is properly divided into paragraphs.* Remember that a paragraph is a unit of thought. If a story is carried mainly by conversation, these divisions are simply marked by the changes in speakers. Otherwise, a new paragraph should begin each time the topic shifts to a different main idea. The symbol ¶ is used to show where a new paragraph should start.

"Look at that snow coming down!" Joanna called. "I hope it snows like this all day."¶"I hope it snows three feet," Claire added.

Of course, these symbols are to be used for marking corrections on your first draft as you proofread. Before you hand in a finished paper, recopy the paper neatly, making the changes you marked.

Class Practice

Proofread this story, going over the items discussed in this lesson one or two at a time.

At dismisal time, Lois Ann stacked her books on top of her desk with unfinished assinements.

"You cleaning out your desk again?" asked Martha. "Your always so neat."

Lois Ann graoned. "No; I'm just to decide what I must take home and what I can finish tomorrow morning before our first class period."

"You have all that homework!" Eva's face shows the

Lesson 8 Answers

Class Practice

(Corrections are marked.)

At dismi*s*al time, Lois Ann stacked her books ⌐on top of her desk⌐ with unfinished assin*g*ements⌐

"*Are y*"~~You~~ cleaning out your desk again?" asked Martha. "*You're*~~Your~~ always so neat."

Lois Ann gra*o*ned. "No; I'm just *trying* to decide what I must take home and what I can finish tomorrow morning before our first class period."

"You have all that homework!" Eva's face show*ed*s

pity they felt. It pricked Lois Ann's concience. She did deserve any pity.

Hilda surveyed the stack to. "Getting a might lazy, huh?" She laughed as if it were very funny. Lois Ann fumbled in her desk, pretending she had not hear.

Written Exercises

A. Copy these paragraphs as they are. Proofread them, using the proper proofreading marks. You should find fourteen mistakes.

On the summer morning of August 3, I awoke early before the sun was up. My first thout was, "Today we're leaving for Mexico!" We had gone to Mexico several years ago too.

After reading a chapter from the Bible and asking God's direction for the day, I stepped out into the hall. To my surprise, no one else were up. "Father! Mother!" I called. "Aren't leaving soon? Its nearly five-thirty all ready!" "You'd better check your clock again," Father repleid from the bedroom. "Your ahead of schedule this morning."

How could I have misread it—2:27! The numbers glow clearly and distinctly on the nightstand from my digital clock. I crawled back into bed, smiling in spite of myself. I guess I was just a little to anxious to get started on our trip.

B. Proofread the character sketch that you wrote for Lesson 4.

---

9. Chapter 1 Review

Class Practice

A. Answer the following questions about sentences.
1. What is a sentence?
2. What two parts must every sentence have?

Lesson 9

Purpose: To review the material taught in Chapter 1.

NOTE: It would be good to make copies of the original stories in Class Practice and in Written Exercises to give to the students.

---

the pity ~~they~~ *she* felt. It pricked Lois Ann's concience^s. She did *not* deserve any pity.

Hilda surveyed the stack to^o. "Getting a ~~might~~ *mite* lazy, huh?" She laughed as if it were very funny. Lois Ann fumbled in her desk, pretending she had not hear^d.

Written Exercises

A. (Corrections are marked; accept reasonable variations. Check for the correct use of proofreading marks.)

On the ~~summer~~ morning of August 3, I awoke ~~early~~ before the sun was up. My first thou^ght was, "Today we're leaving for Mexico!" ~~We had gone to Mexico several years ago too.~~

After reading a chapter from the Bible and asking God's direction for the day, I stepped out into the hall. To my surprise, no one else ~~were~~ *was* up. "Father! Mother!" I called. "Aren't *we* leaving soon? Its nearly five-thirty *already* ~~all ready~~!" ¶ "You'd better check your clock again," Father reple^id from the bedroom. "~~Your~~ *You're* ahead of schedule this morning."

How could I have misread it—2:27! The numbers glow^ed clearly ~~and distinctly~~ on the nightstand from my digital clock. I crawled back into bed, smiling in spite of myself. I guess I was just a little to^o anxious to get started on our trip.

B. (Individual work.)

Lesson 9 Answers

Class Practice

A. 1. a group of words that expresses a complete thought
2. subject, predicate

3. Can a group of words have these two parts and still be a fragment?
4. What is a run-on error?

B. Identify each word group as a *sentence*, a *fragment*, or a *run-on error*.
1. A young cub walks in circles.
2. It has strong front legs, its back legs are weak and wobbly.
3. Which it drags along behind.
4. This is a good thing, for his hibernating mother would not see him walk away.
5. An older cub may wander away he cries and whines for his mother.

C. Do these exercises about sentence parts.
1. What does the subject of a sentence tell?
2. What two parts of speech can be used for a simple subject?
3. What does the predicate tell about a sentence?
4. What part of speech is the simple predicate?
5. What is a sentence skeleton?
6. What is a complement?
7. Name the two kinds of object complements.
8. Name the two kinds of subjective complements.
9. What questions does a direct object answer?
10. What questions does an indirect object answer?
11. Where will an indirect object normally be found?
12. A subjective complement always follows what kind of verb?
13. What does a predicate nominative do?
14. What does a predicate adjective do?
15. What is a noun of direct address?
16. What is an appositive?

D. Read the sentence skeletons. Give the last word in the complete subject.
1. The lettuce in the garden is green and crisp.
2. We have been having delicious salads.
3. The Green Valley Community Cookbook includes several recipes for salad dressing.
4. Uncle Earl and Aunt Sally eat their salads without any dressing.
5. Some of the mothers diced cheese and sliced hard-boiled eggs into their salads.

E. Give the object complements, and identify each one as a *direct object* or *indirect object*.
1. God gave Solomon wisdom and riches.
2. Make me a little cake first.
3. We must give willingly to the Lord.

3. yes
4. two or more sentences run together as one

B. 1. sentence   4. sentence
   2. run-on error   5. run-on error
   3. fragment

C. 1. *who* or *what* the sentence is about
   2. noun, pronoun
   3. what the subject does or is
   4. verb
   5. the simple subject and the simple predicate
   6. a word that completes a sentence skeleton
   7. direct object, indirect object
   8. predicate nominative, predicate adjective
   9. *whom* or *what* about the sentence skeleton
   10. *to whom or what* or *for whom or what*
   11. between the verb and the direct object
   12. linking verb
   13. renames the subject
   14. modifies the subject
   15. a name or title that names the person or thing to whom one is speaking
   16. a noun or pronoun that immediately follows another noun or pronoun to identify or explain it

D. 1. lettuce is; garden
   2. We have been having; We
   3. Green Valley Community Cookbook includes; Cookbook
   4. Uncle Earl (and) Aunt Sally eat; Sally
   5. Some diced (and) sliced; mothers

E. 1. Solomon—indirect object;
      wisdom—direct object;
      riches—direct object
   2. me—indirect object; cake—direct object
   3. (none)

4. We must follow the Lord and serve Him always.
5. Give God the glory due unto His Name.

F. Give the subjective complements, and identify each one as a *predicate nominative* or *predicate adjective*.
   1. A red fox's fur may be silver or black.
   2. He is the farmer's friend and enemy.
   3. He is valuable for catching mice and rats.
   4. He also eats chickens, turkeys, and eggs.
   5. He remains an elusive creature.

G. Give the nouns of direct address and the appositives, including any modifiers that go with them. Tell where the commas should be added.
   1. "Why are ye fearful O ye of little faith?"
   2. "Son of David have mercy on us."
   3. Lazarus the poor beggar lay at the rich man's gate.
   4. Nathanael we have found the Messiah Jesus of Nazareth.
   5. Simon the son of Jonas became Jesus' disciple.

H. On the chalkboard, diagram the skeletons and complements, along with any appositive or noun of direct address.
   1. Gary, have you ever seen an otter?
   2. The river otter, a playful creature, is an excellent swimmer and diver.
   3. It plays games and hunts food in the water.
   4. A newborn otter is very tiny.
   5. A mother otter gives her babies swimming lessons.

I. Do these exercises on character sketches and proofreading.
   1. What is the purpose of a character sketch?
   2. What are the five steps in writing a character sketch?
   3. Give the five points of proofreading that you studied in this chapter.
   4. Describe or illustrate the proofreading marks that should be used to show corrections in this paragraph.

> The day broak cold and cloudy. The tempature was only twenty degrees wen I came in for braekfast. By 11:00, snow swirling. The wind was gusting up to fifty miles hour. "By the looks of this whether, prayer meeting will be canceled tonite," Father observed. "Indeed, if it doesn't soon let up, we'll be snowed in by evening," Mother ansered.

4. (Corrections are marked.)

> The day ~~broak~~ ^broke^ cold and cloudy. The tem-pature ^er^ was only twenty degrees w^h^en I came in for breakfast. By 11:00, snow ^was^ swirling. The wind was gusting up to fifty miles ^per^ hour. "By the looks of this ~~whether~~ ^weather^, prayer meeting will be can-celed ~~tonite~~ ^tonight^," Father observed. ¶"Indeed, if it doesn't soon let up, we'll be snowed in by evening," Mother ans^w^ered.

4. Lord—direct object; Him—direct object
5. God—indirect object; glory—direct object

F. 1. silver—predicate adjective;
      black—predicate adjective
   2. friend—predicate nominative;
      enemy—predicate nominative
   3. valuable—predicate adjective
   4. (none)
   5. creature—predicate nominative

G. 1. O ye of little faith—noun of direct address;
      fearful,
   2. Son of David—noun of direct address; David,
   3. the poor beggar—appositive; Lazarus, beggar,
   4. Nathanael—noun of direct address; Nathanael,
      Jesus of Nazareth—appositive; Messiah,
   5. the son of Jonas—appositive; Simon, Jonas,

H.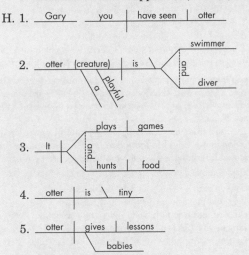

I. 1. to describe one outstanding characteristic of an individual
   2. a. Decide whom you will write about and what characteristic you will emphasize.
      b. List a number of events or examples that illustrate the characteristic you want to emphasize.
      c. Write an introduction for your character sketch.
      d. Write the body of your character sketch.
      e. Write the conclusion of your character sketch.
   3. a. Check for mistakes in spelling, capitalization, punctuation, and grammar.
      b. Delete unnecessary material.
      c. Check for missing words.
      d. Correct any transpositions.
      e. Be sure the composition is properly divided into paragraphs.

Written Exercises

A. Write the name of the sentence part that fits each description.
   1. Tells *to whom or what* or *for whom or what* an action is performed.
   2. A group of words that expresses a complete thought.
   3. A noun or pronoun that follows a linking verb and renames the subject.
   4. A word that names the person or thing to whom one is speaking.
   5. A group of words that does not express a complete thought.
   6. An adjective that follows a linking verb and modifies the subject.
   7. Two or more sentences written incorrectly as one.
   8. Tells what the subject does or is.
   9. A noun or pronoun that immediately follows another noun or pronoun to identify or explain it.
   10. Tells *who* or *what* the sentence is about.
   11. Consists of the simple subject and the simple predicate.
   12. Any word that completes the sentence skeleton.
   13. May be a predicate nominative or a predicate adjective.
   14. Receives the action of a verb.
   15. May be a direct object or an indirect object.

B. Label each item *S* for sentence, *F* for fragment, or *R* for run-on error.
   1. The Old Testament saints loved Jerusalem.
   2. The city of the great King.
   3. Although they might be scattered abroad.
   4. The Jews loved and longed for Jerusalem, the temple was there.
   5. Jewish religious and political life centered on this important city.

C. The following paragraph is not divided into sentences. Show how to correct it by writing the first word and the last word of each sentence, with three dots (...) between them. Use proper capitalization and end punctuation.

   Through the classroom window we could hear excited voices the younger students had found a duck's nest in the nest were five large eggs that afternoon we saw the mother duck on the nest.

D. Copy the direct and indirect objects, and label each one *DO* or *IO*.
   1. Sister Erma will help us with the work today.
   2. We must pick the beans and mow the lawn.
   3. Clifford and Kenneth should give the horses some water.
   4. Maggie may find the baby some toys.
   5. Call Mary Ann and Anna Marie out to the garden.

E. Copy the predicate nominatives and predicate adjectives, and label each one *PN* or *PA*.

Written Exercises
A.   1. indirect object
     2. sentence
     3. predicate nominative
     4. noun of direct address
     5. fragment
     6. predicate adjective
     7. run-on error
     8. predicate
     9. appositive
    10. subject
    11. sentence skeleton
    12. complement
    13. subjective complement
    14. direct object
    15. object complement

B. 1. S   4. R
   2. F   5. S
   3. F

C. Through ... voices. The ... nest. In ... eggs. That ... nest.

D. 1. us—DO
   2. beans—DO; lawn—DO
   3. horses—IO; water—DO
   4. baby—IO; toys—DO
   5. Mary Ann—DO; Anna Marie—DO

1. The soaking rain was a blessing from God.
2. The fields appear fresh and green again.
3. Before the rain, the crops had become wilted.
4. Our primary crops have been corn and cantaloupes.
5. We are thankful to the Lord for the harvest.

F. For each sentence, write *A* or *D* to tell whether it has an appositive or a noun of direct address. (It may have both.) Then write each word that should be followed by a comma, and add the missing comma.
1. Sir we would see Jesus.
2. Peter an unlearned fisherman was used mightily by the Lord.
3. Son of David have mercy on me a poor leper.
4. Do you not understand My words Nicodemus?
5. John the Baptist a prophet of God preached and baptized.

G. Diagram the skeletons and complements along with any appositives or nouns of direct address. Remember to include all the modifiers that go with an appositive or a noun of direct address.
1. Uncle Wesley and Aunt Maggie collect many books.
2. Some of the books are quite old and valuable.
3. Aunt Maggie, who made you these beautiful bookshelves?
4. Grandfather Rutt, my father, was a skilled woodworker.
5. He built these shelves and carved the bookends.

H. Copy this paragraph as it is. Proofread it, using the proper proofreading marks.

"Whose intrested in a change of senery?" Father asked us as he pushed his chair back from the table. "Mrs. Keppel broke her arm, and her garden could some ambitous children." Half hour later, the three of us were across the road, weilding are hoes in the little plot. While we worked, Mrs. Keppel charmed us with stories in Germany of her childhood. After we finished, our kindhearted nieghbor offered us each an ice cream sandwhich and a glass of iced tea.

E. 1. blessing—PN
2. fresh—PA; green—PA
3. wilted—PA
4. corn—PN; cantaloupes—PN
5. thankful—PA

F. 1. D; Sir,   4. D; words,
2. A; Peter, fisherman,   5. A; Baptist, God,
3. D, A; David, me,

G.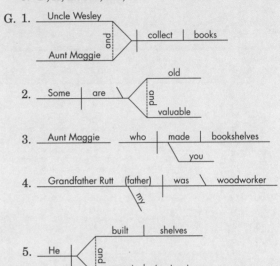

H. (Corrections are marked. Check for the correct use of proofreading marks.)

"~~Whose~~ *Who's* int~~e~~rested in a change of senery? *c* " Father asked us as he pushed his chair back from the table. "Mrs. Keppel broke her arm, and her garden could *use* some amb~~i~~tous children." ¶Half *an* hour later, the three of us were across the road, w~~ei~~lding *our* ~~are~~ hoes in the little plot. While we worked, Mrs. Keppel charmed us with stories ⌐in Germany⌐ of her childhood⌐ After we finished, our kindhearted n~~ie~~ghbor offered us each an ice cream sandwhich and a glass of iced tea.

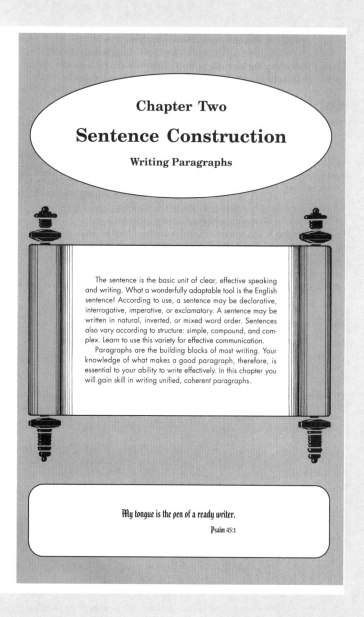

Chapter Two

Sentence Construction

Writing Paragraphs

The sentence is the basic unit of clear, effective speaking and writing. What a wonderfully adaptable tool is the English sentence! According to use, a sentence may be declarative, interrogative, imperative, or exclamatory. A sentence may be written in natural, inverted, or mixed word order. Sentences also vary according to structure: simple, compound, and complex. Learn to use this variety for effective communication.

Paragraphs are the building blocks of most writing. Your knowledge of what makes a good paragraph, therefore, is essential to your ability to write effectively. In this chapter you will gain skill in writing unified, coherent paragraphs.

My tongue is the pen of a ready writer.

Psalm 45:1

10. Types of Sentences

Lesson Survey
- A **declarative sentence** makes a statement.
- An **interrogative sentence** asks a question.
- An **imperative sentence** gives a command or a request.
- An **exclamatory sentence** expresses strong feeling or emotion.

Sentences are classified according to their structure and their use. In this lesson, you will review the four types of sentences according to their use. Later in this chapter, you will study the types of sentences according to their structure.

A *declarative sentence* makes a statement or declares something. This declaration is either true or false. A declarative sentence ends with a period.

The following sentences are both declarative. Notice that one declaration is true, while the other is false.

> Heavy rains fall frequently in tropical forests. (true)
> Heavy rains fall frequently in deserts. (false)

Compare the following examples. They cannot be declarative sentences, because it is not logical to ask "Are these sentences true or false?"

> Do you know Abraham Zimmerman?
>   (A question cannot be true or false.)
> Worship the Lord in the beauty of holiness.
>   (A command cannot be true or false.)

An *interrogative sentence* asks a question. It ends with a question mark. The subject of an interrogative sentence often follows the verb or comes between the parts of a verb phrase.

> <u>Who</u> <u>is coming</u> up the lane?
> <u>Are</u> <u>they</u> our new neighbors?
> <u>Shall</u> <u>we</u> <u>invite</u> them to the church service tonight?

An *imperative sentence* gives a command or a request. The subject of every imperative sentence is *you,* but it is not usually stated in the sentence. An imperative sentence ends with a period unless the command is given with strong emphasis.

Use proper manners at the table.

Lesson 10

Purpose: To teach the four types of sentences according to use.

Oral Review:
1. Name the two kinds of object complements. (direct object, indirect object)
2. Name the two kinds of subjective complements. (predicate nominative, predicate adjective)
3. What is an appositive? (a noun or pronoun that immediately follows another noun or pronoun to identify or explain it)
4. What does a noun of direct address do? (names the person or thing to whom one is speaking)
5. Which words within these sentences should be capitalized? (Answers are underlined.)
   a. <u>The</u> accident happened on a <u>Friday</u> in the spring.
   b. <u>Elijah</u> held a contest on <u>Carmel</u>, a mountain along the <u>Mediterranean Sea</u>.
   c. <u>In</u> history class we learned about <u>George Eastman</u>, who developed the <u>Kodak</u> camera.
6. Tell whether each sentence has a direct or an indirect quotation.
   a. Samuel asked Saul, "What hast thou done?" (direct)
   b. Saul said that he had forced himself and offered a sacrifice. (indirect)
   c. Samuel told Saul that the kingdom would be taken from him. (indirect)
   d. "The Lord hath sought him a man after his own heart," said Samuel. (direct)

Lesson Introduction: On your way to school this morning, you likely passed many different types of buildings. These buildings varied widely in their purposes. A school would not make a good car garage.

Lyndon, you show that plate to your father.

you	show

Sometimes a declarative sentence appears to be a command, and it may even be intended to communicate a command. However, if the sentence is written as a statement that is either true or false, it is declarative.

You should love and obey the Bible. (declarative; a true statement)
Love and obey the Bible. (imperative; a command)

You must always be quiet during fire drills. (declarative; a true statement)
Be quiet during fire drills. (imperative; a command)

Imperative sentences often begin with a noun of direct address. But the subject is still *you;* a noun of direct address is never the subject.

My son, hear the instruction of your father.
Skeleton:

(you)	hear

| *not* | son | hear |

Lucinda, read the first stanza.
Skeleton:

(you)	read

| *not* | Lucinda | read |

An *exclamatory sentence* expresses strong feeling or emotion. It ends with an exclamation point. Any sentence of the first three types may be punctuated as an exclamatory sentence if it is said forcefully.

The electricity went off! (declarative)
Where's the lantern! (interrogative)
Light it quickly! (imperative)

Many exclamatory sentences have a unique word order. In the following sets of examples, notice the differences between exclamatory sentences and other types.

What a day this has been!
    (skeleton last so that *What* can come first)
What kind of day has this been? (interrogative)
This has been quite a day. (declarative)

If only we had followed Father's advice!
    (*If only* clause that would otherwise be a fragment)
Why did we not follow Father's advice? (interrogative)
We should have followed Father's advice. (declarative)

Nor would a church building make a very good house. The purpose of each is specific enough to require a particular type of building.

Likewise in the English language, sentences can be classified according to their use. Each of these four types of sentences has a specific purpose.

Lesson Outline:

1. A declarative sentence makes a statement or declares something.

    a. A statement is either true or false.

    b. A declarative sentence ends with a period.

2. An interrogative sentence asks a question.

    a. An interrogative sentence ends with a question mark.

    b. The subject of an interrogative sentence often follows the verb or comes between the parts of a verb phrase.

3. An imperative sentence gives a command or a request.

    a. The subject of an imperative sentence is *you,* but it is not usually stated in the sentence.

    b. An imperative sentence ends with a period unless the command is given with strong emphasis.

    c. Sometimes a declarative sentence appears to be imperative.

    d. A noun of direct address is never the subject of an imperative sentence.

4. An exclamatory sentence expresses strong feeling or emotion.

    a. An exclamatory sentence ends with an exclamation point.

    b. The other types of sentences may be exclamations if expressed forcefully.

    c. Exclamatory sentences often have a unique word order.

    d. Exclamations should be used sparingly.

Follow Father's advice. (imperative)

How cold that icy water was!
   (skeleton last so that *How* can come first)
How cold was that icy water? (interrogative)
That icy water was cold. (declarative)

Avoid overusing the exclamatory sentence. Most normal writing should contain only a sprinkling of exclamation points.

Class Practice

A. Identify the type of each sentence, and tell what end punctuation is needed.
1. Remember God, your Creator, in your youth
2. The habits of youth influence the character of adulthood
3. Are you cultivating good character
4. How tragic a wasted life is
5. You should be a good example to others
6. If only more people would love the Lord and obey His Word
7. Our lives should show the world the way of godliness
8. Is your Bible on your desk
9. Jonathan, read the words of Paul in 1 Timothy 4:12
10. What a noble example Timothy is

B. On the chalkboard, diagram the skeletons and complements of the sentences in Part A, along with any appositive or noun of direct address.

Written Exercises

A. Label each sentence *dec.* (declarative), *int.* (interrogative), *imp.* (imperative), or *exc.* (exclamatory). Also write the last word of the sentence, followed by the correct end punctuation.
1. Our family's garden is behind the barn
2. Who has the green thumb in your family
3. You should see the beautiful marigolds and zinnias
4. Larry, bring a basket along with you
5. Do you see the rows of tomatoes
6. What a huge tomato this is
7. Is this the biggest one in the garden
8. Give your aunt Verna this large, ripe tomato
9. How the Lord has blessed us
10. Thank God for His bountiful blessings

B. Diagram the skeletons and complements of the sentences in Part A, along with any appositive or noun of direct address.

1–5

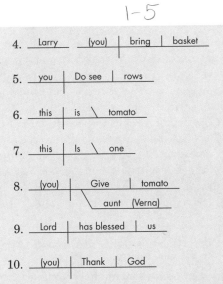

4. Larry | (you) | bring | basket
5. you | Do see | rows
6. this | is \ tomato
7. this | Is \ one
8. (you) | Give | tomato / aunt (Verna)
9. Lord | has blessed | us
10. (you) | Thank | God

Lesson 10 Answers

Class Practice

A.
1. imperative, period
2. declarative, period
3. interrogative, question mark
4. exclamatory, exclamation point
5. declarative, period
6. exclamatory, exclamation point
7. declarative, period
8. interrogative, question mark
9. imperative, period
10. exclamatory, exclamation point

B.
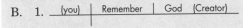
1. (you) | Remember | God (Creator)
2. habits | influence | character
3. you | Are cultivating | character
4. life | is \ tragic
5. You | should be \ example

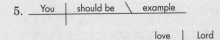
6. people | would < love | Lord / and / obey | Word

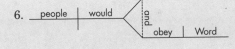
7. lives | should show | way / world

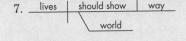
8. Bible | Is
9. Jonathan   (you) | read | words
10. Timothy | is \ example

Written Exercises

A.
1. dec., barn.
2. int., family?
3. dec., zinnias.
  or exc., zinnias!
4. imp., you.
5. int., tomatoes?
6. exc., is!
7. int., garden?
8. imp., tomato.
9. exc., us!
10. imp., blessings.
  or exc., blessings!

B.
1. garden | is
2. who | has | green thumb

(*Green* may be omitted.)

3. You | should see < marigolds / and / zinnias

Review Exercises

These exercises review things that you studied in previous grades. Use the index in the back of this book if you need help.

A. Two words in each sentence have capitalization errors. Write those words correctly.
   1. On wednesday evening we went to prayer meeting at the Glendale Mennonite church.
   2. When Jesus was crucified on mount Calvary, two malefactors were crucified with him.
   3. "Open your Science books," said brother Clair, "to page 132."
   4. The book *Home Fires at the Foot of The Rockies* describes the experiences of a christian family.
   5. On february 26, my father bought a used Ford Truck.
   6. Dr. zarger is much younger than our other Doctor.

B. Copy the sentences with direct quotations, using correct punctuation and capitalization. If a sentence has an indirect quotation, write *indirect*.
   1. When will the corn be ready to pick asked Mother.
   2. Uncle Harvey said that they plan to visit us this evening.
   3. This job would be finished stated Father sternly if you had worked diligently.
   4. Lyle asked if everyone was here.
   5. Charlotte replied the other girls are still in the house.

---

11. Word Order in Sentences

> **Lesson Survey**
> - In a sentence with **natural word order,** the complete subject comes before the complete predicate.
> - In a sentence with **inverted word order,** the complete predicate comes before the complete subject.
> - In a sentence with **mixed word order,** part of the complete predicate comes before the complete subject, and part of it comes after.

For emphasis, effectiveness, and clarity, good writers use a variety of word order in sentences. Read the following paragraphs.

Review Exercises

A. 1. Wednesday, Church
   2. Mount, Him
   3. science, Brother
   4. *the (Rockies),* Christian
   5. February, truck
   6. Zarger, doctor

B. (Corrections are underlined.)
   1. "When will the corn be ready to pick?" asked Mother.
   2. indirect
   3. "This job would be finished," stated Father sternly. "if you had worked diligently."
   4. indirect
   5. Charlotte replied, "The other girls are still in the house."

Lesson 11

Purpose: To teach variety of word order for interesting sentences.

Oral Review:
1. Identify the type of each sentence, and tell what end punctuation is needed.
   a. "Children, obey your parents" (imperative; period)
   b. These words are found in Ephesians 6:1 (declarative; period)
   c. What is the first commandment with promise (interrogative; question mark)
   d. The answer is found in Ephesians 6:2 (declarative; period)
   e. How important it is that young people always honor their parents (exclamatory; exclamation point)

2. What question does a direct object answer? (whom *or* what)
3. What question does an indirect object answer? (to whom or what *or* for whom or what)
4. Where is an indirect object normally found in a sentence? (between the verb and the direct object)
5. What is a predicate nominative? (a noun or pronoun in the predicate that renames the subject)
6. Usually the subject and the —— can be exchanged, and the sentence means the same. (predicate nominative)

Lesson Introduction: Write the following set of sentences on the chalkboard.

   Two eagles soared above the mountain range.
   Above the mountain range soared two eagles.
   Above the mountain range two eagles soared.

Isaac, Nathaniel, and Simon were hoeing weeds in the corn patch. The blazing sun had become hot by midmorning. A welcome break came at 10:30. Rebecca and Sarah brought a treat of iced tea and peanut butter cookies.

*　　*　　*　　*　　*

Isaac, Nathaniel, and Simon were hoeing weeds in the corn patch. By midmorning, the blazing sun had become hot. At 10:30 came a welcome break. Rebecca and Sarah brought a treat of iced tea and peanut butter cookies.

The second example is more effective because of the varied word order in the sentences. A story or an essay is tiresome to read when every sentence is constructed in the usual order of subject followed by predicate.

This arrangement (subject and then predicate) is called normal word order or *natural word order*. In this order, the complete subject comes before the complete predicate. It is the most common order in both speaking and writing.

Judas Iscariot went out into the night.
The cows are grazing in the neighbor's hayfield.

In a sentence with *inverted word order*, the complete predicate comes before the complete subject. This is the least common word order.

Out into the night went Judas Iscariot.
Where are the cows?

Do not think that changing a sentence from active to passive voice will change it from natural to inverted word order. The *subject* changes when the voice changes, but the *word order* of the sentence does not change. If the complete subject still comes before the complete predicate, the sentence still has natural word order.

Jehoiakim destroyed the roll. (active voice; natural order)
The roll was destroyed by Jehoiakim. (passive voice; natural order)

In a sentence with *mixed word order*, part of the complete predicate comes before the complete subject, and part of it comes after. Commas are often used in sentences with mixed word order, especially if a long adverb phrase or an adverb clause comes before the subject.

Out into the night Judas Iscariot went.
Where are the cows grazing?
If we fear God, we need fear no one else.
　　(In determining word order, the entire adverb clause is considered part of the predicate.)

Ask the students to read the skeleton of each sentence. Of course, the skeleton is the same in all three. Point out that exactly the same words are used in each sentence; the only difference is the word order.

Lesson Outline:

1. For emphasis, effectiveness, and clarity, good writers use a variety of word order in sentences.

2. In a sentence with natural word order, the complete subject comes before the complete predicate. This is the most common word order. Sometimes it is called normal word order.

3. In a sentence with inverted word order, the complete predicate comes before the complete subject. This is the least common word order. A shift from active to passive voice must not be confused with a shift from natural to inverted word order.

4. In a sentence with mixed word order, part of the complete predicate comes before the complete subject, and part of it comes after. Commas are often used in sentences with mixed word order, especially if a long adverb phrase or an adverb clause comes before the subject.

5. Not every sentence can be written in each of the three word orders.

6. A sentence that begins with There is written in either inverted or mixed word order. In such a sentence, *There* is an adverb or an expletive.

★ **EXTRA PRACTICE**
Worksheet 5 (*Word Order in Sentences*)

To tell quickly if a sentence has natural, inverted, or mixed word order, find the complete subject. Then see if the complete subject comes at the beginning, at the end, or in the middle of the sentence.

Natural: The axhead flew into the water.
Inverted: Into the water flew the axhead.
Mixed: Into the water the axhead flew.

Not every sentence can be written in each of the three word orders. As you read more and more, you will develop sentence sense to help you decide what makes good sentence variation.

He never eats canned fish. (acceptable natural order)
Canned fish never eats he. (unacceptable inverted order)
Canned fish he never eats. (acceptable mixed order)

The Lord of hosts is on the throne. (acceptable natural order)
On the throne is the Lord of hosts. (acceptable inverted order)
On the throne the Lord of hosts is. (unacceptable mixed order)

Sentence variety is good if it improves communication and readability. But sometimes a writer works so hard at varying his sentences that he does more harm than good. Consider how unnatural the following example sounds. While some of the sentences are all right, the paragraph as a whole is not effective.

Slowly down the road moved the crowd. Near the front, Jesus was walking. Under a sycamore tree to a halt came Jesus. Up this tree had climbed Zacchaeus. Because he was so short, he could not see Jesus. At Jesus' bidding, down he came. Because he repented, Jesus could say, "This day is salvation come to thy house."

A sentence that begins with *There* is written in either inverted or mixed word order. Remember that *There* is never the subject of a sentence. Sometimes *There* is an adverb telling *where*. More often, *There* is an *expletive* (ek′·spli·tiv). An expletive is not part of the subject or predicate. It is simply an introductory word that points forward to the subject.

Inverted word order:
There are the missing keys!
   (*There* is an adverb that tells *where* the keys are.)
There are many excuses for carelessness.
   (*There* is an expletive. It does not tell *where* excuses are!)
Mixed word order:
There the missing keys are! (*There* is an adverb.)
There are different excuses given by different people.
   (*There* is an expletive.)

When used frequently, the expletive *There* weakens the force and clarity of a composition. So an effective writer avoids using this construction too often. Notice how the last example on page 56 is more direct and forceful when it is written without the expletive.

> Different excuses are given by different people.
> Different people give different excuses.

Class Practice

A. Change these sentences to natural word order.
1. "Blessed are the peacemakers."
2. "By their fruits ye shall know them."
3. "In the beginning God created the heaven and the earth."
4. "In his law doth he meditate day and night."
5. "Great deliverance giveth he to his king."

B. Change these sentences to inverted word order.
1. The fir tree shall come up instead of the thorn.
2. Jesus came into this sin-cursed world.
3. A large map hung on each wall of the classroom.

C. Change these sentences to mixed word order. Tell where commas are needed.
1. The Holy Spirit filled the believers on the day of Pentecost.
2. Peter preached to the people with great boldness.
3. Many were convicted of their sins as he preached.

D. Change some of these sentences to inverted word order and some to mixed word order. Tell which order you used. If a comma is needed, tell where it should be added.
1. The teacher drew a picture on the chalkboard.
2. The woods were dark and deep.
3. The church was well filled for the evening service.
4. The congregation waited quietly for the service to begin.
5. A puppy walked through the open door.

E. Change these sentences so that they do not begin with the expletive *There*.
1. There are many mansions in my Father's house.
2. There are promised rich blessings for God's children.
3. There is an innumerable host of angels in heaven.
4. There will enter into that holy place nothing that defiles.

F. On the chalkboard, diagram the skeletons and complements of these sentences.
1. Around the table gathered the family.
2. Father thanked the Lord for their daily bread.

Lesson 11 Answers

Class Practice

A. (Pronouns referring to God may be capitalized.)
1. The peacemakers are blessed.
2. Ye shall know them by their fruits.
3. God created the heaven and the earth in the beginning.
4. He doth meditate in his law day and night.
   or He doth meditate day and night in his law.
5. He giveth great deliverance to his king.
   or He giveth to his king great deliverance.

B. 1. Instead of the thorn shall come up the fir tree.
2. Into this sin-cursed world came Jesus.
3. On each wall of the classroom hung a large map.

C. 1. On the day of Pentecost, the Holy Spirit filled the believers.
2. With great boldness, Peter preached to the people. (Comma is optional.)
3. As he preached, many were convicted of their sins.

D. 1. On the chalkboard, the teacher drew a picture. (mixed)
2. Dark and deep were the woods. (inverted)
3. For the evening service, the church was well filled. (mixed)
4. Quietly the congregation waited for the service to begin. (mixed)
5. Through the open door walked a puppy. (inverted)

E. (Word order may vary.)
1. In my Father's house are many mansions.
   or Many mansions are in my Father's house.
2. Rich blessings are promised for God's children.
3. An innumerable host of angels is in heaven.
4. Nothing that defiles will enter into that holy place.

F. 1.

family	gathered

2.

Father	thanked	Lord

3. There were several small dishes on the table.
4. Carefully, Mother rationed the meager supply of food to the family.
5. After the meal, the children were still hungry.

Written Exercises

A. Change these sentences to natural word order.
   1. "In quietness and in confidence shall be your strength."
   2. "My voice shalt thou hear in the morning."
   3. "In the morning will I direct my prayer unto thee."
   4. "True and righteous are his judgments."
   5. "Holy and reverend is his name."

B. Change these sentences to inverted word order.
   1. The power of our God is great.
   2. The two cherubim were above the mercy seat.
   3. The four and twenty elders sat around the throne.
   4. Lazarus lay at the rich man's gate.
   5. The way of life is found in Jesus Christ.

C. Change these sentences to mixed word order. Be sure to add any needed commas.
   1. We will not sell the truth.
   2. Our congregation sang at the Hilltop Rest Home on Sunday afternoon.
   3. We visited with Mr. Letzer after the service.
   4. God has certainly revealed Himself to man.
   5. We illustrated a song in art class.

D. Change some of these sentences to inverted word order and some to mixed word order. Write which order you used. Be sure to add any needed commas.
   1. Thick, tough vines grew around the old tree.
   2. Our house was damaged during the storm.
   3. We saw a beautiful rainbow after the storm.
   4. A huge rattlesnake lives in this rock pile.
   5. Father carefully examined the sick cow.

E. Rewrite these sentences so that they do not begin with the expletive *There.*
   1. There came to Job many severe trials.
   2. There were some things about Job that Satan did not know.
   3. There was anchored in Job's heart a deep loyalty to the Lord.
   4. There are many statements of Job's strong faith in this inspiring book.

F. Diagram the skeletons and complements of these sentences.

3. <u>dishes</u> | <u>were</u>

4. <u>Mother</u> | <u>rationed</u> | <u>supply</u>

5. <u>children</u> | <u>were</u> \ <u>hungry</u>

Written Exercises

A. 1. Your strength shall be in quietness and in confidence.
   2. Thou shalt hear my voice in the morning.
   3. I will direct my prayer unto thee in the morning.
   4. His judgments are true and righteous.
   5. His name is holy and reverend.

B. 1. Great is the power of our God.
   2. Above the mercy seat were the two cherubim.
   3. Around the throne sat the four and twenty elders.
   4. At the rich man's gate lay Lazarus.
   5. In Jesus Christ is found the way of life.

C. (Allow variation in the use of commas.)
   1. The truth we will not sell.
   2. On Sunday afternoon, our congregation sang at the Hilltop Rest Home.
   3. After the service, we visited with Mr. Letzer.
   4. Certainly God has revealed Himself to man.
   5. In art class we illustrated a song.

D. (Allow variation in the use of commas.)
   1. Around the old tree grew thick, tough vines. (inverted)
      or Around the old tree, thick, tough vines grew. (mixed)
   2. During the storm, our house was damaged. (mixed)
   3. After the storm, we saw a beautiful rainbow. (mixed)
   4. In this rock pile lives a huge rattlesnake. (inverted)
      or In this rock pile, a huge rattlesnake lives. (mixed)
   5. Carefully Father examined the sick cow. (mixed)

E. (Word order may vary.)
   1. Many severe trials came to Job.
   2. Satan did not know some things about Job.
   3. A deep loyalty to the Lord was anchored in Job's heart.
      or In Job's heart was anchored a deep loyalty to the Lord.

4. Many statements of Job's strong faith are in this inspiring book.
   or In this inspiring book are many statements of Job's strong faith.

1. The evil of dishonesty we should abhor.
2. By diligent effort, you should finish your chores in time.
3. "Faithful are the wounds of a friend."
4. Into the hen house crept the fox.
5. Boldly Jeremiah proclaimed God's message.

Review Exercises

Copy each complement, and label it *DO* for direct object, *IO* for indirect object, *PN* for predicate nominative, or *PA* for predicate adjective. [5, 6] (Turn to the lesson numbers in brackets if you need help.)

1. Pennsylvania's state bird is the ruffed grouse.
2. These birds occupy many areas of North America.
3. A ruffed grouse has a ruff of shiny black feathers around its neck.
4. God has not given the grouse the ability for long flights.
5. Their takeoff, however, is thunderous and powerful.
6. In the summer, ruffed grouse eat many insects and berries.
7. Buds of trees are their main winter diet.
8. Conifers provide the grouse their primary place of roosting and shelter.
9. Their winter nest, however, may actually be a snowbank.
10. Under the snow they remain cozy and warm.

---

12. Clauses in Sentences

> **Lesson Survey**
> • A **clause** is a group of words that contains a skeleton and functions as a specific part of a sentence.
> • An **independent clause** expresses a complete thought. It can stand alone as a complete sentence.
> • A **dependent clause** does not express a complete thought. It must be connected to an independent clause.

A phrase is a group of related words that has no subject or predicate. It functions as one part of speech and fills a specific place in a sentence. The following sentence is divided into four phrases: a noun phrase used

F. 1. we | should abhor | evil

2. you | should finish | chores

3. wounds | are \ Faithful

4. fox | crept

5. Jeremiah | proclaimed | message

Review Exercises

1. ruffed grouse—PN
2. areas—DO
3. ruff—DO
4. grouse—IO; ability—DO
5. thunderous—PA; powerful—PA
6. insects—DO; berries—DO
7. diet—PN
8. grouse—IO; place—DO
9. snowbank—PN
10. cozy—PA; warm—PA

Lesson 12

Purpose: (1) To teach the recognition of clauses. (2) To teach the difference between independent and dependent clauses.

Oral Review:

1. Tell whether the following sentences are in natural, inverted, or mixed word order.
   a. Through the tall grass slithered an enormous snake. (inverted)
   b. In fright I turned and fled. (mixed)
   c. Straight to the house I ran. (mixed)
   d. My breath was coming in gasps. (natural)
2. Which of the four sentence types
   a. always has *you* as the subject? (imperative)
   b. must be either true or false? (declarative)
   c. often has a unique word order? (exclamatory)
   d. often has the subject between two parts of the verb? (interrogative)
   e. can be any of the other three if it is said forcefully? (exclamatory)
3. What is a subjective complement that modifies the subject? (predicate adjective)
4. What is a subjective complement that renames the subject? (predicate nominative)

Lesson Introduction: Write on the board several phrases and several clauses in two columns.

between the two posts
will be seeing
Alexander the Great

that we have seen and heard
as the Lord has said
whose friendship we miss

as the subject, a verb phrase, a prepositional adverb phrase, and a prepositional adjective phrase.

> John the Baptist | was preaching | in the desert | by the Jordan River.

Another group of related words is the clause. A *clause* contains a skeleton and functions as a specific part of a sentence. Study the italicized parts of the following sentences to compare phrases and clauses.

> We watched the deer *in the evening twilight.* (adverb phrase)
> We watched the deer *as darkness spread* across the sky. (adverb clause)
>
> The man *in that black van* is our neighbor. (adjective phrase)
> The man *who is driving* that black van is our neighbor. (adjective clause)

Clauses are in two general categories: independent clauses and dependent clauses. An *independent clause* expresses a complete thought, and it can stand alone as a complete sentence. In fact, every simple sentence is an independent clause. But the term *independent clause* is generally used only when a sentence contains more than one clause.

> Carbon monoxide is produced from incompletely burned fuel. (one independent clause; a complete sentence)
> It has no color or odor, but it is a deadly gas. (two independent clauses; each could stand alone as a complete sentence)

A *dependent clause* does not express a complete thought. It cannot stand alone as a complete sentence. Rather, it must be connected to an independent clause, and it fills a specific place in that clause.

> The Law was fulfilled. (independent clause; a sentence)
> When Jesus came. (dependent clause; not a sentence)
> The Law was fulfilled *when Jesus came.* (dependent clause used as an adverb to tell *when* the Law was fulfilled)
>
> The message brought joy to the shepherds. (independent clause; a sentence)
> That the angels proclaimed. (dependent clause; not a sentence)
> The message *that the angels proclaimed* brought joy to the shepherds. (dependent clause used as an adjective to tell *which* message)

Look again at the last example. It shows that a dependent clause is sometimes found between the parts of an independent clause.

What do the word groups in the second column have that those in the first column do not have? Students should recognize that each item in the second column contains a skeleton. Point out that the first column contains three different kinds of phrases, but the second contains clauses.

Lesson Outline:

1. A clause is a group of words that contains a skeleton and functions as a specific part of a sentence.

2. An independent clause expresses a complete thought and can stand alone as a complete sentence.

3. A dependent clause does not express a complete thought; it must be connected to an independent clause.

Class Practice

A. Say *yes* or *no* to tell whether each group of words is a clause. If it is a clause, read the skeleton.
   1. fell into the pond behind the barn
   2. by the apostle Paul
   3. where Peter ran
   4. had been singing all morning
   5. after the house had been built
   6. King Saul was Israel's first king
   7. that God had commanded
   8. after the heavy rain
   9. whose leprosy was cured
   10. had forgotten his memory verse

B. Tell whether each clause is *dependent* or *independent*. Read the skeleton of the clause.
   1. since we saw the bear
   2. the boys built a bird feeder
   3. which the teacher gave
   4. although we had tried our best
   5. the pigs ruined the back yard
   6. the baby cried
   7. whom we met yesterday
   8. it was too hot
   9. where the Lord leads us
   10. we will faithfully follow the Lord

C. Read each clause, and identify it as an *independent* or a *dependent* clause.
   1. We love God because He first loved us.
   2. If we love the Lord, we will love His Word.
   3. The Lord God, whose throne is in the heavens, rules over all.
   4. The truth that God exists is clearly demonstrated by the created world.
   5. The movements of the sun, moon, and stars are amazingly precise.
   6. Astronomers predict eclipses years in advance, and space scientists plan long flights into outer space.
   7. Although scientists cannot fully explain gravity, God designed this force for the successful operation of the universe.
   8. Magnetism is another force that scientists cannot completely understand.
   9. God, who so wisely planned this world, deserves our worship and praise.

Lesson 12 Answers

Class Practice

A. 1. no
    2. no
    3. yes; Peter ran
    4. no
    5. yes; house had been built
    6. yes; King Saul was
    7. yes; God had commanded
    8. no
    9. yes; leprosy was cured
    10. no

B. 1. dependent; we saw
    2. independent; boys built
    3. dependent; teacher gave
    4. dependent; we had tried
    5. independent; pigs ruined
    6. independent; baby cried
    7. dependent; we met
    8. independent; it was
    9. dependent; Lord leads
    10. independent; we will follow

C. 1. We love God—independent; because He first loved us—dependent
    2. If we love the Lord—dependent; we will love His Word—independent
    3. The Lord God rules over all—independent; whose throne is in the heavens—dependent
    4. The truth is clearly demonstrated by the created world—independent; that God exists—dependent
    5. The movements of the sun, moon, and stars are amazingly precise—independent
    6. Astronomers predict eclipses years in advance—independent; space scientists plan long flights into outer space—independent
    7. Although scientists cannot fully explain gravity—dependent; God designed this force for the successful operation of the universe—independent
    8. Magnetism is another force—independent; that scientists cannot completely understand—dependent
    9. God deserves our worship and praise—independent; who so wisely planned this world—dependent

10. Today many deny the Lord, but someday they will meet Him in judgment.

Written Exercises

A. If the word group is a clause, copy the skeleton. If the word group is not a clause, write *not a clause.*
   1. Abraham went into the tent
   2. across the stormy sea
   3. which none understood
   4. although he showed kindness and consideration
   5. because He had performed the miracle
   6. under these circumstances
   7. where he was
   8. if you had come sooner
   9. because of God's love
   10. whose favor the servant sought

B. Label each clause *independent* or *dependent.* Copy the skeleton.
   1. the army ants are coming
   2. which bloomed so beautifully
   3. these peaches are delicious
   4. the squirrel scampered up the tree
   5. that Columbus discovered
   6. when Squanto came

C. Copy each clause separately, and label it *I* for independent or *D* for dependent.
   1. The people mocked as the prophet spoke of their sins.
   2. Now the day is over, and night is drawing nigh.
   3. While the persecution lasted, the Christians hid in dens and caves.
   4. The tabernacle, which God had chosen as His dwelling place with Israel, contained many types of Christ.
   5. Because Haman hated Mordecai, he sought to kill all the Jews.
   6. God delivered them through Esther, who had become queen earlier.
   7. Peter, James, and John were fishermen on the Sea of Galilee.
   8. Saul, whose persecution of the Christians was well known, met Jesus on the road to Damascus.

Review Exercises

A. Write whether each sentence has *natural, inverted,* or *mixed* word order. [11]
   1. The road is still under construction.
   2. There was a pile of gravel blocking the original road surface.

10. Today many deny the Lord—independent; someday they will meet Him in judgment—independent

Written Exercises

A. 1. Abraham went
   2. not a clause
   3. none understood
   4. he showed
   5. He had performed
   6. not a clause
   7. he was
   8. you had come
   9. not a clause
   10. servant sought

B. 1. independent; army ants are coming
   2. dependent; which bloomed
   3. independent; peaches are
   4. independent; squirrel scampered
   5. dependent; Columbus discovered
   6. dependent; Squanto came

C. 1. The people mocked—I;
      as the prophet spoke of their sins—D
   2. Now the day is over—I;
      night is drawing nigh—I
   3. While the persecution lasted—D;
      the Christians hid in dens and caves—I
   4. The tabernacle contained many types of Christ—I;
      which God had chosen as His dwelling place with Israel—D
   5. Because Haman hated Mordecai—D;
      he sought to kill all the Jews—I
   6. God delivered them through Esther—I;
      who had become queen earlier—D
   7. Peter, James, and John were fishermen on the Sea of Galilee—I
   8. Saul met Jesus on the road to Damascus—I;
      whose persecution of the Christians was well known—D

Review Exercises

A. 1. natural
   2. mixed

3. Off to the side was a temporary surface.
4. By next month the road should be much improved.

B. Rewrite each sentence in mixed or inverted word order, using correct punctuation. Write which order you used. [11]
1. The letter from Uncle Fred's has finally arrived.
2. You must never hand in such a sloppy paper!
3. The anxious family gathered around the sick child's bed.
4. We heard Father singing above the noise of the tractor.

C. Rewrite each sentence in natural word order. [11]
1. From the telephone pole, a mockingbird trilled his notes.
2. There was heard a collective sigh of relief as the last peas were shelled.
3. Gratefully Aunt Barbara accepted our offer of help.
4. To its high nest soared the bald eagle.

----

13. Topic Sentences and Paragraph Unity

Lesson Survey
- A paragraph should have proper **form**. The first line should be indented, the left margin should be straight, and the right margin should be as straight as possible.
- The main idea of a paragraph is stated in the **topic sentence.**
- A paragraph should have **unity.** Every sentence should help to develop the topic sentence.

When the earth was without form and void, it was neither attractive nor useful. But God changed that during the six days of Creation. He gave structure and purpose to the world. A paragraph too must be constructed with proper form and unity if it is to communicate effectively.

Proper paragraph *form* has to do with the appearance of a paragraph. The first line is indented to show where a new paragraph begins. The left margin should be kept straight. The right margin should be kept as straight as possible, without crowding words at the ends of lines. Sometimes you may need to hyphenate words in order to keep the right margin reasonably straight.

A paragraph usually has a *topic sentence* that states the main idea of

Lesson 13

Purpose: (1) To teach form and unity in paragraphs.
(2) To teach proper paragraph divisions.

Oral Review:
1. Demonstrate how to proofread the following sentences. (*Teacher:* Write them on the chalkboard.)
   a. The cruel brothers were unmoved by Joseph's grief ~~and sorrow.~~
   b. Jesus spent the ^night in prayer on the mountain.
   c. Jesus asked, "Where shall we buy bread for all these people?" ¶Philip replied, "Lord, two hundred pennyworth of bread would not be enough so that each one could have even a little."
2. Give some rules of good outline form.
   (a. Use Roman numerals for topics, capital letters for subtopics, and Arabic numerals for points. Place a period after each numeral or letter.

3. inverted
4. mixed

B. (Allow reasonable variation.)
1. Finally the letter from Uncle Fred's has arrived. (mixed)
2. Such a sloppy paper you must never hand in! (mixed)
3. Around the sick child's bed gathered the anxious family. (inverted)
   or Around the sick child's bed, the anxious family gathered. (mixed)
4. Above the noise of the tractor, we heard Father singing. (mixed)

C. 1. A mockingbird trilled his notes from the telephone pole.
2. A collective sigh of relief was heard as the last peas were shelled.
3. Aunt Barbara gratefully accepted our offer of help.
   or Aunt Barbara accepted gratefully our offer of help.
4. The bald eagle soared to its high nest.

----

   b. Have at least two items in each group—no *A* without a *B*, no *1* without a *2*, and so on.
   c. Make all the items in each group as nearly parallel as possible.
   d. Indent each subtopic and each point.)

Lesson Introduction: A glance at any prose material shows the importance of the paragraph. Paragraphs are the basic building blocks of stories, articles, and letters. If building blocks are not cut straight and laid properly, the wall will not serve its function well. Likewise, if paragraphs are not carefully constructed, the finished product will not communicate well.

Lesson Outline:
   1. A paragraph should have proper form.
   a. The first line should be indented.
   b. The left margin should be straight.
   c. The right margin should be as straight as possible.

the paragraph. The topic sentence often comes first, though it may also be at the end of the paragraph or even in the middle. The following paragraphs illustrate topic sentences in various positions. Consider how each underlined sentence states the main idea of the paragraph.

A partial vacuum is a space from which most of the air or other gas has been taken. The pressure is extremely low. Man cannot make an absolute vacuum, because it is impossible for him to take all the air out of an enclosed space. Although scientists have created partial vacuums that have only a few million molecules per cubic inch, no manmade vacuum is perfect.

Have you ever flown in an airplane? The top of an airplane's wing is curved so that the air flowing across the top must travel farther than that flowing across the bottom. Since it must travel farther, it has to move faster. This rapidly moving air creates a partial vacuum above the wing, allowing the atmospheric pressure below the wing to lift the airplane. A partial vacuum must be produced to enable the marvel of airplane travel.

Does your mother know how to can? Creating a partial vacuum is essential to canning. She heats the jars of food to kill unwanted bacteria. As the jars are heated, the space between the lid and the food is filled with steam. As the jars cool, the steam condenses, creating a partial vacuum. The lid is pushed down and held tight by atmospheric pressure.

The topic sentence must be constructed carefully so that it does express the main idea of the paragraph clearly.

A partial vacuum is important to the operation of a vacuum cleaner. The blades on the motor remove some of the air from the canister, creating a partial vacuum inside. Atmospheric pressure pushes air into that vacuum. As the air rushes up the intake hose, it draws dirt along with it.

Look at this sentence: *A vacuum cleaner is a useful appliance.* Why would it not be an effective topic sentence for the paragraph above? You should readily see that the paragraph is written to explain how a vacuum cleaner puts a partial vacuum to work. Its purpose is not to explain different ways that vacuum cleaners are useful. Only the last sentence hints at the actual usefulness of this appliance.

On the other hand, a topic sentence should not say too much. It should not summarize all the details of the paragraph. For that reason, the following example would also make a poor topic sentence: *A vacuum cleaner's blades create a partial vacuum that draws air and dirt into the canister.*

2. *The main idea of a paragraph is stated in the topic sentence.*

    a. The topic sentence often comes first, but it may also be at the end of the paragraph or even in the middle.

    b. The topic sentence must be constructed so that it clearly expresses the main idea of the paragraph.

    c. The topic sentence should not summarize all the details of the paragraph.

3. *Some paragraphs do not have topic sentences.* This is true especially in dialogue, where a new paragraph begins every time the speaker changes.

4. *A paragraph should have unity.*

    a. Any unrelated sentence must be removed from a paragraph.

    b. A new paragraph must be started whenever a different topic is introduced.

★ ***EXTRA PRACTICE***
Worksheet 6 (*Topic Sentences and Paragraph Unity*)

Some paragraphs do not have topic sentences. This is true especially in narratives that include dialogue, where a new paragraph begins every time the speaker changes. Such a paragraph may consist of only one sentence and sometimes only a sentence fragment. In Chapter 10 you will learn more about paragraphs in stories.

The topic sentence states the main idea of the paragraph, and the rest of the sentences develop that idea. Thus, a properly written paragraph represents a single unit of thought. This quality of a paragraph is called *unity*.

In order to achieve paragraph unity, you must remove any unrelated sentence from a paragraph. As you read over a paragraph you have written, keep asking yourself the question, "Does this sentence directly support the topic sentence?" Read the following paragraph, and find the sentence that should be removed because it does not support the underlined topic sentence.

> *¹*Everyone probably knows that a plant holds to the earth by its roots. *²*The roots keep the plant stable and upright. *³*<u>But roots have a variety of purposes.</u> *⁴*Even though they are hidden underground, roots take in water and minerals for every leaf on a tree. *⁵*Most plants also store food in their roots for the seasons when no food can be produced. *⁶*In spring, for example, trees make a surge of growth that depends on food stored in the roots since the previous summer. *⁷*Other plants, like the cabbage, store food in their stems and leaves.

The topic is that *roots have a variety of purposes*. Sentences *1* and *2* describe one purpose—anchoring the plant in the ground. Sentence *4* mentions a second purpose—taking in water and minerals for the leaves. Sentences *5* and *6* state and illustrate a third purpose—storing food. But look at sentence 7. It may seem like a natural extension of the idea in sentences *5* and *6*, but *it does not support the topic sentence*. Therefore, sentence 7 mars the unity of the paragraph and should be removed.

To achieve paragraph unity, you must also divide paragraphs at the right place. Some may be short and some longer, but each paragraph must have only one topic. Very long paragraphs can usually be divided into two or more paragraphs, each with a single topic.

The following example should be written as two paragraphs. Where should the division be made? Which sentences are the topic sentences?

> *¹*A bald eagle in flight is a bird of imposing majesty. *²*With a wingspan of six to eight feet, the eagle is twice the size of the largest hawks. *³*Its great wings allow the eagle to catch rising air currents and soar effortlessly for long periods of time. *⁴*The eagle also uses

those wings to make power dives after its prey, sometimes reaching speeds up to one hundred miles per hour. [5]But an eagle is not always gliding and diving. [6]The eagle also presents a majestic appearance when it is perched high in a tree. [7]A large female, which is slightly larger than the male, may be over three feet long and stand two feet high. [8]Its distinctive white head and neck feathers gleam brilliantly in the sunshine. [9]As this bird of prey watches for its dinner, its keen eyes take on a fierce look. [10]Surely the bald eagle is an impressive reminder of the greatness of our Creator.

You should see that sentences *1–4* develop the topic of the bald eagle's majesty in flight. This topic is stated in sentence *1*. Sentence *5* introduces a shift, so a new paragraph should begin with that sentence. However, the second topic is not actually stated until sentence *6*. Sentences *7–10* further develop the second topic—the bald eagle's majesty as it is perched high in a tree.

Class Practice

A. Tell which sentence would make the best topic sentence for each of the following paragraphs. Why are the other choices not satisfactory?
   1. a. Saturn, the second largest planet, possesses great beauty.
      b. Saturn, the second largest planet, is surrounded by seven flat rings.
      c. Saturn is the second largest planet.
      d. Saturn's rings consist of many ringlets, each made of pieces of ice.
         The rings make Saturn one of the most beautiful objects in the solar system. They consist of thousands of narrow ringlets, each containing billions of pieces of ice. These ice pieces range from the size of dust particles to huge chunks more than ten feet in diameter.
   2. a. Michael Sattler was an Anabaptist of the early 1500s.
      b. Before being burned at the stake, Michael Sattler had part of his tongue cut out and several chunks of flesh torn from his body.
      c. Michael Sattler was an Anabaptist who suffered a cruel martyrdom.
      d. Michael Sattler was severely persecuted in his lifetime.
         First he had part of his tongue cut out to prevent him from testifying to the people. Then, while still inside the city, two chunks of flesh were torn from his body with red-hot tongs. Five more chunks were torn from his body after he was brought outside the city gate. Finally, he was burned at the stake.

B. Suggest a good topic sentence for each of the following paragraphs.
   1.   One of these is the meat and eggs group. The foods in this group

Lesson 13 Answers

Class Practice

A. 1. The best topic sentence is *b*.
      (a) The beauty of the planet itself is not described.
      (c) The size of the planet is a separate topic.
      (d) This sentence has too many details for a good topic sentence.
   2. The best topic sentence is *c*.
      (a) This sentence is too general for the specific details that follow.
      (b) This sentence has too many details for a good topic sentence.
      (d) Sattler's lifetime persecutions are a separate topic.

B. (Possible topic sentences.)
   1. For a balanced diet, we should eat foods from the four basic food groups.
      Four basic food groups supply our nutritional needs.
      We need foods from the four basic food groups.

supply most of the protein for building new tissues and healing damaged tissues. Another group is the fruit and vegetable group, which provides most of the vitamins and many of the minerals that keep our bodies healthy. A third group includes milk and milk products, which supply various vitamins and minerals. The last group is the bread and cereal group. Included in this group are all breads, pastries, and anything produced from grains like wheat, rye, rice, and oats. These foods are especially important in supplying energy-giving starch.

2.   Among these commands is the familiar verse, "Remember now thy Creator in the days of thy youth" (Ecclesiastes 12:1). Another command for youth, given first in the Ten Commandments, is repeated by the apostle Paul. "Children, obey your parents in the Lord: for this is right. Honour thy father and mother" (Ephesians 6:1, 2). To the young man Timothy, Paul gave another command: "Let no man despise thy youth; but be thou an example of the believers" (1 Timothy 4:12).

C. Read the paragraph, and do the following exercises.
  1. Read the sentences that should begin the second and the third paragraphs.
  2. Read the topic sentence of each paragraph.
  3. Read the sentences that mar the unity of the paragraphs.

  A tornado is a powerful, twisting windstorm. The winds of a tornado are the most violent winds that occur on earth. They may whirl around the center of the storm at speeds of more than 300 miles per hour. Hurricane winds rarely exceed 160 miles per hour. Most tornadoes measure several hundred yards or less in diameter and last less than an hour. Yet many have caused widespread destruction and death. How are tornadoes formed? First a dense, rolling cloud forms, and the rotating air at the bottom of the cloud becomes a narrow cloud called a funnel. Then this funnel extends toward the earth's surface. When it touches the surface of the earth, the funnel raises a huge dust cloud and destroys almost everything in its path. A storm cellar offers the best protection against a tornado. The storm cellar can also be used to store foods like potatoes, carrots, and onions. A basement is the next best place to take shelter. In a basement, you should crouch under a table on the side of the room from which the tornado is approaching. Where there is no basement, you should lie flat under a bed or table away from windows. Mobile homes that are not anchored should be vacated, for they offer no protection. If you are outside, you should lie flat in a ditch or ravine to keep debris

2. The Bible directs some specific commands to young people.
Some specific Bible commands are given to young people.

C. 1. *Paragraph 2:* How are tornadoes formed?
    Paragraph 3: A storm cellar offers the best protection against a tornado.
  2. *Paragraph 1:* A tornado is a powerful, twisting windstorm.
    Paragraph 2: How are tornadoes formed?
    Paragraph 3: Wherever you are, you should seek a place of protection immediately when a tornado approaches.
  3. *Paragraph 1:* Hurricane winds rarely exceed 160 miles per hour.
    Paragraph 3: The storm cellar can also be used to store foods like potatoes, carrots, and onions.

from hitting you. Wherever you are, you should seek a place of protection immediately when a tornado approaches.

Written Exercises

A. Write the letter of the sentence that would make the best topic sentence for each paragraph.

1. a. The Dead Sea lies at the southern end of the Jordan Valley.
   b. The Jordan River empties into the Dead Sea.
   c. The name *Dead Sea* well describes this sunken spot at the southern end of the Jordan Valley.
   d. The Dead Sea is lifeless because its main source is salty, and it has no outlet.

   No fish swim in its waters, and very little plant life graces its banks. The main source of the sea, the Jordan River, carries with it more than the average amount of minerals. Add to this the fact that the Dead Sea has no outlet, and you can easily understand why this is the most salty and barren sea in the world. In fact, while ocean water averages about 5 percent mineral content, the Dead Sea averages about 25 percent!

2. a. Christians are not to take part in the affairs of civil government.
   b. Because Christians are separated, nonresistant citizens of heaven, they are not to take part in civil government.
   c. Christians are to be nonresistant.
   d. Christians belong not to this world but to the heavenly kingdom.

   The church is clearly established as a people separate from this world. Also, Christians are to be nonresistant. Since civil government operates by force, how can a Christian take part in any of its functions? Furthermore, Christians are citizens of the heavenly kingdom. They are called to be ambassadors for Christ in this world. No ambassador living in a foreign country has any right to become involved in the civil affairs of that country.

B. Write a good topic sentence for each of the following paragraphs.

1. Cold fronts move fast, often giving only a few hours' notice of their approach by cloud formations. Slow-moving warm fronts may give their cloud announcements a day or two in advance. The precipitation caused by cold fronts is usually heavy and stormy, but it does not last long. Warm fronts bring steady precipitation that may last for several days. Cold fronts are followed by a sharp drop in temperature, but warm fronts bring warmer weather.

2. They are the only animals that nurse their young. Compared to most other animals, mammals give much care to their young. They

Written Exercises

A. 1. c
   2. a

B. (Possible topic sentences.)
   1. Warm fronts and cold fronts bring different kinds of weather.
      Warm fronts and cold fronts are quite different.
   2. Mammals are different from other animals in several ways.
      Several characteristics set mammals apart from other animals.

are also the only animals that have hair. Mammals breathe with lungs by means of a diaphragm. Finally, their brains are larger and more complex than those of most other animals.

C. Read the paragraph, and do these exercises.
   1. Copy the sentence that should begin the second paragraph.
   2. Copy the topic sentence of each paragraph.
   3. Copy the sentence that mars the unity of the paragraphs.

   From the Mediterranean Sea on the west to the Arabian Desert on the east, Palestine averages a width of about 70 miles. From the Leontes River and Mount Hermon on the north to the Negev on the south, it stretches about 150 miles. These boundaries enclose only about twelve thousand square miles of land. As you can see, the land of Palestine is smaller than we tend to think. Palestine is divided into four geographical regions. The Coastal Plain, bordering the Mediterranean Sea on the west, includes some of the most fertile areas of Palestine. The Central Range is actually an extension of the Lebanon Mountains. This mountainous area is commonly called the "hill country" in the Bible. East of the Central Range lies the Jordan Valley, of which a large part is below sea level. On the eastern edge of Palestine is the Eastern Range, which includes some fertile plateaus and highlands. The mountains here are higher and steeper than those of the Central Range. East of Palestine stretch thousands of square miles of desert country.

Review Exercises

Copy the following outline, and expand it with points from the list. Follow the rules that you studied in previous grades. If you need help, use the index in the back of this book.

The Pennsylvania Bobcat
I. The body of a bobcat
  A. Is not very large
  B. Has a beautiful pelt
  C. Is well equipped to be a predator
II. The behavior of a bobcat
  A. Hunts mainly at night
  B. Marks definite territory
  C. Runs in high-tailed, bouncing manner

Average weight fifteen to twenty pounds
Gray-brown fur with dark spots and bars
Retractable, hooked claws on its feet

C. 1. Palestine is divided into four geographical regions.
   2. *Paragraph 1:* As you can see, the land of Palestine is smaller than we tend to think.
      Paragraph 2: Palestine is divided into four geographical regions.
   3. East of Palestine stretch thousands of square miles of desert country.

Review Exercises

(Order of points may vary. Check for correct outline form.)

The Pennsylvania Bobcat

I. The body of a bobcat
  A. Is not very large
    1. Average length thirty-six inches, including six-inch tail
    2. Average weight fifteen to twenty pounds
  B. Has a beautiful pelt
    1. Gray-brown fur with dark spots and bars
    2. White lips, chin, underside of neck, and belly
    3. Ruff of fur extending downward and outward from ears
  C. Is well equipped to be a predator
    1. Sharp sense of sight, smell, and especially hearing
    2. Four large canine fangs to hold prey
    3. Retractable, hooked claws on its feet
II. The behavior of a bobcat
  A. Hunts mainly at night
    1. Surveys area from high vantage point for prey
    2. Searches into rock crevices, brush piles, thickets, and stumps
  B. Marks definite territory
    1. Territory may overlap that of other bobcats
    2. Size of territory varies according to game available
  C. Runs in high-tailed, bouncing manner

Territory may overlap that of other bobcats
Average length thirty-six inches, including six-inch tail
Surveys area from high vantage point for prey
Sharp sense of sight, smell, and especially hearing
White lips, chin, underside of neck, and belly
Searches into rock crevices, brush piles, thickets, and stumps
Four large canine fangs to hold prey
Size of territory varies according to game available
Ruff of fur extending downward and outward from ears

---

14. Simple and Compound Sentences

> **Lesson Survey**
> - A **simple sentence** contains only one independent clause.
> - A **compound sentence** contains two or more independent clauses.

In Lesson 10 you saw that sentences are classified into four types according to their use. Sentences are also classified into four types according to their structure. They are *simple, compound, complex,* and *compound-complex* sentences. This lesson reviews simple and compound sentences. In Lesson 15 you will study complex sentences. You will study compound-complex sentences later in this English series.

A *simple sentence* contains only one independent clause. That is, a simple sentence has only one skeleton. To say that a sentence is *simple* or that it has only *one* independent clause does not necessarily mean that it is short. Both of the following examples are simple sentences because each has only one skeleton.

A <u>moose</u> <u>stood</u> beside the road.
A bull <u>moose</u> with a majestic spread of antlers <u>stood</u> silently in the shadow of a large pine tree beside the road.

Do not confuse compound parts in a simple sentence with a compound sentence. A sentence may have a compound subject or verb, but it is still a simple sentence if it has only one clause.

<u>Moose</u>, <u>elk</u>, and <u>caribou</u> <u>are</u> all in the deer family. (compound subject)

Lesson 14

Purpose: (1) To teach simple and compound sentences. (2) To teach the difference between compound parts and compound sentences.

Oral Review:
1. Tell whether each word group is a clause or not a clause.
   a. on the first three benches (not a clause)
   b. which we had not considered (clause)
   c. the fire has died down (clause)
   d. beyond the far horizon (not a clause)
   e. because the pigs rooted under the fence (clause)
2. Tell whether each clause is dependent or independent.
   a. until the rain stops (dependent)
   b. that the song leader had announced (dependent)
   c. the service will soon start (independent)
   d. if the Lord will (dependent)
   e. she told an interesting story (independent)
3. Where should a noun of direct address appear in a sentence diagram? (on a separate horizontal line to the left of the main base line)
4. Where should an appositive appear in a sentence diagram? (in parentheses right after the word it explains)
5. Define each term.
   a. sentence (a group of words that expresses a complete thought)
   b. fragment (a group of words that does not express a complete thought)
   c. run-on error (two or more sentences incorrectly written as one)

Lesson Introduction: Many ideas come in pairs that are closely related. Those ideas often are

The <u>wolves</u> <u>attacked</u> and <u>killed</u> the wounded moose. (compound verb)

The <u>ravens</u> and the <u>vultures</u> <u>swooped</u> in and <u>devoured</u> the remains. (compound subject and compound verb)

A *compound sentence* contains two or more independent clauses. These clauses are usually joined by a coordinating conjunction, such as *and, but, or, for, nor,* or *yet.* Remember to use a comma before the conjunction unless the two clauses are very short.

"<u>I</u> <u>had</u> many things to write, *but* <u>I</u> <u>will</u> not with ink and pen <u>write</u> unto thee."

"<u>God</u> <u>dwelleth</u> in us, *and* his <u>love</u> <u>is perfected</u> in us."

<u>Job</u> <u>suffered</u> pain and misunderstanding, *yet* <u>he</u> <u>maintained</u> his faith.

The <u>Lord</u> <u>spoke</u> *and* the <u>world</u> <u>came</u> into existence. (acceptable with or without the comma)

Of course, not every pair of clauses can be joined into a compound sentence. The two clauses must be related in a sensible way.

The children hoed the corn, and the mailman came. (The two actions are completely unrelated.)

The children hoed the corn, and Father cultivated the beans. (Hoeing corn and cultivating beans are related.)

Honesty is always appreciated in others, yet many people are impatient and irritable. (Honesty has little to do with impatience and irritability.)

Honesty is always appreciated in others, yet many people are deceitful themselves. (Honesty is the opposite of deceitfulness.)

Since the clauses of a compound sentence are both independent, the skeletons are diagramed side by side. The conjunction is placed on a broken line between the clauses.

The men have worked hard, and we appreciate their efforts.

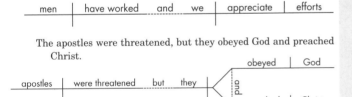

The apostles were threatened, but they obeyed God and preached Christ.

communicated more clearly if they are joined together than if they are expressed as two separate sentences. Here is one example.

Cain was a tiller of the ground. Abel was a shepherd.

Cain was a tiller of the ground, but Abel was a shepherd.

Putting the two ideas together helps to show the relationship between them. Sometimes they are joined as compound sentences (as in today's lesson), and sometimes they are joined as complex sentences (to be studied in Lesson 15).

Lesson Outline:

1. A simple sentence contains one independent clause.

    a. It has only one skeleton.

    b. A sentence may have a compound subject or verb, but it is still a simple sentence if it has only one clause.

2. A compound sentence contains two or more independent clauses.

    a. These clauses are usually joined by a coordinating conjunction.

    b. The conjunction is usually preceded by a comma.

    c. The two clauses must be related in a sensible way.

★ **EXTRA PRACTICE**

Worksheet 7 (*Simple and Compound Sentences*)

Class Practice

A. Join these choppy simple sentences with coordinating conjunctions.
1. The horse ran away. The goat stayed in the pasture.
2. Father will need to help us. We will not finish on time.
3. The girls sang up the scale. The boys sang down the scale.
4. Mother packed a large lunch. Our trip would take most of the day.
5. The owl swooped out of the night sky. The mouse escaped under a rock.

B. Tell whether the two clauses in each sentence are *related* or *unrelated*.
1. Mother prepared a delicious breakfast, and we walked to school.
2. Henry pulled weeds in the garden, but we could not find the book.
3. Yesterday we watered the garden, and today the peas are up.
4. Several deer have been seen in the woods near the farm, yet they have not disturbed our corn patch.
5. The load of topsoil has not arrived, nor has Mother called Aunt Lorene.

C. Tell whether each sentence is *simple* or *compound*. Then diagram the skeletons and complements on the chalkboard.
1. Abram left Ur of the Chaldees, for God had called him.
2. He did not know his destination, but he did trust the Lord.
3. Gideon's three hundred men blew their trumpets and broke their pitchers.
4. Moses and Elijah came and talked with Jesus.
5. The disciples marveled at Jesus' glory, yet they did not fully understand His words.

Written Exercises

A. Join these choppy simple sentences with coordinating conjunctions. Be sure to use correct punctuation.
1. The breadbox was empty. No more loaves were in the freezer.
2. Most moths have feathery antennae. Butterflies have smooth ones.
3. The day was hot and sweltering. The night stayed warm and humid.
4. We cleaned the wound thoroughly. It became swollen and sore.
5. You must do your work more neatly. You will need to recopy it.

B. Write whether the two clauses in each sentence are related (*R*) or unrelated (*U*).
1. The cows contentedly chewed their cuds, but Father worked on the tractor.
2. The wind howled through the trees, and the baby was asleep in the crib.

Lesson 14 Answers

Class Practice

A. 1. The horse ran away, but the goat stayed in the pasture.
2. Father will need to help us, or we will not finish on time.
3. The girls sang up the scale, and (but) the boys sang down the scale.
4. Mother packed a large lunch, for our trip would take most of the day.
5. The owl swooped out of the night sky, but the mouse escaped under a rock.

B. 1. unrelated   4. related
2. unrelated   5. unrelated
3. related

C. 1. compound

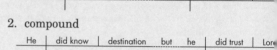

2. compound

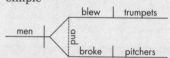

3. simple

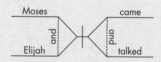

4. simple

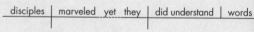

5. compound

Written Exercises

A. 1. The breadbox was empty, and no more loaves were in the freezer.
2. Most moths have feathery antennae, but butterflies have smooth ones.
3. The day was hot and sweltering, and the night stayed warm and humid.
4. We cleaned the wound thoroughly, yet (but) it became swollen and sore.
5. You must do your work more neatly, or you will need to recopy it.

B. 1. U
2. U

3. Felix Manz suffered martyrdom for his faith, but Conrad Grebel died of the plague.
4. Achan's conscience troubled him, or he would not have hidden the stolen things.
5. Moses was the meekest man on earth, but the children of Israel wandered forty years in the wilderness.
6. We went to the evening service at Yellow Creek, and a bus had a flat tire along Route 194.
7. Several severe snowstorms buffeted our valley, yet we were never without electricity.
8. Alligators live in fresh water, and their powerful jaws are frightening to see.
9. Young alligators fall prey to birds and turtles, but the adults have few natural enemies.
10. Most crocodiles live in the Eastern Hemisphere, and some live in salt water.

C. Write whether each sentence is *simple* or *compound*. Then diagram the skeletons and complements.
1. We can know the truth, for God has revealed Himself to us.
2. The Son of God shed His blood and brought redemption.
3. "A false balance is abomination to the Lord: but a just weight is his delight."
4. The Christian may be tempted, yet God supplies His grace.
5. Uncle Leonard and Aunt Elizabeth flew to Seattle but missed their next flight.
6. They missed an appointment, but the Lord had more important plans for them.
7. They met a man in distress, and he asked them many questions.
8. The man returned with them and spent a week in their home.
9. He moved his family to their community, and they are coming to church now.
10. God's ways are best, for He knows all things.

Review Exercises

A. Label each item *S* for sentence, *F* for fragment, or *R* for run-on error. [2]
1. Extending upward many miles.
2. An ocean of air surrounds the earth.
3. This ocean of air is called the atmosphere.
4. Which is actually divided into several layers.
5. Closest to the earth is the troposphere, in this layer weather conditions are formed.

---

3. R   7. R
4. R   8. U
5. U   9. R
6. U   10. U

C. 1. compound
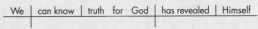

2. simple
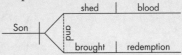

3. compound
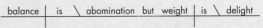

4. compound
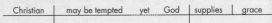

5. simple
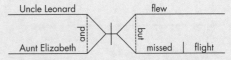

6. compound
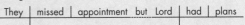

7. compound
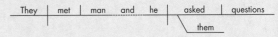

8. simple
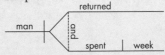

9. compound
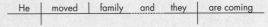

10. compound
ways | are \ best   for   He | knows | things

Review Exercises

A. 1. F   4. F
   2. S   5. R
   3. S

6. Because the troposphere is shallow, only five to ten miles deep.
7. As you climb higher and higher in this layer.
8. The air becomes sharply colder the temperature outside a jet may be minus forty degrees.
9. Above the troposphere is the stratosphere.
10. Which extends about thirty miles beyond the troposphere.
11. Because the air does not circulate.
12. Little change in temperature occurs in the lower part.
13. Although the upper part may reach thirty degrees or more.

B. Correct these fragments and run-on errors. If an item is a correct sentence, write *correct*. [2]
1. The longest book in the Bible.
2. This book is a collection of Hebrew poems, many of them were written by King David.
3. Psalm 22 is unique it contains many prophecies about the Messiah.
4. One of the favorite psalms is Psalm 23.
5. Since it describes the Lord as a shepherd.
6. Psalm 78 is rather long, the psalmist recounts many lessons from Israel's history.
7. Psalm 119 is the longest one it refers to the Bible in almost every verse.
8. Called testimonies, commandments, law, precepts, and statutes.

---

15. Complex Sentences

> **Lesson Survey**
> - A **complex sentence** has one independent (main) clause and one or more dependent clauses.
> - The dependent clause in a complex sentence may be an adjective clause or an adverb clause.
> - An adjective or adverb clause is diagramed on a separate horizontal line beneath the main clause.

An effective writer must be able to write more than simple sentences. He must understand when two independent clauses are closely related and can be joined into a compound sentence. He must also sense when one clause expresses a dependent idea that should be written as an adjective or an adverb clause.

Lesson 15

Purpose: To identify complex sentences that have adjective or adverb clauses.

Oral Review:
1. A compound sentence must contain at least two ———. (independent clauses)
2. The two clauses of a compound sentence are joined by a ———. (coordinating conjunction)
3. Name some common coordinating conjunctions. (and, but, or, for, nor, yet)
4. Tell whether each sentence is simple or compound.
   a. The squirrel scampered up the tree and chattered noisily. (simple)
   b. Soon the dog went away, and the squirrel came down again. (compound)
   c. The busy squirrel gathered a few nuts, but the dog came running after him. (compound)

6. F		10. F	
7. F		11. F	
8. R		12. S	
9. S		13. F	

B. (Corrections are underlined. Words in italics will vary.)
1. The longest book in the Bible *is the Book of Psalms.*
2. This book is a collection of Hebrew poems. Many of them were written by King David.
3. Psalm 22 is unique. It contains many prophecies about the Messiah.
4. correct
5. Since it describes the Lord as a shepherd, *it is called the Shepherd Psalm.*
6. Psalm 78 is rather long. The psalmist recounts many lessons from Israel's history.
7. Psalm 119 is the longest one. It refers to the Bible in almost every verse.
8. *The Scriptures are* called testimonies, commandments, law, precepts, and statutes.

---

5. What kind of clause expresses a complete thought and can stand alone as a sentence? (independent clause)
6. What kind of clause does not express a complete thought and cannot stand alone as a sentence? (dependent clause)
7. Name the four kinds of sentences according to use, and tell what end punctuation should be used with each. (declarative, period; interrogative, question mark; imperative, period; exclamatory, exclamation point)

Lesson Introduction: The word *complex* often means "complicated and difficult," but that is not always the case. Consider the following examples.

housing complex   inferiority complex

Complex in these phrases refers to something that includes more than one part. That is its sense in the

A *complex sentence* has one independent (main) clause and one or more dependent clauses. The dependent clause in a complex sentence does not express a complete thought. It depends on the independent clause for its meaning.

      Jesus, whom we love and worship, is the King of kings.
          Independent clause:
              Jesus is the King of kings (complete thought)
          Dependent clause:
              whom we love and worship (incomplete thought)
      After He arose from the dead, Jesus appeared to His disciples.
          Independent clause:
              Jesus appeared to His disciples (complete thought)
          Dependent clause:
              After He arose from the dead (incomplete thought)

If the dependent clause is used as an adjective, it is usually introduced and linked to the main clause by a relative pronoun (who, whom, whose, which, that).

      The lad *(who) gave his lunch to Jesus* is not named in the Bible.
        (adjective clause telling *which* lad)
      A multitude ate the food *(that) Jesus blessed*.
        (adjective clause telling *which* food)

An adjective clause is diagramed on a separate horizontal line beneath the main clause. A broken line connects the relative pronoun to the word that the clause modifies. Notice that a relative pronoun does more than merely link the two clauses; it fills a definite place in the dependent clause.

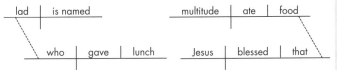

If the dependent clause is used as an adverb, it is introduced and linked to the main clause by a subordinating conjunction. Common subordinating conjunctions include the following: *after, although, as, as if, as though, because, before, even if, how, if, since, so that, than, that, though, till, unless, until, when, whenever, where, wherever, while.*

      (Before) the flood came, God shut the door of the ark.
        (adverb clause telling *when* God shut the door)

phrase *complex sentence;* such a sentence is a "complex" of clauses. A compound sentence also contains more than one clause; but they are each independent clauses, whereas a complex sentence contains at least one dependent clause.

Lesson Outline:

   1. A complex sentence has one independent clause and one or more dependent clauses.

   2. A complex sentence may contain an adjective clause.
      a. An adjective clause is usually introduced by a relative pronoun. (*Teacher:* It may also be introduced by a relative adverb, but that is not taught at this point.)
      b. An adjective clause is diagramed on a separate horizontal line beneath the main clause.

   3. A complex sentence may contain an adverb clause.
      a. An adverb clause is introduced by a subordinating conjunction.
      b. An adverb clause is diagramed on a separate horizontal line beneath the main clause.

★ **EXTRA PRACTICE**
Worksheet 8 (*Complex Sentences*)

Others <u>could have been saved</u> *(if) they <u>had</u> only <u>believed</u>* God.
    (adverb clause telling *under what condition* others could have
    been saved)
<u>Noah</u> <u>built</u> an altar *(when) he <u>came</u> out of the ark.*
    (adverb clause telling *when* Noah built an altar)

The diagram of an adverb clause is similar to that of an adjective clause. However, the broken line always connects the verb of the dependent clause to the word that the clause modifies. The subordinating conjunction fills no specific place in the dependent clause; therefore, it is written on the broken line.

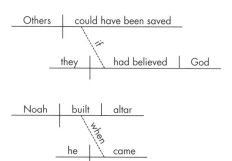

Class Practice

A. Read each clause separately, and identify it as an *independent* or a *dependent* clause.
1. Mother washed the dishes after the babies were asleep.
2. While James waited for the doctor, he read the Bible.
3. Our neighbor, who is a retired carpenter, fixed our leaky roof.
4. Before we start the hike, Brother Victor will describe the vegetation and wildlife that you might observe.
5. These bountiful rains, which the Lord has been giving, promise us fruitful harvests.

B. Tell whether the word that introduces each underlined clause is a *relative pronoun* or a *subordinating conjunction*. Also tell whether the clause is an *adjective* or an *adverb* clause.

Lesson 15 Answers

Class Practice

A. 1. Mother washed the dishes—independent;
    after the babies were asleep—dependent
2. While James waited for the doctor—dependent;
    he read the Bible—independent
3. Our neighbor fixed our leaky roof—independent;
    who is a retired carpenter—dependent
4. Before we start the hike—dependent;
    Brother Victor will describe the vegetation and wildlife—independent;
    that you might observe—dependent
5. These bountiful rains promise us fruitful harvests—independent;
    which the Lord has been giving—dependent

1. The Lord God, <u>who created the heaven and the earth</u>, is worthy of our worship.
2. God created light <u>before He created any form of life</u>.
3. <u>After God had created Adam and Eve</u>, the Creation was finished.
4. The creation, <u>which God finished in six days</u>, is a marvelous testimony of God's wisdom and power.
5. <u>While they lived in Eden</u>, Adam and Eve walked with God, <u>whose presence they enjoyed</u>.

C. Tell whether each sentence is *simple, compound,* or *complex.* Then on the chalkboard, diagram the skeletons and complements of all the clauses.
   1. Squirrels of all kinds can climb trees very well.
   2. When they jump from treetop to treetop, they use their large tails for balance.
   3. The eyes of a squirrel can see no color, but they quickly detect movement.
   4. Their senses of hearing and smell are keen.
   5. The flying squirrel is a nocturnal animal, but other squirrels are most active in early mornings and late afternoons.
   6. Squirrels eat tree buds, which are high-energy foods.
   7. Although a squirrel may reach an age of ten years, most live for only two or three years.

Written Exercises

A. Write the first and last word of each dependent clause, with three dots (...) in between.
   1. John's message, which gripped the hearts of many, prepared the way for Christ.
   2. Because he grieved for the sins of Judah, Jeremiah is called the weeping prophet.
   3. On the isle of Patmos, the apostle John received striking revelations, which he wrote in the Book of Revelation.
   4. Matthew was a tax collector before Jesus called him.
   5. Jehoshaphat, whose life was generally upright, became dangerously friendly with Ahab, a wicked king of Israel.
   6. Although Daniel knew the law, he prayed regularly as usual.

B. Write whether each underlined clause begins with a *relative pronoun* or a *subordinating conjunction.* Also label the clause *adjective* or *adverb.*
   1. The places <u>that were seeded in new grass</u> are looking attractive.
   2. <u>Until we get more rain</u>, we will irrigate <u>so that the crop is not lost</u>.
   3. That elderly man, <u>whom I did not recognize</u>, had known my grandfather <u>when they both were young men</u>.

B. 1. relative pronoun, adjective
   2. subordinating conjunction, adverb
   3. subordinating conjunction, adverb
   4. relative pronoun, adjective
   5. subordinating conjunction, adverb; relative pronoun, adjective

C. 1. simple

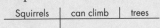

2. complex

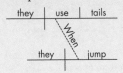

3. compound

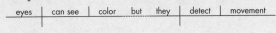

4. simple

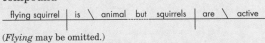

5. compound

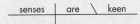

(*Flying* may be omitted.)

6. complex

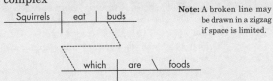

Note: A broken line may be drawn in a zigzag if space is limited.

7. complex

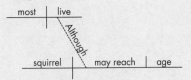

Written Exercises

A. 1. which . . . many
   2. Because . . . Judah
   3. which . . . Revelation
   4. before . . . him
   5. whose . . . upright
   6. Although . . . law

B. 1. relative pronoun, adjective
   2. subordinating conjunction, adverb; subordinating conjunction, adverb
   3. relative pronoun, adjective; subordinating conjunction, adverb

4. This book, <u>which Aunt Grace gave us</u>, is a gripping story of some pioneers <u>who were almost killed in a mountain storm</u>.
5. <u>Since the ground hogs have found our garden</u>, we will not harvest many peas.

C. Write whether each sentence is *simple, compound,* or *complex.* Then diagram the skeletons and complements of all the clauses (dependent and independent).
 1. The tabernacle, which was designed by God Himself, became the center of Jewish worship.
 2. An open courtyard surrounded the tabernacle.
 3. The outer appearance was drab, but the inner beauty must have been dazzling.
 4. The furnishings in the courtyard, which included the altar of burnt offering and the laver, were made with brass.
 5. Before the priests entered the tabernacle, they washed their hands and feet at the laver.
 6. The priest who stepped inside the tabernacle saw furnishings of gold.
 7. A beautiful veil hung from four pillars and divided the tabernacle into two rooms.
 8. Although the priests could enter the first room, only the high priest could enter the second.
 9. This veil was rent at Jesus' death, and the way to God was opened.
10. Because Jesus has shed His blood, we no longer worship in the tabernacle.

Review Exercises

Label each sentence *dec.* (declarative), *int.* (interrogative), *imp.* (imperative), or *exc.* (exclamatory). Also write the last word of the sentence, followed by the correct end punctuation. [10]
 1. Do you know what an ellipse is
 2. An ellipse is actually an oval
 3. How hard it must be to draw an accurate ellipse
 4. If you follow these directions, you can draw one quite easily
 5. You will need a piece of heavy cardboard, a pencil, two thumbtacks, and a piece of string tied in a loop
 6. Push the two thumbtacks into the cardboard, and loop your string around them
 7. Now you must put your pencil into the loop and pull the string tight
 8. The two thumbtacks and the pencil should form a triangle
 9. Move your pencil in a circular motion, keeping the string tight
10. Have you drawn a neat ellipse

10. complex

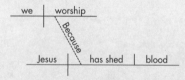

Review Exercises
 1. int., is?   6. imp., them.
 2. dec., oval.   7. dec., tight.
 3. exc., ellipse!   8. dec., triangle.
 4. dec., easily.   9. imp., tight.
 5. dec., loop.   10. int., ellipse?

4. relative pronoun, adjective;
   relative pronoun, adjective
5. subordinating conjunction, adverb

C. 1. complex

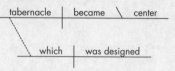

2. simple

3. compound

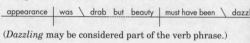

(*Dazzling* may be considered part of the verb phrase.)

4. complex

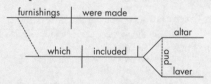

5. complex

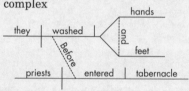

6. complex

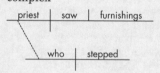

7. simple

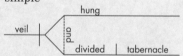

8. complex

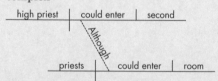

9. compound

| veil | was rent | and | way | was opened |

11. Is your ellipse almost a circle, or is it long and narrow
12. You can draw ellipses of different shapes
13. Move your thumbtacks closer together or farther apart
14. What happens to the shape of your ellipses
15. What a variety of ellipses you have drawn

11. int., narrow?
12. dec., shapes.
13. imp., apart.
14. int., ellipses?
15. exc., drawn!

---

16. Sentence Order and Paragraph Coherence

> **Lesson Survey**
> * A paragraph has **coherence** when all the sentences fit together smoothly in a logical order.
> * Sentence order can help bring coherence to a paragraph.

As you learned in Lesson 13, a paragraph needs unity. But just because every sentence supports the topic sentence does not guarantee a good paragraph. The sentences must also be written in a clear, sensible order, and they must flow smoothly from one to the next. These characteristics give *coherence* to a paragraph.

Compare the following two paragraphs. Both have unity, but the first one lacks coherence. Notice how the adjusted sentence order makes the second paragraph much more effective.

Incoherent:

Standing on the foot bridge over the Cedar Glen Creek, I surveyed the peaceful scene before me. The right bank was low and smooth. Downstream, a dense patch of briers thrust out their threatening arms at any trespasser who might dare to venture among them. The left bank was higher and rougher than the right bank. Next to the bridge, two scraggly cedar trees clung precariously to the bank, dangling their roots into the water. A patch of wild violets surrounded the foot of the bridge on the right bank. About twenty feet beyond the cedars, the West Cedar Glen Creek poured its tribute of water into the main creek. Beyond the brier patch, the stream disappeared in a sharp right turn around a large boulder. A zigzag wooden rail fence came down the western branch and followed the curve of the main stream out of sight.

Lesson 16

Purpose: (1) To define paragraph coherence. (2) To teach the order of sentences as a means of achieving coherence. *(Previous experience:* Concept of chronological order, without use of the term.)

Oral Review:

1. Give some details about proper paragraph form. (first line indented, left margin straight, right margin as straight as possible)
2. When does a paragraph have unity? (when every sentence directly supports the topic sentence)
3. Tell whether each sentence is true or false.
   a. A good topic sentence summarizes the details of a paragraph. (false)
   b. A topic sentence may be found almost anywhere in a paragraph. (true)
   c. Topic sentences are especially important in

---

narrative paragraphs. (false)

4. a. An adverb clause is introduced by a ———. (subordinating conjunction)
   b. An adjective clause is introduced by a ———. (relative pronoun)
5. a. A ——— sentence has only one clause. (simple)
   b. A ——— sentence has a main clause and a dependent clause. (complex)
   c. A ——— sentence has two independent clauses. (compound)

Lesson Introduction: Imagine school life with no coherence or order. You would never know which class was coming next. Recess or lunch might be announced at any time of the day. What a frustrating and inefficient time that would be!

Coherence and order are essential in almost everything we do. In this lesson, we will study the importance of coherence in writing.

Coherent:

> Standing on the foot bridge over the Cedar Glen Creek, I surveyed the peaceful scene before me. The right bank was low and smooth. A patch of wild violets surrounded the foot of the bridge. Farther downstream, a dense patch of briers thrust out their threatening arms at any trespasser who might dare to venture among them. Beyond the brier patch, the stream disappeared in a sharp right turn around a large boulder. The left bank was higher and rougher than the right bank. Next to the bridge two scraggly cedar trees clung precariously to the bank, dangling their roots into the water. About twenty feet beyond the cedars, the West Cedar Glen Creek poured its tribute of water into the main creek. A zigzag wooden rail fence came down the western branch and followed the curve of the main stream out of sight.

As you can see, the order in which sentences are written can help determine whether or not a paragraph is coherent. Most paragraphs use one of three orders of development: chronological order, spatial order, or order of importance.

Paragraphs in stories are usually written in the order that things happened. This is called *chronological order,* or the order of time. Be careful to write the paragraph clearly so that the reader can well understand what happened first, second, third, and so on to the end.

Read this short paragraph from Luke 4:38, 39. Notice how easy it is to follow the sequence of events.

> And he arose out of the synagogue, and entered into Simon's house. And Simon's wife's mother was taken with a great fever; and they besought him for her. And he stood over her, and rebuked the fever; and it left her: and immediately she arose and ministered unto them.

Paragraphs that give directions or explain a process must also follow chronological order. Imagine trying to make a birdhouse or bake some cookies if the steps were not presented in proper chronological order!

A descriptive paragraph is usually written in *spatial order,* or the order of space. The paragraph describes one thing at a time in a logical sequence of position. Depending on the scene you are describing, you may present the details from near to far, far to near, left to right, or right to left. You may use a circular sweep, giving the details in clockwise or counterclockwise order. Perhaps one particular item in the scene stands out. You may describe that item and then give the rest of the details in relationship to that thing. And you may well use a combination of these methods.

Consider again the coherent example near the beginning of this lesson.

Lesson Outline:

1. A paragraph has coherence when all the sentences fit together smoothly in a logical order.

2. Sentence order can help bring coherence to a paragraph.

   a. Paragraphs in stories are usually written in chronological order, or the order of time. This is the order in which things happened.

   b. A descriptive paragraph is usually written in spatial order, or the order of space. The details of the scene are described from near to far, from left to right, or in some other logical sequence of position.

   c. A paragraph of information or explanation should be written in the order of importance. The most effective arrangement is usually to build up from the least important to the most important.

★ *EXTRA PRACTICE*
Worksheet 9 (*Sentence Order and Coherence*)

The stream divided the scene into two sections. First the author described the right bank, giving the details from near to far. Then he described the left bank, using the same order.

A paragraph of information or explanation should be written in the *order of importance*. One method is to arrange the details from the most important to the least important. But the detail given last usually makes the strongest impression. Therefore, a paragraph is usually more effective if the ideas build up from the least important to the most important.

Topic	<u>A young person should cultivate good work habits.</u> For one
Reason 1	thing, diligence and carefulness are generally needed to do satisfactory work and earn good grades. A good worker also makes
Reason 2	a worthwhile contribution to his surroundings. When everyone is working well, there is a pleasant atmosphere at home or at school. Each person's chores are done right, and others are not hindered in their work. Furthermore, developing good work
Reason 3	habits in youth prepares one to contribute to society and to the church as he grows older. Usually, the habits of youth follow a person into his adulthood. Above all, doing one's work well is
Reason 4	essential to pleasing the Lord. The Bible says, "Whatsoever thy hand findeth to do, do it with thy might." This surely applies to a young person's work habits.

As you write a paragraph, consider the order of your sentences. With chronological order, will the reader find it easy to follow the sequence of events? With spatial order, will he be able to picture the scene clearly in his mind? With the order of importance, will he sense a logical progression of thought? Do your best to present the details in the most logical, coherent way that you can.

Class Practice

A. Tell whether these paragraphs are written in *chronological order, spatial order,* or *order of importance.*

1. As we approached the house, we could tell that Sister Lillian loves flowers. From the left side of the gate to the edge of her small lot, a row of black-eyed Susans nodded their heads at us. Around the corner from them were several rows of hollyhocks in various sizes and colors. On the right side of the gate, a row of Shasta daisies extended to the corner, with some tiger lilies down the side. Both sides of the short walk to the house were lined with beautiful beds of marigolds, petunias, zinnias, and snapdragons.

2. From the moment we walked through the gate, we had an enjoyable time with Sister Lillian. The elderly lady bustled down the walk

Lesson 16 Answers

Class Practice

A. 1. spatial order
   2. chronological order

to meet us, and with her usual zest, she was soon showing us her outside flowers. Then we turned to her house, which one might have mistaken for a flower shop. As we moved from room to room, Sister Lillian sounded much like the biology teacher she had been years before. Later we sat in the parlor and visited, and Sister Lillian asked us to sing a few songs. Before long Father announced that it was high time to head for home. And, indeed, the evening had passed quickly!

3.   On the way home, Father reminded us of several reasons for Sister Lillian's pleasant ways. For one thing, she has always loved people, especially children. This was well demonstrated during her thirty years of teaching school. Also, she keeps herself busy. Even at eighty-five years of age, she allows herself no leisure to sit around idly and brood. Most important, she had become a Christian five years earlier. Now her life is filled with the joy of the Lord.

3. order of importance

B. Give the sentence numbers in the correct order to make each paragraph coherent.

1.   ¹A window shade operates in a very simple way. ²A little catch holds the spring in place when you stop pulling. ³Then when you want to put the shade back up, you give it a tug. ⁴When you pull the shade down, you wind up a spring inside the roller. ⁵As the spring unwinds, it pulls the shade up. ⁶This tug releases the catch and allows the spring to unwind.

2.   ¹The heating apparatus takes up the entire north wall of the basement. ²The furnace itself, which is the largest part of the apparatus, stands almost against the wall on the right. ³To the far left is the electric motor that runs the two augers. ⁴Next to the motor is the coal bin. ⁵Below the firebox in the furnace, a second auger carries the ashes through the wall to the ash bin outside. ⁶A large auger carries the coal from the bin to the furnace.

3.   ¹Keeping fresh bedding in a calf hutch is especially important in the summer. ²Most important, a clean hutch is healthier for calves than a dirty one. ³In addition, a clean hutch smells much fresher. ⁴Of course,

B. 1. 1, 4, 2, 3, 6, 5
   2. 1, 3, 4, 6, 2, 5 (The left-to-right sequence reflects spatial order, and the coal-to-ashes sequence reflects chronological order.)
   3. 1, 4, 5, 3, 6, 2

clean straw is always more pleasant to look at than mud and muck. ⁵The calves will also stay much cleaner this way. ⁶Even more important, the fly population will be noticeably lower around a clean hutch.

Written Exercises

A. Write a paragraph explaining a process or describing a series of events in a short happening. Be sure to give your details in clear chronological order.

B. Write a paragraph describing a scene or the layout of a room. Use spatial order to make the scene easy to picture.

C. Choose one of the following topic sentences, or write your own to develop a paragraph using the order of importance. Include at least three details to support the topic sentence.
   1. Getting out of bed promptly is the best way to start the day.
   2. In a few simple ways, a person can keep himself tidy and neat.
   3. Every student should keep his desk orderly.
   4. My first choice for a pet is a dog (cat, parakeet, or other animal).
   5. My favorite subject in school is English (history, math, or other subject).

Review Exercises

A. Write *adjective* or *adverb* for each underlined clause. [15]
   1. Jesus, <u>who is the Son of God</u>, lived a sinless life <u>while He was in the world</u>.
   2. <u>Because Jesus is divine</u>, He could read the hearts of all men.
   3. His humanity is shown by the physical needs <u>that He suffered</u>.
   4. Jesus went to Jerusalem <u>when it was time for Him to die</u>.

B. Label each sentence *S* for simple, *Cd* for compound, or *Cx* for complex. [14, 15]
   1. Peter and John went to the temple at the hour of prayer.
   2. A certain man, who had been lame all his life, was brought to the temple every day.
   3. When he saw Peter and John, he asked alms of them.
   4. The apostles had no silver or gold to give him, but they did have something much better to offer.
   5. They told him about Jesus and healed him.
   6. The healed man praised God, and the people were filled with amazement.
   7. When the people saw this, they gathered around the apostles and the man.
   8. Peter preached a powerful message, and many of the people believed.

Written Exercises

A. (Individual work. Check especially for chronological order.)

B. (Individual work. Check especially for spatial order.)

C. (Individual work. Check for proper order of importance.)

Review Exercises

A. 1. adjective, adverb
   2. adverb
   3. adjective
   4. adverb

B. 1. S
   2. Cx
   3. Cx
   4. Cd
   5. S
   6. Cd
   7. Cx
   8. Cd

17. Sentence Transitions and Paragraph Coherence

> **Lesson Survey**
> - A **transitional word** builds coherence by showing the relationship of one sentence to the next.
> - The **repetition of key words** builds coherence by emphasizing the main idea.
> - The use of **pronoun reference** builds coherence by referring to something mentioned earlier in the paragraph.

By paying careful attention to the order of the sentences within a paragraph, a writer naturally tends to make smooth transitions from one sentence to the next. *However, he* may employ *other devices* to *achieve coherence.* In this lesson, you will learn about three such *tools* that help a *writer* in *this important task.*

In the paragraph above, the italicized words illustrate the three tools mentioned at the end. Perhaps the simplest tool to use is *transitional words,* which link sentences together and show the relationships between them. The word *However* in the previous paragraph is an example of a transitional word.

You must choose transitional words carefully. You want the word that will convey exactly the proper relationship between two ideas. The following chart shows a number of transitional words in various categories.

Time

first	next	later
second	then	eventually
now	after	at last
soon	meanwhile	finally

Space

near	ahead	outside
beyond	behind	to the right (left)
around	above	in the distance
next	inside	in the center
below	along	followed by

Addition

and	moreover	furthermore
and then	likewise	again
too	in addition	also
besides	further	

Lesson 17

Purpose: To show additional methods of achieving coherence in paragraphs, including *repetition of key words and *pronoun reference.

Oral Review:

1. The sentence that states the main idea of a paragraph is the ——— sentence. (topic)
2. When every sentence in a paragraph directly supports the topic sentence, the paragraph has ———. (unity)
3. In what kind of writing do paragraphs often have no clear topic sentences? (narrative writing, especially dialogue)
4. When the sentences in a paragraph flow smoothly from one to the next, the paragraph has ———. (coherence)
5. When details in a paragraph are given in the order of importance, the most important detail should usually be given ———. (last)
6. What two points describe good paragraph form? (first line indented; margins as straight as possible)
7. Name three types of sentence order used in paragraph development. (chronological, spatial, order of importance)

Lesson Introduction: Read 1 Kings 4:29–34 to the students. Ask what important word is repeated a number of times in the passage. (wisdom) Then ask what character is mentioned in each verse. (Solomon) Point out, however, that he is not called by the name *Solomon* each time, but usually by a pronoun. Finally, point out several specific words that help link the sentences together: *and* (several times), *for,* and *also.* This lesson teaches the use of these means to provide coherence in paragraphs.

Contrast

but	otherwise	nevertheless
yet	though	on the other hand
still	although	on the contrary
however		

Example or Illustration

| for example | to illustrate | specifically |
| for instance | in fact | in other words |

Result or Conclusion

| therefore | in summary | consequently |
| thus | in conclusion | as a result |

Notice how the underlined transitional words in the following paragraphs help the sentences to flow smoothly.

> The creek had already overflowed its banks three times that summer. <u>With this in mind</u>, Father decided to reinforce the aging bridge in our lane. <u>But</u> it was all in vain; the <u>next</u> flood swept the bridge off its foundations and scattered the pieces down through the valley.

*   *   *   *   *

> Lois Ann looked around the room. Bunches of dried herbs hung <u>on the wall</u> close to the wood-burning cookstove. There was a sink with only one basin. <u>Above</u> the sink and <u>below</u> it were two-door metal cabinets. A small refrigerator was <u>beside the door</u>. <u>Opposite</u> the door was a table pushed <u>against the wall</u>. The table was littered with old newspapers and carving tools.

Transitional words should be used with discretion. You may discover that tacking such words onto sentence beginnings is an easy way to link sentences. In a well-written paragraph, however, you will not use a transitional word in every sentence. In fact, if you use too many such expressions, your paragraphs will not sound natural.

You can also build coherence into a paragraph by the *repetition of key words.* This is especially effective because the repetition does more than merely link the sentences; it also emphasizes the main idea. Of course, if you use this method carelessly, the repetition will be tiresome rather than helpful.

As you use repetition, remember two important things. First, repeat *key words* that will indeed emphasize the main idea. Second, use *synonyms* instead of always repeating the same word. This preserves coherence while preventing tiresome repetition.

Lesson Outline:

1. One way to build coherence into paragraphs is by using transitional words.
   a. Transitional words show relationships between sentences.
   b. The words chosen must convey proper relationships.
   c. A transitional word must not be used in every sentence.

2. A second way to build coherence into paragraphs is by repeating key words.
   a. The repetition links the sentences and also emphasizes the main idea.
   b. The repeated words must truly emphasize the main idea of the paragraph.
   c. Synonyms should be used to avoid overworking any one word.

3. A third way to build coherence into paragraphs is by using pronoun reference.
   a. This is another form of repetition since the pronouns refer to something mentioned earlier in the paragraph.
   b. Pronoun reference also helps to keep the main thought in focus.

4. Working for paragraph coherence should be done mainly in the revising and proofreading stage of writing.

★ **EXTRA PRACTICE**
Worksheet 10 (*Sentence Transitions and Coherence*)

Poor: Main idea not repeated

Stepping into the replica of the pioneer cabin, we were immediately impressed with its <u>smallness</u>. Its rough-hewn walls enclosed one room barely ten feet by fifteen feet. A gnarled ladder pointed to a loft on the one side. Only a rugged table and two rough-hewn benches furnished the room.

Improved:

Stepping into the replica of the pioneer cabin, we were immediately impressed with its <u>smallness</u>. Its rough-hewn walls enclosed one <u>little</u> room barely ten feet by fifteen feet. A <u>narrow</u> ladder pointed to a loft on the one side. Only a <u>small</u> table and two <u>low</u> benches furnished the room.

Poor: Forms of the same word repeated too often

Jesus was <u>kind</u> to everyone He met. He <u>kindly</u> healed the sick and comforted the sorrowing. He had <u>kind</u> words for small children who came to Him. Even when enemies opposed Him, Jesus <u>kindly</u> tried to show them the right way. Truly Jesus is an example of <u>kindness</u> for us.

Improved:

Jesus was <u>kind</u> to everyone He met. He <u>graciously</u> healed the sick and comforted the sorrowing. He had <u>gentle</u> words for small children who came to Him. Even when enemies opposed Him, Jesus <u>patiently</u> tried to show them the right way. Truly Jesus is an example of <u>kindness</u> for us.

Pronoun reference can also be used to achieve coherence. Actually, this is a form of repetition since the pronouns refer to something mentioned earlier in the paragraph. These pronouns also keep the main thought in focus.

Melinda was puzzled. Why would <u>her</u> friend say such a thing? <u>She</u> still felt the sting of those words. True, the others had admired <u>her</u> picture. But <u>she</u> did not think <u>herself</u> better than everyone else!

Coherence is an essential part of a well-written paragraph. Though it is not so easily defined as unity, a reader can easily tell when coherence is absent. You should probably not put much effort into building coherence as you write the first draft of a composition. But as you proofread and revise, use the following questions to test for coherence.

1. Do the sentences follow a logical order?
2. Do the sentences flow smoothly from one to the next?
3. Have I made effective use of transitional words, repetition, and pronoun reference?

Class Practice

A. Read the paragraphs, and do these exercises.
1. Give the transitional words used in these three paragraphs.
2. In the first paragraph, what two pronouns are used? What is the antecedent of these pronouns?
3. Give two examples of pronoun reference in the third paragraph.
4. The second paragraph illustrates the repetition of key words. What key words are repeated?

   The bottle-nosed dolphin is the best known of the dolphin species. With its short beak, the dolphin always looks as if it is smiling. Its color is predominantly gray. Its back, however, is a bit darker than its underside.

   This water-loving mammal shows great friendliness toward man. Often it swims alongside ships. The dolphin also adapts well to captivity. Most zoos with any marine animals will have some bottle-nosed dolphins. In fact, these unique creatures are often trained to perform tricks.

   *   *   *   *   *

   The highlight of our visit to Hager Pottery was watching a master craftsman at work. First he took a glob of clay and put it on a spinning potter's wheel. Skillfully he molded his vessel. After the vessel was completed, he used a sharp, threadlike instrument to smooth out the imperfections. Finally he took it to the kiln room, where it was baked in intense heat to cure the clay.

B. Suggest suitable transitional expressions to fill in the blanks.
1. Heavy rains have fallen since yesterday morning. ——, the creek has not yet overflowed.
2. We had no snow in December. In the first week of January, ——, we had nine inches of snow.
3. In the center of the front wall is the large clock. —— it, the alphabet cards are arranged.
4. Harvey and Kevin were running in the hall. ——, they must stay in their seats during recess.
5. Uncle Leonard's raise hogs and chickens. ——, they have a number of goats and sheep.
6. I have several problems to do in math. I must study my Bible memory ——.

Written Exercises

A. Read the paragraphs, and do these exercises.
1. Write the transitional words used in these paragraphs.
2. What three related pronouns are used throughout the paragraphs? What is the antecedent of those pronouns?

Lesson 17 Answers

Class Practice

A. 1. *paragraph 1:* however
      paragraph 2: also, In fact
      paragraph 3: First, After, Finally
   2. its, it; bottle-nosed dolphin
   3. he—craftsman; it—glob, vessel
   4. water-loving mammal, dolphin (twice), unique creatures

B. 1. However, Nevertheless
   2. however, though
   3. Above, Below, Around, Near
   4. Therefore, Consequently, As a result
   5. Also, In addition, Furthermore, Moreover
   6. too, also

Written Exercises

A. 1. *paragraph 1:* Soon after, therefore
      paragraph 2: later, Moreover, Finally
   2. he, him, his; David

3. In the second paragraph, what key words are repeated? Answer by copying three synonyms.

> When David entered the camp, he must have recognized quickly that something was wrong. Soon after his arrival, he heard the bellowed challenge of Goliath. He saw the Israelite soldiers fleeing before the giant. He must have sensed, therefore, the cloud of fear enveloping the camp that day.
>
> Despite the fear surrounding him, David maintained and displayed his trust in the Lord. David asked why a heathen Philistine was allowed to defy the armies of the living God. To King Saul he later expressed his confidence that he could defeat Goliath with God's help just as he had killed the lion and the bear. Moreover, he declared to Goliath himself that he was coming in the Name of the Lord of hosts. Finally he said with absolute faith, "This day will the Lord deliver thee into mine hand."

3. trust, confidence, faith

B. Write a different transitional expression to fill in each of the following blanks.

1. Godly fear is the beginning of wisdom. ———, we should rejoice in the privilege of a Christian education.
2. The way of wisdom is to flee from evil. ———, the way of foolishness is to play with temptation.
3. God's Word gives many principles for victory. ———, it states many promises for the overcomer.
4. Abraham laid the wood in order on the altar. ——— he bound Isaac and laid him on the wood.
5. The Book of Psalms is the longest book in the Bible. It ——— contains the longest chapter in the Bible.
6. God commanded King Saul to destroy the Amalekites and all that they had. ———, the king spared the best of the animals.
7. Four of Jesus' disciples wrote accounts of His life. Matthew, the ——— one, records more of Jesus' words than do the others.
8. Honesty places a person in the way of God's blessing. ———, this virtue usually earns the appreciation of men.
9. The people of God have often suffered in this world. Many Anabaptists, ———, were martyred for their faith.
10. Christians long for the return of their Lord. ———, they diligently labor in His kingdom.

B. (Sample answers.)

1. Therefore, Consequently
2. But, However, In contrast, On the other hand
3. Moreover, In addition, Furthermore, Also
4. Then, Next, Afterward
5. also, further
6. However, But, Yet, Nevertheless, Still
7. first
8. In addition, Furthermore, Moreover, Also, Besides
9. for example, for instance, in fact
10. Meanwhile, Therefore, Consequently, Furthermore, Moreover

C. Using details from Genesis 22:5–10, develop the following topic sentence into a paragraph: *Isaac showed great respect for his father on that memorable event at Mount Moriah.* Be sure to put to practice the things you have learned in these two lessons on paragraph coherence.

C. (Individual work.)

Review Exercises

2 verses

A. Read the following Scripture passages. Write *chronological, spatial,* or *order of importance* to identify the order of development that is used. [16]

1. Nehemiah 2:1–8
2. Nehemiah 3
3. Exodus 28:31–35
4. Hebrews 12:5–11

B. Copy the first three words of the topic sentence in each paragraph. [13]

1.   Did you know that the Roman Empire played a pivotal role in world history? For many years, she united the Mediterranean world under one stable government with one common language. During these years, the Romans built a system of good roads for the movement of their armies. Finally, the pagan religion of the Romans was proving unsatisfactory to the masses. In all these ways, God was using the Roman Empire to prepare the world for the coming of Christ.

2.   The Romans, of course, were seeking their own selfish interests. But God used their efforts in each area for His own purposes. The stable government and common language simplified the spread of the Gospel throughout the world then known. An "army" of Christian missionaries traveled those Roman roads to evangelize the world. And the dissatisfaction with pagan religion caused a yearning for true peace and meaning in life that the Saviour now offered.

C. Copy the first three words of the unrelated sentence in the following paragraph. [13]

   A number of writing skills contribute to coherence in a paragraph. The order in which the sentences are written should be carefully planned to produce coherence. In addition, the sentences must all support the topic sentence. Another device to help hold the paragraph together is the use of transitional expressions. The repetition of key ideas and the use of pronoun references also help to achieve coherence.

---

18. Chapter 2 Review

Class Practice

A. Tell what is described by each definition.
1. A sentence that asks a question.
2. A sentence that expresses strong feeling.
3. A sentence that states a fact.
4. A sentence that gives a command or a request.

Lesson 18

Purpose: To review the concepts taught in Chapter 2.

Review Exercises

A. 1. chronological   3. spatial
   2. spatial   4. order of importance

B. 1. Did you know *or* In all these
   2. But God used

C. In addition, the

Lesson 18 Answers

Class Practice

A. 1. interrogative sentence
   2. exclamatory sentence
   3. declarative sentence
   4. imperative sentence

5. Order in which the complete predicate comes before the complete subject.
6. Order in which the complete subject comes before the complete predicate.
7. Order in which part of the complete predicate comes before the complete subject and part comes after.
8. A group of words that contains a subject and a predicate.
9. A clause that does not express a complete thought.
10. A clause that expresses a complete thought and can stand alone as a sentence.
11. A sentence that contains one independent clause and one or more dependent clauses.
12. A sentence that contains only one independent clause.
13. A sentence that contains two or more independent clauses.

B. Identify the following sentences as *declarative, interrogative, imperative,* or *exclamatory.* Tell what end punctuation is needed.
1. God spoke to Jonah
2. Cry against the wickedness of the city of Nineveh
3. Jonah decided to go in the opposite direction
4. Why did God send a mighty tempest
5. How amazing it is that Jonah slept in such a storm

C. Change each sentence to the order named in parentheses after it. If a comma is needed, tell where it should be placed.
1. The disobedient prophet slept down inside the ship. (inverted)
2. There were lots cast to see who was the cause of the distress. (natural)
3. The lot fell upon Jonah. (inverted)
4. The men tried desperately to spare Jonah's life. (mixed)
5. The sea became calm as soon as Jonah was thrown overboard. (mixed)

D. Identify each item as a *dependent clause* or an *independent clause.*
1. After Jonah had run away from God.
2. A great fish had been prepared.
3. While he was in the belly of the fish.
4. Jonah cried unto the Lord.
5. Whom he had disobeyed.
6. The fish vomited out Jonah.
7. Now he was ready to go to Nineveh.
8. Because the people of Nineveh repented of their wickedness.

E. Identify these sentences as *simple, compound,* or *complex.*
1. Down the rough mountain road, the four brethren cautiously made their way with the sick child.

5. inverted word order
6. natural word order
7. mixed word order
8. clause
9. dependent clause
10. independent clause
11. complex sentence
12. simple sentence
13. compound sentence

B. 1. declarative, period
2. imperative, period
3. declarative, period
4. interrogative, question mark
5. exclamatory, exclamation point

C. 1. Down inside the ship slept the disobedient prophet.
2. Lots were cast to see who was the cause of the distress.
3. Upon Jonah fell the lot.
4. Desperately the men tried to spare Jonah's life.
5. As soon as Jonah was thrown overboard, the sea became calm.

D. 1. dependent clause
2. independent clause
3. dependent clause
4. independent clause
5. dependent clause
6. independent clause
7. independent clause
8. dependent clause

E. 1. simple

2. Because the child had a high fever, she was dangerously ill.

3. The doctor diagnosed the illness that caused the fever.

4. He prescribed some antibiotics, and now the child is getting better.

F. Tell whether each underlined item is a *dependent* or an *independent* clause.

1. The title "King of the Mountain" is sometimes given to the bighorn sheep, <u>which is designed specifically to run and jump in the mountains</u>.

2. <u>Although some bighorns live as far south as Mexico</u>, most of them live in British Columbia and Alberta.

3. If we tried to climb the slippery rocks that the bighorn climbs so easily, <u>we would soon be sliding and bouncing down the mountainside</u>.

4. <u>When a bighorn must cross a wide gap</u>, it makes use of its famed jumping ability.

5. If a ridge crumbles as a bighorn lands, <u>it can turn in midair and still land safely</u>.

G. Tell whether each underlined item is an *adjective* or *adverb* clause.

1. The pictures <u>that we drew in art class</u> are hanging on the wall.

2. The parents will be able to see them <u>when they come to the school meeting tonight</u>.

3. <u>Because the pictures are so colorful</u>, the room looks especially attractive.

4. The picture <u>that is hanging in the corner</u> must have been drawn by a talented student.

5. Even Mrs. Snow, <u>who is a professional artist</u>, commented about it.

H. On the chalkboard, diagram the skeletons and complements of these sentences. Include the introductory words of all dependent clauses.

1. Through the forest sounded the cries of the hungry panthers.

2. What an eerie screech they have!

3. When panthers are hungry, they can be dangerous.

4. Check the doors of the sheep barn.

5. The windows, which are strongly barred, should be safe.

6. The panthers may be hungry, but they will hardly catch any sheep here.

Written Exercises

A. Label each sentence *dec.* (declarative), *int.* (interrogative), *imp.* (imperative), or *exc.* (exclamatory). Also write the last word of the sentence, followed by the correct end punctuation.

1. Did you study your Sunday school lesson

2. Fill in the answers carefully and completely

3. These lessons should inspire loyalty to the Lord

---

2. complex

3. complex

4. compound

F. 1. dependent

2. dependent

3. independent

4. dependent

5. independent

G. 1. adjective   4. adjective

2. adverb   5. adjective

3. adverb

H. 1.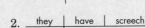

2.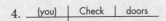

3.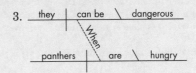

4.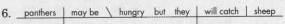

5.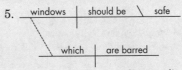

(*Barred* may be diagramed as a predicate adjective.)

6. panthers | may be \ hungry but they | will catch | sheep

Written Exercises

A. 1. int., lesson?

2. imp., completely.

3. dec., Lord.

4. How well God deserves our obedience and service
5. Which verse in the lesson commands us to love the Lord
6. You should learn that verse by memory

B. Rewrite each sentence in the order named in parentheses after it. Be sure to punctuate properly.
1. We had an exciting game of prisoner's base this morning. (mixed)
2. In the first few minutes, we lost four of our best runners. (natural)
3. There were two good runners guarding the prisoners. (natural)
4. James slid right under Henry's arm. (inverted)
5. He freed all six prisoners because he tagged the prisoner at the base line. (mixed)

C. Write whether each clause is *dependent* or *independent*.
1. When King Solomon asked God for wisdom.
2. God had richly blessed the king.
3. While he loved and served the Lord.
4. That he had built in Jerusalem.
5. Later he married many strange wives.

D. Write whether each sentence is *simple, compound,* or *complex.*
1. The Lord fully enables the one whom He calls into special service.
2. He does not always make life easy, but He does provide His grace.
3. Through every circumstance of life, His Spirit indwells and guides His people.
4. God's Word, which contains many promises, is a source of great comfort.

E. Write whether each underlined clause is *dependent* or *independent*.
1. Because we love the Lord, we seek to obey Him.
2. The lowly ant, which works hard to prepare for the winter, is used as an example for the slothful.
3. Two cannot walk together unless they are agreed.
4. If a person does not work, he should not eat.
5. We should choose friends who will help us to think right and do right.

F. Write whether each underlined item is an *adjective* or an *adverb* clause.
1. Leon Shank's, who are going to Maryland, spent the night at our place.
2. Brother Leon is a man whose company I truly enjoy.
3. Although his parents were not Christians, he did attend services at a small Mennonite mission.
4. After he became a Christian, his parents started attending church too.

G. Read the paragraphs, and do these exercises.
1. Write the first three words of the topic sentence in each paragraph.
2. In one paragraph, the unity is marred by a sentence that does not

4. exc., service! 6. dec., memory.
5. int., Lord?

B. 1. This morning we had an exciting game of prisoner's base.
2. We lost four of our best runners in the first few minutes.
3. Two good runners were guarding the prisoners.
4. Right under Henry's arm slid James.
5. Because he tagged the prisoner at the base line, he freed all six prisoners.

C. 1. dependent   4. dependent
2. independent   5. independent
3. dependent

D. 1. complex
2. compound
3. simple
4. complex

E. 1. dependent
2. dependent
3. independent
4. dependent
5. independent

F. 1. adjective
2. adjective
3. adverb
4. adverb

G. 1. *paragraph 1:* A colony of
paragraph 2: Building a prairie
paragraph 3: But these mounds
2. *paragraph 2:* This mound is

develop the main idea. Write the first three words of that sentence.
3. For each paragraph, write what kind of sentence order is used: *chronological order, spatial order,* or the *order of importance.*
4. Copy three transitional expressions used in the second and third paragraphs.
5. For each paragraph, write the key word that is repeated.
6. What pronouns are used in the second paragraph? What is the antecedent?

    A colony of prairie dogs lives in an amazing complex of tunnels. The entrance hole opens into a tunnel that angles underground for six to eight feet. The entrance tunnel leads to the main tunnel, which may connect several burrows. Branching off from this main tunnel are numerous side tunnels. These smaller tunnels lead to rooms used for various purposes in the prairie dog town.

    Prairie dogs dig out their tunnels with their strong, clawed front feet, kicking the dirt away with their back feet. When they finish digging out the tunnels, they scrape up soil from around the hole, adding it to the loose dirt. Finally, they pack this dirt into a firm mound that circles the entrance hole. This mound is quite important to the colony. Building a prairie dog town, as you can see, involves much hard work.

    If you cautiously creep up to a prairie dog town, you may see a few guards sitting on their haunches on top of their mounds. Rising a few feet above the surrounding prairie, each mound serves as a good lookout post. But these mounds have several useful functions. They form an effective dam against runoff from heavy rains. On a sunny day, the mounds will likely be occupied by many prairie dogs sunning themselves. The young ones also enjoy the mounds. They spend much time climbing these miniature mountains.

H. Diagram the skeletons and complements of these sentences. Include the introductory words of all dependent clauses.
1. While Mother dished up the oatmeal, the family gathered around the table.
2. In devotions this morning, we read Matthew 4, which tells the story of Jesus' temptation.
3. Are the boys still cleaning the milk house?
4. Girls, feed the chickens and the calves.
5. How quickly the summer days have passed!
6. In the shade of the maple tree lay the exhausted children.

---

3. *paragraph 1:* spatial order
   paragraph 2: chronological order
   paragraph 3: order of importance
4. Finally, as you can see, But, also
5. *paragraph 1:* tunnel
   paragraph 2: dirt
   paragraph 3: mounds
6. their, they; prairie dogs

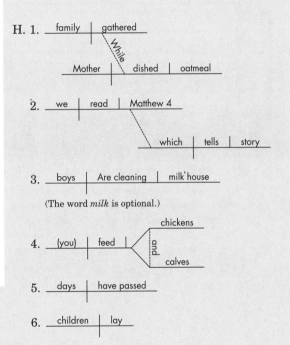

H. 1. family | gathered   While   Mother | dished | oatmeal

2. we | read | Matthew 4   which | tells | story

3. boys | Are cleaning | milk house
(The word *milk* is optional.)

4. (you) | feed | chickens _and_ calves

5. days | have passed

6. children | lay

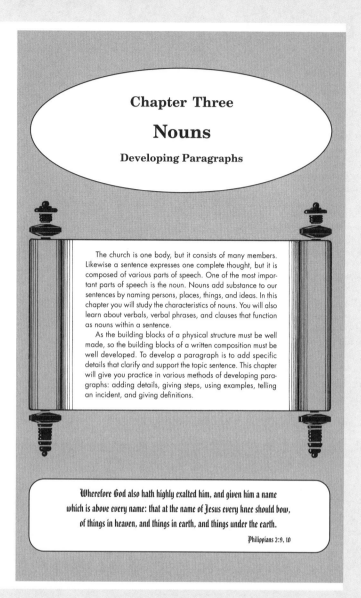

Chapter Three

Nouns

Developing Paragraphs

The church is one body, but it consists of many members. Likewise a sentence expresses one complete thought, but it is composed of various parts of speech. One of the most important parts of speech is the noun. Nouns add substance to our sentences by naming persons, places, things, and ideas. In this chapter you will study the characteristics of nouns. You will also learn about verbals, verbal phrases, and clauses that function as nouns within a sentence.

As the building blocks of a physical structure must be well made, so the building blocks of a written composition must be well developed. To develop a paragraph is to add specific details that clarify and support the topic sentence. This chapter will give you practice in various methods of developing paragraphs: adding details, giving steps, using examples, telling an incident, and giving definitions.

Wherefore God also hath highly exalted him, and given him a name which is above every name: that at the name of Jesus every knee should bow, of things in heaven, and things in earth, and things under the earth.

Philippians 2:9, 10

19. Identifying Nouns

> **Lesson Survey**
> - A **noun** is a word that names a person, place, thing, or idea.
> - A noun may be **concrete** (naming something with definite, physical substance) or **abstract** (naming something with no physical substance).
> - All nouns have **gender**: masculine, feminine, neuter, or common.
> - Nouns can be identified by noun-forming suffixes and by their use in a sentence.

The Bible contains many thousands of words. But these words can all be classified into the eight parts of speech: nouns, pronouns, verbs, adjectives, adverbs, prepositions, conjunctions, and interjections. In Chapters 3–9 of this book, you will review and study these parts of speech.

One of the "workhorses" of the English language is the noun. A *noun* names a person, place, thing, or idea. Notice the underlined nouns in these sentences.

> <u>God</u> created the <u>world</u> by the <u>power</u> of His <u>Word</u>.
> <u>Adam</u> and <u>Eve</u> lived in <u>Eden</u>, a <u>garden</u> that the <u>Lord God</u> had planted.
> <u>God</u> gave them <u>responsibility</u> for the <u>care</u> of this beautiful <u>garden</u>.

Nouns are naming words. Many nouns name things that you can see, touch, smell, hear, or taste. Because such things generally have definite, physical substance, they are called *concrete nouns*. Other nouns name things that you cannot perceive through the five senses. They name conditions, qualities, or ideas. Because these things have no physical substance, they are called *abstract nouns*.

Concrete nouns:
Jesus, King David, Jerusalem, Canaan, prophet, priest, altar, bullock, garment, staff

Abstract nouns:
chaos, order, health, sickness, love, mercy, grace, justice, holiness, courage, faith, memory, thought, attitude

Nouns have four *genders:* masculine, feminine, neuter, and common. Some nouns have different forms for masculine gender and for feminine gender. Notice how the italicized clauses in the following sentences are

Lesson 19

Purpose: (1) To teach the definition of a noun. (2) To identify concrete and abstract nouns. (3) To teach noun gender.

Oral Review:

1. Tell whether each sentence is simple, compound, or complex.
   a. The Israelites crossed over safely, but the Egyptians were destroyed. (compound)
   b. When the last Israelite had reached the other side, the waters came crashing down upon the Egyptians. (complex)
   c. Moses wrote a song that celebrated this great victory. (complex)
   d. Exodus 15 records Moses' song of deliverance. (simple)
2. What is the difference between a fragment and a sentence? (A fragment does not express a complete thought, but a sentence does.)
3. Tell whether each item is a fragment or a sentence.
   a. Through the Red Sea. (fragment)
   b. The children of Israel walked across on dry ground. (sentence)
   c. Which God had parted by a strong east wind. (fragment)
4. What is a run-on error? (two or more sentences incorrectly written together as one)

Lesson Introduction: In Chapter 1 we studied such sentence parts as subjects, predicates, complements, appositives, and nouns of direct address. With the exception of predicates, these sentence parts all need words that name persons, places, things, or ideas. Such words, you should remember, are *nouns*.

repetitious. The meaning of each underlined noun includes the information in the italicized clause.

A underline{prophet}, *who is a man,* spoke God's word to the people.

God commanded that all underline{witches}, *who are women,* should be put to death.

Nouns of *masculine* gender name persons or animals that are male. Nouns of *feminine* gender name persons or animals that are female. A large class of nouns is of *neuter* gender. These nouns name things or ideas that are neither male nor female. Many concrete nouns and all abstract nouns are of neuter gender.

Some nouns name persons or animals that may be either male or female, or a group that might include any combination of genders. Such nouns are of *common* gender. For some words with related meanings, there are nouns of masculine, feminine, and common gender. There are no such related words for nouns of neuter gender. Study the following table.

Masculine	Feminine	Common	Neuter
man	woman	person	book
son	daughter	child	coat
king	queen	ruler	desk
rooster	hen	chicken	idea
prophet	prophetess		law
waiter	waitress		creation
John	Jane		

You probably have little difficulty with identifying most concrete nouns, but abstract nouns may be less obvious. However, many of them can be identified by noun-forming suffixes, such as *-ment, -ion, -ation, -(i)ty, -ness, -dom, -ance, -ence, -ude,* and *-er, -or,* or *-ar.* Note how the second word in each of the following pairs is a noun formed by adding one of these suffixes.

settle—settlement	guide—guidance
express—expression	indulge—indulgence
condemn—condemnation	fortify—fortitude
scarce—scarcity	lead—leader
righteous—righteousness	credit—creditor
free—freedom	beg—beggar

Of course, the use of a word in a sentence determines its part of speech. Many words can be used as more than one part of speech. Which of the underlined words in the following sentences are used as nouns?

Lesson Outline:

1. A noun is a word that names a person, place, thing, or idea.

2. A noun may be concrete or abstract.

    a. Concrete nouns generally name things with definite, physical substance. These things can be perceived through the senses.

    b. Abstract nouns generally name things with no physical substance, such as conditions, qualities, or ideas. These things cannot be perceived through the senses.

3. All nouns have gender.

    a. Nouns of masculine gender name persons or animals that are male.

    b. Nouns of feminine gender name persons or animals that are female.

    c. Nouns of neuter gender name things or ideas that are neither male nor female.

    d. Nouns of common gender name persons or animals that may be either male or female, or a group that might include any combination of genders.

(*Teacher:* Gender in English does not have nearly the significance that it has in many other languages. In German, for instance, there are three definite articles: *der* [masculine], *die* [feminine], and *das* [neuter]. The gender of the article must agree with the gender of the noun that follows it. For example, the word *Hand* [for "hand"] is feminine in German. So the feminine article must be used with it [*die Hand*], any pronoun referring to *Hand* must be feminine, and any adjective describing *Hand* must have a feminine ending. When a person learns German, Spanish, Russian, or any other language in which gender has this significance, he must learn more

I shall answer[1] your question[1], but you must not question[2] my answer[2]!
Doris will cut[1] the tape[1], and I will tape[2] the cut[2].
Job was a just[1] man. The just[2] shall live by faith.
Rich[1] people often despise poor[1] people. But in God's sight, the rich[2] have no special advantage over the poor[2].

You should recognize the following as nouns because they fill noun functions: question[1], answer[2], tape[1], and cut[2] (direct objects); just[2] and rich[2] (subjects); and poor[2] (object of a preposition).

Class Practice

A. Read the nouns in these sentences, and identify each one as *concrete* or *abstract*.
1. The magnitude of even the smallest star staggers the imagination.
2. The Lord will reward your faithfulness in service.
3. The widow cast her two mites into the treasury.
4. King Saul was filled with envy against faithful David.
5. The loyal do not compromise with any evil.

B. Read the nouns in these sentences, and tell their gender.
1. Abraham offered a ram on the altar.
2. Hannah prayed for a child when she was at the tabernacle.
3. Eli gave her the assurance of an answer to her prayer.
4. When the cock crowed, Peter remembered the words of his Master.
5. A follower of Jesus must obey the Bible.

C. Say the numbers of the underlined words that are used as nouns.
1. If you saw[1] into this file[2], you will need to file[3] the dull saw[4].
2. Never feed an envious[5] spirit, for the envious[6] fill their minds with evil thoughts.
3. We should daily ask God to set a watch[7] before our lips. Then we must watch[8] carefully what we think and say.
4. If we honestly search[9] the promises[10] of the Bible, God promises[11] that our search[12] will be fruitful.

D. Use a noun-forming suffix to change each word in parentheses so that it fits in the sentence.
1. The (magnify) of the hurricane's (destroy) amazed us.
2. Christian parents are a youth's most important (counsel), giving (guide) for the (perplex) of life.
3. Our (converse) should always display (kind), (polite), and (honest).
4. The (write) of the Book of James emphasized the (important) of faith and works in (combine).

than just the meaning of each noun. He must also learn its gender so that he can use the noun correctly in a sentence.

The only gender in English is natural gender. That is, if a word is masculine or feminine, it usually refers to a person or animal that is actually male or female. The only definite article is *the,* and it is used before nouns regardless of their gender. Thus, gender in a grammatical sense does not exist in modern English.)

  4. Several tests are helpful in identifying nouns.

  a. Many nouns end with noun-forming suffixes, such as *-ment, -ion, -ation, -(i)ty, -ness, -dom, -ance, -ence, -ude,* and *-er, -or,* or *-ar.*

  b. Nouns fill noun functions in sentences— subjects, complements, appositives, and nouns of direct address.

Lesson 19 Answers

Class Practice

A. 1. magnitude—abstract; star—concrete; imagination—abstract
2. Lord—concrete; faithfulness—abstract; service—abstract
3. widow—concrete; mites—concrete; treasury—concrete
4. King Saul—concrete; envy—abstract; David—concrete
5. loyal—concrete; evil—abstract

B. 1. Abraham—masculine; ram—masculine; altar—neuter
2. Hannah—feminine; child—common; tabernacle—neuter
3. Eli—masculine; assurance—neuter; answer—neuter; prayer—neuter
4. cock—masculine; Peter—masculine; words—neuter; Master—masculine
5. follower—common; Jesus—masculine; Bible—neuter

C. 1. 2, 4   3. 7
2. 6   4. 10, 12

D. (Corrections are underlined.)
1. The magnitude of the hurricane's destruction amazed us.
2. Christian parents are a youth's most important counselors, giving guidance for the perplexities of life.
3. Our conversation should always display kindness, politeness, and honesty.
4. The writer of the Book of James emphasized the importance of faith and works in combination.

★ **EXTRA PRACTICE**
Worksheet 11 (*Identifying Nouns*)

Written Exercises

A. Copy the nouns in these sentences, and label them *C* (concrete) or *A* (abstract).
1. The saints of all ages lived by faith.
2. The walls of Jericho fell according to the will of God.
3. When Moses returned from the mount, a dazzling glory shone on his face.
4. The loyalty of Daniel helped to inspire faithfulness in his friends.
5. Because of her iniquity, Israel lost her independence.

B. Copy each noun, and label it *M, F, N,* or *C* to identify its gender.
1. Father led the family in worship.
2. One bull, ten cows, and four calves are in the pasture.
3. Our family, along with the uncles and aunts and cousins, gathered in the large kitchen.
4. Grandfather led in an earnest prayer of thankfulness and supplication.
5. The simple meal that Grandmother had prepared satisfied our needs.

C. Write the numbers of the words that are used as nouns.
1. While Bethany covers[1] some boxes[2] with decorative paper, Anna boxes[3] the blankets and covers[4] in large cartons.
2. The proud[5] world despises the meek[6] and lowly Christian. But the meek[7] will inherit the earth, while the proud[8] will fall in judgment.
3. They who fear[9] the Lord need not be snared by the fear[10] of man.
4. If our gardens produce[11] plenty of vegetables, we will sell some with Uncle Benjamin's produce[12] at his market.
5. Father will cart[13] the tomato plants[14] to the garden. Then while Mother plants[15] them, he will take the cart[16] back for the water buckets.

D. Use a noun-forming suffix to change each word in parentheses so that it fits in the sentence.
1. The (serene) on Grandmother's face spoke of her (confide) in the Lord.
2. We should express (gratify) in every (pray).
3. The (sail) did not take enough (provide) for their voyage and were faced with (starve).
4. (Sick) and death swept through the pioneer (settle), taxing the (endure) of the healthy.
5. In the (solitary) of exile, John received the (reveal) of Jesus Christ.

Written Exercises

A.
1. saints—C; ages—A; faith—A
2. walls—C; Jericho—C; will—A; God—C
3. Moses—C; mount—C; glory—A; face—C
4. loyalty—A; Daniel—C; faithfulness—A; friends—C
5. iniquity—A; Israel—C; independence—A

B.
1. Father—M; family—C; worship—N
2. bull—M; cows—F; calves—C; pasture—N
3. family—C; uncles—M; aunts—F; cousins—C; kitchen—N
4. Grandfather—M; prayer—N; thankfulness—N; supplication—N
5. meal—N; Grandmother—F; needs—N

C.
1. 2, 4
2. 7, 8
3. 10
4. 12
5. 14, 16

D.
1. serenity, confidence
2. gratitude, prayer
3. sailors, provisions, starvation
4. Sickness, settlement, endurance
5. solitude, revelation

Review Exercises

A. Label each item *S* for sentence, *F* for fragment, or *R* for run-on error. [2]

1. The clever coyote rarely goes hungry.
2. When two coyotes hunt together.
3. One attracts a rabbit's attention the other pounces on it from behind.
4. If a coyote sees vultures circling in the sky.
5. It may find the dead animal and drive the vultures away.
6. A coyote may steal a badger's dinner too.
7. As the badger digs furiously into the burrow of some small animal.
8. The sly coyote stands watching, it pounces on the mouse or squirrel.
9. Escaping through another hole.
10. A coyote may even pretend to be dead, a hungry crow that investigates too closely may become the coyote's dinner.

B. Rewrite the following paragraph, correcting the fragments and run-on errors. [2]

English is our means of communication, a study of it should increase our ability to grasp and express ideas. God wants us to understand the rich truths of His Word. And express these truths to others. A study of English is not the most important help in knowing truth. God enables the honest seeker. Even though he may be quite ignorant of English. But when God provides us with opportunities for further help. We are responsible to use them for His glory. Through your continued study of English, you will learn to better understand and express ideas, you will also be better fitted to serve God.

20. Common and Proper Nouns

Lesson Survey

- A **common noun** is a general name for a person, place, or thing. It is not capitalized.
- A **proper noun** is the name of a specific person, place, or thing. It must always be capitalized.

What different pictures come to your mind as you read each of the following pairs of words? Which word gives you a general picture?

Lesson 20

Purpose: To teach the identification of common and proper nouns, and the capitalization of proper nouns.

Oral Review:

1. Change these words to nouns by adding a noun-forming suffix.
   a. sanctify (sanctification, sanctifier)
   b. instant (instance, instancy, instantness)
   c. sensitive (sensitivity, sensitiveness)
   d. prayerful (prayerfulness)
   e. invest (investment, investor)
   f. certain (certainty, certitude)
2. Give the gender of each noun.
   a. priest (masculine)
   b. prophetess (feminine)
   c. loyalty (neuter)

Review Exercises

A.
1. S
2. F
3. R
4. F
5. S
6. S
7. F
8. R
9. F
10. R

B. (Corrections are marked.)

English is our means of communication. A study of it should increase our ability to grasp and express ideas. God wants us to understand the rich truths of His Word/ and express these truths to others. A study of English is not the most important help in knowing truth. God enables the honest seeker/ even though he may be quite ignorant of English. But when God provides us with opportunities for further help, we are responsible to use them for His glory. Through your continued study of English, you will learn to better understand and express ideas. You will also be better fitted to serve God.

d. drake (masculine)
e. lamb (common)

3. How is a subjective complement diagramed differently than a direct object? (A direct object is placed after a vertical line, but a subjective complement is placed after a line that slants toward the subject.)
4. With which kind of subjective complement does the linking verb act like an equal sign? (predicate nominative)
5. Which kind of object complement answers the questions *whom* or *what*? (direct object)
6. Which kind of object complement tells *to whom or what* or *for whom or what* an action is performed? (indirect object)
7. Tell whether these sentences are in natural, inverted, or mixed word order.

Which gives a more specific picture?

woman—Mother   country—Guatemala
dog—Shep   book—Bible

Nouns are in two main classes—common nouns and proper nouns. A *common noun* is a name belonging to all persons, places, or things with certain qualities or characteristics. A *proper noun* is a specific name that distinguishes one person, place, or thing from others in its class.

Remember to capitalize all proper nouns. If a proper noun includes more than one word, capitalize each important word. Study the following groups of proper nouns.

1. *Names of specific persons, including initials and titles.* A title of respect (such as *president, doctor,* and *brother*) or a word that shows relationship (such as *brother, grandmother,* and *uncle*) is a proper noun when it is part of a name. It is also a proper noun when it is used instead of an actual name, but not when it comes after a possessive pronoun like *my, your,* or *his.*

Menno Simons   Brother John   Mr. M. A. Reinford

Paul testified for Christ before <u>King Agrippa</u>.
Agrippa was a <u>king</u> in the family of Herod.

Did <u>Mother</u> say that <u>Grandpa</u> and <u>Uncle Peter</u> are here?
Did my <u>mother</u> say that my <u>grandpa</u> and my <u>uncle</u> Peter are here?
    (In the phrase "my uncle Peter," *Peter* is an appositive of *uncle.*)

2. *Names of God and words referring to the Bible or to parts of the Bible.*

the Lord God   Jesus Christ   the Word of God
Jehovah   the Messiah   the New Testament
the Almighty   His only begotten Son the Scriptures

When words like *god* or *lord* refer to idols or people, they are not capitalized.

the gods of the Amorites   the lords of the Philistines

3. *Names of geographical features such as cities, states, countries, mountains, rivers, lakes, oceans, deserts, islands, continents, and regions.*

Philadelphia   Bethlehem   Pacific Ocean
Oregon   Mount Sinai   Andros Island
Syria   Nile River   South America
Balkan Peninsula Sea of Galilee   Panama Canal
the South   Wilderness of Judea Middle Atlantic States
the Northeast   Plain of Shinar   Near East

a. To the shepherds outside Bethlehem was made the glorious announcement. (inverted)
b. With fear and wonder, the shepherds came to behold the newborn Saviour. (mixed)
c. They found the Babe, wrapped in swaddling clothes and lying in a manger. (natural)
d. In recognition of His wonderful birth, they praised God. (mixed)

Lesson Introduction: Write the following sentences on the board, and have the students supply names to replace the underlined words.

<u>A man</u> took <u>his son</u> to <u>a mountain</u>.
    (*Abraham* took *Isaac* to *Mount Moriah*.)
<u>A woman</u> plotted to have <u>a man</u> killed in order to get a vineyard for <u>her husband</u>.
    (*Jezebel* plotted to have *Naboth* killed in order to get a vineyard for *Ahab*.)

Ask: "What kind of nouns did we replace?" (common nouns) "What kind of nouns did we use as replacements?" (proper nouns)

Lesson Outline:

1. A common noun is a general name for a person, place, or thing. It is not capitalized.

2. A proper noun is the name of a specific person, place, or thing. It must always be capitalized.

3. Nouns in the following groups are proper nouns and should be capitalized.
    (1) *Names of specific persons, including initials and titles.*
    (2) *Names of God and words referring to the Bible or to parts of the Bible.*
    (3) *Names of geographical features such as cities, states, countries, mountains, rivers, lakes, oceans, deserts, islands, continents, and regions.*

Words like *south* and *northeast* are not proper nouns when they name directions. They are proper nouns only when they refer to geographical regions. When these words are used as proper nouns, *the* usually comes before them.

Wise men came from <u>the East</u> to see Jesus.
The Dead Sea lies <u>east</u> of Jerusalem.
When we lived in <u>the North</u>, we had to prepare for cold winters.
We were traveling <u>north</u> on Interstate 81.

4. *Titles of books, newspapers, magazines, stories, poems, and songs.* Capitalize the first word, last word, and every important word in the title. Do not capitalize an article (*a, an, the*), a conjunction (*and, but, or*), or a preposition of fewer than four letters unless it is the first or last word.

The Demands of Love	*Worth Dying For*
Safe in His Care	"The Arrow and the Song"
Nature Friend	"Oh, Happy Is the Man"

5. *Names of groups, nationalities, organizations, churches, schools, and branches of civil government.* Articles, conjunctions, and prepositions are treated the same as in titles of books.

American Cancer Society	Rod and Staff Publishers, Inc.
Kyner's Country Store	Bethel Christian Fellowship
Pineview Mennonite Church	Oak Ridge Christian School
Department of Agriculture	United States Supreme Court

6. *Names of specific ships, airplanes, trains, buildings, and monuments.*

the *Mayflower* (ship)	the White House
the *Spirit of St. Louis* (airplane)	the Lincoln Memorial
the *General* (train)	

7. *Names of parks, historic sites, and historic events, eras, and documents.*

the Exodus	Civil War
Middle Ages	Glacier National Park
Mayflower Compact	Abraham Lincoln Birthplace
Schleitheim Confession of Faith	

8. *Brand names.* Remember to capitalize only the specific brand name and not any common noun that may follow it.

Paper Mate pen	Frigidaire freezer	Lawn Boy mower

(4) *Titles of books, newspapers, magazines, stories, poems, and songs.*
(5) *Names of groups, nationalities, organizations, churches, schools, and branches of civil government.*
(6) *Names of specific ships, airplanes, trains, buildings, and monuments.*
(7) *Names of parks, historic sites, and historic events, eras, and documents.*
(8) *Brand names.* Capitalize only the brand name and not any common noun associated with it.
(9) *Names of school subjects derived from proper nouns.*
(10) *Calendar items such as months, days of the week, and holidays.* Do not capitalize the names of the four seasons.

9. *Names of school subjects derived from proper nouns.* Most school subjects are common nouns and are not capitalized. If a subject name includes a word derived from a proper noun along with a common noun, do not capitalize the common noun.

reading	English	American geography
spelling	Bible	Anabaptist history

10. *Calendar items such as months, days of the week, and holidays.* Remember that the names of the four seasons are not capitalized.

January	Thanksgiving Day	spring
Sunday	Good Friday	winter

Class Practice

A. Tell how to correct the capitalization of each item. If an item is correct, say *correct.*
1. Sister Janet Friesen
2. the five Brethren on the board
3. the book *The Story is now Told*
4. two sunbeam mixers
5. Bible History
6. the Countries of the Far East
7. Mr. L. A. Hayes, the new Doctor
8. Harrison Christian day school
9. the Empire State Building
10. March 21, the first day of Spring

B. Tell which words have capitalization errors.
1. When we visited several Churches in the northwest, we drove through the Banff national park in the Rocky mountains.
2. The Old Testament scriptures give us a few details of the History of the World before the flood.
3. We were relieved when father and mother came out to the garden and helped to pick the beans.
4. For an opening song, brother Daniel chose "Fresh from the Throne Of Glory."
5. I have finished my Science and Math assignments; now I must do my Bible lesson.
6. The *savannah* was the first steam-powered ship to cross the Atlantic ocean.
7. The Dutch mennonites drew up the Dortrecht confession of faith in 1632.

Lesson 20 Answers

Class Practice

A. (Corrections are underlined.)
1. correct
2. the five <u>b</u>rethren on the board
3. the book *The Story <u>Is</u> <u>N</u>ow Told*
4. two <u>S</u>unbeam mixers
5. Bible <u>h</u>istory
6. the <u>c</u>ountries of the Far East
7. Mr. L. A. Hayes, the new <u>d</u>octor
8. Harrison Christian <u>D</u>ay <u>S</u>chool
9. correct
10. March 21, the first day of <u>s</u>pring

B. 1. churches, Northwest, National, Park, Mountains
2. Scriptures, history, world, Flood
3. Father, Mother
4. Brother, From, of
5. science, math
6. *Savannah,* Ocean
7. Mennonites, Confession, Faith

8. Hawaii, with its many Islands, and Alaska, with its high Mountains, were admitted as states of the united states of america in 1959.
9. The Enoch Brown schoolhouse near greencastle, Pennsylvania, marks the site of an Indian massacre.
10. The ten plagues were designed to prove that the god of israel was sovereign over the gods of egypt.

Written Exercises

A. Write these items correctly. If an item is correct, write *correct*.
1. on mother's day
2. the new Teacher, Brother Eby
3. a rugged mountain range
4. aunt Frances
5. waiting for my grandfather
6. *spelling by sound and structure*
7. in the Winter of 1990
8. weaver's chicken hot dogs
9. the Susquehanna river
10. the Boston tea party of 1773

B. Write correctly each noun that has a capitalization error. If the error is in a proper noun phrase, write the whole phrase.
1. Read *tip lewis and his lamp,* and write a report on it by tuesday afternoon, february 15.
2. Several of my Aunts came to help Mother clean the new house we bought in horse valley.
3. We attended a Bible Conference at the Kingston mennonite church on ascension day.
4. We ate a quick meal of Kinzer's Fish Sticks, Mueller's Egg Noodles, and beans.
5. The statue of liberty on liberty island has welcomed many immigrants into the united states of america.
6. The *great eastern,* a ship powered by both steam and wind, was used in laying the first Telegraph Cable across the atlantic ocean in 1866.
7. The older students are studying spanish, bookkeeping, and church history with brother Lamar.
8. The shenandoah national park is a wilderness reserve in the Blue Ridge mountains of virginia.
9. The Gods of the canaanites became a spiritual threat to the israelites.
10. When pioneers settled the west, they had to cross the rocky mountains before reaching the beautiful land of the oregon territory.

8. islands, mountains, United, States, America
9. Schoolhouse, Greencastle
10. God, Israel, Egypt

Written Exercises

(According to standard practice, a book title like *The Story Is Now Told* should be underlined in handwriting. That rule may be disregarded until after it is introduced in Lesson 111.)

A. (Corrections are underlined.)
1. on Mother's Day
2. the new teacher, Brother Eby
3. correct
4. Aunt Frances
5. correct
6. *Spelling by Sound and Structure*
7. in the winter of 1990
8. Weaver's chicken hot dogs
9. the Susquehanna River
10. the Boston Tea Party of 1773

B.
1. *Tip Lewis and His Lamp,* Tuesday, February
2. aunts, Horse Valley
3. conference, Kingston Mennonite Church, Ascension Day
4. fish sticks, egg noodles
5. Statue of Liberty, Liberty Island, United States of America
6. *Great Eastern,* telegraph cable, Atlantic Ocean
7. Spanish, Brother Lamar
8. Shenandoah National Park, Blue Ridge Mountains, Virginia
9. gods, Canaanites, Israelites
10. West, Rocky Mountains, Oregon Territory

Review Exercises

A. Write whether each sentence has *natural, inverted,* or *mixed* word order. [11]
   1. A person can be guilty of dishonesty in more than one way.
   2. There are some people guilty of telling outright lies.
   3. Behind the boaster's tongue lurks a dishonest heart.
   4. One can slip into the sin of dishonesty by exaggerating.
   5. By saying nothing at all, a person can also be dishonest!

B. Change these sentences to the word order indicated in parentheses. [11]
   1. Through intentionally leaving the wrong impression, a person can act a lie. (natural)
   2. A person can also act a lie by refusing to give information requested by parents or teachers. (mixed)
   3. According to some people's ideas, some lies are innocent and insignificant. (natural)
   4. The lie of the father of lies is found in such ideas. (inverted)
   5. We must avoid the snare of dishonesty at all costs. (mixed)

Review Exercises

A. 1. natural
   2. mixed
   3. inverted
   4. natural
   5. mixed

B. (Allow reasonable variation.)
   1. A person can act a lie through intentionally leaving the wrong impression.
   2. By refusing to give information requested by parents or teachers, a person can also act a lie.
   3. Some lies are innocent and insignificant, according to some people's ideas.
   4. In such ideas is found the lie of the father of lies.
   5. At all costs, we must avoid the snare of dishonesty.

---

21. Developing Paragraphs by Adding Details or Giving Steps

> **Lesson Survey**
> - A paragraph is developed by clarifying and supporting the topic sentence.
> - A paragraph may be developed by adding details to expand the thought of the topic sentence.
> - A paragraph may be developed by giving the steps in a process.

An artist's preliminary sketch shows the basic outlines of the picture he is drawing. But his picture is neither meaningful nor attractive until the details are filled in. Likewise, the topic sentence of a paragraph may sketch the general outline of a writer's main idea. But a topic sentence does not give much detailed information, and it is not likely to be very interesting by itself. Just as an artist must add details to fill out his picture, so a writer must add details to develop his paragraph.

You have learned that a good paragraph is one unit of thought. Generally, the main idea of a paragraph is stated in the topic sentence. A paragraph

Lesson 21

Purpose: To teach paragraph development by adding details or giving steps.

Oral Review:
1. Define paragraph coherence. (all the sentences flowing smoothly together from one to the next)
2. Define paragraph unity. (every sentence directly supporting the topic sentence)
3. List several details important for proper paragraph form. (first line indented, left margin straight, right margin as straight as possible)
4. For each kind of paragraph, tell which order should be used: chronological, spatial, or importance.
   a. a paragraph of description (spatial)
   b. a paragraph that tells a story (chronological)
   c. a paragraph of information (importance)
   d. a paragraph that gives directions (chronological)

Lesson Introduction: Read the following composition to the students.

The Platypus—an Unusual Mammal

Certain characteristics are common to all mammals. The platypus shares many of these characteristics, but it is unique in some ways.

The body of a platypus looks like a strange combination of animals. This animal spends much time in the water and finds its food underwater. But the platypus actually lives on land.

Have someone tell you what is wrong with the composition. You might point out that this example is extreme, but that the failure to develop paragraphs well is a common problem.

is developed by clarifying and supporting that topic sentence. The topic sentence may make a general statement; the rest of the sentences then give specific ideas that add force and meaning to the topic. Sometimes a topic sentence may not make sense by itself; it may even appear to be false. The other sentences are necessary to illustrate and verify the truth of the topic sentence.

One method of developing a paragraph is adding details to expand the thought of the topic sentence. Remember to keep the paragraph unified by writing only details that contribute to the topic. And be sure your sentences do actually add details. Sometimes a writer intends to add details, but he merely rewords the topic sentence several times.

Poor: Rewords topic sentence; includes no specific details

A walk outdoors in the morning is a wholesome experience. It is much better than just staying inside. Few morning activities provide as much benefit as a walk outdoors. If you have never gone on such a walk, you do not know what you are missing. Start taking walks in the morning, and you will be truly glad you did.

Better: Adds specific details

A walk outdoors in the morning is a wholesome experience. No wake-up call is more invigorating than the bright rays of the rising sun, the cheerful singing of birds, and the fresh coolness of the morning air. A morning walk is also an excellent time to receive inspiration through communion with the heavenly Father. In this way, one's whole being—body, soul, and spirit—is energized and prepared for the new day.

A writer who develops a paragraph by adding details must know his subject, for he must do more than make a few comments. He must both stimulate and satisfy the reader's curiosity. By adding specific details and explaining their importance, the author writes a paragraph that is interesting and worthwhile.

Poor: Gives details without explaining their importance

God has given the horse eyes that are different from ours. Its eyes are located toward the side of its head. It can move its eyes independently. Its pupils can open wider than ours can.

Better: Gives clear, well-explained details

God has given the horse eyes that are different from ours. Because its eyes are located toward the side of its head instead of at the front, the horse can see all around, even behind itself. A horse can also move its eyes independently. Therefore, it can focus in two directions at once. The pupils of a horse's eyes open

Lesson Outline:

1. A paragraph is developed by clarifying and supporting the topic sentence.

2. A paragraph may be developed by adding details to expand the thought of the topic sentence.

   a. To keep the paragraph unified, write only details that contribute to the topic.
   b. Do not merely reword the topic sentence several times.
   c. Know your subject so that you can add specific details.

3. A paragraph may be developed by giving the steps in a process.

   a. Present the steps in chronological order.
   b. Avoid a simple numbering of the steps because that will likely produce a choppy, uninteresting style.

★ *EXTRA PRACTICE*
Worksheet 12 (*Developing Paragraphs by Adding Details or Giving Steps*)

wider than ours. These wide-open pupils admit plenty of light, enabling the horse to see much better in the dark than we can.

The first sample is unsatisfactory in several ways. What is the advantage of eyes on the side of the head? How is it useful to have eyes that can move independently, or pupils that can open wide? The second paragraph is much better because it answers these questions.

Another method of paragraph development is to give the steps in a process. When you write such a paragraph, you must first think through the process so that you can present the steps in chronological order.

As with other kinds of writing, transitional expressions may fill a useful role. However, they should not be overused. A simple numbering of the steps will likely produce a choppy, uninteresting style. Smoother transitions are achieved by using expressions like *next, after that,* and *when this is finished.* And many times the order is so logical that specific transitional expressions are not needed.

Poor: Simple, choppy transitions

When you want to start a coal fire, you must realize that a match will not raise the temperature of coal to its kindling temperature. First, you build a stack of fuels with paper on the bottom, wood next, and coal on top. Second, as you strike the match, the heat of friction ignites it. Third, the burning match raises the paper to its kindling temperature. Fourth, the burning paper produces enough heat to raise the wood to its kindling temperature. Finally, the coal is ignited from the heat of the burning wood. In this way, one small match can be the beginning of a very hot fire.

Better: Smoother transitions

When you want to start a coal fire, you must realize that a match will not raise the temperature of coal to its kindling temperature. You first build a stack of fuels with paper on the bottom, wood next, and coal on top. As you strike the match, the heat of friction ignites it. The burning match raises the paper to its kindling temperature. The burning paper produces enough heat to raise the wood to its kindling temperature. Finally, the coal is ignited from the heat of the burning wood. In this way, one small match can be the beginning of a very hot fire.

Class Practice

Tell what is wrong with these paragraphs. Suggest ways to improve them.

1.   On a hot summer afternoon, a thunderstorm can develop quickly. First, moist air rises from the hot earth, forming convectional currents. Second, this moist air cools and condenses as it rises. Third, the high, billowing clouds of the thunderhead form.

Lesson 21 Answers

Class Practice

A. 1. Simple numbering of the steps produces choppy transitions.

On a hot summer afternoon, a thunderstorm can develop quickly. It begins as moist air rises from the hot earth, forming convectional currents. As these currents rise, the moisture in the air cools and condenses. This condensation forms the high, billowing clouds of the thunderhead.

2.	Covetousness is a serious evil. Greed for things that are not rightfully ours is always wrong. God condemns covetousness as idolatry.

3.	Pharaoh was troubled by his two dreams. In the first dream, he had seen seven fat cattle and seven lean cattle. In the second dream, he had seen seven good ears of grain and seven withered ears. Pharaoh was quite disturbed, for the meaning of the dreams was a complete mystery to him.

Written Exercises

A. Develop a paragraph for one of these topic sentences by adding details.
   1. God has specially designed most birds with the ability to fly. (Or choose some other animal, and describe some unique feature.)
   2. The construction of Noah's ark was a great undertaking.
   3. Ants work hard for their living.
   4. "Hast thou entered into the treasures of the snow?"

B. Develop a paragraph for one of these topic sentences by giving steps.
   1. Making good charcoal requires careful planning.
   2. The life cycle of a butterfly is a marvelous process.
   3. Before we plant our garden, we carefully prepare the soil.
   4. It requires much effort to give our kitchen a thorough cleaning.

22. Nouns With Regular Plural Forms

Lesson Survey
- For the plural form of most nouns, simply add -s.
- For most nouns ending with s, sh, ch, x, or z, add -es.
- For a noun ending with o after a vowel, add -s.
- For a noun ending with o after a consonant, add -s or -es.
- For a noun ending with y after a vowel, simply add -s.
- For a noun ending with y after a consonant, change the y to i and add -es.
- For many nouns ending with f or fe, change the f or fe to v and add -es.
- For most compound nouns, change the most important word to its plural form.

Lesson 22

Purpose: To teach the rules for making the plural forms of nouns.

Oral Review:
1. Tell which words in these sentences are proper nouns. (Answers are underlined.)
   a. The <u>God</u> of <u>Abraham</u>, <u>Isaac</u>, and <u>Jacob</u> called <u>Moses</u> at the burning bush.
   b. Our breakfast consisted of fried eggs with <u>Kunzler's</u> bacon, <u>Kellogg's</u> corn flakes, and <u>Minute Maid</u> orange juice.
   c. Before the <u>Pilgrims</u> left the *Mayflower*, they formulated the <u>Mayflower Compact</u>.
   d. We had math, <u>English</u>, and reading classes on <u>Tuesday</u> morning.
   e. Helen's mother was born in southern <u>Ontario</u>, but her father comes from the <u>Midwest</u>.

2. The topic sentence is simply reworded several times.

   Covetousness is a serious evil. In the Ten Commandments, God clearly forbids covetousness of any form. Many of the prophets spoke out against the covetousness of Israel and the wickedness it produced. Jesus emphasized the seriousness of this evil by warning, "Take heed, and beware of covetousness." The apostle Paul declares that covetousness is actually a form of idolatry.

3. Specific details are lacking.

   Pharaoh was troubled by his two dreams. In the first dream, he had seen seven fat cattle and seven lean cattle. The lean cattle devoured the fat cattle, but they were just as thin as before. In the second dream, Pharaoh had seen seven good ears of grain and seven withered ears. The withered ears devoured the good ears, but they were just as withered as before. Pharaoh was quite disturbed, for the meaning of the dreams was a complete mystery to him.

Written Exercises

A. (Individual work. Check especially for adequate details.)

B. (Individual work. Check especially for clear steps.)

2. *Load* is used two times in the following sentence. Which time is it a noun? (Answer is underlined.)

   If we load all this feed on your truck, you will have too big a <u>load</u>.

3. Change these words to noun forms.
   a. serene (serenity)
   b. abominable (abomination)
   c. magnify (magnifier, magnitude)
   d. permanent (permanence)

4. Tell whether these sentences have adjective or adverb clauses.
   a. Since it has rained again, the grass has become green. (adverb)
   b. This book, which Grandmother gave for my birthday, contains an interesting story about a family's move by covered wagon. (adjective)

The form of a noun shows several things. It always shows whether the noun is common or proper, usually whether its *number* is singular or plural, and sometimes whether its gender is masculine or feminine.

The eight rules in this lesson will help you to write the plural forms of nouns.

1. *For the plural form of most nouns, simply add* -s.

   Bible—Bibles   consolation—consolations
   prophet—prophets

2. *For most nouns ending with* s, sh, ch, x, *or* z, *add* -es.

   trellis—trellises   ash—ashes
   princess—princesses   ax—axes
   church—churches   adz—adzes

3. *For a noun ending with* o *after a vowel, add* -s.

   curio—curios   patio—patios

4. *For a noun ending with* o *after a consonant, add* -s *or* -es. A few may be spelled either way. For musical terms that end with *o*, the plural is generally formed by adding *-s*.

   silo—silos   volcano—volcanoes *or* volcanos
   potato—potatoes   soprano—sopranos
   motto—mottoes *or* mottos solo—solos

5. *For a noun ending with* y *after a vowel, simply add* -s.

   birthday—birthdays   journey—journeys   alloy—alloys

6. *For a noun ending with* y *after a consonant, change the* y *to* i *and add* -es.

   liberty—liberties   quality—qualities
   activity—activities

7. *For many nouns ending with* f *or* fe, *change the* f *or* fe *to* v *and add* -es. For others, simply add *-s*. A few are spelled either way.

   self—selves   belief—beliefs
   loaf—loaves   hoof—hoofs *or* hooves
   thief—thieves   staff—staffs *or* staves
   proof—proofs

8. *For most compound nouns, change the most important word (usually the last word) to its plural form. If a noun ends with* -ful, *add* -s *after* -ful. Both parts are made plural in a few compound nouns.

5. Tell what punctuation is needed in each sentence. (*Teacher:* Write the sentences on the board without the underlined punctuation.)
   a. Girls, be sure you are ready by 10:00 A.M.
   b. Joyce asked, "Where are we going?"
   c. Mother said that Carol, Joyce, and I would go shopping with her in Hagerstown, Maryland.

Lesson Introduction: Write the following nouns on the board, and ask how the two in each pair are different.

   pole—Pole (first is common, second is proper—names a person from Poland)

   prince—princess (first is masculine, second is feminine)

   pony—ponies (first is singular, second is plural)

It is usually easy to tell whether a noun is common or proper. Generally it is also easy to tell whether a noun is singular or plural. In this lesson we will study various regular ways of forming plural nouns; in the next lesson we will study some irregular ways.

Lesson Outline:

1. For the plural form of most nouns, simply add -s.

2. For most nouns ending with s, sh, ch, x, *or* z, *add* -es.

3. For a noun ending with o *after a vowel, add* -s.

4. For a noun ending with o *after a consonant, add* -s *or* -es.

   a. The plural forms of musical terms are generally made by adding *-s*.
   b. Some words are correct either way.

brother-in-law—brothers-in-law
mail carrier—mail carriers
postmaster general—postmasters general
handful—handfuls
manservant—menservants

Perhaps the most important rule to remember is to check the dictionary whenever you are in doubt. If no plural form is shown, it is formed by adding -s or -es.

Class Practice

A. On the chalkboard, write the plural form of each noun.

1. principle
2. pass
3. wife
4. shelf
5. donkey
6. coach
7. sky
8. Eskimo
9. tornado
10. high priest

B. On the chalkboard, write the singular form of each noun.

1. groves
2. hoaxes
3. waitresses
4. cruelties
5. potatoes
6. sheaves
7. cupfuls
8. buses

Written Exercises

A. Write the plural form of each singular noun and the singular form of each plural noun. Use a dictionary if you are not sure of the correct spelling.

1. city
2. roof
3. taxes
4. candies
5. instances
6. wolves
7. calf
8. secretary-general
9. knives
10. armful
11. brush
12. wrench
13. piano
14. cargo
15. lens
16. reef
17. alto
18. lasso
19. strifes
20. jack-in-the-pulpit

B. Use these words in original sentences, first in the singular form and then in the plural form.

1. patch
2. cliff
3. leaf
4. sister-in-law
5. pocketful

5. *For a noun ending with* y *after a vowel, simply add* -s.

6. *For a noun ending with* y *after a consonant, change the* y *to* i *and add* -es.

7. *For many nouns ending with* f *or* fe, *change the* f *or* fe *to* v *and add* -es. For others, simply add -s. A few are spelled either way.

8. *For most compound nouns, change the most important word (usually the last word) to its plural form.*
   a. For a noun ending with -ful, add -s after -ful.
   b. For a few nouns, each part is made plural.

Lesson 22 Answers

Class Practice

A. 1. principles
   2. passes
   3. wives
   4. shelves
   5. donkeys
   6. coaches
   7. skies
   8. Eskimo *or* Eskimos
   9. tornadoes *or* tornados
   10. high priests

B. 1. grove
   2. hoax
   3. waitress
   4. cruelty
   5. potato
   6. sheaf
   7. cupful
   8. bus

Written Exercises

A. 1. cities
   2. roofs
   3. tax
   4. candy
   5. instance
   6. wolf
   7. calves
   8. secretaries-general
   9. knife
   10. armfuls
   11. brushes
   12. wrenches
   13. pianos
   14. cargoes *or* cargos
   15. lenses
   16. reefs
   17. altos
   18. lassos *or* lassoes
   19. strife
   20. jack-in-the-pulpits *or* jacks-in-the-pulpit

B. (Individual sentences. Check the plural forms: patches, cliffs, leaves, sisters-in-law, pocketfuls.)

Review Exercises

A. Find each word that has an error in capitalization, and write it correctly. [20]
   1. On the way to British columbia, we crossed the Rocky mountains.
   2. Our old Farmall Tractor is over at Holtry's Machine shop for repairs.
   3. "I owe the Lord a Morning Song" was written by a mennonite man from Lancaster county, Pennsylvania.
   4. The visiting Minister is brother Harold, my Uncle from north Carolina.

B. These sentences have missing commas, colons, and end punctuation. Copy the words or numbers with which these marks should be used, and place the needed marks where they belong. (Use the index if you need help.)
   1. Are you sure Benjamin that you have the right book
   2. Cornelius a Roman centurion was rewarded for his sincere faith
   3. Father is staking the tomatoes and the boys are hoeing the beans
   4. We left for Bethel Mennonite Church at 7 00 A M and arrived at 8 45 A M
   5. Our grandparents uncles aunts and cousins have come to our place
   6. Leon my oldest brother owns a farm near Maugansville Maryland
   7. How much the Lord deserves our praise
   8. In Hebrews 13 2 we are encouraged to be hospitable to strangers

C. Copy each sentence that has a direct quotation, using correct punctuation and capitalization. If a sentence has an indirect quotation, write *indirect*. (Use the index if you need help.)
   1. Gloria told us that the lima beans are ready to be picked.
   2. Children, get your buckets Father directed and come to the garden.
   3. I'll bring out some cold lemonade after a while promised Mother.
   4. Aunt Sue said that she wanted to help.
   5. Melinda shouted let's race to the garden.

Review Exercises

A. 1. Columbia, Mountains
   2. tractor, Shop
   3. Owe, Mennonite, County
   4. minister, Brother, uncle, North

B. 1. sure, Benjamin, book?
   2. Cornelius, centurion, faith.
   3. tomatoes, beans.
   4. 7:00 A.M.   8:45 A.M.
   5. grandparents, uncles, aunts, place.
   6. Leon, brother, Maugansville, Maryland.
   7. praise!
   8. 13:2(,) strangers.

C. (Corrections are underlined.)
   1. indirect
   2. "Children, get your buckets," Father directed, "and come to the garden."
   3. "I'll bring out some cold lemonade after a while," promised Mother.
   4. indirect
   5. Melinda shouted, "Let's race to the garden."

---

23. Nouns With Irregular Plural Forms, and Collective Nouns

> **Lesson Survey**
> - To make some nouns plural, you must change the vowel.
> - Some plural nouns have an archaic -*en* ending.

Lesson 23

Purpose: To study the rules for making some irregular plural forms of nouns, including *foreign plurals.

Oral Review:

1. Spell the plural form of each noun.
   a. monkey (monkeys)
   b. coach (coaches)
   c. muff (muffs)
   d. berry (berries)
   e. postmaster general (postmasters general)
   f. motto (mottoes *or* mottos)
   g. half (halves)
   h. puddle (puddles)
2. Give the gender of each noun.
   a. matron (feminine)
   b. maidservant (feminine)
   c. policeman (masculine)
   d. calf (common)
   e. bench (neuter)
   f. parents (common)
3. Tell whether each sentence is declarative, interrogative, imperative, or exclamatory.
   a. How much we need the help of the Lord! (exclamatory)
   b. Why was Daniel cast into the lions' den? (interrogative)
   c. "Bear ye one another's burdens." (imperative)
   d. God created the world in six days. (declarative)
4. Tell what kind of line is placed before each complement on a sentence diagram.
   a. predicate nominative (a line slanting toward the subject)
   b. direct object (a vertical line)

- Some nouns have identical singular and plural forms.
- Some nouns look like plural forms, but they are singular.
- Some nouns are usually considered plural whether they name one thing or more than one.
- A noun borrowed from another language may have a foreign plural ending.
- A **collective noun** is singular when it refers to a group as a whole, and plural when it refers to the individual members of the group.

Although the majority of nouns have regular plural forms, some do not. These irregular forms present special spelling challenges.

1. *To make some nouns plural, you must change the vowel.* Seven words follow this pattern.

foot—feet	louse—lice	man—men
goose—geese	mouse—mice	woman—women
tooth—teeth		

Of course, any compound words formed with these root words will also follow this pattern.

nobleman—noblemen	flatfoot—flatfeet
eyetooth—eyeteeth	

2. *Some plural nouns have an archaic -en ending.*

child—children
ox—oxen
brother—brethren (used especially within the church)
hose—hosen (found once in the King James Version of the Bible)

3. *Some nouns have identical singular and plural forms.*

deer—deer	salmon—salmon
sheep—sheep	series—series

4. *Some nouns look like plural forms, but they are singular.* There is no plural for these nouns.

measles	news	mathematics
mumps	phonics	checkers (a game)

<u>Measles</u> <u>is</u> a disease.
The <u>news</u> <u>was</u> quite a surprise.

c. predicate adjective (a line slanting toward the subject)

5. Pick out the appositives in these sentences. (Answers are underlined.)
   a. Menno Simons, <u>an outstanding leader of the Dutch Anabaptists</u>, died in 1561.
   b. Pilgram Marpeck, <u>a skilled engineer</u>, designed a series of aqueducts to bring water to Strasburg, <u>the City of Hope</u>.

6. In the following sentences, tell which words are used in direct address. (Answers are underlined.)
   a. "And thou, <u>Solomon my son</u>, know thou the God of thy father."
   b. "Hearken, <u>my beloved brethren</u>, Hath not God chosen the poor of this world rich in faith?"
   c. "The impotent man answered him, <u>Sir</u>, I have no man . . . to put me into the pool."

Lesson Introduction: Why do we write:

<u>goose</u>—<u>geese</u> but not <u>moose</u>—<u>meese</u>?
<u>mouse</u>—<u>mice</u> but not <u>house</u>—<u>hice</u>?
<u>tooth</u>—<u>teeth</u> but not <u>booth</u>—<u>beeth</u>?
<u>man</u>—<u>men</u> but not <u>pan</u>—<u>pen</u>?
<u>ox</u>—<u>oxen</u> but not <u>fox</u>—<u>foxen</u>?
<u>brother</u>—<u>brethren</u> but not <u>mother</u>—<u>methren</u>?

These questions have no simple answers, but they do highlight the fact that many English nouns have irregular plural forms.

Lesson Outline:

1. To make some nouns plural, you must change the vowel. Seven words, and compounds formed with these roots, follow this pattern.

2. Some plural nouns have an archaic -en ending.

5. *Some nouns are usually considered plural whether they name one thing or more than one.* Most nouns of this kind name something made of two parts.

pliers	glasses (an aid to eyesight)
scissors	tongs
trousers	tweezers

The <u>scissors</u> <u>are</u> in the desk drawer.

My <u>glasses</u> <u>were lying</u> beside the book.

6. *A noun borrowed from another language may have a foreign plural ending.* These plural forms are irregular only in the English language; they follow the regular pattern of the native language. For some of these words, the regular English pattern has also become acceptable. Generally speaking, the foreign spelling is retained in formal English.

Nouns With Foreign Plural Endings

Singular ending: is
Plural ending: -es, pronounced (ēz)
Examples: axis—axes; basis—bases; crisis—crises; oasis—oases

Singular ending: ex *or* ix
Plural ending: -ices, pronounced (i·sēz)
Examples: index—indices *or* indexes; vertex—vertices *or* vertexes

Singular ending: a
Plural ending: -ae, pronounced (ē)
Examples: alga—algae; larva—larvae *or* larvas

Singular ending: us
Plural ending: -i, pronounced (ī)
Examples: cactus—cacti *or* cactuses; radius—radii *or* radiuses

---

Another challenge in noun number is the use of collective nouns. A *collective noun* names a group of individuals. Words like *class, congregation, group, herd, swarm, flock, family,* and *team* are collective nouns.

Usually a collective noun is singular because it refers to *one group* as a whole. The one group is acting as a unit, doing one thing together.

3. Some nouns have identical singular and plural forms. Many of these are animal names.

4. Some nouns look like plural forms, but they are singular. There is no plural for these nouns.

5. Some nouns are usually considered plural whether they name one thing or more than one.

6. A noun borrowed from another language may have a foreign plural ending.

   a. For a noun ending with *is,* the plural form ends with -*es.* This plural ending is pronounced (ēz).

   b. For a noun ending with *ex* or *ix,* the plural form ends with -*ices.* This plural ending is pronounced (i·sēz). The plural form may also be made by simply adding -*es.*

   c. For a noun ending with *a,* the plural form ends with -*ae.* This ending is pronounced (ē). The plural form may also be made by simply adding -*s.*

   d. For a noun ending with *us,* the plural form ends with -*i.* This ending is pronounced (ī). The plural form may also be made by simply adding -*es.*

7. A collective noun is singular when it refers to a group as a whole, and plural when it refers to the individual members of the group.

★ **EXTRA PRACTICE**
Worksheet 13 (*Plural Nouns*)

Sometimes, however, a collective noun is used in a plural sense. The focus is on the *individual members* of the group rather than on the group as a unit. Instead of the whole group doing one thing together, each individual is acting separately.

The <u>family</u> <u>sings</u> a new song for family worship every week.
   (Singular: group acting as a unit)
The <u>family</u> <u>recite</u> *their* memory verses by turn.
   (Plural: individuals acting separately)

The <u>flock</u> of sheep <u>was grazing</u> contentedly.
   (Singular: group acting as a unit)
The <u>flock</u> of sheep <u>were fleeing</u> wildly from *their* enemies.
   (Plural: individuals acting separately)

The <u>congregation</u> <u>gathers</u> reverently each Lord's Day morning.
   (Singular: group acting as a unit)
The <u>congregation</u> <u>are sharing</u> *their* testimonies of answered prayers.
   (Plural: individuals acting separately)

Class Practice

A. Give the correct plural spellings of these nouns.
1. trousers   4. oasis   7. louse
2. cactus   5. salmon   8. index
3. fireman   6. larva   9. brother (two forms)

B. Read these sentences, making improvements as needed.
1. Mumps are a contagious disease.
2. Oasises provide welcome relief for desert travelers.
3. The tweezers is lying on the kitchen floor.
4. Mathematics have always been difficult for me.
5. How many salmons are in this creek?

C. In each sentence, tell whether the collective noun is *singular* or *plural* in its use. Then read the sentence, using the correct verb in parentheses.
1. The congregation (is, are) expressing their opinions on the matter.
2. The flock of swallows (have, has) made their nests high on the cliff.
3. The crowd (was, were) shouting, "Away with Him."
4. The team (is, are) putting forth all its effort to win the game.
5. The class (work, works) on this special project every Friday afternoon.

Written Exercises

A. Write the plural forms of these nouns. Use the foreign spellings for numbers 5–12.

Lesson 23 Answers

Class Practice

A. 1. trousers   6. larvae
   2. cacti *or* cactuses   7. lice
   3. firemen   8. indices *or* indexes
   4. oases   9. brothers *or* brethren
   5. salmon

B. (Answers are underlined.)
1. Mumps <u>is</u> a contagious disease.
2. <u>Oases</u> provide welcome relief for desert travelers.
3. The tweezers <u>are</u> lying on the kitchen floor.
4. Mathematics <u>has</u> always been difficult for me.
5. How many <u>salmon</u> are in this creek?

C. (Corrections are underlined.)
1. plural; The congregation <u>are</u> expressing their opinions on the matter.
2. plural; The flock of swallows <u>have</u> made their nests high on the cliff.
3. singular; The crowd <u>was</u> shouting, "Away with Him."
4. singular; The team <u>is</u> putting forth all its effort to win the game.
5. singular; The class <u>works</u> on this special project every Friday afternoon.

1. mailman
2. dormouse
3. tenderfoot
4. goose
5. stimulus
6. basis
7. fungus
8. vertebra
9. alga
10. appendix
11. analysis
12. thesis

B. Write these sentences correctly. If a sentence has no error, write *correct*.
1. The news of Christ's miracles have stirred much excitement.
2. Our neighbor's sheeps became infected with louses.
3. My scissors are too dull to cut the plastic neatly.
4. Measles are the cause of Gloria's absence.
5. A new series of stories have started in the *Christian Pathway*.
6. These pliers always slips before the coupling turns.
7. The blue trousers on the table is for Clarence.
8. The policemen were patrolling the busy highways.

C. Write the verb form that agrees with the use of these collective nouns.
1. A large herd of buffalo (was, were) stampeding across the plains.
2. Now the crowd (go, goes) their separate ways.
3. The family (is, are) scattered over the farm, doing their chores.
4. The assembly (listen, listens) in quiet reverence to the minister.
5. The chorus (watch, watches) the leader closely.
6. The class (is, are) not all finished with their stories.
7. The class (is, are) reading the poem chorally.
8. The bee colony (have, has) been busily working at their different tasks.

Review Exercises

A. Label each sentence *dec.* (declarative), *int.* (interrogative), *imp.* (imperative), or *exc.* (exclamatory). Write the last word, followed by the correct end punctuation. [10]
1. "Go to the ant, thou sluggard"
2. "A word spoken in due season, how good is it"
3. "A wise son heareth his father's instruction"
4. "In all thy ways acknowledge him"
5. "Oh that men would praise the Lord for his goodness, and for his wonderful works to the children of men"
6. "Wilt thou set thine eyes upon that which is not"

B. Diagram the skeletons and complements in the following sentences, along with any appositive or noun of direct address. [5–7]
1. What a mighty God we serve!
2. Observe the beauty of His handiwork.
3. He is the Creator and Sustainer of all things.
4. Kendra, can you quote Psalm 19?

Written Exercises

A.
1. mailmen
2. dormice
3. tenderfeet
4. geese
5. stimuli
6. bases
7. fungi
8. vertebrae
9. algae
10. appendices
11. analyses
12. theses

B. (Corrections are underlined.)
1. The news of Christ's miracles <u>has</u> stirred much excitement.
2. Our neighbor's <u>sheep</u> became infected with <u>lice</u>.
3. correct
4. Measles <u>is</u> the cause of Gloria's absence.
5. A new series of stories <u>has</u> started in the *Christian Pathway*.
6. These pliers always <u>slip</u> before the coupling turns.
7. The blue trousers on the table <u>are</u> for Clarence.
8. correct

C.
1. was
2. go
3. are
4. listens
5. watches
6. are
7. is
8. have

Review Exercises

A.
1. imp., sluggard.
2. exc., it!
3. dec., instruction.
4. imp., him.
5. exc., men!
6. int., not?

B.
1.

| we | serve | God |

2.

| (you) | Observe | beauty |

3.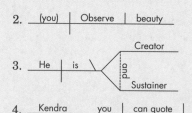

4.

| Kendra | you | can quote | Psalm 19 |

5. The heavens, with an innumerable host of stars, are an impressive sight.
6. Our closest star, the sun, seems quite large.
7. It is, however, one of the smallest stars.
8. We should give the Lord much glory and honor.

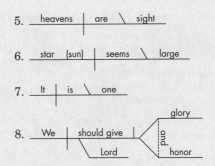

---

24. Possessive Nouns

> **Lesson Survey**
>
> - A **possessive noun** usually functions as an adjective.
> - For most singular nouns and for plural nouns not ending with -s, the possessive form is made by adding 's.
> - For a plural noun ending with -s, the possessive form is made by adding only an apostrophe.
> - Only nouns naming persons or animals are normally written in the possessive form.
> - To show that two or more persons or things have joint ownership, add an apostrophe to only the last word of the compound.
> - To show that two or more persons or things have separate ownership of two similar items, add an apostrophe to each word in the compound.

The use of possessive nouns simplifies and smoothes our language. Consider the following pairs of sentences.

Jesus taught from the boat of Peter.
Jesus taught from Peter's boat.

The barns of the rich man were filled to overflowing.
The rich man's barns were filled to overflowing.

Possessive nouns are usually adjectives that show ownership or relationship. They always answer the question *whose.*

The <u>high priest's</u> garments were beautifully made.
<u>Abraham's</u> willingness to offer Isaac showed his love for God.

Sometimes a possessive noun stands alone. The word that it would

---

Lesson 24

Purpose: To teach the formation and use of possessive nouns.

Oral Review:
1. Spell the plural form of each noun.
   a. clutch (clutches)
   b. basis (bases)
   c. candy (candies)
   d. alga (algae)
   e. sheaf (sheaves)
   f. volcano (volcanoes *or* volcanos)
   g. deer (deer)
   h. vertex (vertices *or* vertexes)
   i. nucleus (nuclei *or* nucleuses)
   j. son-in-law (sons-in-law)
2. Tell which words in these phrases should be capitalized. (Answers are underlined.)

a. *An <u>Index</u> of <u>Weather</u> <u>Facts</u>*
b. the <u>Strait</u> of <u>Magellan</u>
c. the <u>War</u> <u>Between</u> the <u>States</u>
d. <u>Department</u> of <u>Transportation</u>
e. "<u>It</u> <u>May</u> <u>Be</u> at <u>Morn</u>"
f. <u>J</u>. <u>F</u>. <u>Funk</u>
3. Give the skeletons and complements of these sentences.
   a. An angelic host announced the birth of Jesus. (host announced birth)
   b. Each martyr had remained faithful unto death. (martyr had remained faithful)
   c. All of us gave Mother a hearty greeting. (All gave Mother greeting)

Lesson Introduction: Not all languages have possessive forms for nouns. In English we use the phrase *Peter's book*. But a Spanish-speaking person must

normally modify is not stated, so the possessive noun functions as a noun.

Goliath's confidence was in his own might, but David's was in the Lord.
(*Goliath's* is an adjective modifying *confidence. David's,* meaning *David's confidence,* is the noun subject in the second clause.)
I have Galen's coat. Who has Leroy's?
(*Galen's* is an adjective modifying *coat. Leroy's,* meaning *Leroy's coat,* is the direct object in the second sentence.)

There are three simple rules for the formation of possessive nouns.

1. *The possessive form of most singular nouns is made by adding* 's. This includes nouns that end with a single *s* or *z* sound. For a compound noun spelled with or without a hyphen, *'s* is added to the last word.

angel's message	platypus's feet
shepherd's fear	James's letter
brother-in-law's car	Matthias's lot

Words like *Moses* and *Jesus* contain two *s* or *z* sounds in the last syllable. Adding a third *s* or *z* sound makes the word awkward to pronounce.

Moses' choice	Jesus' sufferings

2. *The possessive form of plural nouns not ending with* -s *is made by adding* 's. This includes compound nouns spelled with or without a hyphen.

children's hosannas	sisters-in-law's voices
larvae's appetite	mule deer's antlers
mice's squeaks	

3. *The possessive form of plural nouns ending with* -s *is made by adding only an apostrophe.* For a compound noun spelled with or without a hyphen, the apostrophe is added to the last word.

pupils' answers	great-grandparents' house
disciples' amazement	mail carriers' duties

Singular	Singular Possessive	Plural	Plural Possessive
prophet	prophet's	prophets	prophets'
child	child's	children	children's
fly	fly's	flies	flies'
donkey	donkey's	donkeys	donkeys'
thief	thief's	thieves	thieves'

Only nouns naming persons or animals are normally written in the possessive form. If a noun names an inanimate object, it is better to use a prepositional phrase.

use the equivalent of "the book of Peter"—*el libro de Pedro.* Possessive nouns simplify and smooth our language.

Lesson Outline:

1. A possessive noun usually functions as an adjective that shows ownership or relationship. Sometimes it stands alone and functions as a noun.

2. There are three simple rules for the formation of possessive nouns.

(1) *The possessive form of most singular nouns is made by adding* 's. Words like *Moses* and *Jesus* are exceptions because they contain two *s* or *z* sounds in the last syllable. Adding a third *s* or *z* sound makes the word awkward to pronounce.

(2) *The possessive form of plural nouns not ending with* -s *is made by adding* 's.

(3) *The possessive form of plural nouns ending with* -s *is made by adding only an apostrophe.*

3. Only nouns naming persons or animals are normally written in the possessive form.
   a. Exceptions are made in poetic or figurative language.
   b. Exceptions are also made with measures of time and money and a few other common expressions.

4. To show joint ownership with a compound form, add an apostrophe to only the last word.

5. To show separate ownership with a compound form, add an apostrophe to each word.

The chair's back is beautifully hand-carved.
  Better: The back of the chair is beautifully hand-carved.
The oak's roots have lifted the shed's foundation.
  Better: The roots of the oak have lifted the foundation of the
    shed.

However, the possessive form of inanimate objects is common in poetic or figurative language.

Oh, happy is the man who hears <u>Instruction's</u> warning voice.
The blazing reds, oranges, and yellows are <u>Autumn's</u> glory.
The <u>town's</u> only claim to fame is the underground mine fire.

Other exceptions to this rule are measures of time and money and a few other common expressions.

Measures:
  an hour's drive   a day's wages   a week's rainfall
Other common expressions:
  the earth's surface   a stone's throw

To show that two or more persons or things have joint ownership, add an apostrophe to only the last word of the compound.

Carol and Joy's garden is neat. (one garden owned by two people)
The horse and cow's pen needs cleaning. (one pen for two animals)

To show that two or more persons or things have separate ownership of two similar items, add an apostrophe to each word in the compound.

Hezekiah's and Josiah's reigns were marked by revival.
  (two kings with separate reigns)
Brother Melvin's and Brother Ivan's cars were damaged.
  (two cars of separate ownership)

Class Practice

A. Copy this chart on the board, and fill it in. (Plural forms do not need to be given for numbers 5 and 6.)

Singular	Singular Possessive	Plural	Plural Possessive
1. cattleman	——	——	——
2. lady	——	——	——
3. monkey	——	——	——
4. fox	——	——	——
5. Mrs. Lane	——		
6. Moses	——		

Lesson 24 Answers

Class Practice

A. (Words in italics are given in the pupil's text.)

1. *cattleman*	cattleman's	cattlemen	cattlemen's
2. *lady*	lady's	ladies	ladies'
3. *monkey*	monkey's	monkeys	monkeys'
4. *fox*	fox's	foxes	foxes'
5. *Mrs. Lane*	Mrs. Lane's		
6. *Moses*	Moses'		

B. Read these sentences, changing the underlined words to expressions with possessive forms.
1. The disciples of Jesus could not heal the demon-possessed son.
2. We answered the questions of our teacher carefully.
3. Do you know the address of Lois?
4. We visited in the home of our friends yesterday.

C. Read each sentence, changing the singular possessive expression (such as *boy's cap*) to a plural possessive expression (such as *boys' caps*). Also change other words as needed.
1. Their child's letter was welcome.
2. The baby's cry was pitiful.
3. The calf's pen must be cleaned today.
4. The ostrich's kick is powerful.

D. Read each sentence, using the possessive form of the underlined phrase. The first two should show joint ownership, and the last two should show separate ownership.
1. Jacob and Esau father was Isaac.
2. Joshua and Caleb report was good.
3. Adam and Eve eyes were opened.
4. The herdsmen of Abram and Lot cattle quarreled.

Written Exercises

A. Write the possessive form of each noun.

1. sailor	6. friends	11. mouse	16. waitress
2. babies	7. chief	12. soldiers	17. prince
3. calf	8. uncles	13. fathers	18. hobo
4. geese	9. sisters	14. fox	19. son-in-law
5. Doris	10. Moses	15. fly	20. sons-in-law

B. Rewrite the underlined expressions, using possessive forms.
1. The books of the pupils are stored in the closet over summer.
2. The rebuilding should be finished in the time of three days.
3. From the throne of God proceeds a pure river.
4. The knife of Jehoiakim could not destroy God's Word.

C. Rewrite each sentence, changing the singular possessive expression (such as *boy's cap*) to a plural possessive expression (such as *boys' caps*). Also change other words as needed.
1. The student's desk was well organized.
2. The speaker's message was inspiring.
3. That Anabaptist's deed is a noble example.
4. The child's mother was busy with the quilt.

B. (Answers are underlined.)
1. Jesus' disciples could not heal the demon-possessed son.
2. We answered our teacher's questions carefully.
3. Do you know Lois's address?
4. We visited in our friends' home yesterday.

C. (Answers are underlined.)
1. Their children's letters were welcome.
2. The babies' cries were pitiful.
3. The calves' pens must be cleaned today.
4. The ostriches' kicks are powerful.

D. (Answers are underlined.)
1. Jacob and Esau's father was Isaac.
2. Joshua and Caleb's report was good.
3. Adam's and Eve's eyes were opened.
4. The herdsmen of Abram's and Lot's cattle quarreled.

Written Exercises

A.
1. sailor's	11. mouse's
2. babies'	12. soldiers'
3. calf's	13. fathers'
4. geese's	14. fox's
5. Doris's	15. fly's
6. friends'	16. waitress's
7. chief's	17. prince's
8. uncles'	18. hobo's
9. sisters'	19. son-in-law's
10. Moses'	20. sons-in-law's

B. 1. the pupils' books
2. three days' time
3. God's throne
4. Jehoiakim's knife

C. 1. The students' desks were well organized.
2. The speakers' messages were inspiring.
3. Those Anabaptists' deeds are noble examples.
4. The children's mothers were busy with the quilt.

D. Write each underlined phrase correctly, using a possessive form. The first two should show joint ownership, and the last two should show separate ownership.
1. <u>John and Jake bicycle</u> has a flat tire.
2. Have you seen <u>Mahlon and Peter new store</u>?
3. We enjoyed looking at <u>Freda and Beverly pictures</u>.
4. <u>Father and Mother prayers</u> followed us through the day.

Review Exercises

A. Copy the object complements in these sentences. Label them *DO* for direct object or *IO* for indirect object. [5]
1. Jeremiah told the people God's message.
2. The Babylonians brought death and destruction to Jerusalem.
3. God gave Adam and Eve a few simple commands.
4. Lot pitched his tent toward Sodom.

B. Copy the subjective complements in these sentences. Label them *PN* for predicate nominative or *PA* for predicate adjective. [6]
1. The children of Israel often seemed ungrateful and rebellious.
2. David had been king for forty years.
3. The Old Testament tabernacle was a divine sanctuary.
4. The Gibeonites appeared sincere, but they were actually deceptive.

C. Diagram the skeletons and complements of these sentences. [5, 6]
1. Judas gave his Master a kiss of betrayal.
2. The church at Laodicea had become spiritually destitute.
3. The hills around Jerusalem were a natural protection for the city.
4. Jesus healed the lame, the deaf, and the blind.
5. The Jordan River appeared swollen and muddy.

---

25. Developing Paragraphs by Using Examples or Telling an Incident

> **Lesson Survey**
> - A paragraph may be developed by using examples to support the topic sentence.
> - A paragraph may be developed by telling an incident to illustrate the topic sentence.

Lesson 25

Purpose: To teach paragraph development by using examples or telling an incident.

Oral Review:
1. What do we do when we develop a paragraph? (clarify and support the topic sentence)
2. List several important points to remember when developing a paragraph by adding details. (Use details that actually support the topic sentence; do not merely reword the topic sentence. Know your subject well enough to add specific, meaningful details.)
3. Which kind of sentence order is used when developing a paragraph by giving steps? (chronological order)
4. Where is the topic sentence usually located in a paragraph? (at the beginning)

D. 1. John and Jake's bicycle
2. Mahlon and Peter's new store
3. Freda's and Beverly's pictures
4. Father's and Mother's prayers

Review Exercises

A. 1. people—IO; message—DO
2. death—DO; destruction—DO
3. Adam—IO; Eve—IO; commands—DO
4. tent—DO

B. 1. ungrateful—PA; rebellious—PA
2. king—PN
3. sanctuary—PN
4. sincere—PA; deceptive—PA

C. 1.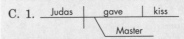
2.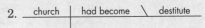
3.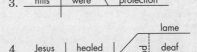
4.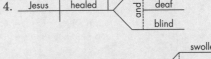
5.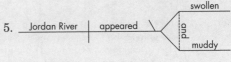

5. List several devices that will help to achieve paragraph coherence. (sentence order, transitional words, repetition of key words, pronoun reference)
6. Should a character sketch emphasize one or several characteristics of an individual? (one)
7. Name the three main parts of a character sketch. (introduction, body, conclusion)
8. The setting of a character sketch may either reflect or ——— the emphasis of the sketch. (contrast)

Lesson Introduction: Do you appreciate when a person makes strong statements but then has nothing to back up what he says? Maybe he says, "John Deere tractors are no good." Then when you ask him why he thinks that, he answers, "I just don't like them," or "They're junk," or "They're the wrong color." Unless he can give some definite reasons for his statement, he will not be very convincing. This

In Lesson 21 you learned that paragraphs may be developed by adding details or by giving steps to explain a process. This lesson teaches two other methods of paragraph development: using examples and telling an incident.

A topic sentence by itself may be vague or unconvincing. But if a writer presents specific evidence to support his topic sentence, he will be much more likely to convince the reader. Even if the reader still disagrees, he will not be left wondering what the writer meant.

When you develop a paragraph by using examples, be sure your examples are clear and specific. The paragraph may include a few examples that are described in considerable detail. Or it may contain a number of examples with fewer details about each one.

Poor: A few examples without enough details

Topic	God is able to use the small resources of the faithful to accomplish His purposes. David used his simple shepherd's
Example 1	sling to answer Goliath's challenge. The widow of Zarephath
Example 2	used her little bit of oil and meal. Both of these used their
Conclusion	little, and God multiplied the small resources into great blessings.

Better: A few examples well described

Topic	God is able to use the small resources of the faithful to accomplish His purposes. David's youthful figure contrasted
Example 1	sharply with Goliath's towering frame. But he wisely refused the armor that King Saul wanted him to wear. Rather, David used his simple shepherd's sling and a few small stones to answer Goliath's challenge. The widow of Zarephath had
Example 2	only a little oil and a little meal. But when Elijah told her to make him a little cake first, she obeyed. Day after day, God multiplied those small resources to sustain the prophet, the woman, and her son during the great famine. Both of these
Conclusion	used their little, and God multiplied the small resources into great blessings.

Better: A number of examples briefly described

Topic	God is able to use the small resources of the faithful to accomplish His purposes. Moses had a simple rod in his hand.
Example 1	But God turned it into a rod of power involved in many miracles. Shamgar had merely an oxgoad, but with God's help he
Example 2	delivered Israel from the Philistines. David wisely answered
Example 3	Goliath's challenge with a simple shepherd's sling that he knew God had used before. The widow of Zarephath gave
Example 4	Elijah a little cake made from her last bit of oil and meal, which

lesson will show how to develop paragraphs by using good examples as well as by telling an incident.

Lesson Outline:

1. A paragraph may be developed by using examples to support the topic sentence.

    a. The examples must be clear and specific.

    b. The paragraph may contain a few examples described in detail.

    c. The paragraph may contain more examples with fewer details.

2. A paragraph may be developed by telling an incident to illustrate the topic sentence.

    a. Telling an incident is actually taking one example and developing it as a brief story.

    b. The story must be long enough to illustrate the point, but not so long as to be distracting.

★ *EXTRA PRACTICE*
Worksheet 14 (*Developing Paragraphs by Using Examples or Telling an Incident*)

Example 5	kept multiplying for many days. The lad's five barley loaves and two small fish were given to Jesus, and He fed a huge multitude with this one lunch. Each of these used the little
Conclusion	he had, and God multiplied the small resources into great blessings.

A paragraph may also be developed by telling an incident to illustrate the topic sentence. Instead of giving several examples, such a paragraph uses only one example. This one example is developed thoroughly enough to well illustrate the main idea.

Using an incident to develop a paragraph is like telling a brief story. The story must be long enough to illustrate the point. But if it is too long or too full of narrative details, it will distract the reader from the point of the topic sentence.

Poor: Insufficient details

Topic	The faithful are willing to use their small resources to accomplish God's purpose. When David heard Goliath's challenge
One incident	thundering across the valley, his faith stirred him to action. He took his simple shepherd's sling and five smooth stones. God
Conclusion	used his small resources to bring a great victory to Israel.

Better: Sufficient details

Topic	The faithful are willing to use their small resources to accomplish God's purpose. When David heard Goliath's challenge
	thundering across the valley, his faith stirred him to action. He refused the armor of King Saul, taking rather the simple shepherd's sling that he knew God had blessed before. After choos-
One incident	ing five smooth stones, he ran confidently to meet the giant. To the contemptuous boast of Goliath, David declared, "I come to thee in the Name of the Lord of hosts." God directed that very first stone to its mark, where it brought low the man who had dared to defy the armies of the living God. David used
Conclusion	his little, and God multiplied it into great blessing.

Class Practice

Tell what is wrong with each paragraph. Suggest ways to improve it.

1.   The faithful saints are often in a minority. Noah and his family were very much alone as a godly remnant. Of the many Hebrew captives, Daniel and his three friends are the only ones mentioned in the Book of Daniel as remaining faithful. The road of faith is not traveled by the multitudes.

Lesson 25 Answers

Class Practice

1. The paragraph should either give more examples or tell more about each one.

(Sample paragraph.)

The faithful saints are often in a minority. Noah and his family were very much alone as a godly remnant. Joshua and Caleb stood alone when the other ten spies declared that Canaan could not be conquered. Although he was wrong, Elijah thought that he was the only one left in all Israel who had not bowed to Baal. Of the many Hebrew captives, Daniel and his three friends are the only ones mentioned in the Book of Daniel as remaining faithful. The road of faith is not traveled by the multitudes.

2.   The sin of covetousness can quickly send a person on a course of disaster. Gehazi coveted Naaman's gifts, and in a short time he told several lies. As a result, God punished him with the leprosy of Naaman.

Written Exercises

A. Choose two of these topic sentences, and write paragraphs developed by using examples. One paragraph should have two or three examples, each described in detail. The other should have five or six examples described more briefly.
1. A rainy day can be an enjoyable day.
2. Our family has several ways of preserving food.
3. The sufferings of man moved Jesus to compassion.
4. The prophets of God often faced persecution.
5. Home accidents may result from children's carelessness.
6. Moses is well known as the meekest man who ever lived.

B. Choose one of these topic sentences, and write a paragraph developed by telling an incident.
1. Having unexpected guests can be embarrassing.
2. A mistake can be profitable if you learn from it.
3. Procrastination can bring painful results.
4. A true friend is a valuable blessing.
5. Jesus had a keen interest in the needs of individual persons.
6. Daniel is a noble example of unswerving loyalty.

---

26. Verbals as Nouns

> **Lesson Survey**
> - A **verbal** is a verb form that is used as another part of speech.
> - A **gerund** is the *-ing* form of a verb used as a noun.
> - An **infinitive** is the basic form of a verb preceded by *to*. It may be used as a noun.
> - A verbal used as a noun is diagramed on a pedestal.

Some words seem to be two different parts of speech at the same time. A possessive noun is an example of this. It functions as a noun in that it names a person, place, or thing. But it also functions as an adjective in

2. The paragraph does not have enough details to illustrate the point.

(Sample paragraph.)

The sin of covetousness can quickly send a person on a course of disaster. Gehazi, Elisha's trusted servant, surely must have been a godly man. Yet the sight of Naaman's gifts sparked an unholy desire to take some things for himself. Within a short time, Gehazi had added lie upon lie. He told Naaman that Elisha had sent him, he deceitfully hid the gifts, and he told Elisha that he had not gone away. As a result, God punished him with the leprosy of Naaman.

Written Exercises

A. (Individual work.)

B. (Individual work.)

Lesson 26

Purpose: To teach the definition and identification of a *gerund and of an *infinitive used as a noun.

Oral Review:
1. For what kind of nouns is the possessive form made by adding *'s*? (most singular nouns, and plural nouns not ending with *-s*)
2. The possessive form of a plural noun ending with *-s* is formed by adding ———. (only an apostrophe)
3. Spell the possessive forms of these nouns.
   a. ladies (ladies')   c. Moses (Moses')
   b. brethren (brethren's)   d. mouse (mouse's)
4. Choose the better verb in each sentence. (Answers are underlined.)
   a. The scissors (is, <u>are</u>) on the shelf.
   b. Because of vaccination, measles (<u>is</u>, are) not as common today as long ago.
   c. Mathematics (have, <u>has</u>) always been my favorite subject.
   d. John's trousers (was, <u>were</u>) torn when he fell.
5. Spell the foreign plural form of each noun.
   a. nucleus (nuclei)
   b. vertex (vertices)
   c. pupa (pupae)

Lesson Introduction: Have the students identify the root word of *verbal*. (verb) Then point out that one meaning of the suffix *-al* is "having the characteristics of." A verbal is a verb form used as another part of speech while retaining some of the characteristics of a verb.

Lesson Outline:
1. A verbal is a verb form that is used as another part of speech.

hat it tells *whose* about some other noun.

> Jesus used the <u>widow's</u> mites to teach an important lesson.
>> (*Widow's* acts as a noun by naming a person. It acts as an adjective by telling *whose* mites.)

Verbals also seem like two different parts of speech at the same time. A *verbal* is a verb form that is used as another part of speech. Two kinds of verbals are used as nouns: the gerund and the infinitive.

A *gerund* is the *-ing* form of a verb used as a noun. Since a gerund is a noun, it must function as a noun. Instead of expressing action performed by a noun or pronoun, a gerund *names* an action. A gerund must also have a noun function within a sentence. It may be the subject, the complement after a verb, or the object of a preposition.

> <u>Singing</u> is a good way to chase away discouragement.
>> (What is? Singing. *Singing* names an action and is the subject.)
>
> Sharon especially enjoys <u>baking</u>.
>> (Sharon enjoys what? Baking. *Baking* names an action and is the direct object.)
>
> My father's occupation is <u>farming</u>.
>> (Occupation is what? Farming. *Farming* names an action and is the predicate nominative.)
>
> We seek God's help by <u>praying</u>.
>> (By what? Praying. *Praying* names an action and is the object of a preposition.)

There is an important clue to help you decide whether an *-ing* word is a verb or a gerund. If a word ending with *-ing* is used as a verb, it must be preceded by a form of *be* as a helping verb.

> The <u>children</u> <u>are hoeing</u> in the garden.
>> (*Are hoeing* is a verb phrase.)
>
> The <u>children</u> <u>enjoy</u> hoeing in the garden.
>> (There is no form of *be*; *hoeing* is a gerund used as a direct object.)

Of course, if the gerund is used as a predicate nominative, it may also be preceded by a form of *be*. However, the gerund will be naming an action that renames the subject. Reading the skeleton should help you decide whether the *-ing* form is part of the verb phrase.

> The <u>congregation</u> <u>is singing</u> a hymn.
>> **Think:** <u>Congregation</u> <u>is singing</u> is sensible.
>>> *Singing* does not rename the subject *congregation*.
>>> *Singing* is part of the verb phrase.

> **2. A gerund is the -ing *form of a verb used as a noun.***
>> a. As a noun, a gerund names an action and fills a noun function in a sentence.
>> b. Unlike a verb ending with *-ing,* a gerund is not used with a form of *be* as a helping verb.

> **3. An infinitive is the basic form of a verb preceded by to.**
>> a. Many infinitives name actions and fill noun functions in a sentence. (*Teacher:* They may also be used as modifiers, as in "We have no time *to lose*"; but that is not taught here.)
>> b. An infinitive must not be confused with a prepositional phrase beginning with *to.*

> **4. A verbal used as a noun is diagramed on a pedestal.**

In worship, one important <u>part</u> <u>is</u> singing hymns.
> **Think:** <u>Part</u> <u>is singing</u> is not sensible. (A part cannot sing.)
> *Singing* renames the subject *part*.
> *Singing* is a gerund.

The <u>ship</u> <u>had been sailing</u> across the ocean for several weeks.
> **Think:** <u>Ship</u> <u>had been sailing</u> is sensible.
> *Sailing* does not rename the subject *ship*.
> *Sailing* is part of the verb phrase.

Their only <u>method</u> of travel <u>was</u> walking.
> **Think:** <u>Method</u> <u>was walking</u> is not sensible. (A method cannot walk.)
> *Walking* renames the subject *method*.
> *Walking* is a gerund.

Another verbal is the infinitive. An *infinitive* is the basic form of a verb preceded by *to*. Like the gerund, an infinitive used as a noun names an action and fills a noun function in the sentence.

> "Behold, <u>to obey</u> is better than sacrifice."
> (What is? To obey. *To obey* names an action and is the subject.)
> These children like <u>to sing</u>.
> (Children like what? To sing. *To sing* names an action and is the direct object.)
> Paula's job this evening will be <u>to clean</u>.
> (*To clean* renames the subject *job*. *To clean* names an action and is the predicate nominative.)

The word *to* is also a common preposition. So you must be careful not to confuse an infinitive with a prepositional phrase. If *to* is used with the basic form of a verb, the combination is an infinitive. If *to* is followed by a noun or pronoun, the combination is a prepositional phrase.

> The weary prisoners' only thought was <u>to rest</u>.
> (*to* + verb = infinitive)
> They were on the way <u>to the galley ship</u>.
> (*to* + noun = prepositional phrase)

All verbals are diagramed across the angle of a slanting and a horizontal line. If a verbal is used as a noun, it is put on a pedestal above the place where a single-word noun would normally go.

Praying brings strength
to a tempted soul.

One important weapon
  is praying.

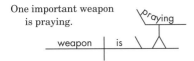

We seek God's will by praying.

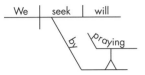

To pray can be hard work.

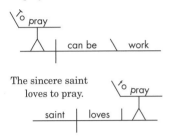

The sincere saint
  loves to pray.

Class Practice

A. Find each verbal in these sentences, and identify it as a *gerund* or an *infinitive*. Tell how it is used in the sentence.
 1. Washing is enjoyable work.
 2. Our goal is to win.
 3. Are you learning to rejoice even in unpleasant circumstances?
 4. Gehazi brought God's judgment on himself by lying.
 5. Most little puppies like to play.
 6. Good listening is difficult if we are talking most of the time.

B. Tell whether each underlined group of words is an *infinitive* or a *prepositional phrase*.
 1. Do all the children want <u>to go</u> along <u>to the berry patch</u>?
 2. <u>To His people</u>, Jesus' command is <u>to watch</u>.
 3. David hurried <u>to Nob</u>.
 4. God has the power <u>to create</u> and <u>to destroy</u>.

Lesson 26 Answers

Class Practice
A. 1. Washing—gerund, subject
   2. to win—infinitive, predicate nominative
   3. to rejoice—infinitive, direct object
      (*Learning* is part of the verb phrase.)
   4. lying—gerund, object of a preposition
   5. to play—infinitive, direct object
   6. listening—gerund, subject
      (*Talking* is part of a verb phrase.)

B. 1. infinitive, prepositional phrase
   2. prepositional phrase, infinitive
   3. prepositional phrase
   4. infinitive, infinitive

C. On the chalkboard, diagram the skeletons, complements, and prepositional phrases.
1. The Christlike way is to forgive.
2. Do you enjoy reading?
3. She is gaining skill in typing.
4. Deceiving is the devil's work.
5. Your responsibility this morning will be baking.

Written Exercises

A. Copy each verbal, and label it *gerund* or *infinitive*. Also write how it is used in the sentence.
1. God's great desire is to bless.
2. Rewriting is usually necessary for a good composition.
3. Gutenberg's occupation had been printing.
4. In art class we are learning to paint.
5. The little lost boy did not want to cry.
6. You might discover the answer by asking.
7. Through sharing, we are showing our love to others.
8. Persevering will bring you to your goal.
9. Everyone must try to sing.
10. To hunt was the hungry panther's need.

B. Diagram the skeletons and complements of these sentences.
1. Carving has always been Roger's talent.
2. Everyone should seek to serve.
3. To endure takes faith in the Lord.
4. One of Mother's jobs is sewing.
5. Have you enjoyed practicing?
6. Every Christian's interest is to grow.

Review Exercises

A. Write the plural forms of these nouns. Use the foreign spellings for numbers 9–12. [22, 23]

1. lady	7. piano
2. hutch	8. bucketful
3. patrolman	9. index
4. cargo	10. radius
5. wharf	11. alga
6. salmon	12. oasis

B. Identify the gender of the nouns in Part A by writing *M, F, N,* or *C* after each of your answers. [19]

C. Write the possessive forms of these singular and plural nouns. [24]

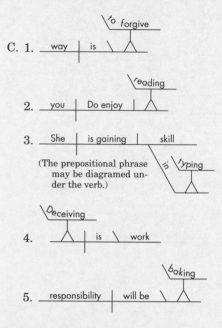

C. 1. way | is \ to forgive

2. you | Do enjoy \ reading

3. She | is gaining | skill — in \ typing
(The prepositional phrase may be diagramed under the verb.)

4. Deceiving | is \ work

5. responsibility | will be \ baking

Written Exercises

A. 1. to bless—infinitive, predicate nominative
2. Rewriting—gerund, subject
3. printing—gerund, predicate nominative
4. to paint—infinitive, direct object
5. to cry—infinitive, direct object
6. asking—gerund, object of a preposition
7. sharing—gerund, object of a preposition
8. Persevering—gerund, subject
9. to sing—infinitive, direct object
10. To hunt—infinitive, subject

B. 1. Carving | has been \ talent
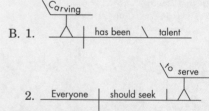

2. Everyone | should seek \ to serve

3. To endure | takes | faith

4. One | is \ sewing
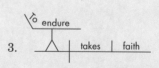

5. you | Have enjoyed \ practicing
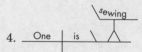

6. interest | is \ to grow
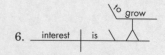

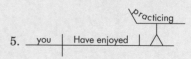

Review Exercises

A and B.

1. ladies—F	7. pianos—N
2. hutches—N	8. bucketfuls—N
3. patrolmen—M	9. indices—N
4. cargoes *or* cargos—N	10. radii—N
5. wharves *or* wharfs—N	11. algae—N
6. salmon—C	12. oases—N

1. firemen
2. horse
3. bees
4. Suzette
5. students
6. larvae
7. mice
8. Moses
9. sister-in-law

D. Rewrite sentences 1 and 2 so that they show joint ownership. Rewrite sentences 3 and 4 so that they show separate ownership. [24]
1. Peter's and Paul's calves were well fed.
2. Mary's and Bernice's quilts are finished.
3. Susan and Mary's book is still new.
4. Nevin and Clarence's chickens have gotten into the garden.

C. 1. firemen's
2. horse's
3. bees'
4. Suzette's
5. students'
6. larvae's
7. mice's
8. Moses'
9. sister-in-law's

D. 1. Peter and Paul's calves were well fed.
2. Mary and Bernice's quilts are finished.
3. Susan's and Mary's books are still new.
4. Nevin's and Clarence's chickens have gotten into the garden.

---

27. Verbal Phrases as Nouns

> ### Lesson Survey
> - A **verbal phrase** consists of a verbal and its complements and modifiers.
> - A verbal phrase used as a noun is diagramed on a pedestal.

You learned in the previous lesson that a verbal is a verb form used as another part of speech. But verbals still have many characteristics of verbs. They may have object complements, subjective complements, and adverb modifiers. These words work with a gerund or an infinitive to make a gerund phrase or an infinitive phrase.

A *verbal phrase* consists of a verbal and its complements and modifiers. Notice how a simple verbal can be expanded to become a verbal phrase.

> Standing can become wearisome. (*Standing* is a simple gerund.)
> Standing quietly in one spot can become wearisome.
>> (The gerund *Standing* is modified by the adverb *quietly* and the adverb phrase *in one spot. Standing quietly in one spot* is a gerund phrase.)
>
> Joanne's favorite job is to wash. (*To wash* is a simple infinitive.)
> Joanne's favorite job is to wash the dishes.
>> (The infinitive *to wash* has the direct object *dishes. To wash the dishes* is an infinitive phrase.)

Like a simple gerund or infinitive, a gerund phrase or an infinitive phrase can be used as the subject, direct object, predicate nominative, or object of a preposition within a sentence. The entire phrase functions as a noun.

Lesson 27

Purpose: To teach the definition and identification of a *gerund phrase and of an *infinitive phrase used as a noun.

Oral Review:

1. What is a verbal? (a verb form used as another part of speech)
2. What kind of verbal is composed of *to* and the basic form of a verb? (infinitive)
3. What kind of verbal ends with *-ing* and is used as a noun? (gerund)
4. Identify the complements in these sentences, and tell what kind they are.
   a. Father is bringing another load of hay. (load—direct object)
   b. Surely he must be quite thirsty. (thirsty—predicate adjective)
   c. Mother will give him some lemonade and a doughnut. (him—indirect object; lemonade—direct object; doughnut—direct object)
   d. That will be a welcome treat. (treat—predicate nominative)
5. Identify each sentence as simple, compound, or complex. If it is complex, tell whether the dependent clause is used as an adjective or an adverb.
   a. Mary, Martha, and Lazarus lived in Bethany. (simple)
   b. When Lazarus became sick, his sisters sent a message to Jesus. (complex; adverb clause)
   c. Jesus, who had healed many others, did not go to Bethany until later. (complex; adjective clause)
   d. Jesus called to Lazarus, and Lazarus came out of the tomb. (compound)

Gerund phrases:

Obeying God's commands is our delight.

(What is our delight? Obeying God's commands. *Obeying God's commands* is the subject.)

We should enjoy seeking the welfare of others.

(We should enjoy what? Seeking the welfare of others. *Seeking the welfare of others* is the direct object.)

Mary's wise choice was sitting quietly at Jesus' feet.

(Choice was what? Sitting quietly at Jesus' feet. *Sitting quietly at Jesus' feet* is the predicate nominative.)

Infinitive phrases:

To rejoice in the Lord is always important.

(What is important? To rejoice in the Lord. *To rejoice in the Lord* is the subject.)

We must seek to develop noble character.

(We must seek what? To develop noble character. *To develop noble character* is the direct object.)

Jesus' mission was to save the world.

(Mission was what? To save the world. *To save the world* is the predicate nominative.)

A verbal phrase used as a noun is diagramed on a pedestal, the same as a simple verbal. The direct object of a verbal is diagramed on the line after the verbal, with a vertical line in between. Adverbs and adverb phrases modifying the verbal are placed on slanted lines beneath the verbal. The example sentences above are diagramed here.

Obeying God's commands is our delight. *Commands* is the direct object of *Obeying*.

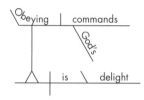

We should enjoy seeking the welfare of others.

Welfare is the direct object of *seeking*. (This gerund phrase *is* a direct object and *contains* a direct object.)

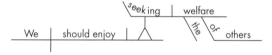

Lesson Introduction: Write the following pairs of sentences on the board.

"The plowing of the wicked is sin."
Paul's goal in life was to win Christ.

Have someone pick out the verbal in the first sentence. (plowing) Ask if simply plowing is sin. Then see if someone can tell which other words work along with the word *plowing*. Do the same for the second sentence. Tell the students that they have identified verbal phrases, which is the topic of today's lesson.

Lesson Outline:

1. A verbal phrase consists of a verbal and its complements and modifiers. The entire phrase often functions as a noun. (*Teacher:* Verbal phrases are also used as modifiers.)

2. A verbal phrase used as a noun is diagramed on a pedestal. Any complements and modifiers are diagramed with the verbal as if it were a verb.

★ **EXTRA PRACTICE**

Worksheet 15 (*Verbal Phrases as Nouns*)

Mary's wise choice was sitting quietly at Jesus' feet.
Quietly and *at Jesus' feet* are modifiers of *sitting*.

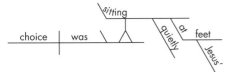

To rejoice in the Lord is always important.
In the Lord is a modifier of *To rejoice*.

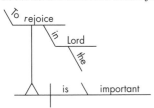

We must seek to develop noble character.
Character is the direct object of *to develop*.

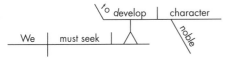

Jesus' mission was to save the world.
World is the direct object of *to save*.

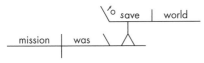

Class Practice

A. Read each verbal phrase, and tell whether it is a *gerund phrase* or an *infinitive phrase*. Also tell how it is used in the sentence.
1. Studying your lesson thoroughly will give you a grasp of its concepts.
2. Immediately after class, you should start to do the new assignment.
3. A basic need of every student is to budget his time well.
4. Your goal should be completing your lessons promptly.

Lesson 27 Answers

Class Practice
A. 1. Studying your lesson thoroughly—gerund phrase, subject
2. to do the new assignment—infinitive phrase, direct object
3. to budget his time well—infinitive phrase, predicate nominative
4. completing your lessons promptly—gerund phrase, predicate nominative

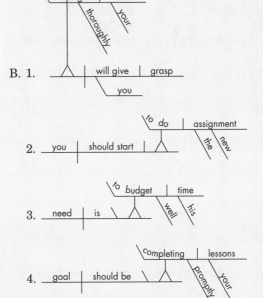

5. Realizing this goal requires good use of your time.
6. To have unfinished work should be an embarrassment.

B. On the chalkboard, diagram the skeletons and complements of the sentences in Part A. Be sure to include the verbal phrases.

Written Exercises

A. Copy each verbal phrase, and write whether it is a *gerund phrase* or an *infinitive phrase*. Also write how it is used in the sentence.
1. Wandering through the wilderness was a punishment for Israel's unbelief.
2. One of Israel's most serious sins was worshiping the golden calf.
3. Moses tried to make atonement for his people.
4. To complain about the manna dishonored God who gave it.
5. The gracious Lord continued to bless His people.
6. A frequent problem was finding sufficient water.
7. Getting to the Promised Land required trust in the Lord's guidance.
8. In the battle against Amalek, Moses needed to raise his arms to heaven.
9. Aaron and Hur's role was holding Moses' arms up.
10. Balaam's desire was to die the death of the righteous.

B. Diagram the skeletons and complements of these sentences. Be sure to include the verbal phrases.
1. Our work this morning was picking these peas.
2. Our neighbors wanted to see the big buck.
3. Collecting stamps of various countries can be quite educational.
4. Aunt Lillie's goal has been to use a different stamp on each letter.
5. To visit with Grandfather is always enjoyable.
6. Watching the playful squirrels provided good entertainment.

Review Exercises

A. Identify the underlined clauses as *adjective* or *adverb* clauses. [15]
1. Only animals that were unblemished were accepted for offerings.
2. After the Jews went into captivity, they never turned to idolatry again.
3. Cyrus, whom God called His anointed, allowed the Jews to go back home.
4. The Jews who returned to Jerusalem faced opposition from the Samaritans.
5. Nehemiah was deeply burdened when he heard about conditions at Jerusalem.

B. Identify these sentences as *simple, compound,* or *complex.* [14, 15]
1. The musk ox is actually not classed with oxen, but with sheep and goats.

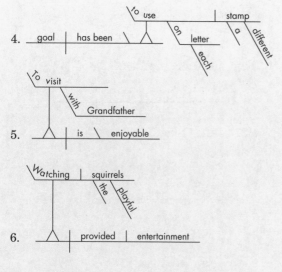

(Review Exercises are on page 131.)

5. Realizing this goal—gerund phrase, subject
6. To have unfinished work—infinitive phrase, subject

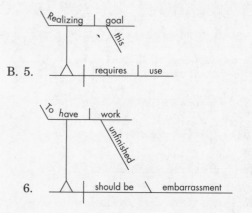

B. 5.

6.

Written Exercises

A. 1. Wandering through the wilderness—gerund phrase, subject
2. worshiping the golden calf—gerund phrase, predicate nominative
3. to make atonement for his people—infinitive phrase, direct object
4. To complain about the manna—infinitive phrase, subject
5. to bless His people—infinitive phrase, direct object
6. finding sufficient water—gerund phrase, predicate nominative
7. Getting to the Promised Land—gerund phrase, subject
8. to raise his arms to heaven—infinitive phrase, direct object
9. holding Moses' arms up—gerund phrase, predicate nominative
10. to die the death of the righteous—infinitive phrase, predicate nominative

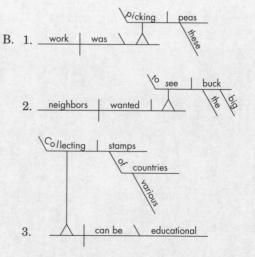

B. 1.

2.

3.

2. Because musk oxen live in Arctic areas, they need good protection against the cold.
3. God has given these creatures heavy fur coats of two layers.
4. The inner layer is a thick fleece of soft fur, and the outer layer is a bulky coat of long guard hairs.
5. The inner layer covers most of the animal's body.
6. At the front of its body, the coat of the musk ox is especially thick.
7. When the winter winds howl, the musk ox faces the wind.
8. This thick coat is pressed tightly against its body, and not much of its body heat is lost.

---

28. Identifying Noun Clauses

> **Lesson Survey**
> - A **noun clause** is a dependent clause that may be used as a subject, direct object, or predicate nominative in a complex sentence.

By now you can readily recognize nouns, those common words that name persons, places, things, or ideas. You will immediately recognize that *work* is a noun used as the subject in the following sentence.

Diligent <u>work</u> should accomplish a good job.
  (What should accomplish a good job? *Work* is a single-word noun used as a subject.)

Further, you learned in this chapter that nouns are sometimes phrases; they may be noun phrases, gerund phrases, or infinitive phrases. Note how *work* becomes a phrase in the following sentence.

<u>Working diligently</u> should accomplish a good job.
  (What should accomplish a good job? *Working diligently* is a gerund phrase used as a subject.)

A *noun clause* may be a noun in the same way as a single word or a phrase. The following example expresses much the same thought as the two sentences above, but this time the subject is a clause because it contains a skeleton.

<u>Whoever works diligently</u> should accomplish a good job.
  (Who should accomplish a good job? *Whoever works diligently* is a clause used as a subject. Note its skeleton: <u>Whoever</u> <u>works</u>.)

Review Exercises

A. 1. adjective   4. adjective
    2. adverb   5. adverb
    3. adjective

B. 1. simple   5. simple
    2. complex   6. simple
    3. simple   7. complex
    4. compound   8. compound

Lesson 28

Purpose: To teach noun clauses and their function in complex sentences.

Oral Review:

1. A gerund is a verbal that ———. (ends with *-ing* and is used as a noun)
2. How can you tell the difference between an infinitive and a prepositional phrase beginning with *to*? (*to* + verb = infinitive; *to* + noun = prepositional phrase)
3. Change these words to nouns by using noun-forming suffixes.
  a. happy (happiness)
  b. prudent (prudence)
  c. alternate (alternation)
  d. better (betterment)
  e. local (locality)
  f. magnify (magnitude, magnifier)
4. Correct the errors in capitalization and punctuation. (*Teacher:* Write the sentences on the board as shown, but without punctuation.)
  a. The beans, potatoes, and tomatoes are wilting; it hasn't rained for six weeks.
  b. Thunderheads are on the Western horizon.
  c. Let us pray that the lord may send some much-needed rain.
5. Tell whether each sentence is simple, compound, or complex.
  a. God is on the throne, and He controls the world. (compound)
  b. If we trust Him, we need not fear. (complex)
  c. God does many things that we do not understand. (complex)
  d. We simply trust His sovereign power. (simple)

A sentence containing a noun clause is a complex sentence because it has one independent clause and one dependent clause. In the complex sentences you have studied before, the dependent clause was either an adjective or an adverb. Look at this complex sentence with an adverb clause.

> Brother Merle stated his concern <u>when the brethren met together</u>.
> (*When the brethren met together* tells *when* Brother Merle stated his concern. It is an adverb clause.)

Now compare the complex sentence below. It looks much the same, but the dependent clause fills a completely different function. Instead of serving as an adverb, it now serves as a noun.

> Brother Merle stated <u>when the brethren would meet together</u>.
> (*When the brethren would meet together* tells *what* Brother Merle stated. It is the direct object of *stated* and is therefore a noun clause.)

A noun clause may be used as a subject, direct object, or predicate nominative. Here is a list of words that commonly introduce noun clauses.

how	wherever	that	whom
why	when	what	whose
whether	whenever	whatever	whoever
where	if	who	

When a sentence contains a noun clause used as a direct object or predicate nominative, you can readily find the two distinct skeletons of the complex sentence. The challenge is to understand how the two clauses fit together. In the following examples, the noun clauses are in brackets.

> <u>Brother Ira</u> <u>has decided</u> [when <u>they</u> <u>will begin</u> the house].
> **Think:** Brother Ira has decided what? When they will begin the house. *When they will begin the house* is the direct object of *has decided*.

> <u>Mother's</u> <u>concern</u> <u>is</u> [that the <u>children</u> <u>may be</u> too cold].
> **Think:** Concern is what? That the children may be too cold. *That the children may be too cold* is the predicate nominative.

A sentence with a noun clause used as a subject is also a complex sentence with two skeletons. However, the two skeletons may not be apparent, because the subject of the main clause is the entire noun clause!

In the following sentences, the noun clauses are again in brackets. Notice how these clauses function as subjects.

Lesson Introduction: On the chalkboard, write the following two sentences (from Oral Review). Underline the clauses as shown. Ask, "What parts of speech are the underlined dependent clauses?"

> God does many things <u>that we do not understand</u>. (adjective clause)
> <u>If we trust Him</u>, we need not fear. (adverb clause)

Tell the class that a clause may also serve as a noun. And since a noun clause is a dependent clause, a sentence with a noun clause is a complex sentence.

Lesson Outline:

1. A noun clause is a dependent clause used as a noun in a complex sentence.

    a. A sentence with a noun clause used as a direct object or predicate nominative has two distinct skeletons.

    b. If the noun clause is used as a subject, the two skeletons are not as obvious, because the subject of the main clause is the entire noun clause.

    c. Two common types of noun clauses are direct and indirect quotations. These usually function as direct objects.

      (*Teacher:* A quotation is sometimes a predicate nominative. Example: Jesus' <u>reply</u> <u>was</u>, "<u>I</u> <u>am</u> the way, the truth, and the life.")

2. Three tests can help to determine if a clause is a noun clause.

    (1) *Does the clause name a person, place, thing, or idea?*

    (2) *Does the clause serve a noun function in the sentence?*

    (3) *Is it sensible to replace the clause with a pronoun?*

★ **EXTRA PRACTICE**
Worksheet 16 (*Noun Clauses*)

[Whoever baked this bread] has done a good job.
  (Who has done a good job? Whoever baked this bread.)
[What you have done] will surely help us.
  (What will help us? What you have done.)

Two common types of noun clauses are direct and indirect quotations. These usually function as direct objects.

Jesus said, "[I am the way, the truth, and the life]."
  (Jesus said what? The direct quotation is the direct object of *said.*)
Jesus stated [that the rich shall hardly enter heaven].
  (Jesus stated what? The indirect quotation is the direct object of
    stated.)
The people asked, "[Who then shall be saved]?"
  (People asked what? The direct quotation is the direct object of
    asked.)

Most of the words that introduce noun clauses can also be used to introduce adjective or adverb clauses. Three tests can be used to distinguish a noun clause from an adjective or adverb clause.

Test 1: *Does the clause name a person, place, thing, or idea?*

I did not hear when Mr. Smith drove in.
  (names the *thing* that I did not hear; noun clause)
Mr. Smith came when you were in the barn.
  (does not name anything; not a noun clause)

His main reason for coming is that he wants to buy some corn.
  (names the *thing* that is his reason; noun clause)
Another reason that he came is to look at the tractor.
  (does not name anything; not a noun clause)

Whose truck he brought is a mystery to me.
  (names the *thing* that is a mystery; noun clause)
His brother, whose truck he has used before, was busy today.
  (does not name anything; not a noun clause)

Test 2: *Does the clause serve a noun function in the sentence?*

I did not hear when Mr. Smith drove in.
  (direct object of *did hear;* noun clause)
Mr. Smith came when you were in the barn.
  (modifies verb *came* by telling *when;* adverb clause)

His main reason for coming is that he wants to buy some corn.
  (predicate nominative renaming *reason;* noun clause)

Another reason <u>that he came</u> is to look at the tractor.
    (modifies *reason* by telling *what kind of;* adjective clause)

<u>Whose truck he brought</u> is a mystery to me.
    (subject of sentence; noun clause)
His brother, <u>whose truck he has used before</u>, was busy today.
    (modifies *brother* by telling *which;* adjective clause)

Test 3: *Is it sensible to replace the clause with a pronoun?* Pronouns like *he, that,* or *it* can replace noun clauses in the same way that they replace one-word nouns.

I did not hear <u>when Mr. Smith drove in</u>.
I did not hear <u>it</u>. (sensible; noun clause)

Mr. Smith came <u>when you were in the barn</u>.
Mr. Smith came <u>it</u>. (not sensible; not a noun clause)

His main reason for coming is <u>that he wants to buy some corn</u>.
His main reason for coming is <u>this</u>. (sensible; noun clause)

Another reason <u>that he came</u> is to look at the tractor.
Another reason <u>it</u> is to look at the tractor. (not sensible; not a noun clause)

Class Practice

A. These sentences contain noun clauses used as direct objects. Read the skeleton of the main clause, and then read the noun clause.
  1. Today we discovered where the old cabin had been located.
  2. Paul certainly should know who the speaker is.
  3. The man said, "Can you give me directions to Fannetsburg?"
  4. Did you see if the cows have come in from the meadow?

B. These sentences contain noun clauses used as predicate nominatives. Read the skeleton of the main clause, and then read the noun clause.
  1. This book is what we need.
  2. The leader should be whoever knows the way through these woods.
  3. The happiest place in life is wherever God wants us.
  4. The question is whether the bridge will be safe to cross.

C. These sentences contain noun clauses used as subjects. Read the noun clause and the verb of the main clause.
  1. Whose horses are running around the neighborhood remains a mystery.
  2. Whoever stacked this wood did a careful job.
  3. How the fire started has been the subject of an extensive investigation.

Lesson 28 Answers

Class Practice

A. 1. we discovered; where the old cabin had been located
  2. Paul should know; who the speaker is
  3. man said; Can you give me directions to Fannetsburg?
  4. you Did see; if the cows have come in from the meadow

B. 1. book is; what we need
  2. leader should be; whoever knows the way through these woods
  3. place is; wherever God wants us
  4. question is; whether the bridge will be safe to cross

C. 1. Whose horses are running around the neighborhood; remains
  2. Whoever stacked this wood; did
  3. How the fire started; has been

4. That the reformers compromised for political reasons disappointed the Anabaptists.

D. Read the noun clause in each sentence, and tell whether it is the *subject, direct object,* or *predicate nominative* of the main clause.
1. That God loves all men is clearly taught in the Scriptures.
2. Christ's great love is what kept Him on the cross.
3. How He prayed for His enemies emphasizes the greatness of His love.
4. We can never comprehend why He loves us so much.

Written Exercises

Copy the noun clause in each sentence, and write whether it is the *subject, direct object,* or *predicate nominative* of the main clause.
1. That Aunt Lavina loves others is demonstrated by her helpfulness.
2. I have read that rattlesnake meat is tasty.
3. How gravity works defies man's understanding.
4. Lydia's answer was what I expected.
5. Sheldon asked whose book you are reading.
6. Where the missing sheep have gone is a strange thing.
7. Whatever Linford does is done carefully.
8. Mother does not know whether Anna Marie feels better yet.
9. What we should do next has not been explained.
10. Lamar explained why we gave Loyal the best bicycle.
11. Father said that we should mow the grass this evening.
12. One of the marvels of the Bible is how exactly the details are fulfilled.
13. Whoever obeys God's Word experiences God's blessing.
14. Eileen declared, "This is a delicious vanilla pie!"
15. The best time to develop good habits is when a person is young.

Review Exercises

A. Find each word that has an error in capitalization, and write it correctly. [20]
1. Abraham, a faithful Patriarch, walked perfectly before the almighty.
2. Forever will i praise thee, o my lord!
3. The most populous nation in the World is china.
4. A mennonite music teacher, joseph funk, compiled *harmonia sacra,* his first music book in the english language.
5. The book was originally published in 1832 near harrisonburg, virginia, under the title *a compilation of genuine church music.*
6. Many of the songs depict the christian life as a journey toward heaven; years later, several became part of a hymnal called *psalms, hymns, and spiritual songs.*

4. That the reformers compromised for political reasons; disappointed

D. 1. That God loves all men—subject
2. what kept Him on the cross—predicate nominative
3. How He prayed for His enemies—subject
4. why He loves us so much—direct object

Written Exercises
1. That Aunt Lavina loves others—subject
2. that rattlesnake meat is tasty—direct object
3. How gravity works—subject
4. what I expected—predicate nominative
5. whose book you are reading—direct object
6. Where the missing sheep have gone—subject
7. Whatever Linford does—subject
8. whether Anna Marie feels better yet—direct object
9. What we should do next—subject
10. why we gave Loyal the best bicycle—direct object
11. that we should mow the grass this evening—direct object
12. how exactly the details are fulfilled—predicate nominative
13. Whoever obeys God's Word—subject
14. This is a delicious vanilla pie—direct object
15. when a person is young—predicate nominative

Review Exercises
A. 1. patriarch, Almighty
2. I, Thee, O, Lord
3. world, China
4. Mennonite, Joseph Funk, *Harmonia Sacra,* English
5. Harrisonburg, Virginia, *A Compilation of Genuine Church Music*
6. Christian, *Psalms, Hymns, and Spiritual Songs*

B. These sentences have missing commas, colons, and semicolons. Copy the words or numbers with which the missing punctuation should be used, and add the needed marks. (Use the index if you need help.)
   1. Matthew Mark Luke and John wrote the four Gospels.
   2. Paul the apostle to the Gentiles wrote several New Testament epistles.
   3. Lazarus, the man who had suffered much on earth, was carried to paradise but the rich man, who had lived selfishly, lifted up his eyes in hell.
   4. Leroy turn to Romans 1 1 Sarah turn to 1 Corinthians 1 1.

C. These sentences have missing apostrophes and hyphens. Copy the word with the missing punctuation, and add the needed mark. (Use the index if you need help.)
   1. Havent you seen Jonathans pink eyed, albino guinea pig?
   2. My brother in law said that his great grandparents have sixty three grandchildren.
   3. You wont receive credit for your spelling words if your *os* look like *as*.
   4. If youve learned self discipline, you shouldnt need as much correction.

B. 1. Matthew, Mark, Luke,
   2. Paul, Gentiles,
   3. paradise;
   4. Leroy, 1:1; Sarah, 1:1

C. 1. Haven't, Jonathan's, pink-eyed
   2. brother-in-law, great-grandparents, sixty-three
   3. won't, *o*'s, *a*'s
   4. you've, self-discipline, shouldn't

---

29. Diagraming Noun Clauses

> **Lesson Survey**
> - The word that introduces a noun clause usually serves as a subject, a direct object, an adjective, or an adverb within the noun clause.
> - The introductory words *that*, *if*, and *whether* serve only to introduce noun clauses.
> - When a noun clause is a direct quotation, it has no introductory word.
> - A noun clause is diagramed on a pedestal above the place where a single-word noun would normally go.

Various words are used to introduce noun clauses. Such a word usually does more than introduce the clause; it also serves a specific function within the noun clause. The following chart classifies these introductory words according to their functions.

Lesson 29

Purpose: To teach how to diagram complex sentences with noun clauses.

Oral Review:
1. Name three common functions of noun clauses within a complex sentence. (subject, direct object, predicate nominative)
2. Explain why the two skeletons are not obvious if a complex sentence has a noun clause used as the subject. (The subject of the main clause is the entire noun clause.)
3. What three tests can be used to determine whether a clause is a noun clause and not an adjective or adverb clause? (Does the clause name a person, place, thing, or idea? Does the clause serve a noun function? Is it sensible to replace the clause with a pronoun?)
4. Identify the noun clauses in these sentences, and tell how they are used. (Clauses are underlined.)
   a. Father cannot understand <u>why the cows are so restless</u>. (direct object)
   b. <u>How we respond to life</u> determines <u>what our course of life will be</u>. (subject; direct object)
   c. Mother's answer was <u>what I expected it to be</u>. (predicate nominative)
5. Identify the appositive or noun of direct address in each sentence. Tell which it is and where commas should be placed. (Commas are underlined.)
   a. Is it true<u>,</u> my friend<u>,</u> that you will be leaving us? (my friend; direct address)
   b. I will be visiting David<u>,</u> my oldest brother<u>,</u> for two days. (my oldest brother; appositive)

Lesson Introduction: You learned in Lesson 28 that a whole clause can act as a single noun. On a

Pronouns: (subject, direct object)

who	whom	what
whoever	whomever	whatever

Adjectives: (modifying a subject or complement)

whose	which

Adverbs: (modifying the verb)

how	when	whenever
why	where	wherever

Introductory: (no specific function)

that	if	whether

To determine the function of an introductory word, find it on the chart above. Then see what place it fills in the clause. A pronoun like *who, whom,* or *what* may serve as a subject or a direct object.

His answer was seemingly <u>whatever came to his mind first</u>.
(Skeleton of clause is <u>whatever</u> <u>came</u>; *whatever* is the subject.)
Nobody knew <u>who the stranger was</u>.
(Skeleton of clause is <u>stranger</u> <u>was</u>; *who* is the predicate nominative.)
<u>Whomever God blesses</u> is truly blessed.
(Skeleton of clause is <u>God</u> <u>blesses</u>; *Whomever* is the direct object.)

The introductory words *whose* and *which* almost always serve as adjectives that modify subjects or complements.

Do you see <u>whose papers are on the floor</u>?
(Skeleton of clause is <u>papers</u> <u>are</u>; *whose* modifies the subject.)
I know <u>which book you have found</u>.
(Skeleton of clause is <u>you</u> <u>have found</u>; *book* is the direct object; *which* modifies the direct object.)

The introductory words *how, when, where,* and *why* serve as adverbs modifying verbs.

<u>How the Lord views an action</u> should guide our behavior.
(Skeleton of clause is <u>Lord</u> <u>views</u>; *action* is the direct object; *How* modifies the verb.)
Peter saw <u>where Jesus' body had lain</u>.
(Skeleton of clause is <u>body</u> <u>had lain</u>; *where* modifies the verb.)
Mrs. Baker's question is <u>when the service will be held</u>.
(Skeleton of clause is <u>service</u> <u>will be held</u>; *when* modifies the verb.)

The introductory words *that, if,* and *whether* merely introduce noun

sentence diagram, how can you squeeze a whole clause into the little space normally used for a subject or direct object? Well, how do you diagram a verbal phrase used as a noun? (on a pedestal) A pedestal is also used to diagram a noun clause.

Lesson Outline:

1. The word that introduces a noun clause usually serves as a subject, a direct object, an adjective, or an adverb within the noun clause.

   a. The words *who, whoever, whom, whomever, what,* and *whatever* serve as subjects or direct objects.

   b. The words *whose* and *which* almost always serve as adjectives that modify the subject or a complement.

   c. The words *how, when, where,* and *why* serve as adverbs that modify the verb.

2. The introductory words that, if, *and* whether *serve only to introduce noun clauses.*

3. When a noun clause is a direct quotation, it has no introductory word.

4. A noun clause is diagramed on a pedestal above the place where a single-word noun would normally go.

   a. An introductory word that serves a specific function within the clause is diagramed to show that function.

   b. An introductory word that merely introduces the clause is placed on the vertical line of the pedestal.

★ **EXTRA PRACTICE**
Worksheet 17 (*More Noun Clauses*)

clauses. They serve no specific function within the clauses.

> That truth always prevails is the assurance of God's people.
> (Skeleton of clause is truth prevails; *That* merely introduces.)
> God's people do not know whether their physical lives will be preserved. (Skeleton of clause is lives will be preserved; *whether* merely introduces.)
> They do not question if God's way is right.
> (Skeleton of clause is way is; *right* is the predicate adjective; *if* merely introduces.)

When a noun clause is a direct quotation, it has no introductory word. Even if the quotation begins with one of the words listed in the chart, that word does not introduce the noun clause as in other cases.

> The men declared, "That we cannot do!"
> (Skeleton of clause is we can do; *That* is the direct object.)

A noun clause is diagramed on a horizontal line that rests on a pedestal. The pedestal stands on the base line where a single-word noun would normally go. If an introductory word serves a specific function in the clause (such as a subject, direct object, adjective, or adverb), it is diagramed to show that function in the noun clause. If the introductory word serves no function other than introducing the noun clause, it is placed on the vertical line of the pedestal.

> What God has spoken is worthy of our attention.
> (Skeleton of clause is God has spoken; *What* is the direct object.)

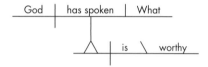

Many Jews did not realize that the Messiah had come.
(Skeleton of clause is Messiah had come; *that* merely introduces.)

The best time for meditation is when your mind is alert.
  (Skeleton of clause is <u>mind</u> <u>is</u>; *alert* is the predicate adjective;
    when modifies the verb.)

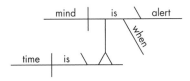

Whoever humbles himself before the Lord finds true joy.
  (Skeleton of clause is <u>Whoever</u> <u>humbles</u>; *himself* is the direct
    object.)

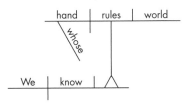

We know whose hand rules the world.
  (Skeleton of clause is <u>hand</u> <u>rules</u>; *world* is the direct object; *whose*
    modifies the subject.)

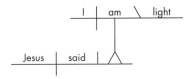

Jesus said, "I am the light of the world."
  (Skeleton of clause is <u>I</u> <u>am</u>; *light* is the predicate nominative; no
    introductory word because the clause is a direct quotation.)

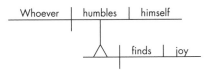

Class Practice

A. Read each noun clause. Say *subject*, *direct object*, *adjective*, or *adverb* if the introductory word has one of those functions; *introduces* if it simply introduces the clause; or *none* if there is no introductory word.
1. I do not know why he did it.
2. Whether we shall leave tonight depends on the weather.
3. Mother said, "I have assigned the boys several chores."
4. We must decide which chores are the most important.
5. Our first consideration must be what the Bible says about the issue.
6. Whatever is accomplished must glorify God.

B. On the chalkboard, diagram the skeletons and complements of the clauses in Part A. Include the introductory words of the noun clauses.

Written Exercises

A. Copy each noun clause. Write *subject*, *direct object*, *adjective*, or *adverb* if the introductory word has one of those functions; *introduces* if it simply introduces the clause; or *none* if there is no introductory word.
1. Paul did not write that money is the root of all evil.
2. Wherever God leads is the right place to go.
3. Obedience to Jesus' command is why Christians cannot fight.
4. Whomever God has placed over us deserves our respect.
5. God does not tell us if the road ahead holds sorrow or joy.
6. Apparently the others did not suspect which disciple would betray Jesus.
7. Jesus' words and miracles convinced whoever was open to the truth.
8. The centurion at the cross declared, "Truly this was the Son of God."

B. Diagram the skeletons and complements of the main clauses and the noun clauses. Include the introductory words of the noun clauses.
1. What Gerald said to Merle reveals his interest in poetry.
2. My contribution to the project will be whatever the teacher asks.
3. Louisa probably knows whose sweater you have found.
4. Barbara has not decided whether she will write the story.
5. Where the skunks nested was very undesirable!
6. Whoever wants a drink must stand quietly in line.
7. The teacher has clearly stated how the answers should be written.
8. Do you know what causes geysers?

Review Exercises

A. Copy each appositive. Also copy each noun of direct address and any modifier that goes with it. Label each item you copy. [7]
1. Starface, our newest calf, has a starlike mark on her face.
2. Thelma, take these bones out to the dogs.

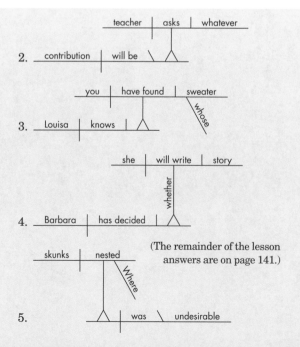

(The remainder of the lesson answers are on page 141.)

Lesson 29 Answers

Class Practice

A. 1. why he did it; adverb
2. Whether we shall leave tonight; introduces
3. I have assigned the boys several chores; none
4. which chores are the most important; adjective
5. what the Bible says about the issue; direct object
6. Whatever is accomplished; subject

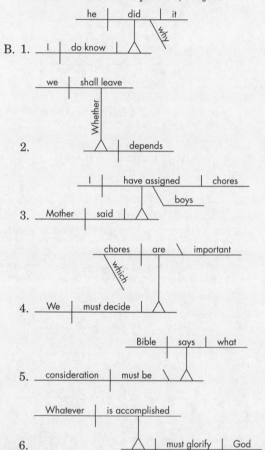

Written Exercises

A. 1. that money is the root of all evil; introduces
2. Wherever God leads; adverb
3. why Christians cannot fight; adverb
4. Whomever God has placed over us; direct object
5. if the road ahead holds sorrow or joy; introduces
6. which disciple would betray Jesus; adjective
7. whoever was open to the truth; subject
8. Truly this was the Son of God; none

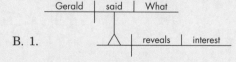

3. Did you know, Nevin, that a true albino always has pink eyes?
4. My sister Anna teaches school in the Philippines.
5. Haiti, a Caribbean nation, is a poverty-stricken land.
6. "My little children, these things write I unto you, that ye sin not."

B. Copy each word that should be followed by a comma, and add the missing comma. If no comma is needed, write *correct*. [7]
1. Come in weary traveler for some rest and refreshment.
2. *Martyrs Mirror* the work of a Dutch Mennonite leader describes the sufferings of many saints.
3. Our dog Princess is always gentle with little children.
4. Do you have any little kittens Joyce?
5. Jesus went to Sychar a city of the despised Samaritans.
6. Timothy hold the door open for your mother.

---

30. Substantives

> **Lesson Survey**
> - A **substantive** is any word or word group that names something.
> - A substantive may be a single word, a phrase, or a clause.
> - A substantive may be used as a subject, a direct object, an indirect object, a predicate nominative, or any other sentence part where a noun can be used.

As you have learned in previous grades, the English language has eight parts of speech. Two of them, nouns and pronouns, are used in referring to persons, places, things, and ideas. There are many words that you should recognize as nouns or pronouns.

Nouns: God, saints, heaven, Jerusalem, ark, Bible, honesty, gratitude

Pronouns: he, hers, themselves, who, somebody, this

Remember, though, that the part of speech of a word is determined mainly by its use in a sentence. Words that you would not identify as nouns or pronouns may be used to name something in a particular sentence. Any word or word group that names something is a *substantive*. A substantive is not another part of speech; it is merely a term that means "any word or word group used as a noun."

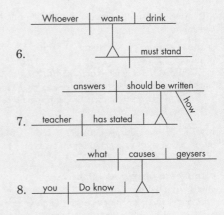

6.
7.
8.

Review Exercises

A. 1. our newest calf—appositive
2. Thelma—direct address
3. Nevin—direct address
4. Anna—appositive
5. a Caribbean nation—appositive
6. My little children—direct address

B. 1. in, traveler,   4. kittens,
2. *Mirror*, leader,   5. Sychar,
3. correct   6. Timothy,

Lesson 30

Purpose: To teach the definition of a *substantive.

Oral Review:
1. A noun clause is diagrammed on a ———. (pedestal)
2. If the introductory word of a noun clause serves no function in the clause, where is it diagrammed? (on the vertical line of the pedestal)
3. Identify the nouns of direct address in these sentences. (Answers are underlined.)
   a. What do you know, <u>Susan</u>, about these papers?
   b. "<u>Little children</u>, keep yourselves from idols."
   c. Are you ready to go, <u>Mother</u>?
4. Identify the appositives in these sentences. (Answers are underlined.)
   a. My friend <u>Larry</u> made this whistle for me.
   b. Marcus, <u>my cousin from Guatemala</u>, will live with us this summer.
   c. Have you met Linda, <u>the new student in our room</u>?
5. Spell the plural form of each noun.
   a. cupful (cupfuls)   c. quality (qualities)
   b. proof (proofs)   d. soprano (sopranos)
6. Give the foreign plural spellings of these words.
   a. index (indices)   c. larva (larvae)
   b. crisis (crises)   d. radius (radii)
7. Reword these expressions, using possessive forms. Tell how to spell the possessive forms.
   a. the brother of Mary and Martha (Mary and Martha's brother)
   b. the descendants of Esau and Jacob (Esau's and Jacob's descendants)

Lesson Introduction: Write two headings on the board: *Substance* and *Not a Substance*. Have students tell where to place the following words and phrases: *chalkboard, write, sing, pencil, desk, eraser,*

Most substantives are single words. Look at the underlined words in the following sentences.

Substantives as single words:
We should not show partiality toward the rich.
(*We* and *rich* name persons; *partiality* names an idea.)
The Bible teaches the importance of kindness to animals.
(*Bible* and *animals* name things; *importance* and *kindness* name ideas.)

Substantives can also be phrases. Proper nouns are often phrases. In addition, you have learned in this chapter about verbal phrases used as nouns.

Substantives as proper noun phrases:
John the Baptist preached near the Jordan River.
(*John the Baptist* names a person; *Jordan River* names a place.)
Yosemite National Park is in the Sierra Nevada.
(*Yosemite National Park* and *Sierra Nevada* name places.)
Substantives as verbal phrases:
Obeying your parents will bring you many blessings.
(*Obeying your parents* names an action.)
Mother decided to bake a batch of cookies.
(*To bake a batch of cookies* names an action.)

Substantives can also be clauses. You have worked with noun clauses in the last two lessons.

Substantives as clauses:
What God says will always come to pass.
(*What God says* names an idea.)
Have you studied how God preserved His Word through the ages?
(*How God preserved His Word through the ages* names an idea.)

A substantive may be used as a subject, a direct object, an indirect object, a predicate nominative, or any other sentence part where a noun can be used. The substantives in the following sentences are underlined.

That Jesus was willing to die is a marvel of divine love.
(*That Jesus was willing to die* is a noun clause used as a subject; *marvel* is a single-word predicate nominative; *love* is a single-word object of a preposition.)
Jesus wanted to help Zacchaeus.
(*Jesus* is a single-word subject; *to help Zacchaeus* is a verbal phrase used as a direct object.)

---

subtract, is adding, Mr. Lewis Gardner. Ask the students what part of speech the words in the first column are. When they identify them as nouns, ask for the definition of a noun. Point out that persons, places, and things have physical *substance*. All words that name these things of substance are substantives. Words that name ideas are also substantives.

Lesson Outline:

1. A substantive is any word or word group that names something. Substantive does not name another part of speech.

2. Substantives may be words, phrases, or clauses.

a. Most substantives are single words (nouns and pronouns).

b. Some substantives are phrases (such as proper noun phrases and verbal phrases).

c. Some substantives are clauses (noun clauses).

3. A substantive may be used as a subject, a direct object, an indirect object, a predicate nominative, or any other sentence part where a noun can be used.

★ *EXTRA PRACTICE*
Worksheet 18 (*Substantives*)

Anna, an aged widow, saw the Lord Jesus and gave God much glory.
(*Anna* is a single-word subject; *an aged widow* is a phrase used
as an appositive; *Lord Jesus* is a phrase used as a direct object;
God is a single-word indirect object; *glory* is a single-word
direct object.)

"Simon, son of Jonas, lovest thou me?"
(*Simon* is a single-word noun of direct address; *son of Jonas* is a
phrase used as an appositive; *thou* is a single-word subject;
me is a single-word direct object.)

Class Practice

A. Give the function of each underlined substantive: *subject, direct object,
indirect object, predicate nominative, object of a preposition, noun of
direct address,* or *appositive.*
1. Daniel purposed to obey the Lord at any cost.
2. Eating food from the king's table would have brought defilement.
3. Ashpenaz, the prince of the eunuchs, feared to grant Daniel his request.
4. Daniel then entreated Melzar, whom Ashpenaz had set over the four
young men.
5. This man agreed to test them for ten days.
6. The result of the test was that these four faithful Jews were the
healthiest of all.
7. Three years later, these were ten times wiser than all the wise men
of Babylon.
8. Do you, my friend, have such loyalty to the Lord God?

B. Give the substantives in these sentences. Do not identify separately
the substantives within a phrase or clause.
1. Who lent you that book, Carol?
2. What we read will shape our thoughts.
3. Thinking good thoughts will produce good habits and actions of life.
4. Jesus stated that a person's thoughts will be expressed in his words.
5. An important principle for life is to guard the mind diligently.

Written Exercises

A. Write the function of each underlined substantive: *subject, direct object,
indirect object, predicate nominative, object of a preposition, noun of
direct address,* or *appositive.*
1. The Lord Jesus was praying in Gethsemane, an olive grove.
2. He prayed that the cup of suffering might pass from Him.
3. The most important thing to Jesus was to do His Father's will.
4. While He prayed in agony, His sweat was as great drops of blood.

Lesson 30 Answers

Class Practice

A. 1. direct object
2. subject
3. appositive, indirect object, direct object
4. subject, direct object, object of a preposition
5. direct object
6. object of a preposition, predicate nominative
7. subject, object of a preposition
8. subject, noun of direct address, direct object,
object of a preposition

B. 1. Who, you, book, Carol
2. What we read, thoughts
3. Thinking good thoughts, habits, actions, life
4. Jesus, that a person's thoughts will be expressed in his words
5. principle, life, to guard the mind diligently

Written Exercises

A. 1. subject, object of a preposition, appositive
2. subject, direct object
3. predicate nominative
4. object of a preposition, subject

5. Jesus knew <u>how intensely the devil wanted to defeat Him</u>.
6. <u>Facing this struggle victoriously</u> was an essential <u>requirement</u> for mankind's salvation.
7. Through His shed blood, Jesus offers the <u>world</u> the <u>potential</u> of <u>salvation</u>.
8. <u>We</u> thank <u>Thee</u>, <u>O Father</u>, for the abundant life in Jesus, <u>our great Redeemer</u>.

B. Copy the substantives in these sentences. Do not copy separately the substantives within a phrase or clause.
1. Singing hymns of praise gives God's people inspiration.
2. The congregation listened reverently to the message.
3. All must learn to pay attention.
4. Each person must decide if he will worship sincerely.
5. Following along in the Bible is a good aid to concentration.
6. Worship the Lord, all people, in the beauty of holiness.

Review Exercises

A. Write the plural forms of these nouns. Use the foreign spellings for numbers 9–12. [22, 23]
1. basketful   4. sheep   7. tornado   10. alga
2. squash   5. roof   8. shelf   11. appendix
3. soprano   6. louse   9. basis   12. cactus

B. Rewrite the underlined expressions, using possessive forms. If no possessive form should be used, write *correct*. [24]
1. <u>The doubts of Thomas</u> were removed by <u>the appearance of Jesus</u>.
2. The <u>prints of the nails</u> were visible in His hands.
3. <u>The answers of the disciples</u> showed that they failed to understand <u>the words of Christ</u>.
4. In Bible times, <u>the wages of a day</u> amounted to a "penny," or denarius.
5. <u>The appearance of a denarius</u> is similar to that of a United States dime.

C. Rewrite the underlined expressions, using possessive forms. Sentences 1 and 2 should show joint ownership, and sentences 3 and 4 should show separate ownership. [24]
1. <u>The friendship of David and Jonathan</u> was a rich blessing to both.
2. Jesus often visited in <u>the home of Mary and Martha</u>.
3. God saw a vast difference between <u>the offerings of Cain and of Abel</u>.
4. Joseph interpreted <u>the dreams of the butler and the baker</u>.

5. direct object
6. subject, predicate nominative
7. indirect object, direct object, object of a preposition
8. subject, direct object, noun of direct address, appositive

B. 1. Singing hymns of praise, people, inspiration
2. congregation, message
3. All, to pay attention
4. person, if he will worship sincerely
5. Following along in the Bible, aid, concentration
6. Lord, all people, beauty, holiness

Review Exercises

A. 1. basketfuls   7. tornadoes *or* tornados
2. squashes *or* squash   8. shelves
3. sopranos   9. bases
4. sheep   10. algae
5. roofs   11. appendices
6. lice   12. cacti

B. 1. Thomas's doubts, Jesus' appearance
2. correct
3. The disciples' answers, Christ's words
4. a day's wages
5. correct

C. 1. David and Jonathan's friendship
2. Mary and Martha's home
3. Cain's and Abel's offerings
4. the butler's and the baker's dreams

31. Developing Paragraphs by Giving Definitions

Lesson Survey
- A paragraph may be developed by giving a definition.
- Many paragraphs are developed by a combination of methods.

What does the word *perseverance* mean? A dictionary may define it as "persistence in a condition or an action in spite of difficulty." A thesaurus may list these synonyms: *steadfastness, constancy, persistence, tenacity, effort, endurance, determination.* Although these definitions and synonyms help us to understand this word, we should have an even clearer understanding after reading the following paragraph.

> <u>Perseverance</u> means "the ability to persist in a condition or an action in spite of difficulty." In everyday terms, this is the quality that keeps you hoeing those weeds when your muscles cry for relief. It enables you to keep trying your best even though your team is badly losing a game. If a long, difficult assignment threatens to discourage you, perseverance motivates you to see it through to completion. When temptations wear you down, perseverance says, "Don't give up!" The devil's easy roads may hold great appeal, and the road of godliness may seem hardly worth the effort; but perseverance will keep you pressing right on toward the goal.

A paragraph may be developed by giving a definition. This method is suitable especially for abstract nouns like *perseverance, honesty,* and *courage,* or for detailed explanations of scientific or Biblical words.

Like every good paragraph, a paragraph developed by definition needs a topic sentence. It is the first sentence in the example above. Notice how the topic sentence states the definition in brief form. The other sentences develop the topic with details showing what is involved in perseverance.

A paragraph developed by definition may begin with the topic sentence, as in the example above. Or it may begin with an introductory question, and the second sentence may be the topic sentence that states the brief definition. The following example illustrates this second pattern.

> What is matter? Matter is anything that has weight and takes up space. This includes the food you eat, the water you drink, the air you breathe, and your physical body. It is easy to see that food, water, and your body have weight and take up space. Air has weight too. For

Lesson 31

Purpose: To teach paragraph development by giving a definition.

Oral Review:
1. What do we do when we develop a paragraph? (clarify and support the topic sentence)
2. A paragraph developed by telling an incident is like a ———. (brief story)
3. Which kind of sentence order is used when developing a paragraph by giving steps? (chronological order)
4. If all the sentences of a paragraph directly support the topic, the paragraph has ———. (unity)
5. If the sentences flow smoothly from one to the next, the paragraph has ———. (coherence)
6. If a paragraph included the words *gentle, considerate, kind,* and *tender,* the writer apparently

made good use of ———. (repetition of key words)

Lesson Introduction: Write on the board two nouns, one concrete (like *protractor*) and one abstract (like *independence*). Ask for definitions, first of the concrete noun and then of the abstract noun. You will likely have much more variation in definitions of the abstract noun. Point out that the various definitions (and other details) could be used to develop a paragraph.

Lesson Outline:

1. A paragraph may be developed by giving a definition.

    a. The most suitable topics for this method are abstract nouns and detailed explanations of scientific or Biblical words.

    b. A clear topic sentence is needed.

2. Many paragraphs are developed by a combination of several methods.

example, an inflated ball weighs slightly more than the same ball when it is deflated. Air also takes up space. If you push an inverted glass into water, the water cannot enter the glass because the air in the glass takes up space. But if you tilt the glass, you will see bubbles of air coming out and being replaced by water rising inside the glass.

In the composition lessons of this chapter, you have studied paragraph development by adding details, by giving steps, by using examples, by telling an incident, and now by giving a definition. Actually, many paragraphs are developed by a combination of several methods. The paragraph about matter is developed mainly by definition. But you also notice a number of examples in the third sentence. And the last two sentences give steps in doing a demonstration.

Class Practice

Tell which method of development is used for each paragraph: *details, steps, examples, incident, definition,* or *combination.*

1.　A healthy body is the best defense against disease. A well-balanced diet; plenty of rest; regular, vigorous exercise; pure living; and good mental hygiene are essential to good physical health. Besides these, the habit of cleanliness and the use of medicine are also basic to maintaining healthy bodies. All these areas are suggested in the Bible as being proper care for the body. Although many of the heathen civilizations around God's people were superstitious in their treatment of disease, God gave sound instructions to His people for their protection from diseases.

2.　David had learned the importance of seeking God's direction. Soon after he was anointed king over all Israel, the Philistines marched in force against him. But before David went out to meet them, he prayed, "Shall I go up to the Philistines?" At God's direction he attacked the Philistines and routed them. They fled so swiftly that they abandoned their idols, which the men of Israel gathered up and burned. Because he had carefully followed God's direction, David won a decisive victory over his enemies.

3.　What is faith? Faith is not vaguely supposing that there is a heavenly reward in the end; it is the "substance," or full assurance, of "things hoped for." Faith is not a hazy notion about the existence of God, of heaven and hell, of angels, or of the soul of man; it is the "evidence," or positive conviction, of "things not seen." Because of the absolute sureness of God and His Word, those things that we can only anticipate now are just as real as those things that we can actually see and touch now.

Lesson 31 Answers

Class Practice
1. details
2. incident
3. definition

4.   Some regions beneath the earth's crust are extremely hot. In fact, a very deep mine may need special ventilation to protect the workers from the great heat. The temperature of the earth rises about one degree for every sixty feet of descent below the surface. At a depth of about twenty miles, the heat may be so intense that the rocks actually melt. Sometimes this molten material, called magma, forms a volcano by forcing its way through a crack in the earth's crust. As the magma rises to the surface, it bursts into the air with great force, releasing tons of ashes, molten rock, and searing vapors.

Written Exercises

A. Develop a paragraph of definition for one of these terms or some other topic that your teacher approves.

   1. honesty   3. osmosis   5. republic
   2. courtesy   4. stewardship   6. submission

B. Write a paragraph based on one of these topic sentences. Develop your paragraph by any of the methods discussed in this chapter: *details, steps, examples, incident, definition,* or *combination.* Identify the method that you use to develop your paragraph.

   1. The character of Job (or some other person) was severely tested in several ways.
   2. God told the Israelites exactly how they should keep the first Passover (or do some other thing).
   3. Isaac Watts (or some other person) was one of the most productive hymn writers of his time.
   4. It is not hard to replace a small windowpane (or to do some other task).
   5. What is a rain shadow (or some other geographical item)?

---

32. Chapter 3 Review

Class Practice

A. Tell which words are nouns. Tell whether each noun is *concrete* or *abstract,* and identify its gender.

   1. Our family receives much inspiration from Grandmother Lavina, an elderly woman in our neighborhood.
   2. The two lambs huddled close to the ewe until the danger had passed.
   3. Father and Jay are cleaning out the stables.

Lesson 32

Purpose: To review the concepts taught in Chapter 3.

4.   combination

Written Exercises

A. (Individual work.)

B. (Individual work.)

Lesson 32 Answers

Class Practice

A. 1. family—concrete, common;
     inspiration—abstract, neuter;
     Grandmother Lavina—concrete, feminine;
     woman—concrete, feminine;
     neighborhood—concrete, neuter *or* common
  2. lambs—concrete, common;
     ewe—concrete, feminine;
     danger—abstract, neuter
  3. Father—concrete, masculine;
     Jay—concrete, masculine;
     stables—concrete, neuter

B. Give the numbers of the underlined words that are used as nouns.
  1. If you can't <u>stand</u>¹ so long, take a chair along to the produce <u>stand</u>².
  2. Lay up <u>treasure</u>³ in heaven; do not <u>treasure</u>⁴ the things of this earth.

B. 1. 2
   2. 3

C. Tell which words have capitalization errors.
  1. Rod and staff publishers seeks to provide Literature that promotes obedience to the bible.
  2. Ferdinand magellan sailed west in order to reach the Lands of the east.
  3. Our Science assignment is short, but our English assignment is long.
  4. We saw a mack truck creeping up town hill.

C. 1. Staff, Publishers, literature, Bible
   2. Magellan, lands, East
   3. science
   4. Mack, Town Hill

D. Give the correct spelling of words to fill in this chart. (Plural forms do not need to be given for numbers 7 and 8.)

Singular	Singular Possessive	Plural	Plural Possessive
1. donkey	——	——	——
2. wife	——	——	——
3. pony	——	——	——
4. high priest	——	——	——
5. child	——	——	——
6. Eskimo	——	——	——
7. Jesus	——		
8. Charles	——		

D. (Words in italics are given in the pupil's text.)

1. *donkey*	donkey's	donkeys	donkeys'
2. *wife*	wife's	wives	wives'
3. *pony*	pony's	ponies	ponies'
4. *high priest*	high priest's	high priests	high priests'
5. *child*	child's	children	children's
6. *Eskimo*	Eskimo's	Eskimos	Eskimos'
7. *Jesus*	Jesus'		
8. *Charles*	Charles's		

E. Read these sentences correctly.
  1. My glasses was off, so I didn't see those five deers you saw.
  2. Chicken pox are spreading throughout the community.
  3. Checkers are my favorite game, and mathematics are my favorite subject.
  4. News from our friends are welcome when we are away from home.

E. (Corrections are underlined.)
  1. My glasses <u>were</u> off, so I didn't see those five <u>deer</u> you saw.
  2. Chicken pox <u>is</u> spreading throughout the community.
  3. Checkers <u>is</u> my favorite game, and mathematics <u>is</u> my favorite subject.
  4. News from our friends <u>is</u> welcome when we are away from home.

F. Decide whether these collective nouns are used in a *singular* or *plural* sense, and tell which verb is correct.
  1. The flock of sheep (is, are) grazing in the meadow.
  2. The congregation (have, has) voiced their opinions on the question.
  3. Our class (have, has) scattered across the hillside to try their skill at identifying plants.

F. 1. singular, is
   2. plural, have
   3. plural, have

G. Read these expressions, using possessive forms. Spell the possessive words. If the noun should not normally be made possessive, say *correct*.
  1. the time of an hour
  2. the papers of the students
  3. the hutch of the rabbit
  4. the seat of the chair
  5. the face of Moses
  6. the squeaks of the mice

G. 1. an hour's time
   2. the students' papers
   3. the rabbit's hutch
   4. correct
   5. Moses' face
   6. the mice's squeaks

H. Read these sentences, using possessive forms in the underlined expressions to give the meanings shown in parentheses.
1. We went to <u>the new house of Paul and Susan</u> for dinner. (joint ownership)
2. <u>The messages of Brother Joel and Brother Aaron</u> were inspiring. (separate ownership)

I. Read each verbal phrase, and tell whether it is a *gerund phrase* or an *infinitive phrase*. Then tell how it is used in the sentence.
1. Judith's job is weeding the strawberry patch.
2. Last year we tried to raise watermelons.
3. We want to praise the Lord, whose delight is giving good things to His children.

J. Read the noun clause in each sentence, and tell how it is used in the sentence.
1. Do you know why toads should be welcomed in your garden?
2. The benefit that makes them welcome is that they eat harmful insects.
3. Whoever wants a good garden should protect these little creatures.
4. Father said that praying mantises are also good friends to the gardener.

K. Read the substantives in these sentences. Do not read separately the substantives within phrases or clauses.
1. Stanley, have you read the book *Home Fires Beneath the Northern Lights*?
2. Figuring out today's math problems required patience and hard work.
3. I haven't heard whether the building plans have been approved.
4. Christian Burkholder came to the New World from his native Palatinate.

L. Do these exercises relating to the composition lessons.
1. What do we do when we develop a paragraph?
2. List several important points to remember when developing a paragraph by adding details.
3. Which kind of sentence order is used for developing a paragraph by giving steps?
4. Describe two ways of developing a paragraph by using examples.
5. Which kind of paragraph development is like telling a brief story?
6. Paragraph development by definition is most suitable for what kinds of words?

H. 1. Paul and Susan's new house
2. Brother Joel's and Brother Aaron's messages

I. 1. weeding the strawberry patch—gerund phrase, predicate nominative
2. to raise watermelons—infinitive phrase, direct object
3. to praise the Lord—infinitive phrase, direct object;
giving good things to His children—gerund phrase, predicate nominative

J. 1. why toads should be welcomed in your garden—direct object
2. that they eat harmful insects—predicate nominative
3. Whoever wants a good garden—subject
4. that praying mantises are also good friends to the gardener—direct object

K. 1. Stanley, you, book, *Home Fires Beneath the Northern Lights*
2. Figuring out today's math problems, patience, work
3. I, whether the building plans have been approved
4. Christian Burkholder, New World, Palatinate

L. 1. clarify and support the topic sentence
2. Add only details that contribute to the topic. Do not merely reword the topic sentence. Know your subject well enough to add specific, meaningful details.
3. chronological order
4. giving two examples with many details about each; giving a number of examples with only a few details about each
5. telling an incident
6. abstract nouns, scientific and Biblical words

Written Exercises

A. Copy each noun, and label it *concrete* or *abstract*. Also label its gender.
   1. If you cover these books, use a clear plastic cover.
   2. The Bible commends the faithfulness of Abraham and Sarah.
   3. The descendants of Cain were noted for their iniquity.

B. Change each word in parentheses to a noun by adding a noun-forming suffix.
   1. Your (persevere) has helped bring the job to its (complete).
   2. In the (solitary) of the Garden, Jesus expressed His (submit) to the Father.
   3. The children's (excite) produced much (restless).

C. Write correctly each word that has a capitalization error.
   1. The ℭedars that grew on the lebanon mountains were prized through-out palestine.
   2. A severe storm overtook the Disciples on the sea of Galilee.
   3. At the close of the Service, we sang "now the day is over."
   4. Jonathan's birthday is in the Winter, december 29 to be exact.

D. Write the plural form of each word.
   1. tomato
   2. salmon
   3. belief
   4. fireman
   5. spoonful
   6. oasis
   7. worry
   8. radius
   9. wife
   10. daughter-in-law

E. Write the possessive form of each word.
   1. women
   2. father
   3. mice
   4. travelers
   5. brother-in-law
   6. sisters
   7. Moses
   8. ladies

F. Write the better verbs.
   1. Mumps (make, makes) a person's neck swollen.
   2. The tongs from the altar (have, has) picked up a live coal.
   3. Ethan's team (have, has) the most points.
   4. The group (is, are) inviting their neighbors to the revival meetings.
   5. (Do, Does) your pliers have a wire cutter?
   6. The herd of cows (was, were) grazing, chewing their cuds, and sleeping.

G. Rewrite these expressions, using possessive forms. If the noun should not normally be made possessive, write *correct*. Show joint ownership for numbers 5 and 6, and separate ownership for numbers 7 and 8.

Written Exercises

A. 1. books—concrete, neuter; cover—concrete, neuter
   2. Bible—concrete, neuter; faithfulness—abstract, neuter; Abraham—concrete, masculine; Sarah—concrete, feminine
   3. descendants—concrete, common; Cain—concrete, masculine; iniquity—abstract, neuter

B. 1. perseverance, completion
   2. solitude, submission
   3. excitement, restlessness

C. 1. cedars, Lebanon Mountains, Palestine
   2. disciples, Sea
   3. service, "Now (the) Day Is Over"
   4. winter, December

D. 1. tomatoes
   2. salmon
   3. beliefs
   4. firemen
   5. spoonfuls
   6. oases
   7. worries
   8. radii *or* radiuses
   9. wives
   10. daughters-in-law

E. 1. women's
   2. father's
   3. mice's
   4. travelers'
   5. brother-in-law's
   6. sisters'
   7. Moses'
   8. ladies'

F. 1. makes
   2. have
   3. has
   4. are
   5. Do
   6. were

1. the rainfall of a month
2. the cars of our uncles
3. the food of the larvae
4. the shelves of the cupboard
5. the bicycle of Nora and Darlene
6. the help of Daniel and Arnold
7. the warnings of Father and Mother
8. the gloves of Herbert and Wayne

H. Copy the verbal phrases and noun clauses. Label each one *gerund phrase, infinitive phrase,* or *noun clause.*
  1. Chopping raw onions makes my eyes water.
  2. Father says that there is a beautiful rainbow.
  3. To listen to my great-aunt Hettie's stories is to get a glimpse of life long ago.
  4. Whether we should go now or wait until later is the question.
  5. The hardest part of this job will be emptying the old bin.

I. Copy the substantives in these sentences. Do not copy separately the substantives within phrases or clauses.
  1. God resists the proud, but He gives grace to the humble.
  2. They did not say if the work is all finished.
  3. Keeping the Lord's Day holy is a Biblical principle.
  4. Mrs. A. H. Evans came for some eggs, and she also decided to buy some sweet corn.

J. Diagram the skeletons and complements of all the clauses in these sentences. Include the verbals and their complements.
  1. Whatever God promises will surely be fulfilled.
  2. Worshiping the Lord must include doing His will.
  3. The apostle Paul admitted that he was not perfect.
  4. To wait patiently often becomes quite difficult.

G. 1. a month's rainfall
   2. our uncles' cars
   3. the larvae's food
   4. correct
   5. Nora and Darlene's bicycle
   6. Daniel and Arnold's help
   7. Father's and Mother's warnings
   8. Herbert's and Wayne's gloves

H. 1. Chopping raw onions—gerund;
      eyes water—noun clause
   2. that there is a beautiful rainbow—noun clause
   3. To listen to my great-aunt Hettie's stories—infinitive;
      to get a glimpse of life long ago—infinitive
   4. Whether we should go now or wait until later—noun clause
   5. emptying the old bin—gerund

I. 1. God, proud, He, grace, humble
   2. They, if the work is all finished
   3. Keeping the Lord's Day holy, principle
   4. Mrs. A. H. Evans, eggs, she, to buy some sweet corn

J. 1.

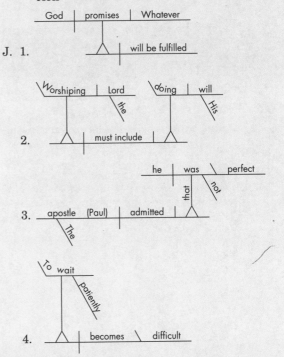

   2.

   3.

   4.

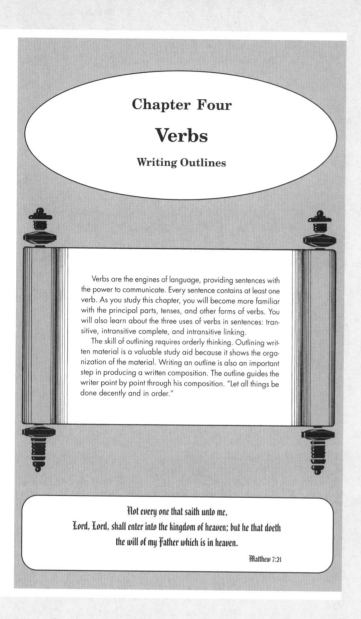

Chapter Four

Verbs

Writing Outlines

Verbs are the engines of language, providing sentences with the power to communicate. Every sentence contains at least one verb. As you study this chapter, you will become more familiar with the principal parts, tenses, and other forms of verbs. You will also learn about the three uses of verbs in sentences: transitive, intransitive complete, and intransitive linking.

The skill of outlining requires orderly thinking. Outlining written material is a valuable study aid because it shows the organization of the material. Writing an outline is also an important step in producing a written composition. The outline guides the writer point by point through his composition. "Let all things be done decently and in order."

Not every one that saith unto me,
Lord, Lord, shall enter into the kingdom of heaven; but he that doeth
the will of my Father which is in heaven.

Matthew 7:21

33. Identifying Verbs

> **Lesson Survey**
> - A **verb** expresses action or being to tell what the subject does or is.
> - The verb of every sentence is the **simple predicate.**
> - A **verb phrase** consists of a main verb and any **helping verbs.**
> - Two or more verbs joined by a conjunction make a **compound verb.**

In Chapter 3 you studied the noun, one of the hardest-working words in the English language. Another prominent "workhorse" is the verb. Whereas the noun is a naming word, the *verb* is an expressing word. It expresses action or being to tell what the subject does or is.

Action:
The boys gathered stones from the field.
The girls were weeding the flower beds.
Being:
Everyone is quite tired from the hard work.
Their muscles will feel sore tomorrow.

Every sentence has two main parts—the subject and the predicate. In the first example sentence above, the complete predicate is *gathered stones from the field.* The *simple predicate* is *gathered.* The simple predicate is often called the verb in a sentence, whether it is one word or more than one.

Besides the main verb, a sentence may contain one or more *helping verbs.* A main verb and its helpers make a *verb phrase* (such as *were weeding* in the example above). In any verb phrase, the main verb always comes last. You should recognize these helping verbs from former years.

Helping verbs:
Forms of *be*:   am, is, are, was, were, be, been, being
Forms of *have*: have, has, had
Forms of *do*:   do, does, did
Forms of *may*:   may, might, must
Others: can—could, shall—should, will—would
Verb phrases:
The peonies are blooming beautifully.
The children have picked a bouquet for the table.

Other words may separate a helping verb from a main verb. The

---

Lesson 33

Purpose: To teach the basic facts about verbs.

Oral Review:
1. Define *substantive.* (any word, phrase, or clause used to name something)
2. Give the noun clause in this sentence: *Jesus asked, "Who touched me?"* ("Who touched me")
3. Give the gerund phrase in this sentence: *Blaming others for our mistakes is a serious error.* (Blaming others for our mistakes)
4. Give the infinitive phrase in this sentence: *My desire is to do a careful job.* (to do a careful job)
5. Tell whether each sentence is in natural, inverted, or mixed word order.
   a. Up the river steamed a large boat. (inverted)
   b. There are many boats traveling on this river. (mixed)
   c. Last year we toured a large ocean vessel. (mixed)
   d. The tour was very interesting. (natural)
6. With which of these three word orders is a comma often needed? (mixed)

Lesson Introduction: The verb is an indispensable part of every sentence. It is the only part of speech that must be found in every sentence, and the only part of speech that can stand alone as a sentence. Can you imagine trying to tell a person to do something without using a verb?

He will come. (only pronoun and verb)
The package has arrived. (only adjective, noun, and verb)
Go! (only verb)

Lesson Outline:
1. A verb expresses action or being to tell what the subject does or is.

following words are closely associated with verb phrases, but they are never verbs: *not, never, hardly, always, ever, surely*. These words are always adverbs.

Our school <u>has</u> hardly ever <u>been closed</u> because of snow.
We <u>have</u> not <u>had</u> any measurable snow for four years.
This year <u>has</u> surely <u>been</u> unusual with its big blizzard.

A verb phrase may be interrupted by other adverbs as well. And in a question, the verb phrase is often interrupted by the subject.

The Anabaptists <u>had</u> quietly <u>gathered</u> in the small clearing.
The soldiers <u>were</u> stealthily <u>surrounding</u> the small group.
<u>Did</u> anyone <u>escape</u> the ruthless captors?

Two or more verbs joined by a conjunction make a *compound verb*. The various parts of a compound verb share the same subject. Sometimes the main verbs also share the same helping verb, which is only expressed once.

The chipping sparrow <u>hopped</u> and <u>flitted</u> about on the lawn.
The hungry cat <u>was staring</u> at it and <u>inching</u> closer.
The cat <u>pounced</u> but <u>caught</u> only a few feathers.

Class Practice

A. Read all the verbs and verb phrases in these sentences.
   1. During the Middle Ages, Europeans were receiving products from the Far East.

2. *The verb of every sentence is the simple predicate.*

3. *A verb phrase consists of the main verb and any helping verbs.*
   a. The main verb always comes last in a verb phrase.
   b. The following list shows all the helping verbs.

   Forms of *be*:   am, is, are, was, were, be, been, being
   Forms of *have*: have, has, had
   Forms of *do*:   do, does, did
   Forms of *may*:   may, might, must
   Other helping verbs:
   can—could, shall—should, will—would

   c. Other words may separate a helping verb from a main verb. The following words commonly interrupt a verb phrase: *not, never, hardly, always, ever, surely*.

4. *Two or more verbs joined by a conjunction make a compound verb.*

Lesson 33 Answers

Class Practice

A. 1. were receiving

2. Even the Romans had been buying silks and spices from China and India.

3. But most European merchants did not get these things directly from the producers.

4. Others usually bought them in the East and sold them again in the West.

5. Sometimes the precious goods were bought and sold several times between India and Italy.

6. They could be loaded on camels, or they might be stowed aboard a ship.

7. Because travel to the Far East was dangerous, the products were extremely expensive.

8. The Arabs and Italians were becoming rich, but most European merchants could not find a way which would bypass the middlemen.

9. Then Columbus said, "I shall sail west and arrive in the East."

10. A way will be found; we can reach China by ship and avoid the hazards and expenses of the land routes!

B. Tell whether each word is *always* a verb or *never* a verb.
1. imagine
2. excitement
3. reasonable
4. hesitate
5. probably
6. confound
7. division
8. personal
9. restrict
10. analyze

C. On the chalkboard, diagram the skeletons and complements of these sentences. Put any adverbs on slanted lines beneath the verbs.
1. My brother can hardly climb this tree.
2. Does Brother Elmer always answer your questions?
3. The snow has been accumulating rapidly.
4. Copy the poem on the chalkboard and memorize it.
5. The old cat should have seen the hole in the floor.
6. We were singing and did not notice the time.

Written Exercises

A. List all the verbs and verb phrases in these sentences. Underline the main verb in each verb phrase.
1. Mourning doves are closely related to domestic pigeons.
2. Sometimes they are called wild pigeons.
3. Doves are smaller and have a more streamlined design than pigeons.
4. Adults may weigh up to five ounces and measure up to thirteen inches.
5. Doves eat thousands of weed seeds, and they usually do not damage crops.

2. had been buying
3. did get
4. bought, sold
5. were bought, sold
6. could be loaded, might be stowed
7. was, were
8. were becoming, could find, would bypass
9. said, shall sail, arrive
10. will be found, can reach, avoid

B. 1. always
2. never
3. never
4. always
5. never
6. always
7. never
8. never
9. always
10. always

C. 1.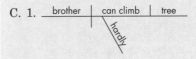

2.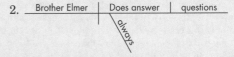

3.

4.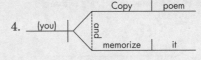

5.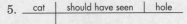

6.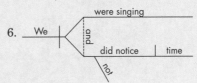

Written Exercises

A. 1. are <u>related</u>
2. are <u>called</u>
3. are, have
4. may <u>weigh</u>, (may) <u>measure</u>
5. eat, do <u>damage</u>

6. If you see doves along the road, they are probably picking up grit.
7. Grit, such as gravel and small stones, aids in grinding their food.
8. Mourning doves' calls may be considered mournful.
9. Mourning doves have adapted well to higher populations of man.
10. In fact, they avoid dense forests and thrive in populated areas.

B. Diagram the skeletons and complements of these sentences. Put any single-word adverbs on slanted lines beneath the verbs.
1. Have you already seen Julie's beautiful picture?
2. These boxes have not been opened.
3. The sun has burst through the clouds and is shining on the refreshed earth.
4. We could scarcely believe our eyes.
5. Several bees are buzzing around the apple trees.
6. Should we have a beehive near our orchard?

Review Exercises

A. Write whether these sentences are written in *natural, inverted,* or *mixed* word order. [11]
1. After a morning shower, the day was bright and sunny.
2. Into their holes scurried the mice.
3. Have the children finished their chores yet?
4. The tidy lawn and neat house looked attractive.

B. Change each sentence to the order indicated in parentheses. [11]
1. Several skunks live in this abandoned shack. (inverted)
2. After such a scare, we had to sit down and gather our wits! (natural)
3. Through the twilight air sounded the booming call of an owl. (natural)
4. We should be picking peas by the end of the week. (mixed)
5. Some geese flew over the house. (inverted)

C. Rewrite these sentences so that they do not begin with the expletive *There.* [11]
1. There are some strange-looking bugs crawling on the walks.
2. There seems to be something wrong with my car.
3. There is found a thorough discussion on the tongue in the Book of James.

---

6. see, are <u>picking</u>   9. have <u>adapted</u>
7. aids   10. avoid, thrive
8. may be <u>considered</u>

B. 1.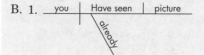

2.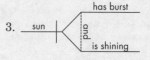

3.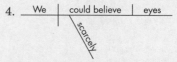

4.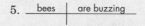

5.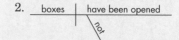

6.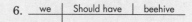

Review Exercises

A. 1. mixed   3. mixed
   2. inverted   4. natural

B. 1. In this abandoned shack live several skunks.
   2. We had to sit down and gather our wits after such a scare!
   3. The booming call of an owl sounded through the twilight air.
   4. By the end of the week, we should be picking peas.
   5. Over the house flew some geese.

C. 1. Some strange-looking bugs are crawling on the walks.
      or Crawling on the walks are some strange-looking bugs.
   2. Something seems to be wrong with my car.
   3. A thorough discussion on the tongue is found in the Book of James.
      or In the Book of James is found a thorough discussion on the tongue.

Principal Parts of Common Verbs

First (Present)	Second (Past)	Third (Past Participle)	First (Present)	Second (Past)	Third (Past Participle)
awake	awoke	(have) awoke	kneel	knelt	(have) knelt
	or awaked	(have) awaked		or kneeled	(have) kneeled
be (is)	was	(have) been	know	knew	(have) known
begin	began	(have) begun	*lay	laid	(have) laid
bid	bade	(have) bidden	*leave	left	(have) left
	or bid	(have) bid	*let	let	(have) let
blow	blew	(have) blown	*lie	lay	(have) lain
break	broke	(have) broken	put	put	(have) put
bring	brought	(have) brought	*raise	raised	(have) raised
*burst	burst	(have) burst	read	read	(have) read
buy	bought	(have) bought	ride	rode	(have) ridden
catch	caught	(have) caught	ring	rang	(have) rung
choose	chose	(have) chosen	*rise	rose	(have) risen
*come	came	(have) come	run	ran	(have) run
cost	cost	(have) cost	*see	saw	(have) seen
creep	crept	(have) crept	seek	sought	(have) sought
cut	cut	(have) cut	send	sent	(have) sent
dig	dug	(have) dug	*set	set	(have) set
*do	did	(have) done	shake	shook	(have) shaken
*drag	dragged	(have) dragged	shine	shone	(have) shone
draw	drew	(have) drawn		or shined	(have) shined
drink	drank	(have) drunk	shoot	shot	(have) shot
*drown	drowned	(have) drowned	shut	shut	(have) shut
eat	ate	(have) eaten	sing	sang	(have) sung
fight	fought	(have) fought	sink	sank	(have) sunk
find	found	(have) found	*sit	sat	(have) sat
fly	flew	(have) flown	slay	slew	(have) slain
forbid	forbade	(have) forbidden	sleep	slept	(have) slept
	or forbad	(have) forbid	speak	spoke	(have) spoken
forget	forgot	(have) forgotten	steal	stole	(have) stolen
freeze	froze	(have) frozen	swim	swam	(have) swum
give	gave	(have) given	*swing	swung	(have) swung
*go	went	(have) gone	*tag	tagged	(have) tagged
grow	grew	(have) grown	take	took	(have) taken
hang	hung (suspend)	(have) hung	teach	taught	(have) taught
			tear	tore	(have) torn
hang	hanged (execute)	(have) hanged	think	thought	(have) thought
			throw	threw	(have) thrown
hold	held	(have) held	wear	wore	(have) worn
hurt	hurt	(have) hurt	weep	wept	(have) wept
keep	kept	(have) kept	write	wrote	(have) written

*These troublesome verbs are often used incorrectly.

NOTE: *Hanged* for "executed" is a formal usage. Informal usage allows *hung,* especially in a sentence like "He hung himself."

34. Principal Parts of Verbs

> **Lesson Survey**
> - A verb has three **principal parts,** which are used to show tense.
>   1. The first principal part (present form).
>   2. The second principal part (past form).
>   3. The third principal part (past participle).
> - The second and third principal parts of most verbs are made by adding *-ed* to the first principal part.
> - The second and third principal parts of some verbs are formed irregularly.

In Proverbs 4:7 the wise man counsels us, "Wisdom is the principal thing; therefore get wisdom." Of all the different aspects of life, heavenly wisdom is the *principal* (most important) thing that we can get.

With verbs, there are three forms that are the most important—the three *principal parts.* These verb forms are used to show different verb tenses. The first principal part, called the *present* form, is used to make the present and future tenses. The second principal part, called the *past* form, is used to make the past tense. The third principal part, called the *past participle,* is used to make the perfect tenses. The following set of sentences will help you to remember the three principal parts of verbs.

Present:
  Today I <u>work</u>.
  Today I <u>study</u>.
Past:
  Yesterday I <u>worked</u>.
  Yesterday I <u>studied</u>.
Past participle:
  Every day I <u>have worked</u>.
  Every day I <u>have studied</u>.

The second and third principal parts of most verbs are made by adding *-ed* to the first principal part. Be sure to make any spelling changes necessary when adding *-ed.* If a verb ends with *e,* drop the *e.* If a verb ends with *y* after a consonant, change the *y* to *i.* If a one-syllable verb ends with a single consonant after a short vowel, double the final consonant.

Lesson 34

Purpose: To teach the principal parts of verbs, and their uses.

Oral Review:

1. Say the twenty-three helping verbs. (am, is, are, was, were, be, been, being; have, has, had; do, does, did; may, might, must; can—could, shall—should, will—would)
2. Give the verb or verb phrase in each sentence.
   a. We will hardly finish our art project today. (will finish)
   b. Have you seen the solar eclipse? (Have seen)
   c. God certainly hears our prayers. (hears)
   d. The father must surely have been watching daily for his son's return. (must have been watching)
3. Give the correct plural spellings for these nouns.
   a. fireman (firemen)
   b. vertex (vertices *or* vertexes)
   c. country (countries)
   d. postmaster general (postmasters general)
   e. vertebra (vertebrae *or* vertebras)
   f. patio (patios)
4. Give the correct possessive spellings for these nouns.
   a. brother (brother's)
   b. children (children's)
   c. visitors (visitors')
   d. Jesus (Jesus')
   e. major general (major general's)
   f. cows (cows')
5. Tell whether each expression shows joint or separate ownership.
   a. Mary and Martha's house (joint ownership)
   b. Stephen's and Larry's poems (separate ownership)

Today I <u>wash</u> dishes.
Yesterday I <u>washed</u> dishes.
Every day I <u>have washed</u> dishes.

Today I <u>hope</u> in the Lord.
Yesterday I <u>hoped</u> in the Lord.
Every day I <u>have hoped</u> in the Lord.

Today I <u>tidy</u> my room.
Yesterday I <u>tidied</u> my room.
Every day I <u>have tidied</u> my room.

Today I <u>stop</u> the auger.
Yesterday I <u>stopped</u> the auger.
Every day I <u>have stopped</u> the auger.

The second and third principal parts of some verbs are formed irregularly. There is no rule to follow in forming their second and third principal parts. These verb forms must simply be memorized.

Many irregular verbs—like *bring, find,* and *dig*—have the same spelling for the second and third principal parts. Others—like *begin, draw,* and *sing*—have three different forms. Some—like *come* and *run*—have the same spelling for the first and third principal parts. And a few—like *burst, put,* and *set*—have the same spelling for all three principal parts.

First (Present)	Second (Past)	Third (Past Participle)
bring	brought	(have) brought
find	found	(have) found
dig	dug	(have) dug
begin	began	(have) begun
draw	drew	(have) drawn
sing	sang	(have) sung
come	came	(have) come
run	ran	(have) run
burst	burst	(have) burst
put	put	(have) put
set	set	(have) set

Whenever a past participle is used to form a perfect tense, the helping verb *have, has,* or *had* must be used with it. A form such as *seen* or *done* must not be used alone as the main verb. If a single helping verb is used in a compound predicate, it may apply to only the first verb or to both verbs.

Lesson Introduction: Ask the students to define the word *principal* (most important; chief). Perhaps your school has a *principal.* What does he do? Can you name the *principal* town or city in your area? What are the *principal* industries or products from your area? These questions should demonstrate the meaning of *principal* as used in referring to the *principal parts* of verbs.

Lesson Outline:

1. A verb has three principal parts which are used to show tense.

    a. The first principal part (present form) is used to make the present and future tenses.

    b. The second principal part (past form) is used to make the past tense.

    c. The third principal part (past participle) is used to make the perfect tenses. This form must be used with a helping verb.

2. The second and third principal parts of most verbs are made by adding -ed *to the first principal part.*

    a. If a verb ends with e, drop the e.

    b. If a verb ends with y after a consonant, change the y to i.

    c. If a one-syllable verb ends with a single consonant after a short vowel, double the final consonant.

3. The second and third principal parts of some verbs are formed irregularly. These must be memorized.

★ *EXTRA PRACTICE*
Worksheet 19 (*Principal Parts of Verbs*)

John <u>had seen</u> the empty tomb and <u>knew</u> that Jesus was not there.
(*Had knew* is incorrect; *had* applies to only the first main verb.)
John <u>had seen</u> and <u>spoken</u> with Jesus after His resurrection.
(*Had* is needed with *seen* and *spoken; had* applies to both main verbs.)

The chart before this lesson shows the principal parts of many irregular verbs. Whenever you are not sure about the correct form of a verb, look at this chart or use a dictionary. Most dictionaries show the forms of the second and third principal parts of irregular verbs. If no forms are shown, the verb is regular.

Class Practice

A. Say the three principal parts of each verb. Include *have* with the third principal part.

1. break	4. drag	7. know	10. swim
2. burst	5. draw	8. let	11. swing
3. choose	6. grow	9. rise	12. think

B. Give the correct form of each verb in parentheses. Use the third principal part if there is a helping verb in the sentence.
1. Paul (write) several epistles while he was in prison.
2. Paul himself had (drag) many Christians to prison.
3. Has Jonathan (go) up to the Philistine garrison?
4. How many wells had Isaac (dig) before the Philistines (leave) him in peace?
5. Jesus (teach) as one who had authority.
6. By the rivers of Babylon, the Jewish captives (sit) down and (weep).
7. When Gideon's army had (blow) their trumpets and (break) their pitchers, the Midianites (run) away in wild confusion.
8. A star has (shine) over Bethlehem, announcing that the Saviour has (come).

Written Exercises

A. Write the correct form of each underlined verb. If the verb is correct, write *correct.*
1. We have <u>knowed</u> this man for years.
2. The boys <u>drug</u> the tree off the road.

Lesson 34 Answers

Class Practice

A. 1. break, broke, (have) broken
2. burst, burst, (have) burst
3. choose, chose, (have) chosen
4. drag, dragged, (have) dragged
5. draw, drew, (have) drawn
6. grow, grew, (have) grown
7. know, knew, (have) known
8. let, let, (have) let
9. rise, rose, (have) risen
10. swim, swam, (have) swum
11. swing, swung, (have) swung
12. think, thought, (have) thought

B. 1. wrote   5. taught
2. dragged   6. sat, wept
3. gone   7. blown, broken, ran
4. dug, left   8. shone *or* shined, come

Written Exercises

A. 1. known
2. dragged

3. Nobody <u>seen</u> the accident happen.
4. The cow has <u>swum</u> across the river.
5. The chickens <u>growed</u> rapidly.
6. Uncle Kenneth has <u>given</u> the children a new ball.
7. He has <u>did</u> the best he could do.
8. The hailstones have <u>broke</u> some windows in our house.
9. Where has Father <u>went</u> this afternoon?
10. I should have <u>chose</u> an easier picture.
11. Cousin Mary <u>done</u> a lot of work for us this fall.
12. Our sister has <u>flew</u> to Paraguay.
13. The muskrat <u>swum</u> under the ice and <u>come</u> out on the other shore.
14. He has not <u>spoke</u> about his trip.
15. Charles has <u>knew</u> the answer all along.
16. I think something has <u>fell</u> on the roof.
17. My grandfather has <u>gave</u> me this book.
18. Our dog has <u>drug</u> something into the yard and has <u>forgot</u> about it.
19. Marjorie has <u>wrote</u> us a letter from Mexico.
20. Have you ever <u>rode</u> in a train?
21. The wind has <u>blown</u> the cold air into the barn, and the pipes have <u>froze</u>.
22. Fixing up this old car has <u>costed</u> more than I <u>think</u> it would.
23. The bell has <u>rang</u>, and the children have <u>ran</u> in from the playground.
24. Have you ever <u>wore</u> that coat before?
25. The children have all <u>took</u> their seats.

B. Be prepared for a quiz on the principal parts of verbs, as shown on the chart at the beginning of this lesson.

Review Exercises

A. Find the misspelled plural nouns, and write them correctly. [22, 23]
1. The three donkies standing by those bushs are mine.
2. How many oasises are in these desert countrys?
3. A giraffe's long neck actually has fewer vertebraes than yours does!
4. The rooves over two patioes were damaged by tornadoes.
5. We have three sopranoes and two altoes in our class.

B. Find the misspelled possessive nouns, and write them correctly. [24]
1. The childrens' praise of Jesus stirred the Jewish rulers' anger.
2. Jesus's miracles inspired many peoples' hopes.
3. Judas' covetousness apparently motivated his betrayal of Jesus.
4. The baby's mothers were glad to have Jesus bless them.
5. The three disciple's sleepiness kept them from sharing in their Master's sorrow and struggle.

3. saw
4. correct
5. grew
6. correct
7. done
8. broken
9. gone
10. chosen
11. did
12. flown
13. swam, came
14. spoken
15. known
16. fallen
17. given
18. dragged, forgotten
19. written
20. ridden
21. correct, frozen
22. cost, thought
23. rung, run
24. worn
25. taken

B. (Give a quiz on principal parts. Be sure to include any verbs misused by your students or by people in your community.)

Review Exercises
A. 1. donkeys, bushes
2. oases, countries
3. vertebrae *or* vertebras
4. roofs, patios
5. sopranos, altos

B. 1. children's
2. Jesus', people's
3. Judas's
4. babies'
5. disciples'

C. Write the letter of the correct sentence in each pair. [24]
1. a. The tree's branches hung over the road.
   b. The branches of the tree hung over the road.
2. a. James's and John's father was Zebedee.
   b. James and John's father was Zebedee.
3. a. The wise man's and the foolish man's houses had contrasting foundations.
   b. The wise man and the foolish man's houses had contrasting foundations.
4. a. Curtis's report was about a walrus's life.
   b. Curtis' report was about a walrus' life.
5. a. Josiah and Hezekiah's reigns were marked by revivals.
   b. Josiah's and Hezekiah's reigns were marked by revivals.

C. 1. b
   2. b
   3. a
   4. a
   5. b

---

35. Simple Verb Tenses

> **Lesson Survey**
> - **Tense** means "time." A verb has three simple tenses.
> - The **present tense** shows action or existence that occurs in the present.
> - The **past tense** shows action or existence that occurred in the past.
> - The **future tense** shows action or existence that will occur in the future.
> - A **conjugation** is a listing of all the forms of a verb.

God wants us to be conscious of time because of its importance to life and to eternity. The first three words in the Bible call attention to time: "*In the beginning* God created the heaven and the earth" (Genesis 1:1). Time began with the creation of this earth, and it will end with its destruction. Time is the short parenthesis between eternity past and eternity future.

Since time is always moving, it is divided into three parts: the present, the past, and the future. Time unfolds in the present; but as time moves on, what is present time changes to past time, and what had been future time becomes present time.

A unique characteristic of verbs is their ability to show time. *Tense* means "time." Verbs change form to show whether they refer to action or

Lesson 35

Purpose: (1) To teach the concept of tense. (2) To teach the formation of the three simple tenses.

Oral Review:
1. Which principal part is always used with a helping verb? (third principal part, or past participle)
2. What ending is used to form the second and third principal parts of most verbs? (*-ed*)
3. Give the second and third principal parts of each verb. Include the helping verb *have* with the third principal part.
   a. blow (blew, [have] blown)
   b. bring (brought, [have] brought)
   c. burst (burst, [have] burst)
   d. do (did, [have] done)
   e. drag (dragged, [have] dragged)
   f. drown (drowned, [have] drowned)
   g. freeze (froze, [have] frozen)
   h. go (went, [have] gone)
   i. lie (lay, [have] lain)
   j. ring (rang, [have] rung)
   k. see (saw, [have] seen)
   l. tag (tagged, [have] tagged)
4. Tell whether each item is a sentence, fragment, or run-on error.
   a. When the work is finished. (fragment)
   b. This is a beautiful day to pick corn. (sentence)
   c. Down by the creek on Grandfather's farm. (fragment)
   d. The long trip is over, I am ready to get out and stretch. (run-on error)

Lesson Introduction: Read Hebrews 13:8 to the class ("Jesus Christ the same yesterday, and to day, and for ever"). What is unusual about this verse? It

existence in the past, present, or future. English verbs have three simple tenses and three perfect tenses.

The *present tense* shows action or existence that occurs in the present. The first principal part (present form) is used for the present tense. The third person singular form of the present tense ends with -*s*.

First person: I <u>work</u> at home today.
Second person: You <u>work</u> on your lessons now.
Third person: He <u>works</u> at Glen's Garden Shop.
              (Note the added -*s*.)

The present tense is also used for statements of general truth.

God <u>is</u> love.   Robins <u>fly</u> south in the fall.
We <u>go</u> to church on Sunday.   Water <u>is</u> more dense than air.

The *past tense* shows action or existence that occurred in the past. The second principal part (past form) is used for the past tense.

The Israelites <u>crossed</u> the Red Sea safely, but the Egyptians <u>drowned</u>
      in its waters.
God <u>brought</u> Israel into the Promised Land.

The *future tense* shows action or existence that will occur in the future. The first principal part (present form), along with the helping verb *shall* or *will,* is used for the future tense. In formal writing, *shall* is used for the first person and *will* is used for the second and third persons. In general usage, *will* is used for all three persons. Follow the rule for formal usage when you make tables of verb tenses like the ones in the rest of this lesson.

First person: shall
    I <u>shall visit</u> you tomorrow.
    We <u>shall see</u> the King in His beauty.

Second and third persons: will
    You <u>will be</u> surprised.
    The saints <u>will serve</u> God in heaven.

A *conjugation* is a listing of all the forms of a verb. Here are partial conjugations of the verbs *be* and *hear.*

Be

Person	Singular	Plural
		Present Tense
First:	I am.	We are.
Second:	You are.	You are.
Third:	He is.	They are.

has no verb to show time. Yet all three elements of time are clearly pointed out with the words *yesterday, to day,* and *for ever.* This verse emphasizes that Jesus Christ, as part of the Godhead, is timeless and changeless. In contrast, we are bound to time. That is why we need to study verb tenses and understand their relationships to time.

Lesson Outline:

1. Tense means "time." A verb has three simple tenses.

2. The present tense shows action or existence that occurs in the present. The first principal part (present form) is used for the present tense. The third person singular form ends with -*s*.

3. The past tense shows action or existence that occurred in the past. The second principal part (past form) is used for the past tense.

4. The future tense shows action or existence that will occur in the future. The first principal part (present form), along with the helping verb *shall* or *will,* is used for the future tense. In formal writing, *shall* is used for the first person and *will* for the second and third persons.

5. A conjugation is a listing of all the forms of a verb.

Past Tense

First:	I was.	We were.
Second:	You were.	You were.
Third:	He was.	They were.

Future Tense

First:	I shall be.	We shall be.
Second:	You will be.	You will be.
Third:	He will be.	They will be.

Hear

Person	*Singular*	*Plural*

Present Tense

First:	I hear.	We hear.
Second:	You hear.	You hear.
Third:	He hears.	They hear.

Past Tense

First:	I heard.	We heard.
Second:	You heard.	You heard.
Third:	He heard.	They heard.

Future Tense

First:	I shall hear.	We shall hear.
Second:	You will hear.	You will hear.
Third:	He will hear.	They will hear.

Class Practice

A. Give the verb or verb phrase in each sentence. Tell whether the tense is *present, past,* or *future.*
1. He learned his verse last evening.
2. Grandmother lives with us.
3. We shall soon arrive at church.
4. She dusted the living room.
5. We ate outside.
6. Jesus will come again, and He will take us home.
7. The sky is blue.
8. We go to church every Sunday.
9. I shall write the words on the board.
10. Abraham offered Isaac to God.

B. Read each sentence, using the verb form for the tense shown in italics.
1. John (enjoy) riding his bicycle. *present*
2. The shepherd (seek) his lost sheep. *past*
3. The angel of the Lord (encamp) around those who fear God. *present*

Lesson 35 Answers

Class Practice

A. 1. learned—past
2. lives—present
3. shall arrive—future
4. dusted—past
5. ate—past
6. will come—future; will take—future
7. is—present
8. go—present
9. shall write—future
10. offered—past

B. (Corrections are underlined.)
1. John enjoys riding his bicycle.
2. The shepherd sought his lost sheep.
3. The angel of the Lord encamps around those who fear God.

4. The Lord (give) grace to those in need. *future*
5. Satan (tempt) Eve to disobey. *past*

C. Read each sentence. Next read it in the past tense, beginning with *Yesterday*. Then read it in the future tense, beginning with *Tomorrow*.
1. Mother freezes some peaches.
2. I think through my hard science lesson.
3. Darlene swings on the tire swing.
4. Ronald bursts one of the balloons with a message inside.
5. The little girl plays on her tricycle.

D. Conjugate the verb *teach* in the three simple tenses.

Written Exercises

A. Copy the verb or verb phrase in each sentence, and write whether its tense is *present, past,* or *future.*
1. The leaves stirred slightly in the breeze.
2. The moon will rise soon.
3. A little wild rabbit hopped across the trail.
4. The night air is alive with the hum of insects.
5. We shall watch for some wildlife here.
6. Most animals have a keen sense of smell.
7. They will likely smell us.
8. Here comes a skunk family!
9. They ambled down the trail only a few feet from us.
10. Thankfully, they never saw us.
11. Cindy hears a coyote howling in the distance.
12. I heard an owl hooting earlier.
13. Maybe it will catch a mouse or rabbit close by.
14. God cares for all His creation.
15. We shall sing a song of praise to the Maker of all things.

B. Write the past and future tenses of each verb.
1. serve   3. carry   5. fly
2. buy   4. set   6. drown

C. Conjugate the verb *drag* in the three simple tenses.

Review Exercises

A. Identify each item as a sentence (*S*), a fragment (*F*), or a run-on error (*R*). [2]
1. Because we want to respect the feelings of others.
2. We are careful how we say things.
3. We can hurt others' feelings by speaking unkindly.

4. The Lord <u>will give</u> grace to those in need.
5. Satan <u>tempted</u> Eve to disobey.

C. 1. Mother freezes some peaches.
Yesterday Mother froze some peaches.
Tomorrow Mother will freeze some peaches.
2. I think through my hard science lesson.
Yesterday I thought through my hard science lesson.
Tomorrow I shall think through my hard science lesson.
3. Darlene swings on the tire swing.
Yesterday Darlene swung on the tire swing.
Tomorrow Darlene will swing on the tire swing.
4. Ronald bursts one of the balloons with a message inside.
Yesterday Ronald burst one of the balloons with a message inside.
Tomorrow Ronald will burst one of the balloons with a message inside.
5. The little girl plays on her tricycle.
Yesterday the little girl played on her tricycle.
Tomorrow the little girl will play on her tricycle.

D.
Teach

Person	Singular	Plural
Present Tense		
First:	I teach.	We teach.
Second:	You teach.	You teach.
Third:	He teaches.	They teach.
Past Tense		
First:	I taught.	We taught.
Second:	You taught.	You taught.
Third:	He taught.	They taught.
Future Tense		
First:	I shall teach.	We shall teach.
Second:	You will teach.	You will teach.
Third:	He will teach.	They will teach.

Written Exercises

A. 1. stirred—past   9. ambled—past
2. will rise—future   10. saw—past
3. hopped—past   11. hears—present
4. is—present   12. heard—past
5. shall watch—future   13. will catch—future
6. have—present   14. cares—present
7. will smell—future   15. shall sing—future
8. comes—present

B. 1. served, will serve   4. set, will set
2. bought, will buy   5. flew, will fly
3. carried, will carry   6. drowned, will drown

C.
Drag

Person	Singular	Plural
Present Tense		
First:	I drag.	We drag.
Second:	You drag.	You drag.
Third:	He drags.	They drag.
Past Tense		
First:	I dragged.	We dragged.
Second:	You dragged.	You dragged.
Third:	He dragged.	They dragged.
Future Tense		
First:	I shall drag.	We shall drag.
Second:	You will drag.	You will drag.
Third:	He will drag.	They will drag.

Review Exercises
A. 1. F   3. S
2. S

4. Unkind words can hurt, a harsh tone of voice can sting.
5. The fact that one's speech is an index to his heart.

B. Correct these fragments by adding words of your own. [2]
1. after the sun went down
2. who came for some strawberries
3. the girls who put up this bulletin board

C. Correct these run-on errors by adding proper punctuation and conjunctions. [2]
1. The sky was overcast all day, a raw wind chilled us to the bone.
2. By late afternoon snow was falling thickly we had three feet of snow before morning.
3. The highway crews tried their best they could not keep ahead of the fast-falling snow.

---

4. R
5. F

B. (Individual answers.)

C. (Sample answers.)
1. The sky was overcast all day, and a raw wind chilled us to the bone.
2. By late afternoon snow was falling thickly, and we had three feet of snow before morning.
3. The highway crews tried their best, but they could not keep ahead of the fast-falling snow.

36. Outlining

Lesson Survey
- An **outline** is an orderly summary of a composition. It may be a **topical outline** or a **sentence outline.**
- An outline must follow a definite pattern.

Before a speaker delivers a sermon or gives a talk, he generally prepares an outline to guide his thoughts. An author usually follows an outline in writing a book, article, or story. A listener or reader may write an outline as an aid in remembering what he hears or reads. Outlines fill an important role in many forms of communication.

An *outline* is an orderly summary of a composition. It includes the title, the main topics, and the subtopics. An outline may be further divided into points, subpoints, and details as needed.

Title of Composition
I. Main topic
  A. Subtopic
  B. Subtopic
    1. Point
      a. Subpoint
        (1) Detail about subpoint *a*

Lesson 36

Purpose: To teach the basic methods and rules of outlining.

Oral Review:
1. Answer *true* or *false*.
  a. Many paragraphs are written by using only one method of development. (false)
  b. A paragraph developed by telling an incident is like a brief story. (true)
  c. A paragraph developed by using examples should have at least four or five examples. (false; One or two examples can be good if they are well developed.)
  d. In a paragraph developed by giving steps, the steps should be clearly numbered. (false; results in choppy transitions)
2. List several devices that will help to achieve paragraph coherence. (sentence order, transitional words, repetition of key words, pronoun reference)
3. What quality does a paragraph lack if a sentence does not support the topic sentence? (unity)
4. What is the most common location of the topic sentence within a paragraph? (first sentence)

Lesson Introduction: A carpenter follows a blueprint, a seamstress follows a pattern, and a writer follows an outline. Impress on your students that writing an outline is not just busywork or an extra job to do. It is an important step in planning and organizing the material for the composition. A carpenter who ignores his blueprint, a seamstress who ignores her pattern, and a writer who ignores his outline will likely all share something in common—failure!

                (2) Detail about subpoint *a*
                    (a) Detail about detail *(2)*
                    (b) Detail about detail *(2)*
            b. Subpoint
        2. Point
    II. Main topic
        A. Subtopic
        B. Subtopic
            1. Point
            2. Point

An outline may be either a topical outline or a sentence outline. A *topical outline* has words or brief phrases to express each idea. This form is an advantage for a speaker because the basic ideas are more quickly seen. For a listener or reader, the advantage is that the ideas can be jotted down quickly. A *sentence outline* has a complete sentence to express each idea. This form is an advantage for a writer because sentences for the composition can often be copied directly from the outline.

Compare the following two outlines. They give exactly the same information; but the first is a topical outline, and the second is a sentence outline.

Topical outline:
Metamorphosis in Insects

    I. Incomplete metamorphosis
        A. Found in only a few insects, such as grasshoppers, crickets, cicadas, and roaches
        B. Involves three basic stages
            1. Egg
            2. Nymph
                a. Looks similar to adult
                b. Cannot fly or reproduce
                c. Develops through several molts
                    (1) Grows until external skeleton is too small
                    (2) Sheds old skeleton and grows new and larger one
                d. Emerges from final molt as mature adult
            3. Adult
    II. Complete metamorphosis
        A. Found in insects like flies, bees, mosquitoes, moths, and butterflies
        B. Involves four stages
            1. Egg
            2. Larva
                a. Looks somewhat like a segmented worm

Lesson Outline:

1. An outline is an orderly summary of a composition. (See skeleton outline in pupil's book.)

2. An outline may be either a topical outline or a sentence outline.

    a. A topical outline has words or brief phrases to express each idea.
       1) Speaker can see basic ideas quickly.
       2) Listener or reader can jot down ideas quickly.
    b. A sentence outline has a complete sentence to express each idea. A writer can often use these sentences in his composition.

3. The form of an outline must follow a definite pattern.

    (1) *The title is centered above the outline.*
    (2) *Each level (main topic, subtopic, point, and so on) is indented equally.*
    (3) *Each line begins with a capital letter.*
    (4) *Each numeral or letter that marks an item is either followed by a period (main topics, subtopics, points, and subpoints) or placed within parentheses (details).*
    (5) *An outline should be either all sentences or all topics.* On a sentence outline, each sentence ends with a period. On a topical outline, the words and phrases do not end with periods.

4. The content of an outline must also follow a definite pattern.

    a. The ideas should be arranged in a logical order, with a definite progression from the beginning of the outline to the end.
    b. When subordinate ideas come under an item on an outline, there must be at least

b. Has different names in different insects
　(1) Maggots for flies
　(2) Grubs for beetles
　(3) Wrigglers for mosquitoes
　(4) Caterpillars for butterflies and moths
c. Spends almost all its time eating
3. Pupa
　a. Enters a resting stage
　b. Forms a hard chrysalis or weaves a silken cocoon
　c. Goes through complete changing of body structures
4. Adult

Sentence outline: (first main topic)

Metamorphosis in Insects

I. Some insects go through incomplete metamorphosis.
　A. This is found in insects like grasshoppers, crickets, cicadas, and roaches.
　B. Incomplete metamorphosis involves three basic stages.
　　1. First is the egg stage.
　　2. Second is the nymph stage.
　　　a. A nymph looks similar to the adult.
　　　b. It cannot fly or reproduce.
　　　c. It develops through several molts.
　　　　(1) The nymph grows until its external skeleton is too small.
　　　　(2) It sheds the old skeleton and grows a new and larger one.
　　　d. The nymph emerges from its final molt as a mature adult.
　　3. Third is the adult stage.

The form of an outline must follow a definite pattern. Compare these rules with the sample outlines above.

1. *The title is centered above the outline.*
2. *Each level (main topic, subtopic, point, and so on) is indented equally.*
3. *Each line begins with a capital letter.*
4. *Each numeral or letter that marks an item is either followed by a period (main topics, subtopics, points, and subpoints) or placed within parentheses (details).*
5. *An outline should be either all sentences or all topics. On a sentence outline, each sentence ends with a period. On a topical outline, the words and phrases do not end with periods.*

　two parts. (If there is an *A*, there must be a *B*. If there is a *1*, there must be a *2*.) When a subordinate idea has only one part, it is included in the item above it.
c. On a topical outline, the items of each level should be as nearly parallel as possible. All the items in a set should have a similar structure, such as by starting with the same part of speech.
d. An outline should not have headings with overlapping ideas.

The content of an outline must also follow a definite pattern. The ideas should be arranged in a logical order, with a definite progression from the beginning of the outline to the end. On the outlines in the lesson, the first main topic covers the three stages of incomplete metamorphosis in order, and the second main topic covers the four stages of complete metamorphosis in order. This is an orderly, logical arrangement for these related ideas.

When subordinate ideas come under an item on an outline, there must be at least two parts. (If there is an *A,* there must be a *B.* If there is a *1,* there must be a *2.*) When a subordinate idea has only one part, it is included in the item above it.

Incorrect: (only one item under *B*)

A. Gospels
   1. Matthew
   2. Mark
   3. Luke
   4. John
B. Church history
   1. Acts
C. Epistles
   1. Romans
   2. 1 Corinthians

Correct:

A. Gospels
   1. Matthew
   2. Mark
   3. Luke
   4. John
B. Church history—Acts
C. Epistles
   1. Romans
   2. 1 Corinthians

On a topical outline, the items of each level should be as nearly parallel as possible. All the items in a set should have a similar structure, such as by starting with the same part of speech. The following examples are based on the topical outline in the lesson.

Not parallel: Subpoints begin with different parts of speech.

   2. Nymph
      a. Appearance similar to adult
      b. Cannot fly or reproduce
      c. Several molts in its development
      d. Finally emerges as mature adult

Parallel: All subpoints begin with verbs.

   2. Nymph
      a. Looks similar to adult
      b. Cannot fly or reproduce
      c. Develops through several molts
      d. Emerges from final molt as mature adult

An outline should not have headings with overlapping ideas. Compare the following outlines.

Incorrect: Overlapping ideas	Correct: Ideas properly categorized
Books of the Bible	**Books of the Bible**
I. Old Testament	I. Old Testament
II. New Testament	A. History
III. History	B. Prophecies
IV. Prophecies	II. New Testament
V. Gospels	A. Gospels
VI. Epistles	B. Epistles

Class Practice

Tell how to correct this outline. Each item that needs improvement is marked with a star.

Early Mennonite Settlements in America

I. The Germantown settlement (1683)
  A. Early days of the settlement itself
     *1. was not primarily a Mennonite settlement
      2. Included nearly 40 Mennonite families by 1708
     *3. A mixture of Dutch and Swiss Mennonites
  *B. The Mennonite Church leaders of early days
      1. Leadership before 1708
         a. No ordained leaders before 1690
            (1) Gathered for fellowship and admonition
            (2) Read old sermons from Europe
            (3) Had no baptisms or Communion services
        *b. Two leaders were ordained in 1690.
            (1) William Rittenhouse as minister
            (2) Jan Neuss as deacon
         c. William Rittenhouse authorized to serve as bishop sometime before 1708
            *(1) Died before assuming the position
        *d. Jacob Gottschalk ordained as minister in 1702
      2. Leadership in 1708 and later
         a. Two ministers and three deacons ordained
         b. Rittenhouse's office assigned to Jacob Gottschalk
            (1) Eleven new members baptized on May 9
            *(2) On May 23 first Communion observed
*II. The settlement at Skippack (1702)
  A. Located about 15 miles northwest of Germantown
  *B. Attractive to Mennonites because of better farmland
  C. Produced the renowned schoolteacher, Christopher Dock
  *D. It became one of two main centers of early American Mennonites.

Lesson 36 Answers

Class Practice

(Corrections are underlined. Refer to the rules in the lesson to make sure pupils understand the reasons for the changes.)

Early Mennonite Settlements in America

I. The Germantown settlement (1683)
  A. Early days of the settlement itself
     1. <u>Was</u> not primarily a Mennonite settlement
     2. Included nearly 40 Mennonite families by 1708
     3. <u>Represented</u> a mixture of Dutch and Swiss Mennonites
  B. <u>Early leaders of the Mennonite Church</u>
      1. Leadership before 1708
         a. No ordained leaders before 1690
            (1) Gathered for fellowship and admonition
            (2) Read old sermons from Europe
            (3) Had no baptisms or Communion services
         b. <u>Two leaders ordained in 1690</u>
            (1) William Rittenhouse as minister
            (2) Jan Neuss as deacon
         <u>c.</u> Jacob Gottschalk ordained as minister in 1702
         d. William Rittenhouse authorized to serve as bishop sometime before 1708, <u>but died before assuming the position</u>
      2. Leadership in 1708 and later
         a. Two ministers and three deacons ordained
         b. Rittenhouse's office assigned to Jacob Gottschalk
            (1) Eleven new members baptized on May 9
            (2) First Communion observed <u>on May 23</u>
II. The <u>Skippack settlement</u> (1702)
  A. Located about 15 miles northwest of Germantown
  B. <u>Attracted</u> Mennonites because of better farmland
  C. Produced the renowned schoolteacher, Christopher Dock
  D. <u>Became</u> one of two main centers of early American Mennonites

III. The Lancaster settlement (1710)
  A. Started by Swiss Mennonites settling along Pequea Creek, south of Lancaster City
  *B. Largest Mennonite community in world by mid-1700s
  C. Spread west and north into York, Adams, and Lebanon Counties

Written Exercises

A. Copy this outline, following the rules for proper form. Each item that needs improvement is marked with a star.

The North American Wild Turkey

I. History
  *A. hunted for food since Indian days
  B. Suggested by Benjamin Franklin as national emblem instead of eagle
  *C. The turkey has become a symbol of Thanksgiving Day.
*II. Its appearance
  A. The tom (male)
    1. His size
      a. Up to 3 feet in height and 4 feet in length
      *b. Weighs up to 16 pounds
    *2. Plumage
      a. Color
        (1) Appears almost black when in shade
        *(2) In sunlight, gleams copper, blue, green, and mahogany
      b. Other features
        (1) Distinctive "beard" of feathers protruding from breast
        *(2) Makes distinctive display by fanning out tail feathers
    3. His head
      a. Is practically bare
      *b. Pencillike wattle dangling between eyes
  B. The hen (female)
    1. Her size
      *a. Measures about 1 foot in height and a little over 1 foot in length
      b. About 9 pounds in weight
    2. Her plumage
      *a. Is not as shiny as a tom's
    3. Her head
      a. Covered with hair and fine feathers
      *b. The wattle lacking

B. Here is the rest of the outline from Part A. Copy it and add the missing

---

III. The Lancaster settlement (1710)
  A. Started by Swiss Mennonites settling along Pequea Creek, south of Lancaster City
  B. <u>Became</u> largest Mennonite community in world by mid-1700s
  C. Spread west and north into York, Adams, and Lebanon Counties

Written Exercises

A. (Corrections are underlined. Allow reasonable variation.)

The North American Wild Turkey

I. History
  A. <u>Hunted</u> for food since Indian days
  B. Suggested by Benjamin Franklin as national emblem instead of eagle
  C. <u>Has</u> become a symbol of Thanksgiving Day
II. <u>Appearance</u>
  A. The tom (male)
    1. His size
      a. Up to 3 feet in height and 4 feet in length
      b. Up to 16 pounds <u>in weight</u>
    2. <u>His</u> plumage
      a. Color
        (1) Appears almost black when in shade
        (2) Gleams copper, blue, green, and mahogany <u>in sunlight</u>
      b. Other features
        (1) Distinctive "beard" of feathers protruding from breast
        (2) <u>Distinctive display made</u> by fanning out tail feathers
    3. His head
      a. Is practically bare
      b. <u>Has</u> pencillike wattle dangling between eyes
  B. The hen (female)
    1. Her size
      a. <u>About</u> 1 foot in height and a little over 1 foot in length
      b. About 9 pounds in weight
    2. Her plumage <u>not as shiny as a tom's</u>
    3. Her head
      a. Covered with hair and fine feathers
      b. <u>Lacks</u> the wattle

details, choosing from the lists given after the outline.

III. Diet
  A. In spring
    1. Leftover nuts
    2.
    3.
  B. In summer
    1. Consists primarily of vegetation
    2. Includes many insects
  C. In fall
    1.
    2.
  D. In winter
    1.
    2.

IV. Behavior
  A. Getting food
    1.
    2.
  B. Giving calls
    1.
    2.
    3.
  C. Escaping danger
    1.
    2.
    3.
    4.

Details for III:
Fruits, seeds, and nuts left from fall
Tender early growth
Fruits of dogwood, grape, thorn apple, and cherry
Greens and insect larvae around springs that stay open
Seeds of grasses, corn, oats, and weeds
Early insects

Details for IV:
May travel several miles a day in search of food
Can fly up to 55 m.p.h.
Soft cluck for an assembly call
Can run up to 18 m.p.h.
Can hide cleverly
Loud gobble of tom for attracting mate and proclaiming territory
Scratches for food like a chicken
Can swim well
Harsh cry of alarm

B. (Added details are underlined. Under main topic IV, note the progression of *soft, loud, harsh* in subtopic B and of *hide, swim, run, fly* in subtopic C. Arrangements other than the ones shown may also be acceptable.)

III. Diet
  A. In spring
    1. Leftover nuts
    2. Tender early growth
    3. Early insects
  B. In summer
    1. Consists primarily of vegetation
    2. Includes many insects
  C. In fall
    1. Fruits of dogwood, grape, thorn apple, and cherry
    2. Seeds of grasses, corn, oats, and weeds
  D. In winter
    1. Fruits, seeds, and nuts left from fall
    2. Greens and insect larvae around springs that stay open

IV. Behavior
  A. Getting food
    1. May travel several miles a day in search of food
    2. Scratches for food like a chicken
  B. Giving calls
    1. Soft cluck for an assembly call
    2. Loud gobble of tom for attracting mate and proclaiming territory
    3. Harsh cry of alarm
  C. Escaping danger
    1. Can hide cleverly
    2. Can swim well
    3. Can run up to 18 m.p.h.
    4. Can fly up to 55 m.p.h.

37. Perfect Tenses of Verbs

> **Lesson Survey**
> - In the **perfect tenses,** the third principal part of the main verb is used with a form of *have* as a helping verb.
> - In the **present perfect tense,** the helping verb is *have* or *has.*

Lesson 37

Purpose: To teach the concept of perfect tenses and the formation of the three perfect tenses.

Oral Review:
1. What does *tense* mean? (time)
2. Say each verb, and tell what tense it is.
  a. Eldon comes every day to help with the chores. (comes—present)
  b. The Yutzy family will leave for their new home tomorrow. (will leave—future)
  c. The sharp snap of a twig broke the silence. (broke—past)
3. Give the second and third principal parts of these verbs. Use *have* with the past participle.
  a. begin (began, [have] begun)
  b. come (came, [have] come)
  c. lay (laid, [have] laid)
  d. shoot (shot, [have] shot)
  e. sleep (slept, [have] slept)
  f. burst (burst, [have] burst)
  g. tag (tagged, [have] tagged)
  h. swing (swung, [have] swung)
  i. go (went, [have] gone)
  j. give (gave, [have] given)
4. Tell whether these sentences are simple, compound, or complex.
  a. The dishes that Geraldine washed are sparkling clean. (complex)

- In the **past perfect tense,** the helping verb is *had.*
- In the **future perfect tense,** the helping verbs are *shall have* or *will have.*

In Lesson 35 you learned about the three simple tenses. There are also three *perfect tenses,* which are used to express *completed action.* In the perfect tenses, the third principal part of the main verb is used with a form of *have* as a helping verb.

In the *present perfect tense,* the helping verb *have* or *has* is used. Whenever a verb phrase contains the helping verb *have* or *has* and the past participle of the main verb, it is in the present perfect tense.

"I have glorified thee on the earth."
The Lord has spoken to mankind through His Son.
Have the disciples understood Jesus' words?

In the *past perfect tense,* the helping verb *had* is used. Whenever a verb phrase contains the helping verb *had* and the past participle of the main verb, it is in the past perfect tense.

Simon had bewitched the people before Philip brought the Gospel.
Many people had regarded him highly until they learned about Jesus.

In the *future perfect tense,* the helping verbs *shall have* or *will have* are used. Whenever a verb phrase contains the helping verbs *shall have* or *will have* and the past participle of the main verb, it is in the future perfect tense. Remember to use *shall* with first person subjects and *will* with second and third person subjects.

With tomorrow's picking, we shall have picked strawberries four times.
By the time we have breakfast, Uncle Leonard's will have left.

Here are the conjugations of the verbs *be* and *hear* in the perfect tenses.

Be

Person	Singular	Plural
	Present Perfect Tense	
First:	I have been.	We have been.
Second:	You have been.	You have been.
Third:	He has been.	They have been.
	Past Perfect Tense	
First:	I had been.	We had been.
Second:	You had been.	You had been.
Third:	He had been.	They had been.

b. After the rain, the garden looked fresh and beautiful. (simple)
c. Because spring was so cool, we were ill prepared for the sudden heat wave. (complex)
d. Hard work is good for the muscles, and deep study is good for the mind. (compound)
e. What the Bible tells us is very important. (complex)

Lesson Introduction: Water is a common but valuable substance. One thing that makes it so valuable is that we can use it in different forms. As a solid (ice), we can use it to make things cold. As a gas (steam), we can use it to drive machinery. And as a liquid, we can use it for washing, drinking, irrigating, and many other purposes. In fact, water is so important that natural life could not continue without it.

In a similar way, no sentence can "live" without a verb. And verbs, like water, are especially valuable because they have different forms that we can use for different purposes. Today we will study the forms used to make the perfect tenses of verbs.

Lesson Outline:

1. The perfect tenses express completed action. By contrast, the simple tenses merely indicate the time of happening.

2. The helping verb **have** *or* **has** *is used in the present perfect tense.*

3. The helping verb **had** *is used in the past perfect tense.*

4. The helping verbs **shall have** *or* **will have** *are used in the future perfect tense.* Use *shall* with first person subjects and *will* with second and third person subjects.

Future Perfect Tense

First: I shall have been.   We shall have been.
Second: You will have been.   You will have been.
Third: He will have been.   They will have been.

Hear

Person	*Singular*	*Plural*

Present Perfect Tense

First: I have heard.   We have heard.
Second: You have heard.   You have heard.
Third: He has heard.   They have heard.

Past Perfect Tense

First: I had heard.   We had heard.
Second: You had heard.   You had heard.
Third: He had heard.   They had heard.

Future Perfect Tense

First: I shall have heard.   We shall have heard.
Second: You will have heard.   You will have heard.
Third: He will have heard.   They will have heard.

Class Practice

A. Read the verb phrase in each independent clause, and tell whether its tense is *present perfect, past perfect,* or *future perfect.*
  1. Before Isaac was born, the Lord had appeared to Abraham several times.
  2. By the end of this term, Sister Mildred will have taught here for five years.
  3. Had you forgotten about your chores this morning?
  4. We have had plenty of rain this spring.
  5. God has never failed to care for His own.
  6. Will you have finished the letter before the mail goes?

B. Read each verb or verb phrase, and tell which of the six tenses it is.
  1. Charlotte washed the dishes this morning.
  2. What have you done?
  3. What had you done before lunch?
  4. What will you have done by 3:00 P.M.?
  5. These peaches look delicious.
  6. Shall we buy a bushel of them?
  7. Some friends have helped with the extra work.
  8. God will surely reward them for their kindness.

C. Read each sentence, using the verb form for the tense shown in italics.

Lesson 37 Answers

Class Practice

A. 1. had appeared—past perfect
   2. will have taught—future perfect
   3. Had forgotten—past perfect
   4. have had—present perfect
   5. has failed—present perfect
   6. Will have finished—future perfect

B. 1. washed—past
   2. have done—present perfect
   3. had done—past perfect
   4. will have done—future perfect
   5. look—present
   6. Shall buy—future
   7. have helped—present perfect
   8. will reward—future

1. The package (arrive) in the mail. *present perfect*
2. Father (give) clear instructions before he left. *past perfect*
3. Before he returns, we (weed) the watermelon patch. *future perfect*

D. Conjugate the verb *begin* in the three perfect tenses.

Written Exercises

A. Copy each verb or verb phrase, and write which of the six tenses it is.
1. Jesus willingly left His home in glory.
2. He has shed His blood for the salvation of mankind.
3. Before Christ's death, the blood of animals had atoned for sin.
4. Now the precious blood of Christ is the provision of a fuller salvation.
5. Jesus has ascended back to the Father.
6. When will He return for His purchased people?
7. Before His return, He will have prepared a place for His own.
8. Ananias and Sapphira had agreed to lie before coming with the money.
9. Has anyone ever deceived the Lord?
10. By this time tomorrow, Brenda will have finished the lettering for the bulletin board.

B. For each sentence, write the verb in the tense that is shown in italics.
1. The visitor (choose) Psalm 23 for devotions. *present perfect*
2. Last week Brother Keith (choose) the same psalm. *past perfect*
3. The Brougher family (come) this evening for a visit. *future*
4. When we arrived at Claremont, we (go) half the way. *past perfect*
5. If the Troyers come, they (come) three times since they moved. *future perfect*
6. This morning we (drag) the old pea vines over to the cows. *past*
7. Marcia (finish) the pictures before she left. *past perfect*
8. My sister (teach) the lower grades at Oakdale Christian School. *present*
9. Several birds (investigate) the houses we made. *present perfect*
10. Before the sun came up, we (pick) several bushels of beans. *past perfect*

C. Conjugate the verb *go* in the three perfect tenses.

Review Exercises

A. Label these sentences *simple, compound,* or *complex.* [14, 15]
1. True beauty is the inner beauty of noble character.
2. We can have this beauty, but we must develop it.
3. We must always do what is right.
4. If we keep a clear conscience, we will have noble character.

Review Exercises

A. 1. simple   3. complex
   2. compound   4. complex

C. (Corrections are underlined.)
1. The package <u>has arrived</u> in the mail.
2. Father <u>had given</u> clear instructions before he left.
3. Before he returns, we <u>shall have weeded</u> the watermelon patch.

D.

Begin

Person	Singular	Plural
	Present Perfect Tense	
First:	I have begun.	We have begun.
Second:	You have begun.	You have begun.
Third:	He has begun.	They have begun.
	Past Perfect Tense	
First:	I had begun.	We had begun.
Second:	You had begun.	You had begun.
Third:	He had begun.	They had begun.
	Future Perfect Tense	
First:	I shall have begun.	We shall have begun.
Second:	You will have begun.	You will have begun.
Third:	He will have begun.	They will have begun.

Written Exercises

A. 1. left—past
    2. has shed—present perfect
    3. had atoned—past perfect
    4. is—present
    5. has ascended—present perfect
    6. will return—future
    7. will have prepared—future perfect
    8. had agreed—past perfect
    9. Has deceived—present perfect
   10. will have finished—future perfect

B. 1. has chosen   6. dragged
   2. had chosen   7. had finished
   3. will come   8. teaches
   4. had gone   9. have investigated
   5. will have come   10. had picked

C.

Go

Person	Singular	Plural
	Present Perfect Tense	
First:	I have gone.	We have gone.
Second:	You have gone.	You have gone.
Third:	He has gone.	They have gone.
	Past Perfect Tense	
First:	I had gone.	We had gone.
Second:	You had gone.	You had gone.
Third:	He had gone.	They had gone.
	Future Perfect Tense	
First:	I shall have gone.	We shall have gone.
Second:	You will have gone.	You will have gone.
Third:	He will have gone.	They will have gone.

B. Use suitable conjunctions to make compound sentences from these simple sentences. If a pair of sentences should not be joined, write *unrelated*. [14]

1. We stopped in at Grandma Martha's place. She was not at home.
2. We could go and visit Mr. Pellman. We could go back home.
3. Mr. Pellman stays at Curfman Nursing Home. His son's name is Stanley.

C. Join each pair of sentences into a complex sentence, using the subordinating conjunction or relative pronoun in parentheses. [15]

1. We will wait till Monday to pick tomatoes. We don't do garden work on Sunday. (because)
2. Mr. Thompson wants two bushels this week. He bought three bushels of tomatoes last week. (who)
3. He acted quite unhappy about them last week. Here he is for some more! (although)

B. 1. We stopped in at Grandma Martha's place, but she was not at home.
2. We could go and visit Mr. Pellman, or we could go back home.
3. unrelated

C. 1. We will wait till Monday to pick tomatoes because we don't do garden work on Sunday.
2. Mr. Thompson, who bought three bushels of tomatoes last week, wants two bushels this week.
3. Although he acted quite unhappy about them last week, here he is for some more!

---

38. Using Perfect Verb Tenses

> **Lesson Survey**
> - The present perfect tense indicates an action or a condition that began in the past and is completed as of the present time or continues into the present.
> - The past perfect tense indicates an action or a condition that was completed by a certain time in the past.
> - The future perfect tense indicates an action or a condition that will be completed by a certain time in the future.

An archaic meaning of *perfect* is "mature or complete." God tells us to "let patience have her perfect work, that ye may be perfect and entire, wanting nothing." In other words, the exercise of patience helps a person to be mature, to be complete, and to lack nothing.

In English grammar, *perfect* still means "completed." The perfect tenses express action completed at a definite time. In contrast to the simple tenses, which merely show the *time* of an action, the perfect tenses indicate the *completion* of an action.

Remember that in the perfect tenses, the third principal part of the

Lesson 38

Purpose: To review and reinforce the time relationships expressed by the three perfect tenses.

Oral Review:
1. Name the three perfect tenses, and give the helping verbs for each. (present perfect—have *or* has; past perfect—had; future perfect—shall have *or* will have)
2. Give the verb phrase in each sentence, and tell which of the perfect tenses it is.
   a. Jesus has come to Bethany. (has come—present perfect)
   b. When Martha had heard of His arrival, she went to Him. (had heard—past perfect)
   c. Many have gathered to mourn the death of Lazarus. (have gathered—present perfect)
   d. Before the final resurrection, Lazarus will have risen from the dead. (will have risen—future perfect)
3. Tell which words in these phrases should be capitalized. (Answers are underlined.)
   a. Dr. Roberts
   b. Whirlpool washer
   c. "A Child Is Born" (poem)
   d. music, English, and science classes
   e. the gods of the Amorites
   f. the first day of summer
4. When should a compound sentence be joined with a semicolon and a conjunction instead of a comma and a conjunction? (when one clause already has a comma in it)
5. Tell where commas should be placed in these sentences. (*Teacher:* Write the sentences on the board.)
   a. I called and called, but there was no answer.

main verb is used with a form of *have* as a helping verb. Use *have* or *has* to form the present perfect tense, *had* to form the past perfect tense, and *shall have* or *will have* to form the future perfect tense.

The present perfect tense indicates an action or a condition that began in the past and is completed as of the present time or continues into the present.

> The second coat of paint <u>has been applied</u>.
>> (The action of applying began in the past and is now completed.)
> Grandmother <u>has been</u> sick for two weeks.
>> (The condition of sickness began in the past and continues into the present.)

The simple past tense and the present perfect tense both refer to actions or conditions in the past. How are they different? An action expressed in the simple past tense could have happened in the near or the distant past. And it could have lasted for a brief time or for a long time. In contrast, an action expressed in the present perfect tense *began* in the past, but it is either completed at the present moment or continues into the present time.

Simple past tense:
> The children <u>sang</u> three songs.
>> (At some time in the past—this morning, yesterday, or last week—the children sang. They are not singing now, at the present time.)

Present perfect tense:
> The children <u>have sung</u> three songs.
>> (They began singing in the recent past and apparently finished just now.)

Simple past tense:
> My father <u>worked</u> at Byler's Machine Shop for five years.
>> (At some time in the past—a year ago or thirty years ago—my father worked there, but apparently he no longer does.)

Present perfect tense:
> My father <u>has worked</u> at Byler's Machine Shop for five years.
>> (He began working there five years ago and apparently still does.)

Sometimes either the simple past tense or the present perfect tense may be suitable, depending on the purpose of the speaker or writer. If he simply wants to state that the action occurred in the past, he may use the simple past tense. But if he wants to emphasize that an action is completed

---

b. My cousin, the boy with red hair, is visiting us.

c. Jessica, will you set the table for dinner?

Lesson Introduction: Call the students' attention to the definition of *perfect* as used in this lesson. You can use a green apple to illustrate. In the past, the apple *had reached* perfection when it was a blossom. In the present, it *has reached* perfection as a green apple. In the future, it *will have reached* perfection when it is a ripe apple.

The apple is perfect in every stage. However, its past perfection would no longer do now. Had it remained a blossom, it would not have remained perfect, for it could not have fulfilled its purpose. The final perfection of the green apple is a ripe apple, which will come in due time.

Lesson Outline:

1. The present perfect tense indicates an action or a condition that began in the past and is completed as of the present time or continues into the present.

a. Distinguish between the simple past tense and the present perfect tense.

1) An action expressed in the simple past tense could have happened in the near or the distant past. And it could have lasted for a brief time or for a long time.

2) An action expressed in the present perfect tense began in the past, but it is either completed at the present moment or continues into the present time.

b. The simple past tense and the present perfect tense emphasize different aspects of the action.

1) The simple past tense merely states that the action occurred in the past.

as of the present time or continues into the present, he must use the present perfect tense.

> Jesus <u>brought</u> salvation to mankind.
> (merely states that this action occurred in the past)
> Jesus <u>has brought</u> salvation to mankind.
> (emphasizes that this action is completed as of now, with effects that continue into the present)

The past perfect tense indicates an action or a condition that was completed by a certain time in the past. Therefore, whenever the past perfect tense is used, two past actions or conditions must be stated or implied.

> **Incomplete:** Only one past action
> We <u>had picked</u> the beans.

> **Complete:** Two past actions stated
> We <u>had picked</u> the beans before we <u>ate</u> breakfast.

> **Complete:** Two past actions, the second one implied
> We <u>had picked</u> the beans before breakfast.

Sometimes a sentence has two verbs expressing two past actions, with one action occurring before the other. The past perfect tense provides a useful way of showing the order of the actions. The action that occurred *first* is expressed in the past perfect tense.

> **Unclear:** Karen <u>realized</u> what a mistake she <u>made</u>.
> (sounds as if she realized the mistake at the same time she made it)
> **Clear:** Karen <u>realized</u> what a mistake she <u>had made</u>.
> (clarifies that making the mistake came first)

The future perfect tense indicates an action or a condition that will be completed by a certain time in the future. As the past perfect tense must state or imply two past actions or conditions, so the future perfect tense must state or imply two future actions or conditions.

> **Incomplete:** Only one future action
> Uncle John <u>will have helped</u> us every day.

> **Complete:** Two future actions stated
> If Uncle John <u>helps</u> us tomorrow, he <u>will have helped</u> us every day.

> **Complete:** Two future actions, the second one implied
> After tomorrow, Uncle John <u>will have helped</u> us every day.

The future perfect tense, like the past perfect tense, provides a useful way of showing the order of two actions. The action that comes *first* is

2) The present perfect tense emphasizes that an action is completed as of the present time or continues into the present.

2. *The past perfect tense indicates an action or a condition that was completed by a certain time in the past.*

    a. With the past perfect tense, two past actions or conditions must be stated or implied.

    b. When a sentence refers to two past actions or conditions, the past perfect tense provides a useful way of showing the order of the actions. The action that occurred first is expressed in the past perfect tense. (*Teacher:* The same thing can be shown by the subordinating conjunction used in a complex sentence, but that is not taught here.)

3. *The future perfect tense indicates an action or a condition that will be completed by a certain time in the future.*

    a. With the future perfect tense, two future actions or conditions must be stated or implied.

    b. The future perfect tense provides a useful way of showing the order of two actions. The action that comes first is expressed in the future perfect tense. The other action may be expressed in the simple future tense or the present tense. (*Teacher:* Again, the same thing can be shown by the subordinating conjunction in a complex sentence.)

★ *EXTRA PRACTICE*
Worksheet 20 (*Using Verbs in Perfect Tenses*)

expressed in the future perfect tense. The other action may be expressed in the simple future tense or the present tense.

> **Unclear:** When we <u>arrive</u> there, we <u>shall travel</u> over five hundred miles. (sounds as if we shall travel five hundred miles after we arrive)
>
> **Clear:** When we <u>arrive</u> there, we <u>shall have traveled</u> over five hundred miles. (clarifies that the traveling comes first)

Class Practice

A. Read each sentence, using the tense shown in italics for the verb in parentheses.
1. Father (return) from Missouri yesterday afternoon. *past*
2. Mother (return) just now from helping Aunt Betty. *present perfect*
3. By this time tomorrow, I (rake) the leaves. *future perfect*
4. After Ellen (study) for half an hour, she went to the library. *past perfect*
5. You (answer) many questions about that broken arm before it heals. *future perfect*

B. In each sentence, tell which verb expresses the action that occurred first. Then read the sentence, changing that verb to a perfect tense so that the relationship is clear.
1. When everyone ate enough, Mother passed the toothpicks.
2. At the doctor's office, the receptionist said that we came on the wrong day.
3. We shall finish cleaning the guest room when Brother Seth arrives for the night.
4. When Edward copied his poem neatly on notebook paper, he handed it in.
5. The healed man told everyone what Jesus did for him.

C. Read each of these complex sentences, changing one verb to a perfect tense. Compare the meaning of that sentence and the original sentence.
1. The grass was dry and brown before it rained.
2. After we washed the dishes, we visited together.
3. When you learn to behave wisely, you will demonstrate acceptable maturity.
4. Aaron told the Israelites what God said to Moses at the burning bush.
5. When we arrive in heaven, we shall escape temptation forever.

Written Exercises

A. Each sentence has a verb in parentheses. Write that verb in the tense shown in italics.

Lesson 38 Answers

Class Practice
A. 1. returned   4. had studied
2. has returned   5. will have answered
3. shall have raked

B. (Corrections are underlined.)
1. ate; When everyone <u>had eaten</u> enough, Mother passed the toothpicks.
2. came; At the doctor's office, the receptionist said that we <u>had come</u> on the wrong day.
3. shall finish; We <u>shall have finished</u> cleaning the guest room when Brother Seth arrives for the night.
4. copied; When Edward <u>had copied</u> his poem neatly on notebook paper, he handed it in.
5. did; The healed man told everyone what Jesus <u>had done</u> for him.

C. (Corrections are underlined. Comparisons are in parentheses.)
1. The grass <u>had been</u> dry and brown before it rained. (This sentence indicates more strongly that the dry and brown condition belonged to the time before the rain came.)
2. After we <u>had washed</u> the dishes, we visited together. (This sentence emphasizes the completion of washing dishes before visiting.)
3. When you <u>will have learned</u> to behave wisely, you will demonstrate acceptable maturity. (This sentence emphasizes the completion of learning before the demonstrating is done.)
4. Aaron told the Israelites what God <u>had said</u> to Moses at the burning bush. (This sentence clarifies that God's speaking preceded Aaron's telling.)
5. When we arrive in heaven, we <u>shall have escaped</u> temptation forever. (This sentence emphasizes the completeness of the escape and that temptation will forever be a thing of the past.)

1. After we (finish) the quiz, Brother Eugene collected our papers. *past perfect*
2. By the time we arrive at McBride, we (drive) for twenty-six hours. *future perfect*
3. Yesterday Susan (bring) some seashells from the Bahamas. *past*
4. So far this week, Brother Isaac (start) every message with a lesson for the children. *present perfect*
5. I hope I (find) the answer by tomorrow. *future perfect*

B. One verb in each sentence should be changed to a perfect tense so that the relationship is clear. Find that verb, and write it in the correct tense.
1. When evening comes, we shall drive into Texas.
2. We went outside to see the damage that the storm did.
3. By the time these chicks begin laying eggs, we shall spend hundreds of dollars on feed.
4. The students busily took notes, for history class began.
5. They will learn many interesting facts when this class is over.

C. Write each of these sentences, using a perfect tense to express the action or condition that occurred first.
1. The train will stop several times before we reach our destination.
2. The rising water covered the road after we arrived at Grandfather's house.
3. The Philistines stopped several wells, but Isaac reopened them.
4. We shall finish packing the suitcases by the time the others arrive.
5. She knitted baby clothes until her fingers became stiff with arthritis.

Review Exercises

Use the index if you need help with any of the following exercises.

A. Write correctly all the words with capitalization errors.
1. let the people from east and from west
   their creator extol,
   yea, from north and from south give their best
   to his sovereign control.
2. "Examine me, o lord, and prove me."
3. When John the baptist baptized jesus, the spirit of God came upon Him.
4. My Father bought a Maytag Washer at Lingo's appliances.
5. Snow occasionally falls in jerusalem during Winter.

B. These sentences have missing commas, colons, and semicolons. Write the words or numbers with which the missing punctuation should be used, and add the needed marks.

Written Exercises

A. 1. had finished
   2. shall have driven
   3. brought
   4. has started
   5. shall have found

B. 1. shall have driven *or* has come
   2. had done
   3. shall have spent
   4. had begun
   5. will have learned

C. 1. The train will have stopped several times before we reach our destination.
   2. The rising water covered the road after we had arrived at Grandfather's house.
   3. The Philistines had stopped several wells, but Isaac reopened them.
   4. We shall have finished packing the suitcases by the time the others arrive.
   5. She had knitted baby clothes until her fingers became stiff with arthritis.

Review Exercises

A. (Corrections are underlined.)
1. Let, East, West, Their, Creator, Yea, North, South, To, His, (Capitalizing *east, west, north,* and *south* is optional in this context.)
2. O, Lord
3. Baptist, Jesus, Spirit
4. father, washer, Appliances
5. Jerusalem, winter

1. Carla has brought our jackets scarves and mittens and Father has started the car already.
2. This picture shows my grandfather's first car a 1921 Willys Knight.
3. Leroy's mother, Martha Steiner, was born near Zanesville Ohio and his father, Amos King, was born near Lancaster Pennsylvania.
4. Graybill Kraybill and Kriebel are all variations of the same original last name.
5. Although the morning dawned clear the sky was overcast by 10 00.
6. The account of Jesus' temptation is recorded in Matthew 4 1–11.

C. Decide whether each sentence has a direct or an indirect quotation. Copy the sentences, punctuating them correctly.
   1. Come out to the grape arbor called Father and see this hummingbird nest
   2. I didn't realize it would be so tiny exclaimed Sarah
   3. Mark told us that he had read about hummingbirds just the other day

B. 1. jackets, scarves, mittens;
   2. car,
   3. Zanesville, Ohio; Lancaster,
   4. Graybill, Kraybill,
   5. clear, 10:00
   6. 4:1–11

C. 1. "Come out to the grape arbor," called Father, "and see this hummingbird nest."
   2. "I didn't realize it would be so tiny!" exclaimed Sarah.
   3. Mark told us that he had read about hummingbirds just the other day.

---

39. Progressive and Emphatic Verb Forms

Lesson Survey
- The **progressive verb form** shows action or condition in progress.
- The **emphatic verb form** gives added emphasis.

Suppose your teacher has asked the class, "Are you studying your Bible memory carefully?" The following statements would give the same basic answer in several different ways.

> I study the passage carefully.
> I am studying the passage carefully.
> I do study the passage carefully.

Notice that the verb in each sentence is in the present tense. It states that an action is taking place now.

> I study (now).   I am studying (now).   I do study (now).

This shows that a verb can have several different forms and still be in the same tense. The first sentence has the basic, or simple, form of the present tense verb; the second has the progressive form of the present

Lesson 39

Purpose: To teach the *progressive and *emphatic forms of verbs.

Oral Review:
1. What does *perfect* mean in English grammar? (completed)
2. Give the helping verbs for each of the perfect tenses. (present perfect—have *or* has; past perfect—had; future perfect—shall have *or* will have)
3. How is the present perfect tense different from the simple past tense? (An action expressed in the simple past tense could have happened in the near or the distant past. An action expressed in the present perfect tense began in the past, but it is completed at the present moment or continues into the present time.)
4. When a sentence refers to two actions, what is a

good way to show which action occurred first? (by using a perfect tense)
5. Give the principal parts of these verbs.
   a. begin (began, [have] begun)
   b. read (read, [have] read)
   c. fly (flew, [have] flown)
   d. choose (chose, [have] chosen)
   e. write (wrote, [have] written)
   f. swim (swam, [have] swum)
   g. sing (sang, [have] sung)
   h. bring (brought, [have] brought)

Lesson Introduction: Write this sentence on the board: *Marie sweeps the floor.* Ask the class what this sentence suggests to them. (It suggests that sweeping the floor is Marie's regular job.) Ask them to give a sentence that says Marie is at the job right now. (*Marie is sweeping the floor.*) What might they say if someone suggests that Marie neglected to sweep the

tense verb; and the third has the emphatic form of the present tense verb.

The *simple form* of a verb is just what it says—simple. It states the action or condition as simply as possible.

Simple form:
> I <u>study</u> the passage carefully.

The *progressive form* of a verb shows action or condition in progress. It is made by adding *-ing* to the first principal part of the verb and using a form of *be* as a helping verb. The *-ing* verb form is called the *present participle*.

Progressive form:
> I <u>am studying</u> the passage carefully.
>> (The helping verb is *am*; *-ing* is added to the first principal part of *study*.)

In contrast to the simple form, the progressive form emphasizes that the action is continuing. Notice the shift in emphasis in these pairs of sentences.

> I <u>study</u> the passage carefully.
>> (simple form—general statement of action in the present)
> I <u>am studying</u> the passage carefully.
>> (progressive form—action in progress now)

> I <u>feed</u> the calves.
>> (simple form—general statement of action in the present)
> I <u>am feeding</u> the calves.
>> (progressive form—action in progress now)

The progressive form of a verb can be used in all six tenses. In the perfect tenses, the verb phrase includes both a form of *be* and a form of *have* as helping verbs.

> She <u>is singing</u>. (present progressive)
> She <u>was singing</u>. (past progressive)
> She <u>will be singing</u>. (future progressive)
> She <u>has been singing</u>. (present perfect progressive)
> She <u>had been singing</u>. (past perfect progressive)
> She <u>will have been singing</u>. (future perfect progressive)

The *emphatic form* of a verb gives added emphasis. In this form, the helping verb *do, does,* or *did* is used with the first principal part of the main verb.

Emphatic form:
> We <u>do help</u> those in need.
>> (The helping verb *do* is used with the first principal part of *help.*)

floor, even though she had actually done it? (*Marie did sweep the floor.*) The last two examples illustrate progressive and emphatic verb forms, which are taught in this lesson. Your students use these forms easily without much thought; now it is time for them to learn more precisely their formation and exact usage.

Lesson Outline:

1. The progressive verb form shows action or condition in progress.

    a. The main verb is made by adding *-ing* to the first principal part. This *-ing* verb form is called the present participle.

    b. A form of the verb *be* is always used as a helping verb.

    c. The progressive verb form emphasizes that the action is continuing.

    d. The progressive form can be used in all six tenses.

2. The emphatic verb form gives added emphasis.

    a. The helping verb *do, does,* or *did* is used with the first principal part of the main verb.

    b. The emphatic form exists only in the present and past tenses.

    c. A sentence with the emphatic form should be spoken or read more emphatically than a similar sentence with the simple form.

    d. The helping verbs *do, does,* and *did* are also used in questions and negative statements. In those cases, they are not emphatic verb forms.

A sentence with the verb in its emphatic form would naturally be spoken or read more emphatically than a similar sentence with the simple form. Consider the difference in emphasis in these pairs of sentences.

I <u>study</u> my lessons. (simple form—no particular emphasis)
I <u>do study</u> my lessons. (emphatic form—forceful answer, perhaps to a question or a doubt)

I <u>finished</u> my assignment. (simple form—no particular emphasis)
I <u>did finish</u> my assignment. (emphatic form—forceful answer, perhaps when student cannot find his paper)

The emphatic form exists only in the present and past tenses.

Brother Allen <u>does appreciate</u> his godly heritage. (present emphatic)
Brother Allen <u>did appreciate</u> his godly heritage. (past emphatic)

Although *do, does,* and *did* are always used to make the emphatic form of a verb, this is not the only time they are used. They may also be used in questions and in simple negative statements. These types of sentences are not emphatic.

<u>Did</u> Martha <u>know</u> the answer? (question—not emphatic)
She <u>did</u> not <u>know</u> the answer then. (negative statement—not emphatic)
She <u>does know</u> the answer now. (emphatic statement)

Here are the conjugations of *learn* in the progressive and emphatic forms.

Learn

Person	Singular	Plural
	Present Tense, Progressive Form	
First:	I am learning.	We are learning.
Second:	You are learning.	You are learning.
Third:	He is learning.	They are learning.
	Past Tense, Progressive Form	
First:	I was learning.	We were learning.
Second:	You were learning.	You were learning.
Third:	He was learning.	They were learning.
	Future Tense, Progressive Form	
First:	I shall be learning.	We shall be learning.
Second:	You will be learning.	You will be learning.
Third:	He will be learning.	They will be learning.

Present Perfect Tense, Progressive Form

First: I have been learning.   We have been learning.
Second: You have been learning.   You have been learning.
Third: He has been learning.   They have been learning.

Past Perfect Tense, Progressive Form

First: I had been learning.   We had been learning.
Second: You had been learning.   You had been learning.
Third: He had been learning.   They had been learning.

Future Perfect Tense, Progressive Form

First: I shall have been   We shall have been learning.
        learning.
Second: You will have been   You will have been learning.
        learning.
Third: He will have been   They will have been learning.
        learning.

Learn

Person	*Singular*	*Plural*

Present Tense, Emphatic Form

First: I do learn.   We do learn.
Second: You do learn.   You do learn.
Third: He does learn.   They do learn.

Past Tense, Emphatic Form

First: I did learn.   We did learn.
Second: You did learn.   You did learn.
Third: He did learn.   They did learn.

Class Practice

A. Read each sentence, changing the verb to the progressive form. Do not change the tense of the verb.
   1. These plants look healthy.
   2. Mother prepared the dinner.
   3. Who has drawn these pictures?
   4. By this time next year, I shall have learned the language.
   5. We had watched the sun set.
   6. We shall see you tomorrow, the Lord willing.

B. Read each sentence, changing the verb to the emphatic form. Do not change the tense of the verb.
   1. Judith has chicken pox.
   2. The wind blew until noon.

Lesson 39 Answers

Class Practice

A. 1. These plants are looking healthy.
   2. Mother was preparing the dinner.
   3. Who has been drawing these pictures?
   4. By this time next year, I shall have been learning the language.
   5. We had been watching the sun set.
   6. We shall be seeing you tomorrow, the Lord willing.

B. 1. Judith does have chicken pox.
   2. The wind did blow until noon.

3. The men worked on the shed today.
4. The Thorntons went on a trip yesterday.
5. Your parents teach you many important things.
6. I appreciate the help that they have given me.

C. Give the tense of each verb phrase. If the verb form is *progressive* or *emphatic*, also state that.
1. We do want God's approval in everything.
2. The grass had grown fast during the wet weather.
3. The boys have been cleaning the garage.
4. They will burn the rubbish.
5. Brother Lynn was giving us some good advice.
6. I have never seen a real meteorite.
7. We students did surprise the teacher by our early arrival.
8. By six o'clock they will have been traveling for nine hours.

D. Conjugate the verb *speak* in the progressive form of all six tenses.

E. Conjugate the verb *speak* in the emphatic form of the present and past tenses.

Written Exercises

A. Write the progressive form of the verb in each sentence. Do not change the tense.
1. In heaven Jesus intercedes for the saints.
2. Brother Leroy spoke about the mission work in Mexico.
3. The visitors have helped with the dishes.
4. Before morning, the snow had melted.
5. We shall sing our theme song tomorrow morning.
6. The temperature had risen until noon.
7. Sister Eileen went to the store in the morning.
8. The men had cut the wood before your arrival.
9. By suppertime, the children will have stacked wood for two hours.
10. We have burned wood in our fireplace every winter.

B. Write the emphatic form of the verb in each sentence. Do not change the tense.
1. Jesus brought many changes to the world.
2. He works through the church today.
3. The angels serve as ministering spirits to the saints.
4. The Holy Spirit brings Scripture verses to our remembrance.
5. The needs of people stirred Jesus' compassion.
6. Today many people seek the way of truth.

3. The men did work on the shed today.
4. The Thorntons did go on a trip yesterday.
5. Your parents do teach you many important things.
6. I do appreciate the help that they have given me.

C. 1. present, emphatic
2. past perfect
3. present perfect, progressive
4. future
5. past, progressive
6. present perfect
7. past, emphatic
8. future perfect, progressive

D.   **Speak**

Person	Singular	Plural
Present Tense, Progressive Form		
First:	I am speaking.	We are speaking.
Second:	You are speaking.	You are speaking.
Third:	He is speaking.	They are speaking.
Past Tense, Progressive Form		
First:	I was speaking.	We were speaking.
Second:	You were speaking.	You were speaking.
Third:	He was speaking.	They were speaking.
Future Tense, Progressive Form		
First:	I shall be speaking.	We shall be speaking.
Second:	You will be speaking.	You will be speaking.
Third:	He will be speaking.	They will be speaking.
Present Perfect Tense, Progressive Form		
First:	I have been speaking.	We have been speaking.
Second:	You have been speaking.	You have been speaking.
Third:	He has been speaking.	They have been speaking.
Past Perfect Tense, Progressive Form		
First:	I had been speaking.	We had been speaking.
Second:	You had been speaking.	You had been speaking.
Third:	He had been speaking.	They had been speaking.
Future Perfect Tense, Progressive Form		
First:	I shall have been speaking.	We shall have been speaking.
Second:	You will have been speaking.	You will have been speaking.
Third:	He will have been speaking.	They will have been speaking.

E.   **Speak**

Person	Singular	Plural
Present Tense, Emphatic Form		
First:	I do speak.	We do speak.
Second:	You do speak.	You do speak.
Third:	He does speak.	They do speak.
Past Tense, Emphatic Form		
First:	I did speak.	We did speak.
Second:	You did speak.	You did speak.
Third:	He did speak.	They did speak.

Written Exercises
A. 1. is interceding
2. was speaking
3. have been helping
4. had been melting
5. shall be singing
6. had been rising
7. was going
8. had been cutting
9. will have been stacking
10. have been burning

(Part B is on page 186.)

C. Write the tense of each verb. Also write *progressive* or *emphatic* if the verb is in one of those forms.
1. The corn is growing rapidly.
2. Plentiful rain and fertile soil do make a difference.
3. Mr. White had been raising hay in that field earlier.
4. He did allow it to lie fallow last year.
5. He was cultivating the corn a few weeks ago.
6. Now it has grown too tall to be cultivated.
7. Soon he will be putting some corn into his silos.
8. He will have harvested all the corn before winter.

D. Conjugate the verb *come* in the progressive form of all six tenses.

E. Conjugate the verb *come* in the emphatic form of the present and past tenses.

Review Exercises

A. Write the second and third principal parts of these verbs. Include the helping verb *have* with the past participle. [34]
1. weep
2. tag
3. go
4. break
5. drink
6. lie
7. set
8. tear

B. Write the correct form of each underlined verb. If the underlined verb is correct, write *correct*. [34]
1. The creek is <u>froze</u> hard enough to walk on.
2. Yesterday I <u>run</u> an errand for Mother.
3. Father told us that Cluck and her baby chicks <u>drownded</u> in the flood.
4. Have you <u>seen</u> what the little children are doing?
5. You <u>swang</u> last; now it's Noah's turn.
6. Have you <u>went</u> to visit your new neighbors?
7. One of Mother's new dishes is <u>broke</u>.
8. The dog <u>dragged</u> a dead rabbit into the yard.
9. Father decided that the bicycle <u>costed</u> too much.
10. Nobody else had <u>tooken</u> the piece with the shiny wrapper, so I did.

B. 1. did bring
2. does work
3. do serve
4. does bring
5. did stir
6. do seek

C. 1. present, progressive
2. present, emphatic
3. past perfect, progressive
4. past, emphatic
5. past, progressive
6. present perfect
7. future, progressive
8. future perfect

D.

Come

Person	Singular	Plural
Present Tense, Progressive Form		
First:	I am coming.	We are coming.
Second:	You are coming.	You are coming.
Third:	He is coming.	They are coming.
Past Tense, Progressive Form		
First:	I was coming.	We were coming.
Second:	You were coming.	You were coming.
Third:	He was coming.	They were coming.
Future Tense, Progressive Form		
First:	I shall be coming.	We shall be coming.
Second:	You will be coming.	You will be coming.
Third:	He will be coming.	They will be coming.
Present Perfect Tense, Progressive Form		
First:	I have been coming.	We have been coming.
Second:	You have been coming.	You have been coming.
Third:	He has been coming.	They have been coming.
Past Perfect Tense, Progressive Form		
First:	I had been coming.	We had been coming.
Second:	You had been coming.	You had been coming.
Third:	He had been coming.	They had been coming.
Future Perfect Tense, Progressive Form		
First:	I shall have been coming.	We shall have been coming.
Second:	You will have been coming.	You will have been coming.
Third:	He will have been coming.	They will have been coming.

Past Tense, Emphatic Form

First:	I did come.	We did come.
Second:	You did come.	You did come.
Third:	He did come.	They did come.

Review Exercises

A. 1. wept, (have) wept
2. tagged, (have) tagged
3. went, (have) gone
4. broke, (have) broken
5. drank, (have) drunk
6. lay, (have) lain
7. set, (have) set
8. tore, (have) torn

B. 1. frozen
2. ran
3. drowned
4. correct
5. swung
6. gone
7. broken
8. correct
9. cost
10. taken

E.

Come

Person	Singular	Plural
Present Tense, Emphatic Form		
First:	I do come.	We do come.
Second:	You do come.	You do come.
Third:	He does come.	They do come.

40. Outlining Written Material

> **Lesson Survey**
> - Outlining is a good study aid.
> - The first step in outlining written material is to pick out the main ideas.
> - The second step in outlining written material is to fill in the subtopics and the details at other levels.

You saw in Lesson 36 that an outline is an orderly summary of a composition. It shows the organization of the main ideas as well as the lesser ideas. Having that organization put into the brief form of an outline helps one to see how the various parts of the composition are related to each other.

Outlining is a good study aid. It helps the reader understand what he is reading because it forces him to analyze the material carefully. He must identify the main ideas as well as the lesser ideas. The value of the outline continues indefinitely. For one thing, the work of making the outline helps the reader to remember what he has read. And later, since the outline is a summary of the written material, it helps him to recall the main ideas when he wants to review the material.

The first step in outlining written material is to pick out the main ideas. In a short composition, each topic on the outline generally corresponds to a paragraph. In a longer composition, each topic on the outline may extend over several paragraphs. In that case, the subtopics should correspond to the paragraph divisions.

After you have worked out the main topics of the outline, the second step is to fill in the subtopics and the details at other levels.

Read this short composition. Pay special attention to the topic sentences, which will give you the main topics.

Investigating Indonesia

Do you know where Indonesia is located? The Republic of Indonesia lies along the equator southeast of Asia. Its 13,600 islands stretch from the Indian Ocean on the west to the Pacific Ocean on the east. To its north is Malaysia, and to its south is Australia.

Among the nations of the world, Indonesia ranks fifth in population. The people are concentrated on the island of Java, where more than three-fifths of the Indonesians live. Three of its four largest cities

Lesson 40

Purpose: To teach how to write an outline of written material.

Oral Review:
1. What is an outline? (an orderly summary of a composition)
2. a. What are the two kinds of outlines? (topical outlines, sentence outlines)
   b. What is the difference between these two kinds of outlines? (A topical outline has words or brief phrases to express each idea. A sentence outline has complete sentences to express each idea.)
3. Complete these statements of outlining rules.
   a. If an item is divided, there must be ———. (at least two parts)
   b. The title is ——— above the outline. (centered)
   c. Each line begins with a ———. (capital letter)
   d. On a sentence outline, each sentence ends with ———. (a period)
   e. Each level is indented ———. (equally)
   f. At each level of a topical outline, the form of the items is as nearly ——— as possible. (parallel)
   g. An outline should be either all ———. (sentences or all topics)
   h. For main topics, subtopics, points, and subpoints, the numerals and letters should be ———. (followed by periods)
   i. For details, the numerals and letters should be ———. (placed within parentheses)

Lesson Introduction: George would like to be a carpenter, and he thinks he is well on the way. He can identify a claw hammer, a tape measure, a planer, a router, and a miter saw. But George has

are on this island. On Java the population density is over seventeen hundred persons per square mile. Indonesia is a heavily populated nation.

What kind of land does Indonesia have? A belt of tropical rain forest stretches across the more northerly islands, and there are grasslands in the east. But much of Indonesia is mountainous, with a number of peaks more than ten thousand feet above sea level. Among the mountains are sixty active volcanoes, making this the most active volcanic region in the world.

Indonesia has a variety of natural resources even though it is a rather poor country. Over half of Indonesia's workers are employed in agriculture. Less than 10 percent of the land is cultivated, yet much of that land has soil made fertile by volcanic ash. Among the chief export crops are rubber, tea, coffee, sugar, and spices. Important mineral resources are also found in Indonesia. The country produces so much oil that this is its most valuable export. Nickel, tin, bauxite, coal, and copper are some of the other minerals from Indonesia.

Did you recognize the topic sentence in each paragraph above? It is the first sentence in paragraphs 1, 3, and 4, and the last sentence in paragraph 2. With this information, we are ready to write the main topics of an outline.

Investigating Indonesia
    I. The location
   II. The population
  III. The land
  IV. The natural resources

Now that the main topics are outlined, we are ready to fill in the details. The outline for the first three paragraphs appears below. You will do paragraph 4 in Class Practice.

Investigating Indonesia
  I. The location
    A. Lies along the equator southeast of Asia
    B. Stretches from the Indian Ocean to the Pacific Ocean
    C. Lies between Malaysia and Australia
  II. The population
    A. Ranks fifth among world nations
    B. Is concentrated on the island of Java
      1. Has three-fifths of the population
      2. Includes three of the four largest cities
      3. Has population density of over 1,700 persons per square mile

never actually used any of these tools. Would you hire him to build something for you?

Outlines are a bit like these carpenter tools. You have learned about their correct form, but that does not make you skilled at using them in speaking and writing. This lesson gives direction for one of the main uses of outlines—as an aid in studying written material.

Lesson Outline:
  1. Outlining is a good study aid.
    a. It forces the reader to analyze what he is reading.
    b. It helps the reader to remember what he has read.
    c. It serves as a useful summary for reviewing material.

  2. The first step in outlining written material is to pick out the main ideas.
    a. In short compositions, each topic on the outline generally corresponds to a paragraph.
    b. In longer compositions, topics may extend over several paragraphs and the subtopics should correspond to the paragraph divisions.

  3. The second step in outlining written material is to fill in the subtopics and the details at other levels.

★ **EXTRA PRACTICE**
Worksheet 21 (*Outlining Written Material*)

III. The land
  A. Tropical forests in northerly islands
  B. Grasslands in the east
  C. Mountains over much of the islands
    1. A number of peaks over 10,000 feet above sea level
    2. Sixty active volcanoes, making this the most active volcanic region of the world

Class Practice

Finish the outline "Investigating Indonesia."

Written Exercises

Outline this composition.

The Roots of Plants

Although you may not often see the roots, they are very important to the life of a plant. Root systems are of two kinds: the taproot system and the fibrous root system. A taproot system is composed of one main root with few smaller branches. The taproot can reach deep into the soil below the water table. A fibrous root system branches out into a tangled mass of roots. This mass holds the soil together quite well.

Roots grow both in length and in diameter. Three different regions are involved in the lengthening of a root. The first step occurs in the cell-forming region, located at the very tip of the root. New cells are produced there in a process called cell division. The second step occurs in the cell-growing region, located just above the cell-forming region. Here root length is increased as individual cells grow. The third step occurs in the cell-maturing region, above the cell-growing region, where the full-grown cells develop into functioning cells. Growth in diameter takes place only in mature roots, and it occurs as new layers of cells are formed in the center of the roots. This growth accounts for the large size of tree roots.

Roots serve a number of functions for the plant. Probably the most obvious function is absorbing water. The water is drawn from the soil into the root hairs, where it first fills the outer cells. Then the water moves into the center of the root, and from there it goes to the rest of the plant. The roots also anchor the plant. It is attached to the soil by the root hairs. Some plants are further supported by prop roots growing from the stem into the ground. Another function of the roots is storing food. This occurs to a small degree in almost all plants, but it is most obvious in plants that live for more than one season.

III. The function of roots
  A. Absorbing water
    1. Drawn from soil into outer cells of root hairs
    2. Moves into center of root
    3. Goes to rest of plant
  B. Anchoring the plant
    1. Attached to soil by root hairs
    2. May be further supported by prop roots
  C. Storing food
    1. Occurs to small degree in almost all plants
    2. Is most obvious in plants that live more than one season

Lesson 40 Answers

Class Practice

IV. The natural resources
  A. Agricultural resources
    1. Over half the workers employed in agriculture
    2. Less than 10 percent of the land cultivated
    3. Chief export crops: rubber, tea, coffee, sugar, spices
  B. Mineral resources
    1. Oil, the most valuable export
    2. Nickel, tin, bauxite, coal, copper

Written Exercises

(Sample outline.)

The Roots of Plants

I. The kinds of root systems
  A. Taproot system
    1. Is composed of one main root with few smaller branches
    2. Can reach deep into soil below the water table
  B. Fibrous root system
    1. Branches into tangled mass of roots
    2. Holds soil together quite well
II. The growth of roots
  A. In length
    1. The cell-forming region
      a. Location is tip of root
      b. New cells produced by cell division
    2. The cell-growing region
      a. Location is just above cell-forming region
      b. Root length increased as individual cells grow
    3. The cell-maturing region
      a. Location is above cell-growing region
      b. Full-grown cells develop into functioning cells
  B. In diameter
    1. Takes place only in mature roots
    2. Occurs as new layers of cells are formed in center of roots
    3. Accounts for large size of tree roots

41. Transitive Verbs

> ### Lesson Survey
> - A **transitive verb** passes its action to a noun or pronoun in the sentence.
> - A transitive verb usually passes its action to a direct object.
> - A transitive verb with a direct object may also have an indirect object.
> - A transitive verb may pass its action back to the subject.

Most English verbs are action verbs like *reward, reveal,* and *fulfill.* Many of these verbs must pass their action to some noun or pronoun; they do not express a complete thought by themselves.

> God always <u>rewards</u>. (incomplete thought)
> God always <u>rewards</u> the faithful *saints.* (complete thought)
>
> God <u>has revealed</u>. (incomplete thought)
> God <u>has revealed</u> His *will* to man. (complete thought)

A *transitive verb* passes its action to a noun or pronoun in the sentence. *Transitive* means "passing over." Look at the second sentence in each pair above. God rewards whom or what? The action of *rewards* is passed to *saints.* God has revealed whom or what? The action of *has revealed* is passed to *will.*

The action of a transitive verb may be passed to either of two different sentence parts.

The Direct Object as the Receiver

A transitive verb usually passes its action to a direct object. In a sentence with a direct object, the subject performs the action and the direct object receives the action. You can find a direct object by saying the skeleton and asking *whom* or *what* after it. The direct object is diagramed on the horizontal line after the skeleton, separated from the verb by a vertical line.

> Abraham carefully obeyed the Lord of all the earth.
>   (<u>Abraham</u> <u>obeyed</u> whom? The Lord. The subject *Abraham* did the action of obeying; the direct object *Lord* received the action of obeying.)

Abraham	obeyed	Lord

Lesson 41

Purpose: To teach that transitive verbs always pass action to a noun or pronoun in the sentence.

Oral Review:

1. What does the progressive form of a verb show? (continuing action or condition)
2. Emphatic verb forms give ———. (added emphasis)
3. What helping verb is always used in the progressive verb forms? (a form of *be*)
4. What helping verb is always used in the emphatic verb forms? (do, does, *or* did)
5. Name the six verb tenses. (present, past, future, present perfect, past perfect, future perfect)
6. Name the kind of sentence described by each phrase, and tell what kind of end punctuation that sentence requires.

   a. Makes a statement. (declarative; period)
   b. Expresses strong feeling or emotion. (exclamatory; exclamation point)
   c. Asks a question. (interrogative; question mark)
   d. Gives a command or request. (imperative; period)

Lesson Introduction: The English prefix *trans-* means "over" or "across." When we *transplant* tomatoes, we take the small plants and *plant* them *over* into a garden plot. When something is *transformed,* its *form* is changed *over* to something different. A *transcontinental* railroad goes *across* the *continent* from one end to the other. And a *transitive* verb passes its action *over* or *across* to some noun or pronoun.

Lesson Outline:

1. A transitive verb passes its action to a noun or pronoun in the sentence.

God blessed Abraham for his faithful obedience.
　　(God blessed whom? Abraham. The subject *God* did the action of
　　　blessing; the direct object *Abraham* received the action of
　　　blessing.)

A verb may have a compound direct object, and a subject may have a
compound verb with a direct object for each verb.

God led Abraham and Sarah for many years.
　　(The subject *God* did the action of leading; the compound direct
　　　object *Abraham* and *Sarah* received the action of leading.)

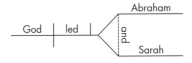

Lot chose the well-watered plains and pitched his tent toward Sodom.
　　(The subject *Lot* did the actions of choosing and pitching; the
　　　direct object *plains* received the action of choosing, and the
　　　direct object *tent* received the action of pitching.)

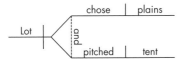

A transitive verb with a direct object may also have an indirect object.
Many sentences have a direct object without an indirect object. But no sentence can have an indirect object without also having a direct object.

An indirect object comes between the verb and the direct object. To find
an indirect object, say the skeleton and the direct object. Then ask *to whom
or what* or *for whom or what.*

Father gave the boys a list of chores.
　　(Say: Father gave list. Ask: Father gave list *to whom*? The indi-
　　　rect object is *boys.*)
The girls made Father and Mother a special gift.
　　(Say: Girls made gift. Ask: Girls made gift *for whom*? The com-
　　　pound indirect object is *Father* and *Mother.*)

**2. A transitive verb usually passes its action
to a direct object.**

　　a. The subject performs the action, and the
　　　direct object receives the action.

　　b. Find a direct object by saying the skeleton
　　　and asking *whom* or *what* after it.

　　c. A verb may have a compound direct object,
　　　and a subject may have a compound verb
　　　with a direct object for each verb.

　　d. A direct object is diagramed on the hori-
　　　zontal line after the skeleton, separated
　　　from the verb by a vertical line.

**3. A transitive verb with a direct object may
also have an indirect object.**

　　a. An indirect object comes between the verb
　　　and the direct object.

　　b. To find an indirect object, say the skeleton
　　　and the direct object. Then ask *to whom or
　　　what* or *for whom or what.*

　　c. An indirect object is diagramed on a hori-
　　　zontal line beneath the base line, connected
　　　to the verb by a slanted line.

**4. A transitive verb may pass its action back
to the subject.** When the subject receives the action, the main verb must be the past participle, and
a form of *be* must be used as a helping verb.

★ EXTRA PRACTICE
Worksheet 22 (*Transitive Verbs*)

Now compare the following two sentences.

Mother prepared her <u>family</u> a delicious meal.
Mother prepared a delicious meal for her <u>family</u>.

These sentences mean exactly the same, but *family* is an indirect object in only the first one. In the second sentence, *family* is the object of the preposition *for*. Remember: An indirect object comes between the verb and the direct object, and it is never the object of a preposition.

An indirect object is diagramed on a horizontal line beneath the base line. A slanted line connects the indirect object to the verb. The examples above are diagramed here.

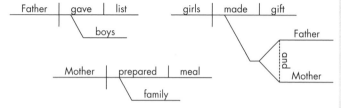

The Subject as the Receiver

A transitive verb may pass its action back to the subject of the sentence. In each pair of sentences below, the same word receives the action of the same verb. But notice how the receiver shifts from the direct object to the subject.

Duane cleaned the calf <u>hutches</u>.
The calf <u>hutches</u> were cleaned by Duane.
  (In both sentences, Duane performed the action of cleaning, and
    the hutches received the action of cleaning.)

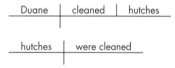

Rover has brought the <u>cow</u> home.
The <u>cow</u> has been brought home by Rover.
  (In both sentences, Rover performed the action of bringing, and
    the cow received the action of bringing.)

| Rover | brought | cow | | cow | has been brought |

Look again at the second sentence in each pair on page 192. Notice how the verb changes when the receiver of the action shifts from the direct object to the subject. When the subject receives the action, the main verb must be the past participle, and a form of *be* must be used as a helping verb.

hutches | were cleaned
cow | has been brought

Class Practice

A. Read each verb, and tell which word receives the action of the main verb. Tell whether the receiver is the *subject* or the *direct object*.
1. These houses were built by Brother Alvin's carpenter crew.
2. The masons carefully laid the blocks.
3. The intermediate class was taught by Brother Wilbur.
4. The cat was chased up the tree by Shep.
5. The trucks have dumped gravel in the driveway.
6. The Lord has revealed His will to us.
7. Because of the heavy snowstorm, the service has been canceled.
8. The Bible shows us the path of life.

B. Read the skeleton and the direct object in each sentence. If there is an indirect object, read it last.
1. The girls are crocheting baby sweaters.
2. The boys are making some beautiful wooden lamps.
3. Roger is giving Skippy some lessons in obedience.
4. Sister Verna made pies and cookies for the cleanup crew.
5. The men cleaned away the branches and repaired the barn roof.
6. Marcus told him and me an interesting story.

C. On the chalkboard, diagram the skeletons, direct objects, and indirect objects of the sentences in Part B above.

Written Exercises

A. Write the verbs, direct objects, and indirect objects. Label the direct objects *DO* and the indirect objects *IO*.
1. God gives us strength for each temptation.
2. We must resist the devil.
3. Satan tells people many lies.
4. Mother baked some muffins and fried some eggs for breakfast.
5. Kevin drove the tractor for Father.
6. Aunt Kathryn will make Susan and her a quilt.
7. The children played checkers and Scrabble.
8. The queen of Sheba asked Solomon many hard questions.

Lesson 41 Answers

Class Practice

A. 1. were built; houses—subject
2. laid; blocks—direct object
3. was taught; class—subject
4. was chased; cat—subject
5. have dumped; gravel—direct object
6. has revealed; will—direct object
7. has been canceled; service—subject
8. shows; path—direct object

B. 1. girls are crocheting sweaters
2. boys are making lamps
3. Roger is giving lessons;
   Skippy—indirect object
4. Sister Verna made pies (and) cookies
5. men cleaned branches (and) repaired roof
6. Marcus told story;
   him (and) me—indirect object

C.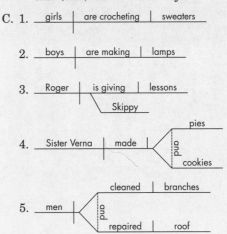

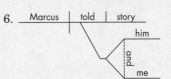

Written Exercises

A. 1. gives, us—IO; strength—DO
2. must resist, devil—DO
3. tells, people—IO; lies—DO
4. baked, muffins—DO; fried, eggs—DO
5. drove, tractor—DO
6. will make, Susan—IO; her—IO; quilt—DO
7. played, checkers—DO; Scrabble—DO
8. asked, Solomon—IO; questions—DO

B. Write the verb and the word that receives the action of the main verb. Label the receiver as *subject* or *direct object*.
1. The accident seriously injured the young man.
2. The students learned their English lesson quite well.
3. All were rewarded with satisfaction.
4. The boys were found in the library with Brother Samuel.
5. The Lord is fulfilling His promises.

C. Diagram the skeletons, direct objects, and indirect objects of these sentences.
1. This book was written by my grandmother.
2. Mr. Carson sold Father and Uncle Floyd some hay.
3. The hunters tracked the wolves and killed two of them.
4. The letter was translated by Johann Goetz.
5. Marie has written many poems and stories.
6. Uncle Galen's gave the orphans a good home.

Review Exercises Orally

A. Label each sentence *declarative, interrogative, imperative,* or *exclamatory.* Also write the last word of the sentence and the correct end punctuation. [10]
1. Iowa is in the Midwest
2. Are there many mountains in Iowa
3. No; Iowa lies mostly in the plains
4. Look at this relief map
5. In 1912 a temperature of -47° was recorded, and in 1934 a temperature of 118° was recorded
6. What a vast range of temperature that is
7. Find some information about the wildlife in Iowa
8. Do you know anyone who lives there

B. Diagram the skeletons and complements of these sentences. [5, 6]
1. Our family took an evening walk through the woods.
2. Father, see this flower.
3. It is a lovely yellow flower.
4. What delicate petals it has!
5. Over here are some more flowers like it.
6. How sweet they smell!
7. May we pick a bouquet?
8. Pick a few for Grandmother's room.

B. 1. injured; man—direct object
2. learned; lesson—direct object
3. were rewarded; All—subject
4. were found; boys—subject
5. is fulfilling; promises—direct object

C. 1. book | was written

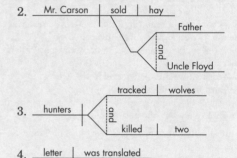

2. Mr. Carson | sold | hay — Father *and* Uncle Floyd

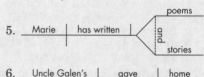

3. hunters | tracked | wolves *and* killed | two

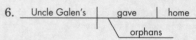

4. letter | was translated

5. Marie | has written | poems *and* stories

6. Uncle Galen's | gave | home / orphans

Review Exercises

A. 1. declarative; Midwest.
2. interrogative; Iowa?
3. declarative; plains.
4. imperative; map.
5. declarative; recorded.
6. exclamatory; is!
7. imperative; Iowa.
8. interrogative; there?

B. 1. family | took | walk
2. (you) | see | flower
3. It | is \ flower
4. it | has | petals
5. flowers | are
6. they | smell \ sweet
7. we | May pick | bouquet
8. (you) | Pick | few

42. Intransitive Complete Verbs

Lesson Survey

- An **intransitive complete verb** does not pass action to any receiver, but is complete in itself.
- Some verbs may be either transitive or intransitive complete, depending on their use in a sentence.

In Lesson 41 you worked with action verbs that pass their action to a direct object or to the subject of a sentence. However, not all action verbs are transitive. An *intransitive complete verb* does not pass action to any receiver, but is complete in itself.

> We bought several young calves.
> > (*We* performed the action of buying; *calves* received the action of buying; the verb is transitive.)
> The cat was walking through the tall grass.
> > (*Cat* performed the action of walking; nothing received the action of walking; the verb is intransitive complete.)

Many verbs that express the position or movement of the subject are intransitive complete verbs.

> The eagles <u>soared</u> through the air.
> > (Nothing receives the action of soaring.)
> A cheetah <u>can run</u> very fast.
> > (Nothing receives the action of running.)
> Our cat often <u>lies</u> on the front step.
> > (Nothing receives the action of lying.)

A sentence with an intransitive complete verb may contain modifiers that tell *how, when, where,* or *why.* Such words do not receive the action of the verb and are not necessary to complete the meaning of the verb.

> Clair waited patiently for his friend.

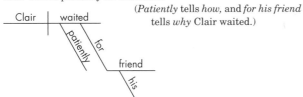

> (*Patiently* tells *how,* and *for his friend* tells *why* Clair waited.)

Lesson 42

Purpose: To teach *intransitive verbs that are complete in themselves. (*Previous experience:* Term *transitive* but not *intransitive.*)

Oral Review:

1. What does *transitive* mean? (passing over)
2. A transitive verb may pass its action to either of what two sentence parts? (subject, direct object)
3. Answer the following questions about a transitive verb that passes action back to the subject.
   a. What is the form of the main verb? (past participle)
   b. What kind of helping verb is used? (a form of *be*)
4. Tell which word receives the action of the transitive verb, and tell whether it is the subject or the direct object. (Words that receive the action are underlined.)
   a. The princes cast <u>Jeremiah</u> into a dungeon. (direct object)
   b. Ebed-melech heard the distressing <u>news</u>. (direct object)
   c. <u>Jeremiah</u> was drawn out of the dungeon by cords. (subject)
   d. <u>Ebed-melech</u> was blessed for his kindness to Jeremiah. (subject)
5. Name the six verb tenses. (present, past, future, present perfect, past perfect, future perfect)
6. Name the helping verbs for each of the perfect tenses. (present perfect—have *or* has; past perfect—had; future perfect—shall have *or* will have)
7. When a sentence refers to two past actions, which one is often expressed in the past perfect tense? (the action that occurred first)

A solitary steer stood by the road.

(*By the road* tells *where* a steer stood.)

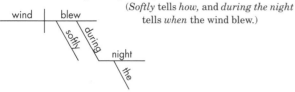

The wind blew softly during the night.

(*Softly* tells *how,* and *during the night* tells *when* the wind blew.)

With some intransitive complete verbs, it almost seems as if the subject receives the action when, actually, the subject is doing the action. The subject receives the action only if there is a past participle as the main verb and a form of *be* as the helping verb.

The window broke with a crash.
> (*Window* did the breaking; the verb is the past form with no form of *be* as the helping verb; the verb is intransitive complete.)

The window was broken by the softball.
> (*Softball* did the breaking; *window* received the action of breaking; the verb is transitive.)

The house shook during the earthquake.
> (*House* did the shaking; the verb is the past form with no form of *be* as the helping verb; the verb is intransitive complete.)

The house was shaken by the earthquake.
> (*Earthquake* did the shaking; *house* received the action of shaking; the verb is transitive.)

Some verbs may be either transitive or intransitive complete, depending on their use in a sentence.

The teacher <u>rang</u> the *bell*.
> (The action of ringing is passed to *bell;* the verb is transitive.)

8. When a sentence refers to two future actions, which one is often expressed in the future perfect tense? (the action that comes first)
9. What helping verbs are used in progressive verb forms? (forms of *be*)
10. What helping verbs are used in emphatic verb forms? (do, does, did)

Lesson Introduction: In the previous lesson, the students saw that *transitive* means "passing over." Now ask them what the prefix *in-* means. They should know that one meaning is "not." Point out that the term *intransitive complete* emphasizes the two main facts about these verbs: first, they do not pass action to any receiver; and second, they are complete in themselves.

Lesson Outline:

1. An intransitive complete verb does not pass action to any receiver, but is complete in itself.

a. Many verbs that express the position or movement of the subject are intransitive complete verbs.

b. A sentence with an intransitive complete verb may contain modifiers that tell *how, when, where,* or *why.*

c. With some intransitive complete verbs, it almost seems as if the subject receives the action when, actually, the subject is doing the action. The subject receives the action only if there is a past participle as the main verb and a form of *be* as the helping verb.

2. Some verbs may be either transitive or intransitive complete, depending on their use in a sentence.

★ *EXTRA PRACTICE*
Worksheet 23 (*Intransitive Complete Verbs*)

The bell <u>rang</u> loudly.

(*Bell* did the ringing; *loudly* modifies *rang* by telling *how;* no action is passed; the verb is intransitive complete.)

We <u>sang</u> a *hymn* after prayer.

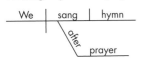

(The action of singing is passed to *hymn;* the verb is transitive.)

We <u>sang</u> fervently.

(*We* did the singing; *fervently* modifies *sang* by telling *how;* no action is passed; the verb is intransitive complete.)

Class Practice

A. Read the verbs in these sentences, and tell if each is *transitive* or *intransitive complete.* If it is transitive, tell what word receives the action.
1. Lester saw through the puzzle.
2. Lester saw the solution to the puzzle.
3. The cat can climb into the tree.
4. Every tree in our back yard has been climbed by the boys.
5. Doris turned her chair toward her teacher.
6. Everyone turned toward the strange noise.
7. This note was slid under the door by our neighbor.
8. Calvin slid on the icy walk.

B. Make up two sentences for each verb. Use it as a transitive verb in the first sentence and as an intransitive complete verb in the second sentence.
1. spoke   2. has blown   3. read

C. On the chalkboard, diagram the skeletons, complements, and verb modifiers of these sentences.
1. Red flames danced along the rooftop.
2. Billowy clouds were blown across the blue sky.
3. A green beetle scurried into the crack.
4. The spider caught a large mosquito.

Teacher: Intransitive complete verbs usually express action. But they may also express existence (with forms of *be*) and be complete in themselves.

God *is*.

The children *were* in school.

Lesson 42 Answers

Class Practice

A. 1. saw—intransitive complete
2. saw—transitive, solution
3. can climb—intransitive complete
4. has been climbed—transitive, tree
5. turned—transitive, chair
6. turned—intransitive complete
7. was slid—transitive, note
8. slid—intransitive complete

B. (Sample answers.)
1. Naomi spoke those words.
Naomi spoke in a soft voice.
2. The engineer has blown the whistle.
The whistle has blown to warn oncoming motorists.
3. Patricia read the story to the children.
Patricia read for a while.

C.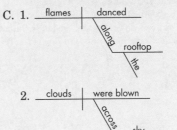

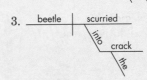

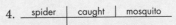

5. Large snowflakes drifted against our faces.
6. Our little boat floated down the narrow ditch.

Written Exercises

A. Copy the verb in each sentence, and label it *T* for transitive or *IC* for intransitive complete. If it is transitive, write the word that receives the action of the main verb.
1. The stones for the temple were laid with care.
2. Who went with Jesus to Gethsemane?
3. David lived at Bethlehem for many years.
4. In obedience to God, Noah built the ark.
5. Abigail gave good advice to David.
6. The trumpet sounded clearly over the valley.
7. Our entire class read the poem in unison.
8. The train is coming into the station now.
9. The house was rebuilt by willing men.
10. Many geese flew toward the south.

B. Write two sentences for each verb. Use it as a transitive verb in the first sentence and as an intransitive complete verb in the second sentence.
1. will leap   3. has bounced
2. hurried   4. bit

C. Diagram the skeletons, complements, and verb modifiers of these sentences.
1. The baby cried loudly for his mother.
2. We watched the meteor shower.
3. Samuel was walking across the rope bridge.
4. Many grapes are grown in our neighborhood.
5. Mother brought us a dish of vegetable stew.
6. The family of ducks waddled slowly across the road.

Review Exercises

A. Copy the verb in each main clause, and label its tense. [35, 37]
1. The geese have migrated south for the winter.
2. The leaves fall every day.
3. Will the first frost strike soon?
4. Before summer was over, we had tired of the hot, humid weather.
5. Last night was a cool, refreshing night.
6. We were glad for a good night of rest.
7. Before the winter is over, we shall have tired of the numbing cold.
8. The Lord has promised the continual changing of the seasons.

Review Exercises

A. 1. have migrated—present perfect
2. fall—present
3. Will strike—future
4. had tired—past perfect
5. was—past
6. were—past
7. shall have tired—future perfect
8. has promised—present perfect

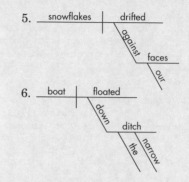

Written Exercises

A. 1. were laid—T, stones   6. sounded—IC
2. went—IC   7. read—T, poem
3. lived—IC   8. is coming—IC
4. built—T, ark   9. was rebuilt—T, house
5. gave—T, advice   10. flew—IC

B. (Sample answers.)
1. The deer will leap the fence gracefully.
   The deer will leap into the forest.
2. Father hurried the children with their chores.
   Father hurried into the house.
3. Darwin has bounced the ball to Joseph.
   The ball has bounced into the road.
4. I bit off a piece of the apple.
   I bit into the apple.

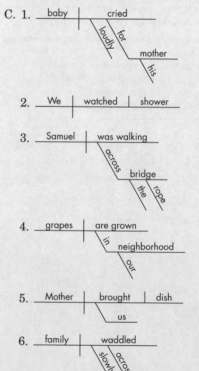

B. For each sentence, write one verb in a perfect tense to show a clearer relationship. [38]
1. Pilate asked the Jews what evil Jesus did.
2. By the time the Reinfords leave, they will help us with many jobs.
3. The guests arrived, and now we must serve dinner.
4. When Janet washed the last dirty kettle, she sat down to rest.

C. Copy each verb, and name its tense. Also write *progressive* or *emphatic* if the verb is in one of those forms. [35–39]
1. God did create the world in six days.
2. Many scientists in the world are denying the existence of God.
3. However, a number of scientists do believe in a Creator.
4. We have not doubted the Word of the Lord.
5. Long before recent times, God had already been giving clear evidence of His eternal power.

B. 1. had done
2. will have helped
3. have arrived
4. had washed

C. 1. did create—past, emphatic
2. are denying—present, progressive
3. do believe—present, emphatic
4. have doubted—present perfect
5. had been giving—past perfect, progressive

43. Intransitive Linking Verbs

Lesson Survey
- An **intransitive linking verb** expresses a condition or state of being. It has no action to pass to a receiver.
- An intransitive linking verb may link the subject to a predicate nominative or a predicate adjective.
- A linking verb followed by an adjective must not be confused with an action verb followed by a direct object or an adverb.

In the last two lessons, you have studied transitive verbs and intransitive complete verbs. The verbs you studied in those lessons are action verbs. As you know, however, not all verbs express action.

An *intransitive linking verb* expresses a condition or state of being; therefore, it has no action to pass to a receiver. The following pairs of sentences show the difference between action verbs and intransitive linking verbs.

Brother Jerry <u>teaches</u> the intermediate class.
    (*Teaches* expresses action; Brother Jerry *does* something.)
Brother Jerry <u>is</u> my Sunday school teacher.
    (*Is* expresses condition; Brother Jerry *is* something.)

Lesson 43

Purpose: To teach *intransitive linking verbs, predicate nominatives, and predicate adjectives. (*Previous experience:* Linking verbs, without using the term *intransitive linking.*)

Oral Review:
1. What does *transitive* mean? (passing over)
2. A transitive verb may pass its action to either of what two sentence parts? (subject, direct object)
3. The past participle and a form of *be* are used when a transitive verb passes action to the ———. (subject)
4. If an action verb does not pass action to the subject or the direct object, it is ———. (intransitive complete)
5. A sentence that has only one clause is a ——— sentence. (simple)
6. A sentence that has one independent clause and one or more dependent clauses is a ——— sentence. (complex)
7. The dependent clause in a complex sentence may be used as what three parts of speech? (adjective, adverb, noun)
8. A sentence that has two independent clauses is a ——— sentence. (compound)
9. Tell whether the following sentences are simple, compound, or complex.
   a. The Lord, who is our heavenly Father, is gracious. (complex)
   b. He understands us perfectly, and He is able to meet our needs. (compound)
   c. We give Him glory and serve Him willingly. (simple)
   d. We know that He will come again. (complex)

Anita <u>has been writing</u> good poetry.
> (*Has been writing* expresses action; Anita has been *doing* something.)

Anita <u>has been</u> a good poet.
> (*Has been* expresses condition; Anita has *been* something.)

An intransitive linking verb may link the subject to a predicate nominative, which is a noun or pronoun in the predicate that renames the subject. Since the subject and the predicate nominative name the same person or thing, the linking verb can be considered an equal sign. The subject equals the predicate nominative. Forms of the verb *be* (*am, is, are, was, were, be, been, being*) are the most common linking verbs.

God <u>will be</u> the ultimate *victor.*
> (*Victor* renames *God;* <u>God</u> = <u>victor</u>.)

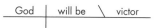

The eternal <u>King</u> <u>is</u> *He.*
> (*He* renames *King;* <u>King</u> = <u>He</u>.)

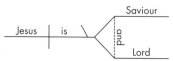

<u>Jesus</u> <u>is</u> *Saviour* and *Lord.*
> (*Saviour* and *Lord* rename *Jesus;* <u>Jesus</u> = <u>Saviour</u> and <u>Lord</u>.)

An intransitive linking verb may also link the subject to a predicate adjective. A predicate adjective is an adjective in the predicate that modifies the subject. These adjectives follow not only forms of *be* but also verbs of sense (*taste, feel, smell, sound, look, appear*) and other linking verbs (*grow, seem, stay, become, remain*).

Since the predicate adjective modifies the subject, it is usually sensible to say the adjective before the subject. This is one way to identify predicate adjectives.

The <u>clouds</u> <u>were</u> *beautiful.*
> (*Beautiful* modifies *clouds:* <u>beautiful clouds</u>.)

Lesson Introduction: Write the following phrases on the board.

> Solomon the king
> Wise Solomon

Ask the students what basic sentence part is missing. (the verb) Have them make a complete sentence from each phrase by adding only a verb.

> Solomon was the king.
> Solomon was wise.

The verbs that are added serve simply to link the sentence parts together. They are intransitive linking verbs.

Lesson Outline:

1. An intransitive linking verb expresses a condition or state of being.
   a. It has no action to pass to a receiver.

   b. The most common linking verbs are forms of *be.*

2. An intransitive linking verb may link the subject to a predicate nominative.
   a. The predicate nominative is a noun or pronoun in the predicate that renames the subject.
   b. The linking verb can be considered an equal sign between the subject and the predicate nominative.

3. An intransitive linking verb may link the subject to a predicate adjective.
   a. A predicate adjective is an adjective in the predicate that modifies the subject. It is usually sensible to say the adjective before the subject.
   b. Predicate adjectives may follow forms of

These <u>mottoes</u> <u>look</u> especially *attractive.*
(*Attractive* modifies *mottoes:* <u>attractive mottoes</u>.)

<u>Joel</u> <u>has become</u> *thoughtful* and *patient.*
(*Thoughtful* and *patient* modify *Joel:* <u>thoughtful, patient Joel</u>.)

Do not confuse a linking verb followed by an adjective with an action verb followed by a direct object or an adverb. Remember that a linking verb expresses a condition or state of being, not an action. When a verb is not a form of *be,* it is a linking verb if it could be replaced by a form of *be* without changing the meaning of the sentence.

The <u>milk</u> <u>tastes</u> *good.*
(*Tastes* expresses the condition of *milk:* <u>good milk</u>. *The milk is good* is sensible. *Tastes* is a linking verb.)
<u>We</u> <u>tasted</u> the *milk.*
(*Tasted* expresses the action of *We; milk* is the direct object that receives the action. *We were the milk* is not sensible. *Tasted* is a transitive verb.)

The <u>grass</u> <u>grew</u> *lush* and *green.*
(*Grew* expresses the condition of *grass:* <u>lush, green grass</u>. *The grass was lush and green* is sensible. *Grew* is a linking verb.)
The <u>grass</u> <u>grew</u> rapidly.
(*Grew* expresses the action of *grass; rapidly* is an adverb telling *how* the grass grew. *The grass was rapidly* is not sensible. *Grew* is an intransitive complete verb.)

Class Practice

A. Read each linking verb, and tell what words it links together.
1. Lazarus became very sick.
2. He was Mary and Martha's brother.
3. Mary seemed troubled and distressed at Jesus' absence.
4. Jesus felt sorrowful at the sadness of others.
5. Jesus is the Resurrection and the Life.
6. The best Friend of all is He.

Lesson 43 Answers

Class Practice
A. 1. became; Lazarus—sick
   2. was; He—brother
   3. seemed; Mary—troubled (and) distressed
   4. felt; Jesus—sorrowful
   5. is; Jesus—Resurrection (and) Life
   6. is; Friend—He

be, verbs of sense (*taste, feel, smell, sound, look, appear*), and other linking verbs (*grow, seem, stay, become, remain*).

4. A linking verb followed by an adjective must not be confused with an action verb followed by a direct object or an adverb.

a. A linking verb expresses a condition or state of being, not an action.

b. When a verb is not a form of *be,* it is a linking verb if it could be replaced by a form of *be* without changing the meaning of the sentence.

★ **EXTRA PRACTICE**
Worksheet 24 (*Intransitive Linking Verbs*)

B. Tell which sentence in each pair has a linking verb.
1. a. The fingers of a man's hand appeared suddenly on the wall.
   b. The guests appeared badly frightened.
2. a. David felt guilty for his sin.
   b. Isaac felt Jacob's hands.
3. a. The travelers grew weary.
   b. The people grew vegetables in Egypt.
4. a. Abner looked behind him.
   b. The tomato plants look healthy.
5. a. Pine trees stay green all year.
   b. The little girl stayed inside.

C. On the chalkboard, diagram the skeletons and complements of these sentences.
1. The morning sky looked bright.
2. Anna's brother was strong and energetic.
3. Gerald was growing tired.
4. Soon the brook became a muddy torrent.
5. My father is a writer and farmer.

Written Exercises

A. Write each linking verb and the words it links together.
1. The boards felt smooth.
2. Sister Annette has been our teacher for the last three years.
3. The peaches tasted sweet and delicious.
4. The dog looked vicious.
5. Can our new neighbors be they?
6. Arlin's favorite pets are hamsters and gerbils.
7. Your room has not appeared this messy for a long time.
8. The peonies have grown big and bushy this year.

B. Write the letter of the sentence in each pair that has a linking verb.
1. a. The children tasted the doughnuts.
   b. The doughnuts tasted delicious.
2. a. The jug felt cold and wet.
   b. Henry felt the jug.
3. a. The fireman sounded alarmed.
   b. The fire alarm sounded urgently across the town.
4. a. We can smell the mulberries from the house.
   b. Those mulberries smell very sweet.
5. a. A stray dog appeared suddenly at our door.
   b. He appeared hungry and shaggy.

C. Diagram the skeletons and complements of these sentences.

B. 1. b   4. b
   2. a   5. a
   3. a

C. 1.
   sky | looked \ bright

   2. brother | was \ strong (and) energetic

   3. Gerald | was growing \ tired

   4. brook | became \ torrent

   5. father | is \ writer (and) farmer

Written Exercises

A. 1. felt; boards—smooth
   2. has been; Sister Annette—teacher
   3. tasted; peaches—sweet (and) delicious
   4. looked; dog—vicious
   5. Can be; neighbors—they
   6. are; pets—hamsters (and) gerbils
   7. has appeared; room—messy
   8. have grown; peonies—big (and) bushy

B. 1. b
   2. a
   3. a
   4. b
   5. b

1. The milk will soon become sour in this hot weather.
2. Those animals are bighorn sheep or mountain goats.
3. The ugly caterpillar has become a beautiful butterfly.
4. A Saint Bernard is huge but gentle.
5. In his hunger, the wolf grew bold.

Review Exercises

A. Label each sentence *simple, compound,* or *complex.* [14, 15]]
1. The smallest birds in the world are hummingbirds.
2. The hummingbird family, which can be found in North and South America, includes over three hundred species.
3. The bee hummingbird, a native of Cuba, measures a mere two inches.
4. The hummingbird eats small insects and drinks nectar from flowers.
5. Its slender bill reaches deep into a flower, and its long, sticky tongue curls into a tube.
6. Because their wings beat as rapidly as seventy times a second, they make a humming sound in the air.
7. Our teacher said that hummingbirds can fly backward.
8. Most hummingbirds live in Central and South America, but some range as far north as southern Canada.

B. Diagram all the skeletons and complements in these compound and complex sentences. [14, 15, 29]
1. Because Ezra trusted the Lord, he did not ask for the king's protection.
2. God blessed their journey, and they reached Jerusalem safely.
3. The temple, which had been destroyed by Nebuchadnezzar, was rebuilt under Ezra's leadership.
4. What Ezra did for his people helped them greatly.

---

44. Using an Outline to Write a Composition

> **Lesson Survey**
> - An outline is needed to provide an orderly plan for a composition.
> - A composition must have a clear introduction and conclusion, even though they may not show on the outline.
> - A sentence outline is especially useful in writing a composition because many sentences can be copied right from the outline.

Lesson 44

Purpose: To teach the use of an outline in writing a composition.

Oral Review:
1. What are some ways that outlining written material is a good study aid? (It forces the reader to analyze the material and identify main ideas and less important ideas. It helps the reader to remember what he read. It provides a good way to recall main ideas when reviewing the material later.)
2. When outlining written material, what should be the first step? (Pick out the main ideas.)
3. What are the two kinds of outlines? (topical outlines, sentence outlines)
4. What is the difference between these two kinds of outlines? (A topical outline has words or brief

C. 1.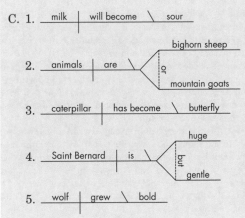

milk | will become \ sour

2. animals | are \

bighorn sheep

or

mountain goats

3. caterpillar | has become \ butterfly

4. 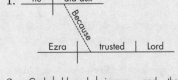 Saint Bernard | is \

huge

but

gentle

5. wolf | grew \ bold

Review Exercises

A. 1. simple   5. compound
2. complex   6. complex
3. simple   7. complex
4. simple   8. compound

B. 1.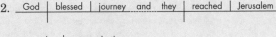

he | did ask

Because

Ezra | trusted | Lord

2. God | blessed | journey   and   they | reached | Jerusalem

3. 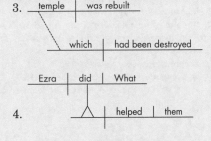 temple | was rebuilt

which | had been destroyed

Ezra | did | What

4. △ | helped | them

---

phrases to express each idea. A sentence outline has complete sentences to express each idea.)

Lesson Introduction: Two families were planning to leave for a trip at 8:00 this morning. It's 8:30, and chaos reigns at the Haphazard household. Several times Mr. Haphazard has had to dig a suitcase or a box out of the trunk to make sure an important item has been packed. Mrs. Haphazard has been frantically ironing a few clothes. The Haphazard children are scurrying about, trying to find some books to read and a few games to play in the car. Everyone is edgy because of the disorder and delay.

At 8:30 the Orderly family is twenty miles down the road. Mr. and Mrs. Orderly had carefully made

In Lesson 40 you learned that outlining written material is a good study aid. Preparing an outline is also an important step in writing a composition. A writer's outline is very much like a builder's blueprint; it is the plan from which he composes the finished product.

An outline is needed to provide an orderly plan for a composition. In making an outline, you are forced to take several important steps. You choose and limit your topic. You set down main ideas and list details to support them. And you organize the basic material in the way it should appear in the finished composition.

Always write an outline before trying to write a composition. You may be tempted to think that you can write a composition without making an outline first. But how many carpenters do you suppose build houses without blueprints? Most effective authors, even those with considerable writing experience, outline their material before they begin writing the actual composition. Making an outline is not just an extra job; it actually makes the work of writing easier.

A composition must have a clear introduction and conclusion, even though they may not show on the outline. In a short composition, these parts usually consist of only one sentence each, or one paragraph at the most. The outline itself covers the information for the body of the composition.

A sentence outline is especially useful in writing a composition. The sentences at the main divisions can often be used as topic sentences, and the other sentences can often be used within the paragraphs. The writer needs to do little more than add transitions and provide sentence variety.

Here is part of an outline from Lesson 36, written in sentence outline form. In the partial composition that follows, notice that some sentences are copied right from the outline. But notice also that some are changed to provide smoother transitions and better sentence variety.

Early Mennonite Settlements in America

I. The Germantown settlement was begun in 1683.
   A. What was the early settlement like?
      1. It was not primarily a Mennonite settlement.
      2. It included nearly 40 Mennonite families by 1708.
      3. It represented a mixture of Dutch and Swiss Mennonites.
   B. How was leadership provided in the early days of the Mennonite Church?
      1. Several steps were taken before 1708.
         a. No leaders were ordained before 1690.
            (1) The members gathered for fellowship and admonition.

lists, and these had governed much of the activity the day before and this morning. The whole family had gotten to bed early last night, and they are in good spirits as they go on their way!

When it comes to writing compositions, there are too many Mr. Haphazards and too few Mr. Orderlys. Starting with a good plan is basic to orderly writing and a worthwhile finished composition.

Lesson Outline:

1. An outline is needed to provide an orderly plan for a composition.
   a. The topic is chosen and limited.
   b. The main ideas and supporting details are listed.
   c. The basic material is organized in the way it should appear in the finished composition.

2. Always write an outline before trying to write a composition. Even most experienced writers work from an outline.

3. A composition must have a clear introduction and conclusion, even though they may not show on the outline.
   a. In a short composition, these parts usually consist of only one sentence each, or one paragraph at the most.
   b. The outline covers the information for the body of the composition.

4. A sentence outline is especially helpful in writing a composition. Many of the sentences are already written. The writer needs to do little more than add transitions and provide sentence variety.

        (2) They read old sermons from Europe.
        (3) They had no baptisms or Communion services.
      b. Two leaders were ordained in 1690.
        (1) William Rittenhouse became the first minister.
        (2) Jan Neuss became the first deacon.
      c. Jacob Gottschalk was ordained as minister in 1702.
      d. William Rittenhouse was authorized to serve as bishop sometime before 1708, but he died before assuming the position.
  2. Further steps were taken in 1708.
      a. Two ministers and three deacons were ordained.
      b. Jacob Gottschalk was assigned to Rittenhouse's office.
        (1) Eleven new members were baptized on May 9.
        (2) The first Communion was observed on May 23.

Early Mennonite Settlements in America

When the first Mennonites set foot on the coast of America, most of the human inhabitants there were Indians. Philadelphia, which would soon become a bustling center of American life, had been founded just the year before. Only a few houses had been built and a few streets laid out. Germantown, which is now part of Philadelphia, was then seven miles away.

The Germantown settlement was begun in 1683. What was the early settlement like? Actually, it was not primarily a Mennonite settlement. By 1708 nearly forty Mennonite families had arrived. These families represented a mixture of Dutch and Swiss Mennonites.

How was leadership provided in the early days of the Mennonite Church? Several steps were taken before 1708. There had been no ordained leaders before 1690. The members gathered for fellowship and admonition, and someone would read old sermons from Europe. But no baptisms or Communion services were held. Then in 1690, two leaders were ordained. William Rittenhouse became the first minister, and Jan Neuss became the first deacon. Jacob Gottschalk was ordained as another minister in 1702. Sometime before 1708, Rittenhouse was authorized by church leaders in Europe to serve as bishop, but he died before assuming that position.

Class Practice

Work together at writing the next paragraph of the composition "Early Mennonite Settlements in America," using point 2 of the outline.

Teacher: Be sure to give pupils enough time to complete the large assignment in Written Exercises.

Lesson 44 Answers

Class Practice

(Sample paragraph.)

Further leadership was provided in 1708 when two ministers and three deacons were ordained. Jacob Gottschalk was assigned to Rittenhouse's office, and on May 9 eleven new members were baptized. The first Communion was observed on May 23.

Written Exercises

Write a composition entitled "Metamorphosis in Insects," based on the topical outline in Lesson 36. Use the following sentences to introduce and conclude your composition.

Introduction:

One of the most awe-inspiring demonstrations of God's creative ability is the metamorphosis of insects.

Conclusion:

The next time you see a tiny grasshopper nymph or a homely caterpillar, remember the tremendous changes God planned for that little creature.

---

45. Reviewing Basic Sentence Patterns

Lesson Survey

- A verb is related to the **basic pattern** used in a sentence.

- A sentence of Pattern 1 has an intransitive complete verb. The sentence follows this pattern: *subject—action verb.*

- A sentence of Pattern 2 has a transitive verb whose action is received by a direct object. The sentence follows this pattern: *subject—action verb—direct object.* A Pattern 2 sentence may also have an indirect object.

- A sentence of Pattern 3 has a transitive verb whose action is received by the subject. The sentence follows this pattern: *subject—action verb.*

- A sentence of Pattern 4 has an intransitive linking verb that connects the subject to a subjective complement. The sentence follows this pattern: *subject—linking verb—predicate nominative* or *subject—linking verb—predicate adjective.*

In Lessons 41–43 you studied three kinds of verbs: *transitive, intransitive complete,* and *intransitive linking.* These verbs are related to the *basic patterns* used in sentences.

Lesson 45

Purpose: (1) To review transitive and intransitive verbs. (2) To show their relationship to *the four basic sentence patterns. (*Previous experience:* Various sentence patterns taught and diagrammed but not identified as such.)

Oral Review:

1. In a progressive verb form, the main verb must end with ———, and the helping verb must be ———. (*-ing,* a form of *be*)

2. What kind of action is showed by a progressive verb form? (continuing)

3. What helping verb is always used in the emphatic verb forms? (do, does, *or* did)

4. Give the second and third principal parts of these verbs.

    a. blow (blew, [have] blown)

Written Exercises

(A sample composition is shown.)

Metamorphosis in Insects

One of the most awe-inspiring demonstrations of God's creative ability is the metamorphosis of insects. There are two kinds of metamorphosis: incomplete and complete. Only a few insects, like grasshoppers, crickets, cicadas, and roaches, go through incomplete metamorphosis.

Incomplete metamorphosis involves three basic stages. First is the egg stage. When the egg hatches, the insect goes into the nymph stage. A nymph looks similar to an adult, but it cannot fly or reproduce. It develops through several molts. The nymph grows until its external skeleton is too small. Then it sheds the old skeleton and grows a new and larger one. The nymph emerges from the final molt as a mature adult, which is the third stage.

Complete metamorphosis is much more common in the insect world. It is found in insects like flies, bees, mosquitoes, moths, and butterflies.

Complete metamorphosis involves four stages, of which the first is the egg stage. When the egg hatches, the insect enters the larva stage and looks somewhat like a segmented worm. The larvae of different insects have different specific names. Maggots are the larvae of flies, grubs of beetles, wrigglers of mosquitoes, and caterpillars of butterflies and moths. A larva spends almost all its time eating.

After the larva stage is the pupa, or resting, stage. The insect either forms a hard chrysalis or weaves a silken cocoon. During this time the insect goes through a complete changing of its body structures. Finally it emerges from its cocoon or chrysalis and enters the fourth stage of its life as a mature adult. The next time you see a tiny grasshopper nymph or a homely caterpillar, remember the tremendous changes God planned for that little creature.

---

b. choose (chose, [have] chosen)

c. dig (dug, [have] dug)

d. read (read, [have] read)

e. steal (stole, [have] stolen)

f. burst (burst, [have] burst)

g. do (did, [have] done)

Pattern 1 Sentences

A sentence of Pattern 1 has an intransitive complete verb. It follows the simplest sentence pattern: *subject—action verb*. Of course, a sentence of Pattern 1 may include an adverb or adverb phrase. Be sure not to mistake these words as complements.

The crow's wings flapped lazily.

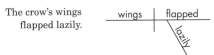

The horse galloped swiftly across the pasture.

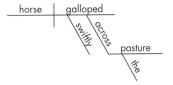

Pattern 2 Sentences

A sentence of Pattern 2 has a transitive verb whose action is received by a direct object. Such a sentence follows this pattern: *subject—action verb—direct object*. Remember that a direct object is diagramed on the base line after the verb, separated by a vertical line.

Mary Lou is gathering the eggs.

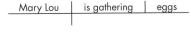

Merle will stack the firewood.

The pattern above is expanded if the sentence also has an indirect object. Remember to diagram the indirect object on a horizontal line under the base line, with a slanted line connecting it to the verb.

Charlene read the little children a story.

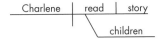

h. keep (kept, [have] kept)
i. shoot (shot, [have] shot)
j. write (wrote, [have] written)

Lesson Introduction: Through careful study, scientists have identified the *wind patterns* of the air around the earth. By careful observation, transportation officials can determine the *traffic patterns* on roads in a certain area. And since you have had several lessons on verbs, you should now be able to identify the various *sentence patterns* that go with these verbs.

What good does it do to know such patterns? Knowledge of wind patterns allows scientists to make useful weather predictions. Knowledge of traffic patterns helps officials to put up road signs and traffic signals intelligently. Knowledge of sentence patterns will enable you to speak and write more effectively.

Lesson Outline:

1. A verb is related to the basic pattern used in a sentence.

2. A sentence of Pattern 1 has an intransitive complete verb. It follows this pattern: *subject—action verb*. An adverb or adverb phrase may modify the verb, but it must not be mistaken for a complement.

3. A sentence of Pattern 2 has a transitive verb whose action is received by a direct object.
  a. The sentence follows this pattern: *subject—action verb—direct object*. The direct object is diagramed on the base line after the verb, with a vertical line between it and the verb.
  b. This pattern can be expanded to include an indirect object. An indirect object is diagramed on a horizontal line under the base line, with a slanted line connecting it to the verb.

Mother will take the neighbors a casserole.

Pattern 3 Sentences

A sentence of Pattern 3 has a transitive verb whose action is received by the subject. Such a sentence follows this pattern: *subject—action verb*. You may think this is the same as Pattern 1, but there is an important difference. When the subject receives the action, there is always a verb phrase in which the main verb is a past participle and the helping verb is a form of *be*.

The neighbor lady was injured in a bad fall.

Her housework has been done by helpful neighbors.

Pattern 4 Sentences

A sentence of Pattern 4 has an intransitive linking verb that connects the subject to a subjective complement. If the complement is a predicate nominative, the sentence follows this pattern: *subject—linking verb—predicate nominative*. If the complement is a predicate adjective, the sentence follows this pattern: *subject—linking verb—predicate adjective*.

When you diagram a Pattern 4 sentence, separate the linking verb from the complement with a slanted line that leans toward the subject. This should remind you that the complement relates to the subject by renaming or modifying it.

A good book can be a wonderful friend.

| book | can be \ friend |

The warm sunshine felt quite welcome.

| sunshine | felt \ welcome |

4. A sentence of Pattern 3 has a transitive verb whose action is received by the subject. The sentence follows this pattern: *subject—action verb*. There is always a verb phrase in which the main verb is a past participle and the helping verb is a form of *be*.

5. A sentence of Pattern 4 has an intransitive linking verb that connects the subject to a subjective complement.

    a. If the complement is a predicate nominative, the sentence follows this pattern: *subject—linking verb—predicate nominative*.

    b. If the complement is a predicate adjective, the sentence follows this pattern: *subject—linking verb—predicate adjective*.

    c. On a sentence diagram, the subjective complement is separated from the linking verb by a slanted line that leans toward the subject.

★ **EXTRA PRACTICE**
Worksheet 25 (*Basic Sentence Patterns*)

Class Practice

A. Tell whether each sentence follows *Pattern 1, Pattern 2, Pattern 3,* or *Pattern 4.*
1. The apostles were talking among themselves.
2. Jesus could tell their thoughts exactly.
3. Which disciple was most important in the kingdom of heaven?
4. A little child was placed before them.
5. The Master taught them a lesson from the little child.
6. You must be humble and teachable like children.
7. Do not rise to a high place.
8. The humble are useful in the Lord's kingdom.

B. On the chalkboard, diagram the skeletons and complements of these sentences.
1. Dorcas had made the poor people many garments.
2. A man was going down to Jericho.
3. Joseph was the husband of Mary.
4. The disciples felt perplexed and disappointed.
5. Jesus multiplied the loaves and the fish.
6. The attention of the crowd was focused on Jesus.

Written Exercises

A. Write *1, 2, 3,* or *4* to identify the pattern of each sentence, as shown in the lesson.
1. The visitors remained here overnight.
2. The Bible remains the eternal Word of God.
3. The boy looked at the birds through his binoculars.
4. The birds are looking for worms.
5. Goldfinches are named for their bright yellow feathers.
6. A bear suddenly appeared in town.
7. The bear did not appear very dangerous.
8. Will you taste this stew?
9. It tastes too salty.
10. We smelled the delicious aroma of baking cookies.
11. The cookies smelled sweet and spicy.
12. John grew three large pumpkins.
13. Sharon grew pink with embarrassment.
14. My favorite dessert is rhubarb pie.
15. Rose is helping the neighbors today.

B. Diagram the skeletons and complements of these sentences.
1. These bananas have been damaged slightly.
2. They are quite brown.

Lesson 45 Answers

Class Practice

A. 1. Pattern 1   5. Pattern 2
   2. Pattern 2   6. Pattern 4
   3. Pattern 4   7. Pattern 1
   4. Pattern 3   8. Pattern 4

B. 1. Dorcas | had made | garments
        \ people

2. man | was going

3. Joseph | was \ husband

4. disciples | felt \ perplexed *and* disappointed

5. Jesus | multiplied \ loaves *and* fish

6. attention | was focused

Written Exercises

A. 1. 1   9. 4
   2. 4   10. 2
   3. 1   11. 4
   4. 1   12. 2
   5. 3   13. 4
   6. 1   14. 4
   7. 4   15. 2
   8. 2

B. 1. 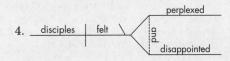 bananas | have been damaged

2.  They | are \ brown

3. We will bake banana cakes and banana bread.
4. Give Father a slice of this banana bread.
5. The dessert will be banana cake and banana ice cream.
6. Some of the baked goods can be given to Grandmother.

Review Exercises

A. Write the three principal parts of these verbs. Include *have* with the third principal part. [34]

1. buy
2. shut
3. drink
4. teach
5. leave
6. tag
7. lay
8. swing
9. weep
10. drown

B. Write the correct form of each underlined verb. If the verb is correct, write *correct*. [34]

1. Has Gerald <u>went</u> along with Nelson?
2. Melinda <u>brang</u> a hummingbird's nest to school today.
3. Our feet <u>sank</u> into the deep mud.
4. Miriam <u>done</u> a good job with her motto.
5. A little sparrow has <u>flew</u> into the classroom.
6. Noah and Leroy <u>swung</u> for a while this afternoon.
7. We <u>seen</u> a doe and two fawns crossing the meadow.
8. From Guatemala, William has <u>wrote</u> a letter to our class.
9. Have the chicken waterers all <u>frozen</u>?
10. Some pipes in the barn <u>busted</u>.

46. Taking Notes on a Sermon

Lesson Survey

- Note-taking helps you to obtain the greatest benefit from a sermon.
- Notes should have a heading that includes the date, the name of the speaker, the place of the service, and the sermon title.
- Notes should be an orderly summary of the speaker's main points.
- Notes should be written as neatly as possible.

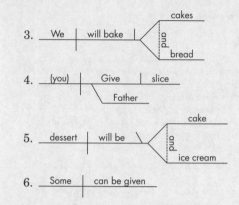

Review Exercises

A.
1. buy, bought, (have) bought
2. shut, shut, (have) shut
3. drink, drank, (have) drunk
4. teach, taught, (have) taught
5. leave, left, (have) left
6. tag, tagged, (have) tagged
7. lay, laid, (have) laid
8. swing, swung, (have) swung
9. weep, wept, (have) wept
10. drown, drowned, (have) drowned

B.
1. gone
2. brought
3. correct
4. did
5. flown
6. correct
7. saw
8. written
9. correct
10. burst

Lesson 46

Purpose: To teach *how to take notes from a sermon.

IMPORTANT: Allow enough time for the written work so that your students can listen to several sermons. Then they can hand in an outline or a list of statements from the sermon they found easiest to take notes on. You may also give immediate practice by having students take notes on devotional periods at school.

Oral Review:

1. What is an outline? (an orderly summary of a composition)
2. What are some ways that outlining written material is a good study aid? (It forces the reader to analyze the material and identify main ideas and less important ideas. It helps the reader to remember what he read. It provides a good way to recall main ideas when reviewing the material later.)
3. Why is outlining an important first step in writing? (It gives the writer an orderly plan for his composition.)
4. For each item, state a rule for proper outlining form.
   a. Placement of title. (The title is centered above the outline.)
   b. Indentation. (Each level is indented equally.)
   c. Use of capital letters. (Each line begins with a capital letter.)
   d. Use of periods and parentheses. (Each numeral or letter that marks an item is either followed by a period [main topics, subtopics, points, and subpoints] or placed within parentheses [details].)

The most important message ever written is the Bible. This is the message from the almighty God to mortal man. In this Word are the answers to all man's deepest needs. The Word is the map from earth to heaven. It is the only piece of literature that is always up-to-date and applies equally to every culture.

God has chosen that the preaching of the Word should be central in Christian worship. Therefore, we should cultivate seriousness and reverence. We should seek to obtain all the benefit we can as we receive this message from heaven.

Taking notes on a sermon has some important advantages. In the first place, note-taking helps you to better understand a sermon. The physical effort of writing helps to keep you alert. You will not fall asleep or daydream as easily while you are disciplining yourself to write notes. Furthermore, the discipline of listening for the next point to write in your notes will help you to grasp the main points of the sermon much better.

Your notes can be a benefit after the sermon as well. You remember those things that you write much better than those things that you merely hear. Of course, you will not remember everything you write, but your notes can be kept for future reference. In addition to your personal benefit, these notes can benefit others. By reading your notes, someone who was not at the service might gain some of the inspiration of the sermon.

What is the best way to take notes on a sermon? First, you should write a heading near the top of the paper. The heading should include the date, the name of the speaker, and the place of the service. Of course, the sermon title should also be placed at the top of the paper. And if the speaker gives a Scripture text, that reference should be included with the title.

The notes themselves should be an orderly summary of the speaker's main points. Often the most effective summary is an outline. Listen carefully for the speaker's arrangement of topics, subtopics, and details. Words like "In the next place..." or "Now we will consider..." or "Moving on..." are clues that the speaker is moving on to a new main point.

However, not all notes need to be written as a formal outline. Sometimes the speaker's outline may be hard for you to identify. His own notes may not even be in outline form; rather, he may simply have a list of basic principles or lessons. In such cases, your notes may be only a list of statements or ideas that have especially impressed you. Whether you have an outline or a list of statements, you should include the Scripture references the speaker gives with his points. Whatever the form of the notes, remember that they should summarize the speaker's main points.

e. Use of periods at the end of items. (On a sentence outline, each sentence ends with a period. On a topical outline, the words and phrases do not end with periods.)

f. Division of items. (If an item is divided into subordinate ideas, there must be at least two parts. If there is only one part, it is included in the item above it.)

g. The form of items in a set. (On a topical outline, the form of items at each level should be as nearly parallel as possible.)

5. How many characteristics should you write about in a character sketch? (one main characteristic)

6. The introduction of a character sketch may either —— or —— the main characteristic. (reflect, contrast)

7. What are some ways to show rather than merely tell about a person's character? (Use specific words and picturesque language. Have the person speak and act.)

Lesson Introduction: Review with the students some points of a recent sermon or school devotional. If possible, have your own set of notes to summarize the main points. Have students read Isaiah 30:8, which says, "Now go, write it before them in a table, and note it in a book, that it may be for the time to come for ever and ever." This verse speaks of God telling Isaiah to use notes.

Lesson Outline:

1. Note-taking helps you to obtain the greatest benefit from a sermon while it is being preached.

a. It helps you to better understand the sermon.

b. The physical effort of writing will help to keep you from sleeping or daydreaming.

Finally, notes should be written as neatly as possible. The original notes, which likely were written hurriedly, may need to be recopied. As you recopy them, write out any abbreviations that may be unclear, check for misspellings, fill in any missing words, and check Bible references for accuracy. The best time to do this is shortly after the preaching, while the sermon is still fresh in your mind.

Note-taking is a skill. As with any other skill, the more you practice, the better you will become. Do not be discouraged if you miss some points or if the sermon seems to be "over your head." But do determine to develop this skill for the glory of God.

Here are two sets of notes taken from the same sermon. The first is written in outline form, and the second is a list of statements.

Sermon Notes: Outline form

Advice for the New Year   January 3, 1993
Philippians 3:13, 14   Carl Morgan
                                         Bethel Mennonite Church

I. Be forgetful
  A. Of past failures and misunderstandings
    1. Because God promises to forgive and forget (Isa. 43:25)
    2. Because moping over mistakes has no benefit
    3. Because our forgiveness depends on our willingness to forgive (Matt. 6:12–15)
    4. Because a bitter spirit is unbecoming to a child of God (Eph. 4:31–5:2)
  B. Of past good deeds
    1. Because of the temptation to do good for hypocritical reasons (Matt. 6:1–4)
    2. Because true good deeds are found in humble service (Matt. 25:37–40)
    3. Because even our best is less than what God deserves (Luke 17:10)

II. Be ambitious
  A. In performing natural duties
    1. As part of God's basic plan for man (Gen. 2:15; 3:17–19)
    2. As an index to faithfulness in spiritual things (Rom. 12:11)
  B. In pursuing spiritual goals
    1. Because God deserves our whole being (Rom. 12:1)
    2. Because entrance into life demands urgency (Luke 13:24)
    3. Because we need to win the crown (1 Cor. 9:25)

    c. The discipline of listening for the next point to write will help you to grasp the main points.

2. Notes on a sermon can be a benefit after the preaching.
    a. Taking notes aids your ability to remember what you have heard.
    b. The notes can be kept for future reference.
    c. The notes can be shared with someone who did not attend the service.

3. Notes on a sermon should include a heading.
    a. Write the date, the name of the speaker, and the place of the service near the top of the paper.
    b. Write the title of the sermon at the top of the paper.

    c. Include a Scripture text if the speaker gives one.

4. The notes themselves should be an orderly summary of the speaker's main points.
    a. An outline is often the most effective summary of a sermon.
    b. Notes may simply be a list of major statements or ideas.
    c. Notes should include the Scripture references that the speaker gives with his points.

5. Notes should be written as neatly as possible.
    a. Recopy the original notes if necessary.
    b. Write out any abbreviations that may be unclear, check for misspellings, fill in any missing words, and check Bible references for accuracy.
    c. Do this checking and revising shortly after the preaching, while the sermon is still fresh in your mind.

Sermon Notes: List of statements

Advice for the New Year   January 3, 1993
    Philippians 3:13, 14   Carl Morgan
                             Bethel Mennonite Church

1. We should forget our past failures because God promises to forgive and forget them (Isa. 43:25).
2. Moping about our mistakes will never benefit us.
3. Our forgiveness depends upon our willingness to forgive others in misunderstandings (Matt. 6:12–15).
4. A bitter spirit is unbecoming to a child of God (Eph. 4:31–5:2).
5. If we think too much about past good deeds, we may be tempted to do good for hypocritical reasons (Matt. 6:1–4).
6. True good deeds are found in humble service now, not in boasting of the past (Matt. 25:37–40).
7. Even our best is less than what God deserves (Luke 17:10).
8. God's basic plan for man involves man's industry in natural pursuits (Gen. 2:15; 3:17–19).
9. Faithfulness in natural pursuits is an index to faithfulness in spiritual things (Rom. 12:11).
10. We must pursue spiritual goals because God deserves our whole being (Rom. 12:1).
11. Entrance into life demands urgency (Luke 13:24).
12. We need spiritual ambition to win the crown (1 Cor. 9:25).

Class Practice

Answer the following questions.
1. What benefits can you receive from taking notes on a sermon (a) during the preaching itself? (b) after the sermon?
2. How can the notes on a sermon be a benefit to others?
3. a. What should be included in the heading of a set of notes?
   b. What should be included in the notes themselves?
4. What are some clues that a speaker is moving on to a new main point?
5. In what two forms may notes on a sermon be written?
6. a. Why is it a good idea to recopy your original notes on a sermon?
   b. How should you check and improve your notes as you recopy them?
   c. When is the best time to do this?

Written Exercises

Take notes on one of the next sermons you hear or on a devotional in school. Recopy the notes with neat penmanship and good organization.

Lesson 46 Answers

Class Practice

1. a. Note-taking helps you to better understand the sermon. The physical effort of writing will help to keep you from sleeping or daydreaming. The discipline of listening for the next point to write will help you to grasp the main points.
   b. Taking notes aids your ability to remember what you have heard. The notes can be kept for future reference.
2. By reading the notes, someone who was not at the service might gain some of the inspiration of the sermon.
3. a. the date, the name of the speaker, the place of the service, the sermon title, and the reference of the Scripture text that the speaker uses
   b. an orderly summary of the speaker's main points
4. words like "In the next place . . ." or "Now we will consider . . ." or "Moving on . . ."
5. a formal outline or a list of important statements
6. a. The original notes, which likely were written hurriedly, may not be very neat and may contain various mistakes.
   b. Write out any abbreviations that may be unclear, check for misspellings, fill in any missing words, and check Bible references for accuracy.
   c. shortly after the preaching, while the sermon is still fresh in your mind

Written Exercises

(Individual work.)

Review Exercises

Write a character sketch about someone you know well. Choose a different character from the one you wrote about in Lesson 4. [4]

---

47. Chapter 4 Review

Class Practice

A. Answer these questions about verbs.
1. What is the definition of a verb?
2. Which principal part must be used to form a perfect tense?
3. What are the six verb tenses?
4. What helping verbs are used with each of the perfect tenses?
5. When a sentence contains two verbs showing past actions, which one is often expressed in the past perfect tense?
6. When a sentence contains two verbs showing future actions, which one is often expressed in the future perfect tense?
7. What kind of action is expressed by the present perfect tense?
8. What kind of action is expressed by progressive verb forms?
9. What do the emphatic verb forms show?
10. What kind of verb phrase is used for a progressive verb form?
11. What are the helping verbs for the emphatic verb forms?
12. What does a transitive verb do?
13. A transitive verb may pass its action to what two sentence parts?
14. If a transitive verb passes its action to the subject, what helping verb will it have?
15. If an action verb does not pass its action to a receiver, what is it called?
16. What are some common intransitive linking verbs?

B. Give the answers to these exercises on outlines and note-taking.
1. If an item is divided, there must be ———.
2. The title is ——— above the outline.
3. Each line begins with a ———.
4. On a sentence outline, each sentence ends with ———.
5. Each level is indented ———.
6. As much as possible, the items at each level of a topical outline should be ———.
7. An outline should be either all ———.

Lesson 47

Purpose: To review the concepts taught in Chapter 4.

Review Exercises

(Individual work.)

Lesson 47 Answers

Class Practice

A. 1. A verb expresses action or being to tell what the subject does or is.
2. the past participle, or third principal part
3. present, past, future, present perfect, past perfect, future perfect
4. present perfect—have *or* has; past perfect—had; future perfect—shall have *or* will have
5. the one that occurred first
6. the one that occurs first
7. action that began in the past and is completed as of the present time or that continues into the present
8. continuing action
9. added emphasis
10. The main verb ends with -*ing,* and the helping verb is a form of *be.*
11. do, does, did
12. It passes action to a noun or pronoun in the sentence.
13. subject, direct object
14. a form of *be*
15. intransitive complete
16. **Forms of *be*:** am, is, are, was, were, be, been, being
    Verbs of sense: taste, feel, smell, sound, look, appear
    Other linking verbs: grow, seem, stay, become, remain

B. 1. at least two parts
2. centered
3. capital letter
4. a period
5. equally
6. parallel in form
7. sentences or all topics

8. For main topics, subtopics, points, and subpoints, the numerals and letters should be ———.
9. For details, the numerals and letters should be ———.
10. Name some advantages in taking notes on a sermon.
11. What information should appear near the top of a paper of sermon notes?
12. What should the sermon notes consist of?

C. Give the three principal parts of each verb. Use *have* with the past participle.
1. come
2. drown
3. lie
4. wear
5. read
6. drag

D. Read each verb or verb phrase, and tell which tense it is. If the verb form is *progressive* or *emphatic,* also state that.
1. The stranger has been asking for some Gospel tracts.
2. As a small boy, he had learned a few things about the Bible.
3. However, his parents taught him little about God.
4. We do keep a variety of tracts on hand.
5. We shall be showing him the way of truth.
6. By bedtime, we shall have discussed many Bible truths with him.

E. Tell whether each underlined verb is *transitive, intransitive complete,* or *intransitive linking.* If it is transitive, tell which word receives the action of the main verb. If it is linking, tell what words are linked.
1. God <u>gave</u> Jonah a message for Nineveh.
2. Jonah <u>fled</u> in the opposite direction.
3. Jonah <u>had become</u> a disobedient prophet.
4. A severe storm <u>was sent</u> on the sea.
5. The sailors <u>grew</u> desperate in their struggle for life.
6. Finally Jonah <u>was cast</u> overboard by the sailors.

F. On the chalkboard, diagram the skeletons of the sentences in Part E.

Written Exercises

A. Write the correct form of the underlined verb. If it is correct, write *correct.*
1. Our class has <u>sang</u> a different theme song every week.
2. The deer <u>drug</u> its wounded leg behind.
3. The wolf has <u>swum</u> across the creek.
4. How many swine <u>drownded</u> in the sea?
5. We <u>seen</u> some interesting displays at the museum.
6. Have you <u>chose</u> the biggest and the best again?
7. Marjorie <u>knew</u> the solution to the puzzle.

Written Exercises

A. 1. sung
2. dragged
3. correct
4. drowned
5. saw
6. chosen
7. correct

---

8. followed by periods
9. placed within parentheses
10. Taking notes helps one to better understand a sermon, to prevent sleepiness and daydreaming, to grasp the main points, and to remember the sermon. The notes serve as a future reference and can be shared with others.
11. the date, the name of the speaker, the place of the service, the sermon title, and the reference of the Scripture text
12. the speaker's main points and the Scripture references used with them

C. 1. come, came, (have) come
2. drown, drowned, (have) drowned
3. lie, lay, (have) lain
4. wear, wore, (have) worn
5. read, read, (have) read
6. drag, dragged, (have) dragged

D. 1. has been asking—present perfect, progressive
2. had learned—past perfect
3. taught—past
4. do keep—present, emphatic
5. shall be showing—future, progressive
6. shall have discussed—future perfect

E. 1. transitive; message
2. intransitive complete
3. intransitive linking; Jonah—prophet
4. transitive; storm
5. intransitive linking; sailors—desperate
6. transitive; Jonah

F.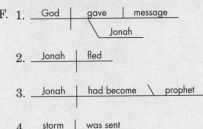
1. God | gave | message \ Jonah
2. Jonah | fled
3. Jonah | had become \ prophet
4. storm | was sent
5. sailors | grew \ desperate
6. Jonah | was cast

8. Randy <u>bursted</u> out the door with some hornets after him.
9. The sun has <u>risen</u> to another beautiful day.
10. The children <u>done</u> a lot of work today.

B. Copy each verb or verb phrase, and write which tense it is.
1. By the end of the school year, you will have spent many hours in school.
2. The first graders are learning how to read.
3. Have you attended this same school since first grade?
4. We studied some geometry last year in math class.
5. Tomorrow we shall have an interesting science demonstration.
6. We do study hard for these science lessons.
7. Before last week, Jeannette had missed school only once.
8. Several visitors have come today.

C. From Part B, copy the verb forms that are described here.
1. a progressive verb form
2. an emphatic verb form

D. In each sentence, one of the verbs should be changed to a perfect tense to make a clearer relationship. Write that verb in the correct perfect tense.
1. By the time Satan is cast into the lake of fire, he will fight hard against God.
2. The minister commented on the hymn that the song leader selected.
3. When Brother Jonas preached the sermon, Brother Elmer made a few announcements.
4. We shall build the forms when the concrete arrives.
5. We gave my grandparents the raspberries that we picked.
6. Merlin came back home because he forgot his suitcase.

E. Write numbers as shown to identify the patterns of these sentences. If the verb is transitive, write the word that receives the action. If the verb is intransitive linking, write the words that are linked.
  Pattern 1: intransitive complete verb
  Pattern 2: transitive verb; action passed to direct object
  Pattern 3: transitive verb; action passed to subject
  Pattern 4: intransitive linking verb
1. These floors were washed just yesterday.
2. They have become dirty already.
3. The children are coming in with muddy boots.
4. Children, you must wash your boots at the outside faucet.
5. After all that rain, the field was a lake.

8. burst
9. correct
10. did

B. 1. will have spent—future perfect
2. are learning—present
3. Have attended—present perfect
4. studied—past
5. shall have—future
6. do study—present
7. had missed—past perfect
8. have come—present perfect

C. 1. are learning
2. do study

D. 1. will have fought
2. had selected
3. had preached
4. shall have built
5. had picked
6. had forgotten

E. 1. 3; floors
2. 4; They—dirty
3. 1
4. 2; boots
5. 4; field—lake

F. Diagram the skeletons, complements, and verb modifiers of these sentences.
1. The cedar tree is a conifer.
2. Have you done a careful job?
3. The snake has gone back into the brush.
4. The bull did not appear mean or dangerous.
5. Bonita wrote us an interesting letter.
6. This meal has been provided by kind friends.

G. Copy and improve this outline. Be sure to use parallel form for all items of the same level.

Moses—the Man of God

I. His birth
　A. born to faithful parents
　B. born in a time of great need
　C. He was preserved in a miraculous manner.
II. His choice
　A. Rejected the world of Egypt
　　1. its prestige
　　2. pleasures
　　3. its wealth
　B. accepted the way of God's people
　　1. A way of affliction and reproach
　　2. Victory
　　3. A dangerous way
　　4. A way of faith
III. He had contact with God.
　A. divine revelation
　B. He was divinely commissioned.
　　C. Divine enabling

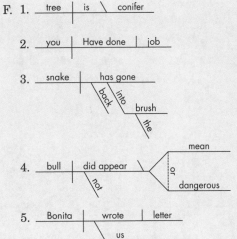

F. 1. tree | is \ conifer
2. you | Have done | job
3. snake | has gone / back / into / brush / the
4. bull | did appear / not \ mean / or / dangerous
5. Bonita | wrote | letter / us
6. meal | has been provided / by / friends / kind

G. (Corrections are underlined.)

Moses—the Man of God

I. His birth
　A. <u>B</u>orn to faithful parents
　B. <u>B</u>orn in a time of great need
　C. <u>Preserved in a miraculous manner</u>
II. His choice
　A. Rejected the world of Egypt
　　1. <u>I</u>ts prestige
　　2. <u>I</u>ts pleasures
　　3. <u>I</u>ts wealth
　B. <u>A</u>ccepted the way of God's people
　　1. A way of affliction and reproach
　　2. <u>A way of</u> victory
　　3. A way <u>of danger</u>
　　4. A way of faith
III. <u>His contact with God</u>
　A. <u>D</u>ivine revelation
　B. <u>Divine commission</u>
　<u>C</u>. Divine enabling

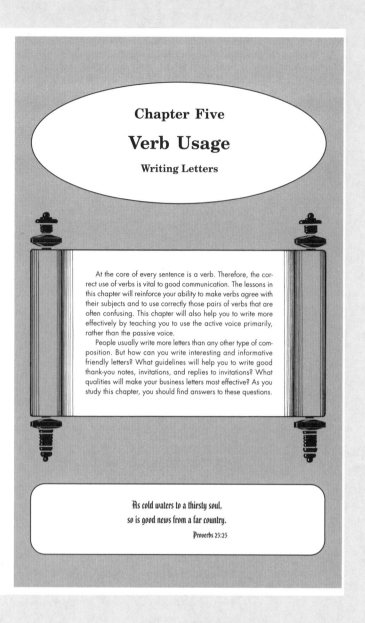

Chapter Five

Verb Usage

Writing Letters

At the core of every sentence is a verb. Therefore, the correct use of verbs is vital to good communication. The lessons in this chapter will reinforce your ability to make verbs agree with their subjects and to use correctly those pairs of verbs that are often confusing. This chapter will also help you to write more effectively by teaching you to use the active voice primarily, rather than the passive voice.

People usually write more letters than any other type of composition. But how can you write interesting and informative friendly letters? What guidelines will help you to write good thank-you notes, invitations, and replies to invitations? What qualities will make your business letters most effective? As you study this chapter, you should find answers to these questions.

As cold waters to a thirsty soul,
so is good news from a far country.

Proverbs 25:25

48. Subject–Verb Agreement

> **Lesson Survey**
> - The subject and verb must always agree in number. Be especially careful in the following cases.
>   1. When the verb precedes the subject.
>   2. When the subject is followed by a prepositional phrase.
>   3. When using *don't* and *doesn't*.
>   4. When two subjects are joined by *and.*
>   5. When two subjects are joined by *or* or *nor.*
>   6. When the subject is an indefinite pronoun.
>   7. When the subject looks like a plural noun but is singular in meaning.
>   8. When the subject is usually considered plural.
>   9. When the subject is a collective noun.

In most cases you naturally make the verb agree in number with its subject. However, there are a number of problem areas for many people. This lesson will give you practice with subject–verb agreement in some of these areas.

1. *When the verb precedes the subject, think ahead to the subject and make the verb agree with it.* The verb (or a helping verb) often precedes the subject in questions, such as the following examples.

> Where <u>is</u> the <u>story</u> of the Rechabites?
> Why <u>were</u> <u>they</u> <u>living</u> in Jerusalem?

The verb also precedes the subject in most sentences beginning with *there* or *here*. Remember that *there* and *here* are never subjects.

> There <u>is</u> a <u>balm</u> in Gilead.
> There <u>was</u> <u>Jesus</u>, sitting among the teachers.
> Here <u>come</u> the <u>children</u>.

In informal usage such as conversations, we often use contractions like *there's, here's, where's,* and *how's.* These contractions combine a word with the singular verb *is;* therefore, you should use them only when a singular subject follows.

> **Incorrect:** There's (There <u>is</u>) some <u>potatoes</u> left in the dish.
> How's (How <u>is</u>) your <u>parents</u> planning to travel?
> When's (When <u>is</u>) the <u>robins</u> coming back?

Lesson 48

Purpose: To teach the rules for subject–verb agreement.

Oral Review:
1. Give the meaning of each word as used in English grammar.
   a. tense (time)
   b. perfect (completed)
   c. transitive (passing over)
2. A transitive verb may pass its action to either of what two sentence parts? (subject or direct object)
3. What term refers to an action verb that does not pass its action to another word? (intransitive complete)
4. What term refers to a verb that does not pass action, but simply joins the subject to a subjective complement? (intransitive linking)

5. What is the word order of a sentence in which the complete predicate precedes the complete subject? (inverted)
6. What is the word order of a sentence in which part of the predicate comes before the subject and part comes after? (mixed)
7. What is the word order of a sentence in which the complete subject precedes the complete predicate? (natural)

Lesson Introduction: The prophet Amos asked, "Can two walk together, except they be agreed?" When two people are agreed, they are able to walk together and enjoy meaningful conversation. When two people who are not agreed try to walk together, they may have considerable difficulty in communicating. In a similar manner, the two main parts of a sentence, the subject and the predicate, cannot "walk together" unless they agree. When they disagree, our speaking and writing lose effectiveness.

Correct: There <u>are</u> some <u>potatoes</u> left in the dish.
How <u>are</u> your <u>parents</u> <u>planning</u> to travel?
When <u>are</u> the <u>robins</u> <u>coming</u> back?

2. *When the subject is followed by a prepositional phrase, make the verb agree with the subject, not with the object of the preposition.* Remember that the subject is never part of a prepositional phrase.

This <u>dish</u> of peas <u>is</u> ready to be passed. (not *are*)
The <u>bags</u> of feed <u>have been torn</u>. (not *has been torn*)
<u>Clyde</u>, as well as Mary Beth, <u>has</u> a pet guinea pig. (not *have*)
<u>Stephen</u>, along with six others, <u>was ordained</u> a deacon. (not *were ordained*)

3. *Use* doesn't *with most singular subjects, and* don't *with plural subjects and with the pronouns* I *and* you. The most frequent error with these contractions is the use of *don't* with a singular noun or with a third person singular pronoun (*he, she, it*). Be especially careful to use *doesn't* with these singular subjects. To decide which contraction is correct, think of the two words from which the contraction is made—*do not* or *does not*.

Incorrect:
Laura <u>don't</u> live far away. (Compare: Laura do not...)
She <u>don't</u> see us. (Compare: She do not...)
It <u>don't</u> rain much here. (Compare: It do not...)
Correct:
Laura <u>doesn't</u> live far away. (Compare: Laura does not...)
She <u>doesn't</u> see us. (Compare: She does not...)
It <u>doesn't</u> rain much here. (Compare: It does not...)

I <u>don't</u> know why they <u>don't</u> come often.

4. *If two subjects are joined by* and, *use a plural verb.* The conjunction *and* means that the verb expresses action or condition for all parts of the subject.

<u>Michael</u> and <u>Gabriel</u> <u>are</u> angels. (<u>Both</u> <u>are</u> angels.)
<u>He</u>, <u>she</u>, and <u>I</u> <u>have</u> an appointment.
(Three <u>persons</u> <u>have</u> an appointment.)
The <u>carpenter</u> and the <u>mason</u> <u>are</u> here. (<u>Both</u> <u>are</u> here.)

Sometimes a compound subject names only one person or thing. This is especially common when one person holds two positions or occupations. In such a sentence, the verb is singular.

Lesson Outline:

*1. **When the verb precedes the subject, think ahead to the subject and make the verb agree with it.***
   a. The words *there* and *here* are never subjects.
   b. An informal contraction that combines a word with the singular verb *is* should be used only when followed by a singular subject.

*2. **When the subject is followed by a prepositional phrase, make the verb agree with the subject, not with the object of the preposition.***

*3. **Use** doesn't **with most singular subjects, and** don't **with plural subjects and with the pronouns** I **and** you.** The most frequent error with these contractions is the use of *don't* with a singular noun or with a third person singular pronoun (*he,*

she, it). To decide which contraction is correct, think of the two words from which the contraction is made—*do not* or *does not*.

*4. **If two subjects are joined by** and, **use a plural verb.***
   a. The conjunction *and* means that the verb expresses action or condition for all parts of the subject.
   b. If a compound subject names only one person or thing, the verb is singular. Then an article is used only before the first noun.
   c. If a compound subject names two persons or things, the verb is plural. Then an article is used before each noun.

*5. **If two singular subjects are joined by** or **or** nor, **use a singular verb.*** The conjunction *or* means that the verb expresses action or condition for only one or the other of the compound parts.

Ham and eggs is my favorite breakfast.
(One dish is my favorite breakfast.)
The carpenter and mason is Brother Leon.
(One person is Brother Leon.)

Take special notice of the last sentence. Since one person holds two occupations, an article (*the*) is used only before the first noun. But if two different people hold two occupations, an article is used before each of the nouns. Then the subject is plural, and a plural verb is used. Consider again the following sentence.

The carpenter and the mason are here. (Two people are here.)

5. *If two singular subjects are joined by* or *or* nor, *use a singular verb.* The conjunction *or* means that the verb expresses action or condition for only one or the other of the compound parts, but not for both.

Carla or Karen is going along with Mother.
(Just one is going along with Mother.)
Neither lead nor mercury is heavier than gold.
(Neither one is heavier than gold.)

6. *Always use singular verbs with singular indefinite pronouns.* These include *each, either, neither, one, another,* and any compounds with *one* or *body.* Often such a pronoun is followed by a prepositional phrase. Remember that the verb must agree with the subject, not with the object of the preposition.

Each of the children has a pencil. (Each one has a pencil.)
Either of these songs fits well. (Either one fits well.)
Everyone is ready to start. (Every one is ready to start.)

7. *Singular verbs are commonly used with nouns that look like plural nouns but are singular in meaning.* These nouns include words like *news* and *gallows;* names of diseases like *measles, mumps, chicken pox,* and *rickets;* and words ending with *-ics* like *electronics, mathematics,* and *phonics.*

The news of Lucy's healing causes us to rejoice.
Rickets is caused by a lack of vitamin D.
Mathematics is used in counting and measuring.

8. *Some nouns are usually considered plural whether they name one thing or more than one. Usually plural verbs are used with them.* Most of these nouns name things that come in pairs, like *shears, scissors, trousers, pliers, glasses,* and *tongs.*

These shears have been used on many sheep.

6. *Always use singular verbs with singular indefinite pronouns. These include* each, either, neither, one, another, *and any compounds with* one *or* body. Be careful when these pronouns are followed by prepositional phrases.

7. *Singular verbs are commonly used with nouns that look like plural nouns but are singular in meaning.*
   a. Nouns like *news* and *gallows*
   b. Names of diseases like *measles, mumps, chicken pox,* and *rickets*
   c. Words ending with *-ics* like *electronics, mathematics,* and *phonics*

8. *Some nouns are usually considered plural whether they name one thing or more than one. Usually plural verbs are used with them.*
   a. Nouns like *shears, scissors, trousers, pliers, glasses,* and *tongs* are usually considered plural.
   b. If the subject is *pair* followed by one of these words in a prepositional phrase, the verb should be singular.

9. *Use either a singular or a plural verb with a collective noun, depending on the sentence.*
   a. If the collective noun refers to the group acting as a unit, use a singular verb.
   b. If the collective noun refers to the individual members of the group acting separately, use a plural verb.
   c. Any pronoun referring to the collective noun must also agree in number.

★ **EXTRA PRACTICE**
Worksheet 26 (*Subject–Verb Agreement*)

My <u>trousers</u> <u>are</u> too small for you.
Your <u>glasses</u> <u>do slide</u> down your nose too easily.

Of course, if the subject is *pair* followed by one of these words in a prepositional phrase, the verb should be singular.

This <u>pair</u> of trousers <u>has become</u> too small.
My new <u>pair</u> of glasses <u>helps</u> me to see much better.

9. *Use either a singular or a plural verb with a collective noun, depending on the sentence.* A collective noun names a group of individuals. If the group acts as a unit, doing one thing together, use a singular verb. But if the individual members of the group act separately, use a plural verb.

The <u>family</u> <u>is singing</u> its theme song.
   (singular: group acting as a unit)
The <u>family</u> <u>are singing</u> their different parts.
   (plural: individuals acting separately)

The <u>swarm</u> of bees <u>is protecting</u> its queen.
   (singular: group acting as a unit)
The <u>swarm</u> of bees <u>are</u> busily <u>doing</u> their different jobs.
   (plural: individuals acting separately)

Be sure any pronoun that refers to the collective noun also agrees in number. In the sentences in which *family* and *swarm* are singular, you see the singular pronoun *its*. But in the sentences in which *family* and *swarm* are plural, you see the plural pronoun *their*.

Class Practice

A. Read each sentence, using the correct form in parentheses.
1. His brother (don't, doesn't) know how to multiply.
2. There (is, are) three pigs in the pen.
3. The scissors (was, were) sharp.
4. Measles (is, are) contagious.
5. The congregation (is, are) waiting reverently for the service to begin.
6. James and John (was, were) the sons of Zebedee.
7. Either Kay or her mother (is, are) coming.
8. The fleet of ships (was, were) battered by a severe storm.
9. Each of the students (appear, appears) ready for the test.
10. (How's, How are) the sick cows doing this morning?

B. Read these sentences, changing the singular subjects and verbs to plural and the plural ones to singular.
1. The cow was in the pasture.
2. Where does the monkey live?

Lesson 48 Answers

Class Practice

A. 1. doesn't   6. were
   2. are   7. is
   3. were   8. was
   4. is   9. appears
   5. is   10. How are

B. (Corrections are underlined.)
1. The <u>cows were</u> in the pasture.
2. Where <u>do</u> the <u>monkeys</u> live?

3. There are two jugs of milk in the refrigerator.
4. Why aren't the jars of peaches full?

C. Read each sentence, following the directions in parentheses and changing the verb to agree with the subject if necessary.
1. The teachers have finished averaging report card grades. (Change *The teachers* to *Each of the teachers.*)
2. A seventh grader and an eighth grader are making the bulletin board display. (Change *and* to *or.*)
3. There's a definite difference between crocodiles and alligators. (Change *a definite difference* to *definite differences.*)
4. The polar bear or the grizzly bear is a dangerous beast to disturb. (Change *or* to *and.*)

Written Exercises

A. Choose the correct form of the verb in parentheses.
1. Fox and geese (is, are) a winter game that many children enjoy.
2. A good horse trainer (don't, doesn't) beat and scold his horses.
3. Each of the training lessons (is, are) important.
4. Considerate riders (don't, doesn't) neglect their horses' needs.
5. There (is, are) many kinds of horses.
6. The grooming of horses (is, are) an important part of good care.
7. The mane and the tail (help, helps) protect the horse from flies.
8. A colt or a horse (lie, lies) down flat on its side.
9. Each diagonal pair of legs (is, are) lifted in trotting.
10. Not everyone (is, are) familiar with the horse.
11. A herd of wild mustangs (is, are) thundering across the plains.
12. Electronics (is, are) the basis of much modern technology.
13. (When's, When are) the next bus scheduled?
14. (There's, There are) few good reasons for tardiness.
15. The large wolf, together with his mate, (is, are) stalking an elk.
16. The faculty (take, takes) their students on hikes at different times.
17. Father's pliers (have, has) disappeared from this toolbox.
18. Each of the boys (need, needs) a haircut.
19. Phonics (deal, deals) with the sounds of letters in the alphabet.
20. My new pair of glasses (have, has) broken already.

B. Rewrite these sentences, changing the singular subjects and verbs to plural and the plural ones to singular.
1. The kittens play very cleverly.
2. The cow doesn't give much milk.
3. Where's the goat?

3. There is one jug of milk in the refrigerator.
4. Why isn't the jar of peaches full?

C. (Corrections are underlined.)
1. Each of the teachers has finished averaging report card grades.
2. A seventh grader or an eighth grader is making the bulletin board display.
3. There are definite differences between crocodiles and alligators.
4. The polar bear and the grizzly bear are dangerous beasts to disturb.

Written Exercises

A.
1. is
2. doesn't
3. is
4. don't
5. are
6. is
7. help
8. lies
9. is
10. is
11. is
12. is
13. When's
14. There are
15. is
16. take
17. have
18. needs
19. deals
20. has

B. (Corrections are underlined.)
1. The kitten plays very cleverly.
2. The cows don't give much milk.
3. Where are the goats?

4. There's a rat in the chicken house.
5. When do the donkeys bray?

C. Rewrite each sentence, following the directions in parentheses and changing the verb to agree with the subject if necessary.
1. Spanish and typing need to be taken by the tenth graders. (Change *and* to *or.*)
2. The students are learning sign language. (Change *The students* to *Everyone in the class.*)
3. Leroy or Henry makes these benches. (Change *or* to *and.*)
4. Where's the songbook? (Change *songbook* to *songbooks.*)

Review Exercises

A. Write whether each sentence has *natural, inverted,* or *mixed* word order. [11]
1. Out of the tall grass slithered a huge snake.
2. Its enormous size made me shudder with revulsion.
3. Without a backward glance, I fled in terror.
4. I rushed into the house and collapsed on the sofa.
5. There I gradually calmed down.

B. Change these sentences to the order given in parentheses. [11]
1. Elijah fled from Israel at Jezebel's threat. (mixed)
2. The weary prophet lay under a juniper tree. (inverted)
3. There were many people coming and going. (natural)
4. Jesus and the disciples sailed across the Sea of Galilee. (inverted)

---

49. Using *Lay—Lie, Set—Sit, and Raise—Rise*

> **Lesson Survey**
> - *Lay* is a transitive verb that means "to put or place (something)."
> - *Lie* is an intransitive verb that means "to rest or recline."
> - *Set* is usually a transitive verb that means "to put or place (something)." It may also be an intransitive verb that means "to move below the horizon, "to keep eggs warm for hatching," or "to become firm."

Lesson 49

Purpose: To teach the correct usage of the following pairs of transitive and intransitive verbs: *lay—lie, set—sit, raise—rise.*

Oral Review:
1. For the following sentences, if there is a mistake in subject–verb agreement, repeat the sentence correctly. If it is correct, say *correct.*
   a. Neither the sun nor the moon were visible for several days. (was)
   b. Fred don't plan to go along after all. (doesn't)
   c. Where's my books? (Where are)
   d. This pair of tweezers are not where it belongs. (is)
   e. The scissors aren't put away either. (correct)
   f. Each of these tools have a definite place to be. (has)

---

4. There <u>are rats</u> in the chicken house.
5. When <u>does</u> the <u>donkey</u> bray?

C. (Corrections are underlined.)
1. Spanish or typing <u>needs</u> to be taken by the tenth graders.
2. Everyone in the class <u>is</u> learning sign language.
3. Leroy and Henry <u>make</u> these benches.
4. <u>Where are</u> the songbooks?

Review Exercises

A. 1. inverted
   2. natural
   3. mixed
   4. natural
   5. mixed

B. 1. At Jezebel's threat, Elijah fled from Israel.
   2. Under a juniper tree lay the weary prophet.
   3. Many people were coming and going.
   4. Across the Sea of Galilee sailed Jesus and the disciples.

g. The herd of cows are grazing contentedly. (is)
h. The herd of cows are finding their separate ways home. (correct)
i. Luella, together with her friends, has planned an interesting scrapbook. (correct)

2. Give the correct verb form for each sentence.
   a. The men drug the heavy bags across the floor. (dragged)
   b. Rover swum across the stream. (swam)
   c. Lemuel seen a red fox. (saw)
   d. Irene has went to stay with Grandmother tonight. (gone)
   e. How much have these shoes costed before? (cost)

Lesson Introduction: Because some words have similar spellings and meanings, they are often confused. Three such pairs are *lay—lie, set—sit,* and *raise—rise.* If you frequently make mistakes with

- *Sit* is an intransitive verb that means "to rest or be seated."
- *Raise* is a transitive verb that means "to cause (something) to go up or grow up."
- *Rise* is an intransitive verb that means "to get up or go up."

Have you ever seen twins who looked so much alike that at first you could not tell them apart? Perhaps even after you knew them fairly well, you still confused them sometimes. Of course, the better acquainted you became with them, the more easily you could tell them apart.

In this lesson, you will be studying verb twins that are also frequently confused. Put forth the effort to learn them well, and you will be able to use these verbs correctly.

The following chart lists these pairs in two columns to show which are transitive and which are intransitive. The definition and the principal parts of each are given.

Transitive Verbs	**Intransitive Verbs**
Lay	*Lie*
Definition	*Definition*
To put or place (something)	To rest or recline
Principal parts	*Principal parts*
lay, laid, (have) laid	lie, lay, (have) lain
Set	*Sit*
Definition	*Definition*
To put or place (something)	To rest or be seated
Principal parts	*Principal parts*
set, set, (have) set	sit, sat, (have) sat
Raise	*Rise*
Definition	*Definition*
To cause (something) to go up or grow up	To get up or go up
Principal parts	*Principal parts*
raise, raised, (have) raised	rise, rose, (have) risen

Lay—Lie

Lay is a transitive verb that means "to put or place (something)." Its principal parts are *lay, laid, (have) laid.* As a transitive verb, *lay* must pass its action either to the direct object or to the subject.

Satan <u>lays</u> his charges against God's people.
    (Satan *places* his charges. *Charges* receives the action of *lays.*)

these verbs, you may need to think carefully about their usage until you have mastered them. If you concentrate on whether the verb is transitive or intransitive and on the meanings of the words, you should be able to establish the habit of using them correctly.

Lesson Outline:

1. Lay is a transitive verb that means "to put or place (something)."
    a. Its principal parts are *lay, laid, (have) laid.*
    b. As a transitive verb, *lay* must pass its action to the direct object or to the subject.

2. Lie is an intransitive verb that means "to rest or recline."
    a. Its principal parts are *lie, lay, (have) lain.*
    b. As an intransitive verb, *lie* never passes action to another word in the sentence.

3. Set is usually a transitive verb that means "to put or place (something)."
    a. Its principal parts are *set, set, (have) set.*
    b. As a transitive verb, *set* must pass its action to the direct object or to the subject.
    c. *Set* also has the special meanings "to move below the horizon," "to keep eggs warm for hatching," and "to become firm." It is an intransitive verb when it is used with one of these meanings.

4. Sit is an intransitive verb that means "to rest or be seated."
    a. Its principal parts are *sit, sat, (have) sat.*
    b. As an intransitive verb, *sit* never passes action to another word in the sentence.

5. Raise is a transitive verb that means "to cause (something) to go up or grow up."

Joseph <u>laid</u> Jesus' body in the grave.
  (Joseph *put* Jesus' body. *Body* receives the action of *laid*.)
God's standard of holiness <u>has been laid</u> down in the Bible.
  (The standard *has been placed*. *Standard* receives the action of
    has been laid.)

Lie is an intransitive verb that means "to rest or recline." Its principal parts are *lie, lay, (have) lain*. As an intransitive verb, *lie* never passes action to another word in the sentence.

The sick calf just <u>lies</u> in its hutch.
  (The calf *rests* in its hutch. No action is passed.)
The cows <u>lay</u> under the shade trees in yesterday's heat.
  (The cows *rested* under the shade trees. No action is passed.)
Lewis <u>has lain</u> in a hospital bed for three weeks since the accident.
  (Lewis *has reclined* in a hospital bed. No action is passed.)

Whenever you must choose between a form of *lay* and a form of *lie*, consider whether the sentence needs a transitive or an intransitive verb and which definition fits the sentence.

Problem: Christine (lays, lies) on the ground to play with her
        kittens.
  Think: No action is passed; an intransitive verb is needed.
        Christine *reclines* on the ground.
Solution: Christine <u>lies</u> on the ground to play with her kittens.

Problem: Father has been (laying, lying) plastic in the garden.
  Think: Action is passed to *plastic;* a transitive verb is needed.
        Father has been *placing* plastic.
Solution: Father has been <u>laying</u> plastic in the garden.

The form *lay* is both the first principal part of the transitive verb *lay* and the second principal part of the intransitive verb *lie*. Therefore, you must be especially careful not to confuse these two meanings of *lay*. Note that *lay* is used as a transitive verb only in the present and future tenses, and as an intransitive verb only in the past tense.

I <u>lay</u> the produce on the shelves. (transitive verb, present tense)
I <u>shall lay</u> the produce on the shelves. (transitive verb, future tense)
I <u>lay</u> on the floor yesterday. (intransitive verb, past tense)

Set—Sit

Set is usually a transitive verb that means "to put or place (something)." Its principal parts are *set, set, (have) set*. As a transitive verb, *set* must pass its action to the direct object or to the subject.

  a. Its principal parts are *raise, raised, (have) raised*.

  b. As a transitive verb, *raise* must pass its action to the direct object or to the subject.

6. Rise *is an intransitive verb that means "to get up or go up."*

  a. Its principal parts are *rise, rose, (have) risen*.

  b. As an intransitive verb, *rise* never passes action to another word in the sentence.

★ EXTRA PRACTICE

Worksheet 27 (*Using* Lay—Lie, Set—Sit, *and* Raise—Rise)

The horses <u>must set</u> each foot down carefully on the slippery path.
(The horses *must put* each foot down carefully. *Foot* receives the action of *must set*.)
A clear choice <u>was set</u> before the people.
(A clear choice *was placed* before the people. *Choice* receives the action of *was set*.)
The Lord <u>has set</u> the laws of nature into force.
(The Lord *has put* the laws of nature into force. *Laws* receives the action of *has set*.)

Set also has some special meanings that are intransitive. When it is used with one of these meanings, there is no receiver of the action.

Special intransitive meanings of *set*:
To move below the horizon.
The sun always <u>sets</u> in the west.
To keep eggs warm for hatching.
A hen was <u>setting</u> in the hay.
To become firm.
Concrete <u>sets</u> in a few hours.

Sit is an intransitive verb that means "to rest or be seated." Its principal parts are *sit, sat, (have) sat*. As an intransitive verb, *sit* never passes action to another word in the sentence.

Jesus <u>sits</u> at the Father's right hand.
(Jesus *is seated* at the Father's right hand. No action is passed.)
Jesus <u>sat</u> on a colt to enter Jerusalem.
(Jesus *was seated* on a colt. No action is passed.)
That huge rock <u>has sat</u> there for many years.
(That huge rock *has rested* there.)

Whenever you must choose between a form of *set* and a form of *sit*, consider whether the sentence needs a transitive or an intransitive verb and which definition fits the sentence.

Problem: The books were (set, sat) on the shelf.
Think: Action is passed to *books;* a transitive verb is needed.
The books were *placed* on the shelf.
Solution: The books were <u>set</u> on the shelf.

Problem: An old car was (setting, sitting) beside the road.
Think: No action is passed; an intransitive verb is needed.
An old car was *resting* beside the road.
Solution: An old car was <u>sitting</u> beside the road.

Problem: This pudding is not (setting, sitting) very well.
  Think: No action is passed; an intransitive verb is needed.
    This pudding is not *becoming firm* very well.
Solution: This pudding is not <u>setting</u> very well.

Raise—Rise

Raise is a transitive verb that means "to cause (something) to go up or grow up." Its principal parts are *raise, raised, (have) raised.* As a transitive verb, *raise* must pass its action to the direct object or to the subject.

 We <u>are raising</u> feeder pigs.
  (We *are causing* pigs *to grow up. Pigs* receives the action of *are raising.*)
 Eric <u>raised</u> his hand.
  (Eric *caused* his hand *to go up. Hand* receives the action of *raised.*)
 The shades <u>have been raised</u> to brighten the room.
  (The shades *have been caused to go up. Shades* receives the action of *have been raised.*)

Rise is an intransitive verb that means "to get up or go up." Its principal parts are *rise, rose, (have) risen.* As an intransitive verb, *rise* never passes action to another word in the sentence.

 The sun <u>rises</u> in the east.
  (The sun *goes up* in the east. No action is passed.)
 The smoke <u>rose</u> lazily from the chimneys.
  (The smoke *went up* lazily. No action is passed.)
 Jesus <u>has risen</u> from the dead.
  (Jesus *has gotten up* from the dead. No action is passed.)

Again, whenever you must choose between a form of *raise* and a form of *rise,* consider whether the sentence needs a transitive or an intransitive verb and which definition fits the sentence.

Problem: The bread has (raised, risen) long enough.
  Think: No action is passed; an intransitive verb is needed.
    The bread has *gone up* long enough.
Solution: The bread has <u>risen</u> long enough.

Problem: Our spirits were (raised, risen) by the good news.
  Think: Action is passed to *spirits;* a transitive verb is needed.
    Our spirits were *caused to go up.*
Solution: Our spirits were <u>raised</u> by the good news.

Class Practice

A. Read each sentence, using the proper form of *lay* or *lie*. If you use a form of *lay*, tell which word receives the action.
   1. The masons were ——— bricks.
   2. Pigs ——— in the mud to cool off.
   3. ——— the baby in her crib.
   4. Each spoonful of batter was ——— in the pan carefully.
   5. The wolf pups ——— in the den until the danger had passed.
   6. The children will ——— down to rest after dinner.
   7. Mother has ——— all the winter clothes on the shelves.
   8. Hazel ——— on the couch after she had fallen off the swing.

B. Read each sentence, using the proper form of *set* or *sit*. If you use a form of *set*, tell which word receives the action, or give the special intransitive meaning of *set*.
   1. The psalmist wrote that God had ——— his feet on a solid rock.
   2. The proud Pharisees ——— in judgment against Jesus.
   3. When will the sun ——— this evening?
   4. ——— the boxes in the utility room.
   5. He has ——— at the bus station for two hours.
   6. Dawn is ——— by the window with her sewing.
   7. Did you ——— the dishes on the table?
   8. After the gelatin is partly ———, we will mix in the fruit.
   9. Do not ——— on that broken chair.
   10. The teacher had not ——— at her desk long before the fire alarm rang.

C. Read each sentence, using the proper form of *raise* or *rise*. If you use a form of *raise*, tell which word receives the action.
   1. Father ——— corn every year to sell.
   2. The eastern horizon is pink, so the sun will soon ———.
   3. The quality of Darla's work has ——— steadily this month.
   4. The dead saints will be ———, and the living saints will be changed.
   5. We must ——— our vision to eternal things.
   6. Our hopes of a bountiful crop were ——— by the good rain.
   7. The full moon ——— slowly from the eastern horizon as we walked home.
   8. A mist is ——— from the warm earth as the air cools.

Written Exercises

A. Write the proper form of *lay* or *lie*.
   1. Lazarus's body had ——— in the grave for several days.
   2. They showed Jesus where they had ——— him.

Lesson 49 Answers

Class Practice

A. 1. laying, bricks
   2. lie
   3. Lay, baby
   4. laid, spoonful
   5. lay
   6. lie
   7. laid, clothes
   8. lay

B. 1. set, feet
   2. sat
   3. set; move below the horizon
   4. Set, boxes
   5. sat
   6. sitting
   7. set, dishes
   8. set; become firm
   9. sit
   10. sat

C. 1. raises, corn
   2. rise
   3. risen
   4. raised, saints
   5. raise, vision
   6. raised, hopes
   7. rose
   8. rising

Written Exercises

A. 1. lain
   2. laid

3. The men were ——— blocks.
4. Levi always ——— them very straight.
5. I shall ——— down and rest awhile.
6. You may use the pencil that is ——— on my desk.
7. The papers had been ——— on the desk yesterday.
8. There they ——— until this morning.
9. Several large trees have ——— across the road since the storm.
10. Have you ——— your work aside?

B. Write the proper form of *set* or *sit*.
1. The dishes are still ——— on the table.
2. How long have you been ——— there?
3. Why have you ——— the bucket in such a precarious place?
4. Albert was ——— his hopes on a new bicycle.
5. The cage was ——— on the table by someone.
6. We ——— out some cabbage plants today.
7. You should never ——— things on the stairs.
8. Never pull the chair away from someone who is ——— down.
9. A duck ——— for five weeks before the eggs hatch.
10. Aurelia may ——— in this chair by the window.
11. The old man ——— down with a sigh.
12. Some stars never ———.

C. Write the proper form of *raise* or *rise*.
1. While Moses ——— his hands, Israel prevailed over Amalek.
2. Gilbert will ——— rabbits to sell.
3. The sun has ——— for another day that the Lord has made.
4. The fog ——— as the sun shines.
5. The walls were ——— by a large crane.
6. Since hot air ———, the ceiling is warmer than the floor.
7. The money is being ——— for the building project.
8. Is the bread dough still ———?
9. The temperature had been ———, but it is falling now.
10. Please ——— the shade so that I can see out.

Review Exercises

A. Write the second and third principal parts of each verb. Write a helping verb with the third principal part. [34]

1. run
2. swim
3. break
4. do
5. tag
6. freeze
7. swing
8. hurry
9. bring
10. cost

3. laying
4. lays *or* laid
5. lie
6. lying
7. lying *or* laid
8. lay
9. lain
10. laid

B. 1. sitting
2. sitting
3. set
4. setting
5. set
6. set
7. set
8. sitting
9. sets
10. sit
11. sat
12. set

C. 1. raised
2. raise
3. risen
4. rises
5. raised
6. rises
7. raised
8. rising
9. rising
10. raise

Review Exercises

A. 1. ran, (have) run
2. swam, (have) swum
3. broke, (have) broken
4. did, (have) done
5. tagged, (have) tagged
6. froze, (have) frozen
7. swung, (have) swung
8. hurried, (have) hurried
9. brought, (have) brought
10. cost, (have) cost

B. If the underlined verb is incorrect, write the correct verb. If it is correct, write *correct*. [34]
1. The pipes <u>bursted</u> in the sub-zero weather.
2. The owl <u>seen</u> a slight movement in the underbrush.
3. Newton <u>done</u> his chores already.
4. Have you <u>wrote</u> your composition yet?
5. Leland <u>tagged</u> Darwin after a difficult chase.
6. The cows have <u>went</u> back out to the pasture.
7. Amy has <u>took</u> her pictures home.
8. Several sheep <u>drownded</u> in the flooded pasture.

B. 1. burst
2. saw
3. did
4. written
5. correct
6. gone
7. taken
8. drowned

50. Using Other Problem Verbs

Lesson Survey
- *Can* means "to be able to."
- *May* means "to be permitted to."
- *Let* means "to allow or permit."
- *Leave* means "to depart, go away from, or allow to remain."
- Do not use *of* for the helping verb *have*.
- Be careful to use the second and third principal parts of these verbs correctly: *attack, blow, break, bring, burst, cost, drag, drown, know, tag, take, throw.*

The pairs of verbs you studied in Lesson 49 are similar in spelling and meaning. The pairs of verbs in this lesson are not quite as similar, yet they are frequently confused by many people.

Can—May

Can means "to be able to." Use this helping verb to express ability rather than permission.

Surely God <u>can</u> do anything.
(Surely God *is able to* do anything.)
<u>Can</u> a mortal man understand God fully?
(*Is* a mortal man *able to* understand God fully?)

Lesson 50

Purpose: (1) To study other problem verbs. (2) To give practice with their correct use.

Oral Review:
1. Give the definitions of the six verbs you studied in Lesson 49.
   a. lay (to put or place [something])
   b. lie (to rest or recline)
   c. set (to put or place [something]; *special meanings:* to move below the horizon; to keep eggs warm for hatching; to become firm)
   d. sit (to rest or be seated)
   e. raise (to cause [something] to go up or grow up)
   f. rise (to go up or get up)
2. Which of these six verbs are transitive? (lay, set, raise)

3. Tell which verb fits in each sentence. (Correct verbs are underlined.)
   a. The doctor's report (<u>raised</u>, rose) our hopes.
   b. You should be (setting, <u>sitting</u>) up straight.
   c. The kite is (raising, <u>rising</u>) high in the sky.
   d. Brian (laid, <u>lay</u>) in bed all morning.
4. Of the verbs *lay, lie, set, sit, raise,* and *rise,* which ones are usually transitive? Which ones are usually intransitive? (transitive—lay, set, raise; intransitive—lie, sit, rise)
5. Name the three perfect tenses, and give the helping verbs for each. (present perfect—have *or* has; past perfect—had; future perfect—shall have *or* will have)
6. What does the progressive form of a verb show? (continuing action or condition)
7. In which tenses can progressive forms be used? (all six tenses)

May means "to be permitted to." Use this helping verb to express permission rather than ability.

> He <u>may</u> go outside today.
>   (He *is permitted to* go outside today.)
> You <u>may</u> read a library book.
>   (You *are permitted to* read a library book.)

The following sentence illustrates the difference between these two verbs.

> I don't think Roy <u>can</u> move these boxes, but he <u>may</u> try if he wishes.
>   (I don't think Roy *is able to* move these boxes, but he *is permitted to* try if he wishes.)

Sometimes either verb would fit in a sentence, depending on the intended meaning.

> Crystal <u>can</u> use this sewing machine.
>   (Crystal *is able to* use this sewing machine.)
> Crystal <u>may</u> use this sewing machine.
>   (Crystal *is permitted to* use this sewing machine.)

The main problem with *can* and *may* is the tendency to use *can* for both meanings and neglect *may* altogether. Whenever you must choose between *can* and *may*, decide whether you want to express ability or permission.

> <u>May</u> I get a drink? (a question about permission, not ability)
> Father said that we <u>may</u> take a short break. (a statement about permission, not ability)

Let—Leave

Let means "to allow or permit." Unlike *can* and *may*, *let* is a main verb. Its principal parts are *let, let, (have) let*. The verb *let* is always used with another verb form. Notice the two verb forms in the following examples. Note also that when the sentence is reworded with *allow* or *permit,* the second verb form is an infinitive.

> Brother Daniel <u>let</u> us *finish* our drawings.
>   (Brother Daniel *permitted* us *to finish* our drawings.)
> Please <u>let</u> him *come* in.
>   (Please *allow* him *to come* in.)

Sometimes the second verb form is not expressed. However, you can usually add it to the sentence quite easily.

> <u>Let</u> me in. (*Let* me *come* in.)
> Father <u>let</u> us *choose* a piece of candy at the store.

8. What does the emphatic form of a verb show? (added emphasis)
9. In which tenses can emphatic forms be used? (past and present)
10. Change the verb in this sentence to the progressive and emphatic forms: *Father baled hay.* (Father was baling hay. Father did bale hay.)

Lesson Introduction: Write the following items on the board, and ask the questions below.

> You can get a drink of water.
> You may get a drink of water.

> attackted   busted   drug
> blowed   costed   tooken
> brang   drownded   tug
> brought

1. On a warm September afternoon, which of the two statements would you prefer your teacher to make? (The second would be preferred, for it gives you permission to get a drink. The first one merely says that you have the ability to get it.)
2. Which verbs listed are not even proper English words? (attackted, blowed, brang, busted, costed, drownded, tooken)
3. Which two can be present forms of verbs, but never past forms? (drug, tug)
4. Which one is a proper past form? (brought)

This lesson will give you practice with these problem verbs.

Lesson Outline:

1. **Can** *means "to be able to."* Use this helping verb to express ability rather than permission.

2. **May** *means "to be permitted to."* Use this helping verb to express permission rather than ability.

He does not <u>let</u> us every time, though.

(He does not *let* us *choose* every time.)

Leave means "to depart, go away from, or allow to remain." Its principal parts are *leave, left, (have) left. Leave* is not used with another verb form.

The summer birds will <u>leave</u> soon.

(The summer birds will *depart* soon.)

We <u>left</u> the house at 7:30 in the morning.

(We *went away from* the house at 7:30 in the morning.)

Aunt Margaret has <u>left</u> some books here for us.

(Aunt Margaret has *allowed* some books *to remain* here for us.)

Whenever you must choose between a form of *let* and a form of *leave* in a sentence, ask yourself these two questions: (1) "Which definition fits?" and (2) "Is there a second verb form?" Answering these questions will sometimes take careful thinking because both definitions include the idea of allowing and because the second verb form with *let* may not be expressed.

Problem: This bologna was (let, left) out overnight.

Think: Was the bologna *permitted* out, or was it *allowed to remain* out? (It was allowed to remain out.)

Is there a second verb form? (no)

Solution: This bologna was <u>left</u> out overnight.

Problem: Kathryn (lets, leaves) the little children play with her toys.

Think: Does Kathryn *permit* them, or does she *allow them to remain*? (She permits them.)

Is there a second verb form? (yes: *play*)

Solution: Kathryn <u>lets</u> the little children play with her toys.

Other Problem Verbs

Do not use *of* for the helping verb *have.* When phrases like *could have, should have, would have,* and *might have* are said hurriedly and carelessly, they sound like *could of, should of, would of,* and *might of.* But *of* can never be a verb.

Incorrect: David <u>would of</u> spared Absalom if he <u>could of</u>.

Correct: David <u>would have</u> spared Absalom if he <u>could have</u>.

Verbs that express past action are sometimes mispronounced or

a. Sometimes either *can* or *may* would fit in a sentence, depending on the intended meaning.

b. The main problem with *can* and *may* is the tendency to use *can* for both meanings and neglect *may* altogether.

3. **Let *means "to allow or permit."***

a. The principal parts of *let* are *let, let, (have) let.*

b. The verb *let* is always used with another verb form.

(*Teacher:* In the definition of *let* as given in this lesson, the verb is transitive. The second verb form, which is actually an infinitive with *to* omitted, is the direct object. The noun or pronoun that is usually found between *let* and the infinitive is the subject of the infinitive.)

c. Sometimes the second verb form is not expressed.

4. **Leave *means "to depart, go away from, or allow to remain."*** Its principal parts are *leave, left, (have) left.*

5. **Do not use *of* for the helping verb *have.*** When phrases like *could have, should have, would have,* and *might have* are said hurriedly and carelessly, they sound like *could of, should of, would of,* and *might of.*

6. **Be careful to use the second and third principal parts of these verbs correctly: attack, blow, break, bring, burst, cost, drag, drown, know, tag, take, throw.**

★ **EXTRA PRACTICE**

Worksheet 28 (*Using* Can—May *and* Let—Leave)

Worksheet 29 (*Using Other Problem Verbs*)

otherwise used wrongly. The following chart shows the principal parts for a number of problem verbs.

Present	Past	Past Participle
attack	attacked [*not* attackted]	(have) attacked [*not* attackted]
blow	blew [*not* blowed]	(have) blown [*not* blowed]
break	broke	(have) broken [*not* broke]
bring	brought [*not* brang]	(have) brought [*not* brung]
burst	burst [*not* bursted]	(have) burst [*not* bursted]

(Do not use forms of *bust* for forms of *burst*.)

cost	cost [*not* costed]	(have) cost [*not* costed]
drag	dragged [*not* drug]	(have) dragged [*not* drug]
drown	drowned [*not* drownded]	(have) drowned [*not* drownded]
know	knew [*not* knowed]	(have) known [*not* knowed]
tag	tagged [*not* tug]	(have) tagged [*not* tug]
take	took [*not* taken]	(have) taken [*not* tooken]
throw	threw [*not* throwed]	(have) thrown [*not* throwed]

If you make mistakes with any of the verbs in this lesson, put forth special effort to overcome the wrong speech habits. An interest in doing your best and a desire to communicate clearly are signs of a worthy character.

Class Practice

Orally

A. Read each sentence, using the correct word.
1. Father said that we (can, may) go fishing tomorrow.
2. (Can, May) Susan make the meal by herself, or does she need Mother's help?
3. (Can, May) I please open the window?
4. We (can, may) not ride our bicycles on this busy highway.
5. He has not (let, left) us enter the room.
6. The neighbors (let, left) us use their truck.
7. Clifford (let, left) his car at the repair shop.
8. We should not (let, leave) the baby outside by himself.

B. Read these sentences correctly.
1. The people who had refused Noah's warnings drownded in the Flood.
2. When the dove had brung an olive branch, Noah must of rejoiced.
3. Lot's selfish choice costed him very dearly.
4. Lot should of stayed out of Sodom.
5. The Midianites attackted the Israelites.
6. Hiram's servants drug cedars out of the Lebanon Mountains for David.
7. King Saul throwed his javelin at his own son.

Lesson 50 Answers

Class Practice

A.
1. may
2. Can
3. May
4. may
5. let
6. let
7. left
8. leave

B. (Corrections are underlined.)
1. The people who had refused Noah's warnings <u>drowned</u> in the Flood.
2. When the dove had <u>brought</u> an olive branch, Noah must <u>have</u> rejoiced.
3. Lot's selfish choice <u>cost</u> him very dearly.
4. Lot should <u>have</u> stayed out of Sodom.
5. The Midianites <u>attacked</u> the Israelites.
6. Hiram's servants <u>dragged</u> cedars out of the Lebanon Mountains for David.
7. King Saul <u>threw</u> his javelin at his own son.

8. When the south wind blowed softly, the shipowner and the captain decided to sail to a better harbor.
9. Mildred has tooken the message to Father.
10. Nobody knowed what the answer was supposed to be.
11. The old burlap sack busted at the seams.
12. Philip had tug Roger before he was on base.
13. The jar bursted when we placed it in hot water.
14. Mother would of answered if she could of heard.
15. Connie brang some pictures of their trip to the Philippines.

C. Read each sentence, changing the verb to the past tense and the present perfect tense.
1. Bradley wears my sweater.
2. This ball glove costs too much for me.
3. The pipes burst under pressure.
4. The winds blow the ship off course.
5. That hawk attacks our chickens.

Written Exercises

A. Write the correct verb for each sentence.
1. We must never (let, leave) our hearts become discouraged.
2. With God's help, we (can, may) do whatever He calls us to do.
3. Paul wrote, "Ye (can, may) all prophesy one by one."
4. God has never (let, left) His people defenseless before the enemy.
5. At Satan's suggestion, some people have (let, left) the truth of God's Word slip from their understanding.
6. They (can, may) no longer interpret the Word accurately.
7. We must (let, leave) the Bible direct our thoughts, words, and actions.
8. All (can, may) take a turn at guessing the number of beans in the jar.

B. Find each incorrect word, and write the word that should replace it. If a sentence has no error, write *correct*.
1. Mary set at Jesus' feet, hearing His gracious words.
2. We too should leave the Master's words feed our souls.
3. Can His words truly meet our needs?
4. God has left many saints go through severe trials of faith.
5. Our prayers raise to the throne of grace.
6. We should leave our burdens at the place of prayer.
7. Christians can do some things that were forbidden for Jews.
8. The sun rises and sets on the just and the unjust.
9. Rehoboam should of listened to the advice of the older men.
10. Like a contented sheep, the child of God lays down in pastures of peace.

8. When the south wind <u>blew</u> softly, the shipowner and the captain decided to sail to a better harbor.
9. Mildred has <u>taken</u> the message to Father.
10. Nobody <u>knew</u> what the answer was supposed to be.
11. The old burlap sack <u>burst</u> at the seams.
12. Philip had <u>tagged</u> Roger before he was on base.
13. The jar <u>burst</u> when we placed it in hot water.
14. Mother would <u>have</u> answered if she could <u>have</u> heard.
15. Connie <u>brought</u> some pictures of their trip to the Philippines.

C. 1. Bradley wore my sweater.
   Bradley has worn my sweater.
2. This ball glove cost too much for me.
   This ball glove has cost too much for me.
3. The pipes burst under pressure.
   The pipes have burst under pressure.
4. The winds blew the ship off course.
   The winds have blown the ship off course.
5. That hawk attacked our chickens.
   That hawk has attacked our chickens.

Written Exercises

A. 1. let   5. let
   2. can   6. can
   3. may   7. let
   4. left   8. may

B. 1. sat   6. correct
   2. let   7. may
   3. correct   8. correct
   4. let   9. have
   5. rise   10. lies

11. Our songs of thanksgiving have raised to the Giver of all things.
12. Jesus left His disciples with the promise of the Comforter.
13. God has lain many opportunities at our feet.
14. We can overcome every temptation by the power of God.
15. Only God could of devised the plan of redemption.

C. Write the correct past form for each one that is incorrect. If a sentence has no error, write *correct*.
   1. The winds blowed and the rains fell, but the house on the rock stood firm.
   2. Pharaoh and his army were drownded in the Red Sea.
   3. The children of Israel burst forth in praise to their Redeemer.
   4. The influence of the heathen drug Israel into idolatry.
   5. Daniel was throwed into the lions' den because of his loyalty to God.
   6. The Lord brang His people into the Promised Land.
   7. Gideon and his men broke the pitchers and blowed the trumpets.
   8. The Midianites thought they had been attackted by a great army.
   9. It has always tooken faith and courage to live for the Lord.
   10. Living for self has always cost more than living for the Lord.
   11. Jesus knowed the bitter thoughts of the Pharisees.
   12. If you have been tagged, you must go to the prison.
   13. Lloyd's arm was broke after he fell off the ladder.
   14. We drug the heavy sacks over to the door.
   15. Has Brother Sidney brung the surprise he promised?
   16. Emily already knowed how to type.
   17. Have you taken your books home?
   18. The dry branches bursted into flames.

Review Exercises

A. Write which of the six tenses each underlined verb is. [35, 37]
   1. Before David subdued the Philistines, they often <u>had attacked</u> Israel.
   2. A clear conscience <u>makes</u> a peaceful heart.
   3. Jesus <u>performed</u> many miracles of healing.
   4. By the time we get home, Uncle Nathan's likely <u>will have arrived</u>.
   5. They <u>will stay</u> at our place for a week.
   6. They <u>have</u> not <u>visited</u> us since they moved to Wisconsin.

B. Write each underlined verb in the progressive form. Do not change the tense. [39]
   1. Mother and the girls <u>clean</u> the kitchen.
   2. Father and the boys <u>baled</u> hay.
   3. We replaced the hose that <u>had leaked</u>.

---

11. risen
12. correct
13. laid
14. correct
15. have

C. 1. blew
   2. drowned
   3. correct
   4. dragged
   5. thrown
   6. brought
   7. blew
   8. attacked
   9. taken
   10. correct
   11. knew
   12. correct
   13. broken
   14. dragged
   15. brought
   16. knew
   17. correct
   18. burst

Review Exercises
A. 1. past perfect
   2. present
   3. past
   4. future perfect
   5. future
   6. present perfect

B. 1. are cleaning
   2. were baling
   3. had been leaking

4. By Sunday we <u>shall have held</u> services in the new building for a year.
5. Tomorrow morning we <u>shall pick</u> blueberries.
6. The cows <u>have eaten</u> more hay than usual.

C) Write each underlined verb in the emphatic form. Do not change the tense. [39]
1. God <u>created</u> all things in six days.
2. Jesus <u>intercedes</u> for the believers.
3. The angels of the Lord <u>minister</u> to the saints.

4. shall have been holding
5. shall be picking
6. have been eating

C. 1. did create
2. does intercede
3. do minister

---

51. Writing Friendly Letters

> **Lesson Survey**
> - The **heading** of a **friendly letter** contains your address and the date of the letter.
> - The **greeting** contains the name of the person to whom you are writing.
> - The **body** is the message of the letter.
> - The **closing** should be a meaningful expression of your feelings.
> - The **signature** may be merely your first name.
> - An envelope should include a return address and a mailing address.

Of the twenty-seven books of the New Testament, twenty-one are specifically identified as epistles or letters. Many of these letters are addressed to groups of people. Some of them, like Philemon and 3 John, are addressed to individuals. In these letters, the apostles give encouragement and warning as well as personal information about their plans.

Many other letters of godly people have been preserved. The *Martyrs Mirror* contains a number of letters written by persecuted Christians to their families and friends. Today letters still fill an important role among God's people.

A *friendly letter* has five main parts: *heading, greeting, body, closing,* and *signature*. The following example illustrates a friendly letter with good form and content. Refer to this example as you study the descriptions of the letter parts.

Lesson 51

Purpose: To study the rules for writing friendly letters.

Oral Review:
1. What are some ways that outlining written material is a good study aid? (It forces the reader to analyze the material and identify main ideas and less important ideas. It helps the reader to remember what he read. It provides a good way to recall main ideas when reviewing the material later.)
2. Why is outlining an important first step in writing? (It gives the writer an orderly plan for his composition.)
3. Name some advantages in taking notes on a sermon. (helps one to better understand the sermon, helps to prevent sleepiness and daydreaming; helps one to grasp the main points; helps one to remember the sermon; serves as a future reference; can be shared with others)
4. What information should appear near the top of a paper of sermon notes? (the date, the name of the speaker, the place of the service, the sermon title, and the reference of the Scripture text)
5. What should the sermon notes consist of? (the speaker's main points and the Scripture references used with them)
6. Tell which words in these phrases should be capitalized. (Answers are underlined.)
   a. <u>Kellogg's</u> corn flakes
   b. <u>June</u> 21, the first day of summer
   c. some mountains in <u>Argentina</u>
   d. "<u>Fresh From</u> the <u>Throne</u> of <u>Glory</u>"

Lesson Introduction: "As cold waters to a thirsty soul, so is good news from a far country" (Proverbs

Heading	Route 2, Box 15 Barnett, MO 65011 May 12, 20—
Greeting	Dear Clifford,

"God moves in a mysterious way, His wonders to perform." Our class sang this as a theme song a few weeks ago. And it is interesting how many examples of His wonders we have observed since then.

I suppose you heard about the heavy rains we have had. Our orchard looked more like a river than an orchard! During the second day of the rain, I was outside sloshing around when I saw our hen in some shallow water. I went to rescue her, but she was already dead. But under her wings were her five little chicks, warm and dry! I had to think of Jesus' words about wanting to help the people of Jerusalem as a hen gathers her chicks under her wings. I think I'll always remember this when I read that verse.

Body   Then last week Brendon brought a five-foot-long black snake to school. The snake had somehow gotten into their house, and Brendon's father managed to catch it. The next day Clyde brought a big rat he had caught in his live-animal trap. Was it ever interesting to watch the snake swallow that rat! I never saw a snake's mouth open so wide before. I did feel almost sorry—even for a rat!—when I saw how it struggled as the snake slowly drew it into its mouth. Some of the girls wouldn't even watch it!

Is your school year almost finished? We have only two more weeks. It was a pleasant year, but I do look forward to being at home more and helping with the summer work. Father says we boys may build that tree house we talked about last summer when you were here! Wouldn't it be fun if your family could visit us again this summer? Maybe you could even help us build it!

Write soon, and let me know if there is any chance you might come in the next few months.

Closing	Your cousin,
Signature	Kenneth

The heading appears in the upper right-hand corner of the letter and consists of three lines: two lines for your address and one for the date. Notice how the rules of capitalization and punctuation are followed in the heading of the sample letter.

The greeting, which is written at the left margin, contains the name of the person to whom you are writing. Capitalize the first word and all the nouns, and place a comma after the greeting.

25:25). Perhaps you have spent several weeks away from your family. Or maybe a close friend has moved to a distant community. If so, you likely know the eager anticipation of expecting a letter.

Have you made excuses for not writing letters? Maybe you have said that you are not a good writer or that you just don't know what to write. Like any other skill, letter writing can be developed. And since it is an important way for friends to communicate, it is a skill you should seek to develop.

Lesson Outline:

1. A friendly letter has five main parts: **heading, greeting, body, closing,** *and* **signature.**

2. The heading contains your address and the date of the letter.

    a. Write the heading in the upper right-hand corner.

    b. Follow the rules of capitalization and punctuation for the address and the date.

3. The greeting contains the name of the person to whom you are writing.

    a. Write the greeting at the left margin.

    b. Capitalize the first word and all the nouns.

    c. Place a comma after the greeting.

4. The body is the message of the letter.

    a. Give your letters a definite tone of friendliness.

    b. Before you begin writing, make a list of things you want to be sure to include in the letter.

      (1) *Begin with a fitting Scripture verse or a few lines of poetry.*

      (2) *Start at once to say what you want to say.*

Dear Margaret,   Dear Mrs. Strite,
Dear Uncle Dale,   Dear Friends at Midvale School,

The body is the message of the letter. Give your letters a definite tone of friendliness. Write the way you would talk to your friend, as much as possible. Show a genuine interest in and courtesy toward the other person. Follow the Golden Rule: write a letter like one that you would enjoy receiving.

Before you begin writing, make a list of things you want to be sure to include in the letter. The following checklist may help you.

1. *Begin with a fitting Scripture verse or a few lines of poetry.*

2. *Start at once to say what you want to say.*

   Poor: "I'm finally getting around to writing."
   "How are you? What are you doing?"
   Good: "I was glad to hear that you're recovering from your accident."

3. *Answer any questions that were directed to you in a previous letter.* If you cannot answer the question, at least acknowledge it and explain why you are not able to answer it.

4. *Tell about interesting events that have happened to you or to others whom the person knows.* Do not assume too much, or you will leave the reader wondering or guessing about details you failed to give.

5. *Write an interesting and worthwhile ending.*

   Poor: "It is almost time for the mailman, so I had better close."
   "I seem to be out of news, so I'll close."
   Good: "I am always glad to hear from you and about you."
   "We will always remember your kindness to us."
   "I'll look forward to hearing from you soon."

The closing should be a meaningful expression of your feelings. Place it below the last line of the letter, with its left edge directly below the left edge of the heading. Capitalize only the first word of the closing, and place a comma after it.

Here are some good closings for a friendly letter.

Sincerely,   In Christian love,   Your friend,
Sincerely yours,   With love and prayers,   Your loving son,

In a friendly letter, the signature may be merely your first name. Always write the signature by hand, even if you have typed the letter. The signature should be directly below the closing.

An envelope should include a return address and a mailing address. The return address should be placed in the upper left-hand corner of the

(3) *Answer any questions that were directed to you in a previous letter.*

(4) *Tell about interesting events that have happened to you or to others whom the person knows.* Do not assume too much and leave the reader wondering or guessing about details you failed to give.

(5) *Write an interesting and worthwhile ending.*

5. **The closing should be a meaningful expression of your feelings.**
   a. Place it below the last line of the letter, with its left edge directly below the left edge of the heading.
   b. Capitalize only the first word of the closing, and place a comma after it.

6. **The signature may be merely your first name.** Always write the signature by hand.

7. **An envelope should include a return address and a mailing address.**
   a. The return address should be placed in the upper left-hand corner of the envelope.
   b. The mailing address should be placed slightly below the center and toward the right.
   c. The mailing address should be typed or printed carefully with all capital letters and no punctuation.

envelope. The mailing address should be placed slightly below the center and toward the right. If the mailing address is typed or printed carefully with all capital letters and no punctuation, the postal service will be able to handle the letter most efficiently.

If you mail the letter in a large envelope, first fold the bottom third of the paper up; then fold the top third down. If you are using a small envelope, first fold the lower half of the paper up; then fold it in thirds. Always place the letter in the envelope with the last fold line at the bottom.

To use a large envelope:

fold paper in thirds   ready for large envelope   insert like this

To use a small envelope:

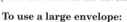

fold paper in half   fold in thirds   ready for small envelope

insert like this

Teacher: In the time since this book was originally published, the value of all capital letters and no punctuation in mailing addresses has diminished. Shift the emphasis to neatness and to printing each part precisely as the official source gave the address. This contributes the most toward efficient mailing service.

Class Practice

Tell what is wrong with the following friendly letter.

                                         3213 west Overbrook drive
                                         Peoria Il. 61604

Dear Judith

    Well, how are you? I'm fine and I hope you are too.

    We went on our school trip last week. I thought it was really interesting. Did you go on yours yet?

    Nanny, our pet goat, had twin kids yesterday. They are cute. I hope you can come while they are young and playful.

    Well, I can't think of anything else to say, so I'll close.

                                                      Hilda

Written Exercises

Write a friendly letter to a friend, a grandparent, or another relative. Address an envelope, and place your letter in it.

Review Exercises

Write the letter of the item that is capitalized correctly. [20]

1. a. false Gods named in the Old testament
   b. false gods named in the Old Testament
2. a. assignments for spelling and Canadian history
   b. assignments for Spelling and Canadian History
3. a. with my uncle and my neighbor John
   b. with my Uncle and my Neighbor John
4. a. the Nile river or the Amazon river
   b. the Nile River or the Amazon River
5. a. at Snyder's Farm Market
   b. at Snyder's Farm market
6. a. Campbell's Tomato Soup
   b. Campbell's tomato soup
7. a. Let Not Your Heart Be Troubled
   b. Let not Your Heart be Troubled
8. a. three miles South of Versailles, Missouri
   b. three miles south of Versailles, Missouri
9. a. in late spring or early summer
   b. in late Spring or early Summer
10. a. after we ask Mother and Father
    b. after we ask mother and father

Grandmama

52. Writing Social Notes

Lesson Survey

- A thank-you note should express sincere gratitude for a pleasant visit or a gift.
- An invitation must be specific to avoid misunderstandings.
- A reply to an invitation should express appreciation for the thoughtfulness of the one who invited you.

A friendly letter may cover a wide range of topics. But sometimes you may send only a brief letter to express thanks, to give an invitation, or to reply to an invitation. These social notes contain the same five parts as other friendly letters, but the body is brief and concise.

A thank-you note should express sincere gratitude for a pleasant visit or a gift. The Bible commands us to be thankful. We should be prompt in expressing our thankfulness when others show kindness to us. We should also be specific with our thanks, telling exactly when the visit was and what we enjoyed, or telling exactly why we appreciate a gift. Specific details make your note meaningful because they help to show the sincerity of your gratitude.

Thank-you note:

506 White Oak Road
New Holland, PA 17557
February 2, 20—

Dear Aunt Mildred,

Thank you very much for your gift! The stationery is beautiful, and the Scripture verses on it are well chosen. You can see that I'm making use of it already.

I sincerely hope you have received a measure of the joy that you have given me.

Affectionately yours,
Mary Ann

Even if the gift is something you do not want or like, you can be thankful that the person thought enough of you to give it. And you can express appreciation for that thoughtfulness. Perhaps you can comment on something that you do like about the gift. However, do not be dishonest and pretend you really appreciated a gift when you did not. On the other hand, you must be careful not to hurt the feelings of the giver.

In the example above, suppose Mary Ann had recently received several

Lesson 52

Purpose: To teach the proper form and content of a thank-you note, an invitation, and a reply to an invitation. (*Previous experience:* These social notes as variants of friendly letters.)

Oral Review:

1. Name the five parts of a friendly letter in order. (heading, greeting, body, closing, signature)
2. What two things are included in the heading? (the writer's address, the date on which the letter is written)
3. What kinds of information should be included in a friendly letter? (a fitting Scripture verse or a few lines of poetry, answers to any questions the other person may have asked, news about events that will be interesting to the receiver)
4. Tell where commas or semicolons are needed in these sentences, and why. (Commas and semicolons are underlined.)
   a. The kind, courteous children helped the visitor find his way around. (two descriptive adjectives used together)
   b. Marlene, you should see Frisky, our little puppy. (noun of direct address; appositive)
   c. Our pets include dogs, cats, and rabbits. (words in a series)
   d. If it hadn't rained, we could have finished today; but now we must wait until another day. (comma after subordinate clause before main clause; semicolon between items if one item contains a comma)
5. When should a semicolon be used instead of a comma in joining the two clauses of a compound sentence? (when there is already a comma in one or both of the clauses)

boxes of identical stationery. Perhaps Aunt Mildred had indicated that she might give a book which Mary Ann really wanted. What should she do? The following body of a thank-you note expresses a good attitude.

Thank you very much for your thoughtfulness in sending the gift! The stationery is beautiful, and the Scripture verses on it are well chosen.

A note of invitation must be specific to avoid misunderstandings. Tell the receiver exactly *what, when,* and *where.* Mention any activities, such as cleaning or painting, that may require suitable clothes.

Note extending an invitation:

> 150 Washington Rd.
> East Greenville, PA 18041
> June 2, 20—

Dear Leonard,

I understand that your father is planning to come to our church for a topic on Thursday evening, July 5. My parents have given their permission for me to invite you to our farm for Friday, Saturday, and Sunday. My father is scheduled to preach at your church on Sunday evening, July 8, so we would take you home then.

If you come, be sure to bring several sets of old clothes along because there are lots of chores to do around here. I'm eager to see you again!

> Your friend,
> Marvin

When you write a reply to an invitation, be sure to express appreciation for the thoughtfulness of the one who invited you. You should also repeat the information so that there is surely no misunderstanding. If you must decline, give a good reason why you cannot accept the invitation.

Note accepting an invitation:

> Route 1, Box 135
> Dover, DE 19901
> June 10, 20—

Dear Marvin,

Thank you for the invitation to come to your farm on Thursday evening, July 5, with my father. Father and Mother say it should suit for me to come. I don't want to just stand around and watch you work, so I'll be sure to bring some work clothes along! The Lord willing, I'll see you in a few weeks. I'm looking forward to it.

> Sincerely,
> Leonard

Lesson Introduction: When Jesus healed the ten lepers, what was it that set the Samaritan apart from the other nine? (He was the only one in the group who returned to thank Jesus.) God's people are thankful people; therefore, thank-you notes should be a fairly common form of friendly letters among them.

Lesson Outline:

1. A thank-you note should express sincere gratitude for a pleasant visit or a gift. If the gift is something you do not want or like, you should still express appreciation for the giver's thoughtfulness.

2. An invitation must be specific to avoid misunderstandings.
    a. Tell the receiver exactly *what, when,* and *where.*
    b. Mention any activities, such as cleaning or painting, that may require suitable clothes.

3. A reply to an invitation should express appreciation for the thoughtfulness of the one who invited you.
    a. Repeat the information so that there is no misunderstanding.
    b. If you must decline, give a good reason why you cannot accept the invitation.

★ *EXTRA PRACTICE*
Worksheet 30 (*Writing Social Notes*)

Note declining an invitation: (body)

Thank you for the invitation to come to your farm on Thursday evening, July 5, with my father. I'm very sorry, but I will not be able to stay this time. Our broilers will be shipped out on Tuesday, July 3, and the next batch will come in on Monday, July 9. In the meantime we will be busy cleaning out the chicken house and making the usual preparations.

I'm really disappointed, but Father says maybe something will work out some other time. Our whole family plans to come along to the meeting on July 5, so at least we'll get to visit a little while.

We could use the telephone to express thanks, or to give or accept an invitation. But a letter of thanks can be put away and read again later. It is visible proof that you remembered to express your gratitude. A letter of invitation presents all the details in writing, and it gives the other person plenty of time for things like checking schedules and discussing the matter with his parents. It can also serve as a written record of a memorable time shared by you and your friend. Using the telephone may seem more convenient, but writing a letter still has a number of advantages.

Class Practice

A. Tell what is wrong with the following thank-you note.

Dear Aunt Lucinda:

Thank you for the gift you sent me. I have been wanting a blue sweater, but I guess brown is all right too. It's rather bulky, so I suppose I'll wear it around the house sometimes. Or maybe one of my younger sisters will like it better. Thank you anyway.

Sincerely,
Bonnie

B. Tell what is wrong with the following invitation.

6877 Brink Rd.
Laytonsville, MD 20882

Eugene,

Would it suit you to come to my place next week? You could come along with Brother Glenn when he comes to preach at our church. I'm looking forward to seeing you again.

Your Cousin,
Melvin

Written Exercises

A. Write a thank-you note to someone who has given you something or has done something for you, or to someone whom you have visited recently.

Lesson 52 Answers

Class Practice

A. 1. There is no heading.
  2. The greeting is followed by a colon rather than a comma.
  3. The tone of the letter is not courteous. Bonnie should not mention that she had wanted a blue sweater or that the sweater is bulky. If she cannot truthfully thank Aunt Lucinda for the sweater, she should at least express appreciation for her aunt's thoughtfulness.

B. 1. The heading does not include a date.
  2. The greeting should say, "Dear Eugene."
  3. The invitation does not specifically say when Eugene would come or go. No suggestion is given for how Eugene would return home.
  4. In the closing, *cousin* should not be capitalized.

Written Exercises

A and B.
  (Individual work.)

B. Write two replies to this invitation, one accepting and one declining.

Route 1, Box 68
Dongola, IL 62926
May 25, 20—

Dear Curtis,

My parents have given me permission to invite you for a visit in our home from June 14 through June 20. I understand that your family is planning to come to the ordination at the Glenwood Mennonite Church on June 14. We plan to be there too, and we could pick you up then. Brother Edwin, one of our ministers, plans to travel to your community on June 20 for the weekend meetings scheduled at your church. We have talked with him, and it suits for him to take you along back.

Bring some old clothes along because we plan to paint the garage that week. I hope we'll be able to hike back to the waterfalls again too.

I am eagerly waiting to hear from you, and I surely hope it will suit.

Your cousin,
Eldon

Review Exercises

Write the letter of the sentence that is punctuated correctly. (If you need help, turn to Lessons 104, 106, and 110.)

1. a. Because the Lord has richly blessed us we have more than enough.
   b. Because the Lord has richly blessed us, we have more than enough.
2. a. Seek to develop the traits of honesty, kindness, and dependability.
   b. Seek to develop the traits of honesty, kindness and dependability.
3. a. Paul, the apostle to the Gentiles, wrote much of the New Testament.
   b. Paul the apostle to the Gentiles wrote much of the New Testament.
4. a. My grandfather, the third in a family of eleven children, was born on May 20, 1921, and my grandmother, the youngest in a family of nine, was born on May 5, 1923.
   b. My grandfather, the third in a family of eleven children, was born on May 20, 1921; and my grandmother, the youngest in a family of nine, was born on May 5, 1923.
5. a. These straight smooth boards should work fine.
   b. These straight, smooth boards should work fine.

Review Exercises

1. b
2. a
3. a
4. b
5. b

53. Active and Passive Voice

> **Lesson Survey**
> - A transitive verb that passes its action to a direct object is in the **active voice.**
> - A transitive verb that passes its action to the subject is in the **passive voice.**
> - A simple predicate in the passive voice is always a verb phrase, with a form of *be* as a helping verb and a past participle as the main verb.
> - The passive voice can be used in all six tenses.

In Chapter 4 you learned about transitive verbs—verbs that pass their action to some other word in the sentence. You should remember that the action may be passed either to a direct object or to the subject of the sentence.

A transitive verb that passes its action to a direct object is in the *active voice.* In such a sentence, the subject is *active,* performing the action of the verb. The direct object receives the action of the verb. Most transitive verbs are in the active voice.

Jesus <u>told</u> many parables.
   (Direct object *parables* receives the action of *told.*)

These <u>stories</u> <u>teach</u> spiritual truths.
   (Direct object *truths* receives the action of *teach.*)

A transitive verb that passes its action to the subject is in the *passive voice.* Instead of the subject being *active,* it is *passive.* Instead of *performing* the action, the subject *receives* the action of the verb.

Many <u>parables</u> <u>were told</u> by Jesus.
   (*Parables* receives the action of *were told,* but it is now the subject.)

```
  parables  |  were told
_____|_____
            |
```

Lesson 53

Purpose: To teach the concept of voice for transitive verbs.

Oral Review:

1. Identify the wrong use of verbs in these sentences.
   a. Leslie tug Donald just in time. (tagged)
   b. Last year the sweet corn costed more than this. (cost)
   c. You should of known better than to jump from that height. (have)
   d. Can I please get a drink? (May)
   e. Leave Loretta answer the phone. (Let)
   f. The fog should raise after the sun shines warmly. (rise)
   g. We must set still in church. (sit)
   h. The sick calf laid around in the barnyard all day. (lay)
   i. The shelf in my closet has broke down. (broken)
   j. We drug the heavy feed bags over to the feeders. (dragged)

2. Tell whether these sentences are simple, compound, or complex.
   a. The young person who develops good habits will avoid many problems. (complex)
   b. My friend, you should remember your Creator and give Him your service. (simple)
   c. Bad habits will become powerful masters, but good habits often are useful servants. (compound)
   d. Because we cannot find our way alone, we need the Bible, God's message to us. (complex)

3. On the chalkboard, diagram the skeletons, complements, and appositives in the sentences in number 2.

Spiritual <u>truths</u> <u>are taught</u> by these stories.
   (*Truths* receives the action of *are taught,* but it is now the subject.)

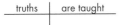

Notice that the direct objects of the active voice verbs (*parables* and *truths*) become the subjects of the passive voice verbs. The original subjects in these examples (*Jesus* and *stories*) are retained as objects of prepositions. Many subjects are retained in this way, but that is not required. The sentence is complete without the prepositional phrase.

> The weathermen forecast severe thunderstorms for our area.
> Severe thunderstorms were forecast for our area.

A simple predicate in the passive voice is always a verb phrase, with a form of *be* as a helping verb and a past participle as the main verb. All the following verb phrases are in the passive voice.

Verb phrases in the passive voice:

am seen	are told	were found
is known	was kept	will be heard

A form of *be* is also a helping verb in the progressive verb forms, but then the main verb is the *present* participle rather than the *past* participle. Compare the following verb phrases with the ones above.

Verb phrases in progressive forms:

am seeing	are telling	were finding
is knowing	was keeping	will be hearing

The past participle is also the main verb in the perfect tenses, but then the helping verb is a form of *have.* Compare the following verb phrases with the ones above.

Verb phrases in perfect tenses:

have seen	have told	has found
has known	had kept	had heard

The passive voice can be used in all six tenses. In every tense, a form of *be* is used as a helping verb. Other helping verbs may be needed as well. For example, a perfect tense in the passive voice needs a form of *have* and a form of *be.* And for the future perfect tense in the passive voice, the verb phrase includes *shall* or *will,* a form of *have,* and a form of *be.*

The following chart shows a conjugation of the verb *keep* in the passive voice for all six tenses.

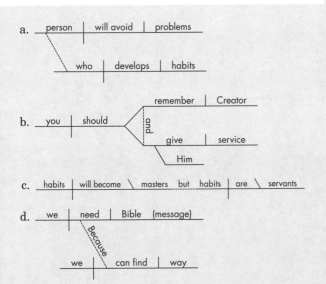

Lesson Introduction: *Active* and *passive* are antonyms that are used in various ways, as illustrated by the following sentences.

> On a job, an active <u>person</u> often <u>tells</u> others what to do.
>
> A passive <u>person</u> <u>is told</u> what to do.
>
> In active solar heating, special <u>devices</u> <u>collect</u> and <u>distribute</u> heat from the sun.
>
> In passive solar heating, a <u>house</u> <u>is warmed</u> by sunshine streaming through large windows.

In these examples, the words *active* and *passive* are used in sentences with active and passive verbs respectively. This lesson deals with the active and passive voice of transitive verbs.

Keep

Person	Singular	Plural

Present Tense

First: I am kept. / We are kept.
Second: You are kept. / You are kept.
Third: He is kept. / They are kept.

Past Tense

First: I was kept. / We were kept.
Second: You were kept. / You were kept.
Third: He was kept. / They were kept.

Future Tense

First: I shall be kept. / We shall be kept.
Second: You will be kept. / You will be kept.
Third: He will be kept. / They will be kept.

Present Perfect Tense

First: I have been kept. / We have been kept.
Second: You have been kept. / You have been kept.
Third: He has been kept. / They have been kept.

Past Perfect Tense

First: I had been kept. / We had been kept.
Second: You had been kept. / You had been kept.
Third: He had been kept. / They had been kept.

Future Perfect Tense

First: I shall have been kept. / We shall have been kept.
Second: You will have been kept. / You will have been kept.
Third: He will have been kept. / They will have been kept.

Class Practice

A. Read each verb, and tell whether it is in the *active* or *passive* voice. Tell what word receives the action of the verb.

1. God has given His message to mankind.
2. The Old Testament was given before the New Testament.
3. God is giving us many good and perfect gifts.
4. The sheep are sheltered by a roof.
5. A hammer can break a stone in pieces.
6. You are being called by Mother.
7. The same carpenters built four other houses in the area.
8. Oil is pumped for many miles in large underground pipes.
9. The children were playing a game under the tree.
10. Our lunches were being prepared before breakfast.

Lesson 53 Answers

Class Practice

A.
1. has given—active, message
2. was given—passive, Old Testament
3. is giving—active, gifts
4. are sheltered—passive, sheep
5. can break—active, stone
6. are being called—passive, You
7. built—active, houses
8. is pumped—passive, Oil
9. were playing—active, game
10. were being prepared—passive, lunches

Lesson Outline:

1. A transitive verb that passes its action to a direct object is in the active voice.

a. The subject performs the action, and the direct object receives the action of the verb.
b. Most transitive verbs are in the active voice.

2. A transitive verb that passes its action to the subject is in the passive voice.

3. A simple predicate in the passive voice is always a verb phrase, with a form of be as a helping verb and a past participle as the main verb.

4. The passive voice can be used in all six tenses.

B. Change each sentence so that the verb is in the active voice. Do not change the tense.
  1. Lazarus has been raised to life by the Master.
  2. Jesus was denied three times by Peter.
  3. The wise men had been led by a star.
  4. All wickedness will be punished by the Lord.

C. Change each sentence so that the verb is in the passive voice and the original subject is in a prepositional phrase. Do not change the tense.
  1. Caesar had ordered a great census.
  2. Moses led the Israelites through the wilderness.
  3. A kind Samaritan will rescue the victim.
  4. Jesus speaks words of comfort.

Written Exercises

A. Write whether each verb is in the *active* or *passive* voice. Write the word that receives the action of the verb.
  1. Rehoboam ignored the advice of the older men.
  2. The advice of younger men was sought by the new king.
  3. The men of the northern tribes have rejected Rehoboam.
  4. Jeroboam has been anointed as king of the Northern Kingdom.
  5. Several golden calves were set up by King Jeroboam.
  6. The people are led away from true worship.
  7. God will punish Jeroboam for his wickedness.
  8. A prophet was sent to Jeroboam with a warning from God.
  9. Jeroboam's resentment of the message is seen by his reaction.
  10. His outstretched hand was rendered useless by the Lord.

B. Rewrite each sentence so that the verb is in the active voice. Do not change the tense.
  1. A simple meal was prepared by the hostess.
  2. The plates have been set neatly on the table by the children.
  3. Our lives are richly blessed by God.
  4. The clocks will be fixed by Mr. Daley.
  5. The leaves were blown by the wind.

C. Rewrite each sentence so that the verb is in the passive voice and the original subject is in a prepositional phrase. Do not change the tense.
  1. That loud noise disturbs Grandmother.
  2. Dallas had rung the bell.
  3. Our congregation has sung this song.
  4. Gloria is cutting the pie.
  5. Raymond ate the last piece of cake.

D. Conjugate the verb *see* in the passive voice for all six tenses.

Past Perfect Tense

Person	Singular	Plural
First:	I had been seen.	We had been seen.
Second:	You had been seen.	You had been seen.
Third:	He had been seen.	They had been seen.

Future Perfect Tense

Person	Singular	Plural
First:	I shall have been seen.	We shall have been seen.
Second:	You will have been seen.	You will have been seen.
Third:	He will have been seen.	They will have been seen.

B. 1. The Master has raised Lazarus to life.
   2. Peter denied Jesus three times.
   3. A star had led the wise men.
   4. The Lord will punish all wickedness.

C. 1. A great census had been ordered by Caesar.
   2. The Israelites were led through the wilderness by Moses.
   3. The victim will be rescued by a kind Samaritan.
   4. Words of comfort are spoken by Jesus.

Written Exercises

A. 1. active, advice
   2. passive, advice
   3. active, Rehoboam
   4. passive, Jeroboam
   5. passive, calves
   6. passive, people
   7. active, Jeroboam
   8. passive, prophet
   9. passive, resentment
  10. passive, hand

B. 1. The hostess prepared a simple meal.
   2. The children have set the plates neatly on the table.
   3. God richly blesses our lives.
   4. Mr. Daley will fix the clocks.
   5. The wind blew the leaves.

C. 1. Grandmother is disturbed by that loud noise.
   2. The bell had been rung by Dallas.
   3. This song has been sung by our congregation.
   4. The pie is being cut by Gloria.
   5. The last piece of cake was eaten by Raymond.

D.

See

Person	Singular	Plural
	Present Tense	
First:	I am seen.	We are seen.
Second:	You are seen.	You are seen.
Third:	He is seen.	They are seen.
	Past Tense	
First:	I was seen.	We were seen.
Second:	You were seen.	You were seen.
Third:	He was seen.	They were seen.
	Future Tense	
First:	I shall be seen.	We shall be seen.
Second:	You will be seen.	You will be seen.
Third:	He will be seen.	They will be seen.
	Present Perfect Tense	
First:	I have been seen.	We have been seen.
Second:	You have been seen.	You have been seen.
Third:	He has been seen.	They have been seen.

Review Exercises

A. Label these sentences *simple, compound,* or *complex.* [14, 15]
1. "A wise son maketh a glad father."
2. "He that walketh uprightly walketh surely."
3. "When pride cometh, then cometh shame."
4. "He heard my voice out of his temple, and my cry came before him."
5. The heavenly Shepherd feeds us in green pastures and leads us beside still waters.

B. Diagram the skeletons, complements, appositives, and nouns of direct address. [7]
1. Our Father in heaven, grant us Thy blessing.
2. Several pieces of paper have become wrinkled and dirty.
3. The corn has been picked, but it has not been husked.
4. After you finish the picture, you should letter it neatly.
5. Clinton Zimmerman's, our former neighbors, will spend the night here.
6. Brother Chester's, whom we have not seen for two years, have returned from Paraguay.

54. Using the Active and Passive Voice

Lesson Survey
- The active voice is more direct and forceful than the passive voice.
- The passive voice may be suitable when there is no clear doer of the action or when there is a good reason not to name the doer of the action.

In Lesson 53 you studied the active and passive voice of transitive verbs. Although both of these voices are important, the active voice is more direct and forceful than the passive voice. In your writing, therefore, the large majority of your sentences should have verbs in the active voice.

The passive voice is overused in the following paragraph. Read the paragraph, and decide which sentences would be more effective in the active voice.

Poor: Too many verbs in the passive voice

1Our garden has been invaded by Japanese beetles. 2Some traps were bought by Father to catch them. 3Each trap is made of

A. 1. simple
2. complex
3. complex
4. compound
5. simple

B. 1.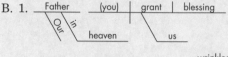
2.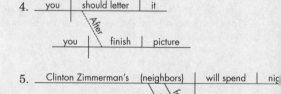
3. corn | has been picked | but | it | has been husk
4. you | should letter | it / After / you | finish | picture
5. Clinton Zimmerman's | (neighbors) | will spend | nig / our / former
6.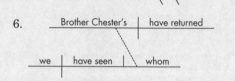

Lesson 54

Purpose: To teach that the active voice is usually better than the passive voice, but that the passive voice may be suitable in a few cases.

Oral Review:
1. Tell whether the verbs are in the active or passive voice.
   a. An angel shut the lions' mouths. (active)
   b. Balaam smote his donkey. (active)
   c. Peter was delivered from prison. (passive)
   d. Paul preached the Gospel to the Gentiles. (active)
2. If the verb is incorrect, give the correct form. If it is correct, say *correct*.
   a. An injured goose drownded in our pond. (drowned)
   b. We throwed the moldy bread to the chickens. (threw)
   c. A swarm of bees attackted the children. (attacked)
   d. The parts for the lawn mower cost less than Father feared. (correct)
   e. We busted out laughing at the monkey's antics. (burst)
   f. The injured cat dragged its one leg along. (correct)
   g. We brung some fresh corn for Mrs. Andrews. (brought)
3. Tell whether the verbs in these sentences are transitive, intransitive complete, or intransitive linking.
   a. Freshly baked bread smells delicious. (intransitive linking)

two flat pieces of plastic and a plastic bag. ⁴The plastic pieces <u>were assembled</u> by Father to form a baffle. ⁵The disposable bag <u>was hung</u> below. ⁶Each trap <u>is provided</u> with a lure by which the beetles <u>are attracted</u>. ⁷When they <u>fly</u> against the baffles, they <u>fall</u> into the bag. ⁸The bag <u>is made</u> with a narrow opening by which the beetles <u>are kept</u> from escaping.

Of the eleven verbs in this paragraph, the two in sentence *7* are the only ones in the active voice! Compare the following paragraph, which has eight verbs in the active voice. The passive verbs in sentences *3, 6,* and *8* are acceptable because we cannot say who made the trap, who provided the lure, or who made the bag. But all the other sentences are better with active verbs; there is no good reason to use the passive voice.

Improved: Most verbs in the active voice
¹Japanese beetles <u>have invaded</u> our garden. ²Father <u>bought</u> some traps to catch them. ³Each trap <u>is made</u> of two flat pieces of plastic and a plastic bag. ⁴Father <u>assembled</u> the plastic pieces to form a baffle. ⁵He <u>hung</u> the disposable bag below. ⁶Each trap <u>is provided</u> with a lure that <u>attracts</u> the beetles. ⁷When they <u>fly</u> against the baffles, they <u>fall</u> into the bag. ⁸The bag <u>is made</u> with a narrow opening that <u>keeps</u> the beetles from escaping.

One case when the passive voice may be suitable is when there is no clear doer of the action expressed by the verb. If a *by* phrase follows a passive verb (as in sentence *2* above), you can easily change it to the active voice. But this may be hard to do if no *by* phrase is there (as in sentences *3, 6,* and *8*). In fact, the active voice may be illogical because no one can tell who or what performed the action. Here are two more examples.

Africa <u>has been divided</u> into many countries.
  (Who or what divided Africa? There is no clear answer, so the passive voice is suitable.)
Reptiles <u>are hatched</u> from tough-shelled eggs.
  (Who or what hatched the reptiles? There is no clear answer.)

But think again! Does the last verb above really have to be passive? No; the sentence is just as clear in the following form. And since the subject is now *performing* the action instead of *receiving* it, this sentence is better.

Reptiles <u>hatch</u> from tough-shelled eggs.

The passive voice is also suitable when there is a good reason not to name the doer of the action.

  b. This poem was written by Isaac Watts. (transitive)
  c. Nathaniel Hawthorne wrote a number of short stories. (transitive)
  d. Several deer bounded over the fence. (intransitive complete)

Lesson Introduction: Often the word *passive* is associated with weakness. A person may be too passive to overcome a bad habit. A businessman may be too passive to make his business successful. A parent may be too passive to discipline his children. In English grammar, passive verbs also tend to be weak and ineffective.

But being passive is sometimes a definite advantage. If disaster strikes, it is better to accept it calmly and passively than to become upset and actively rebel against the situation. Passive animals (like turtles and crocodiles) live longer than active, aggressive animals (like lions and wolves). Just so, passive verbs are sometimes suitable, even though active verbs are usually better. This lesson gives some pointers on the use of verb voice.

Lesson Outline:
  1. The active voice is more direct and forceful than the passive voice. Therefore, the large majority of the sentences written in compositions should have verbs in the active voice.
  2. The passive voice may be suitable when there is no clear doer of the action expressed by the verb. But even then, the active voice is often better.
  (*Teacher:* When a sentence with a passive verb is changed so that the subject performs the action, the resulting verb is *active* [acting] but is not always in

Harold's question has not been answered.
> (Perhaps you would rather not say who should have answered Harold's question.)

This incorrect answer was not marked wrong.
> (It may be better not to say who failed to mark it.)

Remember: The active voice is more expressive because it is more direct and forceful than the passive voice. The passive voice is suitable in a few cases, but otherwise the active voice is usually better. Therefore, you should examine each passive verb that you find in your writing, and see if you can replace it with a verb in the active voice.

Class Practice

A. Read each sentence, changing the verb to the active voice. Do not change the tense.
   1. The people had been deceived by false teachers.
   2. These verses will be memorized by the students.
   3. A number of New Testament epistles were written by the apostle Paul.
   4. The flowers were planted by Mother this morning.
   5. These bicycles have been fixed by Father.
   6. A stirring message has been preached by Brother Mervin.

B. Say *yes* or *no* to tell whether the passive voice in each sentence is suitable. If it is not, read the sentence with the verb in the active voice.
   1. Jonah, the disobedient prophet, was cast into the water by the sailors.
   2. Christ was sought by multitudes from the towns of Galilee.
   3. The early church was severely persecuted.
   4. Lazarus was raised from the dead by Jesus.
   5. A large crowd was fed with five loaves and two fish.
   6. The last doughnuts have already been eaten!
   7. Some new books have been bought for the school library.
   8. The dog was fed by Karen.

Written Exercises

A. Rewrite these sentences, changing the verbs to the active voice. Do not change the tense.
   1. A coat of many colors was given to Joseph by Israel.
   2. This wicked world will be destroyed by God.
   3. Several wells were dug by Isaac.
   4. In heaven all tears will be wiped away by God.
   5. Salvation has been provided by the blood of Jesus.
   6. Divine grace is given to the faithful by God.

the *active voice*. It may be an intransitive complete verb, which does not have voice. [Compare "Eggs are hatched" with "Eggs hatch."] This technicality has little significance here. The main emphasis is to *use the passive voice only when there is a good reason for it.*)

   3. The passive voice may be used when there is a good reason not to name the doer of the action.

★ **EXTRA PRACTICE**
Worksheet 31 (*Active and Passive Voice*)

Lesson 54 Answers

Class Practice

A. 1. False teachers had deceived the people.
   2. The students will memorize these verses.
   3. The apostle Paul wrote a number of New Testament epistles.
   4. Mother planted the flowers this morning.
   5. Father has fixed these bicycles.
   6. Brother Mervin has preached a stirring message.

B. 1. no; The sailors cast Jonah, the disobedient prophet, into the water.
   2. no; Multitudes from the towns of Galilee sought Christ.
   3. yes (But the following form is also possible: The early church suffered severe persecution.)
   4. no; Jesus raised Lazarus from the dead.
   5. no; Jesus fed a large crowd with five loaves and two fish.
   6. yes (You may not wish to tell who ate them.)
   7. yes (You may not know who the buyer is.)
   8. no; Karen fed the dog.

Written Exercises

A. 1. Israel gave a coat of many colors to Joseph.
   2. God will destroy this wicked world.
   3. Isaac dug several wells.
   4. In heaven God will wipe away all tears.
   5. The blood of Jesus has provided salvation.
   6. God gives divine grace to the faithful.

B. The passive voice is used in the numbered sentences. For each one, write the letter of the statement which correctly describes that sentence.

    a. The active voice would be more effective.

    b. There is no clear doer of the action.

    c. There is a good reason not to name the doer.

1. Our chain saw was stolen last night.
2. A proper attitude was displayed by my father.
3. We have been taught to love our enemies.
4. A thief should be pitied rather than hated by us.

C. Rewrite this paragraph, changing all the passive verbs to active verbs unless there is a good reason to use the passive voice.

    Abram's and Lot's herdsmen were quarreling over pastureland. That they must separate was decided by Abram. Because Abram was unselfish, the first choice was left to Lot by Abram. Lot's attention was attracted by the well-watered plain of Jordan. Soon Lot's tent was pitched toward Sodom, and before long his family was living right in that wicked city! Part of his family was lost in the judgment of Sodom. Apparently most of his possessions were also burned up. A forceful warning is given to us by this Bible account.

Review Exercises

A. Write whether each verb is transitive (*T*), intransitive complete (*IC*), or intransitive linking (*IL*). [41–43]

1. Baruch was a scribe for Jeremiah.
2. He wrote the message from God through Jeremiah.
3. Jehoiakim was sitting in his winter house.
4. A message of divine judgment was read to Jehoiakim.
5. Jehoiakim burned the roll piece by piece in his hearth fire.
6. The king and his servants did not feel alarmed at this wicked deed.

B. Write whether each verb is *active* or *passive*. [53]

1. Jehoiakim sought Jeremiah and Baruch.
2. These godly men were hidden by the Lord.
3. At God's command, Jeremiah and Baruch wrote the message again.
4. Additional words were written on this second roll.
5. Jehoiakim was severely punished by the Lord for his wickedness.
6. Man rejects God's Word only to his own ruin.

B. 1. c
  2. a
  3. b
  4. a

C. (Sample paragraph. The one passive verb is underlined.)

    Abram's and Lot's herdsmen were quarreling over pastureland. Abram decided that they must separate. Because Abram was unselfish, he left the first choice to Lot. The well-watered plain of Jordan attracted Lot's attention. Soon Lot pitched his tent toward Sodom, and before long his family was living right in that wicked city! Part of his family <u>was lost</u> in the judgment of Sodom. Apparently most of his possessions also burned up. This Bible account gives a forceful warning to us.

Review Exercises

A. 1. IL   4. T
  2. T   5. T
  3. IC   6. IL

B. 1. active   4. passive
  2. passive   5. passive
  3. active   6. active

55. Writing Business Letters

> **Lesson Survey**
> - The form of a **business letter** is slightly different from that of a friendly letter.
>   1. A business letter has an **inside address**.
>   2. The greeting is more formal and is followed by a colon.
>   3. The closing is more formal.
> - The body of a business letter should be courteous, clear, and concise.
> - A blank space should be left between each part of the letter and the next.

Friendly letters and social notes fill an important role in communicating with our friends. As you grow older, you may communicate more and more with businesses or large organizations. Perhaps you will order something by mail or inquire about an order. You may request information about products or services that the business offers. For such purposes, you need to know how to write a business letter.

The following example illustrates a *business letter* with good form and content. Refer to this example as you study the descriptions of the letter parts.

Heading
> Route 3, Box 247
> Brookfield, IL 60513
> February 6, 20—

Inside Address
> University of Chicago
> 64 East Lake Street
> Chicago, IL 60601

Greeting
> Dear Sirs:

Body
> Please send me the following pamphlets, as advertised in your agricultural newsletter.
>
> | | | |
> | --- | --- | --- |
> | Number 64, *Home Gardening in Illinois* | | $0.50 |
> | Number 83, *Pest Control Without Pesticides* | | 0.50 |
> | | Total | $1.00 |
>
> Enclosed is a check for $1.00 to cover the cost of the order.

Closing
> Very truly yours,
>
> *Grant Hooley*
> **Signature** Grant Hooley

Lesson 55

Purpose: To teach the rules for writing business letters.

Oral Review:
1. Name the five parts of a friendly letter in order. (heading, greeting, body, closing, signature)
2. What two things are included in the heading? (the writer's address, the date on which the letter is written)
3. What punctuation mark follows the greeting? (comma)
4. How should the mailing address be written on the envelope? (with all capital letters and no punctuation)
5. Tell which method of paragraph development you would use for each of the following, as you studied in Chapter 3.

a. to explain how to draw an ellipse (giving steps)
b. to tell why the Bible is the best book (adding details)
c. to tell what *charity* means (giving definitions)
d. to describe a beautiful flower garden (adding details)
e. to show the danger of gossip by telling about an embarrassing experience (telling an incident)

Lesson Introduction: When your mother makes gelatin-based salads or desserts, she may put them into molds. Perhaps she has several different shapes of molds. When we write letters, we "pour them into a certain mold" to give them form and shape. As this lesson teaches, the mold that you use for a business letter is not quite the same as the one that you use for a friendly letter.

The form of a business letter is slightly different from that of a friendly letter. Both kinds have a heading, greeting, body, closing, and signature. In addition to these five parts, a business letter also has an *inside address*. The inside address is the name and address of the person or company that you are writing to. It is exactly the same as the mailing address on the envelope. The inside address should be placed at the left-hand margin of the letter, between the heading and the greeting.

The greeting is more formal than for a friendly letter, and it is followed by a colon. If you are writing to a person whose name you know, you may use that name, such as *Dear Mr. Gray:*. Use *Dear Sir:* if you write to a man whose name you do not know (such as the owner of a business). A suitable greeting for writing to a company is *Dear Sirs:* or *Gentlemen:*. If you write a business letter to a woman, you may use *Dear Madam:*.

The closing is also more formal. Here are some appropriate closings.

Very truly yours,   Cordially yours, (for an acquaintance)
Yours truly,   Respectfully yours, (for a very formal letter)

The body of a business letter should be courteous, clear, and concise. (These may be called the three C's of a business letter.) A tone of courtesy should be maintained by polite expressions, even if you are making a complaint.

Poor:
Send me a copy...
I need to know...
You sure mixed up my order. Send me what I ordered immediately.

Courteous:
Please send me a copy...
I would appreciate information about...
Please note the following problems about the shipment I received. I would appreciate your promptness in making the necessary adjustments.

Clearly state exactly what you want to say. If you are ordering something, state all the necessary information about each item, such as catalog number, size, color, and quantity. If you are requesting information, be specific about what information you want.

Vague:
I would like some information about your business.
Please send some information about your state.

Lesson Outline:

1. The form of a business letter is slightly different from that of a friendly letter.
   a. A business letter has an inside address.
     1) The inside address is the name and address of the person or company that you are writing to.
     2) It should be placed at the left-hand margin, between the heading and the greeting.
   b. The greeting is more formal and is followed by a colon.
   c. The closing is more formal.

2. The body of a business letter should be courteous, clear, and concise.
   a. Maintain a tone of courtesy, even when making a complaint.
   b. Clearly state exactly what you want to say, giving all necessary information.
   c. Keep the letter concise. Be sure to include all necessary information, but do not include extra information not essential to the point of the letter.

3. A blank space should be left between each part of the letter and the next. For best appearance, leave extra space at the top and bottom so that the letter is nicely centered on the paper.

Specific:

I would like some information about the history of your business.

I would like some information about the styles and prices of the storage sheds you sell.

Please send some information about historical sites in your state.

Please send some information about caves in your state.

Keep a business letter concise. Businessmen may need to read many letters every day. Be sure to include all necessary information, but do not include extra information not essential to the point of the letter.

A blank space should be left between each part of the letter and the next. For best appearance, leave extra space at the top and bottom so that the letter is nicely centered on the paper.

Class Practice

Tell what is wrong with the following business letter.

300 Harbaugh Valley Rd.
Fairfield PA 17320

Dear Friends,

Send me two bird feeders and five birdhouses. We just moved to a beautiful mountainside home and are seeing lots of birds. We hope that we will be able to attract some of them.

Affectionately yours,
Brian McClure
Brian McClure

Written Exercises

A. Write a business letter to order one copy each of the following books: *Traveling the Way,* #2445, for $6.55; *The Man in Bearskin,* #6295, for $3.65; and *In a Whale's Belly,* #6241, for $5.20. The receiver's address is Rod and Staff Publishers, Inc., P.O. Box 3, Hwy. 172, Crockett, Kentucky 41413. (Use your home address and today's date in the heading.)

B. Write a business letter, using one of the suggestions here.

1. Write to a local business for information on a specific kind of product or service that it offers. Perhaps you can write to a brother in the church who owns a business.

2. Write for information about historical sites or state parks in a certain state. (To get an address, find an encyclopedia article on that state and look under a heading such as "Places to Visit." Often you can obtain free seals, brochures, and other interesting items.)

Lesson 55 Answers

Class Practice

1. In the heading, the comma between *Fairfield* and *PA* is missing, and the date is missing.

2. The inside address is missing.

3. The greeting is not appropriate for a business letter, and it should end with a colon.

4. The body lacks a courteous tone and specific information. It includes unnecessary information.

5. The closing is not appropriate for a business letter.

6. There are no spaces between the different parts of the letter.

Written Exercises

A. (Individual work.)

Note: This exercise is intended for student practice. If the letter will actually be sent to Rod and Staff, please check the catalog or call for current prices and shipping charges.

B. (Individual work.)

3. Write to a local place of interest. Ask about their visiting hours, special tours, and other information that would help to make a visit enjoyable.

Review Exercises

A. Write whether the following paragraphs are developed by *adding details, giving steps, using examples, telling an incident,* or *giving a definition.* [21, 25, 31]

1. The Waldenses prized the Word of God. Accordingly, they were among the first to translate the Scriptures into the common languages. They copied many portions of the Bible by hand, for the printing press had not yet been invented. They also memorized long passages of God's Word and were able to recite them to their persecutors. In fact, many of these people could repeat whole books of the Bible by memory. The deepest desire of the Waldenses was to live by the Word of God.

2. What were the indulgences that helped to spark the Protestant Reformation? Originally, an indulgence was supposed to excuse the punishment in purgatory for sins already confessed. By their pure lives, saints have supposedly accumulated in heaven an enormous treasury of grace. An indulgence was like a bank check that drew on this grace to pardon someone not quite as holy. Soon this idea was distorted into a license to sin. A person could buy an indulgence to pardon a sin he was planning to commit in the future.

3. The beginning of the Swiss Brethren movement in Zurich occurred on January 21, 1525. Conrad Grebel, Felix Manz, George Blaurock, and a number of others met after the passing of a mandate forbidding further Bible study groups. As they shared together, these men found themselves united in faith. They spent time in earnest prayer, and then George Blaurock asked Conrad Grebel to baptize him with true Christian baptism. George, in turn, baptized Conrad and the rest of the group. After the baptisms, some were chosen to be ministers of the Gospel. These men knew that they would face strong opposition, but they were determined to obey the Word of God at any cost.

B. Answer the following questions about the paragraphs in Part A.
1. What are some transitional expressions used in paragraph 1?
2. What key word is repeated effectively in paragraph 2?

Review Exercises

A. 1. adding details
   2. giving a definition
   3. telling an incident

B. 1. Accordingly, also, In fact
   2. indulgence

56. Chapter 5 Review

Class Practice

A. Give the answers.
1. Tell which of these verbs are usually transitive: *lay, lie, set, sit, raise, rise.*
2. Of the verbs *can* and *may,* which one is used to ask permission? Which one is used to express ability?
3. Of the verbs *let* and *leave,* which one is usually followed by another verb form?
4. Does the subject receive the action in the active voice or in the passive voice?
5. In which voice does the direct object receive the action?
6. What helping verb is always used in the passive voice?
7. What form of the main verb is used in the passive voice?
8. Why should you try to use the active voice more than the passive voice?
9. In what two cases may the passive voice be suitable?

B. Choose the verb that agrees with the subject.
1. There (is, are) six chapters in the Book of Ephesians.
2. The Christian's armor, as well as his sword, (is, are) described in chapter 6.
3. (Don't, Doesn't) God's faithfulness inspire us?
4. The armor and God's grace (provide, provides) victory.
5. The devil's trickery or his persistence (bring, brings) many to defeat.
6. Everyone in Christ's army (is, are) called to alertness and diligence.
7. Mathematics (prepare, prepares) students for practical problem solving.
8. These pruning shears (work, works) well on small branches.
9. The flock of migrating birds (find, finds) its way back to the right place.
10. The flock of birds (choose, chooses) their nesting sites.

C. Read each sentence, choosing the correct verb and using it in the proper form.
1. Each contented sheep (lay, lie) daily in green pastures.
2. Jesus (lay, lie) fast asleep in the boat while the storm raged.
3. The men who stoned Stephen (lay, lie) their coats at Saul's feet.
4. The women beheld the place where Jesus had (lay, lie) before His resurrection.
5. We should never (set, sit) in the seat of the scornful.
6. God has (set, sit) the members in the body as it pleased Him.
7. Have you ever (set, sit) next to the window of an airplane?
8. Some albatrosses (set, sit) for more than two months before the eggs hatch.

Lesson 56 Answers

Class Practice

A. 1. lay, set, raise
    2. may; can
    3. let
    4. passive voice
    5. active voice
    6. a form of *be*
    7. the past participle
    8. The active voice is more direct and forceful than the passive voice.
    9. when there is no clear doer of the action expressed by the verb; when there is a good reason not to name the doer of the action

B. 1. are
    2. is
    3. Doesn't
    4. provide
    5. brings
    6. is
    7. prepares
    8. work
    9. finds
    10. choose

C. 1. lies *or* lay
    2. lay
    3. laid
    4. lain
    5. sit
    6. set
    7. sat
    8. set

Lesson 56

Purpose: To review the concepts taught in Chapter 5.

9. (Set, Sit) the boxes of paper inside the closet.
10. God's people (raise, rise) above the world's allurements.
11. If we have (raise, rise) our eyes to the Lord, we will not become discouraged.
12. Each prayer of faith (raise, rise) to the throne of grace.
13. Did you pray for God's blessing as you (raise, rise) for the new day?
14. Abram (let, leave) his homeland and went where God led him.
15. We should never (let, leave) jealousy grow in our hearts.
16. Father has (let, leave) us each pick one book from the Rod and Staff catalog.
17. Uncle Norman's have (let, leave) for a year of service in the Dominican Republic.

D. Read these sentences, using *can* or *may*.
1. The Lord ——— answer every prayer of faith.
2. No leper ——— dwell within the city.
3. Each of these children ——— read well.
4. Mother said that each of us ——— choose one piece of candy.

E. Read each sentence correctly.
1. Achan should have knowed better than to take the garment and gold.
2. When Israel attackted Ai, they were driven back.
3. The sin of Achan had drug the whole nation to defeat.
4. Sin has always costed more than man likes to admit.
5. Father had to quit plowing because one of the hydraulic lines bursted.
6. We brang Aunt Hetty along to the meeting this evening.
7. It looks as if raccoons might of been in our cornfield.
8. Have you tooken any corn to market yet?
9. The mainspring of this clock has broke.
10. Although the mother hen drownded, the chicks under her wings were safe.

F. Tell which word receives the action, and tell whether the verb is *active* or *passive*.
1. The worlds were framed by the Word of God.
2. The power of Christ daily sustains our own lives.
3. Each rainbow reminds us of God's faithfulness.
4. God's promises can never be broken.

G. Read each sentence, changing the verb from passive to active voice.
1. Jesus was rejected by many of the Jewish leaders.
2. Their hypocrisy was sternly denounced by Jesus.
3. Their eyes were blinded by religious pride.
4. Jeremiah was accused of disloyalty by the princes.

9. Set	14. left
10. rise	15. let
11. raised	16. let
12. rises	17. left
13. rose	

D. 1. can   3. can
   2. may   4. may

E. (Corrections are underlined.)
1. Achan should have <u>known</u> better than to take the garment and gold.
2. When Israel <u>attacked</u> Ai, they were driven back.
3. The sin of Achan had <u>dragged</u> the whole nation to defeat.
4. Sin has always <u>cost</u> more than man likes to admit.
5. Father had to quit plowing because one of the hydraulic lines <u>burst</u>.
6. We <u>brought</u> Aunt Hetty along to the meeting this evening.
7. It looks as if raccoons might <u>have</u> been in our cornfield.
8. Have you <u>taken</u> any corn to market yet?
9. The mainspring of this clock has <u>broken</u>.
10. Although the mother hen <u>drowned</u>, the chicks under her wings were safe.

F. 1. worlds, passive
   2. lives, active
   3. us, active
   4. promises, passive

G. 1. Many of the Jewish leaders rejected Jesus.
   2. Jesus sternly denounced their hypocrisy.
   3. Religious pride blinded their eyes.
   4. The princes accused Jeremiah of disloyalty.

5. Permission to cast him into a dungeon was granted by Zedekiah.
6. He was rescued from the dungeon by Ebed-melech.

H. Tell why the passive voice is suitable in each sentence.
   1. Three of our windows were broken yesterday.
   2. The Book of the Law had been lost for many years.

I. Answer these questions about letter writing.
   1. What are the five parts of a friendly letter?
   2. What sixth part does a business letter have, and where is it located?
   3. How is the greeting of a business letter different from that of a friendly letter?
   4. What are several appropriate closings for a friendly letter? for a business letter?
   5. What are the three C's of a business letter?
   6. How should you respond if you receive a gift that you do not like or cannot use?
   7. What should be the form of the mailing address on the envelope?

Written Exercises

A. Most of these sentences have mistakes in subject–verb agreement. Write the correct verb, or write *correct*.
   1. Where's the stories of Joseph in the Bible?
   2. Lot, in addition to other inhabitants of Sodom, were taken captive.
   3. My trousers need to be pressed.
   4. Chicken pox have been spreading throughout the community.
   5. Our class is going on a hike tomorrow.
   6. A young person don't have as much experience as an older person.
   7. There's several visitors at school today.
   8. Each of the visitors has taught school.
   9. The crew is working at their various jobs.
   10. Leonard or Nevin are in charge of the building project.

B. Most of these sentences have mistakes in the use of problem verbs. Write the correct verb, or write *correct*.
   1. Songs of joy are raising from the group of workers.
   2. We must never leave ourselves yield to a temptation to cheat.
   3. The boys are setting up chairs in the assembly room.
   4. These beans have laid out in the sun too long.
   5. The children can be excused from the table now.
   6. The fawn lay motionless in the brush until the fox went away.
   7. We have left five dozen ears of corn for Widow Henson and her family.
   8. We had set at the airport for two hours before the late flight arrived.

5. Zedekiah granted permission to cast him into a dungeon.
6. Ebed-melech rescued him from the dungeon.

H. 1. There is a good reason not to name the doer.
   2. There is no clear doer of the action.

I. 1. heading, greeting, body, closing, signature
   2. inside address; below the heading, at the left-hand margin
   3. It is more formal and is followed by a colon instead of a comma.
   4. *friendly letter:* Sincerely, With love and prayers Sincerely yours, Affectionately yours, Your friend, In Christian love, Your loving son,
      business letter: Very truly yours, Yours truly, Cordially yours, (for an acquaintance) Respectfully yours, (for a very formal letter)
   5. courteous, clear, concise
   6. You should express your thanks. You can always express appreciation for the giver's thoughtfulness. If possible, say something you like about the gift, but do not be dishonest. Do not say anything that might hurt the giver's feelings.
   7. It should have all capital letters and no punctuation.

Written Exercises

A. 1. (Where) are
   2. was
   3. correct
   4. has
   5. correct
   6. doesn't
   7. (There) are
   8. correct
   9. are
   10. is

B. 1. rising
   2. let
   3. correct
   4. lain
   5. may
   6. correct
   7. correct
   8. sat

9. The prolonged drought will rise the price of produce.

10. Brother Ivan, can we eat outside today?

C. These sentences have mistakes in the forms of problem verbs. Write the correct forms.

1. Have you brung your troubles to the Lord?

2. Satan has attackted the work of God throughout time.

3. By His death on the cross, Jesus has broke the power of sin.

4. A severe storm blowed across the Sea of Galilee.

5. No one drownded, for Jesus stilled the storm.

6. The disciples brang some food for Jesus from the town.

7. Bernice has already tug Joyce, Sharon, and Darwin.

8. Last year peaches costed more than they do this year.

9. You should of seen the beautiful sunrise this morning.

10. Pedro has tooken the sheep up to the mountain pasture.

D. Write whether the verbs in these sentences are *active* or *passive*.

1. "Honour the Lord with thy substance."

2. "So shall thy barns be filled with plenty."

3. "The Lord by wisdom hath founded the earth."

4. "The wicked shall be cut off from the earth."

5. "The liberal soul shall be made fat."

E. In the following paragraph, find four sentences that are ineffective because the verb is passive. Rewrite those sentences, changing the verb to the active voice.

¹The people were called together by Moses. ²A strict warning was given by the Lord. ³The mountain dare not be touched! ⁴Moses ascended the mount, and God talked with him there. ⁵The Law was given to Moses by God. ⁶While Moses was gone, the people became ensnared in idol worship. ⁷Many earrings of gold were given by them to Aaron. ⁸A golden calf was fashioned out of that gold. ⁹The people shamefully worshiped the idol, feasted, and played.

F. Write an invitation for the following situation. Use your own name and address and today's date.

You want to invite a friend (use a real name if you wish) to spend the weekend in your home. You understand that your friend's father is planning to be in your church for a parent–teacher meeting on Friday evening (use an actual date). Your father is scheduled to lead a song service in your friend's church on the following Sunday evening.

———————————

9. raise

10. may

C. 1. brought   6. brought

2. attacked   7. tagged

3. broken   8. cost

4. blew   9. have

5. drowned   10. taken

D. 1. active   4. passive

2. passive   5. passive

3. active

E. (Any four of these sentences may be changed.)

1. Moses called the people together.

2. The Lord gave a strict warning.

5. God gave the Law to Moses.

7. They gave many earrings of gold to Aaron.

8. He fashioned a golden calf out of the gold.

F. (Sample body.)

I would like to invite you to our home for the weekend of March 15–17. I understand that your father is planning to be in our church for a parent–teacher meeting on Friday evening, March 15. We can take you back home on Sunday, March 17, because my father is scheduled to lead a song service in your church that evening.

I am looking forward very much to seeing you again. Please let me know soon whether it will suit for you to come.

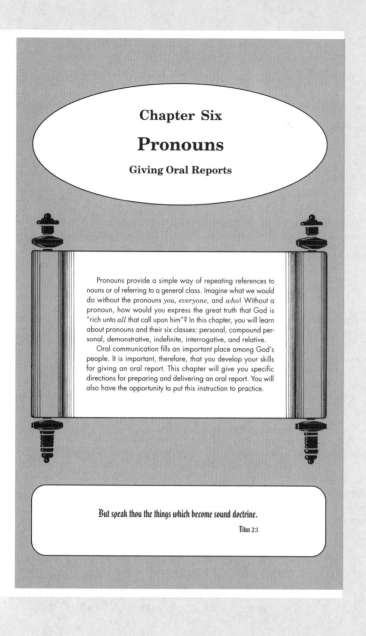

Chapter Six

Pronouns

Giving Oral Reports

Pronouns provide a simple way of repeating references to nouns or of referring to a general class. Imagine what we would do without the pronouns *you, everyone,* and *who*! Without a pronoun, how would you express the great truth that God is "rich unto *all* that call upon him"? In this chapter, you will learn about pronouns and their six classes: personal, compound personal, demonstrative, indefinite, interrogative, and relative.

Oral communication fills an important place among God's people. It is important, therefore, that you develop your skills for giving an oral report. This chapter will give you specific directions for preparing and delivering an oral report. You will also have the opportunity to put this instruction to practice.

But speak thou the things which become sound doctrine.

Titus 2:1

Personal Pronouns
Nominative Case

	Singular	Plural
First person:	I	we
Second person:	you (thou)	you (ye)
Third person:	he, she, it	they

Objective Case

	Singular	Plural
First person:	me	us
Second person:	you (thee)	you
Third person:	him, her, it	them

Possessive Case

	Singular	Plural
First person:	my, mine	our, ours
Second person:	your, yours (thy, thine)	your, yours
Third person:	his, her, hers, its	their, theirs

(Archaic pronouns are in parentheses.)

57. Personal Pronouns

Lesson Survey

- A **pronoun** is a word that takes the place of a noun. The noun for which a pronoun stands is its **antecedent.**

- **Personal pronouns** have different forms to indicate person, number, case, and gender.

- The **person** of a pronoun is first person, second person, or third person.

- The **number** of a pronoun is singular or plural.

- The **case** of a pronoun is nominative, objective, or possessive.

- The **gender** of a pronoun is masculine, feminine, neuter, or common.

- A pronoun must agree with its antecedent in person, number, and gender.

Lesson 57

Purpose: To teach the definition, recognition, and antecedents of personal pronouns.

Oral Review:

1. Tell whether the verb in each sentence is transitive, intransitive complete, or intransitive linking.
   a. A clerk gives customers their change. (transitive)
   b. A clerk should appear pleasant. (intransitive linking)
   c. Clerks are hired by the manager. (transitive)
   d. Clerks must arrive at the store on time. (intransitive complete)

2. Tell whether the voice of each verb is active or passive.
   a. We were inspired by the devotional meditation. (passive)
   b. Did you see that streak of lightning? (active)
   c. Which freezer can hold the most food? (active)
   d. Twenty jars of peaches have been canned. (passive)

3. Why is the active voice better than the passive voice? (It is more direct and forceful.)

4. Name two situations in which it may be suitable to use the passive voice. (when there is no clear doer of the action, when there is a good reason not to name the doer of the action)

Lesson Introduction: Our communication would be quite cumbersome if there were no pronouns. Notice how much better the second sentence sounds than the first.

> Adam blamed Adam's wife for causing Adam to sin.
>
> Adam blamed his wife for causing him to sin.

Your students might enjoy constructing some

In Chapter 3 you learned that a substantive is any word or word group that names something. Substantives may be single words, phrases, or clauses. The most common ones are nouns and pronouns.

A *pronoun* is a word that takes the place of a noun. After something has been identified with a noun, we frequently refer to it by using pronouns instead of repeating the noun.

> God planted a garden eastward in Eden. In <u>it</u> <u>He</u> placed Adam, the man <u>He</u> had formed. Later <u>He</u> made a wife for Adam. Adam called <u>his</u> wife Eve. <u>They</u> lived in perfect harmony with <u>their</u> Creator and with the rest of creation.

The noun for which a pronoun stands is its *antecedent.* Generally that noun is found in the same sentence as the pronoun or in the sentence before. Occasionally, however, it may not be stated.

> Caleb was quite old, but <u>he</u> wanted the mountain for <u>his</u> inheritance.
> (*Caleb* is the antecedent of *he* and *his.*)
> Wendy, have <u>you</u> turned to Joshua 14?
> (*Wendy* is the antecedent of *you.*)
> <u>I</u> did not know <u>he</u> was that old!
> (No antecedent is stated for *I; Caleb* is the antecedent of *he.*)

Personal pronouns have different forms to indicate *person, number, case,* and *gender.* You need to study these forms so that you can use personal pronouns correctly.

Person

The *person* of a pronoun shows the relationship between the pronoun and the speaker. When the speaker refers to himself, he uses the *first person pronouns.* He uses the *second person pronouns* in referring to the person he is speaking to, and the *third person pronouns* in referring to the person or thing he is speaking about.

> Father said, "James, <u>I</u> told <u>you</u> to help Lucinda with <u>her</u> work."
> (*I,* first person, refers to Father, who is speaking.
> *You,* second person, refers to James, whom Father is speaking to.
> *Her,* third person, refers to Lucinda, whom Father is speaking about.)

Number

As with nouns, the *number* of a pronoun shows whether the pronoun is singular or plural. A singular pronoun refers to a singular noun, and a plural pronoun refers to a plural noun.

"pronounless" sentences. Can they reword the following sentences so that they contain no pronouns?

> Is their family coming to your house tonight? We know that our planet is traveling swiftly through space.

This may be more difficult than they first think!

Lesson Outline:

1. A pronoun is a word that takes the place of a noun. The noun for which a pronoun stands is its antecedent.

2. Personal pronouns have different forms to indicate person, number, case, and gender.

3. The person of a pronoun shows the relationship between the pronoun and the speaker.

    a. First person pronouns refer to the speaker himself.

    b. Second person pronouns refer to the one spoken to.

    c. Third person pronouns refer to the one spoken about.

4. The number of a pronoun shows whether the pronoun is singular or plural.

    a. A singular pronoun refers to a singular noun.

    b. A plural pronoun refers to a plural noun.

    c. Second person pronouns may be either singular or plural, depending on their antecedents.

5. The case of a pronoun has to do with how the pronoun is used in a sentence. (Pronoun case is treated in detail in the next lesson.)

6. The gender of a pronoun is either masculine, feminine, neuter, or common.

One <u>girl</u> has finished <u>her</u> quilt block.
(*Girl* and *her* are singular.)
The <u>girls</u> have finished <u>their</u> quilt blocks.
(*Girls* and *their* are plural.)

The pronouns *you, your,* and *yours* may be either singular or plural, depending on their antecedents. To determine the number of these pronouns, you must decide what the antecedent is.

Judith, <u>you</u> have a beautiful rose embroidered on <u>your</u> quilt block.
(Antecedent *Judith* is singular; *you* and *your* are singular.)
Darlene and Lydia, have <u>you</u> put roses on <u>your</u> quilt blocks too?
(Antecedent *Darlene and Lydia* is plural; *you* and *your* are plural.)

Case

The *case* of a pronoun has to do with how the pronoun is used in a sentence, such as subject, direct object, or predicate nominative. The three cases are *nominative, objective,* and *possessive.* You will study pronoun case in the next lesson.

Gender

The *gender* of a pronoun is either *masculine, feminine, neuter,* or *common.* Nouns also have these four genders, as you studied in Chapter 3.

1. Masculine gender *refers to persons or animals that are male.*

    he   him   his

2. Feminine gender *refers to persons or animals that are female.*

    she   her   hers

3. Neuter gender *refers to things or ideas that are neither male nor female.*

    it   its

4. Common gender *refers to persons, animals, or things that may be male, female, or neuter, or to a group that includes more than one gender.* The only pronouns with different forms according to gender are third person singular pronouns (like *he, she,* and *it*). All other pronouns are of common gender.

Sometimes a third person pronoun is needed to stand for a singular noun of common gender, such as *person.* Since there is no special pronoun for this purpose, a masculine pronoun (*he*) is commonly used. A neuter pronoun (*it*) may also be used for an animal, especially a small one. These pronouns are then common, not masculine or neuter.

(1) Masculine gender *refers to persons or animals that are male.*
(2) Feminine gender *refers to persons or animals that are female.*
(3) Neuter gender *refers to things or ideas that are neither male nor female.*
(4) Common gender *refers to persons, animals, or things that may be male, female, or neuter, or to a group that includes more than one gender.*

If a third person pronoun is needed to stand for a singular noun of common gender, a pronoun of masculine or neuter gender is used.

7. A pronoun must agree with its antecedent in person, number, and gender.

★ **EXTRA PRACTICE**
Worksheet 32 (*Personal Pronouns*)

If a *student* wants to succeed, <u>he</u> must discipline <u>himself</u> to study hard.
The *elephant* squirted water into <u>his</u> (or *its*) mouth.
A baby *lion* was washing <u>its</u> face.

A pronoun must agree with its antecedent in person, number, and gender.

Conrad fed <u>his</u> *heifer*. <u>She</u> had been bawling hungrily.
    (*His* is third person, singular, masculine gender to agree with
    Conrad. *She* is third person, singular, feminine gender to agree
    with *heifer*.)
Sherrie fed <u>her</u> *kittens*. The playful *kittens* drank <u>their</u> milk.
    (*Her* is third person, singular, feminine gender to agree with
    Sherrie. *Their* is third person, plural, common gender to agree
    with *kittens*.)

Class Practice

A. Identify each personal pronoun, and give its person and number.
   1. "I know that my redeemer liveth."
   2. "And while they looked stedfastly toward heaven as he went up,
      behold, two men stood by them in white apparel."
   3. "And beholding the man which was healed standing with them, they
      could say nothing against it."
   4. "But if our gospel be hid, it is hid to them that are lost."
   5. "Let not the sun go down upon your wrath."

B. Identify each personal pronoun, and give its gender.
   1. Simeon held baby Jesus in his arms.
   2. The Bible is the best Book; it reveals God to man.
   3. Dorcas spent her time doing good for others.
   4. King Nebuchadnezzar recognized that he was subject to the sovereign God.
   5. We love and serve our great God.
   6. I want to read the Bible and obey its precepts.

C. Read each underlined pronoun, and give its antecedent.
   1. Several students have finished <u>their</u> tests.
   2. Melinda does not remember where <u>she</u> found <u>her</u> information.
   3. Brother Zimmerman told Anita, "<u>I</u> want <u>you</u> to report on <u>your</u> family's visit to Old Faithful."
   4. This geyser is very regular; <u>it</u> shoots <u>its</u> water into the air about
      every sixty-five minutes.

Written Exercises

A. Copy each personal pronoun. After it, write *1, 2,* or *3* to identify its person, and write *S* or *P* to identify its number.

Lesson 57 Answers

Class Practice

A. 1. I—first, singular; my—first, singular
   2. they—third, plural; he—third, singular;
      them—third, plural
   3. them—third, plural; they—third, plural;
      it—third, singular
   4. our—first, plural; it—third, singular;
      them—third, plural
   5. your—second, plural (*Thy* would be used if the
      number were singular.)

B. 1. his—masculine
   2. it—neuter
   3. her—feminine
   4. he—masculine
   5. We—common; our—common
   6. I—common; its—neuter

C. 1. their—students
   2. she—Melinda; her—Melinda
   3. I—Brother Zimmerman; you—Anita;
      your—Anita
   4. it—geyser; its—geyser

1. The Rechabites followed the teachings of their father.
2. The publican prayed, "Lord, be merciful to me a sinner."
3. The angels said to the shepherds, "We bring you good tidings."
4. Our grandparents came to visit us.
5. Eric and Darren, if your chores are finished, please help me with mine.
6. Melissa, did you hear that Loretta broke her leg?
7. Curvin, you must help Lisa fix her bicycle since you broke it.
8. They seemed surprised that we offered to help them after the storm.

B. Copy each personal pronoun. Identify its gender by writing *M, F, N,* or *C* after it.
1. God clearly states that He hates pride and resists it.
2. A virtuous woman guides her household with the law of kindness.
3. A godly father teaches his children and guides them in the right way.
4. We are commanded to obey our parents in all things.
5. When Rover saw the woodchuck, he raced after it.
6. My calf has a crescent-shaped white mark on her forehead.

C. Copy each personal pronoun and its antecedent.
1. Abraham and Sarah sent Hagar away with her son.
2. God gave Abraham and Sarah a promise, and they believed it.
3. Jesus told His disciples, "I go to prepare a place for you."
4. As the dog barked, the squirrel flicked its tail and chattered.
5. The hungry lioness patiently stalked her prey.
6. The children have picked a lovely bouquet for their mother, and she has placed it in a vase.

Review Exercises

A. For each sentence, write *T* if the verb is transitive, *IC* if the verb is intransitive complete, or *IL* if the verb is intransitive linking. [41–43]
1. All the rivers are flowing toward the sea.
2. The zipper on this coat is unusable.
3. These vegetables are planted in even rows.
4. The children bought a bookcase for their parents.
5. Georgia is a southern state.
6. The hammer is lying on the table.

B. Rewrite each sentence, changing the verb from passive to active voice. Do not change the tense. [53]
1. The showers have been sent by the Lord.
2. The text of his message has been announced by the minister.
3. We are being guided by the truth of God's Word.

Written Exercises

A. 1. their—3, P
   2. me—1, S
   3. We—1, P; you—2, P
   4. Our—1, P; us—1, P
   5. your—2, P; me—1, S; mine—1, S
   6. you—2, S; her—3, S
   7. you—2, S; her—3, S; you—2, S; it—3, S
   8. They—3, P; we—1, P; them—3, P

B. 1. He—M; it—N   4. We—C; our—C
   2. her—F   5. he—M; it—C
   3. his—M; them—C   6. My—C; her—F

C. 1. her—Hagar
   2. they—Abraham and Sarah; it—promise
   3. His—Jesus; I—Jesus; you—disciples
   4. its—squirrel
   5. her—lioness
   6. their—children; she—mother; it—bouquet

Review Exercises

A. 1. IC
   2. IL
   3. T
   4. T
   5. IL
   6. IC

B. 1. The Lord has sent the showers.
   2. The minister has announced the text of his message.
   3. The truth of God's Word is guiding us.

4. Many questions about Guatemala were answered by Brother Roberto.

C. The passive voice is used in the numbered sentences. For each one, write the letter of the statement which correctly describes that sentence. [54]
   a. The active voice would be more effective.
   b. There is no clear doer of the action.
   c. There is a good reason not to name the doer.
   1. My message apparently was not repeated correctly.
   2. A detailed account of the fire was given by Donna.
   3. Lake Huron was named after the Huron Indians.
   4. A tremendous roar was uttered by the mighty lion.

4. Brother Roberto answered many questions about Guatemala.

C. 1. c
   2. a
   3. b
   4. a

58. Pronoun Case

> **Lesson Survey**
> - The **case** of a pronoun has to do with how the pronoun is used in a sentence.
> - A pronoun in the **nominative case** is used as a subject or a predicate nominative.
> - A pronoun in the **objective case** is used as a direct object, an indirect object, or the object of a preposition.
> - A pronoun in the **possessive case** is used to show ownership.

= predicate noun
completes a linking verb and re names the subject
★ always a noun or pronoun

You saw in the previous lesson that personal pronouns have different forms to show person, number, case, and gender. The person of a pronoun shows the relationship between the pronoun and the speaker. The number of a pronoun shows whether the pronoun is singular or plural. The gender of a pronoun is masculine, feminine, neuter, or common.

The *case* of a pronoun has to do with how the pronoun is used in a sentence. The three cases are nominative, objective, and possessive.

Nominative Case

A pronoun in the *nominative case* is used as a subject or a predicate nominative. The following pronouns are in the nominative case: *I, you, he, she, it, we, they;* archaic: *thou, ye.* You have little difficulty in using the correct pronoun for the subject.

Lesson 58

Purpose: To study personal pronouns in the nominative, objective, and possessive case.

Oral Review:
1. Identify the personal pronouns in these sentences. Give the person, number, and gender of each.
   a. God created us for His glory. (us—first person, plural, common; His—third person, singular, masculine)
   b. Mary, is she your first cousin? (she—third person, singular, feminine; your—second person, singular, common)
   c. I did not see the ball until it almost hit me. (I—first person, singular, common; it—third person, singular, neuter; me—first person, singular, common)
2. Identify the tense of each verb.

   a. We shall have gone to the store before Friday. (future perfect)
   b. The puppy's tail wagged excitedly. (past)
   c. The rain has filled the rain gauge to the top! (present perfect)
   d. A tornado causes much damage to trees and buildings. (present)
   e. By evening several refreshing showers had fallen. (past perfect)
   f. The carpenters will finish the house by next month. (future)
3. Change the verb in each sentence to the progressive form. Do not change the tense.
   a. Mary Ellen cleans the furniture. (Mary Ellen is cleaning the furniture.)
   b. We have held cottage meetings at Freda Baer's

"I will praise thee, O Lord,
with my whole heart."

| I | will praise | thee |

"He delivered me from my
strong enemy."

| He | delivered | me |

In the King James Bible, the archaic forms *thou* and *ye* are used as second person pronouns in the nominative case. *Thou* is singular and *ye* is plural.

"Lord, remember me when <u>thou</u> comest into thy kingdom."
(Antecedent of *thou* is the singular noun *Lord*.)
"And he saith to his disciples, Sit <u>ye</u> here, while I shall pray."
(Antecedent of *ye* is the plural noun *disciples*.)

You are much more likely to use an incorrect pronoun for the predicate nominative in a sentence. In fact, the correct nominative case pronoun may even sound awkward to you. Nevertheless, a predicate nominative must be in the nominative case.

"But straightway Jesus spake unto them, saying, Be of good cheer; it is <u>I</u>; be not afraid." (Predicate nominative is the pronoun *I*, not *me*.)

Remember that in a sentence with a predicate nominative, the linking verb is like an equal sign. Also remember that the predicate nominative and the subject can usually be exchanged, and the sentence still means the same. Therefore, the same pronouns that are used as subjects must be used as predicate nominatives.

The only seventh grade boy in our school is <u>I</u> (not *me*).
Reworded: <u>I</u> (not *me*) am the only seventh grade boy in our school.)

My younger sister is <u>she</u> (not *her*).
Reworded: <u>She</u> (not *her*) is my younger sister.

My parents are <u>they</u> (not *them*).
Reworded: <u>They</u> (not *them*) are my parents.

home. (We have been holding cottage meetings at Freda Baer's home.)
c. Next week Vincent will stay at our place. (Next week Vincent will be staying at our place.)
4. Change the verb in each sentence to the emphatic form. Do not change the tense.
a. Mr. Berry makes durable brooms. (Mr. Berry does make durable brooms.)
b. Mrs. Conrad lived here for fifty years. (Mrs. Conrad did live here for fifty years.)

Lesson Introduction: In English, pronouns are the main words with different forms according to case (such as *he, him,* and *his*). For nouns, the only form that shows a special case is a possessive form (such as *boy's*). Some other languages have four different case forms, for nouns as well as pronouns. Consider the following comparisons between modern English and New Testament Greek.

Nominative:
<u>Paul</u> (Paulos) saw a great light. <u>He</u> (autos) saw a great light.
Objective:
Jesus spoke to <u>Paul</u> (Paulon). Jesus spoke to <u>him</u> (auton).
Possessive:
<u>Paul's</u> (Paulou) life was changed. <u>His</u> (autou) life was changed.
Dative:
God gave <u>Paul</u> (Paulō) a vision. God gave <u>him</u> (autō) a vision.

Case in modern English does require some attention, but it is not nearly as complicated as in some other languages.

Objective Case

A pronoun in the *objective case* is used as a direct object, an indirect object, or the object of a preposition. Notice that each of these terms includes the word *object*. That will help you to remember that they must be in the *objective* case. The following pronouns are in the objective case: *me, you, him, her, it, us, them;* archaic: *thee.*

"He shall hide <u>me</u> in his pavilion."
(*Me* is the direct object of *shall hide.*)

| He | shall hide | me |

"My son, give <u>me</u> thine heart."
(*Me* is the indirect object of *give.*)

(you) | give | heart
me

"My grace is sufficient for <u>thee</u>."
(*Thee* is the object of the preposition *for.*)

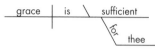

The archaic form *thee* is used in the King James Bible as the second person singular pronoun in the objective case. The plural form is *you.*

"Man, thy sins are forgiven <u>thee</u>." (Antecedent of *thee* is the singular noun *Man.*)
Jesus said to the apostles, "This is my body which is given for <u>you</u>." (Antecedent of *you* is the plural noun *apostles.*)

The pronouns *you* and *it* are the same in both nominative and objective case. You can tell the case of these pronouns only by their use in a sentence.

<u>You</u> called for <u>it</u>. (*You,* the subject, is nominative. *It,* the object of a preposition, is objective.)
<u>It</u> came to <u>you</u>. (*It,* the subject, is nominative. *You,* the object of a preposition, is objective.)

Possessive Case

A pronoun in the *possessive case* is used to show ownership. The following pronouns are in the possessive case: *my, mine, your, yours, his, her, hers, its, our, ours, their, theirs;* archaic: *thy, thine.* When a possessive case pronoun modifies a noun, it is an adjective. When a possessive case pronoun stands alone, it is a pronoun.

Lesson Outline:

1. The case of a pronoun has to do with how the pronoun is used in a sentence.

2. Nominative case pronouns are used as subjects or predicate nominatives.

   a. The nominative case pronouns are as follows: *I, you, he, she, it, we, they;* archaic: *thou, ye.*

   b. The archaic forms *thou* and *ye* are used in the King James Bible as second person pronouns in the nominative case. *Thou* is singular and *ye* is plural.

   c. For a predicate nominative, be careful to use a nominative case pronoun.

3. Objective case pronouns are used as direct objects, indirect objects, or objects of prepositions.

   a. The objective case pronouns are as follows: *me, you, him, her, it, us, them;* archaic: *thee.*

   b. The archaic form *thee* is used in the King James Bible as the second person singular pronoun in the objective case. The plural form is *you.*

   c. The pronouns *you* and *it* are the same in both nominative and objective case. Their case is determined by their use in a sentence.

4. Possessive case pronouns are used to show ownership.

   a. The possessive case pronouns are as follows: *my, mine, your, yours, his, her, hers, its, our, ours, their, theirs;* archaic: *thy, thine.*

   b. When a possessive case pronoun modifies a noun, it is an adjective.

Adjectives:
"My glory will I not give to another."
"We are his people."

Pronouns:
"Vengeance is mine; I will repay, saith the Lord."
"The sea is his, and he made it."

Do not use apostrophes with personal pronouns in the possessive case. Apostrophes are used with possessive forms of nouns and some other classes of pronouns, but not with personal pronouns. The only way an apostrophe is used with a personal pronoun is to form a contraction. If you are not sure whether to use an apostrophe, think of the two words from which the contraction would be made.

Problem: (Its, It's) building (its, it's) nest.
Think: *It is building* is sensible; *it is nest* is not.
Solution: It's building its nest.

Problem: (Your, You're) sister said that (your, you're) raising rabbits.
Think: *You are sister* is not sensible; *you are raising* is.
Solution: Your sister said that you're raising rabbits.

Problem: (Their, They're) helping (their, they're) mother quite well.
Think: *They are helping* is sensible; *they are mother* is not.
Solution: They're helping their mother quite well.

The archaic forms *thy* and *thine* are used in the King James Bible as second person singular pronouns in the possessive case. *Thy* is used before a consonant sound, and *thine* is used before a vowel sound. In archaic usage, *my* is also used only before a consonant sound and *mine* is used before a vowel sound.

"Save thy people, and bless thine inheritance."
"Look upon mine affliction and my pain."

Class Practice

A. Identify each personal pronoun, give its case, and tell how it is used in the sentence.
1. "We are your rejoicing, even as ye also are ours."
2. "Put them in mind to be subject to principalities."
3. "Wherefore I desire that ye faint not at my tribulations for you, which is your glory."
4. "We are bound to thank God always for you."
5. "And if any man obey not our word by this epistle, note that man, and have no company with him, that he may be ashamed."

c. When a possessive case pronoun stands alone, it is a pronoun.
d. Do not use an apostrophe with a personal pronoun in the possessive case.
e. The archaic forms *thy* and *thine* are used in the King James Bible as second person singular pronouns in the possessive case. *Thy* is used before a consonant sound, and *thine* is used before a vowel sound.
f. In archaic usage, *my* is used only before a consonant sound and *mine* is used before a vowel sound.

★ **EXTRA PRACTICE**
Worksheet 33 (*Pronoun Case*)

Lesson 58 Answers

Class Practice
A. 1. We—nominative, subject;
your—possessive, adjective;
ye—nominative, subject;
ours—possessive, predicate nominative
2. them—objective, direct object
3. I—nominative, subject;
ye—nominative, subject;
my—possessive, adjective;
you—objective, object of preposition;
your—possessive, adjective
4. We—nominative, subject;
you—objective, object of preposition
5. our—possessive, adjective;
him—objective, object of preposition;
he—nominative, subject

6. We are taking care of his hamster while they are visiting their friends in Texas.

7. Your picture is beautiful; mine and hers are not shaded as well.

B. Read each sentence, exchanging the subject and the direct object.

1. They see us.
2. He knows me well.
3. You will tell her.
4. She has paid me.
5. I helped them.
6. They are calling him.

C. Tell whether the personal pronouns in each pair differ in *person, number, case,* or *gender.*

1. he, she
2. we, they
3. its, hers
4. them, theirs
5. me, us
6. it, its

D. Choose the correct pronouns in parentheses.

1. The people hardest hit by the storm must have been (we, us).
2. (We, Us) can help (she, her).
3. Are you anxious for (their, they're) help?
4. (Its, It's) quite early for the duck to be building (its, it's) nest.
5. (Your, You're) paper looks as if (your, you're) hurrying too much.
6. The next person up to bat is (I, me).
7. The ones we should have helped were (they, them).
8. He is talking to (they, them).

Written Exercises

A. Copy each personal pronoun, and identify its case as nominative (*N*), objective (*O*), or possessive (*P*). Also identify its use as a subject (*S*), a direct object (*DO*), an indirect object (*IO*), a predicate nominative (*PN*), the object of a preposition (*OP*), or an adjective modifier (*M*).

1. We praise Him for His goodness to us.
2. You should always seek to do your best.
3. I want to express my gratitude to you for your kindness.
4. Our friends will milk the cows so that we can go to my uncle's wedding.
5. When their car passed ours, we waved.
6. Hand him the level, and then bring me a bag of nails.
7. Her helper was she.
8. It was he who gave us the idea.

B. Write a personal pronoun to fit each description.

1. third person, singular, nominative case, feminine gender
2. second person, possessive case
3. third person, plural, objective case

6. We—nominative, subject;
   his—possessive, adjective;
   they—nominative, subject;
   their—possessive, adjective

7. Your—possessive, adjective;
   mine—possessive, subject;
   hers—possessive, subject

B. 1. We see them.
   2. I know him well.
   3. She will tell you.
   4. I have paid her.
   5. They helped me.
   6. He is calling them.

C. 1. gender
   2. person
   3. gender
   4. case
   5. number
   6. case

D. 1. we
   2. We, her
   3. their
   4. It's, its
   5. Your, you're
   6. I
   7. they
   8. them

Written Exercises

A. 1. We—N, S; Him—O, DO; His—P, M; us—O, OP
   2. You—N, S; your—P, M
   3. I—N, S; my—P, M; you—O, OP; your—P, M
   4. Our—P, M; we—N, S; my—P, M
   5. their—P, M; ours—P, DO; we—N, S
   6. him—O, IO; me—O, IO
   7. Her—P, M; she—N, PN
   8. It—N, S; he—N, PN; us—O, IO

B. 1. she
   2. your *or* yours
   3. them

Case = nominative objective possessive

4. first person, singular, nominative case
5. third person, singular, possessive case, neuter gender

C. If there is an error in pronoun usage, write the correct pronoun. If the sentence is correct, write *correct*.
1. Them are visitors at our home.
2. The song leader was him.
3. It might be them who brought the dessert.
4. The artist for this book was she.
5. It was me who noticed the rainbow.
6. They're garden is almost perfectly free of weeds.
7. I wish our's would look just as clean.
8. If you're determined to get it weeded, you can do it.
9. Its time to get these potatoes peeled.
10. Since mine is broken, may I use yours?

Review Exercises

A. Change each verb in parentheses to the form shown in italics. [37–39]
1. The tomatoes (ripen) fast in this warm weather. *future tense*
2. Before today, we (find) only three ripe tomatoes. *past perfect tense*
3. Aunt Louella (write) a poem. *past tense, progressive form*
4. Jonathan (ride) his bicycle to school. *present tense, emphatic form*
5. Brian (teach) his puppy to shake hands. *present perfect tense*
6. Most of the peaches (pick) by the time we return. *future perfect tense, passive voice*

B. Rewrite each sentence, changing the verb to the progressive form. Do not change the tense. [39]
1. Philip hammered a nail into the wood.
2. Sandra keeps a record of the song numbers.
3. My brothers have built a doghouse.

C. Rewrite each sentence, changing the verb to the emphatic form. Do not change the tense. [39]
1. Marlene sings soprano.
2. The wind blew the cornstalks down.
3. Ronald and Stanley collect stamps.

---

4. I
5. its

C. 1. They   6. Their
2. he   7. ours
3. they   8. correct
4. correct   9. It's
5. I   10. correct

Review Exercises

A. 1. will ripen
2. had found
3. was writing
4. does ride
5. has taught
6. will have been picked

B. 1. Philip was hammering a nail into the wood.
2. Sandra is keeping a record of the song numbers.
3. My brothers have been building a doghouse.

C. 1. Marlene does sing soprano.
2. The wind did blow the cornstalks down.
3. Ronald and Stanley do collect stamps.

59. Taking Notes for an Oral Report

Lesson Survey

- To prepare for an oral report, follow these basic steps.
  1. Choose a suitable topic.
  2. Use various reference sources to find information.
  3. Write notes on your topic.

In grade 6 you learned how to take notes for a written report. In this lesson you will learn how to take notes in preparation for a brief oral report.

Whenever you receive information and share it with others, you are giving a report. As with most things in life, the effectiveness of your report will depend partly on how well you prepare beforehand.

Step 1: *Choose a suitable topic.* Your topic should be interesting and worthwhile to you and to others. It should also be a topic that you can cover well in three to five minutes. The first topic you decide to use may be suitable, but it may be too broad. In that case, you must limit the topic to a small part of the general idea. Remember, you want to give a brief report, not a long speech.

For example, suppose you consider the topic "The Life of David." It does not take much thinking to realize that this topic is too broad. In one brief report, you could not possibly cover all the main events in David's long and busy life. You could not even do justice to the topic "David's Life in the Wilderness." You must limit the topic to something quite narrow. "David and Jonathan's Friendship" would be one good possibility. Another suitable topic would be "David's Respect for King Saul."

The following sets of examples show how to limit broad subjects. The underlined topics would be suitable for brief oral reports.

Countries of Asia
China
The Geography of China
<u>The Geography of Southeast China</u>
<u>Major Rivers of China</u>

The Starry Heavens
<u>The Marvels of a Comet</u>
<u>The Precision of Earth's Location in the Solar System</u>

The Roman Empire
The Roman Empire of Jesus' Day

Lesson 59

Purpose: To teach how to take notes for an *oral report. (*Previous experience:* Taking notes for a written report.)

Teacher: This lesson teaches the use of note cards in doing research for an oral report. While many adults do not use this method, they do follow the basic procedure taught in the lesson. They are able to omit some of the technical steps because they are organized in their minds—which is not true of most seventh grade students at this point. But as the students use note cards, they will be learning the steps of organization; and later they too may use a different method for gathering and organizing information.

Oral Review:

1. Tell whether these statements are true or false.
   a. When taking notes on a sermon, you should write as much of the message as you can. (False; you should write main ideas or points that especially impress you.)
   b. On an outline, the first letter of a subpoint should begin with a small letter. (False; every item on an outline should begin with a capital letter.)
   c. If you have a subtopic labeled *A,* you must have a subtopic labeled *B;* and if you have a point labeled *1,* you must have a point labeled *2.* (True)
   d. Items on a topical outline should be followed by periods. (False; use periods only for items on a sentence outline.)
   e. When outlining written material, first pick out the main ideas. (True)

2. Why is outlining an important first step in writing? (It gives the writer an orderly plan for his composition.)

The Roman Empire Prepares the World for Christ
The Organization of the Roman Empire

Step 2: *Use various reference sources to find information.* The most important source is the Bible, which contains specific information about many subjects as well as important principles that relate to every subject. Information on many Bible-related subjects is found in Bible atlases, Bible dictionaries, and Bible handbooks. Encyclopedias give a wealth of information about hundreds of different topics. Nature books, textbooks, and even storybooks are other valuable resources.

You should use more than one reference source to find information. This will make your report more balanced than if all your ideas come from just one source. Combining material from several sources also requires you to express ideas in your own words. This will help you to understand your topic better, with the result that you can give a better report.

Step 3: *Write notes on your topic.* Be selective. Include only information that relates directly to your topic. Write only short phrases, not whole sentences or paragraphs. Use your own words unless you intend to quote directly from the reference source in your report. Any quoted material should be placed in quotation marks.

Write plenty of notes; it is easier to discard some than to go back through the reference books looking for more information. Be sure to specify with the notes exactly where you found the information. This will be helpful later for checking the accuracy of your notes or for finding other details that you may want to add.

Using small note cards, such as three-by-five-inch index cards, is a practical method for taking notes. The cards are small, so you can easily place one specific note on each card. And the cards are easy to shuffle when you are ready to organize your notes into an outline. Two sample note cards are shown here.

God's Glory in the Stars

Unger's Bible Dictionary, p. 1219

Unger, Merrill F.

Bible term *stars* includes planets and other heavenly bodies, but not sun and moon

God's Glory in the Stars

Investigating God's Orderly World, Book 7, p. 113

Double stars generally revolve around each other

Suppose you are taking notes on the topic "Life in Colonial New England," and you find the following article on pages 125 and 126 of a book entitled *A History of the United States.* Read the paragraphs shown,

3. What are some ways that outlining written material is a good study aid? (It forces the reader to analyze the material and identify main ideas and less important ideas. It helps the reader to remember what he read. It provides a good way to recall main ideas when reviewing the material later.)

4. What are some advantages of a topical outline? (enables speaker to see main ideas quickly; enables listener or reader to jot down ideas quickly)

5. What advantage does a sentence outline have to a writer? (Sentences can often be copied directly from the outline.)

Lesson Introduction: Have you ever picked a bouquet of wild flowers for your mother? As you went from one place to another, you did not pick every flower you saw. You may have looked for some specific kinds or simply for a pleasing variety. You tried to find flowers that blended together into an attractive bouquet. Those that did not suit your purpose, you left behind.

Taking notes for a report is somewhat like that. You must have a purpose in mind. You need to be selective, picking out only what suits that purpose. When you finish, you should have a pleasing variety of information.

Lesson Outline:

1. To prepare for an oral report, first choose a suitable topic.

   a. Your topic should be interesting and worthwhile to you and to others.

   b. If the first topic you decide to use is too broad, limit it to a small part of the general idea.

2. Use various reference sources to find information.

and study the notes following them.

Colonial Life

In 1750 there was no United States of America. The thirteen colonies were home to just over one million settlers. By today's standards, life throughout these colonies was slow and primitive. Yet there was much variety from one region of the colonies to another.

Religion was an important element in many people's lives. The New England colonies were influenced by strict Puritan thought. To the Puritans, life was a serious matter, not a game to be filled with fun and pleasure. Education was highly promoted because of their strong emphasis on Bible reading. In most New England colonies, membership in the established state church was a requirement for holding political office.

There was much more variation in the middle colonies, which had no state churches. The presence of the Quakers, Amish, and Mennonites helped to produce a sober, religious climate. Religion had less influence in the South. Most people along the frontier were widely scattered, so religious services were infrequent. Yet many frontier families maintained a strong sense of religion in their homes.

Occupations varied from one region to another. The New England colonies, with their rocky soil and shorter growing seasons, were less than ideal for farming. But their many streams and good harbors were excellent for fishing, manufacturing, and trading. The middle colonies had a mixture of small farms, large plantations, and manufacturing. In the South a small but influential group owned large plantations with many slaves. Yet most people in the South had small farms with few or no slaves. Many frontiersmen, living far away from towns and cities, were almost entirely self-sufficient. Some of them farmed, and many of them sold furs.

People of different regions lived in different kinds of houses. The colonists in New England needed sturdy houses to withstand the harsh winters. Wealthy businessmen owned spacious houses in the larger towns. Otherwise, the houses were generally small but comfortable.

People in the middle colonies had houses very similar to those in New England. The large plantation owners of the South had luxurious mansions, but many of those with small farms had little more than a shack. The symbol of the frontier was the one- or two-room log cabin. On the prairies, the frontiersmen often built sod houses or lived in hollows dug out of hillsides. . . .

a. The Bible is the most important source because it contains specific information about many subjects as well as important principles that relate to every subject.

b. Bible atlases, Bible dictionaries, and Bible handbooks give information about many Bible-related subjects.

c. Encyclopedias give information about hundreds of different subjects.

d. Nature books, textbooks, and storybooks are other valuable resources.

e. Use more than one reference source.

   1) This will make your report more balanced than if all your ideas come from just one source.

   2) Combining material from several sources requires you to express ideas in your own words, which will help you to understand your topic better and to give a better report.

3. **Write notes on your topic.**

a. Include only information that relates directly to your topic.

b. Write short phrases, not whole sentences or paragraphs.

c. Use your own words unless you intend to quote directly from a reference source. Be sure to place quoted words in quotation marks.

d. Write plenty of notes.

e. Specify where you found each item of information.

f. Using small note cards is a practical method for taking notes. Write one specific note on each card. The cards are easy to shuffle when you are ready to write an outline from your notes.

The four note cards read:

Card 1:
Life in Colonial New England
A History of the United States, p. 125
strict Puritan religion kept life serious; little pleasure seeking

Card 2:
Life in Colonial New England
HUS, p. 125
membership in state church required for holding political office

Card 3:
Life in Colonial New England
HUS, p. 125
education promoted because of strong emphasis on Bible reading

Card 4:
Life in Colonial New England
HUS, p. 126
farming difficult because soil and climate not suitable

The illustration above shows how you can use abbreviations to save time and space. The first card gives the full title of the book from which these notes are taken. But the other cards have only the letters *HUS,* which stand for *A History of the United States.* This abbreviation is enough to identify the reference source if you want to recheck a given fact.

Class Practice

A. Suggest wording for more notes on the topic "Life in Colonial New England," which could be taken on the partial article in the lesson.

B. For each broad subject, give several topics limited enough for a brief oral report.
1. The Life of Abraham
2. Good Manners
3. Dogs

Written Exercises

A. In each set of topics, only one or two is limited enough to be covered in a brief oral report. Write the titles of those limited topics.
1. Notable Prayers of Moses
   The Life of Moses
   Moses and the Wilderness Wanderings
   Three Parallels Between Moses and Christ
2. Honeybees
   The Life of a Drone
   The Inside Workings of a Beehive
   Bees of North America

Lesson 59 Answers

Class Practice

A. fishing, manufacturing, and trading common because of many streams and good harbors;
colonists had strong houses for protection in cold winters;
wealthier town dwellers built large houses;
other houses small but comfortable

B. (Sample answers.)
1. Abraham's Altars;
   Outstanding Examples of Abraham's Faith;
   Abraham's Concern for Lot
2. Politeness in the Schoolroom;
   Good Manners at the Table;
   Good Manners at Church
3. How Seeing Eye Dogs Are Trained;
   Saint Bernards at Work in the Alps;
   How Rover Won Our Hearts

Written Exercises

A. 1. Notable Prayers of Moses;
   Three Parallels Between Moses and Christ
2. The Life of a Drone

3. Generating and Using Electricity
   The Development of Electricity
   Electricity Has Greatly Changed Our Homes
   Generating Electricity Through Solar Power

3. Electricity Has Greatly Changed Our Homes;
   Generating Electricity Through Solar Power

B. Each numbered item represents information to be put on note cards. How many cards should be used for each number?

1. **Topic:**
   "The Hanging Gardens of Babylon"
   Information:
   one of the seven wonders of the ancient world; built for Nebuchadnezzar's wife who was homesick for her native mountains; consisted of great terraces of masonry; filled with plants and trees of Babylon and Persia; high enough to be visible above buildings

2. **Topic:**
   "The Water Tunnel Built by Hezekiah"
   Information:
   built to assure water supply from spring of Gihon to Jerusalem even when city was besieged; dug out of solid rock for nearly six hundred yards; workers dug from both ends and met in middle

3. **Topic:**
   "What Causes Colored Leaves in the Fall?"
   Information:
   triggered by shortening days and cool nights, not by frost; happens when sap is cut off because layer of cells between leaf and branch dies; green chlorophyll breaks down; other colors always present in leaves, but formerly hidden by more abundant chlorophyll

B. 1. 5
   2. 3
   3. 4

C. Take notes from at least two sources on a topic suitable for an oral report of three to five minutes. Choose one of the following or one of your own that is approved by your teacher. Save your notes for later lessons in this chapter.
   1. God Chooses a Small Army (Judges 7)
   2. David Responds to a "No" (1 Chronicles 17)
   3. Preparing Meals for a Colonial Frontier Family
   4. Chemical Changes Produced by Light Energy
   5. Drawing Up the Mayflower Compact
   6. How Honeybees Make Honey

C. (Individual work.)

Review Exercises

A. Write correctly all the words with capitalization errors. [20]
   1. Read the poem "In all the Lord Sends."
   2. When father and i were in town, we bought a Sunbeam Mixer.

Review Exercises
A. 1. All
   2. Father, I, mixer

3. We visited with sister Marie from the North Lawrence mennonite church.
4. After lunch, we study Music and European History.

3. These sentences have missing commas and end punctuation. Write the word before the missing punctuation, and add the needed mark. [7, 10, 14]
1. Our neighbors Randall Black's are moving to Denbigh Virginia
2. When will our reports be due Brother Arthur
3. No the floors have not been swept and the windows have not been washed
4. If only we had read the directions

3. Sister, Mennonite, Church
4. music, history

B. 1. neighbors, Black's, Denbigh, Virginia.
2. due, Arthur?
3. No, swept, washed.
4. directions!

---

60. Using Personal Pronouns Correctly

Lesson Survey

- Use the proper case when a pronoun is in a compound sentence part.
- Use the proper case when a pronoun is part of an appositive.
- Use the proper case when a pronoun is followed by an appositive.
- Be sure the antecedent of a pronoun is clear.
- Be sure a pronoun agrees in number with its antecedent.
- When you speak about another person and yourself, refer to the other person first and yourself last.

You are not likely to hear someone say, "*Him* had something better than gold for the lame man." But you just might hear someone say, "Peter and *him* had something better than gold for the lame man." No doubt you would not say, "*Us* read the story of the ten lepers." But you just might say, "*Us students* read the story of the ten lepers." In this lesson you will study some areas of pronoun usage in which you may not naturally use the correct pronoun.

1. *Use the proper case when a pronoun is in a compound sentence part.* Decide how the compound structure is used in the sentence. If it is a subject or a predicate nominative, use a nominative case pronoun. If it is a direct object, an indirect object, or the object of a preposition, use an

---

Lesson 60

Purpose: To teach the correct use of personal pronouns.

Oral Review:
1. Give the nominative case personal pronouns. (I, you, he, she, it, we, they; *archaic:* thou, ye)
2. Give the objective case personal pronouns. (me, you, him, her, it, us, them; *archaic:* thee)
3. Give the possessive case personal pronouns. (my, mine, your, yours, his, her, hers, its, our, ours, their, theirs; *archaic:* thy, thine)
4. Name the sentence parts that require nominative case pronouns. (subject, predicate nominative)
5. Name the sentence parts that require objective case pronouns. (direct object, indirect object, object of a preposition)

6. How can you tell whether a possessive case pronoun is used as an adjective or as a pronoun? (If the pronoun is used as an adjective, it comes right before the noun it modifies. If it is used as a pronoun, it stands alone.)
7. Tell whether the nouns in this group are singular or plural: *shears, scissors, trousers.* (plural)
8. Tell whether the nouns in this group are usually considered singular or plural: *phonics, mathematics, measles.* (singular)
9. With a collective noun, when should you use (*a*) a singular verb? (*b*) a plural verb? (*a.* Use a singular verb when the collective noun refers to the group doing one thing together. *b.* Use a plural verb when the collective noun refers to the individual members doing different things.)

Lesson Introduction: Some people make it sound as if a lot of other people are mean. At least when

objective case pronoun. Check the pronoun you choose by reading the sentence with that pronoun alone.

Problem: Mary and (she, her) did not understand Jesus' delay.
Think: The pronoun is part of a compound subject.
Use the nominative case.
Solution: Mary and <u>she</u> did not understand Jesus' delay.
Check: <u>She</u> did not understand Jesus' delay. (sounds right)

Problem: The godly characters in the story are Daniel and (they, them).
Think: The pronoun is part of a compound predicate nominative.
Use the nominative case.
Solution: The godly characters in the story are Daniel and <u>they</u>.
Check: The godly characters in the story are <u>they</u>. (sounds right)

Problem: God used Moses and (he, him).
Think: The pronoun is part of a compound direct object.
Use the objective case.
Solution: God used Moses and <u>him</u>.
Check: God used <u>him</u>. (sounds right)

Problem: God has given you and (I, me) many promises.
Think: The pronoun is part of a compound indirect object.
Use the objective case.
Solution: God has given you and <u>me</u> many promises.
Check: God has given <u>me</u> many promises. (sounds right)

Problem: We read the story about Deborah and (he, him).
Think: The pronoun is part of a compound object of a preposition.
Use the objective case.
Solution: We read the story about Deborah and <u>him</u>.
Check: We read the story about <u>him</u>. (sounds right)

2. *Use the proper case when a pronoun is part of an appositive.* An appositive is a noun or pronoun that renames another noun or pronoun; therefore, the appositive must be in the same case as the word it renames. Check the pronoun you choose by using it alone to replace the noun that is renamed.

Problem: It was my sisters, Bertha and (she, her).
Think: The appositive renames *sisters,* a predicate nominative.
Use the nominative case.
Solution: It was my sisters, Bertha and <u>she</u>.
Check: It was <u>she</u>. (sounds right)

you hear them talking, they say things like the following:

"Mean Sharon picked a bouquet of flowers."
"Mean James went along with Father to town."

Of course, what they intend to say is this:

"Me and Sharon picked a bouquet of flowers."
"Me and James went along with Father to town."

Running "me and" together is not the only thing wrong with these statements. They also use the wrong pronoun case, and they refer to the speaker before the other person. This lesson addresses a number of common problems with pronoun usage.

Lesson Outline:

1. Use the proper case when a pronoun is in a compound sentence part.

a. Decide how the compound structure is used in the sentence.
b. Use the correct case for that sentence part.
c. Check by reading the sentence with the pronoun alone.

2. Use the proper case when a pronoun is part of an appositive. The pronoun must be in the same case as the word it renames.

3. Use the proper case when a pronoun is followed by an appositive.

a. Decide how the pronoun is used in the sentence.
b. Use the correct case for that sentence part.
c. Check by reading the sentence without the appositive.

4. Be sure the antecedent of a pronoun is clear. If the antecedent is not clear, change the sentence so that it is.

Problem: Aunt Heather helped the girls, Jean and (I, me), while Uncle Eli helped the boys.

Think: The appositive renames *girls,* a direct object.
Use the objective case.

Solution: Aunt Heather helped the girls, Jean and <u>me</u>, while Uncle Eli helped the boys.

Check: Aunt Heather helped <u>me</u> while Uncle Eli helped the boys. (sounds right)

3. *Use the proper case when a pronoun is followed by an appositive.* Again, decide how the pronoun is used in the sentence. Check the pronoun you choose by reading the sentence without the appositive.

Problem: (We, Us) students memorized Psalm 1.

Think: The pronoun is the subject.
Use the nominative case.

Solution: <u>We</u> students memorized Psalm 1.

Check: <u>We</u> memorized Psalm 1. (sounds right)

Problem: Father gave (we, us) boys an assignment.

Think: The pronoun is an indirect object.
Use the objective case.

Solution: Father gave <u>us</u> boys an assignment.

Check: Father gave <u>us</u> an assignment. (sounds right)

4. *Be sure the antecedent of a pronoun is clear.* Sometimes two nouns precede a pronoun in a sentence, and either may logically be the antecedent. Such a sentence should be changed so that the antecedent is clear.

Unclear: John told Robert that his shoe was lost.
(Whose shoe was lost?)

Clear: John said, "Robert, my shoe is lost."
John said, "Robert, your shoe is lost."

Unclear: Mother called Sister Ruth after she came home from the hospital. (Who came home from the hospital?)

Clear: After Sister Ruth came home from the hospital, Mother called her.
After Mother came home from the hospital, she called Sister Ruth.

5. *Be sure a pronoun agrees in number with its antecedent.* A compound antecedent joined by *and* is usually plural and requires a plural pronoun. If an article is used only before the first part of the compound, it refers to one individual and requires a singular pronoun.

5. Be sure a pronoun agrees in number with its antecedent.

a. A compound antecedent joined by *and* is usually plural and requires a plural pronoun.

b. If an article is used only before the first part of the compound, it refers to one individual and requires a singular pronoun.

c. If a compound antecedent is composed of two singular nouns joined by *or* or *nor,* it is singular and requires a singular pronoun.

6. When you speak about another person and yourself, refer to the other person first and yourself last.

★ **EXTRA PRACTICE**
Worksheet 34 (*Using Personal Pronouns Correctly*)

The plumber and the electrician finished <u>their</u> jobs.
>   (Two *men,* the plumber and the electrician, finished *their* jobs.)

The plumber and electrician finished <u>his</u> job.
>   (One *man,* who is both a plumber and an electrician, finished *his* job.)

If a compound antecedent is composed of two singular nouns and joined by *or* or *nor,* it is singular and requires a singular pronoun.

>   Either Robert or Ryan will bring <u>his</u> ball.
>   (Only *one* boy will bring *his* ball.)

>   Neither Father nor Uncle Lyndon could start <u>his</u> car.
>   (Neither *one* could start *his* car.)

6. *When you speak about another person and yourself, refer to the other person first and yourself last.* By doing this, we are not only using correct grammar but also following the rule "In honour preferring one another."

>   **Incorrect:**   I and Miriam walked to school.
>   Andrew ate lunch with me and Ralph.
>   **Correct:**   Miriam and I walked to school.
>   Andrew ate lunch with Ralph and me.

Class Practice

A. Read these sentences, using the correct words in parentheses.
 1. Cultivating good character is important for you and (I, me).
 2. Abraham and (he, him) separated.
 3. Naomi told Ruth and (she, her) to return to Moab.
 4. God severely punished them, Ahab and (she, her), for their wickedness.
 5. Jehoshaphat is a familiar name to (we, us) Bible readers.
 6. Neither Stephen nor James was afraid to die for (his, their) Lord.
 7. Who was that? Was it (he, him)? No, it was (they, them).
 8. (We, Us) students must study diligently.
 9. The secretary and the treasurer gave (his report, their reports).
 10. The secretary and treasurer gave (his report, their reports).

B. Reword these sentences to make the pronouns clear and correct.
 1. Mother helped Aunt Marie while she was visiting.
 2. Either Susan or Mabel will finish their report first.
 3. I and Albert like to fish in our little creek.
 4. Bernice asked Marilyn if her cake was baked yet.
 5. These books are for me and you.

Lesson 60 Answers

Class Practice

A. 1. me
 2. he
 3. her
 4. her
 5. us
 6. his
 7. he, they
 8. We
 9. their reports
 10. his report

B. 1. While Mother was visiting, she helped Aunt Marie.

 or While Aunt Marie was visiting, Mother helped her.

 2. Either Susan or Mabel will finish her report first.

 3. Albert and I like to fish in our little creek.

 4. Bernice asked, "Marilyn, is your cake baked yet?"

 or Bernice asked, "Marilyn, is my cake baked yet?"

 5. These books are for you and me.

Written Exercises

A. If the underlined word or phrase contains a mistake, write it correctly. If it is correct, write *correct*.

1. Neither Jeremiah nor Joel could inspire <u>their</u> fellow Jews to repent.
2. <u>Them and their messages</u> brought bitter opposition.
3. <u>Us students</u> listed all the persecutions Jeremiah endured.
4. The eighth grade girls, <u>Erma and she</u>, made this bulletin board display.
5. Grandfather told <u>me and Donald</u> a story about his childhood.
6. Mother brought some lemonade out for <u>us bean pickers</u>.
7. The fastest pickers are <u>Leon and them</u>.
8. The carpenter and mason started <u>their</u> work today.
9. Harold and James will give <u>their oral reports</u> tomorrow.
10. Harold or James will give <u>their oral reports</u> tomorrow.
11. Father surprised <u>me and Phoebe</u> by bringing home a puppy.
12. My parents invited the visitors, <u>Jonas and he</u>, home for the night.
13. <u>We girls</u> defeated the boys in prisoner's base this morning.
14. Seventh grade students like <u>you and I</u> should be good models for younger students.
15. Our team caught everyone except them, <u>Barton and he</u>.

B. Rewrite these sentences to make the pronouns clear and correct.
1. Sharon told Linda that her sweater was torn.
2. Harvey learned to know Joseph when his father preached here.
3. Sister Lila told Sister Cheryl that her students had played nicely.
4. John tagged Daniel just as he slipped on the wet grass.

Review Exercises

A. Write the better words in parentheses. [48]
1. (There's, There are) many challenges for us in the story of Joseph.
2. We can always pray to God, for He (don't, doesn't) ever grow weary.
3. Peter, along with the other disciples, (was, were) puzzled by Jesus' words.
4. Absalom's army (was, were) scattering in defeat before their pursuers.
5. Every one of the students (know, knows) where to go in a fire drill.
6. A printed paper and a blank paper (lie, lies) on each desk.
7. Smallpox (is, are) much more serious than chicken pox.
8. Judith or Kathryn (wash, washes) the dishes this week.
9. The large shears just (fit, fits) into this box.
10. (How's, How are) the supply of paper towels?

Written Exercises

A.
1. his
2. They and their messages
3. We students
4. correct
5. Donald and me
6. correct
7. Leon and they
8. his
9. correct
10. his oral report
11. Phoebe and me
12. Jonas and him
13. correct
14. you and me
15. Barton and him

B.
1. Sharon said, "Linda, your sweater is torn."
   or Sharon said, "Linda, my sweater is torn."
2. When Harvey's father preached here, Harvey learned to know Joseph.
   or When Joseph's father preached here, Harvey learned to know Joseph.
3. Sister Lila said, "Sister Cheryl, your students played nicely."
   or Sister Lila said, "Sister Cheryl, my students played nicely."
4. Just as Daniel slipped on the wet grass, John tagged him.
   or Just as John slipped on the wet grass, he tagged Daniel.

Review Exercises

A.
1. There are
2. doesn't
3. was
4. were
5. knows
6. lie
7. is
8. washes
9. fit
10. How's

B. Diagram the skeletons, complements, appositives, and nouns of direct address in these sentences. Include all the modifiers that go with an appositive or a noun of direct address.

1. Josiah, a godly king of Judah, inspired a great revival.
2. He ordered the repair of the temple, and soon the Book of the Law was found.
3. Shaphan brought Josiah the precious scroll.
4. When the king heard the words of the Law, he rent his clothes.
5. He realized that God's wrath against them was very great.
6. Dear youth of today, never turn away from the principles of the Bible.

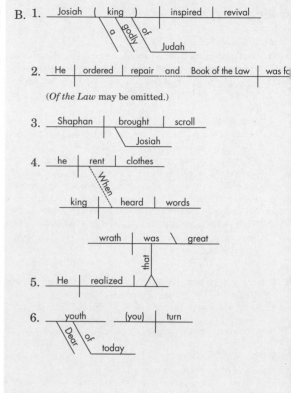

B. 1. Josiah (king) | inspired | revival
         a / godly / of
                    Judah

2. He | ordered | repair and Book of the Law | was fo
   (*Of the Law* may be omitted.)

3. Shaphan | brought | scroll
                    Josiah

4. he | rent | clothes
      When
   king | heard | words

5. He | realized
      wrath | was \ great
         that

6. youth (you) | turn
   Dear / of
          today

---

61. Compound Personal Pronouns and Demonstrative Pronouns

> ### Lesson Survey
> - A **compound personal pronoun** ends with *-self* or *-selves*.
> - A compound personal pronoun can be used intensively to add emphasis.
> - A compound personal pronoun can be used reflexively to refer to the subject.
> - Do not use a compound personal pronoun to replace a personal pronoun.
> - The **demonstrative pronouns** are *this, that, these,* and *those.* They are used to point out specific persons or things.

The personal pronouns you studied in previous lessons of this chapter are the most common pronouns. Beginning in this lesson, you will study five other classes of pronouns. Two of these other classes are compound personal pronouns and demonstrative pronouns.

Compound Personal Pronouns

A *compound personal pronoun* ends with *-self* or *-selves*. Like personal pronouns, these pronouns must agree with their antecedents in person and number. There are eight compound personal pronouns in all, as shown in the table.

Lesson 61

Purpose: (1) To teach *compound personal pronouns and demonstrative pronouns.

Oral Review:

1. When a pronoun is used in a compound sentence part, how can you decide the correct case of the pronoun? (Decide what sentence part it is; then read the sentence with the pronoun alone.)
2. When a pronoun is part of an appositive, it must be in what case? (in the same case as the word it renames)
3. How can you determine which case to use when a pronoun is followed by an appositive? (Decide how the pronoun is used in the sentence; then read the sentence without the appositive.)
4. Tell which pronouns are correct in the following sentences.

a. The carpenter or the mason left some of (his, their) tools.
b. The carpenter and the mason left some of (his, their) tools.
c. The carpenter and mason left some of (his, their) tools.

5. In a sentence about yourself and another person, what rule should you remember? (Speak of yourself last.)
6. Give the second and third principal parts of each verb.

a. do (did, [have] done)
b. tag (tagged, [have] tagged)
c. cut (cut, [have] cut)
d. lay (laid, [have] laid)
e. become (became, [have] become)
f. swing (swung, [have] swung)

Compound Personal Pronouns

	Singular	*Plural*
First person:	myself	ourselves
Second person:	yourself	yourselves
Third person:	himself, herself, itself	themselves

The following forms are sometimes used as compound personal pronouns, but they are not proper English words. Note that the first one improperly combines a plural pronoun with the singular word *self*.

themself   hisself   theirselves

A compound personal pronoun can be used *intensively* to add emphasis. Since it merely adds emphasis, the sentence is complete without it. In the following pairs of sentences, notice how the compound personal pronoun adds emphasis.

Jesus drew near, and went with them.
"Jesus <u>himself</u> drew near, and went with them."

I will awake early.
"I <u>myself</u> will awake early."

We dug the well.
We dug the well <u>ourselves</u>.

A compound personal pronoun can be used *reflexively* to refer to the subject. This is done when the name of a person or thing is the subject as well as the direct object, the indirect object, or the object of a preposition. With the reflexive use of a compound personal pronoun, the same noun does not need to be repeated.

Lena quickly excused <u>herself</u>. (Compare: Lena quickly excused *Lena.*)

Lena	excused	herself

The boys made <u>themselves</u> some sandwiches. (Compare: The boys made *the boys* some sandwiches.)

Marlin wrote a story about <u>himself</u>.
(Compare: Marlin wrote a story about *Marlin.*)

Marlin	wrote	story

about himself

Lesson Introduction: Write the following sentences on the board. Then have some students find these references: Ezra 4:3; 1 Thessalonians 4:16; Ecclesiastes 2:14. Have students compare the sentences on the board with the wording in the Scriptures.

We together will build unto the Lord God. ("We ourselves together will build . . .")
For the Lord shall descend from heaven with a shout. ("For the Lord himself shall descend . . .")
I perceived also that one event happeneth to them all. ("I myself perceived also . . .")

What special effect is produced by the wording in the Bible? Do the pupils sense the added emphasis given by the extra words? This added emphasis is one function that is filled by compound personal pronouns.

Lesson Outline:

1. A compound personal pronoun ends with -self or -selves.

  a. The following words are proper compound personal pronouns: *myself, yourself, himself, herself, itself, ourselves, yourselves, themselves.*

  b. The following forms are sometimes used as compound personal pronouns, but they are not proper English words: *themself, hisself, theirselves.*

(*Teacher: Ourself* is not included in the list, because it does have an accepted use in referring to the "editorial *we.*" Example: "This is a common belief, but we do not accept it ourself." However, the pupils' exercises include sentences with *ourself* because that form is incorrect in most everyday uses.)

Do not use a compound personal pronoun to replace a personal pronoun. Compound personal pronouns should be used only to give added emphasis or to refer to the subject.

Incorrect:
Lela and <u>himself</u> visited the elderly couple.
If you have a question, just call <u>myself</u>.
No one was there except <u>ourselves</u>.

Correct:
Lela and <u>he</u> visited the elderly couple.
If you have a question, just call <u>me</u>.
No one was there except <u>us</u>.

Demonstrative Pronouns

The *demonstrative pronouns* are *this, that, these,* and *those.* They are used to point out specific persons or things. *This* and *that* are singular; *these* and *those* are plural. *This* and *these* are used to point out nearby objects; *that* and *those* are used to point out distant objects.

<u>This</u> is a pine sapling. (singular, near)
<u>That</u> is a mature pine tree. (singular, distant)

<u>These</u> are acorn squash. (plural, near)
<u>Those</u> are zucchini. (plural, distant)

These four words are pronouns only if they stand alone. When they are used before nouns to tell *which,* they are adjectives.

<u>These</u> are Jerry's. (pronoun)
<u>These</u> *books* are Jerry's. (adjective)

I found <u>those</u> in the closet. (pronoun)
I found <u>those</u> *shirts* in the closet. (adjective)

You should never use *them* as a demonstrative pronoun. Neither should you say *this here* or *that there.*

Incorrect:
These apples are green, but <u>them</u> are ripe.
<u>This here</u> is my new hammer.
<u>That there</u> could cause you serious problems.

Correct:
These apples are green, but <u>those</u> are ripe.
<u>This</u> is my new hammer.
<u>That</u> could cause you serious problems.

2. *A compound personal pronoun can be used intensively to add emphasis.* Such a compound personal pronoun merely adds emphasis, so the sentence is complete without it.

3. *A compound personal pronoun can be used reflexively to refer to the subject.* This is done when the name of a person or thing is the subject as well as the direct object, the indirect object, or the object of a preposition.

4. *Do not use a compound personal pronoun to replace a personal pronoun.*

5. *The demonstrative pronouns are* this, that, these, *and* those. *They are used to point out specific persons or things.*

    a. *This* and *that* are singular; *these* and *those* are plural.

    b. *This* and *these* are used to point out nearby objects; *that* and *those* are used to point out distant objects.

    c. These four words are also used as adjectives.

    d. Do not use *them* as a demonstrative pronoun.

    e. Do not say *this here* or *that there.*

★ **EXTRA PRACTICE**
Worksheet 35 (*Compound Personal Pronouns and Demonstrative Pronouns*)

Class Practice

A. Tell whether each compound personal pronoun is used *intensively* or *reflexively*.
1. Mary Magdalene herself had been healed by Jesus.
2. "Keep yourselves in the love of God."
3. The birds are propelling themselves with their wings.
4. Mildred herself had picked two bushels of lima beans.
5. We do not purposely injure ourselves.

B. Read each sentence, using one of the demonstrative pronouns.
1. ———— is quite a surprise for us.
2. The best tomatoes we found are ———— right here on the stand.
3. The sheep in this pen are healthy; ———— in the other pen seem sick.
4. Look down the lane. ———— must be Grandpa's new car!

C. Tell whether each underlined word is used as a *pronoun* or an *adjective*.
1. <u>This</u> window is made from plastic.
2. <u>That</u> is a long, hard job for one person.
3. <u>These</u> on the shelf are the cheapest screwdrivers.
4. What are <u>those</u> brown spots?

D. Read each sentence correctly.
1. Jesus Hisself knew what He would do.
2. We are always inspired by this here story of Caleb's faith.
3. The disciples boldly declared that they would be loyal to Jesus, but they did not understand theirselves.
4. James and myself will wait for you.
5. That there mountain is snowcapped all year.

Written Exercises

A. If the underlined part of the sentence contains a mistake, rewrite it correctly. If it is correct, write *correct*.
1. The children of Israel prepared <u>themself</u> for the battle.
2. We too must arm <u>ourselves</u> for a spiritual battle.
3. Abraham built <u>hisself</u> an altar.
4. <u>This here</u> song tells of Jesus' words on the cross.
5. This tree is a hemlock, but <u>them</u> are mostly fir trees.
6. The teacher told <u>ourselves</u> the story.
7. Mother made lunch for Sarah and <u>myself</u>.
8. They <u>theirselves</u> knew that the answer was wrong.
9. <u>These here</u> holes were made by a woodpecker.
10. Uncle George <u>himself</u> played hide-and-seek with us for a little.

Summit Gateway
947-7070

11. We must discipline <u>ourself</u> to study diligently.
12. I never saw <u>that there</u> book before.
13. Most people give <u>themself</u> the benefit of the doubt.
14. These are my papers, and <u>those</u> are Jonathan's.
15. <u>Them</u> on the stack have not been graded yet.

B. Write one sentence with a compound personal pronoun used intensively, and one sentence with a compound personal pronoun used reflexively.

Review Exercises

A. Write the second and third principal parts of each verb. Include *have* with the third principal part. [34]

1. burst	6. come
2. break	7. write
3. drink	8. ring
4. bring	9. lie
5. rise	10. give

Second = past
third = past partic.

B. Write the correct form of each verb in parentheses. [34]
1. God never (forget) His promises.
2. Moses wisely (choose) to identify with God's people.
3. "I have (fight) a good fight."
4. Jesus (weep) over Jerusalem.
5. "Let him that (steal) steal no more."
6. The children who mocked Elisha were (tear) by two bears.
7. Have you (write) your book report yet?
8. Uncle Leland (raise) feeder pigs.
9. As we drove up the Rocky Mountains, we (leave) the hot weather behind.
10. For many years, a variety of fish have (swim) in these waters.

11. ourselves
12. that
13. themselves
14. correct
15. Those

B. (Individual work.)

Review Exercises

A.
1. burst, (have) burst
2. broke, (have) broken
3. drank, (have) drunk
4. brought, (have) brought
5. rose, (have) risen
6. came, (have) come
7. wrote, (have) written
8. rang, (have) rung
9. lay, (have) lain
10. gave, (have) given

B.		
1. forgets		6. torn
2. chose		7. written
3. fought		8. raises *or* raised
4. wept		9. left
5. stole		10. swum

62. Organizing Your Notes

> **Lesson Survey**
> - To organize your notes, divide them into groups that relate to several main topics.
> - Arrange the main topics in a logical order.
> - Write an outline based on your groups of notes.

Lesson 62

Purpose: To teach how to organize notes into an outline. (*Previous experience:* Outlining for a written report.)

Oral Review:
1. Why should you take notes from more than one reference source? (to have a balanced report; to become well familiar with the topic)
2. What should you do if you write exact words from a reference source? (Put quotation marks around the exact words.)
3. What information should appear on a note card? (title of your topic, source of information, item of information)
4. What are the advantages of using small cards for taking notes? (One item of information can be put on each card. Cards can easily be shuffled to organize the notes.)

Lesson Introduction: An efficient housewife has her equipment and foodstuffs well organized. Her kettles are stacked neatly, with large ones on the bottom and smaller ones on top. Her flour, sugar, spices, and other ingredients are neatly arranged and easily accessible. Plates, cups, and saucers stand in orderly stacks on her cabinet shelves, and silverware is kept in drawers with individual compartments for the various kinds.

An efficient speaker has his notes organized so that he can present his ideas in an orderly way. This lesson will give you direction in organizing your notes into an outline for an oral report.

Lesson Outline:
1. To organize your notes, divide them into groups that relate to several main topics. Any unrelated notes should be laid aside.

God commands that "all things be done decently and in order." Order in speaking is pleasant and effective; instead of a meaningless mixture of ideas, there is a sensible sequence of thought.

The first step in this organization is to review carefully the notes that you have taken. Look for main topics, and divide the notes into groups accordingly. Perhaps you will lay aside some notes because they are not closely related to any main topic.

Study the following cards, and try to pick out several main topics into which to group them. The cards are numbered for simple reference.

The Marvel of Man's Body #1

Bible: Genesis 2:7

made from dust of ground, but houses a living soul

The Marvel of Man's Body #5

Bible: 1 Corinthians 15:53

will be changed into immortal body fit for eternal world

The Marvel of Man's Body #2

Bible: Matthew 4:4

soul must be fed on God's Word

The Marvel of Man's Body #6

Biology: God's Living Creation, p. 247

new bone cells grow to replace damaged cells in a fracture

The Marvel of Man's Body #3

Bible: Philippians 3:21

Christian's body will be changed into likeness of Christ's glorious body

---

The Marvel of Man's Body #7

Science Is Explaining, p. 276

elements in 100-lb. body: 65 lb. oxygen, 18 lb. carbon, 10 lb. hydrogen, 3 lb. nitrogen, 1 lb. phosphorus

---

The Marvel of Man's Body #4

Bible: 1 Corinthians 12:14-17

made of many parts that work together

The Marvel of Man's Body #8

Investigating God's Orderly World, Book 1, p. 330

white blood cells devour harmful germs

---

2. **Arrange the main topics in a logical order.**

3. **Write an outline based on your groups of notes.**

    a. Such an outline is a basic plan that shows main topics and subtopics. It does not have to include every detail that you will use.

    b. The items on the outline will be like topic sentences in paragraphs, which must be supported by specific details. You must be well prepared to use specific details to develop your main ideas. Then you can use your outline simply as a guide that shows your main ideas and the order in which you plan to cover them.

The Marvel of Man's Body #9

IGOW, Book 1, p. 331

antibodies help destroy germs or coun-
teract poisons produced by germs

The Marvel of Man's Body #10

IGOW, Book 1, pp. 318–319

bandages and antiseptics may help, but
God created the body to heal itself

Quotation from SoL, p. 286, to go with #7

"A 100-pound human body contains enough
water to fill an 8-gallon barrel, enough iron
to make a nail, one teaspoon of sugar, enough
fat to make several bars of soap, enough carbon to make about six thousand pencils, enough
calcium to whitewash a small chicken coop,
enough sulfur and phosphorus to make a small
box of matches, and enough potassium to make
the powder of a small shotgun shell."

Do you recognize three main topics in these cards? Cards 1, 4, and 7
give details about the creation and material makeup of the body. Cards 3
and 5 have to do with the future of the body. And cards 6, 8, 9, and 10 deal
with the healing ability of the body. These related cards should be grouped
together. Card 2 is not directly related to the theme of the report. It speaks
about man's soul rather than his body, so it should be laid aside.

You now have three main topics: the creation and material makeup of
the body, the future of the body, and the healing ability of the body. These
main topics need to be arranged in a logical order. Probably the best arrangement in this case is a chronological order: first the past (the creation and
material makeup of the body), then the present (the healing ability of the
body), and finally the future of the body.

Here then is the basic outline of your report.

The Marvel of Man's Body

   I. Creation and material makeup of the body
  II. Healing ability of the body
 III. Future of the body

Now that you have your basic outline, you are ready to fill it in with more detailed information. You will get this information from your note cards. From cards 1, 4, and 7, which were all about your first topic, you might arrange details on an outline like the following example.

The Marvel of Man's Body

I. Creation and material makeup of the body
   A. Made by God from dust
   B. Made of many elements; 100-lb. body contains the following:
      1. 65 lb. oxygen
      2. 18 lb. carbon
      3. 10 lb. hydrogen
      4. 3 lb. nitrogen
      5. 1 lb. phosphorus
      6. Quotation from *SIE* about things in 100-lb. body
   C. Contains many parts that work together
   D. Given a living soul

Can you see how all these details fit together? After considering that the body is made from dust (point A), you look at the elements the body is made of (point B). Then you look at the many body parts working together (point C). You conclude with the most important point of all, the fact that the body contains a living soul.

After organizing the details for the first topic, you must do the same thing for each of the other main topics of your report. That will put all your information into a clear, brief, logical form. This outline will be the basis from which you will give your report to the class.

Class Practice

A. Using cards 6, 8, 9, and 10, organize the details for the second main topic of the outline on "The Marvel of Man's Body."

B. Using cards 3 and 5, organize the details for the third main topic of the outline on "The Marvel of Man's Body."

Written Exercises

A. Organize the notes you gathered in Lesson 59, and write a basic outline of three or four main topics. Show your outline to your teacher before you do Part B.

B. Use the information from your notes to make a more detailed outline.

_____

Lesson 62 Answers

Class Practice

A. (Sample answer.)
   II. Healing ability of the body
      A. Created to heal itself, though bandages and antiseptics may help
      B. Has white blood cells that devour harmful germs
      C. Has antibodies that destroy germs or counteract poisons produced by germs
      D. Produces new bone cells to replace damaged cells in a fracture

B. (Sample answer.)
   III. Future of the body
      A. Every human body to be changed into immortal body
      B. Christian's body to be changed into likeness of Christ's glorious body

Written Exercises
   (Individual work.)

63. Indefinite Pronouns

Lesson Survey

- An **indefinite pronoun** does not refer to a definite person, place, thing, or idea.

- The following indefinite pronouns are always singular: *each, either, neither, one, another, anybody, anyone, everybody, everyone, somebody, someone, nobody, no one.*

- The following indefinite pronouns are always plural: *both, few, many, others, several.*

- The following indefinite pronouns may be either singular or plural: *some, any, none, all, most.*

- The possessive form of an indefinite pronoun is made by adding *'s.*

- An indefinite pronoun is an adjective when it comes just before a noun and modifies that noun.

A personal pronoun usually has a specific antecedent. The pronouns in the large group of *indefinite pronouns,* however, are often used without any antecedents. These pronouns do not refer to definite persons, places, things, or ideas.

> Noah built an ark to the saving of <u>his</u> house. (personal pronoun referring to a specific person; antecedent is *Noah*)
>
> <u>Many</u> perished in the Flood. (indefinite pronoun not referring to specific persons; no antecedent)

The following indefinite pronouns are always singular: *each, either, neither, one, another, anybody, anyone, everybody, everyone, somebody, someone, nobody, no one.* For many of these pronouns, notice that one part is singular—such as *other, one,* or *body.* Also, when these pronouns are used as adjectives, they always modify singular nouns.

> another person (*not* another persons)
> each girl (*not* each girls)
> either boy (*not* either boys)

When a singular indefinite pronoun is used as a subject, it is sometimes followed by a prepositional phrase with a plural object. Be careful to make the verb agree with the indefinite pronoun, not with the object of the preposition. Also be sure that any personal pronoun referring to a

Lesson 63

Purpose: To teach the correct use of indefinite pronouns.

Oral Review:

1. Compound personal pronouns end with ——— or ———. (-self, -selves)

2. Tell whether the following are proper compound personal pronouns.
   a. themselves (yes)   e. myself (yes)
   b. yourself (yes)   f. hisself (no)
   c. themself (no)   g. theirselves (no)
   d. itself (yes)   h. ourselves (yes)

3. Give the four demonstrative pronouns. (this, that, these, those)

4. Give personal pronouns to fit the following descriptions.
   a. first person, singular, nominative case, common gender (I)

   b. third person, plural, possessive case, common gender (their *or* theirs)
   c. second person, plural, objective case, common gender (you)
   d. second person, plural, nominative case, common gender (you)
   e. third person, singular, nominative case, feminine gender (she)

5. Tell whether each sentence is simple, compound, or complex. If it is complex, tell whether the subordinate clause is an adjective, an adverb, or a noun.
   a. The place where Jesus was crucified was near Jerusalem. (complex, adjective)
   b. Satan tried his worst to destroy Jesus, but Jesus' death destroyed Satan's power. (compound)
   c. When John heard the women's story, he ran to the sepulcher. (complex, adverb)
   d. John stooped down and looked into the sepulcher. (simple)

singular indefinite pronoun is singular.

Incorrect: <u>Everyone</u> <u>are</u> expected to bring *their* own pencil.
Correct: <u>Everyone</u> <u>is</u> expected to bring *his* own pencil.

Incorrect: <u>Each</u> of the plants <u>have</u> produced several large tomatoes.
Correct: <u>Each</u> of the plants <u>has</u> produced several large tomatoes.

Incorrect: <u>Somebody</u> <u>are</u> forgetting *their* manners.
Correct: <u>Somebody</u> <u>is</u> forgetting *his* manners.

Incorrect: <u>Either</u> of the girls <u>make</u> good bread.
Correct: <u>Either</u> of the girls <u>makes</u> good bread.

Incorrect: <u>Another</u> of the students <u>have</u> finished *their* project.
Correct: <u>Another</u> of the students <u>has</u> finished *his* project.

Incorrect: <u>No one</u> remembered to express *their* gratitude.
Correct: <u>No one</u> remembered to express *his* gratitude.

The following indefinite pronouns are always plural: *both, few, many, others, several.* These words clearly refer to more than one person, place, thing, or idea. Also, when these pronouns are used as adjectives, they always modify plural nouns.

both cows (*not* both cow)
few notes (*not* few note)
many Bibles (*not* many Bible)

When these indefinite pronouns are used as subjects, be sure to use plural verbs. Also be sure that any personal pronouns referring to them are plural.

<u>Both</u> of you <u>are</u> doing a good job.
A <u>few</u> of the natives <u>have</u> been persecuted by *their* families.
<u>Others</u> <u>find</u> *their* families quite open to the Gospel.

The following indefinite pronouns may be either singular or plural: *some, any, none, all, most.* When these words are used as adjectives, they may modify singular or plural nouns.

some meat *or* some carrots
all water *or* all rocks
most grass *or* most flowers

When one of these indefinite pronouns is used as a subject, you must decide whether it refers to a singular or a plural noun. That noun is often the object in a prepositional phrase that comes right after the indefinite

e. The angel declared that Jesus had risen from the dead. (complex, noun)

Lesson Introduction: Read these two stanzas of the song "Somebody Did a Golden Deed."

Somebody did a golden deed,
Proving himself a friend in need;
Somebody sang a cheerful song,
Bright'ning the sky the whole day long:
     Was that somebody you?
     Was that somebody you?

Somebody idled all the hours,
Carelessly crushed life's fairest flowers;
Somebody made life loss, not gain,
Thoughtlessly seemed to live in vain:
     Was that somebody you?
     Was that somebody you?
                              —John R. Clements

Do you suppose the author had a specific person in mind when he penned these stanzas? Probably not, for the word *somebody* does not refer to a definite person. It could be *Jason* or *Susanna* who did the golden deed—we cannot tell. All we know is that it was *some body,* which is quite indefinite.

Lesson Outline:

1. An indefinite pronoun does not refer to a definite person, place, thing, or idea.

2. The following indefinite pronouns are always singular: **each, either, neither, one, another, anybody, anyone, everybody, everyone, somebody, someone, nobody, no one.**

a. When a singular indefinite pronoun is used as a subject, the verb must agree with the pronoun, not with the object of a prepositional phrase that may come between the subject and the verb.

pronoun. If the object of the preposition is singular, the indefinite pronoun is singular; if the object is plural, the indefinite pronoun is plural.

> Some of the *cake* <u>has</u> been eaten.
> (*Some* refers to singular *cake* and is singular.)
> Some of the *cookies* <u>have</u> been eaten.
> (*Some* refers to plural *cookies* and is plural.)
>
> Most of the *work* <u>is</u> finished already.
> (*Most* refers to singular *work* and is singular.)
> Most of the *chores* <u>are</u> finished already.
> (*Most* refers to plural *chores* and is plural.)
>
> <u>Has</u> any of the *corn* been sold?
> (*Any* refers to singular *corn* and is singular.)
> <u>Have</u> any of the *peaches* been sold?
> (*Any* refers to plural *peaches* and is plural.)

The possessive forms of indefinite pronouns are made by adding *'s*. Remember this rule: To make possessive forms, *never* use apostrophes with personal pronouns, but *always* use apostrophes with indefinite pronouns.

> Someone<u>'s</u> book is on the floor.
> No one<u>'s</u> composition is finished yet.

An indefinite pronoun is an adjective when it comes just before a noun and modifies that noun. It is a pronoun when it stands alone.

> *Many* of the early Christians <u>died</u> as martyrs. (pronoun used as the subject)
> *Many* early <u>Christians</u> <u>died</u> as martyrs. (adjective modifying the subject)

Class Practice

A. Choose the correct words in parentheses.
1. Each of the disciples (was, were) sent out to serve (his, their) Lord.
2. One of Peter's epistles (contain, contains) a discussion on apostasy.
3. Both of the epistles to Timothy (was, were) written by Paul.
4. Some of the Bible (is, are) ignored by people today.
5. Some of the Bible teachings (is, are) ignored by people today.
6. Neither of the girls (need, needs) (her, their) glasses to read.
7. All of the corn (have, has) been eaten.
8. All of the pellets (have, has) been eaten.
9. Few of the towns (remain, remains) undamaged after the hurricane.

b. Any personal pronoun referring to a singular indefinite pronoun must be singular.

3. The following indefinite pronouns are always plural: both, few, many, others, several.

a. If a plural indefinite pronoun is used as a subject, the verb must be plural.

b. Any personal pronoun referring to a plural indefinite pronoun must be plural.

4. The following indefinite pronouns may be either singular or plural: some, any, none, all, most. The number of such a pronoun is determined by the noun it refers to. That noun is often the object in a prepositional phrase that comes right after the indefinite pronoun.

5. The possessive form of an indefinite pronoun is made by adding 's.

Lesson 63 Answers

Class Practice

A. 1. was, his
   2. contains
   3. were
   4. is
   5. are
   6. needs, her
   7. has
   8. have
   9. remain

6. An indefinite pronoun is an adjective when it comes just before a noun and modifies that noun.

★ **EXTRA PRACTICE**
Worksheet 36 (*Indefinite Pronouns*)

10. Everyone (find, finds) (his, their) work easier when he has a good attitude toward it.

B. Tell which word in each sentence needs an apostrophe.
   1. Somebodys lunch box is in the van; is it yours?
   2. Nobodys answer was better than theirs.
   3. Ours were later than anyones from the other room.
   4. After his plan failed, people expected no ones to work.

C. Tell whether each underlined word is used as a *pronoun* or an *adjective*.
   1. <u>Each</u> promise in the Bible is absolutely certain.
   2. <u>All</u> who trust in them will be blessed.
   3. God takes orders from <u>nobody</u>.
   4. <u>Each</u> of His attributes is divinely perfect.
   5. Man cannot comprehend <u>some</u> aspects of God's character.

Written Exercises

A. If a pronoun or a verb is used incorrectly, write the correct word. If the sentence is correct, write *correct*.
   1. Apparently no one in Sodom was turned from their sin by Lot's influence.
   2. Each of his sons-in-law were unconvinced by Lot's warning to flee.
   3. One of the fleeing group has become a memorial against looking back.
   4. All of the inhabitants in Sodom was destroyed by fire and brimstone.
   5. Someone apparently was here already this morning.
   6. Has anybody brought their binoculars along?
   7. None of the oatmeal is left in the dish.
   8. None of the raisins is left either.
   9. Everybody's help was certainly appreciated.
   10. A few of these books was treated carelessly.
   11. Most of the crop seem ready to harvest.
   12. Either of the girls may bring their colored pencils tomorrow.
   13. Any of these mottoes are for you to choose.
   14. No ones except yours would be as pretty as this.
   15. Most of the apples has been blighted by the fungus.

B. Write whether each underlined word is a *pronoun* or an *adjective*.
   1. <u>None</u> of the devil's attacks defeated Jesus.
   2. <u>Some</u> lives are warped by wrong choices in youth.
   3. Bad habits bind <u>some</u> in strong chains to Satan's power.
   4. Maintaining a clear conscience should be <u>one</u> of your primary goals.
   5. <u>One</u> important way to do this is to share freely with godly parents.

10. finds, his

B. 1. Somebody's
   2. Nobody's
   3. anyone's
   4. no one's

C. 1. adjective
   2. pronoun
   3. pronoun
   4. pronoun
   5. adjective

Written Exercises

A. 1. his
   2. was
   3. correct
   4. were
   5. correct
   6. his
   7. correct
   8. are
   9. correct
   10. were
   11. seems
   12. her
   13. correct
   14. No one's
   15. have

B. 1. pronoun
   2. adjective
   3. pronoun
   4. pronoun
   5. adjective

Review Exercises

A. Write whether each underlined clause is an *adjective,* an *adverb,* or a *noun.* [15, 28]

1. Nebuchadnezzar learned <u>that God rules supremely in the kingdoms of men</u>.
2. <u>After God had brought him low</u>, he acknowledged this fact.
3. "He <u>that hath the Son</u> hath life."
4. <u>How God created the world out of nothing</u> defies man's understanding.

B. Write whether each sentence is *simple, compound,* or *complex.* [14, 15]

1. The Master has come and is calling for you.
2. Our outward man perishes, yet the inward man can be renewed daily.
3. We know that Jesus lives.
4. Cornelius, who was a centurion, feared God.
5. Jesus not only died but also rose again.
6. Because he was dropped, Mephibosheth was lame all his life.
7. Teach a just man, and he will increase in learning.
8. Sow good seeds in youth, and reap godly character in adulthood.

Review Exercises

A. 1. noun
   2. adverb
   3. adjective
   4. noun

B. 1. simple
   2. compound
   3. complex
   4. complex
   5. simple
   6. complex
   7. compound
   8. compound

64. Interrogative and Relative Pronouns

Lesson Survey

- The pronouns *who, whom, whose, which,* and *what* are **interrogative pronouns** when they are used to introduce questions.

- The pronouns *who, whom, whose, which,* and *that* are **relative pronouns** when they are used to introduce adjective clauses.

- *Who* and *whom* must be used correctly. If the pronoun is a subject or predicate nominative, use the nominative case *who*. If the pronoun is a direct object, an indirect object, or the object of a preposition, use the objective case *whom*.

- The relative pronouns *who* and *whom* refer only to people, *which* refers only to things, and *that* and *whose* refer to either people or things.

You remember that an interrogative sentence asks a question. The first word in many questions is a pronoun. Because the pronoun introduces an

Lesson 64

Purpose: To teach the correct uses of interrogative and relative pronouns.

Oral Review:

1. Tell whether these indefinite pronouns are always singular, always plural, or sometimes singular or plural.
   a. all, any, most, none, some (sometimes singular or plural)
   b. another, each, anyone, somebody (always singular)
   c. few, both, several, many (always plural)
2. Which two demonstrative pronouns refer to things at a distance? (that, those)
3. Which two demonstrative pronouns refer to things nearby? (this, these)
4. Tell whether the compound personal pronouns in

these sentences are used intensively or reflexively.
   a. God has revealed Himself to man. (reflexively)
   b. God Himself shall wipe away all tears. (intensively)
5. Tell whether each verb is transitive, intransitive linking, or intransitive complete. If it is transitive, tell whether its voice is active or passive.
   a. The Good Shepherd provides for His sheep. (intransitive complete)
   b. Loving care is extended to each sheep. (transitive; passive voice)
   c. He feeds them in green pastures. (transitive; active voice)
   d. Jesus is the Good Shepherd. (intransitive linking)

Lesson Introduction: The Anabaptists often faced interrogations when they were captured by the state

interrogative sentence, it is called an *interrogative pronoun*. The pronouns *who, whom, whose, which,* and *what* are interrogative pronouns when they are used to introduce questions.

"<u>Who</u> is God, save the Lord? and <u>who</u> is a rock, save our God?"
"<u>Whom</u> have I in heaven but thee?"
"<u>Whose</u> son art thou, thou young man?"
"<u>Which</u> of you by taking thought can add one cubit unto his stature?"
"<u>What</u> is man, that thou art mindful of him?"

An interrogative pronoun not only introduces a question but also serves some function in the sentence. The following diagrams illustrate the functions of the pronouns in the sentences above.

"<u>Who</u> is God, save the Lord? and <u>who</u> is a rock, save our God?" (*who* as subject)

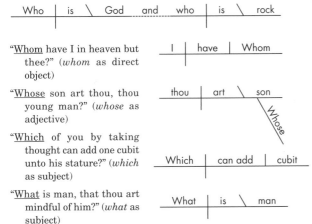

"<u>Whom</u> have I in heaven but thee?" (*whom* as direct object)

"<u>Whose</u> son art thou, thou young man?" (*whose* as adjective)

"<u>Which</u> of you by taking thought can add one cubit unto his stature?" (*which* as subject)

"<u>What</u> is man, that thou art mindful of him?" (*what* as subject)

The pronouns *who, whom, whose, which,* and *that* are *relative pronouns* when they are used to introduce adjective clauses. These pronouns are the same as the interrogative pronouns except that the relative pronoun *that* replaces the interrogative pronoun *what*. A *relative* pronoun has its name because it *relates* the adjective clause to an antecedent in the main clause.

The youth <u>who learns self-discipline</u> is prepared for a useful life.
   (*Who* relates the clause to the antecedent *youth*.)
Jesus Christ, <u>whom we can trust fully</u>, has promised His divine aid.
   (*Whom* relates the clause to the antecedent *Jesus Christ*.)

church authorities. These "question sessions" were designed to get information about other Anabaptists and to break down the arrested person. Here is a sampling of the kinds of questions that they were sometimes asked. These questions begin with interrogative pronouns.

> Who baptized you? Who are your leaders? What do you do at your meetings? Which of these men do you know: Hans Leib, Jacob Schneider, Michael Reublin?

Lesson Outline:
   1. The pronouns who, whom, whose, which, *and* what *are interrogative pronouns when they are used to introduce questions.* An interrogative pronoun also serves as a subject, a direct object, a predicate nominative, an adjective, or the object of a preposition in the sentence.

   2. The pronouns who, whom, whose, which, *and* that *are relative pronouns when they are used to introduce adjective clauses.*
   a. A *relative* pronoun has its name because it *relates* the adjective clause to an antecedent in the main clause.
   b. A relative pronoun serves as a subject, a direct object, a predicate nominative, an adjective, or the object of a preposition in the clause it introduces.

   3. The pronouns who *and* whom *must be used correctly.*
   a. If the pronoun is a subject or predicate nominative, use the nominative case *who*.
   b. If the pronoun is a direct object, an indirect object, or the object of a preposition, use the objective case *whom*.

Serve the Lord, _whose_ power is sovereign.

(_Whose_ relates the clause to the antecedent _Lord._)

The gold _which_ the people had brought to Aaron was made into an idol. (_Which_ relates the clause to the antecedent _gold._)

The people broke the first two commandments _that_ God had given. (_That_ relates the clause to the antecedent _commandments._)

A relative pronoun serves a definite function in the clause it introduces. The following diagrams illustrate the functions of the relative pronouns in the sentences above.

The youth _who learns self-discipline_ is prepared for a useful life. (_who_ as subject)

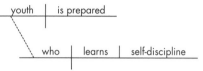

Jesus Christ, _whom_ we can trust fully, has promised His divine aid. (_whom_ as direct object)

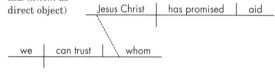

Serve the Lord, _whose_ power is sovereign. (_whose_ as adjective)

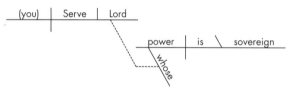

The gold _which_ the people had brought to Aaron was made into an idol. (_which_ as direct object)

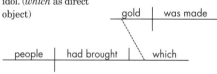

4. The relative pronouns who and whom re-fer only to people, which refers only to things, and that and whose refer to either people or things.

★ **EXTRA PRACTICE**

Worksheet 37 (_Interrogative and Relative Pronouns_)

The people broke the first two commandments *that* God had given.
(*that* as direct object)

```
  people  |  broke  |  commandments
          |              \
                          \ (that)
  God  |  had given  |  that  \
```

Be sure to use *who* and *whom* correctly. If the pronoun is a subject or predicate nominative, use the nominative case *who*. If the pronoun is a direct object, an indirect object, or the object of a preposition, use the objective case *whom*.

Interrogative pronouns:

(Who, Whom) is asking for help? (subject; use nominative *Who*)

```
  Who  |  is asking
```

(Who, Whom) are you asking for help? (direct object; use objective *Whom*)

```
  you  |  are asking  |  Whom
```

The helper was (who, whom)? (predicate nominative; use nominative *who*)

```
  helper  |  was  \  who
```

For (who, whom) did you ask? (object of preposition; use objective *whom*)

```
  you  |  did ask
           \
          for\
              whom
```

Relative pronouns:

We met a man (who, whom) had visited China. (subject in clause; use *who*)

```
  We  |  met  |  man
                    \
                     \
                      who  |  had visited  |  China
```

We serve a God (who, whom) we love. (direct object in clause; use *whom*)

Praise God, by (who, whom) we live. (object of preposition; use *whom*)

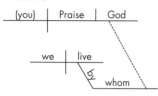

The relative pronouns *who* and *whom* refer only to people, *which* refers only to things, and *that* and *whose* refer to either people or things.

Substandard:
A *person* <u>which</u> is considerate does not stare at strangers.
A *dog* <u>who</u> is trained early can learn many tricks.

Standard:
A *person* <u>who</u> is considerate does not stare at strangers.
A *dog* <u>which</u> is trained early can learn many tricks.
The *man* <u>that</u> drove the old tractor also has a steam *engine* <u>that</u> works.
That *car* <u>whose</u> tire is flat belongs to a *lady* <u>whose</u> name I do not remember.

Class Practice

A. Tell whether the underlined pronouns are *interrogative* or *relative* pronouns.
   1. Gossip is the wood <u>that</u> feeds the fire of strife.
   2. <u>Whom</u> did Jesus heal at Capernaum?
   3. To <u>what</u> is wisdom compared?
   4. Did Solomon always use the wisdom <u>which</u> God gave him?

B. Read the adjective clauses. Give the antecedent of the relative pronoun.
   1. Jeroboam was the king whose arm was dried up.
   2. Ezra, who was a scribe, read from the Law distinctly.

Lesson 64 Answers

Class Practice

A. 1. relative
   2. interrogative
   3. interrogative
   4. relative

B. 1. whose arm was dried up—king
   2. who was a scribe—Ezra

3. We are grateful for a government that allows us religious freedom.
4. Mr. Kerr's house, which we painted last year, is the oldest in town.
5. The man from whom we bought our goat also raises sheep and cattle.

C. Read each sentence, using the correct pronoun in parentheses.
1. Jesus healed the man (who, which) had been born blind.
2. The demoniac, (who, whom) Jesus had delivered, became an effective witness.
3. The prodigal son, (whom, which) the father welcomed back, could not regain his squandered inheritance.
4. (Who, Whom) did Miriam watch by the Nile River?

D. Read each pronoun in these sentences, and identify it as *personal, compound personal, demonstrative, indefinite, interrogative,* or *relative.* Include the possessive pronouns used as adjectives.
1. This is a collie, and that is a poodle.
2. Both of you may go along with me if your mother has no work for you now.
3. He cut himself when he fell over my feet.
4. Who must have his report ready tomorrow?
5. We could see most of their garden from our lawn.
6. Lester himself told us the things which had happened to them.
7. Many of the people will fail; a few will succeed.
8. Which is the book that they asked me to buy?

Written Exercises

A. Copy each relative pronoun and its antecedent.
1. We must understand and obey the Bible, which is God's message to us.
2. Godly parents, whose counsel we appreciate, are a priceless blessing.
3. The wisdom that the world offers is foolishness to God.
4. A friend who is thoughtful and unselfish is a valuable asset.
5. The friends whom we seek tell something about our own character.

B. Write the correct pronouns in parentheses.
1. (Who, Whom) invented the printing press?
2. Johann Gutenberg was the man (who, whom) God used for this important invention.
3. The girl (who, which) is visiting school today is my cousin.
4. Our kittens, (who, which) are six weeks old, are active and playful.
5. (Who, Whom) shall we ask to go along?

C. Copy each pronoun in these sentences, and write whether it is personal (*P*), compound personal (*CP*), demonstrative (*D*), indefinite (*ID*),

3. that allows us religious freedom—government
4. which we painted last year—house
5. from whom we bought our goat—man

C. 1. who   3. whom
2. whom   4. Whom

D. 1. This—demonstrative; that—demonstrative
2. Both—indefinite; you—personal; me—personal; your—personal; you—personal
3. He—personal; himself—compound personal; he—personal; my—personal
4. Who—interrogative; his—personal
5. We—personal; most—indefinite; their—personal; our—personal
6. himself—compound personal; us—personal; which—relative; them—personal
7. Many—indefinite; few—indefinite
8. Which—interrogative; that—relative; they—personal; me—personal

Written Exercises

A. 1. which—Bible
2. whose—parents
3. that—wisdom
4. who—friend
5. whom—friends

B. 1. Who
2. whom
3. who
4. which
5. Whom

interrogative (*IR*), or relative (*R*). Include the possessive pronouns used as adjectives.
1. Who was that?
2. It must have been she.
3. We saw them ourselves.
4. Many who were there bought one.
5. This is a larger elephant than most.
6. The man whom we were helping had cut himself with his saw.
7. Your apples are sweeter than ours; theirs are better than the others.
8. These are my pencils, but whose are those?
9. Are they his?
10. Somebody should tell him.

Review Exercises

A. Label the verbs in these sentences with the abbreviations shown. Each set of four sentences has one of each kind. [41–43, 53]
   TA—transitive verb, active voice
   TP—transitive verb, passive voice
   IC—intransitive complete verb
   IL—intransitive linking verb
1. a. A pencil can write for a long time.
   b. One end of a pencil is sharp.
   c. This pencil was given to me by Stanley.
   d. I sharpened the pencil.
2. a. Some flowers are growing in the garden.
   b. They were planted by my sister.
   c. The gladiolas look very pretty.
   d. My sister waters these flowers.

B. Rewrite each sentence in the passive voice. Do not change the tense. [53]
   1. Such loud noise disturbs Grandmother.
   2. Dallas had rung the bell.
   3. The congregation is singing the opening song.

C. Rewrite each sentence in the active voice. Do not change the tense. [53]
   1. The clock has been fixed by Peter.
   2. The leaves are being blown by the wind.
   3. Our lunches were packed by Aunt Helen.

C. 1. Who—IR; that—D
   2. It—P; she—P
   3. We—P; them—P; ourselves—CP
   4. Many—ID; who—R; one—ID
   5. This—D; most—ID
   6. whom—R; we—P; himself—CP; his—P
   7. Your—P; ours—P; theirs—P; others—ID
   8. These—D; my—P; whose—IR; those—D
   9. they—P; his—P
   10. Somebody—ID; him—P

Review Exercises
A. 1. a. IC   2. a. IC
      b. IL   b. TP
      c. TP   c. IL
      d. TA   d. TA

B. 1. Grandmother is disturbed by such loud noise.
   2. The bell had been rung by Dallas.
   3. The opening song is being sung by the congregation.

C. 1. Peter has fixed the clock.
   2. The wind is blowing the leaves.
   3. Aunt Helen packed our lunches.

65. Developing Your Report From an Outline

Lesson Survey
- Decide how you will describe and illustrate the facts on your outline.
- Write down enough of the added descriptions and illustrations to keep your report going smoothly.

In Lesson 62, you were given the following partial outline for an oral report.

The Marvel of Man's Body
I. Creation and material makeup of the body
  A. Made by God from dust
  B. Made of many elements; 100-lb. body contains the following:
    1. 65 lb. oxygen
    2. 18 lb. carbon
    3. 10 lb. hydrogen
    4. 3 lb. nitrogen
    5. 1 lb. phosphorus
    6. Quotation from *SIE* about things in 100-lb. body
  C. Contains many parts that work together
  D. Given a living soul

With this outline, are you ready to give your report? No, certainly not. If you were to go to the front of the room and use this outline, your report would go like this:

> The body was made by God from the dust. It contains many elements. Here are the elements in a 100-pound body: 65 pounds of oxygen, 18 pounds of carbon, 10 pounds of hydrogen, 3 pounds of nitrogen, and 1 pound of phosphorus. Here is what one book says:
>
> > A 100-pound human body contains enough water to fill an 8-gallon barrel; enough iron to make a nail; one teaspoon of sugar; enough fat to make several bars of soap; enough carbon to make about six thousand pencils; enough calcium to whitewash a small chicken coop; enough sulfur and phosphorus to make a small box of matches; and enough potassium to make the powder of a small shotgun shell.
>
> The body contains many parts that work together. God has given this body a living soul.

Lesson 65

Purpose: To show how to add interesting details in preparing an outline for an oral report.

Oral Review:
1. What should you do if you write exact words from a source? (Put quotation marks around the exact words.)
2. What should be your first step in organizing your notes? (Look for main topics.)
3. What should be your next steps in organizing your notes? (Arrange the main topics in a logical order. Write an outline based on your groups of notes.)
4. Identify each item as a sentence, a fragment, or a run-on error.
  a. The peace of God goes beyond all understanding. (sentence)
  b. And keeps our hearts and minds. (fragment)
  c. Because we want to keep that peace. (fragment)
  d. We must not yield to temptation, we must avoid anything that displeases God. (run-on error)

Lesson Introduction: Suppose your mother gets out her roaster and puts in a piece of meat, some potatoes, and some vegetables. Is she ready to put it into the oven? No, indeed! She must add water, salt, and perhaps some other seasonings. The basic ingredients are all there, but that is not enough.

That is where your outline from Lesson 62 stands now too. The basic facts are all there, but it is hardly ready to "feed" to your listeners as an oral report. You still need to do some work on developing it.

Would that make an interesting report? Hardly. About half of it is a quotation from a science book! That quotation is interesting though, and you will surely want to include it in your report. But the rest is simply a list of facts.

You need more material to describe and illustrate the facts of your outline. You might think of it this way: The facts you have gathered are the meat and potatoes of your report. Now you must prepare some seasonings and sauces to add a distinctive flavor and appeal.

Begin by reconsidering the first point: "Made by God from dust." What more can you say? Well, what comes to your mind when you think about dust? Dust storms? Mother dusting furniture? The dustpan hanging in the school closet? That's an idea. The dustpan might remind you of the dirt (the dust of the earth) which you sweep off the floor. What do you do with it? You throw it away because it is worthless. The dust that makes man's body would be worthless too if God had not worked with it and made it into something special.

Can you see how you could use these additional thoughts to make your first point more interesting? You might say something like this:

> The body was made by God from dust. Really, dust by itself is worthless. We sweep up the dust in our schoolroom and throw it into the trash can because we don't even want it. But when God touched the dust and formed Adam, He turned dust into something of very great value.

That is much better. It takes the bare idea and rounds it out, adding something with a little more flavor. What you must do now is go through the entire outline and consider each point. What descriptions or illustrations can you bring in? How can you develop each point so that it will hold the interest and attention of your listeners?

In presenting point B, you might refer to someone who weighs about one hundred pounds. That will give your listeners a better grasp of what the figures mean. Mention the fact that the sixty-five pounds of oxygen is more than half of the entire body weight.

In presenting point C, you would do well to point out some of the body parts and show how they work together. For example, consider how your arm, hand, and fingers work together when you write. Each muscle and bone must move exactly right and in agreement with the others. And think what would happen if one of the body parts refused to cooperate with the others. What if your little finger refused to bend when you tried to write, insisting instead on remaining straight? As a matter of fact, you can find several interesting examples in 1 Corinthians 12, which talks

Lesson Outline:

1. Decide how you will describe and illustrate the facts on your outline. Go through the outline point by point, trying to think of ideas that will add flavor and interest to your report.

2. Write down enough of the added descriptions and illustrations to keep your report going smoothly.

about the body members working together.

Take plenty of time to think over the different points on your outline. If you do this, you should find numerous related ideas coming to your mind—ideas that will do much to add life and meaning to your report.

How many of these extra ideas should you write on the outline that you take with you to give your report? If you do not write any, you may forget them. If you write them all, your outline will no longer be an outline; it will be more like a written report! The answer then is that you must write down enough of the added descriptions and illustrations to keep your report going smoothly. Most of the ideas will come to your mind when you glance at the points on your outline. Be sure to write the ones you are afraid you will forget and those you want to say in a specific way.

Here is what the main part of your outline might look like when you are ready to give your report.

The Marvel of Man's Body

I. Creation and material makeup of the body
  A. Made by God from dust
    — dust alone worthless; dustpan in closet
    — God's touch turned dust into something of great value
  B. Made of many elements; 100-lb. body contains the following things
    — my brother Thomas weighs about 100 lb.
    1. 65 lb. oxygen—over half the weight
    2. 18 lb. carbon
    3. 10 lb. hydrogen
    4. 3 lb. nitrogen
    5. 1 lb. phosphorus
    6. Quotation from *SIE* about things in 100-lb. body
  C. Contains many parts that work together
    — talk about writing
  D. Given a living soul (most important of all)
    — makes man different from animals
    — means man is more than merely so much oxygen, carbon, etc.

This outline is brief, but it contains all the points you plan to cover. Other than an introduction and a conclusion (which are taught in the next lesson), you will not need any additional notes. As you give your report, you will be able to look at your outline and remember each point. Then you can look up at your listeners as you say the things you were planning to say about each point. You will not look down at your outline all the while you are speaking. Instead, you will glance at your outline, remember the next point, and look up to present it.

Class Practice

Suggest some interesting descriptions and illustrations that could add flavor to this partial outline.

The Life of the North American Beaver
I. Protection from danger
  A. Can swim very well
    1. Webbed hind feet act as oars
    2. Large, flat tail acts as rudder
  B. Can stay under water up to 15 minutes
    1. Heart slows down, so needs less oxygen
    2. Valves close ears and nostrils for added protection
  C. Builds well-protected lodge
    1. Only entrance is under water
    2. Surrounding water keeps away most enemies
    3. When ice allows enemies to approach, frozen mud is too hard for them to dig up
II. Habitat
  A. Prefers small streams that can be dammed easily
  B. Needs plenty of cottonwood, aspen, or willow trees
    1. Adult cuts up to 300 trees per year
    2. One acre of trees can support 6-member colony for 1 or 2 years

Written Exercises

Go through your outline from Lesson 62, adding ideas for descriptions and illustrations to flavor your report.

Review Exercises

A. Write whether each item is a *sentence, fragment,* or *run-on error.* [2]
  1. Primates, mostly tree-dwelling mammals.
  2. They have five fingers and toes, their hands and feet are designed for grasping.
  3. Instead of claws, they have nails.
  4. Monkeys, apes, and lemurs are among the primates that may be seen in a zoo.

B. Correct these run-on errors, either by writing them as two sentences or by joining them correctly. [2, 14]

Lesson 65 Answers

Class Practice

(Sample ideas are underlined.)

The Life of the North American Beaver
I. Protection from danger
  A. Can swim very well
    1. Webbed hind feet act as oars
      — <u>much like a duck</u>
    2. Large, flat tail acts as rudder
  B. Can stay under water up to 15 minutes
      — <u>length of our morning recess</u>
    1. Heart slows down, so needs less oxygen
    2. Valves close ears and nostrils for added protection
  C. Builds well-protected lodge
    1. Only entrance is under water
      — <u>can't get in unless you can swim</u>
    2. Surrounding water keeps away most enemies
    3. When ice allows enemies to approach, frozen mud is too hard for them to dig up
      — <u>hard to dig into frozen ground</u>
II. Habitat
  A. Prefers small streams that can be dammed easily
    — <u>about the size of stream flowing past the church</u>
  B. Needs plenty of cottonwood, aspen, or willow trees
    1. Adult cuts up to 300 trees per year
      — <u>1 tree per day, 6 days a week = 312 trees in a year</u>
    2. One acre of trees can support 6-member colony for 1 or 2 years
      — <u>school property about 1 acre</u>

Written Exercises

(Individual work.)

Review Exercises

A. 1. fragment   3. sentence
   2. run-on error   4. sentence

1. Primates that have no tails are apes, the largest ape is the mountain gorilla of eastern Africa.
2. These animals may stand as tall as a man and weigh as much as four hundred fifty pounds, they are remarkably gentle.
3. Gorillas are not quick to fight they can defend their families very effectively.
4. Gorillas are mainly vegetarian some eat insects and small lizards.

---

66. Giving an Oral Report

Lesson Survey

- In preparing to give an oral report, become thoroughly familiar with your topic.
- Write down the exact words for the introduction and the conclusion.
- Practice giving your report at home.
- In giving an oral report, try to relax before you stand up.
- Look at your audience as you speak.
- Speak loudly and distinctly enough so that everyone can hear you easily.
- Maintain good posture at all times, and avoid distracting habits.

Does it make you nervous to think of giving an oral report before the class? It should! That nervousness will help to motivate you to do your best. Even those who have taught Sunday school or preached sermons for years admit to feeling nervous before getting up to face their audience. Of course, nervousness can become so intense that it hinders one's performance. The points in this lesson should help you to avoid that extreme.

To eliminate excessive nervousness at the time of the report, prepare well beforehand. Become thoroughly familiar with your topic. Go over your outline often enough that the main points stick in your mind. Think about your report for several days before it is due.

Another important part of the preparation is to write down the exact words for the introduction and the conclusion. These two parts of the

Lesson 66

Purpose: To teach how to give an *oral report. (*Previous experience:* Writing a report.)

Oral Review:

1. Why should you take notes from more than one reference source? (to have a balanced report; to become well familiar with the topic)
2. After you have decided on the main topics in your notes, what are the next steps? (Arrange the main topics in a logical order. Write an outline based on your groups of notes.)
3. In addition to the basic facts, what else should appear on your outline? (Ideas for descriptions and illustrations that will add life and meaning to your report.)
4. How many of these extra ideas should you write on your outline? (Write enough of the added

B. (Accept reasonable variation.)

1. Primates that have no tails are apes. The largest ape is the mountain gorilla of eastern Africa.
2. These animals may stand as tall as a man and weigh as much as four hundred fifty pounds, yet they are remarkably gentle.
3. Gorillas are not quick to fight, but they can defend their families very effectively.
4. Gorillas are mainly vegetarian, but some eat insects and small lizards.

---

descriptions and illustrations to keep your report going smoothly.)

Lesson Introduction: This lesson teaches how to give an oral report. Will the pupils ever do this in later life? Yes, in various ways: teaching school or Sunday school, having a devotional, and giving a topic are a few examples. A few of the boys may even preach sermons someday. Now is the time to prepare themselves for public speaking in the future.

Lesson Outline:

1. In preparing to give an oral report, become thoroughly familiar with your topic.

    a. Go over the outline until the main points stick in your mind.

    b. Think about the report for several days before it is due.

2. Write down the exact words for the introduction and the conclusion.

report deserve careful attention. The introduction sets the tone, either sparking or extinguishing the listeners' interest. You may begin with an interesting observation, a thought-provoking question, or a familiar quotation. The title of your report should be woven smoothly into the introduction. Here are some sample introductions for a report on "The Marvel of Man's Body."

Observation:

After God had created plant and animal life, He saw that "it was good." But after He had created man, He saw that "it was very good." Clearly, man is the crown of creation.

In this topic, "The Marvel of Man's Body," we will first note the materials that our bodies are made of. . . .

Question:

Have you ever considered what a marvel your own body is? If you cut your finger, it takes only a few days or weeks for the cut to heal—all on its own. The body of man is more wonderful and complex than the most elaborate machine that has ever been invented.

Let us consider the topic "The Marvel of Man's Body." We will first note the materials that our bodies are made of. . . .

Quotation:

In Psalm 139:14 we read, "I will praise thee; for I am fearfully and wonderfully made." We find that this is certainly true as we consider the topic "The Marvel of Man's Body."

We will begin by noting the materials that our bodies are made of. . . .

You may begin your oral report with an effective introduction and proceed with main points that are well developed with supporting details. But if you conclude like a car running out of fuel, the overall effect of your report will be weakened. The conclusion should be very brief. You may summarize the main points of the report, or you may give a call to some response or action.

Summary:

The material makeup of the body, its ability to heal itself, and its future immortality all show that man's body is indeed a marvel of creation.

Call to response:

As we consider the marvel of man's body, we should be moved to praise and serve the Creator of our bodies.

a. The introduction sets the tone, either sparking or extinguishing the listeners' interest.

b. Begin with an interesting observation, a thought-provoking question, or a familiar quotation.

c. The title of your report should be woven smoothly into the introduction.

d. The conclusion should briefly summarize the main points or give a call to some response or action.

3. *Practice giving your report at home.*

a. Let others give you helpful suggestions.

b. Time yourself, but remember that greater nervousness at school may increase your speed.

4. *Try to relax before standing for the report.*

a. Breathe deeply and evenly several times before standing up.

b. Be well prepared, and become so involved in your topic that you forget yourself.

5. *Look at your audience as you speak.* Do not constantly look at your outline, and do not look at the floor, the ceiling, or the walls.

6. *Speak with proper volume.*

a. Your voice should not be so loud that your listeners feel uncomfortable nor so soft that they must strain to hear what you are saying.

b. Do not lower your voice at the end of sentences so much that your listeners miss the last few words.

7. *Speak distinctly.*

a. Be sure you know how to pronounce each word you plan to use.

b. Do not mumble your words through half-closed lips.

You should practice giving your report at home. Perhaps you can practice before your parents or other people. They may be able to point out ways in which you can improve. You should definitely time yourself as you practice your report so that you can adjust the amount of material that you plan to cover. But remember that you may well be more tense when you give the report at school, and therefore you may talk faster there than at home.

When the time arrives to actually give your report, there are several things to remember. Try to relax before standing to your feet. Too much tension will prevent you from looking and speaking naturally. You can help yourself to relax by breathing deeply and evenly several times. Be well prepared, and be enthusiastic about the points you will present. Try to become so involved in your topic that you forget yourself.

In giving your report, do not begin speaking before you have turned around to face the audience. Look at your listeners as you speak. Let your eyes meet theirs, and talk directly to them. Do not constantly look at your outline, and do not look at the floor, the ceiling, or the walls. Remember, you are giving the listeners a *report* about an interesting topic that you have studied.

Speak with proper volume. Your voice should not be so loud that your listeners feel uncomfortable nor so soft that they must strain to hear what you are saying. Do not lower your voice at the end of each sentence so much that your listeners miss the last few words.

Speak distinctly. Be sure you know how to pronounce each word, especially if you use any scientific or Biblical words that are uncommon. Do not mumble your words through half-closed lips, and do not start walking back to your seat before you have finished your last sentence.

Maintain good posture at all times. As you take your place for the report and as you take your seat, you should neither rush nor shuffle slowly. While giving your report, stand straight, with both feet flat on the floor, and hold your head erect.

Avoid distracting habits. Filling your pauses with *uh*'s and *ah*'s and clearing your throat continually will reduce the effectiveness of your report. Your listeners will also be distracted if you frequently pull at your glasses, nose, or ears; if you put your hands into and out of your pockets; or if you shuffle your feet.

Here is an evaluation chart that summarizes many of the specific points you should remember. Your teacher will likely use this or a similar means to grade your oral report.

8. *Maintain good posture at all times.*
   a. Do not rush or shuffle as you walk to the front of the room or back to your seat.
   b. Stand straight, with both feet flat on the floor, and hold your head erect.

9. *Avoid distracting habits.*
   a. Do not fill your pauses with *uh*'s and *ah*'s or clear your throat continually.
   b. Do not pull at your glasses, nose, or ears.
   c. Do not put your hands into and out of your pockets.
   d. Do not shuffle your feet.

Discuss the evaluation chart in the lesson, and suggest to your students that they use it to evaluate themselves as they practice. This chart or a similar one may be used to grade the students' oral reports.

Evaluation of Oral Report

Points possible	Points earned	
5	____	**Introduction**

No clear introduction (3 points)
Introduction weak or poorly related to topic (4 points)
Clear, interesting introduction (5 points)

| 5 | ____ | **Eye contact** |

Looked constantly at outline (3 points)
Looked up occasionally (4 points)
Looked at audience frequently (5 points)

| 5 | ____ | **Posture** |

Slouched; head down; feet askew (3 points)
Had fairly good posture most of the time (4 points)
Stood straight; head up; feet flat on floor (5 points)

| 5 | ____ | **Enunciation** |

Many words mumbled or mispronounced (3 points)
Occasional words hard to understand (4 points)
Words pronounced clearly and correctly (5 points)

| 5 | ____ | **Volume** |

Almost inaudible or uncomfortably loud (3 points)
Fairly comfortable (4 points)
Pleasant, consistent volume (5 points)

| 5 | ____ | **Organization** |

Illogical order; no clear main points (3 points)
Logical order; some main points unclear (4 points)
Logical order; all main points clear (5 points)

| 5 | ____ | **Preparation** |

Often fumbled for words; many awkward pauses (3 points)
Occasionally hesitated for words (4 points)
Spoke with little hesitation (5 points)

| 5 | ____ | **Mannerism** |

Distracting habits throughout report (3 points)
Occasional distracting habits (4 points)
No distracting habits (5 points)

| 5 | ____ | **Conclusion** |

Stopped without a definite conclusion (3 points)
Weak conclusion (4 points)
Clear, well-defined conclusion (5 points)

| 5 | ____ | **Time** |

Less than two minutes (3 points)
From two to three minutes (4 points)
From three to five minutes (5 points)

| 50 | ____ | **Total points** |

Class Practice

A. Tell what is wrong with these beginnings.
  1. The first point on my outline is "What is gravity?"
  2. Everyone is affected by gravity. After we have considered how gravity affects our lives, I'm sure you will agree that gravity is very important. The first thing we will look at is what gravity is.

B. Tell what is wrong with this ending.
  So gravity, you can see, is very important to our lives.

Written Exercises

Give your oral report at your teacher's direction.

Review Exercises

A. Write the first three words of the topic sentence of each paragraph. [13]
  1.   God's will for man from the Creation was that he subdue the earth and have dominion over every living thing (Genesis 1:28). Man needs an understanding of true science in order to use God's creation as He intended. Such an understanding will help him to be a good steward of the many gifts that God has given him in this world. It will also help him to prepare for the day when God will call him to give account for the way he has used these gifts.
  2.   Another reason we study science is to learn lessons about God and life. When God wanted to teach Job about His greatness and man's ignorance, He asked Job one hard question after another about the created world. The writer of Proverbs advised the sluggard to learn from the ant. Christ said we should learn lessons about life from the lilies of the field and the fowls of the air. Many other passages in the Bible use facts about the earth to help us learn spiritual lessons.

B. What device of coherence is illustrated in each of these paragraphs? [16, 17]
  1.   Science books contain many theories. Some of them are probably true and are very useful to know and apply to God's world. The atomic theory is an example of a useful theory. The atomic theory tells us that all matter is made of very small atoms. This idea does not contradict the Bible or scientific knowledge. The atomic theory has been found to be very useful in working with chemicals.
  2.   It is also true that a decrease in pressure lowers the boiling point of a liquid. It takes a longer time to cook potatoes on the top of a high mountain than it does in the valley. This is because water boils at a lower temperature on the mountain where the air pressure is

---

Lesson 66 Answers

Class Practice

A. 1. There is no introduction.
   2. The introduction is weak. It will not spark the listeners' interest.

B. The ending neither summarizes the main points nor calls the listeners to a response.

Written Exercises

(Individual work.)

Review Exercises

A. 1. Man needs an . . .
   2. Another reason we . . .

B. 1. repetition of key words
   2. transitional words

less. Of course, a pressure cooker solves the problem of low pressure on a mountain top. The heated air and steam in the cooker creates its own pressure.

---

67. Chapter 6 Review

Class Practice

A. Identify the class of pronouns that each list represents.
1. who, whom, whose, which, that
2. somebody, no one, few, many, several
3. he, they, ours, we, her
4. who, whom, whose, which, what
5. myself, themselves, herself, itself, yourselves
6. this, that, these, those

B. Name personal pronouns to fit these descriptions. Some have two answers, as shown by the numbers in parentheses.
1. third person, plural, nominative case
2. first person, singular, possessive case (2)
3. third person, singular, objective case, feminine gender
4. second person, singular, possessive case (2)
5. third person, singular, nominative case, neuter gender

C. Choose the correct words in parentheses.
1. Two men, King Balak and (he, him), viewed the Israelites.
2. Both Joseph and Nicodemus declared (his, their) loyalty to Jesus.
3. Jesus told Peter and (they, them) to watch with Him.
4. The deacon and evangelist gave (his life, their lives) for the Gospel.
5. Brother Lamar helped the regular teachers, Sister Anita and (she, her).
6. (We, Us) seventh graders must study hard.

D. Reword these sentences, making the pronoun usage clear and correct.
1. Brother Clifford talked to Mr. Marlowe before he moved away.
2. Ann told Wilma that her tomatoes were wilting.
3. Me and Melvin have come to help with the chores.

E. Read each sentence, filling in a compound personal pronoun. Tell whether the pronoun is used *intensively* or *reflexively*.
1. The publican smote ——— on the breast.
2. Mary ——— did not understand everything that Jesus would do.
3. We must discipline ——— to study diligently.

Lesson 67 Answers

Class Practice

A. 1. relative pronouns
2. indefinite pronouns
3. personal pronouns
4. interrogative pronouns
5. compound personal pronouns
6. demonstrative pronouns

B. 1. they   4. your, yours
2. my, mine   5. it
3. her

C. 1. he   4. his life
2. their   5. her
3. them   6. We

D. 1. Before Brother Clifford moved away, he talked to Mr. Marlowe.
   or Before Mr. Marlowe moved away, Brother Clifford talked to him.
2. Ann said, "Wilma, your tomatoes are wilting."
   or Ann said, "Wilma, my tomatoes are wilting."
3. Melvin and I have come to help with the chores.

E. 1. himself—reflexively
2. herself—intensively
3. ourselves—reflexively

Lesson 67

Purpose: To review the concepts taught in Chapter 6.

F. Choose the correct words to agree with the indefinite pronouns.
1. Most of the chickens (have, has) roosted for the night.
2. Each of these kittens (have, has) five toes on (its, their) front paws.
3. Some of the sky (is, are) covered with clouds.
4. A few of the peaches (was, were) rotting.
5. Neither of the Christians (appear, appears) ready to give up (his, their) faith.

G. Choose the correct relative pronoun in each sentence.
1. Aunt Christine's pet cat, (who, which) she has had for years, acts as if he owns the house.
2. Cousin Lily, (who, whom) we have not seen for two years, has just returned from the Philippines.
3. Our uncle, (who, which) was crippled as a child, does much writing.

H. Read each adjective clause, and give the antecedent of the relative pronoun.
1. Paul, whose thorn in the flesh was not removed, trusted God's grace.
2. The promise that he received from the Lord must have comforted him.
3. This man, whom God used mightily, was a zealous leader of the church.

I. Give the answers.
1. Why should you take notes from more than one reference source?
2. What should you do if you copy words directly from a reference source?
3. How much information should be included on one note card?

F. 1. have
    2. has, its
    3. is
    4. were
    5. appears, his

G. 1. which
    2. whom
    3. who

H. 1. whose thorn in the flesh was not removed—Paul
    2. that he received from the Lord—promise
    3. whom God used mightily—man

I. 1. to have a balanced report; to become well familiar with the topic
    2. put quotation marks around the exact words
    3. one item of information

4. Name three good ways to introduce an oral report.
5. What are two good ways to conclude a report?
6. Name some things that are included in speaking distinctly.

J. Tell which is the best introduction. Tell what is wrong with the other two.
   1. Study fills an important role in a person's life. That's why school students should learn how to study. In this report on "Study Habits for Seventh Graders," we will first look at some hindrances to good study habits.
   2. Why should we seventh graders learn to study well? What difference will it make when we are farming or cooking? In this report on "Study Habits for Seventh Graders," we will first look at some hindrances to good study habits.
   3. Why should we seventh graders learn to study well? What difference will it make when we are farming or cooking? First, let us look at some hindrances to good study habits.

Written Exercises

A. Copy each personal pronoun. Label its person, number, case, and gender.
   1. Jesus commissioned <u>His</u> disciples, and <u>they</u> went out two by two.
   2. Children, have <u>you</u> seen the new calf and named <u>it</u>?
   3. <u>We</u> have named <u>her</u> Freckles.

B. If the underlined part of the sentence contains a mistake in the usage of a personal pronoun, rewrite it correctly. If it is correct, write *correct*.
   1. The two missionaries, <u>Silas and him</u>, were severely beaten.
   2. The great king and poet had inclined <u>his</u> heart to keep God's Word.
   3. Jesus spoke comforting words to <u>Martha and she</u>.
   4. The busy mother and writer worked on <u>their stories</u> during the evening.
   5. Today there are many good books available for <u>us readers</u>.
   6. <u>Duane and him</u> baled the hay.
   7. <u>Us girls</u> weeded the garden.
   8. Either Joyce or Naomi will give <u>their</u> copy of the school newspaper to Grandmother.
   9. <u>Me and Paul</u> were looking for crayfish in the creek.
   10. The cabinetmaker and the painter gave <u>his estimate</u> to Father.

C. If the underlined part of the sentence contains a mistake in the usage of a compound personal pronoun or a demonstrative pronoun, rewrite it correctly. If it is correct, write *correct*.
   1. During the Feast of Tabernacles, the Israelites made booths for <u>theirselves</u>.

4. with an interesting observation, with a thought-provoking question, with a familiar quotation
5. with a summary of the main points, with a call to some response or action
6. pronouncing words correctly; not mumbling

J. Number 2 is the best. Number 1 says nothing to stir the listeners' interest. Number 3 fails to state the topic of the report.

Written Exercises

A. 1. His—third person, singular, possessive case, masculine gender;
      they—third person, plural, nominative case, common gender
   2. you—second person, plural, nominative case, common gender;
      it—third person, singular, objective case, common gender
   3. We—first person, plural, nominative case, common gender;
      her—third person, singular, objective case, feminine gender

B. 1. Silas and he   6. Duane and he
   2. correct   7. We girls
   3. Martha and her   8. her
   4. her story   9. Paul and I
   5. correct   10. their estimates

C. 1. themselves

2. In this way they reminded <u>themselves</u> of the wilderness wanderings.
3. <u>These here</u> pictures are interesting and helpful.
4. I like <u>these</u> cookies, but <u>them</u> look even better.
5. Jerry and <u>myself</u> will help you with your chores.
6. We helped <u>ourself</u> to the treats that the new store was offering.

D. Write the correct words in parentheses.
1. Will everyone have (his, their) report ready for tomorrow?
2. All of the room (have, has) been cleaned.
3. All of the rooms (have, has) been cleaned.
4. Both of the rooms (have, has) been cleaned.
5. Each of the rooms (have, has) been cleaned.
6. We tried to get (everyones, everyone's) opinion on the matter.

E. Write the correct relative pronoun for each sentence.
1. The man (who, whom) Father talked to on the train had been a soldier.
2. The animals (who, which) we saw in the meadow were llamas.
3. The man (who, which) talked to us is from Australia.

F. Copy each pronoun in these sentences, and write whether it is personal (*P*), compound personal (*CP*), demonstrative (*D*), indefinite (*ID*), interrogative (*IR*), or relative (*R*). Include the possessive pronouns used as adjectives.
1. Which of these are mine?
2. Many are called, but few are chosen.
3. The magpie watched itself in the mirror, forgetting its danger from the hungry cat which crept nearer.
4. That was not the answer that I expected.
5. What do you suppose the men figured out for themselves?
6. No one can kill time without injuring himself.

G. Draw rectangles to represent enough note cards for the following information on the topic "The City of Corinth in Paul's Day." Fill in the note cards properly.
— Situated south of the isthmus between central Greece and the Peloponnesus (*Unger's Bible Dictionary*, page 255)
— had two harbors; was part of an important Roman trade route; became the home to people of many nationalities (*The Bible Digest*, page 667)

———————————

2. correct   5. I
3. These   6. ourselves
4. correct, those

D. 1. his   4. have
   2. has   5. has
   3. have   6. everyone's

E. 1. whom   3. who
   2. which

F. 1. Which—IR; these—D; mine—P
   2. Many—ID; few—ID
   3. itself—CP; its—P; which—R
   4. That—D; that—R; I—P
   5. What—IR; you—P; themselves—CP
   6. No one—ID; himself—CP

G.

| The City of Corinth in Paul's Day |
| Unger's Bible Dictionary, p. 255 |
| situated south of the isthmus between central Greece and the Peloponnesus |

| The City of Corinth in Paul's Day |
| The Bible Digest, p. 667 |
| had two harbors |

| The City of Corinth in Paul's Day |
| IBD, p. 667 |
| was part of an important Roman trade route |

| The City of Corinth in Paul's Day |
| IBD, p. 667 |
| became the home to people of many nationalities |

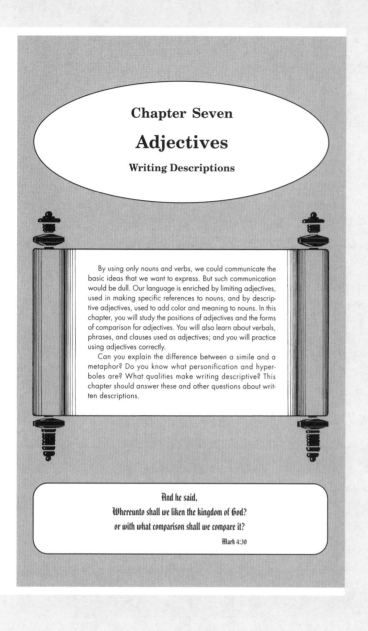

Chapter Seven

Adjectives

Writing Descriptions

By using only nouns and verbs, we could communicate the basic ideas that we want to express. But such communication would be dull. Our language is enriched by limiting adjectives, used in making specific references to nouns, and by descriptive adjectives, used to add color and meaning to nouns. In this chapter, you will study the positions of adjectives and the forms of comparison for adjectives. You will also learn about verbals, phrases, and clauses used as adjectives; and you will practice using adjectives correctly.

Can you explain the difference between a simile and a metaphor? Do you know what personification and hyperboles are? What qualities make writing descriptive? This chapter should answer these and other questions about written descriptions.

And he said,
Whereunto shall we liken the kingdom of God?
or with what comparison shall we compare it?

Mark 4:30

68. Recognizing Adjectives

> **Lesson Survey**
> * An **adjective** modifies a noun or pronoun by telling *which, whose, how many,* or *what kind of.*
> * A **limiting adjective** limits a noun or pronoun by telling *which, whose,* or *how many.*
> * A **descriptive adjective** describes a noun or pronoun by telling *what kind of.*

Nouns and verbs are the "workhorses" of the English language; very little communication occurs without using them. Adjectives and adverbs may not be as basic as the nouns and verbs they modify, but they are important because they dress up and identify those "workhorses."

Adjectives modify nouns and pronouns by telling *which, whose, how many,* and *what kind of.* When something is modified, it is changed. Notice how adjectives can change the meanings of nouns. The nouns and verbs in the following sentences are the same; only the adjectives are different.

A wild, fierce wind blew through several gnarled, straggly trees.
A cool, refreshing wind blew through the four tall, stately trees.

Limiting Adjectives

Adjectives are divided into two general classes: limiting adjectives and descriptive adjectives. A *limiting adjective* limits a noun or pronoun by telling *which, whose,* or *how many.* Limiting adjectives do what the name suggests: they limit the meaning of the modified word in various ways. There are several particular kinds of limiting adjectives.

1. *The articles* a, an, *and the are always limiting adjectives. The* restricts the meaning to a specific noun, but *a* and *an* do not.

   Please bring me the book. (refers to a specific book)
   Please bring me a book. (does not refer to a specific book)

2. *Number words are often used as limiting adjectives.*
   a. Cardinal numbers—like *one, two,* and *three*—tell *how many.* These are the numbers that you see on flash cards (*card—cardinal*).

      one pencil   five girls

   b. Ordinal numbers—like *first, second,* and *third*—tell *which.* These

Lesson 68

Purpose: (1) To define adjectives. (2) To teach their uses.

Oral Review:
1. Compound personal pronouns end with ——— or ———. (-self, -selves)
2. Which of the demonstrative pronouns refer to singular persons or things? (this, that)
3. Which two demonstrative pronouns refer to objects nearby? (this, these)
4. Tell whether each set of indefinite pronouns is always singular, always plural, or sometimes singular or plural.
   a. some, any, none, all, most (sometimes singular or plural)
   b. each, neither, one, everybody (always singular)
   c. both, several, few, many (always plural)

5. Give a personal pronoun to fit each description.
   a. third person, singular, possessive case, feminine gender (her *or* hers)
   b. second person, possessive case (your *or* yours)
   c. third person, plural, objective case (them)
   d. third person, singular, nominative case, masculine gender (he)
   e. first person, plural, objective case (us)

Lesson Introduction: Write the following sentence on the board.

   The hands grasped a sack.

Without adjectives to dress up the nouns, this sentence gives only a vague picture. Paint a more vivid picture together, as the students suggest adjectives to adorn the two nouns. If time permits, have students dress up the nouns first with attractive adjectives and then with unattractive adjectives.

are the numbers that you use to tell the order of items (*order—ordinal*).

<u>seventh</u> grade   the <u>third</u> book

3. *Indefinite pronouns are sometimes used as limiting adjectives that tell* which *or* how many. These adjectives modify without being exact.

<u>each</u> king   <u>few</u> answers
<u>another</u> try   <u>many</u> students

4. *Demonstrative pronouns are sometimes used as limiting adjectives that tell* which. *This* and *these* refer to objects nearby; *that* and *those* refer to objects at a distance. *This* and *that* are singular; *these* and *those* are plural.

<u>this</u> prophet   <u>those</u> disciples

5. *Several of the interrogative pronouns are used as limiting adjectives.* The pronouns *whose, which,* and *what* are used in this way.

<u>whose</u> advice   <u>which</u> trees   <u>what</u> method

6. *Possessive nouns and pronouns are often used as limiting adjectives that tell* whose. Remember that apostrophes are used with nouns and indefinite pronouns, but never with personal pronouns.

<u>Anna's</u> words   <u>everyone's</u> help
the <u>birds'</u> feathers   <u>their</u> knowledge

Descriptive Adjectives

Descriptive adjectives describe nouns and pronouns by telling *what kind of.* They do what their name indicates: they *describe.* In the following examples, notice how much more meaningful the sentences are when descriptive adjectives are used.

Without descriptive adjectives:
The honey soaked into the bread.
God justified the publican rather than the Pharisee.

With descriptive adjectives:
The <u>sweet</u> honey soaked into the <u>fresh</u> <u>homemade</u> bread.
God justified the <u>humble</u>, <u>repentant</u> publican rather than the <u>proud</u>, <u>boasting</u> Pharisee.

Many descriptive adjectives are adjectives in their simplest form. These include words like *wise, kind, strong, rough, blue,* and *warm.* Other descriptive adjectives are made from other parts of speech.

1. *Some descriptive adjectives are formed by adding suffixes to nouns or other parts of speech.*

Lesson Outline:

1. An adjective modifies a noun or pronoun by telling **which, whose, how many, *or* what kind of.**

2. Limiting adjectives limit nouns and pronouns by telling **which, whose, *or* how many.**

   (1) *The articles* a, an, *and* the *are always limiting adjectives.*

   (2) *Number words are often used as limiting adjectives.*

      (a) Cardinal numbers—like *one, two,* and *three*—tell *how many.*

      (b) Ordinal numbers—like *first, second,* and *third*—tell *which.*

   (3) *Indefinite pronouns are sometimes used as limiting adjectives that tell* which *or* how many.

   (4) *Demonstrative pronouns are sometimes used as limiting adjectives that tell* which.

   (5) *Several of the interrogative pronouns are used as limiting adjectives.*

   (6) *Possessive nouns and pronouns are often used as limiting adjectives that tell* whose.

3. Descriptive adjectives describe nouns and pronouns by telling **what kind of.**

   (1) *Some descriptive adjectives are formed by adding suffixes to nouns or other parts of speech.*

   (2) *Some descriptive adjectives are formed by changing the spelling of nouns in other ways.*

   (3) *In some cases, nouns are used as descriptive adjectives without any spelling change.* (*Teacher:* These are called attributive nouns.)

   (4) *Some descriptive adjectives are verbals. These adjectives usually end with* -ing *or* -ed.

-ish:	selfish, childish, foolish, feverish, Danish, Spanish
-like:	Godlike, Christlike, lifelike, homelike
-ic:	angelic, artistic, metric, Arabic, Icelandic
-y:	earthy, roomy, stony, rusty, chilly
-ful:	faithful, sinful, needful, playful
-less:	faithless, fearless, timeless, godless
-ary:	elementary, secondary, visionary
-al:	Biblical, spiritual, optional, critical, musical
-some:	awesome, burdensome, lonesome, tiresome
-ive:	permissive, decisive, constructive, exclusive
-en, -an:	golden, wooden, Roman, European
-ent, -ant:	omniscient, permanent, repentant, significant
-able, -ible:	acceptable, peaceable, sensible, corruptible

2. *Some descriptive adjectives are formed by changing the spelling of nouns in other ways.* Most of these are formed from proper nouns.

Greece—Greek
France—French

3. *In some cases, nouns are used as descriptive adjectives without any spelling change.*

<u>Bible</u> doctrine   <u>brick</u> house
<u>telephone</u> wires   <u>farm</u> buildings

4. *Some descriptive adjectives are verbals.* Remember that a verbal is a verb form used as another part of speech. These adjectives usually end with *-ing* or *-ed*.

<u>barking</u> dogs   <u>answered</u> prayers
<u>praying</u> saints   <u>broken</u> dishes

Since there are thousands of descriptive adjectives, you should be selective in using them. Choose adjectives that clearly show what you mean to say. Do not be satisfied to call everything *nice, good, big, pretty, funny,* or *awful.* Adorn your "workhorse" nouns with specific, descriptive adjectives.

Class Practice

A. Form an adjective from each of these words.
1. permanence
2. silk
3. fool
4. music
5. cloud
6. earth
7. comfort
8. Guatemala
9. Switzerland
10. Mexico

Lesson 68 Answers

Class Practice

A. 1. permanent
2. silken, silky
3. foolish
4. musical
5. cloudy, cloudlike, cloudless
6. earthy, earthen, earthly
7. comfortable
8. Guatemalan
9. Swiss
10. Mexican

B. Identify all the adjectives in these sentences, and tell whether they are *limiting* or *descriptive*.
1. God gives faithful care to all His saints.
2. The Bible way is the best way.
3. The sixth book of the New Testament is Romans.
4. Several soft, billowy clouds sailed across the blue sky.
5. The African violet needs some water.
6. This huge tree is a California redwood.

C. Give five descriptive adjectives to adorn each noun.
1. stream   2. trail   3. puppy   4. book

Written Exercises

A. Copy each adjective, and write whether it is limiting (*L*) or descriptive (*D*). Numbers in parentheses show how many you should find.
1. The last tedious stretch still lay before the weary travelers. (5)
2. Two old men, a young woman, and a crippled boy composed this group. (7)
3. Bits of cruel, icy sleet blew in the harsh wind. (4)
4. The narrow, muddy road stretched across a gloomy, desolate plain. (6)
5. All four travelers were burdened with various bags and packages, their meager earthly possessions. (6)
6. Even the boy grasped a brown bag in his left hand, and a flat wooden box was slung onto his thin back. (10)
7. This boy stumbled wearily on with his two worn crutches. (4)
8. In another thirty minutes, the pitiful group would arrive safely at the home of their waiting friends. (7)

B. Write an adjective to answer each question in parentheses.
1. The (*what kind of?*) door swings slowly on its (*what kind of?*) hinges.
2. (*How many?*) (*what kind of?*) deer jumped over (*whose?*) fence and dashed into the (*what kind of?*) forest.
3. The (*which?*) deer was a (*what kind of?*) buck.
4. The (*how many?*) books on this pile are (*whose?*) books.

C. Write an adjective formed from each word in parentheses.
1. Whether one lives in (Canada), (Spain), or (France) society, (faith) Christian living requires obedience to (Bible) principles.
2. A (thunder) roar filled our ears as the (mud) river flooded the valley.
3. (Mother) (love) hand rested on the (child) (fever) forehead.
4. The (depend) girl gave an (artist) touch to the (remark) bulletin board.
5. The (rush) stream turned the (wood) shaft of the old mill.

C. 1. Canadian, Spanish, French, faithful, Bible *or* Biblical
2. thundering *or* thunderous, muddy
3. Mother's, loving, child's, feverish
4. dependable, artistic *or* artist's, remarkable
5. rushing, wooden

B. 1. faithful—descriptive; all—limiting; His—limiting
2. The—limiting; Bible—descriptive; the—limiting; best—descriptive
3. The—limiting; sixth—limiting; the—limiting
4. Several—limiting; soft—descriptive; billowy—descriptive; the—limiting; blue—descriptive
5. The—limiting; African—descriptive; some—limiting
6. This—limiting; huge—descriptive; a—limiting; California—descriptive

C. (Sample adjectives.)
1. narrow, mountain, sparkling, flowing, clear, cool, rippling, winding, muddy, flooding
2. winding, steep, mountain, narrow, rough, pleasant, dusty, muddy, overgrown, rocky, sloping, animal
3. little, playful, bouncy, cute, friendly, active, noisy, spotted, fat, scrawny, shivering, brown
4. heavy, interesting, helpful, small, big, useful, worthwhile, boring, damaged, historical, picture

Written Exercises

A. 1. The—L; last—L; tedious—D; the—L; weary—D
2. Two—L; old—D; a—L; young—D; a—L; crippled—D; this—L
3. cruel—D; icy—D; the—L; harsh—D
4. The—L; narrow—D; muddy—D; a—L; gloomy—D; desolate—D
5. All—L; four—L; various—D; their—L; meager—D; earthly—D
6. the—L; a—L; brown—D; his—L; left—L; a—L; flat—D; wooden—D; his—L; thin—D
7. This—L; his—L; two—L; worn—D
8. another—L; thirty—L; the—L; pitiful—D; the—L; their—L; waiting—D

B. (Sample adjectives.)
1. heavy, old, wooden; rusty, squeaking
2. (any cardinal number); graceful, white-tailed, mule; (any possessive noun or pronoun); dense, small, large, dark
3. (any ordinal number); large, majestic, watchful
4. (any cardinal number); (any possessive noun or pronoun)

Review Exercises

A. Write a pronoun to fit each description.
1. third person, plural, objective case
2. first person, plural, nominative case
3. third person, singular, possessive case, masculine gender
4. second person, possessive case
5. first person, singular, objective case
6. third person, singular, nominative case, feminine gender

B. Write whether each pair of pronouns differs in *person, number, case,* or *gender.*
1. his, him
2. we, they
3. his, its
4. us, them
5. I, we
6. it, its
7. I, me
8. she, he

Review Exercises

A.
1. them
2. we
3. his
4. your *or* yours
5. me
6. she

B.
1. case
2. person
3. gender
4. person
5. number
6. case
7. case
8. gender

69. Using Figures of Speech

> **Lesson Survey**
> - A **simile** makes a figurative comparison by using *like* or *as.*
> - A **metaphor** makes a figurative comparison without using *like* or *as.*
> - In **personification,** a thing or quality is pictured as having human characteristics.
> - A **hyperbole** is a figurative exaggeration for the purpose of emphasis.
> - Try to use fresh, original figures of speech in your writing.

One of the most effective ways to add interest and color to your speaking and writing is to use figurative language. Often in figurative language, something abstract is compared to a literal person or thing in such a way that a vivid picture is painted in the imagination.

For example, the psalmist could have said simply, "Thy word tells me how to live." But instead he said, "Thy word is a lamp unto my feet." How much more vivid and expressive!

A *simile* makes a figurative comparison by using *like* or *as.* This is the

Lesson 69

Purpose: To teach the identification and use of similes, metaphors, personification, and *hyperboles.

IMPORTANT: Tell your pupils to choose a book, get it approved, and read it in preparation for writing a book report. (See Lesson 81.) They should read the entire book carefully, looking for information to include in the book report.

Oral Review:
1. Name the five parts of a friendly letter. (heading, greeting, body, closing, signature)
2. What additional part does a business letter have? (inside address)
3. What specific details should be included in an invitation? (what the event is, when and where it is to be, information about any preparations the invited person needs to make)
4. What are the three C's of business letters? (courteous, clear, concise)

Lesson Introduction: The scene was a seventh grade classroom on a warm spring afternoon. Susan was sitting in the back row, but she was miles away. When Brother Mark called her name, she jumped as if she had been hit by a rock, and her face turned as red as a ripe strawberry. Thoroughly embarrassed, she stammered, "I-I'm sorry, Brother Mark. I didn't hear your question."

Which of the statements above are true only in a figurative sense?

Lesson Outline:

1. A simile makes a figurative comparison by using like *or* as.

2. A metaphor makes a figurative comparison without using like *or* as.

simplest figure of speech. Consider the following Bible similes.

"The devil, as a roaring lion, walketh about, seeking whom he may devour."

"A merry heart doeth good like a medicine."

We know that a lion is vicious, strong, and cunning in catching its prey. Since the devil is like that, we realize that he is dangerous indeed! The second simile is meaningful because we know how beneficial it is to take the right medicine for a sickness. This helps us to understand the benefit of being merry (cheerful).

By the use of similes that paint vivid pictures in our minds, the sentences above are made effective and impressive. They communicate much better than sentences like "The devil is extremely fierce and dangerous" and "Cheerfulness is good for you." The sentences with figurative language also stick much better in the memory.

A *metaphor* makes a figurative comparison without using *like* or *as*. Many metaphors contain a form of the verb *be* and say that one thing is another thing. Other metaphors say that something happens in a literal, physical way when it actually happens only in a figurative sense. Consider the following examples.

"Israel is an empty vine."

Courtesy lubricates the gears of everyday living.

Israel was a nation, not a vine. But in her apostasy, she was just as disappointing to God as a fruitless vine is to a vinedresser. Everyday living is not a machine with gears that need lubrication. But as oil helps machinery to run smoothly, so courtesy helps people to get along pleasantly in everyday life. Again, the figurative language puts vivid pictures into our minds.

In *personification,* a thing or quality is pictured as having human characteristics. This figure may take the form of a thing or quality talking or acting in a way that only humans can. Or it may refer to something abstract as having human features like hands or feet. Extended personification is sometimes found in allegories and parables, such as the parable of the trees in Judges 9. Consider the following examples of personification.

"The heavens declare the glory of God."

Opportunity is usually dressed in work clothes.

Again notice the figurative nature of these statements. The heavens cannot literally speak about God's glory, and opportunity does not wear literal clothes. Yet these figures communicate truth in a clear, forceful way. The first one emphasizes how clearly the heavenly bodies express

a. Many metaphors contain a form of the verb *be* and say that one thing is another thing.

b. Other metaphors say that something happens in a literal, physical way when it actually happens only in a figurative sense.

3. In personification, a thing or quality is pictured as having human characteristics.

a. This figure may take the form of a thing or quality talking or acting in a way that only humans can.

b. It may refer to something abstract as having human features like hands or feet.

c. Extended personification is sometimes found in allegories and parables.

4. A hyperbole is a figurative exaggeration for the purpose of emphasis.

a. The exaggeration is often so great that it is amusing, and in this way it impresses the hearer or reader with an important truth.

b. A hyperbole is used to impress people with truth, whereas a simple exaggeration is used to impress people with one's abilities or experiences.

5. Try to use fresh, original figures of speech in your writing. You should seldom use the first figurative comparison that comes to your mind, for it may well be stale and tasteless.

he majesty of God. The second one tells us that an opportunity is seldom
n easy way to make progress. Usually we must work hard to take advan-
age of it.

A *hyperbole* (hī·pėr′·bə·lē) is a figurative exaggeration for the purpose
f emphasis. The exaggeration is often so great that it is amusing, and in
his way it impresses the hearer or reader with an important truth. Consider
he following hyperbole from the Bible.

> "And why beholdest thou the mote that is in thy brother's eye, but
> considerest not the beam that is in thine own eye?"

Can you imagine someone with a beam (log) in his eye, who tries to
emove a mote (speck) from someone else's eye? The exaggeration is amus-
ng, but it gives powerful emphasis to a sober truth. It shows how foolish
ve are if we try to help someone with a minor problem when we have a
najor problem ourselves.

Here is another example of a hyperbole.

> Don't burn the house down to get rid of the mice.

We could express the same idea by saying, "Don't take drastic action to
olve a minor problem." But that sounds flat in comparison to the hyperbole!

As you can see, a hyperbole is not the same as a simple exaggeration.
Someone who exaggerates tries to make something bigger, better, or more
xciting than it really is, usually to draw attention to himself. But the use
f a hyperbole gives a vivid mental picture to put strong emphasis on an
mportant fact. An exaggerator seeks to impress people with his abilities
r experiences. A hyperbole is used to impress people with truth.

Figures of speech are like spice. You do not use spice in every dish, neither should you use a figure of speech in every sentence. Both must be
used sparingly. Also, spice may become stale and lose its flavor, and the
ame is true of many common figures of speech. Therefore, you should
eldom use the first figurative comparison that comes to your mind; it
nay well be stale and tasteless. Some trite, worn-out figures of speech
re listed here.

busy as a bee	quick as a flash	straight as an arrow
neat as a pin	quiet as a mouse	white as a sheet

The following sentences contain figures of speech that are fresh and
riginal. Do you see how they add flavor and color to the sentences?

> This man had nine children, all as healthy as acorns.
> Folding his wings, the falcon dropped like a black meteor.
> The bear's heart turned to water, and he fled like a frightened rabbit.

Class Practice

A. Identify the figure of speech that is used in each sentence. Discuss its meaning.
1. "The Lord is my light."
2. "The sun . . . rejoiceth as a strong man to run a race."
3. "It is easier for a camel to go through the eye of a needle, than for a rich man to enter into the kingdom of God."
4. "Beware of false prophets, which come to you in sheep's clothing, but inwardly they are ravening wolves."
5. "As the hart panteth after the water brooks, so panteth my soul after thee, O God."

B. Suggest a fresh, meaningful figure of speech to complete these sentences.
1. The sunflowers . . . in the gentle breeze. (personification)
2. The wind roared through the trees like . . . (simile)
3. Far down in the valley was the . . . of the highway. (metaphor)
4. By the time we had loaded all the apples, each crate . . . (hyperbole)

Written Exercises

A. Identify the figure of speech in each sentence: *simile, metaphor, personification,* or *hyperbole.*
1. "Ephraim is a cake not turned."
2. "Israel slideth back as a backsliding heifer."
3. "He brought me up also out of an horrible pit."
4. "For all the Athenians . . . spent their time in nothing else, but either to tell, or to hear some new thing."
5. "Righteousness and peace have kissed each other."
6. "Thou shalt not be afraid . . . for the pestilence that walketh in darkness."
7. Falsehood travels around the world while truth is putting his boots on.
8. The playful wind tossed the boys' caps into the air.
9. The floodwaters rushed down the narrow valley like a train out of control.
10. The threatening sky muttered to itself and scowled down at us.
11. Each thorn was a dagger protecting the precious treasure of berries.
12. Snowflakes drifted like downy feathers out of the sky.

B. Write a fresh, expressive figure of speech to complete each sentence.
1. Cumulus clouds like . . . sailed across the sky. (simile)
2. The sick fawn's body . . . (hyperbole)
3. The busy squirrels . . . as they gathered their winter's store of nuts. (personification)
4. The full moon was a (an) . . . in the night sky. (metaphor)

Lesson 69 Answers

Class Practice

A. 1. metaphor—The Lord is the source of our understanding.
2. personification—As the sun rises, it seems to be glowing with ambition to run its race across the sky.
3. hyperbole—Jesus was emphasizing the great difficulty of entering God's kingdom if one is cumbered with riches. (He said further that this is impossible with men, but that "with God all things are possible.")
4. metaphor—The false prophets resemble true believers, but they are actually destructive to the Christian faith.
5. simile—As the deer longs for a drink of water from a cool stream, so the saint longs for communion with God.

B. (Sample answers.)
1. nodded their heads, waved, smiled
2. a freight train, an angry bear, a raging lion
3. narrow ribbon, thread
4. weighed a ton

Written Exercises

A.
1. metaphor	8. personification
2. simile	9. simile
3. metaphor	10. personification
4. hyperbole	11. metaphor
5. personification	12. simile
6. personification	
7. personification *or* hyperbole	

B. (Sample answers.)
1. mounds (balls) of cotton candy; huge pieces of popcorn
2. wasted away; became a mere skeleton; was reduced to skin and bones
3. chattered excitedly; scolded noisily
4. huge silver dollar; great orange ball

Review Exercises

Write the correct verbs. [48]

1. Honesty, along with trustworthiness, (is, are) important to a useful life.
2. One (don't, doesn't) have to be around a dishonest person to appreciate the worth of honesty.
3. Each of the Bible books (give, gives) an important message to man.
4. The angelic chorus (proclaim, proclaims) the good news.
5. The congregation (have, has) arisen for the benediction.
6. Either Martha or Susan (bake, bakes) bread today.
7. (What's, What are) the answers to the math puzzles?
8. Mathematics (is, are) the study of numbers.
9. English and spelling (deal, deals) with words.
10. The herd of elk (was, were) scattering across the plains to find their food.
11. (There's, There are) numerous small cedar trees on our farm.
12. (Have, Has) chicken pox spread through your school this year?
13. Good shears (stay, stays) sharp for a considerable time.
14. He still (don't, doesn't) have the right answer.
15. A book of facts (sit, sits) on the shelf.

---

70. Positions of Adjectives

> ### Lesson Survey
> - An **attributive adjective** precedes the word it modifies.
> - An **appositive adjective** immediately follows the word it modifies. When appositive adjectives are used in pairs, they are set off by commas.
> - A **predicate adjective** follows a linking verb and modifies the subject.
> - When two or more descriptive adjectives modify the same noun, they may need to be separated by commas.

Descriptive adjectives may be placed in various positions in relation to the nouns they modify. The following sentences communicate the same idea, but notice the different positions of the adjectives.

Lesson 70

Purpose: To teach the position of adjectives in sentences, and the use of commas with adjectives. (*Previous experience:* Concept of attributive adjectives, without use of the term.)

Oral Review:

1. Use a suffix to change each word to an adjective.
   a. comfort (comfortable)
   b. sense (sensible)
   c. offend (offensive)
   d. dust (dusty)
   e. pain (painful, painless)
   f. music (musical)
   g. Greece (Greek)
   h. Italy (Italian)
2. List the six classes of limiting adjectives. (articles, number words—cardinal and ordinal, indefinite

Review Exercises

1. is
2. doesn't
3. gives
4. proclaims
5. has
6. bakes
7. What are
8. is
9. deal
10. were
11. There are
12. Has
13. stay
14. doesn't
15. sits

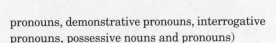

pronouns, demonstrative pronouns, interrogative pronouns, possessive nouns and pronouns)
3. Give at least five descriptive adjectives to modify each noun. (Sample answers given.)
   a. fence (white, picket, wooden, stone, wire, straight, zigzag, sturdy, strong, weak, rotten)
   b. cake (chocolate, delicious, tasty, burned, beautiful, decorated, frosted, moist, dry, crumbly)
   c. calf (clean, dirty, dry, wet, active, healthy, sick, playful, weaned)
4. Give several pronouns for each of the following six classes.
   a. personal (*Samples:* I, you, he, she, them, ours, theirs)
   b. compound personal (*Samples:* myself, yourself, ourselves, themselves)
   c. demonstrative (this, that, these, those)
   d. indefinite (*Samples:* each, everyone, any, both, many, some)
   e. interrogative (who, whom, whose, which, what)
   f. relative (who, whom, whose, which, that)

The <u>tall</u>, <u>lovely</u> palms are in the front lawn.
The palms, <u>tall and lovely</u>, are in the front lawn.
The palms in the front lawn are <u>tall and lovely</u>.

An *attributive adjective* precedes the word it modifies. The quality expressed by the adjective is *attributed* (assigned) to the noun that follows. This is the most common position of adjectives.

Three <u>slender</u>, <u>agile</u> deer grazed in <u>the</u> <u>lush</u>, <u>tranquil</u> meadow.

An *appositive adjective* immediately follows the word it modifies, just as an appositive noun follows another noun. In addition to providing sentence variety, the appositive position tends to place greater emphasis on the adjectives.

Appositive adjectives almost always come in pairs, and they are set off by commas. One exception is adjectives that refer to position, which are commonly used as single adjectives in the appositive position.

Three deer, <u>slender</u> and <u>agile</u>, grazed in the meadow, <u>lush</u> and <u>tranquil</u>.
God made the heavens <u>above</u> and the earth <u>beneath</u>.

Attributive adjectives and appositive adjectives are diagramed on slanted lines below the noun or pronoun they modify. If they come in pairs, the conjunction is placed on a broken horizontal line between the adjectives.

Three <u>slender</u>, <u>agile</u> deer grazed in <u>the</u> <u>lush</u>, <u>tranquil</u> meadow.

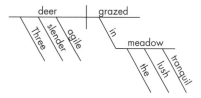

Three deer, <u>slender</u> and <u>agile</u>, grazed in the meadow, <u>lush</u> and <u>tranquil</u>.

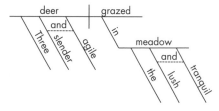

Lesson Introduction: Would you enjoy sitting at the same position in the classroom all year? Probably all of us enjoy variety enough to appreciate a change of position. Sometimes those small changes help to spark some interest. The position of adjectives can be changed as well. This variety helps to produce interesting sentences and paragraphs.

Lesson Outline:

1. An attributive adjective precedes the word it modifies.

a. This is the most common position of adjectives.

b. Attributive adjectives are diagramed on slanted lines below the noun or pronoun they modify.

2. An appositive adjective immediately follows the word it modifies.

a. The appositive position tends to place greater emphasis on the adjectives.

b. Appositive adjectives almost always come in pairs, and they are set off by commas. One exception is adjectives that refer to position, which are commonly used as single adjectives in the appositive position.

c. Appositive adjectives are diagramed on slanted lines below the noun or pronoun they modify. If they come in pairs, the conjunction is placed on a broken horizontal line between the adjectives.

3. A predicate adjective follows a linking verb and modifies the subject.

a. It is usually sensible to move a predicate adjective to the attributive position.

b. Predicate adjectives are diagramed on the horizontal base line after the linking verb.

God made the heavens <u>above</u> and the earth <u>beneath</u>.

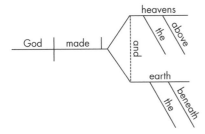

A *predicate adjective* follows a linking verb and modifies the subject. You know that it modifies the subject because usually it is sensible to move the predicate adjective to the attributive position.

The corn on the stand looked <u>fresh</u>.
    Think: *Fresh corn* is sensible.
The book on the table was <u>torn</u> and <u>dusty</u>.
    Think: *Torn and dusty book* is sensible.

Predicate adjectives are subjective complements (as predicate nominatives are). Therefore, they are diagramed on the horizontal base line after the linking verb.

The corn on the stand looked <u>fresh</u>.

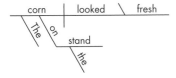

The book on the table was <u>torn</u> and <u>dusty</u>.

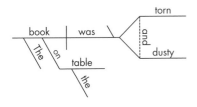

4. When two or more descriptive adjectives modify the same noun, they may need to be separated by commas.

    a. Never place a comma between two limiting adjectives or between a limiting adjective and a descriptive adjective.

    b. Never place a comma after the last adjective in a series, which comes just before the word that the adjectives modify.

    c. If the final adjective is closely connected to the noun, do not place a comma before the last adjective.

    d. Three tests are helpful in deciding whether to use a comma between two descriptive adjectives.

        1) *Do you pause between the adjectives as you read them?*

        2) *Does it sound right to use* and *between the adjectives?*

        3) *Does it sound right to change the order of the adjectives?*

When two or more descriptive adjectives modify the same noun, they may need to be separated by commas. Never place a comma between two limiting adjectives or between a limiting adjective and a descriptive adjective. Never place a comma after the last adjective in a series, which comes just before the word that the adjectives modify.

> **Incorrect:**   <u>Marie's, three</u> dresses are worn and patched.
>
> My grandmother made <u>those, beautiful</u> mottoes.
>
> The cold drinks were welcomed by the <u>dusty, tired,</u> workers.
>
> **Correct**:   <u>Marie's three</u> dresses are worn and patched.
>
> My grandmother made <u>those beautiful</u> mottoes.
>
> The cold drinks were welcomed by the <u>dusty, tired</u> workers.

Sometimes the final adjective in a series is closely connected to the noun, forming a unit much like a noun phrase. In such cases, do not place a comma before the last adjective.

> **Incorrect:**   A <u>young, song</u> leader directed the singing.
>
> (*Song leader* should be considered a unit.)
>
> **Correct:**   A <u>young song</u> leader directed the singing.

> **Incorrect:**   On the front porch stood a <u>large, iron</u> kettle.
>
> (*Iron kettle* should be considered a unit.)
>
> **Correct:**   On the front porch stood a <u>large iron</u> kettle.

Three tests will help you decide whether to use a comma between two descriptive adjectives. If the answers are *yes,* the adjectives should be separated by a comma.

> **Test 1:**   *Do you pause between the adjectives as you read them?*
>
> **Test 2:**   *Does it sound right to use* and *between the adjectives?*
>
> **Test 3:**   *Does it sound right to change the order of the adjectives?*

> **Problem:**   A <u>steep narrow</u> path zigzagged over the mountain.
>
> *Think:*   Do you pause between *steep* and *narrow* as you read them? (yes)
>
> Does it sound right to say "*steep and narrow* path"? (yes)
>
> Does it sound right to say "*narrow steep* path"? (yes)
>
> **Solution:**   A <u>steep, narrow</u> path zigzagged over the mountain.

> **Problem:**   My father works at a <u>large stone</u> quarry.
>
> *Think:*   Do you pause between *large* and *stone* as you read them? (no)

Does it sound right to say *"large and stone* quarry"? (no)

Does it sound right to say *"stone large* quarry"? (no)

Solution: My father works at a <u>large stone</u> quarry.

Problem: The children recited a <u>long memory</u> passage.

Think: Do you pause between *long* and *memory* as you read them? (no)

Does it sound right to say *"long and memory* passage"? (no)

Does it sound right to say *"memory long* passage"? (no)

Solution: The children recited a <u>long memory</u> passage.

Class Practice

A. Identify each adjective, and tell whether it is *attributive, appositive,* or *predicate.*

1. Our God can deliver His people from every distressing trouble.
2. Many shining angels became visible to the frightened servant.
3. The Lord, merciful and gracious, sent His Son into the world below.
4. The children's game outside sounded lively and exciting.

B. Read each sentence, adding adjectives for the underlined nouns according to the directions in parentheses. Tell where commas should be used.

1. The <u>horses</u> plodded across the prairie with the heavily loaded Conestoga wagon. (two descriptive adjectives in the appositive position)
2. The <u>girls</u> who came to help Mother were certainly ———. (two descriptive adjectives in the predicate position)
3. We watched the <u>kittens</u>. (three descriptive adjectives in the attributive position)
4. The <u>dogs</u> were playing with an old shoe. (one limiting and one descriptive adjective in the attributive position, and one adjective in the appositive position)

C. Combine these sentence pairs by the correct use of appositive adjectives. Tell where commas are needed.

1. The dog was young and alert. He quickly spotted the squirrel.
2. Shirley carried a kitten to the house. It was soft and fluffy.
3. Several rules are written on the board. They are short and clear.

D. Tell where commas are needed in these sentences.

1. Haman conceited and spiteful plotted against the Jews.
2. The beautiful godly queen had been raised by Mordecai.
3. This simple inexpensive machine will help the overworked mechanic.
4. One of the ropes rotten and ragged finally let loose.

Lesson 70 Answers

Class Practice

A. 1. Our—attributive; His—attributive; every—attributive; distressing—attributive
   2. Many—attributive; shining—attributive; visible—predicate; the—attributive; frightened—attributive
   3. The—attributive; merciful—appositive; gracious—appositive; His—attributive; the—attributive; below—appositive
   4. The—attributive; children's—attributive; outside—appositive; lively—predicate; exciting—predicate

B. (Sample answers. Added items are underlined.)
   1. The horses, <u>strong and steady,</u> plodded across the prairie with the heavily loaded Conestoga wagon.
   2. The girls who came to help Mother were certainly <u>eager and industrious</u>.
   3. We watched the <u>small, fluffy, playful</u> kittens.
   4. The <u>two</u> <u>small</u> dogs <u>outside</u> were playing with an old shoe.

C. (Commas are underlined.)
   1. The dog, young and alert, quickly spotted the squirrel.
   2. Shirley carried a kitten, soft and fluffy, to the house.
   3. Several rules, short and clear, are written on the board.

D. (Commas are underlined.)
   1. Haman, conceited and spiteful, plotted against the Jews.
   2. The beautiful, godly queen had been raised by Mordecai.
   3. This simple, inexpensive machine will help the overworked mechanic.
   4. One of the ropes, rotten and ragged, finally let loose.

E. On the chalkboard, diagram these sentences.
1. The butterfly's wings, beautiful and delicate, fanned the air.
2. The ripe berries underneath were large and juicy.
3. The three young children, hungry and weary, followed their mother.

Written Exercises

A. Copy each adjective, and write whether it is attributive (*AT*), appositive (*AP*), or predicate (*P*).
1. The Bible is unchanging and authoritative.
2. The prophet, courageous and dedicated, boldly proclaimed God's message.
3. You will never regret a harsh word unspoken or an evil deed undone.
4. Beautiful singing birds trilled their notes in the morning air, clear and fresh.
5. An Arctic wind blasted bitter cold into the southern states.
6. This new book is interesting and worthwhile.

B. Copy these sentences, replacing each word in parentheses with an adjective of the kind indicated. Use correct punctuation.
1. The birdsongs filling the air were (predicate) and (predicate).
2. We stood on the porch (appositive), silently watching the (attributive) (attributive) northern lights.
3. They fed the (limiting) (descriptive) puppies.
4. Snowflakes (appositive) and (appositive) filled the air.

C. Combine these sentence pairs by the correct use of appositive adjectives. Use commas as needed.
1. The woman climbed out of her car. She was weak and shaky.
2. Two men came to her aid. They were polite and helpful.
3. The car had slid on the icy road. It was scratched and dented.

D. Copy each word that should be followed by a comma, and add the missing comma.
1. A lion silent and hungry had sneaked up and caught one of David's lambs.
2. The courageous godly shepherd trusted in the Lord's help.
3. David strong and skillful rescued his frightened helpless lamb.
4. The excited restless sheep were calmed by David's gentle voice.

E. Diagram these sentences.
1. Lot, selfish and greedy, chose the best land.
2. Isaac must have been humble and peaceable.
3. Elijah was a bold, zealous prophet.
4. The Hebrews' courageous response infuriated the king.

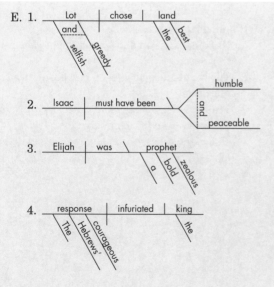

E. 1.

2.

3.

4.

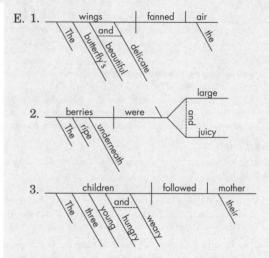

E. 1.

2.

3.

Written Exercises

A. 1. The—AT; unchanging—P; authoritative—P
2. The—AT; courageous—AP; dedicated—AP; God's—AT
3. a—AT; harsh—AT; unspoken—AP; an—AT; evil—AT; undone—AP
4. Beautiful—AT; singing—AT; their—AT; the—AT; morning—AT; clear—AP; fresh—AP
5. An—AT; Arctic—AT; bitter—AT; the—AT; southern—AT
6. This—AT; new—AT; interesting—P; worthwhile—P

B. (Added commas and sample adjectives are underlined.)
1. The birdsongs filling the air were <u>clear</u> and <u>melodious</u>.
2. We stood on the porch <u>outside</u>, silently watching the <u>gorgeous</u>, <u>colorful</u> northern lights.
3. They fed the <u>three</u> <u>lively</u> puppies.
4. Snowflakes<u>,</u> <u>huge</u> and <u>fluffy,</u> filled the air.

C. (Commas are underlined.)
1. The woman<u>,</u> weak and shaky<u>,</u> climbed out of her car.
2. Two men<u>,</u> polite and helpful<u>,</u> came to her aid.
3. The car<u>,</u> scratched and dented<u>,</u> had slid on the icy road.

D. 1. lion, hungry,
2. courageous,
3. David, skillful, frightened,
4. excited,

Review Exercises

Copy each pronoun, and write whether it is personal (*P*), compound personal (*CP*), demonstrative (*D*), indefinite (*ID*), interrogative (*IR*), or relative (*R*). [57–64]

1. When some wanted to throw Jesus over a cliff, He passed safely through their midst.
2. Who has power to heal all of our sicknesses?
3. This was He of whom the prophets had spoken for many years.
4. Jesus proved Himself the Messiah by the miracles that He performed.
5. Those who did not believe Him had to ignore many of the Old Testament prophecies.
6. We should acquaint ourselves with the Bible.
7. Whose life is the perfect example for everyone to follow?
8. This is found only in Jesus Christ.

71. Forms of Comparison for Adjectives

Lesson Survey

- Many descriptive adjectives have three degrees of comparison: **positive, comparative,** and **superlative.**
- The positive degree is the simplest form of an adjective.
- To form the comparative and superlative degrees of most adjectives, add *-er* and *-est* to the positive degree, or use *more* and *most* with the positive degree.
- Some common adjectives have irregular forms of comparison.
- Use the positive degree to describe without making a comparison. Use the comparative degree to compare two items. Use the superlative degree to compare more than two items.
- Do not use *more* or *most* with an adjective that is already a form of comparison. The result is an improper double comparison.
- If an adjective expresses an absolute quality, it cannot logically have degrees of comparison.

By today's life expectancy, Adam was a very *old* man when he died at 930 years of age. His great-great-great-grandson Jared was even *older*

Lesson 71

Purpose: To teach the formation and use of the three degrees of comparison for adjectives.

Oral Review:

1. Tell what kind of adjective is found in each position.
   a. directly after the noun it modifies (appositive)
   b. just before the noun it modifies (attributive)
   c. after a linking verb, where it modifies the subject (predicate)
2. Which of these three positions usually requires the use of commas? (appositive)
3. What three tests can you use to decide if two descriptive adjectives should be separated by a comma? (Do you pause between the adjectives as you read them? Does it sound right to use *and* between the adjectives? Does it sound right to

Review Exercises

1. some—ID; He—P; their—P
2. Who—IR; all—ID; our—P
3. This—D; He—P; whom—R
4. Himself—CP; that—R; He—P
5. Those—D; who—R; Him—P; many—ID
6. We—P; ourselves—CP
7. Whose—IR; everyone—ID
8. This—D

change the order of the adjectives?)
4. Give sentences with the subject *he* and the verb *find* in all six tenses. (He finds. He found. He will find. He has found. He had found. He will have found.)
5. Change each sentence so that the verb is a progressive form. Do not change the tense.
   a. The Lord called Samuel. (The Lord was calling Samuel.)
   b. A steadfast person will serve the Lord in all circumstances. (A steadfast person will be serving the Lord in all circumstances.)
6. Change each sentence so that the verb is an emphatic form. Do not change the tense.
   a. Our choice of friends influences our character. (Our choice of friends does influence our character.)
   b. The prophet warned the people. (The prophet did warn the people.)

when he died at 962 years of age. And Jared's grandson Methuselah, who died at the age of 969 years, was the *oldest* man who ever lived.

Many descriptive adjectives have three degrees of comparison: positive, comparative, and superlative. These three degrees are illustrated by the italicized words in the paragraph above. The *positive degree* is the simplest form of an adjective. This form is used to describe without comparing.

To form the *comparative* and *superlative* degrees of most one-syllable and some two-syllable words, add *-er* and *-est* to the positive degree. If necessary, double the final consonant or change the *y* to *i* before adding the suffix. For most two-syllable words and for all longer words, use *more* and *most* with the positive degree. *Less* and *least* are used if a negative comparison is made.

Positive	Comparative	Superlative
tall	taller	tallest
glad	gladder	gladdest
holy	holier	holiest
modern	more modern	most modern
interesting	more interesting	most interesting
beautiful	less beautiful	least beautiful

Some common adjectives have irregular forms of comparison.

Positive	Comparative	Superlative
good, well	better	best
bad, ill	worse	worst
far	farther	farthest
much, many	more	most
little	less	least

Littler and *littlest* are correct forms when they refer to size. Use the irregular *less* and *least* when referring to an amount.

> Saul felt himself the <u>least</u> (in amount of worth), but he was certainly not the <u>littlest</u> (in size).

Be careful when you use the three degrees of comparison. Use the positive degree to describe without making a comparison. Use the comparative degree to compare two items, and use the superlative degree to compare more than two.

> **Positive degree:** No comparison
> Lake Victoria, covering 26,828 square miles, is a <u>large</u> lake.
> Chicago, which has nearly three million

---

inhabitants, is a <u>populous</u> city of the United States.

Comparative degree: Compares two items

Lake Superior, covering 31,700 square miles, is <u>larger</u> than Lake Victoria.

Los Angeles, which has over three million inhabitants, is <u>more populous</u> than Chicago.

Superlative degree: Compares more than two items

The Caspian Sea, covering 143,244 square miles, is the <u>largest</u> lake in the world.

New York City, which has over seven million inhabitants, is the <u>most populous</u> city of the United States.

The most common mistake in using forms of comparison is to use the superlative form when only two things are compared. When you compare only two items, be especially careful to use the comparative degree.

Incorrect: Minerva is the <u>tallest</u> of the two seventh grade girls.
Correct: Minerva is the <u>taller</u> of the two seventh grade girls.

Incorrect: Of Uncle Milton's two ponies, Star is <u>most beautiful</u>.
Correct: Of Uncle Milton's two ponies, Star is <u>more beautiful</u>.

Do not use *more* or *most* with an adjective that is already a form of comparison. The result is an improper double comparison.

Incorrect: The Bible is <u>more better</u> than any other book.
Correct: The Bible is <u>better</u> than any other book.

Incorrect: This is the <u>most delightfulest</u> story in the book.
Correct: This is the <u>most delightful</u> story in the book.

If an adjective expresses an absolute quality, it cannot logically have degrees of comparison. For example, something dead is absolutely dead; one thing cannot be deader than another. Something square is absolutely square; one thing cannot be squarer than another. However, one sick calf may be *more nearly dead* than another, and one student's diagram may be *more nearly square* than another's. The same is true of words like *unique, perfect, straight, fatal, true,* and *round.*

b. Use the comparative degree to compare two items.

c. Use the superlative degree to compare more than two items.

6. Do not use more or most with an adjective that is already a form of comparison. The result is an improper double comparison.

7. If an adjective expresses an absolute quality, it cannot logically have degrees of comparison.

(*Teacher:* Many adjectives that express absolute qualities also have meanings that are not absolute, and then these adjectives may have forms of comparison. One example is *square* in the expression "a square meal." The form *squarest* is correct in the following sentence: It was the squarest meal he had eaten in many days.)

★ **EXTRA PRACTICE**
Worksheet 38 (*Forms of Comparison for Adjectives*)

Anita's circles are <u>more nearly round</u>, and her lines are <u>more nearly straight</u>, than mine.

As it turned out, Lillian's account was <u>more nearly true</u> than Jerry's.

Class Practice

A. Give the comparative and superlative degrees of these adjectives.

1. soft
2. far
3. hot
4. much
5. little, in amount
6. lovely
7. expensive
8. courteous
9. ill
10. well

B. Read each sentence correctly.

1. Both Israel and Judah were sinful, but Israel was the most corrupt.
2. The wounded king was more dead than his armorbearer was.
3. The older we grow, the more humbler we should become.
4. Of the two kings, Jehoshaphat was most interested in knowing what God said.
5. On Monday Susanna felt quite ill, but on Tuesday she felt even iller.
6. I think Lorna's picture is beautifuller than mine.
7. My score on the history quiz today is worser than it was yesterday.
8. Arlan has the littlest amount of homework to do tonight.
9. After looking over the six puppies, we chose the one with the longer fur.
10. Although the two school buildings are nearly the same size, you can quickly see that Hickory Grove School has the most students.

Written Exercises

A. Write correctly each adjective that is written in the wrong form. If a word should be left out, copy it and draw a line through it.

1. Of the two daughters-in-law, Ruth was most devoted to Naomi.
2. Abel's offering was more better than Cain's, and God accepted it.
3. Zimri's reign was the shorter one in all the history of the northern kingdom.
4. This doughnut is rounder than that one.
5. This is a pleasanter day for our trip than yesterday would have been.
6. Carl's dog is bigger than mine, but mine is the fastest runner.
7. Carol can make littler *e*'s than I, but my *r*'s are more neater than hers.
8. Fred is usually the more curious of all the boys in the class.
9. This is the goodest story I've read for months!
10. The corners in this old house are more square than what we had expected.

Lesson 71 Answers

If an adjective has two syllables, and if *-er* and *-est* may be added, the answer key gives only those forms of comparison (such as *nobler* and *noblest*). Students may also make the forms of comparison by using *more* and *most* (such as *more noble* and *most noble*).

Class Practice

A.
1. softer, softest
2. farther, farthest
3. hotter, hottest
4. more, most
5. less, least
6. lovelier, loveliest
7. more expensive, most expensive
8. more courteous, most courteous
9. worse, worst
10. better, best

B. (Corrections are underlined.)

1. Both Israel and Judah were sinful, but Israel was the <u>more corrupt</u>.
2. The wounded king was <u>more nearly dead</u> than his armorbearer was.
3. The older we grow, the <u>humbler</u> we should become.
4. Of the two kings, Jehoshaphat was <u>more interested</u> in knowing what God said.
5. On Monday Susanna felt quite ill, but on Tuesday she felt even <u>worse</u>.
6. I think Lorna's picture is <u>more beautiful</u> than mine.
7. My score on the history quiz today is <u>worse</u> than it was yesterday.
8. Arlan has the <u>least</u> amount of homework to do tonight.
9. After looking over the six puppies, we chose the one with the <u>longest</u> fur.
10. Although the two school buildings are nearly the same size, you can quickly see that Hickory Grove School has the <u>more</u> students.

Written Exercises

A.
1. more devoted
2. ~~more~~
3. shortest
4. more nearly round
5. more pleasant
6. faster
7. ~~more~~
8. most curious
9. best
10. more nearly square

11. Aunt Mae brought the most tastiest cookies of all.
12. I thought the peach ice cream was the best of the two kinds.
13. Of the two years that we farmed in Missouri, that year was the best.
14. Since Uncle Curvin's moved to Alberta, they have littler opportunity to come to our family gatherings.

3. For each adjective, write three sentences illustrating the three degrees of comparison. For the comparative and the superlative degrees, be sure to write sentences that show comparisons of two things or of three or more.

1. hot   2. friendly   3. delicious

Review Exercises

A. Write six meaningful sentences, using the verb *teach* in all six tenses. Be sure to include two actions or conditions in the sentences with verbs in the past perfect and future perfect tenses. [35, 37, 38]

B. Change the verb in each sentence to a progressive form. Do not change the tense. [39]
1. God's angels watch over God's people.
2. Jesus had prepared His disciples before His death.
3. Jonathan will type his story this evening.
4. Brother Noah has taught at our school for five years.

C. Change the verb in each sentence to an emphatic form. Do not change the tense. [39]
1. God answers the prayers of the saints.
2. Jesus arose from the dead.

---

72. Verbals as Adjectives

Lesson Survey

- One kind of verbal used as an adjective is the **participle.** It may be a past participle or a present participle.

- Another kind of verbal used as an adjective is the **infinitive.**

- A verbal used as an adjective is diagramed across the angle of a slanting and a horizontal line, below the noun or pronoun it modifies.

Lesson 72

Purpose: To teach the identification of *verbals used as adjectives.

Oral Review:

1. Give the comparative and superlative forms of these adjectives.
   a. good (better, best)
   b. holy (holier, holiest)
   c. many (more, most)
   d. soft (softer, softest)
   e. marvelous (more marvelous, most marvelous)
   f. delightful (more delightful, most delightful)
   g. far (farther, farthest)
   h. little, in size (littler, littlest)
2. Tell whether the word *delighted* is in the attributive, appositive, or predicate position in these sentences.

11. ~~most~~
12. better
13. better
14. less

B. (Individual work.)

Review Exercises
A. (Individual work.)

B. 1. are watching
   2. had been preparing
   3. will be typing
   4. has been teaching

C. 1. does answer
   2. did arise

a. Joseph seems delighted with his toy truck. (predicate)
b. Christa, delighted and happy, came running to the car. (appositive)
c. The delighted boys hurried to the house with the news. (attributive)

3. Change each word to an adjective by using a suffix.
   a. tire (tiresome, tireless)
   b. shine (shiny)
   c. tolerance (tolerant)
   d. star (starry, starlike)
   e. England (English)
   f. France (French)
   g. Alaska (Alaskan)
   h. Bible (Biblical)
4. For the passive voice, what helping verb and which principal part are always used? (a form of *be* with the past participle)

You know that a past participle is a verb form that is used with a helping verb. It is one of the three principal parts of a verb—the form that often ends with *-ed* or *-en*.

First	**Second**	**Third**
(Present)	*(Past)*	*(Past Participle)*
break	broke	(have) broken

John has <u>broken</u> the window. (past participle used as main verb)

A past participle may also be used as an adjective.

John paid for the <u>broken</u> window. (past participle used as adjective)

In the last example, *broken* modifies *window* by telling *what kind of.* It is no longer a true verb but a verbal—a verb form used as another part of speech (an adjective in this case). This kind of verbal is called a *participle.* It may be a past participle or a present participle (the *-ing* form of a verb).

The <u>falling</u> leaves covered the <u>fallen</u> log.
(*Falling* tells *what kind of* leaves. *Fallen* tells *what kind of* log.)
God gives us many <u>comforting</u> promises.
(*Comforting* tells *what kind of* promises.)
Nehemiah, <u>grieved</u> and <u>concerned</u>, was mourning over Jerusalem.
(*Grieved* and *concerned* describe Nehemiah by telling *what kind of.*)

Do not confuse participles used as adjectives with participles used as main verbs. When a participle is the main verb, it always expresses action or being in relation to the subject and it is always used with a helping verb. A participle that ends with *-ing* may also be a gerund. But then it names an action and serves a noun function, such as the subject, direct object, or predicate nominative. To be an adjective, a participle must modify a noun or pronoun that comes immediately before or after it.

Look at each of the following sentences. Is the underlined participle used as an adjective or as some other part of speech?

Problem: The faithful prophet was <u>warning</u> the people.
  Think: Does *warning* modify a noun or pronoun? (no)
            Does *warning* serve a noun function? (no)
            Is *warning* used with a helping verb to express action or being in relation to the subject? (yes; used with *was* to express action of the subject *prophet*)
Solution: <u>Warning</u> is the main verb, not an adjective.

Problem: The <u>persecuted</u> martyr saw Jesus at God's right hand.
  Think: Does *persecuted* modify a noun or pronoun? (yes; modifies *martyr*)

5. Name two situations in which it may be suitable to use the passive voice. (when there is no clear doer of the action, when there is a good reason not to name the doer of the action)

Lesson Introduction: Write the following sentence on the board.

Those leaping salmon should make delicious fish to fry.

Have students pick out the adjectives that modify *salmon*. Do the same for *fish*. If *to fry* is not mentioned, ask if that phrase describes *fish*. *To fry* is a verbal used as an adjective to describe *fish*.

Lesson Outline:

1. One kind of verbal used as an adjective is the participle.
   a. A past participle often ends with *-ed* or *-en*. It is the form used with a helping verb when it is the main verb in a sentence.
   b. A present participle ends with *-ing*.
   c. Not every word that ends with *-ing* is a participle used as an adjective. It may be a main verb or a gerund.

2. Another kind of verbal used as an adjective is the infinitive.
   a. An infinitive is the basic form of a verb preceded by *to*.
   b. Not every infinitive is an adjective. It may also be a noun or an adverb.
   c. Do not confuse infinitives (*to* and a verb form) with prepositional phrases (*to* and a noun).

3. A verbal used as an adjective is diagramed across the angle of a slanting and a horizontal line, below the noun or pronoun it modifies.

Does *persecuted* serve a noun function? (no)

Is *persecuted* used with a helping verb to express action or being in relation to the subject? (no)

Solution: <u>Persecuted</u> is an adjective modifying <u>martyr</u>.

Problem: <u>Studying</u> demands concentration and diligence.
  Think: Does *Studying* modify a noun or pronoun? (no)

Does *Studying* serve a noun function? (yes; serves as subject)

Is *Studying* used with a helping verb to express action or being in relation to the subject? (no)

Solution: <u>Studying</u> is a gerund used as the subject.

Problem: Angels are <u>created</u> beings.
  Think: Does *created* modify a noun or pronoun? (yes; modifies *beings*)

Does *created* serve a noun function? (no)

Is *created* used with a helping verb to express action or being in relation to the subject? (no; verb is not *are created* but *are,* which links subject *Angels* to predicate nominative *beings*)

Solution: <u>Created</u> is an adjective modifying <u>beings</u>.

Another kind of verbal used as an adjective is the *infinitive*. An infinitive is the basic form of a verb preceded by *to*. An infinitive used as an adjective usually answers the question *which* or *what kind of.*

The need <u>to worship</u> is native to every human being.
  (*To worship* tells *what kind of* about the subject *need.*)

Jesus Christ is our true Example <u>to follow</u>.
  (*To follow* tells *what kind of* about the predicate nominative *Example.*)

Not every infinitive is an adjective. It may also be a noun (as you studied in Chapter 3) or an adverb. But an infinitive used as an adjective always modifies a noun or pronoun, and it always comes right after that noun or pronoun.

Look at each of the following sentences. Is the underlined infinitive used as an adjective or as some other part of speech?

Problem: <u>To complain</u> will do no good.
  Think: Does *To complain* follow and modify a noun or pronoun? (no)

Solution: <u>To complain</u> is not an adjective but a noun (the subject).

★ *EXTRA PRACTICE*
Worksheet 39 (*Verbals as Adjectives*)

Problem: We must resist every temptation <u>to cheat</u>.
   Think: Does *to cheat* follow and modify a noun or pronoun? (yes)
Solution: <u>To cheat</u> is an adjective telling <u>what kind of</u> temptation.

Problem: We know that Jesus was willing <u>to die</u>.
   Think: Does *to die* follow and modify a noun or pronoun? (no)
Solution: <u>To die</u> is not an adjective but an adverb modifying *willing*.

Problem: A lamb <u>to sacrifice</u> was carefully selected.
   Think: Does *to sacrifice* follow and modify a noun or pronoun?
           (yes)
Solution: <u>To sacrifice</u> is an adjective telling <u>what kind of</u> lamb.

Do not confuse infinitives (*to* and a verb form) with prepositional phrases (*to* and a noun).

The house <u>to paint</u> is near the airport. (*to* + verb form = infinitive)
We went <u>to the house</u> near the airport. (*to* + noun = prepositional
   phrase)

The cake <u>to ice</u> is on the counter. (*to* + verb form = infinitive)
Water turns <u>to ice</u> at 32 degrees. (*to* + noun = prepositional phrase)

A verbal used as an adjective is diagrammed across the angle of a slanting and a horizontal line, below the noun or pronoun it modifies.

The <u>singing</u> birds praise their Creator.
   (*Singing* tells *what kind of* birds.)

The neighborhood dogs, <u>barking</u> and <u>howling</u>, made a great disturbance. (*Barking* and *howling* tell *what kind of* dogs.)

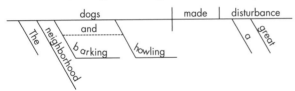

Isaac quietly surrendered the <u>disputed</u> wells.
   (*Disputed* tells *which* wells.)

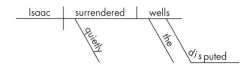

We have many opportunities <u>to share</u>.
(*To share* tells *what kind of* opportunities.)

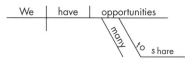

The right way <u>to take</u> is sincere obedience to the Lord.
(*To take* tells *which* way.)

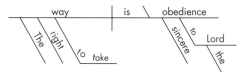

The last sentence contains both an infinitive and a prepositional phrase beginning with *to*. Note carefully the difference in the way these are diagramed. For the infinitive, the two words are written across the angle of the slanting and the horizontal line. But for the prepositional phrase, the preposition is placed on the slanting line and its object on the horizontal line.

Class Practice

A. Identify each participle used as an adjective, and the word it modifies.
  1. Paul and Silas, singing and praying, impressed the jailer.
  2. The trembling jailer asked them what he should do.
  3. The jailer washed their beaten backs.
  4. The departing apostles were comforting the saints.
  5. The boys, lost and despairing, sought shelter in a cave.
  6. A driving rain had chilled their exhausted bodies.

B. Identify each infinitive used as an adjective, and the word it modifies. Not every sentence has such an infinitive.
  1. The best book to study is the Bible.
  2. The way to heaven has been opened by the blood of Jesus.
  3. The potatoes to peel are in the bowl.
  4. To lie never solves a problem.

Lesson 72 Answers

Class Practice

A. 1. singing—Paul and Silas;
       praying—Paul and Silas
   2. trembling—jailer
   3. beaten—backs
   4. departing—apostles
   5. lost—boys; despairing—boys
   6. driving—rain; exhausted—bodies

B. 1. to study—book   3. to peel—potatoes
   2. (none)   4. (none)

5. Brother Ernest would be the best one to ask.
6. Several jobs to finish are listed on the board.

C. On the chalkboard, diagram these sentences.
1. We should recognize our need to pray.
2. The crucified Saviour has arisen!
3. Doubting Thomas has declared his restored faith.
4. The smiling sun warmed the earth, washed and refreshed.

Written Exercises

A. Copy each participle used as an adjective, and the word it modifies.
1. The burning bush arrested Moses' attention.
2. The Israelites, despised and oppressed, needed a deliverer.
3. Because God pitied His groaning people, He called Moses.
4. The chirping bird is a robin.
5. The nails, bent and twisted, were discarded.
6. The lost child was found after a determined search.
7. The remaining walls, blackened and charred, told of the recent fire.
8. The blowing snow and the drifted roads kept everyone at home.

B. Copy each infinitive used as an adjective, and the word it modifies.
1. Proverbs describes many foolish ways to avoid.
2. Our crosses to bear are never greater than the cross Jesus bore.
3. If we have enough food to eat and clothes to wear, we should be content.
4. The goal to seek is to please the Lord.
5. This week's passage to memorize is Matthew 7:1–5.
6. Report to Sister Ellen, and she will give you something to do.
7. The corn to hoe stretched to the far end of the patch.
8. Our garden has many weeds to pull.

C. Diagram these sentences.
1. The ascended Christ has conquered every foe.
2. Theresa, laughing and waving, was enjoying her tractor ride.
3. This would be a good poem to read.
4. The smiling boys have three large pumpkins to sell.
5. The starred items are the ones to correct.

Review Exercises

A. Rewrite these sentences, changing the verbs to the active voice. Do not change the tense. [53]
1. A blind man was healed by Jesus.
2. A golden calf was fashioned by Aaron.
3. A beautiful display was put on the bulletin board by Sister Charlene.

Review Exercises
A. 1. Jesus healed a blind man.
2. Aaron fashioned a golden calf.
3. Sister Charlene put a beautiful display on the bulletin board.

5. to ask—one
6. to finish—jobs

C. 1.
2.
3.
4.

Written Exercises

A. 1. burning—bush
2. despised—Israelites; oppressed—Israelites
3. groaning—people
4. chirping—bird
5. bent—nails; twisted—nails
6. lost—child; determined—search
7. remaining—walls; blackened—walls; charred—walls
8. blowing—snow; drifted—roads

B. 1. to avoid—ways
2. to bear—crosses
3. to eat—food; to wear—clothes
4. to seek—goal (*To please the Lord* is a noun.)
5. to memorize—passage
6. to do—something
7. to hoe—corn
8. to pull—weeds

C. 1.
2.
3.
4.
5.

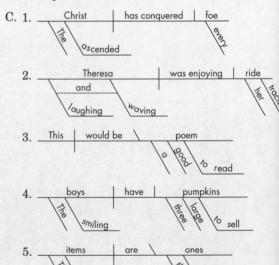

4. The broken door latch has been fixed by Brother Arnold.
5. Family worship was led by Mother during Father's absence.

3. The passive voice is used in the numbered sentences. Write the letter of the statement that correctly describes each sentence. [54]
    a. The active voice would be more effective.
    b. There is no clear doer of the action.
    c. There is a good reason not to name the doer.
1. My bicycle was badly scratched last evening.
2. A story was told to the children by Brother Leland.
3. This calligraphy was done by Curtis.
4. Many frogs are eaten in the tadpole stage.

---

4. Brother Arnold has fixed the broken door latch.
5. Mother led family worship during Father's absence.

B. 1. c
   2. a
   3. a
   4. b

---

73. Descriptive Writing

> **Lesson Survey**
> - **Descriptive writing** paints colorful word pictures.
> - **Exact nouns** help to paint clear, specific pictures.
> - **Expressive adjectives** clarify nouns.
> - **Lively verbs** help to paint vivid pictures.
> - **Figurative language** puts rich sparkle into descriptive writing.

An attractive painting must have clearly formed pictures and vivid colors. If the colors are dull, the painting is drab. If you must guess what the painting is to represent, the painting is worthless.

Descriptive writing paints colorful word pictures. The words may picture a scene or a happening. Like a painting, descriptive writing must be clear and specific; the reader should not need to guess about details. It should also be vivid and sparkling; the reader should enjoy the description.

You can do several things to make your writing clear and lively. First, using *exact nouns* will help to paint clear, specific pictures. Consider the following two sentences.

    Ahab coveted Naboth's <u>land</u>.
    Ahab coveted Naboth's <u>vineyard</u>.

Vineyard is more specific than *land*. It gives a clearer, more definite picture of what is being named. *Land* can be covered with grass, planted

Lesson 73

Purpose: (1) To teach recognition of descriptive writing. (2) To give practice in writing descriptive sentences and paragraphs.

Oral Review:

1. Name the figure of speech that fits each description.
    a. It is an obvious exaggeration to emphasize a truth. (hyperbole)
    b. It compares two things by using *like* or *as*. (simile)
    c. It compares two things without using *like* or *as*. (metaphor)
    d. It refers to a thing or quality as having human characteristics. (personification)
2. How is a hyperbole different from a simple exaggeration? (An exaggeration is used to impress people with one's abilities or experiences. A hyperbole is used to impress people with an important truth.)
3. Tell which word in each phrase should be capitalized. If no word needs a capital letter, say *none*.
    a. living in the northeast (Northeast)
    b. eating kellogg's corn flakes (Kellogg's)
    c. the high school in elkton (Elkton)
    d. happened in the spring (none)
    e. studying algebra and spanish (Spanish)
    f. my uncle on the home farm (none)
4. Tell where commas are needed in the following sentences. (Commas are underlined.)
    a. Moses, the son of Pharaoh's daughter, chose to suffer with God's people.
    b. Because of Pharaoh's anger, Moses fled to Midian.
    c. Moses, I have heard the groanings of My people, and I am sending you to deliver them.

in trees, grown up in briers, or a hundred other things. But when the reader sees *vineyard,* he knows immediately that the land is planted in grapevines.

Sometimes there is no single noun that tells exactly what we want to say. In those cases we must use descriptive adjectives to clarify the nouns we use. But we should not write a general noun with an adjective when we could use a specific noun to say exactly what we mean. Look at the following sentences. In which one could the underlined expression be replaced by a specific noun?

The rich man lived in a <u>very large, expensive house</u> beside the lake.
The shelves of the <u>produce stand</u> were loaded with vegetables.

No single noun means the same as *produce stand.* But the single noun *mansion* means the same as *very large, expensive house,* so it should be used to replace those words.

Even when you have chosen exact nouns, you should include the *expressive adjectives* that are needed to make your writing clear and interesting. In the example above, the shelves of the produce stand were loaded with vegetables. What kind of vegetables? Dry, tasteless vegetables? Fresh vegetables? Many colorful vegetables? Be specific. Better yet, tell exactly what vegetables were there. Note how much more descriptive the following sentence is than the one above.

The shelves of the <u>small</u> produce stand were loaded with <u>fresh corn, crisp green beans, and ripe red tomatoes.</u>

Another way to paint colorful pictures is by using *lively verbs.* Vivid images are conveyed much better by strong action verbs than by linking verbs, verbs in the passive voice, or weak action verbs modified by adverbs. Look at the following sentence, which contains a linking verb.

The sky <u>was</u> deep blue and cloudless.

Even though the descriptive words *deep blue* and *cloudless* are used, the verb *was* lacks life. How can we get some action into the sentence? The following reworded sentence also tells about the deep blue and cloudless sky, but it is more interesting because it includes an action verb.

Not one cloud <u>drifted</u> across the deep blue sky.

Here are two more sentences with weak verbs, along with the improved sentences.

Poor: Weak verbs
The small creek <u>was spanned</u> by a quaint covered bridge. (passive voice)
As the car <u>came slowly</u> to a stop before our house, its horn <u>blew</u>

Lesson Introduction: Read the following paragraphs. If they were the opening paragraphs of stories, which story would promise to be more interesting? Why?

As Marjorie stood on the porch steps, she looked at the evening sky. The sunset had almost faded away. A few stars shone in the sky.

*   *   *   *   *

As Marjorie stood on the porch steps, she glanced up at the darkening sky. The last tints of the fast-fading sunset still glowed on the western horizon. A few stars twinkled bravely overhead.

Lesson Outline:

1. Descriptive writing paints colorful word pictures.
   a. It describes a scene or a happening.
   b. The details should be given clearly and specifically.
   c. The description should be vivid and sparkling.

2. Exact nouns help to paint clear, specific pictures. Do not write a general noun with an adjective if a specific noun says what you mean.

3. Expressive adjectives clarify nouns. Include the adjectives that are needed to make your writing clear and interesting.

4. Lively verbs help to paint colorful pictures. Vivid images are conveyed much better by strong action verbs than by linking verbs, verbs in the passive voice, or weak action verbs modified by adverbs.

5. Figurative language puts rich sparkle into descriptive writing.

loudly for attention. (weak action verbs modified by adverbs)
Improved: Lively verbs
    A quaint covered bridge <u>spanned</u> the small creek. (active voice)
    As the car <u>drifted</u> to a stop before our house, its horn <u>blared</u> for
        attention. (exact verbs that need no modifiers)

Well-chosen adjectives and adverbs also add color to your writing.
Adverbs of degree should be used sparingly. Usually a single expressive
adjective or adverb can replace a weak one modified by an adverb of degree.

Poor: Adjective modified by an adverb of degree
    Because of the <u>extremely cold</u> wind, the skaters soon left the ice.
Improved: Expressive adjective
    Because of the <u>bitter</u> wind, the skaters soon left the ice.

A device that puts rich sparkle into descriptive writing is *figurative language*. In Lesson 69 you studied similes, metaphors, personification, and
hyperboles. These figures of speech not only add appealing variety but also
paint specific pictures by their effective comparisons. Do you agree that
the second description here is more interesting than the first one?

Fair: Simple description
    Lois Ann swallowed. She took several deep breaths. Her feet felt
        heavy, and her heart beat rapidly as she slowly approached
        the dark house.
Improved: Description with figurative language
    Lois Ann swallowed. She took several deep breaths. Her feet felt
        like heavy rocks, and her heart fluttered like a trapped spar-
        row as she slowly approached the dark house.

Read the following paragraph, in which some of the descriptive wording is underlined. You should be able to identify each item as an exact noun,
an action verb, a descriptive adjective, or figurative language.

By late afternoon, black <u>thunderheads</u> were <u>rolling</u> in from the
west. One <u>bolt of lightning</u> after another <u>flashed its brilliant search-
light</u> across the <u>thirsty</u> fields as the farmer <u>trudged</u> toward his <u>rustic
cabin</u>. Soon the first drops of rain were <u>splattering</u> his <u>dusty hat</u> and
streaking his <u>sweat-stained shirt</u>. By the time he reached the <u>sagging
porch</u>, the <u>rain was a waterfall</u> <u>pounding</u> on the <u>cabin roof</u>. "Helen,"
he called to his <u>young wife</u>, "thank God, the rain has come!"

Class Practice

A. Give an exact noun or lively verb for each underlined word or phrase.
    1. Sirens <u>made a lot of noise</u> as the <u>vehicles</u> <u>went</u> to the fire.
    2. A small creek <u>flowed</u> down the mountainside.

Lesson 73 Answers

Class Practice
A. (Sample answers.)
    1. wailed, screamed; fire trucks;
        raced, rushed, sped, hurried
    2. tumbled, cascaded, splashed, twisted

3. A <u>bunch of animals</u> stampeded across the open <u>flat land</u>.
4. As Sarah <u>came</u> through the door, her <u>things</u> <u>went</u> out of her hands.
5. The children talked in <u>very quiet voices</u> while Mother <u>was</u> on the couch.
6. The <u>birds</u> cooed to each other from the roof of the <u>building</u>.

B. Think of a figurative way to describe each action.
1. A teakettle making noise because of boiling water inside.
2. A narrow trail twisting and turning down a mountain.
3. Leaves swirling about in the wind.
4. A large oak tree standing beside a small cottage.

Written Exercises

A. Write a sentence describing each of these items, using exact nouns and lively verbs. Use figurative language for at least two of them.
1. a snowy day
2. a skyscraper
3. an April afternoon
4. a pleasant classroom
5. a rooster

B. Write a descriptive paragraph about one of these subjects, using exact nouns and expressive verbs. Use figurative language in at least one sentence.
1. a waterfall
2. a young child
3. an old truck
4. a flower garden

Review Exercises

A. Write the letter of the sentence with correct capitalization. [20]
1. a. Jesus is the son of God.
   b. Jesus is the Son of God.
2. a. Our family is planning a trip to the Southwest.
   b. Our family is planning a trip to the southwest.
3. a. School begins in the fall.
   b. School begins in the Fall.
4. a. We finished the chores before my Father and Mother came home.
   b. We finished the chores before my father and mother came home.
5. a. We bought a new Sunbeam mixer.
   b. We bought a new Sunbeam Mixer.
6. a. Our Music class comes just before the last recess.
   b. Our music class comes just before the last recess.

B. Write the letter of the sentence with correct punctuation. [7, 14, 15]
1. a. God may not always give us what we want, but He does give us what is best for us.

---

3. herd of buffalo (*or* caribou, elk); prairie, plain
4. rushed, stumbled; books, dishes, shoes; flew, dropped
5. whispers; lay, rested, slept
6. pigeons, doves; barn, shed, church, school

B. (Sample answers.)
1. A teakettle whistled merrily.
2. A narrow trail snaked down a mountain.
3. Leaves were playing tag in the wind.
4. A large oak spread its branches protectingly over a small cottage.

Written Exercises

A. (Individual work.)

B. (Individual work.)

Review Exercises

A. 1. b
   2. a
   3. a
   4. b
   5. a
   6. b

B. 1. a

b. God may not always give us what we want but He does give us what is best for us.

2. a. Peter one of the twelve disciples, was also called Cephas.

   b. Peter, one of the twelve disciples, was also called Cephas.

3. a. Do you know, Karen, which is the longest book in the Bible?

   b. Do you know, Karen which is the longest book in the Bible?

4. a. While we children shelled peas Grandfather told us stories from his childhood.

   b. While we children shelled peas, Grandfather told us stories from his childhood.

5. a. Father filled the fuel tank, and checked the oil.

   b. Father filled the fuel tank and checked the oil.

2. b

3. a

4. b

5. b

---

74. Adjective Phrases

> **Lesson Survey**
> - An **adjective phrase** may be a **prepositional phrase, a participial phrase,** or an **infinitive phrase.**
> - When a verbal phrase is diagramed, a direct object is placed on the line after the verbal, with a vertical line in between. Any adverb modifier is placed under the verbal.
> - Be careful to avoid misplaced adjective phrases.

You have learned that a phrase is a group of related words that has no subject or predicate and that functions as one part of speech. An *adjective phrase,* then, is a group of related words that modifies a noun or pronoun. Three kinds of phrases can function as adjectives: prepositional phrases, participial phrases, and infinitive phrases.

Prepositional Phrases

A *prepositional phrase* can serve as an adjective. Remember that a prepositional phrase begins with a preposition and ends with the object of the preposition. The phrase includes all the words in between, which modify the object of the preposition.

A prepositional phrase used as an adjective always comes right after the noun or pronoun it modifies. It usually tells *which* or *what kind of.*

Lesson 74

Purpose: (1) To identify prepositional phrases used as adjectives, and *verbal phrases used as adjectives. (2) To show the error of misplaced adjective phrases.

Oral Review:

1. A present participle always ends with ———. (*-ing*)
2. A past participle usually ends with ———. (*-ed*)
3. What is an infinitive? (the word *to* and the basic form of a verb)
4. Identify the participles in these sentences. (Participles are underlined.)
   a. The wind, <u>howling</u> and <u>shrieking</u>, piled the <u>falling</u> snow into huge drifts.
   b. What an <u>amazing</u> sight were the <u>drifted</u> roads!
5. Identify the infinitives in these sentences. (Infinitives are underlined.)
   a. The potatoes <u>to sprout</u> are in the root cellar.

b. Anita has a new kitten <u>to hold</u> and <u>to enjoy</u>.

6. Spell (or write on the board) the singular possessive, the plural, and the plural possessive form of each word.
   a. larva (larva's, larvae, larvae's)
   b. workman (workman's, workmen, workmen's)
   c. sister (sister's, sisters, sisters')
   d. pony (pony's, ponies, ponies')

Lesson Introduction: Write this pair of sentences on the board.

> The girl in the blue sweater is my cousin.
> The girl wearing the blue sweater is my cousin.

Ask the following questions.

> Do the sentences suggest the same picture or different pictures? (same)
> Read the phrase modifying *girl* in the first sentence. (*in the blue sweater*)

The angel of God brought the shepherds in the field a message of hope.

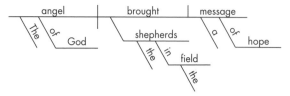

Anyone with a servant's heart can be a helper of great value.

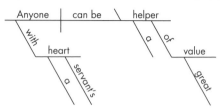

In the examples above, the phrases all modify basic sentence parts (subjects and complements). A prepositional phrase used as an adjective can also modify the object of a preceding prepositional phrase.

The faithful examples of the saints in the past inspire us.
   (*In the past* is diagramed under *saints* because it tells *which* saints.)

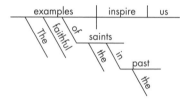

Moses fled into the land of Midian.
   (*Of Midian* is diagramed under *land* because it tells *which* land.)

What kind of phrase is it? (prepositional)
Read the similar phrase modifying *girl* in the second sentence. (*wearing the blue sweater*)
What kind of word is *wearing*? Remember Lesson 72. (participle)
Can you tell what kind of phrase this is? (participial phrase)

This lesson teaches three kinds of adjective phrases. The sentences on the board contain two of those kinds.

Lesson Outline:

   1. A prepositional phrase can serve as an adjective.
      a. A prepositional phrase begins with a preposition, ends with the object of the preposition, and includes all the words in between.
      b. A prepositional phrase used as an adjective always comes right after the noun or pronoun it modifies. It usually tells *which* or *what kind of.*

   2. A participial phrase serves as an adjective.
      a. A participle is either a present participle (*-ing* form of a verb) or a past participle (third principal part of a verb).
      b. A participial phrase is a participle with all its modifiers and complements.

   3. An infinitive phrase can serve as an adjective.
      a. An infinitive phrase is an infinitive with all its modifiers and complements.
      b. An infinitive phrase is not always an adjective. It may be a noun or an adverb.

Participial Phrases

A *participial phrase* serves as an adjective. A participle, as you studied in Lesson 72, is either a present participle, such as *doing,* or a past participle, such as *done.* Since participles are verb forms, they can have adverb modifiers and object complements. A participial phrase is a participle with all its modifiers and complements.

Singing, the girls cleaned the kitchen. (participle modifying *girls*)
Singing cheerfully, the girls cleaned the kitchen.
(participial phrase modifying *girls* and including adverb)
Singing songs cheerfully, the girls cleaned the kitchen.
(participial phrase modifying *girls* and including complement
and adverb)

Each sentence above begins with a participle or participial phrase modifying the subject. Of course, participial phrases can modify nouns and pronouns anywhere in a sentence.

We watched the clouds floating overhead.
(participial phrase modifying direct object)
The first story, written carefully, is a good one.
(participial phrase modifying subject)
The Gospel is a message bringing hope and cheer.
(participial phrase modifying predicate nominative)

Infinitive Phrases

An *infinitive phrase* can serve as an adjective. Like the participial phrase, an infinitive phrase is an infinitive with all its modifiers and complements.

Grandfather has a story to tell. (infinitive modifying *story*)
Grandfather has a story to tell now.
(infinitive phrase modifying *story* and including adverb)
Grandfather has a story to tell us now.
(infinitive phrase modifying *story* and including adverb and complement)

An infinitive phrase, like a participial phrase, can modify a noun or pronoun anywhere in the sentence.

The paper to give Father is in this envelope.
(infinitive phrase modifying subject)
Lynette's sketch is the best one to use here.
(infinitive phrase modifying predicate nominative)

An infinitive phrase, like an infinitive, is not always an adjective. It

4. **A verbal is always diagramed across the angle of a slanting and a horizontal line.**
   a. A direct object of the verbal is diagramed on the line after it, with a vertical line in between.
   b. Each modifier of the verbal or its object is placed on a slanted line beneath the word it modifies.

5. **Be careful to avoid misplaced adjective phrases.** A misplaced phrase appears to modify the wrong word in the sentence.

★ **EXTRA PRACTICE**
Worksheet 40 (*Adjective Phrases*)

may be a noun (as you studied in Chapter 3), or it may be an adverb. But remember: An infinitive phrase used as an adjective always modifies a noun or pronoun, and it always comes right after that noun or pronoun.

Look at each of the following sentences. Is the underlined phrase used as an adjective or as some other part of speech?

Problem: We love <u>to sing praises</u>.
Think: Does *to sing praises* follow and modify a noun or pronoun? (no)
Solution: <u>To sing praises</u> is not an adjective but a noun (direct object).

Problem: We have many reasons <u>to praise God</u>.
Think: Does *to praise God* follow and modify a noun or pronoun? (yes)
Solution: <u>To praise God</u> is an adjective (modifies direct object).

Problem: <u>To remove this rock</u> may take all afternoon.
Think: Does *To remove this rock* follow and modify a noun or pronoun? (no)
Solution: <u>To remove this rock</u> is not an adjective but a noun (subject).

Remember that a verbal is always diagramed across the angle of a slanting and a horizontal line. A direct object of the verbal is diagramed on the line after it, with a vertical line in between. Each modifier of the verbal or its object is placed on a slanted line beneath the word it modifies.

The boys, <u>seeing their mistake</u>, were sorry. (present participle with direct object)

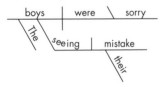

Bring in all those boots <u>left outside</u>. (past participle with adverb)

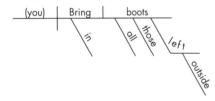

Paul's courage <u>to preach the Gospel</u> inspired others. (infinitive with direct object)

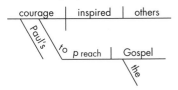

These are the mottoes <u>to be lettered today</u>. (infinitive with adverb modifier)

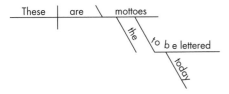

Misplaced Phrases

A misplaced phrase is one that appears to modify the wrong word. It is easy to misplace adjective phrases. To avoid this, you must place every adjective phrase right before or after the word it modifies. Look at these examples.

Misplaced:
The box was given to the man <u>with several songbooks inside</u>.
(The man did not have several songbooks inside.)
Two girls handed out the candy <u>in blue sweaters</u>.
(The candy was not in blue sweaters.)
The children drew sketches of the playful lambs <u>sitting outside</u>.
(The lambs were not sitting outside.)
We saw much trash on the ground <u>to pick up</u>.
(The ground was not to be picked up.)

Clear:
The box <u>with several songbooks inside</u> was given to the man.
Two girls <u>in blue sweaters</u> handed out the candy.
<u>Sitting outside</u>, the children drew sketches of the playful lambs.
On the ground we saw much trash <u>to pick up</u>.

In the last example, the adverb phrase *on the ground* is moved to the beginning of the sentence. This allows the infinitive phrase to come right after the word it modifies.

Class Practice

A. Read each prepositional phrase used as an adjective, and tell what word it modifies.
  1. The first king of Israel came from the tribe of Benjamin.
  2. Melanie's reputation for thoughtfulness is well deserved.
  3. The shelves in the basement were loaded with jars of food.
  4. In the bucket on the porch are two large bass from the pond.

B. Read each participial phrase, and tell what word it modifies.
  1. Sitting at Jesus' feet, Mary had chosen the better part.
  2. John the Baptist, preaching repentance, prepared the way for Christ.
  3. Persecuting the church, Saul tried to stamp out Christianity.
  4. The dog snapped at the kitten climbing a tree.

C. Read each infinitive phrase used as an adjective, and tell what word it modifies.
  1. "They cried, but there was none to save them."
  2. Abram was not a man to enjoy strife.
  3. In His life, Jesus pointed man to the Father; in His death, He made a way to redeem man.
  4. The Bible is a book to read daily.

D. On the chalkboard, diagram these sentences.
  1. Hardening his heart, Pharaoh pursued the Israelites.
  2. The man from France painted that picture on the wall.
  3. You must correct the problems marked wrong.
  4. Father left instructions to do the chores.

Written Exercises

A. Copy each prepositional phrase used as an adjective, and the word it modifies.
  1. The prophet from Anathoth was the son of Hilkiah.
  2. No one with a careless attitude can serve the Lord acceptably.
  3. The book after Psalms is Proverbs, with its many wise sayings.
  4. Mother bought a motto with a saying about prayer.

B. Copy each participial phrase, and the word it modifies.
  1. An angel appeared to the shepherds watching their sheep.
  2. Grieved deeply, Jesus wept over Jerusalem.
  3. The man lying there was helped by the Good Samaritan.
  4. Following Christ's example, Stephen prayed for his persecutors.
  5. The water flowing past us will finally reach the ocean.
  6. Chattering excitedly, the children quickly finished their work.

Lesson 74 Answers

Class Practice

A. 1. of Israel—king; of Benjamin—tribe (*From the tribe* is an adverb phrase.)
  2. for thoughtfulness—reputation
  3. in the basement—shelves; of food—jars
  4. on the porch—bucket; from the pond—bass (*In the bucket* is an adverb phrase.)

B. 1. Sitting at Jesus' feet—Mary
  2. preaching repentance—John the Baptist
  3. Persecuting the church—Saul
  4. climbing a tree—kitten

C. 1. to save them—none
  2. to enjoy strife—man
  3. to redeem man—way
  4. to read daily—book

D. 1.
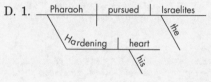

2.
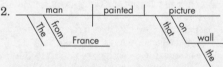

3.
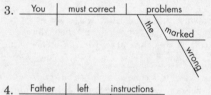

4.
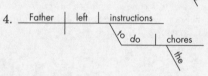

Written Exercises

A. 1. from Anathoth—prophet; of Hilkiah—son
  2. with a careless attitude—No one
  3. after Psalms—book;
     with its many wise sayings—Proverbs
  4. with a saying—motto; about prayer—saying

B. 1. watching their sheep—shepherds
  2. Grieved deeply—Jesus
  3. lying there—man
  4. Following Christ's example—Stephen
  5. flowing past us—water
  6. Chattering excitedly—children

C. Copy each infinitive phrase used as an adjective, and the word it modifies.
1. The Bible is a map to guide our way.
2. One habit to overcome daily is the tendency to laziness.
3. True wisdom to make proper choices is found in the Bible.
4. Paul's decision to serve Christ changed his life dramatically.
5. This looks like a good place to eat our lunch.
6. The boys caught some fish to fry later.

D. Diagram these sentences.
1. David was a man after God's own heart.
2. His ability to use a sling must have been remarkable.
3. Accepting Goliath's challenge, David faced the fearsome giant.
4. David, trusting God's help, defeated the Philistine.
5. The whole Israelite army gained the courage to fight valiantly.

E. Rewrite each sentence, putting the misplaced adjective phrase where it belongs.
1. The math problems were hard for the students on the chalkboard.
2. Sanded smoothly, Father brought the boards into the shop.
3. Mr. Jones delivered a load of feed to the farmer weighing a ton.
4. We gave the puppy to our neighbors with long ears.
5. Flying overhead, all the children watched the huge airplane.

Review Exercises

A. Write the plural forms of these nouns. Use the foreign spellings for numbers 7–10. [22, 23]
1. candy
2. eyetooth
3. salmon
4. ox
5. wolf
6. policeman
7. cactus
8. index
9. pupa
10. oasis

B. Rewrite these expressions, using possessive forms. Number 5 should indicate joint ownership, and number 6 should indicate separate ownership. [24]
1. the lowing of the cow
2. the cackling of the chickens
3. the neighing of the ponies
4. the efforts of the firemen
5. the rabbits of Jay and Ray
6. the notes of Vera and Mae

C. 1. to guide our way—map
2. to overcome daily—habit
3. to make proper choices—wisdom
4. to serve Christ—decision
5. to eat our lunch—place
6. to fry later—fish

D. 1.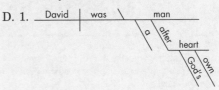

2.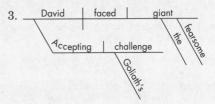

3.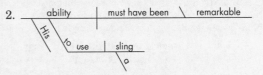

4.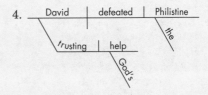

5.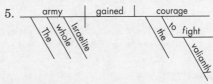

B. 1. the cow's lowing
2. the chickens' cackling
3. the ponies' neighing
4. the firemen's efforts
5. Jay and Ray's rabbits
6. Vera's and Mae's notes

E. (Repositioned phrases are underlined.)
1. The math problems <u>on the chalkboard</u> were hard for the students.
2. Father brought the boards, <u>sanded smoothly</u>, into the shop.
3. Mr. Jones delivered a load of feed <u>weighing a ton</u> to the farmer.
4. We gave the puppy <u>with long ears</u> to our neighbors.
5. All the children watched the huge airplane <u>flying overhead</u>.

Review Exercises

A. 1. candies
2. eyeteeth
3. salmon
4. oxen
5. wolves
6. policemen
7. cacti
8. indices
9. pupae
10. oases

75. Adjective Clauses

Lesson Survey
- An **adjective clause** is a dependent clause that modifies a noun or pronoun. It usually begins with a relative pronoun.
- An adjective clause is diagramed on a horizontal line below the independent clause, with a broken line connecting the relative pronoun to the word modified.

In Chapter 2 you learned that a clause is a group of words that contains a skeleton and functions as a specific part of a sentence. You also learned that an independent clause expresses a complete thought, but a dependent clause does not.

An *adjective clause* is a dependent clause that modifies a noun or pronoun. Notice that the following sentences both communicate the same basic idea. But the modifier of the italicized noun changes from a phrase to a clause.

> Daniel was a *man* <u>with great faith</u>. (adjective phrase)
> Daniel was a *man* <u>who had great faith</u>. (adjective clause)

Most adjective clauses begin with one of the relative pronouns: *who, whom, whose, which, that*. They are called *relative* pronouns because they *relate* the clause to a noun or pronoun in the main clause. The entire dependent clause is also called a *relative clause.*

> <u>Cornelius</u> <u>was</u> a centurion. (independent clause)
> <u>who</u> <u>prayed</u> often (dependent clause)
> Cornelius was a centurion <u>who prayed often</u>.
>   (Adjective clause tells *what kind of* centurion.)

> <u>This</u> <u>is</u> the day. (independent clause)
> which the <u>Lord</u> <u>hath made</u> (dependent clause)
> This is the day <u>which the Lord hath made</u>.
>   (Adjective clause tells *which* day.)

> The <u>man</u> <u>appealed</u> to Jesus. (independent clause)
> whose <u>son</u> <u>was</u> ill (dependent clause)
> The man <u>whose son was ill</u> appealed to Jesus.
>   (Adjective clause tells *which* man.)

Remember to use *who* and *whom* only for people and *which* only for things. *That* and *whose* may be used for people or things.

Incorrect:
> A <u>man</u> *which* came by gave us directions.

Lesson 75

Purpose: To teach the recognition and diagraming of adjective clauses.

Oral Review:
1. Tell what kind of adjective phrase modifies *road* in each sentence.
   a. The road over the mountains is icy this morning. (prepositional)
   b. It is not the best road to use today. (infinitive)
   c. This narrow road, winding through the mountains, is a scenic route. (participial)
2. Give the comparative and superlative forms of these adjectives.
   a. good (better, best)
   b. far (farther, farthest)
   c. near (nearer, nearest)
   d. many (more, most)
   e. ill (worse, worst)
   f. delightful (more delightful, most delightful)
   g. little, in amount (less, least)
   h. little, in size (littler, littlest)
3. Tell whether the adjectives *soft and fluffy* are in the attributive, appositive, or predicate position in these sentences.
   a. The kittens, soft and fluffy, settled peacefully in my lap. (appositive)
   b. These kittens are soft and fluffy. (predicate)
   c. The soft, fluffy kittens are hungry. (attributive)
4. Which verb in each pair is transitive?
   a. set, sit (set)   c. lay, lie (lay)
   b. raise, rise (raise)
5. Which verb expresses permission, *can* or *may*? (may)
6. Which verb is always used with another verb form, *let* or *leave*? (let)

The <u>goat</u> *whom* we bought must be penned up when Mother washes.
Correct:
A <u>man</u> *who* (or *that*) came by gave us directions.
The <u>goat</u> *which* (or *that*) we bought must be penned up when Mother washes.

A relative pronoun fills a specific function in a relative clause. The nominative case *who* should be used for the subject or predicate nominative in the clause, and the objective case *whom* should be used for the direct object, indirect object, or object of a preposition. The possessive case *whose* is a modifier in the adjective clause.

There is the little girl <u>*who* was setting</u> the table.
(*Who* is the subject in the adjective clause.)
The little girl *whom* <u>we met</u> was cheerful and friendly.
(*Whom* is the direct object in the adjective clause.)
She is the little girl *whose* <u>father</u> <u>is</u> the teacher.
(*Whose* is a modifier in the adjective clause.)

Sometimes the relative pronoun is not directly stated. Although it is omitted, its meaning is understood.

An idea <u>we find often in Proverbs</u> is that wisdom has great value.
(Meaning: An idea <u>which</u> we find often in Proverbs...)
Much of the wisdom <u>this world offers</u> is actually foolishness.
(Meaning: Much of the wisdom <u>that</u> this world offers...)

An adjective clause is diagramed on a horizontal line below the independent clause, with a broken line connecting the relative pronoun to the word modified. Be sure to determine the function of the relative pronoun within the clause. It may be a subject, direct object, predicate nominative, object of a preposition, or modifier.

People <u>who love the Lord</u> obey His commandments.
(The pronoun *who* is the subject in the adjective clause.)

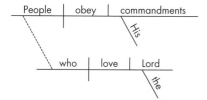

Lesson Introduction: Write the following sentences on the board.

This is a job for a patient girl.
This is a job for a girl with patience.
This is a job for a girl who has patience.

Have someone read the words that modify *girl* in each sentence. As you can see, a noun can be modified by a word, a phrase, or a clause.

Lesson Outline:
1. An adjective clause is a dependent clause that modifies a noun or pronoun. It usually begins with a relative pronoun, and it is also called a relative clause.
   a. The relative pronouns are *who, whom, whose, which,* and *that.*
   b. *Who* and *whom* should be used for people, and *which* for things. *That* and *whose* may be used for people or things.
   c. *Who* should be used for the subject or predicate nominative in the adjective clause, and *whom* for the direct object, indirect object, or the object of a preposition.
   d. Sometimes the relative pronoun is not stated, but understood.

2. An adjective clause is diagramed on a horizontal line below the independent clause, with a broken line connecting the relative pronoun to the word modified.
   a. Carefully determine the function of the relative pronoun within the clause.
   b. If the relative pronoun is not directly stated in the sentence, it is placed within parentheses on the diagram.

The God <u>whom we serve</u> hears our prayers.
(The pronoun *whom* is the direct object in the adjective clause.)

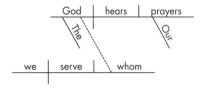

One <u>whose mind is disciplined</u> avoids many temptations.
(The pronoun *whose* modifies the subject in the adjective clause.)

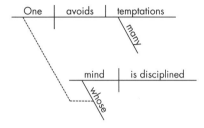

If the relative pronoun is not directly stated in the sentence, it is placed within parentheses on the diagram.

The book <u>you gave me</u> is interesting.
(The understood pronoun *that* is the direct object in the adjective clause.)

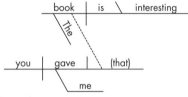

Class Practice

A. Read each adjective clause, and tell what word it modifies.
1. "But the path of the just is as the shining light, that shineth more and more unto the perfect day."
2. Commonplace decisions, which we make every day, determine the course that our lives will follow.

3. God, who cannot lie, will fulfill every promise that the Bible gives.
4. The picture that shows trotting horses was painted before cars were known.
5. The lesson we learned today was very costly.

B. Tell which relative pronouns are correct. Also give the function of the relative pronoun in each adjective clause.
1. The children had a dog (who, which) was lively and playful.
2. Uncle Jacob, (who, whom) we visited yesterday, is an invalid.
3. We spoke with a man (who, which) was touring our area.
4. Our neighbors, (who, whom) we have often invited to church, have come tonight.
5. They are the ones (who, whom) get milk and eggs from us.

C. On the chalkboard, diagram these sentences.
1. Jesus fed the people who were following Him.
2. The people whom Jesus fed were amazed.
3. The boy whose lunch fed the multitude would remember this event.
4. The bread that Jesus provided was the main attraction for many people.
5. The true bread we must seek is spiritual bread.

Written Exercises

A. Copy each adjective clause and the word it modifies.
1. "He that gathereth in summer is a wise son."
2. "Narrow is the way, which leadeth unto life."
3. Jesus died for a reason that everyone should understand.
4. The children saved the money they had earned.
5. We helped the family whose barn had burned.
6. Some boys whom we met in Maryland have written us a letter.
7. The farm that Uncle Benjamin bought is right next to our farm.
8. Helen, who is confined to a wheelchair, writes many stories and poems.

B. Write the correct pronoun for each sentence. Also write whether that pronoun is the subject (*S*), the direct object (*DO*), or a modifier (*M*) in the adjective clause.
1. Elymas was a man (who, whom, which) lived on the island of Cyprus.
2. This man, (whom, whose) other name was Bar-jesus, was a sorcerer.
3. Sergius Paulus, (who, whom, which) was a deputy, wanted to hear the Word of God.
4. Elymas tried to turn the deputy away from the faith (who, whom, which) Paul was preaching.
5. Paul severely rebuked the sorcerer, (who, whom, which) he called a child of the devil.

3. who cannot lie—God;
   that the Bible gives—promise
4. that shows trotting horses—picture
5. (that) we learned today—lesson

B. 1. which, subject   4. whom, direct object
   2. whom, direct object   5. who, subject
   3. who, subject

C. 1.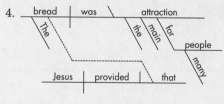

2.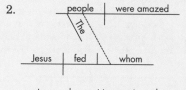

3.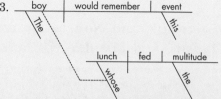

4.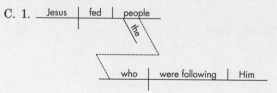

5.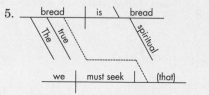

Written Exercises

A. 1. that gathereth in summer—He
   2. which leadeth unto life—way
   3. that everyone should understand—reason
   4. (that) they had earned—money
   5. whose barn had burned—family
   6. whom we met in Maryland—boys
   7. that Uncle Benjamin bought—farm
   8. who is confined to a wheelchair—Helen

B. 1. who—S   4. which—DO
   2. whose—M   5. whom—DO
   3. who—S

6. Sudden blindness fell upon this man (who, whom) Paul had denounced.
7. Sergius Paulus, (who, whom, which) was greatly astonished, believed in the Lord.

C. Diagram these sentences.
1. God's grace, which He has provided, is sufficient.
2. The lame man, whose body was healed, praised the Lord.
3. Father will buy the house that Grandfather owns.
4. The watermelons we bought were delicious.
5. The children were selling the melons that they had raised.

Review Exercises

Write the correct verbs. [49, 50]
1. Father said he would (let, leave) us use his tools for this project.
2. (Can, May) we please work inside that building?
3. Yes, if we (can, may) get the door open.
4. These boards have (laid, lain) out in the weather too long.
5. A great plume of black smoke (raised, rose) high into the air.
6. A large hawk is (setting, sitting) in the top of that dead tree.
7. It must (of, have) been there for half an hour already.
8. Hawks must (set, sit) for three weeks or more before their eggs hatch.

---

76. Restrictive and Nonrestrictive Clauses, and Misplaced Clauses

> **Lesson Survey**
> - A **restrictive adjective clause** is essential to the meaning of the sentence.
> - A **nonrestrictive adjective clause** is not essential to the meaning of the sentence.
> - Be careful to avoid misplaced adjective clauses.

Restrictive and Nonrestrictive Clauses

There are two classes of adjective clauses: restrictive and nonrestrictive. A *restrictive adjective clause* does exactly what its name indicates: it

Lesson 76

Purpose: (1) To teach the recognition and proper punctuation of *restrictive and nonrestrictive clauses. (2) To teach the avoidance of misplaced adjective clauses.

Oral Review:
1. What word usually introduces an adjective clause? (a relative pronoun: *who, whom, whose, which, that*)
2. Identify the relative pronouns that are described.
   a. They refer only to people. (who, whom)
   b. It refers only to things. (which)
   c. It refers to people or things. (that; *also* whose)
   d. It is used as a modifier. (whose)
3. Consider this sentence: *You are the one I want to see.*
   a. What is the adjective clause? (I want to see)

6. whom—DO
7. who—S

C. 1.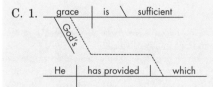

2.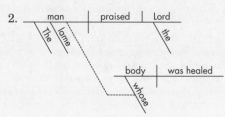

3.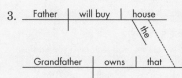

4.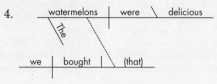

5.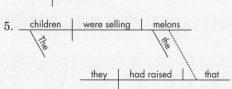

Review Exercises

1. let
2. May
3. can
4. lain
5. rose
6. sitting
7. have
8. set

---

b. What word is not stated, but understood? (whom *or* that)
c. How should the missing word be diagramed? (within parentheses)
4. Tell whether these sentences are simple, compound, or complex.
   a. "Wise men lay up knowledge: but the mouth of the foolish is near destruction." (compound)
   b. "He that loveth pleasure shall be a poor man." (complex)
   c. "The fear of the Lord is a fountain of life." (simple)

restricts the meaning of the noun or pronoun it modifies. Compare the meaning of the following noun with and without the adjective clause.

people
people <u>who love the Lord</u>

By itself, *people* refers to all human beings. But when *people* is followed by the clause *who love the Lord,* it refers to a much smaller group of human beings. Thus the adjective clause restricts, or limits, the meaning of the noun *people.* Now consider a sentence in which the noun and the restrictive clause are used together.

All people <u>who love the Lord</u> obey God's commandments.

Without the adjective clause, the sentence would say, "All people obey God's commandments." That statement is not even true. The adjective clause restricts the meaning of the noun so that the sentence is clear and accurate. It limits the noun *people* by telling *which* people obey God's commandments. The adjective clause is essential to the meaning of the sentence.

By contrast, a *nonrestrictive adjective clause* does not restrict the meaning of the noun or pronoun it modifies. The noun or pronoun means the same whether or not the adjective clause is used with it. Consider the following example.

Alvin Kline
Alvin Kline, <u>whom we brought along</u>

Does *whom we brought along* restrict the meaning of *Alvin Kline* by telling *which* Alvin Kline is meant? No, *Alvin Kline* refers to the same person whether or not an adjective clause is used. Therefore, the clause is nonrestrictive; it does not restrict the meaning of the noun it modifies. The clause merely gives additional information about the noun.

A nonrestrictive clause gives information that is nonessential to the meaning of a sentence. For this reason, it is set off by commas, the same as an appositive. But a restrictive clause contains information that is needed to make the meaning clear. Therefore, a restrictive clause is *not* set off by commas.

All people <u>who love the Lord</u> obey God's commandments. (restrictive)
Alvin Kline, <u>whom we brought along</u>, is our neighbor. (nonrestrictive)

It is not always easy to tell whether a clause is restrictive or nonrestrictive, but with careful thinking you can usually decide. Study the following examples.

The projects <u>that are finished</u> should be placed on the table.
    (Clause is needed to tell *which* projects. There are other projects,

Lesson Introduction: The Bible contains many statements that bring comfort and encouragement. But very few apply to all people unconditionally; most are restricted to those who meet certain requirements. Here are a few examples.

"Every one <u>that asketh</u> receiveth; and he <u>that seeketh</u> findeth" (Matthew 7:8).
"All things are possible to him <u>that believeth</u>" (Mark 9:23).
"All things work together for good to them <u>that love God</u>" (Romans 8:28).
"Every one <u>that doeth righteousness</u> is born of him" (1 John 2:29).
"He <u>that overcometh</u> shall inherit all things" (Revelation 21:7).

In each verse above, the condition is stated in a restrictive adjective clause (underlined). This lesson teaches restrictive and nonrestrictive clauses.

Lesson Outline:
  1. One kind of adjective clause is the restrictive clause.
      a. A restrictive clause restricts the meaning of the modified noun or pronoun.
      b. No commas are used to separate it from the rest of the sentence.

  2. Another kind of adjective clause is the nonrestrictive clause.
      a. A nonrestrictive clause merely gives additional information about the modified noun or pronoun.
      b. Commas are used to separate it from the rest of the sentence.

(*Teacher:* In deciding whether commas are needed, it is helpful to notice whether one pauses in reading

but they are not to be placed on the table. Clause is restrictive; should not be set off by commas.)

I admire my oldest brother, <u>who is learning to drive</u>.
    (Clause is not needed to tell *which* brother; I have only one oldest brother. Clause is nonrestrictive; should be set off by commas.)

The seventh graders, <u>who have just received their assignment</u>, are starting to do the written work.
    (Clause is not needed to tell *which* seventh graders; they have all received their assignment. Clause is nonrestrictive; should be set off by commas.)

The seventh graders <u>who failed the test</u> must correct their papers.
    (Clause is needed to tell *which* seventh graders; only those who failed the test are included. Clause is restrictive; should not be set off by commas.)

Misplaced Clauses

Be careful to avoid misplaced adjective clauses. An adjective clause should be placed immediately after the word it modifies, the same as an adjective phrase.

Misplaced:
The book was badly damaged that I left out in the rain.
The volcano is described in this article which erupted last week.

Clear:
The book that I left out in the rain was badly damaged.
The volcano which erupted last week is described in this article.

Class Practice

A. In each pair of sentences, tell which underlined clause is *restrictive* and which is *nonrestrictive*. Tell where commas are needed.

  1. a. The Bible <u>which we know is God's Word</u> is the most precious book.
      b. The Bible <u>that my parents gave me</u> is treasured in a special way.
  2. a. Mary Magdalene was the first person <u>who saw the risen Christ</u>.
      b. Mary Magdalene <u>who first saw the risen Christ</u> had gone to the tomb early that morning.
  3. a. Great-aunt Maggie <u>who is over ninety years old</u> still knits beautifully.
      b. A lady <u>who is over ninety years old</u> made this knitted scarf.
  4. a. Mother is mopping the floors <u>that were tracked with mud</u>.
      b. Mother is mopping the kitchen floor <u>which had been tracked with mud</u>.
  5. a. Henry <u>who lives next door</u> visits me often.
      b. The boy <u>who lives next door</u> visits me often.

Lesson 76 Answers

Class Practice

A. 1. a. nonrestrictive; Bible, Word,
      b. restrictive
   2. a. restrictive
      b. nonrestrictive; Magdalene, Christ,
   3. a. nonrestrictive; Maggie, old,
      b. restrictive
   4. a. restrictive
      b. nonrestrictive; floor,
   5. a. nonrestrictive; Henry, door,
      b. restrictive

a sentence with an adjective clause. Another clue is that if the modified noun is a proper noun, or if it is preceded by an adjective [not an article], the adjective clause is often nonrestrictive.)

3. Be careful to avoid misplaced adjective clauses. An adjective clause should be placed immediately after the word it modifies.

★ **EXTRA PRACTICE**
Worksheet 41 (*Adjective Clauses*)

B. The following sentences have misplaced clauses. Read them correctly.
1. The car was in a minor accident that has a dented fender.
2. This house is over one hundred years old which has beautiful stonework.
3. These boys live in Oklahoma, who are good friends of Leroy.
4. The tree was uprooted in the storm that my grandfather planted.
5. The service was postponed until the next week that was planned for Sunday evening.

Written Exercises

A. For each pair of sentences, write which underlined clause is restrictive (*R*) and which is nonrestrictive (*N*). Also write each word that should be followed by a comma, and add the comma.
1. a. God's Word <u>which He has preserved to our day</u> is unchanging.
   b. The words <u>which God spoke to Israel from Mount Sinai</u> were the Ten Commandments.
2. a. The disciples <u>whom Jesus took along to the Mount of Transfiguration</u> were Peter, James, and John.
   b. Peter, James, and John <u>whom Jesus took along to the Mount of Transfiguration</u> were His closest disciples.
3. a. Assyria <u>which God used to punish Israel</u> was once a great empire.
   b. The empire <u>which God used to punish Israel</u> was Assyria.
4. a. The queen <u>who threatened Elijah</u> was Jezebel.
   b. Elijah <u>who had boldly challenged the prophets of Baal</u> fled in fear.
5. a. Harold and James <u>whom you saw yesterday</u> were running an errand.
   b. The two boys <u>whom you saw yesterday</u> were running an errand.
6. a. The poem <u>that I recited</u> is not original with me.
   b. That poem <u>which I have recited several times</u> is not original with me.

B. The following sentences have misplaced clauses. Rewrite each sentence, placing the adjective clause where it belongs and adding any needed commas.
1. Father spotted the lost steer who was driving past the woods.
2. These apples taste delicious which George has sent us.
3. A woman was speaking to my sister whom I did not know.
4. The book was about toads and frogs that we read.
5. Carl quickly called the fire department who saw the smoke.

Review Exercises

A. Write whether each sentence is *simple, compound,* or *complex.* [14, 15]
1. The oranges looked delicious, but they were too expensive.
2. The oranges that looked delicious were too expensive.

B. (Repositioned clauses are underlined.)
1. The car <u>that has a dented fender</u> was in a minor accident.
2. This house, <u>which has beautiful stonework</u>, is over one hundred years old.
3. These boys, <u>who are good friends of Leroy</u>, live in Oklahoma.
4. The tree <u>that my grandfather planted</u> was uprooted in the storm.
5. The service <u>that was planned for Sunday evening</u> was postponed until the next week.

Written Exercises

A. 1. a. N; Word, day,
      b. R
   2. a. R
      b. N; John, Transfiguration,
   3. a. N; Assyria, Israel,
      b. R
   4. a. R
      b. N; Elijah, Baal,
   5. a. N; James, yesterday,
      b. R
   6. a. R
      b. N; poem, times,

B. 1. Father, who was driving past the woods, spotted the lost steer.
   2. These apples, which George has sent us, taste delicious. (Commas are optional.)
   3. A woman whom I did not know was speaking to my sister.
   4. The book that we read was about toads and frogs.
   5. Carl, who saw the smoke, quickly called the fire department.

Review Exercises

A. 1. compound
   2. complex

3. The man thanked us for our help and wanted to give us some money.
4. The man whom we helped wanted to give us some money.
5. Because the roads were drifted, school was canceled for two days.
6. Because of the heavy snow, school was canceled for two days.

B. Combine each pair of clauses into a compound or complex sentence, according to the directions in parentheses. [14, 15]
   1. The students were studying diligently. They were expecting a hard test. (complex sentence with adverb clause)
   2. We must pick the peas today. They will become too old. (compound sentence)
   3. It rained for two days. The creek did not overflow. (compound sentence)
   4. Stephen made the lamp. It is on the table. (complex sentence with adjective clause)

3. simple
4. complex
5. complex
6. simple

B. 1. The students were studying diligently because they were expecting a hard test. (Clauses may be transposed.)
   2. We must pick the peas today, or they will become too old.
   3. It rained for two days, but (or yet) the creek did not overflow.
   4. Stephen made the lamp that is on the table.

---

77. Using Adjectives Correctly

Lesson Survey

• Use an adjective only when it contributes something worthwhile.

• Use articles correctly in referring to one or more individuals.

• Do not use *a* or *an* after *kind of* or *sort of.*

• Do not use *this here, that there,* or *them* as adjectives.

• Use *less* to indicate *how much* about a singular noun, and *fewer* to indicate *how many* about a plural noun.

Adjectives fill an important role in our communication. But like other valuable things, they must be used properly. Here are some rules for the correct usage of adjectives.

1. *Use an adjective only when it contributes something worthwhile.* In the following expressions, the idea of each underlined adjective is included in the noun. These adjectives should be omitted because they add nothing to the meaning of the expressions.

> little midget (All midgets are little.)
> rich millionaire (All millionaires are rich.)

Sometimes a noun is modified by several adjectives that mean the same

Lesson 77

Purpose: To teach some additional rules for adjective usage.

Oral Review:
1. Name the five relative pronouns. (who, whom, whose, which, that)
2. Which may be needed to make a statement true: a restrictive or a nonrestrictive clause? (restrictive)
3. What does a nonrestrictive clause do? (gives additional information)
4. Which kind of adjective clause must be set off by commas? (nonrestrictive)
5. Name three kinds of phrases that may function as adjectives. (prepositional, participial, infinitive)
6. Name and describe the three degrees of comparison. (positive—modifies without comparison;

comparative—compares two items; superlative—compares more than two items)
7. Name and describe the three positions of adjectives. (attributive—comes just before the noun; appositive—comes right after the noun; predicate—comes after a linking verb and modifies the subject)

Lesson Introduction: Write the following sentences on the board.

> The three tired old horses plodded up the steep, winding, treacherous gravel trail.
> A tired, weary man carried a heavy, bulky backpack.

Do the students think these sentences are effective? Can they tell what is wrong with them? (The first one is "overstuffed with adjectives," and the second one uses repetitious adjectives.)

thing. Such repetition adds nothing worthwhile; it merely produces wordy language.

> a <u>brave, courageous</u> girl (*Brave* and *courageous* are synonyms.)
> the <u>big, huge</u> redwood tree (*Big* and *huge* are synonyms.)

Some adjectives fail to add any worthwhile meaning. They may be so overused that they are worn out, or they may be too general to add much meaning. Use fresh, descriptive adjectives that say exactly what you mean.

> an <u>awful</u> storm (terrifying? destructive? severe?)
> an <u>awful</u> mistake (embarrassing? shocking? serious? costly?)

> a <u>nice</u> gift (useful? rare? beautiful? practical?)
> a <u>nice</u> dog (friendly? gentle? beautiful?)

> a <u>real</u> surprise (actual? genuine? Or do you mean complete? pleasant?)
> a <u>real</u> story (actual? genuine? Or do you mean impressive? fascinating?)

In the following list are some more overused adjectives, with suggestions of more meaningful adjectives.

> **big:**   bulky, heavy, massive, mountainous, impressive, important
> **funny:** amusing, humorous, laughable, witty
>   (Do not use *funny* to mean "strange" or "unusual.")
> **good:** helpful, valuable, useful, profitable, interesting, excellent
> **great:** huge, strong, high, vast, notable, outstanding
>   (Do not use *great* to mean "excellent.")

2. *Use articles correctly in referring to one or more individuals.* When one individual is described by two adjectives or named by two nouns, use only one article.

> <u>The</u> rich and powerful king coveted Judah's wealth.
>   (one king who was both rich and powerful)
> <u>The</u> preacher and schoolteacher came for a visit.
>   (one person who was both a preacher and a schoolteacher)

When more than one individual is described by two adjectives or named by two nouns, use an article for each individual.

> <u>The</u> rich and <u>the</u> powerful king coveted Judah's wealth.
>   (two kings, one rich and one powerful)
> <u>The</u> preacher and <u>the</u> schoolteacher came for a visit.
>   (two persons, one a preacher and one a schoolteacher)

3. *Do not use* a *or* an *after* kind of *or* sort of.

Lesson Outline:

   1. Use an adjective only when it contributes something worthwhile.
   > a. Do not use an adjective to modify a noun if the noun includes the idea of the adjective.
   > b. Avoid the meaningless repetition of synonymous adjectives modifying one word.
   > c. Use fresh, descriptive adjectives that say exactly what you mean.

   2. Use articles correctly in referring to one or more individuals.
   > a. When one individual is described by two adjectives or named by two nouns, use only one article.
   > b. When more than one individual is described by two adjectives or named by two nouns, use an article for each individual.

   3. Do not use a *or* an *after* kind of *or* sort of.

   4. Do not use this here, that there, *or* them *as adjectives.*

   5. Use less *to indicate how much* about a singular noun, and *fewer to indicate* how many *about a plural noun.*

Incorrect:
> What <u>kind of a</u> tree was Lebanon famous for?
> Do not boast; that <u>sort of a</u> response indicates a proud heart.

Correct:
> What <u>kind of</u> tree was Lebanon famous for?
> Do not boast; that <u>sort of</u> response indicates a proud heart.

4. *Do not use* this here, that there, *or* them *as adjectives.*

Incorrect:
> <u>This here</u> command told Israel to destroy all the Canaanites.
> <u>That there</u> disobedience was a serious mistake.
> <u>Them</u> people later became a snare to Israel.

Correct:
> <u>This</u> command told Israel to destroy all the Canaanites.
> <u>That</u> disobedience was a serious mistake.
> <u>Those</u> people later became a snare to Israel.

5. *Use* less *to indicate* how much *about a singular noun, and* fewer *to indicate* how many *about a plural noun.* Avoid the common error of using *less* with plural nouns.

> We have <u>less cake</u> and <u>fewer cookies</u> than we had expected.

Incorrect:
> I had <u>less spelling words</u> wrong this week than last week.
> This pizza has <u>less mushrooms</u> than that one.

Correct:
> I had <u>fewer spelling words</u> wrong this week than last week.
> This pizza has <u>fewer mushrooms</u> than that one.

Class Practice

A. Read these sentences, omitting the unnecessary or repetitious adjectives.
   1. Zacchaeus was a small, little man.
   2. A poor, needy widow woman cast two mites into the treasury.
   3. The cold snow numbed our hands.
   4. The naughty, mischievous puppy chewed up the shoe.

B. Suggest several descriptive adjectives to replace each underlined adjective.
   1. Mark is a <u>nice</u> friend.
   2. It was an <u>awful</u> picture.
   3. Sharon's <u>funny</u> illustration made us laugh.

C. Tell whether the subject of each sentence is *singular* or *plural.*
   1. The kind and loving shepherd sought the lost lamb.
   2. The old and the young shepherd sought the lost lamb.

Lesson 77 Answers

Class Practice

A. (Corrections are marked.)
   1. Zacchaeus was a small (*or* little) man.
   2. A poor (*or* needy) widow ~~woman~~ cast two mites into the treasury.
   3. The ~~cold~~ snow numbed our hands.
   4. The naughty (*or* mischievous) puppy chewed up the shoe.

B. (Sample answers.)
   1. kind, thoughtful, affectionate, close
   2. shocking, horrifying, sloppy, messy
   3. amusing, humorous, comical

C. 1. singular
   2. plural

3. The hunter and trapper walked through the woods.
4. The gray and the white carpet had been cleaned.
5. A gray and white house stood by the roadside.

D. Read each sentence correctly. If the sentence has no mistake, say *correct*.
1. Them Egyptians pursued Israel right into the Red Sea.
2. What kind of a king was Jehoshaphat?
3. When that there donkey spoke to Balaam, he should have been shocked.
4. When Lot and his possessions were captured, Abram rescued them.
5. This here coat is Jonathan's.
6. Does William have less sheep than John?
7. Them horses galloped down the road.
8. Many nations have fewer cars per person than the United States does.
9. What sort of a plant is this?
10. We have less quizzes in math than in history.

Written Exercises

A. Copy each sentence, omitting the unnecessary or repetitious adjectives.
1. The old antique reminded Grandfather of his childhood.
2. This city has many tall skyscrapers.
3. The repair bill includes two costly, expensive parts.
4. The main part of this design includes five round circles.
5. This book has an attractive, appealing design.

B. Write a descriptive adjective to replace each underlined adjective.
1. Christopher Dock must have been a <u>great</u> teacher.
2. Being unable to read is a <u>real</u> disadvantage today.
3. After my fall, I had a <u>bad</u> headache for a while.
4. Lucy had a <u>big</u> decision to make before the next day of school.

C. Write whether the subject of each sentence is *singular* or *plural*.
1. The skilled singer and brave shepherd gained Jonathan's admiration.
2. The fugitive and the prince met in the woods.
3. The red-haired and the fair-skinned son of Isaac sought the blessing.
4. The brown and the blue songbook had been on the shelf.
5. The pink and orange tulip added to the beauty of the flower arrangement.

D. Rewrite enough of each sentence (two to four words) to show what words should be changed or omitted. If a sentence has no error, write *correct*.
1. What kind of an animal did Jesus ride into Jerusalem?
2. That there colt had never been ridden before.

3. singular   5. singular
4. plural

D. (Corrections are marked.)
1. <u>Those</u> Egyptians pursued Israel right into the Red Sea.
2. What kind of ~~a~~ king was Jehoshaphat?
3. When that ~~there~~ donkey spoke to Balaam, he should have been shocked.
4. correct
5. This ~~here~~ coat is Jonathan's.
6. Does William have <u>fewer</u> sheep than John?
7. <u>Those</u> horses galloped down the road.
8. correct
9. What sort of ~~a~~ plant is this?
10. We have <u>fewer</u> quizzes in math than in history.

Written Exercises

A. 1. The antique reminded Grandfather of his childhood.
2. This city has many skyscrapers.
3. The repair bill includes two expensive (*or* costly) parts.
4. The main part of this design includes five circles.
5. This book has an attractive (*or* appealing) design.

B. (Sample answers.)
1. excellent, effective, successful, noble
2. serious, major, extreme
3. severe, painful, serious
4. important, major, weighty

C. 1. singular   4. plural
2. plural   5. singular
3. plural

D. 1. kind of animal
2. That colt

3. Them Jewish leaders hated the honor Jesus was receiving.
4. A few days later, there were far fewer people honoring Jesus.
5. This sort of a flower needs plenty of water.
6. The raspberries in this patch have less berries than those.
7. I would like some of that kind of ice cream, please.
8. Where can we get some more of this here material?
9. Do you like them erasable ink pens?
10. Even Mr. Bates could not tell what kind of a bird we heard.

Review Exercises

A. Write the second and third principal parts of these verbs. [34]

1. think
2. burst
3. lay
4. drink
5. swing
6. run
7. tag
8. rise

B. Write the correct verb forms. [34, 50]

1. When God (blowed, blew) with a strong wind, the sea parted.
2. Though the Israelites had (went, gone) through the sea safely, the Egyptians did not.
3. The Egyptians were (drowned, drownded) in the Red Sea.
4. The strength of Egypt was effectively (broke, broken).
5. Have you ever (ran, run) in a relay race?
6. After the storm, we (drug, dragged) a lot of branches off the road.
7. The monkeys (swang, swung) from tree to tree.
8. Have you (wrote, written) your penmanship lesson yet?

3. Those Jewish leaders
4. correct
5. sort of flower
6. fewer berries
7. correct
8. this material
9. those erasable ink pens
10. kind of bird

Review Exercises

A. 1. thought, (have) thought
   2. burst, (have) burst
   3. laid, (have) laid
   4. drank, (have) drunk
   5. swung, (have) swung
   6. ran, (have) run
   7. tagged, (have) tagged
   8. rose, (have) risen

B. 1. blew
   2. gone
   3. drowned
   4. broken
   5. run
   6. dragged
   7. swung
   8. written

78. Writing a Descriptive Composition

Lesson Survey

- A descriptive composition describes a scene or an event.

- A descriptive composition uses exact nouns, lively verbs, and figurative language to paint a colorful picture.

- To write an effective description, you must choose specific details that produce the impression you want to make.

- When you describe a scene, organize your description by using spatial order.

Lesson 78

Purpose: To give practice with writing a descriptive composition.

Oral Review:

1. What are some things that help to make descriptive writing? (exact nouns, expressive verbs, and figures of speech)

2. Name four kinds of figures of speech. (simile, metaphor, personification, hyperbole)

3. Identify the figures of speech that have these descriptions.
   a. Speaking of a thing or quality as having human characteristics. (personification)
   b. Saying that one thing is another thing, or using literal terms to describe something that happened only in a figurative sense. (metaphor)
   c. Using a figurative exaggeration for the purpose of emphasis. (hyperbole)
   d. Making a figurative comparison by using *like* or *as*. (simile)

Lesson Introduction: Have you ever had to miss an exciting event because of illness or some other reason? Perhaps you were especially grateful for someone who took the time to describe for you, in words or in writing, what you missed. Maybe you were disappointed because you knew that the actual event had been far more interesting than the description you were given. The ability to describe vividly is an important composition skill.

Lesson Outline:

1. A descriptive composition describes a scene or an event.

In Lesson 73 you learned that descriptive writing uses exact nouns, lively verbs, and figurative language to paint a colorful picture. Now you may be asking, When do I write a descriptive composition? Often, descriptive writing is included within a story or some other kind of writing. For example, a person may write a story about something that happened when he was visiting his grandparents. When he writes about arriving there, he may use descriptive writing to tell about their home. This description will show the setting where his story takes place. The specific details will help to stir the reader's feelings and create a mood for the story.

Though description often makes up only part of a larger piece of writing, an entire composition may consist of description. Such a composition is not a story; it has no conflict, and it does not seek to teach a lesson. It simply describes a scene or an event in order to put clear, vivid pictures in the reader's mind.

A description of a scene will show a place or a physical object, such as a seashore, a house, or a school building. It will probably not describe much action taking place. A description of an event tells about something that is taking place. It may describe a barn fire, a public auction, or a visit to the dentist. In this kind of description, the writer shows as clearly and vividly as he can the various things that are happening.

To write descriptively, you must use many specific details. What shall you include? Use your senses. What do you see that is interesting and meaningful? Open your ears; what do you hear? Can you smell anything? Taste anything? Does your sense of touch contribute anything special? All these stimulations coming through your senses provide things that can be included in your description.

However, you should not write everything you can think of. You must be selective in the details you choose. Actually, writing a description is similar to writing a character sketch as you did in an earlier lesson. In writing a character sketch, your purpose is to leave a specific impression in the reader's mind; so you select details to give that impression. In the same way, a description should include only those details that contribute to one main impression.

Suppose, for example, that you are describing your grandparents' house. What impression do you want to give? Is their home a friendly, comfortable place? It probably is, so you should consider some details that make it that way. You may write about the aroma of freshly baked bread. (Your sense of smell picks this up!) You could tell about the worn recliner where Grandpa sits as he tells his interesting stories. (This involves your senses of sight and hearing.) Will you tell about their noisy refrigerator or their new vinyl floor covering? Not likely, unless these

2. A descriptive composition uses exact nouns, lively verbs, and figurative language to paint a colorful picture.

3. To write an effective description, you must choose specific details that produce the impression you want to make.

4. When you describe a scene, organize your description by using spatial order.

details somehow add to the feeling of warmth and comfort in their home. Remember: Select your details carefully so as to produce the one main impression you want to give.

Remember one other thing. If you are describing a scene, you should organize your description by using spatial order. Describe the scene from what is nearest to what is farthest away, from one side to the other, or in some other orderly way. Avoid jumping from one part of the scene to another in a disorganized way that will confuse the reader.

Now read the following descriptive composition, and notice the vivid, descriptive language that is used. Observe also how the entire composition serves to leave you with a single impression—the friendly appeal of the nighttime outdoors.

A Walk in the Night

It was bedtime on a warm, humid night after a day that had been even more sultry and oppressive. "We probably won't go right to sleep anyway in this heat," Father commented. "Why don't we take a little walk before we go to bed? Maybe it will be cooler by the time we come back."

An owl called enticingly from the woods as we followed Father out into the soft moonlight. A cool breeze fanned my cheeks and left the dampness of dew. Another breeze came to tease my hair, bringing a tempting whiff of peppermint from the tea bed.

My eyes rose to meet the gaze of the stars overhead. They seemed so wise up there. I searched among them to somehow capture their wisdom. I found only the Big Dipper.

We walked silently down the back lane, along the field where corn leaves rustled in the breeze. I could see nothing but a silvery rolling blackness like the rippling of a lake in a soft wind. Beyond the corn stood an inky mound of trees, their towering forms rising in unflinching, irresistible strength.

As we stood still in the darkness, the owl's challenging call sounded again, this time much closer. Then came a soft thud, promptly followed by a high-pitched squeak. I stared into the night but saw nothing. There! I caught the flick of a wing and a dark object sailing through the air. I grinned in the darkness. "Old Mouser" was getting his evening breakfast.

Finally we turned and retraced our steps. I drew a deep breath, savoring the sweetness of the honeysuckle that covered the fence. The soft grass tickled my bare feet as we approached the house. That stroll in the dark had been just what we needed to prepare for a good night's sleep.

Class Practice

A. In the sample description, find exact nouns that are used instead of the following general phrases.
1. a light wind
2. a slight smell
3. a dull sound
4. a bird
5. a high-pitched sound
6. a constellation
7. vines with fragrant flowers
8. a meal

B. Find the descriptive verbs or verbals that express the following ideas.
1. The owl seemed to invite the family outside.
2. The breeze blew across the author's face.
3. The author's eyes turned upward.
4. The moving corn leaves made a soft sound.
5. The corn leaves moved gently up and down. (two words)
6. The trees appeared tall.
7. The author tried to see the owl.
8. The owl moved swiftly through the air.
9. The author enjoyed a sweet smell.
10. The grass felt good to the author's feet.

C. Go through the composition by paragraphs, finding figures of speech. Tell which kind of figure each one is.

Written Exercises

Write a descriptive composition of at least three hundred words. Choose one of the following topics or one of your own that your teacher approves.
1. A trail through the forest
2. An airplane ride
3. A busy store
4. The lunch area at an all-day church service
5. A kitchen on a busy baking day
6. Sheep shearing
7. A cluttered bedroom

79. Chapter 7 Review

Class Practice

A. Give the term that fits each description.
1. An adjective that modifies a noun or pronoun by telling what kind of.

Lesson 79

Purpose: To review the concepts taught in Chapter 7.

2. An adjective that modifies a noun or pronoun by telling *which, whose,* or *how many.*
3. A number word that tells *how many.*
4. A number word that tells *which.*
5. An adjective that comes after a linking verb and modifies the subject.
6. An adjective that comes just before a noun.
7. An adjective that comes right after a noun.
8. A verbal used as an adjective, often ending with *-ing* or *-ed.*
9. A verbal that may be used as an adjective, consisting of *to* and the basic form of a verb.
10. An adjective clause that limits the meaning of a noun.
11. An adjective clause that simply gives additional information.
12. Speaking of a thing or quality as having human characteristics.
13. A figurative comparison that uses *like* or *as.*
14. A figurative exaggeration for the purpose of emphasis.
15. A figurative comparison that does not use *like* or *as.*

B. Form an adjective from each word by adding a suffix.
1. rock 3. comfort 5. offend
2. Bible 4. Mexico 6. trouble

C. Identify the adjectives in these sentences, and tell whether each is *descriptive* or *limiting.* Also tell in which position it is.
1. The bleating sheep outside told the prophet that Saul had sinned.
2. A godly person is peaceable toward other people.
3. The two children, excited and happy, will have first choice.

D. Give the comparative and superlative forms of these adjectives.
1. little, in size 3. close 5. dependable
2. bad 4. much 6. far

E. Read each adjective phrase, and tell whether it is a *prepositional,* a *participial,* or an *infinitive* phrase.
1. The multitudes, seeking the Master, took the road around the sea.
2. Traveling Palestine's dusty road, Jesus taught in many towns of Galilee.
3. Christ's purpose to redeem mankind was finally fulfilled in His willingness to shed His blood.

F. Read the adjective clauses. Tell which one of each pair is *restrictive* and which is *nonrestrictive.* Also tell where commas are needed.
1. a. Every student who applies himself diligently will receive great benefit from school.

---

2. limiting adjective
3. cardinal number
4. ordinal number
5. predicate adjective
6. attributive adjective
7. appositive adjective
8. participle
9. infinitive
10. restrictive clause
11. nonrestrictive clause
12. personification
13. simile
14. hyperbole
15. metaphor

B. 1. rocky, rocklike 4. Mexican
2. Biblical 5. offensive
3. comfortable 6. troublesome, troublous

C. 1. The—limiting, attributive;
bleating—descriptive, attributive;
outside—limiting *or* descriptive, appositive;
the—limiting, attributive
2. A—limiting, attributive;
godly—descriptive, attributive;
peaceable—descriptive, predicate;
other—limiting, attributive
3. The—limiting, attributive;
two—limiting, attributive;
excited—descriptive, appositive;
happy—descriptive, appositive;
first—limiting, attributive

D. 1. littler, littlest 5. more dependable,
2. worse, worst most dependable
3. closer, closest 6. farther, farthest
4. more, most

E. 1. seeking the Master—participial;
around the sea—prepositional
2. Traveling Palestine's dusty road—participial;
of Galilee—prepositional (*In many towns* is an adverb phrase.)
3. to redeem mankind—infinitive;
to shed His blood—infinitive (*In His willingness* is an adverb phrase.)

F. 1. a. who applies himself diligently, restrictive (no commas)

b. Little Clarence who is applying himself diligently will receive great benefit from school.

2. a. We appreciate our Christian school which promotes good study skills.

b. School is an institution which promotes good study skills.

3. a. Timothy whose mother and grandmother were godly women became a faithful church leader.

b. The young man whose father is a bishop has been ordained to the ministry.

G. Give several descriptive adjectives to replace each underlined adjective.
1. We had a <u>great</u> time when Uncle Lloyd's came.
2. Myra has an <u>awful</u> case of the flu.

H. Read these sentences, omitting the unnecessary or repetitious adjectives.
1. The hot molten iron was poured into some huge, enormous molds.
2. Several small dwarf apple trees stood in the back yard.

I. Tell whether the subject of each sentence is *singular* or *plural*.
1. The mechanic and writer found little time for hobbies.
2. The red and the blue dictionary could not be found.

J. Read each sentence correctly.
1. Robert brought the wrong kind of a wrench.
2. Them pigs have gotten out again.
3. Mother canned less pears than usual this year.
4. This here pear is one of the biggest I have ever seen.

K. Complete each sentence with the figure of speech indicated.
1. The puddle of water in the back yard became . . . (hyperbole)
2. The mountain range rose like . . . from the valley floor. (simile)
3. The . . . plants . . . the rain. (personification)
4. Lori's feet were . . . across the lawn. (metaphor)

Written Exercises

A. Copy each underlined adjective, and label it *D* for descriptive or *L* for limiting. Also write *AT* for attributive, *AP* for appositive, or *PR* for predicate.
1. <u>David's</u> actions, <u>decisive</u> and <u>courageous</u>, demonstrate <u>his</u> trust in God.
2. King Saul, <u>weak</u> and <u>fearful</u>, shows the <u>final</u> result of not trusting God.
3. Because of <u>the</u> courage of <u>one</u> man, the whole army became <u>courageous</u>.

B. Copy each word that should be followed by a comma, and add the comma.
1. Three young men helped to clean up the slimy smelly mud.
2. The windows old and worn-out will be replaced.

b. who is applying himself diligently, nonrestrictive, commas after *Clarence* and *diligently*

2. a. which promotes good study skills, nonrestrictive, comma after *school*

b. which promotes good study skills, restrictive (no comma)

3. a. whose mother and grandmother were godly women, nonrestrictive, commas after *Timothy* and *women*

b. whose father is a bishop, restrictive (no commas)

G. (Sample answers.)
1. interesting, exciting, pleasant, enjoyable
2. serious, severe, dangerous

H. 1. The molten iron was poured into some huge (*or* enormous) molds.
2. Several dwarf apple trees stood in the back yard.

I. 1. singular   2. plural

J. 1. Robert brought the wrong kind of wrench.
2. Those pigs have gotten out again.
3. Mother canned fewer pears than usual this year.
4. This pear is one of the biggest I have ever seen.

K. (Sample answers.)
1. an ocean; a lake; a sea   3. thirsty, drank in
2. a wall; a fortress   4. flying

Written Exercises

A. 1. David's—L, AT; decisive—D, AP; courageous—D, AP; his—L, AT
2. weak—D, AP; fearful—D, AP; final—D *or* L, AT
3. the—L, AT; one—L, AT; courageous—D, PR

B. 1. slimy,
2. windows, worn-out,

3. Monday morning sunny and cool held the promise of a pleasant enjoyable school trip.

C. Find each error in these sentences, and write enough words to show how the error should be corrected. If a sentence has no error, write *correct*.
1. Mother's cookies always get rounder than mine.
2. Who is tallest, Glen or James?
3. This peach ice cream is the goodest of all.
4. The blue can has the littlest oil in it.
5. These roses are more lovelier than mine.
6. It was the delightsomest day we had all summer.
7. The Bible states that this here earth will be burned up some day.
8. There have always been less people serving God than living for self.
9. What kind of tree did Zacchaeus climb?
10. Jezebel was furious to learn that them prophets had been killed.
11. These buns have less white flour and more whole-wheat flour than ours.
12. Do you know what sort of a tractor your grandfather had?
13. We were startled when that there quail burst up in front of us.
14. Did you get a good look at them bees with their full pollen baskets?

D. Identify each underlined adjective phrase as prepositional (*prep.*), participial (*part.*), or infinitive (*inf.*). Write *N* if it is not an adjective phrase.
1. Zacchaeus, (*a*) <u>repenting sincerely</u>, promised (*b*) <u>to make restitution</u>.
2. (*a*) <u>Serving the Lord</u> includes service (*b*) <u>to our fellow men</u>.
3. The cool air (*a*) <u>of the morning</u> was a pleasure (*b*) <u>to breathe deeply</u>.
4. A warm breeze, (*a*) <u>blowing gently</u>, brought strange smells (*b*) <u>to intrigue the dog</u>.

E. For each pair, write which underlined clause is restrictive (*R*) and which is nonrestrictive (*N*). Also write each word that should be followed by a comma, and add the comma.
1. a. The shepherd's keen vigilance <u>which he exercises day and night</u> is vital to the welfare of the sheep.
   b. The care <u>that a good shepherd gives his sheep</u> is symbolic of Jesus' care for His followers.
2. a. Easter is the day <u>that is observed in memory of Christ's resurrection</u>.
   b. The resurrection of Christ is commemorated on Easter <u>which comes on the first Sunday after the first full moon after the first day of spring</u>.
3. a. The students <u>whose assignments are finished</u> may do some work for Sister Thelma.

3. morning, cool, pleasant,

C. 1. more nearly round
2. taller
3. best
4. least
5. are lovelier
6. the most delightsome
7. this earth
8. fewer people
9. correct
10. those prophets
11. correct
12. sort of tractor
13. that quail
14. those bees

D. 1. a. part.   3. a. prep.
      b. N   b. inf.
   2. a. N   4. a. part.
      b. prep.   b. inf.

E. 1. a. N; vigilance, night,
      b. R
   2. a. R
      b. N; Easter,
   3. a. R

b. These students <u>whose assignments are finished</u> are doing some work for Sister Thelma.

7. Copy each sentence, putting the misplaced phrase or clause where it belongs.
1. Blowing across the school yard, I managed to catch the hat.
2. The cold drinks were very welcome that Mother brought to the garden.
3. Hidden behind a loose board, Karen found the nest of kittens.

3. Write a more exact noun or a more expressive verb for each underlined word.
1. When the <u>insects</u> came buzzing out, we <u>went</u> away at top speed.
2. We usually park that <u>thing</u> in this <u>building</u>.
3. Several horses <u>went</u> down the road.

4. Write what kind of figurative language is contained in each sentence.
1. A mountain of dishes was stacked on the counter top.
2. My head was spinning with all the strange words.
3. The children, chattering like excited squirrels, headed in from recess.
4. The briers reached out with sharp claws to hinder our progress.

. Diagram these sentences.
1. The tender shepherd watched his flock of sheep.
2. Romping friskily about, a lamb had left the safety of the flock.
3. A roaming bear saw something to eat!
4. The shepherd's quick actions to rescue the lamb were successful.

---

b. N; students, finished,

F. 1. I managed to catch the hat blowing across the school yard.
2. The cold drinks that Mother brought to the garden were very welcome.
3. Karen found the nest of kittens hidden behind a loose board.

G. (Sample answers.)
1. bumblebees, yellow jackets, hornets; dashed, ran
2. car, truck, tractor, riding mower; garage, shed, barn
3. walked, trotted, cantered, galloped

H. 1. hyperbole   3. simile
2. metaphor   4. personification

I. 1.

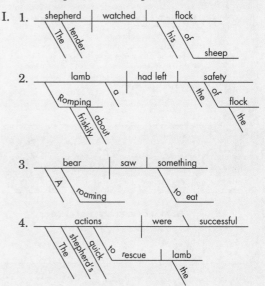

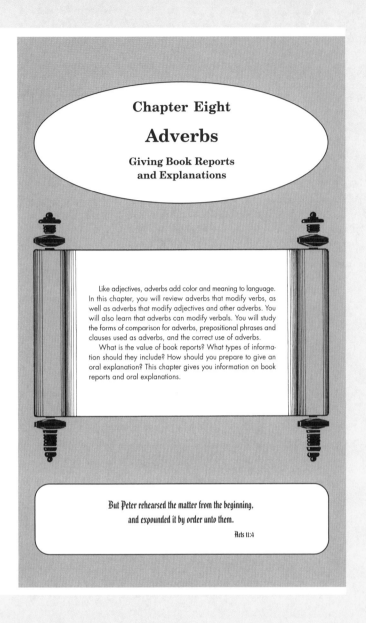

Chapter Eight

Adverbs

Giving Book Reports and Explanations

Like adjectives, adverbs add color and meaning to language. In this chapter, you will review adverbs that modify verbs, as well as adverbs that modify adjectives and other adverbs. You will also learn that adverbs can modify verbals. You will study the forms of comparison for adverbs, prepositional phrases and clauses used as adverbs, and the correct use of adverbs.

What is the value of book reports? What types of information should they include? How should you prepare to give an oral explanation? This chapter gives you information on book reports and oral explanations.

But Peter rehearsed the matter from the beginning,
and expounded it by order unto them.

Acts 11:4

80. Recognizing Adverbs

Lesson Survey

- Most **adverbs** modify verbs.
- An adverb of degree modifies an adjective or another adverb.
- An adverb may also modify a verbal.
- An adverb is diagrammed on a slanted line under the word it modifies.

Adverbs, like adjectives, are modifiers. Adjectives modify the "workhorse" nouns; adverbs modify the "workhorse" verbs.

Most *adverbs* modify verbs. They tell *how, when,* and *where* things happened or existed. Many adverbs, but not all, end with *-ly*. An adverb that modifies a verb may be placed at various positions. It may come right before or right after the verb it modifies. It may come at the beginning or the end of the sentence.

Elijah prayed <u>earnestly</u> to God.   <u>Earnestly</u> Elijah prayed to God.
Elijah <u>earnestly</u> prayed to God.   Elijah prayed to God <u>earnestly</u>.

The words *not, never, ever, almost, always, hardly, scarcely,* and *seldom* are always adverbs. These words often interrupt the verb phrases they modify.

God <u>can *never* lie</u>, for His Word <u>is *ever* settled</u> in heaven.
His promises <u>are *always* fulfilled</u>.

The words *how, when, where,* and *why* are also adverbs. They often introduce questions. Notice that when you answer questions beginning with these adverbs, you often replace them with other adverbs.

<u>How</u> did Micaiah answer the king? Micaiah answered the king <u>boldly</u>.
<u>When</u> should we pray? We should pray <u>daily</u>.

Adverbs of degree modify adjectives and other adverbs. They are called adverbs of degree because they answer the question *to what degree*. Adverbs of degree usually come immediately before the words they modify. The following words are commonly used as adverbs of degree.

very	somewhat	extremely
so	surely	especially
too	partly	dangerously
rather	unusually	thoroughly
quite		

Lesson 80

Purpose: (1) To define adverbs. (2) To teach their uses.

Oral Review:

1. What parts of speech do adjectives modify? (nouns, pronouns)
2. Name and describe the three positions of adjectives. (attributive—right before noun; appositive—right after noun; predicate—after linking verb, modifying subject)
3. If two descriptive adjectives are used before a noun, how can you tell when they should be separated by a comma? (when you pause between them in reading, when it sounds right to use *and* between them, when it sounds right to change the order of the adjectives)
4. What kind of adjective clause needs to be separated from the rest of the sentence with commas? (nonrestrictive)
5. Name the three kinds of word order found in sentences. (natural, inverted, mixed)
6. Tell which order is used for this sentence: *Smoothly the sled glided down the hill.* (mixed)
7. Now read that sentence in natural and inverted order. (*Natural:* The sled glided smoothly down the hill. *Inverted:* Smoothly down the hill glided the sled.)

Lesson Introduction: What is the root word of *adverb*? (verb) The verb may be considered the most important word in a sentence; it is the only part of speech that can make a complete sentence by itself. So the adverb, as it adds color and meaning to the verb, also fills an important place in the sentence.

In this chapter on adverbs, you will discover that adjectives and adverbs have a number of things in

Idol-worshiping neighbors were <u>dangerously</u> *deceptive* to Israel. (*Dangerously* tells *to what degree* about the predicate adjective *deceptive*.)

Israel's <u>partly</u> *successful* efforts did not destroy them all. (*Partly* tells *to what degree* about the adjective *successful*.)

The Israelites accommodated themselves <u>too</u> *well* to these enemies. (*Too* tells *to what degree* about the adverb *well*.)

Adverbs may also modify verbals. As you should recall, a verbal is a verb form used as another part of speech, but it still retains some characteristics of a verb. One such characteristic is that it can be modified by an adverb.

Verbal (gerund) used as a noun:
> <u>Thinking</u> *clearly* is important. (*Thinking clearly* is the subject. *Clearly* tells *how* about *thinking*.)

Verbal (infinitive) used as a noun:
> We plan <u>to leave</u> *soon*. (*To leave soon* is the direct object. *Soon* tells *when* about *to leave*.)

Verbal (participle) used as an adjective:
> <u>Pouncing</u> *quickly*, the cat caught the mouse. (*Pouncing quickly* modifies *cat*. *Quickly* tells *how* about *pouncing*.)

Verbal (infinitive) used as an adjective:
> We have much work <u>to do</u> *today*. (*To do today* modifies *work*. *Today* tells *when* about *to do*.)

Adverbs are diagramed on slanted lines beneath the words they modify. In the word *cannot* and in contractions with *n't*, the *not* or *n't* is diagramed separately as the adverb *not*.

God <u>graciously</u> answers our prayers. (adverb modifying verb)

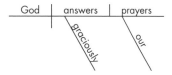

<u>Daily</u> God blesses us <u>richly</u> and <u>freely</u>. (compound adverb modifying verb)

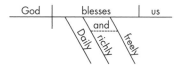

common. Both are modifiers; both may come as single words, as phrases, or as clauses; both have three degrees of comparison; and both need to be used sparingly.

Lesson Outline:
1. *Most adverbs modify verbs.*
   a. They tell *how, when,* and *where* things happened or existed.
   b. Many adverbs end with *-ly*.
   c. An adverb that modifies a verb can be placed right before the verb, right after the verb, at the beginning of the sentence, or at the end of the sentence.
   d. The words *not, never, ever, almost, always, hardly, scarcely,* and *seldom* are always adverbs, often interrupting the verb phrase.
   e. The words *how, when, where,* and *why* are also adverbs, often introducing questions.

2. *Adverbs of degree modify adjectives and other adverbs.*
   a. They answer the question *to what degree.*
   b. They usually come immediately before the words they modify.
   (*Teacher:* Adverbs of degree should be used sparingly, since they often do little more than add emphasis to other words that are not specific and meaningful. This point is taught in Lesson 73.)

3. *Adverbs may also modify verbals.* Verbals may be used as nouns (gerunds and infinitives) or as adjectives (participles and infinitives).
   (*Note:* An infinitive may itself be an adverb, as in the sentence *Jesus died to save us.* This point will be taught later.)

4. *Adverbs are diagramed on slanted lines beneath the words they modify.*

We <u>cannot</u> fully understand God's ways.   (adverb *not* or *n't*
We <u>can't</u> fully understand God's ways.   joined to verb)

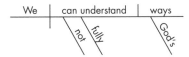

Praying <u>regularly</u> is important. (adverb modifying verbal)

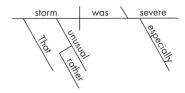

An adverb that modifies an adjective or another adverb is placed on a slanted line beneath the word it modifies. This also applies to a predicate adjective, which is diagramed on the base line.

Adverbs modifying adjective and predicate adjective:
That rather unusual storm was especially severe.

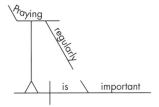

Adverb modifying another adverb:
I spoke too soon.

a. In the word *cannot* and in contractions with *n't,* the *not* or *n't* is diagramed separately as the adverb *not*.
b. An adverb that modifies an adjective or another adverb is placed on a slanted line under the word it modifies. This also applies to a predicate adjective, which is diagramed on the base line.

★ **EXTRA PRACTICE**
Worksheet 42 (*Recognizing Adverbs*)

Class Practice

A. Identify each single-word adverb, and tell what word it modifies.
1. Privately, Ananias and Sapphira agreed to a definitely dishonest plan.
2. They were punished very severely.
3. At Peter's words, they fell down and immediately died.
4. Wendell was always very friendly.
5. This exceptionally dull knife cannot be used effectively.
6. Roaming too freely, the dog had soon become a nuisance.
7. Eagerly the students went outside.
8. Where were they going so fast?

B. Tell whether each underlined adverb modifies a *verb,* an *adjective,* an *adverb,* or a *verbal.* Also tell what question it answers.
1. Jesus was <u>always</u> <u>entirely</u> submissive to the Father's will.
2. One reason for laying <u>down</u> His life was to defeat Satan <u>completely</u>.
3. <u>Finally</u> the smoke cleared <u>away</u>.
4. We learned to sing <u>correctly</u> in music class.
5. We <u>already</u> are doing it <u>much</u> <u>better</u>.
6. Looking <u>carefully</u>, we <u>finally</u> found a way to get <u>out</u>.

C. On the chalkboard, diagram these sentences.
1. Faithfully and bravely, Ehud led his people.
2. We cannot turn around now.
3. Slowly Henry trudged home.
4. Watching intently, the hawk almost immediately caught a mouse.
5. Someone failed to sweep the floor properly.

Written Exercises

A. Write each single-word adverb and the word it modifies.
1. Subtly but persistently, Satan led Eve into thinking wrongly.
2. The large buck moved very slowly through the exceptionally dense forest.
3. Indians have never lived here.
4. Ostriches cannot fly, but they can run quite fast.
5. The horns, blaring too loudly, easily attracted our attention.
6. Quite often, the children tenderly cuddled the baby.
7. How is the work coming today?
8. Yesterday we had scarcely begun.

B. Copy each underlined adverb, and write whether it modifies a *verb,* an *adjective,* an *adverb,* or a *verbal.* Also write what question it answers.
1. George Blaurock <u>often</u> preached <u>quite</u> <u>boldly</u>.
2. The temple was <u>completely</u> destroyed because Israel had sinned <u>grievously</u>.

Lesson 80 Answers

Class Practice

A. 1. Privately—agreed; definitely—dishonest
2. very—severely; severely—were punished
3. down—fell; immediately—died
4. always—was; very—friendly
5. exceptionally—dull; not—can be used; effectively—can be used
6. too—freely; freely—Roaming; soon—had become
7. Eagerly—went; outside—went
8. Where—were going; so—fast; fast—were going

B. 1. always—verb, when; entirely—adjective, to what degree
2. down—verbal, where; completely—verbal, how
3. Finally—verb, when; away—verb, where
4. correctly—verbal, how
5. already—verb, when; much—adverb, to what degree; better—verb, how
6. carefully—verbal, how; finally—verb, when; out—verbal, where

C. 1.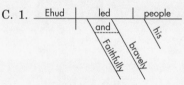

2.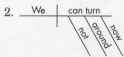

3.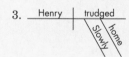

4.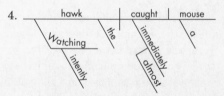

5.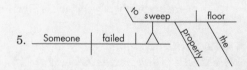

Written Exercises

A. 1. Subtly—led; persistently—led; wrongly—thinking
2. very—slowly; slowly—moved; exceptionally—dense
3. never—have lived; here—have lived
4. not—can fly; quite—fast; fast—can run
5. too—loudly; loudly—blaring; easily—attracted
6. Quite—often; often—cuddled; tenderly—cuddled
7. How—is coming; today—is coming
8. Yesterday—had begun; scarcely—had begun

B. 1. often—verb, when; quite—adverb, to what degree; boldly—verb, how
2. completely—verb, how; grievously—verb, how

3. <u>Softly</u> and <u>quietly</u>, the worshipers came <u>in</u>.
4. <u>Now</u> they are worshiping <u>reverently</u>.
5. Brother Paul remembered <u>perfectly</u> the names of each youth in the <u>rather</u> large group.
6. Practicing <u>regularly</u>, Mabel has learned to quilt <u>exceptionally</u> <u>well</u>.
7. Some of the quiz questions were <u>surprisingly</u> simple, but most of them were <u>quite</u> difficult.
8. Studying <u>diligently</u> is a requirement for learning <u>successfully</u>.

C. Diagram these sentences.
1. Very graciously, the Lord extends His mercy today.
2. The angels cannot fully understand redemption.
3. We are not planning to go away today.
4. Practicing daily, we memorized the poem almost perfectly.
5. These pancakes taste unusually sweet.

Review Exercises

A. Write whether each sentence has *natural*, *inverted*, or *mixed* word order. [11]
1. In all his sufferings, Job trusted God.
2. That trust preserved him in the time of severe testing.
3. Seldom have men been tested so severely.
4. Through this man's life was displayed the power of faith.
5. Job's faith meant Satan's defeat.

B. Rewrite each sentence in the order named in parentheses. [11]
1. A small pony stood under the old oak. (inverted)
2. The falling snowflakes swiftly covered the ground. (mixed)
3. Across the valley sounded the howl of a coyote. (natural)
4. Up in the haymow, the heat was almost unbearable. (natural)
5. A large rattlesnake lay under the rock. (inverted)
6. We worked in the garden after supper. (mixed)

C. Rewrite these sentences, removing the expletive *There*. [11]
1. There are many examples of faithfulness given in the Bible.
2. There came some wise men to Jerusalem, seeking the newborn King.
3. There is a song service planned for Sunday evening.
4. There are still too many weeds in the garden.

C. 1. Many examples of faithfulness are given in the Bible.
2. Some wise men came to Jerusalem, seeking the newborn King.
3. A song service is planned for Sunday evening.
4. Too many weeds are still in the garden.

3. Softly—verb, how; quietly—verb, how; in—verb, where
4. Now—verb, when; reverently—verb, how
5. perfectly—verb, how; rather—adjective, to what degree
6. regularly—verbal, how *or* when; exceptionally—adverb, to what degree; well—verbal, how
7. surprisingly—adjective, to what degree; quite—adjective, to what degree
8. diligently—verbal, how; successfully—verbal, how

C. 1.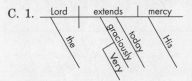

2.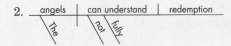

3.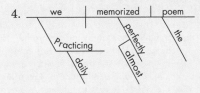

4.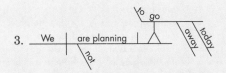

5.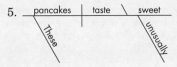

Review Exercises

A. 1. mixed   4. inverted
2. natural   5. natural
3. mixed

B. 1. Under the old oak stood a small pony.
2. Swiftly the falling snowflakes covered the ground.
3. The howl of a coyote sounded across the valley.
4. The heat was almost unbearable up in the haymow.
5. Under the rock lay a large rattlesnake.
6. After supper, we worked in the garden.

81. Writing a Book Report

Lesson Survey

- A **book report** should include the following kinds of information.
  1. Basic facts such as the title, author, and publisher.
  2. The setting of the story.
  3. The main characters and their characteristics.
  4. The theme and main events of the story.
  5. Lessons that can be learned from the story.
  6. An evaluation of the book.

- Use the following steps to write a book report.
  1. Read an approved book.
  2. List details for the six kinds of information to be included.
  3. Write your book report.
  4. Proofread your report.

In writing a *book report,* you do several things. First of all, you show how well you have actually read the book. You also share with others some of the enjoyment and inspiration that you received from the book. And if your book report is well written, it should stimulate in others a desire to read the book too.

Sample book report:

Basic facts

Tip Lewis and His Lamp is an old story, written by an author identified simply as "Pansy." The revised edition, copyrighted in 1987, was published by Rod and Staff Publishers.

Setting

The setting of the story is possibly the state of New York, as the city of Albany is mentioned. Several details suggest that the story took place quite a few years ago. There is no mention of cars, electricity, or other modern conveniences. And in school, the students used slates.

Main characters

The main character is Tip Lewis, whose first name was actually Edward. He lived in a poor, dirty house with his father, mother, younger sister, and younger brother. His father was sick in bed. His mother had to work to support the family, so she often seemed tired and cross. His sister Kitty was very short-tempered and irritable. Little Johnny was a neglected baby who died early in the story. Mr. Holbrook, the minister, and Mr. Burrows, the schoolteacher, helped Tip in many different ways.

The main theme of the story is how Tip Lewis learned to use the Bible as his lamp. A visiting teacher had come one

Lesson 81

Purpose: To teach how to write book reports for the purpose of inspiring others to read good books.

Oral Review:

1. Name the figure of speech that fits each description.
   a. It is an obvious exaggeration to emphasize a truth. (hyperbole)
   b. It compares two things without using *like* or *as.* (metaphor)
   c. It compares two things by using *like* or *as.* (simile)
   d. It refers to things or qualities as having human characteristics. (personification)

2. How is a hyperbole different from a simple exaggeration? (A hyperbole is used to impress people with an important truth, whereas an exaggeration

is used to impress people with one's abilities or experiences.)

3. Proofread these sentences, and mark the corrections. (Write the sentences on the board for pupils to correct.)
   a. We should learn to ~~right~~ carfully and neatly.
   b. Doing our best what God expects of us.
   c. We should beleive that what says God He means.

Lesson Introduction: Have you ever looked at a book, trying to decide whether it is worth reading? Perhaps you laid it aside, and later someone else described the book enthusiastically or gave a report about the book at school. You decided that at the next chance you would read the book. That is one purpose of a book report.

Theme and main events

Sunday and had told a story about another boy from an unhappy home, who became a Christian and later became a minister. This set Tip to thinking and longing to enjoy the beauties of heaven that the teacher had described. Some time later, after the funeral of his little brother Johnny, he prayed for the first time that God would help him to be different and to get to heaven where Johnny was.

But Tip Lewis had always been so full of mischief that he had a hard time convincing people that he was really different. When school started four weeks later, his friend Bob tried hard to drag him into the same wrongdoing that the two had been in before. In one case Tip was accused of throwing a paper ball, and the teacher would not believe his word against that of Ellis Holbrook, the minister's son.

However, people did notice the change in Tip. How did that change affect his home? How did it affect his school friends? What other struggles did he face? How did God bless his sincere efforts to do what he knew was right?

Lessons taught

Reading this book has helped me to appreciate a Christian home where I have been taught to know and love the Bible. I was impressed with the way Tip always found help by reading his Bible.

Evaluation of the book

Tip Lewis and His Lamp is a very interesting story. The author uses uncommon and humorous expressions. On getting out of bed, Tip Lewis said, "I wish getting up wasn't such hard work—spoils all the fun of going to bed." His room, his bed, and Tip himself are described as looking "about as bad as dust and rags and poverty could make them look." You will enjoy reading this fascinating and worthwhile book.

A book report should include six main kinds of information. Notice where the different kinds are found in the sample book report above.

First, you must give the basic facts about the book. Name the title, the author, the publisher, and the copyright date. Tell where the reader may be able to find the book.

The report should give some brief information about the setting of the story. The setting includes the place and time of the story. Does the story take place on a Pennsylvania farm, at a Guatemala mission, in a Swiss village, or deep in an African jungle? Does it occur in the early 1900s, in the middle 1800s, in Anabaptist times, in the time of Christ, or in the time of the judges of Israel?

A book report should describe the main characters—those who are the

Lesson Outline:

1. A book report should include six main kinds of information.

    a. The basic facts: the title, author, publisher, copyright date, and place to find the book

    b. The setting of the story, which includes the place and the time

    c. The main characters and their characteristics

    d. The theme and main events of the story
       1) This should be the largest part of the report.
       2) Show what the theme is by describing the main events rather than merely giving a general statement of the theme.
       3) Do not give away the outcome of the story.

    e. Some of the lessons or benefits you have received from the book

    f. Your own evaluation of the book
       1) Describe a part of the book you especially enjoyed.
       2) Give some examples of exceptionally descriptive language.
       3) Tell why others should read the book.

2. Use the following steps to write a book report.

    a. Read an approved book.
       1) Read the entire book carefully before you write your report.
       2) Discipline your mind to be alert for information to put into your report.

    b. List ideas for the six kinds of information that you should include.

    c. Write your report.
       1) Stick to your main ideas.
       2) Write the report in your own words.

most important to the main events and the outcome of the story. You do not need to write a character sketch of them, but you should give a few details that are especially important in understanding the theme of the story.

The largest part of a book report should describe the theme and main events of the story. The theme is the central idea or main thrust of the things that happen. Does the book show how nonresistant Christians responded to persecution or other threats? Does it describe the conflict the main character has in doing what he knows is right, even when severely tempted? Does it describe the main character's struggles to be a faithful, growing Christian? These are just a few of the many possible themes in worthwhile stories.

Your report must do more than merely give a general statement of the theme. It should also describe the main events in order to *show* what the theme is. However, be sure that you do not give away the outcome of the story. Leave your readers in suspense so that they will want to read the story too.

A good book is beneficial in that it teaches certain lessons. Does the book challenge you to be more patient, more respectful, more zealous, more thoughtful of others, more thankful for freedoms? Has it helped you to understand people in a different setting better than you did before? Has it helped you to understand the Bible better? Does it inspire you with the way in which God works to accomplish His purposes? Be sure to express those lessons or benefits in your book report.

Finally, your report should give your own evaluation of the book. Perhaps you can describe a part of the book that you especially enjoyed. Did the author use exceptionally descriptive language? Is there any other good reason why others should read the book?

Writing a book report is much like writing other forms of composition. You need to follow some definite steps. The first step, of course, is to read an approved book. Obviously, you cannot give an accurate, fair report on the book unless you have recently read the entire book. Reading a book to give a report on it is different from your normal, casual reading. You must discipline your mind to be alert for information to put into your report.

The second step is to list details and ideas for the six kinds of information that you should include. As with other forms of compositions, the success of the final product depends in part on the gathering and organizing of material before you start the actual writing.

After your ideas are organized, you are ready to write the report. Stick to the main ideas; do not attempt to rehearse the whole story. Write the report in your own words. Occasionally, you may quote directly from the book, but direct quotations should be few and short. Be sure to enclose quotations within quotation marks.

The final step is to proofread your report. Look for errors in spelling

      3) Keep direct quotations few and short. Use quotation marks.
   d. Proofread your report.
      1) Check for errors in spelling and grammar.
      2) Check for details of all six kinds of information.
      3) Ask yourself if your report will stimulate an interest in reading the book.
      4) Check whether you have given away the outcome of the story.

and grammar as you studied in Lesson 8. But also check your report with these questions.

1. Have I included all six kinds of information, with enough details for each?
2. Have I written my report in such a way that it will stimulate an interest in reading the book?
3. Have I avoided giving away the outcome of the story?

Class Practice

Answer these questions about book reports.

1. What are six kinds of information that you should include in a book report?
2. What two things are included in the setting?
3. What should be the largest part of the book report?
4. What one thing must you *not* give in a book report?
5. In what ways is writing a book report like writing any other composition?

Written Exercises

Write a report on an approved book that you have read recently.

---

82. Forms of Comparison for Adverbs

Lesson Survey

- Many adverbs have three degrees of comparison: **positive, comparative,** and **superlative.**

- The positive degree is the simplest form of an adverb.

- The comparative and superlative degrees are formed by adding *-er* and *-est*, by using *more* and *most*, or by using irregular forms of comparison.

- Use the positive degree to modify without making a comparison, the comparative degree to compare two actions, and the superlative degree to compare more than two actions.

- Do not make a double comparison by both adding *-er* or *-est* and using *more* or *most*. Do not change an adverb to an adjective in forming the comparative and superlative degrees.

Lesson 82

Purpose: To teach the three degrees of comparison for adverbs.

Oral Review:

1. Name four kinds of words that adverbs may modify. (verbs, adjectives, other adverbs, verbals)
2. What question is answered by adverbs that modify adjectives and other adverbs? (to what degree)
3. What questions do other adverbs answer? (how, when, where)
4. Name several adverbs that often interrupt a verb phrase. (not, never, ever, almost, always, hardly, scarcely, seldom)
5. Name some adverbs that often begin questions. (how, when, where, why)
6. Tell whether the verb described in each sentence

Lesson 81 Answers

Class Practice

1. (1) Basic facts, including title, author, publisher, and copyright date
   (2) Setting, including place and time
   (3) Main characters and their characteristics
   (4) Main plot or theme
   (5) Lessons or benefits of the story
   (6) Your evaluation of the story
2. the place and the time
3. the main plot or theme
4. the outcome of the story
5. You need to gather and organize information before writing. You need to proofread after writing.

Written Exercises

(Individual work.)

---

is transitive, intransitive complete, or intransitive linking.
   a. It passes action to some other word. (transitive)
   b. It does not express action but connects a subjective complement to the subject. (intransitive linking)
   c. It expresses action but needs no complement. (intransitive complete)
7. Tell whether each sentence refers to active or passive voice.
   a. Action is passed to the subject. (passive)
   b. Action is passed to the direct object. (active)

Lesson Introduction: Large cumulus clouds float *high* in the sky. The patchwork of *altocumulus* clouds floats quite a bit *higher* than the cumulus clouds. But the thin wisps of cirrus clouds float *highest* of all the clouds in the sky.

Those sentences illustrate the three degrees of comparison for the adverb *high*.

Like adjectives, many adverbs have three degrees of comparison: *positive, comparative,* and *superlative.* These three degrees are illustrated in the following sentences.

Peter worked <u>carefully</u>.
Jonathan worked <u>more carefully</u> than Peter.
William worked the <u>most carefully</u> of all the boys.

The positive degree is the simplest form of an adverb. The comparative and superlative degrees of some one-syllable and two-syllable adverbs are formed by adding -*er* and -*est* to the positive degree. For longer adverbs, the degrees of comparison are formed by using *more* and *most* with the positive degree. This is especially true of adverbs ending with -*ly*. *Less* and *least* may also be used to state comparisons.

Positive	Comparative	Superlative
fast	faster	fastest
near	nearer	nearest
early	earlier	earliest
cheerfully	more cheerfully	most cheerfully
hastily	less hastily	least hastily

Some common adverbs have irregular forms of comparison. Notice that all of these are identical or nearly identical to irregular adjective forms. Their use in a sentence determines whether they are adjectives or adverbs.

Positive	Comparative	Superlative
well	better	best
badly	worse	worst
ill	worse	worst
far	farther	farthest
little	less	least
much	more	most

Be sure to use the three degrees of comparison correctly. Use the positive degree to modify without making a comparison. Use the comparative degree to compare two actions, and the superlative degree to compare more than two actions.

Positive degree: No comparison
    The lion, clocked at fifty miles per hour, can run <u>fast</u>.
    Saturn travels <u>far</u> in its orbit around the sun.
Comparative degree: Compares two actions
    The pronghorn antelope, clocked at sixty-one miles per hour, can run <u>faster</u> than a lion.
    Uranus travels <u>farther</u> than Saturn in its orbit around the sun.

Lesson Outline:

1. Many adverbs have three degrees of comparison: positive, comparative, and superlative.

2. The positive degree is the simplest form of an adverb.

3. The comparative and superlative degrees of adverbs are formed in three ways.

   a. For some one-syllable and two-syllable adverbs, -*er* and -*est* are added to the positive degree.

   b. For most adverbs, *more* and *most* are used with the positive degree. *Less* and *least* may also be used to state comparisons.

   c. Some common adverbs have irregular forms of comparison. These include *well, badly, ill, far, little,* and *much.*

4. Be sure to use the three degrees of comparison correctly.

   a. Use the positive degree to modify without making a comparison. Use the comparative degree to compare two actions, and the superlative degree to compare more than two.

   b. Do not make a double comparison by both adding -*er* or -*est* and using *more* or *most.*

   c. Do not change an adverb to an adjective in forming the comparative and superlative degrees.

Superlative degree: Compares more than two actions

 The cheetah, clocked at seventy miles per hour, can run the <u>fastest</u> of all animals.

 Neptune travels the <u>farthest</u> of all the planets in its orbit around the sun.

As with adjectives, using the superlative form when only two actions are compared is the most common mistake made in using the degrees of comparison. When comparing only two actions, be especially careful to use the comparative degree.

Incorrect: Which of the two girls usually writes <u>most neatly</u>?
Correct: Which of the two girls usually writes <u>more neatly</u>?

Incorrect: Of James and Joshua, James can hit the ball <u>hardest</u>.
Correct: Of James and Joshua, James can hit the ball <u>harder</u>.

Do not make a double comparison by both adding -er or -est and using more or most.

Incorrect:

 We have come <u>more nearer</u> to your base than you have to ours.

Correct:

 We have come <u>nearer</u> to your base than you have to ours.

Do not change an adverb to an adjective in writing a comparative or superlative form. If an adverb ends with -ly in the positive degree, you must not form the comparative or superlative degree by dropping the -ly and adding -er or -est. Instead, you must use more or most with the adverb.

Incorrect: Linda painted her birdhouse <u>neater</u> than Lyle painted his.
Correct: Linda painted her birdhouse <u>more neatly</u> than Lyle painted his.

Incorrect: Lawrence painted his birdhouse the <u>neatest</u> of all.
Correct: Lawrence painted his birdhouse the <u>most neatly</u> of all.

Class Practice

A. Give the comparative and superlative degrees of these adverbs.

1. close
2. easily
3. much
4. fondly
5. little
6. well
7. commonly
8. badly
9. far
10. courteously

B. Read each sentence correctly.
1. Of the kings Manasseh and Josiah, Josiah lived the most righteously.

Lesson 82 Answers

Class Practice

A. 1. closer, closest
 2. more easily, most easily
 3. more, most
 4. more fondly, most fondly
 5. less, least
 6. better, best
 7. more commonly, most commonly
 8. worse, worst
 9. farther, farthest
 10. more courteously, most courteously

B. (Corrections are marked.)
 1. Of the kings Manasseh and Josiah, Josiah lived the <u>more righteously</u>.

2. Rehoboam said he would deal even harsher with the people than Solomon had done.
3. The bird's call is coming fainter now than it had.
4. Of all the pictures, this one is smudged worse.
5. The wind blew calmer when the storm had passed.
6. We could not tell who was hurt most badly, Claude or Melinda.
7. This dog barks the most loudest of all our dogs.
8. As the cold crept in, we tried to get more nearer to the little fire.

Written Exercises

A. Write correctly each adverb that is written in the wrong form. If a word should be left out, copy it and draw a line through it.
   1. Of the two dispensations, God revealed Himself most fully in the New Testament.
   2. Ezra lived more later than Isaiah did.
   3. King David lived humbler than King Saul did.
   4. Who traveled farthest from home, Jacob or Esau?
   5. Which of the three houses was damaged the badliest?
   6. Marie petted her kitten fondlier as each day passed.
   7. Susan and Ada both bake bread, but Susan can do it best.
   8. Marvin can say the tongue twister quicklier than I can.
   9. Denise jumped rope more faster than Lydia.
   10. Of Lyndon and Vernon, Lyndon walked least noisily through the woods.
   11. Phyllis drew the picture neater this time than the other time.
   12. You thought Sparky was an ill-behaved dog, but Duke actually does worst.
   13. Stacy has been obeying promptlier since Mother's talk with her.
   14. You must speak more louder to be heard with this machinery running!
   15. Of Abram and Lot, Abram served God most faithfully.

B. Write three sentences to illustrate the three degrees of comparison for each adverb. For the comparative and the superlative degrees, be sure your sentences show specific comparisons.
   1. well   2. close   3. quietly

Review Exercises

A. For each sentence, write whether the verb is transitive active (*TA*), transitive passive (*TP*), intransitive linking (*IL*), or intransitive complete (*IC*). Each set has one of each kind. [41–43, 53]
   1. a. The Lord is my shepherd.
      b. My needs are abundantly supplied by Him.

2. Rehoboam said he would deal even <u>more harshly</u> with the people than Solomon had done.
3. The bird's call is coming <u>more faintly</u> now than it had.
4. Of all the pictures, this one is smudged <u>worst</u>.
5. The wind blew <u>more calmly</u> when the storm had passed.
6. We could not tell who was hurt <u>worse</u> (or <u>more badly</u>), Claude or Melinda.
7. This dog barks the ~~most~~ loudest of all our dogs.
8. As the cold crept in, we tried to get ~~more~~ nearer to the little fire.

Written Exercises

A.
1. more fully	9. ~~more~~ faster
2. ~~more~~ later	10. less noisily
3. more humbly	11. more neatly
4. farther	12. worse
5. worst	13. more promptly
6. more fondly	14. ~~more~~ louder
7. better	15. more faithfully
8. more quickly	

B. (Individual sentences.)

Review Exercises

A. 1. a. IL
        b. TP

c. Daily He restores my soul.

d. His presence abides with me.

2. a. He prepares a table before me in the presence of my enemies.

b. My head is anointed with oil.

c. My cup of joy runs over.

d. Heaven will be my eternal home.

B. Rewrite each sentence, changing the verb to the passive voice. Do not change the tense. [53]

1. David's army defeated the Philistines.

2. Moses had set up the brazen serpent.

3. Jesus has calmed the wind and the waves.

C. Rewrite each sentence, changing the verb to the active voice. Do not change the tense. [53]

1. Stern warnings were given by the prophet Jeremiah.

2. The worlds are upheld by the hand of God.

3. The way of truth will often be despised by the multitudes.

c. TA

d. IC

2. a. TA   c. IC

   b. TP   d. IL

B. 1. The Philistines were defeated by David's army.

2. The brazen serpent had been set up by Moses.

3. The wind and the waves have been calmed by Jesus.

C. 1. The prophet Jeremiah gave stern warnings.

2. The hand of God upholds the worlds.

3. The multitudes will often despise the way of truth.

83. Prepositional Phrases Used as Adverbs

Lesson Survey

- A prepositional phrase that modifies a verb or verbal usually tells *how, when, where,* or *why.*

- A prepositional phrase that modifies an adjective or adverb usually tells *to what degree, how,* or *how much.*

- An adverb phrase must be put at a place where it clearly modifies the right word.

- Several prepositional phrases in a row may all be adverbs modifying the same word.

- A prepositional phrase used as an adverb may contain a prepositional phrase used as an adjective.

In Lesson 74 you studied prepositional phrases used as adjectives. They can also be used as adverbs.

A prepositional phrase used as an adverb, like a single-word adverb, can modify a verb, an adjective, or another adverb. Adverb phrases can

Lesson 83

Purpose: To teach the recognition, placement, and diagraming of prepositional phrases used as adverbs.

Oral Review:

1. Name and describe the three degrees of comparison. (positive—modifies without comparison; comparative—compares two items; superlative—compares more than two items)

2. Give the comparative and superlative degrees of these adverbs.

   a. badly (worse, worst)

   b. well (better, best)

   c. near (nearer, nearest)

   d. easily (more easily, most easily)

   e. fast (faster, fastest)

   f. softly (more softly, most softly)

3. Identify the adverbs in these sentences. (Adverbs are underlined.)

   a. We shall not stay here.

   b. Go very quietly.

   c. Yesterday we found an unusually long snake.

4. With a collective noun, when should you use (a) a singular verb? (b) a plural verb? (a. Use a singular verb when the collective noun refers to the group doing one thing together. b. Use a plural verb when the collective noun refers to the individual members doing different things.)

5. In each pair of words, tell which one should be used with a singular verb. (Answers are underlined.)

   a. mathematics, shears

   b. few, each

   c. trousers, electronics

   d. pliers, measles

answer the main adverb questions *how, when,* and *where.* They can also tell things like *why, to what degree,* and *how much.*

Adverb prepositional phrases most frequently modify verbs or verbals, as in the following sentences.

In the morning, Abraham arose.
   (*In the morning* tells *when* about the verb *arose.*)

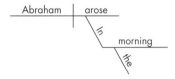

Abraham, trusting in God's promise, obeyed His command.
   (*In God's promise* tells *where* about the verbal *trusting.*)

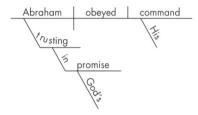

God blessed Abraham for his faithfulness.
   (*For his faithfulness* tells *why* about the verb *blessed.*)

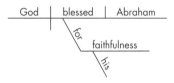

When prepositional phrases modify adjectives or adverbs, they usually tell *to what degree, how,* or *how much.* These phrases are more difficult to evaluate. But by orderly, step-by-step thinking, we can understand the place they fill in a sentence. Study these examples.

The little donkey was suitable for the Master's use.
   Think: Does the prepositional phrase modify *was* or *suitable?*

---

e. news, glasses
f. chicken pox, scissors

Lesson Introduction: Write the following question and partial sentence on the board.

Where was Jesus born?
He was born ———.

Ask the students if they can give a satisfactory ending by using only single-word adverbs. (*There* is not satisfactory.) Of course they cannot, so have them suggest any words that are suitable. Prepositional phrases used as adverbs fill an important place in our language.

Lesson Outline:

1. A prepositional phrase that modifies a verb or verbal usually tells how, when, where, *or* why.

2. A prepositional phrase that modifies an adjective or adverb usually tells to what degree, how, *or* how much.

3. An adverb phrase must be put at a place where it clearly modifies the right word.

4. Several prepositional phrases in a row may all be adverbs, each serving as an independent modifier of the same word. Then each phrase is diagramed separately under the word it modifies.

5. A string of prepositional phrases may all work together as one adverb. The "main" adverb phrase is the first one, and the other phrases are adjectives that modify objects in previous phrases. Each adjective phrase is diagramed under the object that it modifies.

★ *EXTRA PRACTICE*
Worksheet 43 (*Adverb Phrases*)

Was for the Master's use is sensible, but that is not what the sentence means.

Suitable for the Master's use is what the sentence means.

For the Master's use modifies the adjective *suitable* by telling *how.*

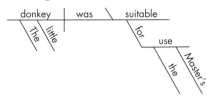

God is great <u>beyond our understanding</u>.

Think: Does the prepositional phrase modify *is* or *great*?

Is beyond our understanding is sensible, but that is not what the sentence means.

Great beyond our understanding is what the sentence means.

Beyond our understanding modifies the adjective *great* by telling *to what degree.*

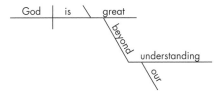

Jesus' mother stood near <u>to His cross</u>.

Think: Does the prepositional phrase modify *stood* or *near*?

Stood to His cross is not sensible.

Near to His cross is sensible; it is what the sentence means.

To His cross modifies the adverb *near* by telling *where.*

Take special notice of the last example. The diagram of the prepositional phrase is similar to that of a single-word adverb that modifies another adverb.

An adverb phrase can be placed at different locations in a sentence. However, you must be careful to put it at a place where it clearly modifies the word you intend.

Unclear: We could see a bear sitting there <u>with Father's binoculars</u>. (Did the bear have Father's binoculars?)

Clear: <u>With Father's binoculars</u>, we could see a bear sitting there.

Unclear: We watched the process of making paper <u>with keen interest</u>. (Was the paper being made with keen interest?)

Clear: <u>With keen interest</u>, we watched the process of making paper.

Many sentences contain several prepositional phrases in a row. Sometimes these phrases are all adverbs, each serving as an independent modifier of the same word. Look at this example.

Prayer was made <u>without ceasing</u> <u>of the church</u> <u>unto God</u> <u>for Peter</u>.

The following sentences show that each phrase modifies the verb independently. Therefore, each phrase is diagramed separately under the verb.

Prayer was made <u>without ceasing</u>.   Prayer was made <u>unto God</u>.
Prayer was made <u>of the church</u>.   Prayer was made <u>for Peter</u>.

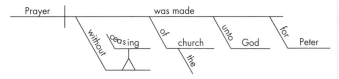

At other times, a string of prepositional phrases all work together as one adverb. The "main" adverb phrase is the first one, and the other phrases are adjectives that modify objects in previous phrases.

Jesus sat <u>in a boat</u> <u>near the edge</u> <u>of the lake</u>.

Think: The entire phrase tells *where* about the verb *sat,* so it is an adverb phrase.
Near the edge is an adjective phrase telling *which boat.*
Of the lake is an adjective phrase telling *which edge.*

The following sentences show that each phrase does *not* modify the verb independently.

Jesus sat <u>in a boat</u>. (sensible because this phrase directly modifies
     the verb)
Jesus sat <u>near the edge</u>. (sensible, but not the original meaning)
Jesus sat <u>of the lake</u>. (not sensible)

On the sentence diagram, only the first phrase is connected directly to
he verb. Each of the other phrases is diagramed under the object that it
modifies.

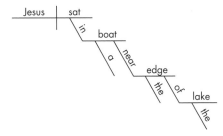

Class Practice

A. Read each adverb phrase, including any adjective phrase that may be
in it. Tell what word the adverb phrase modifies, and give the part of
speech of the modified word.
1. Nehemiah was sad about the news from Jerusalem.
2. Nehemiah prayed to the God of heaven for wisdom.
3. The king sent him to Jerusalem.
4. Nehemiah went by the brook during the night and viewed the wall.
5. Jerusalem lay in the ruins of its destruction.
6. Nehemiah was ready for the challenge of rebuilding.
7. We can read the account of this great work later in the Book of
Nehemiah.

B. Read these sentences, placing the adverb phrases where they are sensible.
1. The man had a bag of apples for the children on his back.
2. We took the cookies that Mother had frosted in a small brown bag.
3. Today our neighbor came to church upon our special invitation.
4. I finally escaped from the bees in a boat.

C. On the chalkboard, diagram these sentences.
1. The cow had fallen into a large sinkhole.
2. On the banks of the stream, we searched for animal tracks.
3. From the window we watched, with intense curiosity, the bear's antics.

Lesson 83 Answers

Class Practice

A. 1. about the news from Jerusalem—sad, adjective
2. to the God of heaven—prayed, verb;
for wisdom—prayed, verb
3. to Jerusalem—sent, verb
4. by the brook—went, verb;
during the night—went, verb
5. in the ruins of its destruction—lay, verb
6. for the challenge of rebuilding—ready, adjective
7. in the Book of Nehemiah—later, adverb (*Of
this great work* is an adjective phrase.)

B. 1. On his back, the man had a bag of apples for
the children.
or The man had a bag of apples on his back
for the children.
2. In a small brown bag, we took the cookies that
Mother had frosted.
3. Upon our special invitation, our neighbor came
to church today.
4. In a boat, I finally escaped from the bees.

C.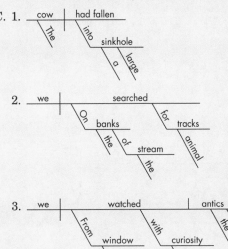

4. In this new van, we will drive through the night to Grandfather's house.

Written Exercises

A. Copy each adverb phrase, including any adjective phrase that may be in it. Write the word that the adverb phrase modifies.
1. Jesus stood in the boat and spoke to the people on the shore.
2. Along the way to Emmaus, Jesus talked about many things in the Scriptures.
3. Jesus rode into Jerusalem on a young donkey.
4. Jesus was crucified outside Jerusalem on a Roman cross at the Jews' insistence.
5. We fished in the stream in the meadow at Grandfather's farm.
6. Our attention was attracted to Orion's bright band.
7. Harry's story was wrong in several details.
8. Brother Noah wrote a word in big, bold letters on the blackboard.
9. After her punishment, Lorna was more careful with her words.
10. Jay's radiant smile seemed like bright sunshine.

B. Rewrite these sentences, placing the adverb phrases where they are sensible.
1. We declined the invitation to visit Uncle Wesley's family with regret.
2. We children learned where our forefathers had lived at Grandfather's home this morning.
3. Charles swatted an enormous mosquito with a shoe.
4. Jeff has an apple for the pony in his pocket.
5. We found a clean set of clothes for my cousin in the old chest in the attic.

C. Diagram these sentences.
1. The angels spoke to the shepherds about the birth of the Saviour.
2. In the fullness of time, Jesus was born into this world.
3. The disciples in the boat grew anxious about the severe storm.
4. Jesus slept soundly in the bottom of the boat.
5. The water poured over the dam in a thunderous roar.
6. Joy is ahead by a few feet.

Review Exercises

A. Write the correct words for these sentences. [48]
1. The gallows that Haman built (was, were) seventy-five feet high.
2. (There's, There are) many warnings against pride in the story about Haman.
3. Mordecai and Esther (is, are) good examples of godliness in action.

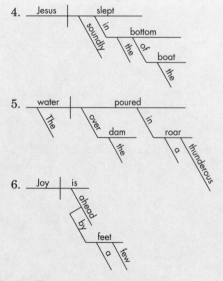

(Review Exercises are on page 391.)

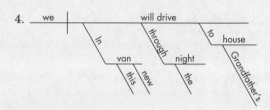

Written Exercises

A. 1. in the boat—stood;
to the people on the shore—spoke
2. Along the way to Emmaus—talked;
about many things in the Scriptures—talked
3. into Jerusalem—rode;
on a young donkey—rode
4. outside Jerusalem—was crucified;
on a Roman cross—was crucified;
at the Jews' insistence—was crucified
5. in the stream in the meadow at Grandfather's farm—fished
6. to Orion's bright band—was attracted
7. in several details—wrong
8. in big, bold letters—wrote;
on the blackboard—wrote
9. After her punishment—was;
with her words—careful
10. like bright sunshine—seemed

B. 1. With regret, we declined the invitation to visit Uncle Wesley's family.
or We declined with regret the invitation to visit Uncle Wesley's family.
2. At Grandfather's home this morning, we children learned where our forefathers had lived.
3. With a shoe, Charles swatted an enormous mosquito.
4. In his pocket, Jeff has an apple for the pony.
5. In the old chest in the attic, we found a clean set of clothes for my cousin.

C.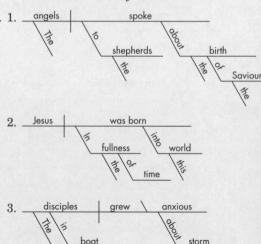

4. Neither of them (was, were) too fearful to do what was necessary.
5. The congregation (is, are) listening to the inspiring sermon.
6. The congregation (have, has) dispersed to their homes.
7. The shears (belong, belongs) in the top drawer.
8. This pair of shears (is, are) too dull.
9. Hilda or Rachel (have, has) the book now.
10. (Don't, Doesn't) Mary want it next?

. If the underlined expression has no error, write *correct*. If it has an error, write the expression correctly. [77]
1. Brother Benjamin has <u>less cows</u> now than he did a few years ago.
2. <u>Them blue jays</u> are making a lot of noise.
3. <u>What sort of a bird</u> sings like that?
4. The small stream has <u>less water</u> than the one on our property.
5. <u>This here stream</u> does provide good fishing though.

Review Exercises

A. 1. was   6. have
   2. There are   7. belong
   3. are   8. is
   4. was   9. has
   5. is   10. Doesn't

B. 1. fewer cows   4. correct
   2. Those blue jays 5. This stream
   3. What sort of bird

84. Adverb Clauses

Lesson Survey

• An **adverb clause** is a dependent clause that modifies a verb, an adjective, or an adverb. It begins with a **subordinating conjunction.**

• Adverb clauses can answer the main adverb questions *how, when,* and *where.* They can also tell *why, how long, how much, to what degree, in spite of what,* and *under what condition.*

• An adverb clause, like other adverbs, can be placed at different locations in a sentence.

• An adverb clause is diagramed on a horizontal line below the main clause, with a broken line connecting the verb of the dependent clause to the modified word in the main clause.

You should remember that a dependent clause is a group of words that ontains a skeleton and functions as a single sentence part. You studied oun clauses in Chapter 3 and adjective clauses in Chapter 7. Now you re ready to study clauses used as adverbs.

An *adverb clause* is a dependent clause used as an adverb. The folowing sentences communicate the same basic idea, but the modifier of

Lesson 84

Purpose: To teach the identification and diagraming of adverb clauses.

Oral Review:
1. Tell whether these statements are true or false.
   a. A phrase that modifies a verb or verbal usually answers the question *how, when, where,* or *why.* (true)
   b. An adverb phrase must come right after the word it modifies. (false)
   c. An adverb phrase may contain an adjective phrase within it. (true)
   d. If several adverb phrases come in a row, the second one usually modifies the object of the preposition in the first. (false)
2. Identify each prepositional phrase used as an adverb, and tell what word it modifies. (Adverb

phrases are underlined; modified words are italicized.)
   a. The angel *spoke* <u>to Mary</u> <u>about the birth of the Saviour</u>.
   b. <u>In six days</u>, God *created* the world.
   c. The Name of Jesus is *excellent* <u>above every other name</u>.
3. Give the verb forms that should replace the wrong ones in these sentences.
   a. Wayne tug Ray before he was on base. (tagged)
   b. We swang on Grandfather's tree swing. (swung)
   c. Brother Melvin has wrote the assignments on the board. (has written)
   d. Our water pipes busted in the sub-zero weather. (burst)
   e. The geese have all went south for the winter. (have gone)

the italicized verb changes from a word to a phrase to a clause. The word, the phrase, and the clause are all adverbs because they modify the verb *have*.

> We *have* our family worship <u>early</u>. (single-word adverb telling *when*)
> We *have* our family worship <u>before breakfast</u>. (adverb phrase telling *when*)
> We *have* our family worship <u>before we eat breakfast</u>. (adverb clause telling *when*)

An adverb clause begins with a *subordinating conjunction*. The following list contains the most common subordinating conjunctions.

after	as though	how	than	unless	where
although	because	if	that	until	wherever
as	before	since	though	when	while
as if	even if	so that	till	whenever	

Adverb clauses can answer the main adverb questions *how, when,* and *where.* They can also tell *why, how long, how much, to what degree, in spite of what,* and *under what condition.*

Most adverb clauses modify verbs. Study the following sentences in which the adverb clauses are underlined and the subordinating conjunctions are italicized.

> "I will praise thee with uprightness of heart, <u>*when* I shall have learned thy righteous judgments</u>." (The underlined clause tells *when* about the verb *will praise.*)
> "I love the Lord, <u>*because* he hath heard my voice and my supplications</u>." (The underlined clause tells *why* about the verb *love.*)
> "<u>*Though* he slay me</u>, yet will I trust in him." (The underlined clause tells *in spite of what* about the verb *will trust.*)

In the examples above, the adverb clauses all modify verbs. But adverb clauses, like other adverbs, can also modify adjectives and adverbs.

> New Testament blessings are greater <u>*than* Old Testament blessings were</u>. (The underlined clause tells *how much* about the adjective *greater.*)

An adverb clause, like other adverbs, can be placed at different locations in a sentence. Usually if it is at the end of a sentence, you do not need to set it off with a comma. But if it is at the beginning or in the middle of a sentence, you must use commas.

Lesson Introduction: Write the following sentences on the board.

> A thunderstorm moved across the valley <u>later</u>.
> A thunderstorm moved across the valley <u>in the evening</u>.
> A thunderstorm moved across the valley <u>while the evening service was closing</u>.

Which of these sentences gives the least specific information? (first) Which gives the most specific information? (third) Adverb clauses are often necessary for clear, specific communication.

Lesson Outline:

1. An adverb clause is a dependent clause that modifies a verb, an adjective, or an adverb. It begins with a subordinating conjunction.

2. Adverb clauses can answer the main adverb questions **how, when,** *and* **where.** *They can also tell* **why, how long, how much, to what degree, in spite of what,** *and* **under what condition.**

3. An adverb clause, like other adverbs, can be placed at different locations in a sentence.
   a. An adverb clause at the end of a sentence is usually not set off with a comma.
   b. An adverb clause at the beginning or in the middle of a sentence must be set off with commas.

4. An adverb clause is diagramed on a horizontal line below the main clause, with a broken line connecting the verb of the dependent clause to the modified word in the main clause. The subordinating conjunction is written on the broken line.

★ **EXTRA PRACTICE**
Worksheet 44 (*Adverb Clauses*)

The people of Nineveh were spared from destruction <u>because they repented</u>.

The people of Nineveh, <u>because they repented</u>, were spared from destruction.

<u>Because they repented</u>, the people of Nineveh were spared from destruction.

An adverb clause is diagramed on a horizontal line below the main clause, with a broken line connecting the verb of the dependent clause to the modified word in the main clause. The subordinating conjunction is written on the broken line.

Jesus acted as though He would go farther.

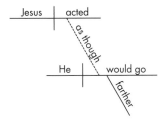

Because he was a short man, Zacchaeus climbed a tree.

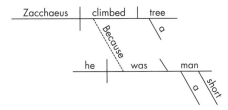

The peas have ripened sooner than we had expected.

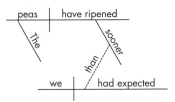

Class Practice

A. Tell what question each adverb clause answers, what word it modifies, and what part of speech that word is.
1. Lot was taken captive <u>when Sodom was defeated</u>.
2. Abraham pursued the raiders <u>until he overtook them</u>.
3. Abraham's concern for Lot was greater <u>than Lot deserved</u>.
4. <u>After he was rescued</u>, Lot lived in Sodom <u>as if nothing had happened</u>.
5. <u>Because Abraham interceded for him</u>, Lot was delivered from Sodom <u>before God destroyed the city</u>.
6. Abraham's intercession, fervent <u>as man's prayer has ever been</u>, could not spare the city <u>because not enough righteous souls were there</u>.

B. Read each adverb clause, and tell what word it modifies.
1. Because He knew their unbelief, Jesus did not confide in the people.
2. Such miracles have not been seen since the world began.
3. Although they saw His miracles, many people still rejected the Messiah.
4. Since we had a flat tire, we arrived at church later than we ever did before.
5. If the ground is not too wet, we will plow the garden tomorrow.
6. This garden soil is much better than it had been.

C. Tell where commas are needed in these sentences. If a sentence needs no commas, say *correct*.
1. As the sun rose above the horizon the birds began to sing.
2. The weary refugees ate the moldy bread and spoiled soup because they were so hungry.
3. Before anyone could catch him Blue Boy had flown out the open window.
4. The boys after they had a roaring bonfire decided to roast hot dogs.

D. On the chalkboard, diagram these sentences.
1. I have not seen James since he visited us in September.
2. If we do not leave soon, we shall surely be late.
3. The kitten cried pitifully until Father rescued it.
4. The package arrived later than we had hoped.
5. Saul, zealous as a persecutor has ever been, relentlessly pursued the believers.

Written Exercises

A. Copy the conjunction and the last word of each adverb clause, with three dots (...) between them. Write the word that the clause modifies, and what part of speech that word is.

Lesson 84 Answers

Class Practice

A. 1. when, was taken—verb
   2. how long, pursued—verb
   3. how much, greater—adjective
   4. when, lived—verb; how, lived—verb
   5. why, was delivered—verb;
      when, was delivered—verb
   6. to what degree, fervent—adjective;
      why, could spare—verb

B. 1. Because He knew their unbelief, did confide
   2. since the world began, have been seen
   3. Although they saw His miracles, rejected
   4. Since we had a flat tire, arrived;
      than we ever did before, later
   5. If the ground is not too wet, will plow
   6. than it had been, better

C. 1. horizon,   3. him,
   2. correct   4. boys, bonfire,

D. 1.

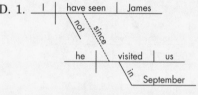

2.

3.

4.

5.

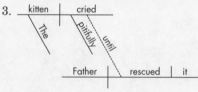

1. We never eat before we have given thanks to the Lord.
2. Because tomorrow is Sunday, we must do extra work today.
3. This morning our family worship was longer than it usually is.
4. After Father had read the Bible passage, we had a lengthy discussion on what it means for us.
5. We must keep the sick cow in the stall so that the veterinarian can treat her.
6. The sun rises higher now than it does in December.
7. The girls, while they were doing the dishes, memorized a new song.
8. Although the fence had been broken, the cows did not get out.
9. Whenever we have a thunderstorm, our dog Ginger hides in the barn.
10. Juanita sang as if nothing had gone wrong all day.
11. We discussed our plans while we ate lunch.
12. Until this latch is fixed, we should keep this door closed.
13. As we walked through the woods, we saw many birds and small animals.

B. Copy each word that should be followed by a comma, and add the missing comma. If no comma is needed, write *correct*.
1. We love the Lord because He first loved us.
2. If we love the Lord we will keep His commandments.
3. Jesus after He had suffered and died ascended back to the Father.
4. Though He is not here in bodily form His presence is always with us.
5. Before He went away He promised to send the Comforter.

C. Diagram these sentences.
1. We should always live as if this day were our last day.
2. Because a pure conscience is a precious possession, we must never ignore it.
3. Our friends, if they are chosen well, can be a valuable asset.
4. While we are young, we should appreciate godly examples.
5. Life is shorter than we often realize.
6. God has blessed us more than we deserve.

Review Exercises

A. Write the second and third principal parts of these verbs. Use *has* with the past participle. [34]
1. send
2. go
3. lay
4. cut
5. bring
6. weep
7. lie
8. leave
9. forget
10. swing

6.

Review Exercises

A. 1. sent, (has) sent
   2. went, (has) gone
   3. laid, (has) laid
   4. cut, (has) cut
   5. brought, (has) brought
   6. wept, (has) wept
   7. lay, (has) lain
   8. left, (has) left
   9. forgot, (has) forgotten
   10. swung, (has) swung

Written Exercises

A. 1. before . . . Lord, eat—verb
   2. Because . . . Sunday, must do—verb
   3. than . . . is, longer—adjective
   4. After . . . passage, had—verb
   5. so that . . . her, must keep—verb
   6. than . . . December, higher—adverb
   7. while . . . dishes, memorized—verb
   8. Although . . . broken, did get—verb
   9. Whenever . . . thunderstorm, hides—verb
   10. as if . . . day, sang—verb
   11. while . . . lunch, discussed—verb
   12. Until . . . fixed, should keep—verb
   13. As . . . woods, saw—verb

B. 1. correct   4. form,
   2. Lord,   5. away,
   3. Jesus, died,

C. 1.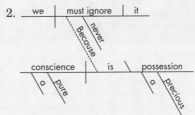

   2.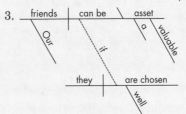

   3.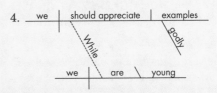

   4.

   5.

B. Write the correct verb for each sentence. [34, 50]
1. How much have the supplies (cost, costed) so far?
2. Scott (knowed, knew) the story quite well.
3. The water on the creek has (froze, frozen) solid this week.
4. Roxanne has (forgot, forgotten) her lunch.
5. A frightened deer (burst, bursted) out of the brush.
6. The Indian hunters (slayed, slew) several buffalo.
7. They (dragged, drug) the valuable hide and meat back to camp.
8. Wilfred has (wrote, written) a fine piece of poetry.
9. Laurene had already (chose, chosen) a design for her motto yesterday.
10. Albert has (tooken, taken) the responsibility to clean out the shed.

B. 1. cost
    2. knew
    3. frozen
    4. forgotten
    5. burst
    6. slew
    7. dragged
    8. written
    9. chosen
    10. taken

85. Giving an Oral Explanation

> **Lesson Survey**
>
> • When you prepare to give an **oral explanation,** limit the subject to a specific topic.
>
> • Organize your explanation clearly.
>   1. Outline the steps of the explanation in a logical order.
>   2. Prepare an introduction that both catches the interest of your listeners and tells them what process you will be explaining.
>   3. Plan to use a diagram or other visual aid.
>   4. Prepare a suitable conclusion.
>
> • Follow the rules for speaking well before a group.
>   1. Try to relax before standing to your feet.
>   2. Look at your listeners as you speak.
>   3. Speak with proper volume.
>   4. Speak distinctly.
>   5. Maintain good posture at all times.
>   6. Avoid distracting habits.

No doubt you have already explained a process in an informal setting. Perhaps you showed a younger brother or sister how to tie his shoes or how to feed the chickens. Or you may have explained to a friend how you made a birdhouse or an apron. In such informal settings, your listener's questions may prompt you to fill in and clarify details. But when you give an oral

Lesson 85

Purpose: To teach how to give an oral explanation of how to do something or how something works. (*Previous experience:* Grade 5—giving directions orally; Grade 6—writing a set of directions)

Oral Review:
1. What are some things a good book report does? (shows that the reader has read the book carefully, shares with others some of the enjoyment and inspiration of the book, stimulates in others a desire to read the book)
2. Name the six kinds of information that a book report should include. (basic facts such as title, author, and publisher; setting; main characters and their characteristics; theme and main events; some lessons; personal evaluation of the book)

3. Proofread the following sentences, using the marks you learned in Chapter 1. (*Teacher:* Write the sentences on the board as given, and have students mark corrections.)
   a. A Christain book should set good examples us. *for*
   b. My brother gave me a good book who lives in Ontario.
   c. ~~Your~~ certainly welcome read intresting book. *You're* *to* *this e*

Lesson Introduction: Read this explanation of a reflex action to the students.

> What makes your hand jerk back from a hot stove when you touch it? Your nervous system has interpreted an urgent message that you are touching something hot. In your skin are many nerve endings; some of them are sensitive to heat. Your muscles are response organs. So these muscles jerked your hand

xplanation before a group, you must be much better prepared beforehand.

The first step in preparing for an *oral explanation* is to limit the subject to a specific topic. Choose a topic in which you are interested so that ou can give the explanation enthusiastically. Be sure you know your topic horoughly so that you can give the explanation meaningfully. For this lesson, choose a process that you can explain in three to five minutes.

Too General	Specific Topics
Gardening	Making a cold frame
	Raising potatoes
Ironing	How to organize your ironing
	How to iron a shirt
Internal-combustion engines	How a four-cycle gasoline engine works
	How a diesel engine works

After you have chosen and limited your topic, you must organize your xplanation clearly. Outline the steps of the explanation in a logical order. Most likely, you will explain a process that must be understood in chronological order. If you explain how something works, you might describe it n spatial order or in a combination of spatial and chronological order.

Be sure you do not omit any steps that are necessary in understanding he process. Describe each step with enough details to be well understood. Jse specific names of tools or ingredients.

Suppose you plan to explain how to make a cold frame. The following xample shows the main points that may be on your outline.

Making a Cold Frame
I. Gathering materials and tools
II. Building the main box
III. Putting on the lid
IV. Preparing the soil and planting the seeds

Expand your outline with specific details. Exactly what materials and cools are needed? What shape and size should the main box be, and how should it be put together? Add details about making the lid, putting it on, preparing the soil, and planting the seeds. Plan to make your explanation so clear that it can be understood by someone who has never seen such a ching before.

Prepare an introduction that both catches the interest of your listeners and tells them what process you will be explaining. The introduction sets the tone of your entire explanation, either sparking or extinguishing the listeners' interest. A thought-provoking question or an interesting statement is often effective.

away from the hot stove.

Could you follow this explanation clearly? What is wrong with it? (It is not well organized. It lacks specific details.)

This lesson will give some instructions on how to prepare and give an effective explanation.

Lesson Outline:

1. When you prepare to give an oral explanation, limit the subject to a specific topic.
   a. Choose a topic in which you are interested.
   b. Know your topic thoroughly.
   c. Choose a process that you can explain in three to five minutes.

2. Organize your explanation clearly.
   a. Outline the steps of the explanation in a logical order.
      1) Use chronological or spatial order.
      2) Do not omit any steps.
      3) Describe each step in sufficient detail.
   b. Prepare an introduction that both catches the interest of your listeners and tells them what process you will be explaining.
      1) A thought-provoking question or an interesting statement is often effective.
      2) You should write out the exact words of the introduction because of the importance of getting started smoothly.
   c. Plan to use a diagram or other visual aid.
   d. Prepare a suitable conclusion.
      1) You may end with a summary of the main steps in the process or with a specific impression of the explanation you have given.
      2) Write out the exact words of the conclusion so that you can close your explanation satisfactorily.

Because of the importance of getting started smoothly, you should write out the exact words of the introduction. The following introductions would be effective for the topic "Making a Cold Frame."

Question:
Would you like to enjoy fresh, homegrown lettuce before spring frosts are past? Making a cold frame is the answer. Use the following steps, and you can enjoy some fresh lettuce early next spring.

Statement:
You can enjoy fresh, homegrown lettuce before spring frosts are past! Making a cold frame is the answer. Use the following steps, and you can enjoy some fresh lettuce early next spring.

A visual aid will greatly improve the effect of your presentation. You may be able to use real objects and actually go through the steps as you explain them. You might also prepare a diagram on a poster or draw one on the chalkboard as you speak. Your listeners will remember the explanation much better if they can see how things are done rather than just hearing about them.

Your explanation may begin with an effective introduction and proceed with clear, logical steps. But if your conclusion is poor, the overall effect of your explanation will be weakened. So you also need to write out the exact words of a suitable conclusion. You may end with a summary of the main steps in the process or with a specific impression of the explanation you have given. The following examples would be effective conclusions for the topic "Making a Cold Frame."

Summary of steps:
So get together the materials and tools that you need. Build the main box of the cold frame, and put on the lid. Then prepare the soil, plant the seeds, and get ready to enjoy some fresh, early-spring lettuce!

Specific impression:
A cold frame is simple to construct and easy to use. It may open a world of gardening pleasure to you and your family.

Remember to follow the rules for speaking well before a group. Try to relax before standing to your feet. Too much tension will prevent you from looking and speaking naturally. You can help yourself to relax by breathing deeply and evenly several times. Be well prepared, and be enthusiastic about the points you will present. Try to become so involved in your explanation that you forget your nervousness.

In giving your explanation, do not begin speaking before you have turned

3. *Follow the rules for speaking well before a group.*
    a. Try to relax before standing to your feet.
        1) Breathe deeply and evenly several times.
        2) Be well prepared and enthusiastic.
        3) Become so involved in your explanation that you forget your nervousness.
    b. Look at your listeners as you speak.
        1) Do not begin speaking before you have turned around to face the audience.
        2) Look at your listeners directly.
        3) Do not constantly look at your outline, and do not look at the floor, the ceiling, or the walls.
    c. Speak with proper volume.
        1) Your voice should not be so loud that your listeners feel uncomfortable nor so soft that they must strain to hear what you are saying.
        2) Do not lower your voice at the end of each sentence so much that your listeners miss the last few words.
    d. Speak distinctly.
        1) Know how to pronounce each word you use.
        2) Do not mumble.
        3) Do not start walking back to your seat before you have finished your last sentence.
    e. Maintain good posture at all times.
        1) As you take your place to give the explanation and as you take your seat, you should neither rush nor shuffle slowly.
        2) While speaking, stand straight, with both feet flat on the floor, and hold your head straight.

around to face the audience. Look at your listeners as you speak. Let your eyes meet theirs, and talk directly to them. Do not constantly look at your outline, and do not look at the floor, the ceiling, or the walls.

Speak with proper volume. Your voice should not be so loud that your listeners feel uncomfortable nor so soft that they must strain to hear what you are saying. Do not lower your voice at the end of each sentence so much that your listeners miss the last few words.

Speak distinctly. Be sure you know how to pronounce each word, especially if you use any technical terms that are uncommon. Do not mumble your words through half-closed lips, and do not start walking back to your seat before you have finished your last sentence.

Maintain good posture at all times. As you take your place to give the explanation and as you take your seat, you should neither rush nor shuffle slowly. While speaking, stand straight, with both feet flat on the floor, and hold your head straight.

Avoid distracting habits. Filling your pauses with *uh*'s and *ah*'s and clearing your throat continually will reduce your effectiveness. Your listeners will also be distracted if you frequently pull at your glasses, nose, or ears; put your hands into and out of your pockets; or shuffle your feet. Forget yourself and concentrate on *clearly explaining how to do something*, and you will do well.

Class Practice

Tell what is wrong with the following set of notes for an oral explanation. Suggest ways to improve the weaknesses.

Our Sense of Hearing

Introduction: I am planning to describe the process of how we hear.
 I. In the outer ear, which gathers the vibrations
  A. Large flap of cartilage and skin to catch sound waves
  B. Sound waves traveling through air
   1. Are produced by vibrations from vocal cords, creaking hinges, the wind, etc.
   2. Make up all sounds we hear
  C. The small, narrow ear canal
   1. Ends with the eardrum
    a. Consists of tough piece of skin stretched tightly across canal
    b. Vibrates as the sound waves push against it
   2. Acts as a funnel to carry sound waves into the middle ear
 II. In the middle ear, which amplifies the vibrations
  A. Consists of three tiny bones
  B. Multiplies the force of the vibrations up to twenty-two times

---

 f. Avoid distracting habits.
  1) Do not fill your pauses with *uh*'s and *ah*'s or clear your throat continually.
  2) Do not frequently pull at your glasses, nose, or ears; put your hands into and out of your pockets; or shuffle your feet.

NOTE: It would be good to make copies of the original story in Review Exercises to give to the students.

Lesson 85 Answers

Class Practice

1. The introduction is not effective. (*Possible introduction:* "God gave us two small organs that do an extremely important job for us. The process of how we hear is interesting to study.")
2. The point about sound waves traveling through the air (I-B) should precede the point about the flap of cartilage and skin that catches the sound waves (I-A).
3. The point about the ear canal acting as a funnel (I-C, point 2) should precede the point about it ending with the eardrum (I-C, point 1).
4. The point about the three tiny bones in the middle ear (II-A) should be more specific. Name the bones: malleus (or hammer), incus (or anvil), and stapes (or stirrup bone).

III. In the inner ear, which transforms the vibrations
  A. The main part of the inner ear
    1. What it is like
      a. Looks like a spiral snail shell
      b. Is filled with fluid
      c. Contains thousands of tiny hairlike nerve cells

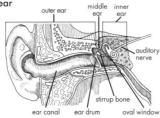

    2. How it works
      a. Vibrating fluid causes the hairlike nerve cells to wave
      b. Vibrations from the stirrup bone of the middle ear pass through the oval window
      c. Vibrating nerve cells produce small electrical impulses
  B. The auditory nerve
    1. Picks up the electrical impulses
    2. Carries them to the brain, which interprets them

Written Exercises

A. Prepare a set of notes on how to do something or how something works. Include a written introduction and conclusion. Here are some suggestions.

How to make candy or cookies	How to mow a lawn
How to arrange a flower bed	How an engine works
How to prepare a meal	How an electric motor works
How to iron a shirt	How to tan leather

B. Give your explanation orally to the class.

Review Exercises

Copy these paragraphs as they are. Proofread them and correct the mistakes, using the proper proofreading marks. [8]

As I steped around the corner of barn, my younger borther Daryl ran into me. "Th-There's a snake in the haymow!" he stamered. Its curled up on that I was ready to pull down!" "Are you shore?" I asked.

"Yes," he insisted. "Come and see it!" "Well, it's dark rather up there. Let me go and get a first," I answered. "Ill be write back."

---

5. The point about the main part of the inner ear (III-A) should be more specific. Give the name: cochlea.
6. The point about vibrations from the stirrup passing through the oval window (III-A, point 2-b) should precede the point about vibrating fluid causing hairlike nerve cells to wave (III-A, point 2-a).

Written Exercises

(Individual work.)

Review Exercises

As I stepped around the corner of *the* barn, my younger brother Daryl ran into me. "Th-There's a snake in the haymow!" he stammered. Its curled up on that *hay bale* I was ready to pull down!" ¶"Are you ~~shore~~ *sure*?" I asked.

"Yes," he insisted. "Come and see it!" ¶"Well, it's dark rather up there. Let me go and get a *flashlight* first," I answered. "Ill be ~~write~~ *right* back."

I climed the ladder with the flashlight that leads up to the haymow. Daryl came right behind me. "Over there! See it?" Daryl wispered horsely.

When I shone my light on the dark spot that he was pionting to, I busted out laughing. In spight of hisself, Daryl had to luagh to. The "snake" turned out to be Daryl's cap!

I climed the ladder ^b with the flashlight ^W that leads up to the haymow. Daryl came right behind me. "Over there! See it?" Daryl wispered ho^arsely.

When I shone my light on the dark spot that he was pio^hnting to, I ~~busted~~ *burst* out laughing. In s~~pight~~ *pite* of hisself, Daryl had to l^muagh ~~to~~ *too*. The "snake" turned out to be Daryl's cap!

---

86. Distinguishing Between Adjectives and Adverbs

> ### Lesson Survey
> - Many adjectives and adverbs cannot be distinguished by their form. Their part of speech is determined by their function in a sentence.
> - To distinguish an adjective from an adverb, the most important tests are *what part of speech the word modifies* and *what question it answers.*
> - The same two tests can be used to distinguish between adjective and adverb phrases and clauses.

You have learned many things about both adjectives and adverbs. Can you always tell the difference between the two? By this time you should have little difficulty in most cases. However, there are likely some times when you still are not sure or when you label a word wrongly.

Many adjectives and adverbs cannot be distinguished by their form. It is true that many adverbs end with *-ly*, while most adjectives do not. In fact, many descriptive adjectives are changed to adverbs by adding *-ly*.

Adjectives		Adverbs
gentle + ly	=	gently
heavy + ly	=	heavily
perfect + ly	=	perfectly

However, there are also a number of adjectives that end with *-ly*.

Lesson 86

Purpose: To teach how to distinguish between adjectives and adverbs.

Oral Review:
1. What kind of word begins an adverb clause? (a subordinating conjunction)
2. Name several subordinating conjunctions. (*Sample answers:* after, although, as, as if, as though, because, before, even if, how, if, since, so that, than, that, though, till, unless, until, when, whenever, where, wherever, while)
3. An adverb clause may come at the beginning, in the middle, or at the end of a sentence. In which positions does it need to be set off with commas? (beginning, middle)
4. Name several categories of nouns that are capitalized because they are proper nouns. (names of particular people; names of God and words referring to the Bible; names of geographical features; titles of books, poems, etc.; names of groups, organizations, etc.; names of particular ships; names of parks, historic sites, etc.; brand names; names of school subjects derived from proper nouns; calendar items)
5. When may the comma be omitted in a compound sentence? (when the two clauses are very short)
6. Which kind of adjective clause must be set off with commas: restrictive or nonrestrictive? (nonrestrictive)

Lesson Introduction: Write the following words on the board. (*Teacher:* The material in parentheses is for your own information.)

diligently (adverb)	friendly (adjective)
near (both)	kindly (both)

Consider the following expressions, in which the underlined words are adjectives.

a <u>friendly</u> girl   a <u>godly</u> remnant
with <u>fatherly</u> concern   the <u>pearly</u> gates
on a <u>lonely</u> path   our <u>daily</u> bread

Furthermore, not all adverbs end with -ly. In the following expressions, the underlined words are adverbs.

have worked <u>well</u>   can see <u>far</u>
don't fall <u>off</u>   will draw <u>near</u>
go <u>slow</u>   is going <u>past</u>

To further complicate things, many modifiers can be either adjectives or adverbs. Look at the underlined words in these columns. The modified words are in italics.

Adjectives: **Adverbs:**
Leo was <u>early</u>.   He *came* to school <u>early</u>.
The *floors* are <u>clean</u>.   The furniture *is dusted* <u>clean</u>.
The <u>past</u> *days* have been busy.   The days *flew* <u>past</u> swiftly.

All of this shows that many adjectives and adverbs cannot be distinguished by their form. Rather, we must decide what part of speech a modifier is by its function in a sentence. There are two tests that we can use.

Test 1: *What part of speech does the word modify?*
An adjective modifies a noun or pronoun.
An adverb modifies a verb, an adjective, an adverb, or a verbal.

Test 2: *What question does the word answer?*
Adjectives answer the questions *which, whose, how many,* and *what kind of.*
Adverbs answer questions like *how, when, where, why, how long, how much, to what degree, in spite of what,* and *under what condition.*

Now study the following sentences. Are the underlined words adjectives or adverbs? Use the two tests to decide.

The <u>early</u> Anabaptists endured persecution <u>steadfastly</u>.
  Test 1: *What part of speech does the word modify?*
  Early modifies the noun *Anabaptists.* It is an adjective.
  Steadfastly modifies the verb *endured.* It is an adverb.

Ask the students which of the words are adjectives and which are adverbs. If a student gives a wrong answer, ask him to give a sentence using the word as the part of speech he said. For *near* and *kindly,* use the word as the other part of speech from the one named. These words illustrate the difficulty in identifying words as adjectives or adverbs.

Lesson Outline:
  1. Many adjectives and adverbs cannot be distinguished by their form.
      a. Many adverbs end with -ly.
      b. Some adjectives also end with -ly.
      c. Some adverbs do not end with -ly.
      d. Some words can be either adjectives or adverbs.

  2. To distinguish an adjective from an adverb, the most important tests are what part of speech the word modifies *and* what question it answers.

  3. The same two tests can be used to distinguish between adjective and adverb phrases.
      a. Also, an adjective phrase must come right after the word it modifies, but an adverb phrase usually can be moved to a different place without changing the meaning of the sentence.
      b. An adverb phrase may contain one or more adjective phrases.

  4. The same two tests can be used to distinguish between adjective and adverb clauses. Also, an adjective clause usually begins with a relative pronoun, whereas an adverb clause begins with a subordinating conjunction. Another clue is that an adverb clause can be moved to a different position without changing the meaning of the sentence.

★ **EXTRA PRACTICE**
Worksheet 45 (*Distinguishing Between Adjectives and Adverbs*)

Test 2: *What question does the word answer?*
   Early tells *which.* It is an adjective.
   Steadfastly tells *how.* It is an adverb.

The bears have <u>often</u> been coming <u>quite</u> <u>close</u> to the house.
   Test 1: *What part of speech does the word modify?*
      Often modifies the verb *have been coming.* It is an adverb.
      Quite modifies the adverb *close.* It is an adverb.
      Close modifies the verb *have been coming.* It is an adverb.
   Test 2: *What question does the word answer?*
      Often tells *when.* It is an adverb.
      Quite tells *to what degree.* It is an adverb.
      Close tells *where.* It is an adverb.

You may also tend to confuse prepositional phrases. The same prepositions are used for adjective and adverb phrases. In fact, the very same phrase might be an adjective in one sentence and an adverb in another.

To decide whether a prepositional phrase is an adjective or an adverb, use the same two tests: "What part of speech does the phrase modify?" and "What question does the phrase answer?" Also consider the position of the prepositional phrase. An adjective phrase must come right after the word it modifies, but an adverb phrase usually can be moved to a different place without changing the meaning of the sentence.

Every story <u>in the Bible</u> is true and accurate.
   (*In the Bible* modifies the noun *story* by telling *which.* Also, the
      phrase must come right after *story.* It is an adjective phrase.)
<u>In the Bible</u> we can read the story of the Creation.
   (*In the Bible* modifies the verb *can read* by telling *where.* Also,
      the phrase can be moved to a different position. It is an adverb
      phrase.)
The visitors <u>from Ohio</u> bought several bushels <u>of peaches.</u>
   (*From Ohio* modifies the noun *visitors* by telling *which.* Also, the
      phrase must come right after *visitors.* It is an adjective phrase.)
   (*Of peaches* modifies the noun *bushels* by telling *what kind of.*
      Also, the phrase must come right after *bushels.* It is an adjective phrase.)

Remember that an adverb phrase may contain one or more adjective phrases. The adjective phrases modify previous objects of prepositions.

<u>After the sacrifice of Christ's blood,</u> the Old Testament sacrifices became
   meaningless. (*After the sacrifice of Christ's blood* modifies the verb

became by telling *when;* it is an adverb phrase. *Of Christ's blood* modifies the noun *sacrifice* by telling *what kind of;* it is an adjective phrase.)

You must also distinguish between adjective and adverb clauses. Again the tests are the same: "What part of speech does the clause modify?" and "What question does the clause answer?" Also remember that an adjective clause usually begins with a relative pronoun: *who, whom, whose, which,* or *that.* An adverb clause begins with a subordinating conjunction, such as *after, because, if, though,* or *while.*

> The man <u>whose younger son had left home</u> yearned for his return.
> > (*Whose younger son had left home* modifies the noun *man* by telling *which.* Also, it begins with the relative pronoun *whose,* so it is an adjective clause.)
> <u>After the prodigal son returned,</u> the elder son was bitter and jealous.
> > (*After the prodigal son returned* modifies the verb *was* by telling *when.* Also, it begins with the subordinating conjunction *After,* so it is an adverb clause.)

Remember too that an adverb clause can be moved to a different position without changing the meaning of the sentence. Any word, phrase, or clause that can be moved about in this way is an adverb.

> The angels rejoice <u>when a sinner repents</u>.
> <u>When a sinner repents</u>, the angels rejoice.
> > (Both sentences mean the same.)

Class Practice

A. Tell whether each underlined word is an *adjective* or an *adverb.*
1. The Good Samaritan exercised true <u>brotherly</u> love to the <u>hurt</u> man.
2. He was not <u>too</u> <u>proud</u> to stoop <u>down</u> and help the man.
3. Because he treated the man <u>kindly</u>, he stands as a <u>worthy</u> example to us.
4. His <u>kindly</u> deeds will <u>surely</u> be remembered <u>often</u>.

B. Tell whether each underlined phrase is an *adjective* or an *adverb.* A phrase that is part of another phrase is underlined twice and should be identified separately.
1. A little boy <u>with a small lunch</u> was quite useful <u>to the Master</u>.
2. Our thanks <u>to the Lord</u> should come <u>from a sincere heart</u>.
3. <u>Through the storms <u>of life</u></u>, we should trust <u>in the Lord</u>.
4. The dog <u>on the ground</u> was barking <u>at the large red squirrel <u>on the branch <u>above him</u></u></u>.

Lesson 86 Answers

Class Practice

A. 1. brotherly—adjective; hurt—adjective
   2. too—adverb; proud—adjective; down—adverb
   3. kindly—adverb; worthy—adjective
   4. kindly—adjective; surely—adverb; often—adverb

B. 1. with a small lunch—adjective; to the Master—adverb
   2. to the Lord—adjective; from a sincere heart—adverb
   3. Through the storms of life—adverb; of life—adjective; in the Lord—adverb
   4. on the ground—adjective; at the large red squirrel on the branch above him—adverb; on the branch—adjective; above him—adjective

5. In the middle of the afternoon, the girls took a treat out <u>to the field for the hardworking crew</u>.

C. Tell whether each underlined clause is an *adjective* or an *adverb*.
   1. <u>Because God is still on the throne</u>, we need not fear the circumstances of life <u>which are beyond our control</u>.
   2. The Book <u>that always gives us courage</u> is the Bible.
   3. John was in exile <u>when he received a glorious revelation from God</u>.
   4. He saw the saints <u>whose robes were washed in the blood of the Lamb</u>.
   5. <u>After Satan is defeated</u>, the Lord will reign forever with the saints <u>whom He has redeemed</u>.

D. On the chalkboard, diagram these sentences.
   1. These boys almost always do good work.
   2. The bird in the tree is a meadowlark.
   3. A meadowlark is singing sweetly in the tree.
   4. When we see the stars, we should feel very small.
   5. Those deer beside the stream are the ones that we saw.

Written Exercises

A. Write whether each underlined word is an adjective (*adj.*) or an adverb (*adv.*).
   1. Josiah, <u>a</u> <u>godly</u> king of Judah, sought <u>the</u> Lord <u>early</u> in life.
   2. With <u>deep</u> <u>fatherly</u> concern, David <u>earnestly</u> prepared Solomon for the <u>kingly</u> duties that he would assume <u>shortly</u>.
   3. <u>Boldly</u>, Sennacherib declared that he would <u>completely</u> overthrow Jerusalem.
   4. The Lord dealt <u>very</u> <u>kindly</u> with Ruth when she chose to <u>wholly</u> follow the Lord.
   5. <u>Two</u> <u>large</u> dogs barked <u>furiously</u> as we came <u>too</u> <u>close</u> to the gate.
   6. <u>This</u> <u>recently</u> <u>discovered</u> cave is <u>already</u> <u>famous</u>.
   7. <u>His</u> <u>tiny</u> <u>baby</u> brother could <u>not</u> talk <u>yet</u>.

B. Write whether each underlined phrase is an adjective (*adj.*) or an adverb (*adv.*). If a phrase is underlined twice, write a separate label for it.
   1. God formed man <u>from the dust</u> <u>of the earth</u>.
   2. Set your affection <u>on things above</u>, keep your eyes <u>upon Jesus</u>, and keep traveling <u>toward heaven</u>.
   3. All <u>of the pre-Flood patriarchs</u> <u>except Enoch</u> died <u>after a long life</u>.
   4. Three black bears emerged <u>from the den</u> and peered <u>around the rock</u> <u>beside the waterfall</u>.
   5. The boy <u>between Glen and Lavern</u> is Glen's cousin <u>from Iowa</u>.

B. 1. adv., adj.
   2. adv., adv., adv.
   3. adj., adj., adv.
   4. adv., adv., adj.
   5. adj., adj.

5. In the middle of the afternoon—adverb; of the afternoon—adjective; to the field—adverb; for the hardworking crew—adverb

C. 1. Because God is still on the throne—adverb; which are beyond our control—adjective
   2. that always gives us courage—adjective
   3. when he received a glorious revelation from God—adverb
   4. whose robes were washed in the blood of the Lamb—adjective
   5. After Satan is defeated—adverb; whom He has redeemed—adjective

D. 1.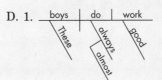

   2.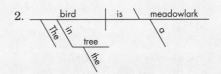

   3.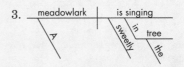

   4.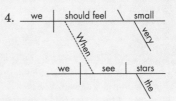

   5.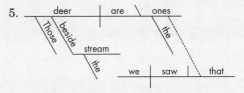

Written Exercises
A. 1. adj., adj., adj., adv.
   2. adj., adj., adv., adj., adv.
   3. adv., adv.
   4. adv., adv., adv.
   5. adj., adj., adv., adv., adv.
   6. adj., adv., adj., adv., adj.
   7. adj., adj., adj., adv., adv.

6. <u>During that time</u>, my parents worked <u>among the Indians in Guatemala</u>.

C. Write *adj.* or *adv.* for each underlined clause.
1. <u>When Abraham was ninety-nine years old</u>, the Lord appeared to him.
2. God promised him the land <u>that he was in</u>.
3. <u>If God be for us</u>, we need not fear the devil, <u>who seeks our ruin</u>.
4. All <u>who truly fear the Lord</u> will live <u>as He commands in the Bible</u>.
5. Jesus prayed in Gethsemane, <u>which was on the Mount of Olives</u>.
6. Peter was released from prison <u>while the saints were gathered in prayer</u>.
7. <u>Because Father was preaching in a distant community</u>, the responsibility of the farm fell on Joel, <u>who was now seventeen years old</u>.

D. Diagram these sentences.
1. Jesus was led by the Spirit into the wilderness.
2. When He was in the wilderness, Jesus was sorely tempted by the devil.
3. During the temptation, He repeatedly quoted the Scriptures, which always lead man to victory.
4. The incredibly detailed replica of an old gristmill was quite small.
5. The old mill stood on the spot that is now the location of a much newer mill.

Review Exercises

A. Copy correctly each word with a capitalization error. [20]
1. Uncle Seth is my oldest Uncle on mother's side.
2. He teaches at the Mountville Mennonite school.
3. We traveled through several States in the northeast last Spring.
4. In our Reading class, we studied the poem "The Blind Men And the Elephant."
5. On Thanksgiving day, grandmother served Pennsupreme Ice Cream with her apple pie.

B. Copy each word that should be followed by a comma, a semicolon, or an end mark, and add the missing punctuation. (Use the index if you need help.)
1. What a mighty God we serve
2. He created the whole world and now He upholds it by His power
3. Since He is so great should we not worship and adore Him
4. He deserves our love our loyalty and our service
5. Jesus Christ who is part of the triune Godhead condescended to be

B. 1. serve!
2. world, power.
3. great, Him?
4. love, loyalty, service.
5. Christ, Godhead, man; earth, mankind.

6. adv., adv., adj.
C. 1. adv.   5. adj.
2. adj.   6. adv.
3. adv., adj.   7. adv., adj.
4. adj., adv.

D. 1.
2.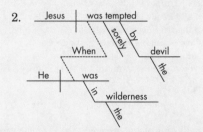
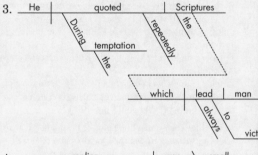
3.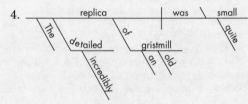
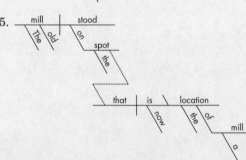

Review Exercises
A. 1. (oldest) uncle, Mother's
2. School
3. states, Northeast, spring
4. reading, and
5. Day, Grandmother, ice cream

born as a man and while He was here on earth He lived and died for mankind

---

87. Using Adverbs Correctly

> ### Lesson Survey
> - Use an adverb only when it communicates effectively.
> - Do not use adverbs unnecessarily.
> - Use *good, well, bad,* and *badly* in the right way.
> - Do not use the adjectives *real, sure,* and *easy* for the adverbs *really, surely,* and *easily.*
> - Do not use two negative words to express one negative thought.
> - Do not use *kind of* or *sort of* for *rather* or *somewhat.*

Adverbs, like adjectives, are important in our communication. But if we want to benefit from their usefulness, we must learn to use them correctly. The following rules will help you.

1. *Use an adverb only when it communicates effectively.* Do not use adverbs to modify weak verbs and adjectives, when you could use expressive verbs and descriptive adjectives that express your ideas much more clearly.

Weak: The two boys <u>ran rapidly</u> to the tree.
Better: The two boys <u>raced</u> to the tree.

Weak: A lonely ox <u>called loudly</u> from the meadow.
Better: A lonely ox <u>bawled</u> from the meadow.

Weak: We were <u>extremely wet</u> in the sudden downpour.
Better: We were <u>drenched</u> in the sudden downpour.

Of course, this does not mean that you should avoid using adverbs. They do often improve communication. In the examples above, other adverbs could be used with the more expressive verbs and adjectives.

The two boys <u>raced excitedly</u> to the tree.
A lonely ox <u>bawled dolefully</u> from the meadow.
We were <u>miserably drenched</u> in the sudden downpour.

Lesson 87

Purpose: To teach some additional rules for adverb usage.

Oral Review:

1. Identify the single-word adverbs in these sentences. (Adverbs are underlined.)
   a. The early Christians were <u>often</u> persecuted <u>severely</u> for their faith.
   b. <u>Finally</u> Darla found the <u>cleverly</u> hidden thimble.
   c. Do <u>not</u> go <u>too near</u> to the edge.
2. Identify the adverb phrase in this sentence: *The monkey in the tree is holding a banana in his paw.* (in his paw)
3. Identify the adverb clause in this sentence: *After the meeting was over, we ate lunch in the room that the intermediate Sunday school class uses.* (After the meeting was over)

4. Tell whether each sentence is simple, compound, or complex.
   a. Did you know that today is the first day of spring? (complex)
   b. The clouds are hiding the sun, and a cold wind is blowing. (compound)
   c. Now the sun is shining brightly and chasing the chills away. (simple)
   d. After the sun had shone for a while, the day became quite pleasant. (complex)

Lesson Introduction: By not following the rules of proper usage, people sometimes say things they really do not mean. For instance, a person who has been sick may say, "I feel good again." He probably means that he no longer feels sick; actually he has said that he no longer feels unhappy or upset. Another may say, "I wasn't involved in none of that mischief." Probably he means that he is innocent of

2. *Do not use adverbs unnecessarily.* In the following expressions, the underlined adverbs usually add nothing to the meaning.

Do Not Say	**Say**
connect <u>up</u>	<u>Connect</u> these two hoses.
divide <u>up</u>	We shall <u>divide</u> the candy among the children.
end <u>up</u>	I wonder how the story will <u>end</u>.
wash <u>up</u>	Clyde is <u>washing</u> the car.
continue <u>on</u>	We shall <u>continue</u> with our original plans.
farther <u>on</u>	The boys rested before going <u>farther</u>.
later <u>on</u>	We shall finish this project <u>later</u> in the week.
seek <u>after</u>	Do you <u>seek</u> peace with all men?
leave <u>from</u>	Jay <u>left</u> St. Louis this morning.
refer <u>back</u>	This <u>refers</u> to an earlier event.

3. *Use* good, well, bad, *and* badly *in the right way. Good* and *bad* are always adjectives; use them only to modify nouns and pronouns.

Some of these boards are still <u>good</u>.
Replace the <u>bad</u> ones.

Well can be used as an adjective meaning "healthy," "proper," or "prudent."

Aunt Susan had been sick, but now she is <u>well</u> again.
It is <u>well</u> (*or* <u>good</u>) that you came early.

Well is usually an adverb; *badly* is always an adverb.

Father plows <u>well</u>, but I plowed quite <u>badly</u> the first time.
This picture, <u>well</u> detailed but <u>badly</u> proportioned, should be improved.

4. *Do not use the adjectives* real, sure, *and* easy *for the adverbs* really, surely, *and* easily.

Incorrect: The geese are <u>real</u> excited.
The boys <u>sure</u> made a mistake!
We should finish <u>easy</u> today.
Correct: The geese are <u>really</u> excited.
The boys <u>surely</u> made a mistake!
We should finish <u>easily</u> today.

5. *Do not use two negative words to express one negative thought.* The following list contains some common negative words, which mean "not" or "almost not."

all the mischief; actually he has said that he is guilty of some of the mischief.

Lesson Outline:

1. Use an adverb only when it communicates effectively. Do not use adverbs to modify weak verbs and adjectives, when you could use expressive verbs and descriptive adjectives that express your ideas much more clearly.

2. Do not use adverbs unnecessarily.

(*Teacher:* The "unnecessary" adverbs listed in the lesson are acceptable when they are part of idioms with meanings of their own. For example, *end up* is proper when it refers to an ultimate outcome, as in this sentence: If you act too hastily, you will end up regretting it.)

3. Use **good, well, bad,** *and* **badly** *in the right way.*

a. *Good* and *bad* are always adjectives.
b. *Well* can be used as an adjective meaning "healthy," "proper," or "prudent."
c. *Well* is usually an adverb; *badly* is always an adverb.

4. Do not use the adjectives **real, sure,** *and* **easy** *for the adverbs* **really, surely,** *and* **easily.**

5. Do not use two negative words to express one negative thought.

6. Do not use **kind of** *or* **sort of** *for* **rather** *or* **somewhat.**

★ *EXTRA PRACTICE*
Worksheet 46 (*Using Adverbs Correctly*)

no	never	nothing	barely
not	nobody	neither	hardly
none	no one	nowhere	scarcely

Incorrect: Uncle Harvey ca<u>n't hardly</u> hear anymore.
Correct: Uncle Harvey can <u>hardly</u> hear anymore.

A sentence with a double negative can often be corrected in two ways.

Incorrect: I ca<u>n't</u> find <u>no</u> mistake in this work.
Correct: I ca<u>n't</u> find <u>any</u> mistake in this work.
I <u>can</u> find <u>no</u> mistake in this work.

6. *Do not use* kind of *or* sort of *for* rather *or* somewhat.

Incorrect: We were <u>sort of</u> sleepy.
Correct: We were <u>rather</u> (*or* <u>somewhat</u>) sleepy.

Incorrect: This soup is <u>kind of</u> salty.
Correct: This soup is <u>somewhat</u> (*or* <u>rather</u>) salty.

Class Practice

A. Read these sentences, replacing the underlined words with more expressive verbs or adjectives.
1. David and Jonathan were <u>really good</u> friends.
2. The temple that Solomon built was <u>very nice</u>.
3. It <u>rained slowly</u> all day.
4. The bitter man <u>walked angrily</u> away.

B. Read these sentences correctly.
1. The Lord does all things good.
2. We sure should be thankful to Him for His blessings to us.
3. Did Joseph continue on serving the Lord faithfully?
4. Aaron's explanation of the golden calf was kind of foolish.
5. The New Testament Scriptures often refer back to the Old Testament.
6. Eli didn't place no restrictions on his evil sons.
7. The priests had to wash up carefully before entering the tabernacle.
8. Naaman was sort of surprised at the prophet's instructions.
9. He couldn't scarcely bring himself to wash in the Jordan River.
10. After obeying the prophet, Naaman became good again.
11. It was so foggy that Father couldn't barely see where he was going.
12. The boy worked so bad that he was reprimanded.
13. The carpenter could easy see that he was not interested in working.
14. How shall we divide up the work this evening?

Lesson 87 Answers

Class Practice
A. (Sample answers.)
1. close, devoted
2. beautiful, glorious, magnificent
3. sprinkled, drizzled
4. stalked, stomped

B. (Corrections are marked.)
1. The Lord does all things <u>well</u>.
2. We <u>surely</u> should be thankful to Him for His blessings to us.
3. Did Joseph continue ~~on~~ serving the Lord faithfully?
4. Aaron's explanation of the golden calf was <u>rather</u> (<u>somewhat</u>) foolish.
5. The New Testament Scriptures often refer ~~back~~ to the Old Testament.
6. Eli didn't place <u>any</u> restrictions on his evil sons.
   or Eli <u>placed</u> no restrictions on his evil sons.
7. The priests had to wash ~~up~~ carefully before entering the tabernacle.
8. Naaman was <u>rather</u> (<u>somewhat</u>) surprised at the prophet's instructions.
9. He could~~n't~~ scarcely bring himself to wash in the Jordan River.
10. After obeying the prophet, Naaman became <u>well</u> again.
11. It was so foggy that Father could~~n't~~ barely see where he was going.
12. The boy worked so <u>badly</u> that he was reprimanded.
13. The carpenter could <u>easily</u> see that he was not interested in working.
14. How shall we divide ~~up~~ the work this evening?

Written Exercises

A. Write a more expressive verb or adjective to replace the underlined words in each sentence.
   1. The frightened girl <u>called loudly</u> for help.
   2. The screen door <u>shut quickly</u> after Timothy as he bounded into the house.
   3. This redwood tree is <u>extremely big</u>.
   4. A horse <u>ran swiftly</u> across the yard.
   5. Hummingbird eggs are <u>really small</u>.

B. Write the correct words in parentheses.
   1. Jesus knew perfectly (good, well) what the Pharisees were thinking.
   2. They wanted very (bad, badly) to trap Him in His words.
   3. The common people (sure, surely) flocked to Jesus.
   4. Many sick people came to Jesus, and He made them (good, well) again.
   5. Some of these apples taste (bad, badly).
   6. Edith's poems are (real, really) interesting.
   7. Nathan (easy, easily) beat Harvey in the race.
   8. These nails are still (good, well); put them in a box.

C. Write these sentences correctly.
   1. The crown is only for those who continue on faithfully until the end.
   2. Daniel's enemies couldn't find no fault in his life.
   3. They sought after some excuse to remove him.
   4. Elijah must have felt kind of afraid of Jezebel.
   5. He left from Jezreel to flee for his life.
   6. Jerry couldn't find the keys to the tractor nowhere.
   7. Refer back to the chart if necessary.
   8. The refugees never had no real home.

Review Exercises

A. Write whether each sentence is *simple, compound,* or *complex.* [14, 15]
   1. "A city that is set on an hill cannot be hid."
   2. "If thou wilt, thou canst make me clean."
   3. "The leprosy departed from him, and he was cleansed."
   4. "My servant lieth at home sick of the palsy, grievously tormented."
   5. "I will come and heal him."
   6. We never know what a new day may bring forth.
   7. Mammals are warm-blooded animals, but reptiles are cold-blooded.
   8. A mammal has a backbone, is covered with hair, and provides milk for its young.

Written Exercises

A. (Sample answers.)
   1. screamed, yelled, cried
   2. slammed, banged
   3. gigantic, huge, enormous
   4. galloped, raced, bolted
   5. tiny

B. 1. well   5. bad
   2. badly   6. really
   3. surely   7. easily
   4. well   8. good

C. (Corrections are marked.)
   1. The crown is only for those who continue ~~on~~ faithfully until the end.
   2. Daniel's enemies could~~n't~~ find no fault in his life.
      or Daniel's enemies couldn't find <u>any</u> fault in his life.
   3. They sought ~~after~~ some excuse to remove him.
   4. Elijah must have felt <u>somewhat</u> (rather) afraid of Jezebel.
   5. He left ~~from~~ Jezreel to flee for his life.
   6. Jerry couldn't find the keys to the tractor <u>anywhere</u>.
      or Jerry could~~n't~~ find the keys to the tractor nowhere.
   7. Refer ~~back~~ to the chart if necessary.
   8. The refugees never had <u>any</u> real home.
      or The refugees ~~never~~ had no real home.

Review Exercises

A. 1. complex   5. simple
   2. complex   6. complex
   3. compound   7. compound
   4. simple   8. simple

3. For each pair, write the letter of the sentence that is better. [77]
  1. a. What sort of a mushroom is this beautiful red one?
     b. What sort of mushroom is this beautiful red one?
  2. a. These mushrooms are poisonous.
     b. Them mushrooms are poisonous.
  3. a. Those behind the woodpile are edible.
     b. Those there behind the woodpile are edible.
  4. a. These tiny, small mushrooms are glistening inky caps.
     b. These tiny mushrooms are glistening inky caps.
  5. a. This year we found fewer mushrooms to eat than we did last year.
     b. This year we found less mushrooms to eat than we did last year.
  6. a. A cold rain fell all day.
     b. A cold, wet rain fell all day.
  7. a. We bought a nice recipe box for Mother.
     b. We bought a decorative recipe box for Mother.
  8. a. A raccoon is a curious and clever animal.
     b. A raccoon is a curious and a clever animal.
  9. a. Brother Merle, the secretary and the treasurer, gave his report.
     b. Brother Merle, the secretary and treasurer, gave his report.
  10. a. Leslie had an awful time with his chores tonight.
      b. Leslie had a difficult time with his chores tonight.

B. 1. b
    2. a
    3. a
    4. b
    5. a
    6. a
    7. b
    8. a
    9. b
    10. b

---

88. Chapter 8 Review

Class Practice

A. Identify each single-word adverb, and tell which word it modifies.
  1. The Rechabites still followed their father's teachings very faithfully.
  2. Peter declared too boldly his willingness to die for Jesus.
  3. Soon he had shamefully denied his Master.
  4. When the test actually came, he was not very courageous after all.

B. Identify each adverb phrase, and tell which word it modifies.
  1. Paul preached to the disciples at Troas late into the night.
  2. Eutychus sat in the window during Paul's sermon.
  3. He sank down with sleep and fell from the third loft.
  4. In his fall, Eutychus was killed, but Paul raised him to life.

C. Identify each adverb clause, and tell which word it modifies. Also tell

Lesson 88

Purpose: To review the concepts taught in Chapter 8.

Lesson 88 Answers

Class Practice

A. 1. still—followed; very—faithfully; faithfully—followed
   2. too—boldly; boldly—declared
   3. Soon—had denied; shamefully—had denied
   4. actually—came; not—was; very—courageous

B. 1. to the disciples at Troas—preached; into the night—late (*At Troas* is an adjective phrase.)
   2. in the window—sat; during Paul's sermon—sat
   3. with sleep—down; from the third loft—fell
   4. In his fall—was killed; to life—raised

where any missing commas need to be placed.

1. As the night grew dark the sound of insects filled the air.
2. Some of God's creatures are active at night because it is unsafe for them in the daytime.
3. A mouse while it searches for food must be on the lookout for a hungry weasel, which is also looking for a meal.
4. God designed each creature so that it would fill the right place in this world.

D. Tell whether each underlined modifier is an *adverb* or an *adjective*.
1. The friendly visitor spoke kindly to the sickly girl, who lay in bed all the time.
2. The canal boats that once carried much cargo have now been replaced with more modern means of transportation.
3. Canals quickly went out of business when railroads began crisscrossing the countryside.
4. The jars in these boxes should be placed in the basement.

E. Read each sentence, using the correct form of the adverb in parentheses.
1. Of our two augers, this one runs (fast).
2. Sound travels (far) and (fast) through solids than through gases.
3. Of all those who refused to take a tract, Mr. Bindle spoke the (rudely) and treated us the (badly).
4. Aluminum will melt (quickly) than copper.

F. Read these sentences, replacing the underlined words with more expressive verbs or adjectives.
1. The fishermen talked loudly over the roar of the wind.
2. Mrs. Sipes lives in a very small apartment.

G. Read each sentence correctly.
1. The mechanic couldn't find nothing wrong with the car.
2. The car had certainly not been running good for us though.
3. He will continue on checking a few other things.
4. Even though Arthur's softball glove is kind of old, it sure works well.

H. On the chalkboard, diagram these sentences.
1. A pleasant breeze blew softly through the partly opened window.
2. The far windows should remain completely shut.
3. Because the dog strayed too far, it was killed on the road.
4. These books on my desk should be laid on the shelf before lunch.

I. Answer these questions about giving oral explanations.
1. What two orders are the most commonly used in giving explanations?

C. 1. As the night grew dark—filled; comma after *dark*
2. because it is unsafe for them in the daytime—are
3. while it searches for food—must be; commas after *mouse* and *food*
4. so that it would fill the right place in this world—designed

D. 1. friendly—adjective; kindly—adverb; sickly—adjective;
who lay in bed all the time—adjective
2. that once carried much cargo—adjective; now—adverb; with more modern means of transportation—adverb
3. quickly—adverb; when railroads began crisscrossing the countryside—adverb
4. in these boxes—adjective;
in the basement—adverb

E. 1. faster   3. most rudely, worst
2. farther, faster   4. more quickly

F. (Sample answers.)
1. yelled, shouted
2. tiny

G. (Corrections are marked.)
1. The mechanic couldn't find anything wrong with the car.
   or The mechanic couldn't find nothing wrong with the car.
2. The car had certainly not been running well for us though.
3. He will continue on checking a few other things.
4. Even though Arthur's softball glove is rather (somewhat) old, it surely works well.

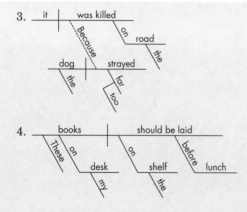

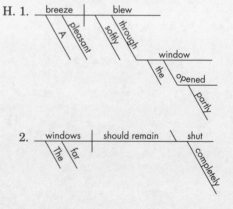

I. 1. chronological and spatial

2. Why should you write the exact words of the introduction and the conclusion?

3. What are two good ways to introduce your explanation?

4. What are two good ways to conclude your explanation?

Written Exercises

A. Write each single-word adverb and the word it modifies.
1. Jesus turned and looked sadly at Peter.
2. Peter immediately recognized his sin and wept very bitterly.
3. True godly fear always moves one to draw near to the Lord.
4. The students are filing in quietly now.
5. Today we have a rather difficult assignment.

B. Write each adverb phrase and the word it modifies.
1. Beneath God's watchful eye, the saints dwell in perfect security.
2. We can always live under God's approval.
3. The turmoil in the world should turn our minds to God's sovereignty.
4. After our last recess, a visitor with an artificial leg came to school.
5. The deer leaped over the fence, crashed through the underbrush, and disappeared into the forest.

C. Copy the conjunction and the last word of each adverb clause, with three dots (…) between them. Also write the word that it modifies.
1. Because we believe the Bible, we know the way that pleases the Lord.
2. People are drawn into deception when they do not obey the Bible.
3. The house that stands across the road belonged to Brother Dale before his family moved to British Columbia.
4. During the busy season, our family picked strawberries until our backs ached.
5. For a few weeks, we were busier than we had expected to be.

2. These two parts are important in setting the tone of the explanation and in closing the explanation effectively.

3. with a thought-provoking question or an interesting statement

4. with a summary of the main steps or a specific impression of the explanation

Written Exercises

A. 1. sadly—looked
2. immediately—recognized; very—bitterly; bitterly—wept
3. always—moves; near—to draw
4. in—are filing; quietly—are filing; now—are filing
5. Today—have; rather—difficult

B. 1. Beneath God's watchful eye—dwell; in perfect security—dwell
2. under God's approval—can live
3. to God's sovereignty—should turn
4. After our last recess—came; to school—came
5. over the fence—leaped; through the underbrush—crashed; into the forest—disappeared

C. 1. Because … Bible—know
2. when … Bible—are drawn
3. before … Columbia—belonged
4. until … ached—picked
5. than … be—busier

D. Write the correct words in parentheses.
1. This (easy, easily) assignment is a pleasant surprise.
2. It (sure, surely) should not take long!
3. I did yesterday's lesson so (bad, badly) that I had to do it over.
4. Which of the two girls wrote (more, most) neatly?
5. Carl feels sick today, but Carol feels (good, well) again.
6. Mary Louise has ironed these shirts very (good, well).

E. Write each underlined expression correctly.
1. The speaker <u>referred back to something</u> he had said earlier.
2. There <u>isn't no outlet</u> from the Dead Sea.
3. Would Nicodemus <u>continue on seeking</u> the way of truth?
4. We <u>couldn't scarcely understand</u> the stranger's speech.
5. Of our two goats, Flop-ear pulls a wagon the <u>most willingly</u>.
6. We were <u>sort of surprised</u> when a strange goat came to our farm.
7. Both Warren and Wayne are good pitchers, but Wayne <u>can pitch farthest</u>.
8. The weather became cold <u>kind of early</u>.
9. Sarah finished her math lesson <u>quicklier than</u> Elizabeth did.
10. After we <u>connected up the two wires</u>, the lights worked again.

F. Diagram these sentences.
1. These springs have always been unusually strong.
2. They have never failed since Grandfather moved here in 1930.
3. A bitterly cold air mass moved in rapidly yesterday.
4. Father greatly surprised us when he brought a puppy home.

G. Answer these questions about book reports.
1. What are six kinds of information that a book report should include?
2. What two things are included in the setting?
3. What should the largest part of the book report tell about?
4. What is one thing you should not state in a book report?
5. How should you prepare for writing a book report?
6. As with any other composition, what should you do after writing the book report?

D. 1. easy   4. more
2. surely   5. well
3. badly   6. well

E. 1. referred to something
2. isn't any outlet *or* is no outlet
3. continue seeking
4. could scarcely understand
5. more willingly
6. rather (somewhat) surprised
7. can pitch farther
8. rather (somewhat) early
9. more quickly than
10. connected the two wires

F. 1.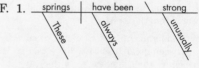

2.

3.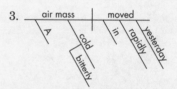

4.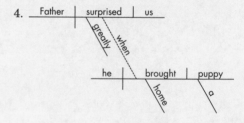

G. 1. (1) Basic facts, including title, author, publisher, and copyright date
(2) Setting, including place and time
(3) Main characters and their characteristics
(4) Theme and main events
(5) Lessons or benefits of the story
(6) Your evaluation of the story
2. the place and the time
3. the theme and main events
4. the outcome of the story
5. You need to gather and organize information before writing.
6. You need to proofread after writing.

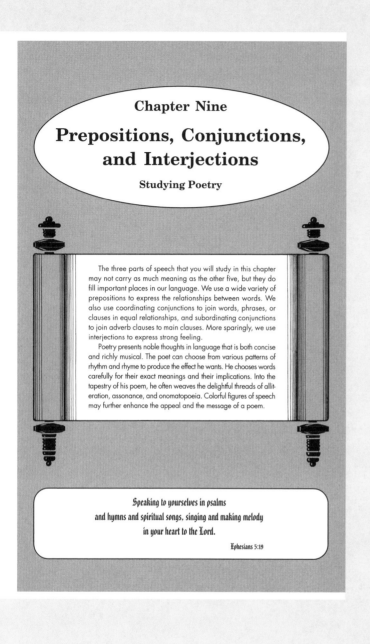

Chapter Nine

Prepositions, Conjunctions, and Interjections

Studying Poetry

The three parts of speech that you will study in this chapter may not carry as much meaning as the other five, but they do fill important places in our language. We use a wide variety of prepositions to express the relationships between words. We also use coordinating conjunctions to join words, phrases, or clauses in equal relationships, and subordinating conjunctions to join adverb clauses to main clauses. More sparingly, we use interjections to express strong feeling.

Poetry presents noble thoughts in language that is both concise and richly musical. The poet can choose from various patterns of rhythm and rhyme to produce the effect he wants. He chooses words carefully for their exact meanings and their implications. Into the tapestry of his poem, he often weaves the delightful threads of alliteration, assonance, and onomatopoeia. Colorful figures of speech may further enhance the appeal and the message of a poem.

Speaking to yourselves in psalms
and hymns and spiritual songs, singing and making melody
in your heart to the Lord.

Ephesians 5:19

89. Prepositions

> ### Lesson Survey
> - A **preposition** is a word that shows the relationship between its object and some other word in the sentence.
> - A **prepositional phrase** includes the preposition, its object, and any adjectives that modify the object.
> - A prepositional phrase can be used as an adjective or an adverb.
> - Prepositions must not be confused with adverbs.
> - A prepositional phrase is diagramed beneath the word it modifies.

Most prepositions are simple, basic words. Sometimes a preposition consists of more than one word. Study the following chart so that you are thoroughly familiar with the common prepositions.

aboard	below	in	since	within
about	beneath	inside	through	without
above	beside	into	throughout	according to
across	besides	like	to	along with
after	between	near	toward	because of
against	beyond	of	under	due to
along	by	off	underneath	in addition to
among	despite	on	until	in spite of
around	down	out	unto	instead of
as	during	outside	up	on account of
at	except	over	upon	out of
before	for	past	with	with regard to
behind	from			

A *preposition* is a word that shows the relationship between its object and some other word in the sentence. The prepositions in the following sentences show three different relationships between the verb *moved* and the noun *Sodom* (the object of the preposition).

Lot moved <u>toward</u> Sodom.
Lot moved <u>into</u> Sodom.
Lot moved <u>out of</u> Sodom.

A *prepositional phrase* includes the preposition, its object, and any adjectives that modify the object. Remember that the phrase always begins with a preposition and ends with an object that tells *whom* or *what* about the

Lesson 89

Purpose: To teach the rudiments of prepositions.

Oral Review:

1. Label the parts of speech for the words in these sentences. (*Teacher:* Write on the board and do together, or dictate for the students to do individually.)

    n.   adv.   v.   adj.   n.
  a. Jeremiah boldly proclaimed God's message.

    adj. n. v. adv. v. pron.
  b. The wicked did not appreciate him.

    pron. v. adj. adj. n.
  c. Somebody did a golden deed.

    adj. adj. n. v. adv. adj.
  d. The broken toys were still useful.

2. Using the verb *see*, make a short sentence for each of the six tenses. (*Teacher:* Write the following form sentence on the board: *I ——— the stars.*)

  a. present (I *see* the stars.)
  b. past (I *saw* the stars.)
  c. future (I *shall see* the stars.)
  d. present perfect (I *have seen* the stars.)
  e. past perfect (I *had seen* the stars.)
  f. future perfect (I *shall have seen* the stars.)

3. Using the same basic sentence, give the progressive form of the verb *see* in all six tenses.

  a. present progressive (I *am seeing* the stars.)
  b. past progressive (I *was seeing* the stars.)
  c. future progressive (I *shall be seeing* the stars.)
  d. present perfect progressive (I *have been seeing* the stars.)
  e. past perfect progressive (I *had been seeing* the stars.)
  f. future perfect progressive (I *shall have been seeing* the stars.)

preposition. Can you find three prepositional phrases in the following sentence?

The Son of God was born into the world as a little baby.

You should recognize the three common prepositions—*of, into,* and *as.* Now find the entire phrases by finding the objects and then including all the adjectives that modify the objects.

The Son <u>of God</u> was born <u>into the world</u> <u>as a little baby</u>.

A preposition may have two objects (a compound object).

John, the son <u>of Zacharias and Elisabeth</u>, was the forerunner of Christ.
All the spies <u>except Joshua and Caleb</u> brought back an evil report.

Prepositions normally come before their objects, but sometimes they come after. This is especially common with the pronouns *what, whom, which,* and *that.*

<u>What</u> are you talking <u>about</u>? (You are talking *about what*?)
<u>Which cage</u> do these hens belong <u>in</u>? (These hens belong *in which cage*?)

When the object of a preposition is a pronoun, it must be in the objective case. Be especially careful to use the correct pronoun when the preposition has a compound object.

Incorrect: We received a letter <u>from Harold and they</u>.
Father bought a bicycle <u>for David and I</u>.
Correct: We received a letter <u>from Harold and them</u>.
Father bought a bicycle <u>for David and me</u>.

Prepositional phrases can be used as adjectives and adverbs. You have already studied such phrases in Chapters 7 and 8. When a prepositional phrase is used as an adjective, it must come right after the noun or pronoun it modifies.

The boy <u>with a brown shirt</u> is my brother.
(*With a brown shirt* modifies the noun *boy.*)
Someone <u>in a stylish car</u> requested some information.
(*In a stylish car* modifies the pronoun *Someone.*)

When a prepositional phrase is used as an adverb, it modifies a verb, an adjective, an adverb, or a verbal. An adverb phrase can be placed at different locations in a sentence.

4. Using the same basic sentence, give the emphatic form of the verb *see* in the present and past tenses.
   a. present emphatic (I *do see* the stars.)
   b. past emphatic (I *did see* the stars.)

Lesson Introduction: Sometimes one little word can make a vast difference in the meaning of a sentence. In the following example, the only change from the first sentence to the second is a change of the preposition. But that makes such a difference that the second sentence is not even true.

Jesus came to save His people <u>from</u> their sins.
Jesus came to save His people <u>in</u> their sins.

In the sentences above, the prepositions show the relationship between *save* and *sins*. *From* shows a proper relationship, but *in* does not; therefore, the second sentence is false.

Lesson Outline:

1. A preposition is a word that shows the relationship between its object and some other word in the sentence. Most prepositions are simple, basic words. Sometimes a preposition consists of more than one word.

2. A prepositional phrase includes the preposition, its object, and any adjectives that modify the object.
   a. The phrase begins with a preposition and ends with an object that tells *whom* or *what* about the preposition.
   b. A preposition may have a compound object.
   c. Sometimes a preposition follows its object. This is especially common with the pronouns *what, whom, which,* and *that.*

The fire raged <u>in the forest</u> <u>throughout the week</u>.
  (*In the forest* and *throughout the week* modify the verb *raged*.)
<u>Until yesterday</u>, these bins were completely empty <u>of potatoes</u>.
  (*Until yesterday* modifies the verb *were; of potatoes* modifies the
    adjective *empty*.)
Praying <u>in faith</u> pleases God better <u>by far</u> than merely praying.
  (*In faith* modifies the verbal *Praying; by far* modifies the adverb
    better.)

Prepositions must not be confused with adverbs. Many of the words in the chart at the beginning of this lesson can be used as adverbs and as prepositions. If the word is used alone to tell *when* or *where,* it is an adverb. If it is followed by an object, it is a preposition.

Adverbs:
  The passenger climbed <u>aboard</u>.
  I wrote a poem <u>before</u>.
  Several boats sailed <u>past</u>.

Prepositions:
  The passenger climbed <u>aboard the ship</u>.
  I wrote a poem <u>before lunch</u>.
  Several boats sailed <u>past the island</u>.

A prepositional phrase is diagramed beneath the word it modifies. The preposition is placed on a slanted line, and its object is placed on a horizontal line connected to it. Any adjectives are placed on slanted lines below the object that they modify.

Mother baked these loaves of bread after supper.

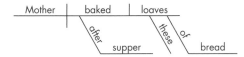

In spite of a late frost, we had a bountiful crop of apples.

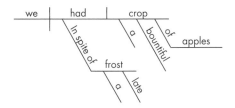

d. When the object of a preposition is a pronoun, it must be in the objective case. Be especially careful to use the correct pronoun when the preposition has a compound object.

3. A prepositional phrase can be used as an adjective or an adverb.
  a. When a prepositional phrase is used as an adjective, it must come right after the noun or pronoun it modifies.
  b. When a prepositional phrase is used as an adverb, it modifies a verb, an adjective, an adverb, or a verbal. An adverb phrase can be placed at different locations in a sentence.

4. Prepositions must not be confused with adverbs.
  a. If the word is used alone to tell *when* or *where,* it is an adverb.

  b. If it is followed by an object, it is a preposition.

5. A prepositional phrase is diagramed beneath the word it modifies.
  a. If a preposition has a compound object, the objects are diagramed on a fork.
  b. If several phrases are written in succession, you must decide if each phrase modifies the same word or if the second phrase modifies the object of the first preposition.

★ **EXTRA PRACTICE**
Worksheet 47 (*Prepositions*)

If a preposition has a compound object, the objects are diagramed on a fork.

This train goes through Lexington and Louisville.

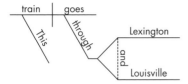

Sometimes several phrases are used in succession. Then you must decide if each phrase modifies the same word or if the second phrase modifies the object of the first preposition.

The family worked in the garden until noon.
(*In the garden* tells *where* about the verb *worked,* and *until noon* tells *how long* about the verb *worked.*)

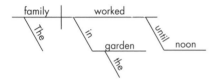

Laura looked under the sofa in the family room.
(The whole expression *under the sofa in the family room* tells *where* about the verb *looked. In the family room* tells *which* about *sofa,* the object of the first preposition.)

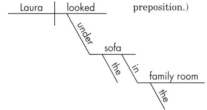

Class Practice

A. Read each prepositional phrase, tell what word or words it modifies, and tell whether the phrase is an *adjective* or an *adverb.* If a phrase is part of a longer phrase, include it with the longer phrase and also treat it separately.

Example: Daniel was cast into the den of lions.
Answer: into the den of lions, was cast, adverb; of lions, den, adjective

1. "The memory of the just is blessed: but the name of the wicked shall rot."
2. "Heaviness in the heart of man maketh it stoop."
3. "The eyes of the Lord are in every place, beholding the evil and the good."
4. "By mercy and truth iniquity is purged: and by the fear of the Lord men depart from evil."
5. After the storm, limbs from the trees lay on the drive and the road, and water stood in the lawn.
6. The eggs in the tiny nest on the porch will hatch in a few days.
7. The path through the forest passes a pond full of frogs and fish.
8. Because of Uncle Calvin's hospital stay, we helped with the chores around the house and the barn.
9. Who is the writer of that story, and what is it about?
10. Grandfather can hardly get out of his chair because of his arthritis.

B. Read these sentences correctly.
1. Between you and I, I think Marion's poem was really interesting.
2. While Aunt Lucinda was visiting Uncle Ira's in Missouri, we received a letter from them and she.
3. This package comes from Henry, Susan, and he.

C. Tell whether each underlined word is an *adverb* or a *preposition*.
1. Daniel knelt <u>down</u> and prayed <u>before</u> his window as he always had done.
2. The priest walked <u>past</u> the hurt man and went <u>on</u> his way.
3. We will not be alarmed <u>by</u> life's troubles if we look <u>up</u> to the Lord.
4. When Sheldon fell <u>off</u>, we rushed <u>over</u> to see if he had been hurt.

D. On the chalkboard, diagram these sentences.
1. These grapefruit came from Florida or Texas.
2. The children played in the yard behind the house.
3. Which house do you live in?
4. We walked over to the accident along with our guests.

Written Exercises

A. Copy each prepositional phrase and the word or words it modifies. If a phrase is part of a longer phrase, include it with the longer phrase and

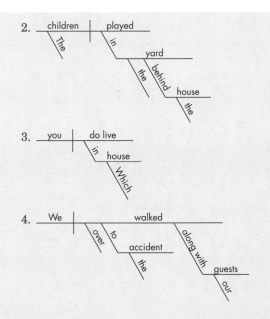

Lesson 89 Answers

Class Practice

A. 1. of the just, memory, adjective;
       of the wicked, name, adjective
    2. in the heart of man, Heaviness, adjective;
       of man, heart, adjective
    3. of the Lord, eyes, adjective;
       in every place, are, adverb
    4. By mercy and truth, is purged, adverb;
       by the fear of the Lord, depart, adverb;
       of the Lord, fear, adjective;
       from evil, depart, adverb
    5. After the storm, lay, adverb;
       from the trees, limbs, adjective;
       on the drive and the road, lay, adverb;
       in the lawn, stood, adverb
    6. in the tiny nest on the porch, eggs, adjective;
       on the porch, nest, adjective;
       in a few days, will hatch, adverb
    7. through the forest, path, adjective;
       of frogs and fish, full, adverb
    8. Because of Uncle Calvin's hospital stay, helped, adverb;
       with the chores around the house and the barn, helped, adverb;
       around the house and the barn, chores, adjective
    9. of that story, writer, adjective;
       about what, is, adverb
   10. out of his chair, can get, adverb;
       because of his arthritis, can get, adverb

B. (Corrections are underlined.)
1. Between you and <u>me</u>, I think Marion's poem was really interesting.
2. While Aunt Lucinda was visiting Uncle Ira's in Missouri, we received a letter from them and <u>her</u>.
3. This package comes from Henry, Susan, and <u>him</u>.

C. 1. down—adverb; before—preposition
   2. past—preposition; on—preposition
   3. by—preposition; up—adverb
   4. off—adverb; over—adverb

D. 1.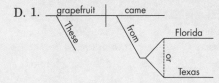

also copy it separately. Label each phrase *adj.* or *adv.*
1. "Ye are the light of the world."
2. "Whosoever shall smite thee on thy right cheek, turn to him the other also."
3. "Lay up for yourselves treasures in heaven."
4. What sermon are these words of Jesus quoted from?
5. Jesus gave many stern warnings to the proud scribes and Pharisees.
6. During the three years of His public ministry, Jesus traveled by foot throughout Palestine.
7. How many verses in the Bible can you quote from memory?
8. According to many statements in the Bible, God's people must be separate from the world.
9. Which book is the great faith chapter in?
10. In addition to faith and hope, charity is essential to God's people.

B. Copy each underlined word, and label it *adv.* or *prep.*
1. The sun sank <u>down</u> <u>toward</u> the horizon.
2. The water rose <u>above</u> the dam and spilled <u>over</u>.
3. The fish swam <u>around</u> <u>inside</u> the aquarium.
4. The rat poked its head <u>into</u> the hole and squeezed <u>through</u>.

C. Diagram these sentences.
1. In Bible times, writers often wrote their names at the beginning of their letters.
2. Because of Father's illness, we could not go along.
3. Whom are you sending this package of papers to?
4. On our way to school, we drive past two stores and one shop.
5. During the spring and the fall, we often have many rainy days.

Review Exercises

A. Change each verb in parentheses to the tense given in italics. [35, 37]
1. God (give) us a clear revelation of truth. *present perfect*
2. The Bible (show) man the way to God. *present*
3. Jesus (come) as the supreme revelation of God to man. *past*
4. In heaven God (continue) to reveal Himself to man. *future*
5. The apostle John saw a great multitude who (make) their robes white in the blood of the Lamb. *past perfect*
6. When we (finish) our course of life, we shall move to the next world. *future perfect*

B. Change each underlined verb to the progressive or emphatic form, as indicated in parentheses. [39]
1. God's people <u>have faced</u> conflict with evil throughout time. (progressive)

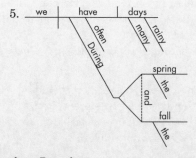

Review Exercises
A. 1. has given   4. will continue
   2. shows   5. had made
   3. came   6. shall have finished

B. 1. have been facing

Written Exercises
A. 1. of the world, light, adj.
2. on thy right cheek, shall smite, adv.; to him, turn, adv.
3. for yourselves, Lay, adv.; in heaven, Lay, adv.
4. of Jesus, words, adj.; from What sermon, are quoted, adv.
5. to the proud scribes and Pharisees, gave, adv.
6. During the three years of His public ministry, traveled, adv.; of His public ministry, years, adj.; by foot, traveled, adv.; throughout Palestine, traveled, adv.
7. in the Bible, verses, adj.; from memory, can quote, adv.
8. According to many statements in the Bible, must be, adv.; in the Bible, statements, adj.; from the world, separate, adv.
9. in Which book, is, adv.
10. In addition to faith and hope, is, adv.; to God's people, essential, adv.

B. 1. down—adv.; toward—prep.
2. above—prep.; over—adv.
3. around—adv.; inside—prep.
4. into—prep.; through—adv.

C.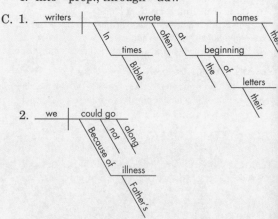
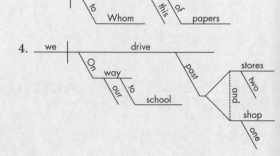

2. God <u>provides</u> abundant grace for His people. (emphatic)
3. The devil <u>fights</u> a losing battle against God. (progressive)
4. Jesus <u>bruised</u> the serpent's head at Calvary. (emphatic)

2. does provide
3. is fighting
4. did bruise

0. Poetry

Lesson Survey

- **Prose** is written in sentences and paragraphs; **poetry** is written in lines and stanzas.
- Most poetry has distinct rhythm and rhyme.
- Poetry makes effective use of descriptive words and figurative language.
- Poetry has a special beauty that affects our feelings.

The two main types of literature are prose and poetry. *Prose* is written in sentences and paragraphs; *poetry* is written in lines and stanzas. Each line of a poem begins with a capital letter. Compare these two examples.

Prose:

The Simple Truth
We always tell the simple truth because we love it. Nothing is ever so bad or so big that it can overcome the truth. A lie, like a shadow or a bubble, is worthless. In fact, it brings only trouble. On the other hand, truth is like a golden robe that brings honor. Nothing shall ever spoil its beauty; no lie shall ever destroy it.

Poetry:

The Simple Truth
We always tell the simple truth,
    We do so, for we love it.
There's nothing bad or big enough
    To get the better of it.

A lie is like a shadow, or
    A wordy, windy bubble;
It holds no good, it has no use,
    It brings us only trouble.

Lesson 90

Purpose: (1) To recognize the characteristics of poetry. (2) To compare poetry with prose.

Oral Review:

1. What are some things a good book report does? (shows that the reader has read the book carefully; shares with others some of the enjoyment and inspiration of the book; stimulates in others a desire to read the book)
2. Name the six kinds of information that a book report should include. (basic facts such as title, author, and publisher; setting; main characters and their characteristics; theme and main events; some lessons; personal evaluation of the book)
3. In giving an oral explanation, you will likely follow ——— or ——— order. (chronological, spatial)

4. Why should you give careful attention to the introduction of an oral explanation? (The introduction sets the tone of the whole explanation, either sparking or extinguishing the listeners' interest.)
5. The ——— voice of a verb is more effective than the ——— voice. (active, passive)
6. Name two situations in which it may be suitable to use the passive voice. (when there is no clear doer of the action, when there is a good reason not to name the doer of the action)

Lesson Introduction: Have you ever considered what the world would be like if there were no poetry? The Book of Job would consist of the brief account of chapters 1, 2, and 42. Psalms, Proverbs, Ecclesiastes, the Song of Solomon, and Lamentations would be nonexistent. There would be little if any music, for most songs are poems set to music. How

> The truth is like a golden robe
> That honors those who wear it.
> Its beauty never shall be spoiled;
> No lie shall ever tear it.
> —*Mary Tate*

What makes the poetry different from the prose? The same basic ideas are expressed in both forms. In fact, much of the language is identical. But poetry has special characteristics that prose does not have. Several of these characteristics are reviewed briefly in this lesson. You will study them further in later lessons of this chapter.

Most poetry has distinct rhythm and rhyme. *Rhythm* is a regular pattern of accented and unaccented syllables, with a certain number of syllables in each line. Here is the first stanza of the poem above, with its rhythm pattern marked.

We always tell the simple truth,
We do so, for we love it.
There's nothing bad or big enough
To get the better of it.

Rhyme is a regular arrangement of syllables that end with the same sounds. In this poem, the last two syllables of the rhyming lines sound alike: *love it—of it, bubble—trouble,* and *wear it—tear it.* A more common pattern is for only the last syllables in each set of rhyming lines to sound alike.

Poetry makes effective use of descriptive words and figurative language. In the example poem, the similes "like a shadow or a bubble" and "like a robe" stir our imagination. The descriptive words *wordy, windy,* and *golden* add to the poetic feel of the poem.

Poetry can say much in a few words. The first stanza of this familiar hymn by Isaac Watts is a good example.

When I Survey the Wondrous Cross
When I survey the wondrous cross
On which the Prince of Glory died,
My richest gain I count but loss,
And pour contempt on all my pride.

What a tremendous amount of meaning is packed into these few lines! Where the poet said, "When I survey the wondrous cross," the prose writer might have written, "When I carefully consider the wonderful cross." Instead drab life would be if God had not given us the gift of poetry!

When was poetry first used? If Adam's words in Genesis 2:23 were a poem (as arranged in some Bibles), man's first recorded words were poetry.

Lesson Outline:

1. Prose is written in sentences and paragraphs; poetry is written in lines and stanzas. Each line of a poem begins with a capital letter.

2. Most poetry has distinct rhythm and rhyme.
  a. Rhythm is a regular pattern of accented and unaccented syllables, with a certain number of syllables in each line.
  b. Rhyme is a regular arrangement of syllables that end with the same sounds.

3. Poetry makes effective use of descriptive words and figurative language.

4. Poetry has a special beauty that affects our feelings.
  a. It can be an effective means of conveying truth.
  b. It is often set to music and becomes an important part of our worship services.
  c. It is easier to memorize than prose.

of "My richest gain I count but loss," the prose writer might have written, "I see the most important things in life as having little worth." And instead of "pour contempt on all my pride," the prose writer might have said, "hate the tendency to become proud."

All these characteristics give poetry a special beauty that affects our feelings. Even if we could not understand the words, the rhythm and rhyme of a poem would still give it a certain beauty. Because of this beauty, poetry can be an effective means of conveying truth. Poetry is often set to music and becomes an important part of our worship services. And the special way in which the words of a poem are put together makes poetry easier to memorize than prose.

Class Practice

A. Tell whether each of the following could be lines of *poetry* or of *prose*.
   1. The path of the new year stretches out ahead of us. Where does it lead? What will it unfold?
   2. The Bible is my blessed guide that charts the narrow way. In Christ it leads me to abide and cleanse my life each day.
   3. This path we tread may be quite rough, with rocks and thorns to pierce our feet.
   4. Even though not every experience is pleasant or easy, we know that God has designed a perfect pattern for our lives.

B. Read the following poem, and do the exercises.

Trust
Build a little fence of trust
   Around today;
Fill the space with loving deeds
   And therein stay.

Look not through the sheltering bars
   Upon tomorrow;
God will help thee bear what comes
   Of joy or sorrow.

—Mary Frances Butts

   1. Tell which pairs of words rhyme.
   2. a. Write the first two lines of the poem on the board, and mark the rhythm.
      b. Do the rest of the lines follow that pattern?
   3. What do lines 1 and 2 suggest that trust provides for us?
   4. How do we "fill the space with loving deeds"?
   5. Give the idea of lines 5 and 6 in a prose sentence.

Lesson 90 Answers

Class Practice

A. 1. prose
   2. poetry
   3. poetry
   4. prose

B. 1. today—stay; morrow—sorrow
   2. a. Build a little fence of trust
         Around today;
      b. yes (except that lines 6 and 8 each have one more syllable than lines 2 and 4)
   3. security or protection
   4. by being busy with doing kind and thoughtful things for others today
   5. Do not look beyond the security of today and worry about tomorrow.

Written Exercises

A. Write whether each of the following could be lines of *poetry* or of *prose*.

1. The Lord is my Shepherd; He guides me each day. He guards me from evil and lights up life's way.
2. Too many people would like to wear a crown of glory in heaven, but they do not want to bear the cross today.
3. I am made in a way that should cause me to praise my omnipotent Maker throughout all my days.
4. O Father, may Thy blessing rest on those who show to us Thy way.

B. Read the following poem, and do the exercises.

Breaking a Habit

"How shall I a habit break?"
As you did that habit make.
   As you gathered, you must lose;
   As you yielded, now refuse.
Thread by thread the strands we twist
Till they bind us neck and wrist;
   Thread by thread the patient hand
   Must untwine ere free we stand.

As we builded, stone by stone,
We must toil unhelped, alone,
Till the wall is overthrown.
   But remember, as we try,
   Lighter every test goes by;
Wading in, the stream grows deep
Toward the current's downward sweep;
   Backward turn, each step toward shore
   Shallower is than that before.
               —*John Boyle O'Reilly*

1. Write all the sets of rhyming words. (One is a set of three.)
2. a. Copy the first line of stanza 1, and mark the rhythm pattern.
   b. How many syllables are in each line of stanza 1?
   c. Does the whole poem follow this pattern?
3. Breaking a habit is compared to all the following things *except*
   a. untwisting a rope.
   b. untying a difficult knot.
   c. tearing down a stone wall.
   d. wading out of a deep stream.
4. Several thoughts from the poem are expressed as prose in the following sentences. Copy a line from the poem to match each one.

Written Exercises

A. 1. poetry
   2. prose
   3. poetry
   4. poetry

B. 1. break—make; lose—refuse; twist—wrist; hand—stand;
   stone—alone—overthrown; try—by; deep—sweep; shore—before

   2. a. "How shall I a habit break?"
      b. seven
      c. yes (except for a slight variation in the last line)

   3. b

a. As we continue in a habit, it gradually becomes stronger.
b. We must break the habit by ourselves; others cannot break it for us.
c. Every temptation to fall back will be easier to resist.

5. What quality must we have in order to break a habit successfully? (See stanza 1.)

C. You will be assigned to write an original poem later in this chapter. It is to have two or three stanzas of at least four lines each. You will be expected to use good rhyme, smooth rhythm, and descriptive words, and to try to include figures of speech. The poem will be due by the time you finish the chapter.

Begin thinking now of ideas to put into your poem. Here are some suggestions.

Describe something in nature.
Describe something you enjoy doing.
Describe something that teaches a lesson.
Describe an interesting experience you have had.

Review Exercises

A. The passive voice is used in the numbered sentences. Write the letter of the statement that correctly describes each sentence. [54]
   a. The active voice would be more effective.
   b. There is no clear doer of the action.
   c. There is a good reason not to name the doer.
1. The Book of Esther was written to show how God preserved His people.
2. Mother's china dish was broken this morning.
3. A poem was read with good expression by Brother James.
4. A magnificent temple was built in Jerusalem by Solomon.

B. Rewrite each sentence in the active voice. Do not change the tense. [54]
1. The apostles were severely threatened by the council.
2. The apostles had been released by an angel before the rulers could harm them.
3. This bulletin board has been designed by the girls.
4. The lines on the playground will be marked by Brother Daniel tomorrow.

4. a. Thread by thread the strands we twist
      or Wading in, the stream grows deep
   b. We must toil unhelped, alone,
   c. Lighter every test goes by;
5. patience ("the patient hand")

C. (Individual work.)

Review Exercises

A. 1. b
   2. c
   3. a
   4. a

B. 1. The council severely threatened the apostles.
   2. An angel had released the apostles before the rulers could harm them.
   3. The girls have designed this bulletin board.
   4. Brother Daniel will mark the lines on the playground tomorrow.

91. Using Prepositions Correctly

> **Lesson Survey**
> - Learn the correct usage of similar prepositions, such as *in* and *into*.
> - Avoid nonstandard expressions containing prepositions, such as *different than* for *different from*.
> - Do not use unnecessary prepositions.
> - If two words require different prepositions, do not omit the first one.

Most prepositions are simple words, but they can make a big difference in a sentence. Therefore, we must learn to use them correctly to say exactly what we mean.

A number of prepositions are similar to other prepositions or to other words. Because of this close similarity, the words are sometimes interchanged and used incorrectly. Be especially careful when using the following pairs of similar expressions.

1. In *refers to location.* Into *refers to entrance or movement to a point of contact.*

Incorrect:
   Jesus came <u>in</u> this world as the Saviour.
Correct:
   Jesus came <u>into</u> this world as the Saviour.
      (He entered this world.)
   As He lived <u>in</u> this world, He taught and preached.
      (He was already in this world.)
   In the crowd, many people bumped <u>into</u> the Master.
      (They came to a point of contact with Him.)

2. Beside *means "by the side of."* Besides *means "other than or in addition to."*

   The cabin is <u>beside</u> the road. (It is by the side of the road.)
   No one <u>besides</u> the girls is coming. (No one other than the girls is coming.)

3. Accept *is a verb that means "to receive."* Except *is usually a preposition that means "not including."* As a verb, *except* means "to omit or leave out."

Incorrect:
   Most of the Jewish rulers <u>accept</u> Nicodemus and Joseph hated Jesus.

Lesson 91

Purpose: To teach the proper use of various prepositions and related words that are often used incorrectly.

Oral Review:
1. What does a preposition do? (It shows the relationship between its object and some other word in the sentence.)
2. Pick out the prepositional phrases in these sentences. (Phrases are underlined.)
   a. The children <u>of Israel</u> were trapped <u>between the Egyptian army and the Red Sea</u>.
   b. God delivered them <u>from the Egyptians</u> <u>in a miraculous way</u>.
   c. Pharaoh's army was drowned <u>in the midst of the Red Sea</u>.
3. Give the person, number, case, and gender of these personal pronouns.
   a. she (third person, singular, nominative, feminine)
   b. us (first person, plural, objective, common)
   c. yours (second person, singular or plural, possessive, common)
   d. them (third person, plural, objective, common)
   e. his (third person, singular, possessive, masculine)
4. Tell what class of pronouns each set belongs to.
   a. each, none, somebody, several (indefinite)
   b. who, whom, whose, which, that (relative)
   c. who, whom, whose, which, what (interrogative)
   d. I, you, she, them, theirs (personal)
   e. this, that, these, those (demonstrative)
   f. myself, himself, themselves (compound personal)

Correct:
Most of the Jewish rulers <u>except</u> Nicodemus and Joseph hated Jesus. (not including Nicodemus and Joseph)
They would not <u>accept</u> His claim of being the Messiah. (would not receive His claim)
The Pharisees paid tithes but <u>excepted</u> more important things like mercy and faith. (left out more important things)

4. Between *refers to just two things.* Among *refers to more than two things.*

Incorrect: The chores were divided <u>between</u> the three boys.
Correct: The chores were divided <u>among</u> the three boys.
                Do not eat <u>between</u> meals. (two meals in focus at one time)

Also be careful to avoid nonstandard expressions containing prepositions. These expressions may seem to be sensible; but they are not considered good usage, and we must learn to avoid them.

1. *Use* different from *instead of* different than.

Incorrect: These flowers are <u>different than</u> those.
Correct: These flowers are <u>different from</u> those.

This rule applies when *different* is followed by a prepositional phrase. When a clause follows *different* (or *differently*), it may be introduced by the conjunction *than*.

Correct: Everything was <u>different than</u> I had expected.
             Jesus taught <u>differently than</u> the scribes taught.

2. *Do not use* in back of *for* behind.

Incorrect: Father is <u>in back of</u> the house.
Correct: Father is <u>behind</u> the house.

3. *Do not use* by *for* at *or* to. When *by* is used with a verb like *come, go, or drive,* it speaks of continuous motion past a place.

Incorrect:
Brother Ervin will come <u>by</u> our house and pick up Brian.
    (It sounds as if he does not plan to stop.)
Correct:
Brother Ervin will come <u>to</u> our house and pick up Brian.
We drove <u>by</u> Kentucky Lake.

Another problem is the use of unnecessary prepositions. When a

Lesson Introduction: Write the following pair of sentences on the board.

The dog jumped far in the water and retrieved the pheasant.
The dog jumped far into the water and retrieved the pheasant.

Which sentence probably states an impossibility? Why? (The first. Many dogs can swim and perhaps jump or bob around a bit. But it is highly unlikely that a dog can jump far after it is in the water.)

Lesson Outline:
1. Learn the correct usage of similar prepositions.
    (1) In *refers to location.* Into *refers to entrance or movement to a point of contact.*
    (2) Beside *means "by the side of."* Besides *means "other than or in addition to."*
    (3) Accept *is a verb that means "to receive."* Except *is usually a preposition that means "not including."* As a verb, *except* means "to omit or leave out."
    (4) Between *refers to just two things.* Among *refers to more than two things.*

2. Avoid nonstandard expressions containing prepositions.
    (1) *Use* different from *instead of* different than. This rule applies when *different* is followed by a prepositional phrase. When a clause follows *different* (or *differently*), it may be introduced by *than.*
    (2) *Do not use* in back of *for* behind.
    (3) *Do not use* by *for* at *or* to. When *by* is used with a verb like *come, go,* or *drive,* it speaks of continuous motion past a place.

preposition is not needed, leave it out of your sentence.

1. *Do not use* of *with* off, inside, *or* outside.

Incorrect: Stay off <u>of</u> the wet concrete.
We stayed outside <u>of</u> the fence and hoped the bull would
stay inside <u>of</u> his pen.
Correct: Stay off the wet concrete.
We stayed outside the fence and hoped the bull would
stay inside his pen.

2. *Do not use* at *or* to *with* where.

Incorrect: Where is he <u>at</u>? Where did he go <u>to</u>?
Correct: Where is he? Where did he go?

3. *Do not use* with *after* over.

Incorrect: Is the game over <u>with</u>?
Correct: Is the game over?

Look at the following sentence. The preposition *to* is correct after both
talking and *listening,* so only one preposition is needed before *doctors.*

The boy Jesus was talking and listening <u>to</u> the doctors of the Law.

However, two words sometimes require different prepositions. Then
both prepositions must be stated; it is not correct to omit the first one.

Incorrect:
The prophet <u>prayed and preached to</u> his people.
(He *preached to* his people but did not *pray to* them.)
Correct:
The prophet <u>prayed for and preached to</u> his people.

Incorrect:
Noah's life is a strong <u>encouragement and example of</u> faith.
(His life is an *example of* faith but not an *encouragement of* faith.)
Correct:
Noah's life is a strong <u>encouragement to and example of</u> faith.

Class Practice

Read these sentences correctly. Some are already correct.
1. God loves to dwell among His people.
2. None of the spies beside Joshua and Caleb gave a good report.
3. Where did Naomi and Ruth go to?
4. Abraham's outlook was quite different from Lot's.
5. When the small Israelite army came by Ai, they were badly defeated.

Lesson 91 Answers

Class Practice
(Corrections are underlined.)
1. (correct)
2. None of the spies <u>besides</u> Joshua and Caleb
gave a good report.
3. Where did Naomi and Ruth go <s>to</s>?
4. (correct)
5. When the small Israelite army came <u>to</u> Ai, they
were badly defeated.

---

3. *Do not use unnecessary prepositions.*
(1) *Do not use* of *with* off, inside, *or* outside.
(2) *Do not use* at *or* to *with* where.
(3) *Do not use* with *after* over.

**4. *If two words require different preposi-
tions, do not omit the first one.***
(*Teacher:* If pupils wonder how two prepositions
can have the same object, explain that the first object is understood. The understood object is placed
in parentheses on a sentence diagram.)

★ ***EXTRA PRACTICE***
Worksheet 48 (*Using Prepositions Correctly*)

6. A pot of manna was put inside of the ark of the covenant.
7. The prodigal son's return was different than he had expected.
8. The Jews often found fault and worked against Jesus.
9. All the disciples except Judas became apostles in the Christian church.
10. Divide the cherries between the six girls.
11. The dog is on the porch; do not let him go in the house.
12. That car has been sitting besides the road all week.
13. Harold fell off of the ladder and broke his leg.
14. There was no righteous man in Sodom accept Lot.
15. Uncle Clarence's garden is in back of the barn.
16. If you hit a home run, we may win before recess is over with.
17. We walked by a little pond in the meadow.
18. The plans and work of the building project kept Father busy.
19. A family from Germany moved into our neighborhood last week.
20. We could not guess what was inside of the package.

Written Exercises

Write correctly each underlined expression that contains a mistake. If the expression is correct, write *correct*.

1. The story of Jonah is found between the books of the Minor Prophets.
2. The land of Canaan was divided between the tribes by casting lots.
3. Jesus was crucified outside of Jerusalem.
4. Jesus is now sitting besides the throne of God.
5. All the Gospels accept John record the parable of the sower.
6. Many Old Testament prophets wrote and looked for the Messiah.
7. When Paul came to a new city, he often went in a synagogue first.
8. Ananias and Sapphira agreed between themselves to lie.
9. My answers are all different than yours.
10. The children sat beside the road and waited for their grandparents.
11. Put all your clothes in this suitcase.
12. We have everything accept nails and glue.
13. Where did you put my hammer at?
14. The house looked different than I had remembered.
15. The playground is in back of the school.
16. We plan to go by Aunt Mabel's cottage and visit her.
17. Because we were delayed in a traffic jam, the first message was over with before we arrived at church.
18. The flowerpot fell off the windowsill with a crash.
19. Where are we going to on our school trip?
20. The clothes hanging in back of the stove should soon be dry.
21. Lucy's book looks different from ours.
22. As we drove by the sawmill, we saw acres of logs ready to be sawed.

6. A pot of manna was put inside ~~of~~ the ark of the covenant.
7. (correct)
8. The Jews often found fault <u>with</u> and worked against Jesus.
9. (correct)
10. Divide the cherries <u>among</u> the six girls.
11. The dog is on the porch; do not let him go <u>into</u> the house.
12. That car has been sitting <u>beside</u> the road all week.
13. Harold fell off ~~of~~ the ladder and broke his leg.
14. There was no righteous man in Sodom <u>except</u> Lot.
15. Uncle Clarence's garden is <u>behind</u> the barn.
16. If you hit a home run, we may win before recess is over ~~with~~.
17. (correct)
18. The plans <u>for</u> and work of the building project kept Father busy.
19. (correct)
20. We could not guess what was inside ~~of~~ the package.

Written Exercises

1. among the books
2. among the tribes
3. outside Jerusalem
4. beside the throne
5. except John
6. wrote about and looked for
7. into a synagogue
8. correct
9. different from yours
10. correct
11. into this suitcase
12. except nails
13. put my hammer
14. correct
15. behind the school
16. to Aunt Mabel's cottage
17. was over
18. correct
19. Where are we going
20. behind the stove
21. correct
22. correct

Review Exercises

A. Write *person, number, case,* or *gender* to tell how the pronouns in each pair are different. [57, 58]

1. he, she
2. we, us
3. we, they
4. I, we
5. its, his
6. them, theirs

B. Copy each underlined word. If it is used as a pronoun, identify its class with the label *P* (personal), *CP* (compound personal), *D* (demonstrative), *ID* (indefinite), *IR* (interrogative), or *R* (relative). If the word is not used as a pronoun, write *none.* [57–64]

1. Adam and Eve made <u>themselves</u> aprons of leaves, but God made <u>them</u> coats of animal skins.
2. <u>Who</u> shut the door of the ark <u>which</u> Noah had built?
3. <u>Nobody</u> except Pharaoh <u>himself</u> had more power than Joseph.
4. <u>These</u> verses are from the Old Testament, but <u>those</u> are from the New Testament.
5. <u>What</u> is <u>everyone</u> doing with the papers <u>that</u> the guide gave to <u>us</u>?
6. In <u>what</u> way is <u>that</u> better than <u>this</u>?

92. Coordinating Conjunctions

> **Lesson Survey**
> - A **conjunction** joins words, phrases, or clauses in a sentence.
> - A **coordinating conjunction** joins sentence parts of parallel structure and function.
> - **Correlative conjunctions** are coordinating conjunctions that work in pairs.

Conjunctions do not name, they show no action, and they do not modify other words. Yet they are important words in our language. A *conjunction* joins words, phrases, or clauses in a sentence. There are two main classes of conjunctions: coordinating conjunctions, which you will study in this lesson, and subordinating conjunctions, which you will study in Lesson 95.

Coordinating conjunctions join sentence parts of parallel structure and function. *Parallel structure* means that the joined parts are both words, both phrases, or both clauses. Furthermore, the phrases must be both prepositional phrases or both verbal phrases, and the clauses must be both

Review Exercises

A.
1. gender
2. case
3. person
4. number
5. gender
6. case

B.
1. themselves—CP; them—P
2. Who—IR; which—R
3. nobody—ID; himself—CP
4. These—none; those—D
5. What—IR; everyone—ID; that—R; us—P
6. what—none; that—D; this—D

Lesson 92

Purpose: To teach the basic concepts of coordinating and correlative conjunctions.

Oral Review:

1. Pick out the prepositional phrases in these sentences. (Phrases are underlined.)
   a. "<u>Out of the depths</u> have I cried <u>unto thee</u>, O Lord."
   b. We must stay <u>on the road</u> <u>to glory</u> <u>in spite of present difficulties</u>.
   c. The angels <u>of God</u> minister <u>to the saints</u>.
2. Tell how to correct these sentences.
   a. We must continue on in the service of the King. (omit *on*)
   b. No sin will ever get in heaven. (not *in* but *into*)
   c. Error may appear very little different than truth. (not *than* but *from*)

d. Canaan was divided between the various tribes. (not *between* but *among*)
3. Tell whether these nouns are used with a singular or a plural verb.
   a. glasses (plural)
   b. phonics (singular)
   c. news (singular)
   d. measles (singular)
   e. scissors (plural)
   f. mathematics (singular)
4. Tell whether each group of pronouns is always singular, always plural, or either.
   a. some, all, most (either)
   b. each, everyone, either (always singular)
   c. few, both, several (always plural)
5. With a collective noun, when should you use (*a*) a singular verb? (*b*) a plural verb? (*a.* Use a singular verb when the collective noun refers to the group doing one thing together. *b.* Use a plural verb when the collective noun refers to the individual members doing different things.)

ndependent or both dependent clauses. *Parallel function* means that the parts are used in the same way: both are subjects, both are verbs, both are modifiers, and so forth.

The simple coordinating conjunctions are *and, but, or, for, nor, yet,* and *so.* These conjunctions do more than merely join; they also show a variety of relationships. *And* shows addition or continuing thought; *but* and *yet* show contrast or unexpected outcome; *or* and *nor* show choice or option; and *for* and *so* show cause and effect.

> *Jesus* <u>and</u> His *disciples* traveled throughout the land. (*And* joins subjects that are words; shows addition)
>
> A strong bad habit is not a *servant* <u>but</u> a *master*. (*But* joins predicate nominatives that are words; shows contrast)
>
> The hogs are *in the shed* <u>or</u> *behind the barn*. (*Or* joins adverb prepositional phrases; shows choice)
>
> The car tire was flat, <u>so</u> we rode our bicycles. (*So* joins independent clauses; shows cause and effect)
>
> Did you stop mowing *because you have finished* <u>or</u> *because something broke*? (*Or* joins dependent adverb clauses; shows choice)

Sometimes a writer or speaker uses a coordinating conjunction to join word to a phrase or a phrase to a clause. This is an error because the parts joined must be parallel in structure.

> **Incorrect:**
> We worked *quietly* <u>but</u> *in haste*. (word joined to phrase)
> It rained *during the night* <u>and</u> *after the sun rose*. (phrase joined to clause)
>
> **Correct:**
> We worked *quietly* <u>but</u> *hastily*.
> It rained *during the night* <u>and</u> *after sunrise*.

When a coordinating conjunction joins two independent clauses in a compound sentence, a comma is usually needed before the conjunction. The comma may be omitted if the clauses are short and closely related.

> We knocked on the door<u>, but</u> no one answered.
> The store is prospering<u>, yet</u> it will soon be closed.
> The door slammed<u>, and</u> I jumped. *or* The door slammed <u>and</u> I jumped.

Correlative conjunctions are coordinating conjunctions that work in pairs. The common correlative conjunctions are listed here.

both—and	neither—nor	whether—or
either—or	not only—but also	

Lesson Introduction: Have you ever been on a see-saw with someone thirty pounds lighter or heavier than yourself? Likely your ride was not very smooth. Perhaps you have tried to lift a heavy crate with a strong twenty-year-old, and your end dragged along the ground. How much more smoothly the work would have been with two twenty-year-olds! Because the weight and the strength were not parallel, there was imbalance and inconvenience. In language, too, problems result when a coordinating conjunction joins sentence parts that are not parallel.

Lesson Outline:

1. A conjunction joins words, phrases, or clauses in a sentence.

2. A coordinating conjunction joins sentence parts of parallel structure and function.

    a. *Parallel structure* means that the joined parts are both words, both phrases, or both clauses.

    b. *Parallel function* means that the parts are used in the same way in the sentence.

    c. Coordinating conjunctions show a variety of relationships.

      1) *And* shows addition or continuing thought.

      2) *But* and *yet* show contrast or unexpected outcome.

      3) *Or* and *nor* show choice or option.

      4) *For* and *so* show cause and effect.

    d. When a coordinating conjunction joins two independent clauses in a compound sentence, a comma is usually needed before the conjunction. The comma may be omitted if the clauses are short and closely related.

Like other coordinating conjunctions, the correlative conjunctions must join sentence parts of parallel structure and function.

<u>Neither</u> the *priest* <u>nor</u> the *Levite* helped the hurt man. (one-word subjects joined by *Neither—nor*)

Anabaptists worshiped <u>not only</u> *in their homes* <u>but also</u> *in secret places*. (prepositional phrases used as adverbs, joined by *not only—but also*)

<u>Either</u> *he had misunderstood me,* <u>or</u> *he did not care to answer.* (independent clauses joined by *Either—or*)

Incorrect:

I hardly knew <u>whether</u> I should run for help first <u>or</u> to battle the flames myself. (noun clause *I should run for help first* joined to verbal phrase *to battle the flames myself*)

Correct:

I hardly knew <u>whether</u> *to run for help first* <u>or</u> *to battle the flames myself.*

When using the correlative conjunctions, be especially careful to place them just before the parts that they join. Otherwise, they will appear to join parts that are not parallel.

Incorrect:

Brother Smith had <u>both</u> seen the animals <u>and</u> the buildings. (appears to join verb *seen* and direct object *buildings*)

Correct:

Brother Smith had seen <u>both</u> the *animals* <u>and</u> the *buildings*.

Incorrect:

<u>Either</u> you mislaid the book <u>or</u> lost it. (appears to join clause *you mislaid the book* and verb *lost*)

Correct: <u>Either</u> *you mislaid the book,* <u>or</u> *you lost it.*

You <u>either</u> *mislaid* the book <u>or</u> *lost* it.

Incorrect:

<u>Neither</u> the boys could solve the problem <u>nor</u> the girls. (appears to join clause *the boys could solve the problem* and subject *girls*)

Correct: <u>Neither</u> the *boys* <u>nor</u> the *girls* could solve the problem.

Incorrect:

We <u>not only</u> sang <u>but also</u> we prayed. (appears to join verb *sang* and clause *we prayed*)

Correct: We <u>not only</u> *sang* <u>but also</u> *prayed*.

When you use *not only—but also,* be careful not to omit the word *also*.

3. Correlative conjunctions are coordinating conjunctions that work in pairs.

    a. Like other coordinating conjunctions, the correlative conjunctions must join sentence parts of parallel structure and function.

    b. Correlative conjunctions must be placed just before the parts that they join.

    c. When *not only—but also* is used, the word *also* must not be omitted.

        (*Teacher:* The combination "not only . . . but" is correct in sentences like the following examples.

           I was not only tired but sick.

           Solomon was not only a wise king but a king wiser than any other.

        In these sentences, the words after *but* serve to intensify the thought of the preceding noun or adjective, and they are heavily emphasize[d] in speaking. *Not only* is not part of a correlative conjunction in such a construction; it i[s] simply a combination of modifiers equal to *no[t] just* or *not merely.*)

    d. When a compound subject is joined by *an[d]* or *both—and,* the verb is always plural.

    e. When *but, or, nor, either—or, neither—no[r]* or *not only—but also* is used to join com[pound subjects, one singular and one plura[l] the verb must agree with the subject tha[t] is nearer to it.

★ *EXTRA PRACTICE*

Worksheet 49 (*Coordinating Conjunctions*)

Incorrect:
> The drought affected <u>not only</u> our crops <u>but</u> the wildlife.

Correct:
> The drought affected <u>not only</u> our crops <u>but also</u> the wildlife.

When a compound subject is joined by *and* or *both—and,* it always refers to more than one. Therefore, the verb is always plural.

> Both the <u>man</u> and his <u>son</u> <u>were</u> here.

Compound subjects can also be joined by the conjunctions *but, or, nor, either—or, neither—nor,* and *not only—but also.* Then the verb must be singular if both parts of the subject are singular, or plural if both parts are plural. If one part is singular and one is plural, the verb must agree with the part that is nearer to it.

> <u>Bread</u> or <u>cake</u> <u>was</u> on the table.
> <u>Rolls</u> or <u>cookies</u> <u>were</u> on the table.
>
> Not <u>cookies</u> but <u>cake</u> <u>was</u> on the table.
> Not <u>cake</u> but <u>cookies</u> <u>were</u> on the table.
>
> Neither the <u>boys</u> nor <u>Father</u> <u>was injured</u> by the bull.
> Neither <u>Father</u> nor the <u>boys</u> <u>were injured</u> by the bull.

Class Practice

A. Give the coordinating conjunctions, and tell how the joined parts are parallel both in structure and in function.
  1. Joseph and Mary anxiously sought for Jesus.
  2. Our words must be both true and kind.
  3. The disciples became greatly afraid, so they finally awoke Jesus.
  4. Jesus brought salvation not only to the Jews but also to the Gentiles.
  5. Mother hardly knew whether to patch the trousers or to throw them away.
  6. The keys are here somewhere, but I cannot find them.
  7. Both the mother and her daughter can make delicious pies.
  8. Oatmeal, either cooked or baked, makes a delicious breakfast.

B. Read each sentence correctly.
  1. Jesus both taught His disciples and the multitudes.
  2. Daniel not only prayed as before but opened his window toward Jerusalem.
  3. King Darius certainly wanted to spare Daniel but the law of the Medes and Persians could not be altered.
  4. We were not only the first to arrive but also had traveled the farthest.

Lesson 92 Answers

Class Practice

A. 1. and; joins words that are subjects
  2. both—and; joins words that are predicate adjectives
  3. so; joins independent clauses
  4. not only—but also; joins prepositional phrases used as adverbs
  5. whether—or; joins infinitive phrases used as direct objects
  6. but; joins independent clauses
  7. Both—and; joins words that are subjects
  8. either—or; joins words that are adjectives

B. (Corrections are underlined.)
  1. Jesus <u>taught both</u> His disciples and the multitudes.
  2. Daniel not only prayed as before <u>but also</u> opened his window toward Jerusalem.
  3. King Darius certainly wanted to spare Daniel (<u>comma</u>) but the law of the Medes and Persians could not be altered.
  4. We <u>not only arrived the first</u> but also had traveled the farthest.
     or We were not only the first to arrive but also <u>the ones who</u> had traveled the farthest.

5. Either these calves need different feed or some medication.
6. We walked across the meadow and where the old cemetery is.
7. The book both was expensive and rare.
8. Our visitors either started late, or they have lost their way.
9. An old shed, dilapidated and without paint, stood beside the barn.
10. Neither the teacher had seen the mouse nor the students.

C. Choose the correct verb for each sentence.
1. Neither God's grace nor His promises (have, has) ever failed.
2. Both the mercies and the love of God (is, are) renewed daily.
3. Either the cookies or the cake (is, are) for our lunches.
4. Both the cat and her kittens (was, were) waiting on the porch.
5. Not only the lane but also the road (was, were) flooded.

Written Exercises

A. Copy the coordinating conjunctions. Write how the joined parts are parallel in structure and in function.
1. "In the beginning God created the heaven and the earth."
2. God created man in His own image, yet man soon defiled that image.
3. We serve the great and mighty God.
4. The apostle Paul wanted to glorify God whether by life or by death.
5. Father planted both a white pine and a Norway spruce in the back yard.
6. Robert Greene or his brother will probably buy the tractor.
7. Over the hill and into the forest raced the escaped antelope.
8. We searched all day but found nothing.
9. I would enjoy not only some cookies but also some milk.
10. Either this room is cold, or I must be getting sick.

B. Write each sentence correctly.
1. Not only should we fear the Lord but also obey Him.
2. Joseph did not feel bitter toward either God or toward his brothers.
3. Jesus spent the night in prayer for He had a great work to do.
4. Our singing should inspire not only ourselves but others.
5. Either trials increase a person's faith or make him bitter against God.
6. The wise men both adored Jesus and they offered Him gifts.
7. The blizzard raged throughout the morning and as the afternoon passed.
8. I must study my Bible memory now or I will not be ready for class.
9. The dog barked loudly and with a fierce sound.
10. Uncle Aaron has not only bought a house, but his family has moved already.

5. These calves need either different feed or some medication.
6. We walked across the meadow and into the old cemetery.
7. The book was both expensive and rare.
8. Our visitors either started late, or they have lost their way.
   or Either our visitors started late, or they have lost their way.
9. An old shed, dilapidated and unpainted, stood beside the barn.
10. Neither the teacher nor the students had seen the mouse.

C. 1. have   4. were
   2. are   5. was
   3. is

Written Exercises

A. 1. and; joins words that are direct objects
2. yet; joins independent clauses
3. and; joins words that are adjectives
4. whether—or; joins prepositional phrases used as adverbs
5. both—and; joins words that are direct objects
6. or; joins words that are subjects
7. and; joins prepositional phrases used as adverbs
8. but; joins words that are verbs
9. not only—but also; joins words that are direct objects
10. Either—or; joins independent clauses

B. (Some answers may vary. Corrections are underlined.)
1. We should not only fear the Lord but also obey Him.
2. Joseph did not feel bitter either toward God or toward his brothers.
3. Jesus spent the night in prayer, for He had a great work to do.
4. Our singing should inspire not only ourselves but also others.
5. Trials either increase a person's faith or make him bitter against God.
6. The wise men both adored Jesus and offered Him gifts.
7. The blizzard raged throughout the morning and the afternoon.
8. I must study my Bible memory now, or I will not be ready for class.
9. The dog barked loudly and fiercely.
10. Not only has Uncle Aaron bought a house, but also his family has moved already.

C. Write the correct verb for each sentence.
1. Not only the students but also Brother Mark (was, were) startled by the noise.
2. Neither the children nor their father (have, has) arrived yet.
3. Both the plow and the disk (is, are) for sale.
4. Either James or his sisters (have, has) made a snowman.
5. Mother or the girls (is, are) baking some bread.

Review Exercises

Find each sentence that has a mistake in subject–verb agreement, and write its skeleton correctly. If there is no such mistake, write *correct*. [48]
1. Where's some Bible verses that tell us how to speak?
2. Elaborate houses don't fit with godly people.
3. Each of these promises encourage us to faithfulness.
4. Phonics are a valuable help in learning to read.
5. The cleanup crew has started to do their various jobs.
6. Here's the papers that you had asked for.
7. This basket of apples is for Grandfather.
8. Robert's trousers are covered with grass stains.
9. A large flock of geese have descended on our pond.
10. My pliers has been lost.

C. 1. was
2. has
3. are
4. have
5. are

Review Exercises
1. verses are
2. correct
3. Each encourages
4. Phonics is
5. crew have started
6. papers are
7. correct
8. correct
9. flock has descended
10. pliers have been lost

---

93. Conjunctive Adverbs

Lesson Survey
- A **conjunctive adverb** is an adverb that can join and relate independent clauses.
- When a conjunctive adverb is used in a compound sentence, a semicolon must divide the two clauses. The conjunctive adverb is often followed by a comma.
- A conjunctive adverb is diagramed as an adverb beneath the verb in the second clause.

Coordinating conjunctions are commonly used to connect sentence parts of parallel structure and function. A connector with a more limited use is the *conjunctive adverb*. This is an adverb that can join and relate independent

Lesson 93

Purpose: (1) To introduce *conjunctive adverbs.(2) To teach their proper use and punctuation.

Oral Review:
1. Name seven common coordinating conjunctions. (and, but, or, for, nor, yet, so)
2. Name five correlative conjunctions. (both—and, either—or, neither—nor, not only—but also, whether—or)
3. What is meant by parallel structure? (having the same structure, as is true of two words, two phrases, or two clauses)
4. What is meant by parallel function? (having the same function, as is true of two subjects, two verbs, two modifiers, etc.)
5. Diagram these sentences on the board.

a. George, my youngest uncle, is a schoolteacher.

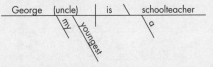

b. This motto, my dear mother, is a birthday gift that I made for you.

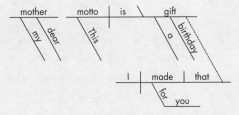

clauses. The following words are often used as conjunctive adverbs.

accordingly	henceforth	namely
afterward	however	nevertheless
also	indeed	otherwise
anyway	instead	still
besides	likewise	then
consequently	meanwhile	therefore
furthermore	moreover	thus
hence		

The following examples show how conjunctive adverbs are used to join independent clauses into compound sentences.

David spared Saul's life. Saul still hated David.
David spared Saul's life; <u>nevertheless,</u> Saul still hated David.

Saul had rejected God. The Spirit of God departed from him.
Saul had rejected God; <u>consequently,</u> the Spirit of God departed from him.

By 8:00 Father had picked a trailer load of sweet corn. The work started in earnest.
By 8:00 Father had picked a trailer load of sweet corn; <u>afterward,</u> the work started in earnest.

Nevin was mowing the lawn. Joyce was weeding the flower bed.
Nevin was mowing the lawn; <u>meanwhile,</u> Joyce was weeding the flower bed.

When a conjunctive adverb is used in a compound sentence, a semicolon must divide the two clauses. The conjunctive adverb is often followed by a comma.

God has promised to supply all our needs<u>; however,</u> He has not promised to supply all our wants.

Remember that a conjunctive adverb must be preceded by a semicolon when it joins two independent clauses. If you use a comma instead, your sentence will be a run-on error with a comma splice.

Incorrect: Mocking another's abilities is cruel<u>, furthermore,</u> it reproaches the Creator.
Correct: Mocking another's abilities is cruel<u>; furthermore,</u> it reproaches the Creator.

Incorrect: Elsie dreaded making the apology<u>, still,</u> she knew her conscience would not have rest until she did.

c. The sign, painted brightly, caught our attention as we drove into the lane.

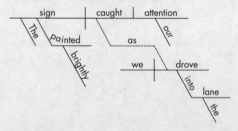

d. We could see that a severe storm was brewing in the west.

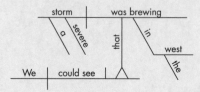

Lesson Introduction: Write the following sentences on the board.

Tomorrow is the day for our school trip, and you should bring your lunches in disposable bags.
Since tomorrow is the day for our school trip, you should bring your lunches in disposable bags.
Tomorrow is the day for our school trip; therefore, you should bring your lunches in disposable bags.

Ask the following questions.

Which of the three sentences are compound sentences? (first and third)
What is the coordinating conjunction that joins the clauses in the first sentence? (and)
What is the coordinating conjunction that joins

Correct: Elsie dreaded making the apology; still, she knew her conscience would not have rest until she did.

The words listed at the beginning of the lesson are not always conjunctive adverbs. They are conjunctive adverbs only when they join independent clauses. Such a word may also function as a single-word adverb. When it is used in that way, no semicolon is needed.

Conjunctive adverbs:
Lloyd worked diligently all morning; consequently, Father was much surprised when he returned home.
This is beautiful spring weather; indeed, it bids us to spend the whole day outdoors!

Simple adverbs:
Lloyd worked diligently all morning and consequently surprised Father.
This is beautiful spring weather indeed!

You have learned that coordinating conjunctions, correlative conjunctions, and conjunctive adverbs can be used to join independent clauses into compound sentences. On a sentence diagram, a coordinating conjunction or a correlative conjunction is placed on a broken line between the two independent clauses. But a conjunctive adverb should be diagramed as an adverb beneath the verb in the second clause.

Jesus rose from the dead, and then He ascended into heaven.

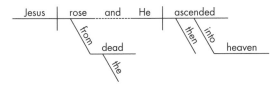

Not only did Jesus rise from the dead, but also He ascended into heaven.

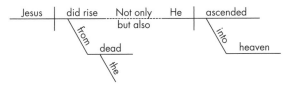

the clauses in the third sentence? (There is no coordinating conjunction; rather, the clauses are joined by *therefore,* a conjunctive adverb.)

In this lesson, you will learn about conjunctive adverbs.

Lesson Outline:

1. A conjunctive adverb is an adverb that can join and relate independent clauses. It acts as both a conjunction and an adverb. (*Teacher:* A conjunctive adverb is not a true conjunction, because it can be moved to different positions. In a sense, the two clauses are simply joined by a semicolon, with the conjunctive adverb modifying the verb of the second clause.)

2. When a conjunctive adverb is used in a compound sentence, a semicolon must divide the two clauses. The conjunctive adverb is often followed by a comma. (*Teacher:* The comma may be omitted if the clause reads smoothly without it, but that point is not taught until grade 8.)

a. If a comma instead of a semicolon is used before the conjunctive adverb, the sentence will have a comma splice.

b. Words used as conjunctive adverbs do not always join independent clauses. They may also be used as simple adverbs.

3. A conjunctive adverb is diagramed as an adverb beneath the verb in the second clause. It is not written on the broken line as a coordinating conjunction or a correlative conjunction is.

Jesus rose from the dead; <u>moreover</u>, He ascended into heaven.

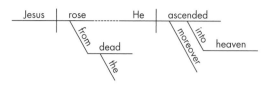

Class Practice

A. Find the conjunctions and conjunctive adverbs in these sentences. Tell where semicolons and commas should be added.
   1. Several disciples were busy fishermen nevertheless they followed Jesus.
   2. Peter boldly declared his loyalty to Jesus yet he denied his Lord.
   3. Peter repented of his sin accordingly his relationship with Christ was restored.
   4. The bridge was closed otherwise we would have arrived sooner.
   5. Either this tractor is not working right or I don't know how to run it.

B. Combine each pair of sentences, using a suitable conjunctive adverb. Tell where semicolons and commas are needed.
   1. The lame man asked for money. Peter and John had something better to give him.
   2. Jesus quietly disappeared through the crowd. He might have been thrown over the brow of the hill.
   3. Jesus sternly condemned the hypocrisy of the Pharisees. His strongest denunciations were directed to them.
   4. Over the last two days, twenty inches of snow blanketed the earth. Last night a strong north wind whipped it into huge drifts.
   5. A huge bull moose stepped onto the highway in front of us. Father slammed on the brakes.

C. On the chalkboard, diagram these sentences.
   1. The longest book in the Bible is Psalms; moreover, it contains the longest chapter in the Bible.
   2. God had marvelously led the Hebrews, yet they soon murmured.
   3. Balaam could not curse Israel; however, he obviously wanted the king's reward.
   4. The fruit clearly identifies the tree; likewise, your actions clearly identify your character.
   5. Either the ferry had left early, or our clocks showed the wrong time.

Lesson 93 Answers

Class Practice

A. (Answers are underlined.)
   1. Several disciples were busy fishermen<u>; nevertheless,</u> they followed Jesus.
   2. Peter boldly declared his loyalty to Jesus<u>, yet</u> he denied his Lord.
   3. Peter repented of his sin<u>; accordingly,</u> his relationship with Christ was restored.
   4. The bridge was closed<u>; otherwise,</u> we would have arrived sooner.
   5. <u>Either</u> this tractor is not working right<u>, or</u> I don't know how to run it.

B. (Answers are underlined.)
   1. The lame man asked for money<u>; however,</u> Peter and John had something better to give him.
   2. Jesus quietly disappeared through the crowd<u>; otherwise,</u> He might have been thrown over the brow of the hill.
   3. Jesus sternly condemned the hypocrisy of the Pharisees<u>; indeed,</u> His strongest denunciations were directed to them.
   4. Over the last two days, twenty inches of snow blanketed the earth<u>; moreover (or furthermore, then, also),</u> last night a strong north wind whipped it into huge drifts.
   5. A huge bull moose stepped onto the highway in front of us<u>; consequently (or therefore, accordingly),</u> Father slammed on the brakes.

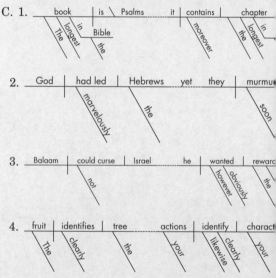

Written Exercises

A. Copy the conjunction or conjunctive adverb in each sentence. Label it *CC* for common coordinating conjunction, *Cor* for correlative conjunction, or *CA* for conjunctive adverb.
  1. A dishonest person can seldom be trusted; moreover, he ruins his own conscience.
  2. Most people hate pride in others, yet many harbor it in themselves.
  3. Jesus was not the victim at Calvary; indeed, there He destroyed the works of the devil.
  4. Not only did Jesus have the power to heal men's sicknesses, but also He had the authority to forgive men's sins.
  5. The wicked may seem to live comfortably today; nevertheless, we know that their end will be bitter.
  6. This world is not our final home; instead, we are pilgrims and strangers here.

B. Copy each word that should be followed by a semicolon or comma, and add the missing punctuation.
  1. Saturday was cold and rainy consequently our family picnic had to be postponed.
  2. Either the cattle are out of hay or something has disturbed them.
  3. We have several fields of hay that should be mowed also we have two fields that need to be planted with corn.
  4. The leaves are swiftly changing colors for the hours of sunlight are decreasing.
  5. Arlene enjoys reading poetry nevertheless she does not enjoy writing poems.

C. Combine each pair of sentences, using a suitable conjunctive adverb. Be sure to use correct punctuation.
  1. The Old Testament sacrificial lamb was to be without blemish. Jesus offered Himself without spot to God.
  2. The Old Testament high priest had to sanctify himself first. The Son of God was already perfect in holiness.
  3. Jesus was willing to shed His precious blood. A new and living way has been opened.

D. Diagram these sentences.
  1. You can teach a just man, and he will become wiser.
  2. A fool despises reproof; indeed, he may resist it quite angrily.
  3. We must develop good character; therefore, we need wholesome friendships.

Written Exercises

A. 1. moreover—CA
   2. yet—CC
   3. indeed—CA
   4. Not only—but also—Cor
   5. nevertheless—CA
   6. instead—CA

B. 1. rainy; consequently,
   2. hay,
   3. mowed; also,
   4. colors,
   5. poetry; nevertheless,

C. (Conjunctive adverbs may vary.)
  1. The Old Testament sacrificial lamb was to be without blemish; likewise, Jesus offered Himself without spot to God.
  2. The Old Testament high priest had to sanctify himself first; however, the Son of God was already perfect in holiness.
  3. Jesus was willing to shed His precious blood; consequently (therefore, accordingly), a new and living way has been opened.

D. 1.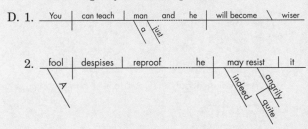

   2.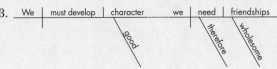

   3.

4. Not only must we choose good friends, but also we must read good books.

5. We must carefully guard our lives; otherwise, our character will be marred.

Review Exercises

Diagram these sentences.
1. Stephen, the first Christian martyr, had boldly preached the Gospel.
2. Before his death, he saw the Lord Jesus.
3. He prayed that God would forgive his persecutors.
4. Devout men buried Stephen and mourned over him.
5. Because persecution greatly increased, the Christians were scattered.
6. Philip, who had been ordained with Stephen, went down to the city of Samaria.
7. Many Samaritans, hearing the Gospel, became Christians.
8. Dear Lord, give us faith today!

---

94. Rhythm in Poetry

Lesson Survey
- **Rhythm** is produced by a regular pattern of accented and unaccented syllables.
- A **poetic foot** contains one accented syllable and the unaccented syllable or syllables associated with it.
- The four common types of poetic feet are **iambic, trochaic, anapestic,** and **dactylic.**
- **Bible poetry** and **free verse** have no regular pattern of rhythm.

In Lesson 90 you were reminded that *rhythm* is one characteristic of poetry. The words of the English language have naturally occurring accented and unaccented syllables; however, in normal speech these do not form a regular pattern.

Saviour, we pray Thy blessing this evening before we go to sleep.

We confess our sin and unworthiness. Thou canst save and heal.

Lesson 94

Purpose: To teach four common rhythm patterns used in poetry, and to introduce *free verse. (Previous experience:* Concepts of anapestic and dactylic feet, without use of the terms.)

Oral Review:
1. What are the two main types of literature? (prose, poetry)
2. Name several characteristics that distinguish poetry from prose. (Poetry is written in lines and stanzas, usually has rhythm and rhyme, makes effective use of descriptive words and figurative language, can say much in a few words, and has a special beauty that affects our feelings.)
3. These sentences have errors in pronoun usage. Tell how to correct them.
   a. Brother Larry helped Clifford and I. (Clifford and me)

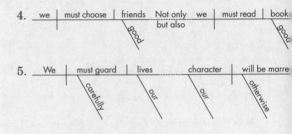

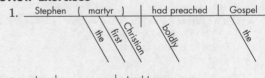

Review Exercises

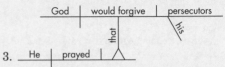

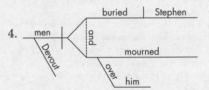

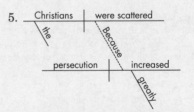

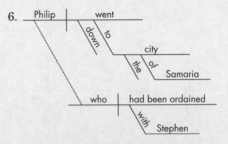

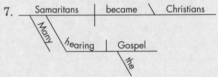

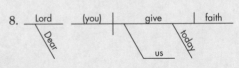

In poetry, words are so arranged that the naturally occurring accents produce a regular, pleasing rhythm. Notice how this is done in the following poem. Of the one-syllable words, the more important ones (*breathe, Ere, Sin,* and so on) are accented, and the less important ones (like *an, our,* and *we*) are unaccented. The two- and three-syllable words (such as *Saviour, evening,* and *confessing*) are so placed that their natural accents match the rhythm of the poem.

> ´ ˘ ´ ˘ ´ ˘ ´ ˘
> Saviour, breathe an evening blessing,
>   ´ ˘ ´ ˘ ´ ˘ ´
>   Ere repose our spirits seal;
> ´ ˘ ´ ˘ ´ ˘ ´ ˘
> Sin and want we come confessing;
>   ´ ˘ ´ ˘ ´ ˘ ´
>   Thou canst save and Thou canst heal.
>   —*James Edmeston*

The accented syllables are the most important ones. They are used to divide lines of poetry into units called feet. A *poetic foot* contains one accented syllable and the unaccented syllable or syllables associated with it. To count the feet in a line of poetry, count the accented syllables. The example above has four feet in each line. How many feet are in each line of the following poem?

> When I shall reach the more excellent glory,
>   And all my trials are past,
> I shall behold Him, O wonderful story!
>   I shall be like Him at last.
>   —*W. A. Spencer*

Did you recognize the rhythm pattern above? The first and third lines have four feet each, and the second and fourth lines have three feet each.

There are four common types of poetic feet: iambic, trochaic, anapestic, and dactylic. Each of these is explained and illustrated here.

1. *The* iambic (ī·am´·bik) *foot consists of one unaccented syllable followed by one accented syllable.* This is the most common pattern used in English poetry. In fact, iambic rhythm is the pattern that most closely matches the normal rhythm of speech. Page through a hymnal, and you will find more poems with this pattern than any other. Its light, cheerful rhythm is well suited to themes of praise, joy, and beauty.

> ˘ ´ ˘ ´ ˘ ´ ˘ ´
> My heart leaps up when I behold
>   ˘ ´ ˘ ´ ˘ ´
>   A rainbow in the sky;

b. Us children planned a surprise for Mother. (We children)

c. The fastest runners are those two, Donald and him. (Donald and he)

d. The plumber and electrician has finished their job. (his job)

e. Father wants me and Roland out in the barn. (Roland and me)

f. Leland and myself visited the elderly neighbor. (Leland and I)

g. The stranger helped hisself to a tract. (himself)

h. Them are our rabbits. (Those are)

i. The men which were here yesterday have returned. (who)

4. These sentences have errors in adverb usage. Tell how to correct them.

a. David responded bolder than the rest of Israel to Goliath's challenge. (more boldly)

b. Father draws faces very good. (very well)

c. We left from the store at 4:00. (left the store)

d. The explosion made a real loud noise. (really)

e. Yesterday was sort of drizzly and dreary. (somewhat *or* rather)

Lesson Introduction: God created rhythm. The heavenly bodies move with such precise rhythm that man can predict eclipses, meteor showers, and the appearance of comets for years in the future. Those who live near the ocean soon learn the rhythm of the tides. The seasons come and go, fulfilling in their rhythm God's covenant with the earth. Our hearts beat rhythmically day and night, year after year. And as this lesson teaches, God's gift of rhythm is used in language to enhance the beauty of poetry.

Lesson Outline:

   1. Rhythm is produced by a regular pattern of accented and unaccented syllables. In poetry,

So was it in my childhood days,

So be it till I die!

2. *The* trochaic (trō·kā′·ik) *foot consists of one accented syllable followed by one unaccented syllable.* This pattern, the exact opposite of the iambic rhythm pattern, has a heavier rhythm that is well suited to sober, thoughtful themes.

Though the mills of God grind slowly,

Yet they grind exceeding small;

Though with patience He stands waiting,

With exactness grinds He all.

3. *The* anapestic (an′·ə·pes′·tik) *foot consists of two unaccented syllables followed by one accented syllable.* This pattern produces a flowing, almost galloping rhythm that is well suited to themes of hope, joy, and earnestness.

Oh, how sweet is the shepherd's sweet lot!

From the morn to the evening he strays;

He shall follow his sheep all the day,

And his tongue shall be gladsome with praise.

For he hears the lamb's innocent call,

And he hears the ewe's tender reply;

He is watchful, while they are in peace,

For they know when their shepherd is nigh.

—*William Blake*

4. *The* dactylic (dak·til′·ik) *foot consists of one accented syllable followed by two unaccented syllables.* Like the anapestic foot, the dactylic foot produces a flowing rhythm that is suited to themes of hope, joy, and earnestness.

God is in every tomorrow;

Therefore I live through today,

words are so arranged that the naturally occurring accents produce a regular, pleasing rhythm. More important one-syllable words are accented, and less important ones are unaccented. Two- and three-syllable words are so placed that their natural accents match the rhythm of the poem.

2. A poetic foot contains one accented syllable and the unaccented syllable or syllables associated with it.

3. The four common types of poetic feet are iambic, trochaic, anapestic, and dactylic.

(1) *The* iambic *foot consists of one unaccented syllable followed by one accented syllable.*

a) This is the most common pattern used in English poetry.

b) It is the pattern that most closely matches the normal rhythm of speech.

c) Its light, cheerful rhythm is well suited to themes of praise, joy, and beauty.

(2) *The* trochaic *foot consists of one accented syllable followed by one unaccented syllable.* This pattern has a heavier rhythm that is well suited to sober, thoughtful themes.

(3) *The* anapestic *foot consists of two unaccented syllables followed by one accented syllable.* This pattern produces a flowing, almost galloping rhythm that is well suited to themes of hope, joy, and earnestness.

(*Note:* The word *anapestic* is pronounced with anapestic rhythm.)

(4) *The* dactylic *foot consists of one accented syllable followed by two unaccented syllables.* This flowing rhythm, like that of the anapestic foot, is suited to themes of hope, joy, and earnestness.

´ ‿ ‿ ´ ‿ ‿ ´ ‿
Certain of finding at sunrise

´ ‿ ‿ ´ ‿ ‿ ´ ‿ ‿ ´
Guidance and strength for the way.
—*Laura A. Barter Snow*

Bible poetry and *free verse* have no regular pattern of rhythm or rhyme. Such poetry is divided into lines according to the thoughts, not according to a pattern of rhythm.

Bible poetry:
Surely there is a vein for the silver,
And a place for gold where they fine it.
Iron is taken out of the earth,
And brass is molten out of the stone.
—*Job 28:1, 2*

Observe the "thought rhythm" in the lines above. Instead of a pattern of accented and unaccented syllables, there is a pattern of words with matching ideas. This can be illustrated as shown here.

Surely there is a <u>vein</u> for the <u>silver</u>,

And a <u>place</u> for <u>gold</u> where they fine it.

<u>Iron</u> is <u>taken</u> out of the <u>earth</u>,

And <u>brass</u> is <u>molten</u> out of the <u>stone</u>.

Free verse:
Dawn
The promise of a new day faintly touches the eastern horizon.

Slowly the dull red glow broadens and brightens
To fill the sky with bold splashes of red, orange, and magenta.

In the distance the wild coyotes bid the night farewell;
In the pasture a friendly cow lows her welcome to the dawn;
In the tree outside my open window a mockingbird bursts forth
      in its medley of an awakening chorus.
In my heart I echo and exceed nature's praise for nature's God.

The flaming colors fade from the eastern sky,
Swallowed in a dazzling brightness. And then—!

Triumphant, the sun pours its rays of light into the chalice of a
      new day!
—*Anonymous*

(*Note:* A dactyl is a finger. The dactylic foot, like a finger, has one "longer" part—the accented syllable—followed by two "shorter" parts—the unaccented syllables.)

4. Bible poetry and free verse have no regular pattern of rhythm or rhyme. Both of these poetic forms illustrate that the most important aspect of poetry is its language rather than its mechanics (rhythm and rhyme).

★ *EXTRA PRACTICE*
Worksheet 50 (*Rhythm in Poetry*)

Even though this example does not have rhythm and rhyme, it is obviously a poem and not prose. The words are carefully arranged in lines that are similar in length, content, and structure. (Note how each line of stanza 3 begins with an *In* phrase.) The language includes many colorful poetic expressions: "dull red glow broadens and brightens," "bold splashes of red, orange, and magenta," "flaming colors," and so on. And there are several vivid figurative expressions: "promise of a new day faintly touches," "swallowed in a dazzling brightness," and "the sun pours its rays of light into the chalice." Rhythm and rhyme add to the appeal of poetry, but its true beauty is found in vivid language that paints clear, colorful pictures in the reader's mind.

Class Practice

A. On the chalkboard, copy these stanzas, and mark their rhythm patterns.
   1. Assembled with the saints, O Lord,
         I love to worship Thee,
      To meditate upon Thy Word
         And let it speak to me.
                              —*Anonymous*

   2. O wonderful, marvelous treasure, great gift,
         Worth more than the earth's store of gold!
      The story of love, let it ever be told,
      For nothing can bridge that great rift,
         That deep, yawning gulf that divides God and man,
         Except God's provision—salvation's great plan.
                              —*Anonymous*

B. Tell which kind of poetic foot is used in each stanza.
   1. Before you push a brother down,
         Think twice.
      Before at others' sins you frown,
         Think twice.
                              —*Author unknown*

   2. How firm a foundation, ye saints of the Lord,
      Is laid for your faith in His excellent Word!
         What more can He say than to you He hath said,
         Who unto the Saviour for refuge have fled?
                              —*George Keith*

   3. Over the ocean wave, far, far away,
      There the poor heathen live, waiting for day,
         Groping in ignorance, dark as the night,
         No blessed Bible to give them the light.
                              —*Julia Sampson Haskell*

Lesson 94 Answers

Class Practice

A. 1. Assembled with the saints, O Lord,
         I love to worship Thee,
      To meditate upon Thy Word
         And let it speak to me.

   2. O wonderful, marvelous treasure, great gift,
         Worth more than the earth's store of gold
      The story of love, let it ever be told,
      For nothing can bridge that great rift,
         That deep, yawning gulf that divides God and man
         Except God's provision—salvation's great plan

B. 1. iambic
   2. anapestic
   3. dactylic

4. The bread that bringeth strength I want to give,
   The water pure that bids the thirsty live;
       I want to help the fainting day by day;
       I'm sure I shall not pass again this way.
                                        —*Anonymous*

5. The fear of the Lord
       Is the fountain of life:
   It gives us great strength
       To o'ercome in the strife.
                                        —*Anonymous*

6. Anywhere with Jesus I can safely go,
   Anywhere He leads me in this world below;
       Anywhere without Him dearest joys would fade;
       Anywhere with Jesus I am not afraid.
                                        —*Jessie Brown Pounds*

C. Suggest a line of poetry to match the thought and the rhythm of each line. It does not need to rhyme.
   1. A rainbow is a lovely thing (iambic)
   2. Lord, as there dawns once again a new year (dactylic)
   3. What a treasure is friendship, a joy to the heart (anapestic)
   4. Jesus left His home in glory (trochaic)

Written Exercises

A. Copy the first two lines of each stanza, and mark the rhythm pattern.
   1. When you think, when you speak, when you read, when you write,
      When you sing, when you walk, when you seek for delight—
          To be kept from all evil at home and abroad,
          Live always as under the "eye of the Lord."
                                        —*Author unknown*

   2. When days appear so cold and dim,
      Your path has grown quite hard and grim,
          Then stop and pray, along the way,
          For strength divine to last all day.
                                        —*Anonymous*

   3. God of all wisdom and knowledge, we pray,
      Bless Thou our studies again through this day;
          May every concept and skill we attain
          Be to Thy glory, and be to our gain.
                                        —*Anonymous*

   4. Jesus, bless us with Thy Spirit,
          Give Thou strength for weary feet;

4. iambic
5. anapestic
6. trochaic

C. (Sample answers.)
   1. A lofty arch that spans the sky.
   2. Help us to trust Thee for grace every day.
   3. It's a pleasure in which we can all have a part.
   4. For this world of sin and sadness.

Written Exercises

A. 1. When you think, when you speak, when you read, when you write,
      When you sing, when you walk, when you seek for delight—
   2. When days appear so cold and dim,
      Your path has grown quite hard and grim,
   3. God of all wisdom and knowledge, we pray,
      Bless Thou our studies again through this day;
   4. Jesus, bless us with Thy Spirit,
          Give Thou strength for weary feet;

> O refresh us with Thy manna
> So divinely pure and sweet!
> —*Jacob D. Toews*

B. Write whether each stanza has *iambic, trochaic, anapestic,* or *dactylic* rhythm.

1. To the promised home in glory,
      To that land of blissful rest,
     My Redeemer's gone before me,
      To prepare a mansion, blest.
    —*Author unknown*

2. I am so glad that our Father in heav'n
     Tells of His love in the Book He has giv'n;
       Wonderful things in the Bible I see,
       This is the dearest, that Jesus loves me.
     —*Philip P. Bliss*

3. The roses red upon my neighbor's vine
    Are owned by him, but they are also mine.
      His was the cost, and his the labor too,
      But mine as well as his the joy, their loveliness to view.
    —*Abraham L. Gruber*

4. Far and near the fields are teeming
      With the waves of ripened grain;
     Far and near their gold is gleaming
      O'er the sunny slope and plain.
    —*J. O. Thompson*

5. See the splashing, clear stream with its silvery gleam,
      Where the sun and the waterdrops play,
     As the cold waters shock over pebble and rock,
      Sending forth their prismatic, rich spray.
    —*Anonymous*

6.   Be strong!
    We are not here to play, to dream, to drift,
    We have hard work to do, and loads to lift,
    Shun not the struggle, face it, 'tis God's gift.
    —*Maltbie D. Babcock*

C. Write a line of poetry to match the thought and the rhythm of each line. It does not need to rhyme.
1. What a beautiful sight are the stars in the sky (anapestic)
2. As I gaze upon the mountain (trochaic)
3. The Bible is God's message clear (iambic)
4. List to the birds as they sing in the trees (dactylic)

B. 1. trochaic
    2. dactylic
    3. iambic
    4. trochaic
    5. anapestic
    6. iambic

C. (Sample answers.)
1. As they twinkle all night in the heavens above.
2. And behold its lofty height.
3. Revealing what no man could show.
4. Warbling and trilling their songs of delight.

D. Begin looking for a poem to read aloud to the class in Lesson 99. Get it approved by your teacher before that lesson.

Review Exercises

A. Write the letter of the sentence with proper pronoun usage. [60–64]
1. a. The secretary and treasurer gave their report.
   b. The secretary and treasurer gave his report.
2. a. Mother called for us girls.
   b. Mother called for we girls.
3. a. Aaron and me finished the chores.
   b. Aaron and I finished the chores.
4. a. The plumbers were they, Merle and him.
   b. The plumbers were they, Merle and he.
5. a. Clara and I are going to Uncle Marvin's for the weekend.
   b. Clara and me are going to Uncle Marvin's for the weekend.
6. a. Us students are working on an interesting project.
   b. We students are working on an interesting project.
7. a. Father and myself unloaded the hay from the wagon.
   b. Father and I unloaded the hay from the wagon.
8. a. Three little coneys were sunning themselves on the rocks.
   b. Three little coneys were sunning theirselves on the rocks.
9. a. Somebodys book fell on the floor.
   b. Somebody's book fell on the floor.
10. a. These are my books; those must be yours.
    b. These are my books; them must be yours.
11. a. These goats, whom we bought last spring, are very playful.
    b. These goats, which we bought last spring, are very playful.
12. a. The boys which made this clutter must clean it up quickly.
    b. The boys who made this clutter must clean it up quickly.

B. Write the letter of the sentence with proper adverb usage. [82, 87]
1. a. Mary Anne felt iller today than she did yesterday.
   b. Mary Anne felt worse today than she did yesterday.
2. a. This printing press runs more swiftly than our old one.
   b. This printing press runs swifter than our old one.
3. a. An ostrich sure can run fast.
   b. An ostrich surely can run fast.
4. a. Connect the hoses quickly and spray this fire!
   b. Connect up the hoses quickly and spray this fire!
5. a. Everybody did quite good on the test today.
   b. Everybody did quite well on the test today.

D. (Individual work.)

Review Exercises

A. 1. b
   2. a
   3. b
   4. b
   5. a
   6. b
   7. b
   8. a
   9. b
   10. a
   11. b
   12. b

B. 1. b
   2. a
   3. b
   4. a
   5. b
   6. a

6. a. On the way home, we all walked rather slowly.
   b. On the way home, we all walked kind of slowly.

_____

95. Subordinating Conjunctions

> **Lesson Survey**
> - A **subordinating conjunction** joins a dependent adverb clause to an independent main clause.
> - When an adverb clause introduces a sentence, it is separated from the main clause by a comma.
> - When the conjunction *as* or *than* introduces an adverb clause of comparison, the clause is often shortened and may be hard to recognize.
> - The preposition *like* must not be used for the conjunction *as* or *as if* in formal English.

The two main classes of conjunctions are coordinating conjunctions and subordinating conjunctions. Whereas coordinating conjunctions join items that are parallel in structure and in function, subordinating conjunctions do not. Coordinating conjunctions may join words, phrases, or clauses; subordinating conjunctions join only clauses.

Subordinating conjunctions join clauses that are not parallel in function. Something that is *subordinate* is of a lower rank than another thing. Subordinating conjunctions introduce subordinate (dependent) clauses that are used as adverbs, and they join those clauses to independent clauses in complex sentences.

There are many subordinating conjunctions; the following list shows some of the most common ones. Some of these words may also be used as adverbs or prepositions. They are subordinating conjunctions only when they introduce adverb clauses.

after	even though	than	when
although	how	that	whenever
as	if	though	where
as if	in order that	till	wherever
because	since	unless	whether
before	so that	until	while

Lesson 95

Purpose: To teach the basic concepts of subordinating conjunctions.

Oral Review:

1. Give seven common coordinating conjunctions. (and, but, or, for, nor, yet, so)
2. Give five correlative conjunctions. (both—and, either—or, neither—nor, not only—but also, whether—or)
3. Identify the conjunctive adverb in each sentence. (Answers are underlined.)
   a. The giant sequoia and redwood trees produce a vast number of seeds; <u>however</u>, only a few of them germinate and grow to maturity.
   b. These amazing trees grow to an enormous height; <u>indeed</u>, the tallest redwood recorded is over 364 feet tall.
   c. The wood of the redwood tree is highly resistant to insects, decay, and fire; <u>consequently</u>, it is prized for outdoor furniture and lumber.
4. Identify the prepositions in these sentences. (Prepositions are underlined.)
   a. <u>Before</u> 1912, most natural rubber came <u>from</u> the Amazon rain forest <u>in</u> South America.
   b. Rubber trees have been transplanted <u>to</u> Southeast Asian countries, which today produce most <u>of</u> the world's natural rubber.
5. Give the correct plural spellings of these words.
   a. monkey (monkeys)
   b. solo (solos)
   c. louse (lice)
   d. story (stories)
   e. bluff (bluffs)
   f. marsh (marshes)
   g. fish (fish)
   h. volcano (volcanoes, volcanos)
   i. sheaf (sheaves)
   j. flatfoot (flatfeet)
6. Give the foreign plural spellings of these words.

In the following sentences, the subordinating conjunctions are in italics and the subordinate clauses are underlined.

"We love him, <u>*because* he first loved us</u>."
(The underlined clause tells *why* about the verb *love*.)

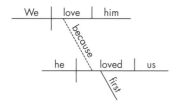

We should be kind to others <u>*even though* they have mistreated us</u>.
(The underlined clause tells *in spite of what* about the verb *should be*.)

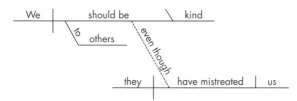

The work went much better <u>*after* we took a cheerful attitude about it</u>.
(The underlined clause tells *when* about the verb *went*.)

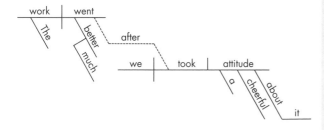

a. crisis (crises) c. vertex (vertices)
b. alga (algae) d. nucleus (nuclei)
7. Give the possessive spellings of these words.
a. prophet (prophet's) c. calves (calves')
b. Moses (Moses') d. man (man's)

Lesson Introduction: Children in a family have a coordinate relationship with each other: they are equals. They share equally in the security and love of the home. They are equally responsible to their parents. However, children have a subordinate relationship to their parents: they are not equals. The child is not independent; he depends on his parents for the needs of physical life and for proper training in moral and spiritual life.

In some sentences, two clauses have an equal or parallel relationship. Then we use a coordinating conjunction to join them. In other sentences, one clause cannot stand alone but depends on another clause. Then we use a subordinating conjunction to join the two.

Lesson Outline:
1. A subordinating conjunction joins clauses that are not parallel in function.
  a. It introduces a subordinate (dependent) clause that is used as an adverb, and joins that clause to an independent clause in a complex sentence.
  b. There are many subordinating conjunctions. (Students should become familiar with those listed in the text.)

2. When an adverb clause introduces a sentence, it is separated from the main clause by a comma.

3. When the conjunction as *or* than *introduces an adverb clause of comparison, the*

The job was finished more quickly *than we had expected*.

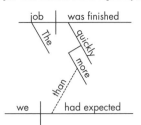

(The underlined clause tells *to what degree* about the adverb *more*.)

When an adverb clause introduces a sentence, it is separated from the main clause by a comma.

> *While Adam slept,* God took a rib from his side.
> *Wherever Jesus went,* crowds flocked around Him.

When the conjunction *as* or *than* introduces an adverb clause of comparison, the clause is often shortened and may be hard to recognize. Some words are understood rather than directly stated.

> George is not as strong <u>as his brother</u>.
>   (Meaning: George is not as strong *as his brother is strong*.)
> Eugene is taller <u>than his sister</u>.
>   (Meaning: Eugene is taller *than his sister is tall*.)
> We feed these heifers more grain <u>than those calves</u>.
>   (Meaning: We feed these heifers more grain *than we feed those calves*.)

When you use a pronoun in a clause of comparison, be sure to choose the correct pronoun case. First, you must complete the construction in your mind and decide whether the pronoun is a subject or an object in the clause. Then choose the correct pronoun case.

> **Problem:** Arlene seemed as delighted <u>as (I, me)</u> about the plans.
>   *Think:*   Completed construction: <u>as I was delighted</u> (I = subject).
> **Solution:** Arlene seemed as delighted <u>as I</u> about the plans.

> **Problem:** Baby Esther asks for Lydia more <u>than (I, me)</u>.
>   *Think:*   Completed construction: <u>than she asks for me</u> (me = object of the preposition).
> **Solution:** Baby Esther asks for Lydia more <u>than me</u>.

Now consider these two sentences. Can they both be correct? What does each one mean?

clause is often shortened and may be hard to recognize.

    a. Some words of the clause are understood rather than directly stated.

    b. The correct pronoun case must be used for a pronoun in a clause of comparison.

      1) Complete the construction in your mind, and decide whether the pronoun is a subject or an object in the clause.

      2) Choose the correct pronoun case.

  4. The preposition* like *must not be used for the conjunction* as *or* as if *in formal English. In informal usage, *like* has become accepted as a conjunction.

★ ***EXTRA PRACTICE***
Worksheet 51 (*Subordinating Conjunctions*)

Norma writes to Alice more <u>than I</u>.
Norma writes to Alice more <u>than me</u>.

Both sentences could be correct. Notice the different meanings, though, as shown by the completed constructions.

Norma writes to Alice more <u>than I write to Alice</u>.
Norma writes to Alice more <u>than she writes to me</u>.

Like is a preposition; do not use it for the conjunction *as* or *as if* in formal English. In informal usage, *like* has become accepted as a conjunction.

Informal: They behaved <u>like they were taught to behave</u>.
This corn tastes <u>like it needs more salt</u>.

Formal: They behaved <u>as they were taught to behave</u>.
This corn tastes <u>as if it needs more salt</u>.

Class Practice

A. Identify each subordinating conjunction, and read the subordinate clause that it introduces. If a comma is needed, tell what word it should follow.
 1. Lot was captured when Sodom was defeated.
 2. Although Lot had chosen the best land Abraham rescued him.
 3. Melchizedek met Abraham after he had defeated the kings.
 4. Lot returned to Sodom as if nothing had happened.
 5. Before the Lord destroyed Sodom Lot was brought out of the city.
 6. Lot's loss was much greater than his gain was.

B. On the chalkboard, diagram the sentences in Part A.

C. Read the following sentences, filling in the words that are understood. If the clause includes a choice of pronouns, choose the correct one.
 1. The watch is worth as much as the calculator.
 2. Alma has more work than (I, me), so you should help her more than (I, me).
 3. Keith can run faster than (I, me).
 4. We have science classes more often than music classes.

D. If the underlined word is incorrect or informal, give the word that should be used instead. If it is correct, say *correct*.
 1. We must recognize that the devil is stronger than <u>us</u>.
 2. We must honor our parents, but we must honor God even more than <u>them</u>.
 3. Melanie answered <u>like</u> she knew what we were talking about.
 4. Rhoda is only three months older than <u>me</u>.
 5. We try to sing the songs exactly <u>like</u> they are written.

 3. Keith can run faster than <u>I</u> (can run).
 4. We have science classes more often than (we have) music classes.

D. 1. we (we are strong)   4. I (I am old)
 2. correct (we honor them) 5. as
 3. as if

Lesson 95 Answers

Class Practice

A. (Conjunctions are underlined.)
 1. <u>when</u> Sodom was defeated (no comma)
 2. <u>Although</u> Lot had chosen the best land (comma after *land*)
 3. <u>after</u> he had defeated the kings (no comma)
 4. <u>as if</u> nothing had happened (no comma)
 5. <u>Before</u> the Lord destroyed Sodom (comma after *Sodom*)
 6. <u>than</u> his gain was (no comma)

B. 1.

 2.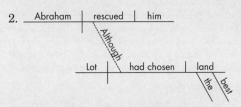

 3.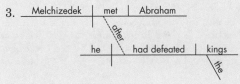

 4.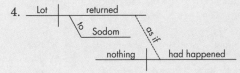

 5.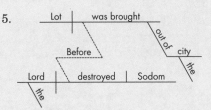

 6.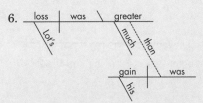

C. (Understood words are in parentheses. Correct pronouns are underlined.)
 1. The watch is worth as much as the calculator (is worth).
 2. Alma has more work than <u>I</u> (have), so you should help her more than (you help) <u>me</u>.

Written Exercises

A. Copy the subordinate clauses, and underline the subordinating conjunctions.
1. Whenever we resist temptation, we strengthen our character.
2. We need to love noble things so that we can better resist temptation.
3. Even though many others choose wrong, a person of strong character chooses right.
4. We are truly blessed as we live in the favor of the Lord.
5. Nathan pulled weeds while Mother picked beans.
6. Because we forgot to water the flowers, they withered.

B. If the underlined word is incorrect or informal, write the word that should be used instead. If it is correct, write *correct*.
1. The Pharisees reviled the man who had been born blind, but he actually knew more of the truth than <u>them</u>.
2. They acted <u>like</u> they had nothing to learn from others.
3. Several of the fifth graders are as tall as <u>me</u>.
4. Naturally, Father plays with the little children more than <u>us</u>.
5. Little Conrad colored the picture <u>like</u> his big sister had showed him.

C. Diagram these sentences.
1. After Joseph revealed himself, his brothers were afraid.
2. Our labors will always fail unless the Lord blesses them.
3. Thankful people are happier than wishful dreamers are.
4. While the girls unpacked the food, the boys gathered firewood.
5. The weather was quite warm even though it was already October.

Review Exercises

A. Write the correct plural spellings of these nouns. Use foreign spellings for numbers 17–20. [22, 23]
1. quality
2. motto
3. adz
4. brother-in-law
5. ox
6. salmon
7. nobleman
8. belief
9. high priest
10. sandwich
11. eyetooth
12. soprano
13. journey
14. bucketful
15. loaf
16. manservant
17. cactus
18. larva
19. index
20. oasis

B. Write the possessive form of each noun. [24]
1. Israel
2. children
3. donkeys
4. Jesus
5. sister-in-law
6. disciples
7. Brother Clyde
8. thief
9. James
10. mail carrier

15. loaves
16. menservants
17. cacti
18. larvae
19. indices
20. oases

B. 1. Israel's
2. children's
3. donkeys'
4. Jesus'
5. sister-in-law's
6. disciples'
7. Brother Clyde's
8. thief's
9. James's
10. mail carrier's

Written Exercises

A. 1. <u>Whenever</u> we resist temptation
2. <u>so that</u> we can better resist temptation
3. <u>Even though</u> many others choose wrong
4. <u>as</u> we live in the favor of the Lord
5. <u>while</u> Mother picked beans
6. <u>Because</u> we forgot to water the flowers

B. 1. they
2. as if *or* as though
3. I
4. correct
5. as

C. 1.
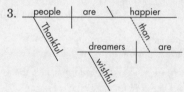

2.
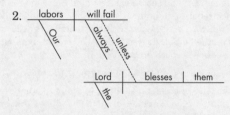

3.
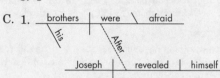

4.
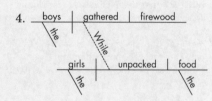

5.
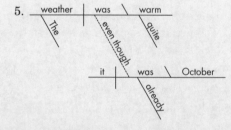

Review Exercises

A. 1. qualities
2. mottoes *or* mottos
3. adzes
4. brothers-in-law
5. oxen
6. salmon
7. noblemen
8. beliefs
9. high priests
10. sandwiches
11. eyeteeth
12. sopranos
13. journeys
14. bucketfuls

C. Write the underlined phrases correctly, using possessive forms. The first two should show joint ownership, and the last two should show separate ownership. [24]
1. <u>Uncle Ray and Aunt Faye farm</u> is an interesting place to visit.
2. <u>Lori and Lisa pet lamb</u> skipped across the meadow.
3. <u>Ahab and Naboth properties</u> bordered each other.
4. <u>Ahab and Jezebel reactions</u> were quite different.

C. 1. Uncle Ray and Aunt Faye's farm
2. Lori and Lisa's pet lamb
3. Ahab's and Naboth's properties
4. Ahab's and Jezebel's reactions

---

96. Interjections

Lesson Survey

- An **interjection** is a word that expresses strong feeling or emotion.
- Use only those interjections that are suitable for God's people.
- A mild interjection is followed by a comma, and a more emphatic one by an exclamation point.
- An interjection is diagramed on a line separate from the rest of the sentence.

In earlier lessons of this book, you have studied seven of the eight parts of speech: nouns, pronouns, verbs, adjectives, adverbs, prepositions, and conjunctions. In this lesson you will study the last one, interjections.

An *interjection* expresses strong feeling or emotion. It is a cry or exclamation to express pleasure, admiration, adoration, surprise, pain, or some other feeling. Some common interjections are shown here.

ah	behold	ho	ouch	whew
alas	ha	lo	well	why
amen	hallelujah	oh	what	

"<u>Ho</u>, every one that thirsteth, come ye to the waters."
"<u>Behold</u>, how great a matter a little fire kindleth!"

<u>What</u>! The chores are finished already?
<u>Whew</u>! This is hard work on a warm day!

Words that represent sounds are often interjections. Actually, any word used as an independent exclamation can be an interjection.

<u>Bang</u>! The door slammed shut in my face.
<u>Crash</u>! The thunder shook the whole house.

Lesson 96

Purpose: To teach the definition, use, and punctuation of interjections.

Oral Review:

1. What kind of word joins two clauses that are not parallel? (subordinating conjunction)
2. What part of speech is a clause introduced by a subordinating conjunction? (adverb)
3. Name and explain the two ways in which the sentence parts joined by a coordinating conjunction must be parallel. (in structure—both parts are words, phrases, or clauses; in function—both parts are subjects, verbs, modifiers, etc.)
4. What punctuation must precede a coordinating conjunction that joins two independent clauses? (comma)
5. What punctuation must precede a conjunctive adverb that joins two independent clauses? (semicolon)
6. Tell whether the second word in each phrase is an adjective or an adverb.
   a. the scholarly book (adj.)
   b. with friendly interest (adj.)
   c. arrived early today (adv.)
   d. has kindly spoken (adv.)
   e. comes close to the truth (adv.)
   f. the far mountains (adj.)
7. Tell whether the second word in each phrase is an adverb or a preposition.
   a. come in now (adv.)
   b. arrived in Michigan (prep.)
   c. went across the lake (prep.)
   d. went across on the ferry (adv.)
   e. is under God's care (prep.)
   f. dived under and disappeared (adv.)

<u>Rabbits</u>! What will I do with rabbits?
<u>Down</u>! Get down, Rover.
<u>Surprise</u>! Here's a gift for your birthday.

Use only those interjections that are suitable for God's people. Using God's Name as an interjection is a form of taking His Name in vain. This includes not only the names *God* and *Jesus* but also words that are alterations of these names. Neither is it right to use interjections that refer to goodness, graciousness, holiness, or any other characteristic of God.

Interjections that refer to heaven, the earth, the stars, or any other part of God's creation should also be avoided. And of course we must never use exclamations that refer to hell, Satan, or any part of his kingdom. Interjections that give sinful expression to feelings of anger or disgust are likewise wrong. Neither is it proper to use a common word as an interjection that has nothing to do with its normal meaning. Words like *boy, man,* and *rats* are sometimes used in that way.

A mild interjection is followed by a comma, and a more emphatic one by an exclamation point. If an exclamation point is used, the interjection stands as a complete sentence by itself. The next word begins a new sentence and should be capitalized. Many interjections are used mildly sometimes and emphatically at other times. The difference is determined by the manner in which they are expressed.

<u>Good,</u> that job is finished.
<u>Good</u>! Now we can go home.

If the whole sentence shows strong feeling, a comma may be used after the interjection and an exclamation point at the end of the sentence.

<u>Oh,</u> what a beautiful sunset<u>!</u>
<u>Why,</u> we hardly recognized him anymore<u>!</u>

An interjection has no direct relationship to the rest of the sentence. Therefore, it is diagramed on a line separate from the rest of the sentence.

Well, what shall we do next?

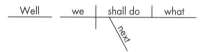

Alas! It was too late.

Lesson Introduction: Write the following sentences on the board. Have the students tell what part of speech the word *well* is in each.

> Because of the drought, our <u>well</u> went dry yesterday.
> We had thought we were <u>well</u> situated with a good water supply.
> It is <u>well</u> that we have a strong spring at the barn.
> <u>Well</u>, we surely are praying for rain.

Students should recognize the first three quite easily: *noun, adverb, adjective.* Perhaps they will not remember interjections. If not, ask which of the eight parts of speech they have not studied this year.

Lesson Outline:

1. An interjection is a word that expresses strong feeling or emotion. Students should become familiar with the common interjections listed in the lesson.

    a. Words that represent sounds are often interjections.

    b. Any word used as an independent exclamation can be an interjection.

2. Use only those interjections that are suitable for God's people.

    a. Using the names *God* and *Jesus* as interjections (as well as alterations of these) is taking God's Name in vain. It is also wrong to use interjections that refer to goodness, graciousness, holiness, or any other characteristic of God.

    b. All the following interjections should also be avoided.

      1) Interjections that refer to heaven, the earth, the stars, or any other part of God's creation.

      2) Exclamations that refer to hell, Satan, or any part of his kingdom.

      3) Interjections that give sinful expression to feelings of anger or disgust.

Class Practice

A. Identify each interjection, and tell whether it should be followed by a comma or an exclamation point. Say *yes* or *no* to tell whether the next word should be capitalized.
1. "Behold we put bits in the horses' mouths, that they may obey us."
2. "Lo the star, which they saw in the east, went before them."
3. Say look at this strange bug.
4. Oh you must have misunderstood what I said.
5. Excellent these pieces should fit just right.

B. On the chalkboard, diagram these sentences.
1. "Behold, God is mine helper."
2. What! None of the others have come yet?
3. Well, they must have had some delays.
4. Alas! What shall we do?
5. Why, here are those missing papers!

Written Exercises

A. Copy each interjection, and put a comma or an exclamation point after it. Also copy the next word, and capitalize it if necessary.
1. Hallelujah the Lord is on the throne.
2. "Lo they that are far from thee shall perish."
3. Ah you do know the answer!
4. Ouch my ankle must be sprained.
5. Look it's snowing hard now.
6. Wonderful we are going to Uncle Leonard's place this evening.
7. Well let's get the chores done quickly.
8. Say they must have gotten a new bicycle.

B. Diagram these sentences.
1. What! Is this experience discouraging you?
2. Lo, God will help us in every experience of life.
3. Behold, if we pray in faith, He will give us His aid.
4. Alas! Many people never pray to the Lord.
5. Ah, we must pray for them!

Review Exercises

A. Copy each underlined word, and label it *adj.* or *adv.* [86]
1. The design for the <u>priestly</u> garments was given <u>directly</u> by God.
2. A <u>godly</u> person stays <u>far</u> from whatever our <u>holy</u> God disapproves.
3. A <u>miserly</u> person <u>selfishly</u> hoards things to himself.
4. We should <u>freely</u> share our <u>earthly</u> possessions with those in need.
5. In the <u>far</u> corner of the room stands a <u>friendly</u> man who often shares <u>kindly</u> with others.

4) Common words used as interjections that have nothing to do with their normal meanings.

3. A mild interjection is followed by a comma, and a more emphatic one by an exclamation point.
a. If an exclamation point is used, the next word should be capitalized.
b. Many interjections are used mildly sometimes and emphatically at other times. The difference is determined by the manner in which they are expressed.

4. If the whole sentence shows strong feeling, a comma may be used after the interjection and an exclamation point at the end of the sentence.

5. An interjection is diagramed on a line separate from the rest of the sentence.

Lesson 96 Answers

Class Practice
A. 1. Behold, no   4. Oh, no
2. Lo, no   5. Excellent! yes
3. Say! yes

B. 1.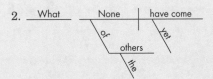
2.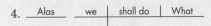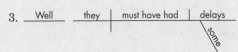
3.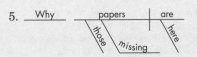
4.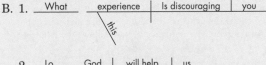
5.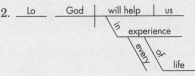

Written Exercises
A. (Allow reasonable variation.)
1. Hallelujah! The   5. Look! It's
2. Lo, they   6. Wonderful! We
3. Ah, you   7. Well, let's
4. Ouch! My   8. Say! They

B. 1.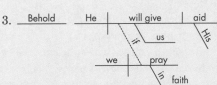
2.
3.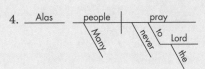
4.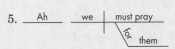
5.

(Review Exercises are on page 458.)

B. Copy each underlined word, and label it *prep.* or *adv.* [89]

1. When we feel troubled, we should look <u>up</u> to the Lord <u>in</u> faith.
2. Nevin went <u>outside</u> to bring <u>in</u> the cows.
3. The family sat <u>around</u> the table and asked God's blessing <u>on</u> the meal.
4. Yesterday we hiked <u>up</u> the steep hill <u>behind</u> our house and looked <u>out</u> <u>over</u> the valley.
5. Why don't you come <u>over</u> next week and look <u>around</u> <u>for</u> a while?

---

97. Review of the Parts of Speech

> **Lesson Survey**
> - Know the definitions and abbreviations of all the eight parts of speech.
> - The use of a word in a sentence determines its part of speech. When labeling words in a sentence, be especially careful with words that may be two different parts of speech.

Every word of every English sentence can be classified as one of the eight parts of speech. You should be familiar with the following definitions and abbreviations by now.

1. A **noun** (n.) names a person, place, thing, or idea.
2. A **pronoun** (pron.) takes the place of a noun.
3. A **verb** (v.) expresses action or being.
4. An **adjective** (adj.) modifies a substantive by telling *which, whose, how many,* or *what kind of.*
5. An **adverb** (adv.) modifies a verb or verbal, an adjective, or another adverb by telling *how, when, where,* or *to what degree.*
6. A **preposition** (prep.) shows the relationship between its object and some other word in the sentence.
7. A **conjunction** (conj.) joins words, phrases, or clauses.
8. An **interjection** (interj.) expresses strong feeling or emotion.

Be sure not to confuse the *parts of speech* with the *parts of a sentence.* For example, a noun may be used as a subject, a direct object, or a predicate nominative. But as a part of speech, it is a noun no matter which of these places it fills—and it should be labeled that way. However, most other words are labeled the same way whether you are identifying parts of speech or parts of a sentence. Compare the labels above the following sentences.

Lesson 97

Purpose: To review the eight parts of speech.

Oral Review:

1. What is an interjection? (a word that expresses strong feeling or emotion)
2. How is an interjection set off from the rest of a sentence? (A mild interjection is set off by a comma, and a strong interjection by an exclamation point.)
3. Name the two general classes of conjunctions. (coordinating, subordinating)
4. What is the name for coordinating conjunctions that come in pairs? (correlative conjunctions)
5. When words like *however, nevertheless,* and *consequently* are used to join two clauses, what are they called? (conjunctive adverbs)
6. Answer the following questions about capitalization.

Review Exercises

A. 1. priestly—adj.; directly—adv.
  2. godly—adj.; far—adv.; holy—adj.
  3. miserly—adj.; selfishly—adv.
  4. freely—adv.; earthly—adj.
  5. far—adj.; friendly—adj.; kindly—adv.

B. 1. up—adv.; in—prep.
  2. outside—adv.; in—adv.
  3. around—prep.; on—prep.
  4. up—prep.; behind—prep.; out—adv.; over—prep.
  5. over—adv.; around—adv.; for—prep.

a. When are words like *uncle* and *brother* capitalized, and when are they not? (capitalized when used with or instead of actual names; not capitalized when preceded by possessive pronouns)
b. When are words like *north* and *west* capitalized, and when are they not? (capitalized when used to name geographic regions; not capitalized when used to name directions)
c. Which words should be capitalized in this title: "Day Is Dying in the West"? (Shown correctly.)
d. Should the names of school subjects be capitalized? (only if they are derived from proper nouns, like *English* or *American history*)
e. Which of the following items should be capitalized: Ascension Day, February, spring? (Shown correctly.)

Sentence parts labeled:

<pre>
sub. v.   adv.   v. conj. v. adj. d.o. prep. adj. adj. o.p.
</pre>
We shall always obey and serve the Lord with our whole heart.

Parts of speech labeled:

<pre>
pron. v.   adv.   v. conj. v. adj. n.   prep. adj. adj. n.
</pre>
We shall always obey and serve the Lord with our whole heart.

Generally you can look at a word and immediately recognize its part of speech. When you see the word *student,* you know it is a noun. You recognize *them* as a pronoun. And you know that *speak* is a verb. But what part of speech is *light*? It may be a noun, naming a thing that shines (like the sun); a verb, expressing the action of the sun; or an adjective, describing a room with the sun shining into it.

These examples show that the use of a word in a sentence determines its part of speech. With certain kinds of words, you need to be especially careful to label the parts of speech correctly. Some of these are described in this lesson.

1. *Some words can be either prepositions or adverbs.* Remember that an adverb stands alone and modifies a verb or verbal, an adjective, or another adverb. But a preposition always has an object, and it shows the relationship of its object to some other word in the sentence. Say the word, and ask *whom* or *what.* If there is a noun, pronoun, or other substantive to answer the question, the word is a preposition. If there is none, the word is an adverb.

We are going <u>over</u> to Aunt Lela's house to sing this evening.
>   **Think:** Over whom or what? There is no answer.
>   *Over* is an adverb.

I looked <u>over</u> Betty's shoulder to see the songbook.
>   **Think:** Over whom or what? Object is *shoulder.*
>   *Over* is a preposition.

Lesson Introduction: The would-be mechanic has been learning about the parts of an engine. He has learned what the spark plugs do and where they are located. Likewise, he knows a little about the pistons, the valves, the crankshaft, and other important parts. He has only one problem—a rather major problem though. He has a bit of difficulty distinguishing the crankshaft from the drive shaft, and he is constantly confusing the oil dipstick with the power steering dipstick. He has much to learn before he can be a master mechanic, does he not?

You have learned many things about the eight parts of speech. But are you like that would-be mechanic? Do you get mixed up when you try to distinguish an adjective from an adverb, or a preposition from a conjunction? This lesson should help to clarify your overall understanding of the eight parts of speech.

Lesson Outline:

1. Know the definitions and abbreviations of all the eight parts of speech.

2. The use of a word in a sentence determines its part of speech. Many words can be used as more than one part of speech. Be especially careful in the following cases.

(1) *Some words can be either prepositions or adverbs.*
   a) An adverb stands alone and modifies a verb or verbal, an adjective, or another adverb.
   b) A preposition always has an object, and it shows the relationship of its object to some other word in the sentence.
   c) Test by saying the word and asking *whom* or *what.*

2. *Some words can be either adjectives or adverbs.* You studied this difference just recently. Words like *early, kindly, close, near,* and *slow* are commonly used as either part of speech. You can tell which they are by remembering the definitions of adjectives and adverbs. An adjective modifies a noun, pronoun, or other substantive and answers the question *which, whose, how many,* or *what kind of.* An adverb modifies a verb or verbal, an adjective, or another adverb and answers the question *how, when, where,* or *to what degree.*

> We must go to bed <u>early</u> tonight.
> > **Think:** *Early* modifies the verb *must go* and tells *when.*
> > *Early* is an adverb.
> We need an <u>early</u> start for our trip tomorrow.
> > **Think:** *Early* modifies the noun *start* and tells *what kind of.*
> > *Early* is an adjective.

3. *Some words can be either prepositions or conjunctions.* To tell the difference, look at the words that follow. If they make up a phrase with no skeleton but with an object, the word is a preposition. If they make up a clause with a skeleton, the word is a conjunction.

> Brother Lamar looked in the dictionary <u>for</u> the correct pronunciation.
> > **Think:** *For* is followed by *the correct pronunciation.*
> > There is no skeleton, but there is an object.
> > For *what*? For *pronunciation.*
> > *For* is a preposition.
> Brother Lamar looked in the dictionary, <u>for</u> he was not sure of the correct pronunciation.
> > **Think:** *For* is followed by *he was not sure of the correct pronunciation.*
> > There is a skeleton: <u>he</u> <u>was</u>.
> > *For* is a conjunction.

4. *Some words can be either pronouns or adjectives.* This is especially true of the possessive case *his;* the demonstrative pronouns *this, that, these,* and *those;* and indefinite pronouns like *each, both, several,* and *few.* Remember that a pronoun names something and takes the place of a noun. By contrast, an adjective only modifies a noun, pronoun, or other substantive. Generally, if one of these words immediately precedes a substantive, it is an adjective. Otherwise, it is a pronoun.

> Darren has checked <u>both</u> fans this morning.
> > **Think:** *Both* immediately precedes and modifies *fans.*
> > *Both* is an adjective.

(2) *Some words can be either adjectives or adverbs.*
  a) An adjective modifies a noun, pronoun, or other substantive and answers the question *which, whose, how many,* or *what kind of.*
  b) An adverb modifies a verb or verbal, an adjective, or another adverb and answers the question *how, when, where,* or *to what degree.*
(3) *Some words can be either prepositions or conjunctions.* To tell the difference, look at the words that follow.
  a) If they make up a phrase with no skeleton but with an object, the word is a preposition.
  b) If they make up a clause with a skeleton, the word is a conjunction.

(4) *Some words can be either pronouns or adjectives.* This is especially true of the possessive case *his,* the demonstrative pronouns, and the indefinite pronouns.
  a) If it names something and takes the place of a noun, it is a pronoun.
  b) If it only modifies a noun, pronoun, or other substantive, it is an adjective.
  c) These kinds of words are usually adjectives if they immediately precede substantives; otherwise, they are usually pronouns.
(5) *Sometimes nouns are used as adjectives.* A noun becomes an adjective when it is used to describe another noun.
(6) *Sometimes adjectives are used as nouns.*
  a) Such an adjective usually describes a particular characteristic of a person. But

Two fans had not worked, but Darren fixed <u>both</u> this morning.
Think: *Both* names something and takes the place of *both fans.*
It does not immediately precede a noun.
Both is a pronoun.

The girls have written their poems, but Brian has not done <u>his</u> yet.
Think: *His* names something and takes the place of *his poem.*
It does not immediately precede a noun.
His is a pronoun.

<u>His</u> poem will have eight stanzas when it is finished.
Think: *His* immediately precedes and modifies *poem.*
His is an adjective.

5. *Sometimes nouns are used as adjectives.* When a word that is normally a noun is used to describe another noun, it becomes an adjective. For example, the words *brick, slate,* and *stone* are normally nouns. In the following sentences, however, they are adjectives telling *what kind of* about the nouns that follow them.

Grandfather Burkholders live in a <u>brick</u> house with a <u>slate</u> roof.
A large <u>stone</u> barn stands behind the house.

6. *Sometimes adjectives are used as nouns.* Such an adjective usually describes a particular characteristic of a person. But instead of modifying a noun like *man* or *person,* the adjective itself is used to name someone with that characteristic. Thus, wise people are called the *wise,* and rich people are called the *rich.* Generally, when an adjective is used as a noun, you could sensibly insert a noun after it.

"Forsake the <u>foolish</u>, and live; and go in the way of understanding."
(the foolish *person*)
"The <u>righteous</u> shall never be removed: but the <u>wicked</u> shall not inhabit the earth." (the righteous *people;* the wicked *people*)

7. *Any word can be used as an interjection.* As you have just studied in Lesson 96, an interjection is any word spoken with strong feeling and set off by a comma or an exclamation point.

<u>Broken</u>! What shall we do now? (*Broken* is normally a verb.)
<u>Heaven</u>! How glorious it must be. (*Heaven* is normally a noun.)

Class Practice

A. Name the part of speech for each underlined word.
1. The Bible is an <u>anchor</u> <u>for</u> the soul <u>in</u> <u>times</u> like <u>these</u>.
2. As we <u>trust</u> the Lord, we can <u>chart</u> a <u>steady</u> <u>course</u> through life.

instead of modifying a noun, the adjective itself is used to name someone with that characteristic.
   b) Generally, when an adjective is used as a noun, you could sensibly insert a noun after it.
(7) *Any word can be used as an interjection.*

Lesson 97 Answers

Class Practice
A. 1. anchor—n.; for—prep.; in—prep.; times—n.; like—prep.; these—pron.
   2. trust—v.; chart—v.; steady—adj.; course—n.

3. Anchor your life in the Bible, and your soul is secure regardless of life's billows.
4. Never give up, for the eternal rewards are well worth any sacrifice.
5. If I sacrifice my will to the Lord, He will surely reward me.
6. In the early morning, our minds should turn to God.

B. Name the part of speech for each word.
1. The faithful, despised and persecuted, are always under God's watchful eye.
2. Indeed, if a sparrow never falls to the ground without God's notice, His people surely do not suffer without His care.
3. Did you notice the way those cats eye that dog?
4. Mark brought one too, but his did not go into the box.
5. The glowing embers were still hot after several hours.
6. Some are glowing quite weakly; however, others are surprisingly hot.
7. Marshmallows! We should have thought of marshmallows before we left.
8. A friendly boy helped us kindly, and now we are close friends.

Written Exercises

A. Write the part of speech for each underlined word.
1. Jesus spoke to the woman at the well.
2. He understood her needs perfectly well.
3. Her spiritual life was not well before she met Jesus.
4. Well, she certainly found something more satisfying than water!
5. Satan will blind the hearts of all that he can.
6. The blind beggars called out to Jesus.
7. Jesus had compassion on the blind, and He healed many of them.
8. Do you welcome the return of warm weather?
9. We received a hearty welcome when we arrived in Guatemala.
10. Aunt Geraldine sent a welcome letter to us.
11. Welcome! We are pleased to have you here.
12. Clean your bedroom carefully.
13. Is the floor clean under your bed?
14. Linda, bring the wash in.
15. Mother is in the house.
16. After the chores are finished, we will have a snack.
17. After supper, we shall visit Uncle Amos.
18. The mother duck led the way, and her ducklings waddled after.
19. This is quite a surprise.
20. Do you know where this sweater belongs?
21. Father is singing as he plows.

3. Anchor—v.; secure—adj.; billows—n.
4. up—adv.; for—conj.; rewards—n.; well—adv.; sacrifice—n.
5. sacrifice—v.; will—n.; will—v.; reward—v.
6. In—prep.; early—adj.; minds—n.; turn—v.

B. 1. The faithful, despised and persecuted, are always under God's watchful eye.
    (adj.) (n.) (adj.) (conj.) (adj.) (v.) (adv.) (prep.) (adj.) (adj.) (n.)

2. Indeed, if a sparrow never falls to the ground without God's notice, His people surely do not suffer without His care.
    (interj.) (conj.) (adj.) (n.) (adv.) (v.) (prep.) (adj.) (n.) (prep.) (adj.) (n.) (adj.) (n.) (adv.) (v.) (adv.) (v.) (prep.) (adj.) (n.)

3. Did you notice the way those cats eye that dog?
    (v.) (pron.) (v.) (adj.) (n.) (adj.) (n.) (v.) (adj.) (n.)

4. Mark brought one too, but his did not go into the box.
    (n.) (v.) (pron.) (adv.) (conj.) (pron.) (v.) (adv.) (v.) (prep.) (adj.) (n.)

5. The glowing embers were still hot after several hours.
    (adj.) (adj.) (n.) (v.) (adv.) (adj.) (prep.) (adj.) (n.)

6. Some are glowing quite weakly; however, others are surprisingly hot.
    (pron.) (v.) (v.) (adv.) (adv.) (adv.) (pron.) (v.) (adv.) (adj.)

7. Marshmallows! We should have thought of marshmallows before we left.
    (interj.) (pron.) (v.) (v.) (v.) (prep.) (n.) (conj.) (pron.) (v.)

8. A friendly boy helped us kindly, and now we are close friends.
    (adj.) (adj.) (n.) (v.) (pron.) (adv.) (conj.) (adv.) (pron.) (v.) (adj.) (n.)

Written Exercises

A.
1. n.		8. v.		15. prep.	
2. adv.		9. n.		16. conj.	
3. adj.		10. adj.		17. prep.	
4. interj.		11. interj.		18. adv.	
5. v.		12. v.		19. pron.	
6. adj.		13. adj.		20. adj.	
7. n.		14. adv.		21. v.	

22. The <u>singing</u> birds are pleasant to hear.
23. In <u>His</u> Word, God has revealed the origin of the world.
24. The earth and all it contains are <u>His</u> by right of creation.
25. A flight of <u>concrete</u> steps leads up to the museum.
26. Mr. Lawson will <u>concrete</u> the basement floor this summer.
27. <u>Concrete</u> is a useful building material.
28. <u>Concrete</u>! Did he fall on the concrete?
29. I must do the evening chores alone, <u>for</u> I dawdled this morning.
30. Mother is making ham and cheese sandwiches <u>for</u> lunch.

B. Copy these sentences, and label the part of speech for each word.
1. Good! We are having a cherry pie for dessert.
2. You left one cherry on your plate.
3. My left hand hurts, for it was smashed under a block.
4. The running water cleaned the dirt from the wound.
5. I was running the tractor, which is one of my favorite jobs.
6. Those are the chickens that we will butcher.
7. If we shun the wrong and lead a holy life, God will make a way for us.
8. Lift up your eyes, place your trust in the Lord, and stay close to His side.

Review Exercises

A. Write the letter of the item that is capitalized correctly. [20]
1. a. study math and English
   b. study Math and English
2. a. an old Farmall Tractor
   b. an old Farmall tractor
3. a. what mother said
   b. what Mother said
4. a. lived in the Southwest
   b. lived in the southwest
5. a. the Countries of Asia
   b. the countries of Asia
6. a. a project for the Winter
   b. a project for the winter
7. a. At Rest under the Stars
   b. At Rest Under the Stars
8. a. the long-awaited Messiah
   b. the long-awaited messiah
9. a. visited the Indian Echo Caverns
   b. visited the Indian Echo caverns
10. a. traveled west on Interstate 64
    b. traveled West on Interstate 64

B. Write the letter of the sentence that is punctuated correctly. (Use the index if you need help.)
1. a. We grow peaches, pears and apples.
   b. We grow peaches, pears, and apples.
2. a. A squirrel often buries many more nuts than it needs for food; consequently, some of them sprout and grow into trees.
   b. A squirrel often buries many more nuts than it needs for food, consequently, some of them sprout and grow into trees.
3. a. What a strange animal the platypus is!

22. adj.   25. adj.   28. interj.
23. adj.   26. v.   29. conj.
24. pron.   27. n.   30. prep.

B. 1. Good! We are having a cherry pie for dessert.
    interj. pron. v. v. adj. adj. n. prep. n.

2. You left one cherry on your plate.
   pron. v. adj. n. prep. adj. n.

3. My left hand hurts, for it was smashed under a block.
   adj. adj. n. v. conj. pron. v. v. prep. adj. n.

4. The running water cleaned the dirt from the wound.
   adj. adj. n. v. adj. n. prep. adj. n.

5. I was running the tractor, which is one of my favorite jobs.
   pron. v. v. adj. n. pron. v. pron. prep. adj. adj. n.

6. Those are the chickens that we will butcher.
   pron. v. adj. n. pron. pron. v. v.

7. If we shun the wrong and lead a holy life, God will make a way for us.
   conj. pron. v. adj. n. conj. v. adj. adj. n. n. v. v. adj. n. prep. pron.

8. Lift up your eyes, place your trust in the Lord, and stay close to His side.
   v. adv. adj. n. v. adj. n. prep. adj. n. conj. v. adv. prep. adj. n.

Review Exercises

A. 1. a   6. b
   2. b   7. b
   3. b   8. a
   4. a   9. a
   5. b   10. a

B. 1. b   3. a
   2. a

b. What a strange animal the platypus is.
4. a. Gary you are supposed to fill the woodbox.
   b. Gary, you are supposed to fill the woodbox.
5. a. Because we love God, we obey His Word.
   b. Because we love God we obey His Word.
6. a. Imagine, some people have never heard of the Bible.
   b. Imagine! Some people have never heard of the Bible!
7. a. We have been richly blessed, so we should thank God every day.
   b. We have been richly blessed so we should thank God every day.
8. a. The classroom has a quiet studious atmosphere.
   b. The classroom has a quiet, studious atmosphere.
9. a. The students were either studying their Bible memory, or writing out the passage.
   b. The students were either studying their Bible memory or writing out the passage.
10. a. On our trip we visited Nevin Zimmerman, my father's cousin, Alan Gehman, my mother's uncle, and Eugene Fisher, a previous neighbor.
    b. On our trip we visited Nevin Zimmerman, my father's cousin; Alan Gehman, my mother's uncle; and Eugene Fisher, a previous neighbor.

4. b
5. a
6. b
7. a
8. b
9. b
10. b

---

98. Rhyme and Repetition in Poetry

Lesson Survey

- Good rhyme adds to the beauty of poetry. The rhyming pattern can be shown by using a different small letter for each set of rhyming words.

- The intended rhyming words in poetry should be true rhymes.

- The beauty of poetry is also increased by **alliteration** (repetition of beginning consonant sounds), **assonance** (repetition of similar vowel sounds in accented syllables), and **onomatopoeia** (use of words having imitative sounds).

- **Parallelism,** the repetition of thoughts, is a common characteristic of Bible poetry.

Lesson 98

Purpose: To teach rhyming patterns, *alliteration, *assonance, *onomatopoeia, and the parallelism of Bible poetry. (*Previous experience:* Concepts of alliteration and onomatopoeia, without use of the terms.)

Oral Review:

1. What are the two main types of literature? (prose, poetry)
2. Name several characteristics that distinguish poetry from prose. (Poetry is written in lines and stanzas, usually has rhythm and rhyme, makes effective use of descriptive words and figurative language, can say much in a few words, and has a special beauty that affects our feelings.)
3. What is rhythm? (a regular pattern of accented and unaccented syllables)
4. Name the rhythm pattern in each of these lines.

a. "O Life in whom is life indeed" (iambic)
b. "Use me, O God, in Thy great harvest field" (dactylic)
c. "Often weary and worn on the pathway below" (anapestic)
d. "Can you count the stars of evening" (trochaic)
5. How many feet are in each of the lines above? (4)
6. Tell which kind of verb fits each of the following descriptions and examples.

a. Links a predicate nominative or predicate adjective to the subject. "The leaves were red, yellow, and brown." (intransitive linking)
b. Passes action to the subject. "The leaves have been raked into piles." (transitive passive)
c. Passes action to a direct object. "We raked the leaves into piles." (transitive active)
d. An action verb that does not pass action to any word. "We were working for a while this afternoon." (intransitive complete)

In Lesson 90 you were reminded that rhythm and rhyme are two outstanding characteristics that distinguish poetry from prose. Rhyme, the matching of sounds at the ends of lines, adds much to the special beauty of poetry.

Many different rhyming patterns are used in poems. The rhyming pattern can be shown by using a different small letter for each set of rhyming words. In addition, lines of poetry are generally indented according to the rhyming pattern, with lines that rhyme indented equally. The examples below illustrate a few of the possible patterns.

If God should call to you	a
A special work to do,	a
Would you be quick to say,	b
"I'm ready, Lord, today"?	b

Too many people want a crown	a
But do not want to bear their cross;	b
In wealth they want to have renown,	a
So count not all for Christ as loss.	b

The Lord is my Shepherd,	a
He guides me each day;	b
He guards me from evil,	c
And lights up life's way.	b

Though storms be severe,	a
I harbor no fear;	a
The course is quite clear,	a
For Jesus is near.	a

Jesus left His high, heavenly throne	a
And to earth as a low servant came;	b
He allowed men to mock His great Name	b
As He suffered in anguish alone.	a

The intended rhyming words in poetry should be true rhymes. Remember, not every pair of words that looks like a rhyme actually makes a good rhyme. Study the following rules.

1. *The vowel sounds of rhyming syllables must be the same.* Rhyme is a matter of sound, not spelling. So even though two syllables have the same vowels, they do not rhyme unless the vowel sounds are alike.

<u>Truth</u> and <u>youth</u> rhyme; <u>youth</u> and <u>mouth</u> do not.

2. *The final consonant sounds of rhyming syllables must be the same.* It is not enough for only the vowel sounds to be the same.

Lesson Introduction: The quilt maker enjoys using different patterns for her quilts. Occasionally she puts some special touches on the quilt. The woodworker experiments with different designs for his birdhouses. He too puts special touches on his workmanship at times. Like other craftsmen, the poet uses variety and looks for special touches of beauty. The possibilities for variety are much greater in rhyme than in rhythm, as you will see in this lesson.

Lesson Outline:

1. Good rhyme adds to the beauty of poetry. The rhyming pattern can be shown by using a different small letter for each set of rhyming words.

2. The intended rhyming words in poetry should be true rhymes.

  (1) *The vowel sounds of rhyming syllables must be the same.*

  (2) *The final consonant sounds of rhyming syllables must be the same.*

  (3) *The beginning consonant sounds of rhyming syllables must be different.*

  (4) *The rhyming syllables must be accented.*

3. The beauty of poetry is also increased by alliteration (repetition of beginning consonant sounds), assonance (repetition of similar vowel sounds in accented syllables), and onomatopoeia (use of words having imitative sounds).

  (*Note:* The following associations can be used as a help in remembering the meaning of each term.

    a. The root of *alliteration* is Latin *littera* [letter]. Alliteration usually involves "same-first-letter" words.

    b. The root of *assonance* is Latin *sonare* [sound]. Assonance involves "same-vowel-sound" words.

Sound and found rhyme; sound and crown do not.

3. *The beginning consonant sounds of rhyming syllables must be different.* If two different words sound exactly alike, they are homonyms. They are not rhyming words.

Pair and lair rhyme; pair and pear do not.

4. *The rhyming syllables must be accented.* A final unaccented syllable is often pronounced with a schwa or some other unclear sound. Such a sound does not make a good rhyme.

Confer and deter rhyme; confer and enter do not.

Of course, if the next-to-the-last syllable is accented, a good rhyme can be made with the last *two* syllables.

All these words rhyme: enter, center, renter, inventor.
These pairs do not rhyme: enter—rented, seven—level.

There are other kinds of repetition that help to make poetry beautiful. One device is *alliteration,* or the repetition of beginning consonant sounds in words that are close together. Study the following examples.

Alliteration:
Let there be light, Lord God of Hosts!

Let woe and waste of warfare cease.

The repetition of beginning *l* and *w* sounds helps to give these lines a pleasing sound. It also links the words beginning with that sound and emphasizes them in a special way. That effect is particularly strong in the second example, where *woe, waste,* and *warfare* have related meanings.

Alliteration can produce various effects, depending on the sound that is repeated. A repeated *s* sound adds a tone of softness. A repeated *k* sound produces a tone of sharpness or harshness. In any case, alliteration adds to the special beauty and appeal of poetry.

Another device is *assonance* (as′·ə·nəns), or the repetition of similar vowel sounds in accented syllables that are close together. The following lines contain an example of assonance.

Assonance:
One there is above all others,
    Well deserves the name of Friend;
His is love beyond a brother's,
    Costly, free, and knows no end.

c. The root of *onomatopoeia* is Greek *onoma* [name] and *poiein* [to make]. Onomatopoeia involves "making the name" of a sound by imitating it.)

4. *Parallelism, the repetition of thoughts, is a common characteristic of Bible poetry.* The repeated thoughts may be similar or opposite.

★ *EXTRA PRACTICE*
Worksheet 52 (*Rhyme and Repetition in Poetry*)

Assonance, like alliteration, adds a poetic feeling because of the repeated sounds. However, alliteration tends to speed up a poetic passage, while assonance tends to slow it down.

A device called *onomatopoeia* (on′·ə·mat′·ə·pē′·ə) also adds to the beauty of poetry. Onomatopoeia is the use of a word having an imitative sound. Expressions like the *hiss* of escaping steam or a *clap* of thunder make use of onomatopoeia. Read the following lines. Can you hear the sound of the bells as the cows come home? (A dingle is a small, shady valley.)

Onomatopoeia:
> With <u>klingle</u>, <u>klangle</u>, <u>klingle</u>,
> Far down the dusky dingle,
>> The cows are coming home.
>
> Now sweet and clear, now faint and low,
> The airy <u>tinklings</u> come and go,
>> Like <u>chimings</u> from a far-off tower,
>> Or <u>patterings</u> of an April shower
> That makes the daisies grow.
>
> <u>Ko</u>-<u>ling</u>, <u>ko</u>-<u>lang</u>, <u>ko</u>-<u>lingle</u>, <u>lingle</u>,
> Far down the darkening dingle,
>> The cows come slowly home.

In Lesson 94 you saw that Bible poetry does not have the rhythm of accented syllables. Neither does it have the rhyme of repeated sounds. Instead, Bible poetry has a pattern of repeated thoughts called *parallelism*. The parallelism of Bible poetry has "rhythm and rhyme" in thought rather than sound. Sometimes the thoughts are similar, and sometimes they are opposite.

Similar parallelism:
> The Lord reigneth; let the people tremble:
> He sitteth between the cherubims; let the earth be moved. (Psalm 99:1)

Opposite parallelism:
> The light of the righteous rejoiceth:
> But the lamp of the wicked shall be put out. (Proverbs 13:9)

The lines above have "rhythm" in that the thoughts of each pair are expressed in the same order. They have "rhyme" in that the thoughts are expressed by words of similar or opposite meaning. This can be shown by matching the main words in each pair of lines.

The <u>Lord</u> <u>reigneth</u>; <u>let</u> the <u>people</u> <u>tremble</u>:

He <u>sitteth</u> between the cherubims; <u>let</u> the <u>earth</u> <u>be moved</u>.

The <u>light</u> of the <u>righteous</u> <u>rejoiceth</u>:

But the <u>lamp</u> of the <u>wicked</u> shall be <u>put out</u>.

Parallelism is often not as perfect as in the examples above. But this is the general pattern, and it makes the poetry of the Bible truly beautiful.

Class Practice

A. Tell whether the words in each pair are a perfect rhyme. If they are not, tell which of the four rules is broken.

1. throne, done
2. prefer, enter
3. weary, cheery
4. face, bless
5. name, claim
6. vain, vein
7. cost, loss
8. time, thine

B. Give the rhyming pattern of each stanza.

1. O for a faith that will not shrink
   Tho' pressed by many a foe,
   That will not tremble on the brink
   Of any earthly woe.
2. Jesus, my Lord, my God, my All,
   Hear me, blest Saviour, when I call;
   Hear me, and from Thy dwelling place
   Pour down the riches of Thy grace;
   Jesus, my Lord, I Thee adore;
   O make me love Thee more and more.
3. Christ for the world we sing,
   The world to Christ we bring
   With loving zeal;
   The poor and them that mourn,
   The faint and overborne,
   Sin-sick and sorrow-worn,,
   Whom Christ doth heal.
4. Let there be light, Lord God of Hosts!
   Let there be wisdom on the earth!
   Let broad humanity have birth!
   Let there be deeds instead of boasts.

C. Find examples of alliteration, assonance, and onomatopoeia in these lines.

1. The day, departing with the disappearing sun,
       Upon its page a tale of pain and death acclaims.

2. Jesus, keep me near the cross;
   There a precious fountain,
   Free to all, a healing stream,
   Flows from Calv'ry's mountain.
3. Holy Ghost, with light divine,
   Shine upon this heart of mine;
4. Mighty God, while angels bless Thee,
   May a mortal sing Thy Name?
5. Within the maple's shade I sat to rest,
   My ears attuned to every sound of spring;
   The bumblebee's bold buzz told of its quest
   For nectar sweet to bear on tireless wing.

D. Turn to the Book of Proverbs. Tell which kind of parallelism is found in each of these verses.
   1. 1:7   3. 1:13   5. 1:20   7. 4:8
   2. 1:8   4. 1:18   6. 3:35   8. 10:23

Written Exercises

A. If the pair of words is a perfect rhyme, write *perfect*. If it is not, write the number of the rule that is broken.
   1. mourn, morn   5. pray, obey
   2. stood, flood   6. stain, aim
   3. young, sung   7. cease, peace
   4. days, space   8. acorn, adorn

B. Write the rhyming pattern for these stanzas.
   1. My God and Father, while I stray
      Far from my home, on life's rough way,
      O teach me from my heart to say,
      "Thy will be done."
   2. Thou, whose almighty word
      Chaos and darkness heard
      And took their flight;
      Hear us, we humbly pray,
      And where the Gospel day
      Sheds not its glorious ray,
      Let there be light!
   3. It was only a tiny seed,
      Carelessly brushed aside;
      But it grew in time to a noxious weed,
      And spread its poison wide.

2. *assonance:* Jesus, keep, me, Free, healing, stream
3. *assonance:* light, divine, Shine, mine
4. *alliteration:* Mighty, May, mortal
5. *alliteration:* sat, sound, spring; bumblebee's, bold, buzz
   onomatopoeia: buzz

D. 1. opposite   5. similar
   2. similar   6. opposite
   3. similar   7. similar
   4. similar   8. opposite

Written Exercises

A. 1. 3   5. perfect
   2. 1   6. 2
   3. perfect 7. perfect
   4. 2   8. 4

B. 1. aaab
   2. aabcccb
   3. abab

4. Simply trusting ev'ry day,
   Trusting through a stormy way,
   Even when my faith is small,
   Trusting Jesus, that is all.
5. Lord, I stand at the door of another school day:
   Give me wisdom to learn,
   Make the old facts return,
   For some new skills I yearn;
   O Lord, bless me again in my studies, I pray.

C. Name one poetic device that is clearly illustrated by each set of lines: *alliteration*, *assonance*, or *onomatopoeia*. Then copy the words used for that device.
   1. Great ball of brilliancy
        Is blazing from the blue.
   2. The Lord pours eyesight on the blind,
      The Lord supports the fainting mind.
   3. Silently, with padded step and slow,
        A tawny, spotted serval stalks his prey.
   4.   **The Eagle**
      He clasps the crag with crooked hands,
      Close to the sun in lonely lands,
      Ringed with the azure world, he stands.
   5. Rattling o'er the cobblestones and rumbling down the roads,
      Lumbering toward the market are the farmers' wagonloads.

D. Turn to the Book of Psalms. Name the kind of parallelism used in each of these verses.
   1. 32:10   2. 33:8   3. 33:13   4. 34:10

E. Show the parallelism in these lines by following the pattern in the lesson. Copy the lines, underline the three main words or phrases in each, and draw lines to connect the matching words.
   The glory of young men is their strength:
   And the beauty of old men is the grey head. (Proverbs 20:29)

Review Exercises

A. Copy each verb or verb phrase, and label it *TA* for transitive active, *TP* for transitive passive, *IL* for intransitive linking, or *IC* for intransitive complete. [41–43, 53]
   1. Dishonesty is an abomination to the Lord.
   2. Since the beginning of time, Satan has been implanting seeds of lies in men's hearts.

---

4. aabb
5. abbba

C. 1. *alliteration:* ball, brilliancy, blazing, blue
   2. *assonance:* Lord, pours, Lord, supports;
      or eyesight, blind, mind
   3. *alliteration:* Silently, step, slow, spotted, serval, stalks
      or assonance: tawny, spotted, stalks
   4. *alliteration:* clasps, crag, crooked, Close; lonely, lands
      or assonance: clasps, crag, hands, lands, azure, stands
   5. *onomatopoeia:* Rattling, rumbling, Lumbering

D. 1. opposite   3. similar
   2. similar   4. opposite

E. The glory of young men is their strength:

   And the beauty of old men is the grey head.

Review Exercises

A. 1. is—IL
   2. has been implanting—TA

3. Satan is working hard for man's destruction.
4. We must cultivate honesty at all times.
5. Our character is developed by our choices.
6. The pattern of our choices becomes the pattern of our lives.

B. Rewrite these sentences in the passive voice. Do not change the tense. [53]
1. The girls have weeded these rows of beans.
2. Uncle Enos will build the addition to our house.
3. One of my aunts arranged the flowers in this bouquet.

C. Rewrite these sentences in the active voice. Do not change the tense. [53]
1. Some of our corn had been damaged by raccoons before the bad storm.
2. Our road has been flooded by water from the Conestoga River.
3. The rabbits are fed every morning by one of the children.

---

99. The Message of Poetry

> **Lesson Survey**
> - Good poetry deserves the effort needed to understand its message.
> - Poetry should be read clearly and expressively.

Understanding Poetry

One of the characteristics of good poetry is its ability to say much in a few words. Therefore, you may need to read a poem several times to discover the message that the poet wanted to give.

Poets often make use of figurative language. If you would understand the message of the poem, you must consider the meanings of the figures of speech. Perhaps you have sung these words of poetry often: *"Gentle words and deeds of kindness / Fall like sunbeams on the snow."* How are gentle words and kind deeds like sunbeams falling on snow? If you have ever seen sunlight on snow, you know the dazzling, sparkling beauty it produces. Likewise, words and actions of love are outstanding for their beauty in this cold world. And in the same way that warm sunshine melts cold snow, sincere love brings warmth and comfort to hearts that are sad and lonely.

Lesson 99

Purpose: To teach appreciation for good poetry.

Oral Review:
1. Name and describe the four patterns of rhythm. (iambic—one unaccented syllable followed by one accented syllable; trochaic—one accented syllable followed by one unaccented syllable; anapestic—two unaccented syllables followed by one accented syllable; dactylic—one accented syllable followed by two unaccented syllables)
2. What is a poetic foot? (one accented syllable and the unaccented syllable or syllables associated with it)
3. How is the rhyming pattern of a poem shown? (by using a different small letter for each set of rhyming words)
4. Complete these rules for good rhymes.

3. is working—IC
4. must cultivate—TA
5. is developed—TP
6. becomes—IL

B. 1. These rows of beans have been weeded by the girls.
2. The addition to our house will be built by Uncle Enos.
3. The flowers in this bouquet were arranged by one of my aunts.

C. 1. Raccoons had damaged some of our corn before the bad storm.
2. Water from the Conestoga River has flooded our road.
3. Every morning one of the children feeds the rabbits.
   or One of the children feeds the rabbits every morning.

---

a. The vowel sounds of rhyming syllables must be ———. (the same)
b. The final consonant sounds of rhyming syllables must be ———. (the same)
c. The beginning consonant sounds of rhyming syllables must be ———. (different)
d. The rhyming syllables must be ———. (accented)
5. Give the words for the following descriptions.
a. The repetition of thoughts, as often found in Bible poetry. (parallelism)
b. The repetition of beginning consonant sounds in words that are close together. (alliteration)
c. The repetition of similar vowel sounds in accented syllables that are close together. (assonance)

Read this poem, paying attention to the figurative language.

Hypocrisy

Be genuine! Your character
    Is like a picket fence—
It's useless putting on an air
    Or living a pretense;

For if your posts are rotten
    And any pickets split,
All the whitewash in the world
    Will never strengthen it.

—*Margaret Penner Toews*

This poem develops one simile, expressed in lines 1 and 2. In what ways is character like a picket fence? For one thing, the true quality of both cannot be successfully hidden for long. Furthermore, the inner soundness (or lack of it) is far more important to both character and fences than the impression one may try to make. The poem also suggests that people tend to cover failures, rather than honestly taking care of them.

Because poets want to say much in a few words, they must choose their words carefully. Pay attention to the exact meanings of expressive words. The following words are from the song "God Is Love, His Mercy Brightens."

Chance and change are busy ever,
    Worlds decay and ages move;
But His mercy waneth never;
    God is light, and God is love.

What is the poet saying that God's mercy never does? The word *wane* means "to become less." The first two lines declare that this world is marked by change and decline. In contrast, God's mercy never fades or becomes weaker.

Consider these lines from the song "Crown Him With Many Crowns."

Crown Him the Lord of years,
    The Potentate of time;
Creator of the rolling spheres,
    Ineffably sublime.

What does line 2 say about the Lord? A *potentate* is one who has the power of control. The root word is *potent,* which means "powerful." In other words, the "Lord of years" has full control of time. According to line 4, our Creator is sublime (noble and majestic). How sublime is He? *Ineffably* means "inexpressibly." God is more sublime than can be expressed in words.

Lesson Introduction: Read the following poem, first in a monotonous, chanting style and then with good expression. Ask the students which sounded better and which way helped them to understand the meaning of the poem.

Cheerfulness

Do not yield to frowns and tears,
Gloom, self-pity, doubts, and fears.
    It won't help things to complain:
    Grumbling never stopped the rain,
    Changed a menu, softened pain,
    Sweetened sorrow, lightened strain.
Be as cheerful as you can,
For it is a better plan.

Lesson Outline:

1. Good poetry deserves the effort needed to understand its message.

   a. Consider the meanings of the figures of speech.

   b. Pay attention to the exact meanings of expressive words.

   c. Pay attention to what words imply.

   d. Follow the thoughts of the poem, not just the lines.

2. Poetry should be read clearly and expressively.

   a. Read the poem aloud to yourself several times.

   b. Observe the punctuation carefully.

   c. Avoid a monotonous, chanting style of reading.

   d. Read slowly, clearly, and expressively.

Not only should you be sure to know the meanings of words, but also you should pay attention to what words imply. Notice the word *pants* in the song "Break Thou the Bread of Life."

> My spirit pants for Thee,
>   O living Word.

The poet could have used a number of other words, including *longs, yearns, sighs, craves,* and *thirsts.* While these other words are equally expressive, only the word *pants* reminds us of the familiar Scripture verse, "As the hart *panteth* after the water brooks, so *panteth* my soul after thee, O God" (Psalm 42:1).

Follow the thoughts of the poem, not just the lines. Watch the punctuation. What does the following line of poetry mean to a person who reads a poem line by line?

> "Bring love and justice home, and then no more"

But here is the entire stanza. Read it by thoughts, and see how the meaning becomes clear.

> Go not abroad for happiness. For see,
>   It is a flower that blossoms at thy door!
>   Bring love and justice home, and then no more
> Thou'lt wonder in what dwelling joy may be.
> > —*Minot J. Savage*

Reading Poetry

The full beauty of a poem comes out only when it is read or recited orally. Only then can the rhythm and rhyme be well expressed and fully enjoyed. Only then can poetic devices, such as alliteration and assonance, be truly appreciated.

Before you read a poem to others, you should read it aloud to yourself several times. This will ensure that you are familiar with the rhythm so that you can read the poem smoothly. Also be sure you know how to pronounce every word properly. There is little excuse to stumble awkwardly as you read a poem, if you have plenty of time to practice reading it beforehand.

Observing the punctuation carefully is an important part of reading poetry smoothly. Just as you must read a poem by thoughts for your own understanding, so you must read by thoughts for your listeners' benefit. Remember that a comma calls for a short pause, a semicolon or dash calls for a longer pause, and a period or other end mark calls for an even longer pause. If the end of a line has no punctuation mark, do not pause as if it does. And if some mark of punctuation is placed in the middle of a line, do not read through the line as if no punctuation were there. Punctuation marks are placed in a poem to clarify its meaning.

Avoid a monotonous, chanting style of reading. Poetry has rhythm, and that rhythm is a part of its beauty. But sometimes a person emphasizes rhythm so much that his reading becomes wearisome. Do not raise and lower your voice at the same place in each line, with no regard to the words you are reading. Read expressively. Emphasize the important words in each line. Adjust your volume and speed to match the words you are reading.

Read slowly and clearly. A good poem says much in a few words. It may also have words arranged in unusual patterns. Your listeners usually do not have a copy of the poem you are reciting, so you need to give them time to grasp the message of the poem.

Class Practice

Read this poem, and do the exercises that follow.

The Kite

My waking dreams are best concealed,
Much folly, little good, they yield;
   But now and then, I gain, when sleeping,
   A friendly hint that's worth the keeping.
Lately I dreamt of one who cried,
"Beware of self, beware of pride;
   When you are prone to build a Babel,
   Recall to mind this little fable."

Once on a time a paper kite
Was mounted to a wondrous height,
   Where, giddy with its elevation,
   It thus expressed self-admiration:
"See how yon crowds of gazing people
Admire my flight above the steeple:
   How would they wonder if they knew
   All that a kite like me can do!

"Were I but free, I'd take a flight
And pierce the clouds beyond their sight.
   But ah! Like a poor prisoner bound,
   My string confines me near the ground.
I'd brave the eagle's towering wing
Might I but fly without a string."

It tugged and pulled while thus it spoke,
To break the string—at last it broke!
   Deprived at once of all its stay,
   In vain it tried to soar away;
Unable its own weight to bear,
It fluttered downward through the air;
   Unable its own course to guide,
   The winds soon plunged it in the tide.
Ah, foolish kite! Thou had'st no wing;
How could'st thou fly without a string?

My heart replied, "O Lord, I see
How much this kite resembles me!
   Forgetful that by Thee I stand,
   Impatient of Thy ruling hand,
How oft I've wished to break the lines
Thy wisdom for my lot assigns.
   How oft indulged a vain desire
   For something more or something higher!
And, but for grace and love divine,
A fall thus dreadful had been mine."
               —John Newton

1. a. What figure of speech is found in the first stanza?
   b. In addition to being part of a figure, what does the word *Babel* imply?
2. A large part of this poem is an extended use of which kind of figure of speech?
3. What does the word *giddy* mean?
4. a. Sometimes a slight pause is required within a poetic line as you read it. Point out several lines in which this is true.
   b. Which lines deserve longer pauses?
   c. Which lines should be read with *no* pause at the end?
5. Find a few examples of alliteration.
6. Find a few examples of assonance.
7. Which lines in stanza 4 illustrate parallelism?

Written Exercises

A. Read this poem, and do the exercises.

The Red Barn

There is something that is pleasant
   In a barn's simplicity,
The beauty of its sloping roof
   And massive symmetry.

Lesson 99 Answers

Class Practice

1. a. "prone to build a Babel"
   b. It reminds us of the Tower of Babel (Genesis 11). Babel represents pride and rebellion—and the resulting confusion and discomfiture.
2. personification
3. lightheartedly silly; frivolous; dizzy
4. a. stanza 1, lines 2, 3, 6;
    stanza 2, line 3;
    stanza 3, line 1; stanza 4, line 9;
    stanza 5, lines 1, 9
   b. stanza 3, line 3;
    stanza 4, lines 2, 9
   c. stanza 2, lines 1, 5, 7;
    stanza 3, lines 1, 5;
    stanza 5, lines 1, 5, 7
5. *stanza 1:* beware, beware, build, Babel
   stanza 2: would, wonder
   stanza 3: free, flight; poor, prisoner
6. *stanza 1:* dreams, concealed, yield
   stanza 2: time, kite, height; mounted, how, crowds; Admire, flight
   stanza 3: I, flight; I, fly
   (More examples could be found.)
7. lines 5–8

Beneath its eaves, the blue-black wings
  Of swallows flash and soar,
And sun-drenched hay of summertime
  Spills fragrance from the door.

In winter it looms bold and red
  Above white curves of snow,
And hugs the sheltered stalls within,
  Where steaming cattle low.

And through the seasons' weathering,
  The oaken timber stands . . .
A symbol of the farmer's toil,
  The harvest of his land.
                    —*Lois Brandt Phillips*

1. Explain the meaning of each figure of speech.
   a. The hay is "sun-drenched."
   b. The hay "spills fragrance from the door."
   c. The barn "hugs the sheltered stalls within."
2. Define the words *symmetry* and *weathering*.
3. What does the word *loom* imply about the appearance of the barn in snowy weather?
4. What are the "white curves of snow"?
5. Which line in particular would not make sense if the poem were read by lines and not by thoughts?

B. Prepare to read in class the poem that you were told to select in Lesson 94.

C. Finish the poem on which you began working in Lesson 90. It is to have two or three stanzas of at least four lines each. Use good rhyme, smooth rhythm, and descriptive words, and try to include figures of speech.

_____

100. Chapter 9 Review

Class Practice

A. Give the correct term for each definition.
   1. A word that shows strong feeling or emotion.
   2. A word that shows the relationship between its object and another word in the sentence.
   3. A word that joins words, phrases, or clauses.

Lesson 100

Purpose: To review the concepts taught in Chapter 9.

Written Exercises

A. 1. a. The hay had soaked up much sunshine while drying.
       b. The smell of the hay is coming out the door.
       c. The walls of the barn stand protectingly around the stalls within.
   2. *symmetry:* balanced proportions; correspondence in size, shape, and relative position of parts on opposite sides of a dividing line
      weathering: the altering or wearing away of objects exposed to the weather
   3. The barn appears especially large. (It stands out in the snowy landscape.)
   4. snowdrifts
   5. stanza 2, line 1

B. (Individual work.)

C. (Individual work.)

_____

Lesson 100 Answers

Class Practice

A. 1. interjection
   2. preposition
   3. conjunction

4. A conjunction that joins sentence parts of parallel structure and function.
5. A conjunction that joins an adverb clause to an independent clause.
6. Conjunctions that work in pairs.
7. An adverb that joins two independent clauses.
8. A regular pattern of accented and unaccented syllables.
9. One accented syllable and the unaccented syllable or syllables associated with it.
10. The matching of sounds at the ends of lines.
11. The repetition of similar vowel sounds in accented syllables that are close together.
12. The repetition of beginning consonant sounds in words that are close together.
13. The repetition of thoughts in lines of poetry, especially Bible poetry.

B. Read each prepositional phrase and the word it modifies. Tell whether the phrase is an *adjective* or an *adverb*.
1. The study of God's world should turn our minds to the Creator.
2. In the vast regions of outer space, we find many examples of God's greatness.
3. Because of our smallness, we may be tempted to think that God will overlook us.
4. Yet God's tender concern for mankind goes beyond our comprehension.

C. Tell which pronouns are correct.
1. Everybody except you and (I, me) has an assignment now.
2. My sister is going along with Melinda, Sarah, and (she, her).

D. Read these sentences correctly. Some are already correct.
1. The sun is hidden in back of the clouds.
2. We have had showers every day this week accept yesterday.
3. Who is sitting beside Aunt Louella?
4. Albert drove in a tree and wrecked his bicycle.
5. Mother planted a row of marigolds between the garden and the lawn.
6. Your garden arrangement is different than ours.

E. Give the coordinating conjunctions, and tell whether they join *words, phrases,* or *clauses.*
1. Abraham and Sarah are outstanding examples of faith.
2. Not only did God call them to leave their familiar home, but also He called them to go to an unknown land.
3. In Canaan they had no permanent home but lived as pilgrims.
4. Whether in Ur or in Canaan, Abraham was sensitive to God's voice.

4. coordinating conjunction
5. subordinating conjunction
6. correlative conjunctions
7. conjunctive adverb
8. rhythm
9. poetic foot
10. rhyme
11. assonance
12. alliteration
13. parallelism

B. 1. of God's world, study, adjective; to the Creator, should turn, adverb
2. In the vast regions of outer space, find, adverb; of outer space, regions, adjective; of God's greatness, examples, adjective
3. Because of our smallness, may be tempted, adverb
4. for mankind, concern, adjective; beyond our comprehension, goes, adverb

C. 1. me   2. her

D. (Corrections are underlined.)
1. The sun is hidden <u>behind</u> the clouds.
2. We have had showers every day this week <u>except</u> yesterday.
3. (correct)
4. Albert drove <u>into</u> a tree and wrecked his bicycle.
5. (correct)
6. Your garden arrangement is different <u>from</u> ours.

E. 1. and, words
2. Not only—but also, clauses
3. but, words
4. Whether—or, phrases

F. Tell how to correct each sentence.
1. It is both wrong to tell and to act a lie.
2. This student either did not understand the lesson or the directions.
3. Not only does this science book have clear explanations, but our teacher uses interesting illustrations.
4. I must study these lessons carefully for Brother Clyde often gives quizzes.
5. I had thought this lesson was easy, nevertheless, I had a few wrong on the quiz.
6. Although I want to get good grades I know that doing my best is the most important thing.

G. Read each subordinating conjunction and the clause it introduces.
1. Although porpoises live in the water, they are mammals.
2. A baby porpoise is born under water even though he must breathe air.
3. A mother porpoise may help her baby to the surface so that he can get his first breath.

H. Read the following sentences, filling in the understood words. If the clause includes a choice of pronouns, choose the correct one.
1. Katie lives alone, so we should visit her more often than (they, them).
2. Aunt Minerva can wash dishes faster than (I, me).
3. We have baked potatoes more often than mashed potatoes.

I. Identify each interjection, and tell whether it should be followed by a comma or an exclamation point. Also tell whether the next word needs to be capitalized.
1. What have you not heard that Sister Edith is in the hospital?
2. Well she seems to be feeling better now.
3. Good maybe she will come home soon.

J. Give the part of speech for each word.
1. This is the right thing, for the Bible clearly teaches it.
2. God knows all men's lives perfectly because He can see within the heart of everyone.

Written Exercises

A. Copy each prepositional phrase, and label it *adj.* or *adv.*
1. Jonah climbed aboard a ship and headed toward Tarshish.
2. He went down into the sides of the ship.
3. Soon the winds of a great tempest threatened to sink the ship.
4. God sent this storm because of Jonah's disobedience.
5. After Jonah was delivered from the belly of the whale, he went to Nineveh.

F. (Corrections are underlined.)
1. It is <u>wrong both</u> to tell and to act a lie.
2. This student <u>did not understand either</u> the lesson or the directions.
3. Not only does this science book have clear explanations, but <u>also</u> our teacher uses interesting illustrations.
4. I must study these lessons carefully, for Brother Clyde often gives quizzes.
5. I had thought this lesson was easy; nevertheless, I had a few wrong on the quiz.
6. Although I want to get good grades, I know that doing my best is the most important thing.

G. (Conjunctions are underlined.)
1. <u>Although</u> porpoises live in the water
2. <u>even though</u> he must breathe air
3. <u>so that</u> he can get his first breath

H. (Understood words are in parentheses. Correct pronouns are underlined.)
1. Katie lives alone, so we should visit her more often than (we visit) <u>them</u>.
2. Aunt Minerva can wash dishes faster than <u>I</u> (can wash dishes).
3. We have baked potatoes more often than (we have) mashed potatoes.

I. 1. What! Have 3. Good! Maybe
2. Well, she

J. 1.
pron. v. adj. adj. n. conj. adj. n. adv.
This is the right thing, for the Bible clearly
v. pron.
teaches it.

2.
n. v. adj. adj. n. adv. conj.
God knows all men's lives perfectly because
pron. v. v. prep. adj. n. prep. pron.
He can see within the heart of everyone.

Written Exercises

A. 1. aboard a ship—adv.; toward Tarshish—adv.
2. into the sides of the ship—adv.; of the ship—adj.
3. of a great tempest—adj.
4. because of Jonah's disobedience—adv.
5. from the belly of the whale—adv.; of the whale—adj.; to Nineveh—adv.

B. Write the choices that are correct, formal English.
1. This week we will (continue, continue on) memorizing Psalm 19.
2. It looks (as if, like) most of the class will have finished their art projects by the end of the week.
3. We were amazed at the scenery when we went (in, into) Guatemala.
4. The first time we visited (between, among) the natives, we were amazed again.
5. Their way of living is quite different (from, than) ours.

6. What (kind of, kind of a) bird is sitting on that tree stump?
7. Julia worked hard to scrub the stains (off, off of) the sink.
8. She was glad when that job was (over, over with).
9. Neither the cupboards nor the counter top (have, has) been cleaned.
10. Both the refrigerator and the stove (need, needs) to be scrubbed.
11. Either Jerry or the two younger boys (is, are) to help move furniture.
12. Grandmother enjoys quilting more than (I, me).
13. She can stitch a lot more evenly than (I, me).
14. When his brothers came, Joseph honored Benjamin more than (they, them).

C. Copy the coordinating conjunction, subordinating conjunction, or

B. 1. continue
    2. as if
    3. into
    4. among
    5. from

    6. kind of
    7. off
    8. over
    9. has
   10. need
   11. are
   12. I
   13. I
   14. them

conjunctive adverb in each sentence. Label it *CC, SC,* or *CA.*

1. We have our family worship before we eat breakfast.
2. We sing two songs and say our Sunday school verses nearly every morning.
3. Of course, we not only read the Bible but also pray every time.
4. This morning Father plans to till the garden; afterward, we will plant the early garden things.
5. Because of heavy rains, Father could not work in the fields earlier; consequently, he is very busy now.

D. Rewrite these sentences so that the correlative conjunctions are used properly.
1. Ahab not only worshiped idols but married the wicked Jezebel.
2. Jezebel neither respected God nor human life.
3. God seeks those who will both serve Him in spirit and in truth.

E. Copy each word that should be followed by a comma or semicolon, and add the correct punctuation.
1. We searched the pasture but we could not find Brindle and her new-born calf.
2. We had some showers today consequently we cannot work in the garden.
3. Not only was Mother busy with the regular washing but also she had to scrub out the grass stains from the children's clothes.

F. Copy these sentences, and above each word write the abbreviation for its part of speech.
1. Say, did you see all those geese in the back field?
2. Some of the rash has come back, so Mother bought more cream for it.
3. The dishes, washed and dried, were placed on the kitchen counter.
4. Christians should show kindness after mistreatment, although it may be quite difficult.

G. For each stanza, write the name of the poetic foot and write letters to show the rhyming pattern.
1. Elijah's mantle fell upon
   Elisha plowing sod,
   And Gideon was threshing wheat
   When he was called of God.
   —*Sarah Elizabeth Sprouse*

2. Come and watch the shining rain
   Falling where the dust had lain,
   Pouring from our waterspout,
   In a hurry to get out.
   —*Ada Wine*

C. 1. before—SC
   2. and—CC
   3. not only—but also—CC
   4. afterward—CA
   5. consequently—CA

D. 1. Ahab not only worshiped idols but also married the wicked Jezebel.
   2. Jezebel respected neither God nor human life.
   3. God seeks those who will serve Him both in spirit and in truth.

E. 1. pasture,   3. washing,
   2. today; consequently,

F. 1. Say, did you see all those geese in the back field?
   (interj. v. pron. v. adj. adj. n. prep. adj. adj. n.)

   2. Some of the rash has come back, so Mother bought more cream for it.
   (pron. prep. adj. n. v. v. adv. conj. n. v. adj. n. prep. pron.)

   3. The dishes, washed and dried, were placed on the kitchen counter.
   (adj. n. adj. conj. adj. v. v. prep. adj. adj. n.)

   4. Christians should show kindness after mistreatment, although it may be quite difficult.
   (n. v. v. n. prep. n. conj. pron. v. v. adv. adj.)

G. 1. iambic; abcb
   2. trochaic; aabb

3. Saviour! I follow on,
   Guided by Thee,
   Seeing not yet the hand
   That leadeth me;
   Hushed be my heart and still,
   Fear I no further ill;
   Only to meet Thy will
   My will shall be.
                    —*C. S. Robinson*

4. The rabbits, huddled in the shadows, shudder all:
   They've heard the hungry owl hoot out his booming call.
   Then suddenly a ghostly form in silence falls
   And carries to its doom one of those furry balls.

5. 'Twas a heaven below,
   My Redeemer to know;
   And the angels could do nothing more
   Than to fall at His feet,
   And the story repeat,
   And the Lover of sinners adore.
                    —*Charles Wesley*

H. Copy words from Part G, number 4, to illustrate the poetic devices named here.
   1. Two pairs of words that illustrate alliteration.
   2. Two pairs of words that illustrate assonance.
   3. Two words that illustrate onomatopoeia.

I. Write whether the following verses illustrate *similar* or *opposite* parallelism.
   1. "The heart of the wise is in the house of mourning; but the heart of fools is in the house of mirth" (Ecclesiastes 7:4).
   2. "By much slothfulness the building decayeth; and through idleness of the hands the house droppeth through" (Ecclesiastes 10:18).
   3. "Who hath put wisdom in the inward parts? or who hath given understanding to the heart?" (Job 38:36).

----

3. dactylic; abcbdddb
4. iambic; aabb
5. anapestic; aabccb

H. 1. (Any two pairs.)
      shadows—shudder;
      heard—hungry—hoot—his;
      suddenly—silence
   2. rabbits—shadows; huddled—shudder; owl—out
   3. hoot, booming

I. 1. opposite
   2. similar
   3. similar

Chapter Ten

Capitalization and Punctuation

Writing Stories

When we speak, our facial expressions and gestures help to convey the meanings of our words. But when we write, we must use mechanical devices to clarify what we mean. In this chapter, you will review many words and abbreviations that need to be capitalized. You will also review and learn rules for the use of end punctuation, commas, quotation marks, colons, semicolons, italics, apostrophes, and hyphens.

Most people enjoy reading stories. And a story is a good way to present truth. A good story causes the reader to identify with the main character. This chapter teaches how to portray story characters, how to develop story conflict, and how to use good story style.

And with many such parables spake he the word unto them, as they were able to hear it.

Mark 4:33

101. Capitalization

By this time you are so familiar with the rules for capitalization that you probably take them for granted. These rules are a great help in making our writing clear and understandable. They are summarized in this lesson.

1. *Every sentence, line of poetry, and direct quotation begins with a capital letter.* If a direct quotation is interrupted by explanatory material, the second part does not begin with a capital letter unless it begins a new sentence.

Jesus said, "It is I; be not afraid."
"Sit in your seats," directed Father, "and we will have family worship."
"Sit in your seats," directed Father. "We are ready for family worship."

In the morning let your prayers arise
To the Father's throne above the skies.
   Seek His guidance for the newborn day,
   Pray for strength to walk the narrow way.

2. I *and* O *are capitalized when written as words.* You are well familiar with the pronoun *I.* The word *O* is less common. It is used mainly in poetry and in archaic language, such as that in the King James Bible.

In modern prose, *O* and *oh* are different words. *Oh* is an interjection that is capitalized only when it begins a sentence. *O* is used to make a solemn appeal to someone, and it is always followed by a noun of direct address. A comma is used after *oh* but not after *O*.

   Archaic and poetic language:
   "Give ear, O ye heavens, and I will speak" (Deuteronomy 32:1).
   "O that my ways were directed to keep thy statutes!" (Psalm 119:5).
   "O for a faith that will not shrink" (hymn)

Lesson 101

Purpose: To teach some capitalization rules.

Oral Review:

1. Name the part of speech that
   a. shows strong feeling or emotion. (interjection)
   b. shows the relationship of its object to some other word in the sentence. (preposition)
   c. joins words, phrases, or clauses. (conjunction)
2. Of the two main classes of conjunctions, which joins only items that have parallel structure and function? (coordinating conjunctions)
3. What do subordinating conjunctions join? (two clauses—a dependent clause to an independent clause)
4. Tell whether the words in each group are usually considered singular or plural.
   a. each, either, neither, anybody (singular)
   b. shears, scissors, pliers (plural)
   c. news, chicken pox, mathematics (singular)
5. Tell whether each expression names one person or two persons.
   a. the teacher and farmer (one person)
   b. the teacher and the farmer (two people)
6. With a collective noun, when should you use (*a*) a singular verb? (*b*) a plural verb? (*a.* Use a singular verb when the collective noun refers to the group doing one thing together. *b.* Use a plural verb when the collective noun refers to the individual members doing different things.)

Lesson Introduction: Standard rules of capitalization have not always existed in the English language. If you read documents from the American colonial era, for instance, you will see wide variations in capitalization. Here is an excerpt from the *Massachusetts Body of Liberties* (1641).

Modern prose:

To you, <u>O</u> friends, <u>I</u> bring a message of hope; <u>oh</u>, that you would listen to these words.

3. *A proper noun is capitalized.* In Lesson 20 you studied ten groupings of proper nouns. These are briefly reviewed for you here.

  a. Names of specific persons, including initials and titles. Remember that a title is not considered a proper noun unless it is used with a proper name or instead of an actual name. The word *president* is sometimes an exception. If it refers to the current president of the United States, it is always capitalized.

Capitalized:

Where was <u>General Washington</u>?
I asked <u>Father</u> for some help.
The <u>President</u> approved the law.

Not capitalized:

George Washington was a popular <u>general</u>.
I asked my <u>father</u> for some help.
The <u>president</u> of the company is busy.

  b. Names of God, and words referring to the Bible or to parts of the Bible. Pronouns like *He* and *His* are also capitalized when they refer to God. Words like *god* or *lord* are not capitalized when they refer to idols or people.

  c. Names of geographical features. Words like *north* and *southwest* are not capitalized when they refer to directions. But they are capitalized when they refer to specific geographical regions, in which case they are usually preceded by *the*.

Capitalized:

Florida is in the <u>Southeast</u>.

Not capitalized:

We live a few miles <u>southeast</u> of here.

  d. Titles of books, newspapers, magazines, stories, poems, and songs. Do not capitalize an article (*a, an, the*), a conjunction (*and, but, or*), or a preposition of fewer than four letters unless it is the first or last word in the title.

  e. Names of groups, nationalities, organizations, churches, schools, and branches of civil government. Articles, conjunctions, and prepositions are treated the same as in titles of books.

  f. Names of specific ships, airplanes, trains, buildings, and monuments.

All the people of god within this Jurisdiction who are not in a church way, and the orthodox Judgment, and not scandalous in life, shall have libertie to gather themselves into a Church Estaite.

How would your students like this kind of "freedom"? Our standard rules of capitalization save us much trouble!

Lesson Outline:

1. Every sentence, line of poetry, and direct quotation begins with a capital letter. If a direct quotation is interrupted by explanatory material, the second part does not begin with a capital letter unless it begins a new sentence.

2. I and O are capitalized when written as words. O is used mainly in poetry and in archaic language. In modern prose, it is used to make a solemn appeal. It is always followed by a noun of direct address and is not set off with a comma. By contrast, the interjection *oh* is capitalized only when it begins a sentence, and it is set off with a comma. (In the King James Bible, *O* and *oh* are used interchangeably. For example, Job 16:21 and Psalm 119:5 begin with "O that . . . ," whereas Psalm 81:13 and Psalm 107:8 begin with "Oh that . . .")

3. A proper noun is capitalized.
  (a) Names of specific persons, including initials and titles.
  (b) Names of God, and words referring to the Bible or to parts of the Bible.
  (c) Names of geographical features.
  (d) Titles of books, newspapers, magazines, stories, poems, and songs.
  (e) Names of groups, nationalities, organizations, churches, schools, and branches of civil government.

g. Names of parks, historic sites, and historic events, eras, and documents.
h. Brand names. Remember to capitalize only the specific brand name and not any common noun that may follow it.
i. Names of school subjects derived from proper nouns.

Capitalized:
English   Bible   American history
Not capitalized:
math   spelling   reading

j. Calendar items such as months, days of the week, and holidays. The names of the four seasons are not capitalized.

Capitalized:
July   Sunday   Easter
Not capitalized:
spring   summer   fall   winter

4. *A proper adjective is capitalized.* These are adjectives derived from proper nouns.

the <u>Hebrew</u> people   a <u>French</u> city
in the <u>Biblical</u> record   the <u>Canadian</u> government

5. *Many abbreviations are capitalized.* If you are not sure whether to capitalize an abbreviation, check a dictionary or an English handbook. The following groups show some common abbreviations that are capitalized.
   a. Abbreviations of titles used with a person's name.

   Mrs. Arlene Lucas   Dr. Roberts   Alan Martin, Jr.

   b. Abbreviations of professional or college degrees after a person's name.

   Conrad Smith, M.D.—Doctor of Medicine
   Lee Steele, B.A.S.—Bachelor of Agricultural Science

   c. Abbreviations of political and geographical areas.

   Mt. Zion—Mount Zion   U.S.A.—United States of America
   Ont. *or* ON—Ontario   Nile R.—Nile River

   d. Abbreviations of organizations and government agencies.

   MCC—Mennonite Central Committee
   UN *or* U.N.—United Nations
   FBI *or* F.B.I.—Federal Bureau of Investigation

(f) Names of specific ships, airplanes, trains, buildings, and monuments.
(g) Names of parks, historic sites, and historic events, eras, and documents.
(h) Brand names (but not a common noun that may follow a brand name).
(i) Names of school subjects derived from proper nouns.
(j) Calendar items such as months, days of the week, and holidays (but not the names of the four seasons).

4. A proper adjective is capitalized. These are adjectives derived from proper nouns.

5. Many abbreviations are capitalized.
   (a) Abbreviations of titles used with a person's name.
   (b) Abbreviations of professional or college degrees after a person's name.
(c) Abbreviations of political and geographical areas.
(d) Abbreviations of organizations and government agencies.
(e) Abbreviations of Bible translations and parts of the Bible.
(f) Abbreviations used in addresses.
(g) Miscellaneous abbreviations. *A.D.—anno Domini* (in the year of the Lord); *A.M.—ante meridiem* (before midday); *B.C.—*before Christ; *C*—Celsius, centigrade; *F* or *Fahr.—*Fahrenheit; *P.M.—post meridiem* (after midday); *T.* or *tbsp.—*tablespoon

6. The address, date, greeting, closing, and signature of a letter are capitalized.

★ **EXTRA PRACTICE**
Worksheet 53 (*Practice With Capitalization*)

   e. Abbreviations of Bible translations and parts of the Bible.

> KJV—King James Version
> AV—Authorized Version: same as King James Version
> O.T.—Old Testament
> Col.—Colossians

   f. Abbreviations used in addresses.

> Main St.—Main Street   R.D.—Rural Delivery

   g. Miscellaneous abbreviations.

> A.D.—*anno Domini* (in the year of the Lord)
> A.M.—*ante meridiem* (before midday)
> B.C.—before Christ
> C—Celsius; centigrade
> F *or* Fahr.—Fahrenheit
> P.M.—*post meridiem* (after midday)
> T. *or* tbsp.—tablespoon

6. *The address, date, greeting, closing, and signature of a letter are capitalized.*

> 1325 North Main Street   Dear Marion,
> Appleton, WI 54915   Sincerely yours,
> April 28, 20—   Arthur Stevens

Class Practice

Tell which words or abbreviations have capitalization errors.

1. the saviour was born in a Stable in Bethlehem of judea.
2. The town of bethlehem lies South of Jerusalem.
3. the christian governs his life by the new testament scriptures.
4. when solomon was anointed king, he sought the Blessing of God.
5. Later king solomon worshiped the Gods of his Heathen wives.
6. was abraham lincoln the president of the united states during the civil war?
7. before School was dismissed, brother Carl said, "remember to bring your Lunches in disposable bags tomorrow."
8. the Doctor who diagnosed my disease was h. j. kaiser, m.d.
9. the first roman emperor, augustus, reigned from 27 b.c. to a.d. 14.
10. in Geography class we learned that mt. McKinley is the highest Mountain in north america.
11. we have a Frigidaire refrigerator and a hotpoint Stove.
12. is gary reading *all on a mountain day*?

Lesson 101 Answers

Class Practice

1. The, Saviour, stable, Judea
2. Bethlehem, south
3. The, Christian, New Testament Scriptures
4. When, Solomon, blessing
5. King Solomon, gods, heathen
6. Was, Abraham Lincoln, President, United States, Civil War
7. Before, school, Brother, Remember, lunches
8. The, doctor, H. J. Kaiser, M.D.
9. The, Roman, Augustus, B.C., A.D.
10. In, geography, Mt., mountain, North America
11. We, Hotpoint, stove
12. Is, Gary, *All, Mountain, Day*

13. last Winter in bible school we studied the sermon on the mount.
14. this is another day, o lord,
        that thou hast given me;
    may i in every deed and word
        bring glory, lord, to thee.
15.

              1980 blair court
              louisville, ky 40243
              april 6, 20—

dear anna marie,
            (Body of letter.)

              your friend,
              linda garman

Written Exercises

Write correctly each word or abbreviation that has a capitalization error.
1. our god is high above all gods and all powers.
2. During old testament times, the holy spirit did not dwell with God's People in the same way he does today.
3. when king Herod heard the Wise Men's story, he was upset.
4. He did not want any King to threaten his Throne.
5. "Set a watch, o lord, before my mouth; keep the door of my lips."
6. Did i hear that aunt Twila will be here from thanksgiving day through sunday?
7. The fda has approved a new drug to be used by Prescription only.
8. One of my Father's favorite songs is "in the cross of christ i glory."
9. When mother needed her wisdom teeth cut out, she went to h. j. castleman, d.d.s.
10. The president of the united states holds one of the world's most influential jobs.
11. The Yellowstone national park lies mostly in Northwestern Wyoming.
12. The mountains are much higher in the west than in the east.
13. Linford said, "our Pontiac Station Wagon climbed those Mountains well."
14. Label these places on your map: delaware r., tucker is., and the kittatinny mts.
15. The Natives of the Dominican republic speak spanish.
16. "Did i hear correctly," asked sister Lorraine, "That you are leaving for the Philippines in two weeks?"
17. my god—o could i make the claim—
    My father and my friend—
    And call thee mine by every name
    On which thy saints depend!

13. Last, winter, Bible, Sermon, Mount
14. This, O, Lord, That, Thou, May, I, Bring, Lord, Thee
15. Blair Court, Louisville, KY, April, Dear, Anna Marie, Your, Linda Garman

Written Exercises

1. Our, God
2. Old Testament, Holy Spirit, people, He
3. When, King, wise men's
4. king, throne
5. O, Lord
6. I, Aunt, Thanksgiving Day, Sunday
7. FDA, prescription
8. father's, In, Cross, Christ, I, Glory
9. Mother, H. J. Castleman, D.D.S.
10. President, United States
11. National Park, northwestern
12. West, East
13. Our, station wagon, mountains
14. Delaware R., Tucker Is., Kittatinny Mts.
15. natives, Republic, Spanish
16. I, Sister, that
17. My, God, O, I, Father, Friend, Thee, Thy
    (Capitalization of *Friend* is optional.)

18.

　　　　　　　　　　　　　　　route 1, box 300
　　　　　　　　　　　　　　　middletown, de 19709
　　　　　　　　　　　　　　　may 2, 20—

dear melvin,

　　　　　　　(Body of letter.)

　　　　　　　　　　　　　　　sincerely,
　　　　　　　　　　　　　　　abel stauffer

Review Exercises

Copy the correct verb for each sentence. [48]

1. Rosa, along with Joyce and Ella, (help, helps) regularly at the market.
2. This chicken and rice (is, are) delicious.
3. Everybody (have, has) helped quite well with the work this morning.
4. Harold's glasses (was, were) broken in the accident.
5. My new pair of glasses (is, are) a bit stronger than my old pair.
6. Why (is, are) those men running out to the barn?
7. He (don't, doesn't) boast so much anymore.
8. Kathryn or Diane (is, are) coming to help Mother tomorrow.
9. Electronics (is, are) the science that deals with the behavior of electrons.
10. The group of boys (is, are) doing various jobs.
11. The group of boys (is, are) resting under the shade tree.
12. (How's, How are) peaches this year?
13. (There's, There are) some visitors at church today.
14. The carpenter and electrician (have, has) come.
15. Because of modern vaccines, measles (don't, doesn't) afflict many people today.

102. Story Writing: Portraying the Main Character

Lesson Survey
- A **short story** usually has one main character as the central figure.
- The traits of a story character are revealed by his actions, words, and thoughts.

Lesson 102

Purpose: (1) To teach that a short story usually has one main character as the central figure. (2) To show some methods of revealing the traits of story characters.

Oral Review:

1. Name several characteristics that distinguish poetry from prose. (Poetry is written in lines and stanzas, usually has distinct rhythm and rhyme, makes effective use of descriptive words and figurative language, can say much in a few words, and has a special beauty that affects our feelings.)
2. Define *rhythm*. (a regular pattern of accented and unaccented syllables)
3. Tell which of the four rhythm patterns is found in each line.

Review Exercises

18. Route, Box, Middletown, DE, May, Dear Melvin, Sincerely, Abel Stauffer

Review Exercises

1. helps
2. is
3. has
4. were
5. is
6. are
7. doesn't
8. is
9. is
10. are
11. is
12. How are
13. There are
14. has
15. doesn't

---

a. See the clouds in their brightness sail over our heads (anapestic)
b. How clear the voice of nature's praise (iambic)
c. In the Garden Jesus prayed (trochaic)
d. Over the earth a great darkness has come (dactylic)

4. How many feet are in the last line above? (4)
5. Give the word for the following descriptions.
　a. The repetition of thoughts, as found in much Bible poetry. (parallelism)
　b. The repetition of beginning consonant sounds. (alliteration)
　c. The repetition of similar accented vowel sounds. (assonance)
6. Tell how to correct these sentences.
　a. There was a large crowd in back of Jesus. (behind Jesus)
　b. Where are they going to? (going to)

The Bible contains many stories that you have enjoyed over and over again. Think of Abraham moving to Canaan, of Joseph being sold into Egypt, of Miriam watching baby Moses, of Daniel in the lions' den, and of Paul escaping from Damascus in a basket. Each of these stories makes you think of one outstanding person—a main character.

Indeed, almost every good *short story* has one main character as the central figure. As you read the following short story, notice how you live through the story with one of the characters.

Pitch or Patch?

"Oh, Mother!" wailed Evelyn as the storm door closed behind her. "Look what happened!" Evelyn stretched out her dress skirt to show Mother a three-cornered tear.

"How did you do that?" asked Mother, laying her paring knife on the counter. She came to look at the rent.

"I caught it on something as I jumped out of the van. Oh, I feel like just pitching this thing in the trash. I never did like this dress. It's such a weird green." Evelyn clattered her lunch box on the table.

Mother looked at her daughter in surprise. "Pitch it!" she exclaimed. "Of course not! The dress is perfectly all right except for this tear. We'll patch it, and it will be just fine for school."

Now it was Evelyn's turn to be surprised. "Mother, never!" she gasped. "I didn't think we'd pitch it, but I surely thought it would be an everyday dress. Please, Mother. I can't wear a patched dress to school. That would be terrible."

"Now, now," Mother said soothingly with a hint of rebuke. "It's not that bad. The tear is small, the edges are smooth, and it's in the skirt. An iron-on patch will fix it up beautifully. I'm sure it won't be very noticeable. Go up and change your clothes now, and stop complaining."

Without another word, Evelyn went upstairs to change her clothes. "I know Mother will do the neatest job possible with that patching," she mumbled to herself. "But it will be embarrassing to wear a patched dress to school! We're not poor!" She flung the dress into her clothes hamper and dashed downstairs to tackle her regular afternoon chores.

Evelyn forgot all about the torn dress until the next afternoon after school. "I finished my chores," she sang out to Mother. "What shall I do now?"

"Sew the button back on your good sweater," Mother called from the sewing room.

Evelyn came and stood beside Mother. "What are you doing?"

c. Soon they came in Jerusalem with shouts of praise. (into Jerusalem)

d. The Jewish leaders were furious that the crowds treated Him like He was a victorious king. (as if He was)

e. Jesus demonstrated far more dignity and glory than them. (than they)

Lesson Introduction: Read the following paragraph from a story.

> Curtis was a shy thirteen-year-old. His shyness made it very hard for him to make new friends. When visitors came to church, he always felt terribly nervous about talking with them. But after he learned to know a person, Curtis was a fine, loyal friend.

Does that paragraph sound like part of an interesting story? Really, it sounds rather dull, doesn't it?

That is because you cannot see Curtis in a real-life experience. There is nothing in the paragraph that makes him "come alive" and act like a real person.

This lesson will help you to make story characters seem alive and realistic.

Lesson Outline:

1. A short story usually has one main character as the central figure.

    (1) The main character should generally be introduced first and should be mentioned the most often throughout the story.

    (2) All the events and the other characters should be in the story because of their relationship to the main character.

    (3) The point of the story should be a lesson the main character must learn.

    (4) The main character should be the person facing a conflict in the story.

she asked with a puzzled frown.

"Patching Ronald's trousers," Mother replied.

"But it looks like you're patching the patch! Why don't you just pitch them? Won't they look terrible?" Evelyn rummaged in the sewing machine drawer for a needle and thread.

Mother gave her a little smile. "No, I don't think they will look terrible. But my drawer soon will. Here's what you need." Mother quickly handed Evelyn the things she had not been able to find.

"I know," continued Mother, "sometimes it's difficult to tell when things are worn-out and ought to be pitched into the trash. But I do not want to be wasteful. God expects His children to be good stewards of the things He gives to them.

"Like these trousers." Mother held them up for Evelyn to see. "The seat is a bit worn, but it will last a while yet. Neither of the pockets is worn through. It's these knees that have holes again. Certainly it would be wasteful to throw them away because the patch has a hole."

"I guess you're right," Evelyn assented as she struggled to thread her needle. "It's just that it will look ugly."

"No, it won't," Mother disagreed. "A neat patch isn't ugly. It's nothing to be ashamed of."

Evelyn was silent a bit; then she asked, "But won't people think we're poor if we have all these patches?"

"I doubt it," Mother said. "But what if they do? There's nothing wrong with being poor if we're doing what God wants us to do. And if we're doing what God wants us to do, it doesn't matter what they think, right?"

Evelyn smiled. "Right," she said.

Then she spied her green dress hanging on the rod, ready to be taken upstairs. "Patches," Evelyn thought to herself as she guided her needle in and out of the buttonholes. "And now that dress has a patch too. I do dread wearing that thing to school. Wish I could wear it for everyday. But I know what Mother will say if I fuss. Maybe it won't look too bad. Hope it doesn't!" Evelyn snipped her thread. "Done," she announced.

"Good," Mother commended. "Please take these clothes upstairs, and then set the table for supper."

Thursday morning Evelyn slipped the green dress over her head. "Oh, that patch!" She suddenly had a sickening feeling inside. "The patch," she repeated as she searched her skirt for it.

"Oh," she said when she spied it. Yes, you could tell it had been

2. The traits of a story character are revealed in various ways.

    a. By his actions.

    b. By his words. Traits are shown not only by his actual words but also by the explanatory terms that tell how he spoke.

    c. By his thoughts.

torn, and yes, you could tell it was patched. "At least it's not very noticeable," she told herself as she darted down the steps.

That day at school, whenever Evelyn remembered that patch, her stomach twisted uncomfortably. She was glad Mother was a good steward, but still, a patch does look like a patch. How she hoped no one would notice that spot on her green dress!

Then, during study period, Brother Vernon was standing in front of her desk helping Karen with a math problem. With his hands behind his back, he toyed with his red pen. And there, neatly but clearly, was a patch.

Evelyn was startled. Brother Vernon was wearing a patched shirt in school! A patch! Maybe she was being overly sensitive about such things. It did not look bad at all, that little patch on Brother Vernon's shirtsleeve. Maybe Mother was wiser than Evelyn had thought.

Evelyn turned her gaze back to her lessons. There was a warm glow in her heart. She would simply ignore that patch on her skirt. She was sure it did not look any worse than Brother Vernon's. She was glad Mother was teaching her to be a good steward of God's gifts.

—Joyce Good

The main character in this story is obviously Evelyn. Notice how the story revolves around her in a number of ways.

1. The first character introduced in the story is Evelyn. Evelyn is mentioned the most often throughout the story, and the story ends with Evelyn's thoughts.
2. All the events and the other characters are in the story because of their relationship to Evelyn. Mother is the only other character who speaks in the story. All her words are directed to Evelyn and her problem.
3. The point of the story is a lesson that Evelyn must learn.
4. Evelyn is the person facing a conflict in the story. She is the one who has a problem to solve.

Showing Character Traits

When you read a good short story, you feel as if you have learned to know the main character. That is because the author has shown the traits, or characteristics, of that person. The most common ways in which this is done are by showing the main character's actions, words, and thoughts.

A person's *actions* reveal his characteristics. Therefore, you must choose carefully the details of how the main character opens or closes a door, goes up the steps, sweeps the floor, or empties the feed bucket into the feeding trough. In the example story, Evelyn clattered her lunch box on the table, she flung her dress into the hamper, she dashed downstairs, and she rummaged in the sewing machine drawer. These actions all show that Evelyn is rather careless and impulsive. A prim, particular girl would have placed her lunch box quietly on the table, folded her dress and laid it in the hamper, and walked down the stairs.

A person's *words* also reveal his characteristics. The character in your story must say words that reveal the traits you want the story to emphasize about the character. Not only the actual words but also the explanatory terms that tell how he spoke the words are important. Suppose the author of the example story had begun with " 'Oh, Mother!' said Evelyn." The word *said* would not have suggested Evelyn's impulsiveness as the word *wailed* does. Or suppose the author had written that Evelyn sighed or whimpered those opening words. Either of these words would clash with the impression that the rest of the story gives of Evelyn.

Notice how these examples all contribute to the picture of Evelyn's impulsive nature.

"Oh, I feel like just pitching this thing in the trash."
"Mother, never!" she gasped.
"I finished my chores," she sang out to Mother.

Finally, a person's *thoughts* reveal his characteristics. You should show a person's thoughts less often than you show his actions and words. But like actions and words, a character's thoughts must contribute to the characteristics that the rest of the story reveals. Notice how Evelyn's thoughts about the patch on her dress flit impulsively from dread to hopeful optimism.

"And now that dress has a patch too. I do dread wearing that thing to school. Wish I could wear it for everyday. But I know what Mother will say if I fuss. Maybe it won't look too bad. Hope it doesn't!"

Class Practice

A. Tell which sentence best matches the character trait named for each person. Tell what is wrong with the other two.
1. Walter likes to bully others.
   a. Walter reached right into the middle of the plate and grabbed the biggest piece of cake.
   b. Walter shoved aside two pairs of small hands and grabbed the biggest piece of cake.
   c. When Walter saw Sherwin's piece of cake, he scowled angrily.
2. Lucy is known for her cheerfulness.
   a. "Let's tackle this mountain of dishes right away, girls," sang out Lucy. "Then we'll still have time to walk down to the stream."

Lesson 102 Answers

Class Practice

A. 1. b (Choice *a* shows selfishness. Choice *c* shows jealousy. Neither of them necessarily portrays the character as a bully.)

2. a (Choice *b* shows obedience or a sense of duty, but no particular cheerfulness. Choice *c* sounds more silly than cheerful.)

b. "Let's wash these dishes right away, girls," advised Lucy. "Then we'll still have time to walk down to the stream."

c. "Well, I guess we'd better rattle these dishes in a hurry, girls." Lucy giggled. "Then we'll still have time for a quick dash down to the stream."

3. Joshua is a dependable worker.

a. "Well, that's done, and Father's not back yet," Joshua thought. "Let's see, just the other day Father said he should clean up the shop soon. I wonder if there's something I could do there."

b. "Well, that's done, and Father's not back yet," Joshua thought. "Let's see, just the other day Father said he should clean up the shop soon. But that's hardly something I can do myself."

c. "Well, that's done, and Father's not back yet," Joshua thought. "Let's see, just the other day Father said he should clean up the shop soon. Oh, I know! The garden tractor needs an oil change. Father never let me do that by myself, but I'm sure I know how."

3. Tell how the actions, words, or thoughts of each character can be adjusted to make the change described in parentheses.

1. (Change Rhoda from an outgoing girl to a shy girl.)

"Oh, someone else must be visiting Uncle Harold's this evening too," Rhoda declared. "I wonder if there's a girl my age. It's such fun learning to know new friends!"

2. (Change Kevin from a showoff to a conscientious boy.)

Kevin swaggered up to the plate with a smirk on his face. "Just look at them scatter," he thought. Giving the bat a number of vigorous swings, he shouted to Brent, "All right, send that ball across the plate!"

C. Do the following exercises.

1. Larry is in the store with his father. Suggest an action, a statement, and a thought that portray Larry as a considerate boy.

2. Martha is visiting at her friend Katrina's house. Suggest an action, a statement, and a thought that portray Martha as having a problem with envy.

Written Exercises

A. Write the letter of the paragraph that best matches the character trait named for each person.

1. Melissa is a practical-minded girl.

a. "Company coming in about twenty minutes!" Melissa glanced at the floor and headed for the broom. Fifteen minutes later she was putting the broom away as Mother came downstairs with the

3. a (Choice *b* reveals a boy who is unwilling to do what he can. Choice *c* reveals a boy who wants to do something new—even though it is unapproved—rather than try to do something less interesting that he knows he can do.)

B. (Sample answers.)

1. "Oh, someone else must be visiting Uncle Harold's this evening too," Rhoda sighed. "I wonder if there's a girl my age. I feel so nervous around strangers!"

2. Kevin stepped up to the plate with a hopeful smile on his face. "Wonder if I can hit a home run this time," he thought. Giving the bat a few swings, he called to Brent, "All right, I'm ready any time."

C. (Sample answers.)

1. *Action:* Larry moved a shopping cart aside for an elderly man who walked with a cane.

Statement: "I can carry one of those bags, Father," Larry offered.

Thought: "That lady has waited quite a long time," thought Larry. "I hope one of the clerks can help her soon."

2. *Action:* Martha looked longingly at the new carpet in Katrina's room.

Statement: "I wish my room were half as nice as yours," she said.

Thought: "Why are other people's things always so much better than mine?" she thought to herself.

Written Exercises

A. 1. c (In choice *a* Melissa spends so much time making the floors perfect that she neglects the sofas and chairs. In choice *b* she is so overwhelmed that she gets hardly anything accomplished.)

three little ones dressed and combed. "The floors are as neat as a pin, but the sofas and chairs are a mess," Melissa told Mother.

b.   "Company coming in about twenty minutes!" Melissa glanced at the floor and headed for the broom. "Oh, Mother, we'll never have this house looking neat enough for company in twenty minutes! Whatever shall I do?" she wailed as she scurried about in the kitchen.

c.   "Company coming in about twenty minutes!" Melissa glanced at the floor and headed for the broom. Ten minutes later she was whisking some cluttered papers and toys off the sofas and chairs. "I think the kitchen and living room are fit for company," Melissa said as Mother came downstairs with the three little ones dressed and combed.

2. Aaron has a healthy sense of humor.

a.   "You ought to see Flop-ears, my donkey. Whenever I hitch him up to his cart, he shakes his head as if he were saying 'No!' And then his ears flop in the funniest way. You'll just have to laugh!" Aaron chuckled as he led the boys out to the barn.

b.   "You ought to see Flop-ears, my donkey. Whenever I hitch him up to his cart, he shakes his head as if he were saying 'No!' And that makes his ears flop just like Betty's pigtails. You'll just have to laugh!" Aaron snickered as he led the boys out to the barn.

c.   "You ought to see Flop-ears, my donkey. Whenever I hitch him up to his cart, he shakes his head as if he were saying 'No!' His ears flop all over the place. It'll be the funniest thing you've ever seen!" Aaron roared with laughter as he led the boys out to the barn.

3. Susan is determined to do what is right.

a.   "Oh, I do hope Carmen doesn't think of so much mischief on this visit. She's almost sure to get me into trouble again." Susan's thoughts tumbled restlessly as Carmen's family drove in.

b.   "Oh, I do hope Carmen doesn't think of so much mischief on this visit. She can argue so persuasively that sometimes I hardly know how to answer her." Susan's thoughts tumbled restlessly as Carmen's family drove in.

c.   "Oh, I do hope Carmen doesn't think of so much mischief on this visit. Maybe if I first suggest a few daring things that I know won't get us into trouble, I'll make out all right." Susan's thoughts tumbled restlessly as Carmen's family drove in.

B. Rewrite the actions, words, or thoughts of each character to make the changes given in parentheses.

2. a (Choice *b* includes an unkind remark about Betty. Choice *c* includes exaggerations and an exaggerated laugh.)

3. b (In choice *a* Susan blames Carmen for her own failure to do right. In choice *c* she seems to think that she can play with fire and not get burned.)

1. (Change Donald from a complainer to a good sport.)
   "These teams aren't one bit fair! I'm tired of this game anyway. I don't care if we do lose," Donald thought angrily.
2. (Change Doris from a careless girl to a neat girl.)
   When the recess bell rang, Doris shoved her crumpled paper into the book and thrust the book into her desk. With a grab for her sweater, she dashed up the aisle.
3. (Change Steven from a thoughtless boy to a thoughtful boy.)
   "Did you see Irvin? He took quite a funny flip down those steps. He has a scattered pile of books and papers to pick up too," Steven laughed as he headed out the door.

C. Do the following exercises.
1. Dorcas is in church after the service is over. Write a paragraph giving an action, a statement, and a thought that portray Dorcas as a friendly girl.
2. Charles is having trouble with the lawn mower. Write a paragraph giving an action, a statement, and a thought that portray Charles as an impatient boy.

Review Exercises

Write the correct word or phrase for each sentence. [91, 95]
1. No one (accept, except) Father was able to quote the whole passage.
2. Are the other girls still (inside, inside of) the school?
3. Cautiously the refugees stepped (in, into) the icy water.
4. This new school building is quite different (from, than) our old one.
5. What is (behind, in back of) that old shed?
6. It looks (as if, like) this place has been abandoned for years.
7. Jehoshaphat was certainly a more godly man than (he, him).
8. Jehoshaphat wondered if there was no prophet in Israel (beside, besides) the heathen prophets.
9. A stranger stopped (by, at) our house and asked for directions.
10. Talents vary (between, among) the many different members of a family.

B. (Sample answers.)
1. "These teams aren't quite even, so I'll have to work as hard as I can! We can't let the others win without a good fight," Donald thought.
2. When the recess bell rang, Doris placed her neatly folded paper into the book and put the book into her desk. She picked up her sweater and walked up the aisle.
3. "Did you see Irvin? He took quite a bad flip down those steps. Let's help pick up his scattered pile of books and papers," Steven said as he hurried toward Irvin.

C. (Sample answers. Actions, statements, and thoughts may be given in any order.)
1. "I don't remember ever seeing that girl before," Dorcas mused. "I think I'll go over and talk to her." She quickly moved in the direction of the stranger. "Good morning," Dorcas greeted warmly. "My name is Dorcas. What's your name?"
2. "This mower is such a bother!" thought Charles. He yanked peevishly at the starter rope. "It always takes a dozen or more pulls to get this old thing going," he fumed.

Review Exercises
1. except
2. inside
3. into
4. from
5. behind
6. as if
7. he
8. besides
9. at
10. among

103. End Punctuation

Lesson Survey

- Use a **period** after a declarative or an imperative sentence.
- Use a **question mark** after an interrogative sentence or quotation.
- Use an **exclamation point** after a strong interjection and after an exclamatory sentence or quotation.
- Use a period after each initial that is part of a name.
- In most cases, use a period after an abbreviation.
- Use **ellipsis points** to show where material has been left out of a quotation.

Can you easily read and understand the following paragraph?

Elijah mocked the prophets of Baal in desperation they cried aloud and cut themselves later Elijah repaired the altar of the Lord he prayed at the time of the evening sacrifice to his prayer God gave an immediate answer

The paragraph above is hard to read because there are no sentence divisions. As you studied in Lesson 101, each sentence should begin with a capital letter. You also know that every sentence needs some mark of end punctuation. Now read the following paragraph, in which the sentences are properly capitalized and punctuated.

Elijah mocked the prophets of Baal. In desperation they cried aloud and cut themselves. Later Elijah repaired the altar of the Lord. He prayed at the time of the evening sacrifice. To his prayer God gave an immediate answer.

How glad we can be that punctuation marks are used in English writing to divide the thoughts clearly!

Punctuation With the Four Sentence Types

Use a *period* after a declarative or an imperative sentence.

"The Lord by wisdom hath founded the earth."
Send for Simon Peter.

Use a *question mark* after an interrogative sentence or quotation. In the second example, the quotation is a question and ends with a question

Lesson 103

Purpose: (1) To teach the use of periods, question marks, and exclamation points. (2) To teach the use of *ellipsis points.

Oral Review:

1. What two one-letter words are always capitalized? (I, O)
2. When are words like *east* and *south* capitalized? (when they refer to specific geographical regions)
3. When are words like *mother* and *uncle* capitalized? (when they are used with a proper name or instead of an actual name)
4. What words in a title are not capitalized? (articles [*a, an, the*], conjunctions [*and, but, or*], and prepositions of fewer than four letters, unless they are the first or last words of the title)
5. Tell whether the verb in each sentence is transitive active, transitive passive, intransitive complete, or intransitive linking.
   a. A train whistle sounded far in the distance. (intransitive complete)
   b. Soon the whistle sounded loud and clear. (intransitive linking)
   c. The engineer sounded the whistle at each crossing. (transitive active)
   d. The whistle was sounded at each crossing. (transitive passive)

Lesson Introduction: Fifth grader Susan was working on her English lesson. "There are so many rules for commas," she complained. "Sometimes I wish nobody would ever have invented them."

Big sister Janet smiled. "Oh, but commas are necessary," she said. "Sometimes they are very important in a sentence."

mark. But the whole sentence is a statement and ends with a period.

"Am I my brother's keeper?"
"Am I my brother's keeper?" retorted Cain.

Use an *exclamation point* after a strong interjection and after an exclamatory sentence or quotation. In the fourth example below, the quotation is an exclamation and ends with an exclamation point, but the whole sentence is a statement and ends with a period.

How beautiful heaven must be!
Well, what a surprise this is!
What! You don't know who has come?
"Watch that bull!" shouted Mark.

Sometimes a sentence quotes a Bible verse and gives the reference in parentheses after it. In such a sentence, no end punctuation follows the verse unless it is a question or an exclamation. End punctuation for the whole sentence comes *after* the parentheses.

"And God said, Let us make man in our image" (Genesis 1:26).
"Pilate saith unto him, What is truth?" (John 18:38).

Punctuation With Initials and Abbreviations

Use a period after each initial that is part of a name.

A. D. Wenger   J. F. Funk   M. S. Stoltzfus

In most cases, use a period after an abbreviation. If you are not sure whether to use a period, check a dictionary or an English handbook.

1. *Measurement words.*

foot—ft.	pound—lb.
mile—mi.	second—sec.
teaspoon—tsp.	hour—hr.
quart—qt.	week—wk.
peck—pk.	dozen—doz.

2. *Days of the week and most of the months.*

Sunday—Sun.	Wednesday—Wed.	Friday—Fri.
Monday—Mon.	Thursday—Thurs.	Saturday—Sat.
Tuesday—Tues.		

January—Jan.	May	September—Sept.
February—Feb.	June	October—Oct.
March—Mar.	July	November—Nov.
April—Apr.	August—Aug.	December—Dec.

"But they are such little marks," countered Susan. "I don't think they make much difference at all!"

"I'd like to show you something," replied Janet. She wrote the following sentence on a paper.

Susan says Janet is mistaken.

"Now," said Janet, "put one comma after *Susan* and one after *Janet.* Do the commas make any difference?"

Punctuation is always important, and sometimes it makes a great difference in the meaning of what we write!

Lesson Outline:

1. Use a period after a declarative or an imperative sentence.

2. Use a question mark after an interrogative sentence or quotation.

3. Use an exclamation point after a strong interjection and after an exclamatory sentence or quotation.

4. When a Bible verse is quoted with its reference in parentheses, no end punctuation follows the verse unless it is a question or an exclamation. End punctuation for the whole sentence comes after the parentheses.

5. Use a period after each initial that is part of a name.

6. In most cases, use a period after an abbreviation.

7. Use ellipsis points to show where material has been left out of a quotation. Ellipsis points are three spaced periods (. . .).

   a. Several rules should be followed when ellipsis points are used to show omissions.

3. *Titles and degrees with proper names.*

Mrs. Darlene Gray	Dr. Ronald Towers
Leroy Kline, Jr.	Mr. Glenford Zaleski, M.D.

4. *Expressions used in writing a time or date.* Note that if one of these abbreviations (or any other) comes at the end of a sentence, only one period is used there.

7:30 A.M.	3:00 P.M.	800 B.C.	A.D. 1456

The Romans captured Jerusalem in 63 B. C.

5. *Words used in writing addresses.*

Avenue—Ave.	Highway—Hwy.	Street—St.
Boulevard—Blvd.	Road—Rd.	

However, do not use a period with the two-letter abbreviations assigned by the postal service for states and provinces.

Phoenix, AZ 85008	Vancouver, BC V8W 2Y9

6. *Miscellaneous words.*

number—no. *or* No.	cash on delivery—C.O.D.
department—dept.	page—p.
each—ea.	pages—pp.
for example—e.g.	verse—v.
Incorporated—Inc.	verses—vv.
miscellaneous—misc.	versus—vs.

Most abbreviations for organizations and government agencies do not use periods.

United Parcel Service—UPS
General Motors Corporation—GMC
Internal Revenue Service—IRS
Central Intelligence Agency—CIA

Punctuation to Show Omissions

Use three spaced periods, called *ellipsis points* (. . .), to show where material has been left out of a quotation. For example, you should use ellipsis points when you want to copy the beginning and end of a Bible verse and leave out the middle part.

"The earth was . . . void" (Genesis 1:2).

Remember the following rules when you use ellipsis points to show omissions.

(1) *Never change the meaning of a quotation by your omission.*

(2) *If you quote more than one sentence and the first part makes a complete sentence, end the first part with the appropriate punctuation mark. Then use ellipsis points to show the omission, and continue with the quotation.*

(3) *If you quote more than one sentence and the first part does not make a complete sentence, use only the ellipsis points.*

Note: When ellipsis points are used within a sentence, they may indicate the omission not only of words but also of the punctuation used immediately before or after the omitted words. Thus the writer is free to retain or omit this internal punctuation, whichever suits his purpose best. If he chooses to retain the punctuation either before or after the omitted words, that punctuation should correspondingly be placed before or after the ellipsis points.

Original: "Wherefore come out from among them, and be ye separate, saith the Lord, and touch not the unclean thing; and I will receive you" (2 Corinthians 6:17).

Quotations: "Wherefore come out from among them . . . and touch not the unclean thing."

"Wherefore come out . . . and be ye separate, saith the Lord, . . . and I will receive you."

"Wherefore . . . be ye separate, saith the Lord . . . ; and I will receive you."

This information is given mainly for the teacher's benefit. The students will work with

1. *Never change the meaning of a quotation by your omission.* This is dishonest because it makes the quotation say something that the original speaker or writer did not intend.

Original statement:
"And by him all that believe are justified from all things" (Acts 13:39).

Dishonest quotation:
"And by him all . . . are justified from all things" (Acts 13:39).

2. *If you quote more than one sentence and the first part makes a complete sentence, end the first part with the appropriate punctuation mark. Then use ellipsis points to show the omission, and continue with the quotation.*

period ⌐   ⌐ ellipsis points
"And above all these things put on charity. . . . And let the peace of God rule in your hearts" (Colossians 3:14, 15).

3. *If you quote more than one sentence and the first part does not make a complete sentence, use only the ellipsis points.*

"And Jesus, walking by the sea . . . saith unto them, Follow me, and I will make you fishers of men" (Matthew 4:18, 19).

You should also use ellipsis points to show that a sentence trails off without a proper ending.

If that happens, I will . . .

Incomplete sentences are common in dialogue. Such an *elliptical sentence* is not punctuated with ellipsis points, for the quotation includes all the words that the speaker actually said.

"I'm sure they saw it."
"Saw what?" (Meaning: You're sure they saw what?)
"The fire." (Meaning: They saw the fire.)

Class Practice

A. Tell how to divide each group of words into sentences with proper capitalization and punctuation.
1. How the rain comes down it must have rained several inches already do you suppose it will flood
2. Did you hear that what a terrible crash I believe there has been an accident
3. Pick up that tiny screw can you see it how did it get there

ellipsis points in connection with end punctuation but not with internal punctuation.
   b. Also use ellipsis points to show that a sentence trails off without a proper ending.
   c. Do not use ellipsis points to indicate an elliptical sentence.

Lesson 103 Answers

Class Practice

A. 1. How the rain comes down! It must have rained several inches already! Do you suppose it will flood?
   2. Did you hear that? What a terrible crash! I believe there has been an accident. (!)
   3. Pick up that tiny screw. Can you see it? How did it get there?

4. Aren't you about exhausted how long and hard you have worked just sit down here for a few minutes

B. Tell where to place the proper marks of punctuation in these sentences. Also tell if any capitalization is needed.
   1. "Where are the nine" Jesus asked the thankful Samaritan
   2. Praise the Lord How great He is
   3. Suddenly Angela called, "The meadow is burning"
   4. Quick call Father out from his study
   5. "Blessed are they which are persecuted for righteousness' sake: for theirs is the kingdom of heaven Rejoice, and be exceeding glad: for great is your reward in heaven: for so persecuted they the prophets which were before you" (Matthew 5:10, 12)
   6. "For thine is the kingdom for ever. Amen" (Matthew 6:13)
   7. Imagine I would never have expected
   8. My appointment is with A K Palmer, MD
   9. Herod the Great began rebuilding the temple around 20 BC, and it was destroyed in AD 70
   10. Do you know the dimensions of this imposing structure
   11. The temple proper, with its porches and vestibules, was 150 ft long and 150 ft wide
   12. What a magnificent sight the temple presented

Written Exercises

A. Write the first and last word of each sentence or exclamation, using ellipsis points to show omitted words between them. Use correct capitalization and end punctuation.
   1. A great tempest has swept down on the Sea of Galilee how frightened the disciples are doesn't the Master care if they perish
   2. What will the Master do is He actually rebuking the winds and waves how quickly they have quieted
   3. Oh, what a delightful puppy is it yours let me hold it for a minute
   4. What are you looking at why, it's a rattlesnake bring me that shovel
   5. Fresh strawberries we haven't had them for a long time

B. Write the last word and all the punctuation that should follow it.
   1. What a great God we serve
   2. Why do so many refuse to bow down to Him
   3. Have you memorized Psalm 19
   4. In surprise Judith exclaimed, "What a pleasure to see you"
   5. "When did you leave," she asked, "to get here so early"
   6. "We left last night at 10:30," answered Rosalyn
   7. We'll either have to do that or

4. Aren't you about exhausted? How long and hard you have worked! Just sit down here for a few minutes.

B. 1. nine?" Samaritan.
    2. Lord! is!
    3. burning!"
    4. Quick! Call   study. (!)
    5. heaven. . . . 12).
    6. kingdom . . . 13).
    7. Imagine! expected . . .
    8. A. K. M.D.
    9. B.C. A.D. 70.
    10. structure?
    11. ft. ft. wide.
    12. presented!

Written Exercises

A. (Use of exclamation points may vary.)
   1. A . . . Galilee. How . . . are! Doesn't . . . perish?
   2. What . . . do? Is . . . waves? How . . . quieted!
   3. Oh, . . . puppy! Is . . . yours? Let . . . minute.
   4. What . . . at? Why, . . . rattlesnake! Bring . . . shovel!
   5. Fresh strawberries! We . . . time.

B. 1. serve!   5. early?"
    2. Him?   6. Rosalyn.
    3. 19?   7. or . . .
    4. you!"

C. Copy each initial or abbreviation, and punctuate it correctly.
1. Jesus was crucified about 9:00 AM, which was the third hour.
2. The apostle Paul died around AD 68.
3. This book was written by Larry A Snyder, Jr and M F Hunsberger.
4. Paper measuring 8 ½ in by 11 in is of a standard size.
5. Here are the prices you asked for: peaches, $12 a bu; eggs, 90¢ a doz; and tomatoes, 69¢ a lb

D. Look up the following verses in Psalm 19. Then copy each quotation, using ellipsis points and capitalization correctly.
1. "The heavens declare the glory of God; and the firmament sheweth his handywork there is no speech nor language, where their voice is not heard." (verses 1, 3)
2. "The sun rejoiceth as a strong man to run a race." (verses 4, 5)
3. "More to be desired are they than much fine gold." (verse 10)

Review Exercises

Write whether each verb is transitive active (*TA*), transitive passive (*TP*), intransitive complete (*IC*), or intransitive linking (*IL*). [41–43, 53]
1. Mark sees his older sisters in the yard.
2. Mark is my little brother.
3. Mark has been lifted up to the swing.
4. The trees are growing well.
5. Alan is growing some new fruit trees.
6. These apple trees are growing old and weak.
7. Everyone listens to the noise.
8. The wind of the storm is heard within the house.
9. The wind sounds fierce and dangerous.
10. Overnight the water became ice.
11. Our refrigerator makes too much ice.
12. Pamela has fallen through the ice.
13. Mother turned the pancakes in the pan.
14. Father looked up at the sky.
15. The sky looked quite stormy.

C. 1. A.M.
2. A.D.
3. A. Jr. M. F.
4. in. in.
5. bu. doz. lb.

D. 1. "The heavens declare the glory of God; and the firmament sheweth his handywork. . . . There is no speech nor language, where their voice is not heard."
2. "The sun . . . rejoiceth as a strong man to run a race."
3. "More to be desired are they than . . . much fine gold."
   or "More to be desired are they . . . than much fine gold."

Review Exercises
1. TA
2. IL
3. TP
4. IC
5. TA
6. IL
7. IC
8. TP
9. IL
10. IL
11. TA
12. IC
13. TA
14. IC
15. IL

104. Commas

> **Lesson Survey**
> - Use **commas** to separate the parts of dates and addresses.
> - Use a comma after the greeting of a friendly letter and after the closing of any letter.
> - Use commas to separate large numbers into periods of thousands, millions, and so forth.
> - Use a comma to set off an introductory word, such as *yes* or *no*, or a mild interjection.
> - Use a comma to set off a long introductory prepositional phrase.
> - Use a comma after an introductory adverb clause.
> - Use commas to set off most interrupting expressions, such as appositives, nouns of direct address, and parenthetical elements.

The *comma* is one of the most frequently used marks of punctuation. It also has the greatest variety of uses. In this lesson and in Lesson 106, you will study a number of these uses.

1. *Use commas to separate the parts of dates and addresses.*

7190 Pinecrest Drive   Route 1, Box 140
Zanesville, OH 43701   Womelsdorf, PA 19567
March 6, 20—   April 10, 20—

On July 4, 1776, independence was proclaimed in Philadelphia, Pennsylvania.
Harold moved to 123 Holly Avenue, Madison, Wisconsin, on March 12, 1990.

2. *Use a comma after the greeting of a friendly letter and after the closing of any letter.* Remember that the greeting of a business letter is followed by a colon.

Dear friend,   Dear Sister Alice,   Sincerely yours,

3. *Use commas to separate large numbers into periods of thousands, millions, and so forth.*

13,283,504   8,736,209,330

4. *Use a comma to set off an introductory word, such as* yes *or* no, *or a mild interjection.*

Lesson 104

Purpose: To teach rules for using commas.

Oral Review:
1. Which two kinds of sentences end with periods? (declarative, imperative)
2. What are two uses of the exclamation point? (to follow an exclamatory sentence and to follow a strong interjection)
3. (*a*) What are ellipsis points? (b) When are they used? (*a.* three spaced periods; *b.* to show where material is omitted in a quotation, to show that a sentence trails off without a proper ending)
4. When are the words *god* and *lord* capitalized? (when they refer to the true God)
5. When are the names of school subjects capitalized? (when they are derived from proper nouns)
6. Give the second and third principal parts of these verbs. Use the helping verb *have* with the third principal part.
   a. drown (drowned, [have] drowned)
   b. drag (dragged, [have] dragged)
   c. lie (lay, [have] lain)
   d. forbid (forbade *or* forbad, [have] forbidden *or* [have] forbid)
   e. shine (shone *or* shined, [have] shone *or* [have] shined)

Lesson Introduction: What is the difference between a *comma* and a *coma*? Both represent a pause—the comma a short one and the coma a *very long* one. The pause indicated by a comma is significant, but not nearly as significant as that indicated by a coma! This lesson gives direction for using commas to indicate *brief* pauses in your writing.

Yes, I have finished sweeping the floors.
Well, look at the dirt on this floor.
Ah, now I know the answer.

5. *Use a comma to set off a long introductory prepositional phrase.* If an introductory phrase is short, no comma is used unless it is needed to make the sentence clear. Also, no comma is used if the sentence has inverted word order.

Long introductory prepositional phrase: Comma needed
   Out of the dense underbrush of the forest, a majestic buck
      emerged.

Inverted word order: No comma needed
   Out of the dense underbrush of the forest emerged a majestic
      buck.

Short introductory prepositional phrase: No comma needed
   From the porch we watched the beautiful sunset.

Short introductory prepositional phrase: Comma needed
   for clarity
   From the porch, steps lead down to the back yard.
      (Without the comma, the introductory phrase appears to be
         From the porch steps.)

6. *Use a comma after an introductory adverb clause.*

   Because Daniel refused to compromise, he was cast into the den
      of lions.
   Although many godly people have been persecuted, they have cho-
      sen the way of eternal blessing.

7. *Use commas to set off most interrupting expressions, such as appositives, nouns of direct address, and parenthetical elements.* If a single-word appositive is closely related to the preceding noun or pronoun, it is usually not set off with commas.

Appositives:
   Samuel, the Lord's prophet, anointed David to be the next king.
   David was a son of Jesse, a man of Bethlehem.
   David's brother Eliab seemed jealous of David.
   David, ruddy and handsome, offered to fight the giant. (adjec-
      tives in appositive position)
Nouns of direct address:
   Susan, write the next sentence on the board.
   Did you hear, Dorothy, that Grandmother is coming next week?

Lesson Outline:

1. **Use commas to separate the parts of dates and addresses.**

2. **Use a comma after the greeting of a friendly letter and after the closing of any letter.** The greeting of a business letter is followed by a colon.

3. **Use commas to separate large numbers into periods of thousands, millions, and so forth.**

4. **Use a comma to set off an introductory word, such as yes and no, or a mild interjection.**

5. **Use a comma to set off a long introductory prepositional phrase.** If an introductory phrase is short, no comma is used unless it is needed to make the sentence clear. Also, no comma is used if the sentence has inverted word order.

6. **Use a comma after an introductory adverb clause.**

7. **Use commas to set off most interrupting expressions, such as appositives, nouns of direct address, and parenthetical elements.** If a single-word appositive is closely related to the preceding noun or pronoun, it is usually not set off with commas.

Parenthetical elements:
Aunt Naomi, however, will not be along this time.
Nevin's plans, in my opinion, will not work.
Raw turnips, I think, are much better than cooked turnips.
A person's character, not his talents or beauty, is the most important.

Class Practice

A. Tell where commas should be added in this friendly letter.

1.   1330 Mt. Joy Rd.
2.   Manheim PA 17545
3.   March 14 20—
4. Dear Harold
5.   When I watched the beautiful sunrise this morning I was reminded
6. of the great God we serve. It is I'm sure a good reward for getting
7. out of bed early!
8.   On the other side of town a large vegetable farm was sold last
   week. We heard that an out-of-state building developer bought it
9. for $650000. Since the farm contained about 200 acres that comes
10. to $3250 per acre.

         *   *   *   *   *

11.   Well it has been good talking to you again. Please write and tell
12. how things are going for you in Texas.
13.   Your cousin
14.   Daniel

B. Tell where commas should be added in these sentences.

1. Martin Luther a reformer in Germany spoke out against the errors of the Roman Catholic Church.
2. On October 31 1517 he nailed his Ninety-five Theses on the church door at Wittenberg Germany.
3. Do you know William what those theses were about?
4. My father I'm sure will enjoy reading this account.
5. Yes we heard about the fire Martha.
6. At our school students are required to do a lot of writing.
7. After school is over we plan to visit Uncle Lee Mother's oldest brother.
8. Oh Sister Miriam our friends are waiting for us already.

Written Exercises

Copy each word or number that should be followed by a comma, and add the comma. Write the large numbers correctly.

1. Before a skunk sprays it usually gives some warning.
2. It will for example stamp its front feet.

Lesson 104 Answers

Class Practice

A. 1. (none)   8. town,
   2. Manheim,   9. $650,000 acres,
   3. 14,   10. $3,250
   4. Harold,   11. Well,
   5. morning,   12. (none)
   6. is, sure,   13. cousin,
   7. (none)   14. (none)

B. 1. Luther, Germany,
   2. 31, 1517, Wittenberg,
   3. know, William,
   4. father, sure,
   5. Yes, fire,
   6. school,
   7. over, Lee,
   8. Oh, Miriam,

Written Exercises

1. sprays,
2. will, example,

3. No a skunk will not spray if it cannot arch its back and lift its tail.
4. The skunk incidentally is considered a member of the weasel family.
5. Though all animals in the weasel family produce a strong-smelling musk the skunk surely produces the most powerful one.
6. Did you know Charles that a skunk produces only enough musk to spray five or six times a week?
7. By 1990 the world population was approximately 5300000000.
8. Canada has over 3800000 square miles of land; the United States has only a little over 3600000 square miles.
9. The Bible God's eternal Word should guide our lives.
10. There are I suppose you realize many false ideas about God's Word.
11. In those children's school desks were unknown Harry.
12. In the cookbook with the blue covers you should find the recipe.
13. Gerald was born on July 15 1971 at Harrisonburg Virginia.
14. Uncle Lloyd's have moved to 550 White Oak Road New Holland Pennsylvania.
15. Well they have lived there for three months already Margaret.

Review Exercises

A. Write the three principal parts of each verb. Include *have* with the third principal part. [34]
1. bid
2. creep
3. hurt
4. rise
5. shake
6. wear

B. For each sentence, write the correct form of the verb in parentheses. [34]
1. God has (break) the power of the enemy.
2. Jesus (drive) the merchants out of the temple.
3. The words over Jesus' cross were (write) in three languages.
4. Man's redemption (cost) nothing less than Jesus' blood.
5. A lion (slay) the disobedient prophet.
6. The other students have (go) out to the playground.
7. Yesterday we (hang) the chicken feeders from the ceiling.
8. Who has (eat) the cookies from this container?

3. No,
4. skunk, incidentally,
5. musk,
6. know, Charles,
7. 5,300,000,000
8. 3,800,000; 3,600,000
9. Bible, Word,
10. are, realize,
11. school, unknown,
12. covers,
13. 15, 1971, Harrisonburg,
14. Road, Holland,
15. Well, already,

Review Exercises

A. 1. bid, bade *or* bid, (have) bidden *or* (have) bid
2. creep, crept, (have) crept
3. hurt, hurt, (have) hurt
4. rise, rose, (have) risen
5. shake, shook, (have) shaken
6. wear, wore, (have) worn

B. 1. broken
2. drove
3. written
4. cost
5. slew
6. gone
7. hung
8. eaten

105. Story Writing: Developing the Conflict

Lesson Survey

- The **conflict** of a story must portray the main character in conflict with another person, with his circumstances, or with his own self.

- The conflict of a story does not need to be something spectacular.

- The conflict should be introduced early in the story, it should build up in intensity as the story develops, and it should lead to a climax near the end of the story.

- When the conflict is over, the story should end with a brief, pointed conclusion.

In Lesson 102 you learned that a short story usually revolves around one main character. A worthwhile, interesting story tells about a *conflict* or problem that the main character faces. Without a conflict, the "story" merely reports an incident. Conflict is what holds the reader's interest. He reads on to see what the main character does next, how he solves his problem, and what the final outcome is.

There are three main kinds of conflict in short stories.

1. *The main character may be in conflict with another person.* He may be resisting the good influence of his parents, his teacher, or some other person. Or he may be resisting the wrong influence of someone. This kind of conflict also occurs when the main character must endure the ill will or unkindness of another.

The stories of David killing Goliath and of Jeremiah being persecuted are examples of this kind of conflict. Other examples are a young person who struggles to accept his parents' advice, or a student who struggles to get along with a fellow student at school.

2. *The main character may be in conflict with his circumstances.* This kind of conflict occurs when a character must deal with circumstances rather than with another person.

If the cherished plans of the main character are changed because of the weather or someone else's sickness, he is in conflict with his circumstances. If the character must learn to accept the braces in his mouth or the wheelchair to which he is confined, he also faces this kind of conflict.

3. *The main character may be in conflict with his own self.* This kind

Lesson 105

Purpose: To teach how to write stories with good conflict.

Oral Review:

1. How many main characters should a story have? (one)

2. What are three common ways of revealing the traits of a story character? (by the character's actions, words, and thoughts)

3. Tell whether each of these verbs is transitive or intransitive.
   a. set (transitive)
   b. sit (intransitive)
   c. rise (intransitive)
   d. raise (transitive)
   e. lay (transitive)
   f. lie (intransitive)

4. What is the difference in meaning between *can* and *may*? (*Can* speaks of ability; *may* speaks of permission.)

5. Tell how each of the following expressions should be read.
   a. a small dwarf tree (a dwarf tree)
   b. several lively, energetic boys (Omit either *lively* or *energetic.*)
   c. those there mountains look beautiful (those mountains)
   d. a different sort of a plant (a different sort of plant)
   e. instead of them horses (instead of those horses)
   f. with less apples in it (with fewer apples in it)

Lesson Introduction: Have you ever noticed how the parts of a continued story always seem to stop at the most interesting and suspenseful places? Teachers may do that when reading for story time too! How do they manage it? They stop at a point where the conflict is strong—where the main character is perhaps in danger and must take prompt

of conflict occurs when the main character must deal with his own con-science, feelings, and desires.

He may be trying to overcome a bad habit, like complaining too much, or a wrong attitude, like disrespect or jealousy. He may have a guilty con-science because of some wrong he has done or something he should have done and failed to do. Any time the main character knows what is right but finds it hard to do right, he is facing this kind of conflict.

In trying to plan a story, have you ever felt that nothing great or unusual happens to you? "What can *I* write about?" you may have asked. Remember that the conflict of a story does not need to be something spectacular. Look for the three kinds of conflict in the simple happenings of a normal day. The examples given under the previous three points are conflicts that you or your friends have probably faced a number of times.

In Lesson 102 you learned that the main character should be intro-duced at the very beginning of a story. The conflict is the reason that the main character is in the story. It is what holds the reader's interest and makes him want to read on. Of course, the conflict is not fully explained at the beginning of the story; only a hint is given. Read the following story beginnings. Both of them hint at a conflict but do not state it directly.

> "I can hardly wait to play ball again."
> "Softball is so much fun!"
> David listened to the excited talk of his classmates while he slowly chewed his sandwich. "I don't know why they think playing ball is so much fun," he thought miserably. "Maybe if I could bat as well as the other boys . . . but I can't even hit the ball."
>
> *   *   *   *   *
>
> "I don't care," Thelma blurted as she entered the kitchen door. "It's not one bit fair."
> "I don't think so either." And Kathy set her lunch box on the counter with a clatter.
> Mother looked up in surprise from her ironing.

The conflict should build up in intensity as the story develops. Unless the story is very short, the main character often faces his conflict two or more times before it is settled. The very fact that the same problem arises a second or third time increases the reader's interest in how the main char-acter will finally settle the issue. Moreover, each new incident often involves stronger emotion than the previous incident.

Think back to the story "Pitch or Patch?" in Lesson 102. The first inci-dent of the conflict is near the beginning, when Evelyn realizes that she will need to wear the patched dress to school. The second incident occurs when action to solve his problem. This shows the impor-tance of conflict: it makes the reader want to read on and find out what happens next.

Lesson Outline:

1. The conflict of a story must relate directly to the main character in one of three ways.
   (1) *He may be in conflict with another person.*
   (2) *He may be in conflict with his circumstances.*
   (3) *He may be in conflict with his own self.*

2. The conflict of a story does not need to be something spectacular.

3. The conflict should be introduced early in the story. It should not be fully explained; only a hint should be given.

4. The conflict should build up in intensity as the story develops.
  a. The main character often faces his conflict two or more times before it is settled. This increases the reader's interest in how the main character will finally settle the issue.
  b. Each new incident often involves stronger emotion than the previous incident.

5. The conflict should lead to a climax.
  a. The climax is actually the last and most in-tense incident in the conflict.
  b. At this point in the story, the main char-acter's response brings either victory or de-feat.

6. When the conflict is over, the story should end with a brief, pointed conclusion.
  a. The conclusion should be short because the conflict is over and the reader's curiosity is satisfied.
  b. The conclusion should show rather than tell the lesson of the story.

she sees Mother patching Ronald's trousers, and the point is reemphasized that patches do not look terrible. The third incident is when Evelyn puts on the dress and has a sickening feeling of dread about wearing a patched dress to school. Especially in this third incident, Evelyn's feelings about wearing a patched dress are more intense than they were in the previous incidents.

The conflict should lead to a climax. The climax is actually the last and most intense incident in the conflict. At this point in the story, the main character's response brings either victory or defeat.

In the story "Pitch or Patch?" the fourth and climaxing incident in the conflict occurs when Evelyn sees the patch on Brother Vernon's shirtsleeve. Reread the following paragraph, which shows the intensity of her feelings at this point as well as her right response that brings victory.

> Evelyn was startled. Brother Vernon was wearing a patched shirt in school! A patch! Maybe she was being overly sensitive about such things. It did not look bad at all, that little patch on Brother Vernon's shirtsleeve. Maybe Mother was wiser than Evelyn had thought.

When the conflict is over, the story should end with a brief, pointed conclusion. It should be short because the conflict is over and the reader's curiosity is satisfied. The conclusion should show rather than tell the lesson of the story. In the example story, this is done by describing the glow of happiness that Evelyn felt and the renewed appreciation she had for her mother.

Class Practice

A. Tell which story beginning better introduces a conflict.

  1. a.   "Do you know the Rhodes family that is moving here?" Barbara asked her friend Joan after prayer meeting.

         "I don't really know them," Joan replied. "But from what I've seen and heard, it seems like they are a nice family. Do you know them?"

         "No, I just wondered if you knew anything about them," replied Barbara.

    b.   "What do you think of the Rhodes family that is moving here?" Barbara asked her friend Joan after prayer meeting.

         "I don't really know them," Joan replied. "But from what I've seen and heard, it seems like they are a nice family."

         "Well, I heard some things about Cynthia," stated Barbara. She lowered her voice as several ladies passed close by.

  2. a.   Thirteen-year-old Marlene stepped back and critically surveyed the wet kitchen floor. Yes, it was spotless, she was certain. Now her work was done and she could read. Picking up the bucket of dirty water, she went to empty it.

Lesson 105 Answers

Class Practice

A. 1. b
    2. a

The last of the water was gurgling down the drain when she heard a thud and a crash in the kitchen. Marlene hurried to the doorway.

  b.   Thirteen-year-old Marlene stepped back and critically surveyed the wet kitchen floor. Yes, it was spotless, she was certain. Now her work was done and she could read. Picking up the bucket of dirty water, she went to empty it.

As the last of the water was gurgling down the drain, Marlene thought about the book that Grandmother had given her.

3. Tell which of the three kinds of conflict is shown in each of these story excerpts.

  1.   "I thought earlier that we may be in for some snow today, and it looks as though I'm right," Sanford said as the snow came down faster. "Of course, Brent was sure it would *not* snow."

Sanford sighed. "Really, Mother, I find it hard sometimes to love Brent as I should."

Mother looked at Sanford in surprise. "Why?" she asked in concern.

"Well, I guess it's because he is always so sure he's right and that others are wrong," Sanford began.

  2.   Timothy stood leaning dejectedly against the gate of the corral and stared unseeingly at the cattle in it. "What's the matter, son?" asked Father as he came around the corner of the barn.

Timothy did not reply for several moments. Finally he blurted out, "Why do I have such a temper?"

"There is hardly a boy without a temper," Father replied. "But every boy must learn to control that temper of his."

  3.   Entering the kitchen downstairs, Mary Lou asked, "Mother, what does my ringworm look like this morning?"

"I think it's spreading a bit," said Mother after taking a look. "Come, let me treat it with the salve we got from the doctor."

Mary Lou's heart sank, and a few tears slid silently down her cheeks.

B. 1. Main character in conflict with another person.
    2. Main character in conflict with himself.
    3. Main character in conflict with circumstances.

Written Exercises

Read the following story, and do the exercises that follow.

Careless Carla

"Carla, where is my history book?" Michael called urgently, picking up his lunch box from the counter. "I let you look at it last evening, but now where is it? The school van will soon be here."

"I was looking at it in the living room. Let me check among my books," Carla answered breathlessly, hurrying about. A frantic search through her disorderly pile revealed no tenth grade history book.

She hurried to the living room to help her brother search. "Here it is!" she exclaimed in relief as she pulled two books from underneath a sofa cushion. "And my math book too. I would have forgotten it."

"Finally," Michael sighed. "You know I told you to put it back when you finished looking at it." He smoothed his neatly combed hair, picked up his ball glove, and went out the door.

Carla was racing around, gathering up her last things when she realized she did not have her sweater. "May I wear your church sweater, Jolene? I can't find mine," she called to her older sister.

"I suppose. But be careful with it, please," Jolene responded.

"I will," came the hasty promise.

Carla was finally ready, and she hurried out, letting the door slam behind her. She ran to join her two brothers and sister at the end of the lane. "I hope I have everything," she panted as the Millers' blue van rounded the curve.

Michael looked at her wisely. "If you'd plan ahead and be more organized, maybe you'd know for sure," he answered.

The white schoolhouse soon came into view. As the van halted in the driveway, the children jumped out and hurried toward the door.

"Let's play a game of tag before the bell rings," Carla's friend Marie suggested eagerly, joining Carla in the coatroom.

"All right. It's so pleasant outside this morning, I don't feel like staying inside," Carla agreed, hastily depositing her books on her desk.

Carla followed Marie out the front door. A lively game was soon under way.

Smoothing back a stray hair, Carla paused breathlessly at the base to pull off her sweater. "It's warm out here," she commented as Marie joined her.

After devotions, the pupils settled down for arithmetic classes. Carla stared at the problem in front of her. Would it ever come out right? She scratched some more on the eraser-smudged paper. Just as Brother Marlin called for class, Carla glanced out the window. The bright sunshine had disappeared, and large raindrops were beginning to fall.

"Seventh grade may go to the blackboard," Brother Marlin directed. "We'll work at some of these division problems together."

Carla's problem was one of the easier ones, and she finished it with little trouble. "The rain is falling steadily now," she observed as she stood at the board. Then suddenly a thought struck her. Jolene's sweater! It was out there in the rain where she had left it. "Oh, why did I forget it?" she rebuked herself. "And what will Jolene say? It was her new one."

Brother Marlin directed them to their seats. "I must bring that sweater inside at the first recess," she resolved, returning to her seat.

As soon as recess came, Carla asked for permission and then dashed through the pouring rain to the swing set. She picked up the sopping sweater and sprinted back to the schoolhouse. At the sink she paused to squeeze the water out of the rain-soaked sweater. Spreading it on the table, she breathed to herself, "I hope it's dry by this afternoon, but Jolene's still not going to be very happy. I should have remembered it," she thought remorsefully.

Carla joined the other girls in the room for a game of eraser tag. In hot pursuit of someone, she bumped into her own desk, knocking a pen to the floor. "There's that blue pen I borrowed from you the other day!" she exclaimed to Marie. But Carla hurried off after another girl, not bothering to pick it up. "I'll get it later and return it," she reasoned.

Within minutes, the ringing of the buzzer sent the energetic students to their seats. Suddenly remembering the borrowed pen, Carla hunted on the floor for it.

"There it is," she sighed as she discovered the pen under the radiator. She picked it up and was about to place it on Marie's desk when the top came off in her hand. "Oh, no!" exclaimed Carla, slipping into her seat before Brother Marlin rang the tap bell. She examined the special pen. Marie's grandmother had sent it to her from Guatemala for her birthday, and Marie treasured it highly. Now it was broken! Carla placed it in her desk, not sure how or when to return it.

"What will happen next?" she thought wearily. "Mother has told me before to be more careful with borrowed things." She turned to her history book with an impatient sigh.

Bursting into the kitchen after school, Michael, Carla, Jolene, and Stanley slid their lunch boxes onto the counter. Mother turned from the sink to greet them with her usual smile. "Hello, children," said Mother. "Did you have a good day?"

They began telling her about the interesting little incidents of the day as they gathered around the table to munch on cookies and to drink some milk. Carla put off discussing the sweater incident.

After they finished their treat, Mother broke the chatter by saying, "Carla, I thought we could cut a dress out of the material Aunt Rose sent you."

Carla headed for the stairway. "I'll bring the material and pattern down," she called back to Mother.

Soon Mother and Carla were busy cutting out the dress. Just as they finished, Mother was called to the telephone. "Put everything away,

Carla," she said over her shoulder.

Carla gathered the dress, pattern, and pins together, and placed them in the sewing cabinet. Then she settled herself comfortably in a living room chair with a book.

Mother returned from the study with one-year-old Stephen in her arms. She placed him at the toy box. "Carla, I want you to entertain him while I prepare supper," Mother instructed. "Don't let him get into any drawers."

Carla nodded and continued reading. Suddenly she jerked guiltily. Where was Stephen? She soon found him in the sewing room.

"Cut, cut," he laughed happily, holding up a small piece of paper for Carla to see.

"Stephen, no!" exclaimed Carla, jerking the paper from him. "That's my art picture." Stephen's smile disappeared, and he burst into tears. Mother came to the doorway to see what the commotion was about.

"Mother, look what he did!" Carla wailed, nearly in tears herself. "It's my art picture that I had just finished painting for school." She held up several pieces in dismay.

Mother picked up Stephen and came to look. "Where did he get the scissors? And why was your picture on the sewing machine? Hadn't I told you to put everything away?" she asked, looking directly at Carla.

"I must have forgotten," she gulped. Then she burst into tears. "Oh, Mother," sobbed Carla, and she poured out the whole story of all the troubles she had gone through that day. "I am careless with things, even other people's things, and then they get ruined," she finished lamely, hanging her head.

"Well," Mother said firmly, "you will need to apologize to Jolene and Marie and do everything you can to correct those mistakes. And I want you to ask me first before you borrow anything from others. You must learn to be more careful with your own things first. This spoiled picture should be a lesson for you."

Carla nodded and began to gather the scraps together.

"Now finish cleaning this up, and then come and set the table for supper," Mother finished kindly, rising to go to the kitchen.

To make the apologies was not going to be easy. "But," Carla determined staunchly, "I *am* going to do better."

1. Choose two answers: The second and third paragraphs reveal the main character's traits by (actions, words, thoughts).
2. To emphasize Carla's problem, the story shows a contrast between her and Michael. Give one detail about Michael that shows this contrast.

Written Exercises

1. actions, words
2. Michael had "neatly combed hair." He told Carla, "If you'd plan ahead and be more organized, maybe you'd know for sure."

3. Which of the three kinds of conflict does Carla face?

4. The first incident in the conflict is when Carla must quickly find Michael's history book, almost making herself late for the school van. Describe the three other incidents of conflict.

5. Read again the paragraph that begins with the words, "What will happen next?" Which phrase suggests that Carla had not yet learned her lesson at that point?

6. The final incident of conflict shows greater intensity and involves stronger emotion than any previous incident. Support this statement with evidence from the story.

7. Does the climax show a response that brings victory or defeat?

8. Why does the conclusion not describe how Carla made things right? Choose the best answer.
   a. The story is long enough without those details.
   b. Details of that nature should not be included in a story.
   c. Those details are not necessary since the real problem (Carla's careless attitude) has been solved.

Review Exercises

A. Write the correct verb for each sentence. [49, 50]
   1. Jonah (laid, lay) down in the ship.
   2. God did not (let, leave) him run away without dealing with him.
   3. Out on the sea the winds (raised, rose) and threatened the ship.
   4. We will (set, sit) these baskets on the porch.
   5. Father said that we boys (can, may) go fishing this afternoon.
   6. Shep often (sets, sits) beside us on the bank, watching us fish.
   7. Brother James has (laid, lain) the new books on the shelf.
   8. With this strong breeze, our kites should (raise, rise) quickly.

B. If the underlined expression has an error, write it correctly. If it is correct, write *correct*. [77]
   1. A layer of <u>cold, clear ice</u> covered each bucket.
   2. Do you see how <u>them stars</u> are shining brilliantly tonight?
   3. After the moon comes up, <u>fewer stars</u> will be visible.
   4. What <u>kind of an animal</u> makes a noise like that?
   5. There seem to be <u>less coyotes</u> around now than there were years ago.
   6. <u>These old antiques</u> once belonged to my great-grandfather.
   7. <u>A pink and yellow ribbon</u> holds the box shut.
   8. I wonder what is in <u>this here box</u>.

3. Conflict with her own self.

4. *Second incident:* Carla left Jolene's new sweater out in the rain.
   Third incident: She neglected to pick up the pen she had borrowed from Marie, and it was broken when she found it later.
   Fourth incident: She had not put the scissors or her art picture away, and her younger brother cut up the picture.

5. "with an impatient sigh"

6. Carla burst into tears and poured out the whole story of all her troubles that day.

7. victory

8. c

Review Exercises

A. 1. lay
   2. let
   3. rose
   4. set
   5. may
   6. sits
   7. laid
   8. rise

B. 1. clear ice
   2. those stars
   3. correct
   4. kind of animal
   5. fewer coyotes
   6. These antiques
   7. correct
   8. this box

106. More Rules for Using Commas

Lesson Survey

- Use a comma before a coordinating conjunction that joins the clauses of a compound sentence.
- Use commas to separate three or more items in a series.
- Use commas to separate descriptive adjectives.
- Use a comma to separate a direct quotation from the rest of the sentence unless some other punctuation is used.
- Use commas to separate a nonrestrictive adjective clause from the rest of the sentence.

Commas, commas, and more commas. What would we ever do without commas to help make our writing clear? This lesson adds to the rules for commas studied in Lesson 104.

1. *Use a comma before a coordinating conjunction that joins the clauses of a compound sentence.* If the two clauses are very short and closely related, the comma may be omitted.

> Noah warned the wicked people of his day, *but* they refused to listen.
> Jesus spoke *and* the storm ceased.

2. *Use commas to separate three or more items in a series.* Be sure to include the comma after the item just before the coordinating conjunction. If a conjunction is used between each pair of items, do not use any commas.

Single words:
> Peaches, pears, plums, apples, and cherries are common fruits in a temperate climate.
> The trapped dog yelped *and* whined *and* howled.

Phrases:
> Aunt Betty planted flowers in front of the porch, along the fence, and around the garage.

Clauses:
> Andrew read a book, Sarah wrote a letter, and Robert took a nap.

3. *Use commas to separate descriptive adjectives.* Never place a comma between two limiting adjectives or between a limiting adjective and a descriptive adjective. Never place a comma between the last adjective and the word the adjectives modify. If the final adjective is closely connected with the noun, do not use a comma before that adjective.

Lesson 106

Purpose: To teach additional rules for using commas.

Oral Review:

1. Tell whether each statement is true or false.
   a. In an address, a comma is needed between the state and the zip code. (false)
   b. In an address, a comma is needed between the city and the state. (true)
   c. In a business letter, a comma is used after the closing but not after the greeting. (true)
   d. If an introductory adverb clause is short, the comma may be omitted. (false)

2. When should you use a comma after an introductory prepositional phrase? (when the phrase is long)

3. What are the interrupting expressions that need to be set off by commas in these sentences? (Commas are shown.)

   a. This story, I understand, actually happened to my grandfather.
   b. You should do what you can, Galen, to make a visitor feel welcome.
   c. Mr. Smith, our next door neighbor, is in the hospital.

4. Tell whether these sentences are simple, compound, or complex.

   a. A person who trusts the Lord does not need to worry. (complex)
   b. Worry is a miserable companion in life. (simple)
   c. When we are tempted to worry, we should pray. (complex)
   d. Our God is omnipotent, but sometimes we fail to trust Him. (compound)

Lesson Introduction: Write the following sentence on the board without commas, and have someone put in the commas so that the meaning is clear.

Do you remember these three tests from Lesson 70? If the answers to these questions are *yes,* you should use a comma.

(1) Do you pause between the adjectives as you read them?
(2) Does it sound right to use *and* between the adjectives?
(3) Does it sound right to change the order of the adjectives?

In the garage we saw old, rusty, broken bicycles. (three descriptive adjectives)

The three rusty bicycles could be fixed and painted.
(No comma between *The* and *three* because they are both limiting; no comma between *three* and *rusty* because one is limiting and the other descriptive.)

A low brick wall surrounded the cemetery.
(No comma between *low* and *brick* because *brick wall* is a closely related unit.)

4. *Use a comma to separate a direct quotation from the rest of the sentence unless some other punctuation is used.*

Jesus said, "I am the bread of life."
"Go to the garden," Mother instructed, "and pull some radishes."
"Where are the boys?" Father asked. (A question mark is used; no comma.)

5. *Use commas to separate a nonrestrictive adjective clause from the rest of the sentence.* Remember that a nonrestrictive clause does not restrict the meaning of the noun it modifies. It merely gives additional information.

Uncle Raymond, who lives in Georgia, plans to visit us next month.
Harriet Freshen, whom we sang for yesterday, is ninety-two years old.

But:

My uncle who lives in Georgia plans to visit us next month.
(The clause restricts *uncle* by telling which one; no commas used.)

All the students who were running in the hall must stay in their seats. (The clause restricts *students* to certain ones; no commas used.)

Class Practice

Tell where commas should be placed in these sentences.
1. We found supplies of flour sugar salt and baking powder in the pantry.
2. Various animals and birds chirp squeal bark whistle and grunt.
3. Jerusalem which was built in ancient times by the Jebusites became King David's capital city.

The five seventh-grade boys from the Morrisville School are Timothy Dale Weaver, Martin Leroy Frey, Nelson Martin, Mark Horst Shank, and George Lee Burkholder.

Lesson Outline:

1. Use a comma before a coordinating conjunction that joins the clauses of a compound sentence. If the two clauses are very short and closely related, the comma may be omitted.

2. Use commas to separate three or more items in a series.

a. Be sure to include the comma after the item just before the coordinating conjunction.
b. If a conjunction is used between each pair of items, do not use any commas.

3. Use commas to separate descriptive adjectives.

Lesson 106 Answers

Class Practice

1. flour, sugar, salt,
2. chirp, squeal, bark, whistle,
3. Jerusalem, Jebusites,

---

a. Never place a comma between two limiting adjectives or between a limiting adjective and a descriptive adjective.
b. Never place a comma between the last adjective and the word the adjectives modify.
c. If the final adjective is closely connected with the noun, do not use a comma before that adjective.
d. Remember the following three tests. If the answers to these questions are *yes,* you should use a comma.
(1) Do you pause between the adjectives as you read them?
(2) Does it sound right to use *and* between the adjectives?
(3) Does it sound right to change the order of the adjectives?

4. This strong beautiful city was easily defended from enemies.
5. We must learn to handle the small problems of each day or we shall be overwhelmed by the larger ones.
6. "Your patient careful work shows encouraging results" Father said.
7. We have scrubbed the porch picked the tomatoes and mowed the lawn.
8. "Is lunch ready to be served" Lloyd asked "or should I finish raking?"
9. All the calves that are in this pen are ready to be sold and we expect the dealer to come tomorrow.
10. A short timid young man knocked at the door.

Written Exercises

Copy each word that should be followed by a comma, and add the comma.

1. God sent many prophets to the Jews and they foretold the coming of the Messiah.
2. Jesus Christ who was the long-awaited Messiah was rejected by many Jews.
3. Jesus endured more pain shame and sorrow than any other man ever did.
4. Suddenly Joy exclaimed "It's really snowing hard now!"
5. I pushed aside some matted grass and the cold beady eyes of a snake stared straight at me.
6. Any book that has such wickedness in it must be destroyed or it will poison our minds.
7. "The barn floor needs to be swept the car should be washed and the front yard should be raked" Father stated.
8. "These sweet crisp bars are delicious" agreed Ann "but I have had enough."
9. The refugees trudged down the steep hill over the raging stream and onto the wide plain on the other side.
10. Every village that they have passed through has closed its doors to them but their faith in God has not been shaken.
11. The cold weary travelers huddled around the warmth of the campfire.
12. They thanked God for His protecting care they interceded for their persecutors and they prayed for God's continued blessing.

Review Exercises

A. Write whether each sentence is *simple, compound,* or *complex.* [14, 15]
1. If we truly love God, He will always make a way for us.
2. In God's eternal Word, we can find strength and wisdom for each day.
3. The God who made us deserves our worship.

4. strong,
5. day,
6. patient, results,
7. porch, tomatoes,
8. served, asked,
9. sold,
10. short,

Written Exercises
1. Jews,
2. Christ, Messiah,
3. pain, shame,
4. exclaimed,
5. grass, cold,
6. destroyed,
7. swept, washed, raked,
8. sweet, delicious, Ann,
9. hill, stream,
10. them,
11. cold,
12. care, persecutors,

Review Exercises
A. 1. complex
   2. simple
   3. complex

4. Use a comma to separate a direct quotation from the rest of the sentence unless some other punctuation is used.

5. Use commas to separate a nonrestrictive adjective clause from the rest of the sentence.

★ **EXTRA PRACTICE**
Worksheet 54 (*Practice With Commas*)

4. We can take our stand, or we can blindly follow the crowd.
5. Such choices do determine the quality of our character.

B. Combine each pair into a compound sentence, using a suitable coordinating conjunction. [14]
1. The pigs are all over the garden. I neglected to latch the gate.
2. We thought we had all the pigs back in the pen. We soon discovered a few more out in the orchard.
3. You must learn to be more responsible. You will need to be punished.

C. Combine these sentences into complex sentences, with the kind of dependent clause indicated in the parentheses. [76, 84]
1. The paint set is quite detailed. Aunt Beatrice sent it for my birthday. (restrictive adjective clause)
2. The storm passed over. A beautiful rainbow appeared. (adverb clause)
3. Great-uncle Mahlon is an interesting person to visit. He is Grandma Witmer's only brother. (nonrestrictive adjective clause)

---

107. Quotation Marks

> **Lesson Survey**
> - A direct quotation is enclosed in **quotation marks.**
> - If a quotation is divided by explanatory words, the second part does not begin with a capital letter unless it begins another sentence.
> - Quotation marks are used around the titles of short stories, short poems, songs, and chapters of books.

Direct quotations help to make stories interesting and realistic. The characters seem to come alive as we "hear" the exact words they say. In each of the following pairs, both sentences give the same information. But the direct quotations are definitely more appealing than the indirect quotations.

Indirect: Father said that he was pleasantly surprised at our work.
Direct: Father said, "I am pleasantly surprised at your work."

Indirect: Aunt Louise asked when she should come to help us.
Direct: "When should I come to help you?" asked Aunt Louise.

A direct quotation is enclosed in *quotation marks*. Remember to separate

---

4. compound
5. simple

B. 1. The pigs are all over the garden, for I neglected to latch the gate.
2. We thought we had all the pigs back in the pen, but we soon discovered a few more out in the orchard.
3. You must learn to be more responsible, or you will need to be punished.

C. 1. The paint set that Aunt Beatrice sent for my birthday is quite detailed.
2. After the storm passed over, a beautiful rainbow appeared.
3. Great-uncle Mahlon, who is Grandma Witmer's only brother, is an interesting person to visit.
or Great-uncle Mahlon, who is an interesting person to visit, is Grandma Witmer's only brother.

Lesson 107

Purpose: To teach the correct use of quotation marks.

Oral Review:
1. In a compound sentence, when may you omit the comma before the coordinating conjunction? (when the two clauses are very short and closely related)
2. What kind of adjective clauses need to be set off with commas? (nonrestrictive)
3. What are the three tests to help you decide whether to put a comma between descriptive adjectives? (Do you pause between the adjectives as you read them? Does it sound right to use *and* between the adjectives? Does it sound right to change the order of the adjectives?)
4. What two parts of a friendly letter are followed by a comma? (greeting, closing)
5. Which of those parts is followed by a comma in a business letter? (closing)
6. What kind of verb
   a. passes action to some word in the sentence? (transitive)
   b. connects the subject to some word in the predicate? (intransitive linking)
   c. does not pass action to any word and does not join the subject to any word in the predicate? (intransitive complete)
7. What is the difference between the active and the passive voice? (In the active voice, the action is passed to the direct object. In the passive voice, the action is passed to the subject.)

Lesson Introduction: Call the students' attention to the conversation between Jesus and Nicodemus in John 3. Ask if they ever tried to decide exactly

the quotation from the rest of the sentence with a comma unless some other punctuation mark is used.

> "Jesus, have mercy on us," called the ten lepers.
> Jesus commanded, "Go and show yourselves to the priests."
> "Where are the nine?" Jesus asked the thankful man.

If a quotation is divided by explanatory words, the second part does not begin with a capital letter unless it begins another sentence. Notice also that if the second part does not begin another sentence, a comma follows the explanatory words. But if it does begin another sentence, a period is used.

> "We're having a quiz today," said Brother Thomas, "to see how well you have studied your lesson." (One sentence: "We're having a quiz today to see how well you have studied your lesson." To is not capitalized.)
> "Close your books," instructed Brother Thomas. "We're having a quiz today." (Two sentences: "Close your books. We're having a quiz today." *We're* is capitalized.)

Problem: Is the following sentence written correctly?
"When light passes through a prism," said Brother Carl, "the colors of light are separated."

Think: What is the quotation? ("When light passes through a prism, the colors of light are separated.")
Is the quotation one sentence or two? (one sentence)

Solution: The sentence is written correctly.

Problem: Is the following sentence written correctly?
"Raindrops can act like prisms too," he continued, "sunlight shining on them causes a beautiful rainbow."

Think: What is the quotation? ("Raindrops can act like prisms too, sunlight shining on them causes a beautiful rainbow.")
Is the quotation one sentence or two? (two sentences; a run-on error if written together as one sentence)

Solution: The sentence should be rewritten as two sentences.
"Raindrops can act like prisms too," he continued. "Sunlight shining on them causes a beautiful rainbow."

Quotation marks are used around the titles of short stories, short poems, songs, and chapters of books. (The titles of longer writings, such as books, are italicized, as you will study in a later lesson.) In general, no comma is used before a title enclosed in quotation marks.

> Margaret has just finished reading the chapter "Flames in the Night" in *Home Fires Beneath the Northern Lights.*

where the conversation ends. Did Jesus say everything through the end of verse 21? Or did He stop talking at the end of verse 15 or 16? (Then the rest through verse 21 would be the writer's reflections.) There is no way of knowing, for quotation marks were not used in ancient Greek writing. Today we use quotation marks to clearly indicate which words are quoted and which ones are not.

Lesson Outline:

1. A direct quotation is enclosed in quotation marks. Separate the quotation from the rest of the sentence with a comma unless some other punctuation mark is used.

2. If a quotation is divided by explanatory words, the second part does not begin with a capital letter unless it begins another sentence.
   a. If the second part does not begin another sentence, a comma follows the explanatory words.
   b. If the second part does begin another sentence, a period is used.
   c. The following questions can be used to decide how a divided quotation should be written.
      1) What is the quotation? (Read it without the explanatory words.)
      2) Is the quotation one sentence or two? (If it is one sentence, use a comma and no capital letter. If it is two sentences, use a period and a capital letter.)

3. Quotation marks are used around the titles of short stories, short poems, songs, and chapters of books. In general, no comma is used before titles enclosed in quotation marks.

The story "Hidden Blessings" in this week's *Christian Pathway* was very interesting.

In devotions this morning, we sang "I Owe the Lord a Morning Song."

Class Practice

A. Tell whether these sentences contain *direct* or *indirect* quotations. Tell how to punctuate them.
1. What is truth asked Pilate
2. He declared I find no fault in Him
3. The Pharisees asked Jesus if He was really the Messiah
4. Peter asserted that Jesus is the Messiah, the Son of God
5. How can these things be asked Nicodemus

B. Tell how to punctuate these sentences.
1. Who was the youngest man that ever lived asked Carol
2. What do you mean demanded Joel by such a question
3. Paula said your question doesn't even make sense
4. Well declared Joel I know that Methuselah was the oldest man that ever lived
5. The answer said Carol is Adam
6. Only Adam was a man when he was one day old she continued everyone else was still a baby at that age
7. The seventh graders read the poem Spring on the Farm in unison
8. In our next history class, we will have a test on the chapter The Roman World in Christ's Day

Written Exercises

A. Copy these sentences containing direct and indirect quotations. Supply the missing punctuation and capitalization.
1. I came to help you said Lena what shall I do first
2. My work is finished answered Jason all the calves are fed
3. The encyclopedia says that alligators can make a loud bellow
4. Daniel little David begged will you help me play a game
5. Look at that bright rainbow called Peter in fact, it's a double rainbow
6. Did you know asked Henry that our silo is nearly empty
7. Barbara told us that her aunt plans to teach school next year
8. Rosene questioned are you sure that you followed the directions right

B. Copy the titles that should be enclosed with quotation marks, and place the marks properly.
1. Is the song Fresh From the Throne of Glory in the *Church Hymnal*?
2. You will find some information for your report in the chapter

Lesson 107 Answers

Class Practice

A. 1. direct; "What is truth?" asked Pilate.
2. direct; He declared, "I find no fault in Him."
3. indirect; The Pharisees asked Jesus if He was really the Messiah.
4. indirect; Peter asserted that Jesus is the Messiah, the Son of God.
5. direct; "How can these things be?" asked Nicodemus.

B. 1. "Who was the youngest man that ever lived?" asked Carol.
2. "What do you mean," demanded Joel, "by such a question?"
3. Paula said, "Your question doesn't even make sense."
4. "Well," declared Joel, "I know that Methuselah was the oldest man that ever lived."
5. "The answer," said Carol, "is Adam."
6. "Only Adam was a man when he was one day old," she continued. "Everyone else was still a baby at that age."
7. The seventh graders read the poem "Spring on the Farm" in unison.
8. In our next history class, we will have a test on the chapter "The Roman World in Christ's Day."

Written Exercises

A. (Corrections are underlined.)
1. "I came to help you," said Lena. "What shall I do first?"
2. "My work is finished," answered Jason. "All the calves are fed."
3. The encyclopedia says that alligators can make a loud bellow.
4. "Daniel," little David begged, "will you help me play a game?"
5. "Look at that bright rainbow," called Peter. "In fact, it's a double rainbow."
6. "Did you know," asked Henry, "that our silo is nearly empty?"
7. Barbara told us that her aunt plans to teach school next year.
8. Rosene questioned, "Are you sure that you followed the directions right?"

B. 1. "Fresh From the Throne of Glory"
2. "Literature and Hymnody"

Literature and Hymnody in the book *Glimpses of Mennonite History and Doctrine.*

3. The book *Poems for Memorization* includes the poem The Brook.

C. Write five sentences of conversation between two people. Include at least one divided quotation of one sentence and one divided quotation of two sentences.

Review Exercises

A. Write *transitive, intransitive complete,* or *intransitive linking* to tell which kind of verb each sentence has. [41–43]
1. We should always be a noble example to others.
2. A noble example shuns the wrong at all times.
3. The young person of strength never speaks disrespectfully of authority.
4. Moreover, he does not treat other people unkindly.
5. Even youth can grow strong in noble character.

B. Write whether the voice of each verb is *active* or *passive.* [53]
1. The whole sky was lit by a beautiful display of the northern lights.
2. Dennis painted the birdhouse carefully.
3. Lucy prepared a simple meal for her guests.
4. Kenton was surprised by the sudden noise behind him.
5. In the old pine tree, a pair of finches made their nest.

3. "The Brook"

C. (Individual work.)

Review Exercises
A. 1. intransitive linking
   2. transitive
   3. intransitive complete
   4. transitive
   5. intransitive linking

B. 1. passive   4. passive
   2. active   5. active
   3. active

---

108. More Quotation Marks

> **Lesson Survey**
> - A quotation within a quotation is enclosed with single quotation marks.
> - A comma or a period is always placed inside the quotation marks.
> - If a quotation is a question or an exclamation, the question mark or exclamation point is placed inside the quotation marks.
> - If the whole sentence is a question or an exclamation but the quotation is not, the question mark or exclamation point is placed outside the quotation marks.

In Lesson 107 you studied the most common uses of quotation marks. This lesson should help you to use them correctly in more difficult constructions.

Lesson 108

Purpose: To teach the method of writing *a quotation within a quotation.

Oral Review:
1. When should the second part of a divided quotation begin with a capital letter? (only when it begins a new sentence)
2. What are some examples of titles that should be enclosed with quotation marks? (titles of short stories, short poems, songs, and chapters of books)
3. What are some introductory words that should be followed by a comma? (*yes, no,* and mild interjections)
4. What kind of introductory prepositional phrases should be followed by a comma? (long)
5. When should an introductory adverb clause be followed by a comma? (always)

6. Tell how to diagram these sentence parts.
   a. noun of direct address (on a separate line to the left of the main base line)
   b. appositive (in parentheses after the noun or pronoun it explains)
   c. verbal used as a noun (across the angle of a slanting and a horizontal line, resting on a pedestal, above the place where a single-word noun would go)
   d. noun clause (on a horizontal line resting on a pedestal, above the place where a single-word noun would go)

Lesson Introduction: Write the following sentence on the board.

   Did you hear Mary say, "My brother has measles?"

Sometimes a story character quotes someone else's words or states the title of a short story or poem. Such a quotation within a quotation is enclosed with single quotation marks. Be sure to begin this inner quotation with a capital letter. If the inner quotation follows explanatory words such as *Jesus said* or *who asked,* a comma is usually placed before the single quotation mark. But remember that a comma is generally not used before a title.

> "We must remember," replied Father, "that Jesus said, 'In my Father's house are many mansions.'"
> Eunice explained, "We had to practice the chant 'Out of the Depths' a number of times."
> "'Though he slay me, yet will I trust in him' was one of Job's remarkable statements of faith," commented Brother Adrian.
> "When Job said, 'Though he slay me, yet will I trust in him,' he made a remarkable statement of faith," commented Brother Adrian.

Of course, an *indirect* quotation within a quotation is not set off with single quotation marks.

> "Jesus said that He is the Good Shepherd," Brother Marlin said.

Follow these rules for the use of other punctuation marks with quotation marks.

1. *A comma or a period is always placed inside the quotation marks.* This applies to both single and double quotation marks.

> "I have homework this evening," Susan reported, "so I won't be able to help with the project."
> "According to Benjamin Franklin," began Brother Aaron, "'He that is good for making excuses is seldom good for anything else.'"

2. *If a quotation is a question or an exclamation, the question mark or exclamation point is placed inside the quotation marks.*

> Brenda asked, "Have you eaten yet?"
> "The cows are out!" shouted Joseph.

3. *If the whole sentence is a question or an exclamation but the quotation is not, the question mark or exclamation point is placed outside the quotation marks.*

> Did Mary say, "I refuse to eat"?
> (The whole sentence is a question, but the quotation is not.)
> That boy actually had the discourtesy to say, "Your drawing is ugly"!
> (The whole sentence is an exclamation, but the quotation is not.)

Ask, "Is this sentence written correctly?" Students will likely think so because it matches what they studied in the past. Point out, however, that the *whole sentence* is a question, whereas the *quotation* is not. This lesson teaches how to punctuate sentences like that.

Lesson Outline:

1. A quotation within a quotation is enclosed with single quotation marks.
   a. Begin the inner quotation with a capital letter.
   b. If the inner quotation follows explanatory words, a comma is usually placed before the single quotation mark.
   c. In general, do not use a comma before a title.
   d. Do not use single quotation marks for an indirect quotation within a quotation.

(*Teacher:* The comma after *said* or *asked* may be omitted when the quotation is very short or is grammatically closely related to the explanatory words. The main clue is that no pause precedes the quotation in reading the sentence orally. This point is not taught in grade 7.

> Mother asked, "Did you remember to say 'Thank you'?"
> Jesus said that "all things are possible to him that believeth.")

2. Follow these rules for the use of other punctuation marks with quotation marks.
   (1) *A comma or a period is always placed inside the quotation marks.*
   (2) *If a quotation is a question or an exclamation, the question mark or exclamation point is placed inside the quotation marks.*

Class Practice

A. Tell what the mistake is in each sentence.
1. Jeffrey shouted, "It's coming down"!
2. Could you hear him whisper, "I'm over here?"
3. Mary said, "My mother always tells us, 'Your work isn't done until it's done right."
4. "Suddenly I heard him say, 'I think this ladder is falling!' Father explained.
5. Abraham told Lot, "You may choose first.
6. Did God at this time repeat His promise to Abraham: "All the land you see will belong to you'"?

B. Tell how to use correct punctuation and capitalization in these sentences.
1. Grandfather used to say haste makes waste replied Uncle David
2. Let's sing Amazing Grace Aunt May suggested
3. Was it Benjamin Franklin who said early to bed, early to rise, makes a man healthy, wealthy, and wise
4. How much better I felt when Susan said quietly I'm sorry
5. Little Katie announced Jesus Loves Me is my favorite song

Written Exercises

A. Copy these sentences, and supply the missing punctuation and capitalization. Use quotation marks only when explanatory words clearly indicate a direct quotation.
1. I heard Brother Lawrence say hand in your reports by Friday insisted Ralph.
2. Which apostle wrote For the love of money is the root of all evil
3. Washington Irving said a sharp tongue is the only edged tool that grows keener with constant use, Mother commented
4. Brother Clyde asked is the poem The Blind Men and the Elephant familiar to you
5. Just in time, Father shouted stop

B. If the underlined part of the sentence is punctuated incorrectly, write it correctly. If it is correct, write *correct*.
1. As soon as Father stepped into the room, the children all shouted, "Happy birthday"!
2. Esther declared, "Uncle Lloyd will long be remembered for his words, 'Always live with tomorrow in view."
3. "I thought you said, 'That's a home-run hit for sure,'" commented Floyd.

(3) *If the whole sentence is a question or an exclamation but the quotation is not, the question mark or exclamation point is placed outside the quotation marks.*

★ **EXTRA PRACTICE**
Worksheet 55 (*Quotation Marks*)

Lesson 108 Answers

Class Practice

A. (Corrections are underlined.)
1. Jeffrey shouted, "It's coming down!"
2. Could you hear him whisper, "I'm over here"?
3. Mary said, "My mother always tells us, 'Your work isn't done until it's done right.'"
4. "Suddenly I heard him say, 'I think this ladder is falling!'" Father explained.
5. Abraham told Lot, "You may choose first."
6. Did God at this time repeat His promise to Abraham: "All the land you see will belong to you"?

B. (Answers are underlined.)
1. "Grandfather used to say, 'Haste makes waste,'" replied Uncle David.
2. "Let's sing 'Amazing Grace,'" Aunt May suggested.
3. Was it Benjamin Franklin who said, "Early to bed, early to rise, makes a man healthy, wealthy, and wise"?
4. How much better I felt when Susan said quietly, "I'm sorry"! (*Teacher:* This whole sentence is exclamatory, as shown by the word arrangement; but the quotation is not exclamatory, as shown by *quietly*.)
5. Little Katie announced, "'Jesus Loves Me' is my favorite song."

Written Exercises

A. (Corrections are underlined.)
1. "I heard Brother Lawrence say, 'Hand in your reports by Friday,'" insisted Ralph.
2. Which apostle wrote, "For the love of money is the root of all evil"?
3. "Washington Irving said, 'A sharp tongue is the only edged tool that grows keener with constant use,'" Mother commented.
4. Brother Clyde asked, "Is the poem 'The Blind Men and the Elephant' familiar to you?"
5. Just in time, Father shouted, "Stop!"

B. 1. "Happy birthday!"
   2. view.'"
   3. correct

4. John G. Whittier wrote "Dear Lord and Father of <u>Mankind</u>".
5. "Theodore Parker <u>said The</u> books that help you the most are those which make you think the most,'" began Brother Charles.
6. A person should never ask, "Does God really see <u>me</u>"?
7. "The Bible clearly says, 'The eyes of the Lord are in every <u>place</u>'" observed Catherine.
8. "That is a comfort to the people of <u>God</u>", stated Diane.
9. "If these problems aren't done, why did you <u>say, 'I've finished all my homework'</u>?" asked Mother.
10. Father said, "The barn aisles are not swept well <u>enough.</u>
11. Can you explain the line "Though the loss sustained our spirit often <u>grieves?</u>"
12. "Aunt Lillie said that she should arrive this <u>evening,</u>'" Mother said.

Review Exercises

Diagram these sentences.
1. Curvin, have you ever seen a polar bear?
2. The Arctic, a cold, barren region, is their home.
3. Because they live in this bitter climate, God gave them very special bodies.
4. Hugging the skin, a coat of short underhair traps the body's heat.
5. The outer coat, which consists of coarse hair, repels water and snow.
6. Under the skin is a thick layer of fat.
7. Fur on the bottom of their feet insulates their feet and provides good traction.
8. Having small, furry ears also prevents the loss of heat.
9. These bears live in the frigid North, but they survive there quite well.
10. That God designed their bodies is clearly evident.

---

109. Story Writing: Using Good Style

> **Lesson Survey**
> * In a story, use **dialogue** that sounds natural.
> * Use lively action verbs as much as possible.
> * Use exact, descriptive words instead of general ones.

Lesson 109

Purpose: To teach some methods for showing a story rather than merely telling it.

Oral Review:

1. What are the three main kinds of conflict? (main character in conflict with another person, with his circumstances, and with his own self)
2. How can the conflict build up in intensity during the story? (by having more than one incident of the conflict; by having later incidents of the conflict involve stronger emotion)
3. (*a*) What is the most intense incident in the conflict? (*b*) Where should it occur? (*a.* the climax; *b.* near the end of the story)
4. What are three common ways of portraying the traits of the main character? (by the character's actions, words, and thoughts)

4. Mankind."   9. correct
5. said, 'The   10. enough."
6. me?"   11. grieves"?
7. place,'"   12. evening,"
8. God,"

Review Exercises

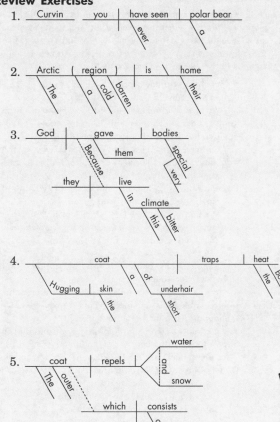

(Numbers 6–10 are on page 524.)

---

5. Name the kind of rhythm found in these lines of poetry. Tell how many feet are in each.
   a. Up the steep mountainside, rocky and dangerous (dactylic, 4 feet)
   b. The Bible is my treasured Lamp (iambic, 4 feet)
   c. Little cotton-ball lambs by the brook (anapestic, 3 feet)
   d. Up the pasture lane the cows come lowing home (trochaic, 6 feet)
6. What is alliteration? (the repetition of beginning consonant sounds in words)
7. What is assonance? (the repetition of similar vowel sounds in accented syllables)

In earlier lessons of this chapter, you studied two important things that make a good story—the way the main character is portrayed and the way the conflict is developed. This lesson will show you how to write stories with an interesting, readable style. Your stories should *show* details rather than merely *telling* about them. Your readers should feel as if they can hear the conversations and see the activities in your story.

Natural Dialogue

One of the most important ways to show the details of a story is to use plenty of *dialogue* (written conversation) and to make sure it sounds natural. Dialogue helps to make the characters and events seem real. Compare the following two story beginnings. Notice how much more natural the dialogue is in the second one than in the first one.

"We have so many beans. I am tired of snapping all these beans," sighed ten-year-old Denise.

"We have finished over half the job." Her older sister Danelle tried to give some encouragement. "Denise, would you like to hang out the laundry? The washer just stopped."

"Certainly, I would like that," Denise replied, eager to take a break from doing beans. Quickly she went to get the laundry basket.

Coming back through the kitchen, she overheard some of what Danelle was saying to Darla and Daryl, the younger helpers.

"Maybe we can do that," she ended.

"Maybe you can do what?" Denise asked with interest.

"Maybe we can do something," answered Darla.

"You will find out later," added Danelle.

*   *   *   *   *

"Beans, beans, beans. I'm tired of snapping all these beans," sighed ten-year-old Denise.

"We've finished over half the job." Her older sister Danelle tried to give some encouragement. "Denise, would you like to hang out the laundry? The washer just stopped."

"Certainly," Denise replied, eager to take a break from doing beans. Quickly she went to get the laundry basket.

Coming back through the kitchen, she overheard some of what Danelle was saying to Darla and Daryl, the younger helpers.

"Maybe we can," she ended.

"Can what?" Denise asked with interest.

"Something," answered Darla abruptly.

"You'll find out later," added Danelle.

Look again at the second sample above. There are several things that

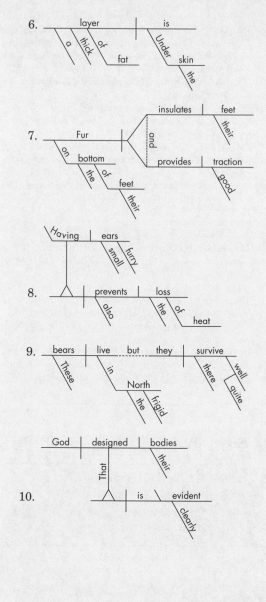

6.

7.

8.

9.

10.

Lesson Introduction: Imagine that ——— (name one of your own students) had come to school this morning and told us about a fire that broke out last evening. Can you imagine him talking like this?

Last evening after the chores were done, we were ready to go into the house. But Father said, "What do I smell?" He thought it came from the silo, so he started climbing up the silo. When he was halfway up, he knew the silage was on fire. He called the fire department. Soon the firemen came and put out the fire, and before long everything was back to normal.

No one would tell that kind of story in such a manner. Yet students sometimes *write* like this. What excitement must have been a part of this experience! But how poorly that excitement is shown! In fact, the story really does not *show* much at all; it merely *tells*. Using a good style calls the writer to *show* the characters and events in a story.

Lesson Outline:

   1. In a story, use dialogue that sounds natural.

   a. Write quotations with contractions and incomplete sentences.

   b. Change speakers frequently. Begin a new paragraph each time a different person begins to speak.

   c. Use descriptive explanatory words.

   d. Avoid quotations with poor grammar and slang.

specially help to make the conversation sound natural. First, *the speak-* *rs use contractions* as we often do in real life. Second, *the speakers use* *ncomplete sentences.* Although these things are not acceptable in formal vriting, they do contribute to natural dialogue. Third, *the speakers change* *requently* from one to another. There should not be many long quotations n a story.

In dialogue, be careful to put quotation marks only where they belong. f a speaker says several sentences together, do not put quotation marks round every sentence. Put them only at the beginning and end of the vhole quotation. The words that simply tell the story should not be inside uotation marks.

Begin a new paragraph in your story each time you begin a new topic. lso begin a new paragraph each time a different person begins to speak.

Another way to write dialogue that shows rather than tells is to use escriptive explanatory words. *Said* is a good word; you should not be afraid o use it sometimes. But it is not very descriptive. Characters should *ask,* *vhisper, shout, complain, demand,* and *suggest* some of their words. Try o think of words that describe exactly *how* the speakers talk.

Sometimes writers think that natural-sounding dialogue should include oor grammar and slang. Although some people do use such expressions n their conversations, they are not necessary to make natural conversa- ions. Such expressions are unsuitable for Christian writing.

Lively Action Verbs

Another way to show the details of the story is to use lively action verbs s much as possible. If you use too many linking verbs and use the pas- ive voice too freely, your characters will seem motionless. Even verbs in he active voice can be used in a way that dulls the action of the story. But f you use lively, active verbs, your story will seem real—as if it were hap- ening right before your reader's eyes.

In each pair of examples, notice how much more effective the second xample is than the first.

Charlene's face <u>was</u> full of smiles again.
Charlene <u>smiled</u> freely again.

Later in the evening Mary Louise <u>was reminded</u> of her faul
Later in the evening Mother <u>reminded</u> Mary Louise of her

The wind <u>grew</u> strong. Soon the windows <u>were rattling</u> and
    branches <u>were tossing</u> in the storm.
The wind <u>increased</u> in strength. Soon the storm <u>rattled</u> the
    and <u>tossed</u> the tree branches.

2. **Use lively action verbs as much as possib**
    a. Too many linking verbs and passive vo
       verbs will make your characters seem r
       tionless.
    b. Poor use of active voice verbs also dulls
       action of the story.
    c. Lively, active verbs make the story s
       real—as if it were happening right be
       your reader's eyes.

3. **Use exact, descriptive words instea**
general ones.

Nominative case = used as a subject or predicate noun

Objective case = used as a direct object, an indirect object, or object of the prep.

Possesive case = used to show awnership

Exact, Descriptive Words

Still another help for showing rather than merely telling the story is to use specific words instead of general ones. Use words that paint definite, concrete word pictures. Specific words help your reader to know exactly what is happening in the story. They add color and interest. Do not write *building* if *woodshed* or *two-car garage* would give the reader a better picture. Do not write *walk* if *trudge, hike,* or *stroll* would show the story better.

Poor: Too general
> The animals in their pen had eaten all their food.
>
> Nevin went into the room, picked something up, and went out to the van in a hurry.

Better: More specific
> The rabbits in their hutch had eaten all their clover.
>
> Nevin dashed into the kitchen, grabbed his books from the table, and hurried out to the school van.

Merely tells:
> As Philip lay on the grass, he saw the clouds moving across the sky.
>
> Nancy felt the cold coming through her coat.

Shows descriptively:
> Philip lay on the warm grass. Above him large cumulus clouds floated across the sky.
>
> Nancy shivered in the bitter cold, which crept through her thin coat.

In some cases you do not need to state the character's relationship to a scene. If the preceding sentences clarify what that relationship is, simply describe the scene. Compare the following examples.

Weak: Too much emphasis on character's relationship to the scene
> Lowell parked his wheelchair before the large family room window. Suddenly he saw a large buck stepping out of the woods. He watched as it bounded across the narrow, rock-strewn meadow and leaped over the board fence.

Better: Proper emphasis on the scene itself
> Lowell parked his wheelchair before the large family room window. Suddenly a large buck stepped out of the woods. It bounded across the narrow, rock-strewn meadow and leaped over the board fence.

Class Practice

A. Tell how to change this dialogue so that it sounds more natural.

"Well, boys, according to the weatherman, we are in line for a big snowstorm," Father said as he came in from the barn.

"We are in line for a big snowstorm? When will it come?" said James.

"It should come sometime this afternoon," said Father. "We will eat a quick breakfast and get to work. There is much to do."

B. Change these sentences to include more lively action verbs.
1. Long before he had hoed all the bean rows, Wesley was tired.
2. Little Grant was pulled back from the fire by Rover's quick action.
3. There are several cars in the ditch on Barne's Hill.
4. Gloria walked across the lawn and looked into the bushes.

C. Change each sentence so that it uses exact, descriptive words.
1. Beth poured the drinks while Annette passed out the snack.
2. Gilbert and Brian saw the two birds making their nest in the tree.
3. As Richard went into the kitchen, he smelled apple pies baking.
4. Edith heard some bees, so she ran into the house.
5. Edward took another spoonful of the homemade ice cream.
6. Geraldine glanced out the window to see if the boys were coming. She saw that rain was pouring down and a strong wind was blowing. (Change the second sentence so that it describes the scene without referring to the character.)

Written Exercises

A. Rewrite this dialogue so that it sounds more natural.

"Did you hear that we are moving to Delaware?" said Mildred.

"No, I did not hear that. When are you moving?" said Anna.

"We will move after school is over," said Mildred. "Father bought a farm with two big chicken houses."

"Is the house big?" said Anna.

"Oh, the house is fairly big. There is a really big lawn out in front," said Mildred.

B. Rewrite these sentences to include more lively action verbs.
1. Little Timmy was excited.
2. Miriam was hit in the back by the fast-moving ball.
3. Although the weather was chilly, it was a sunny day.
4. The firewood was put in a neat stack by Harry and Lee.
5. This part of the garden is the responsibility of Alma and Lisa.

B. (Sample answers.)
1. Little Timmy jumped up and down, clapping his hands in excitement.
2. The swiftly moving ball struck Miriam in the back.
3. The bright sunshine tempered the chilliness of the day.
4. Harry and Lee stacked the firewood neatly.
5. Alma and Lisa tend this part of the garden.

Lesson 109 Answers

Class Practice

(Encourage a variety of answers in these exercises.)

A. (Improvements are underlined.)

"Well, boys, according to the weatherman, we're in line for a big snowstorm," Father announced as he came in from the barn.

"A big snowstorm? When?" James asked.

"Sometime this afternoon," replied Father. "We'll eat a quick breakfast and get to work. There's much to do."

B. (Sample answers.)
1. Long before he had hoed all the bean rows, Wesley's arms and back ached with weariness.
2. With one great bound, Rover reached little Grant and yanked him back from the fire.
3. Several cars slid into the ditch on Barne's Hill.
4. Gloria tiptoed across the lawn and peeked into the bushes.

C. (Sample answers.)
1. Beth poured the lemonade while Annette passed out the pretzels.
2. Gilbert and Brian watched the robins building their nest in the maple tree.
3. As Richard stepped into the kitchen, his nose was teased by the delicious aroma of baking apple pies.
4. The warning buzz of the angry bees chased Edith into the house.
5. As Edward took another spoonful, he savored the cool sweetness of the homemade ice cream.

   or "M-m-m! Homemade ice cream! My favorite dessert!" Edward murmured over another spoonful.
6. The wind-driven rain lashed against the windowpane.

   or In wave after wave, great sheets of rain billowed across the meadow.

Written Exercises

A. (Sample improvements are underlined.)

"Did you hear that we're moving to Delaware?" asked Mildred.

"No! When?" asked Anna.

"After school is over," answered Mildred. "Father bought a farm with two big chicken houses."

"Is the house big?" asked Anna.

"Oh, fairly big. There's a really big lawn out in front," replied Mildred.

C. Rewrite these sentences, replacing the underlined words with more specific words.
1. In the corner of the <u>room</u> stood a <u>stove</u>. Occasionally Amos <u>walked</u> over and <u>put</u> <u>something</u> into it.
2. "Glen, have you fed your <u>pets</u>?" asked Father.
3. After <u>this</u> class we have <u>a time to eat</u>.
4. The two girls <u>talked quietly</u> for <u>a little while</u>. Then they <u>got</u> up and <u>went</u> over to Mother.
5. A <u>nice</u> <u>flower</u> brightened the small kitchen.

D. Rewrite these sentences, using more descriptive language and omitting the mention of story characters.
1. As the wind blew in from the orchard, Gerald could smell the apple blossoms.
2. Marie suddenly heard a loud noise from the basement steps.
3. The family sat on the grass in the meadow. They saw a family of ducks going down to the pond. (Rewrite only the second sentence.)

Review Exercises

Read this poem, and do the exercises. [69, 94, 98]

My Part
O brook and breeze and blossom,
And robin in the tree,
You make a bliss of duty,
A joy of industry.

Teach me to work as blithely,
With willing hand and heart;
The world is full of labor,
And I must do my part.
—*Anonymous*

1. a. Which of the four kinds of rhythm does this poem have?
   b. How many feet are in each line?
2. Show the rhyming pattern of the first stanza.
3. Copy several examples of alliteration from the poem.
4. Copy an example of assonance from the poem.
5. Lines 3 and 4 must be understood at least partly in a figurative sense. Why? (Consider the antecedents of *You*.)

C. (Sample answers.)
1. In the corner of the <u>kitchen</u> stood a <u>wood stove</u>. Occasionally Amos <u>hobbled</u> over and <u>tossed</u> <u>another piece of firewood</u> into it.
2. "Glen, have you fed your <u>puppies</u>?" asked Father.
3. After <u>reading</u> class we have <u>lunch</u>.
4. The two girls <u>whispered</u> for a <u>few minutes</u>. Then they <u>jumped</u> up and <u>skipped</u> over to Mother.
5. A <u>beautiful</u> <u>geranium</u> brightened the small kitchen.

D. (Sample answers.)
1. Drifting in from the orchard, the breeze carried the sweet smell of apple blossoms.
2. Suddenly a loud crash sounded from the basement steps.
3. A mother duck with her six ducklings waddled down to the pond.

Review Exercises
1. a. iambic   b. three
2. abcb
3. brook, breeze, blossom; with, willing; hand, heart
4. blossom, robin
5. A brook, a breeze, and a blossom do not know anything about bliss and joy (or about duty and industry).

110. Colons and Semicolons

Lesson Survey

- Use a **colon** to separate the numbers in Scripture references and in expressions of time.
- Use a colon after the greeting of a business letter.
- Use a colon to introduce a list, statement, question, or formal quotation.
- Use a **semicolon** to join independent clauses when no conjunction is used, when a conjunctive adverb is used, or when commas are already used in one or more of the clauses.
- Use a semicolon to separate items in a series when the individual items contain commas.

Compared with commas, colons and semicolons are not used very often. But they also have important functions.

Colons

1. *Use a colon to separate the numbers in Scripture references and in expressions of time.*

Matthew 1:21	8:30 A.M.
Ephesians 6:10–18	9:02 P.M.

2. *Use a colon after the greeting of a business letter.*

Dear Sir: Dear Mr. Daniels:

3. *Use a colon to introduce a list, statement, question, or formal quotation.* In this use the colon is like an arrow, directing the reader's attention ahead to what comes next. The expression *as follows* or *the following* often comes before a colon used in this way.

A formal quotation is a notable statement, often made by someone of high rank. When a formal quotation follows a colon, the quotation should be enclosed in quotation marks and begin with a capital letter. If a colon is used before some other statement or question, it may also begin with a capital letter, especially if it is long.

Introducing a list:
  For the test you will need the following items: paper, a pencil, and an eraser.

Lesson 110

Purpose: To study the correct use of colons and semicolons.

Oral Review:
1. When are single quotation marks used? (when there is a quotation within a quotation)
2. Which marks of punctuation are always placed inside quotation marks? (comma, period)
3. When is a question mark or an exclamation point placed outside quotation marks? (when the whole sentence is a question or an exclamation, but the quotation is not)
4. What kind of adjective clause needs to be set off with commas? (nonrestrictive)
5. What three tests can you use to decide if two descriptive adjectives should be separated by a comma? (Do you pause between the adjectives as you read them? Does it sound right to use *and* between the adjectives? Does it sound right to change the order of the adjectives?)
6. How can you tell whether a word like *early* is an adjective or an adverb? (It is an adjective if it modifies a substantive; an adverb if it modifies a verb, an adjective, or another adverb.)
7. How can you tell whether a word like *down* is an adverb or a preposition? (It is an adverb if it stands alone; a preposition if it has an object.)
8. How can you tell whether a word like *before* is a preposition or a conjunction? (It is a preposition if it introduces a phrase; a conjunction if it introduces a clause.)

Lesson Introduction: Challenge the students to see how many different valid references they can make from Psalm 1234 by inserting punctuation. Psalm 1:234? (Obviously not.) Psalm 12:34? (No; Psalm 12

Introducing a statement:

The people of Israel had a serious problem: They had learned the way of the heathen. (*or* ... problem: they ...)

Introducing a question:

If you wonder what to do, consider this: What would Jesus do?

Introducing a formal quotation:

Before Abraham Lincoln was elected president, he gave this warning from the Bible: "A house divided against itself cannot stand."

The words before a colon should make a complete thought by themselves. Therefore, a colon must never be used between a verb and its complements or between a preposition and its objects.

Incorrect:	Some qualities of a good worker are: diligence, perseverance, and enthusiasm.
Correct:	Some qualities of a good worker are diligence, perseverance, and enthusiasm.
	Some qualities of a good worker are as follows: diligence, perseverance, and enthusiasm.
Incorrect:	Large deposits of coal have been found in: Asia, North America, and Europe.
Correct:	Large deposits of coal have been found in Asia, North America, and Europe.
	Large deposits of coal have been found in these continents: Asia, North America, and Europe.

Semicolons

1. *Use a semicolon to join independent clauses when no conjunction is used, when a conjunctive adverb is used, or when commas are already used in one or more of the clauses.* A comma is not strong enough to hold two clauses together alone or with just a conjunctive adverb; the semicolon provides a stronger link. When commas are used between small units (words or phrases), semicolons are often used between larger units (clauses).

Anna vacuumed the carpet; Ida washed the windows.
Anna vacuumed the carpet; meanwhile, Ida washed the windows.
Anna, the oldest girl in the family, vacuumed the carpet; and Ida, our cousin from Alberta, washed the windows.

2. *Use a semicolon to separate items in a series when the individual items contain commas.* If only commas are used, it is hard to tell which ones are separating items in the series and which ones are doing something else.

has only eight verses.) Psalm 123:4? (Yes.) Other possibilities are Psalm 1:2–3:4 and Psalm 12:3, 4.

Lesson Outline:

1. *Learn the following rules for using colons.*

   (1) *Use a colon to separate the numbers in Scripture references and in expressions of time.*

   (2) *Use a colon after the greeting of a business letter.*

   (3) *Use a colon to introduce a list, statement, question, or formal quotation.*

   a) The expression *as follows* or *the following* often comes before a colon that introduces a list.

   b) A formal quotation should be enclosed in quotation marks and begin with a capital letter.

   c) The words before a colon should make a complete thought by themselves. Therefore, a colon must never be used between a verb and its complements or between a preposition and its objects.

2. *Learn the following rules for using semicolons.*

   (1) *Use a semicolon to join independent clauses when no conjunction is used, when a conjunctive adverb is used, or when commas are already used in one or more of the clauses.*

   (*Teacher:* Commas within clauses do not always mean that commas between clauses must be replaced by semicolons. For example, when a comma sets off an introductory word or a noun of direct address, the comma between

The semicolons are needed to show clearly the breaks between the items in the series.

> The speakers at the all-day meeting were Conrad Baer, a minister from Pennsylvania; Leland Snyder, a bishop from Indiana; and Henry Showalter, a minister from Wisconsin.

Class Practice

Tell where colons, semicolons, and capital letters are needed in these sentences.

1. The problem is simple to summarize the boys have gotten careless with their chores.
2. We were late, furthermore, we were warm and tired.
3. We finally arrived at 830 in the evening by then most of the work had been done.
4. This morning Brother Richard read from Jeremiah 35 1–17.
5. The Rechabites remained faithful to their father's teaching, therefore, Jeremiah could use them as an object lesson.
6. Jonadab had given the following commandments to the Rechabites drink no wine, build no houses, and plant no vineyards or fields.
7. The seventh grade boys are Vernon, Allen, Marcus, and Edward, and the girls are Linda, Mary, Nancy, Velma, and Ada Mae.
8. Grandmother Beiler is scheduled for tests at the hospital on the following dates Monday, April 6, Wednesday, April 15, and Thursday, April 16.

Written Exercises

A. Write these times and Bible references, using numerals.
1. a quarter to eight
2. twelve minutes after three
3. the eighteenth verse of Psalm 22
4. the first verse of 1 John 3

B. Copy each word that should be followed by a colon or semicolon, and add the correct punctuation mark. You will need to change some commas to colons or semicolons.
1. Brother Melvin began his sermon with these words "Every way of a man is right in his own eyes."
2. We should not stay the same we should grow and improve.
3. Most people do not plan to fail they fail to plan.
4. Success does not come easily we need to persevere to earn it.
5. If we are sad, our work seems long, hard, and tiresome but when we are cheerful, the time moves faster and is more enjoyable.
6. Four kinds of arthropods are as follows insects, arachnids, crustaceans, and myriapods.

two clauses is usually retained.

> Yes, Anna has swept the floor, and Ida has washed the windows.
> Lisa, if it starts raining, please bring in the laundry.)

(2) *Use a semicolon to separate items in a series when the individual items contain commas.*

★ **EXTRA PRACTICE**
Worksheet 56 (*Colons and Semicolons*)

Lesson 110 Answers

Class Practice
(Corrections are underlined.)
1. The problem is simple to summarize: The boys have gotten careless with their chores. (Capitalization is optional.)
2. We were late; furthermore, we were warm and tired.
3. We finally arrived at 8:30 in the evening; by then most of the work had been done.
4. This morning Brother Richard read from Jeremiah 35:1–17.
5. The Rechabites remained faithful to their father's teaching; therefore, Jeremiah could use them as an object lesson.
6. Jonadab had given the following commandments to the Rechabites: drink no wine, build no houses, and plant no vineyards or fields.
7. The seventh grade boys are Vernon, Allen, Marcus, and Edward; and the girls are Linda, Mary, Nancy, Velma, and Ada Mae.
8. Grandmother Beiler is scheduled for tests at the hospital on the following dates: Monday, April 6; Wednesday, April 15; and Thursday, April 16.

Written Exercises
A. 1. 7:45
   2. 3:12
   3. Psalm 22:18
   4. 1 John 3:1

B. 1. words:
   2. same;
   3. fail;
   4. easily;
   5. tiresome;
   6. follows:

7. I know all three girls on this picture Anita Brandt, Cynthia Diller, and Elsie Fisher.
8. Petroleum is used to make products like these gasoline, kerosene, asphalt, paint, and plastic.
9. The school board members are Joseph Wyler, the chairman, Nathan Charlton, the vice-chairman, Clyde Ehst, the secretary, Maurice Sauder, the treasurer, and Ethan Gehman, the assistant secretary-treasurer.
10. It rained for two hours then the sky suddenly cleared.

C. Copy the word just before each punctuation error. Add the correct punctuation mark, or omit any unnecessary mark.
1. If you want peaches, you will find them on the bottom shelf, and if you want cherries, they are on the top shelf.
2. Purple martins migrate far, they fly to Brazil.
3. The three breeds of dogs with the highest registration in the American Kennel Club are: Labrador retrievers, rottweilers, and cocker spaniels.
4. Across the front wall of our schoolroom are lettered these words from Proverbs 4 "Wisdom is the principal thing; therefore get wisdom: and with all thy getting get understanding."
5. The Bible is God's eternal Word, nevertheless, many people reject its authority.

Review Exercises

A. Copy each underlined word, and label it *adj.* or *adv.* [86]
1. Much of David's <u>early</u> youth was spent as a <u>lowly</u> shepherd.
2. As his <u>lovely</u> psalms indicate, he often longed to draw <u>near</u> to God.
3. God dealt <u>kindly</u> with David, and David became a <u>godly</u> man.

B. Copy each underlined word, and label it *adv.* or *prep.* [89]
1. When Mother called us <u>in</u> for lunch, we raced <u>up</u> the lane.
2. <u>In</u> the kitchen we found a delicious meal spread <u>out</u> for us.
3. An eagle soared <u>up</u> <u>above</u> the clouds.

C. Copy each underlined word, and label it *prep.* or *conj.* [89, 95]
1. <u>After</u> Jonah had delivered his message, the people of Nineveh repented <u>before</u> the Lord.
2. Isaiah was told to prophesy <u>until</u> the cities were wasted <u>without</u> inhabitants.
3. The people on the storm-tossed ship waited <u>until</u> dawn <u>before</u> they tried to steer the ship to the land.

---

7. picture:
8. these:
9. chairman; vice-chairman; secretary; treasurer;
10. hours;

C. 1. shelf;   4. 4:
2. far;   5. Word;
3. are

Review Exercises
A. 1. early—adj.; lowly—adj.
2. lovely—adj.; near—adv.
3. kindly—adv.; godly—adj.

B. 1. in—adv.; up—prep.
2. In—prep.; out—adv.
3. up—adv.; above—prep.

C. 1. After—conj.; before—prep.
2. until—conj.; without—prep.
3. until—prep.; before—conj.

11. Italics (Underlining)

> ### Lesson Survey
>
> - Use **italics** for the title of a book, magazine, newspaper, pamphlet, periodical, or book-length poem.
> - Use italics for the specific name of a ship, aircraft, train, spacecraft, and so on.
> - Use italics for a word, letter, number, or symbol that is the subject of discussion.
> - Italics may be used occasionally for special emphasis.

Italics are a special style of lettering used in printed material. Letters printed in italics slant to the right—*like this.* In handwritten or typewritten material, italics are indicated by underlining.

The following rules describe various places where italics (underlining) should be used.

1. *Use italics for the title of a book, magazine, newspaper, pamphlet, periodical, or book-length poem.* If *a, an,* or *the* is the first word in a book title, it should be italicized along with the rest of the title. However, these words are not italicized when they are the first word in the title of a magazine or newspaper. The titles of short stories, short poems, and songs are not written in italics. Instead, they are enclosed in quotation marks (as you learned in Lesson 107).

> Have you read many stories in the *Christian Example?*
> The story "Better Late" in *Cherry Cobbler* illustrates how God cares for His people in unusual ways.
> Mr. Benson said that he had read about the fire in the *Lancaster New Era.*

2. *Use italics for the specific name of a ship, aircraft, train, spacecraft, and so on.*

> Christian Burkholder came to the New World on the ship *Phoenix.*
> The *Shasta Daylight,* a train on the Southern Pacific Railroad, began service on July 10, 1949.

3. *Use italics for a word, letter, number, or symbol that is the subject of discussion.* In other words, you are referring to this item as a word or symbol; you are not using it in its normal sense.

> The word *bury* rhymes with *hairy,* not with *hurry.*
> The *#* before that *5* means "number."

Lesson 111

Purpose: To teach the proper use of *italics (underlining).

Oral Review:

1. Name three standard places where the colon is used. (in Scripture references, in expressions of time, after the greeting of a business letter)
2. A colon should never come between a verb and its ——— or between a preposition and its ———. (complements; objects)
3. In what three cases should a semicolon be used to join independent clauses? (when no conjunction is used, when a conjunctive adverb is used, when commas are already used in one or more of the clauses)
4. When should a semicolon be used to separate items in a series? (when the individual items contain commas)
5. When is a question mark or an exclamation point placed outside quotation marks? (when the whole sentence is a question or an exclamation, but the quotation is not)
6. Which voice of verbs should be used more frequently: active or passive? (active)
7. Name two situations in which it may be suitable to use the passive voice. (when there is no clear doer of the action, when there is a good reason not to name the doer of the action)

Lesson Introduction: Challenge a student to come to the board and write (or print) "How are you?" with *you* in italics. If you have no brave volunteers, assign someone to try it. Then evaluate with the class how clearly the "italics" shows. Since our writing cannot show italics as clearly as a printer can with his special type, what do we do instead? (underline) And even if Susie writes beautifully and thinks she

Your *e*'s and *l*'s look the same. (Italicize only the letter or symbol, not the apostrophe and *s* that may follow.)

4. *Italics may be used occasionally for special emphasis.* This kind of emphasis should be used sparingly. If italics are used too often, they lose their meaning.

Are you *sure* you brought the ball inside yesterday?

Class Practice

A. Tell where italics and quotation marks are needed. A word printed in all capital letters is to receive special emphasis.
1. Jeff gave a report on the book The Lim Family of Singapore.
2. Is Joy to the World in the Christian Hymnal?
3. Be careful to dot your i's and cross your t's.
4. I enjoyed the story Worth More Than Money in the Christian Pathway.
5. Can you use doesn't to start a sentence that is not a question?
6. We were not planning to buy THAT kind of meat.
7. The front page of the Daily Times has a picture of the accident.
8. The Titanic was not unsinkable as her owners had boasted.

B. On the chalkboard, write the following sentence four times: "The Lord is my shepherd." Emphasize a different word in each sentence.

Written Exercises

A. Copy the words that should be written in italics or enclosed in quotation marks, and mark them correctly. A word printed in all capital letters is to receive special emphasis.
1. John Bunyan wrote The Pilgrim's Progress while he was in prison.
2. The poem Others is found in Poems for Memorization.
3. Long ago, the word conversation referred to a person's general conduct.
4. The a in Babel may be pronounced as a long or a short vowel.
5. Though God sees everything, the fool thinks that God will not see HIM.
6. Carefully print Maps on the front cover.
7. Cherubim and seraphim are the plural forms of cherub and seraph.
8. The s in island is silent.
9. Robert E. Peary designed the Roosevelt for his expedition to the North Pole.
10. On January 31, 1958, the United States launched its first man-made satellite, Explorer I.
11. In 1927, Charles Lindbergh flew the Spirit of St. Louis from New York to Paris.
12. I just read It Did Not Pay in the Christian Pathway.

Lesson 111 Answers

Class Practice

A. 1. *The Lim Family of Singapore*
2. "Joy to the World", *Christian Hymnal*
3. *i*'s, *t*'s
4. "Worth More Than Money", *Christian Pathway*
5. *doesn't* (*Teacher:* The following sentence starts with *doesn't* and is not a question: "*Doesn't* is a contraction.")
6. *that*
7. *Daily Times*
8. *Titanic*

B. 1. The Lord is my shepherd.
2. The Lord is my shepherd.
3. The Lord is my shepherd.
4. The Lord is my shepherd.

Written Exercises

A. 1. The Pilgrim's Progress
2. "Others", Poems for Memorization
3. conversation
4. a, Babel
5. him
6. Maps
7. Cherubim, seraphim, cherub, seraph
8. s, island
9. Roosevelt
10. Explorer I
11. Spirit of St. Louis
12. "It Did Not Pay", Christian Pathway

can write in italics, she must still underline! Sorry, no exceptions.

Today's lesson shows various places where italics (underlining) should be used.

Lesson Outline:

1. Use italics for the title of a book, magazine, newspaper, pamphlet, periodical, or book-length poem.

    a. If *a, an,* or *the* is the first word in a book title, italicize it along with the rest of the title.

    b. Do not italicize *a, an,* or *the* when it is the first word in the title of a magazine or newspaper.

    c. The title of a short story, short poem, or song is not written in italics. Instead, it is enclosed in quotation marks.

2. Use italics for the specific name of a ship, aircraft, train, spacecraft, and so on.

3. Use italics for a word, letter, number, or symbol that is the subject of discussion. Italicize only the item itself, not the apostrophe and *s* that may follow.

4. Italics may be used occasionally for special emphasis.

3. Write a sentence to illustrate each of the four rules in this lesson.

Review Exercises

A. Rewrite these sentences, changing the verbs to the active voice. Do not change the tense. [53]
1. The people of Nineveh were moved to repentance by Jonah's preaching.
2. By the time of Nahum, the message of God had been rejected by the Ninevites.
3. The total destruction of Nineveh was prophesied by Nahum.
4. The needed materials will be ordered by the treasurer.
5. Students are assigned by the teacher to help with the cleaning.

B. The passive voice is used in the numbered sentences. For each one, write the letter of the statement which correctly describes that sentence. [54]
   a. The active voice would be more effective.
   b. There is no clear doer of the action.
   c. There is a good reason not to name the doer.
1. The force of gravity is constantly exerted on our bodies.
2. The wood was stacked neatly by the boys.
3. Our shop was broken into last night.
4. The glad news of Uncle Lee's healing was told us by Mother.

---

112. Story Writing: The First Draft

Lesson Survey
- To begin writing a story, make a careful plan to use as a guide.
- Write the first draft of the story.

Now that you have studied several elements of a good story, it is time for you to write a story of your own! This lesson deals with the first draft, showing you how to proceed step by step to write your own story.

Planning

A good story, like most things in life, is not produced automatically. It is accomplished by careful planning, writing, and rewriting. Before you

B. (Individual work.)

Review Exercises

A. 1. Jonah's preaching moved the people of Nineveh to repentance.
   2. By the time of Nahum, the Ninevites had rejected the message of God.
   3. Nahum prophesied the total destruction of Nineveh.
   4. The treasurer will order the needed materials.
   5. The teacher assigns students to help with the cleaning.

B. 1. b
   2. a
   3. c
   4. a

---

conflict involve greater emotion)
6. (a) What is the most intense incident of the conflict? (b) Where should it occur? (a. climax; b. near the end of the story)
7. A good story does not merely *tell;* it ———. (shows)
8. What are some things that help to make dialogue sound natural? (contractions, incomplete sentences, frequent change of speakers, descriptive explanatory words)
9. What are some other things that help you to show, rather than merely tell, a story? (lively action verbs, specific words rather than general ones)

Lesson Introduction: An experienced baker does not take his recipe and immediately begin throwing ingredients into his bowl. He does a bit of planning first. He may check to be sure that all the ingredients are on hand. He may gather his utensils together. Then when the actual mixing process begins, the work progresses smoothly.

Lesson 112

Purpose: To teach how to write the first draft of a story.

Oral Review:
1. How many main characters should a story have? (one)
2. When should the main character be introduced? (at the very beginning)
3. What are three common ways of revealing the traits of a story character? (by the character's actions, words, and thoughts)
4. What are the three main kinds of conflict? (main character in conflict with another person, with his circumstances, and with his own self)
5. How can the conflict build up in intensity during the story? (by having more than one incident of the conflict; by having later incidents of the conflict involve greater emotion)

write a single sentence of your story, you should do some planning to guide your writing process.

1. *Have a definite purpose and conflict in mind.* If your story is to move smoothly and purposefully from beginning to end, you must have a clear idea of what the purpose is and what problem is to be solved in the story. You will find it helpful to write out the purpose and the conflict. Then if you list each incident of the conflict, you will have a clear guide for the actual writing of the story. The following example is for the story "Pitch or Patch?" in Lesson 102.

Purpose:
A girl learns to appreciate the meaning of stewardship.
Conflict:
The girl wonders why her mother must patch torn clothes instead of throwing them away. Her family could afford to buy new clothes.
Incident one:
She tears her dress and realizes that she will need to wear a patched dress to school.
Incident two:
She sees her mother patching her brother's trousers.
Incident three:
She puts on her dress for school and has a sickening feeling of dread about wearing a patched dress to school.
Incident four: Climax
She sees a patch on her teacher's shirtsleeve and comes to realize that there is nothing wrong with patched clothes.

2. *Have a clear picture of the main character and of any other important characters.* You need to know exactly what kind of personality your characters have so that their actions, words, and thoughts are consistent throughout the story.

Writing

After you have the story planned, you are ready to write. The first copy of the story should be written on every other line so that you can more easily proofread it later.

3. *Write a good beginning for the story.* As you learned in Lesson 102, the story beginning should introduce the main character very early. In fact, the first person mentioned should be the main character. You learned in Lesson 105 that the story conflict should also be introduced early. In addition, the first several paragraphs should indicate something about the setting of the

---

In this lesson your students will be the "bakers." Instead of baking beautiful golden loaves of bread, they will be producing stories. (We'll wait until later to decide if they are "beautiful and golden"!) Like the baker, a writer must do some careful planning before he begins actually writing.

Lesson Outline:

1. To write a good story, first have a definite purpose and conflict in mind. It would be good to write out the purpose and the conflict and to list each incident of the conflict.

2. Have a clear picture of the main character and of any other important characters. This enables you to keep each character's actions, words, and thoughts consistent throughout the story.

3. Write a good beginning for the story.
  a. Introduce the main character very early.
  b. Introduce the conflict early.
  c. Indicate something about the setting.

4. Write the middle part of the story.
  a. Develop the various incidents of the conflict.
  b. Build up the intensity of the conflict to the climax, which should be very near the end of the story.

5. Write a short conclusion to the story.
  a. Close the story quickly after the climax.
  b. Do not directly state the lesson of the story.

6. Write an interesting title for the story.
  a. Keep it short, seldom over five words.
  b. Make it catchy so that the reader wants to read the story.
  c. Do not give away the outcome of the story.

story—the place and time that it occurred.

Look again at the sample story in Lesson 102. The first paragraph introduces Evelyn, the main character. It also hints at the conflict by mentioning the tear in her dress skirt. By the third paragraph, you know that the place of the story includes Evelyn's home and school and that the time is during the school term.

4. *Write the middle part of the story.* Here in the main part of the story, the various incidents of the conflict are developed. Remember to make the conflict build up in intensity to the climax, which should be very near the end of the story.

5. *Write a short conclusion to the story.* After the climax is reached, the story should close quickly. Be sure you do not directly state the lesson that the story is to teach. Have the main character *show* the lesson by his actions, words, or thoughts.

6. *Write an interesting title for the story.* Sometimes you may have a good title before you start writing. But more often you will need to think one up later.

A title should seldom be more than five words long. It should catch the reader's attention and make him want to read the story. A good title never gives away the outcome of the story.

Good: Pitch or Patch?
Poor: Evelyn Learns to Appreciate Good Stewardship (too long; gives away the outcome)

Good: Wheelchairs and Braces
Poor: How I Learned to Accept My Braces (too long; gives away the outcome)

Written Exercises

A. Plan a story, following Steps 1 and 2 in the lesson. Show the plan to your teacher before you go on to Part B. Here are some ideas for stories.

A missionary child facing adjustments
A girl baking her first cake
A student's first day at a new school
Apologizing for doing wrong
Two brothers in charge of chores while Father is away

B. Write the first draft of your story, following Steps 3 through 6.

Lesson 112 Answers

Written Exercises
(Individual work.)

Teacher: Since Parts A and B in Written Exercises are both major assignments, you may want to assign them on two separate days.

113. Apostrophes and Hyphens

Lesson Survey

- Use an **apostrophe** to show the possessive case of a noun or an indefinite pronoun.

- Use an apostrophe in a contraction to show where one or more letters have been omitted.

- Use an apostrophe to make the plural form of a letter, symbol, digit, or word used as the subject of discussion.

- Use a **hyphen** to join some compound words.

- Use a hyphen to divide a word between syllables at the end of a line.

- Use a hyphen to show a series of connected verses in a Scripture reference.

Most punctuation marks help to show relationships among words in sentences. Apostrophes and hyphens are different in that they are more directly related to the spelling of individual words.

Apostrophes

1. *Use an apostrophe to show the possessive case of a noun or an indefinite pronoun.* In Lesson 24 you learned the following three rules for the formation of possessive nouns.

a. The possessive form of most singular nouns is made by adding *'s*. This includes nouns that end with a single *s* or *z* sound. Words like *Moses* and *Jesus* contain two *s* or *z* sounds in the last syllable. Adding a third *s* or *z* sound makes the word awkward to pronounce.

    my father's car   Moses' sister
    Charles's glasses   Jesus' disciples

b. The possessive form of plural nouns not ending with *-s* is made by adding *'s*.

    children's songs   brothers-in-law's business

c. The possessive form of plural nouns ending with *-s* is made by adding only an apostrophe.

    girls' bouquets   attorney generals' offices

The possessive form of an indefinite pronoun is made in the same way

Lesson 113

Purpose: To review the correct use of apostrophes and hyphens.

Oral Review:

1. How do you show italics in handwritten or typewritten material? (by underlining)
2. What kinds of titles should be italicized? (titles of books, magazines, newspapers, pamphlets, periodicals, and book-length poems)
3. What kinds of names should be italicized? (names of ships, aircraft, trains, spacecraft, and so on)
4. (*a*) What are ellipsis points? (*b*) When are they used? (*a*. three spaced periods; *b*. to show where material is omitted in a quotation, to show that a sentence trails off without a proper ending)
5. When should commas be used to separate an adjective clause from the rest of the sentence? (when it is nonrestrictive)
6. Tell whether the following groups of words are usually used with singular or plural verbs.
   a. shears, pliers, trousers, glasses (plural)
   b. each, either, one, everybody (singular)
   c. news, mumps, mathematics, electronics (singular)
7. With a collective noun, when should you use (*a*) a singular verb? (*b*) a plural verb? (*a*. Use a singular verb when the collective noun refers to the group doing one thing together. *b*. Use a plural verb when the collective noun refers to the individual members doing different things.)

Lesson Introduction: Write this sentence twice on the board, exactly the same.

"Well work for a while longer," Father said.

as that of a singular noun. However, be sure that you do *not* use *'s* for personal pronouns.

somebody's paper   theirs (*not* their's)
no one's answer   its cage (*not* it's cage)

2. *Use an apostrophe in a contraction to show where one or more letters have been omitted.*

<u>It's</u> too bad <u>they're</u> not coming. <u>It is</u> too bad <u>they are</u> not coming.
<u>Don't</u> worry; <u>we'll</u> do it. <u>Do not</u> worry; <u>we will</u> do it.

3. *Use an apostrophe to make the plural form of a letter, symbol, digit, or word used as the subject of discussion.* Remember to italicize (underline) any of these characters used as the subject of discussion.

Her *T*'s look like *F*'s.
On an electronic calculator, *2*'s are the exact reverse of *5*'s.
Avoid using *&*'s in formal writing; write out the word *and*.
Do not link a string of clauses with *and*'s and *but*'s.

Hyphens

1. *Use a hyphen to join some compound words.* The following groups of words deserve special mention.
   a. Compound number words from *twenty-one* through *ninety-nine*.

   thirty-four   eighty-eight   two hundred sixty-one

   b. Fractions written in words. A hyphen is placed between the numerator and denominator unless either word already contains a hyphen.

   one-half inch
   three-tenths of a mile
   twenty-three hundredths of an inch

   c. Words ending with *in-law*.

   father-in-law   daughters-in-law

   d. Compound words beginning with *great* that refer to relatives.

   great-grandfather   Great-aunt Matilda

   e. Compound words beginning with *self*.

   self-confident   self-reliant
   self-righteous   self-discipline

   f. Many compound adjectives, when the two words form a unit modifying a substantive.

Have one student punctuate the first sentence to say that Father is not helping with the work but is telling someone else to keep working. Have another student punctuate the second sentence to say that Father is helping with the work.

"Well, work for a while longer," Father said.
"We'll work for a while longer," Father said.

Lesson Outline:

1. Learn the following rules for using apostrophes.

(1) *Use an apostrophe to show the possessive case of a noun or an indefinite pronoun.*

(a) The possessive form of most singular nouns is made by adding *'s*. Words like *Jesus* and *Moses* are exceptions.

(b) The possessive form of plural nouns not ending with *-s* is made by adding *'s*.

(c) The possessive form of plural nouns ending with *-s* is made by adding only an apostrophe.

(d) The possessive form of an indefinite pronoun is made in the same way as that of a singular noun. However, do *not* use *'s* for personal pronouns.

(2) *Use an apostrophe in a contraction to show where one or more letters have been omitted.*

(3) *Use an apostrophe to make the plural form of a letter, symbol, digit, or word used as the subject of discussion.* Remember to italicize (underline) any of these characters used as the subject of discussion.

2. Learn the following rules for using hyphens.

(1) *Use a hyphen to join some compound words.*

(a) Compound number words from *twenty-one* through *ninety-nine*.

green-eyed cat   light-footed runner
air-conditioned office

Many compound words are written as one word; others are written as two separate words. Use a dictionary when you are not sure of the correct spelling.

2. *Use a hyphen to divide a word between syllables at the end of a line.* Divide a word at the end of a line only when necessary. When you must divide a word, be sure to divide only between syllables. Do not divide a word in such a way that a single letter is left at the beginning or end of a line. When you are not sure where to divide a word, check a dictionary.

Incorrect	Correct
His brother works at the cre-amery. (not divided between syllables)	His brother works at the cream-ery.
My voice became quite husk-y with my cold. (single letter left alone)	My voice became quite husky with my cold.
Uncle Levi has raised an a-bundance of corn. (single letter left alone)	Uncle Levi has raised an abun-dance of corn.

3. *Use a hyphen to show a series of connected verses in a Scripture reference.* The hyphen means "through." If you want to show a break in the series, use a comma.

We memorized Colossians 3:1–17.
Our lesson was taken from Zechariah 7:5–7, 9–14.

Class Practice

A. Tell how to make these words possessive. If no change is needed, say *none*.
1. princess
2. oxen
3. everybody
4. deer
5. babies
6. theirs
7. students
8. Moses

B. Tell how to spell the contractions for these words.
1. is not
2. you are
3. he will
4. will not
5. who is
6. I have

C. Find each error in the use of apostrophes or hyphens, and tell how to correct it.

(b) Fractions written in words.
(c) Words ending with *in-law.*
(d) Compound words beginning with *great* that refer to relatives.
(e) Compound words beginning with *self.*
(f) Many compound adjectives, when the two words form a unit modifying a substantive.
Use a dictionary when you are not sure how to spell a compound word.
(2) *Use a hyphen to divide a word between syllables at the end of a line.*
a) Divide a word at the end of a line only when necessary.
b) Be sure to divide only between syllables.
c) Do not divide a word in such a way that a single letter is left at the beginning or end of a line.

Lesson 113 Answers

Class Practice

A. 1. princess's
2. oxen's
3. everybody's
4. deer's
5. babies'
6. none
7. students'
8. Moses'

B. 1. isn't
2. you're
3. he'll
4. won't
5. who's
6. I've

d) If you are not sure where to divide a word, check a dictionary.
(3) *Use a hyphen to show a series of connected verses in a Scripture reference.*
(*Teacher:* In printed material, the short dash that means "through" is known as an en-dash [in distinction from the longer em-dash]. But in handwritten and typewritten material, an en-dash and a hyphen are the same punctuation mark.)

★ **EXTRA PRACTICE**
Worksheet 57 (*Italics, Apostrophes, and Hyphens*)

1. Matthew and Acts both have twenty eight chapter's.
2. Marks account of Jesus's life and ministry is the shortest.
3. Peters' self confidence led him to failure.
4. Along with correct pronunciation of words, well emphasize clear e-nunciation.
5. When my great grandparents moved to Virginia, their's was the only house along this road.
6. Nobodys house was in sight then; now theyre almost surrounded by houses.
7. Your es and as are blurred; youll need to clean the type in you're typewriter.
8. This paragraph has too many ands and buts; Im going to rewrite it.

Written Exercises

A. Write these compound words correctly. Use a dictionary if you are not sure of the correct spelling.
1. touchtype
2. carwash
3. blow-torch
4. trade mark
5. threedimensional
6. openminded

B. Write each word, using hyphens to show where you may divide the word at the end of a line.
1. extraordinary
2. consideration
3. apologetic
4. electricity

C. Write contractions for these words.
1. who will
2. does not
3. here is
4. they are

D. Write correctly the items that have errors in the use of apostrophes or hyphens.
1. Gods' people havent always enjoyed freedom from persecution.
2. Were commanded to pray for our ruler's so that we might be able to live quiet and peaceable lives.
3. Forms of the word *persecute* occur forty five times in the New Testament.
4. Of the twenty two pupils in the class, no ones answer was correct.
5. The embarrassment's that come from a persons impulsiveness are actually self inflicted wounds.
6. Several student's papers have been done carefully and neatly; their's are returned with As.
7. The one's who have'nt received a grade must proofread and rewrite their compositions.
8. In *repetitious,* the first two vowels are es and the next two are is.

C. 1. twenty-eight, chapters
2. Mark's, Jesus'
3. Peter's, self-confidence
4. we'll, enunciation
5. great-grandparents, theirs
6. Nobody's, they're
7. *e*'s, *a*'s, you'll, your
8. *and*'s, *but*'s, I'm

Written Exercises

A. 1. touch-type
2. car wash
3. blowtorch
4. trademark
5. three-dimensional
6. open-minded

B. 1. ex-traor-di-nary
2. con-sid-er-a-tion
3. apol-o-get-ic
4. elec-tric-i-ty

C. 1. who'll
2. doesn't
3. here's
4. they're

D. 1. God's, haven't
2. We're, rulers, able
3. forty-five
4. twenty-two, no one's
5. embarrassments, person's, self-inflicted
6. students', theirs, A's
7. ones, haven't
8. e's, i's

Review Exercises

Copy the words in parentheses that give the proper subject–verb agreement. [48]

1. (When's, When are) these assignments due?
2. It (don't, doesn't) look as if we'll be here long anymore.
3. Neither Loren nor Michael (have, has) read this book.
4. Mathematics (is, are) a field that includes arithmetic, geometry, and algebra.
5. Glenda's glasses (is, are) broken.
6. (There's, There are) a job for everyone to do.
7. Nathan, as well as Joshua, (is, are) working in the garden.
8. Esther and Miriam (clean, cleans) the upstairs this time.
9. Everybody (seem, seems) to be busy.
10. The family (have, has) scattered to (its, their) various chores.

---

114. Story Writing: The Second Draft

Lesson Survey

- To finish writing a story, proofread the first draft.
- Rewrite the story, making the changes you have marked.

Unless you are an exceptional writer, your job is by no means finished after you have written the first draft of a story. You must now improve the story by proofreading and rewriting it.

Proofreading

In Lesson 8 you worked with a number of marks that are used in proofreading. You will use the same proofreading marks when you improve a story.

"Oh, mother!" wailed Evelyn as the storm door closed behind her. "Look wat hapened!" Evelyn streched out her dress skirt to show mother a three-cornered tear.

"How did you do that?" asked Mother, laying her paring knife the on counter. She came to look at the rent.

Lesson 114

Purpose: To teach how to write the second draft of a story.

Oral Review:

1. What are the two steps in planning a story? (Have a definite conflict and purpose in mind. Have a clear picture of the main character and of any other important characters.)
2. What kind of written plan is a helpful guide for writing a story? (a plan that includes the purpose of the story, the main conflict, and each incident of the conflict)
3. What are the four steps in writing the first draft of a story? (Write a good beginning for the story. Write the middle part of the story. Write a short conclusion to the story. Write an interesting title for the story.)
4. What are some requirements for a good title? (It

Review Exercises

1. When are
2. doesn't
3. has
4. is
5. are
6. There's
7. is
8. clean
9. seems
10. have, their

---

should be short—seldom more than five words long. It should catch the reader's attention and make him want to read the story. It must not give away the outcome of the story.)

5. What are three ways of *showing* what happens in a story, rather than merely telling it? (Use dialogue that sounds natural. Use lively action verbs as much as possible. Use exact, descriptive words rather than general ones.)

Lesson Introduction: Have you ever written something and later wondered why you wrote such a thing? (This happens especially if we write something when we are upset.) The same thing can happen after we write a story. At the time of writing, our thoughts and feelings are so deeply involved that everything seems perfectly clear. But after the story "cools off," we find that some parts are not clear at all. And we find other mistakes, some of them almost embarrassing.

This is why it is best to write the first draft of a story, lay it aside for a time, and then revise and rewrite the story. Some professional writers admit to rewriting their compositions a dozen times or more!

Lesson Outline:

1. Proofread the first draft of your story. Mark corrections by using the proofreading marks that you worked with earlier. Also ask the following questions.

(1) Are the main character and the conflict introduced early?
(2) Are only necessary details included?
(3) Is the story written in a logical order?
(4) Is the conflict clear, and does it build up in intensity?
(5) Is the climax forceful? Does it occur very near the end of the story?
(6) Is the dialogue natural?
(7) Have you used lively action verbs as much as possible?
(8) Have you used specific words rather than general ones?

2. Write the story in its final form.

a. Write on every line, making the changes you have marked.
b. Have a neat paper, with good penmanship and proper margins.

In addition to things like spelling and punctuation, check the general content and structure of your story. Use the following questions.

1. Are the main character and the conflict introduced early?
2. Are only necessary details included?
3. Is the story written in a logical order?
4. Is the conflict clear, and does it build up in intensity?
5. Is the climax forceful? Does it occur very near the end of the story?
6. Is the dialogue natural?
7. Have you used lively action verbs as much as possible?
8. Have you used specific words rather than general ones?

Rewriting

For this step, you should write on every line, making the changes you have marked. Have your paper as neat as possible. Use good penmanship. Keep the left margin straight and the right margin as straight as possible.

> *"Oh, Mother!" wailed Evelyn as the storm door closed behind her. "Look what happened!" Evelyn stretched out her dress skirt to show Mother a three-cornered tear.*
> *"How did you do that?" asked Mother, laying her paring knife on the counter. She came to look at the rent.*

Written Exercises

A. Proofread the first draft of the story you wrote in Lesson 112. Use the proofreading marks you have learned, as well as the list of questions in this lesson.

B. Write the second draft of your story, making the improvements you have marked. Use every line, and write as neatly as you can.

---

115. Chapter 10 Review

Class Practice

A. Tell which words have errors in capitalization.

1. "But it is good for me to draw near to god: i have put my trust in the lord god" (Psalm 73:28).
2. The last Prophet of the old Testament was malachi.
3. In the year that king Uzziah died, isaiah saw a vision of the lord.
4. One of the gods of the philistines was dagon.

Lesson 115

Purpose: To review the concepts taught in Chapter 10.

Lesson 114 Answers

Written Exercises
(Individual work.)

Lesson 115 Answers

Class Practice
A. 1. God, I, Lord God
   2. prophet, Old, Malachi
   3. King, Isaiah, Lord
   4. Philistines, Dagon

5. My Uncle just bought a Honda Lawn Mower at Upton lawn and garden.
6. The president made a series of speeches in the midwest.
7. The State of Missouri lies just West of the Mississippi river.
8. a. **God gives his best**
   b. God knows, he loves, he cares;
   c. nothing this truth can dim;
   d. he gives his very best to those
   e. who leave the choice to him.

B. Tell where end marks, ellipsis points, and commas should be added.
   1. While you are young you can learn good habits more easily
   2. How much some older people long for power to undo wrong habits
   3. Are you my friend developing noble habits
   4. Well I want to do my best, but
   5. "Lay not up for yourselves treasures upon earth, but lay up for yourselves treasures in heaven" (Matthew 6:19, 20).
   6. The rich young ruler had treasures on earth but he failed to gain treasures in heaven.
   7. The persecuted faithful believers had their treasures in heaven.
   8. The apostle Paul who counted all things loss for Christ surely had his treasures in heaven Gerald.
   9. Peter James and John in fact left their fishing and followed Jesus.
   10. On December 12 1992 Brother Larry preached at our church in Lancaster Pennsylvania about having treasures in heaven.

C. Tell where quotation marks and other punctuation should be added. Also tell which words need capital letters.
   1. Anna asked has it started to rain already
   2. Leonard said I have closed all the doors Aaron reported
   3. Yes agreed Carolyn he was more careful this time
   4. Did Conrad say, I have the books
   5. What a shock to hear her say, "I don't care what the Bible says

D. Tell where colons and semicolons are needed.
   1. My grandfather has owned the following cars a 1918 Ford Model T, a 1921 Willys Knight, and a 1932 Ford Model A.
   2. A bright full moon was shining consequently, we could see the deer.
   3. On our trip we drove through Illinois, Kentucky, West Virginia, Maryland, and Pennsylvania.
   4. Before we moved, we sold Tony, our horse, Frisky, our goat, and Bessy, our cow.
   5. The Bible makes a strong statement about our tongues, "But the tongue can no man tame."

5. uncle, lawn mower, Lawn, Garden
6. President, Midwest
7. state, west, River
8. a. Gives His Best   d. He, His
   b. He, He   e. Who, Him
   c. Nothing

B. 1. young, easily.
   2. habits!
   3. you, friend, habits?
   4. Well, but . . .
   5. earth, . . .
   6. earth,
   7. persecuted,
   8. Paul, Christ, heaven,
   9. Peter, James, John, fact,
   10. 12, 1992, Lancaster, Pennsylvania,

C. (Corrections are underlined.)
   1. Anna asked, "Has it started to rain already?"
   2. "Leonard said, 'I have closed all the doors,'" Aaron reported.
   3. "Yes," agreed Carolyn, "he was more careful this time."
   4. Did Conrad say, "I have the books"?
   5. What a shock to hear her say, "I don't care what the Bible says"!

D. 1. cars:
   2. shining;
   3. (none)
   4. horse; goat;
   5. tongues:

E. Tell which words should be set off by italics or quotation marks.
1. The first song in both the Church Hymnal and the Christian Hymnal is Come, Thou Almighty King.
2. Do not write so carelessly that your 5's look like S's.
3. The Southern and the Royal Palm were two trains on the Southern Railway.
4. The weather map in the Morning Herald showed an approaching cold front.
5. The k in knife was not silent in Old English.

F. Identify the errors in the use of apostrophes and hyphens.
1. The three teacher's cars are parked in front of the building.
2. My brother in laws farm has thirty four acres of woodland.
3. Well stay at home this evening if the roads have become too slippery by then.
4. Sister Doris' great grandfather fled from Virginia to escape the Confederate Army.
5. My self confidence was badly shaken, but their's seemed unaffected.

G. In each pair, tell which sentence more effectively portrays the characteristics of the person. Also tell whether it reveals the character through *actions, words,* or *thoughts.*
1. a. After Brother Carl spoke to Mr. Lesher about the Gospel, he became angry.
   b. "How dare the man talk to me like that!" fumed Mr. Lesher to himself as Brother Carl walked away.
2. a. Annette skipped out the walk in the warm spring sunshine.
   b. The warm spring sunshine made Annette feel happy.
3. a. "Oh, you should never have done that!" interrupted Neil.
   b. Neil said that they should never have done that.

H. For each story described here, tell which of the three kinds of conflict is involved.
1. A girl feels frustrated at the ill will of another girl.
2. A boy is tempted with bitter thoughts because his grandmother's illness means he cannot spend the weekend with his cousin.
3. A boy finds a twenty-dollar bill under the seat of the car, and he wants to keep it without saying anything to his parents.

Written Exercises

A. Write correctly each word or abbreviation that has a capitalization error.
1. Mr. Morgan sipes, jr., lives on blue spruce road.
2. Has uncle lyle bought a new Ford Tractor?
3. Last Spring we memorized the song "Fresh from the throne of Glory."

E. 1. *Church Hymnal, Christian Hymnal,* "Come, Thou Almighty King"
   2. *5's, S's*
   3. *Southern, Royal Palm*
   4. *Morning Herald*
   5. *k, knife*

F. 1. teachers'
   2. brother-in-law's, thirty-four
   3. We'll, slippery
   4. Doris's, great-grandfather
   5. self-confidence, theirs

G. 1. b; thoughts
   2. a; actions
   3. a; words

H. 1. main character in conflict with another person
   2. main character in conflict with his circumstances
   3. main character in conflict with his own self

Written Exercises

A. 1. Sipes, Jr., Blue Spruce Road
   2. Uncle Lyle, tractor
   3. spring, From, Throne

4. after lunch we have Science and American History.

5. Is syracuse farther North than Buffalo?

6. Before the civil war, the south was dominated by Plantation owners.

B. Copy each word or abbreviation that should be followed by a comma, a colon, a semicolon, or an end mark, and add the correct punctuation.

1. Mr J B Knepper who is our neighbor wants to go to church with us today

2. Do you remember children how upset he was when we first invited him

3. What a tremendous change has taken place

4. Daryl help him into the car

5. We have tried to be a good witness indeed we have gone the second mile many times.

6. After the loss of our barn by fire many brethren came to help us.

7. When Mr. Knepper saw this response he was deeply impressed.

8. Yes I still remember his words vividly, "You people make me hungry to know more about Christianity."

9. God is working in the elderly man's life, maybe He will work through us.

10. We can pray testify and urge but only God can lead him to repentance.

C. Copy these sentences, and supply the missing punctuation and capitalization. Use quotation marks only when explanatory words clearly indicate a direct quotation.

1. Do you know where the Aswan High Dam is located asked Kenneth

2. No I don't replied Keith slowly it doesn't sound familiar to me

3. Suddenly Lori exclaimed look at that huge bear

4. Paul was able to say I have learned . . . to be content commented Father

5. Mother responded the Shunammite woman also expressed contentment when she said I dwell among mine own people

6. Where did Paul say in him we live, and move, and have our being

D. Copy the titles in these sentences, either enclosing them with quotation marks or underlining them.

1. Have you read the book Trapped by the Mountain Storm?

2. I used the article Australia in the Encyclopedia International as one of my reference sources.

3. Silent Night is one of the most popular Christmas songs.

4. The poem The Blind Men and the Elephant teaches an excellent lesson.

4. After, science, history

5. Syracuse, north

6. Civil War, South, plantation

B. 1. Mr. J. B. Knepper, neighbor, today.

2. remember, children, him?

3. place!

4. Daryl, car.

5. witness; indeed,

6. fire,

7. response,

8. Yes, vividly:

9. life;

10. pray, testify, urge;

C. (Corrections are underlined.)

1. "Do you know where the Aswan High Dam is located?" asked Kenneth.

2. "No, I don't," replied Keith slowly. "It doesn't sound familiar to me."

3. Suddenly Lori exclaimed, "Look at that huge bear!"

4. "Paul was able to say, 'I have learned . . . to be content,'" commented Father.

5. Mother responded, "The Shunammite woman also expressed contentment when she said, 'I dwell among mine own people.'"

6. Where did Paul say, "In him we live, and move, and have our being"?

D. 1. Trapped by the Mountain Storm

2. "Australia", Encyclopedia International

3. "Silent Night"

4. "The Blind Men and the Elephant"

C. Write correctly each word that should be italicized or that has an error in the use of an apostrophe or a hyphen.
1. Jesus sternly condemned the Pharisee's for their self righteousness.
2. They claimed to be Moses's disciples, but they did'nt live as he had.
3. In the word sepulchre, the l follows the u in spelling and in pronunciation.
4. These two ply paper towels wont crumple as quickly as those cheap ones.
5. Three of the ladies coats have fallen to the floor.
6. My father's parents have forty six grandchildren and twelve great grandchildren.

F. Rewrite this dialogue, making it sound more natural.
"I do not believe it!" said Winfred.
"What do you not believe?" said Thomas.
"Someone broke into Merle Diller's shop while the family was at church last evening. They stole a bunch of tools, and they also messed up the shop," said Winfred.
"Oh, that is terrible! Who would do such a thing?" said Thomas.

E. 1. Pharisees, self-righteousness
2. Moses', didn't
3. <u>sepulchre</u>, <u>l</u>, <u>u</u>
4. two-ply, won't, cheap
5. ladies'
6. forty-six, great-grandchildren

F. (Sample improvement.)
"I don't believe it!" exclaimed Winfred.
"What?" asked Thomas.
"Someone broke into Merle Diller's shop while the family was at church last evening. Stole a bunch of tools and also messed up the shop," stated Winfred.
"Oh, that's terrible! Who'd do such a thing?" asked Thomas.

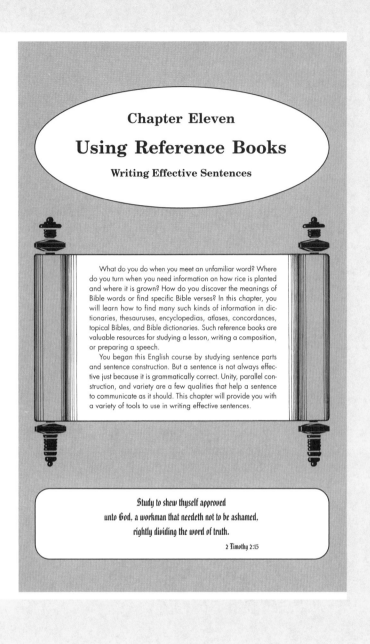

Chapter Eleven

Using Reference Books

Writing Effective Sentences

What do you do when you meet an unfamiliar word? Where do you turn when you need information on how rice is planted and where it is grown? How do you discover the meanings of Bible words or find specific Bible verses? In this chapter, you will learn how to find many such kinds of information in dictionaries, thesauruses, encyclopedias, atlases, concordances, topical Bibles, and Bible dictionaries. Such reference books are valuable resources for studying a lesson, writing a composition, or preparing a speech.

You began this English course by studying sentence parts and sentence construction. But a sentence is not always effective just because it is grammatically correct. Unity, parallel construction, and variety are a few qualities that help a sentence to communicate as it should. This chapter will provide you with a variety of tools to use in writing effective sentences.

Study to shew thyself approved
unto God, a workman that needeth not to be ashamed,
rightly dividing the word of truth.

2 Timothy 2:15

116. Using a Dictionary

Lesson Survey

- Guide words help you to locate words in a dictionary quickly.
- Entry words in a dictionary show spellings and syllable divisions.
- Dictionary entries show pronunciations, parts of speech, inflections, definitions, usage labels, and etymologies of the entry words.
- Some dictionaries supply synonyms and antonyms for certain words.
- Learn to know the specific dictionary you use frequently.

Dictionaries are one of the most common, useful, yet neglected resources for working with the language. Develop the dictionary habit; the time spent in using a dictionary is in no sense wasted! Do not be satisfied to stumble over an unfamiliar word, merely guessing at its pronunciation and meaning. When you meet a familiar word used in an unfamiliar way, do not merely wonder how that word fits. Use a dictionary. Learn to use more effectively the rich and varied vocabulary of the English language.

Guide Words and Entry Words

Guide words help you to locate words in a dictionary quickly. The guide word on the left is the first entry word on the page, and the one on the right is the last entry word on the page.

The entry word in a dictionary shows the correct spelling of a word. Some words have more than one correct spelling. If the alternate spellings are close together in alphabetical order, the more common spelling is used for the entry word and the other one is shown as an alternate spelling. If the two spellings are not close together, each is listed separately as an entry word. Then the entry for the less common spelling refers you to the more common spelling; and the entry for the more common spelling may mention the other as an alternate spelling. In many dictionaries, any option that follows the word *also* is definitely less common.

rick•sha or rick•shaw (rik′·shô), *n.* A small two-wheeled carriage pulled by one man.

cham•ois (sham′·ē), *n. pl.* -ois (sham′·ēz). 1. A small antelope of Europe and Asia. 2. A soft leather made from the skin of the chamois or of a sheep, goat, or deer. Also **chammy** or **shammy** for def. 2.

sham•my (sham′·ē), See **chamois.**

Lesson 116

Purpose: (1) To study types of information found in the dictionary, including *etymologies and *inflections. (2) To promote regular dictionary use.

IMPORTANT: Check your school's supply of the following reference books studied in Lessons 120 and 121. If possible, it would be good to have a copy available for each student.

road atlas
Strong's Exhaustive Concordance
Nave's Topical Bible
Unger's Bible Dictionary

Teacher: Dictionaries vary widely, and language changes over a period of time. This may be especially evident in relation to usage labels for words. Check your school's dictionaries for the labeling of the words used in the exercises. If necessary, find other words to use.

Oral Review:
1. What kind of punctuation indicates that quoted material has been omitted? (ellipsis points)
2. When should a semicolon be used to separate items in a series? (when the individual items contain commas)
3. When is a question mark or an exclamation point placed after the quotation marks? (when the whole sentence is a question or an exclamation, but the quotation is not)
4. Which titles should be set off (*a*) with quotation marks? (*b*) with italics? (*a.* titles of short stories, short poems, songs, and chapters; *b.* titles of books, magazines, newspapers, pamphlets, periodicals, and book-length poems)
5. Name the kind of pronouns in each of the following groups.
   a. who, whom, whose, which, that (relative)
   b. who, whom, whose, which, what (interrogative)
   c. this, that, these, those (demonstrative)
   d. I, he, them, its, hers (personal)

Entry words have syllable divisions, which show where a word may be divided at the end of a line. But be careful! In some dictionaries, the entry words do not show the division for a beginning or ending syllable of only one letter, as in *a-bide* and *dair-y.* This is because of the rule that a word must not be divided so that a single letter is left at the beginning or end of a line. So a word that actually has two syllables may appear to have only one. For such a word, you need to look at the pronunciation to see the two syllables.

Pronunciations

The phonetic spelling shows the correct pronunciation of a word. A complete pronunciation key is found in the front of the dictionary. Most dictionaries also print a short key at the bottom of each right-hand page. Not all use the same key, so you must become familiar with the key of the dictionary you are using.

Many words have more than one correct pronunciation. These variations are shown in different ways. You must check the explanatory notes in the front of the dictionary to discover whether the first option is preferred above the others. Sometimes a specific region is named where alternate pronunciations are used. If only part of the word has varied pronunciations, only those syllables with variations are shown in the alternate pronunciation.

> **chocolate** (chô′·kə·lit, chôk′·lit, chok′-)
> **erase** (i·rās′, *Brit.* -rāz′)
>> (*Brit.* means that the second pronunciation is used in Great Britain.)

Inflections

A dictionary gives some *inflections* of words. These are different forms of a word to show things like number and tense. A dictionary usually shows irregular and unusual plural forms of nouns. If you look up *dolphin* in the dictionary, you will not see the plural form. But if you look up *chamois,* you will probably find *chamois* shown as the plural. (See the entry above.) And if you look up *cherub,* you will find *cherubim.*

Another inflection that most dictionaries show is the principal parts of irregular verbs. If the past and the past participle have the same spelling, only one past form is shown. If they have different spellings, both are shown. Often if the irregular forms are shown, the present participle is shown also.

> **seep** (sēp), *v.* (No principal parts are shown because this is a regular verb.)

e. anybody, someone, each, few (indefinite)
f. myself, herself, ourselves, itself (compound personal)

6. Give a personal pronoun to fit each description.
   a. first person, possessive case, singular (my, mine)
   b. third person, nominative case, singular, feminine gender (she)
   c. second person, possessive case (your, yours)
   d. third person, objective case, plural (them)

Lesson Introduction: Ask these questions to stir your students' interest in the dictionary.

> Does your car have a <u>bonnet</u>? (British for *hood,* as of an automobile)
> Would you appreciate being <u>cashiered</u>? (being dismissed in disgrace, as from a job)
> Do you suppose <u>salvage</u> is more closely related to <u>salve</u> or to <u>safe</u>? (*Salvage* and *safe* both come from Latin *salvus,* which means "safe.")

Write these words on the board, and ask students to pronounce them.

> blaspheme (blas·fēm′)
> blasphemous (blas′·fə·məs)

Have you discovered that you need a dictionary? If you are like most people, you will find a dictionary beneficial in relation to unfamiliar words as well as familiar ones.

Lesson Outline:

(*Note:* Students should be well familiar with points 1–3 and 5. Point 8 will be treated in the next lesson. Plan to spend most of your time on points 4, 6, and 7.)

1. Guide words help you to locate words in a dictionary quickly. The guide word on the left is the first entry word on the page, and the one on the right is the last entry word on the page.

2. Entry words in a dictionary show spellings and syllable divisions.

   a. If alternate spellings are close together in alphabetical order, they are listed together.

seek (sēk), *v.* sought; seeking
see (sē), *v.* saw, seen; seeing

Still another common inflection shown in dictionaries is the irregular forms of comparison for adjectives and adverbs. If you look up *quiet,* you will probably not find any forms of comparison. But if you look up *creaky,* you will find *creakier* and *creakiest.* And if you look up *well,* you will find *better* and *best.*

Definitions

A dictionary gives the part of speech and the meaning of a word. If a word can be used as more than one part of speech, the definitions for each part of speech are grouped together.

Some words with the same spelling come from different sources and have completely different meanings. Separate, numbered entries are used for these words. A few dictionaries have a separate entry for each different part of speech that a word is.

> ¹**pen** (pen), *n.* A small enclosure for animals. [from Old English *penn*]
> ²**pen** (pen), *n.* A writing instrument that uses ink. [from Latin *penna*]

Dictionary A:
> **gaze** (gāz), *v.* To look steadily. —*n.* A steady look. [from Middle English *gazen*]

Dictionary B:
> ¹**gaze** (gāz), *v.* To look steadily. [from Middle English *gazen*]
> ²**gaze** (gāz), *n.* A steady look. [from same source]

Usage Labels

A dictionary gives usage labels to certain words. Some words should be avoided altogether. Words labeled *vulgar* should not be used because of their association with evil. Words labeled *nonstandard, substandard,* or *illiterate* also represent poor English and should be avoided.

Other labels limit the proper usage of words. *Slang* words were invented by people trying to say things in unique ways. Many slang expressions come from the "street language" of immoral people. For this reason, godly people avoid the new, catchy expressions that are constantly showing up. The words *cool* and *grand* are perfectly acceptable when used with their normal meanings. But saying *cool* for "excellent" and *grand* for "thousand dollars" is not appropriate for people professing godliness.

Informal words are acceptable in everyday speaking or writing (such as in notes to yourself or in a friendly letter). They would not be acceptable for use in formal speech (giving a topic or preaching a sermon) or

> b. If alternate spellings are not close together, each is listed separately.
> c. Syllable divisions show where a word may be divided at the end of a line.

3. The phonetic spelling shows the correct pronunciation of a word.
> a. A complete pronunciation key is found in the front of the dictionary.
> b. Most dictionaries also print a short key at the bottom of each right-hand page.
> c. Variant pronunciations are shown in different ways, so check your dictionary.

4. A dictionary gives some inflections of words. These are different forms of a word to show things like number and tense. The following common inflections are shown in most dictionaries.
> a. Irregular plural forms of nouns
> b. Principal parts of irregular verbs
> c. Irregular forms of comparison for adjectives and adverbs

5. A dictionary gives the part of speech and the meaning of a word.
> a. If a word can be used as more than one part of speech, the definitions for each part of speech are grouped together.
> b. Separate, numbered entries are used for words with the same spelling but completely different meanings and different sources. However, some dictionaries have a separate entry for each different part of speech.

6. A dictionary gives usage labels to certain words.
> a. Some labels mark words that should be avoided altogether.
> > 1) Words labeled *vulgar* should not be used because of their association with evil.
> > 2) Words labeled *nonstandard, substandard,* or *illiterate* also represent poor English and should be avoided.
> b. Other labels limit the proper usage of words.

formal writing (schoolwork, articles for publication, or legal papers). Words labeled *regional* or *dialectal* are used in relatively small areas or by a limited group of people. Some dictionaries may even specify regions where certain words are commonly used. The labels *archaic* and *obsolete* are used for words that are no longer in general use. A number of such words are well known to us because we are familiar with the King James Bible.

Etymologies

Many dictionaries also give an *etymology,* or brief history of a word. The etymology is usually placed within brackets [ ]. It traces a word back to its source in Old English or a foreign language, such as Latin. An etymology is especially helpful in comparing words with similar roots or affixes. Here is a typical etymology, followed by an explanation of its meaning. The symbol < means "from."

> **reveal** [< ME *revelen* < OF *reveler* < L *revelare,* to unveil < *re-,* back + *velum,* veil]
> **Meaning:**
> > From Middle English *revelen;* which comes from Old French *reveler;* which comes from Latin *revelare,* meaning "to unveil"; which comes from the prefix *re-,* meaning "back," and the root word *velum,* meaning "veil."

Synonyms and Antonyms

Some advanced dictionaries list synonyms and antonyms for certain words. This helps you to understand the exact meaning of the word you are looking up. It also may show another word that expresses more precisely what you want to say. The next lesson will deal more specifically with synonyms and antonyms.

Dictionaries vary considerably. They have differences in pronunciation symbols, definitions, usage labels, and various other things. Therefore, you need to become well familiar with the specific dictionary that you use frequently. The better you are acquainted with your dictionary, the more you will benefit from this valuable tool.

Class Practice

A. Tell where these words may be divided at the end of a line. Give another correct spelling for each word.
   1. aeon   2. counsellor   3. tzar

B. Pronounce these words correctly. If more than one pronunciation is given in the dictionary, say the word each way.

1) *Slang* words were invented by people trying to say things in unique ways. New and catchy expressions are constantly showing up, but they are not appropriate for people professing godliness.

2) *Informal* words are acceptable in everyday speaking or writing but not in formal speech or formal writing.

3) Words labeled *regional* or *dialectal* are used in relatively small areas or by a limited group of people.

4) Some dictionaries may even specify regions where certain words are commonly used.

5) The labels *archaic* and *obsolete* are used for words that are no longer in general use.

Lesson 116 Answers

NOTE: Dictionaries vary widely. Check your school's dictionaries in order to properly credit your students' work.

Class Practice

A. 1. ae/on; eon
   2. coun/sel/lor; counselor
   3. (no divisions); czar

---

7. *Many dictionaries also give an etymology, or brief history of a word.* The etymology is usually placed within brackets [ ]. It traces a word back to its source in Old English or a foreign language. An etymology is helpful in comparing words with similar roots or affixes.

8. *Some advanced dictionaries list synonyms and antonyms for certain words.* This helps you to understand the exact meaning of the word you are looking up. It also may show another word that expresses more precisely what you want to say. The next lesson will deal more specifically with synonyms and antonyms.

9. *Become familiar with the dictionary that you use frequently.*

★ *EXTRA PRACTICE*
Worksheet 58 (*Using a Dictionary*)

1. rinse
2. congratulate
3. advertisement
4. trespass
5. disputable
6. camaraderie

C. For each of these words, give as many separate definitions as you can find. In each case, tell the part of speech.
1. domestic   2. project   3. thread

D. Give the inflections your dictionary lists for each word.
1. good   2. tread   3. radius

E. Tell what usage labels your dictionary gives for each of these words.
1. critter   2. awful   3. irregardless

F. Tell what you can find about the origins of these words.
1. infant   3. wrestle
2. maintenance

Written Exercises

A. Write another spelling for each word.
1. vizor   3. siphon   5. lovable
2. ameba   4. cookie   6. programme

B. Copy the phonetic spelling for each word.
1. pecan   2. luxury   3. provender

C. Copy the correct definition for the underlined word in each sentence.
1. Joshua, lying prone before the ark of the Lord, agonized over Israel's defeat at Ai.
2. This morning the boys built a crawl.
3. The old man welcomed us into his hutch.
4. Did the hail pit the cars?
5. Is the fell of a mink very valuable?
6. Does the sun verge in the morning or in the evening?
7. You would probably not enjoy a walk in a fen.
8. This material has a nice, thick nap.

D. Copy the inflections your dictionary gives for these words.
1. lose   3. spindly   5. bacterium
2. ferry   4. devise   6. many

E. Copy any usage labels your dictionary gives for these words.
1. petrol   3. turtle   5. twain
2. art   4. ken   6. job

F. Write out the etymology of each word, using no abbreviations.
1. anarchy   2. kerchief   3. volume

Written Exercises

A. 1. visor   4. cooky
   2. amoeba   5. loveable
   3. syphon   6. program

B. 1. pi·kon'; pi·kan'; pē'·kan
   2. luk'·shə·rē; lug'·zhə·rē
   3. prov'·ən·dər

C. 1. in a horizontal position, with face downward
   2. an enclosure made with stakes in shallow water, for holding fish, turtles, lobsters, etc.
   3. a shack; a hut
   4. to dent; to make small indentations in
   5. a pelt
   6. to sink; to incline toward the horizon
   7. a marsh; a bog
   8. the soft, downy surface of cloth

(Parts D–F are on page 554.)

B. 1. (rins)
   2. (kən·grach'·ə·lāt', -graj'-, kəng-)
   3. (ad'·vər·tīz'·mənt; ad·ver'·tis·mənt; ad·ver'·tiz·mənt)
   4. (tres'·pəs; tres'·pas')
   5. (di·spyü'·tə·bəl; dis'·pyə·tə·bəl)
   6. (ko'·mə·ro'·də·rē; kam'·ə·rad'·ə·rē)

C. 1. adj.—related to the household or family; related to one's own country; living naturally in a region; tame; devoted to home duties or pleasures.
   n.—a household servant; cotton cloth; an article made at home or in a native country.
   2. n.—a plan or course of action; an undertaking requiring concerted effort; a problem or task given to a student or group of students; a group of houses or apartments.
   v.—to visualize; to plan for the future; to throw; to propose for consideration; to cause to extend forward or outward; to cause an image or a shadow to fall on a surface; to cause one's voice to be heard clearly at a distance; to jut out; to send out into space; to produce (a projection); to attribute (an emotion) to someone else.
   3. n.—a very slender cord of fibers, metal, or glass; a slender stream (as of water, light, or color); the ridge of a screw; a continuous element (as of thought or theme in writing); feeble support; a thin strand, cord, or filament of natural or manufactured material.
   v.—to pass a thread, yarn, or other small material through a narrow opening (as the eye of a needle); to arrange on a thread or string; to go through or between; to interweave; to form the threads of a screw; to form a threadlike strand when poured from a spoon; to make one's way cautiously; to proceed by a winding course.

D. 1. better, best
   2. trod, treaded; trodden, trod; treading
   3. radii, radiuses

E. 1. (U.S.) dialectal; regional
   2. informal (with meaning "very great"); obsolete (with meaning "terrified")
   3. nonstandard

F. 1. from Latin infans, from in- "not" and fari "to speak"
   2. from Old French maintenir, from Latin manu tenēre "to hold in the hand," from manus "hand" and tenēre "to hold"
   3. from Old English wraēstlian, from wraēstan, "to wrest or twist"

Review Exercises

A. Write four headings on your paper: *Person, Number, Case,* and *Gender.* In each column, write the appropriate label for the following pronouns. [57, 58]

1. him   3. ours   5. its
2. them   4. she   6. your

B. Copy the pronouns in each sentence. Label each one *P* for personal, *CP* for compound personal, *D* for demonstrative, *ID* for indefinite, *IR* for interrogative, or *R* for relative. [57–64]

1. The man whom we will read about this morning is called the Weeping Prophet.
2. Who knows the name of the man that earned this name for himself?
3. Is everyone ready to read about him in Jeremiah 1?
4. Those in seventh grade will take turns reading the first ten verses; then the ones in eighth grade will read verses eleven through sixteen.
5. God Himself had formed the prophet; this was an encouragement in the difficult assignment which he received.

---

117. Groups of Related Words

Lesson Survey

- **Synonyms** are words with similar meanings.
- **Antonyms** are words with opposite meanings.
- **Homophones** are words that are pronounced alike but spelled differently.
- **Heteronyms** are spelled alike but pronounced differently.
- **Homographs** are spelled and pronounced alike, but they have different origins and meanings.

Because the English language has borrowed words from many different languages, it has a rich, varied vocabulary. Therefore it includes many words with almost the same meaning, as well as completely different words with the same spelling or pronunciation. You can help your vocabulary grow as you study such groups of words.

Lesson 117

Purpose: To teach synonyms, antonyms, homonyms, *heteronyms, and *homographs; and to introduce the *thesaurus. (*Previous experience:* Mention of synonym dictionary, but term *thesaurus* not used.)

Oral Review:

1. Are variant spellings always listed separately as entry words? (not if they are close together in alphabetical order)
2. Why do some words have more than one numbered entry? (They may be words with the same spelling that come from different sources and have different meanings. In some dictionaries, there is a separate entry for each different part of speech.)
3. What are three inflections that most dictionaries show? (irregular plural forms of nouns, principal parts of irregular verbs, irregular forms of

D. 1. lost, losing   4. devised, devising
2. ferried, ferrying, ferries   5. bacteria
3. spindlier, spindliest   6. more, most

E. 1. chiefly British
2. archaic; poetic
3. archaic; chiefly British
4. archaic; chiefly dialectal; Scottish and British dialectal
5. archaic
6. chiefly British; informal; archaic

F. 1. from Greek *an-* "without" and *archos* "ruler"
2. from Old French *covrir* "to cover" and *chef* "head"
3. from Latin *volumen* "roll, scroll," from *volvere* "to roll"

Review Exercises

A.

Person	Number	Case	Gender
1. third	singular	objective	masculine
2. third	plural	objective	common
3. first	plural	possessive	common
4. third	singular	nominative	feminine
5. third	singular	possessive	neuter
6. second	singular *or* plural	possessive	common

B. 1. whom—R; we—P
2. Who—IR; that—R; himself—CP
3. everyone—ID; him—P
4. Those—D; ones—ID
5. Himself—CP; this—D; which—R; he—P

---

comparison for adjectives and adverbs)

4. When is it proper to use words labeled *informal?* (in everyday speaking or writing)
5. Tell whether *is* or *are* is the better verb in these sentences.
   a. Where (is, are) the book?
   b. A pen or pencil (is, are) needed.
   c. The pliers (is, are) on the bench.
   d. The news (is, are) quite a surprise.
   e. The class (is, are) finishing their papers.
   f. Each of the students (is, are) working hard.

Lesson Introduction: *Prolong, extend,* and *lengthen* are synonyms. Which word fits best in each of the following sentences?

As the girls grow, Mother must —— their dresses. (lengthen)

Putting off an unpleasant task will only —— your dread. (prolong)

Synonyms

Many people tend to overwork a few common words. Often these words are not as specific or colorful as other words would be. When they write dialogue, most of their characters' words are *said* or *asked*. When they speak or write, skyscrapers and sequoias are no more than *very big*, exciting plans are blandly *nice* or *great*, and people merely *go* from one place to another. How much more effectively they would communicate if they used more exact words!

Synonyms are words with similar meanings. Often they are so nearly the same that they can be interchanged in many sentences. However, no pair of synonyms is perfectly interchangeable in every sentence.

Goliath <u>boldly</u> defied God. *or* Goliath <u>brazenly</u> defied God.
David <u>boldly</u> ran to meet him. *but not* David <u>brazenly</u> ran to meet him.

The crew <u>left</u> the sinking ship. *or* The crew <u>abandoned</u> the sinking ship.
We <u>left</u> Grandpa's at 7:30. *but not* We <u>abandoned</u> Grandpa's at 7:30.

There are various reference sources for finding synonyms. In the previous lesson, you learned that an advanced dictionary may list synonyms for some words. Even more helpful is a thesaurus (thĭ·sôr′·əs) or some other special dictionary of synonyms. Use these reference books to find synonyms as you write.

Suppose after writing a paragraph, you notice that you have overused a certain word. Of course you do want to repeat the main idea, but you do not want to use the same word so often that it becomes tiresome. Look for synonyms to replace some of the repeated words.

Poor: Forms of *watch* used too often
A squirrel is a pleasure to <u>watch</u>. Last evening I <u>watched</u> a squirrel for a while. I <u>watched</u> his quick, jerking motions as he made his way down the tree trunk. As he scampered across the grass, I <u>watched</u> him pick up a nut and scurry back up the tree.

A thesaurus shows the following synonyms for *watch.*

see	observe	view	keep an eye on
look at	spy	notice	

Better: Some forms of *watch* replaced with synonyms
A squirrel is a pleasure to <u>observe</u>. Last evening I <u>watched</u> a squirrel for a while. I <u>noticed</u> his quick, jerking motions as he made his way down the tree trunk. As he scampered across the grass, I <u>saw</u> him pick up a nut and scurry back up the tree.

Another reason for finding synonyms is to use words with exactly the

The storeowner has decided to ——— the sale through next week. (extend)

Write these sentences on the board. Can your students tell what is wrong with each?

You must ring your dishcloth out better. (wring)
A small boat saled down the creak. (sailed, creek)

In this lesson you will study groups of words like the synonyms and homonyms illustrated in these examples.

Lesson Outline:
1. *Synonyms are words with similar meanings.*
   a. There are various reference sources for finding synonyms: an advanced dictionary, a thesaurus, and a dictionary of synonyms.
   b. Using synonyms adds variety to our speaking and writing.
   c. Finding synonyms is important for using words with exactly the meaning we want.
2. *Antonyms are words with opposite meanings.*
   a. The contrast of antonyms can give a strong effect within a sentence. Antonyms can also be used in developing a paragraph.
   b. *Un-, dis-, non-,* and *in-* are common antonym-forming prefixes. When the prefix *in-* is used, the *n* may become the same as the first letter of the root word. (*Teacher:* Assimilation is taught in Grade 7 of *Spelling by Sound and Structure,* Lesson 7.)
   c. A dictionary of synonyms is a good place to find antonyms.
3. *Homophones are words that are pronounced alike but spelled differently.* They often pose a spelling problem, especially when one of the homophones is a contraction.

meaning you want. Suppose you are writing this sentence: "We were fascinated by the ——— of the potter's hands in shaping the intricate pitcher." All you can think of to fill in the blank is the word *cleverness,* but you know this does not sound right. A thesaurus will suggest words like *skill, dexterity,* and *ability.*

Antonyms

Sometimes we can understand a word or an idea better by saying what it is not like. Words that have such opposite meanings are *antonyms.* Antonyms can be used effectively within a single sentence. The contrast gives a strong effect.

> The <u>balmy</u> spring days were rudely interrupted by a <u>frigid</u> north wind.

Antonyms can also be used in developing a paragraph. Suppose you have written this sentence: "Sheep are *social* animals." You could use opposite expressions in the next sentences. "They do not like to be *alone.* A *solitary* sheep cannot defend itself very well from attack."

One common way to form antonyms is to add negative prefixes like *un-, dis-, non-,* or *in-* to a word. When the prefix *in-* is used, the *n* may become the same as the first letter of the root word. (This is called assimilation, as you may remember from spelling class.)

noticed—unnoticed	finite—infinite
organized—disorganized	legal—illegal
perishable—nonperishable	responsible—irresponsible

A dictionary of synonyms may also give antonyms for the entry words. But you can use any dictionary of synonyms to find antonyms. For example, suppose you want to find several antonyms for *quiet.* Think of one antonym, such as *loud,* and look up synonyms for that word. A thesaurus may give *noisy, roaring, deafening,* and *earsplitting.* All these words are antonyms for *quiet.*

Homophones

Homophones are words that are pronounced alike but spelled differently. The English language has many hundreds of homophones in sets of two, three, or even four words. Homophones pose a special spelling problem for many people. If you are not careful, you may write the wrong word. This is especially true when one of the homophones is a contraction.

air, ere, err, heir	die, dye	knead, need
aisle, isle, I'll	ewe, yew, you	pair, pare, pear
brake, break	flour, flower	rain, reign, rein
buy, by, bye	heal, heel, he'll	their, there, they're
coarse, course	its, it's	whose, who's

4. Heteronyms are spelled alike but pronounced differently. They pose a problem with pronunciation rather than with spelling.

5. Homographs are spelled and pronounced alike, but they have different origins and meanings.

(*Note:* Synonyms and antonyms will be familiar to most pupils. To help them distinguish homonyms, heteronyms, and homographs, use the following memory aids.

> *Homo-* means "same" and *phone* means "sound." Homophones are words having the same sound [but spelled differently].

> *Hetero-* means "different" and *nym* means "name or sound." Heteronyms are words having different sounds [but spelled the same].

> *Homo-* means "same" and *graph* means "writing." Homographs are words having the same writing or spelling [and also pronounced the same].)

Grandmother will <u>pare</u> only one <u>pear</u> of this <u>pair</u>.

<u>It's</u> interesting to watch a praying mantis catch <u>its</u> prey.

If you use only the front <u>brake</u> of your bicycle, you might <u>break</u> your nose.

Heteronyms

Heteronyms are spelled alike but pronounced differently. These words pose more of a problem with pronunciation than with spelling. You must understand the meaning of the word in order to know which pronunciation you should use.

Is there a <u>tear</u> (tir) in her eye because of the <u>tear</u> (tar) in her paper?

Brian will <u>mow</u> (mō) the hay while I make some repairs in the <u>mow</u> (mou).

Homographs

Homographs are spelled and pronounced alike, but they have different origins and meanings. These words are usually listed as separate entries in a dictionary, as you learned in Lesson 116. Sometimes homographs result from inflections of a word. For example, one word spelled *bore* is the past tense of *bear* ("to carry"). Another *bore* may be a verb that means "to make a hole" or "to weary with monotony"; or it may be a noun that means "a hole made by a drill," "a tidal flood with a high front," or "a person who causes boredom."

Class Practice

A. Tell whether the underlined words are *synonyms, antonyms, homophones, heteronyms,* or *homographs.*
  1. Their <u>plan</u> calls for a special <u>design</u>.
  2. The vandal paid a <u>fine</u> for throwing <u>fine</u> dust on the <u>fine</u> painting.
  3. William <u>threw</u> the ball <u>through</u> the window.
  4. We will <u>sow</u> oats in the field where the <u>sow</u> is rooting.
  5. John was <u>uninterested</u>, but everyone else seemed <u>attentive</u>.
  6. I <u>do</u> not know if I can sing that high <u>do</u>.

B. Identify the correct words in these sentences.
  1. When Alice spilled a (pail, pale) of milk, her face turned (pail, pale).
  2. The river followed a winding (coarse, course).
  3. The rosebushes have (groan, grown) rapidly.
  4. Does your behavior (meat, meet, mete) your parents' expectations, or will they have to (meat, meet, mete) out punishment to you?
  5. (Its, It's) (to, too, two) dark to tell if the (ewe, yew, you) has (its, it's) (to, too, two) lambs close by.

C. Read these sentences, pronouncing the underlined heteronyms correctly.
1. We bow our heads when we pray.
2. The ribbon around the box was neatly tied into a bow.
3. The hunter fitted an arrow into his bow.
4. The bow of the boat was damaged when it hit the rocks.
5. The aye votes outnumbered the nay votes.
6. In heaven we will live for aye.

D. Use *grade* and *pitch* in pairs of sentences to show two different meanings each may have.

Written Exercises

A. Write whether the underlined words are *synonyms, antonyms, homophones, heteronyms,* or *homographs.*
1. Did you hear that the Martins are here now?
2. Do not lean on the grapevine. Aren't those cattle too lean?
3. While James has been diligent, Leon has been neglectful of his work.
4. We will need to train that dog not to chase the train.
5. Linda was delighted to go, and Martha was pleased to have her along.
6. Please lead me to the closet where the lead pencils are stored.

B. Copy the correct words for these sentences.
1. Did Hezekiah (rain, reign, rein) on the (throne, thrown) of Judah?
2. Jesus was (born, borne) into the world; He has (born, borne) the sins of mankind.
3. A well-trained (hoarse, horse) can be guided by a mere touch of the (rains, reigns, reins).
4. Use the (pail, pale) green (pail, pale) to (bare, bear) the water for cooking the (meat, meet, mete).
5. Elijah carefully laid the (wood, would) on the (altar, alter).
6. (Whose, Who's) calling Israel to forsake (idle, idol) worship and turn (to, too, two) the Lord?
7. Those who (know, no) God's power can (brake, break) any wrong habit.
8. Satan will (seas, sees, seize) every opportunity to (reck, wreck) a person's (sole, soul).

C. Copy each underlined heteronym and the number of the correct pronunciation.
1. The prayer (^{1}prā′·ər, ^{2}prar) must bow (^{1}bō, ^{2}bou) humbly before God.
2. Only then are anyone's prayers (^{1}prā′·ərz, ^{2}prarz) answered.
3. We should sow (^{1}sō, ^{2}sou) righteous seed in our lives (^{1}līvz, ^{2}livz).
4. Jesus lives (^{1}līvz, ^{2}livz) forever enthroned in glory.
5. You can put a beautiful bow (^{1}bō, ^{2}bou) on a sow (^{1}sō, ^{2}sou), but she

C. 1. (bou)   4. (bou)
2. (bō)   5. (ī)
3. (bō)   6. (ā)

D. (Sample sentences.)
Grade: What grade did you receive on your paper?
The teacher will grade our tests.
The truck slowly climbed the steep grade.
We bought a heavier grade of material this time.
You are in seventh grade.
Pitch: Sound your pitch with the song leader.
We will pitch this song a little lower.
Pitch the ball to Stephen.
The sailors smeared pitch into the cracks.
This barn roof has a steep pitch.
Where shall we pitch the tent?

Written Exercises

A. 1. homophones   4. homographs
2. homographs   5. synonyms
3. antonyms   6. heteronyms

B. 1. reign, throne   5. wood, altar
2. born, borne   6. Who's, idol, to
3. horse, reins   7. know, break
4. pale, pail, bear, meat   8. seize, wreck, soul

C. 1. prayer 1, bow 2
2. prayers 2
3. sow 1, lives 1
4. lives 2
5. bow 1, sow 2

will return to her wallowing in the mud.

6. Does (*¹dōz*, *²duz*) the picture show a buck and two <u>does</u> (*¹dōz*, *²duz*)?

D. Write two sentences for each homograph, showing two completely different meanings.

1. fast   2. rent   3. will

Review Exercises

If the underlined verb or contraction does not agree with the subject, write it correctly. If it is correct, write *correct*. [48]

1. The dish of beans <u>are</u> ready to be passed.
2. Chicken and rice <u>makes</u> a delicious meal.
3. Everybody <u>have</u> finished eating now.
4. The shears <u>belong</u> on the shelf in the utility room.
5. A large flock of ducks <u>were</u> flying north.
6. Electronics <u>is</u> a science that has many useful applications.
7. Either snow or rain <u>have</u> been predicted for today.
8. Nelson <u>don't</u> have his answers labeled clearly.
9. There <u>is</u> a sandwich on the counter.
10. The group of students <u>were</u> divided in their opinions.
11. <u>How's</u> your drawings looking by now?
12. Joyce and Joan <u>agrees</u> with our decision.
13. Each of the students <u>has</u> chosen a song.
14. The plumber and electrician <u>are</u> scheduled to come this afternoon.
15. It <u>don't</u> sound like a good answer to me.

---

118. Writing Effective Sentences

> **Lesson Survey**
> - An effective sentence has unity and coherence.
> - Parallel construction adds to sentence effectiveness.
> - An effective sentence is concise.
> - The active voice usually communicates more effectively than the passive voice.
> - A direct quotation usually communicates more effectively than an indirect quotation.

Lesson 118

Purpose: To teach various ways of improving sentence effectiveness, including *conciseness.

Oral Review:

1. What are three common ways of revealing the traits of a story character? (by the character's actions, words, and thoughts)
2. What are the three main kinds of conflict? (main character in conflict with another person, with his circumstances, and with his own self)
3. (*a*) What is the most intense incident in the conflict? (*b*) Where should it occur? (*a*. the climax; *b*. near the end of the story)
4. What are some things that help to make dialogue sound natural? (contractions, incomplete sentences, frequent change of speakers, descriptive explanatory words)

6. Does 2, does 1

D. (Individual work.)

Review Exercises

1. is	9. correct
2. correct	10. correct
3. has	11. How are
4. correct	12. agree
5. was	13. correct
6. correct	14. is
7. has	15. doesn't
8. doesn't	

5. Tell what words in these expressions should be capitalized. (Answers are underlined.)
   a. in the <u>North</u>
   b. a <u>John</u> <u>Deere</u> tractor
   c. <u>God</u> shows us <u>His</u> will.
   d. the song "<u>Shall</u> <u>I</u> <u>Be</u> <u>Ashamed</u>?"
   e. <u>Ascension</u> <u>Day</u> comes in the spring.
   f. <u>King</u> <u>David</u>, a godly king
6. When should a semicolon be used instead of a comma? (when commas are used between smaller units)
7. Tell what punctuation marks are needed within this sentence: *Noah's three sons were as follows: Shem, Ham, and Japheth.* (colon and commas)
8. When should a question mark or an exclamation point be placed outside the quotation marks? (when the whole sentence is a question or an exclamation, but the quotation is not)

The sentence is a basic building block of paragraphs, stories, and compositions. No piece of writing deserves a high rating if the individual sentences are written carelessly and ineffectively.

Unity

Effective sentences have unity; they express only one thought in a clear, logical way. A sentence with a run-on error is not only ungrammatical but also ineffective because it does not communicate clearly. Two unrelated or poorly related clauses should not be joined into one sentence. Such a sentence may not be ungrammatical, but it does lack unity. On the other hand, two closely related clauses should not be separated. They should be combined into one compound or complex sentence to show the unity of thought most effectively.

Run-on error:
>Balaam's donkey saw the angel in the path, later Balaam saw him too.

Two sentences with unity:
>Balaam's donkey saw the angel in the path. Later Balaam saw him too.

Poorly related clauses:
>Balaam was pursuing his own way, but the donkey crushed his foot.

One sentence with unity:
>Balaam was pursuing his own way when the donkey crushed his foot.

Separation of related thoughts:
>Balaam wanted to be righteous at his death. He loved the wages of unrighteousness.

One sentence with unity:
>Balaam wanted to be righteous at his death, but he loved the wages of unrighteousness.

Coherence

A sentence may have unity yet not be clearly understandable. Effective sentences must also have coherence. In Lesson 17 you learned that a paragraph has coherence when the ideas flow smoothly and clearly from one sentence to another. In a similar way, a sentence has coherence when its different parts work together to express the thought smoothly and clearly. One thing that spoils sentence coherence is unclear pronoun reference.

Unclear pronoun reference:
>Barbara told Helen that her mother was at the door.

Lesson Introduction: Write these sentences on the board.

>The walks were lined with flowers.
>Grandmother had planted them.

Are these sentences complete? (yes) Are they effective sentences for a seventh grader? (no) Can someone suggest a more effective way to write this? (The walks were lined with flowers that Grandmother had planted.)

In first grade you learned to write complete sentences. The sentences you wrote then may have been just as correct as the ones you write now; however, the sentences you write now are more effective, no doubt, than those were. What are some things that make sentences effective, not merely correct? This lesson should help you to answer that question.

Lesson Outline:

1. *Effective sentences have unity.*
   a. A sentence with a run-on error does not communicate clearly.
   b. Two unrelated or poorly related clauses should not be joined into one sentence.
   c. Two closely related clauses should be combined into one compound or complex sentence.

2. *Effective sentences have coherence.*
   a. A sentence has coherence when its different parts work together to express the thought smoothly and clearly.
   b. Unclear pronoun reference spoils sentence coherence.
   c. Misplaced modifiers also mar coherence.
   d. Coherence is marred by the careless separation of closely related sentence parts.

Coherent:
Barbara told Helen, "My mother is at the door."
Barbara told Helen, "Your mother is at the door."

Unclear pronoun reference:
In some countries they persecute Christians.
Coherent:
In some countries the government persecutes Christians.
In some countries the Christians are persecuted.

Misplaced modifiers also mar coherence. Be especially careful with modifiers like *almost, even, just, nearly,* and *only.* Their position can make a big difference in the meaning of a sentence. Also be sure that adjective phrases and adjective clauses clearly modify the right words.

Misplaced modifier:
As I just turned on the light, a mouse ran across the floor.
Coherent:
Just as I turned on the light, a mouse ran across the floor.

Misplaced modifier:
Peering from under the cupboard, I saw the mouse a little later.
Coherent:
A little later I saw the mouse peering from under the cupboard.

Another thing that mars sentence coherence is the careless separation of closely related sentence parts. Try to avoid interrupting a verb phrase with a long modifier or parenthetical expression. Also be careful not to split an infinitive unless that is the best way to express your idea clearly and smoothly.

Divided verb phrase:
Marie will be, the way it looks, finishing her motto today.
Better:
The way it looks, Marie will be finishing her motto today.

Split infinitive:
Brother Titus instructed us to neatly letter the motto.
Better:
Brother Titus instructed us to letter the motto neatly.

Parallel Construction

Parallel construction adds to sentence effectiveness. Carefully matching sentence parts makes a sentence easy to understand and smooth to read. Sentence parts joined by a coordinating conjunction should have the same structure: word to word, participial phrase to participial phrase, adverb clause to adverb clause, and so forth.

such as a verb phrase or an infinitive.

3. Parallel construction adds to sentence effectiveness.
   a. Sentence parts joined by a coordinating conjunction should have the same structure: word to word, participial phrase to participial phrase, adverb clause to adverb clause, and so forth.
   b. Avoid a shift in the tense of the verbs or in the person or number of the subjects within a sentence.
   c. When you define a word, use another word of the same part of speech. A *when* or *where* clause usually does not make a good definition.

4. Effective sentences are concise.

5. The active voice usually communicates more effectively than the passive voice.

6. Direct quotations usually communicate more effectively than indirect quotations.

★ **EXTRA PRACTICE**
Worksheet 59 (*Writing Effective Sentences*)

Unparallel:

Mother taught us girls <u>to cook</u> and <u>sewing</u>.

Parallel:

Mother taught us girls <u>to cook</u> and <u>to sew</u>.

Mother taught us girls <u>cooking</u> and <u>sewing</u>.

Sometimes a writer improperly shifts from one verb tense to another within a sentence. Or he may shift the person or number of the subjects within a sentence. Such shifts also produce unparallel sentences.

Unparallel: Shift in verb tense

After Father <u>gave</u> a few parting instructions, he <u>leaves</u> for his meeting.

Parallel:

After Father <u>gave</u> a few parting instructions, he <u>left</u> for his meeting.

Unparallel: Shift in person of the subjects

When <u>one</u> looks at the stars, <u>you</u> are humbled by the Creator's greatness.

Parallel:

When <u>you</u> look at the stars, <u>you</u> are humbled by the Creator's greatness.

Unparallel: Shift in number of the subjects

After a <u>person</u> tells one lie, <u>they</u> find it easier to tell another one.

Parallel:

After a <u>person</u> tells one lie, <u>he</u> finds it easier to tell another one.

Another unparallel construction sometimes occurs in definitions. When you define a word, use another word of the same part of speech. Use nouns to define nouns, verbs to define verbs, and so forth. A *when* or *where* clause usually does not make a good definition.

Unparallel:

The <u>equator</u> is <u>where</u> the Northern and Southern Hemispheres meet.

Parallel:

The <u>equator</u> is the imaginary <u>line</u> between the Northern and Southern Hemispheres.

Unparallel:

To <u>procrastinate</u> is <u>when</u> you put off something that you should do now.

Parallel:

To <u>procrastinate</u> is to <u>put</u> off something that you should do now.

Conciseness

Effective sentences are concise. They are not cluttered with unnecessary or repetitious words.

Wordy:
> As a usual rule, we find it easier to be more cheerful on days when the sun is shining than on days when it is cloudy.

Concise:
> Usually it is easier to be cheerful on sunny days than on cloudy days.

Wordy:
> There was a welcome treat of cold ice cream awaiting us after the hard, strenuous work in the blazing hot sun.

Concise:
> A welcome treat of ice cream awaited us after the hard work in the blazing sun.

Active Voice

The active voice usually communicates more effectively than the passive voice. A verb in the active voice makes a straightforward statement, whereas a verb in the passive voice tends to be weak and indirect. As you studied in Chapter 5, sometimes the passive voice does have a proper use. But in most cases it is better to use the active voice.

Poor: Passive voice
> Our peas were eaten by a woodchuck.

Better: Active voice
> A woodchuck ate our peas.

Direct Quotations

Direct quotations usually communicate more effectively than indirect quotations. Like the active voice, a direct quotation makes a more direct statement than an indirect quotation. Using a speaker's exact words adds to the interest and effectiveness of a sentence.

Poor: Indirect quotation
> Lois said that she would enjoy going along.

Better: Direct quotation
> "I would enjoy going along," Lois replied.

Class Practice

Tell how to improve these sentences.

1. Father asked Uncle Marcus about the car that he had just bought from him.

Lesson 118 Answers

Class Practice

(Sample improvements; encourage variety.)

1. Father asked, "Uncle Marcus, how is the car doing that you just bought from me?"

2. The horse was skillfully carved by Pierre.
3. A thesaurus is where synonyms for many words are listed.
4. Slowly and with much pain, the wounded bear crawled up the trail.
5. He dragged along his one hind leg behind him, and it had been crushed by a huge, big boulder in a landslide.
6. In England they use some words that we do not use.
7. Three monkeys chattered at us swinging from branch to branch.
8. Joshua told the people that as for him and his house, they would serve the Lord.
9. Joshua was nearing the end of his life and the time when he should die. He wanted to challenge Israel to remain true and faithful to God.
10. When someone drives a nail in crooked, they have a harder time making it go straight the next time.
11. Our lives can be like that too, it is harder to do something right after having done it wrong.
12. We should purpose and determine in our hearts to never do things that we know are wrong.

Written Exercises

Rewrite these sentences more effectively. The letters in parentheses tell whether improvement is needed in unity (*U*), coherence (*Coh*), parallel structure (*P*), conciseness (*Con*), or voice of the verb (*V*). You may need to join or divide sentences.

1. The porcupine has been given a highly effective weapon by God. (V)
2. The porcupine has, because of this weapon, been called a walking pincushion. (Coh)
3. Each and every quill in this pincushion is actually a spine made of hardened hairs, at the tip of the end of each quill are many barbs that point backward. (Con, U)
4. When the flesh of an enemy is pierced by a quill, these barbs lie flat. (V)
5. But the enemy tries to pull out the quill, and the barbs hook into the flesh and hold the quill securely in place. (U)
6. These quills cover the porcupine's entire body except parts of the face, the underside of the tail, and on the belly. (P)
7. It is said by some people that a porcupine shoots its quills, but this is not really true and accurate. (V, Con)
8. When an enemy is struck by the porcupine's thrashing tail, the quills stick to its nose or paws. (V)
9. With such an effective defense, there are very few animals that are enemies of the porcupine. (Coh, Con)

2. Pierre skillfully carved the horse.
3. A thesaurus is a book that lists synonyms for many words.
4. Slowly and painfully, the wounded bear crawled up the trail.
5. He dragged along his one hind leg, which had been crushed by a huge boulder in a landslide.
6. People in England use some words that we do not use.
7. Swinging from branch to branch, three monkeys chattered at us.
8. Joshua told the people, "As for me and my house, we will serve the Lord."
9. Joshua was nearing the end of his life, and he wanted to challenge Israel to remain faithful to God.
10. When someone drives a nail in crooked, he has a harder time making it go straight the next time.
11. Our lives can be like that too. It is harder to do something right after having done it wrong.
12. We should purpose in our hearts never to do wrong things.

Written Exercises

(Allow reasonable variation.)

1. God has given the porcupine a highly effective weapon.
2. Because of this weapon, the porcupine has been called a walking pincushion.
3. Each quill in this pincushion is actually a spine made of hardened hairs. At the tip of each quill are many barbs that point backward.
4. When a quill pierces the flesh of an enemy, these barbs lie flat.
5. But when the enemy tries to pull out the quill, the barbs hook into the flesh and hold the quill securely in place.
6. These quills cover the porcupine's entire body except parts of the face, the underside of the tail, and the belly.
7. Some people say that a porcupine shoots its quills, but this is not really true.
8. When the porcupine's thrashing tail strikes an enemy, the quills stick to its nose or paws.
9. With such an effective defense, the porcupine has very few enemies.

10. However, fishers have a plan and way to, in spite of the quills, kill porcupines. (Con, Coh)
11. These animals can, since they are very quick, avoid the quills. They flip the porcupine on its back. (Coh, U)
12. This leaves the belly unguarded and unprotected from attack. (Con)

Review Exercises

A. Write the letter of the item that is capitalized correctly. [101]

1. a. a Bic ball point pen
   b. a Bic Ball Point Pen
2. a. lives in the Southwest
   b. lives in the southwest
3. a. Cloverdale Christian school
   b. Cloverdale Christian School
4. a. the last day of spring
   b. the last day of Spring
5. a. found in the old Testament
   b. found in the Old Testament
6. a. Saul, Israel's first King
   b. Saul, Israel's first king
7. a. "Now the Day Is Over"
   b. "Now the Day is Over"
8. a. Jesus and his disciples
   b. Jesus and His disciples
9. a. across the Jordan river
   b. across the Jordan River
10. a. a river in Syria
    b. a River in Syria

B. Write the letter of the sentence that is punctuated correctly. [106–113]

1. a. The qualities of honesty, kindness, and perseverance are important.
   b. The qualities of honesty, kindness and perseverance are important.
2. a. Dishonesty can be expressed in the following ways, telling an untruth, acting a lie, and failing to tell a necessary truth.
   b. Dishonesty can be expressed in the following ways: telling an untruth, acting a lie, and failing to tell a necessary truth.
3. a. Did Mr. Smith say, "I would like to go along to church?"
   b. Did Mr. Smith say, "I would like to go along to church"?
4. a. John Steiner, who is Father's cousin, is doing the excavation; and Abram Stauffer, who employs several crews, will build the house.
   b. John Steiner, who is Father's cousin, is doing the excavation, and Abram Stauffer, who employs several crews, will build the house.
5. a. Great aunt Sarah made dozens of afghans in her last years.
   b. Great-aunt Sarah made dozens of afghans in her last years.
6. a. Our neighbor, as I understand, planted a self-pollinating apricot.
   b. Our neighbor, as I understand, planted a self pollinating apricot.
7. a. We are memorizing "The Old Lamp" from "Poems for Memorization."
   b. We are memorizing "The Old Lamp" from *Poems for Memorization*.
8. a. A sentence with too many and's sounds stringy.
   b. A sentence with too many *and*'s sounds stringy.

10. However, fishers have a way to kill porcupines in spite of the quills.
11. Since these animals are very quick, they can avoid the quills and flip the porcupine on its back.
12. This leaves the belly unprotected from attack.

Review Exercises

A. 1. a
   2. a
   3. b
   4. a
   5. b
   6. b
   7. a
   8. b
   9. b
   10. a

B. 1. a
   2. b
   3. b
   4. a
   5. b
   6. a
   7. b
   8. b

9. a. Several tall straight pines lined the driveway.
   b. Several tall, straight pines lined the driveway.
10. a. I heard Wanda say, "Mother is calling you," declared Juanita.
    b. "I heard Wanda say, 'Mother is calling you,'" declared Juanita.

9. b
10. b

119. Word Families

Lesson Survey
• Words with the same *root* make up a **word family.**
• A **prefix** is added to the beginning of a word or word root to alter the meaning of the original word.
• A **suffix** is added to the end of a word or word root, usually to change it to a different part of speech.
• A dictionary will help you to use prefixes and suffixes correctly.

Children in the same family often are similar in their appearance, their speech, and their actions. If you have learned to know a boy or girl your age, you will often recognize an older brother or sister as well.

Word Roots

Words also come in families. All the words in a *word family* have the same *root,* or basic word element. The root gives the words in a family a similar appearance and related meanings. If you know the meaning of a word root, you should be able to figure out the meanings of many words in that family.

The following chart shows several word families. Do you see how the words in each family are related?

Root	Meaning	Examples
sci	know	science, scientific, conscience, conscious, omniscient, unscientific
pend, pens	hang, weigh	pendant, pendulum, pension, appendix, compensate, depend, expense, independent
man	hand	manacles, manager, manipulate, manual, manufacture, unmanageable
chron	time	chronic, chronicles, chronograph, chronological, anachronism, synchronize

Lesson 119

Purpose: To teach the study of word families as a means of expanding vocabulary.

Oral Review:
1. What are synonyms? (words with similar meanings)
2. What are antonyms? (words with opposite meanings)
3. What are homophones? (words pronounced alike but spelled differently)
4. What are heteronyms? (words spelled alike but pronounced differently)
5. What are homographs? (words spelled and pronounced alike, but having different origins and meanings)
6. Give nine types of information that many dictionaries show. (spellings, syllable divisions, pronunciations, parts of speech, meanings, inflected forms, usage labels, synonyms and antonyms, etymologies)
7. Tell what part of speech *early* is in each sentence.
   a. Our visitors came <u>early</u> in the evening. (adverb)
   b. The <u>early</u> bird catches the worm. (adjective)
8. Tell what part of speech *through* is in each sentence.
   a. The turnpike goes <u>through</u> a tunnel in the mountain. (preposition)
   b. Those who will be rich pierce themselves <u>through</u> with many sorrows. (adverb)
9. Tell what part of speech *until* is in each sentence.
   a. We worked hard <u>until</u> suppertime. (preposition)
   b. We worked hard <u>until</u> Mother called for supper. (conjunction)

Prefixes

If the same root is used for words in a word family, how are the different words made? Generally the new words are formed by adding prefixes and suffixes. A *prefix* is added to the beginning of a word or word root to alter the meaning of the original word. By learning the meanings of prefixes, you can expand your knowledge of words. In the following examples, the roots are words that you know, so you should be able to figure out the meanings of the words.

Prefix	Meaning	Examples
ante-	before	antechamber, antedate, anteroom
anti-	against	antichrist, antifreeze, antislavery
de-	down, away	de-emphasize, defrost, degrade
dis-	absence, away	disability, discontent, discount
ex-	away, out from	excommunicate, export, express
inter-	between, within	international, interstate, intertropical
pre-	before	prearrange, predawn, preview
pro-	for, forward	pronoun, proslavery, prothorax
re-	again, back	recall, reecho, retell
sub-	below	subaudible, subcabinet, subconscious
super-, sur-	over, above	superheat, supernatural, surtax
trans-	across, over	transcontinental, transmigrate, transplant

Now notice how a knowledge of these prefixes can help you understand the meanings of words with less obvious roots.

Prefix	Root	New Word and Meaning
ante-	pend (hang)	antependium (a hanging before a lectern)
anti-	path (feeling)	antipathy (a strong feeling against something)
de-	cline (lean)	decline (to lean downward)
dis-	pel (drive)	dispel (to drive away)
ex-	cav (hollow)	excavate (to hollow out)
inter-	ject (throw)	interject (to throw in between)
pre-	dict (say)	predict (to say beforehand)
pro-	spect (look)	prospect (a looking forward to something)
re-	deem (buy)	redeem (to buy back)
sub-	script (write)	subscription (a writing below)
super-	flu (flow)	superfluous (overflowing; more than necessary)
trans-	fer (carry)	transfer (to carry across)

Suffixes

Suffixes can also be added to words and word roots. A *suffix* is added to the end of a word or word root, usually to change it to a different part of speech. Suffixes also add specific meanings to roots. The following charts list some common suffixes for nouns, verbs, adjectives, and adverbs.

Lesson Introduction: If possible, use some people your students know quite well as examples of family likenesses. Point out how similar some siblings are in their appearance, speech, or actions. Then point the students to the title of this lesson. Tell them that when they become familiar with a few words in one family, they can often recognize other words in that family.

Lesson Outline:

1. Words with the same root make up a word family.

2. A prefix is added to the beginning of a word or word root to alter the meaning of the original word.

3. A suffix is added to the end of a word or word root, usually to change it to a different part of speech. Suffixes also add specific meanings to word roots.

a. The following are common noun-forming suffixes: *-cy, -ance* or *-ence, -ism, -ar* or *-er* or *-or, -ion* or *-ation, -ment, -ness,* and *-ship.*

b. The following are common verb-forming suffixes: *-ate, -ify,* and *-ize.*

c. The following are common adjective-forming suffixes: *-able* or *-ible, -al* or *-ual, -ant* or *-ent, -ful, -ic, -less, -ous,* and *-ive.*

d. One common adverb-forming suffix is *-ly.*

4. A dictionary will help you to use prefixes and suffixes correctly.

★ **EXTRA PRACTICE**
Worksheet 60 (*Word Families*)

Noun-Forming Suffixes

Suffix	Meaning	Examples
-cy	rank, quality	accuracy, leniency, presidency
-ance, -ence	action or state of	appearance, dependence, preference
-ism	action, state, doctrine	baptism, communism, criticism, Hinduism, monotheism, realism
-ar, -er, -or	one who, that which	beggar, employer, director
-ion, -ation	action or condition of	action, discussion, consolation
-ment	action of	betterment, placement, settlement
-ness	condition, state	godliness, goodness, happiness
-ship	quality, skill, rank	friendship, kingship, penmanship
-ty, -ety, -ity	condition, state	royalty, variety, purity

Verb-Forming Suffixes

Suffix	Meaning	Examples
-ate	do, make, become	activate, elongate, operate
-ify	make	beautify, dignify, identify
-ize	make into, resemble	crystallize, itemize, winterize

Adjective-Forming Suffixes

Suffix	Meaning	Examples
-able, -ible	capable of, tending to	comfortable, dependable, durable, defensible, flexible
-al, -ual	relating to	accidental, personal, spiritual
-ant, -ent	being in a state or position of	assistant, decadent, independent
-ful	full of, characteristic of	careful, masterful, peaceful, wonderful
-ic	relating to, characterized by	allergic, alphabetic, electronic
-ive	performing, tending toward	conclusive, creative, decisive, descriptive, transitive
-less	not having or doing	fadeless, pointless, speechless
-ous	full of, having	continuous, gracious, marvelous

Adverb-Forming Suffix

Suffix	Meaning	Examples
-ly	in such a manner	boldly, carefully, slowly

A dictionary will help you to use prefixes and suffixes correctly. Sometimes two words have the same root and a prefix or suffix with the same meaning, yet the meanings of the two words are different. For example, the suffixes -*ful* and -*ous* both mean "full of." But the words *graceful* and *gracious* do not have the same meanings. *Graceful* usually describes physical motion, and *gracious* refers mainly to words or attitudes.

We enjoyed watching the graceful maneuvers of the barn swallows. The people marveled at the gracious words of Jesus.

Class Practice

A. Tell what the following words mean by the clues given.
1. The prefix *ex-* means "out from," the root *spect* means "look," and the suffix *-ation* means "action or quality of."
   a. What does *expectation* mean?
   b. The prefix *circum-* means "around." What does *circumspect* mean?
   c. The suffix *-or* means "one who." What is a *spectator*?
   d. Give several other words in this family.
2. The prefix *in-* can mean "not," the root *cred* means "believe," the suffix *-ible* means "capable of," and the suffix *-ly* means "in such a manner."
   a. What does *incredibly* mean?
   b. The suffix *-ence* means "action of." What does *credence* mean?
   c. What is a *creed*?
   d. Name several other words in this family.

B. Form new words from the ones given, using the same suffix as that in the underlined word.
1. <u>productive</u>   a. correct   b. support   c. extend   d. corrode
2. <u>polarize</u>   a. final   b. legal   c. real   d. normal
3. <u>persuasion</u>   a. revert   b. immerse   c. conclude   d. revise

C. Name the part of speech for each word, and then add a suffix to make a noun.
1. certain   2. punish   3. kind   4. relate

D. Make adjectives from these verbs by adding suffixes.
1. observe   2. malign   3. describe   4. abhor

E. Make verbs from these nouns by adding or changing suffixes.
1. beauty   2. material   3. alphabet   4. contemplation

Written Exercises

A. Do these exercises on word families. Use a dictionary to check your answers.
1. The root *clam* means "to cry out."
   a. Write a word with this root and the meaning "noisy outcry; hubbub."
   b. The prefix *pro-*, meaning "for or forward," can also mean "forth." When God told a prophet to proclaim His message, what was the prophet to do?
   c. The prefix *ex-* means "out," and the suffix *-ation* means "the action of." Write a word that means "the action of crying out."

Lesson 119 Answers

Class Practice

A. 1. a. the action of looking out from (toward something in the future)
   b. looking around in all directions
   c. one who looks at something
   d. (Sample words.) spectacle, respect, prospect
2. a. in a manner not capable of being believed
   b. the action of believing
   c. a belief
   d. (Sample words.) credit, credible, discredit

B. 1. a. corrective   c. extensive
   b. supportive   d. corrosive
2. a. finalize   c. realize
   b. legalize   d. normalize
3. a. reversion   c. conclusion
   b. immersion   d. revision

C. 1. adjective, certainty
2. verb, punishment
3. adjective, kindness
4. verb, relation

D. 1. observable, observant
2. malignant
3. descriptive, describable
4. abhorrent

E. 1. beautify   3. alphabetize
2. materialize   4. contemplate

Written Exercises

A. 1. a. clamor
   b. cry forth His message
   c. exclamation

2. The root *therm* means "heat."
   a. The root *meter* means "measure," and the root *graph* means "to write." What is the difference between a thermometer and a thermograph?
   b. The root *geo* means "earth." How is geothermal steam produced?
   c. What is thermoelectricity?
3. The root *cede* or *cess* means "to go or yield."
   a. Write a verb that means "to go before."
   b. Does the antecedent of a pronoun usually go before or after the pronoun?
   c. Write a word that means "the action of going forward."
   d. Write a word that means "pertaining to the action of going back." (You need one prefix and two suffixes.)
   e. Write a word that means "one who goes between."

B. Form new words from the ones given, using the same suffix as that in the underlined word. Use a dictionary if you are not sure of the correct spelling.

1. <u>remarkable</u>   a. move   b. describe   c. forget   d. agree
2. <u>settlement</u>   a. content   b. endear   c. case   d. wonder
3. <u>rustic</u>   a. rhythm   b. melody   c. hygiene   d. angel
4. <u>clarify</u>   a. mortal   b. simple   c. ample   d. code

C. Change each word to the part of speech named in parentheses by adding or changing a suffix. Use a dictionary if you are not sure of the correct spelling.

1. sanitary (verb)   6. tense (noun)
2. conceal (noun)   7. circuit (adjective)
3. duty (adjective)   8. considerable (adverb)
4. hard (noun)   9. donor (verb)
5. fortitude (verb)   10. wander (noun)

Review Exercises

A. Copy each underlined word, and label it *adj.* or *adv.* [86]
   1. The Old Testament saint depended upon <u>priestly</u> intercession to draw <u>near</u> to God.
   2. The <u>holy</u> lives of God's people witness to those who are <u>far</u> from God.
   3. Although we left <u>early</u> enough, we arrived <u>late</u> because of a flat tire.
   4. In the <u>far</u> corner stood a <u>lovely</u> philodendron.

B. Copy each underlined word, and label it *adv.* or *prep.* [89]
   1. God came <u>down</u> to see the wickedness of Sodom.
   2. Lot chose the lands <u>near</u> Sodom, and eventually he moved <u>inside</u>.

2. a. A thermometer measures the temperature; a thermograph records the temperature on paper.
   b. with heat from the earth
   c. electricity produced by heat
3. a. precede   d. recessional
   b. before   e. intercessor
   c. procession

B. 1. a. movable *or* moveable   c. forgettable
      b. describable   d. agreeable
   2. a. contentment   c. casement
      b. endearment   d. wonderment
   3. a. rhythmic   c. hygienic
      b. melodic   d. angelic
   4. a. mortify   c. amplify
      b. simplify   d. codify

C. 1. sanitize
   2. concealment, concealer
   3. dutiful, duteous, dutiable
   4. hardness, hardship
   5. fortify
   6. tension, tenseness
   7. circuitous
   8. considerably
   9. donate
   10. wanderer

Review Exercises

A. 1. priestly—adj.; near—adv.
   2. holy—adj.; far—adv.
   3. early—adv.; late—adv.
   4. far—adj.; lovely—adj.

B. 1. down—adv.
   2. near—prep.; inside—adv.

3. We should lift our eyes <u>up</u> to the One whose throne is <u>above</u> all.
4. Though storms roar <u>without</u>, we can trust the Lord.

C. Copy each underlined word, and label it *prep.* or *conj.* [89, 95]
   1. <u>After</u> the thunderstorm, a beautiful rainbow appeared.
   2. We must wait patiently <u>until</u> Grandfather comes.
   3. <u>Before</u> we moved to the farm, Father had taught school.
   4. <u>After</u> my day at the market stand, I am ready to rest.

3. up—adv.; above—prep.
4. without—adv.

C. 1. After—prep.   3. Before—conj.
   2. until—conj.   4. After—prep.

---

120. Encyclopedias and Atlases

> **Lesson Survey**
> - An **encyclopedia** is a helpful source of general information.
> - An encyclopedia needs to be used with caution.
> - An **atlas** is a book of maps.

Encyclopedias

Do you want to know where Abraham Lincoln was born, and when? Would you like to find out which states produce the most coal? Are you interested in how a hygrometer works? Where would you find information about these and hundreds of other subjects? Probably one of the first places you would look is in an encyclopedia.

An *encyclopedia* is a helpful source of general information. A wide range of subjects is treated within its volumes. Some articles are just a few sentences long, and others cover several pages; but all are arranged alphabetically by subject. To find an article on Abraham Lincoln, you would look in the *L* volume.

Most encyclopedias have an index in a separate volume. The index lists all the articles that mention a certain subject. For example, if you look up *Lincoln, Abraham* in the index, you will find the page number of the main article entitled "Abraham Lincoln." But the index entry also directs you to other articles that mention him, such as "Civil War," "Gettysburg Address," "Illinois," and "President of the United States."

The index is also helpful in finding information on subjects for which there is no separate article. For example, in the *World Book Encyclopedia* you will find nothing about the Kootenay River in the *K* volume. However, the index will direct you to the exact page and heading title

Lesson 120

Purpose: To teach the use of *encyclopedias and *atlases.

Oral Review:
1. What is a word root? (a basic word element)
2. How does a prefix usually change a word or word root? (changes its meaning)
3. How does a suffix usually change a word or word root? (changes its part of speech)
4. Name the word group described by each phrase.
   a. Words with opposite meanings. (antonyms)
   b. Words spelled and pronounced alike, but having different origins and meanings. (homographs)
   c. Words with similar meanings. (synonyms)
   d. Words spelled alike but pronounced differently. (heteronyms)
   e. Words pronounced alike but spelled differently. (homophones)
5. Tell what is wrong with each sentence.
   a. Either Mark or Conrad may bring their soccer ball. (his)
   b. My uncles, Oliver and him, will drive the moving truck. (he)
   c. Seventh graders have less subjects than tenth graders. (fewer)
   d. Them apples look delicious. (Those)
   e. The dog looks kind of sick. (rather *or* somewhat)
   f. This has sure been an unusual day! (surely)

Lesson Introduction: Encyclopedias have been around for many centuries. Marcus Terentius Varro, a Roman scholar, compiled perhaps the first set in the last century B.C. Another set was produced in the first century A.D. by Pliny the Elder, also a

in the *B* volume where this river is mentioned.

Many encyclopedia articles have cross-references at the end. The cross-references direct you to articles with information that is closely related to the subject you have looked up.

Encyclopedias need to be used with caution. The articles are not written on a Biblical basis, but from man's point of view. They glorify man's achievements and promote man's theories rather than the truth of God's Word.

Another caution is to avoid using an encyclopedia as your only source of information, especially when doing research for a composition. Do not think that you have gained all the information you need just by reading encyclopedia articles. A book devoted to grafting fruit trees will contain much more information on that subject than you will find in an encyclopedia.

Atlases

An *atlas* is a book of maps. There are many different kinds of atlases: world atlases, road atlases, Bible atlases, and others. A world atlas shows the world geographically and politically. Geographical maps emphasize the physical features of the land, the types of vegetation and land use, the rainfall and climate patterns, and the population density. The political maps emphasize the boundaries of nations, states, and provinces.

A road atlas is a guide for traveling. It has maps that show the different kinds of roads and highways within states, provinces, and cities. Such an atlas also shows places of interest and other information important to travelers.

A Bible atlas includes maps of the Bible lands as they were during various periods of Bible history. Larger Bible atlases, like *Baker's Bible Atlas* or *The Moody Atlas of Bible Lands,* also include detailed information about Bible geography and history.

An atlas usually has an index listing all the place names shown on all the maps in the atlas. The index is keyed to tell you on which maps a place can be found and exactly where the place is located on each map.

Class Practice

A. Answer these questions.
   1. What is the value of the index to an encyclopedia?
   2. Why must you use encyclopedias with caution?
   3. What is the value of the index to an atlas?

B. Give the number of the encyclopedia volume in which you would find an article on each of the following subjects.
   1. Leo Tolstoy   4. Kangaroos
   2. Chief products of Monaco   5. Type of government in Zaire
   3. Barometers   6. Languages of the world

Lesson 120 Answers

Class Practice

A. 1. The index lists all the articles in the encyclopedia that mention a certain subject. It also shows where to find subjects that do not have separate articles in the encyclopedia.
   2. They are written from man's point of view. They glorify man's achievements and promote man's theories rather than the truth of God's Word. Also, they do not contain as much information about a particular subject as one could find in a whole book devoted to that subject.
   3. It lists all the place names that are found on all the maps. It tells on which maps a place can be found and exactly where it is located on each map.

B. (Answers depend on the encyclopedia used.)

Roman scholar. The word *encyclopedia* is derived from three Greek word elements: *en* from the word for "in," *cyclo* from the word for "circle," and *pedia* from the word for "education." So the word means literally "education in the whole circle of knowledge." And that is exactly what makes an encyclopedia so valuable to us.

Lesson Outline:

1. An encyclopedia is a helpful source of general information.
   a. The articles are arranged alphabetically by subject.
   b. An index lists all the articles that mention a certain subject.
   c. Cross-references direct you to articles with information that is closely related to the subject you have looked up.

2. An encyclopedia needs to be used with caution.
   a. The articles are written from man's point of view, glorifying man's achievements and promoting man's theories rather than the truth of God's Word.
   b. Encyclopedias must not be used as one's only source of information.

3. An atlas is a book of maps.
   a. A world atlas has geographical maps that emphasize the physical features of the land, the types of vegetation and land use, the rainfall and climate patterns, and the population density. It also has political maps

Written Exercises

A. Write the number of the encyclopedia volume in which you would find an article on each of the following subjects.
1. The island of Ellesmere
2. Martin Luther
3. Mount McKinley
4. Manufacturing rubber
5. Hot-air balloons
6. How pineapples are harvested
7. Whales
8. How snow is formed

B. Using the index, list three articles in the encyclopedia for each of the following subjects to show where you could find information on them.
1. George Washington
2. Pompeii
3. Plastics
4. Porpoise

C. Using a road atlas, write down the routes you would use to travel to these places.
1. The capital city of your state or province.
2. The capital city of your country.

Review Exercises

A. If the underlined word or phrase contains a mistake in pronoun usage, write it correctly. If it is correct, write *correct*. [60]
1. Three of the disciples, <u>Peter, James, and him</u>, went with Jesus.
2. Neither Peter nor Judas was faithful to <u>their</u> Lord.
3. Uncle Milton brought a surprise for <u>us children</u>.
4. Mother wrote a story about <u>me and you</u> at the barn fire.

B. If the underlined word or phrase contains a mistake in adjective usage, write it correctly. If it is correct, write *correct*. [77]
1. There are <u>less</u> books in the New Testament than in the Old Testament.
2. Therefore, the New Testament takes up much <u>less</u> space.
3. God used <u>them</u> different writers to record His message to man.
4. What <u>kind of a</u> flower is this?
5. <u>That there</u> flower has several beautiful blossoms.

C. These sentences contain mistakes in adverb usage. Write each underlined item correctly. [87]
1. Andrea has a cold and cannot talk very <u>good</u>.
2. Hasn't Harry <u>never</u> missed a day of school yet?
3. This cake is <u>sort of</u> dry.
4. This ice cream is <u>real</u> delicious though.
5. You will have a chapter test <u>later on</u>.

Written Exercises

A. (Answers depend on the encyclopedia used.)

B. (Answers depend on the encyclopedia used. For future reference, you may wish to write the answers from your encyclopedia in the answer key.)

C. (Answers depend on the location of your school.)

Review Exercises

A. 1. Peter, James, and he
2. his
3. correct
4. you and me

B. 1. fewer
2. correct
3. those
4. kind of
5. That

C. 1. well
2. ever
3. rather *or* somewhat
4. really
5. later

that emphasize the boundaries of nations, states, and provinces.
b. A road atlas shows different kinds of roads and highways, places of interest, and other information important to travelers.
c. A Bible atlas includes maps of the Bible lands as they were during various periods of Bible history.
d. An atlas usually has an index listing all the place names shown on all the maps in the atlas.

121. Concordances, Topical Bibles, and Bible Dictionaries

Lesson Survey

- A **concordance** lists Bible words alphabetically and gives references where the words are used.

- Some concordances give the original Hebrew and Greek words from which the English words in the Bible were translated.

- A **topical Bible** is a book of Bible topics arranged in alphabetical order, with verses about each topic.

- A **Bible dictionary** is like a small encyclopedia of Bible information.

- We must use these reference books wisely and compare them carefully with the Bible itself.

The Bible is the most important book in the world. This book contains the direct message of God to man. But the Bible is a whole library of books, containing vast amounts of detailed information. Very few people, if any, have become so thoroughly familiar with the Bible that they can tell where any verse in the Bible is found. Nor has any person ever learned all there is to know about every person, place, or custom mentioned in the Bible. Anyone who studies the Bible will receive much benefit by using concordances, topical Bibles, and Bible dictionaries.

Concordances

A *concordance* lists Bible words alphabetically and gives references where the words are used. Many Bibles have concordances in the back, but they are small and quite limited. A complete concordance, like *Strong's Exhaustive Concordance of the Bible,* is often more satisfactory.

You use a concordance mainly to find verses which contain specific words that you remember. Suppose you are preparing to write a composition on "How Snow Forms." You know there is a Bible verse that mentions the treasures of the snow, and you want to write the exact words. You could look up either *treasures* or *snow* and find that the reference is Job 38:22.

When you use a concordance, try to decide which word that you remember is the least common word. Suppose you want to find the verse that contains the words "A righteous man regardeth the life of his beast." Which word should you look up? *Righteous, man, life,* and *beast* are all very common in the Bible. If you look up one of these words, you will probably need

Lesson 121

Purpose: To teach the use of concordances, *topical Bibles, and Bible dictionaries.

Oral Review:

1. Why should you use the index of an encyclopedia when searching for information? (The index lists every place in the entire set where specific information is found.)

2. What other help do most encyclopedias have for finding information at various places in the set? (cross-references at the end of articles)

3. Why must encyclopedias be used with caution? (They give man's point of view, glorifying man's achievements and promoting man's ideas rather than the truth of God's Word. Also, they do not give information as thoroughly as more detailed sources do.)

4. Tell whether these sentences contain synonyms, antonyms, homophones, heteronyms, or homographs.

   a. Marlene's side of the bedroom is usually <u>neat</u>, but Nellie's is often <u>sloppy</u>. (antonyms)

   b. The <u>lean</u> cow was so weak that she had to <u>lean</u> against the wall. (homographs)

   c. Would Noah and his family <u>bow</u> before the Lord whenever they saw a <u>bow</u> in the sky? (heteronyms)

   d. God <u>talked</u> with Moses; but when He <u>spoke</u> to the people, they feared. (synonyms)

   e. The Israelites were not <u>allowed</u> to talk <u>aloud</u> while marching around Jericho. (homophones)

Lesson Introduction: Ask your students to give some Bible passages that refer to shepherds or sheepherding. Likely they will mention such familiar passages as Psalm 23 and John 10. Under the entries for

to search through many references before you find the one you want. But *regardeth* has only a few references because that word is fairly uncommon in the Bible. So that is the best word to look up.

Some concordances give the original Hebrew and Greek words from which the English words in the Bible were translated, along with the definitions for those words. *Strong's Exhaustive Concordance* is the most common one of this kind. Every reference is followed by a number in the right-hand column. If the word is in an Old Testament reference, the number is in regular type, like this: 3045. If it is in a New Testament reference, the number is in italics, like this: *5426*.

The Old Testament was written in Hebrew and Chaldee, and the New Testament in Greek. Therefore, to look up the original meaning of an Old Testament word, find that number in the "Hebrew and Chaldee Dictionary" in the back of the concordance. To look up the original meaning of a New Testament word, find that number in the "Greek Dictionary of the New Testament."

Perhaps you are reading in Judges 4:19 about Jael opening a bottle of milk. You wonder, "What kind of bottle would she have had?" So you look up *bottle* in *Strong's Concordance* and find the reference, Judges 4:19. Beside that reference is the number 4997. Since this is an Old Testament reference, you turn to the "Hebrew and Chaldee Dictionary." In the entry for number 4997, you find these words: "a (skin or leather) *bag* (for fluids)."

Or suppose you read Jesus' words in John 12:24: "Except a corn of wheat fall into the ground and die, it abideth alone." You wonder, "What is a corn of wheat?" You look up *corn,* find the reference John 12:24, and note that the number for this word is *2848*. This is a New Testament reference, so you turn to the "Greek Dictionary of the New Testament." In the entry for number *2848,* you find these words: "a *kernel* of seed."

Topical Bibles

A *topical Bible* is a book of Bible topics arranged in alphabetical order, with verses about each topic. This book is different from a concordance in that it gives verses about a topic like *prayer* even if they do not actually contain the word *prayer. Nave's Topical Bible* is the most familiar and the most complete topical Bible available. Major topics have the verses printed so that you need not look them up in your regular Bible. Other topics have only the references listed.

Many topics in a topical Bible are subdivided so that it is simpler to find specific references. In *Nave's Topical Bible,* for instance, some of the subheads under the topic "Influence" are "Evil," "Good," and "Political." There are also cross-references that direct the user to "Example" and "Politics."

the various forms of *shepherd, Strong's Concordance* lists eighty-two occurrences of that word. A topical Bible lists several more verses that refer to sheepherding without using any form of the word. A Bible dictionary gives other information about the work of a shepherd in Palestine. We should appreciate the efforts that others have put into compiling reference books like these. They can be a valuable help to our understanding of the Bible.

Lesson Outline:

1. A concordance lists Bible words alphabetically and gives references where the words are used.

    a. Many Bibles have small concordances in the back, but a complete concordance is often more satisfactory.

    b. A concordance is used mainly to find verses which contain specific words that we remember.

    c. When using a concordance, look up one of the least common words in the verse you want to find.

2. Some concordances give the original Hebrew and Greek words from which the English words in the Bible were translated. *Strong's Exhaustive Concordance of the Bible* is the most common one of this kind.

    a. Each Old Testament reference is followed by a number in regular type, which refers to an entry in the "Hebrew and Chaldee Dictionary."

    b. Each New Testament reference is followed by a number in italics, which refers to an entry in the "Greek Dictionary of the New Testament."

3. A topical Bible is a book of Bible topics arranged in alphabetical order, with verses about each topic. Nave's Topical Bible is the most

Bible Dictionaries

A *Bible dictionary* is like a small encyclopedia of Bible information. It gives information about people, places, objects, and customs referred to in the Bible. It also explains Bible doctrines and the meanings of Bible words. Like a regular dictionary, the entry words are arranged alphabetically. But more like an encyclopedia, many entries include several paragraphs of information.

Do you want to know what the pool of Siloam is like? In a Bible dictionary, you will discover that it is about fifty-three feet long, eighteen feet wide, and nineteen feet deep. The water in the pool comes from a spring outside the city of Jerusalem. To bring this water into the city, a channel was cut through solid rock for a distance of 1,780 feet.

Are you planning a report about olives and wanting to include some facts about olives in Bible times or Bible lands? A Bible dictionary is sure to supply the information you need.

All these reference books, of course, are the works of men. They are not perfect as the Bible is. They are valuable sources of information only as we use them wisely and compare them carefully with the Bible itself.

Class Practice

Answer these questions about concordances, topical Bibles, and Bible dictionaries.

1. Which word would be the best to use in looking up these verses in a concordance?
   a. "A good name is better than precious ointment."
   b. "Moreover it is required in stewards, that a man be found faithful."
   c. "Now there was no smith found throughout all the land of Israel."
2. a. Name the original languages of the Old Testament.
   b. Name the original language of the New Testament.
3. In *Strong's Concordance,* how can you tell whether a number refers to a word in the Greek dictionary or in the Hebrew and Chaldee dictionary?
4. How would you benefit by looking up the word *contentment* in a topical Bible rather than in a concordance?
5. How is a long entry in a topical Bible arranged so that it is simpler to find specific references?
6. a. How is a Bible dictionary arranged like a regular dictionary?
   b. How is it more like an encyclopedia?

Written Exercises

A. Using a concordance, find and write the reference for each verse.
1. "I am the Lord thy God which teacheth thee to profit, which leadeth thee by the way that thou shouldest go."

Lesson 121 Answers

Class Practice

1. (As a matter of interest, numbers are given in parentheses to indicate the number of references in *Strong's Concordance.*)
   a. precious (76) *or* ointment (27)
   b. stewards (4) *or* required (22)
   c. smith (3)
2. a. Hebrew and Chaldee
   b. Greek
3. The numbers for the Hebrew and Chaldee dictionary are in regular type. The numbers for the Greek dictionary are in italics.
4. A topical Bible would probably have verses about contentment printed out, rather than just giving the references. A topical Bible would give verses about the topic *contentment,* not just verses that contain the word *contentment.*
5. Long entries usually are subdivided.
6. a. Entry words are listed alphabetically.
   b. Many entries contain several paragraphs of information.

Written Exercises

A. 1. Isaiah 48:17

familiar and the most complete topical Bible available.

   a. Major topics have the verses printed so that you need not look them up in your regular Bible. Other topics have only the references listed.
   b. Many topics in a topical Bible are subdivided so that it is simpler to find specific references.

   4. A Bible dictionary is like a small encyclopedia of Bible information.
   a. It gives information about people, places, objects, and customs referred to in the Bible. It also explains Bible doctrines and the meanings of Bible words.

   b. Like a regular dictionary, the entry words are arranged alphabetically. But more like an encyclopedia, many entries include several paragraphs of information.

   5. We must use these reference books wisely and compare them carefully with the Bible itself.

2. "Let the elders that rule well be counted worthy of double honour, especially they who labour in the word and doctrine."

3. "If the Son therefore shall make you free, ye shall be free indeed."

4. "And the men did so; and took two milch kine, and tied them to the cart, and shut up their calves at home."

B. Use *Strong's Exhaustive Concordance* to do these exercises.
1. Look up the words *unicorn* and *unicorns.*
   a. What is the total number of Bible verses that contain these words?
   b. To find the original word for *unicorn,* turn to the (Hebrew, Greek) dictionary and look up the number ———.
   c. What is the meaning of *unicorn* in the original language?
   d. Read Job 39:9, and explain why Job would have had to say *no* in answer to this question.
2. Look up the word *fierce.*
   a. How many times does this word occur in the New Testament?
   b. Look at the numbers for the Greek words translated *fierce.* Then write the number of the correct sentence in this list.
      (1) *Fierce* is translated from the same Greek word each time.
      (2) *Fierce* is translated from a different Greek word each time.
      (3) *Fierce* is sometimes translated from the same Greek word and sometimes from different Greek words.
   c. Write the original meaning of *fierce* as used in each of the following references.
      (1) Luke 23:5   (2) 2 Timothy 3:3

C. Use a topical Bible to find verses about these subjects. For each one, copy two verses with their references from two different books of the Bible.
1. Forgiveness   3. Creation of man
2. Anointing with oil   4. Horses

D. Use a Bible dictionary to answer the following questions.
1. What does the name *Peter* mean?
2. Why is *Bethel* a common name for churches?
3. a. What tool was John referring to when he said that Christ's *fan* was in His hand (Matthew 3:12)?
   b. What was this tool used for?
   c. What does this speak of Jesus doing?
4. What two kinds of *engines* were used in Bible times?

Review Exercises

A. Write four synonyms for each word. [117]
1. temperance   3. disobedient
2. marsh   4. perambulate

2. 1 Timothy 5:17
3. John 8:36
4. 1 Samuel 6:10

B. 1. a. 9
     b. Hebrew, 7214
     c. a wild bull
     d. Since the unicorn was a wild animal, it would not have been willing to work for Job or to stay with him.
  2. a. 4
     b. 2
     c. (1) To insist stoutly
        (2) Savage

C. (Answers will vary.)

D. (Answers are based on *Unger's Bible Dictionary.*)
1. a rock
2. The name means "house of God."
3. a. a long-handled wooden shovel
   b. to throw grain up into the wind so that the chaff would be separated from the grain
   c. separating the evil from the good
4. the *balista,* used to throw stones; the *catapulta,* used to shoot arrows

Review Exercises

A. (Sample answers.)
1. moderation, self-restraint, self-control, continence, sobriety
2. swamp, morass, fen, bog, slough, wash
3. insubordinate, defiant, unruly, unsubmissive, noncompliant
4. wander, meander, stroll, walk, roam

B. Write an antonym for each word. Do not merely add a prefix. [117]
   1. tarnish   2. facilitate

C. Write a pair of homophones for each of these pronunciations. [117]
   1. far   3. prof´·it
   2. ī´·dəl   4. bōl´·dər

D. Write two different phonetic spellings for each heteronym. [117]
   1. bass   2. close

E. Write two short sentences for each homograph, illustrating the different meanings. [117]
   1. pitcher   2. mean

B. (Sample answers.)
   1. brighten, polish, buff, furbish, gloss, shine
   2. hinder, impede, obstruct

C. 1. fair, fare   3. profit, prophet
   2. idle, idol   4. bolder, boulder

D. (Answers will vary according to dictionary used.)
   1. bās, bas   2. klōs, klōz

E. (Individual work.)

---

122. Sentence Variety in Paragraphs

Lesson Survey
- Good sentence variety produces effective emphasis.
- Sentence variety can be achieved by varying the lengths of sentences, the word order in sentences, the beginnings of sentences, the types of sentences according to structure, and the types of sentences according to use.

An interesting paragraph includes some variety. This lesson emphasizes five ways in which sentences may be varied. Not every paragraph will include all these kinds of variety, but every paragraph should include at least some of them.

Good sentence variety produces effective emphasis. Simply having variety is valuable, but you should strive for variety that emphasizes the important ideas. Generally speaking, the part of a sentence that comes first receives the most emphasis, especially if it is something that is not normally put first. A sentence tends to be emphasized if it is sharply different from the preceding ones. For example, a very short sentence after several longer ones will stand out.

Sentence variety can be achieved in the following ways.

1. *Write sentences of various lengths.* The writing of many people consists mainly of long sentences. But we do not speak that way! In fact, we often use more short sentences than long ones when we speak. A paragraph with some shorter sentences will sound more natural.

Lesson 122

Purpose: To teach various methods of achieving sentence variety in paragraphs.

Oral Review:
1. Tell how to make these sentences more effective.
   a. An intersection is where two line segments meet or cross. (An intersection is a point where two line segments meet or cross.)
   b. Brother Clifford said that the tour of the museum should last about one hour. ("The tour of the museum should last about one hour," stated Brother Clifford.)
   c. We finished the cleaning easily and with great speed. (We finished the cleaning easily and speedily.)
   d. Our plans for a picnic lunch were changed by the stormy weather. (The stormy weather changed our plans for a picnic lunch.)
   e. In some countries they are too poor to own cars. (In some countries the people are too poor to own cars.)

2. Which of the four kinds of poetic feet has each pattern?
   a. two unaccented syllables followed by an accented syllable (anapestic)
   b. one unaccented syllable followed by an accented syllable (iambic)
   c. one accented syllable followed by two unaccented syllables (dactylic)
   d. one accented syllable followed by an unaccented syllable (trochaic)

3. What would these letters tell you about a poem? *abbacc* (The first and fourth lines rhyme; the second and third lines rhyme; and the fifth and sixth lines rhyme.)

Study the following paragraph. Notice that it includes short, medium-ized, and long sentences. Especially notice the shortest sentence, "Courage erseveres." That shortness effectively emphasizes the point that is being made.

> Courage is an important quality. Your circumstances may make it easy for you to cheat or lie, or wrong thoughts may sneak into your mind. Courage will enable you to resist these temptations. Your friends may be deliberately avoiding another person or treating him unkindly. They may be acting irreverent in church or unsubmissive at school. With a courageous heart, you can stand alone for the right. Your teacher may have assigned you a difficult lesson. Your parents may have given you a wearisome, unpleasant task. Courage perseveres. Indeed, very little of true value is accomplished without people who have developed courage.

2. *Write sentences with a variety of word order.* Natural word order is used the most often because it makes statements in the most simple manner. Mixed word order is fairly common as well, but inverted word order is used more sparingly. Therefore, sentences with inverted word order tend to be especially catchy. You may need to put forth definite effort to write good sentences with inverted word order.

Study the following paragraph. Which word order is used for each sentence? Does the sentence with inverted word order catch your attention? Notice that it draws your attention to the most important sentence in the paragraph. By placing the phrase "Into such a camp" first, it also emphasizes the *place* where David came. The *person* is merely introduced in this paragraph.

> Day after day, the blasphemous challenge of Goliath thundered into the camp of Israel. The soldiers of Israel fled like terrified rabbits before the fearsome giant. The king of Israel cowered in his tent, wishing someone would do something about the predicament they faced. Into such a camp walked a young shepherd boy.

3. *Use a variety of sentence beginnings.* Of course, changing the word order results in varied sentence beginnings. Be alert to single-word adverbs, adverb phrases, and adverb clauses that can be placed at the beginning of a sentence. Sometimes a transitional expression can also be placed first in a sentence.

> <u>Suddenly</u> a light from heaven shone upon Saul.
> <u>After the flood</u>, God sent a rainbow.
> <u>Because Abraham loved Lot</u>, he prayed for the deliverance of Sodom.

4. Give the correct term for each description.
   a. The repetition of similar vowel sounds in accented syllables. (assonance)
   b. The repetition of beginning consonant sounds. (alliteration)
   c. The use of words having imitative sounds. (onomatopoeia)

Lesson Introduction: Read this paragraph in a monotone; then read it again expressively.

> Did you know that a loon can take off only from water? Even then it must paddle and flap for a long distance before it can rise into the air. If a loon on a northern lake waits too long in the fall before migrating south, so much of the lake may freeze over that the loon does not have enough open water for a takeoff. Then the loon will fall victim to predators or starvation, for it cannot run fast enough to take off from land.

A paragraph without sentence variety is like a speech without voice inflection. Both will communicate, but neither communicates very effectively.

Lesson Outline:
   1. Good sentence variety produces effective emphasis.
   a. Generally, the part of a sentence that comes first receives the most emphasis.
   b. A sentence tends to be emphasized if it is sharply different from the preceding ones.

   2. Sentence variety can be achieved in a number of ways.
   (1) *Write sentences of various lengths.*
   (2) *Write sentences with a variety of word order.*
   (3) *Use a variety of sentence beginnings.*
   (4) *Vary the types of sentences according to structure.*
   (5) *Vary the types of sentences according to use.*

Mother washed the dishes and cleaned the counter. <u>But</u> by evening she needed to clean up the kitchen again.

4. *Vary the types of sentences according to structure.* You have studied simple, compound, and complex sentences. No doubt, most of your sentences will be simple. But combining sentences often shows relationships more effectively. Thus you can gain not only variety but also clearer communication.

5. *Vary the types of sentences according to use.* Although most of your sentences will be declarative, a sprinkling of interrogative, imperative, and exclamatory sentences adds variety. However, avoid the tendency to write exclamatory sentences when you have nothing truly emphatic to say.

Compare the following two paragraphs. The first one has only simple, declarative sentences. The second has sentences that are varied according to their structure and their use.

Poor: No variety in sentence structure or use

A duck's body is designed for life in the water. Its body is shaped like a boat. It floats high on the water. With its webbed feet, the duck can propel itself easily through the water. An inner layer of soft, fluffy down feathers traps the duck's body heat. An outer layer of smooth feathers keeps out cold and moisture. As further protection against the water, the duck waterproofs its outer feathers with oil from its oil gland. God certainly has created the duck to be a waterfowl.

Better: Improved variety in sentence structure and use

Interrogative   How is a duck's body designed for life in the water?
Complex   Since its body is shaped like a boat, it floats high on the water. With its webbed feet, the duck can propel itself easily through the water. An inner layer of soft, fluffy down
Compound   feathers traps the duck's body heat, and an outer layer of smooth feathers keeps out cold and moisture. As further protection against the water, the duck waterproofs its outer feathers with oil from its oil gland. How evident that God
Exclamatory   has created the duck to be a waterfowl!

Class Practice

A. Change these sentences to different word order.
1. Moses' mother made an ark of bulrushes to hide the baby.
2. She placed the ark at the edge of the Nile River.
3. Pharaoh's daughter came down to the river.

B. Change the beginnings of these sentences.

Lesson 122 Answers

Class Practice

A. 1. To hide the baby, Moses' mother made an ar[k] of bulrushes.
2. At the edge of the Nile River, she placed th[e] ark.
3. Down to the river came Pharaoh's daughter[.]

1. Miriam faithfully watched her baby brother.
2. God rewarded the faith of Moses' parents in a marvelous way.
3. Miriam offered to get a Hebrew nurse when Pharaoh's daughter found the baby.
4. Pharaoh's daughter, in fact, allowed Moses' own mother to raise the child at home.

C. Change these pairs of sentences into either compound or complex sentences.
1. Good work habits must be developed. By nature most people are lazy.
2. A lazy person may have difficulty sleeping well. A hard worker enjoys sweet sleep.
3. Good work habits were evident in the life of Paul. He earned his living by making tents.

Written Exercises

A. Rewrite these paragraphs, making changes as indicated by the following directions.

[a]The migration of birds is a mystery. [b]It baffles the most brilliant scientists. [c]Migrating birds make unbelievably long trips. [d]They go on these journeys without ever getting lost. [e]They have never made such a trip before.

[f]The Atlantic golden plover flies south by one route in the fall. [g]It returns by another route in the spring. [h]The entire route is in the form of a great ellipse. [i]This bird heads out from Canada over the Atlantic Ocean to South America. [j]It returns in the spring by way of the Mississippi valley.

[k]The feat of the Pacific golden plover is equally astonishing. [l]This bird leaves Alaska. [m]It flies hundreds of miles toward the south. [n]It finds the Hawaiian Islands in the middle of the trackless Pacific Ocean. [o]It goes back to Alaska in the spring. [p]It returns the next fall to the same tiny island. [q]The migration of birds truly shows the wisdom and power of our great Creator.

1. Use *that* to join sentences *a* and *b* into a complex sentence.
2. Join sentences *d* and *e* into a complex sentence that ends with an exclamation point. Use *even though* as the conjunction.
3. Join sentences *f* and *g* into a compound sentence.
4. Begin sentence *i* with the prepositional phrase *from Canada.*
5. Join sentences *l, m,* and *n* into a sentence with three verbs in a series. Remember to use commas correctly.
6. Change sentences *o* and *p* so that each begins with a phrase telling *when.* Combine the resulting sentences into a compound sentence that ends with an exclamation point.
7. In sentence *q,* move *truly* to the beginning of the sentence.

B. 1. Faithfully Miriam watched her baby brother.
2. In a marvelous way, God rewarded the faith of Moses' parents.
3. When Pharaoh's daughter found the baby, Miriam offered to get a Hebrew nurse.
4. In fact, Pharaoh's daughter allowed Moses' own mother to raise the child at home.

C. 1. Good work habits must be developed because by nature most people are lazy.
or Good work habits must be developed, for by nature most people are lazy.
2. A lazy person may have difficulty sleeping well, but a hard worker enjoys sweet sleep.
or Although a lazy person may have difficulty sleeping well, a hard worker enjoys sweet sleep.
3. Good work habits were evident in the life of Paul, who earned his living by making tents.

Written Exercises

A. (Wording of sentences may vary somewhat.)

The migration of birds is a mystery that baffles the most brilliant scientists. Migrating birds make unbelievably long trips. They go on these journeys without ever getting lost, even though they have never made such a trip before!

The Atlantic golden plover flies south by one route in the fall, and it returns by another route in the spring. The entire route is in the form of a great ellipse. From Canada this bird heads out over the Atlantic Ocean to South America. It returns in the spring by way of the Mississippi valley.

The feat of the Pacific golden plover is equally astonishing. This bird leaves Alaska, flies hundreds of miles toward the south, and finds the Hawaiian Islands in the middle of the trackless Pacific Ocean. In the spring it goes back to Alaska, and the next fall it returns to the same tiny island! Truly, the migration of birds shows the wisdom and power of our great Creator.

B. Write a paragraph describing an exciting happening or a beautiful scene. Use good sentence variety.

Review Exercises

Read the following poem, and do the exercises that follow. [94–99]

Snowstorm

Just a few lonely flakes floating down through the air—
See them drifting and sifting from dark, leaden skies?
Ah, the deer seeks its shelter, the wolf seeks its lair,
And the bird for a bulwark to thick bushes flies;
For the threat of a storm seems to hover around,
Though as yet those few flakes hardly make any sound.

Now a host of white flakes falling fast fills the sky—
See them blowing and growing to deep, drifted mounds?
Not a beast on the move, not a bird on the fly;
And the roar of the storm as it o'er the earth sounds
Makes us grateful to God for our shelter this night,
And we peacefully rest, all secure in God's sight.

1. Write letters to represent the rhyming pattern.
2. a. Copy the first two lines, and mark the rhythm pattern.
   b. Name the poetic foot that is used.
   c. How many feet does each line have?
3. Copy at least two examples of alliteration.
4. Copy one example of assonance.
5. Copy one example of onomatopoeia.
6. Describe at least three contrasting thoughts between the first and the second stanza of this poem.

---

123. Chapter 11 Review

Class Practice

A. Define these terms. For numbers 3–7, also give a pair of words as an example.

1. inflections
2. etymology
3. synonyms
4. antonyms
5. homophones
6. heteronyms
7. homographs

Lesson 123

Purpose: To review the concepts taught in Chapter 11.

Teacher: The test on Chapter 11 is to be given after this lesson, with the final test to follow Lesson 125.

B. (Individual work.)

Review Exercises

1. ababcc
2. a. Just a few lonely flakes floating down through the air—
      See them drifting and sifting from dark, leaden skies?
   b. anapestic
   c. four
3. (Any two.)
   stanza 1: few, flakes, floating; bird, bulwark, bushes; storm, seems; few, flakes
   stanza 2: flakes, falling, fast, fills; deep, drifted; beast, bird; grateful, God; secure, sight
4. (Any one.) drifting, sifting; blowing, growing; roar, storm, o'er
5. (Any one.) blowing, roar
6. (Any three.) a few flakes versus a host of flakes; flakes falling slowly and softly versus flakes falling rapidly; animals seeking shelter versus animals in their helters; hardly any sound versus the roar of the storm; threat of a storm versus the reality of the storm

---

Lesson 123 Answers

Class Practice

A. (Examples are individual answers.)

1. Different forms of a word that show things like number and tense.
2. A brief description of the origin of a word.
3. Words with similar meanings.
4. Words with opposite meanings.
5. Words that are pronounced alike but spelled differently.
6. Words that are spelled alike but pronounced differently.
7. Words that are spelled and pronounced alike, but they have different origins and meanings.

B. Name the reference book that fits each description.
1. Volumes of information on a wide range of subjects.
2. A special book of synonyms and sometimes of antonyms.
3. A book of Bible topics arranged in alphabetical order, with verses about each topic.
4. A book of maps.
5. An arrangement of Bible words in alphabetical order, with references showing where the words are used.
6. A book of information about Bible words, doctrines, people, places, objects, practices, and customs.

C. Answer these questions about dictionaries.
1. Why does a word like *mean* have more than one numbered entry?
2. What three types of inflections do most dictionaries show?
3. Give a label to fit each description. If more than one label fits, a number is given in parentheses.
   a. Words acceptable in everyday speaking or writing, but not in formal speech or writing.
   b. Words to be avoided because of their evil use.
   c. Words to be avoided because they represent poor English. (3)
   d. Words no longer in general use. (2)
   e. Words invented by people trying to say things in unique ways.
   f. Words used in relatively small areas or by a limited group of people. (2)
4. Use this sample dictionary entry to do the exercises that follow.
   suc•cumb (sə·kum′) *v.* 1. To give way to some force or persuasion. 2. To die. [< OF *succomber* < L *succumbere* < *sub-*, below + *cumbere*, to lie down]
   a. Read the etymology correctly.
   b. How are the modern definitions related to the etymology?

D. Do the following exercises on word families.
1. The prefix *super-* means "over or above," the root *vis* means "to see," and the suffix *-or* means "one who."
   a. What does *supervisor* mean?
   b. The suffix *-ion* means "action or state of." What does *supervision* mean?
2. Add noun-forming suffixes to these words: *social, friendly, teach, create, present.*
3. Add verb-forming suffixes to these words: *clear, lubricant, final.*
4. Add adjective-forming suffixes to these words: *persist, microscope, erase, study, mercy, angel.*

B. 1. encyclopedia   4. atlas
   2. thesaurus   5. concordance
   3. topical Bible   6. Bible dictionary

C. 1. There are several words of different origins that have this spelling. In some dictionaries, a separate entry is used for each different part of speech that a word may be.
2. Irregular and unusual plural forms of nouns; principal parts of irregular verbs; irregular forms of comparison for adjectives and adverbs.
3. a. informal
   b. vulgar
   c. substandard, nonstandard, illiterate
   d. obsolete, archaic
   e. slang
   f. regional, dialectal
4. a. From Old French *succomber,* from Latin *succumbere,* from the prefix *sub-,* meaning "below," and the root *cumbere,* meaning "to lie down."
   b. When one gives way to a force or persuasion, he does not stand up against it but lies down or falls down before it. When one dies, his body lies below the ground.

D. 1. a. One who sees or watches over things to care for them.
      b. The action of seeing or watching over things.
2. socialism; friendliness; teacher; creation, creator; presence, presentness, presenter, presentation
3. clarify, lubricate, finalize
4. persistent; microscopic; erasable; studious; merciful, merciless; angelic, angelical

E. Answer these questions about reference books.
1. What is the value of the index to an encyclopedia set?
2. Why must you use encyclopedias cautiously?
3. What is the value of the index to an atlas?
4. Which word would you use in finding this verse in the Bible? "And Moses was an hundred and twenty years old when he died: his eye was not dim, nor his natural force abated."
5. The words in the "Hebrew and Chaldee Dictionary" of *Strong's Exhaustive Concordance* would be from which part of the Bible?
6. In *Strong's Concordance,* how are the numbers for the Greek dictionary kept separate from the numbers for the Hebrew and Chaldee dictionary?
7. How would you benefit by looking up an entry like *peace* in a topical Bible rather than in a concordance?
8. a. How is a Bible dictionary arranged like a regular dictionary?
   b. How is it more like an encyclopedia?

F. Tell why these sentences are not as effective as they could be. Then change them to more effective sentences.
1. The garden was plowed by Brother Nelson.
2. A concordance is where all Bible words are listed alphabetically.
3. Anita told Cheryl that she had spilled ketchup on her sleeve.
4. In art class this year, we learned to make macramé and doing calligraphy.
5. As a usual rule, March is full of a lot of windy, blustery days.

G. Answer these questions about sentence variety in paragraphs.
1. Which part of a sentence generally has the greatest emphasis?
2. Name five ways to achieve sentence variety.
3. Which kind of word order has the most emphasis, and why?

Written Exercises

A. Do these exercises on dictionary use.
1. Write at least one definition for each entry of the word *tender.*
2. Write at least two phonetic spellings of *despicable.*
3. Write *amenability,* using hyphens to show the syllable divisions.
4. Write the inflections given for these words.
   a. library   b. sparky   c. fight
5. What usage labels are given in the entries for these words?
   a. trow   b. crook   c. bonnet

B. Do these exercises on groups of related words.
1. Write four synonyms for *throw.*
2. Write four antonyms for *cheerful.*

E. 1. It lists all the articles that mention a certain subject.
2. They are written from man's point of view, glorifying man's achievements and promoting man's theories rather than God's Word. They also do not give as much detailed information as other sources can.
3. It lists all the place names shown on all the maps and the specific locations on the maps where the places are shown.
4. dim (9); natural (13); abated (6)
5. Old Testament
6. Numbers for the Hebrew and Chaldee dictionary are in regular type; numbers for the Greek dictionary are in italics.
7. The topical Bible would list all verses that relate to peace whether or not the word *peace* was actually used.
8. a. Entries are arranged alphabetically.
   b. Many entries include several paragraphs of information.

F. 1. unnecessary passive voice; Brother Nelson plowed the garden.
2. unparallel definition; A concordance is an alphabetical list of Bible words, with references showing where the words are used.
3. unclear pronoun reference; Anita told Cheryl, "You have spilled ketchup on your (*or* my) sleeve." *or* Anita told Cheryl, "I have spilled ketchup on my (*or* your) sleeve."
4. unparallel parts joined by a conjunction; In art class this year, we learned to make macramé and to do calligraphy.
5. wordy; March usually has many blustery days.

G. 1. the beginning
2. by varying the lengths of sentences, the word order in sentences, the beginnings of sentences, the types of sentences according to structure, and the types of sentences according to use
3. Inverted order has the most emphasis because it is the most unusual.

5. a. obsolete *or* archaic
   b. informal *or* Australian
   c. Chiefly Scottish *or* British

B. 1. (Sample answers.) propel, project, fling, cast, pitch, toss, hurl, sling
2. (Sample answers.) sad, unhappy, melancholy, gloomy, dejected, sorrowful, mournful, heavyhearted, doleful, woebegone, desolate

Written Exercises

A. (Answers will vary according to the dictionary used.)
1. tender¹, easily damaged; fragile; tender², a formal offer; tender³, one who tends something
2. des'·pi·ka·bəl; di·spik'·ə·bəl
3. a-me-na-bil-i-ty
4. a. libraries
   b. sparkier, sparkiest
   c. fought, fighting

3. Write homophones for each of these words. The number in parentheses tells how many.
   a. straight (1)   b. plain (1)   c. dew (2)
4. Write two sentences showing the two meanings of the heteronyms *wind*.
5. Write two sentences showing the two meanings of the homographs *pound*.

C. Do these exercises on word families. Use the charts in Lesson 119, and check your answers with a dictionary.
   1. The root *duce* means "to lead."
      a. The prefix *pro-* means "forward or forth," and the suffix *-er* means "one who." How is a producer of fruit "one who leads forth"?
      b. Add a prefix to this root to form a word that means "to lead down" or "to form a conclusion by reasoning."
      c. Add a prefix and a suffix to this root to form a word that means "the action of leading back (to a lower condition)."
   2. Change each word to the part of speech given in parentheses by adding or changing suffixes.
      a. act (adjective)   d. teach (adjective)
      b. familiar (verb)   e. consider (noun)
      c. certain (adverb)   f. buoyant (noun)

D. Do these exercises on using encyclopedias.
   1. Write the number of the encyclopedia volume in which you would find the following subjects.
      a. History of printing   c. How magnetism works
      b. Ulysses S. Grant   d. Liechtenstein
   2. Using the index, list the volume and page numbers of every mention of these items.
      a. Menno Simons   b. periodic table

E. Do these exercises on using Bible reference books.
   1. Write the reference for each verse.
      a. "And the Lord rooted them out of their land in anger, and in wrath, and in great indignation, and cast them into another land, as it is this day."
      b. "And the servant of the Lord must not strive; but be gentle unto all men, apt to teach, patient."
   2. From a topical Bible, list the references of three verses that speak about generosity.
   3. Find the Greek word that is translated *subverting* in 2 Timothy 2:14. Which of the following English words comes from that Greek word?
      catastrophe   disaster   perdition

3. a. strait
   b. plane
   c. do, due
4. (Sample sentences.) The wind blew fiercely. Wind the yarn onto spools.
5. (Sample sentences.) We bought one pound of butter. The little boy tried to pound the nail into the board.

C. 1. a. He raises fruit and brings it out to sell.
      b. deduce
      c. reduction
   2. a. actual, active, *or* actable
      b. familiarize
      c. certainly
      d. teachable
      e. consideration, considerer
      f. buoyancy, buoyance

D. 1. (Answers will vary.)
   2. (Answers will vary.)

E. 1. a. Deuteronomy 29:28
      b. 2 Timothy 2:24
   2. (Answers will vary.) Exodus 36:3–6; Proverbs 11:25; 22:9; Luke 6:38; Acts 20:35
   3. catastrophe

4. Using a Bible dictionary, discover what has been built over the cave of Machpelah.

F. Rewrite these sentences more effectively.
1. Brother Glen declared that we should not run in the halls.
2. In our classroom they mostly bring mechanical pencils from home.
3. If a student has finished all the assignments, they may work on the special project.
4. The children spoke respectfully and with courtesy to the elderly man.
5. Elvin has been, as I understand, helping Uncle Merle with the chores.
6. After I had tripped and stumbled over the round ball, my leg was painful and sore.
7. Jumping and barking furiously, I was welcomed home by our two dogs.
8. Much of Pennsylvania was heavily forested, and white men settled there.

G. Rewrite this paragraph, using better sentence variety.

Bamboo is the most important part of a panda's diet. Its life, in fact, depends on this plant. It eats hardly anything else. A panda has plenty of food whenever it stays in a bamboo forest. One panda, however, can eat hundreds of stalks in one day. The bamboo in one area dies out sometimes. The pandas there may face starvation.

---

124. Final Review 1 (Chapters 1–6)

Class Practice

A. Name each sentence part described here.
1. It completes the skeleton by receiving the action of a verb.
2. It tells *who* or *what* the sentence is about.
3. It follows a linking verb and renames the subject.
4. It follows another noun or pronoun and identifies or explains it.
5. It tells *to whom or what* or *for whom or what* an action is performed.
6. It follows a linking verb and modifies the subject.
7. It names the person or thing to whom one is speaking.
8. It tells what the subject does or is.
9. It consists of the simple subject and the simple predicate.

B. Tell whether each item is a *sentence,* a *fragment,* or a *run-on error.*
1. If properly guided and educated.
2. The conscience can be one of our best friends.

Lesson 124

Purpose: To review the concepts taught in chapters 1–6, in preparation for a final test.

4. a Muslim mosque

F. (Allow reasonable variation.)
1. Brother Glen declared, "You shall not run in the halls."
2. In our classroom students mostly bring mechanical pencils from home.
3. If a student has finished all the assignments, he may work on the special project.
4. The children spoke respectfully and courteously (*or* with respect and courtesy) to the elderly man.
5. As I understand, Elvin has been helping Uncle Merle with the chores.
6. After I had stumbled over the ball, my leg was painful.
7. Jumping and barking furiously, our two dogs welcomed me home.
8. Much of Pennsylvania was heavily forested before white men settled there.

G. (Check paragraphs for good sentence variety.)

Bamboo is the most important part of a panda's diet. In fact, its life depends on this plant because it eats hardly anything else. Whenever a panda stays in a bamboo forest, it has plenty of food. However, one panda can eat hundreds of stalks in one day. Sometimes the bamboo in one area dies out, and the pandas there may face starvation.

Lesson 124 Answers

Class Practice
A. 1. direct object
2. subject
3. predicate nominative
4. appositive
5. indirect object
6. predicate adjective
7. noun of direct address
8. verb *or* simple predicate
9. skeleton

B. 1. fragment
2. sentence

3. However, it remains a good friend only if we obey it.
4. A person can ignore its voice, then it becomes hardened and worthless.

C. Tell whether each sentence has *natural, inverted,* or *mixed* word order.
  1. As a lowly servant came the Son of God.
  2. Jesus revealed the Father to mankind.
  3. Through His shed blood He provided salvation.

D. Tell whether each underlined substantive is a *gerund phrase,* an *infinitive phrase,* or a *noun clause.*
  1. <u>That God is all-wise</u> is shown by the marvels of His creation.
  2. Satan's goal is <u>ruining the work of God</u>.
  3. Man chooses <u>to follow either God's or Satan's plan</u>.

E. Say the second and third principal parts of these verbs. Use *have* with the third principal part.
  1. drown   5. lie   8. wear
  2. throw   6. write   9. drag
  3. freeze   7. begin   10. leave
  4. cost

F. Tell what tense each underlined verb or verb phrase is. Also tell if it is a *progressive* or *emphatic* form of the verb.
  1. Grandfather Sauder <u>has made</u> some beautiful weather vanes.
  2. During the winter months, he <u>had worked</u> at them steadily.
  3. He <u>is bringing</u> them to our market to sell.
  4. On a good day he <u>will sell</u> two or three weather vanes.
  5. One day last week he <u>did sell</u> six of them.
  6. By the end of the season, he <u>will have sold</u> several hundred of them.

G. Identify the pronouns in each group as *personal, compound personal, demonstrative, indefinite, interrogative,* or *relative* pronouns.
  1. this, that, these, those
  2. he, I, theirs, our, it
  3. who, whose, whom, which, that
  4. each, everybody, someone, few, both, many
  5. who, whom, whose, which, what
  6. myself, yourself, ourselves, themselves, herself

H. Read each sentence, using the correct choice.
  1. A character sketch should (give one main impression, describe two or three character traits, include as many details as possible).
  2. Proofreading a composition is best done (as soon as you have written it, after you have laid it aside for a while).
  3. A topic sentence can be written (only as the first sentence, only as

3. sentence
4. run-on error

C. 1. inverted   3. mixed
   2. natural

D. 1. noun clause   3. infinitive phrase
   2. gerund phrase

E. 1. drowned, (have) drowned
   2. threw, (have) thrown
   3. froze, (have) frozen
   4. cost, (have) cost
   5. lay, (have) lain
   6. wrote, (have) written
   7. began, (have) begun
   8. wore, (have) worn
   9. dragged, (have) dragged
  10. left, (have) left

F. 1. present perfect   4. future
   2. past perfect   5. past, emphatic
   3. present, progressive   6. future perfect

G. 1. demonstrative   4. indefinite
   2. personal   5. interrogative
   3. relative   6. compound personal

H. 1. give one main impression
   2. after you have laid it aside for a while
   3. anywhere in the paragraph

the first or last sentence, anywhere in the paragraph).

4. When the ideas in a paragraph do not flow smoothly from one sentence to the next, the paragraph lacks (unity, coherence, order).

5. If a paragraph gives directions or explains a process, it should be written in (chronological order, spatial order, order of importance).

6. If a paragraph is developed by giving reasons, it should be written in (chronological order, spatial order, order of importance).

7. All the following are rules of good outline form *except* (each level is indented equally, the title begins in line with the first main topic, each line begins with a capital letter).

8. Both friendly letters and business letters have all the following parts *except* (body, closing, greeting, heading, inside address, signature).

9. In preparing an oral report, you should write out the exact words of all the following *except* (the introduction, any direct quotation, the illustrations for developing your main points, the conclusion).

I. Each starred line on this outline contains an error. Tell how to correct each mistake.

Prayer

I. Reasons for praying
 *A. the command of God
 *B. Protects against temptation
 C. An essential for true life
   *1. "the Christian's vital breath"
*II. What are some conditions for answered prayers?
 A. Submission to God's will
*B. Faith in God
 *C. perseverance in prayer
 *D. Being obedient to God

Written Exercises

A. Write whether each sentence is *simple, compound,* or *complex.*

1. If jealousy is allowed to grow in the heart, it quickly destroys friendships.

2. Not only does jealousy hurt others, but also it mars the life of the jealous person himself.

3. Is this truth not illustrated in the life of Saul, who became jealous of David?

4. What a terrible thing is jealousy!

B. Copy each underlined word, and write what sentence part it is. Use the following abbreviations.

---

4. coherence
5. chronological order
6. order of importance
7. the title begins in line with the first main topic
8. inside address
9. the illustrations for developing your main points

I. (Corrections are underlined.)

Prayer

I. Reasons for praying
 A. <u>The</u> command of God
 B. <u>A protection</u> against temptation
 C. An essential for true life—<u>"the Christian's vital breath"</u>
II. <u>Conditions</u> for answered prayers
 A. Submission to God's will
 <u>B.</u> Faith in God
 C. <u>Perseverance</u> in prayer
 D. <u>Obedience</u> to God

Written Exercises

A. 1. complex
   2. compound
   3. complex
   4. simple

S—subject   PN—predicate nominative
V—verb   PA—predicate adjective
DO—direct object   DA—noun of direct address
IO—indirect object   AP—appositive

1. Joseph <u>remained</u> <u>faithful</u> in many trying circumstances.
2. His father had given <u>him</u> a <u>coat</u> of many colors.
3. Joseph's <u>brothers</u> were not good <u>men</u>.
4. <u>Reuben</u>, the oldest <u>brother</u>, <u>planned</u> to rescue Joseph.
5. My <u>friends</u>, we can hardly imagine the <u>grief</u> that Joseph experienced.

C. Write the possessive form of each word.

1. foxes   5. father-in-law   8. Moses
2. baby   6. child   9. mice
3. ladies   7. larva   10. fireman
4. Carlos

D. Write the plural form of each word. Use foreign plurals for numbers 11–14.

1. louse   6. volcano   11. cactus
2. salmon   7. sister-in-law   12. index
3. ox   8. fireman   13. oasis
4. monkey   9. library   14. alga
5. wolf   10. spoonful

E. Write numbers as shown to identify the patterns of these sentences. If the verb is transitive, write the word that receives the action. If the verb is intransitive linking, write the words that are linked.

Pattern 1: intransitive complete verb
Pattern 2: transitive verb, active voice
Pattern 3: transitive verb, passive voice
Pattern 4: intransitive linking verb

1. The warm spring air was an invitation to go outdoors.
2. A butterfly flew lazily through the open window.
3. A mockingbird poured its medley into the morning air.
4. Several bees were busy at the white clover.
5. The fragrance of the wild roses was carried in by a breeze.

F. Write the better verb for each sentence.

1. One of life's important lessons (is, are) to learn to share.
2. There (come, comes) to everyone many temptations to be selfish.
3. Each morning as we (raise, rise) from bed, we should thank God for another day.
4. Unselfishness and thoughtfulness (go, goes) hand in hand.
5. The news of Laura's accident (was, were) quite a shock.
6. She (don't, doesn't) remember what happened.

B. 1. remained—V; faithful—PA
   2. him—IO; coat—DO
   3. brothers—S; men—PN
   4. Reuben—S; brother—AP; planned—V
   5. friends—DA; grief—DO

C. 1. foxes'   6. child's
   2. baby's   7. larva's
   3. ladies'   8. Moses'
   4. Carlos's   9. mice's
   5. father-in-law's   10. fireman's

D. 1. lice   8. firemen
   2. salmon   9. libraries
   3. oxen   10. spoonfuls
   4. monkeys   11. cacti
   5. wolves   12. indices
   6. volcanoes *or* volcanos   13. oases
   7. sisters-in-law   14. algae

E. 1. 4—air, invitation   4. 4—bees, busy
   2. 1   5. 3—fragrance
   3. 2—medley

F. 1. is
   2. come
   3. rise
   4. go
   5. was
   6. doesn't

7. Yesterday we (laid, lay) in the cool shade to rest.
8. Erma (can, may) pass out the papers now.
9. Smallpox (have, has) been successfully controlled with modern drugs.
10. Our dog (dragged, drug) a dead ground hog into the back yard.
11. Last winter some pipes (busted, burst) in the cold spell.
12. Father (let, left) us go wading in the creek.
13. The bicycle (cost, costed) too much, and Father did not buy it.
14. Spot often (sets, sits) at the front door, waiting for us to come home.
15. This cow must have (laid, lain) in the mud.
16. A flock of blackbirds (raised, rose) noisily from the field.
17. Father's pliers (belong, belongs) on the peg beside his pipe wrench.
18. Fox and geese (was, were) my choice of a game for today.
19. In the second round, both of the foxes (was, were) able to catch three runners.
20. Some of our morning recess (was, were) spent in picking up branches from yesterday's thunderstorm.
21. Have you (forgot, forgotten) your paper again?
22. Lucinda's glasses were (broke, broken) when she fell.
23. Leonard (did, done) a good job on his bird feeder.
24. He (saw, seen) a Baltimore oriole at the feeder yesterday.
25. After we had read the Bible and (sang, sung) a hymn, we stood for prayer.

G. Copy the four headings shown. Then copy each underlined pronoun, and identify its person (*1, 2, 3*), number (*S, P*), case (*N, O, P*), and gender (*M, F, N, C*) in the phrase given.

	Person	Number	Case	Gender
1. in <u>my</u> desk	———	———	———	———
2. things in <u>it</u>	———	———	———	———
3. if <u>she</u> does	———	———	———	———
4. to <u>you</u> children	———	———	———	———
5. <u>their</u> teacher	———	———	———	———
6. found <u>him</u>	———	———	———	———

H. Write the correct words for these sentences.
1. God daily provides many blessings for you and (I, me).
2. God gave them, Abraham and (she, her), a son in their old age.
3. Neither Ruth nor Orpah wanted to desert (her, their) mother-in-law at first.
4. Ruth's response is an inspiration to (we, us) Bible readers today.
5. Nora said that Uncle Galen's drove in. Was it really (they, them)?
6. (We, Us) cousins will enjoy a game of hide-and-seek.

Answers

7. lay
8. may
9. has
10. dragged
11. burst
12. let
13. cost
14. sits
15. lain
16. rose
17. belong
18. was
19. were
20. was
21. forgotten
22. broken
23. did
24. saw
25. sung

G.

	Person	Number	Case	Gender
1. my	1	S	P	C
2. it	3	S	O	N
3. she	3	S	N	F
4. you	2	P	O	C
5. their	3	P	P	C
6. him	3	S	O	M

H. 1. me
2. her
3. her
4. us
5. they
6. We

7. The carpenter and mason gave (his estimate, their estimates).
8. The plumber and the electrician gave (his estimate, their estimates).

I. Read these paragraphs, and answer the questions that follow.

*a*An attitude is the way a person thinks and feels about a certain thing. *b*For example, every person has an attitude about himself. *c*He may think of himself as the center of his own little world, as unable to do anything right, or as a normal person with both strengths and weaknesses. *d*Every attitude is hidden deep inside a person, but it definitely affects everything the person says and does.

*e*If you hear someone complaining about a job, you may conclude that he has a wrong attitude about the place of work. *f*But actually a number of wrong attitudes likely have combined to produce the complaint. *g*The complainer has a wrong attitude about himself: he is selfish or proud or lazy. *h*He also has a wrong attitude about the one who gave him the job to do. *i*He may be bitter toward that person, or at the very least, he is not as respectful as he should be. *j*Furthermore, his attitudes toward God are not right, for God commands each person to be a diligent, willing worker.

1. What is the topic sentence in each paragraph?
2. Which method of paragraph development is used in each?
3. What key word is repeated throughout both paragraphs?
4. Copy some transitional expressions used in the paragraphs.

---

125. Final Review 2 (Chapters 7–11)

Class Practice

A. Name the parts of speech described here.
1. It joins words, phrases, or clauses.
2. It names a person, place, thing, or idea.
3. It modifies a verb, adjective, or adverb.
4. It expresses action or being.
5. It expresses strong feeling or emotion.
6. It takes the place of a noun.
7. It shows the relationship between an object and some other word in the sentence.
8. It modifies a substantive.

B. Tell whether each underlined adjective is *descriptive* or *limiting* and

7. his estimate
8. their estimates

I. 1. *paragraph 1:* sentence *a*
      paragraph 2: sentence *f*
   2. *paragraph 1:* by giving a definition
      paragraph 2: by using examples
   3. attitude(s)
   4. *paragraph 1:* For example
      paragraph 2: But, also, Furthermore

Lesson 125 Answers

Class Practice

A. 1. conjunction   5. interjection
   2. noun   6. pronoun
   3. adverb   7. preposition
   4. verb   8. adjective

Lesson 125

Purpose: To review the concepts taught in chapters 7–11, in preparation for a final test.

whether it is *attributive, appositive,* or *predicate.*
1. <u>The</u> journey through the wilderness, <u>long</u> and wearisome, lasted <u>forty</u> years.
2. During <u>these</u> years, Israel was often faithless and <u>disobedient</u>.

C. Identify each underlined adjective phrase as a *prepositional phrase,* a *participial phrase,* or an *infinitive phrase.*
1. The best way <u>to make good friends</u> is to be a good friend.
2. Any youth <u>desiring a noble character</u> must purpose to maintain a clear conscience at all times.
3. Daniel is an example <u>of a youth</u> <u>with a strong purpose</u>.

D. Tell whether each underlined clause is *restrictive* or *nonrestrictive.* Also tell where commas are needed.
1. Every woodchuck <u>that comes to our farm</u> must contend with Rex.
2. Raymond Rutt <u>who was my grandfather</u> bought this farm in 1940.
3. All children <u>who are under four years</u> may board the train free.

E. Tell whether each underlined conjunction is a *coordinating conjunction,* a *correlative conjunction,* a *conjunctive adverb,* or a *subordinating conjunction.*
1. Every person has the potential to glorify God; <u>however</u>, not everyone chooses to serve Him.
2. God <u>not only</u> desires <u>but also</u> deserves man's loyalty.
3. Did Jacob <u>or</u> Esau seek God's blessing on his life?
4. <u>Both</u> Abram <u>and</u> Jacob had their names changed by God.
5. <u>When</u> men lived by faith, God always blessed their lives.

F. Identify the words that have capitalization errors.
1. Did brother William grow up in the Mountains of west Virginia?
2. Last Spring father bought an Ariens Lawn Mower.
3. We have English, Reading, and Arithmetic in the morning.
4. Have you read the story *The Man In Bearskin*?

G. Name the figure of speech that each sentence contains.
1. The blizzard howled and screamed with relentless fury.
2. Those dark woods held a thousand terrors.
3. Jealousy is a cancer of the soul.
4. The kites soared like eagles in the stiff March breeze.

H. Give the answers.
1. What are three ways of showing the traits of the main character in a story?
2. What are three kinds of conflict that the main story character may face?

B. 1. The—limiting, attributive; long—descriptive, appositive; forty—limiting, attributive
2. these—limiting, attributive; disobedient—descriptive, predicate

C. 1. infinitive phrase
2. participial phrase
3. prepositional phrase, prepositional phrase

D. 1. restrictive
2. nonrestrictive; comma after *Rutt* and *grandfather*
3. restrictive

E. 1. conjunctive adverb
2. correlative conjunction
3. coordinating conjunction
4. correlative conjunction
5. subordinating conjunction

F. (Words with errors are shown correctly.)
1. Brother, mountains, West
2. spring, Father, lawn mower
3. reading, arithmetic
4. in

G. 1. personification
2. hyperbole
3. metaphor
4. simile

H. 1. by the character's actions, words, and thoughts
2. conflict with another person, with his circumstances, or with his own self

3. How should the conflict be treated in the story beginning? in the middle? in the ending?
4. What is the climax of the story, and where should it be found?
5. What are some ways to make dialogue sound natural?
6. A book report should include all the following *except* (information about the title, author, and publisher; the theme and main events; the setting; information about the main characters; the outcome of the story; a lesson that can be learned from the story; your opinion of the story).
7. An encyclopedia must be used carefully for all the following reasons *except* (much of its information may be inaccurate, it emphasizes man's ideas, its information is not as detailed as what other sources may give).

Written Exercises

A. Write the comparative and superlative degrees of these adjectives and adverbs.

1. good
2. delightful
3. fluffy
4. little, in amount
5. smoothly
6. ill
7. close
8. early

B. If the underlined part of the sentence contains an error, write it correctly. If it is correct, write *correct*.

1. Ezekiel must have been awed by <u>them visions</u> he saw.
2. What <u>kind of a man</u> was Manasseh in his last years?
3. The Bible tells about <u>fewer people</u> who started wrong and ended right than who started right and ended wrong.
4. Where do <u>these here books</u> belong?
5. Today I have <u>less books</u> to take home than I did yesterday.
6. Sheldon is <u>washing up the car</u>.
7. We all felt <u>sort of relieved</u> to know that Aaron was not seriously hurt.
8. Even though he fell out of the tree, he didn't have <u>no broken bones</u>.
9. I was surprised at <u>how well I</u> did on the science test.
10. Darrel's report was <u>real interesting</u>.
11. A small shack <u>stood besides</u> the trail.
12. There was plenty of candy to <u>divide between</u> the four boys.
13. The playground <u>is in back of</u> the school.
14. Our new house is <u>quite different from</u> our old one.
15. The parakeet was flying around <u>outside of his</u> cage.
16. Because of the heat, we went <u>in the house</u> for a cool drink.
17. After Brother Lee read both poems, we agreed that the first one <u>was best</u>.

3. The conflict should be introduced promptly in the beginning. It should build up in intensity in the middle. It should be brought to a climax in the ending.
4. The climax is the last and most intense incident in the conflict. It should be found near the end of the story.
5. Use contractions and incomplete sentences. Have frequent changes of speakers.
6. the outcome of the story
7. much of its information may be inaccurate

Written Exercises

A. 1. better, best
2. more delightful, most delightful
3. fluffier, fluffiest
4. less, least
5. more smoothly, most smoothly
6. worse, worst
7. closer, closest
8. earlier, earliest

B. 1. those visions
2. kind of man
3. correct
4. these books
5. fewer books
6. washing the car
7. rather (somewhat) relieved
8. any broken bones
9. correct
10. really interesting
11. stood beside
12. divide among
13. is behind
14. correct
15. outside his
16. into the house
17. was better

C. Identify the conjunction in each sentence. Use the following abbreviations.

    CC—coordinating conjunction   CA—conjunctive adverb
    Cor—correlative conjunction   SC—subordinating conjunction

1. <u>Both</u> seventh <u>and</u> eighth graders are preparing for an English test.
2. <u>After</u> this term of school is over, we will visit my grandparents.
3. The weatherman predicted rain; <u>however</u>, the sun is shining brightly.
4. We worked in the garden <u>until</u> the corn was all planted.
5. We picked strawberries all morning, <u>yet</u> much of the patch was still not finished.

D. Write whether each underlined clause serves as a *noun,* an *adjective,* or an *adverb.*

1. <u>Although everyone faces temptations,</u> God enables each to do the right.
2. In the Bible we learn <u>how God wants us to live.</u>
3. Truth will always triumph <u>because God is omnipotent.</u>
4. The fact <u>that God will triumph</u> should inspire us with courage.

E. Copy each underlined word, and write what part of speech it is. Use abbreviations.

1. <u>Beautiful</u>! <u>This</u> motto is <u>beautiful</u>, <u>and</u> <u>I</u> <u>want</u> to buy it.
2. <u>Because</u> it is raining, we <u>will</u> play <u>inside</u> today.
3. <u>Inside</u> this room the <u>air</u> is <u>warm</u> and stuffy.
4. We will <u>open</u> the windows and <u>air</u> <u>this</u> out.
5. The <u>open</u> windows have <u>changed</u> the atmosphere <u>dramatically</u>.
6. <u>Oh</u>, this story, proofread and <u>improved</u>, is <u>much</u> better.
7. <u>Much</u> of the garden <u>remains</u> <u>under</u> <u>water</u>.
8. It will take <u>much</u> work to clean up the <u>remains</u> of this building.

F. These sentences have errors in the use of end punctuation, commas, colons, semicolons, and ellipsis points. Copy the words or numbers with which the errors occur, and put the correct marks where they belong.

1. "But whoso shall offend one of these little ones which believe in me, it were better that he were drowned in the depth of the sea" (Matthew 186).
2. What a pleasant relaxed walk we had through the woods today
3. My father, Uncle Elmer and Brother Abner are repairing the barn roof, meanwhile, Brother John and Brother Carl are cleaning up around the barn
4. Arlene have you met Carolyn my cousin from Pennsylvania
5. Greta Weber who is staying with her grandparents will be in our class.
6. Yes the committee consists of the following brethren, Rodney Steiner,

C. 1. Cor
  2. SC
  3. CA
  4. SC
  5. CC

D. 1. adverb
  2. noun
  3. adverb
  4. adjective

E. 1. Beautiful—interj.; This—adj.; beautiful—adj.; and—conj.; I—pron.; want—v.
  2. Because—conj.; will—v.; inside—adv.
  3. Inside—prep.; air—n.; warm—adj.
  4. open—v.; air—v.; this—pron.
  5. open—adj.; changed—v.; dramatically—adv.
  6. Oh—interj.; improved—adj.; much—adv.
  7. Much—pron.; remains—v.; under—prep.; water—n.
  8. much—adj.; remains—n.

F. 1. better . . . 18:6
  2. pleasant, today!
  3. Elmer, roof; barn.
  4. Arlene, Carolyn, Pennsylvania?
  5. Weber, grandparents,
  6. Yes, brethren: chairman; vice-chairman;

the chairman, Alvin Wise, the vice-chairman, and John Sauder, the secretary.

G. These sentences have errors in the use of quotation marks, italics, apostrophes, and hyphens. Copy the word or words most closely associated with the error, and make the needed corrections.
1. "This week, Brother Clarence announced, our theme song will be My Body Is God's Temple."
2. We found the needed information in the article Animal Kingdom in Unger's Bible Dictionary.
3. Remember that repetitious has two es first and two is next.
4. Mr. Eagles small airplane, the Royal Eagle, landed safely in our field.
5. As he climbed out, he asked his companion, "Was your self confidence shaken as badly as mine was?
6. Was it your great grandfather who often said, "No one ever got lost following the Lord?

H. Write a poetic term to match each description.
1. The regular pattern of accented and unaccented syllables.
2. The matching of sounds at the ends of lines.
3. An accented syllable and the unaccented syllables associated with it.
4. The following rhythm patterns.
   a. ´ ˘ ˘ ´ ˘ ˘   c. ´ ˘ ´ ˘
   b. ˘ ´ ˘ ´   d. ˘ ˘ ´ ˘ ˘ ´
5. The repetition of thoughts, common in Bible poetry.
6. The use of words having imitative sounds.
7. The repetition of similar accented vowel sounds.
8. The repetition of beginning consonant sounds.

I. Name the reference book that matches each description.
1. A collection of maps.
2. Volumes of information containing articles on a wide range of subjects.
3. A book of Bible topics arranged in alphabetical order, with verses about each topic.
4. A book of synonyms.
5. A book of Bible words and references.
6. A book of words, with various kinds of information about them.

G. 1. week," "our 'My Temple.'"
   2. "Animal Kingdom" *Unger's Bible Dictionary*
   3. *repetitious* *e*'s *i*'s
   4. Eagle's *Royal Eagle*
   5. self-confidence was?"
   6. great-grandfather Lord"?

H. 1. rhythm
   2. rhyme
   3. poetic foot
   4. a. dactylic   c. trochaic
      b. iambic   d. anapestic
   5. parallelism
   6. onomatopoeia
   7. assonance
   8. alliteration

I. 1. atlas
   2. encyclopedia
   3. topical Bible
   4. thesaurus
   5. concordance
   6. dictionary

Name _____   *(Lesson 5)*

Worksheet 1
Direct and Indirect Objects

A. Underline the direct objects and indirect objects in these sentences. Identify each one by writing *DO* or *IO* above it.

                        IO   IO
1. We should send <u>Grandfather</u> and <u>Grandmother</u>
     DO
   a <u>letter</u>.

              DO   DO
2. Read the <u>directions</u>, and do the <u>work</u> carefully.

                  DO
3. An angel announced Jesus' <u>birth</u>.

               DO
4. The shepherds left their <u>flocks</u>.

            DO   DO
5. Wise men followed the <u>star</u> and found <u>Christ</u>.

             IO   DO
6. King Herod gave <u>them</u> a <u>message</u>.

               DO
7. He professed a <u>desire</u> to worship Christ.

             DO
8. God warned the <u>wise men</u> in a dream.

               DO
9. They disobeyed the <u>king</u> and took a different
 DO
 <u>way</u> to their homes.

                   DO
10. In anger, Herod slew many little <u>children</u>.

          IO   DO
11. God gave <u>Joseph</u> a <u>warning</u> in a dream.

                DO
12. Joseph took his <u>family</u> to Egypt.

                 DO
13. Columbus discovered <u>America</u> in 1492.

                DO
14. Many explorers followed <u>him</u> to this land.

                 DO
15. They were seeking a water <u>route</u> to Asia.

            DO   DO
16. These men explored <u>bays</u> and <u>rivers</u>.

            DO   DO
17. They also crossed <u>mountains</u> and <u>plains</u>.

                DO
18. None ever found the desired <u>passageway</u>.

                DO
19. Their explorations opened the <u>New World</u>.

                DO
20. Soon European nations were starting <u>colonies</u>.

            IO   IO
21. God provided many <u>Mennonites</u> and <u>Amish</u> a
 DO
 <u>haven</u> of freedom.

            IO   DO
22. We should give <u>God</u> our sincere <u>praise</u> and
 DO
 <u>thanks</u> for His goodness.

B. Diagram the skeletons and complements of sentences 1–6 in Part A.

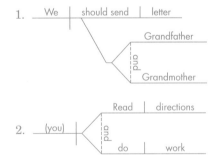

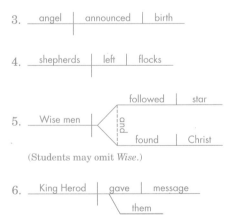

(Students may omit *Wise*.)

Name _____   (Lesson 6)

Worksheet 2
Predicate Nominatives and Predicate Adjectives

A. Underline the predicate nominatives and predicate adjectives. Identify each one by writing *PN* or *PA* above it. (Some sentences have none.)

         PN
1. A glacier is a <u>mass</u> of moving ice and snow.

         PA   PA
2. Glaciers may be quite <u>small</u> or very <u>huge</u>.

         PA
3. Their movement is usually <u>slow</u>.

         PA   PA
4. They may appear <u>serene</u> and <u>beautiful</u>.

         PN
5. These glaciers may become the <u>scenes</u> of fierce

storms.

         PN
6. Sometimes snowbridges are a subtle <u>danger</u>.

         PN
7. A snowbridge is a thin <u>layer</u> of snow over a

crevasse.

         PN
8. Two evidences of heat underground are <u>geysers</u>

    PN
and <u>volcanoes</u>.

         PN
9. A geyser is a <u>fountain</u> of steam and water.

         PN
10. One famous geyser is <u>Old Faithful</u> in Yellow-

stone National Park.

         PA
11. A volcanic eruption is more <u>spectacular</u> and

    PA
<u>dangerous</u>.

         PA
12. A volcano may remain <u>inactive</u> for years.

         PN
13. The Philistines' champion was <u>Goliath</u>.

         PN   PN
14. David's weapons were his <u>staff</u> and his <u>sling</u>.

         PA   PA
15. David appeared <u>weak</u> and <u>helpless</u> to Goliath.

         PN
16. But God was his true <u>source</u> of strength.

         PN
17. The army of Israel became the <u>victor</u>.

         PA   PA
18. The mountain air smelled <u>fresh</u> and <u>woodsy</u>.

    (none)
19. I smelled the catnip tea.

         PA   PA
20. The boys appear <u>hot</u> and <u>tired</u>.

    (none)
21. Susan appeared with a refreshing drink.

         PN
22. This must be fresh <u>lemonade</u>.

B. Diagram the skeletons and complements of sentences 1–6 in Part A.

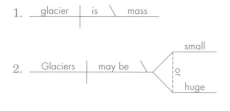

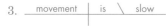

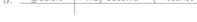

Name _____   *(Lesson 7)*

Worksheet 3
Appositives and Nouns of Direct Address

A. Underline each subject, and put parentheses around each noun of direct address.

   1. ("Lord,) my <u>heart</u> is not haughty."

   2. "Thy <u>name</u>, (O Lord,) endureth for ever."

   3. "Our <u>feet</u> shall stand within thy gates, (O Jerusalem.")

(In numbers 2 and 3, students may omit the interjection O.)

   4. Your <u>help</u>, (my dear friends,) has been greatly appreciated.

   5. (Rosetta,) <u>you</u> may take this lemonade to the boys in the field.

B. Underline each appositive, and draw an arrow from it to the word it explains.

   1. This book, <u>a gift from Grandfather</u>, is special to me.

   2. Do you want to see Caesar, <u>our haughty gander</u>?

   3. Grandfather's first car, <u>a 1921 Willys Knight</u>, has been kept in remarkable condition.

   4. The angel <u>Gabriel</u> announced Jesus' birth.

   5. The angel also announced the birth of John the Baptist, <u>the forerunner of Christ</u>.

C. Add the missing commas to these sentences.

   1. The presidents and princes, cruel and jealous men, watched Daniel.

   2. O king, Daniel, a captive of Judah, does not obey your law.

   3. Darius, king of the Medes and Persians, spent a sleepless night.

   4. Far happier was Daniel, the man in the lions' den.

   5. Have you, my friend, the loyalty of Daniel, the servant of God?

D. Diagram the skeletons, complements, appositives, and nouns of direct address. Remember to include all the modifiers that go with an appositive or a noun of direct address.

   1. Luann, did you meet my cousin Gloria?

       Luann   you | did meet | cousin   (Gloria)

   2. Harvey Daniels, our new neighbor, is a friendly man.

       Harvey Daniels   (neighbor) | is \ man
                 our   new

   3. Did you hear that bird, Gwendolyn?

       Gwendolyn   you | Did hear | bird

   4. Jason, read the Golden Text, John 3:16.

       Jason   (you) | read | Golden Text   (John 3:16)

   5. Have you bumped your head, my little boy?

       boy   you | Have bumped | head
         my   little

Name _____   *(Lesson 8)*

Worksheet 4
Proofreading a Story

Proofread this story. Show all the necessary corrections, using the proper proofreading marks.

(Allow reasonable variation.)

"This ~~seen~~ *scene* is as ~~beutiful~~ as you described it, Father," Mother said softly as

she ~~set~~ *sat* down on an old stump. Christa and I nodded in agreement. When we still

lived in New Jersey, we didn't have a woods to go walking in. Before us ~~laid~~ *lay* a

small lake, almost encircled by the forest ~~all around it~~. To our left, a forlorn

log cabin sat in a small clearing with gaping doors and windows.

"Wouldn't be it *e* intresting to ~~meat~~ *meet* the family that lived in this ~~here~~ cabin?"

Father asked. "Do you suppose they were a Christian fam*i*ly t*o*o?" I wondered.

Just then Mother motion*ed* for us to be quiet. As our eyes turn*ed* in the direction

of ~~his~~ *her* pointed finger, we ~~see~~ *saw* a doe and a ~~baby~~ fawn step up to the lake. The grace-

ful, ~~elegant,~~ beautiful fawn, with its spindly legs, ~~are~~ *was* almost hidden in the tall

grass. After a long drink of the cool, ~~clear,~~ refreshing water, the ~~pare~~ *pair* melt*ed* into

the shadows of the deep, dark forest again.

"I never ~~seen~~ *saw* ~~dear~~ *deer* so close before," I breathed. "I didn't relize that a *a* fawn

was so little ~~and small~~!" added Christa.

"We certainly ~~was~~ *were* blessed with an unusual privilege this evening," stated Father.

"Let's sing 'I'll Praise My Maker.'"

As the last notes fla*o*ted across the twilight air, I thanked *God* for the b*e*a*u*ty of

His creation. As I glanced at Father and Mother and Christa, I thanked God for the

love of a Christian family too.

Worksheet 8, Part B *(Continued)*

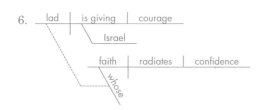

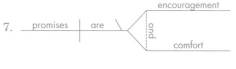

Name _____   *(Lesson 11)*

Worksheet 5
Word Order in Sentences

A. Underline the complete subject in each sentence. Then write whether the word order is natural (*N*), inverted (*I*), or mixed (*M*).

__N__   1. The river flowed steadily into the sea.

__I__   2. Along the river lived many people.

__M__   3. Often the high tide rose swiftly.

__I__   4. Up the river rushed a high wall of water.

__N__   5. This wall of water is called a bore.

__M__   6. There are some tidal bores as high as fifteen feet.

__N__   7. Ocean tides are caused by the moon.

__M__   8. In one place, the tide rises as much as fifty feet.

__I__   9. Where is that?

__N__ 10. It happens in the Bay of Fundy.

B. Change each sentence to the word order shown in parentheses.

1. We went outside after lunch. (mixed) ___After lunch we went outside.___

_____

2. There were many children on the playground. (natural) ___Many children were on the playground.___

_____

3. Dark clouds gathered overhead before long. (mixed) ___Before long, dark clouds gathered overhead.___

_____

4. Then the rain came down. (inverted) ___Then down came the rain.___

C. Rewrite each sentence so that it does not begin with *There.*

1. There was a wounded man lying beside the road. ___A wounded man was lying beside the road.___

_____

2. There came along a priest and a Levite, but they passed by. _____
   ___A priest and a Levite came along, but they passed by.___

3. There came also a Samaritan, and he helped the man. _____
   ___A Samaritan also came, and he helped the man.___

4. There are several important lessons taught by this story. ___Several important lessons are taught by
   this story. *or* This story teaches several important lessons.___

5. There are lying around us many opportunities to do good. _____
   ___Many opportunities to do good are lying around us.___

Name _____   *(Lesson 13)*

Worksheet 6
Topic Sentences and Paragraph Unity

A. Write a good topic sentence for each paragraph.   (Sample topic sentences.)

1.   The young person in a Christian home enjoys many blessings.

Because his parents carefully guard his friendships, the young person in a Christian home is spared from many unwholesome influences. He develops a sense of security and peace in the atmosphere of loving care. Through his parents' consistent discipline, he learns the value and practice of self-discipline. Above all, such a youth learns from his earliest childhood to believe and trust in the Lord God.

2.   Fungi are used in various ways.

To many people, the most familiar use of fungi is found in the delicate flavor of the various edible mushrooms. Other kinds of fungi are involved in making several kinds of cheese, such as Swiss, cheddar, and Limburger. The yeasts that raise bread dough represent another major use of fungi. Fungi are also valuable in medicine. The primary source of penicillin and some other important antibiotics is simple, lowly fungi.

B. Underline the topic sentences. In each paragraph, cross out one sentence that mars the unity.

1.   How can you tell the difference between a sea lion and other seals? ~~Both are pinnipeds, or fin-footed animals.~~ A sea lion has two small ears, but other seals have no visible ears. A sea lion walks clumsily on land, using its four flippers as legs. But other seals crawl across land on their stomachs. *or* These two simple details can be used to easily distinguish a sea lion from most other seals.

2.   A sea lion bull can grow to enormous size. The California sea lion has an average length of nearly eight feet and an average weight of more than five hundred pounds. The northern sea lion is even larger, measuring up to nine feet long. This massive beast may weigh as much as one ton. ~~The elephant seal is not a sea lion, but it may reach a weight of four tons!~~

3.   Many people are aware that a sea lion has a thick layer of fat. This blubber acts as insulation to keep the sea lion warm. Actually, the sea lion has several ways of keeping warm in winter. In addition to the layer of fat, a thick fur coat keeps the heat in and the cold out. The hair grows so close together that water never penetrates to the skin. It traps millions of tiny air bubbles, and these also serve as insulation. ~~Sometimes in summer, the thick fur coat keeps the sea lion too warm.~~

Worksheet 7, Part C *(Continued)*

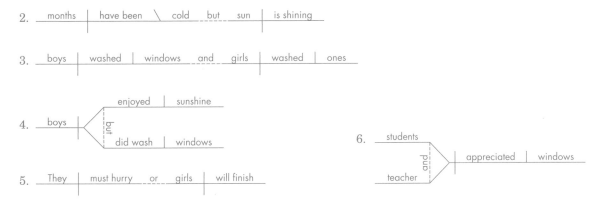

Name _____   *(Lesson 14)*

Worksheet 7
Simple and Compound Sentences

A. Label each sentence *S* for simple sentence or *C* for compound sentence.

   S   1. Paul and Barnabas were called by the Holy Spirit and commissioned by the church at Antioch.

   S   2. These missionaries preached the Gospel and established new churches.

   C   3. They faced many dangers, yet God was their constant companion.

   S   4. The missionaries went to Paphos and met a man named Bar-jesus.

   C   5. Bar-jesus was a Jew, but he was also a sorcerer.

   C   6. He opposed the Gospel, and Paul sternly denounced him.

   S   7. The sorcerer became blind and sought for someone to lead him by the hand.

   C   8. Sergius Paulus was astonished, and he believed the Gospel.

B. Make a compound sentence from each pair. Use correct punctuation.

  1. Ezekiel prophesied to the exiles in Babylon. Jeremiah served those still in Judah.

     Ezekiel prophesied to the exiles in Babylon, but (and) Jeremiah served those still in Judah.

  2. The Babylonian army destroyed Jerusalem. Nebuchadnezzar disgraced King Zedekiah.

     The Babylonian army destroyed Jerusalem, and Nebuchadnezzar disgraced King Zedekiah.

  3. The Jews went to Babylon as destitute captives. They soon prospered greatly in their new homes.

     The Jews went to Babylon as destitute captives, but they soon prospered greatly in their new homes.

  4. The Babylonian rulers grew increasingly wicked and complacent. God brought them to judgment at the hands of the Medes and Persians. The Babylonian rulers grew increasingly wicked and complacent,

     and God brought them to judgment at the hands of the Medes and Persians.

  5. The exiles were permitted by Cyrus to return to Judah. They could remain in Babylon.

     The exiles were permitted by Cyrus to return to Judah, or they could remain in Babylon.

C. Diagram these simple and compound sentences on other paper.
  1. The windows have become dirty, and today is an ideal cleaning time.
  2. The winter months have been cold, but now the sun is shining warmly.
  3. The boys washed the west windows, and the girls washed the south ones.
  4. The boys enjoyed the warm sunshine but did not wash windows very fast.
  5. They must hurry, or the girls will finish first.
  6. The students and the teacher appreciated the clean windows.

  1. windows | have become \ dirty ___ and ___ today | is \ time

(Numbers 2–6 are on page T–601.)

Name _____   *(Lesson 15)*

Worksheet 8
Complex Sentences

A. Underline each dependent clause in these sentences. In the blank, label the clause *adj.* for adjective or *adv.* for adverb.

  adj.   1. The school hike, <u>which is scheduled every fall,</u> is planned for Friday.

  adv.   2. <u>Because we are having showers,</u> the hike will be postponed.

  adv.   3. <u>Although we were disappointed about the change of plans,</u> we tried to study.

  adj.   4. The next Friday, <u>which dawned clear and pleasantly cool,</u> was an ideal day for hiking.

  adj.   5. In the morning we hiked to a small stream <u>that cascades over enormous rock formations.</u>

  adj.   6. The forest ranger <u>who hiked along with us</u> identified numerous trees.

  adv.   7. <u>When we arrived at the falls,</u> we were able to climb up on some of the rocks.

  adv.   8. <u>While the ranger listened with interest,</u> we sang several songs of special praise to the Creator.

  adv.   9. We heartily thanked the ranger <u>after we had returned to his headquarters.</u>

  adj.   10. We also thanked Brother Duane, <u>who had planned this special day.</u>

B. In the blank, label each sentence *S* for simple, *Cd* for compound, or *Cx* for complex. Diagram the skeletons and complements of all the clauses.

  Cx   1. Jesus Christ, whom we adore, has done marvelous things for us.

   S   2. Angels often provide God's people unseen protection.

  Cd   3. The Bible has been carefully preserved, and its message remains unchanged.

  Cx   4. Until John the Baptist boldly preached the kingdom of God, no prophet had stirred the hearts of the Jews for four hundred years.

  Cx   5. Jesus began His public ministry after John had prepared the way.

  Cx   6. This young lad, <u>whose strong faith in God</u> radiates confidence, is giving Israel new courage.

   S   7. The promises of the Bible are an encouragement to the struggling and a comfort to the faithful.

  Cd   8. God has never spoken in vain, nor will His Word fail in the future.

1.
   Jesus Christ | has done | things
   we | adore | whom

2.
   Angels | provide | protection
     people

3.
   Bible | has been preserved   and   message | remains \ unchanged

4.
   prophet | had stirred | hearts
   John the Baptist | Until \ preached | kingdom

5.
   Jesus | began | ministry
   John | after \ had prepared | way

(Numbers 6–8 are on page T–599.)

Name _____   *(Lesson 16)*

Worksheet 9
Sentence Order and Coherence

A. For each Scripture passage, write which kind of sentence order is used: *chronological, spatial,* or order of *importance.*

    spatial   1. Revelation 4:2–8

    importance   2. Proverbs 3:31–35

    chronological   3. Jeremiah 36:20–26

    chronological   4. Acts 18:12–17

B. Number these sentences in a coherent order.   (Allow reasonable variation.)

Sentences for Paragraph 1: (Sequence—center, front, right, left, back)

  1   The Greenview Christian School presents a simple, pleasant appearance.

  7   A cornfield stretches across the entire back side of the school grounds.

  3   Two large maple trees grace the large front lawn.

  5   To the right, a ball diamond fills the only level area on the property.

  4   Under these trees are the swing set and the sliding board.

  6   Rising sharply to a flat summit, a large knoll occupies the school grounds to the left.

  2   The building itself, which dominates the scene, sits back from the road about 150 feet.

Sentences for Paragraph 2:

  3   As the fish opens its mouth, the gill slits behind the mouth close.

  5   Then the fish closes its mouth and opens the slits, forcing the water over the gills.

  2   These movements are actually part of the process of respiration in fish.

  4   This action draws water into its mouth.

  6   As the water flows over the gills, the fish absorbs the oxygen dissolved in the water and releases the waste carbon dioxide.

  1   Have you ever watched a fish in water opening and closing its mouth?

Sentences for Paragraph 3:

  2   For one thing, a certain freedom accompanies going outside without any heavy coats or jackets.

  5   The notes of the mockingbird, the robin, and the meadowlark fill the air with beauty.

  4   Not only the flowers but also the birds cheer the spring atmosphere.

  3   The daffodils brighten the front lawn, and the lilacs sweeten the air.

  1   The arrival of warm spring weather is always welcome.

  6   And best of all, what a pleasure it is to place those first seeds into the freshly tilled soil!

Name _____   *(Lesson 17)*

Worksheet 10
Sentence Transitions and Coherence

A. Write a different transitional expression in each blank.   (Sample answers.)

1. We had expected a difficult hike up the mountain. __On the contrary__, the trail was smooth and the slope was gradual.
   or However

2. A guide led the way down the hall. _____Behind_____ her filed the students.
   or After

3. We anticipated a small snack. We were surprised, _____however_____, to see three kinds of doughnuts, cheese and crackers, and two flavors of punch.
   or though

4. A direct object answers the question *whom* or *what* about the skeleton. __In other words__, it receives the action of the verb.
   Therefore, Consequently, *or* As a result

5. "We should leave shortly after the service," Father stated. "_____Otherwise_____, we won't get home until nearly midnight."
   or Still

6. For now, we have the basic structure of the house finished. _____Eventually_____ we will finish the trim.
   or Later

7. As the Anabaptists arrived, they carefully found their way across the rocky meadow. _____Above_____ them, the moon faintly lit the way.

8. These brown hens lay large brown eggs. _____Also_____, they are less wild and flighty than many Leghorns.
   Furthermore, In addition, *or* Besides

B. What key words are repeated in the following Scripture passages?

1. Luke 11:33–36 ___light___

2. Psalm 24:7–10 ___King (Lord); *also* lift___

3. James 3:5–10 ___tongue___

4. James 5:7–11 ___patient (patience)___

C. From the following Scripture passages, list the pronouns that illustrate pronoun reference. Also write the antecedent for each set of pronouns.

1. Acts 18:24–28 ___he, him—Apollos___

2. Genesis 39:1–3 ___him, he, his—Joseph___

3. 2 Kings 18:1–8 ___he, his, him—Hezekiah___

4. 2 Corinthians 8:1–3 ___their, they, themselves—churches___

D. Write the transitional expressions used in these Scripture passages. (Pronouns are not considered transitional expressions.)

1. 1 Corinthians 10:1–6 (Do not write *and*.) ___Moreover, But, Now___

2. Job 42:7, 8 ___And, after, Therefore___

3. Job 42:10, 11 ___And, also, Then___

4. Hebrews 12:5–11 ___And, But, then, Furthermore, Now, nevertheless___

Name _____   *(Lesson 19)*

Worksheet 11
Identifying Nouns

A. In the first blank, write *C* or *A* to tell whether the noun is concrete or abstract. In the second blank, write *M, F, N,* or *C* to tell whether its gender is masculine, feminine, neuter, or common.

C	M	1. rooster
C	F	2. prophetess
A	N	3. joy
C	F	4. vixen
C	C	5. calves
C	N	6. waterfall

A	N	7. bravery
C	N	8. eraser
C	M	9. ram
A	N	10. consideration
C	C	11. cousin
C	F	12. maid

B. Change these words to nouns by using noun-forming suffixes.

peacefulness	1. peaceful	
organization	2. organize	
disturbance	3. disturb	
establishment	4. establish	
solitariness *or* solitude	5. solitary	
intensity *or* intenseness	6. intense	

invitation	7. invite
roughness	8. rough
declaration *or* declarer	9. declare
frailness *or* frailty	10. frail
permanence permanentness *or* permanency	11. permanent
piety *or* piousness	12. pious

C. Write *X* in the blank before each underlined word that is used as a noun.

1. We must _____ <u>fight</u> the good __X__ <u>fight</u> of faith.

2. _____ <u>Wheel</u> the __X__ <u>cart</u> over here, and _____ <u>cart</u> this __X__ <u>wheel</u> to the truck.

3. Don't _____ <u>squash</u> the pumpkins and the __X__ <u>squash</u>.

4. An Indian __X__ <u>brave</u> would often _____ <u>brave</u> many kinds of danger.

5. Disappointments _____ <u>test</u> our __X__ <u>trust</u> in the Lord. If we sincerely _____ <u>trust</u> Him, we can pass every __X__ <u>test</u> in life.

6. Each person must _____ <u>find</u> his __X__ <u>place</u> in line and then _____ <u>place</u> his __X__ <u>find</u> on the table.

7. _____ <u>Water</u> your flowers with __X__ <u>water</u> from that _____ <u>water</u> hose.

8. This freezing rain will _____ <u>ice</u> the roads. See how the __X__ <u>ice</u> is hanging from the trees!

9. Carefully _____ <u>hoe</u> around each tomato __X__ <u>plant</u>. Then use your __X__ <u>hoe</u> to _____ <u>plant</u> these sweet potatoes.

10. Curtis must _____ <u>wash</u> the car, and Jessica must bring in the __X__ <u>wash</u>.

Name _____   *(Lesson 21)*

Worksheet 12
Developing Paragraphs by Adding Details or Giving Steps

A. In each blank, write *D* or *S* to tell whether the passages are developed by adding details or by giving steps.

   S   1. Leviticus 16:20–28   D   3. 2 Timothy 3:1–9

   S   2. 1 Corinthians 15:22–28   S   4. Joshua 6:1–5

B. Improve these paragraphs by adding specific details. Do some research if necessary so that you will know your subject well enough to be specific.   (Sample paragraphs.)

1.   Hares are different from rabbits. They are different at birth. Their sizes and their habits are also different. The jack rabbit is actually a hare, not a rabbit.

     Hares are different from rabbits. Hares are born with a full coat of fur and with their eyes open, but rabbits are naked and blind at birth. Hares are larger than rabbits, and they do not dig burrows as rabbits do. The jack rabbit is actually a hare, not a rabbit.

2.   Heaven is a glorious place! Its beauty far surpasses anything we can know on earth. The wonders of heaven cannot even be imagined.

     Heaven is a glorious place! The beauty of its golden streets and many mansions far surpasses anything we can know on earth. Imagine the wonder of being in the very presence of God and the Lamb, with the holy angels and the saints of all ages! No taint of sin will defile the glory of this place. Truly the wonders of heaven cannot even be imagined.

C. Improve this paragraph by using smoother transitions.

     Follow an orderly method in cutting out a new apron. First, lay out your material. Second, lay your pattern pieces on the material. Third, adjust the pieces to use the least amount of material possible. Fourth, be sure each pattern piece has a place. Fifth, cut out the pieces. Sixth, fold the pieces, keeping the pattern with each piece for easy identification.

(Sample paragraph.)

     Follow an orderly method in cutting out a new apron. First, lay out your material. Lay your pattern pieces on the material, and adjust them to use the least amount of material possible. After you are sure each pattern piece has a place, cut out the pieces of material. Then fold the pieces, keeping the pattern with each piece for easy identification.

Name _____   *(Lesson 23)*

Worksheet 13
Plural Nouns

A. Write the plural forms of these nouns. For numbers 13–20, use the foreign spellings.

_____brushes_____	1. brush	_____press agents_____	11. press agent
_____businessmen_____	2. businessman	_____contraltos_____	12. contralto
_____series_____	3. series	_____synopses_____	13. synopsis
_____bunnies_____	4. bunny	_____foci_____	14. focus
_____chuckles_____	5. chuckle	_____vortices_____	15. vortex
_____fountain pens_____	6. fountain pen	_____theses_____	16. thesis
_____thieves_____	7. thief	_____formulae_____	17. formula
_____zeros *or* zeroes_____	8. zero	_____stimuli_____	18. stimulus
_____proofs_____	9. proof	_____vertebrae_____	19. vertebra
_____trays_____	10. tray	_____indices_____	20. index

B. Underline the correct words in parentheses.

1. The news of the accidents (have, <u>has</u>) shocked the community.

2. My Sunday trousers (<u>need</u>, needs) to be pressed.

3. Measles (<u>is</u>, are) a highly contagious disease.

4. Red-hot tongs (was, <u>were</u>) used to torture the Christians.

5. My new glasses (<u>help</u>, helps) me to see much better than before.

6. Phonics (<u>is</u>, are) an aid in spelling words correctly.

7. Checkers (demand, <u>demands</u>) strategy and concentration.

8. Chicken pox (<u>is</u>, are) usually a mild disease.

9. (<u>Is</u>, Are) mathematics one of your easier subjects?

10. These pliers (<u>slip</u>, slips) too easily.

C. Underline the verb that agrees with each collective noun as used in the sentence.

1. The fleet of ships (<u>was</u>, were) entering the harbor.

2. Because of the storm, the fleet of ships (<u>have</u>, has) to find their separate ways home.

3. The faculty (meet, <u>meets</u>) regularly with the school board.

4. The faculty (is, <u>are</u>) planning their different special projects.

5. This morning the committee (was, <u>were</u>) trying to reconcile their opposing ideas.

6. Now the committee (have, <u>has</u>) agreed on a course of action.

7. The congregation (have, <u>has</u>) gathered for worship.

8. The congregation (<u>have</u>, has) dispersed to their homes.

Name _____

Worksheet 14
Developing Paragraphs by Using Examples or Telling an Incident

A. In the blanks, write *E* or *I* to tell whether the passages are developed by using examples or by telling an incident.

   E   1. 1 Corinthians 10:1–11   I   3. 2 Corinthians 12:7–10

   I   2. James 5:16–18   E   4. 2 Corinthians 4:7–10

B. Improve this paragraph by supplying more details for each example. See Daniel 4 and 5 for information.

"A man's pride shall bring him low." Nebuchadnezzar was proud of the kingdom he had built. God removed him from the kingdom and caused him to live with the beasts. Belshazzar was likewise a proud man. God used the Medes and Persians to slay Belshazzar and take his kingdom.

(Sample paragraph.)

"A man's pride shall bring him low." Nebuchadnezzar was proud of the kingdom he had built. But as he boasted of his power and majesty, the judgment of God fell. God removed him from the kingdom, and he was driven from men to live with the beasts. Belshazzar was likewise a proud man. Though he knew the story of his grandfather Nebuchadnezzar, he exalted himself against the Lord of heaven. He used the vessels from the holy temple in his unholy feast, and he praised his idols. But God interrupted the feast with a message of judgment. That very night the Medes and Persians killed Belshazzar and took his kingdom.

C. Improve this paragraph by adding at least three additional examples and a conclusion.

Spring is a beautiful time of year! The warming weather means that we can exchange heavy winter coats for lighter jackets and sweaters. The first brave flowers spread some color across the drab winter barrenness.

(Sample paragraph.)

Spring is a beautiful time of year! The warming weather means that we can exchange heavy winter coats for lighter jackets and sweaters. The first brave flowers spread some color across the drab winter barrenness. Instead of brown lawns, there is lush greenness. Back from their southern winter homes flock the beautiful songbirds. The twilight air is again filled with the sweet notes of spring peepers and the hum of insects. Our hearts rise in praise to the Creator for the beauty of spring.

D. On other paper, improve this paragraph by developing the incident more fully. See Mark 6 for additional information.

Jesus never considered His own needs more important than the needs of others. One day He and His disciples needed a time of rest, but the crowd followed them. Jesus took the time to teach them. As evening drew on, He even fed the multitude.

(Sample paragraph is on page T–619.)

Name _____   *(Lesson 27)*

Worksheet 15
Verbal Phrases as Nouns

A. Above each underlined phrase, write *I* or *P* to tell whether it is an infinitive phrase or a prepositional phrase.

             I   P

   1. <u>To go across the mountain</u> is the shortest route <u>to Five Forks</u>.

          P   I

   2. <u>To the three Hebrews</u>, the only response was <u>to not bow before the idol</u>.

B. Above each underlined phrase, write *G* or *V* to tell whether it is a gerund phrase or a main verb with complements or modifiers.

                        V

   1. The boys are <u>hoeing in the garden</u>.

                             G

   2. Their goal is <u>finishing the bean rows before dinner</u>.

                                  G

   3. The Pharisees' intense desire was <u>getting rid of Jesus</u>.

                              V

   4. In their minds, Jesus was <u>attracting too many followers</u>.

C. Underline the verbal phrases. Above each one, write *G* or *I* to tell whether it is a gerund phrase or an infinitive phrase.

              G

   1. <u>Brushing teeth regularly</u> is an important part of good health practices.

                              I

   2. We should not try <u>to impress others with our abilities</u>.

                                                  G

   3. The squirrel is sitting on that branch, and my interest is <u>capturing him in a quick sketch</u>.

     I   I

   4. <u>To serve the Lord</u> is <u>to take the way of the cross</u>.

D. Diagram the skeletons and complements of these sentences. Be sure to include the verbal phrases.
   1. Seeking a water route to the East brought explorers to the New World.
   2. The early explorers wanted only to find a way through this continent.
   3. Magellan's dream was to sail around South America.
   4. Preparing the New World for persecuted Christians may have been God's purpose.
   5. Sailing across the Atlantic Ocean meant taking a long, dangerous voyage.
   6. To undertake such a journey must have called for much prayer.

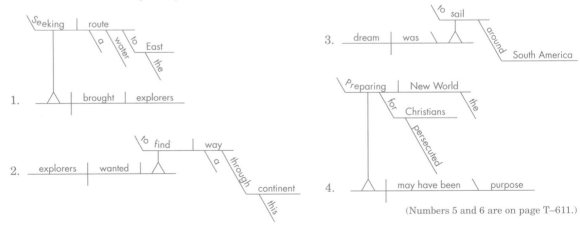

(Numbers 5 and 6 are on page T–611.)

Name _____

Worksheet 16
Noun Clauses

Underline the noun clauses. Above each clause, write *S, DO,* or *PN* to tell whether it is a subject, direct object, or predicate nominative.

1.   ^S
   <u>Whatever God does</u> is done perfectly.

2. The man who lives next door said ^{DO} <u>that the ground hogs ruined his garden</u>.

3. Does anyone know ^{DO} <u>whose servant was named Eliezer</u>?

4. We asked ^{DO} <u>if Brother Daryl was enjoying good health</u>.

5. His standard answer has been ^{PN} <u>that God is always good</u>.

6. An important lesson in life is ^{PN} <u>when we should keep silence</u>.

7. When the cows got out again, Father declared ^{DO} <u>that the fence must be fixed that very day</u>.

8. We cannot always know ^{DO} <u>why God allows suffering and pain in our lives</u>.

9. ^S <u>How magnetism and gravity work</u> defies man's understanding.

10. ^S <u>That God can never fail</u> is a source of comfort to us.

11. The disciples said, ^{DO} <u>"Lord, teach us to pray."</u>

12. Do you realize ^{DO} <u>who has pulled into the driveway</u>?

13. Always remember ^{DO} <u>that God is there too</u>.

14. This bicycle from Grandpa's is ^{PN} <u>what we brought home</u>.

15. "I know ^{DO} <u>whom I have believed</u>."

Worksheet 15, Part D *(Continued)*

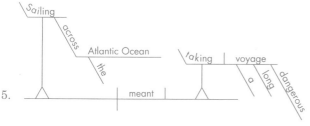

5.

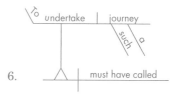

6.

Worksheet 17, Part B *(Continued)*

5.

6.

Name _____   *(Lesson 29)*

Worksheet 17
More Noun Clauses

A. Underline each noun clause. Above the introductory word, write whether that word serves as a *subject, direct object, adjective,* or *adverb.* If the word merely introduces the clause, write *introduces.*

                direct object
   1. "I know <u>whom I have believed</u>."

                   subject
   2. Your speech reveals <u>what is in your heart</u>.

                 adverb
   3. We still do not know <u>how the accident happened</u>.

              adverb
   4. We do not know <u>when Jesus will return for His own</u>.

       introduces
   5. <u>That Brother Nelson truly loves the Lord</u> is seen by his life.

                direct object
   6. I told the teacher <u>what I wanted</u>.

             adjective
   7. Hetty has decided <u>which book she will read</u>.

     introduces
   8. <u>Whether we pick peas</u> depends on Mother's schedule.

   direct object
   9. <u>Whatever we can do for Christ</u> never earns His grace.

                   adverb
  10. The best time to do an assignment is <u>when the lesson is fresh</u>.

           direct object
  11. We must respect <u>whomever the Lord places over us</u>.

           adverb
  12. Have you learned <u>why you cannot walk on quicksand</u>?

   adverb
  13. <u>Whenever the moon is not shining</u> is the best time for stargazing.

       adverb
  14. Do you know <u>where the little kittens are</u>?

B. Diagram the skeletons and complements of all the clauses in these sentences. Include the introductory words of the noun clauses.
   1. Pharaoh boldly said that he did not know the Lord.
   2. How God humbled proud Pharaoh is a thrilling story.
   3. The unmistakable message of the ten plagues was that God is sovereign.
   4. God plainly showed where the Israelites should travel on their journey.
   5. When they should stop was shown by the cloudy pillar.
   6. The Israelites did not always appreciate what God was doing for them.

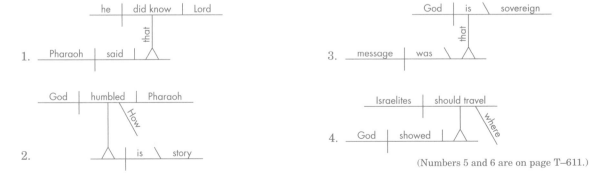

(Numbers 5 and 6 are on page T–611.)

Name _____   (Lesson 30)

Worksheet 18
Substantives

A. Underline the single-word substantives. Above each one, write *S, DO, PN, OP,* or *A* to tell whether it is used as a subject, direct object, predicate nominative, object of a preposition, or appositive.

   1.   ^SEverybody should admit his ^{DO}limitations and ^{DO}faults.

   2.   God's ^Speople do not follow the ^{DO}styles of the ^{OP}world.

   3.   The first Christian ^Smartyr, ^AStephen, was a ^{PN}deacon.

B. Underline the substantive phrases, and label them as in Part A.

   1.   The ^SLord Jesus appeared to ^{OP}John the Revelator while he was in the Spirit on the ^{OP}Lord's Day.

   2.   The church, ^Athe bride of Christ, will continue ^{DO}to serve God in heaven.

   3.   Elymas was influencing ^{DO}Sergius Paulus against the Gospel.

C. Underline the substantive clauses. Above each one, write *S, DO,* or *PN* to tell whether it is used as a subject, direct object, or predicate nominative.

   1.   ^SWhether circumstances are favorable does not determine ^{DO}whether we will be faithful to the Lord.

   2.   The Word of God is ^{PN}what gives us direction and counsel for life.

   3.   The blind man understood ^{DO}that Jesus had the power of God.

   4.   The truly great person is ^{PN}whoever serves willingly and humbly.

D. Underline the substantives in these sentences. Do not underline separately the substantives within phrases or clauses.

   1.   Uncle Wesley is disking the fields, and Father is planting corn.

   2.   Have you met Earl Groff, our new neighbor across the road?

   3.   We read from the Holy Bible and prayed for God's blessing on our lives.

   4.   Treating others fairly is an important part of the Golden Rule.

   5.   All should consider how their actions affect others.

   6.   To work together as a family is a great blessing.

   7.   The evening passed quickly for us, and soon our guests decided to leave for home.

   8.   Whenever you are ready will be fine with me.

   9.   Uncle Roy's moved to Cottonwood Valley and plan to start a small store.

  10. Everyone passed the test, and now we can start the next chapter.

Name _____   *(Lesson 34)*

Worksheet 19
Principal Parts of Verbs

A. Write the missing principal parts. Include *have* with the past participle.

First (Present)	Second (Past)	Third (Past Participle)
1. tarry	tarried	(have) tarried
2. weep	wept	(have) wept
3. drown	drowned	(have) drowned
4. come	came	(have) come
5. put	put	(have) put
6. do	did	(have) done
7. swim	swam	(have) swum
8. freeze	froze	(have) frozen

B. Write the correct form of the verb before the sentence.

drown   1. The ungodly people ____drowned____ in the Flood.

run   2. The horses have _____run_____ in from the field.

burst   3. Has Benny _____burst_____ his balloon on purpose?

shine   4. The flashlight _____shone_____ cheerily on the pathway.
                            shined, *or* shines

cut   5. Will you _____cut_____ me a piece of cake, please?

buy   6. We have regularly _____bought_____ our meats from Weber's Meats.

steal   7. We must forgive the man who _____stole_____ our bicycles.

forget   8. Have you already _____forgotten_____ Father's warning?

cost   9. Because of a late spring frost, peaches have _____cost_____ more this year than last year.

tag   10. I just _____tagged_____ Susie, and she is caught.

C. Write the correct form of each underlined verb. If the verb is correct, write *correct*.

_____did_____ 1. Karen <u>done</u> a good job on her map.

_____dug_____ 2. The dog has <u>digged</u> another hole in the yard.

_____written_____ 3. Have you <u>wrote</u> to your brother at Bible school?

_____saw_____ 4. We <u>seen</u> a beautiful display of the northern lights.

_____knew_____ 5. Mr. Daley <u>knowed</u> how to make a temporary splint.

_____dragged_____ 6. We <u>drug</u> the deer off the road.

_____correct_____ 7. We have often <u>spoken</u> to Barney Shefler as he walks past.

_____gone_____ 8. Mother has <u>went</u> to Dellington this morning.

_____come_____ 9. Has the company <u>came</u> yet?

_____taken_____ 10. The girls have <u>tooken</u> Baby Joan for a walk.

Name _____

Worksheet 20
Using Verbs in Perfect Tenses

A. When perfect tenses are used, two actions or conditions are often stated or implied. Write *yes* or *no* to tell whether perfect tenses are suitable for the underlined verbs in these sentences.

<u>yes</u>   1. I <u>had flown</u> in an airplane only once before my trip to Paraguay.

<u>no</u>   2. Last week I <u>had seen</u> a meteor shower.

<u>yes</u>   3. It is no longer so warm since the sun <u>has gone</u> behind the clouds.

<u>no</u>   4. Charity <u>will have ironed</u> all the shirts.

<u>yes</u>   5. By the time you leave Mexico, you <u>will have learned</u> many Spanish words.

<u>yes</u>   6. So far our work <u>has consisted</u> of feeding the cattle.

<u>yes</u>   7. Charles <u>had cleaned</u> the pens before Merle came home.

<u>no</u>   8. Yesterday the girls <u>had baked</u> pies and cookies.

<u>yes</u>   9. The thief catcher <u>had broken</u> through the thin ice, and Dirk Willems was rescuing him.

<u>no</u> 10. The Stoltzfuses <u>will have left</u> for home.

<u>yes</u> 11. These shelves <u>have been polished</u>, and Kaylene is putting the books back on.

<u>yes</u> 12. The wood fire <u>had become</u> a pile of glowing embers by the time we were ready to roast the hot dogs.

B. In each sentence, one verb should be changed to a perfect tense so that the relationship is clearer. Cross out that verb, and write a suitable perfect tense above it.

1. By the time evening came, three families ~~arrived~~ *had arrived* at our door.

2. When the first frost strikes, we ~~shall pick~~ *shall have picked* many bushels of tomatoes.

3. Father told us about many things that he ~~saw~~ *had seen* in Mexico.

4. When we ~~sketched~~ *had sketched* the outline, we filled in the details.

5. By the time snow comes, most of the migratory birds ~~will leave~~ *will have left*.

6. When I ~~finished~~ *had finished* the chores, I sat down and relaxed with a book.

7. The feed truck ~~arrived,~~ *had arrived* and we hurried to help unload it.

8. After we build this birdhouse, we ~~shall make~~ *shall have made* ten birdhouses in all.

9. All winter the family lived on the food that they ~~stored~~ *had stored* away.

10. When the workers ~~seated~~ *had seated* the old people, the children began singing.

Name _____   *(Lesson 40)*

Worksheet 21
Outlining Written Material

Read this composition, and complete the outline. You may need to copy it on other paper.

Regions of Judea

Many events of Bible history occurred in Judea, located in southern Palestine. Farthest to the west is an area of gently sloping foothills called the Shephelah. This region stretches about forty miles from north to south and up to eight miles from east to west. It served as an important buffer zone between Philistia and Judah, as shown by Biblical events that occurred in its three major valleys. In the Valley of Aijalon, Joshua fought a desperate battle with the Canaanites and commanded the sun and moon to stand still. The Philistines returned the ark of the Lord to Israel by way of the Valley of Sorek. And in the Valley of Elah, David silenced the challenge of the blasphemous Goliath.

East of the Shephelah rise the Judean Hills. This region includes a number of notable towns and cities, from Bethel in the north to Gibeon and Jerusalem in the middle to Hebron in the south. The Judean Hills also include three major clusters of peaks. The Bethel Hills are to the north and the Hebron Hills to the south, all rising well over three thousand feet above sea level. In the middle are the Jerusalem Hills, which rise less than twenty-seven hundred feet above sea level.

Between the Judean Hills and the Dead Sea is the Wilderness of Judah. This wilderness is an extremely rugged, desolate desert. Its Old Testament name is Jeshimon, which means "desolation." The character of this place can be illustrated by several accounts. To this wilderness David fled for his life, seeking to escape Saul's relentless pursuit. In this wilderness, quite likely, Jesus was tempted by the devil. Also in this wilderness the Essenes led their stern lives, leaving behind the renowned Dead Sea Scrolls. A good mental picture of these geographical regions is a significant help to Bible study.

(Sample outline.)   **Regions of Judea**

I. The Shephelah in western Judea

    A. Is an area of gently sloping foothills to the west

    B. Stretches about 40 miles from north to south and up to 8 miles from east to west

    C. Served as an important buffer zone between Philistia and Judah

        1. Includes the Valley of Aijalon, where Joshua fought against the Canaanites and commanded the sun and moon to stand still

        2. Includes the Valley of Sorek, where the Philistines sent the ark of the Lord back to Israel

        3. Includes the Valley of Elah, where David silenced the challenge of Goliath

II. The Judean Hills east of the Shephelah

    A. Includes notable towns and cities

        1. Bethel in the north

        2. Gibeon and Jerusalem in the middle

        3. Hebron in the south

    B. Includes three major clusters of peaks

        1. Bethel Hills to the north, over 3,000 feet above sea level

        2. Hebron Hills to the south, over 3,000 feet above sea level

        3. Jerusalem Hills in the middle, less than 2,700 feet above sea level

III. The Wilderness of Judah between the Judean Hills and the Dead Sea

    A. Is an extremely rugged, desolate desert

    B. Is named Jeshimon, meaning "desolation," in the Old Testament

    C. Has a character illustrated by several accounts

        1. Where David fled to escape from Saul

        2. Where Jesus likely was tempted

        3. Where the Essenes led their stern lives and left behind the Dead Sea Scrolls

Name _____

Worksheet 22
Transitive Verbs

A. The verb in each sentence is transitive. Underline the word that receives the action of the main verb.

1. Aunt Maggie told us a <u>story</u> of her childhood.

2. This <u>story</u> was related with much animation.

3. The <u>snow</u> had been piled into huge drifts.

4. Grandfather had started the <u>chores</u> early that evening.

5. Then he scratched his <u>arm</u> quite badly.

6. That night <u>he</u> was afflicted with blood poisoning.

7. Grandmother called the <u>family</u> together for prayer.

8. God graciously answered those <u>prayers</u>.

9. <u>Grandfather</u> was healed almost immediately.

10. Our <u>hearts</u> were filled with joy from the Lord.

11. We thanked <u>Him</u> for His goodness to us.

12. God does not always grant our <u>requests</u> this way.

13. But our <u>prayers</u> are definitely answered.

14. God may choose a less welcomed <u>answer</u> at times.

15. Truly, God loves His <u>people</u> very dearly.

16. I had finished my <u>homework</u> before supper.

17. The <u>Christian</u> is tempted by the devil.

18. The <u>bridge</u> was rebuilt before summer.

19. The <u>message</u> has been typed in a strange code.

20. God has proven His <u>faithfulness</u> and <u>love</u> many times.

21. Lowell wrote an interesting <u>story</u>.

22. Jean's <u>cake</u> was decorated very nicely.

23. Lynn's pet <u>dog</u> was penned up in the barn.

24. Mother prepared a delicious <u>lunch</u> for our picnic.

25. Brother Chester announced the <u>plans</u> for the school hike.

B. Diagram the skeletons, direct objects, and indirect objects.
1. The achievement tests have been finished.
2. Uncle George brought us some duck eggs to hatch.
3. Electric motors were running the fans and the augers.
4. The water was spilled all over my trousers.
5. The plow cut the sod with a straight furrow.

1. achievement tests | have been finished

(Students may omit *achievement*.)

2. Uncle George | brought | eggs / us

3. motors | were running | fans *and* augers

4. water | was spilled

5. plow | cut | sod

Name _____   *(Lesson 42)*

Worksheet 23
Intransitive Complete Verbs

A. Write *T* or *IC* in each blank to tell whether the verb is transitive or intransitive complete. If the verb is transitive, underline the word that receives its action.

__T__   1. My father runs a <u>dairy.</u>

__IC__   2. My dog runs after ground hogs and rabbits.

__IC__   3. The baby splashed in the water.

__T__   4. She splashed the <u>floor</u> with her bath water.

__T__   5. I ate three small <u>apples.</u>

__IC__   6. Martha ate slowly.

__T__   7. Brent scattered the grass <u>seed.</u>

__IC__   8. The little boys scattered across the lawn.

__IC__   9. The wire snapped under the weight of the fallen branch.

__T__   10. The <u>branch</u> was snapped off by the high wind.

__T__   11. Lorene flashed a <u>signal</u> to the others.

__IC__   12. The signal flashed brightly against the dark sky.

__IC__   13. The kites flew far above the treetops.

__T__   14. The highest <u>kite</u> was flown by Wendell.

__IC__   15. My shirt tore on the nail.

__T__   16. I tore my new <u>shirt</u> on the loose end of wire.

__IC__   17. The window cracked in two places.

__T__   18. The ball cracked the <u>window.</u>

__IC__   19. The paint sprayed all over the ground.

__T__   20. The apple <u>trees</u> were sprayed with a fungicide.

B. On other paper, write two sentences for each verb, one in which the verb is transitive and the other in which it is intransitive complete.   (Individual work.)

1. stopped   2. opened   3. shook   4. prepared

C. Diagram the skeletons, complements, and verb modifiers of these sentences.
   1. The snowplow pushed the snow off the roads.
   2. The big plows pushed through huge drifts.
   3. These beans have not been washed.
   4. Warren tripped over a rock.
   5. The swallows flew swiftly through the air.

Name _____

Worksheet 24
Intransitive Linking Verbs

A. Find each sentence with an intransitive linking verb, and underline the two words that are linked. If there is no linking verb, do not underline anything.

1. This green <u>book</u> is very <u>interesting</u>.

2. Those two <u>brethren</u> are the <u>ministers</u>.

3. This <u>house</u> was a <u>school</u> at one time.

4. The girls are reading quietly.

5. The <u>grass</u> has become <u>brown</u>.

6. <u>David</u> became the <u>king</u> over all Israel.

7. The <u>Christian</u> can be <u>calm</u> even in the face of danger.

8. The first two <u>boxes</u> are much too <u>heavy</u> to carry.

9. <u>Jesus</u> is the perfect <u>God-man</u>.

10. The snow is melting in the sun.

11. These <u>books</u> are all quite <u>attractive</u>.

12. The students turned in their seats.

13. The prophet sounded the message of God to the people.

14. The <u>story</u> sounded <u>unbelievable</u>.

15. This <u>calf</u> looked <u>healthy</u> this morning.

16. The barbecued <u>chicken</u> smelled <u>delicious</u>.

17. Our new <u>assignment</u> will be <u>easy</u> to do.

18. The <u>children</u> have been <u>helpful</u> all day.

19. We smelled the roses on the teacher's desk.

20. <u>Sister Jane</u> had been my <u>teacher</u> at our old place.

21. <u>Prayer</u> is the Christian's vital <u>breath</u>.

22. "The <u>tongue</u> is a little <u>member</u>."

23. A true <u>gentleman</u> must be <u>considerate</u> of others.

24. Bible <u>study</u> is <u>important</u> to the child of God.

25. The Anabaptist <u>preacher</u> became a <u>martyr</u>.

B. Diagram the skeletons and complements of these sentences.
1. Delvin feels satisfied with his new assignment.
2. The brown goat looked around the corner.
3. He looked amusing and mischievous.
4. You would be the best one for this job.
5. Angels are ministering spirits to the saints.

1. Delvin | feels \ satisfied

2. goat | looked

3. He | looked \ amusing and mischievous

4. You | would be \ one

5. Angels | are \ spirits

Worksheet 14, Part D *(Continued)*

    Jesus never considered His own needs more important than the needs of others. One day He and His disciples needed a time of rest, and Jesus called them apart to a place of quietness. But the people, see-ing them go, flocked after them. Jesus had compassion on these sheep without a shepherd, and He patiently taught them many things. By evening the disciples wanted Jesus to send the multitude away, but Jesus said, "Give ye them to eat." Then He used five loaves and two fishes to feed more than five thousand people. The time to "rest a while" had disappeared in a day of service.

Name _____   *(Lesson 45)*

Worksheet 25
Basic Sentence Patterns

Label the sentence patterns as shown.

Pattern 1: intransitive complete verb
Pattern 2: transitive verb; action passed to direct object
Pattern 3: transitive verb; action passed to subject
Pattern 4: intransitive linking verb

2   1. I returned the books to the library.

4   2. Jesus is the Prince of Peace.

2   3. The boy scraped his knee on the stones.

1   4. The men are looking for the broken piece.

4   5. The pictures look very beautiful.

1   6. Jesus died on the cross for us.

4   7. The storm seems very dangerous.

3   8. The papers have been corrected.

2   9. The three girls swept the floors in the house.

3   10. The earth is watered by God's care.

3   11. The Bible was written by holy men of God.

4   12. This man is my good friend.

1   13. Brother Paul preached about the grace of God.

3   14. Daniel was thrown into the lions' den.

4   15. Amos was a herdsman at the time of God's call.

3   16. Brian's lessons were finished before recess.

1   17. The noisy trucks rumbled across the shaky bridge.

3   18. The entire house was searched by the soldiers.

2   19. Susan turned the pages of her book slowly.

3   20. Esau was rejected by God as a profane man.

4   21. The pretty roses became wilted by the end of the day.

1   22. Jesus shall descend from heaven with a shout.

2   23. The bull chased the two boys out of the pasture.

4   24. The ground is too damp and cool to sit on.

4   25. Today's science lesson is intriguing.

1   26. We studied about the force of gravity.

2   27. No scientist can fully explain this mysterious force.

4   28. Gravity is essential to man's very existence.

3   29. Without it, we would be spun right off the earth.

2   30. Gravity overcomes the centrifugal force of the spinning earth.

Name _____

Worksheet 26
Subject–Verb Agreement

A. Underline the correct verbs in parentheses.

1. The congregation (<u>is</u>, are) having its first service in the new building.

2. The number of families (have, <u>has</u>) been increasing over the years.

3. (Is, <u>Are</u>) the benches new?

4. (There's, <u>There are</u>) more benches in this building than in the old one.

5. Each (hold, <u>holds</u>) more people than one of the old benches did.

6. The *Church Hymnal* and the *Life Songs* (<u>fit</u>, fits) nicely in the racks.

7. The larger auditorium, along with the additional Sunday school rooms, (make, <u>makes</u>) a more practical building.

8. A dog or a fox (<u>is</u>, are) running along the fencerow.

9. The ambulance crew (is, <u>are</u>) treating several victims of the accident.

10. She (don't, <u>doesn't</u>) make many mistakes in her computation.

11. Mathematics (<u>is</u>, are) her easiest subject.

12. The pruning shears (<u>don't</u>, doesn't) belong on the shop floor.

13. Ham and eggs (make, <u>makes</u>) a delicious breakfast.

14. (Is, <u>Are</u>) the cows coming in from the pasture?

15. (How's, <u>How are</u>) your rabbits doing?

16. Everybody in the cars (wonder, <u>wonders</u>) why the traffic has stopped.

17. Edward's trousers (is, <u>are</u>) full of burs.

18. Aunt Mary or Grandmother (have, <u>has</u>) plans to help us today.

19. Each of the cookie sheets (<u>is</u>, are) ready for the oven.

20. Measles (<u>is</u>, are) a highly contagious disease caused by a virus.

B. Rewrite these sentences, following the directions in parentheses. Change the verb to agree with the subject if necessary.

1. When's this assignment due? (Change *this assignment* to *the assignments.*)

    When are the assignments due? _____

2. Gordon or Wendell has the materials you need. (Change *or* to *and.*) _____

    Gordon and Wendell have the materials you need. _____

3. The students want to watch the road crew at work. (Change *The students* to *Each of the students.*)

    Each of the students wants to watch the road crew at work. _____

4. Melanie and Kendra are to wash the windows. (Change *and* to *or.*) _____

    Melanie or Kendra is to wash the windows. _____

Name _____   *(Lesson 49)*

Worksheet 27
Using *Lay—Lie, Set—Sit,* and *Raise—Rise*

A. Write the proper form of *lay* or *lie.*

<u>laid *or* lying</u>   1. Fresh shewbread was —— on the table each day.

<u>lay</u>   2. Jacob used a stone for a pillow when he —— down to sleep.

<u>lying</u>   3. Isaac was submissively —— on the altar.

<u>lay</u>   4. This morning Mother —— down for a while.

<u>lie</u>   5. Will the snow melt, or will it —— on the ground?

<u>lain</u>   6. The snow had —— on the mountain slopes until May.

<u>laid</u>   7. Lowell has —— the stakes in neat piles.

<u>lays</u>   8. As I pull the wagon, Miriam —— the onions in it.

<u>lies</u>   9. Baby Kay —— on her back and plays with her toes.

<u>laid</u>   10. The electric line to the house is being —— underground.

B. Write the proper form of *set* or *sit.*

<u>set</u>   1. Haman —— Mordecai on the horse at the king's command.

<u>sit</u>   2. The saints can —— in heavenly places with Christ.

<u>sat</u>   3. After reading from Isaiah, Christ —— down and spoke.

<u>sit</u>   4. Airplane passengers must —— during takeoff and landing.

<u>sets</u>   5. The new moon rises and —— with the sun.

<u>sitting</u>   6. The girls are —— before the fireplace and braiding rugs.

<u>set</u>   7. Do not —— the basket of eggs on the kitchen floor.

<u>Sit</u>   8. —— up to the table for dinner.

<u>sat</u>   9. The visitors have —— in the living room.

<u>sets</u>   10. After a mockingbird —— about twelve days, the eggs hatch.

C. Write the proper form of *raise* or *rise.*

<u>raised</u>   1. At each place on his journey, Abraham —— an altar to God.

<u>rose</u>   2. When he offered sacrifices, the smoke —— into the air.

<u>risen</u>   3. His prayers have —— to the Almighty.

<u>raises</u>   4. Uncle Lester —— much produce when summer comes.

<u>raise *or* raised</u>   5. The sunflowers —— their heads over six feet high.

<u>risen</u>   6. The sweet corn has —— to an unusual height.

<u>rising</u>   7. The river is —— almost to the flood stage.

<u>rising</u>   8. Sales of the new book are —— fast.

<u>raising</u>   9. The congregation is —— funds for a new school.

<u>rose</u>   10. The people —— to their feet for the benediction.

Name _____   *(Lesson 50)*

Worksheet 28
Using *Can—May* and *Let—Leave*

A. Write *can* or *may* for each sentence.

_____can_____   1. God's people ——— always overcome their enemies.

_____may_____   2. Whosoever will ——— come to the fountain of life.

_____can_____   3. The challenge of a giant ——— frighten only the faithless.

_____May_____   4. ——— I please open the door?

_____may_____   5. Lucille ——— pass out the songbooks this time.

B. Write the proper form of *let* or *leave*.

_____left_____   1. God has ——— His people in the world to do His work.

_____Let_____   2. ——— God have His proper place in your life.

_____leave_____   3. Did I ——— my car lights on?

_____let_____   4. This cat has never ——— us pet it yet.

_____left_____   5. Sister Wilma has ——— a message for Mother.

_____let_____   6. Margaret will ——— me ride her bicycle for a while.

leaves *or* left   7. Wayne ——— for Manitoba this morning.

_____letting_____   8. A pinhole is ——— the air escape from the inner tube.

C. Write the correct verb for each verb that is incorrect. If there is no error, write *correct*.

_____let_____   1. Do not leave your faith falter.

_____may_____   2. Please ask Mother if we can eat these cookies.

_____sit_____   3. We should set at Jesus' feet as Mary did.

_____correct_____   4. King David, old and feeble, lay on his bed.

_____rose_____   5. The cry of Abel's blood raised to the Lord in heaven.

_____correct_____   6. Do not let the door slam noisily.

_____risen_____   7. The widow's son had raised to life.

_____sat_____   8. The Shunammite's sick boy had set in her lap all morning.

_____laid_____   9. When her son died, the mother lay him on Elisha's bed.

_____correct_____   10. God's power can bring him back to life.

_____leave_____   11. Never let a hoe on the ground with its blade pointing up.

_____let_____   12. If you leave the tank become empty, you will need to walk for gasoline.

_____rising_____   13. A strong, musty smell was raising from the old cellar.

_____lying_____   14. A large branch was laying across the road.

_____correct_____   15. The chimpanzee had sat on a crate until the keeper went in.

Name _____   (Lesson 50)

Worksheet 29
Using Other Problem Verbs

A. Write the second and third principal parts of each verb.

1. attack	attacked	(have) attacked	7. drag	dragged	(have) dragged
2. blow	blew	(have) blown	8. drown	drowned	(have) drowned
3. break	broke	(have) broken	9. know	knew	(have) known
4. bring	brought	(have) brought	10. tag	tagged	(have) tagged
5. burst	burst	(have) burst	11. take	took	(have) taken
6. cost	cost	(have) cost	12. throw	threw	(have) thrown

B. Write the correct verb for each verb that is incorrect. If there is no error, write *correct*.

brought	1.	A woman had brung her alabaster box of ointment to Jesus.
broken	2.	When she had broke it open, the smell filled the house.
cost	3.	The precious ointment must have costed much money.
knew	4.	The Pharisee knowed that this woman had been a sinner.
attacked	5.	In his thoughts, he attackted Jesus for accepting her devotion.
dragged	6.	Paul and Silas were drug before the rulers.
taken	7.	Then they were tooken to prison.
drowned	8.	At the riot in Ephesus, the mob drownded out all reason.
threw	9.	We throwed the cornhusks to the pigs.
correct	10.	Your bicycle cost too much to use it recklessly.
burst	11.	The aerosol can bursted in the heat.
knew	12.	At first nobody knowed what had happened.
correct	13.	We could not tell who was tagged first.
attacked	14.	The hungry wolves attackted the aging moose.
have	15.	Who would of expected that the tractor cost this much?
drowned	16.	When the Missouri River flooded, all our pigs drownded.
blew	17.	After the tire blowed, Father lost control of the car.
correct	18.	Have you taken the wash off the line?
brought	19.	Susan brang it into the house.
have	20.	Mabel must of washed the dishes herself.

Worksheet 39, Part C *(Continued)*

Name _____

Worksheet 30
Writing Social Notes

The following notes have various errors. Match the small raised letters to the sentences below, which describe the errors. You will not use all the letters.

[a]Route 2, Box 124

October 14, 20—

[b]Uncle James and Aunt Miriam,

[c]Thank you for the enjoyable visit in your home. [d]I am finally writing to tell you how much I appreciated it. [e]You did so many things to make my stay pleasant. [f]I look forward to visiting you again sometime, and I hope you will visit us too when you can.

[g]Sincerely yours

Sharon

＊　　　＊　　　＊　　　＊　　　＊

[h]237 Ranger lane

Danville, Va 24540

july 22, 20—

[i]Dear Jonathan:

[j]I would like to invite you to spend the weekend with me. [k]My oldest brother will be going to your area early the next week, so he could take you back home. [l]We have lots of work to do right now, but we usually have some free time in the evening. [m]I am looking forward to seeing you.

[n]Mark

__d__ 1. The letter was not written promptly enough.

__j__ 2. It does not say how and when the invited person would come.

__i__ 3. The greeting is not punctuated correctly.

__c__ 4. It does not mention the date of the enjoyable visit.

__n__ 5. The closing is omitted.

__h__ 6. The heading has errors in capitalization.

__e__ 7. It mentions no specific things that made the stay pleasant.

__b__ 8. The greeting is not complete.

__k__ 9. It does not say exactly when the invited person would leave.

__g__ 10. The closing is not punctuated correctly.

__a__ 11. The heading is not complete.

__l__ 12. The specific kind of work is not mentioned, in case suitable clothes are needed.

Name _____   *(Lesson 54)*

Worksheet 31
Active and Passive Voice

A. Write whether the verb in each sentence is *active* or *passive*.

    ___active___ 1. True faith produces action.

    ___active___ 2. Abel offered to God an acceptable sacrifice.

    ___passive___ 3. Enoch was translated from this world to the eternal world.

    ___active___ 4. God warned Noah of the coming judgment.

    ___passive___ 5. We have often been inspired by Moses' choice of faith.

    ___passive___ 6. The Passover was observed by the children of Israel.

    ___active___ 7. The Israelites crossed the Red Sea safely.

    ___passive___ 8. The Egyptians were drowned in their attempt to follow.

B. Rewrite each sentence, changing the verb to the active voice. Do not change the tense.

    1. All the animals were named by Adam.   ___Adam named all the animals.___

    2. Our lives have been blessed by God's tender love.   ___God's tender love has blessed our lives.___

    3. The shelves were built by Uncle Alvin.   ___Uncle Alvin built the shelves.___

C. Rewrite each sentence, changing the verb to the passive voice and putting the original subject into a prepositional phrase. Do not change the tense.

    1. My great-uncle had collected these stamps.   ___These stamps had been collected by my great-uncle.___

    2. The children are picking up the potatoes.   ___The potatoes are being picked up by the children.___

    3. A cold front brings cooler weather.   ___Cooler weather is brought by a cold front.___

D. The passive voice is used in the sentences below. Before each one, write the letter of the statement which correctly describes that sentence.

    a. The active voice would be more effective.
    b. There is no clear doer of the action.
    c. There is a good reason not to name the doer.

    ___c___ 1. Mother's best dish has been broken.

    ___a___ 2. Two familiar hymns were led by Brother Vernon.

    ___b___ 3. Saul was also called Paul.

    ___a___ 4. These tomatoes were given us by Grandmother.

Name _____   *(Lesson 57)*

Worksheet 32
Personal Pronouns

A. Label the person, number, and gender of each pronoun, using the numbers and letters shown. For the number of one pronoun, you should write *S or P*.

	Person 1, 2, 3	Number S, P	Gender M, F, N, C
1. hers	3	S	F
2. theirs	3	P	C
3. my	1	S	C
4. he	3	S	M
5. they	3	P	C
6. it	3	S	N *or* C
7. us	1	P	C
8. yours	2	S *or* P	C
9. she	3	S	F
10. him	3	S	M

B. Underline each personal pronoun, and put parentheses around its antecedent.

1. (Jesus) stilled the tempest with <u>His</u> words.

2. (Mary and Martha) mourned the death of <u>their</u> brother.

3. (Rice) swells when <u>it</u> is cooked.

4. Glenda and Lois visited the new (neighbors) and took some food to <u>them</u>.

5. George saw (Lamar) and went over to <u>him</u>.

C. In each blank, write the personal pronoun that would be used to represent the word or phrase in parentheses.

1. ____Hers____ (Alma's) is lying here with ____theirs____ (the other pupils').

2. ____She____ (Mother) and ____they____ (the boys) have sold ____them____ (the beans).

3. ____He____ (Brother Martin) spoke with ____her____ (Sister Agnes) and ____them____ (the children).

4. ____We____ (My sister and I) are using ____his____ (Charles's) right now.

5. ____They____ (The boys) have found ____them____ (the knives).

6. These pencils are ____his____ (Frank's); the blue ones are ____theirs____ (the girls').

Worksheet 41, Part D *(Continued)*

3.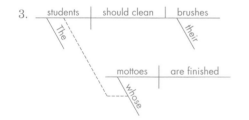

4.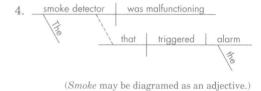

(Smoke may be diagramed as an adjective.)

Name _____   *(Lesson 58)*

Worksheet 33
Pronoun Case

A. Write a personal pronoun to fit each description.

_____me_____   1. first person, singular, objective case

_____they_____   2. third person, plural, nominative case

_____its_____   3. third person, singular, possessive case, neuter gender

your *or* yours   4. second person, possessive case

_____we_____   5. first person, plural, nominative case

_____him_____   6. third person, singular, objective case, masculine gender

B. In each blank, write whether the two pronouns differ in *person, number, case,* or *gender.*

_____case_____   1. us, our   _____gender_____   5. he, she

_____person_____   2. we, they   _____number_____   6. I, we

_____gender_____   3. hers, its   _____person_____   7. us, them

_____case_____   4. he, him   _number *or* gender_ 8. hers, theirs

C. Underline each personal pronoun. Above it, write *N* or *O* to identify its case.

              O   N   O
1. The Lord has blessed <u>us</u>, and <u>we</u> should give <u>Him</u> praise and glory.

                    N   O
2. When the disciples thought that <u>they</u> would sink, Jesus walked to <u>them</u> on the water.

    N   O
3. <u>You</u> should give <u>him</u> something worthwhile.

    N   O   O
4. <u>She</u> will advise <u>you</u> what to do for <u>it</u>.

D. Cross out any incorrect pronoun, and write the correct pronoun above it. Some sentences have no errors.

                        their
1. Jesus came to the disciples and calmed ~~they're~~ fears.

   They
2. ~~Them~~ remained loyal to the Lord.

                 I
3. Nevin answered, "It was ~~me~~ who washed the dishes for you."

                yours
4. I didn't realize that the book is ~~your's~~.

   (correct)
5. We shall meet them at the airport.

   (correct)
6. The work was not difficult, and they finished it by noon.

                they
7. The bean pickers this morning are ~~them~~.

   (correct)
8. You're doing a neat job of crocheting.

          your
9. If you cannot find ~~you're~~ colored pencils, you may use mine.

                they
10. The surprise helpers may have been ~~them~~.

Name _____   *(Lesson 60)*

Worksheet 34
Using Personal Pronouns Correctly

A. Underline the correct words in parentheses.

1. Read Susie and (she, <u>her</u>) the story of Queen Esther.

2. (<u>We</u>, Us) girls are often inspired by her noble example.

3. Haman did not realize that Mordecai and (<u>she</u>, her) were related.

4. Queen Esther invited the king and (he, <u>him</u>) to a banquet.

5. Queen Esther told the king, "The wicked enemy is (<u>he</u>, him)."

6. God used these two Jews, Mordecai and (she, <u>her</u>), to save the Jewish nation from destruction.

7. Will Brother Ben teach (we, <u>us</u>) boys how?

8. Either Debra or Darla will read (<u>her</u>, their) poem first.

9. The crop farmer and mechanic had (<u>his</u>, their) hands full that spring.

10. Two boys, Mervin and (<u>he</u>, him), have figured out the puzzle.

11. Uncle Jesse brought some new books for you and (I, <u>me</u>).

12. The secret helpers must have been Aunt Sue and (<u>they</u>, them).

13. The ones in the back, Rosetta and (<u>she</u>, her), did not get wet.

14. You may go with Elmer and (he, <u>him</u>) if you wish.

15. The baker and the butcher had (his stand, <u>their stands</u>) at the market.

16. The baker and butcher had (<u>his stand</u>, their stands) at the market.

17. Either Andrew or Glen will tell us (<u>his</u>, their) opinion next.

18. (<u>We</u>, Us) bookworms must be careful to do our work diligently.

19. The girls in our family, Barbara and (<u>I</u>, me), do most of the cooking.

20. The next person in line for new shoes is Harvey or (<u>I</u>, me).

B. Rewrite these sentences to make the pronouns clear and correct.

1. The teacher told me and Lorene to clean the chalkboard. _____

    <u>The teacher told Lorene and me to clean the chalkboard.</u> _____

2. Uncle Leonard told Howard that his peach trees were blooming nicely.   <u>Uncle Leonard said, "Howard,</u>

    <u>your peach trees are blooming nicely." *or* Uncle Leonard said, "Howard, my peach trees are blooming nicely."</u>

3. Heidi visited with Catherine when she spent the weekend here.   <u>When Catherine spent the week-</u>

    <u>end here, Heidi visited with her. *or* When Heidi spent the weekend here, she visited with Catherine.</u>

4. The dessert is for me and you to plan.   <u>The dessert is for you and me to plan.</u>

    _____

5. Wilmer asked Harry if his bicycle was fixed yet.   <u>Wilmer asked, "Harry, is your bicycle fixed yet?"</u>

    <u>*or* Wilmer asked, "Harry, is my bicycle fixed yet?"</u>

Name _____   *(Lesson 61)*

Worksheet 35
Compound Personal Pronouns and Demonstrative Pronouns

A. Underline the compound personal pronouns. Above each, write *I* if it is used intensively or *R* if it is used reflexively.

1. The children of Israel prepared <u>themselves</u> ^R for the Passover.

2. Balaam <u>himself</u> ^I said that he wanted to die the death of the righteous.

3. But he never identified <u>himself</u> ^R with the people of God.

4. We must place <u>ourselves</u> ^R in the way of divine blessing.

5. You <u>yourself</u> ^I should know the answer to that question.

B. Label each underlined word as a pronoun (*P*) or an adjective (*A*).

  _P_ 1. <u>Those</u> who are ready to do God's will can know what it is.

  _A_ 2. We must not become bound to <u>these</u> earthly pursuits.

  _A_ 3. <u>This</u> world and everything in it will pass away.

  _P_ 4. <u>That</u> should be a constant reminder to us to lay up treasures in heaven.

  _P_ 5. <u>These</u> are perilous times.

  _P_ 6. <u>This</u> is not our final home.

C. Cross out each wrong word. If another word should be used instead, write the correction above it.

1. Adam and Eve placed ~~theirselves~~ *themselves* under the sentence of death.

2. Adam ~~hisself~~ *himself* knew better than to take the forbidden fruit.

3. That ~~there~~ tree was the only one they were forbidden to take from.

4. We must keep ~~ourself~~ *ourselves* from the snares of the devil.

5. Joel and ~~myself~~ *I* would like to hear about your adventure.

6. ~~Them~~ *Those* boys are talking too loudly.

7. The workers helped ~~themself~~ *themselves* to the cookies and drink.

8. Have you waited long for Lester and ~~myself~~ *me*?

9. These ~~here~~ stalks are loaded with beautiful beans.

10. ~~Them~~ *Those* bushes have lots of lima beans too.

11. Melvin cut ~~hisself~~ *himself* with his pocketknife.

12. Great-uncle Levi told ~~ourselves~~ *us* some stories of his childhood.

13. These are the bicycles we will sell; ~~them~~ *those* are the ones we will keep.

Name _____

Worksheet 36
Indefinite Pronouns

A. Underline the correct words in parentheses.

1. Several of the Ten Commandments (<u>address</u>, addresses) man's relationship to God.

2. One of them (show, <u>shows</u>) God's attitude toward the Sabbath.

3. Each of them (contain, <u>contains</u>) a principle that is still important.

4. Some of the bread (have, <u>has</u>) had (<u>its</u>, their) crust burned.

5. Some of the doughnuts (<u>have</u>, has) had (its, <u>their</u>) glaze put on.

6. (Is, <u>Are</u>) any of the watermelons ripe yet?

7. One of the cantaloupes (<u>is</u>, are) ripe now.

8. All of the cantaloupes (<u>need</u>, needs) to be picked next week.

9. Neither of the rooms (have, <u>has</u>) been cleaned.

10. None of the rooms (<u>have</u>, has) been cleaned.

11. Each of us (need, <u>needs</u>) new shoes before school starts.

12. (<u>Is</u>, Are) anybody in your congregation at least one hundred years old?

13. Several of the boys (<u>remember</u>, remembers) (his, <u>their</u>) promise to help.

14. None of the girls (<u>have</u>, has) forgotten (her, <u>their</u>) promise.

15. Most of the hamburger (have, <u>has</u>) been browned.

16. Most of the hamburgers (<u>have</u>, has) been eaten.

17. (<u>Is</u>, Are) any of the cheese left?

18. (Is, <u>Are</u>) any of the pickles left?

19. Nobody (seem, <u>seems</u>) to know where (<u>he</u>, they) saw the cats last.

20. Each of the students (<u>is</u>, are) expected to keep (<u>his</u>, their) desk neat.

B. Put an apostrophe in each word that needs one.

1. Somebody's car is parked right in front of ours.

2. Yours are stacked on the table; no one's are in the box anymore.

3. After hers worked that well, we expected everyone's to work too.

4. Everybody's is here on time, or haven't theirs come yet?

C. Write whether each underlined word is used as a pronoun (*P*) or an adjective (*A*).

   A   1. <u>Either</u> apple should taste good.

   A   2. <u>One</u> answer on the test was wrong.

   P   3. <u>Most</u> of the trees have lost their leaves.

   P   4. <u>All</u> of the snow has melted.

   P   5. <u>Both</u> have answered the question wisely.

Name _____   *(Lesson 64)*

Worksheet 37
Interrogative and Relative Pronouns

A. Write whether each underlined pronoun is an interrogative pronoun (*I*) or a relative pronoun (*R*).

   I   1. <u>Who</u> is equal in glory to our great God?

   R   2. Has any man on earth seen the glory <u>that</u> surrounds Him?

   R   3. Jesus Christ, <u>whom</u> God sent, revealed a measure of God's glory.

   I   4. <u>Whose</u> image does a godly person reflect?

   R   5. We seek to fill the place <u>which</u> God has designed for us.

B. Underline each relative pronoun, and put parentheses around its antecedent.

1. (Peace) <u>that</u> passes understanding shall keep your hearts and minds.

2. We should never take revenge on (those) <u>who</u> mistreat us.

3. (People) <u>who</u> are jealous cannot live together peaceably.

4. Neighbors helped the (family) <u>whose</u> basement was flooded.

5. The (boy) <u>whom</u> you met was my cousin.

6. The sick girl received some (cards) <u>which</u> gave her encouragement.

C. Underline the correct pronouns in parentheses.

1. Joseph, (who, <u>whom</u>) his brothers hated, became a ruler in Egypt.

2. Joseph, (<u>who</u>, whom) recognized his brothers, decided to test them.

3. Lazarus, (who, <u>whom</u>) Jesus loved dearly, had died.

4. The crowd of people (<u>who</u>, which) gathered at the tomb were amazed.

5. The man (<u>who</u>, whom) had been dead came out of the grave.

6. The people (<u>who</u>, which) stayed up to watch the meteor shower saw a spectacular sight.

7. This goat, (who, <u>which</u>) is getting loose almost every day, is destroying Mother's flowers.

8. This dog, (who, <u>which</u>) is chewing on a towel, must be tied on washdays.

D. Underline each pronoun, including possessive personal pronouns used as adjectives. Above each pronoun, write *P* for personal, *CP* for compound personal, *D* for demonstrative, *ID* for indefinite, *IR* for interrogative, or *R* for relative.

1.   <u>Which</u> of the flowers did <u>you</u> plant last spring?
     IR   P

2.   <u>These</u> are the <u>ones</u>; <u>those</u> are some bushes <u>that</u> <u>we</u> planted before.
     D   ID   D   R P

3.   Did <u>anyone</u> help <u>you</u> with the work, or did <u>you</u> <u>yourself</u> do <u>all</u> of <u>it</u>?
       ID   P   P CP   ID P

4.   <u>This</u> is the climbing rose <u>which</u> <u>I</u> started from <u>one</u> of Grandmother's.
     D   R P   ID

5.   <u>What</u> is <u>that</u> called?
     IR   D

6.   <u>You</u> may pick <u>yourself</u> a bouquet.
     P   CP

Name _____

Worksheet 38
Forms of Comparison for Adjectives

A. Write the comparative and superlative forms of these adjectives.

Positive	Comparative	Superlative
1. tight	tighter	tightest
2. well	better	best
3. bad	worse	worst
4. hungry	hungrier	hungriest
5. far	farther	farthest
6. little, in amount	less	least
7. much	more	most
8. comfortable	more comfortable	most comfortable

B. Correct these sentences by crossing out words or word endings, or by adding words. Show where added words belong by using a caret (∧).

1. Sally and Mary could not decide which of the two plans was ~~best~~ better.

2. Of Judah and Israel, Judah had the ~~largest~~ larger number of good kings.

3. David was a ~~more~~ godlier king than Saul.

4. By the end of Jesus' story, the younger son had become ∧more righteous~~er~~ than the older son.

5. Joseph is a more ∧nearly perfect type of Christ than David is.

6. Of Lucille and Edith, Lucille is the ~~best~~ better singer of alto.

7. Which of these two flower beds is ∧more nearly round~~er~~?

8. Yesterday Marian felt the ~~illest~~ worst she has since getting the flu.

9. Of all the girls, Sandra took the ~~littlest~~ least ice cream.

10. Clair's answer is more ∧nearly correct than Joel's.

11. Nero was one of the ~~most~~ cruelest rulers in history.

12. Of the two English-speaking countries in North America, Canada is ~~greatest~~ greater in size.

13. Daniel and his friends looked ~~more~~ healthier than the other young men.

14. Joseph was a ∧more faithful~~ler~~ son than his older brothers were.

15. Goliath was the ~~most~~ tallest man recorded in the Bible.

16. This battery is ∧more nearly dead~~er~~ than that one.

Name _____   *(Lesson 72)*

Worksheet 39
Verbals as Adjectives

A. Underline each participle used as an adjective. Draw an arrow from it to the word it modifies.

1. The pursuing Egyptians frightened the Israelites.

2. The wearied travelers, murmuring and complaining, were making life hard for Moses.

3. Moses' burdened plea was that God would spare His failing people.

4. Jeremiah is often called the Weeping Prophet.

5. Timon was one of the chosen deacons.

6. Jesus could not open the blinded eyes of the proud Pharisees.

7. The broken bread depicts Christ's broken body.

8. The devoted women had bought spices for anointing Jesus' body.

9. Jesus, crowned and exalted, is now at the Father's right hand.

10. Our risen Saviour makes intercession for the saints.

B. Underline each infinitive used as an adjective. Draw an arrow from it to the word it modifies.

1. Israel had a new song to sing after their deliverance from Egypt.

2. Apart from Jesus, there is no safe way to go, no genuine truth to know, and no eternal life to live.

3. A charge to keep is given to each person.

4. The way to live is to forgive.

5. We have grass to mow and beans to pick.

6. Brother Wenger had some encouraging words to give.

7. We learned a new inside game to play.

8. Brother Martin gave us a poem to read.

9. These quarrelsome children apparently need more work to do.

10. The greatest honor to seek is the knowledge that God is pleased with us.

C. Diagram these sentences.
1. An important lesson to learn is complete obedience.
2. The horses, whinnying and prancing, were awaiting the command to go.
3. The defeated people served their conquerors.
4. Each person has been assigned several chores to do.
5. A growing teenager needs ample time to rest.
6. That flashing light is an airport beacon.

(Numbers 5 and 6 are on page T–624.)

Name _____   *(Lesson 74)*

Worksheet 40
Adjective Phrases

A. Underline each prepositional phrase used as an adjective. Draw an arrow from it to the word it modifies.

1. Moses, the adopted son of Pharaoh's daughter, received the best education of Egypt.

2. His identification with the people of God shows a strong faith in God.

3. His burden for Israel was not appreciated by them.

B. Underline each participial phrase. Draw an arrow from it to the word it modifies.

1. God, sustaining the created worlds, clearly remains in full control.

2. The steadfast Christians, singing joyfully, were led to execution.

3. The two boys playing outside are my brothers.

4. Striking suddenly, the earthquake destroyed many buildings.

C. Underline each infinitive phrase used as an adjective. Draw an arrow from it to the word it modifies.

1. One way to overcome discontentment is to cultivate a thankful attitude.

2. Naboth's desire to keep his vineyard was not based on selfishness.

3. He was following God's command to keep each parcel of land in the family line.

4. One's willingness to do his best affects his ability to serve God well.

D. Underline each misplaced phrase, and draw an arrow from it to the place where it belongs.

1. The herd of thirsty buffalo stampeded to the riverbed, scenting water.

2. Streaking overhead, we were amazed at the brilliant meteor.

3. The people wanted to stone Moses, complaining bitterly.

4. After Jesus ascended, two men spoke to the disciples in white apparel.

E. Diagram these sentences.
1. Jesus, seeking the Father's will, trod the pathway of pain.
2. His willingness to die sacrificially indicates His great love.
3. The Jewish leaders welcomed Judas's offer to betray Jesus.
4. Peter, fearing greatly, denied his knowledge of Jesus.

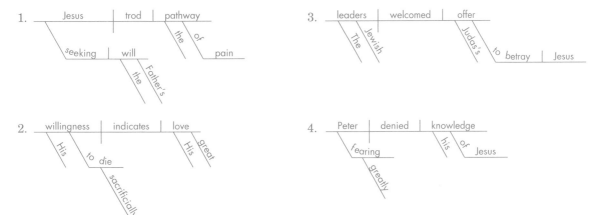

Name _____   *(Lesson 76)*

Worksheet 41
Adjective Clauses

A. Underline each adjective clause, and draw an arrow from it to the word it modifies.

1. Joseph, who stands as a noble example to all youth, fled temptation.

2. Even circumstances which seemed totally unfair did not shake his faith.

3. The butler, whose promise to Joseph had been forgotten, finally remembered Joseph when the king's dream could not be interpreted.

4. The things that Joseph had dreamed in his youth would soon be fulfilled.

5. The brothers, whom Joseph immediately recognized, did not know Joseph.

B. For each pair, write which of the underlined clauses is restrictive (R) and which is nonrestrictive (N). Add any commas that are needed.

___R___ 1. a. The man who fears the Lord departs from evil.

___N___   b. Job, who feared the Lord, refused to speak against Him.

___N___ 2. a. The Lord, whose throne is in heaven, rules over the kingdoms of men.

___R___   b. Nebuchadnezzar was a king who learned this through a hard lesson.

___R___ 3. a. My brother bought the truck which had belonged to my uncle.

___N___   b. That blue truck, which had belonged to my uncle, is now my brother's.

___R___ 4. a. A car which has been driven only eight thousand miles should not burn oil.

___N___   b. This car, which has been driven only eight thousand miles, already burns oil.

___N___ 5. a. Lori Blank, whom we have visited several times, is at a rest home.

___R___   b. The lady whom we have visited several times is at a rest home.

C. Underline each misplaced clause, and draw an arrow from it to the place where it belongs.

1. The flower bed surrounds an old tree stump that Mother planted.

2. This car belongs to my sister, which was dented by hail.

3. Yesterday my uncle and aunt visited us who live near New York.

4. I found the game in the closet that I was looking for.

D. Diagram these sentences.
   1. Our family visited Sister Bertha, who is an invalid.
   2. We planted the watermelon seeds we had saved.
   3. The students whose mottoes are finished should clean their brushes.
   4. The smoke detector that triggered the alarm was malfunctioning.

(Numbers 3 and 4 are on page T–627.)

Name _____

Worksheet 42
Recognizing Adverbs

A. Underline each single-word adverb, and draw an arrow from it to the word or words it modifies. Above the modified word or phrase, write whether it is a verb (*v.*), an adjective (*adj.*), an adverb (*adv.*), or a verbal (*vbl.*).

1. Joseph <u>never</u> became bitter in the <u>extremely</u> difficult trials of life.

2. <u>How</u> was he able to live <u>faithfully</u>?

3. <u>Solidly</u> anchored in the Lord, his faith <u>always</u> kept him strong.

4. <u>Slowly</u> and <u>laboriously</u>, the <u>badly</u> crippled boy inched his way <u>along</u>.

5. <u>Finally</u>, the last field was plowed <u>today</u>.

6. The frightened birds flew <u>away</u> <u>fast</u>.

7. <u>Where</u> was this picture taken, and <u>why</u> are these people smiling <u>so</u> <u>happily</u>?

8. The children worked <u>unusually</u> <u>well</u> <u>yesterday</u>.

B. Underline each single-word adverb. Above each, write what question it answers.

1. The whole world was <u>totally</u> covered with water during the Flood.
   (how)

2. <u>Later</u>, God placed a <u>beautifully</u> colored rainbow in the sky.
   (when — how or to what degree)

3. Noah <u>immediately</u> built an altar, and the family <u>reverently</u> worshiped the Lord God.
   (when — how)

4. <u>Today</u> astronomers can <u>accurately</u> chart the orbits of the planets.
   (when — how)

5. Our <u>almost</u> new car was <u>badly</u> wrecked in the accident.
   (to what degree — how)

6. After driving <u>slowly</u> through the storm, we <u>finally</u> arrived <u>home</u> <u>safely</u>.
   (how — when — where how)

C. Diagram these sentences.
   1. Two amazingly swift airplanes screamed overhead.
   2. Quite often, those squirrels noisily scold the dog.
   3. We had not planned the trip sufficiently.
   4. The refugees are still extremely destitute.

1.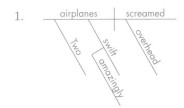

2.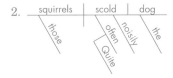

3.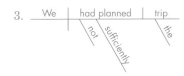

4.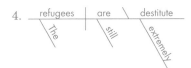

Worksheet 43
Adverb Phrases

A. Underline each adverb phrase, and draw an arrow from it to the word or phrase it modifies. If an adverb phrase includes one or more adjective phrases, underline the entire phrase.

1. We must purpose in our hearts to serve the Lord until the end of our days.

2. The world lay in great darkness, but Jesus brought light into the world.

3. After the death of Jesus, many priests were obedient to the faith.

4. We walked past the old barn and peered through the broken windows.

5. Underneath the large rock, several sow bugs lay in the cool, damp earth.

6. A deer and a wolf raced across the meadow, and the deer remained ahead by only a few yards.

7. We hiked over the little bridge, across the meadow, and into the woods.

8. Along the narrow trail, we identified several plants that we had studied in school.

B. Draw proofreading marks to show where the misplaced adverb phrases should be.

1. Father keeps plenty of tracts for people he meets in the glove compartment of his car.   *or* Father keeps plenty of tracts for people he meets in the glove compartment of his car.

2. There are several sacks of oats for the horses in the feed room.

3. Robert killed the snake with a shovel.

4. The foolish man built his house on the earth without a foundation.

C. Diagram these sentences.
1. The Spirit descended like a dove upon Jesus after His baptism.
2. After a week of absence, I had fallen behind in my work.
3. We should always be kind toward other people.
4. The dog jumped to its feet with a volley of loud barks.

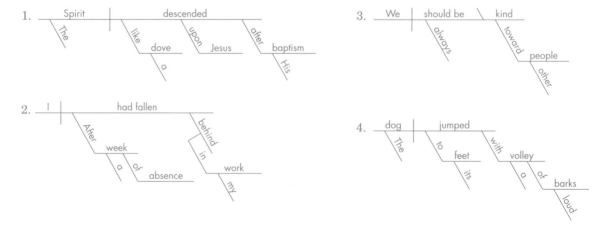

Name _____   *(Lesson 84)*

Worksheet 44
Adverb Clauses

A. Underline each adverb clause, and draw an arrow from it to the word or phrase it modifies. Above the modified word or phrase, write what part of speech it is.

1. <u>When Jesus was born</u>, the heavenly hosts praised the Lord.   *v.*

2. <u>Unless a proud person humbles himself</u>, he can never have God's blessing.   *v.*

3. God hates pride <u>because it places people at enmity against Him</u>.   *v.*

4. God's grace is richer <u>than man can measure</u>.   *adj.*

5. He has dealt with us more kindly <u>than we deserve</u>.   *adv.*

6. These defective books are cheaper <u>than the perfect ones</u>.   *adj.*

7. <u>While the rain soaked into the thirsty ground</u>, we gave thanks to God.   *v.*

8. We needed the rain <u>so that the crops could grow</u>.   *v.*

9. The task was harder <u>than William had expected</u>.   *adj.*

10. Darla had done her work more carelessly <u>than she wanted to admit</u>.   *adv.*

B. Add the missing commas. One sentence is correct as written.

1. Although Caleb was an old man, he was still ready to fight.

2. Moses also retained his physical strength until he was a very old man. (no commas needed)

3. When Paul prayed for the removal of his thorn in the flesh, God assured Paul that His grace was sufficient.

4. The Gospel, wherever it is preached, brings God's power to men.

C. Diagram the following sentences.
1. We finished the chores as the sun slipped below the horizon.
2. We put plastic on the windows so that the cold wind would not blow into the chicken house.
3. Before we eat breakfast, we do the outside chores.
4. Although the days grew quite warm, the nights were very cold.
5. We worked in the garden until the mosquitoes chased us inside.

1.

2.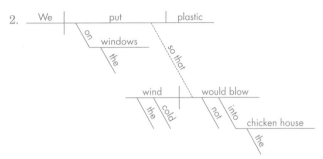

(Numbers 3–5 are on page T–647.)

Name _____   *(Lesson 86)*

Worksheet 45
Distinguishing Between Adjectives and Adverbs

A. Draw an arrow from each underlined word to the word or phrase it modifies. Above the underlined word, write *adj.* or *adv.* to tell what part of speech it is.

1. John 17 records Christ's <u>high-priestly</u> intercession for His disciples.

2. With <u>deep</u> concern, Christ <u>earnestly</u> prayed for their spiritual safety.

3. We can draw <u>near</u> to the <u>holy</u> God only through Jesus.

4. <u>Suddenly</u>, Lee's <u>carefully</u> crafted model boat fell <u>down</u>.

5. We dug <u>deep</u> into the earth, and finally some water sprang <u>up</u>.

6. Mark brought <u>in</u> the heifers from the <u>far</u> corner of the <u>back</u> field.

B. Draw an arrow from each underlined phrase to the word or phrase it modifies. Above the underlined phrase, write *adj.* or *adv.* to tell what part of speech it is.

1. "The wise <u>in heart</u> shall be called prudent."

2. "A friend loveth <u>at all times</u>."

3. The bicycle <u>in the driveway</u> should be kept <u>in the barn</u>.

4. The baby rabbits stayed <u>in their nest</u> while a fox chased the mother <u>through the brush</u>.

5. <u>In the bitter cold</u>, the refugees drew closer <u>to the warm fire</u>.

6. Help <u>for these poor sufferers</u> must come <u>from the Lord Himself</u>.

C. Draw an arrow from each underlined clause to the word or phrase it modifies. Above the underlined clause, write *adj.* or *adv.* to tell what part of speech it is.

1. Jesus was crucified at a place <u>that lay outside Jerusalem</u>.

2. Pilate declared Jesus' innocence <u>after he had examined Him</u>.

3. <u>After he had looked at the book</u>, Father stated several reasons <u>that we should not read it</u>.

4. Mark may take this load in to the barn <u>when the wagon is full</u>.

5. <u>Because so many unusual things happened</u>, I shall always remember the day <u>that followed my birthday last year</u>.

6. We should go <u>where the trail markers direct</u> <u>so that we do not get lost</u>.

Name _____

Worksheet 46
Using Adverbs Correctly

A. In the blank, write an expressive verb or a descriptive adjective to replace the underlined expression.
(Sample answers.)

plunged, dived   1. The hawk <u>went down rapidly</u> toward the earth.

___scribbled___   3. The boy <u>carelessly wrote</u>
scrawled   his name on the paper.

serious, severe   2. Aunt Mildred's injuries in the accident were <u>very bad</u>.

___beautiful___   4. Joan's picture is <u>really nice</u>.
lovely

B. Underline the correct words in parentheses.

1. Jesus illustrated quite (good, <u>well</u>) the way of true service.

2. He (sure, <u>surely</u>) is the highest example of serving others.

3. The Jewish rulers wanted very (bad, <u>badly</u>) to kill Paul.

4. Their vow to eat or drink nothing until they had killed him was (real, <u>really</u>) foolish.

5. This sick goat won't eat (no, <u>any</u>) feed.

6. It has not been feeling (good, <u>well</u>) for several days.

7. Neither of the teachers had (no, <u>any</u>) watch.

8. We were (kind of, <u>rather</u>) surprised when a cat walked into the room.

9. On the windowsill, the cat found a (<u>good</u>, well) place to sun itself.

10. Father was (sort of, <u>somewhat</u>) worried about the icy roads.

11. We couldn't get (none, <u>any</u>) of our neighbors to come to church.

12. The tractor ran so (bad, <u>badly</u>) that Father took it to the shop.

13. The baby has been (kind of, <u>somewhat</u>) fussy all day.

14. Mother (sure, <u>surely</u>) was not able to get much work done today.

15. She (<u>could</u>, couldn't) hardly get supper ready.

16. We can't (never, <u>ever</u>) finish all this work today.

17. The children were (sort of, <u>rather</u>) pleased with how much they had gotten done.

18. Brent couldn't go (nowhere, <u>anywhere</u>) because of his broken leg.

C. Cross out each incorrect word. If it should be replaced, write the correct word above it.

1. Grandfather often refers ~~back~~ to his childhood days.

2. How ~~easy~~ easily we can do our farm work today!

3. Will we leave ~~from~~ Crockett early in the morning?

4. Don't forget to connect ~~up~~ the wires for the trailer.

5. We don't have ~~no~~ any spare tire for this trailer.   *or* We ~~don't~~ have no spare tire for this trailer.

6. The work progressed surprisingly ~~good~~ well this afternoon.

Name _____   *(Lesson 89)*

Worksheet 47
Prepositions

A. Underline each prepositional phrase, and above it write *adj.* for adjective phrase or *adv.* for adverb phrase.
   If one phrase is part of a longer one, underline it twice, and label both clearly.

      adv.   adv.
1. In a worthwhile book, the main character sets a noble example for us.

                                  adv.   adj.
2. We should not judge a book merely by its level of excitement.

                          adv.
3. The influence that it leaves upon us is more important to consider.

    adv.   adj.
4. According to Janet, the bird feeder behind the house has been broken.

                             adv.   adv.
5. Bring it in, and Father will look at it after breakfast.

                  adv.
6. Go out to Father and the boys, and see if they are coming in soon.

B. Underline the correct words in parentheses.

1. You are on this team with Thelma and (she, **her**).

2. You will sit between Homer and (I, **me**).

3. Brian came before either Daniel or (they, **them**).

C. Above each underlined word, write *adv.* if it is an adverb or *prep.* if it is a preposition.

                               adv.   prep.
1. Filled with wonder, we walked around among the huge redwood trees.

         adv.   adv.
2. I glanced out just as Uncle Leon's drove in with their new car.

         prep.   prep.
3. A bear lumbered around the corner and stopped in surprise.

                      adv.   prep.
4. Mother saw the ladder fall down and ran to see if Father had fallen off the roof.

D. Above each underlined *to,* write *prep.* if it is a preposition or *inf.* if it is part of an infinitive. Remember:
   To + noun = prepositional phrase; to + verb = infinitive.

        inf.
1. We plan to visit Grandfather this evening.

       inf.   prep.
2. He likes to tell stories of his family's move to Alberta.

                     prep.   prep.
3. This land was wilderness when they came to it, and they rarely went to the city.

E. Diagram these sentences.
   1. We ate a light lunch in the car.
   2. What are the men talking about?
   3. Electricity flows well through copper or aluminum.
   4. Because of the influence of godly homes, we are spared
      from many evils.
   5. The blessing of God should be the desire of our hearts.

1.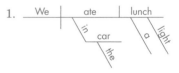

2.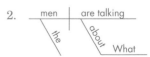

(Numbers 3–5 are on page T–651.)

Name _____

Worksheet 48
Using Prepositions Correctly

Correct each error in one of the ways described below. If a sentence is correct, leave it as it is.

(1) by crossing out an unnecessary word
(2) by adding a missing preposition, using a caret (∧)
(3) by crossing out a wrong expression and writing the correction above it

1. Where was Elijah going ~~to~~ in such a hurry?

2. His terror now surely seems different ~~than~~ ^{from} his boldness on Mount Carmel.

3. When he reached Mount Horeb, he went ~~in~~ ^{into} a cave and lodged there.

4. When Sarah sits ~~besides~~ ^{beside} me, I can sing alto better.

5. Soon recess was over ~~with~~, and we went back to our studies.

6. Sister Anita came ~~by~~ ^{to} our room to get an encyclopedia.

7. The money from the pumpkins was divided equally ~~between~~ ^{among} the four boys.

8. Little Henry looked almost squashed ~~among~~ ^{between} his two big brothers.

9. Does their house look much different than it did before? ^(correct)

10. No one was cleaning the kitchen ~~accept~~ ^{except} Kathleen.

11. With the sun behind the clouds, the breeze is quite chilly. ^(correct)

12. We were excited ∧ and anxious for the surprise that Father was planning. ^{about}

13. Several of the sheep are outside ~~of~~ the fence.

14. The way of God's people is very different from that of the world. ^(correct)

15. Besides a love of the truth, we need a hatred of the evil. ^(correct)

16. We must look ∧ and walk in the way of wisdom. ^{for}

17. Let us watch and pray so that we do not fall ~~in~~ ^{into} temptation.

18. Between you and me, we should be able to have breakfast ready on time. ^(correct)

19. Aunt Ada is in the living room, reading to the little children. ^(correct)

20. Since we were in the area, we drove by our old farm again. ^(correct)

21. The new owners have built a two-car garage ~~in back of~~ ^{behind} the house.

22. Everything seemed much the same ~~accept~~ ^{except} for that new garage.

23. Father almost ran off ~~of~~ the road because he was looking around so much.

Name _____   *(Lesson 92)*

Worksheet 49
Coordinating Conjunctions

A. Write the conjunction in the blank. Underline the words, phrases, or clauses that the conjunction joins.

___Whether—or___ 1. Whether <u>in life</u> or <u>in death</u>, Paul wanted the Lord to be glorified.

___but___ 2. <u>Paul prayed for the removal of his affliction</u>, but <u>God declared the sufficiency of His grace</u>.

___and___ 3. The <u>faith</u> and <u>courage</u> of this man are an inspiration.

___for___ 4. <u>He still influences our lives today</u>, for <u>he wrote many of the New Testament epistles</u>.

___Not only—but also___ 5. Not only <u>the believers</u> but also <u>his enemies</u> recognized the importance of his leadership.

B. Rewrite each sentence correctly.

1. We not only sanded our pieces of wood but stained them today. _____

   We not only sanded our pieces of wood but also stained them today. _____

2. Steven either opened the wrong box, or Father bought the wrong nails. _____

   Either Steven opened the wrong box, or Father bought the wrong nails. _____

3. We knocked on the door but no one answered. ___We knocked on the door, but no one answered.___

4. Clair can neither find his book nor his papers. ___Clair can find neither his book nor his papers.___

5. Clara has not only done the regular assignment but also the extra work. _____

   Clara has done not only the regular assignment but also the extra work. _____

6. Quietly and with patience the panther stalked the big buck. _____

   Quietly and patiently, the panther stalked the big buck. _____

7. I either did not make the directions clear or Paula was not paying attention. _____

   Either I did not make the directions clear, or Paula was not paying attention. _____

C. Underline the correct verbs in parentheses.

1. Not only my fingers but also my hand (<u>was</u>, were) crushed by the block.

2. Both the goat and her kid (<u>enjoy</u>, enjoys) romping in the meadow.

3. Neither the teacher nor the students (<u>remember</u>, remembers) which story that illustration was in.

4. Neither the students nor the teacher (have, <u>has</u>) solved the problem.

5. Either the boys or Father (mow, <u>mows</u>) the grass.

Name _____

Worksheet 50
Rhythm in Poetry

A. Mark the rhythm pattern of the first two lines of each stanza. In the blank to the right of each stanza, write which kind of pattern it is.

  1. Háil the blést mórn when the gréat Mediátor   _____dactylic_____
      Dówn from the régions of glóry descénds;
    Shepherds, go worship the Babe in the manger;
      Lo, for His guard the bright angels attend.

  2. How sháll the yóung secúre their héarts   _____iambic_____
      And guárd their líves from sín?
    Thy Word the choicest rules imparts
      To keep the conscience clean.

  3. Chíldren óf the héavenly Kíng,   _____trochaic_____
    Ás you jóurney, swéetly síng;
      Sing your Saviour's worthy praise,
      Glorious in His works and ways.

  4. Háil, my éver bléssed Jésus,   _____trochaic_____
      Ónly Thée I wísh to síng;
    To my soul Thy Name is precious,
      Thou my Prophet, Priest, and King.

  5. Do you séek for a fríend who is álways the sáme,   _____anapestic_____
      Who will ánswer your sígh and your cáll?
    There is just such a Friend, I will tell you His name—
      It is Jesus, the best Friend of all.

B. Write a line of poetry to match the thought and rhythm of each line.   (Sample answers.)

  1. Splashing and gurgling, the stream rushes down (dactylic)

      Dashing and leaping with boundless delight _____

  2. Tender buds and leaves appear (trochaic)

      Robins call, and bluebirds sing _____

  3. We know our heavenly Father reigns (iambic)

      And sees us from His throne above _____

  4. We rejoice in the care that our God daily shows (anapestic)

      He endows us with blessings abundant and free _____

Name _____   *(Lesson 95)*

Worksheet 51
Subordinating Conjunctions

A. Underline the subordinate clauses, and put parentheses around the subordinating conjunctions.

1. (Because) the Bible is God's Word, we handle it reverently.

2. We obey the Bible (even though) many ignore its teachings.

3. We hide God's Word in our hearts (so that) it may guide our lives.

4. It is much colder now (than) it had been this morning.

5. (When) these jobs are finished, we may have some free time.

6. That horse limps (as if) he has a thorn in his hoof.

B. Underline the correct words in parentheses.

1. Since I am an older student, the teacher helps the other children more than (I, me).

2. Sometimes I feel (as if, like) I need as much help as (they, them).

3. Darlene can surely play checkers better than (I, me).

4. The heifers outside the barn act (as if, like) they have not been fed today.

5. We usually feed the calves inside the barn earlier than (they, them).

C. Diagram these sentences.
1. After the shower passed by, we saw a beautiful rainbow.
2. This tree is more rotten than we had expected.
3. We opened the windows so that the fresh spring breeze could blow into the room.
4. The mottoes were painted as carefully as we could do them.

1.

3.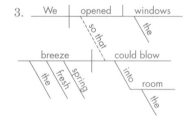

2.

4.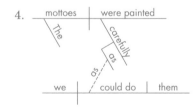

Name _____ *(Lesson 98)*

Worksheet 52
Rhyme and Repetition in Poetry

A. On the lines to the right, show the rhyming pattern of each stanza.

1. Hark! The herald angels sing,   a
   "Glory to the newborn King;   a
   Peace on earth, and mercy mild;   b
   God and sinners reconciled";   b
   Joyful, all ye nations, rise,   c
   Join the triumph of the skies;   c
   With angelic hosts proclaim,   d
   "Christ is born in Bethlehem."   d *or* e

2. With humble heart and tongue,   a
   My God, to Thee I pray;   b
   O make me learn, while I am young, a
   How I may cleanse my way.   b

3. Yes, the Redeemer rose,   a
   The Saviour left the dead;   b
   And o'er our hellish foes   a
   High raised His conquering head.   b
   In wild dismay,   c
   The guards around   d
   Fall to the ground   d
   And sink away.   c

B. Underline examples of alliteration in numbers 1 and 3 above.   (Any one example for each.)

C. Underline one example of assonance in number 2 above.

D. In each blank, write *P* if the words are a perfect rhyme. If they are not, write the number of the rule that is broken.

   __1__ 1. love, move   __3__ 3. fain, feign   __2__ 5. begin, hymn
   __4__ 2. azure, bestir   __P__ 4. view, few   __P__ 6. complaints, restraints

E. Write whether the parallelism in each verse is similar (*S*) or opposite (*O*).

   __S__ 1. Deuteronomy 32:16   __O__ 3. Proverbs 29:11
   __O__ 2. Proverbs 28:1   __S__ 4. Exodus 15:4

Worksheet 44, Part C *(Continued)*

Name _____   *(Lesson 101)*

Worksheet 53
Practice With Capitalization

Cross out each capitalization error, and write the correct letter above it.

1. God tells us in ^H his ^W word that ^H he hates pride.

2. When ^H haman's pride prompted him to seek the ^J jews' destruction, ^G god brought him low.

3. Ben-hadad was the ^k King of ^S syria who fought against ^K king ^A ahab.

4. We sang the little song "Be ^Y ye ^K kind ^O one to Another."

5. My ^f Father is teaching a series of ^l Lessons from ^E ephesians during ^p Prayer ^m Meetings at the Maple View ^M mennonite ^C church.

6. More words are capitalized in the ^G german language than in the English ^l Language.

7. George ^W washington was the first president of the ^U united ^S states.

8. Uncle Donald and ^A aunt Irene visited us on ^T thanksgiving ^D day.

9. Our ^r Reading book states that ^D david ^L livingstone discovered ^V victoria ^F falls along the ^Z zambezi ^R river.

10. Because it does not have an automatic transmission, ^M mother does not like to drive our Dodge ^p Pickup.

11. We bought some supplies at Stickle's ^G general ^S store in ^M mount ^V vernon.

12. The sign above the door said, Martin Heller, ^M.D. m.d.

13. We left for ^h Home at 9:30 ^P.M. p.m.

14. Donald ^K kaisar, the ^p President of Altenwald Industries, lives at 559 ^W west ^M main ^S street, ^C central ^F falls, ^R rhode ^I island.

15. California is a western state, but New Jersey is in the ^E east.

16. Many of the ^p Prophets of the ^O old Testament had spoken of a day when ^G god would visit ^H his people.

17. Although the ^M messiah had come, many of the ^J jewish people rejected ^H him.

18. Jesus of ^N nazareth came as a humble servant, not the mighty king they were looking for.

19. When ^I i face any distress, ^O ^L o lord, help me to trust in ^T thee.

20. Help me not to let the ^g Gods of this world tempt my ^s Soul away from ^T thee.

Name _____

Worksheet 54
Practice With Commas

Add the missing commas. If any unnecessary comma is used, cross it out.

1. Route 1, Box 1689

   Jonestown, PA 17038

   March 18, 20—

2. Yes, Carl, that is the correct heading.

3. This house, as you can see, is an old farmhouse.

4. Surrounding the house, are a wide front lawn, the driveway, a small back yard, and a small orchard.

5. After my grandfather bought this house, he built an addition to it.

6. Dark, rolling, clouds billowed in from the west soon after breakfast.

7. The temperature dropped quickly, and soon it was snowing in earnest.

8. By the middle of the afternoon, the roads were almost impassable.

9. Oh, I forgot to bring my books along, Brother Daniel.

10. The pencils, rulers, and erasers are in the supply closet.

11. While one grade is having a class, the rest of us have study time.

12. Nevada, which has an area of 110,561 square miles, is the seventh largest state.

13. Bordering Nevada are California, Oregon, Idaho, Utah, and Arizona.

14. Mount Whitney, which is the highest peak in the continental United States, is less than one hundred miles from Death Valley, which is the lowest spot.

15. The Mississippi River, which drains a vast area of the Midwest, is the largest river system in the United States.

16. "We finished cleaning out the garage," announced Lester.

17. "I'll be right out," replied Father, "to check your work."

18. Those heifers, in spite of all our efforts, have broken out again!

19. When we go to town tomorrow, we'll have to buy some more flour, sugar, and eggs for baking.

20. Are you sure, Mother, that we have enough baking powder?

21. The rising bread dough spilled out of the pans, over the counter top, and down on the floor.

22. Judith cleared the table, Duane washed the dishes, and Kathryn dried them.

23. Well, they worked efficiently, and soon they had finished their jobs.

24. Soon Jonathan, the baby of the family, was playing with several, dirty spoons.

Name _____   *(Lesson 108)*

Worksheet 55
Quotation Marks

Add single and double quotation marks and related punctuation. Change small letters to capital letters where needed. Use quotation marks to indicate direct quotations only if there are explanatory words.

1. Ahab asked, "Will you help me conquer Ramoth-gilead?"

2. "I am as thou art," replied Jehoshaphat.

3. What a disgrace that godly Jehoshaphat said to wicked Ahab, "We are the same, and our people are the same"!

4. "I heard Myron say, 'The popcorn is ready,'" announced Verna.

5. Chapter 4 of this book is entitled "On the Move Again."

6. "Look at that huge airplane!" shouted Twila excitedly.

7. "Let's sing 'A Morning Prayer,'" requested Annie.

8. "After the dishes are done," announced Father, "we have some special plans."

9. "We'll finish in record time!" exclaimed Donna and Diane.

10. Have you read the story "In the Middle"?

11. "I enjoyed reading the story 'In the Middle,'" said Nelson.

12. "I heard Shirley say, 'This floor is clean enough for me,'" insisted Ada.

13. "For next Friday's class," announced Brother Alvin, "you are to memorize the poem 'Tell Him So.'"

14. Does everyone have a copy of the poem "Tell Him So"?

15. "If you expect to be a decent, dependable adult," Brother Richard commented, "you had better start now."

16. "Young people often fail to realize," he continued, "how much their present habits will influence their later lives."

17. How foolish to say, "I'll wait until I'm older to learn to work carefully and diligently"!

18. "Procrastination," Brother Richard pointed out, "is one of Satan's favorite tricks."

19. "Can someone explain why life is so serious?" asked Brother Richard.

20. Clayton replied, "Because life prepares us for eternity."

21. "We visited Sister Martha last night," said Nevin. "It's hard to complain after seeing her cheerfulness."

22. "Even though she stays in bed all the time," Brian added, "she never complains."

Name _____

Worksheet 56
Colons and Semicolons

A. Write these Bible references, using numerals.

_____John 3:16_____ 1. the sixteenth verse of John 3

_____Genesis 1:1_____ 2. the first verse of Genesis 1

_____2 Kings 19:7_____ 3. the seventh verse of 2 Kings 19

_____Mark 12:17_____ 4. the seventeenth verse of Mark 12

B. Write these expressions of time, using numerals.

___7:22___ 1. twenty-two minutes after seven   ___9:18___ 3. eighteen minutes after nine

___10:57___ 2. three minutes before eleven   ___3:50___ 4. fifty minutes after three

C. Cross out any incorrect punctuation, and add the missing commas, colons, and semicolons.

1. Moses led Israel out of Egypt/; however, he could not lead them into Canaan.

2. God told Moses to speak to the rock/; he struck it instead.

3. The following kings ruled in Israel before the kingdom was divided/: Saul, David, Solomon, and Rehoboam.

4. A Canada goose usually flies about forty miles per hour/; it can fly up to sixty miles per hour when it is being chased.

5. When a goose is on land, it eats grass, grains, berries, and insects/; and when it is in water, it eats underwater plants.

6. We read stories about/ geese, ducks, pelicans, and flamingos.

7. The following girls are assigned to work on the bulletin board/: Arlene, Wilma, Carla, and Rosemary.

8. Samuel Johnson made this noteworthy statement/: "The chains of habit are too weak to be felt until they are too strong to be broken."

9. A person's words reveal the quality of his heart/; furthermore, the tone in which they are said reveals much about his attitude.

10. We must learn what the Bible teaches, and we should pattern our lives after noble examples around us.

Worksheet 47, Part E (Continued)

Name _____   *(Lesson 113)*

Worksheet 57
Italics, Apostrophes, and Hyphens

A. Add underlining or quotation marks where they are needed.

1. We are memorizing the song "Jesus the Teacher" in devotions this week.

2. I am reading sections of <u>Martyrs Mirror</u> for a book report.

3. Is the song "Christ the Lord Cometh?" in the <u>Christian Hymnal</u>?

4. Mr. Bentley talked about a story he had read in the <u>Daily News</u>.

5. Darlene is reading the story "Just an Apple" in the <u>Christian Pathway</u>, which came in today's mail.

B. Draw vertical lines to show where these words may be divided at the end of a line.

1. e v a l|u|a|t i o n   3. o c e a n|o g|r a|p h y

2. s i m|p l i c|i|t y   4. a d o r n|m e n t

C. Add apostrophes, hyphens, and underlining to these sentences. Cross out any incorrect letter or punctuation.

1. God's people have always been in conflict with this world's system.

2. Their's is often a life of suffering at the hand's of the ungodly.

3. The saints' lives have often testified to the world of Jesus's teaching.

4. How often is the word <u>praise</u> used in the New Testament?

5. <u>Strong's Exhaustive Concordance</u> shows twenty-five occurrences.

6. <u>Bookkeeper</u> has three sets of double letters: double <u>o</u>'s, double <u>k</u>'s, and double <u>e</u>'s.

7. George didn't put $'s with his answers.

8. Since these tapered roller bearings are self-lubricating, we shouldn't need to grease them.

9. Great-uncle Eli is ninety-six years old, and Great-aunt Hettie is almost ninety-four years old.

10. Life was surely different years ago when they started housekeeping.

11. My brother-in-law lives on their old farm.

12. This self-supporting bookshelf could be used to divide the room; the others must be placed against a wall.

13. Ellen Zimmerman's good-natured smile helped to quiet the ladies' complaints about the produce prices.

14. The *'s on your paper mark places where you carelessly omitted punctuation marks; you must practice greater self-discipline in your work.

Name _____

Worksheet 58
Using a Dictionary

A. In each blank, write an alternate spelling of the word.

___neighbour___ 1. neighbor   ___check___ 3. cheque

___ouzel___ 2. ousel   ___sulphur___ 4. sulfur

B. Underline each phonetic spelling that is correct, with no usage label.

1. rinse: (rinz) (rins) (rench)   3. grievous: (grē′·vəs) (grē′·vē·əs)

2. deluge: (dē′·lüj) (dē·lüj′) (del′·yüj) (del·yüj′)   4. apostolic: (ap′·ə·stol′·ik) (ə·pos′·tol′·ik)

C. Copy a definition for the underlined word in each sentence.   (Sample answers.)

1. Myra was filled with <u>ruth</u> when she learned how she had hurt my feelings. _____

    ___sorrow, regret___

2. The boys will <u>pick</u> the ice while Mother stirs the ice cream mixture. _____

    ___break with a pointed instrument___

3. Mother <u>bolts</u> the flour from the fifty-pound bag into the large canister. _____

    ___sifts___

4. The <u>mean</u> noon temperature for the month of March was 55°. _____

    ___average___

D. Copy the inflections your dictionary gives for these words.

1. mealy   ___mealier, mealiest___

2. trifle   ___trifled, trifling___

3. index   ___indexes, indices___

4. shelf   ___shelves___

E. Copy any usage labels your dictionary gives for these words.   (Answers may vary.)

1. let   ___archaic; chiefly British___

2. aeroplane ___chiefly British___

3. nowheres ___chiefly dialectal, nonstandard___

4. chapman   ___chiefly British, archaic___

F. Underline the one word in each list that does not have the same root as the others. Read the etymologies for the words.

1. advise, <u>devious</u>, revise, vision, evidence

2. factory, manufacture, <u>facet</u>, fashion, benefactor

3. encourage, discord, <u>cordon</u>, cordial

4. maintenance, obtain, <u>tendon</u>, continuous, content

Worksheet 59
Writing Effective Sentences

Rewrite these sentences more effectively.   (Sample sentences. Accept reasonable variation.)

1. Ten of the spies returned with an evil report. Joshua and Caleb gave a faithful report.

   Ten of the spies returned with an evil report, but Joshua and Caleb gave a faithful report.

2. Faithfully and with boldness, they encouraged Israel to trust the Lord. _____

   Faithfully and boldly, they encouraged Israel to trust the Lord.

3. Their encouragement would not be received by the people. _____

   The people would not receive their encouragement.

4. Israel was ready to almost stone Joshua and Caleb. _____

   Israel was almost ready to stone Joshua and Caleb.

5. A cold, icy wind roared noisily through the trees.   An icy wind roared through the trees.

6. The new books were, as I have been told, shipped last week. _____

   The new books, as I have been told, were shipped last week.

7. In the Bahamas they do not expect freezing temperatures. _____

   People in the Bahamas do not expect freezing temperatures.

8. When I awoke this morning, rain is pounding on the roof. _____

   When I awoke this morning, rain was pounding on the roof.

9. If a student does not work diligently, they can expect poor grades. _____

   If a student does not work diligently, he can expect poor grades.

10. Mrs. White said that she appreciated our help.   Mrs. White said, "I appreciate your help."

11. Yesterday we planted three pounds of peas, and Uncle Nelson called from Guatemala.

    Yesterday we planted three pounds of peas after Uncle Nelson called from Guatemala.

12. An orifice is where a hole allows something to pass through. _____

    An orifice is a hole that allows something to pass through.

13. The heifers have been bedded by Nevin and Brian.   Nevin and Brian have bedded the heifers.

14. After one has worked that hard, you are ready for a break. _____

    After one has worked that hard, he is ready for a break.

15. Soaring high above the house, we saw two bald eagles. _____

    We saw two bald eagles soaring high above the house.

16. To nock is when a notch is made in a bow or an arrow. _____

    To nock is to make a notch in a bow or an arrow.

Name _____   *(Lesson 119)*

Worksheet 60
Word Families

(Use a dictionary if you need help with any of the exercises below.)

A. All the words in this list have the root *litera,* which means "letter." In the blanks below, write the words that match the definitions.

literacy	literalize	literature
literal	literary	subliterature
literalism	literation	transliterate

_____literal_____ 1. Relating to the letter; not figurative, but actual; word for word.

_____literation_____ 2. The action of representing sounds by letters.

____transliterate____ 3. To change over to letters of another alphabet.

____subliterature____ 4. Literature of a lower class or quality.

_____literalism_____ 5. Adherence to the exact meaning of a written record.

_____literacy_____ 6. The ability to read and write.

B. All the words in this list have the root *dict,* which means "say; speak." In the blanks below, write the words that match the definitions.

dictate	contradict	predict
diction	edict	predictable
dictionary	interdictor	verdict

_____diction_____ 1. The action or manner of saying.

_____edict_____ 2. An official command spoken by a ruler.

_____verdict_____ 3. A judgment spoken by a jury.

_____interdictor_____ 4. One who speaks between in order to prohibit.

_____contradict_____ 5. To speak against.

____predictable____ 6. Able to be told beforehand.

C. Change each word to the part of speech given in parentheses by adding or changing a suffix.

1. magnet (v.)	magnetize		7. diction (v.)	dictate	
2. cavern (adj.)	cavernous		8. anticipate (n.)	anticipation	
3. class (v.)	classify		9. mass (adj.)	massive	
4. class (adj.)	classic		10. tender (v.)	tenderize	
5. mystery (v.)	mystify		11. tender (n.)	tenderness	
6. mystery (adj.)	mysterious		12. tender (adv.)	tenderly	

Building Securely

Chapter 1 Test   **Score** _____

Name _____ **Date** _____

A. Circle *T* if the statement is true or *F* if it is false.

(T) F   1. Every sentence must have a subject and a predicate.

(T) F   2. A fragment may contain a skeleton.

T (F)   3. An object complement may follow a linking verb.

T (F)   4. An indirect object is found right after a direct object.

T (F)   5. In a sentence containing a predicate adjective, the verb is much like an equal sign.

(T) F   6. Subjective complements include predicate nominatives and predicate adjectives.

T (F)   7. A good character sketch describes several outstanding characteristics of a person.

T (F)   8. It is usually best to proofread your story as soon as you have finished writing it.

(8 points)

B. Match the terms to the descriptions by writing the letter of the correct choice in the blank. Each set has one choice that you will not use.

___b___ 9. Word group without a complete thought.

___f___ 10. Tells *who* or *what* a sentence is about.

___d___ 11. Two or more sentences joined incorrectly.

___c___ 12. Tells what the subject *does* or *is*.

___a___ 13. Completes the sentence skeleton.

a. complement
b. fragment
c. predicate
d. run-on error
e. skeleton
f. subject

___h___ 14. Receives the action of a verb.

___k___ 15. Modifies the subject.

___m___ 16. Names the person to whom one is speaking.

___i___ 17. Tells *to whom or what* or *for whom or what* an action is performed.

___l___ 18. Renames the subject.

___g___ 19. Immediately follows a noun or pronoun to identify or explain it.

g. appositive
h. direct object
i. indirect object
j. simple predicate
k. predicate adjective
l. predicate nominative
m. noun of direct address

(11 points)

C. Label each item *S* for sentence, *F* for fragment, or *R* for run-on error.

   __F__ 20. Because the weather was beautiful.

   __S__ 21. We took a walk through the woods.

   __F__ 22. Which cover about twenty acres.

   __R__ 23. A rabbit darted across the trail Spotty almost caught it.

(4 points)

D. Draw a vertical line to show the division between the complete subject and the complete predicate. Underline each simple subject once and each simple predicate twice.

24. Man's early <u>home</u> | <u>was</u> the Garden of Eden.

25. <u>God</u> | <u>talked</u> to Adam and Eve in the cool of the evening.

26. The <u>enemy</u> of God | <u>came</u> and <u>tempted</u> them.

27. Their <u>sin</u> against God | <u>brought</u> fear into their hearts.

(12 points)

E. Underline the five direct objects and the four indirect objects. Identify each one by writing *DO* or *IO* above it.

28. Feed the <u>chickens</u>^{DO} and gather the <u>eggs</u>^{DO}.

    IO   DO
29. Tell <u>Gary</u> the good <u>news</u>.

          IO   DO
30. The Lord gives His <u>people</u> <u>grace</u> for each test.

       IO   IO   DO
31. Grandmother sent <u>Linda</u> and <u>Lynette</u> a <u>post card</u>.

(9 points)

F. Underline the two predicate nominatives and the three predicate adjectives. Identify each one by writing *PN* or *PA* above it.

          PN (*Of Glory* may be omitted.)
32. Jesus is the <u>King of Glory</u>.

          PA   PA
33. In His earthly ministry, He was <u>meek</u> and <u>lowly</u>.

         PN
34. In His death, He became the <u>Lamb</u> of sacrifice.

          PA
35. Now in heaven, He will remain highly <u>exalted</u> forever.

(5 points)

G. Underline the three nouns of direct address and the two appositives. Identify each one by writing *D* or *A* above it. Also add the missing commas.

    D
36. "<u>Lord</u>, thou hast been our dwelling place in all generations."

         A
37. The Bible, <u>God's holy Word</u>, reveals to us the way of truth.

38.   D
    Stanley, please read to us from 1 Corinthians 13, the Love Chapter.
                                  A

39. Can you quote the Golden Rule, Rosalie?
                       D

(5 points)

H. Diagram the skeletons and complements, and any appositive or noun of direct address.

40. James, please give your father this book.

41. This volume, a book about Bible customs, is a valuable reference tool.

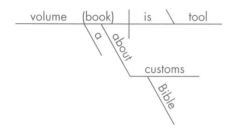

42. The explanations are simple but thorough.

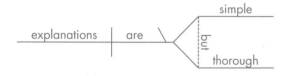

(13 points)

I. Find eight mistakes in these paragraphs. Show the necessary corrections by using the proper proofreading marks.   (Corrections are marked. Check for the correct use of proofreading marks.)

                                           h

While Gideon was threshing weat by the winepress, God called him to deliver

                                               ¶

Israel. The angel said, "The Lord is with you." Gideon, distressed at Israel's

                           is (or be)

bondage ~~and slavery~~, replied, "If God with us, why are we so trubbled by the

Midianites?"

                                                    sign

To assure Gideon that the Lord |with\was| him, the angel gave him a ~~sine~~. When

Gideon brought some food, the angel told him to put the meat and cakes on the rock

and to pour out the broth. Then the angel touched the food with his staff. Fire

   out of
came the rock and consumed all the food.

(8 points)

Total points: 75

Building Securely

Chapter 2 Test   Score _____

Name _____ Date _____

A. Circle *T* if the statement is true or *F* if it is false.

   T Ⓕ   1. A comma is usually needed when inverted word order is used.

   Ⓣ F   2. A clause must contain both a subject and a predicate.

   T Ⓕ   3. A topic sentence should summarize the details of a paragraph.

   T Ⓕ   4. In a well-written paragraph, most of the sentences contain transitional words.

   Ⓣ F   5. An adjective clause usually begins with a relative pronoun.

   Ⓣ F   6. In using repetition of key words, it is wise to use synonyms.

                                                                     (6 points)

B. Match the terms to the descriptions by writing the letters of the correct choices in the blanks. You may not use some choices in a set, and you may use some more than once.

   __b__   7. A sentence that expresses strong feeling.   a. declarative sentence
                                                                   b. exclamatory sentence
   __a__   8. A sentence that states a fact.   c. imperative sentence
                                                                   d. interrogative sentence
   __d__   9. A sentence that asks a question.

   __c__ 10. A sentence that gives a command.

   __c__ 11. A sentence in which the subject is always *you*.

   __b__ 12. A sentence that often has special word order.

   __a__ 13. A sentence that must be either true or false.

   __e__ 14. The complete predicate comes before the complete subject.   e. inverted word order
                                                                            f. mixed word order
   __g__ 15. The complete subject comes before the complete predicate.   g. natural word order

   __f__ 16. The complete subject comes between two parts of the predicate.

   __g__ 17. The word order that is most frequently used.

___j___ 18. A sentence with only one independent clause.

___h___ 19. A sentence with one independent clause and one or more dependent clauses.

___i___ 20. A sentence with two or more independent clauses.

___i___ 21. A sentence with clauses usually joined by a coordinating conjunction.

h. complex sentence
i. compound sentence
j. simple sentence

___n___ 22. Every sentence supports the main idea.

___l___ 23. The first line is indented, and the margins are straight.

___k___ 24. The sentences fit together smoothly.

k. coherence
l. form
m. topic sentence
n. unity

___q___ 25. Sentences arranged in the order of space.

___o___ 26. Sentences arranged in the order of time.

___q___ 27. The order used in describing a scene.

___p___ 28. The order used when several reasons are given to explain something.

___o___ 29. The order used in explaining a process.

o. chronological order
p. order of importance
q. spatial order

(23 points)

C. Label each sentence *dec.* (declarative), *int.* (interrogative), *imp.* (imperative), or *exc.* (exclamatory). Write the correct punctuation mark at the end.

____int.____ 30. Do you know what the two middle verses of the Bible are?

____imp.____ 31. Turn to Psalm 103:1, 2.

____dec.____ 32. These verses have a significant message for their central location.

____exc.____ 33. How important it is for us to bless the Lord!

____dec.____ 34. You should memorize these verses and their reference.

(5 points)

D. Label each sentence *N* for natural word order, *I* for inverted word order, or *M* for mixed word order. Then rewrite the sentence in a different word order. Use correct punctuation.   (Rewritten sentences may vary somewhat.)

___I___ 35. Out in the orchard stands a gnarled apple tree. _____

   _A gnarled apple tree stands out in the orchard._____

___N___ 36. This tree has produced a fine crop for many years. _____

   _For many years, this tree has produced a fine crop._____

___M___ 37. During last year's drought, we were able to irrigate the orchard. _____

_____We were able to irrigate the orchard during last year's drought._____

___M___ 38. There are several bushels of fine red apples on its branches now. _____

_____Several bushels of fine red apples are on its branches now._____

_____

(8 points)

E. Label each sentence *S* (simple), *Cd* (compound), or *Cx* (complex).

___S___ 39. The Bible contains much practical advice for youth.

___Cx___ 40. Because many young people prefer their own plans, God commands them to remember their Creator in their youth.

___Cx___ 41. Paul wrote and encouraged Timothy, who was a young church leader.

___Cd___ 42. Young people can choose wrong habits and attitudes, or they can develop a solid character.

(4 points)

F. Label the underlined clauses *ind.* for independent, *adj.* for adjective, or *adv.* for adverb.

_____adj._____ 43. The Sermon on the Mount, <u>which Matthew records in detail</u>, opens with the Beatitudes.

_____ind._____ 44. <u>This notable sermon describes the life</u> that Jesus wants His followers to live in this world.

_____adv._____ 45. <u>Although such a life is not natural to man</u>, it is possible through the grace of God.

_____adj._____ 46. Those <u>who consistently follow Christ's teachings</u> are building their lives on the Rock.

_____ind._____ 47. Because Jesus taught with authority, <u>the people were astonished at His words</u>.

(5 points)

G. These sentences include simple, compound, and complex sentences. Diagram the skeletons and complements of all the clauses.   (Count 1 point for each simple subject, simple predicate, or complement. A sentence like number 50 is worth 6 points.)

48. The sun is the center of the solar system, and the planets orbit it.

49. The sun is one star in the vast universe.

50. The earth is the planet that God designed for the existence of life.

51. Because no other planet can support life, man inhabits only Earth.

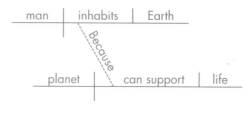

52. We worship our great God, who created this temporary habitation for man.

(27 points)

H. Read the paragraphs below, and do these exercises.

53. Write *chronological*, *spatial*, or *importance* to identify the type of sentence order that is used.

_____spatial_____ a. Paragraph 1   ___chronological___ b. Paragraph 2

54. Write the numbers that identify these sentences.

__1__ a. The topic sentence of Paragraph 1.

__5__ b. The topic sentence of Paragraph 2.

__4__ c. The sentence that mars the unity of Paragraph 2.

55. Copy the words in Paragraph 1 that illustrate the following things.

___monarch___ ___butterfly___ a. Repetition of key words (two synonyms).

_____it_____ _____its_____ b. Pronoun reference (two pronouns).

Paragraph 1:

¹The monarch butterfly is a marvel of creative design. ²Out front it has two antennae, delicately sensing the air to help the monarch find the nectar of its favorite flowers. ³Behind the antennae are two eyes with six thousand lenses each, seeming to bulge out of proportion to the rest of its head. ⁴In the entire creation, these eyes are among the best for sensitivity to motion—as you can readily believe if you ever try to catch a monarch. ⁵This butterfly, like all insects, has six legs. ⁶But the monarch's legs serve the unusual function of tasting its food! ⁷Overspreading most of the monarch's body are its four beautiful wings of orange and black. ⁸Each wing is covered with millions of overlapping scales. ⁹If you touch a wing, these tiny scales rub off and look like powder on your finger.

Paragraph 2:

¹As autumn starts bringing colder weather, lonely monarch butterflies start winging their way south. ²Later these monarchs may congregate in large groups, especially at difficult crossings. ³After a journey of as much as two thousand miles, they reach their winter homes in Florida, California, or Mexico. ⁴The monarchs find their way back to their summer homes when spring arrives. ⁵Of all the species in the butterfly world, only the monarch and a few others migrate south for the winter.

(7 points)

Total points: 85

Building Securely

Chapter 3 Test   **Score** _____

Name _____ **Date** _____

A. Circle *T* if the statement is true or *F* if it is false.

T (F) 1. A good paragraph developed by giving steps has each step numbered.

T (F) 2. For musical terms ending with *o,* you should add *-es* for the plural forms.

(T) F 3. In writing a plural form, you should change a final *y* to *i* if it comes after a consonant.

(T) F 4. A good paragraph developed by using examples might have only two examples if enough details are given about each.

T (F) 5. A paragraph developed by giving a definition is like a brief story.

(T) F 6. A paragraph can be developed by using more than one method.

(6 points)

B. In the first blank, write *C* or *A* to tell whether the noun is concrete or abstract. In the second blank, write *M, F, N,* or *C* to tell whether its gender is masculine, feminine, neuter, or common.

_C_ _N_ 7. road	_C_ _F_ 11. seamstress
_C_ _M_ 8. Michael	_C_ _C_ 12. teacher
_A_ _N_ 9. honesty	_A_ _N_ 13. contentment
_C_ _C_ 10. sheep	_C_ _F_ 14. hen

(8 points)

C. Change each word in parentheses to a noun by using a noun-forming suffix.

15. The (lead) of our tour thanked us for our (cooperate).

_____leader_____   _____cooperation_____

16. The (identify) of God's people is marked by their godly (separate).

identity *or* identification   _separation *or* separateness_

17. The Christian's (fortify) is in his (depend) on the Lord.

fortitude *or* fortification   _____dependence_____

(6 points)

D. Write *X* before the underlined words that are used as nouns.

18. If we do not _____ praise the Lord daily, we cannot live to His __X__ praise.

19. After I _____ box these sheets and this __X__ cover, I want you to _____ cover the __X__ box with

gift-wrapping.

(6 points)

E. Correct the capitalization errors by crossing out each incorrect letter and writing the correct letter above it.

(Count ½ point for each one.)

20. The lord told abram to leave ur and go to a new land.

21. We bought a Baker's Wood Stove in marysville.

22. The Pioneers left the east in a Covered Wagon they named prairie wings.

23. The cedar lake Mennonite Church should be finished by July, and the new School should be ready

by Fall.

(9 points)

F. Write the plural form of each noun. For numbers 32–35, use the foreign spellings.

24. motto _____ mottoes _____

25. journey _____ journeys _____

26. louse _____ lice _____

27. city _____ cities _____

28. shelf _____ shelves _____

29. soprano _____ sopranos _____

30. sister-in-law _____ sisters-in-law _____

31. eyetooth _____ eyeteeth _____

32. oasis _____ oases _____

33. index _____ indices _____

34. vertebra _____ vertebrae _____

35. fungus _____ fungi _____

(12 points)

G. Rewrite these expressions, using possessive forms. If a possessive form should not normally be used, write *correct*. Show joint ownership for numbers 40 and 41, and separate ownership for numbers 42 and 43.

36. the papers of the children _____ the children's papers _____

37. the hands of the clock _____ correct _____

38. the comb of the rooster _____ the rooster's comb _____

39. the time of three weeks _____ three weeks' time _____

40. the rabbits of Lloyd and George _____ Lloyd and George's rabbits _____

41. the idea of Marjorie and Helen _____ Marjorie and Helen's idea _____

42. the answers of Leah and Eugene _____ Leah's and Eugene's answers _____

43. the pencils of Larry and Dorothy _____ Larry's and Dorothy's pencils _____

(8 points)

H. Each sentence contains one verbal phrase or noun clause. Underline it, and in the blank write *G, I,* or *C* to identify it as a gerund phrase, an infinitive phrase, or a noun clause.

   C   44. Mother was wondering <u>if Father had finished the chores</u>.

   I   45. <u>To leave by 5:30</u> is still our goal.

   C   46. <u>Whatever you can do</u> will be appreciated.

   G   47. Mother's only job was <u>combing the girls' hair</u>.

(4 points)

I. Underline the substantives in these sentences. Do not underline separately the substantives within phrases or clauses.   (Count ½ point for each item underlined.)

48. The <u>boys</u> are hoeing the <u>beans</u> in the <u>garden</u>, and <u>you</u> should help <u>them</u>.

49. <u>Raising produce for the market</u> requires hard <u>work</u> from the whole <u>family</u>.

50. <u>We</u> enjoy <u>working together</u>, and <u>we</u> know <u>that God blesses hard work</u>.

51. Our <u>market</u>, <u>Mary</u>, is at <u>Avery Square</u> in <u>Smithsburg</u>.

(8 points)

J. Diagram the skeletons and complements of the clauses in these sentences. Include verbals and their complements and the introductory words of noun clauses.

52. Speaking kindly about others shows a thoughtful attitude.   (3 points)

53. The student's responsibility is to respect his teacher.   (4 points)

54. Lucinda said that she enjoys poetry.   (6 points)

55. How she can write such good poetry is a mystery to me.   *(6 points)*

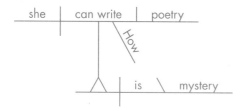

(19 points)

K. Write *X* before the better paragraph in each pair.

56.

_____ a.   God's Word is absolutely sure. Nothing in the Bible can fail or change. Jesus said that not one jot or tittle would pass from the Law until all was fulfilled. And everything in the Bible will certainly be fulfilled, for God's Word is forever settled in heaven. God's Word is completely worthy of our full confidence.

__X__ b.   God's Word is absolutely sure. Many of its prophecies have already come to pass, and we know that all the rest will also be fulfilled. Without fail, Bible promises have encouraged and inspired those who have claimed them. The principles taught in the Bible will never fail if they are applied diligently. God's Word is completely worthy of our full confidence.

57.

__X__ a.   The force of atmospheric pressure can be shown by a simple demonstration. You will need an empty metal can with a tight-fitting cap, some water, and a hot plate or stove. With the cap off the can, heat a small amount of water in the can. After the water is hot, take the can off the burner, put on the cap, and pour cold water over it. As the steam in the can condenses, a partial vacuum is produced. Atmospheric pressure on the outside of the can is so great that it will crush the can.

_____ b.   The force of atmospheric pressure can be shown by a simple demonstration. First, get an empty metal can with a tight-fitting cap, some water, and a hot plate or stove. Second, put a small amount of water into the can and heat it with the cap off the can. Third, take the can off the burner and put on the cap. Fourth, pour cold water over the can so that the steam condenses and a partial vacuum is produced. Atmospheric pressure on the outside of the can is so great that it will crush the can.

(2 points)
Total points: 88

Building Securely

Chapter 4 Test

Score _____

Name _____ Date _____

A. Circle *T* if the statement is true or *F* if it is false.

   Ⓣ F   1. In a sentence about two past actions or conditions, the one that occurred first is often expressed in the past perfect tense.

   T Ⓕ   2. In a sentence about two future actions or conditions, the one that occurs second is often expressed in the future perfect tense.

   T Ⓕ   3. In English grammar, *perfect* means "precise."

   Ⓣ F   4. The emphatic form of a verb can be used only in the present and past tenses.

   Ⓣ F   5. In both topical and sentence outlines, each item should begin with a capital letter.

   T Ⓕ   6. In both topical and sentence outlines, each item should end with a period.

(6 points)

B. Match the terms to the descriptions by writing the letters of the correct choices in the blanks.

   a. present perfect
   b. past perfect
   c. future perfect
   d. transitive verb
   e. intransitive complete verb
   f. intransitive linking verb

__b__   7. Indicates action that was completed by a certain time in the past.

__a__   8. Indicates action that began in the past and is now completed.

__c__   9. Indicates action that will be completed by a certain time in the future.

__a__   10. Helping verb *have* or *has* is used.

__c__   11. Helping verbs *shall have* or *will have* are used.

__b__   12. Helping verb *had* is used.

__e__   13. An action verb that does not pass action.

__f__   14. A form of *be* or some other verb that does not express action.

__d__   15. An action verb that passes action to a receiver.

__f__   16. A verb that acts like an equal sign between the subject and the predicate nominative.

(10 points)

C. Write the missing principal parts. Use a helping verb with the third part.   (Helping verbs may vary.)

First (Present)	Second (Past)	Third (Past Participle)
17. drag	dragged	(have) dragged
18. go	went	(have) gone
19. think	thought	(have) thought
20. do	did	(have) done
21. come	came	(have) come
22. burst	burst	(have) burst

(12 points)

D. Underline each verb or verb phrase. In the blank, write the letter showing the tense of the verb.

a. present   c. future   e. past perfect
b. past   d. present perfect f. future perfect

___a___ 23. The righteous man <u>regards</u> the life of his beast.

___e___ 24. By noon we <u>had cleaned</u> the whole downstairs.

___c___ 25. We <u>shall</u> surely <u>finish</u> the upstairs this afternoon.

___f___ 26. By tomorrow at this time, Grandfather's <u>will have arrived</u>.

___d___ 27. They <u>have</u> never <u>visited</u> us at our new place yet.

___d___ 28. A heifer <u>has broken</u> through the fence.

___b___ 29. The heavy rain <u>washed</u> some deep gullies in the garden.

___c___ 30. <u>Will</u> the carpenters <u>finish</u> the roof today?

(8 points)

E. Write the correct verb or verb phrase in each blank, as indicated in parentheses.

31. Carl _____forgets_____ his books and papers too often. (present tense of *forget*)

32. My brother ___will be teaching___ our class tomorrow. (future tense, progressive form of *teach*)

33. Kevin _____had run_____ to third base before the outfielder threw the ball. (past perfect tense of *run*)

34. I _____did write_____ the assignment in my assignment book. (past tense, emphatic form of *write*)

(4 points)

F. In the blank, write the word that receives the action of the verb.

_____cherries_____ 35. The cherries have been eaten by the birds.

_____goats_____ 36. Father bought two goats at the auction today.

_____box_____ 37. Aden made a beautiful box for Mother's recipe cards.

(3 points)

G. In each sentence, underline the two words that are linked by the verb.

38. <u>Saul</u> was the first <u>king</u> of Israel.

39. This hot <u>stew</u> will taste <u>good</u> to the tired men.

40. The <u>corn</u> has not grown <u>tall</u> during this dry weather.

(3 points)

H. Label the patterns of these sentences.

Pattern 1: intransitive complete verb
Pattern 2: transitive verb; action passed to direct object
Pattern 3: transitive verb; action passed to subject
Pattern 4: intransitive linking verb

___4___ 41. For seventy years the Israelites had been captives.

___1___ 42. Sister Mabel has been writing to us regularly.

___3___ 43. Many inspiring lessons are taken from David's life.

___2___ 44. Harvey did bring his butterfly collection to school.

___4___ 45. The rainbow soon became brilliant.

(5 points)

I. Diagram the skeletons, complements, and verb modifiers of these sentences. (Count 1 point for each subject, verb, complement, and verb modifier.)

46. Seth is proofreading his story.

| Seth | is proofreading | story |

47. Louella has been a good helper.

| Louella | has been \ helper |

48. The airplane was tossed violently by the strong winds.

| airplane | was tossed |
violently by — winds (the, strong)

49. Sally gave us an account of her day with the Smiths.

```
  Sally  |  gave  |  account
         \         us
```

(14 points)

J. Each line on this outline has one mistake. Write it correctly as a topical outline.   (Corrections are marked.)

Nehemiah—a Man of Action

I. The source of his Strength
   A. prayer
      1. when he heard disturbing news
      2. He needed to answer the king
      3. When he faced opposition.
   b. Concern for the welfare of God's people
   C. He knew God's Word.
   D. He was consecrated.
   E. Faith and Trust in God
      1. seen in his many prayers
      2. Seen in his confidence in the hand of God.
II. What the secret of his strength was

Nehemiah—a Man of Action

_____ I. The source of his strength _____

_____ A. Prayer _____

_____ 1. When he heard disturbing news _____

_____ 2. When he needed to answer the king _____

_____ 3. When he faced opposition/ _____

_____ B. Concern for the welfare of God's people _____

_____ C. Knowledge of God's Word _____

_____ D. Consecration _____

_____ E. Faith and trust in God _____

_____ 1. Seen in his many prayers _____

_____ 2. Seen in his confidence in the hand of God/ _____

_____ II. The secret of his strength _____

(12 points)

Total points: 77

Building Securely

Chapter 5 Test

Score _____

Name _____ Date _____

A. Circle *T* if the statement is true or *F* if it is false.

T (F) 1. If two singular subjects are joined by *and,* the verb should be singular.

(T) F 2. A verb in the passive voice passes its action to the subject.

(T) F 3. The passive voice is suitable when there is no clear doer of an action.

T (F) 4. In a friendly letter, the greeting should be followed by a colon.

T (F) 5. In a business letter, the inside address should come before the heading.

(T) F 6. A thank-you note or other social note should have the same five parts as a friendly letter.

(*6 points*)

B. Underline the correct words.

7. Everyone in the nation of Israel (<u>is</u>, are) safely over the Jordan River.

8. (There's, <u>There are</u>) two men spying on Jericho.

9. Rahab (don't, <u>doesn't</u>) want to be destroyed with Jericho.

10. Rahab, as well as those with her, (<u>was</u>, were) delivered.

11. Everybody who was not behind the scarlet line (have, <u>has</u>) been destroyed.

12. A flock of geese (pass, <u>passes</u>) overhead on its way south.

13. With modern medication, smallpox (have, <u>has</u>) been wiped out.

14. My small scissors (<u>have</u>, has) fallen out of my purse.

15. (<u>Do</u>, Does) these clouds foretell snow?

16. Our herd of cows (is, <u>are</u>) contentedly chewing their cuds.

(*10 points*)

C. Choose the correct verb for each sentence, and write it in the proper form.

____rose____ 17. Samuel thought Eli had called, and he (raise, rise) quickly.

____lay____ 18. Samuel returned to his bed and (lay, lie) down again.

___sitting___ 19. Eli was (set, sit) on a bench when the news came.

____let____ 20. Because Eli had (let, leave) his sons persist in evil, his household was severely punished.

_____risen_____ 21. Our hopes of rain have (raise, rise) with the cloudy skies.

_____sets_____ 22. We must hurry and smooth the concrete before it (set, sit).

_____May_____ 23. (Can, May) we take a break afterward?

(7 points)

D. Write the correct verb for each sentence.

_____drowned_____ 24. Pharaoh and his army were drownded in the Red Sea.

_____attacked_____ 25. God's people have often been attackted viciously.

_____cost_____ 26. Solomon's temple costed an enormous amount of money.

_____have_____ 27. The dedication service must of greatly inspired the godly.

_____broken_____ 28. Olen had broke his arm once before.

_____dragged_____ 29. Brendon drug the heavy crate across the barn floor.

_____threw_____ 30. Dallas throwed ten bales of straw down to bed the heifers.

_____brought_____ 31. Barry has brung the pitchforks to spread the straw.

_____burst_____ 32. The blister on my finger has bursted.

_____taken_____ 33. Mother has tooken a treat out for the men in the field.

(10 points)

E. Write whether the verbs in these sentences are *active* or *passive*.

_____passive_____ 34. A person's heart is revealed by his words and actions.

_____active_____ 35. Love always seeks the welfare of others.

_____active_____ 36. Father led the family in a prayer of thanksgiving.

_____passive_____ 37. Our parents' guidance should be appreciated deeply.

_____passive_____ 38. Important training for life is being given daily.

(5 points)

F. The passive voice is used in each sentence below. Before each one, write the letter of the statement which correctly describes that sentence.

    a. The active voice would be more effective.
    b. There is no clear doer of the action.
    c. There is a good reason not to name the doer.

_a_ 39. These pillow tops were crocheted by a friend.

_b_ 40. Bronze is made from copper and tin.

___a___   41. A story was told by our teacher.

___c___   42. A page has been torn out of Leanne's new book.

(4 points)

G. Read the following friendly letter. In the numbered blanks, list three mistakes that you see in the letter.

Route 2, Box 215
Rutherfordton, NC 28139

Dear Sidney,

   Well, I haven't written to you for a while, so I thought I would write again.

   Last week we went to the Philadelphia zoo. That was a lot of fun!

   Have you gotten your rabbit hutches built already? Do you have rabbits too? I'm eager to see your setup. Maybe I'll be able to buy some rabbits from you and start raising some here. I'll ask Father about that.

   Our cantaloupes are almost ready. That means a lot of work for the next several weeks. We've been selling a lot of sweet corn already.

   I hope we can come and see you sometime soon.

Your cousin
Joseph

(Any of these answers.)

43.   The heading does not include a date.

44.   The letter does not have a good beginning, such as a Scripture verse or a worthwhile line of poetry.

45.   The letter is weak in detail, especially about the visit to the zoo.

(3 points)

The closing has no comma.

H. Read the following business letter. In the numbered blanks, list three mistakes that you see in the letter.

Route 1, Box 93
Croghan, NY 13327
March 3, 20—

Dear Sirs,

   I would like some information about the products you sell. Send whatever you can immediately.

Respectfully yours,
Jonas King

(Any of these answers.)

46.   The inside address is missing.

47.   The greeting has a comma instead of a colon.

48.   The body is not specific enough.

(3 points)

Total points: 48

The body is not courteous.

Building Securely

Chapter 6 Test

Score _____

Name _____ Date _____

A. Circle *T* if the statement is true or *F* if it is false.

(T) F   1. Only personal pronouns in the third person have different forms according to gender.

T (F)   2. Apostrophes are used in spelling personal pronouns in the possessive case.

(T) F   3. A compound personal pronoun is used reflexively when it is a direct object naming the same person or thing as the subject.

T (F)   4. The interrogative and the relative pronouns are identical except in their use within a sentence.

T (F)   5. When you prepare note cards for an oral report, you may write two or three items of information on each card.

(T) F   6. The pronouns *who* and *whom* should refer only to persons, and the pronoun *which* should refer to anything except persons.

(6 points)

B. Write whether each pair of pronouns is different in person (*P*), number (*N*), case (*C*), or gender (*G*).

__N__   7. I, we

__C__   8. I, me

__P__   9. theirs, ours

__P or G__ 10. me, him

__G__ 11. him, her

__C__ 12. they, them

(6 points)

C. Write a pronoun for each of the following descriptions.

__you__   13. second person, objective case

__I__   14. first person, singular, nominative case

__them__   15. third person, plural, objective case

__his__   16. third person, singular, possessive case, masculine gender

__us__   17. first person, plural, objective case

__she__   18. third person, singular, nominative case, feminine gender

(6 points)

D. Write *N* or *O* to tell whether each underlined pronoun is in the nominative or objective case.

__N__   19. Moses cast down his rod, and <u>it</u> became a serpent.

__O__   20. Never let hardships discourage <u>you</u>.

___N___ 21. The person taking this test is <u>you</u>.

___O___ 22. When you receive advice, you should benefit from <u>it</u>.

(4 points)

E. Underline the correct choices in parentheses.

23. The gifted poet and storywriter kept (<u>her</u>, their) note pad handy to jot down ideas.

24. The tenor singers, Brent and (<u>he</u>, him), are struggling with this new song.

25. For Alice and (I, <u>me</u>), this was an enjoyable day.

26. Father told (we, <u>us</u>) boys to clean out the calf hutches.

27. Either Julia or Judy had (<u>her</u>, their) quilt block here today.

28. (<u>We</u>, Us) young people must learn to practice good habits.

29. The most surprised persons must have been you and (<u>I</u>, me).

30. Mother gave Charlotte and (she, <u>her</u>) clear directions.

31. The secretary and treasurer gave (<u>his report</u>, their reports).

32. The secretary and the treasurer gave (his report, <u>their reports</u>).

(10 points)

F. Rewrite these sentences to make the pronouns clear and correct.

33. When Harry raced with Dale, he tripped and sprained his ankle. <u>Harry tripped and sprained his</u>
     <u>ankle when he raced with Dale.</u> *or* <u>Dale tripped and sprained his ankle when Harry raced with him.</u>

34. Michael told Raymond that his answer was right. <u>Michael said, "Raymond, your answer is right."</u>
     <u>*or* Michael said, "Raymond, my answer is right."</u>

35. Father said that me and you may walk back to the creek. _____
     <u>Father said that you and I may walk back to the creek.</u>

(3 points)

G. Cross out the wrong word in each sentence. If another word should be used instead, write the correct word
    in the blank.

_____himself_____ 36. Because Moses sinned, he ~~hisself~~ lost the right to enter Canaan.

_____themselves_____ 37. The sons of Eli made ~~theirselves~~ vile.

_____Those_____ 38. ~~Them~~ are the cedars of Lebanon.

_____ 39. Nobody volunteered for that ~~there~~ job.

_____ourselves_____   40. We should discipline ~~ourself~~ to do what we know is right.

_____I_____   41. Jonathan and ~~myself~~ will come to help you.

(6 points)

H. Underline the correct choices in parentheses.

42. Everybody (have, <u>has</u>) been created to glorify God.

43. Nobody can fill this place in only (<u>his,</u> their) own strength.

44. None of God's Word (<u>is,</u> are) ever outdated or false.

45. None of God's promises (is, <u>are</u>) vain.

46. Few of the angels (<u>have</u>, has) names known to man.

47. Each of the patriarchs had (<u>his,</u> their) special trials in life.

(6 points)

I. Underline the relative pronoun in each sentence, and draw an arrow from it to its antecedent.

48. Job, <u>whose</u> life was greatly changed in one day, trusted God.

49. Satan, <u>who</u> falsely accused Job, could not destroy that faith.

50. The unwavering faith <u>that</u> Job had in God was the key to his steadfastness.

51. These troubles, with <u>which</u> Satan intended to destroy Job, only strengthened his faith.

(8 points)

J. Label the underlined pronouns *P* for personal, *CP* for compound personal, *D* for demonstrative, *ID* for indefinite, *IR* for interrogative, or *R* for relative.

_CP_   52. Find <u>yourselves</u> seats while dinner is prepared.

_D_   53. Was <u>that</u> an interesting school trip?

_R_   54. This is the day <u>that</u> the Lord has made.

_P_   55. We must use <u>our</u> abilities to serve the Lord.

_ID_   56. <u>Both</u> of the ideas are worthy of consideration.

_D_   57. I did not ask for <u>these</u>.

_IR_   58. <u>Whom</u> did God choose to be the first king of Israel?

_R_   59. Saul, <u>whom</u> God chose as the first king, soon fell into disobedience.

(8 points)

K. Write the following information on the note cards. The notes are taken for the topic "Coal, an Important Fuel."

— hard anthracite best coal for fuel (*Investigating God's Orderly World*, Book 1, page 226)
— appears to be formed from mainly plant material, fossilized under pressure (*Biology for Christian Schools*, page 187)   (Count 2 points for each card.)

Coal, an Important Fuel

Investigating God's Orderly World, Book 1, p. 226

hard anthracite best coal for fuel

Coal, an Important Fuel

Biology for Christian Schools, p. 187

appears to be formed from mainly plant material,
    fossilized under pressure

(4 points)

L. Write *X* before the two best headings under which the information in Part K and below should be organized.

— soft, brown lignite burns poorly (*Investigating God's Orderly World*, Book 1, page 226)
— soft but blacker bituminous is a better fuel (*Investigating God's Orderly World*, Book 1, page 226)
— not known to be forming in natural world today (*Biology for Christian Schools*, page 187)

_____ 60. The Discovery of Coal

___X___ 61. The Formation of Coal

___X___ 62. The Kinds of Coal

_____ 63. The Uses of Coal

(2 points)
Total points: 69

Building Securely

Chapter 7 Test

Score _____

Name _____ Date _____

A. Circle *T* if the statement is true or *F* if it is false.

T (F)   1. Descriptive adjectives answer the questions *which, whose,* and *how many.*

(T) F   2. A participle is a verb form used as an adjective.

(T) F   3. If two descriptive adjectives are used together, they are often separated by a comma.

T (F)   4. Restrictive clauses should be set off by commas.

(T) F   5. *Less* should be used with singular nouns, and *fewer* with plural nouns.

T (F)   6. *Them* may be used as a pronoun and an adjective.

(6 points)

B. Write the letter of the correct term to match each description. Some letters may be used more than once.

___d___ 7. A figurative exaggeration for emphasis.

___c___ 8. A figurative comparison using *like* or *as.*

___a___ 9. A figurative comparison not using *like* or *as.*

___b___ 10. Giving human characteristics to a thing or quality.

___a___ 11. Saying that one thing is another thing, or using literal terms to describe something that happened only in a figurative sense.

a. metaphor
b. personification
c. simile
d. hyperbole

___g___ 12. An adjective following a linking verb, modifying the subject.

___e___ 13. An adjective coming right after the word it modifies.

___f___ 14. An adjective coming just before the word it modifies.

___e___ 15. Adjectives often coming in pairs and set off by commas.

e. appositive position
f. attributive position
g. predicate position

(9 points)

C. Underline the seven adjectives in these sentences. Above each, write *D* for descriptive or *L* for limiting.

     L   D   L   D
16. One Indian family attended the worship service.

      L   L   D
17. Joseph's coat of many colors must have been beautiful.

(7 points)

D. Cross out each word that should not be used, and write any correction above it. If words are missing, use a caret (∧) to show where they belong, and write the words in the space above the sentence.

18. The Garden of Eden must have been ~~beautifuller~~ than we can imagine.
    more beautiful
    ∧

19. Before the Flood, people grew ~~more~~ older than they do today.

20. According to the lesson, your answer is more ∧ correct than mine.
    nearly

21. Although I felt ill yesterday, I feel even ~~iller~~∧ today.
    worse

22. Both girls explained the game, but Darlene's explanation was ~~clearest~~.
    clearer

23. Leon has ~~littler~~ experience with driving tractors than Ira has.
    less

24. How do you like this ~~here~~ story?

25. A ~~dishonest~~ liar loses the confidence of others.

26. The chickens laid ~~less~~ eggs today than yesterday.
    fewer

27. The ~~loud,~~ noisy children needed something worthwhile to do.   *or* The loud, ~~noisy~~ children needed something worthwhile to do.

28. Eileen copied ~~them~~ recipes from her cousin's collection.
    those

29. Do you know what kind of à squash this is?

(12 points)

E. Underline each adjective phrase. In the blank, write whether the phrase is prepositional (*prep.*), participial (*part.*), or infinitive (*inf.*).

____part.____ 30. Moses and Joshua, <u>nearing the camp</u>, heard a strange sound.

____prep.____ 31. The people <u>in the camp</u> were singing and shouting.

_____inf._____ 32. Aaron's willingness <u>to please the people</u> had led to great sin.

____part.____ 33. <u>Seeing the golden calf</u>, Moses knew that the people had broken their commitment

_____inf._____   <u>to serve the Lord</u>.

(5 points)

F. Add the missing commas to these sentences. For those given in pairs, write *R* or *N* in the blank to tell which sentence has a restrictive clause and which has a nonrestrictive clause.   (Count 1 point for each comma or set of commas, and 1 point for each letter.)

34. The long, low boat sped down the river, muddy and swollen.

__R__ 35. a. The man who owned the boat was taking a load of produce to market.   (no commas)

__N__   b. Philadelphia, which was his destination, was a bustling market town.

___N___ 36. a. The Ten Commandments, which God gave to Moses, are found in Exodus 20.

___R___   b. The teachings that Jesus gave represent even higher standards.   (no commas)

(8 points)

G. Underline each adjective phrase or clause that is misplaced, and draw an arrow from it to the place where it belongs.

37. The lame man asked for alms <u>seeing Peter and John</u>.   *or* The lame man asked for alms <u>seeing Peter and John</u>.

38. The new book is out on the porch <u>that Aunt Faye sent us</u>.

39. This shirt needs to be mended <u>with a big hole</u>.

(3 points)

H. Diagram these sentences.

40. Lightning, striking a nearby tree, killed several cattle.   (5 points)

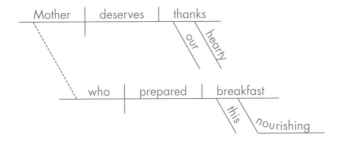

41. Mother, who prepared this nourishing breakfast, deserves our hearty thanks.   (7 points)

42. Barry is the one whom I tagged.   (6 points)

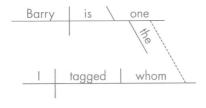

43. The books within these boxes are the ones to take along.   (5 points)

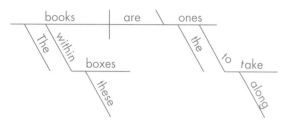

(23 points)

I. Write whether each sentence contains a metaphor (*M*), a simile (*S*), a hyperbole (*H*), or personification (*P*).

   __M__   44. Aunt Velma carries the glow of sunshine wherever she goes.

   __P__   45. The trees whispered together in the breeze, and the flowers nodded to each other.

   __H__   46. Do not make a mountain out of a molehill.

   __S__   47. Clyde's thoughtless words stung like a whip.

   __S__   48. The children, as nervous as mice watched by a cat, waited for Father to return.

(5 points)

J. Write a more exact noun or a more expressive verb for each underlined expression.   (Sample answers.)

   49. Use this <u>white thing</u> to write the problem on the board.   __chalk__

   50. The thunder <u>made a loud noise</u>, and we jumped.   __crashed, boomed, clapped__

   51. Three black <u>animals</u> escaped up the tree as Rover   __cats, kittens__

   <u>came after</u> them.   __chased, pursued__

(4 points)
Total points: 82

Building Securely

Chapter 8 Test

Score _____

Name _____ Date _____

A. Circle *T* if the statement is true or *F* if it is false.

   T (F) 1. *Badly* and *well* are always adverbs.

   (T) F 2. An adverb clause at the beginning of a sentence must be followed by a comma.

   (T) F 3. An adverb clause begins with a subordinating conjunction.

   T (F) 4. A book report should not reveal the theme and main events of the story.

   T (F) 5. In a book report, you should avoid giving your own evaluation of the book.

   (T) F 6. A book report should briefly describe the setting of the story.

   (T) F 7. For giving an explanation of a process, the most common order of development is chronological order.

   T (F) 8. In an oral explanation, the introduction is generally of little importance.

   (8 points)

B. Underline the eight single-word adverbs, and draw an arrow from each one to the word it modifies.

   9. Worldly wisdom too often ignores the true wisdom of God's Word.

   10. Man never finds true wisdom unless he lays aside his own will.

   11. Man quickly became exceedingly wicked in the early history of the world.

   12. One holy family drew near to the Lord and lived faithfully.

   (8 points)

C. Underline the eight adverb phrases, and draw an arrow from each one to the word or words it modifies.

   13. Wise men from the East came into Jerusalem and inquired about the newborn King.

   14. They were sent by Herod to Bethlehem.

   15. In a dream, God warned the wise men about Herod's evil intentions.

   16. They departed into their own country by a different way.

   (8 points)

D. Underline the six adverb clauses, and draw an arrow from each one to the word or words it modifies.

   17. When the wise men did not return to him, Herod was filled with anger.

   18. Jesus was safe from Herod's wrath because God had warned Joseph to flee to Egypt.

19. <u>After Herod died</u>, Joseph returned to the land of Israel <u>as an angel had directed him</u>.

20. <u>Since Joseph paid close attention to God</u>, God could lead him <u>where He wanted him to go</u>.

(6 points)

E. Label each underlined word, phrase, or clause by writing *adj.* or *adv.* above it.

21. That car <u>with the flat tire</u> [adj.] must be moved <u>off the busy road</u> [adv.].

22. The man at the <u>far</u> [adj.] end of the bench has traveled <u>far</u> [adv.] today.

23. Do not drive <u>too</u> [adv.] <u>fast</u> [adv.] on this rough road.

24. The reason <u>that we are late</u> [adj.] will be understood <u>when you hear our story</u> [adv.].

25. The <u>lonely</u> [adj.] man sat down under the <u>stately</u> [adj.] trees.

(10 points)

F. In each blank, write the correct form of the adverb in parentheses.

26. Laura works (well) ____better____ and talks (quietly) __more quietly__ than her sister.

27. The large lion behaved (wildly) __more wildly__ than the lioness did.

28. Of the two neighbor boys, Ronald acted (badly) ____worse____.

29. Towns on the flat prairies can be spotted (far) ____farther____ away than in these rolling hills.

30. Of the four hikers, Albert worried the (little) ____least____ about getting lost.

(6 points)

G. Cross out the incorrect words. If other words should be used instead, write them in the blanks.

____rather____ *or somewhat*   31. Elijah must have been ~~sort of~~ depressed as he lay under the juniper tree.

____could____   32. Pilate ~~couldn't~~ find no fault in Jesus.   *or* Pilate couldn't find ~~no~~ [any] fault in Jesus.

____really____   33. Rehoboam was ~~real~~ harsh with the people.

_____   34. A fruitful branch must be connected ~~up~~ with the vine.

____well____   35. Jesus always answered His enemies too ~~good~~ for them to trap Him.

_____   36. Simon brought no water for Jesus to wash ~~up~~ His feet.

____could____   37. The woman of Sychar ~~couldn't~~ hardly believe that a Jew would speak to her.

____badly____   38. Jews usually treated Samaritans very ~~bad~~.

_____   39. As Jesus spoke, the woman of Sychar sought ~~after~~ the living water.

____rather____ *or somewhat*   40. She was ~~kind of~~ startled that Jesus knew so much about her.

(10 points)

H. Diagram these sentences.

41. Our recently purchased typewriter operates very quietly.   (4 points)

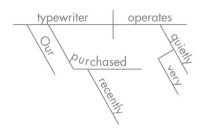

42. The cows are walking slowly across the road to the meadow.   (4 points)

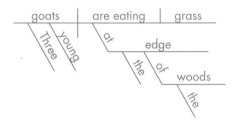

43. Three young goats are eating grass at the edge of the woods.   (4 points)

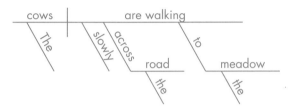

44. After Father marked the rows, we planted the seeds.   (4 points)

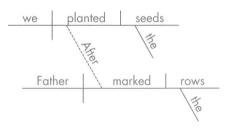

45. The grass has become greener than we had expected.   (4 points)

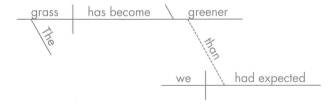

(24 points)
Total points: 80

Building Securely

Chapter 9 Test

Score _____

Name _____ Date _____

A. Write the letter of the correct term to match each description. In each set, one letter must be used twice.

___e___   1. Word that shows strong feeling or emotion.

___d___   2. Connecting words that work in a pair.

___f___   3. Connecting word that introduces a phrase.

___a___   4. Any one of these words: *and, but, or, since, when, because.*

___f___   5. Connecting word that shows relationship between its object and some other word.

___c___   6. Word like *and,* which always joins sentence parts of parallel structure and function.

___g___   7. Connecting word that joins an adverb clause to an independent clause.

___b___   8. Connects two independent clauses and is preceded by a semicolon.

a. conjunction
b. conjunctive adverb
c. coordinating conjunction
d. correlative conjunction
e. interjection
f. preposition
g. subordinating conjunction

___n___   9. Regular pattern of accented and unaccented syllables.

___h___   10. Repetition of beginning consonant sounds.

___m___   11. Repetition of matching sounds at ends of lines.

___i___   12. Repetition of similar vowel sounds in accented syllables.

___k___   13. Repetition of similar or opposite ideas.

___m___   14. Pattern shown with small letters such as *abcb.*

___l___   15. Accented syllable and the unaccented syllable or syllables associated with it.

___j___   16. Use of a word having an imitative sound.

h. alliteration
i. assonance
j. onomatopoeia
k. parallelism
l. poetic foot
m. rhyme
n. rhythm

___o___   17. Two unaccented syllables followed by one accented syllable.

___r___   18. One accented syllable followed by one unaccented syllable.

___q___   19. One unaccented syllable followed by one accented syllable.

___p___   20. One accented syllable followed by two unaccented syllables.

___q___   21. The most common rhythm in English poetry.

o. anapestic
p. dactylic
q. iambic
r. trochaic

(21 points)

B. Underline each prepositional phrase, and above it write *adj.* for adjective phrase or *adv.* for adverb phrase. If one phrase is part of a longer phrase, underline it twice and label both phrases clearly.

               adv.   adv.
22. <u>Before His suffering and death</u>, Jesus went <u>to the Garden</u> to pray.

                                                         adj.
23. His sleeping disciples could not understand His agony <u>of spirit</u>.

                        adv.   adj.   adv.
24. As Peter stood <u>in the group</u> <u>around the fire</u>, one person recognized him <u>by his speech</u>.

                                adv.
25. Peter denied his Lord <u>because of his fear</u>.

(7 points)

C. Underline each conjunction or conjunctive adverb, and label it *CC* for coordinating conjunction, *SC* for subordinating conjunction, or *CA* for conjunctive adverb. Be sure to include all the parts of a correlative conjunction.

                        CC
26. A diligent attitude <u>and</u> a disciplined mind are key ingredients for successful study.

                             CA
27. We must strive for the best; <u>however,</u> we must be content with the abilities that God has given us.

                                CA
28. Youthful habits influence a person's life; <u>therefore,</u> you should develop good habits now.

     SC
29. <u>As</u> a person grows older, habits become harder to change.

                CC   CC
30. All habits work <u>either</u> for the good <u>or</u> for the bad.

(5 points)

D. Underline each interjection. Place a comma or an exclamation point after each one, and capitalize the following word if necessary.

        T
31. <u>Whew</u>! that car almost ran off the road.

        T
32. <u>Rocks</u>! this farm is almost covered with them.

33. <u>Oh</u>, now I understand this problem.

(6 points)

E. Cross out each mistake in word usage, and write any correction above it.

               behind
34. Our garden is ~~in back of~~ the house.

35. The sugar peas will soon be over ~~with~~ for this spring.

36. What kind of ~~a~~ tomato stalk is that?

                      from
37. Its leaves look a bit different ~~than~~ the leaves of the others.

                                     except
38. Insects have been bothering most of the plants ~~accept~~ the tomatoes.

                       beside
39. The salesman parked his car ~~besides~~ the barn.

                    into
40. Did you see that bullfrog leap ~~in~~ the pond?

41. Mother divided the remaining cake ~~between~~ ^{among} us four boys.

42. Father gave this job to you and Ɨ ^{me}, so let's get busy.

(9 points)

F. Underline the correct words in parentheses.

43. No doubt, my great-grandfather worked much harder than (I, me).

44. Since Sharon is handicapped, my parents must help her more than (I, me).

45. The cattle are bawling (as if, like) they are out of hay.

(3 points)

G. Above each underlined word or phrase, write what part of speech it is.

46. The Bible is a guiding light, showing the right way to the godly.
    (adj. n. ... adj. ... n.)

47. Godly people cling to the right, for evil ruins those who fall into it.
    (adj. ... v. ... n. conj. ... v. pron.)

48. For those airplanes that fly through the air, a partial vacuum is necessary.
    (prep. adj. ... v. prep. ... n.)

49. Crash! Mother's treasured dish lies in ruins because of my carelessness.
    (interj. ... adj. n. ... n. prep.)

50. Lois will come in and vacuum the remains off the floor.
    (v. ... adv. ... v. ... n.)

51. The will to do right should be guiding our reactions in difficulties.
    (n. ... v. ... prep.)

52. Because Grandfather took a kindly interest in our activities, we treasured his visits.
    (conj. ... adj. ... v.)

53. Act kindly toward the elderly; they are often weaker than we are.
    (adv. ... n. ... adv. ... conj.)

(34 points)

H. In the blank before each stanza, write which pattern of rhythm it has. In the blanks after the lines, show the rhyming pattern.

54. _____iambic_____

    The snow is like a blanket that   __a__

    God spreads across the land,   __b__

    Where wheat and oats and barley sleep,   __c__

    Awaiting spring's command.   __b__

55. _____anapestic_____

    The Assyrian came down like the wolf on the fold,   __a__

    And his cohorts were gleaming in purple and gold;   __a__

And the sheen of their <u>spears</u> was like <u>stars</u> on the <u>sea</u>,   b

When the blue wave rolls nightly on deep Galilee.   b

56. _____ trochaic _____

When at last I near the shore,   a

And the fearful breakers <u>roar</u>   a

'Twixt me and the peaceful rest,   b

Then, while leaning on Thy breast,   b

May I hear Thee say to me,   c

"Fear not, I will pilot thee."   c

57. _____ dactylic _____

<u>Wisdom</u> is <u>bidding</u> in <u>still</u> and sweet voice,   a

Bidding each one to his soul's solemn choice: a

Wisdom or folly—which <u>way</u> will you <u>take</u>?   b

Wisdom brings true godly honor and joy,   c

Folly the soul of a man will destroy;   c

Wisdom or folly—this choice all must make.   b

58. Draw one line under the simile and two lines under the example of personification in number 54.
59. Underline the words that show alliteration in number 55.
60. Underline the word that shows onomatopoeia in number 56.
61. Underline the words that show assonance in number 57.

(13 points)

I. Write whether the parallelism in each verse is similar (*S*) or opposite (*O*).

___S___ 62. "But he that sinneth against me wrongeth his own soul: all they that hate me love death" (Proverbs 8:36).

___O___ 63. "Reprove not a scorner, lest he hate thee: rebuke a wise man, and he will love thee" (Proverbs 9:8).

___S___ 64. "In the way of righteousness is life; and in the pathway thereof there is no death" (Proverbs 12:28).

(3 points)
Total points: 101

Building Securely

Chapter 10 Test

Score _____

Name _____   Date _____

A. Circle *T* if the statement is true or *F* if it is false.

T (F) 1. A restrictive adjective clause should be set off with commas.

(T) F 2. A question mark is placed outside the quotation marks if the whole sentence is a question but the quotation is not.

T (F) 3. A period is always placed outside the quotation marks.

T (F) 4. If a verb is followed by several direct objects in a list, a colon should be placed after the verb.

(T) F 5. A semicolon may be used between two independent clauses even if no conjunction is used.

(T) F 6. To show what is italicized in print, you underline in writing.

T (F) 7. A story conflict should be introduced in the middle of the story.

T (F) 8. The climax should be described in the last several sentences of the story.

T (F) 9. Dialogue in a story should consist of formal language and complete sentences.

(T) F 10. A good storywriter avoids using many linking verbs and passive voice verbs.

(10 points)

B. Cross out each error in capitalization, and write the correct letter above it.

11. At the store, Mother bought some Mueller's nNoodles on a special sale.

12. The Springville Shoe Sstore is owned by Alfred Bender, Ssr.

13. The Yosemite Nnational Ppark is on the Wwest slope of the Sierra Nevada.

14. Thanksgiving Dday always comes on a Tthursday.

15. My fFather enjoyed mMath when he was a student in sSchool.

16. Every morning, OLo lord, Tthou wilt hear our prayers.

17. We read some vVerses from the Wword of God.

(16 points)

C. Add the missing commas and end marks.   (Count 2 points for each sentence.)

18. Jericho, which lies northeast of Jerusalem, was the hometown of Zacchaeus.

19. Did you know, Marie, that Jericho is eight hundred feet below sea level?

20. Jericho is less than twenty miles from Jerusalem, yet Jerusalem is about twenty-five hundred feet above sea level.

21. What a steep climb that must be!

22. A cool, refreshing breeze made a pleasant day for hoeing in the garden, digging postholes, and picking up stones in the field.

23. Because we wanted to surprise Father, we worked hard, in fact, at all three jobs.

24. Eric was born on July 15, 1970, at Jefferson City, Missouri.

(14 points)

D. Add quotation marks and other related punctuation. Show any correction of capitalization as you did in Part B. Do not put quotation marks around a sentence that has no explanatory words.

(Count 3 points for each sentence.)

25. "In the Bible," began Brother Herbert, "we find the source of all truth."

26. "In His prayer, Jesus said, 'Thy Word is truth,'" he continued.

27. How sad that many people say, "Truth is whatever man discovers"!

28. Pilate asked, "ᵂwhat is truth?"

(12 points)

E. Add underlining or quotation marks where they are needed.

29. Father had read "Four Centuries of Dutch Mennonitism" from the book Glimpses of Mennonite History and Doctrine.

30. At the close of the service, we sang "Now the Day Is Over."

31. Use Strong's Exhaustive Concordance to find the verse.

32. Did you read "Long Days for Leah" in the Christian Pathway?

(6 points)

F. Add the missing colons and semicolons. You will need to replace some commas with these marks.

33. Ralph Waldo Emerson made this statement: "The reward of a thing well done is to have done it."

34. We drove through Washington, the Evergreen State; Oregon, the Beaver State; and California, the Golden State.

35. Our neighbors have lived in the following states: Vermont, Ohio, Iowa, Mississippi, and Florida.

36. Floyd says that it's exciting to live in so many different places; I'm glad to stay here on our farm.

37. I would be willing to move if God calls us somewhere else‚; however, their father moves to find the highest paying jobs he can.

(5 points)

G. Add apostrophes, hyphens, and underlining where they are needed.

38. I don't have any great-grandparents living anymore.

39. Long ago, s's within words looked much like f's.

40. The word <u>shew</u> is pronounced the same as <u>show</u>.

41. Mr. Getz still has twenty-two desks with self-contained lamps.

42. The word <u>parallel</u> has only one set of double l's.

43. Somebody's cows are loose, but they aren't ours.

44. The <u>Flying Eagle</u>, our neighbor's small airplane, was lost during the sudden tempest last week.

(15 points)

H. Improve each sentence so that the dialogue sounds more natural.   (Sample answers. Count 2 points for each sentence.)

45. "There is a beautiful rainbow out here," said Dennis.

46. "Where is the rainbow?" said Lynette.

47. "The rainbow is over the meadow," said Dennis. "Let us go and tell Mother."

45. <u>"There's a beautiful rainbow out here!" shouted Dennis.</u>

46. <u>"Where?" asked Lynette.</u>

47. <u>"Over the meadow," replied Dennis. "Let's go and tell Mother."</u>

(8 points)

I. Rewrite these sentences to include more lively action verbs that show rather than merely tell.

(Sample answers.)

48. It was a bitterly cold day.

<u>We shivered as we stepped out into the sub-zero morning.</u>

49. These books have all been read by me.

<u>I have read all these books.</u>

(4 points)

Total points: 90

Building Securely

Chapter 11 Test

Score _____

Name _____ Date _____

A. Circle *T* if the statement is true or *F* if it is false.

   T (F) 1. The etymology of a word shows its different forms, such as plurals and principal parts.

   (T) F 2. Generally the beginning of a sentence receives the greatest emphasis.

   T (F) 3. One good way to write an emphatic sentence is to separate a verb phrase with a lengthy inter-
ruptive phrase.

   T (F) 4. Prefixes usually change the part of speech of a word, and suffixes change the meaning of a word.

   (T) F 5. The index of an encyclopedia gives more details on finding information than do the cross-
references.

   T (F) 6. Encyclopedias give information on many subjects in greater detail than most books.

   T (F) 7. The Old Testament was written in Greek.

   (T) F 8. Careful speakers and writers avoid using words that the dictionary labels *nonstandard* or
illiterate.

(8 points)

B. Write the letter of the correct term to match each description. You may use a letter more than once.

    a. atlas   d. dictionary   g. topical Bible   j. homographs
    b. Bible dictionary   e. encyclopedia   h. antonyms   k. homophones
    c. concordance   f. thesaurus   i. heteronyms   l. synonyms

   _f_   9. A book of synonyms.

   _c_ 10. A book of Bible words and their references.

   _d_ 11. A book of words, showing pronunciations, meanings, and other information.

   _a_ 12. A book of maps.

   _e_ 13. Volumes of information containing articles on a wide range of subjects.

   _g_ 14. A book of Bible subjects, with verses pertaining to each subject.

   _b_ 15. A book of information on Bible words, places, people, and customs.

   _c_ 16. A book that may have dictionaries of the Hebrew and Greek words from which English words
in the Bible were translated.

   _j_ 17. Words that are spelled and pronounced alike but have different origins and meanings.

   _l_ 18. Words with similar meanings.

   _i_ 19. Words that are spelled alike but pronounced differently.

___h___ 20. Words with opposite meanings.

___k___ 21. Words that are pronounced alike but spelled differently.

(13 points)

C. All the following words have the root *gress,* which means "to go or step." In the blanks below, write the words that match the definitions.

aggressive	progress	regression
digress	progression	transgressor

___progress___ 22. To go forward.

___transgressor___ 23. One who steps across (a boundary line).

___regression___ 24. The action of going back.

___digress___ 25. To go away from (a topic of discussion).

(4 points)

D. Use suffixes to change the following words to the parts of speech indicated.

___hardship___ 26. hard (n.)
or hardness

___permanence___ 27. permanent (n.)
or permanency

___persecution___ 28. persecute (n.)
or persecutor

___sailor___ 29. sail (n.)

___finalize___ 30. final (v.)

___glorious___ 31. glory (adj.)

___colorful___ 32. color (adj.)
or colorless

___absent___ 33. absence (adj.)

___marvelous___ 34. marvel (adj.)

___activate___ 35. active (v.)

(10 points)

E. Make each sentence more effective by using the active voice, using a direct quotation, improving the parallelism, making the pronoun reference clear, removing wordiness, or moving a modifier to a better position.

36. Roxanne must choose to bake brownies or cooking custard. ___Roxanne must choose to bake brownies or to cook custard. or Roxanne must choose baking brownies or cooking custard.___

37. Mother said that Lori must bake some bread. ___Mother said, "Lori must bake some bread." or Mother said, "Lori, bake some bread."___

38. The cleaning will be done by Joyce and Esther this time. ___Joyce and Esther will do the cleaning this time.___

39. When we hit that sharp rock, the tire almost went flat immediately. ___When we hit that sharp rock, the tire went flat almost immediately.___

40. Father told the neighbor man that his wood supply should last all winter. ___Father told the neighbor man, "My (or Your) wood supply should last all winter."___

41. After the starting bell rang, Brother Noah announces the opening song. _____

    After the starting bell rang, Brother Noah announced the opening song. or After the starting bell

    rings, Brother Noah announces the opening song.

42. To expostulate is when you object earnestly but kindly. _____

    To expostulate is to object earnestly but kindly.

43. A ruffed grouse seemed to suddenly appear from nowhere. _____

    A ruffed grouse seemed to appear suddenly from nowhere.

44. A grouse's sudden, abrupt takeoff into flight often surprises and startles people. _____

    A grouse's sudden (abrupt) takeoff often surprises (startles) people.

(9 points)

F. Rewrite the following paragraph, making the changes indicated to give greater sentence variety.

45. Change sentence *a* to an interrogative sentence.
46. Combine sentences *b* and *c* into a compound sentence.
47. Change sentence *d* so that the dependent clause comes first.
48. Combine sentences *e* and *f* into a complex sentence.
49. Change sentence *g* to inverted word order.
50. Change sentence *h* to an exclamatory sentence.

   *a*The Amazon River is the largest river system in the world. *b*This huge river is only the second longest. *c*It carries the greatest volume of water. *d*Over one thousand tributaries join the mighty Amazon before it completes its four-thousand-mile journey to the Atlantic. *e*The river drains an area of 2.5 million square miles. *f*This is over two-thirds of the area of the entire United States. *g*Its fresh water flows far out into the Atlantic Ocean. *h*The Amazon is an amazing river indeed.

   (Sample paragraph.)

   Did you know that the Amazon River is the largest river system in the world? This huge river is only the

   second longest, but it carries the greatest volume of water. Before it completes its four-thousand-mile jour-

   ney to the Atlantic, over one thousand tributaries join the mighty Amazon. The river drains an area of 2.5

   million square miles, which is over two-thirds of the area of the entire United States. Far out into the Atlantic

   Ocean flows its fresh water. What an amazing river the Amazon is!

(6 points)
Total points: 50

Dr. Wise's
275-8882

Dr. Peneul
939-9939

Building Securely

Final Test   **Score** _____

Name _____   **Date** _____

A. Circle *T* if the statement is true or *F* if it is false.

   (T) F   1. If a verb is in a perfect tense, a form of *have* is always used as a helping verb.

   T (F)   2. Modifying words, like adjectives and adverbs, are substantives.

   (T) F   3. A character sketch should give one main impression about a person.

   T (F)   4. A paragraph explaining a process should be developed in the order of importance.

   T (F)   5. In addition to the parts of a friendly letter, a business letter has a heading.

   (T) F   6. A paragraph has coherence when the ideas flow smoothly from one sentence to the next.

   (T) F   7. A topic sentence may be found anywhere within a paragraph.

   (T) F   8. The story conflict should be introduced early in the story.

   T (F)   9. The climax of a story should be found in the middle of the story.

   T (F) 10. One good way to make dialogue sound natural is to use expressions like "he don't" and "we seen."

               (10 points)

B. Before each sentence, write the abbreviation for the part of speech that the underlined word is.

  conj. 11. We surveyed the damage <u>after</u> the storm was over. *conj*

  prep. 12. <u>After</u> the next town, we will see no service stations for a while. *prep*

  adv. 13. The older boys ran, and the younger ones had trouble following <u>after</u>.

  pron. 14. The calves in this pen look well, but <u>those</u> look rather sick. *pron.*

  adj. 15. <u>Those</u> paragraphs were well developed.

  interj. 16. <u>Rich</u>! Solomon must have been richer than we can imagine.

  _n._ 17. The <u>rich</u> are not always the happiest. *n*

  adj. 18. God's blessing is <u>rich</u> even though earthly riches may be scarce. *adj*

  adj. 19. The <u>singing</u> birds sounded very cheerful.

  _n._ 20. <u>Singing</u> can be a good way to encourage yourself. *n* ___v.___ 21. The students are <u>singing</u> the new song quite well.   V

___conj.___ 22. We practiced the song quite often, <u>for</u> it was difficult to learn.

___prep.___ 23. We sang it <u>for</u> the closing song in devotions this morning.

(13 points)

C. In each blank, write what sentence part the underlined word is. Use the following abbreviations.

S—subject	PN—predicate nominative
V—verb	PA—predicate adjective
DO—direct object	DA—noun of direct address
IO—indirect object	AP—appositive

___PA___ 24. You will grow <u>strong</u> in character if you love the truth.

___DO___ 25. Guard carefully your <u>attitudes</u> about right and wrong.

___IO___ 26. Give your <u>parents</u> the respect that God calls you to give.

___PN___ 27. Your present attitudes will become an important <u>key</u> to your future character.

___S___ 28. In the midst of daily temptations, <u>you</u> must determine to be faithful.

___DA___ 29. Do you know if Mother is resting, <u>Twila</u>?

___AP___ 30. Midnight, the <u>cat</u> lying on the step, catches many mice.

___V___ 31. Do you <u>plant</u> string beans every year?

___PA___ 32. The train's whistle sounded <u>loud</u> and clear.

___DO___ 33. A passerby saw the fire and sounded an <u>alarm</u>.

(10 points)

D. In the first blank, write *S* for simple, *Cd* for compound, or *Cx* for complex to identify the structure of the sentence. In the second blank, write *N* for natural, *I* for inverted, or *M* for mixed to identify the word order of the sentence.

___Cd___ ___N___ 34. The way of the world promises pleasure, but it brings misery.

___Cx___ ___M___ 35. When the Jews fell into idolatry, were they better off?

___S___ ___N___ 36. Gehazi coveted this world's goods and suffered for it.

___S___ ___I___ 37. How great was his punishment!

___Cd___ ___N___ 38. Follow the Lord, and love not the world.

(10 points)

E. In each blank, write *prep.* for prepositional, *part.* for participial, *ger.* for gerund, or *inf.* for infinitive to identify the underlined phrase.

   part.   39. Peter, <u>misjudging himself</u>, said that he would die for Jesus.

   inf.   40. The self-confident person fails <u>to seek God's help</u>.

   prep.   41. He trusts rather in the strength <u>of his own heart</u>.

   ger.   42. <u>Trusting one's own self</u> is a sure formula for failure.

   prep.   43. We should pray <u>to the Lord</u> every day.

(5 points)

F. In the first blank, write *D* or *I* to tell whether the underlined clause is dependent or independent. If the clause is dependent, write the abbreviation for noun (*n.*), adjective (*adj.*), or adverb (*adv.*) in the second blank.

  D   adv.   44. <u>Although it is May already</u>, the weather has been quite cool.

  I   45. <u>A large ocean liner was passing under the Bay Bridge</u> while we were driving over it.

  D   n.   46. We saw <u>what the hailstorm did to your corn</u>.

  I   47. <u>A beautiful spring day dawned</u>, but I was sick in bed.

  D   adj.   48. I am returning the books <u>that you loaned me last month</u>.

(5 points)

G. Fill in the blanks of this chart. For the starred words, use the foreign plural spellings.

Singular	Singular Possessive	Plural	Plural Possessive
49. monkey	monkey's	monkeys	monkeys'
50. brother-in-law	brother-in-law's	brothers-in-law	brothers-in-law's
51. calf	calf's	calves	calves'
52. prince	prince's	princes	princes'
53. man	man's	men	men's
54. sheep	sheep's	sheep	sheep's
55. *larva	larva's	larvae	larvae's
56. *fungus	fungus's	fungi	fungi's
57. *crisis		crises	
58. *vertex		vertices	

(10 points)

H. Identify the person (*1, 2, 3*), number (*S, P*), case (*N, O, P*), and gender (*M, F, N, C*) of each underlined pronoun.

	Person	Number	Case	Gender
59. The Bible guides <u>us</u>.	1	P	O	C
60. <u>He</u> sent a Saviour.	3	S	N	M
61. Sue helped <u>her</u> nicely.	3	S	O	F
62. Children, are <u>you</u> ready?	2	P	N	C
63. Look at <u>its</u> torn pages!	3	S	P	N

(10 points)

I. Underline the correct words.

64. Abraham gave them, Hagar and (he, <u>him</u>), food and water for their journey.

65. Isaac's two sons, Jacob and (<u>he</u>, him), were quite different.

66. When the man asked for Mr. Shrock, Father replied, "I am (<u>he</u>, him)."

67. May (<u>we</u>, us) students eat lunch beside the creek at noon?

68. The secretary and treasurer gave (<u>his answer</u>, their answers).

(5 points)

J. In each blank, write the tense of the underlined verb.

future perfect	69.	The Lord willing, we <u>shall have arrived</u> home before evening.
past	70.	The Lord certainly <u>did bless</u> us with safe traveling.
present perfect	71.	Too often we <u>have forgotten</u> to thank Him for His blessings.
future	72.	We <u>shall thank</u> Him before we leave the car.
present	73.	We <u>are seeking</u> His daily blessing on our lives.
past perfect	74.	We <u>had seen</u> four accidents before we left Illinois.

(6 points)

K. From Part J, copy the verbs that fit these descriptions.

are seeking	75.	a verb in a progressive form
did bless	76.	a verb in an emphatic form

(2 points)

L. Write numbers in the blanks to identify the sentence patterns.

Pattern 1: intransitive complete verb
Pattern 2: transitive verb, active voice
Pattern 3: transitive verb, passive voice
Pattern 4: intransitive linking verb

____1____ 77. "My cup runneth over."

____4____ 78. "The word of the Lord is right."

____3____ 79. "All his works are done in truth."

____2____ 80. "I will bless the Lord at all times."

(4 points)

M. Underline the better words.

81. (There's, <u>There are</u>) many examples of sowing and reaping in the Bible.

82. Mother's scissors (<u>have</u>, has) been misplaced.

83. Either Esther or Miriam (<u>was</u>, were) using them this morning.

84. Father said we (can, <u>may</u>) fly our kite after chores.

85. We should (<u>let</u>, leave) the younger ones choose first.

86. Chicken pox (<u>is</u>, are) caused by the same virus as shingles.

87. After the heavy rains, the creek (raised, <u>rose</u>) over its banks.

88. Don't gather the eggs in this nest; this hen is (<u>setting</u>, sitting).

89. Grandfather has been (laying, <u>lying</u>) in bed for two weeks.

90. The bags of feed (<u>have</u>, has) been delivered.

91. The balloon (<u>burst</u>, busted) with a loud pop.

92. Paula has (went, <u>gone</u>) along with Mother to the store.

93. Henry (<u>tagged</u>, tug) Clyde between second and third base.

94. The ice cream has (froze, <u>frozen</u>) hard by now.

95. Please (<u>raise</u>, rise) the shade to let the sun shine in.

(15 points)

N. In the first blank, write *D* for descriptive or *L* for limiting to describe the underlined adjectives. In the second blank, write *AT* for attributive, *AP* for appositive, or *PR* for predicate.

__D__ __AT__ 96. A <u>difficult</u> task awaited Kenneth.

__L__ __AT__ 97. <u>Two</u> calf pens needed to be cleaned out.

__D__ __PR__ 98. The morning air felt <u>fresh</u> and crisp.

__D__ __AP__ 99. The task, difficult but <u>necessary</u>, was soon finished.

__L__ __AT__ 100. The work was made easier by <u>his</u> good attitude toward it.

(10 points)

O. Write the comparative and superlative degrees of these adjectives and adverbs.

101. helpful ____more helpful____ ____most helpful____

102. well ____better____ ____best____

103. holy ____holier____ ____holiest____

104. pleasant ____more pleasant____ ____most pleasant____

105. great ____greater____ ____greatest____

106. far ____farther____ ____farthest____

(6 points)

P. Cross out each word that should not be used, and write any correction above it.

107. ~~Them~~ _Those_ ten spies who brought an evil report lacked faith in God.

108. There were ~~less~~ _fewer_ spies who saw the Lord than who saw the difficulties.

109. But these ~~here~~ two spies, Joshua and Caleb, were richly rewarded by God.

110. Both boys gave correct answers, but Leon's was ~~most~~ _more_ satisfactory.

111. Do you know what kind of ~~a~~ bird whistles like that?

112. How long can the men continue ~~on~~ battling this blazing fire?

113. Mr. Morgan sounded ~~kind of~~ _rather or somewhat_ upset when we invited him to come to church.

114. We will divide these chores ~~between~~ _among_ the five boys.

115. Be careful not to fall off ~~of~~ the ladder.

116. The cows went ~~in~~ _into_ the barn for shelter from the rainstorm.

(10 points)

Q. Cross out each capitalization error, and write the letter correctly above it. Not every item has an error.

117. a warm summer day (correct)

118. a quiz in American History *h*

119. God and his holy angels *H*

120. the song "Now the day is over" *D I O*

121. our Whirlpool Refrigerator *r*

122. the Cedar Ridge Feed and Seed *F S*

123. during the middle Ages *M A*

124. a State in the west *s W*

(8 points)

R. Add the two missing punctuation marks to each sentence. Underlining one or more words counts as one mark.

125. Your diligence today, my friend, will certainly pay off in the future.

126. Did David, who was a man after God's own heart, ever make any mistakes?

127. Yes, he did sin grievously several times, but he always repented afterward.

128. What Bible character said, "I have played the fool"?

129. Although he recognized his folly, he did not sincerely repent; indeed, he finally took his own life.

130. "You are to memorize the poem 'One by One,'" stated Brother John.

131. "You'll find the poem in the book Poems for Memorization," he continued.

132. My great-grandfather Bauman was respected as a man of self-control.

133. There's a large number of and's in that paragraph.

134. The following books make up the Pentateuch: Genesis, Exodus, Leviticus, Numbers, and Deuteronomy.

(10 points)

S. Write the letter of the correct term to match each description. A letter may be used more than once.

___d___ 135. The repetition of thoughts.

___a___ 136. The repetition of beginning consonant sounds.

___b___ 137. The repetition of similar vowel sounds.

___f___ 138. The matching of sounds at the ends of lines.

___c___ 139. The use of words having imitative sounds.

___g___ 140. The regular pattern of accented and unaccented syllables.

___d___ 141. A device more common in Bible poetry than in English poetry.

___e___ 142. An accented syllable and the unaccented syllable or syllables associated with it.

a. alliteration
b. assonance
c. onomatopoeia
d. parallelism
e. poetic foot
f. rhyme
g. rhythm

(8 points)

T. Read this paragraph, and do the exercises below.

[a]You have a four-chambered heart that constantly circulates blood through your body. [b]First, the right ventricle pumps the blood to the lungs, where it is supplied with oxygen. [c]From the lungs the blood returns to the left atrium and empties into the left ventricle. [d]Then the left ventricle pumps the oxygen-rich blood to the various parts of the body. [e]Sometimes germs enter the blood from these body parts. [f]Having delivered its oxygen, the blood returns to the right atrium, flows into the right ventricle, and is pumped to the lungs again. [g]In this way the blood follows a definite path as it flows through the body.

_a or g_ 143. Write the letter of the topic sentence.

___e___ 144. Write the letter of the sentence that mars the unity.

_a or b_ 145. Write whether the paragraph is developed by (a) adding details, (b) giving steps, (c) using examples, (d) telling an incident, or (e) giving a definition.

(3 points)

U. Each starred line on this partial outline contains a mistake. Write the outline correctly on the lines below.

The Process of Digestion
I. In the mouth
  *A. teeth
    *1. Break food into small pieces
  B. Saliva
  *1. Moistens food
    *2. Starches are changed into sugars.
*II. The stomach

The Process of Digestion

I. In the mouth

   A. Teeth—break food into small pieces

   B. Saliva

     1. Moistens food

     2. Changes starches into sugars

II. In the stomach

(5 points)
Total points: 165

Index

A